THE
FAMILY
AND THE
LAW

THE
FAMILY
AND THE
LAW

Problems for decision in
the family law process

Joseph Goldstein <small>YALE UNIVERSITY</small>

Jay Katz <small>YALE UNIVERSITY</small>

THE FREE PRESS, NEW YORK

COLLIER-MACMILLAN LIMITED, LONDON

For Information, address:

THE FREE PRESS

A DIVISION OF THE MACMILLAN COMPANY
60 Fifth Avenue, New York, 10011

COLLIER-MACMILLAN CANADA, LTD., TORONTO, ONTARIO

Designed by Sidney Solomon

Illustrations by Ellen Raskin

Library of Congress Catalog Card Number: 65-10189

To our families present, past, and future

PREFACE

This book is the result of an intensive elbow-to-elbow collaboration. It represents a continuing effort by men of different disciplines—law and psychoanalysis—to understand and challenge each other's experiences, assumptions, and knowledge in furtherance of a common task: the study of the family law process. This collaboration extends beyond the two of us to our students. During the past five years they have contributed to the development of this volume by working through and challenging each of its five drafts. Its final shape has been determined by many rewarding and demanding, although not always satisfying, office, classroom, and seminar hours.

Although we have designed this book for use by law teachers for students of law, we hope that it may stimulate the kind of interdisciplinary teaching we have found so gratifying and that it will be of use to the many disciplines, both theoretical and clinical, concerned with the study of the family.

The book has been divided into three large chapters, each of which is made up of many parts. Chapter I is an introduction to the family and the law and to our methods, concepts, and techniques for analyzing substantive and procedural problems for decision in the family law process. Chapter II provides detailed substantive explorations of decisions concerned with wife–husband relationships, and Chapter III explores decisions concerned with child–parent and parent–child relationships. In our basic course, Family and the Law I, we study most of Chapter I and parts of Chapters II and III. We have also used Chapter III in a seminar devoted to the disposition of children in a variety of legal settings, and sections of Chapter I in a seminar on the family of the future. Our purpose in describing how we have used these materials is not to suggest a formula for their use but rather to indicate our belief and expectation that the permutations for seminar and course design are numerous.

The conventions adopted in the organization of this book follow those initiated in *Criminal Law:** "The NOTES omit string citations and references to other materials easily located through standard indices. Because they raise important issues, NOTES are printed in the same type as the major problem material. To the extent that this book departs from what might be called 'legal' categories, the index provides a means for regrouping the materials in accord with traditional concepts, words, and phrases. In addition, there are three tables of contents: the first provides an over-view of the three major chapters and their parts; the second a detailed analytical breakdown of all the sections, including NOTES; and the third, which appears at the beginning of each chapter, falls in between these two in degree of comprehensiveness. There are also tables of cases, of authors, and of articles."†

* Richard C. Donnelly, Joseph Goldstein, and Richard D. Schwartz, *Criminal Law*. New York: The Free Press (1962).

† *Id.* at v.

This book has been supported in large measure by funds from a grant of the National Institute of Mental Health to the Yale Law School. As the dispenser of these and other funds and as a source of encouragement and understanding, Dean Eugene V. Rostow has been, in the spirit of academic freedom, a silent but ever-present and all-important partner in this collaboration. We are especially indebted to him and to our faculty for making it possible for Dr. Anna Freud to join us in seminar and work sessions in the preparation and teaching of these materials, particularly those concerned with children. These encounters with Dr. Freud have contributed greatly to the shape of Chapter III, have enriched our understanding of childhood, and have given us the rare treat of working with a person and a mind of great beauty. We are intellectually and affectionately in her debt. Others who have provided us with critical stimulation and to whom we are deeply grateful are Alexander M. Bickel, Sonja Goldstein, Fowler V. Harper, and Friedrich Kessler. We appreciate greatly, for calling to our attention materials and for other assistance, the help of Dorothy Burlingham, Elias Clark, Otto Kahn-Freund, Sanford N. Katz, Mary Kohler, Marianne Kris, Harold D. Lasswell, Seymour L. Lustman, Ellen A. Peters, Justine Wise Polier, Abraham Pomerantz, Fredrick C. Redlich, Charles A. Reich, Charles L. Remington, Samuel Ritvo, Roy Schafer, John G. Simon, Albert J. Solnit, and Morris A. Wessel. In this regard we are especially grateful to Joseph Tiefenbrun, who supplied us with much of the material in the Lesser case, to the Department of Social Welfare of the State of California, to the Family Court Center of Toledo, Ohio, and to the Conciliation Court of Los Angeles, California, for providing us with case studies. Throughout we acknowledge many other attorneys, doctors, social agencies, and court personnel who have been cooperative in responding to our request for data and permission to use their comments.

We owe much to the staff of the Yale Law Library, particularly to Harry Bitner, Robert E. Brooks, James M. Golden, and Solomon C. Smith, who met our seemingly unending requests with cheerful and successful searches.

Among the many students, now lawyers, who have played a special role in the preparation of this volume we thank George Driesen, Ernest Ettlinger, Henry Freedman, James O. Friedman, Martin Levine, Donald Marshall, Paul Nejelski, Neil Peck, Ruben Robertson, Bruce Schrager, Roger Tompkins, Louise Trubek, Steven Umin, Jonathan Weiss, David White, Frances White, and Sidney Wolinsky.

We gratefully acknowledge the generous help of Anne Cote, Isabel Malone, Helen Minor, Doris Moriarty, Lucille Siebert, and Ruth Wrisley in the preparation of many mimeographed versions.

We thank Meira G. Pimsleur for providing us with the index, Lily Neurath for her translations, Ellen Raskin for her fine drawings, and Emanuel Geltman, Nat Halebsky, Marlene Mandel, and Wally Schmidt of The Free Press for their fine editorial work; and finally, we thank Jeremiah Kaplan, George D. McCune, and Sidney Solomon for the friendly and understanding direction they gave to the production of this volume.

New Haven, Connecticut   J. G
November, 1964   J. K

Lesser case: 158 NYS 2d 504
Glackner case.

Condensed Table of Contents

Analytical Table of Contents

Part Three. ADMINISTERING AND REORGANIZING PARENT-CHILD RELATIONSHIPS—ON THE SELECTION OF CUSTODIANS FOR WHAT PURPOSES 175

2a. *Painter v. Bannister*

Part Five. IN SEARCH OF FUNCTIONAL DEFINITIONS OF FAMILY 337

Part Six. THE FAMILY LAW PROCESS—THE FUNCTION OF THE STATE IN ESTABLISHING, ADMINISTERING, AND REORGANIZING THE FAMILY AND ADMINISTERING THE REORGANIZED FAMILY 517

Chapter II

Problems for Decision in Establishing, Administering, and Reorganizing Wife-Husband Relationships 563

Part One. FOR WHOM, TO WHAT EXTENT, AND WHY IS PROVIDING OR OBTAINING ECONOMIC GRATIFICATION RELEVANT: 565

Part Two. FOR WHOM, TO WHAT EXTENT, AND WHY IS SEXUAL GRATIFICATION RELEVANT: 639

Part Three.   FOR WHOM, TO WHAT EXTENT, AND WHY IS BEING HEALTHY, HAPPY, AND RESPECTED RELEVANT: 713

Chapter III

Problems for Decision in Establishing, Administering, and Reorganizing Child-Parent and Parent-Child Relationships   831

Part Two. WHEN, WHY, AND HOW SHOULD THE STATE INTERVENE?—FOUR STUDIES IN CHILD CUSTODY 913

PKU

add: Reactions to Parent's Suicide

Part Three. WHEN, WHY, AND HOW SHOULD THE STATE INTERVENE TO DETERMINE THE DISPOSITION OF "ADULT" DEPENDENTS? —THREE PROBLEMS IN PARENTAL CUSTODY 1155

THE
FAMILY
AND THE
LAW

INTRODUCTION

This book examines and evaluates the interaction between two of man's creations for the development and social control of human beings, the Family and the Law.[1]

The law, without explicitly defining family, assumes that "family" is essential to the evolution and growth of a viable society. This assumption rests on another assumption: that family, like law itself, is one of the basic processes for the control of human behavior. Indeed, law may be perceived as a response to "the family's" success or failure in providing each *child* with internal mechanisms of control sufficient for each *adult* to be a law unto himself. Thus perceived, the law shapes and is shaped by the family.

Family law, for the purposes of this book, is defined as the process for deciding what relationships should be labelled "family," under what circumstances such relationships may be established, administered, and reorganized, and what consequences should accompany these determinations. In perceiving the cycle of state and family interaction in terms of the three basic problems for decision—establishment, administration, and reorganization—we further define family law to include the processes for determining to what persons or agencies, should be assigned, under what circumstances, the role of promulgating, invoking, implementing, and appraising these decisions.[2]

The conceptual scheme, of examining problems for decision at each point in the family law process in terms of the establishment, administration, and reorganization of family relation-

---

1. This book follows the method of analysis developed in *Criminal Law*, by Richard C. Donnelly, Joseph Goldstein, and Richard D. Schwartz (New York: The Free Press, 1962). We have consciously been influenced, as this Introduction makes manifest, by that volume, which provided us with a useful frame of reference for exploring problems for decision in the family law process.

2. Harold Lasswell divides the decisionmaking process, for purposes of functional analysis, into seven steps: intelligence, recommendation, prescription, invocation, application, appraisal, and termination. See Lasswell, *The Decision Process* (1956).

ships, has proven to be a useful analytic tool. But, it is nothing more than that. None of the problems for decision can be neatly confined to any single category. Problems of reorganization, for example, must also be viewed as problems concerning the establishment of new relationships, which in turn may become the subject for decision involving issues of administration and reorganization. Specifically, some of the legislative, judicial, and agency decisions which must be analyzed both in terms of *establishment* and *reorganization* of family relationships concern substantive and procedural requisites for becoming married, separated, divorced, and single, as well as becoming a natural, adoptive, foster, neglected, and emancipated parent or child. Furthermore, such decisions must be analyzed in terms of *administration* of established and reorganized family relationships. Thus viewed, administration may concern the requisites, both substantive and procedural, for providing support, maintenance, alimony, welfare benefits, homestead exemptions, education, a name, medical care, conciliation services, supervision of custody, and relief from criminal or tort liability, as well as freedom from the obligations to testify against a member of one's family. We had difficulty finding a relatively neutral term for problems concerned with the function of the state in nourishing, undermining, controlling, maintaining, regulating, and supervising existing and persisting "legal" family relationships. The term "administration" seems to fulfill the need and, at the same time, stimulates—without limiting—inquiry into these considerations. Thus, in terms of the goals of family law, an evaluation of any decision at any point in the process requires an analysis from each of the three vantage points—establishment, administration, and reorganization.

This book presents problems for decision in the family law process that confront or might confront the state in its interaction with the family or, more precisely, with individuals in terms of their relationships to one or more families. To locate and examine these problems, we have selected materials from many sources, including trial transcripts, hearings in chambers, case studies, psychiatric reports, conciliation proceedings, appellate decisions, lawyers' files, private agreements, follow-up communications from parties and attorneys, as well as from legislative records; we have interwoven them with material from psychoanalysis, psychology, anthropology, jurisprudence, philosophy, sociology, political science, economics, genetics, medicine, geriatrics, and religion. These materials should be treated as legal data, whose relevance for decision must be considered at all points in the family law process. The decisionmaker must determine whether, how, why, and for what purposes the data are or are not relevant. Even if relevance is established, there remains the task of subjecting the reliability of such material to critical and unrelenting scrutiny. We share the view of Mr. Justice Frankfurter: "If law is to have a strength adequate to the task, the widest learning—constant cultivation of the legal mind by exposure to every subject of human investigation—is requisite. Thus only can those through whose decisions the law emerges escape shallowness, oversimplification, too quick acceptance of uncritical formulas which, by plating the mind against self-examination, impair its capacity for reasoned judgment."[3]

To identify problems for decision and to evaluate decisions in terms of their consequences, the student of family law may find it useful to consider many of the questions that follow. Although the decisionmaker may not actually pose or be aware of these questions, he answers them, in a very real sense, in the constant flow of decisions as legislator, judge, lawyer, and therapist in the family law process. Possibly he finds it difficult to articulate these questions because he is and has always been a member of one or more families. He may see his personal

3. 49 *A.B.A.J.* 876 ,877 (1963).

resolution of a similar problem as the only answer and thus see no questions that require precise formulation in order to ferret out the problem presented. He may find the problem, either consciously or unconsciously, so emotionally freighted by painful memories that the questions are distorted or obscured because he must deny what is there to be seen or heard.

Although the answers to the general questions which follow may differ from generation to generation, we hope that the questions identify the issues to be resolved in determining the nature and extent of ṣtate interaction with the family. Since this may be a false hope, we must constantly ask of these questions: Are we unconsciously so bound by our experiences and values that the questions demand reformulation in order to reveal the problem for decision?

1. Considering law and family as processes of social control, what goals should men seek to achieve through law and family in a democratic society? What are the functions of the family and the law?

2. Who, under what circumstances and by what procedures, are to be designated members of what family or families?

3. What consequences, for what purposes, should accompany an official designation of membership in a family?

4. Why, how, and under what circumstances should and can the state intervene to establish, administer, or reorganize a family?

   (a) To what extent should and can the law create, nourish, or destroy biological, economic, psychological, geographical, ethical, and historical family ties?

   (b) To what extent can a family relationship be dissolved or destroyed other than possibly by the death of all the members of a family?

5. What alternative to family could "better" fulfill some or all the functions left or assigned by the state to the family?

6. Who, under what circumstances and at what point in the family law process, should have official responsibility for formulating questions similar to the foregoing and giving answers to them?

To facilitate analysis and discussion of these general questions and to illustrate the variety of contexts in which each may arise at every decisionmaking point in the family law process, these more specific questions are posed:

1. To what extent should law establish, administer, and reorganize the family as an enclosure and source of continuity for economic, sexual, and procreative gratification?

2. To what extent should law establish, administer, and reorganize the family as an enclosure and source of continuity for the growth and development of children, for the care of parents, and for the disposition of the dead?

3. To what extent should law establish, administer, and reorganize the family as an enclosure and source of continuity for affection and aggression as well as for collaboration and conflict?

4. To what extent should law establish, administer, and reorganize the family as an enclosure and source of continuity for health, well being, affection, identity, respect, happiness, discipline, and property, as well as for intellectual and vocational stimulation?

5. To what extent should law establish, administer, and reorganize the family as an enclosure and source of continuity for race, religion, morality, law, and state?

6. To what extent should age, sex, blood, religion, education, political affiliation, occupation, ancestry, wealth, happiness, color, health, fault, love, motivation (conscious and unconscious), or criminal record be relevant to becoming engaged, married, separated, or divorced; to obtaining support, alimony, or welfare benefits; and to becoming a natural, foster, or adopting parent, child, or agency?

7. To what extent should "in the child's best interests," "in the parent's best interests," "that which is the least detrimental alternative for the child," or "that which is least unsatisfactory to the parent" be the guide or guides for decision concerning the disposition of children in such proceedings as divorce, separation, juvenile delinquency, neglecting parent, adoption, and foster care?

8. To what extent and how is family defined or reflected in the consequences which accompany the status of "fiance," "fiancee," "wife," "husband," "father," "mother," "son," "daughter," "artificially inseminated parent," "artificially procreated child," "neglecting parent," "neglected child," "child placement agency," "child care institution," "institutionalized child," "foster parent," "foster child," "adopting parent," "adopted child," "divorced parent," "child in custody," "emancipated child," "brother," "sister," "grandparent," "grandchild," "aunt," "uncle," "niece," "nephew," "cousin," or "in-law?"

9. How adequate are the procedures for obtaining, introducing, and determining the relevance of data to the decisions being made throughout the process?

The question underlying all of these general and specific questions is whether, how, and to what extent the state should not or should be authorized to regulate the relations of man. In answering this question the decisionmaker must resolve the important issue of why, when, and how the state ought or ought not to intervene. It should not be assumed, however, that he will respond rationally "[e]ven if the materials are sufficiently relevant and valid to fully support or undermine a given position. Like all human beings he is subject to a variety of internal and external, conscious and unconscious, pressures which may evoke a decision contrary to that sought. Awareness of this makes it all the more important that we seek to design our model of [the family law process] carefully and free from second guesses about possible pressures. For models built on the sand of anticipated compromises obscure and hinder the development of well articulated objectives which ought to be available as guides to and bases for appraising the work of decisionmakers."[4]

The reader who opens himself to these questions and materials will be unable to keep his thoughts from straying to reflections about himself and his families. This may cause feelings of uneasiness, particularly if the boundary between the people in the materials and those in personal fantasy become hazy. Such an experience can be likened to that of the medical student who frequently "suffers" from all of the symptoms he is studying in his text books. "As a matter of fact, it is most unsatisfactory to be immune to 'medical students' disease'. A touch of the ailment is a sign that the reader is really opening himself to his subject, trying to grasp it and feel it rather than just reading about it."[5]

In preparing this book we have come to hope that it might have a place in the tradition for which Mr. Justice Frankfurter spoke in one of his dissents:

---

4. *Criminal Law, op. cit.,* p. iv.
5. White, *The Abnormal Personality* (2d ed.; 1956), p. 58 [copyright 1948 (1956) The Ronald Press Company].

"To be writing [a casebook affecting many] lives after the curtain has been rung down upon them has the appearance of pathetic futility. But history also has its claims. This [book, we hope] is an incident in the long and unending effort to develop and enforce justice according to law. The progress in that struggle surely depends on searching analysis of the past, though the past cannot be recalled, as illumination for the future. Only by sturdy self-examination and self-criticism can the necessary habits for detached and wise judgment be established and fortified so as to become effective when the judicial process is again subjected to stress and strain."[6]

Law, like man, meets the need for continuity and stability by listening to precedent and rule as guides for decision. And law, like man, meets the need for flexibility and adaptability by making available for selection alternative precedents and rules (sometimes called counter-precedent and counterrule)[7] as guides for decision. Thus law, like man, in search of autonomy and identity must integrate these needs and become aware of both the values exerting pressure and the values to be preferred in each decision.[8]

We have designed this book, then, to encourage students and decisionmakers in law to develop the capacity to communicate with and understand the communication of many disciplines, to appraise and assess their relevance, and to speculate about their many wonderful and frightening implications for the future of the family and society. The application of scientific "advances" in theory and technique must be subject to advance thinking by lawyers concerned with the limits of state intervention. Otherwise much knowledge may be too little and too dangerous for the health and well being of the family and the law in a democracy.

---

6. Rosenberg v. U.S., 340 U.S. 273, 310 (1953).

7. See Kessler, F., *Natural Law, Justice And Democracy—Some Reflections On Three Types Of Thinking About Law And Justice* 19 TULANE L. REV. 32, 49 *et seq.* (1944).

8. "No lawyer worthy of the name can ever be either truly a conservative or truly a radical: at one and the same time we must somehow devote ourselves to the preservation of tradition, which we do not greatly respect, and to the promotion of change, in which we do not greatly believe." Gilmore, *The Truth About Harvard and Yale*, YALE L. REP. 8, 9 (Winter 1963).

CHAPTER 1

An Introduction to the
Family Law Process—
The Case of the Lesser Family

PART ONE

ESTABLISHING WIFE-HUSBAND RELATIONSHIPS

A.

Legislative Decision — Requisites for Marriage

It takes three to make a marriage—a male, a female and a state.[1] The legislature of New York, like the legislature of each state, has promulgated a series of statutory requirements for establishing a new family relationship through marriage. These requisites determine a person's legal capacity to form a "family." How a state perceives the functions of family may in part be discovered in its promulgations for obtaining authority to be married and to marry. In examining such provisions we ask: "What does the state deny or grant in forbidding or authorizing a marriage?" and "Why is the state concerned with who marries whom and with the procedures for establishing such a relationship?"

NEW YORK DOMESTIC RELATIONS LAW

Sec. 5. *Incestuous and void marriages.* A marriage is incestuous and void whether the relatives are legitimate or illegitimate between either:

1. An ancestor and a descendant;
2. A brother and sister of either the whole or the half blood;

---

1. In viewing this descriptive statement as a prescription, students of the family and the law must evaluate the assumed preference in this statement for heterosexual relationships. It is, of course, conceivable that decisionmakers may wish to authorize, though not necessarily prefer, a process and criteria for establishing "marital status" for homosexual partners.

3. An uncle and niece or an aunt and nephew.

If a marriage prohibited by the foregoing provisions of this section be solemnized it shall be void, and the parties thereto shall each be fined not less than fifty nor more than one hundred dollars and may, in the discretion of the court in addition to said fine, be imprisoned for a term not exceeding six months. Any person who shall knowingly and wilfully solemnize such marriage, or procure or aid in the solemnization of the same, shall be deemed guilty of a misdemeanor and shall be fined or imprisoned in like manner.

Sec. 6. *Void marriages.* A marriage is absolutely void if contracted by a person whose husband or wife by a former marriage is living, unless either:

    1. Such former marriage has been annulled or has been dissolved for a cause other than the adultery of such person; . . .

    2. Such former husband or wife has been finally sentenced to imprisonment for life; [2] . . .

Sec. 7. *Voidable marriages.* A marriage is void from the time its nullity is declared by a court of competent jurisdiction if either party thereto:

    1. Is under the age of legal consent, which is eighteen years, provided that such nonage shall not of itself constitute an absolute right to the annulment . . .

    2. Is incapable of consenting to a marriage for want of understanding;

    3. Is incapable of entering into the married state from physical cause;

    4. Consents to such marriage by reason of force, duress or fraud;

    5. Has been incurably insane for a period of five years or more.[3] . . .

Sec. 8. *Marriage after divorce for adultery.* Whenever a marriage has been or shall be dissolved, the complainant may marry again during the lifetime of the defendant. But a defendant for whose adultery the judgment of divorce has been granted in this state may not marry again during the lifetime of the complainant, unless the court in which the judgment of divorce was rendered shall in that respect modify such judgment. . . .

*   *   *

Sec. 10. *Marriage a civil contract.* Marriage, . . . continues to be a civil contract, to which the consent of parties capable in law of making a contract is essential.

Sec. 11. *By whom a marriage must be solemnized.* No marriage shall be valid unless solemnized by either:

    1. A clergyman or minister of any religion, or by the senior leader, or any of the other leaders, of The Society for Ethical Culture. . . .

    2. A mayor, recorder, city magistrate, police justice or police magistrate. . . .

---

2. N.Y. Penal Law Sec. 511: "1. A person sentenced to imprisonment for life is thereafter deemed civilly dead; provided, that such a person may marry while on parole, or after he has been discharged from parole, if otherwise capable of contracting a valid marriage. Such capability shall be deemed to exist where the marriage of a person sentenced to imprisonment for life has been terminated by divorce, annulment, or subsequent remarriage of a former spouse. A marriage contracted pursuant to this section by a person while he is on parole, without the prior written approval of the board of parole, shall be a ground for revocation of the parole. 2. This section shall not apply to a person sentenced to imprisonment for an indeterminate term, having a minimum of one day and a maximum of his natural life."

3. On financial provisions for the incurably insane, see Sec. 141 N.Y. Domestic Relations Law (1963); concerning annulment and legitimacy, see Sec. 145 N.Y. Domestic Relations Law (1963).

3. A justice or judge of a court of record, or of a municipal court, a police justice of a village, or a justice of the peace . . . or,

4. A written contract of marriage signed by both parties and at least two witnesses. . . .

Sec. 12. *Marriage, how solemnized.* No particular form or ceremony is required when a marriage is solemnized . . . by a clergyman or magistrate, but the parties must solemnly declare in the presence of a clergyman or magistrate and the attending witness or witnesses that they take each other as husband and wife. In every case, at least one witness besides the clergyman or magistrate must be present at the ceremony.

* * *

Sec. 13. *Marriage licenses.* It shall be necessary for all persons intended to be married . . . to obtain a marriage license . . . and to deliver said license, within sixty days, to the clergyman or magistrate who is to officiate before the marriage ceremony may be performed. . . .

Sec. 13a. *Physician's examination and serological test of applicant for marriage license.*

1. Except as herein otherwise provided, no application for a marriage license shall be accepted by the town or city clerk . . . unless there shall have been filed with him a statement . . . signed by a duly licensed physician . . . that each applicant has been given [an] examination, including a standard serological test . . . and that in the opinion of the physician the person . . . is not infected with syphilis in a communicable stage.

7. This section shall not apply to either the man or woman, when the woman is pregnant at the time of application for the marriage license.

* * *

Sec. 14. *Town and city clerks to issue marriage licenses; form.* The town or city clerk . . . is hereby empowered to issue marriage licenses . . . which license shall be substantially in the following form:

State of New York,   )

County of ....)

City or town of ....)

Know all men by this certificate that any person authorized by law to perform marriage ceremonies within the state of New York to whom this may come, he, not knowing any lawful impediment thereto, is hereby authorized and empowered to solemnize the rites of matrimony between ———— of ———— in the county of ———— and state of New York and ———— of ———— in the county of ———— and state of New York and to certify the same to be said parties or either of them under his hand and seal in his ministerial or official capacity and thereupon he is required to return his certificate in the form hereto annexed. The statements endorsed hereon or annexed hereto, by me subscribed, contain a full and true abstract of all of the facts concerning such parties disclosed by their affidavits or verified statements presented to me upon the application for this license.

In testimony whereof, I have hereunto set my hand and affixed the seal of said town or city at ——— this ——— day of ——— nineteen ———, at ——— m. Seal.

The form of the certificate annexed to said license and therein referred to shall be as follows:

I, ——— a ———, residing at ——— in the county of ——— and state of New York do hereby certify that I did on this ——— day of ——— in the year A.D., nineteen ———, at ——— m., at ——— in the county of ——— and state of New York, solemnize the rites of matrimony between ——— of ——— in the county of ——— and state of New York, and ——— of ——— in the county of ——— and state of New York in the presence of ——— and ——— as witness, and the license therefore is hereto annexed.

Witness my hand ——— in the county of ——— this ——— day of ——— A.D., nineteen _____

In the presence of _____

_____

_____

* * *

Sec. 15. *Duty of town and city clerks.* It shall be the duty of the . . . clerk . . . to require each of the contracting parties to sign and verify a statement . . . containing the following information. From the groom: Full name of husband, color, place of residence, age, occupation, place of birth, name of father, country of birth, maiden name of mother, country of birth, number of marriage. From the bride: Full name of bride, place of residence, color, age, occupation, place of birth, name of father, country of birth, maiden name of mother, country of birth, number of marriage. The said clerk shall also embody in the statement if either or both of the applicants have been previously married, a statement as to whether the former husband or husbands or the former wife or wives of the respective applicants are living or dead and as to whether either or both of said applicants are divorced persons, if so, when and where and against whom the divorce or divorces were granted and shall also embody therein a statement that no legal impediment exists as to the right of each of the applicants to enter into the marriage state. . . .

If it appears from the . . . statements . . . the persons . . . are legally competent to marry the said clerk shall issue such license. . . . If it shall appear . . . that the man is under twenty one years of age and is not under sixteen years of age, or that the woman is under the age of eighteen years and is not under fourteen years of age, then the . . . clerk before he shall issue a license shall require the written consent to the marriage from both parent of the minor or minors. . . . If the marriage of the parents of such minor has been dissolved by decree of divorce or annulment, the consent of the parent to whom the court which granted the decree has awarded the custody of such minor shall be sufficient. . . .

* * *

Sec. 15a. *Marriages of minors under sixteen years of age.* Any marriage in which the man is under . . . sixteen . . . or . . . the woman is under . . . fourteen . . . is . . . prohibited. . . .

* * *

Sec. 17. *Clergyman or officer violating article; penalty.* If any clergyman or other person authorized . . . to perform marriage ceremonies shall solemnize or presume to solemnize any marriage between any parties without a license being presented to him . . . or with knowledge that either party is legally incompetent to contract matrimony as is provided for in this article he shall be guilty of a misdemeanor and on conviction thereof shall be punished by a fine not less than fifty dollars nor more than five hundred dollars or by imprisonment for a term not exceeding one year.

B.

Decision of an Engaged Couple —

Sadie Pepper and Perry Lesser become Wife and Husband

INTERVIEW WITH SADIE LESSER

Q. [W]ere you engaged for any length of time before March 24, 1935, the day you were married? A. Yes, about two and a half years. We were very young when we met.

Q. Your family knew about the engagement? A. Yes, sir.

Q. Were you both living in the Bronx at the time? A. Just a block from each other.

Q. What was the necessity for the elopement? A. I had an older sister who was engaged at the time but her fiance was not working. My father said, from his standpoint, that I must wait until she becomes married before I could get married. My husband did not want to wait. We had already kept company two and a half years, but we were both very young anyway.

Q. Where did you get your marriage license, New York or the Bronx? A. I don't remember.

Q. Where was the wedding performed? A. In New York City, downtown, on the east side somewhere.

Q. Was this at a rabbi's home? A. I believe he lived there or practiced there.

Q. Anyway, there was no large wedding party? A. No, sir. We were the only two there. The only two of the family.

Q. Were any of your friends or relatives there? A. No, sir. This was a strict elopement.

INTERVIEW WITH PERRY LESSER

Q. Would you state . . . as nearly as you could recall what the marriage ceremony performed by Rabbi Bienenfeld consisted of? A. The ceremony was performed in the Hebraic and English language, both. The certificate there is read during the middle of the ceremony.

Q. And that was in the presence and hearing of course of your wife too? A. Yes, sir.

Q. [W]hat else happened after he read that certificate? A. There was a glass of wine. A prayer was said in connection with it. The bride was given a sip of the wine. The groom was too. The glass was put in a napkin or a piece of paper, put on the floor, and smashed. That is part of the ceremony. Directly after that the Rabbi took this marriage certificate and gave it to the bride.

Q. And were any things said or done by the bride and groom? A. Yes, sir. The Rabbi asked questions and the answers were "I do," both by the bride and groom.

In 1939, 1942, and 1950 new family relationships were established with the birth of Dee, Benjamin, and Larry. At least until December 1955 the Lesser family was counted as an "unbroken home" in the vital statistics of the state. At that time Mrs. Lesser invoked the New York statutes concerned with the administration and reorganization of a family in conflict by commencing an action for separation.

PART TWO

ADMINISTERING AND REORGANIZING WIFE-HUSBAND RELATIONSHIPS

A.

Legislative Decision — Marriage without Bed and Board

Like many states, New York provides essentially four courses for officially modifying wife-husband relationships—(1) *annulment*[1] for the reasons set forth in § 7, p. 10; (2) *divorce* for "adultery";[2] (3) *dissolution* by death of either spouse or because one of them had been "absent" for five successive years, could not be found and is believed to be dead;[3] and (4) *separation from bed and board*[4] under Sec. 200 of the New York Domestic Relations Law. That section, under which Sadie Lesser brought the complaint which commenced this action, and related sections provide:

Sec. 200. *Action for separation.* An action may be maintained by a husband or wife against the other party to the marriage to procure a judgment separating the parties from bed and board, forever, or for a limited time, for any of the following causes:

---

1. See also, N.Y. Domestic Relations Law Secs. 140-146 (1963).
2. N.Y. Domestic Relations Law Secs. 170-177 (1963).
3. N.Y. Domestic Relations Law Secs. 220 and 221 (1963).
4. "Although divorce in the modern sense was not permitted, the canon law ... did retain in the Latin word *divortium*. What the canonists called *divortium a vinculo* (divorce from the bonds of matrimony) is in modern parlance annulment; what they called *divortium a mensa et thoro* (divorce from bed and board) is judicial separation, or limited divorce without the privilege of remarriage. Separation from bed and board was the only remedy allowed by the canon law for causes arising after marriage. Three grounds were recognized: adultery, 'spiritual adultery,' and cruelty. Spiritual adultery was a somewhat vague term, but was usually interpreted to mean the heresy or apostacy of one of the parties to the marriage."—[Blake, N.W.: *The Road to Reno*, New York: Macmillan, 1962 (pp. 14-15).]

1. The cruel and inhuman treatment of the plaintiff by the defendant.
2. Such conduct on the part of the defendant towards the plaintiff as may render it unsafe and improper for the latter to cohabit with the former.
3. The abandonment of the plaintiff by the defendant.[5]
4. Where the wife is plaintiff, the neglect or refusal of the defendant to provide for her.
5. The commission of an act of adultery by the defendant; except where such offense is committed by the procurement or with the connivance of the plaintiff or where there is voluntary cohabitation of the parties with the knowledge of the offense or where action was not commenced within five years after the discovery by the plaintiff of the offense charged or where the plaintiff has also been guilty of adultery under such circumstances that the defendant would have been entitled, if innocent, to a divorce.

* * *

Sec. 201. *Proof.* In an action for a separation, a final judgment shall not be entered by default for want of an appearance or pleading, or by consent, or upon trial of an issue, without proof of the grounds for separation.

* * *

Sec. 202. *Defense of justification.* The defendant in an action for separation from bed and board may set up, in justification, the misconduct of the plaintiff; and if that defense is established to the satisfaction of the court, the defendant is entitled to judgment.

* * *

Sec. 203. *Judgment for separation revocable.* Upon the joint application of the parties, accompanied with satisfactory evidence of their reconciliation, a judgment for a separation, forever, or for a limited period . . . may be revoked at any time by the court which rendered it, subject to such regulations and restrictions as the court thinks fit to impose.

* * *

Sec. 235. *Information as to details of matrimonial actions.* An officer of the court with whom the proceedings in an action to annul a marriage or for divorce or separation are filed, or before whom the testimony is taken, or his clerk, either before or after the termination of the suit, shall not permit a copy of any of the pleadings or testimony, or any examination or perusal thereof, to be taken by any other person than a party, or the attorney or counsel of a party who had appeared in the cause, except by order of the court.

If the evidence on the trial of such an action be such that public interest requires that the examination of the witnesses should not be public, the court or referee may exclude all persons from the room except the parties to the action and their counsel and the witnesses, and in such case may order the evidence, when filed with the clerk, sealed up, to be exhibited only to the parties to the action or some one interested, on order of the court. . . .

---

5. N.Y. Decedent Estate Law Sec. 87. *Effect of divorce, abandonment, or refusal to support upon rights of a parent, or of former husband or wife to distributive share*

No distributive share of the estate of a decedent [surviving spouse's right to elect to take not more than one-half the net estate as in intestacy Sec. 18] shall be allowed . . . either

(a) to a spouse against whom or in whose favor a final decree or judgment of divorce recognized as valid by the law of this state has been rendered;

(b) or to a spouse who has procured without the state of New York a final decree or judgment dissolving the marriage with the decedent, where such decree or judgment is not recognized as valid by the law of this state;

(c) or to a husband who has neglected or refused to provide for his wife, or has abandoned her;

(d) or to a wife who has abandoned her husband; . . . .

Sec. 236. *Alimony, temporary and permanent.* In any action or proceeding brought (1) during the lifetime of both parties to the marriage to annul a marriage or declare the nullity of a void marriage, or (2) for a separation, or (3) for a divorce, the court may direct the husband to provide suitably for the support of the wife as, in the court's discretion, justice requires, having regard to the circumstances of the case and of the respective parties. Such direction may require the payment of a sum or sums of money either directly to the wife or to third persons for real and personal property and services furnished to the wife, or for the rental of or mortgage amortization or interest payments, insurance, taxes, repairs or other carrying charges on premises occupied by the wife, or for both payments to the wife and to such third persons. . . . Such direction may be made notwithstanding that the parties continue to reside in the same abode and notwithstanding that the court refuses to grant the relief requested by the wife (1) by reason of a finding by the court that a divorce, annulment or judgment declaring the marriage a nullity had previously been granted to the husband in an action in which jurisdiction over the person of the wife was not obtained, or (2) by reason of the misconduct of the wife, unless such misconduct would itself constitute grounds for separation or divorce, or (3) by reason of a failure of proof of the grounds of the wife's action or counterclaim. . . .

* * *

Sec. 237. *Counsel fees and expenses.* (a) In any action or proceeding brought (1) to annul a marriage . . . or (2) for a separation, or (3) for a divorce, or . . . (6) upon any application to annul or modify an order for counsel fees and expenses made pursuant to this subdivision provided, the court may direct the husband, or where an action for annulment is maintained after the death of the husband may direct the person or persons maintaining the action, to pay such sum or sums of money to enable the wife to carry on or defend the action or proceeding as, in the court's discretion, justice requires, having regard to the circumstances of the case and of the respective parties. . . .

(b) Upon any application to annul or modify an order or judgment for alimony or for custody, visitation, or maintenance of a child, . . . or upon any application by writ of habeas corpus or by petition and order to show cause concerning custody, visitation or maintenance of a child, the court may direct the husband or father to pay such sum or sums of money for the prosecution or the defense of the application or proceeding by the wife or mother as, in the court's discretion, justice requires, having regard to the circumstances of the case and of the respective parties. . . .

* * *

Sec. 238. *Expenses in enforcement proceedings.* In any action or proceeding to compel the payment of any sum of money required to be paid by a judgment or order entered in an action for divorce, separation, annulment or declaration of nullity of a void marriage, . . . the court may in its discretion require the husband to pay the wife's expenses in bringing, carrying on, or defending such action or proceeding. . . .

* * *

Sec. 240. *Custody and maintenance of children.* In any action or proceeding brought (1) to annul a marriage or to declare the nullity of a void marriage, or (2) for a separation, or (3) for a divorce, or (4) to obtain, by a writ of habeas corpus or by petition and order to show cause, the custody of or right to visitation with any child of a marriage, the court must give such direction, between the parties, for the custody, care, education and maintenance of any child of the parties, as, in the court's discretion, justice requires, having regard to the circumstances of the case and of the respective parties and to the best interests of the child. In all cases there shall be no prima facie right to the custody of the child in either parent. Such direction may make provision for the education and maintenance of such child out of the property of either or both of its parents. Such direction may require the payment of a sum or sums of money either directly to the wife or to third persons for goods or services furnished for such child, or for both payments to the wife and to such third persons. Such direction may be made in the final judgment in such action or proceeding, or by one or more orders from time to time before or subsequent to final judgment, or by both such order or orders and the final judgment. Such direction may be made notwithstanding that the court for any reason whatsoever, other than lack of jurisdiction, refuses to grant the relief requested in the action or proceeding. . . . Upon the application of either the husband or the wife, or of any other person or party having the care, custody and control of such child pursuant to such judgment or order, . . . the court may annul or modify any such direction, whether made by order or final judgment, . . .

*   *   *

Sec. 245. *Enforcement by contempt proceedings of judgment or order in action for divorce, separation or annulment.* Where the husband, in an action for divorce, separation, annulment or declaration of nullity of a void marriage, or for the enforcement in this state of a judgment for divorce, separation, annulment or declaration of nullity of a void marriage rendered in another state, makes default in paying any sum of money as required by the judgment or order directing the payment thereof, and it appears presumptively, to the satisfaction of the court, that payment cannot be enforced by means of the sequestration of his property, or by resorting to the security, if any, given as prescribed by statute, the court in its discretion, may make an order requiring the husband to show cause . . . why he should not be punished for his failure to make the payment; and thereupon proceedings must be taken to punish him, . . . for . . . contempt of court . . . and such punishment, either by fine or commitment, shall not be a bar to a subsequent proceeding to punish him as for a contempt for his failure to pay subsequent installments, . . .

*   *   *

Sec. 246. *Persons financially unable to comply with orders or judgments directing the payment of alimony.* . . . Any person may assert his financial inability to comply with the directions contained in an order or judgment . . . if the court, upon the hearing of such contempt proceeding, is satisfied from the proofs and evidence offered and submitted that the defendant is financially unable to comply with such order or judgment, it may, in its discretion, until further order of the court, make an order modifying such order or judgment and denying the application to punish the defendant for contempt. . . .

*   *   *

B.

Decisions of a Wife, a Husband, and their Attorneys to Seek Marriage without Bed and Board — Informing Whom and for What Purpose ?

1.

THE WIFE INVOKES THE PROCESS

a. Summons Husband

Supreme Court
New York County

SADIE LESSER,
                              Plaintiff,
against
PERRY LESSER, [1]
                              Defendant.

Action for Separation

To the above named Defendant:

YOU ARE HEREBY SUMMONED to answer the complaint in this action, and to serve a copy of your answer, within 20 days after the service of this summons ; and in case of your failure to appear, or answer, judgment will be taken against you by default, for the relief demanded in the complaint.

Dated, New York, December 6, 1955.

ERDHEIM & ARMSTRONG,
Attorneys for Plaintiff.

b. Complains about Husband

Plaintiff, by her attorneys, Erdheim & Armstrong, complaining of the defendant, respectfully shows to this Court and alleges:

As and For a First Cause of Action :

First: That at all times hereinafter mentioned, plaintiff and defendant were and still are residents of the State of New York.

Second: That the parties hereto were duly married on the 24th of March, 1935, in the City and State of New York.

Third: That the issue of this marriage, are three (3) children, to wit, Dee, age 16 ; Benjamin, age 12 ; and Larry, age 5.

Fourth: That on or about the 15th of September, 1955, the defendant did wilfully abandon the

---

[1.] This is an actual record. Dates, names of the parties, and their residence have been changed. Without indicating deletions we have edited the record primarily to reduce repetition.

plaintiff and the infant issue of the marriage, and did leave the home maintained by the parties, in Mount Vernon, without justification, and without intention of returning, and did state that he would not return and has failed and refused to return.

Fifth: That during the time that plaintiff has been the wife of the defendant, she has conducted herself towards the defendant with propriety, managed the household affairs of her husband, with prudence and economy, and has treated the defendant with kindness and forebearance, and has not given the defendant any provocation whatsoever.

Sixth: That the defendant's annual earnings are in excess of $40,000 per year, and he is financially able to support and maintain the plaintiff, and the infant issue herein.

As and For a Second Cause of Action :

Seventh: Plaintiff reiterates every allegation as set forth in plaintiff's "First", "Second", "Third", "Fifth" and "Sixth" paragraphs.

Eighth: That prior to the commencement of this action, defendant practiced a course of cruel and inhuman treatment on the plaintiff.

Ninth: Among other things, defendant has been cruel and inhuman as follows:

(a) That on or about the 8th of September, 1942, while transporting plaintiff home from the hospital, wherein she had given birth to Benjamin, the defendant, without just cause or provocation, caused the automobile he was driving to stop and ordered plaintiff into the street ;

(b) That, when plaintiff finally arrived at the marital residence, defendant unjustifiably refused to admit her, keeping the door locked, and only after the intervention of the police, whom plaintiff contacted, was plaintiff able to gain access ;

(c) That on or about the 5th of August, 1947, at [their] home, the defendant, without just cause or provocation, severely beat the plaintiff in and about the face and body causing pain, extensive bruises, abrasions, cuts and other markings, and requiring plaintiff to obtain necessary medical attention ;

(d) That on or about the 15th of January,

1955, at the marital residence, the defendant, unjustifiably struck the plaintiff in the face with his fist, causing the plaintiff's eyeglasses to shatter, all to her detriment, pain and injury;

(e) That on or about March 26 [and May 29, 1955], at the marital residence, defendant, without just cause or provocation, struck and beat the plaintiff with his fists, and physically forced her into the street, in cold weather, without outer clothing, all to her injury and pain and necessitating medical treatment;

*   *   *

(g) That on or about June 1, 1955, at the residence of the parties the defendant again unjustifiably beat and struck the plaintiff in and about her face and body, thereby injuring her, directed foul, profane and obscene language towards her and threatened to kill her, [and] caused plaintiff to flee, in fear of her life and only with the assistance of the police was plaintiff able to return home;

(h) That on or about November 12, 1955, the defendant returned home and beat and struck the plaintiff to such an extent that she required medical treatment;

(i) That since the marriage of the parties, and prior to September 1st, 1955, the defendant unjustifiably has frequently and regularly absented himself from the marital residence, without notice or explanation and without the consent or knowledge of plaintiff for weeks, and months, at a time; on one occasion going to California for 3 weeks, and on another occasion to Europe for 8 weeks, all to the plaintiff's pain and mental anguish;

(j) That since plaintiff has embraced the Christian Science Religion, defendant has openly and notoriously before the children, relatives, and friends, ridiculed the plaintiff and her religion causing plaintiff to be hurt, embarrassed and injured;

(k) That the defendant unjustifiably removed and burned plaintiff's Bible in the fireplace thereby needlessly embarrassing and injuring plaintiff;

(l) That for the past several years in the home and elsewhere, the defendant, without just cause or provocation, has constantly ridiculed and mocked the plaintiff in front of their children, censoring her discipline, refusing to admit plaintiff to family discussions, taking the children to unknown places without the knowledge or consent of plaintiff, countermanding directions given by the plaintiff to said children, and advising them that they need not follow her directions, and in every way possible attempting to discredit and disgrace the plaintiff in the eyes of the children herein, thereby causing plaintiff pain, suffering and mental anguish;

(m) That for the past several months, prior to his abandonment, the defendant unjustifiably refused to sit or eat at the customary dining table with plaintiff but removed himself and the children to the breakfast room, directing them not to join plaintiff at the customary dining table, all to plaintiff's embarrassment and injury;

(n) That prior to the abandonment, the defendant refused to live or cohabit with the plaintiff, but instead removed himself to a separate room where he slept alone.

As and For a Third Cause of Action:

Tenth: Plaintiff reiterates every allegation as set forth in plaintiff's "First", "Second", "Third", "Fifth", "Sixth" and "Ninth" paragraphs.

*   *   *

Twelfth: That by reason of the foregoing cruel and inhuman treatment of plaintiff by defendant, it has become and is now unsafe and improper for plaintiff to cohabit with the defendant.

As and For a Fourth Cause of Action:

Thirteenth: Plaintiff reiterates paragraphs "First" through "Third" inclusive and paragraphs "Fifth", "Sixth" and "Ninth" of the complaint.

Fourteenth: The defendant is a wealthy owner and operator of a kosher food products company; the defendant owns in his name alone, a large one family home, in which the plaintiff and the issue of the marriage reside, which he has recently placed upon the market for sale; has ample funds for prolonged vacations to California, Bermuda, Europe and elsewhere, which he takes alone, and earns upwards of $40,000.00 per year.

Fifteenth: Prior to the extreme beatings the plaintiff received from the defendant $200.00 or more per week to use for normal household expenses, personal purchases, servants, clothing, food and the like.

Sixteenth: Commencing with the events described, the defendant stopped the payments. Instead, he adopted a system of compelling the plaintiff to plead with him for money for basic necessities, and when it suited the defendant's fancy, he would deposit to her credit a sum that he, in his sole discretion, believed adequate, which sums have been far from adequate to properly support the plaintiff and maintain the household. Plaintiff has, at times, not had sufficient funds to purchase food for the home and, at such times as defendant gives sums to plaintiff the same is done only after the plaintiff pleads and exhorts the defendant to do so.

Seventeenth: That plaintiff has no independent income of her own, no position, job or profession, no possibility or expectation of income, no assets of her own and no hope of supporting herself independently.

Eighteenth: Despite the foregoing, the defendant has refused, although requested on numerous occasions, to restore to the plaintiff the customary payments, which were necessary to maintain the plaintiff and the infant issue, in the station in life to which they had been accustomed as the wife and children of a person of the defendant's economic status.

WHEREFORE, plaintiff demands judgment against the defendant for a decree of separation from the bed and board of the defendant; for custody of the infant issue of the marriage; for support and maintenance of herself, and the infant issue of the marriage; and for such other and further relief as to this Court may seem just and proper.

ERDHEIM & ARMSTRONG,
Attorneys for Plaintiff.

2.
THE HUSBAND ANSWERS AND COUNTER-COMPLAINS

Defendant:

1. Admits each and every allegation contained in paragraph "Third" of the complaint, except denies that Benjamin is age 12.

2. Admits so much of paragraph "Fourth" as alleges that defendant did leave the home in Mount Vernon, N.Y., and, except as so admitted, denies each and every allegation contained in said paragraph.

3. Denies each and every allegation contained in paragraph "Fifth" "Eighth, Twelfth, Fifteenth, Sixteenth, Seventeenth, and Eighteenth".

4. Admits so much of paragraph "Sixth" as alleges that defendant is financially able to support and maintain the plaintiff and the infant issue herein and, except as so admitted, denies each and every allegation in said paragraph contained.

6. Denies each and every allegation contained in paragraph "Ninth" except admits so much of sub-paragraph "(j)" as alleges that "plaintiff has embraced the Christian Science Religion."

* * *

8. Admits so much of paragraph "Fourteenth" as alleges that defendant owns and operates a kosher food company and the house in which plaintiff resides, and the defendant proposes to sell said house and, except as so admitted, denies each and every allegation.

* * *

As an Affirmative Defense and Counterclaim:

13. Prior to and after September 15, 1955, the plaintiff engaged in a course of cruel and inhuman treatment of defendant, as hereinafter more fully alleged.

14. Defendant was born and brought up in the Jewish faith. He has all of his life observed and practiced the rules and rituals of the Hebrew religion.

15. Plaintiff was born in the Jewish faith.

16. Their marriage was ceremonialized by an orthodox Rabbi in accordance with the Hebrew religion.

17. Prior to and with a view to their marriage, the parties mutually agreed that they would maintain their home and conduct their lives in accordance with the tenets, practices and rituals of the Jewish faith, observe its High Holy Days, its dietary laws, and, in general, live in the manner prescribed by tradition for persons of that faith. It was further agreed that any children who might be born to the parties were to be brought up in the Jewish faith and were to be taught the history, religion, practices and rituals of the Hebrew religion.

18. Without these promises and agreements defendant would not have married plaintiff.

19. The issue of this marriage are Dee, age 16, Benjamin, age 13, and Larry, age 5.

20. About the time of the birth of the last born child, plaintiff embraced the Christian Science religion.

21. Ever since, plaintiff has brought the practices and preachings of the Christian Science religion into the home of the parties. She has caused Christian Science literature to be left around the house. She physically destroyed or threw away the book containing the Old Testament which defendant presented and inscribed to his two older children. She has implanted and

continues to implant in the minds of the children the teaching and articles of faith of the Christian Science religion which are wholly inconsistent with the Jewish faith, in which the parties agreed their children would be brought up and in which they were brought up. Despite defendant's frequently repeated requests and entreaties, plaintiff has persisted in such conduct, resulting in great injury to the mental peace and health of the children and causing great pain and mental anguish to defendant.

22. Plaintiff has humiliated defendant by stating to him and his friends that the "Jews are a vanishing race" and that the Jewish people are greedy, mercenary, materialistic, and by uttering other words of deprecation.

23. Plaintiff has attempted to proselytize to the Christian Science religion defendant's Jewish friends and acquaintances and in so doing has caused serious embarrassment and humiliation to defendant.

24. Plaintiff has from time to time stated that, as a student and follower of the Christian Science religion, she did not believe in doctors or surgeons, medicines or surgery and that, in the event of the illness of her children, she would minister to them "metaphysically" and, if necessary, call on a Christian Science "Practitioner", a person who is not licensed to practice medicine or surgery.

25. Plaintiff has imperiled the health and lives of the children by failing and refusing to secure needed medical attention from licensed physicians and surgeons. On many occasions, where medication has been prescribed, plaintiff has failed and refused to give such medication to them and has attempted to encourage the children in the belief that medicine was unnecessary. Plaintiff has continued in such course of conduct despite defendant's frequently repeated requests and entreaties, to defendant's great mental pain and anguish.

26. Within the past month licensed physicians and surgeons recommended that the tonsils and adenoids of Larry be removed. Accordingly, defendant made arrangements for an operation at the Mount Vernon Hospital. After Larry had been taken into the hospital and physically and psychologically prepared for the needed operation, plaintiff came into the hospital and insisted that the operation must not take place. As a result of plaintiff's insistence, the hospital anesthetist refused to proceed and Larry suffered a considerable psychological shock and disturbance to his nervous system. Thereupon, defendant had to remove Larry to a hospital in the City of New York where the operation was duly performed

and plaintiff was promptly notified of the fact so that she could be with her child.

27. The children of the parties are in mortal danger should they become ill or in need of medical or surgical attention. The danger is accentuated by the fact that, by reason of the plaintiff's conduct herein set forth, defendant is unable to live, and no longer does live, with the plaintiff but lives separate and apart from her.

28. Upon claimed instructions from the Deity, plaintiff has put her son Benjamin out of the house and stated that he could not come back.

29. In practically all discussions between plaintiff and defendant, plaintiff would continually respond to observations by claiming that there was no use discussing the matter further with defendant; that her attitude was dictated by the "voice of God" to which she claimed to be attuned.

30. Plaintiff has constantly upbraided and nagged defendant, often in the presence of their children, for "oppressing labor" and for being "selfish" and "greedy" and plaintiff has frequently stated that she has been informed by the Deity that he would visit retribution on defendant for his "sins".

31. Repeatedly plaintiff has assaulted the defendant, particularly during the course of acrimonious discussions concerning the plaintiff's attitude towards, and treatment of, the children. Such assaults were on occasion followed by plaintiff securing a summons charging defendant with assault. No conviction has ever resulted against the defendant.

32. As a result of the humiliation suffered by defendant, defendant has left the house but has continued to support plaintiff and their children. Defendant makes frequent visits largely to assure himself of the condition of the health of the children and to make appropriate arrangements for their medical needs.

33. Defendant demands custody of the children on the ground that their continued living with plaintiff presents a threat to their health, safety and lives.

WHEREFORE, defendant demands judgment dismissing the complaint and granting defendant a decree of separation from the bed and board; for custody of the issue of the marriage; and for such other relief as to this Court may seem just and proper.

POMERANTZ, LEVY & HAUDEK,
Attorneys for Defendant.

3.
THE WIFE REPLIES

The plaintiff, by Erdheim & Armstrong, her attorneys:

First: Admits each and every allegation as contained in paragraphs "15", "16", and "19".

Second: Denies each and every allegation as contained in paragraphs "13", "17", "18", "20", "22", "23", "24", "25", "26", "28", "29", "30", "31", "32" and "33".

Third: Denies each and every allegation as contained in paragraph "14", except admits that defendant was born in the Jewish faith.

Fourth: Denies each and every allegation as contained in paragraph "21", except admits Christian Science literature may be found in plaintiff's bedroom.

Fifth: Denies each and every allegation as contained in paragraph "27", except admits defendant lives separate and apart from plaintiff.

WHEREFORE, plaintiff demands judgment for the relief demanded in her complaint, and for judgment dismissing the counterclaim of the defendant, together with the costs and disbursements of this action.

ERDHEIM & ARMSTRONG,
Attorneys for Plaintiff.

C.
Informing the Judge for Decision—Lesser v. Lesser, Trial I—1956

What is the function of the trial?

To facilitate and encourage separate examinations of the state's role in reorganizing and administering adult family relationships and parent-child relationships, we have divided the record of these proceedings into two separate sections. The second half of the proceedings, which is primarily focused on problems concerned with the disposition of the Lesser children, is presented in PART THREE.

Here the proceedings concerned with the husband-wife relationship are the subject for analysis: How would you evaluate these proceedings and the work of the participants? Put somewhat differently, what is or ought to be the function of the trial?

Prior to the trial, which took place before Justice Streit, two judges, for reasons not disclosed in the record, declined to hear this case.

LESSER v. LESSER

Before:

Mr. Justice Saul S. Streit

November 28, 1956.

THE COURT. Would you bring me up-to-date, gentlemen, so far, as to what happened in Special Term?

MR. POMERANTZ. A motion for counsel fees with respect to defending the counterclaim was made by Mr. Erdheim on behalf of the plaintiff.

Upon our withdrawing the defendant's counterclaim Judge Hofstadter denied the motion for a temporary counsel fee award with respect to that counterclaim.

MR. ERDHEIM. I made application for a counsel fee to defend the counterclaim but made no application with respect to the prosecution of the action because I still did not know what services I was going to render.

When I made such application, the defendant then withdrew his counterclaim and then the application became academic, of course.

THE COURT. There is no specific request for a separation on the part of the defendant?

MR. POMERANTZ. That is right. We are merely opposing plaintiff's request.

THE COURT. Have you made application for alimony?

MR. ERDHEIM. No, sir.

MR. POMERANTZ. The weekly payments have been continuing as in the past.

THE COURT. Call the first witness.

1.
SADIE LESSER—PLAINTIFF

a. Direct Examination by Mr. Erdheim

Q. Is the defendant Perry Lesser your husband?
A. Yes, Sir.

Q. Are there any children issue of the marriage?
A. Yes, sir, three. Dee is 17. Benjamin is 14. Larry is 6.

Q. Do you desire the custody of these children? A. Yes, sir.

Q. And do you desire support and maintenance for yourself and children? A. Yes, sir.

Q. Dee, who is now 17 years of age, where is she at the present time? A. She is away at college.

Q. And is the defendant paying for her education and her board? A. Yes, sir.

Q. Now, Benjamin, who is 14 years of age, does he live with you? A. No, sir. He is living with his father.

Q. Is that with your consent? A. No, sir.

Q. And where does Larry reside? A. He lives with me.

Q. Does Benjamin attend school? A. Yes, sir. Junior High School.

Q. And does Larry attend school? A. Yes, sir.

Q. Tell the Court what took place on the 15th of September, 1955. A. My husband told me he was going to leave me and pack most of his things and he said he would not return and he left.

Q. From the 15th to the present date, has your husband come home to live with you and the children? A. No, sir.

Q. Prior to the 15th, did you take care of the household and the children? A. Yes, sir.

Q. Before September 15, 1955, how much money were you receiving for the running of the household? A. $209 a week.

Q. And in addition to the $209 a week, did you pay for the maintenance of the house or was that extra? A. That was paid by my husband.

Q. What was the $209 for, Mrs. Lesser? A. For a maid, laundress, food, my own clothing and some of the children's.

Q. Who paid the taxes on the house and the interest payments on the mortgages? A. My husband did.

Q. Did you own an automobile? A. Yes, sir. A Cadillac.

Q. Did your husband own an automobile? A. Yes, sir. A Lincoln.

Q. After September 15, 1955, did your husband continue to give you the $209 a week? A. No, sir. He gradually decreased it—the first time to $165 a week, then to $125 a week, and then to $100 a week.

Q. When did he start giving you the $100 a week? A. When my daughter left for college in September.

Q. Do you recall an incident taking place on the 8th day of September, 1942? A. Yes, sir.

Q. What, if anything, took place on that date?

MR. POMERANTZ. Instead of objecting, may I ask counsel whether he is referring to any allegation in the complaint? If so, I may want to object to it on the ground of possible condonation. What are you referring to?

MR. ERDHEIM. Paragraph A of the second cause of action.

THE COURT. It is in there. I will allow it.

BY MR. ERDHEIM

THE WITNESS. I was on the way home from the hospital, having given birth to my second child. My husband objected to the way that I held the child and I answered that having had one child, I knew how to hold a child.

He became very abusive and ordered me to put the child down on the seat of the car and leave the car.

Q. Did you leave the car? A. Yes. He insisted that I do so.

Q. What did you do with the eight-day-old baby? A. I left the baby with him.

Q. What happened after that? A. I began to walk—it was a residential district—and I could not find a telephone or a policeman, so I kept on walking until I came to my sister's home. I stayed there a while. Then I decided I would either get a policeman or go home, but I went home, and he refused to allow me into the house.

I heard my three-year-old daughter crying for me, so I pleaded with him to let her come out, which he did.

I walked with her until I found a police car and the policeman came back with me and finally ordered that he let me in.

Q. Do you recall the 5th day of August, 1947? A. Yes, sir. My husband beat me cruelly. He just punched me about the face and neck and he was abusive in every way.

Q. Did you bear any marks on your body as a result of that? A. Yes, sir, for about two or three weeks.

Q. Do you recall doing or saying anything which would cause Mr. Lesser to strike you? A. No, sir.

Q. How do you recall that this incident took place on August 5, 1947? A. Well, my family saw the condition I was in and they advised me to have pictures taken.

Q. Did you consult a lawyer on that occasion? A. Yes, I did.

Q. And was it on the advice of an attorney that you had pictures taken? A. Yes, sir.

MR. ERDHEIM. So that the record may be protected, may I at this time make a formal application on behalf of the plaintiff for a counsel fee. I do not recall that I made such a formal application. At the conclusion of the trial I would like to submit proof with respect to the services rendered.

THE COURT. All right.

BY MR. ERDHEIM

Q. Tell the Court what on the 15th of January

1955, if anything, you or the defendant said to each other or what if anything the defendant did to you. A. Well, we did not speak to each other at all. I was sitting and reading a periodical on Christian Science. My husband walked into the room. Seeing the book I was reading, he struck me in the face, breaking my glasses.

Q. Do you recall the 26th day of March, 1955? A. Yes, sir. I was in the kitchen of my home preparing dinner because the maid was out. My husband asked for a certain book. I said that I had discarded it. He lifted me bodily and threw me out the door and locked the door.

Q. What was the weather condition at the time? A. I would just like to clarify that. He asked for the old Jewish Testament——

MR. POMERANTZ. I object to any clarification.

BY MR. ERDHEIM

Q. What was the weather condition at the time? A. It was a clear cold day. About 7 o'clock in the evening.

Q. And when you were thrown out of the house, what clothing, if any, were you wearing? A. I was wearing a sweater and a skirt.

Q. What happened when you were thrown out in the street? A. I walked to my car and I sat there for five hours because I had no key, no car keys, and no coat. I tried to decide what to do. I was ashamed to go to the neighbors, so I sat there crying for about three hours when my daughter came out with my coat, my car keys and some money.

Q. Now, you said you went to the police? A. Yes, sir. They told me——

Q. You cannot say what they told you.

MR. POMERANTZ. I am not objecting.

BY MR. ERDHEIM

Q. Tell us. A. They told me to go to a hotel for the night and to swear out a warrant or a complaint rather in the morning because there was no one there that night. So I slept at the hotel.

Q. What did you do the next morning? A. I went to the police and I swore out a complaint.

Q. This information was finally withdrawn, is that correct? A. Yes, sir.

Q. Did an incident take place on May 29, 1955? A. Yes, sir. My husband walked in and administered a beating. He abused me generally. He struck me many times.

Q. Did you file an information against your husband on that assault? A. Yes, sir.

Q. Did you finally withdraw that summons, Mrs. Lesser? A. Yes, sir. We had reconciled.

Q. Now, do you recall June 1, 1955, some three days after the May 29th incident? A. My husband came home and beat me again and tore my books. He went into my room, tore my books,

and he proceeded to mistreat me.

Q. Now, at the time he struck you, did he use any language? A. Yes. He said he would kill me. At that time he was quite abusive.

Q. At the time your husband made the statement that he was going to kill you, did it produce any fears in you? A. Yes. I went to the police and they came back to the house with me, but he was not there any longer.

Q. When did your husband return that day or the next day, if at all? A. That evening.

Q. You have testified that on September 15th your husband left you and did not return to the house, is that correct? A. Yes, sir.

Q. Now, on November 12, 1955, did your husband come to your house? A. Yes, sir.

Q. And was that to visit the children? A. Well, he came very late at night, as I recall. He came about two o'clock in the morning and he proceeded to beat me.

Q. Where were you at the time? A. I was in bed.

Q. What did he do or say to you? When you say he beat you, what did he do? A. He threw me on the floor, off the bed, and he proceeded to pummel me.

Q. Did you have any marks about you at that time? A. Just a few black and blue marks.

Q. How long did they last? A. About a week or ten days.

Q. Were you examined by a physician on November 13, 1955? A. Yes, sir. Dr. Reardon.

MR. ERDHEIM. May I consult with Mr. Pomerantz for a moment, your Honor?

THE COURT. Yes.

MR. POMERANTZ. If this will serve to dispense with the calling of the doctor, I have no objection to it.

MR. ERDHEIM. I offer in evidence the medical report of Dr. Reardon in lieu of calling the doctor to testify and Mr. Pomerantz has no objection.

BY MR. ERDHEIM

Q. From the time of your marriage and up to the first day of September 1955, did your husband frequently absent himself, without your knowledge and consent? A. Yes, sir.

Q. Would you take the last few years prior to September 15, 1955—tell the Court where he went and for how long a period of time. A. He went to Israel for eight or ten weeks.

Q. Did you know he was going? A. No, sir.

Q. And in what manner did you find out that your husband was leaving the country and going to Israel? A. I was shopping at a supermarket and I met a woman who is the wife of a doctor and she told me that my husband had gone to her husband for injections prior to going overseas to Europe. That is how I found out.

Q. And when was that before he left, did you discover that? A. About a week.

Q. Did you speak to your husband about that discovery? A. Yes. I said I was packed and that I was ready to go with him.

Q. And what did he say? A. He said, "You cannot go with me." He said, "You cannot go with me and you probably would not want to take those injections because you are a Christian Scientist."

I said I would take them because that is the state law or the law of the country.

Q. Did you go? A. No. He refused to take me anyhow.

Q. Where else did your husband go? A. He went to British Columbia and the Northwestern part of the United States on a tour or visit of some kind, I don't know which, and he took the children to Bermuda, out of school, the two older children.

Q. Did you know that he was taking the children? A. No, sir.

Q. And were you invited along on this trip? A. No, sir.

Q. Did you consent to the children being taken out of school and going with your husband to Bermuda? A. I couldn't do anything about this.

MR. POMERANTZ. I object and move to strike out the answer.

THE COURT. Strike it out.

BY MR. ERDHEIM

Q. Did you object to your husband taking the children? A. No, sir. I felt it would be useless.

Q. How long were they gone to Bermuda? A. Five or six days.

Q. Were there any other trips your husband took without your knowledge or without you being along? A. Oh, yes. He has gone to Florida in the past few months at least 15 or 20 times.

Q. Has he ever taken you on any of these trips? A. No, sir.

Q. Of what religious faith were you some years ago? A. Jewish faith.

Q. Have you since embraced any other religious faith? A. Yes, sir. Christian Scientist.

Q. And would you tell the Court where and when you embraced such faith? A. Well, it is difficult to give you an exact time. I would say about five years ago.

Q. Notwithstanding the fact that you embraced the Christian Science faith, in what manner did you run your house? A. Kosher, according to the way my husband demanded that it be run.

Q. And was your son Benjamin confirmed in accordance with the Hebrew Orthodox faith? A. Yes, sir, he was confirmed.

Q. What if anything took place, will you tell the Court, when the children sat down to eat, were you permitted to sit at the same table? A. No. I was told I could not sit with them while he was eating with the children.

Q. Are you able to fix any dates? A. No, sir.

Q. And why is it that you cannot fix any dates? A. Because it happened one or two nights a week, on the one or two nights a week that he came home for dinner.

BY THE COURT

Q. I assume this happened during the same five years you embraced the Christian Science faith? A. Yes, sir.

BY MR. ERDHEIM

Q. Did any incidents take place when friends did come into your house? A. Well, he insulted me and he insulted them, too.

Q. What did he do or say? A. On one occasion he said to a Christian friend, he made a remark that was not quite right about her religion.

At one time he asked one of my Christian Science friends to leave, pointedly, which she did.

Q. Before September 15, 1955, while your husband was living in the house, did he permit any of your friends into the home? A. No, sir.

Q. When did he direct you that your friends were not allowed to come into the house? A. He said it on quite a number of occasions, when he first began throwing out my books and opposing me about Christian Science—I would say from three years back.

Q. Do you recall an incident when one of your bibles was burnt? A. And other books.

MR. POMERANTZ. I object to the question as being leading.

THE COURT. Well, he has been leading the witness right along with respect to dates and incidents.

MR. POMERANTZ. I know, and in the interest of expediting the trial, I have not objected.

THE COURT. I will sustain the objection.

BY MR. ERDHEIM

Q. Do you recall an incident involving the bible? A. Yes, sir. About two years ago my husband took all the books out of the drawers in my room and from under the bed where I had them hidden.

He had a fire going in the fireplace. He just threw them in there and he burned them.

Q. Did any incidents take place between yourself and your husband in front of the children? A. He belittled me constantly. On numerous occasions he said that they did not have to obey me because I was insane.

Q. And this started when? A. About three years ago.

Q. And as a result of these directions by your husband, to the children, did the children obey you? A. No, sir. They became very rebellious. They became confused, rebellious, insubordinate toward any directions I gave them, or any supervision that was required, in particular, Benjamin.

Q. Did there come a time, Mrs. Lesser, before September 15, 1955, when your husband removed himself to another room? A. Yes, sir—I am sorry—no, sir—he removed me to another room.

BY THE COURT

Q. Are you talking about a bedroom? A. Yes, sir.

Q. Up to that time you had shared a common bedroom? A. On and off, yes. I had been removed a number of times, as I said, in the three years. He removed my clothing.

Q. How many rooms are there in this house in Mount Vernon? A. There are eleven rooms.

Q. How many bedrooms? A. Five and a maid's room.

Q. When things were running smoothly, you both shared a master bedroom? A. Yes, sir.

Q. When you say "removed" did he suggest you go to another room? A. No. He just threw my clothing on top of me while I was in bed, out of the closet, and I had no other closet in that room, so everything lay on the floor for weeks until I joined my son's closet. He locked his door and said I could not come back in.

Q. Let us see if we understand each other. We are talking about the time this sleeping in another room started. This was six or eight months before September 15th. Was that the first time? A. No, sir. There were other times before that when he told me to sleep in the next room and he locked the door or closed it.

Q. Did you go to the other room? A. Yes, sir.

Q. Did you let your clothes lay on the floor for a period of time? A. Yes, sir.

Q. Couldn't you pick them up and put them someplace else? A. Yes, sir, but my children objected to my putting them with their things.

Q. After he left the house, couldn't you go in there and pick up the clothes? A. Yes, sir.

Q. Why should they lay there for any length of time? A. I had no place to put them.

Q. So you left them on the floor? A. No, sir. I put them on the bed.

MR. ERDHEIM. I offer in evidence a photostatic copy of the 1954 individual income tax return of Perry and Sadie Lesser.

MR. POMERANTZ. I have no objection. May I suggest, along the lines of our off the record discussion, that perhaps these financial matters might await the conclusion of the substantive issues of right and wrong involved in this lawsuit?

MR. ERDHEIM. That is going into my fourth cause of action, your Honor.

MR. POMERANTZ. I have no objection. May I state for the record as I have said off the record, that pursuant to a notice to produce served on me last week, I believe we have produced all of the material that Mr. Erdheim requested.

It is available to his inspection. I rather imagine that we can save this court a great deal of time. There will be no controversy about Mr. Lesser's means, both of income and of assets when we are through and if Mr. Erdheim and I will take an hour or two to go through that material I am sure in the form of a stipulation, we will be able to give you in five minutes what might otherwise take a court day to present.

I respectfully urge Mr. Erdheim to desist from making further proof as to Mr. Lesser's means until he has had an opportunity to inspect the material he has requested.

THE COURT. I recommend that procedure.

MR. ERDHEIM. I will go along but I am just trying to make out the fourth cause of action, that's all.

THE COURT. Very well.

BY MR. ERDHEIM

Q. What is your husband giving you at this time weekly? A. He is giving me $100 a week.

Q. Who owns the building in which you are living? A. My husband.

Q. What did your husband do with respect to the house which you and your family were living in after September 15, 1955. A. He placed it with the Realty Board and people began to come to see the house regularly.

Q. Had your husband made any arrangements to move you and your children elsewhere? A. No, sir.

Q. After your husband left the home on September 15, 1955, were there any outstanding bills which your husband refused to pay? A. Yes, sir.

MR. POMERANTZ. To save time, may I ask counsel whether in fact those bills were paid by Mr. Lesser?

MR. ERDHEIM. I don't know. I sent them to you and you returned the bills.

THE COURT. He is obligated to pay them, isn't he?

MR. ERDHEIM. Yes, but I wanted to show that credit was stopped.

MR. POMERANTZ. Since you are not going to prove that they were not and I assert that they were [paid], I object to this line of testimony as wholly irrelevant to the issue, on the basis of your statement that you are not going to prove that the bills were unpaid.

All that you are establishing is that maybe Mr. Lesser is a poor credit risk. If that is your thesis, I believe it is not relevant to this issue.

THE COURT. I do not see that you have to go into that, Mr. Erdheim. Next question.

BY MR. ERDHEIM

Q. In the event that the Court awards you the custody of the children, should the children require medical attention, notwithstanding your religious beliefs, will you call a physician?   A. Yes, sir.

Q. And have you, in the past, since you have adopted the Christian Science faith, called physicians for your children?   A. Yes, sir.

Q. You are not employed, are you?   A. No, sir.

Q. Do you have any income of your own?   A. No, sir.

b. Cross Examination by Mr. Pomerantz

Q. Mrs. Lesser, please try to keep up your voice. If necessary, shout a little, so we can all hear you.

You testified in answer to a question by your lawyer concerning an episode of March 28, 1955, and as I wrote down your testimony you said this:

That you were in the kitchen preparing dinner that day and your husband asked you for a certain book and, I quote you exactly, you said, "a certain book," and you said to your husband "I discarded the book."

That was the day, you recall, when your husband, you testified, put you out in the street.

Will you tell his Honor, what was the name of that certain book which your husband asked you for and which you discarded?   A. The Holy Scriptures.

Q. And is it not the fact, Mrs. Lesser, that the book or books you discarded, the Old Testament, were owned by your children Dee and Benjamin, and were given to them by your husband inscribed by your husband to them? Are all those things true?   A. I don't know of the occasion wherein he gave them to the children.

Q. Is it true at least that your children owned the books that you destroyed?   A. I don't know. I was not in the room when he gave them to the children, but they were in the book case.

Q. Do you know whether those books were ever used by your oldest daughter Dee, the books which you destroyed?   A. No, sir, I don't know.

Q. By the way, is it two books you destroyed or just one?   A. Just one.

Q. And you say you don't know whether Dee ever read out of the Bible?   A. No, sir.

Q. And would you say that Benjamin ever read out of that book which you destroyed?   A. I don't know.

Q. Isn't it true that you heard Benjamin reading out of that book in your presence and hearing?   A. Yes, sir, afterwards, on occasional Friday nights, they would read one or two stanzas at my husband's direction, at the table.

Q. Would you please say what your husband said to these children which constituted the direction that they read the Bible?   A. "Dee, get the Bible."

Q. Well, would they read something out of the Bible?   A. Yes, sir, occasionally, not on every Friday night.

Q. Well, they certainly would not do it when your husband was not around and when you were present, would they?   A. No, sir.

Q. And that is because, isn't it true, you tried to discourage your children from reading the Old Testament? I want the truth.   A. No, sir. I never told them not to read it.

Q. Isn't it true that quite to the contrary you tried to proselytize your children to Christian Science?   A. No, sir. I did not proselytize the children.

Q. Well, let me put it this way: Did you ever discuss with Dee or with Benjamin or with your youngest boy Larry any of the ideology or ideas or theories or precepts or anything concerning Christian Science?   A. No, sir.

Q. You are sure of that?   A. Yes, sir. I will clarify it if you want me to. Regarding Dee, who I thought would understand what I was talking about, I read a few articles from the Christian Science Sentinel to her when she was ill at one time. She listened to me but said, "Mother, I think I would rather have a doctor," and I immediately went to the phone and called a doctor.

Q. You mean you read her the article from the Sentinel in the hope that you could persuade her not to call a doctor, is that right?   A. Yes, sir, in the hope that she would understand it, but I don't think she did.

BY THE COURT

Q. You read some articles in accordance with the Christian Science Faith in an attempt to heal her or assuage her pain, is that what you mean?   A. Also to eliminate her fears.

Q. Concerning her ailment?   A. Yes, sir.

Q. And she said, "I would rather have a doctor"?   A. She allowed me to finish and a few hours later, when she felt that she wanted the doctor, I called the doctor.

Q. What was the matter with her?   A. This is going back quite a while, that I read the Sentinel to her. It was two or three years ago. It must have been a sore throat or an infection, but I don't recall. It is about the only ailment she has had in the last few years.

BY MR. POMERANTZ

Q. What did you mean by saying to his Honor that you read the article for the purpose of eliminating her fears? A. Well, she evidently had an infection, because an infection can turn into blood poisoning, according to present beliefs, and I felt that eliminating fear would be the beginning of eliminating disease.

Q. In other words, it is true, is it not, that the so-called mental healing and practices and preachments by Christian Science is aimed at persuading people who believe they are sick that they are really not sick at all but merely suffering from fears, merely suffering from lack of faith?

Is that a fair summary, and, if it is not, will you please correct it?

MR. ERDHEIM. I object to that as immaterial to the issues herein, what the general theory is. What happened in this case is material.

THE COURT. I will allow her to answer the question.

THE WITNESS. I will do the best I can, your Honor.

BY THE COURT

Q. Go ahead. A. Christian Science is a way of life. It is a way of living honestly and simply and purely, and that is the basis of our way of life.

We do not feel any necessity for doctors because we live that way. The beginning of any ailment, we feel, is the beginning of some mind problem or disease of the mind, and that can be eliminated by first eliminating the fear.

It has nothing to do with lack of faith, because a good many people have lack of faith, but a good many people do have faith.

That is the best I can do in explaining the little I know.

BY MR. POMERANTZ

Q. Perhaps we can apply that practically for the Court in these terms:

There came a time within the past year when your youngest child, then age 5, was ordered to a hospital to have his tonsils removed. Do you recall that occasion? A. Yes, sir. He was not ordered to the hospital, according to my knowledge, because I had him to a physician who said that there was no need and no hurry to have the child's tonsils removed.

Q. Were you in consultation with Dr. Bass as to the necessity of the tonsillectomy which he recommended? A. Yes, sir. He told me he had seen the child upon a previous occasion, perhaps a week or two before, I don't know when my husband took him there, but he did not tell me that the tonsils must come out that week, because I claimed that the child had a cold at the time and that I felt the anesthesia would affect him.

He had mucus in his throat and he was coughing slightly.

Q. And what did Dr. Bass say about your fears? Did he agree with them or did he say the child ought to be operated upon? A. He said that it could wait.

Q. Now, what other doctors, if you know, had examined your son Larry prior to his arrival at the Mount Vernon Hospital for tonsillectomy? A. Dr. Smith.

Q. Now, did you arrive at the Mount Vernon Hospital one morning right on the verge of your son's going into the operating room? A. I arrived while he was in the laboratory with his father.

Q. And do you know whether he had been physically and medically prepared for his operation, I mean specifically by blood tests and so forth? A. I don't know at what stage or point they were in the examination when I arrived.

Q. Did you have any conversations with any doctor, nurse, anesthetist or other persons in the Mount Vernon Hospital? A. Yes, sir. A strange doctor, whose name I did not know, who was in charge of the operating room, appeared while I was waiting for my little boy to come up from the laboratory.

They allowed me to wait there and I asked him whether my son had been operated upon yet and he said no, but his name was on the list.

I said, "Doctor, will you please examine him first, because I feel that he should not be operated upon because of the mucus in his throat and I am afraid of the anesthesia."

He said, "I will do my best to look him over when he arrives in the operating room."

Q. Who else did you speak to in the hospital that morning in connection with your son's proposed operation? A. No one that I recall.

Q. Would it refresh your recollection that you told the nurse who was taking your boy to the operating room that under no circumstances was she to take him up there. A. Oh, no, sir, I don't speak that way to people.

Q. Well, forget my tone of voice, which I can assure you I do not use, but in your probably more ladylike tones what did you say to the nurse about removing your son to the operating room? A. All I asked her was if she knew my son. She said, "He is probably in the laboratory. Wait here."

Then I got impatient and I went down to the laboratory and I saw my husband and child there. I walked over to my child. I think I kissed them. Then I went off with both of them to the receiving room and I stayed there awhile and I read some stories to another little boy, because my husband would not let me go near my boy.

Q. And you did not say to your boy, in words or in substance, something about that if he had faith the operation would not be necessary? A. No, sir.

Q. Cutting across a lot of conversation, did you tell anybody connected with the Mount Vernon Hospital, that they were not to go forward with the operation? A. No, sir, except that I told you the conversation with the first doctor and I did not order him not to go forward. I just asked him to look at the child.

Q. Do you know as a matter of fact that the operation was not performed at the Mount Vernon Hospital? A. Yes, sir.

Q. And thereafter did you receive a telephone call from me or more accurately from your lawyer, who in turn heard from me that the child had been operated upon at Mt. Sinai and you could come down to hold his hand or be with him? A. Yes, sir.

Q. And you came to Mt. Sinai after the operation? A. Yes, sir.

Q. Do you believe your presence at Mount Vernon Hospital that morning had something to do with retarding or delaying or trying to prevent the operation of your son in that hospital that morning? A. Yes, sir. I tried to delay it because I felt there was a danger for my child.

Q. Did any of the doctors in the Mount Vernon Hospital or any nurse therein confirm your apprehension? A. There was one other doctor that I spoke to, but he said if it was his child he would have the child operated upon.

I said, "Well, I have had my child to Dr. Morley Smith and he said there is no need for the operation now, that it can certainly wait."

He is the only other doctor that I spoke to. I believe Mr. Lesser sent him in.

Q. Is it true that over a period of about a year —I am not being strictly accurate with dates— your son Larry suffered from colds rather frequently? A. That is untrue.

Q. Apropos of your statement that your son did not suffer from colds during the year more or less prior to the tonsillectomy, is it true that a Dr. Foreman, during the course of that year, prescribed medicines for your son Larry to take? A. Yes, sir.

Q. And is it also true that the medicines which the doctor prescribed for your son to take were not given to your five-year-old boy by you? A. As I recall, perhaps the first bottle I gave only one teaspoon out of it and my doctor administered some and the maid administered the rest.

Q. Isn't it true that the reason your maid administered medicine to your son Larry was because your husband gave your maid instructions to do so since you refused to do so? That is true, isn't it? A. At one time it was true, but not when I learned better.

BY THE COURT
Q. When you learned better? A. Yes. I learned not to oppose my husband because I was a Christian Scientist and that my thoughts were perhaps different from his, and since he wanted materia medica I felt it was useless to oppose him.

Q. Materia medica is a term applied to those who believe in medicine and want to use medicine as distinguished from Christian Science? A. Yes, sir.

Q. Since he wanted materia medica, you decided to yield and let him have it? A. Yes, sir, to keep the peace, perhaps.

BY MR. POMERANTZ
Q. And you wanted to keep peace in the house? A. Yes, sir. I felt he was the father and he had some rights too over his children.

Q. Well, as a matter of fact, did you feel he had the right to bring up his children as Jews, speaking about his rights? A. Not any more than I had the right to bring up my children as Christian Scientists.

BY THE COURT
Q. There came a time when you felt the children should be brought up as Scientists? A. No, sir.

Q. Was there a clash between you and your husband as to what religious tenets, if any, should be taught the children? A. No, sir. I never objected to the children having the Jewish faith, even though it was against mine.

Q. I am merely referring to some statement you just made in answer to counsel's questions, wherein Mr. Pomerantz said your husband had certain rights in respect to the religious beliefs in which the children were to be brought up and you said that you also had certain rights. A. Yes, sir.

Q. That led me to believe there was some difference between you as to what to teach the children. Was there? A. No, sir.

BY MR. POMERANTZ
Q. Well, let us pursue that a little further. I hold in my hand a batch of pamphlets. As I hand them to you, I ask you to tell me whether or not you brought these pamphlets into your home?

I show you first one pamphlet entitled "The House With The Colored Windows." It shows a picture of two young children on it. A. Yes, sir. I brought that into the home.

MR. POMERANTZ. I offer it in evidence for the purpose of intending to negative the testimony of the witness in the last answer to your Honor's question—for the purpose of showing that this woman was propagandizing her children by pamphlets and literature brought into the home, literature on the art or science of Christian Science, and for the purpose of showing, so far as the issues in this case are concerned, that these children were subjected and are daily subjected to the conflicting talks of mutually antithetic religions, and the last proposition I will bring out in a few minutes.

THE COURT. Of course, no one of you have given me any memoranda or proof on the subject.

I take it now from what you just said that there is a contention on the part of the defendant that the plaintiff had no right, authority or power to endeavor to teach her children and the children of her husband any religion other than that of her husband. Is that your contention?

MR. POMERANTZ. Any religion other than that of their marital religion, not the husband's.

If these children had been born in different faiths, it would be a different problem.

THE COURT. I will put it in the manner you just enunciated. I take it that it is the defendant's contention that these two people, the plaintiff and the defendant, have been married in the Jewish faith and this plaintiff having later adopted the Christian Science faith, that she was without power, right or authority to endeavor to, as you call it, propagandize or teach their children any other faith but that in which they contractually married.

Is that your contention?

MR. POMERANTZ. Yes, your Honor, but let me add to it these additional points. I should have prepared a brief on the subject, because there is a considerable body of law on it.

This is our view. Here are two Jewish people. It is not a case of a mixed religious marriage. They are both Jewish. They were people who were married in the orthodox faith by an orthodox rabbi, who made an orthodox contract that the children would be brought up in the Jewish faith.

THE COURT. Is this an oral or a written contract?

MR. POMERANTZ. This is in writing. Perhaps I should have offered this document before this, but I will in a moment.

Now let me say this: These children were brought up, from circumcision to Bar Mitzvah, as Jewish children. They were brought up in a Jewish dietetic home. They observed all of the Jewish laws and regulations.

I say that with that background it was absolutely, under the cases in the State of New York, and I might say under the cases involving international conventions, absolutely improper, incorrect and a violation of the common law, of

the contract law, of the juridical recognition of religious rights, for the mother, when the eldest girl is twelve, when the boy, now confirmed, was nine, when the youngest child was perhaps one year of age, to shift the rules of the game, if I may lapse into a colloquial expression of the formula, because there is one thing the law has recognized above everything else, and that is that the finest way to make neurotics and even psychotics out of children is to have parents tugging away at them with conflicting——

THE COURT. Now, just a minute. As I understand you now, it is the defendant's contention that at the time of the contracting and at the time of the performance of the marriage ceremony, when the marriage contract was entered into— and you say you have a written contract—that there was an agreement to bring the children up in the Jewish faith.

MR. POMERANTZ. I did say that, your Honor, and I do have it.

THE COURT. Having done so, and thereafter this plaintiff having adopted the Christian Science faith, she was without right, power or authority to attempt to propagandize or to convert these children into the Christian Science faith.

Is that your contention?

MR. POMERANTZ. That is exactly my contention, which I will back up by cases about which there will be no contrariety.

MR. ERDHEIM. That is not the issue in this case.

MR. POMERANTZ. It is not the only issue.

MR. ERDHEIM. First of all, the marriage contract and I have just glanced at it, does not say anything with respect to the bringing up of the children.

MR. POMERANTZ. We are ready to offer external proof to show that that clause means to bring up the children as Jewish children, in accordance with the laws of Israel and Moses.

If it is not conceded, we will offer proof that that means as Jewish children.

MR. ERDHEIM. That is not the issue in this case. The issue in this case is whether or not, on the question of custody, this Court in his own mind can determine:

1. Is this woman a fit and proper person to take care of the children?

2. Will she take care of the children, will she look after these children, the way a mother should?

I do not think religion enters into the question of custody.

THE COURT. I am not going into that at this moment.

The Charge here is: No. 1, abandonment; No. 2, cruel and inhuman treatment; No. 3, conduct rendering it unsafe for her to live and cohabit;

Custody issue [handwritten margin note]

No. 4, inadequate support.

Now, is there a contention here that he was justified in abandoning her?

MR. POMERANTZ. Yes, sir.

THE COURT. Where is that?

MR. POMERANTZ. It is part of the affirmative defense which is still in the case, even though the counterclaim is out.

In other words, the abandonment justified largely by her practices, not by her ideas.

In other words, the affirmative defense sets up the episode of depriving the children of medical care, needed surgical care, trying to proselytize them to her faith and several other episodes which I have yet to put in concerning her relationship with her husband, with the local rabbi, with the whole community.

THE COURT. Is this under the theory of justification of the abandonment? Do you deny the abandonment?

MR. POMERANTZ. No, sir, it is admitted.

THE COURT. Do you contend there was justification for the abandonment?

MR. POMERANTZ. Yes, sir.

THE COURT. And that the justification was because of her actions in connection with the attempt to convert and proselytize the children?

MR. POMERANTZ. Only one small part. May I give you the rest? There was no opening statement or brief, so your Honor is at a disadvantage.

No. 1. That this lady endangers the lives of her children by her faith in Christian Science and to that extent is not a fit custodian for the children.

No. 2. That to the extent that she is attempting to win the children away from the faith of their marital contract, from the faith of both father and mother, from the faith in which all these children have been brought up in a positive sense, as Jews, to that extent she is an unfit custodian for her children.

No. 3. To the extent—and this remains to be shown—that she converted the home into a Christian Science reading room to the point where, by her own admission, she destroyed the Bible of these children.

I submit that is both cruel and inhuman treatment and an aspect that goes to the question of the custody.

As I will show in a moment, that she carried on a daily, hourly and nightly campaign to convert him to her faith, driving him to distraction, to that extent I say there are grounds for a separation and relative elements to the question of custody.

THE COURT. You are not seeking a separation?

MR. POMERANTZ. No, sir, we just want to defeat this action for separation.

Now, under the law, the question of custody is before your Honor even though there is no counterclaim for a separation.

In an action of this kind the statute says that no matter what the disposition or action your Honor decides, your Honor may award such custody of the children as seems fit and proper, having in mind exclusively the interest of the children.

THE COURT. You say there is no issue involved here with respect to that, Mr. Erdheim, where the defendant says, "Yes, I abandoned her but I abandoned her because she was attempting to proselytize my children and convert them into another faith, which I, the defendant, say she had no right to do"?

MR. ERDHEIM. I say there is no issue as to that.

THE COURT. Why?

MR. ERDHEIM. Well, first of all, let us get to the acts before the abandonment.

There is no justification for cruel and inhuman treatment when a man assaults a woman.

THE COURT. I am not talking about that. I am talking about the abandonment action.

He says, "Yes, I abandoned her. I abandoned her for the reason that she"—we are talking about the admissibility of the proof, as to the circulars that she had in her home, that she was attempting to convert the children to the Christian Science faith.

The defendant says, "Yes, I abandoned her, but the reason for it is that I was justified because she was attempting to convert my children to the Christian Science faith. That is the reason I left, and I had a right to do it," says the defendant, "because we had an agreement that the children should be brought up in Jewish faith."

That is his cause of action and that is his defense. You say there is no issue there?

MR. ERDHEIM. I say that is no issue because that is no justification for a man leaving his bed and board.

THE COURT. There is no jury here. I will take it and I will entertain a motion later to strike it out.

Meanwhile, I have no memorandum or brief from either of you, so it will behoove you in the very near future to submit to me such memoranda as will be necessary in this case.

CROSS-EXAMINATION BY MR. POMERANTZ (cont'd.)

Q. Are you familiar with the contents of that book? A. Yes, sir.

Q. And is it true to say that that book is aimed at children? A. Yes, sir.

Q. And did you ever read any portion of that to any of your children? A. Yes, sir, to Larry.

Q. I show you a book entitled "The Capabilities and Possibilities of Youth", published by the

Christian Science Publishing Society, and I ask you if that book was brought by you into your home? A. Yes, sir.

MR. POMERANTZ. I offer it in evidence.

MR. ERDHEIM. Objection.

THE COURT. I will make the same ruling in respect to this. I will pass upon the competency of it later.

BY MR. POMERANTZ.

Q. Now, is it true that there would arrive at your home periodically certain publications or periodicals from the Christian Science Publishing Society or Christian Science movements of one kind or another? A. Yes, sir. One book, The Sentinel, arrived once a week in the mail.

Q. Now, from time to time did you invite into your home and the home of your husband while you were both living together Christian Science practitioners? A. No, sir.

Q. Did you ever invite a Christian Science practitioner into your home? A. Yes, sir, after my husband and I separated.

Q. I thought you testified on direct examination that your husband threw certain of your friends out of the house. I think you used the word "throw" or "threw". Were those practitioners of Christian Science that your husband threw out of the house, as you put it? A. One woman was. After he moved out he suddenly came home from an extended trip. It was 11 o'clock one evening. I was sitting out on the terrace with a friend who happens to be a practitioner. He said to her, "Are you a practitioner?"

She said, "Yes, I am."

He said, "Kindly leave my house."

Q. Is that what you mean when you stated your husband threw her out of the house? A. I did not say "threw", as I recall it.

Q. Now I want to examine briefly into your relationship with your husband, with particular reference to your religious differences.

I will leave the children aside for the moment.

Q. Did you ever discuss Christian Science with your husband? A. No, sir, not per se.

Q. And when you said "not per se"—— A. I know what you mean, but it is very difficult to answer a question like that.

Q. See if I can help you. Did you ever tell your husband that you heard the voice of the Lord and that the voice of the Lord was asking you to tell your husband certain things that he did that were wrong, or for which he would be punished, or anything like that? A. I do not hear voices. I did say that due to the fact that we have the key to the scriptures, which Mrs. Mary Baker Eddy has given us, we are able to interpret the Bible spiritually and, as such, having read from the Bible, I interpreted it to mean—what I was reading—that we all must come to the truth and that he must come, just like everyone else.

Q. Did you ever tell your husband that the Lord has spoken to you about him? A. Yes, sir, because I felt he would not understand if I said it in any other way.

Q. Well, isn't it also true that when you said it that way you believed it? A. Yes, sir. I usually believe what I say.

Q. Or did you ever say to your husband in words or substance—I do not ask you to recall the exact words—that the Lord had told you that there was sorrow in store for him? A. That was the same incident wherein he claims that I said the Lord had spoken to me.

Q. I am asking you is it true that you said that? A. Yes, sir.

Q. And did you curse your husband and say that you were asked to curse him on instructions from the Lord? A. I am not in the habit of cursing, so I don't remember.

Q. Well, did you say to your husband that the Lord was going to bring calamity on him? A. Well, that is the same thing as you just said. Yes, sir, many, many times, perhaps.

Q. And isn't it the fact that the reason you said the Lord would bring calamity upon him is because he was a materialistic person? A. No. I said he was a wicked, materialistic person.

Q. Well, now, isn't it a fact that in connection with your discussions with your husband, discussions of the kind we have been talking about for the past few minutes, you also charged him with belonging to a wicked and materialistic race, the Jewish people? A. No, sir, I never said that. I do not think an entire race is wicked.

Q. You say you never said that? A. No, sir.

Q. Did you ever discuss Judaism with your husband? A. Yes, sir. I said it had a veil up in front of it and because the Jewish people refused to go further—by that I mean because they refuse to accept the Christ, they would never have any good.

Q. When you made that type of statement to your husband, Mrs. Lesser, he did not take it calmly, did he? A. No, sir.

Q. He would get rather violent, would he? A. Not any more than on other occasions, when I did not say those things.

Q. Well, now, let us see. During the five years that you have embraced Christian Science would you say it was a fair and honest thing to say that you were perpetually working upon him in one or another fashion, however it might be, to try to make him see the light, as you had seen it?

Is that an honest statement? And if it is not, you correct me.   A. Yes, sir, I was trying to make a good and honest man out of him.

Q. And he did not want to be an honest man, in your image, did he?   A. I don't know. He has to make his own salvation.

BY THE COURT

Q. Just a moment. Counsel asked you whether you endeavored in some manner, directly or indirectly, to get your husband to embrace Christian Science. Your answer was "Yes, I was trying to make a good and honest man of him."

I don't know what you mean by that. Were you trying to prevail upon him in some fashion to embrace Christian Science?   A. No, sir. I was trying to prevail upon him to acknowledge God and to bring himself closer to God and in that way he would ultimately become a good and honest man.

Q. You have me confused there, Mrs. Lesser. I don't want you to go into the depths of science or theology with me and on the other hand I don't want you to fence with me.   A. I am trying not to.

Q. Now, were you trying to get him to see God as you saw God, to go further and see Christ, or were you just trying to improve his morals, his ethics?   A. Well, there are so many answers. I was trying to improve his morals, but I myself cannot do it.

Q. Were you trying to get him to become a member of the Christian Science faith, yes or no?   A. No, sir.

Q. The answer to that question was "No"?   A. That's right.

BY MR. POMERANTZ

Q. Now, is it true, Mrs. Lesser, that Christian Science is antithetical to Judaism in its preachments? And if there is any question about the meaning of the word "antithetical" I will be glad to clear it up.

What I mean is: Does Christian Science teach that Judaism is a decadent or a materialistic or a sordid or a dying religion?

MR. ERDHEIM. I object to the form of the question.

THE COURT. You have a lot of questions there.

MR. POMERANTZ. I am getting at the purpose of establishing that the mutual antagonism which existed had not only a husband and wife basis but that deeper than that the faith which this woman was trying to propagandize in her home was a faith which was hateful to the Jews.

I do not want to inject any more religion into this lawsuit than I need to, but I need to where the woman says she was trying to make this man see God the way she sees Him——

THE COURT. That in and of itself, the difference in the two faiths, that does not amount to justification for abandonment.

MR. POMERANTZ. That is right, until it is practiced——

THE COURT. Now, wait a minute. You are asking this witness as to whether the tenets of Christian Science are, as you term it, antithetical or inimical or opposed to the tenets of the Jewish race.

Is that what your point is?

MR. POMERANTZ. That is right, but only as a foundation question for the purpose of showing that it was her articles of faith, that hatefulness which she was trying to propagandize——

THE COURT. You have too much in one question. You have the testimony of this witness that she told him that the Jewish people refused to go further, that is, because they refused to accept Christ, that they would never have any good.

I assume that is part of the doctrine of Christian Science.

BY THE COURT

Q. Is that right?   A. Yes, sir. It is also part of the doctrine of other religions as well.

THE COURT. Proceed from there.

BY MR. POMERANTZ

Q. As a matter of fact, didn't you from time to time ask your husband to join you in prayer, meaning in Christian Science prayer?   A. No, sir.

Q. Is this your handwriting (handing witness paper)?   A. Yes, sir, this is my handwriting.

MR. POMERANTZ. I offer it in evidence.

MR. ERDHEIM. I do not see what materiality this has to the case. I object to it.

MR. POMERANTZ. In the light of the witness' last answer, your Honor will see its relevancy.

Q. Whatever the reason for writing it, I call your attention to the statement "Any family that prays together stays together."

Did you intend by that, that your husband join you in Christian Science prayer?   A. No, sir.

MR. ERDHEIM. Objection.

THE COURT. Objection overruled.

Q. You were not intending by that to suggest that you would pray with your husband in the faith of the Jews?   A. No, sir. I was intending that we should try to keep the family together, because it seemed to be splitting up.

Q. But when you admonished or requested your husband that you all pray together——   A. I had no reference to that thought at all when I wrote it. It just appealed to me.

Q. I show you another letter written by you to your husband, I expect. Will you state to the Court when and the circumstances under which you wrote that letter to your husband? A. I do not believe this was written to my husband.

My husband ransacked my drawer regularly and took everything out of it that I copied from the Bible.

MR. POMERANTZ. If your Honor please, I am offering this for the purpose of attacking the credibility of the witness.

I propose to show through this document that she was uttering imprecations upon her husband, that she was threatening him with calamity, that she was deprecating the Jews, that in the last paragraph, where she said, "You shall be utterly broken and your high gates burn with fire and your people shall labor in vain," I want to elicit that this was part of a systematic campaign to berate her husband, her husband and his religion, and the religion of the children.

THE COURT. I do not agree with any of your legal contentions. The objection is sustained. Go to something else.

(Afternoon Session)

BY MR. POMERANTZ

Q. Apropos of your testimony this morning that you called your husband wicked and materialistic, let me pause here in my question—do you recall your testimony to that effect? A. Yes, sir.

Q. Did you come to that belief as to your husband's character by virtue of what you read and what you learned as a Christian Scientist?

MR. ERDHEIM. Objected to as immaterial to the issue.

THE COURT. Objection sustained.

MR. POMERANTZ. I propose to prove that this persistent course of nagging, of imposing her ideology on her husband, of berating him and his religion, is something that comes precisely out of the very writings which this lady had in her home.

THE COURT. I am sustaining the objection to that question.

BY MR. POMERANTZ

Q. As a matter of fact, is it part of the teachings of Christian Science, to your knowledge, that the Jews are a wicked and materialistic people?

MR. ERDHEIM. Objected to as immaterial to the issues.

THE COURT. Objection overruled.

BY MR. POMERANTZ

Q. Is it part of the Christian Science teachings that the Jews are a wicked and materialistic people? A. No, sir.

Q. You have read Mary Baker Eddy's book "Science and Health," have you? A. Yes, sir. The book teaches us the tenets of Christian Science, which we observe.

We pray and we take all our problems to God. We learn to pray, not to a corporeal God, but to a spiritual God.

Is there any further answer that you required?

Q. Do you believe that it correctly sets forth the Christian Science faith? A. To my knowledge, yes, sir.

Q. Now, I read you from that book at page 314, merely for the purpose of asking you whether you do or do not believe in the quotation which I am now to give you:

"The Jews who sought to kill this man of God showed plainly that their material views were the parents of their wicked deeds."

Let me pause there. Is that consonant with your view?

MR. ERDHEIM. Objected to.

THE COURT. Objection sustained.

Now, Mr. Pomerantz, I think you have gone far afield in this particular phase of the inquiry.

I am not interested in her prejudices. I am not interested in her views and her doubts concerning the Jews in general.

I am interested in her conduct as a wife and mother and I am not interested in and I am not going into the theological phase, foundation, or tenets of Christian Science. We are not going into that at all.

If this plaintiff sought to influence the defendant or her children, you may prove it by her or by affirmative proof.

I am not going into the phases and foundations of Christian Science.

MR. POMERANTZ. With all sincere deference, may I make this one offer of proof and then of course I will adhere to your Honor's admonition not to go into this.

I want to show this not for the purpose of getting into an ideological or philosophical discussion of religion.

I want to show it for two reasons: First, this mother has already testified to here, in response to Mr. Erdheim's question, that she wants the right and will persist unless your Honor makes it impossible for her, to bring these children up in the Christian Science faith.

Now, I submit it is wholly immaterial——

THE COURT. You have plenty of time to go into that at another stage of these proceedings, if I should find that there was a prenuptial agreement with respect to the marriage, with respect to the religion of the children, with respect to the religion of the parties to the agreement; if there is such a finding, there will be plenty of time to discuss that phase of it, as to whether or not she is a proper guardian to rear these children at that particular time.

At this particular phase of it, in connection with the separation action as such, we are not going to go into the ephemeral and the theosophical phases of their religions.

MR. POMERANTZ. Then I take it that the question of custody will be tried out at a later date?

THE COURT. No. I will take the testimony later on. There will not be two trials here. There will be but one trial; but in connection with the issues of the separation, we are not going into theosophy at this particular moment.

MR. POMERANTZ. I do not want to maneuver about this. I want to obey your Honor's mandate.

THE COURT. This woman says she is a Christian Scientist. She admits she is a Christian Scientist. Now, your contention is that as a Christian Scientist, under the contractual relationship between these parties, she is not in a position to rear these children, that they should be reared in the Jewish faith.

MR. POMERANTZ. No court, whether this Court or an appellate court, will take judicial notice, I am afraid, of the tenets of the Christian Science religion.

Therefore I feel that it is incumbent upon me or it is certainly important, if not indispensable, to have this record contain some evidence, your Honor, as to why, over and above abstract theosophical or theological questions, it is important for this woman not to be the custodian.

THE COURT. Why don't you lay that aside until you furnish me with a memorandum of law?

My reaction at this particular moment is that if there was an agreement to rear these children in the Jewish faith, we do not have to go into the details of Protestantism, Catholicism or Christian Science, if there was such an agreement, and she is bound to live up to it.

I think it becomes academic if I should hold that these children must be brought up in the Jewish faith, and if I hold to the contrary, then it certainly does not mean anything.

MR. POMERANTZ. Then may we postpone that until I give you a memorandum and I will try to persuade you to the contrary?

THE COURT. All right.

BY MR. POMERANTZ

Q. At the time of your marriage you were Jewish—you were born in the Jewish faith? A. My mother and father are. I suppose I am.

Q. And does the certificate which I show you refresh your recollection that you received that certificate at the time of the wedding ceremony? A. I never had possession of this document, so I am not sure.

Q. Did you see that certificate at the time you

and your husband were married, 21 years ago? A. The names of the witnesses seem to be right. You see, we eloped and so my husband chose the Rabbi. I don't remember his name.

Q. And even in your elopement it was your husband who suggested a Rabbinical marriage, is that right? A. Yes, sir.

Q. In the early years of your marriage and from the very beginning of your marriage, did you maintain a kosher home?

MR. ERDHEIM. Objected to as immaterial to the issues.

THE COURT. Objection overruled.

THE WITNESS. No, sir. It was many years before I awoke to the fact that my husband desired a kosher home. I never knew what a kosher home was because my parents were not kosher.

BY MR. POMERANTZ

Q. And thereafter did you maintain a kosher home throughout your married life? A. I was never taught how but I maintained it to the best of my ability until six or eight months ago.

Q. And then you ceased maintaining a kosher home? A. Yes, sir.

Q. Your youngest child Larry is still living with you? A. Yes, sir.

Q. Was your oldest child Dee taught the Jewish religion? A. She was asked by her father to attend the synagogue, also by myself, five years ago, when we moved to Mount Vernon.

She went for a short time and then she objected. She went to the Sunday school. She said she found nothing in it that she desired, and she stopped going, and her father condoned her.

MR. POMERANTZ. I move to strike out the part about the father condoning her as not responsive to the question.

THE COURT. Strike it out.

BY MR. POMERANTZ

Q. Is it true that your husband caused a religious teacher to come into the home for the purpose of teaching Dee the Jewish religion? A. No, sir.

Q. Did you ever have anybody from the Theological Seminary? A. Yes, sir, in New York City, when they were quite small, this young boy who was studying Jewish theology came to our home once a week, because the children did not go to any Sunday school.

Q. And he taught Dee Judaism? A. No, sir, just Hebrew.

Q. Turning from Dee to Benjamin, did he go to Hebrew school? A. Yes, sir.

Q. And was he, in due course, confirmed or, in the Hebrew language "bar mitzvah'd"? A. Yes, sir.

Q. And after his bar mitzvah, did he continue

to pursue his Hebrew studies, to your knowledge?
A. He went for a while on Sundays to the Bar Mitzvah Club; but as far as I know, he has stopped that.

Of course, he is not living with me now, so I don't know.

Q. Now, as a matter of fact, did your children go to a synagogue on the Hebrew New Year? A. The first two years that we lived in Mount Vernon I went and the children went, every high holy day, and I went as much as I could get them to go with me on other days. Dee refused to go after a while —on the high holy days I think she went with her father once in a while.

Q. Now going back to your home, did you, during most of your married life, until very recently, commemorate the Sabbath by lighting candles Friday nights? A. No, sir.

Q. Were candles lit in your home Friday night? A. We bought our candlesticks about eight years ago and we started then for a short time. Then we stopped and I started again. Father was sometimes not home on Friday night and there was no one to observe it and to me it did not mean that much.

Q. Apropos of your husband having taken your son from you—I think that was the word you used—meaning now your son Benjamin, it is true, is it not, that Benjamin visits you very frequently since he has gone over to your husband's home? A. Not to my way of thinking. It is not very frequent, no.

Q. How often does he visit you? A. He does not often visit me at home, but he looks for my car on the street and he sits in the car and waits for me to come out of wherever I am, so that we can have a talk.

Q. When is the last time you visited Benjamin at his father's home, at the defendant's home, that is? A. Last Thanksgiving, last Thursday.

Q. Both male children were circumsized, weren't they? A. Yes, sir.

Q. You testified earlier that you were quite surprised—I think you said some time in the last couple of years—correct me if I am wrong—you were quite surprised to learn that your husband was taking a trip to Israel and you learned about it quite accidentally. Is that substantially your testimony? A. Yes, sir.

Q. Isn't it true, Mrs. Lesser, that on that occasion your husband offered to take you along and the question of your vaccination came up? A. No, sir, that is untrue.

Q. And at the same time or about the same time, did your husband say to you in words or substance that you could go to Israel with him provided you would stop doing missionary work on him? A. No, sir.

Q. You are sure of that? A. Yes, sir.

Q. Well, the year before that you had gone to Europe with your husband, isn't that right? A. No, sir.

Q. Well, when was it? A. I followed him a week after he arrived there.

He asked me to come there a week later because he had to stop off in Scotland or Ireland.

Q. And you met him in Europe? A. Yes, sir.

Q. Was that the trip upon which you presented your husband with a copy of the New Testament as a present, or a going away gift? A. No, sir.

Q. Did you ever present your husband with a copy of the New Testament? A. Yes, sir. On one of his trips.

Q. You knew, did you not, that your husband prayed and practiced under the Old Testament, is that right? A. Yes, sir.

Q. Did you ever say to either of your children, your older children, in words or in effect, that their father, this defendant, idolized money? A. Yes, sir.

Q. You said it to both Dee and Benjamin? A. I recall saying it to one of the children, perhaps both.

Q. And did you also say to either or both of your older children that the Lord will punish daddy? A. I might have. I don't know.

Q. You believed that the Lord would, did you not? A. If he sinned, yes.

Q. But you have already testified you thought your husband was wicked and materialistic. That was a sin, was it not? A. God is the Judge.

Q. Did you ever try to convert or proselyte or proselytize, whichever way you prefer to say it, any of the defendant's, that is, your husband's friends and acquaintances, to the Christian Science faith?

MR. ERDHEIM. Objected to as immaterial.

MR. POMERANTZ. I submit, your Honor, that on both question of separation and on the question of custody of these children, it is very important to distinguish two types of cases.

If these are purely religious beliefs, o.k., that is one thing.

If these are beliefs which are militantly and actively being propagandized, not only with the children, not only with the husband, but, as I am to show, with the very rabbi of the family and the tradesmen and the people with whom they do business, then that kind of situation is intolerant.

THE COURT. I will allow the question.

A. Did I every proselytize anybody outside of my husband? Is that the question?

BY MR. POMERANTZ

Q. Your husband's friends or acquaintances. A. No, sir.

Q. Now you testified on your direct examination concerning what you claim to be beatings administered to you by your husband. I want to go into one or two or more of them.

One of the episodes, the episode of your being put out or thrown out of the house, occurred the night that you told your husband that you had destroyed the Old Testament. Is that right? A. Yes, sir.

Q. And is it true that your husband picked you up in his arms on that occasion and did deposit you outside the house? A. He threw me out. I fell down, as I landed on the ground outside the house. He threw me out forcibly.

Q. Is it true that while you were outside, a hat and coat were brought to you by one of your children? A. A coat, yes, sir.

Q. And is it true that while you were outside, your husband invited you back into the house? A. Oh, no, sir.

Q. Did you try to get back into the house? A. Once, yes, sir.

Q. And this all happened in the presence of your children, did it not? A. Yes, sir.

Q. On another occasion which you put at November 12, 1955, that is after the occasion that you said the separation occurred, is that right? A. Yes, sir.

Q. On that occasion you testified that late at night, I believe you said about 2 o'clock in the morning, your husband threw you off the bed. Is that right? A. Yes, sir.

Q. Was it his room or your room? A. The guest room.

Q. During the period that you both maintained separate bedrooms, isn't it true that you would, on occasion, come into his bedroom for the purpose of reading out of the Bible? A. No, sir.

Q. Would you ever, in Mr. Lesser's bedroom, discuss Christian Science with him? A. I would go in to talk to him occasionally.

Q. That is not my question. My question is whether you discussed Christian Science with your husband in his bedroom? A. No, sir.

Q. Not ever? A. No, sir.

Q. And this altercation or this controversy or whatever you call it, that occurred at two o'clock in the morning of November 12, 1955, when he threw you off the bed, you say had nothing to do with Christian Science? A. As far as I recall the date, and there were many beatings and many dates that I do not recall too well, I know there was one occasion where he came in at two in the morning and beat me. I believe that was the one. We had no discussion whatever.

Q. You mean he just came home, walked into your room and administered a beating to you and walked out again? A. He may have said a few words, but I know I said nothing.

Q. I say, you do remember that there were several occasions when very violent altercations and controversies between you and your husband came as the result of a prior talk about one or another aspect of Christian Science?

MR. ERDHEIM. I object to the form of the question.

THE COURT. Objection overruled.

THE WITNESS. We had many violent altercations but not from a discussion of Christian Science, because we did not discuss Christian Science. We discussed God. I believe I made that clear.

BY MR. POMERANTZ

Q. And your husband's wickedness? And your husband's materialism too? Is that right? A. Must I answer that, your Honor?

BY THE COURT

Q. Yes. A. Yes, sir.

BY MR. POMERANTZ

Q. Finally, let me ask you this: In connection with your son's tonsillectomy which was finally performed at the Mt. Sinai Hospital, did you or did you not telephone or speak to any doctor connected with the proposed operation and in words or substance say to him that under no circumstances was he to perform that operation? A. No, sir.

Q. You are sure of that? A. Positive.

Q. And specifically did you say that to Dr. Foreman? A. No, sir.

Q. Dr. Foreman has attended your family for many years, hasn't he? A. As long as we are in Mount Vernon, yes, sir.

MR. POMERANTZ. I might say, your Honor, Dr. Foreman is on his way down here and he should be here any minute.

BY MR. POMERANTZ

Q. Was your husband active in the synagogue of Mount Vernon?

MR. ERDHEIM. Objected to as immaterial.

THE COURT. Objection overruled. I will allow it, if she knows.

THE WITNESS. We both were.

BY MR. POMERANTZ

Q. You were active in the synagogue too? A. Extremely.

Q. Well, on the last Jewish New Year, do you recall an episode about Dee going to the synagogue as opposed to going back to school?

MR. ERDHEIM. I object to that.

THE COURT. Sustained.

MR. POMERANTZ. I submit, in an equity action, proof is admissible up to the time of the decree on the issue of custody.

THE COURT. I will allow it.

BY MR. POMERANTZ

Q. On the occasion of the last Rosh Hashonoh or New Year, do you recall a question arising as to whether Dee should go to synagogue or go back to school? A. I was to drive her to Ithaca, New York, which was ten hours from here. The only time I could go was on a certain date with the friend who would help me drive.

Q. And that certain date happened to be the Jewish New Year? A. Yes, sir.

Q. In connection with the few questions your lawyer asked you about support, in addition to the weekly payments your husband is making to you, he is paying the taxes on your home, isn't he? A. Yes, sir.

Q. And the mortgage payments on your home? A. Yes, sir.

Q. He is paying for your daughter's tuition and board at Cornell University? A. Yes, sir, about $2,500 a year, but it is not necessary.

Q. You say it is not necessary? A. No, sir. She has money for her college tuition from her grandparents, if she has to use it.

Q. We will go into the question of necessity at another time perhaps.

Q. And do you concede that your husband is paying for Benjamin's maintenance at this time? A. Yes, sir.

Q. You have an automobile now? A. Yes, sir.

Q. How old is your present automobile? A. Two weeks.

Q. You have no private means of your own, that is to say, whatever means you have, your husband has given you, is that right? A. No, sir. Some bonds I had in the vault. I had saved money and bought them.

MR. POMERANTZ. No further questions.

c. Redirect Examination by Mr. Erdheim

Q. Did you have the boy Larry taken to Dr. Smith before he was operated on? A. Yes, sir.

Q. There has been some testimony here about your not taking your children to doctors. Who is Dr. Dworin? A. He is a doctor that the children would see upon occasion.

Q. And which children have seen Dr. Dworin, do you know? A. Dee and Larry have seen him.

Q. Have you taken your children to Dr. Dworin? A. No, sir, but I have called a Dr. Fordham to my home for the children and I have taken Larry to Dr. Smith for examination.

Q. In other words, if the children are in need of medical attention, would you hesitate to call a doctor or to bring them to a doctor? A. According to my discretion, I would do the best of my ability.

Q. On the occasion that you read to Dee, when Dee was ill, was that your way of curing her? Or what was the reason for your reading to her? A. Well, I just wanted to help her.

Q. And did you intend to indoctrinate Dee with Christian Science by reading to her? A. No, sir.

Q. Is that your intention and has that been your intention with respect to your husband or your children? A. No, sir.

MR. ERDHEIM. That is all.

d. Recross Examination by Mr. Pomerantz

Q. Why then did you bring these pamphlets into the home, if not to have them affect the children? A. For two reasons: One was that I wanted to read the book and see what it was about; and another reason is I have sometimes given those as gifts.

Q. To whom? A. I have given them to children.

Q. But not your own children? A. No, sir.

Q. Larry would understand what you were saying, if you read that book? A. Yes, sir.

Q. And you did read that book? A. Once or twice, yes, sir.

Q. To Larry? A. Yes, sir.

MR. POMERANTZ. That is all.

MR. ERDHEIM. No questions.

2.

CHARLES FOREMAN, M.D.—FOR THE DEFENSE

a. Direct Examination by Mr. Pomerantz

Q. Now, getting right to the point, do you recall an episode at the Mount Vernon Hospital where Larry Lesser was at the hospital with a view to a tonsillectomy? A. Yes, sir. My recommendation was that he have his tonsils and adenoids removed.

Q. And four of you examined the boy prior to the operation? A. Yes, sir.

Q. And did you on that day receive any communication or have any talk with Mrs. Lesser about her son and about the proposed operation? A. Yes, sir. She said she did not approve of having the boy operated on and she refused to sign a paper giving him permission for the operation.

Q. Is it standard hospital procedure to have the parents sign such a paper? A. One of the parents.

b. Cross Examination by Mr. Erdheim

Q. You are an internist? A. Yes, sir.

Q. Do you know a Dr. Morely Thomas Smith? A. Yes, sir.

Q. Does he have an excellent reputation? A. Yes, sir.

Q. When you first examined the boy Larry, what condition did you find him in? A. As I recall, he had abnormally enlarged tonsils and adenoids. He had difficulty swallowing and breathing.

Q. Was there anything urgent with respect to this operation? A. No, sir.

Q. Tell the Court what Mrs. Lesser said to you? A. She told me that she had been to another doctor, Morely Smith, and she said that he felt it was not urgent, as I recall.

However, I had not had an opportunity to speak to Dr. Smith. I also felt it was not urgent that it be done that particular day, but that it was urgent enough that it be done soon, and that that was the opportune moment to have it done.

Q. Why didn't the operation take place at the Mount Vernon Hospital? A. Because the operation is not a procedure that involves one person. It involves the hospital, the surgeon, the anesthetist, the operating room nurses, and the final one who refused to give anesthesia was the anesthetist.

Apparently he was afraid he was liable to a suit.

Q. Why, because the child's throat was infected? Isn't that why the anesthetist did not want to administer anesthesia to this boy, because his throat was infected? A. No, sir.

Q. Isn't that why none of the doctors operated upon the boy? A. No, sir.

Q. Did Perry Lesser, the defendant here, sign the consent to the operation? A. I think he did.

Q. Isn't that the only paper required to be signed? A. Yes, sir.

Q. Why didn't the operation take place then at the hospital? A. Because I went down to the Superintendent of the hospital and I explained to him that the mother expressed a desire that the operation not continue and he passed that communication to two other doctors to examine the child, which I did.

The anesthetist himself was informed that the mother refused. He explained to me then that he did not want to take any chances. An operation is an operation. Anything might happen during an operation. And if the mother protested the operation, he would not have anything to do with it, and he refused to give anesthesia.

Q. What did the other two doctors say? Did they say anything? A. There was nothing wrong with the boy. They said he had enlarged tonsils and large adenoids, difficulty in breathing, and they advised that the tonsils and adenoids be removed as soon as feasible.

Q. Immediately? Did they think it was an emergency operation, that it must be done immediately? A. No, sir.

MR. ERDHEIM. That is all.

MR. POMERANTZ. No further questions.

(Witness excused.)

MR. POMERANTZ. May I proceed now, your Honor?

THE COURT. Yes.

MR. POMERANTZ. May I say that I have invited as my witness a professor at the Theological Seminary. He has to get back to his classroom. When he comes, may I interrupt the testimony of the witness to put him on?

THE COURT. Yes.

3.

PERRY LESSER—DEFENDANT

MR. POMERANTZ. In the light of the colloquy that occurred just before you went on the bench today, that pursuant to Mr. Erdheim's notice to produce, we have produced and there has been constantly available for Mr. Erdheim's inspection and there will continue to be made available for his inspection all material he has asked for . . .

THE COURT. I don't know what this is all about. You people both get together as to what the financial status is and put it in the form of a stipulation, or examine the witness, if you cannot do it by stipulation. Let us proceed with the trial of the action.

a. Direct Examination by Mr. Pomerantz

Q. How old are you? A. Forty-four.

Q. And without going into too much detail, would you say that you were brought up as an orthodox Jew? A. Yes, sir.

Q. And in the home of your parents, all this, of course, prior to your marriage, you observed the dietary laws and the Sabbath? A. Yes, sir.

Q. Now, in connection with the ceremonialization of the marriage by a rabbi, did you have any conversation with your wife?

MR. ERDHEIM. I object to that, your Honor. If it is the defense of this defendant, your Honor, that pursuant to an antenuptial agreement, that this woman breached the same, under the Martin v. Martin case, 308 Court of Appeals 136, that is no defense.

I object to it as immaterial to the issues.

THE COURT. I will send for the case.

MR. ERDHEIM. May we also get the Appellate Division decision, because in the Appellate Division decision are the facts of the case.

Will your Honor also see 141 Supp. 2nd.

MR. POMERANTZ. If it will expedite the case may I withdraw the question at this time and proceed with the examination? Maybe I won't need to press the other question, although I would like to reserve the right to press it, based upon the rest of the testimony.

THE COURT. Very well.

BY MR. POMERANTZ

Q. In connection with this ceremony performed by Rabbi Bienenfeld—and by the way, were there any witnesses to that ceremony? A. Yes, sir.

Q. And how many in number? A. Ten witnesses. In the Hebrew law, there should be a minyon or ten people when you are performing the ceremony, a quorum.

Q. I show you a piece of paper which your wife could not identify yesterday and I ask you to look at it. It is entitled, "Certificate of Marriage". A. Yes, sir.

Q. Was that certificate given to you or your wife in connection with the ceremony performed by Rabbi Bienenfeld? A. Yes, sir.

Q. To whom was it given? A. To my wife directly after the ceremony.

MR. POMERANTZ. I now offer it in evidence.

MR. ERDHEIM. I object to this paper upon the ground that it does not bear any signature of the plaintiff. It is not binding upon her.

THE COURT. I assume you must think it is material or you would not offer it. You are not making an idle gesture. I read this yesterday.

Now, I have been a Judge for almost twenty years and I have performed a number of ceremonies. In some instances, the participants desired a certificate of marriage and the person officiating, performing the ceremony, later on presents them with a certificate of marriage.

The certificate contains a number of statements or details to which the participants or rather, the original contractual parties, are not parties.

They do not sign the certificate.

It is a statement made by the person who performs the ceremony and I cannot conceive how it is binding on the people who have contracted the marriage.

MR. POMERANTZ. Under those circumstances, may I withdraw my offer at this time and show your Honor by the next questions why I think it is, in all deference.

THE COURT. Lay your foundation first before offering it, instead of offering it first and then attempting to lay a foundation.

MR. POMERANTZ. Your Honor is quite right and I should have done so.

BY MR. POMERANTZ

Q. Would you state to the Court as nearly as you could recall what the marriage ceremony performed by Rabbi Bienenfeld consisted of? A. The ceremony was performed in the Hebraic and English language, both. The certificate there is read during the middle of the ceremony.

Q. And that was in the presence and hearing of course of your wife too? A. Yes, sir.

Q. And were any things said or done by the bride and groom? A. Yes, sir. The Rabbi asked questions and the answers were "I do," both by the bride and the groom.

Q. And was that before or after reading the certificate that the Rabbi asked questions and when the statement was made "I do"? A. No. That was while reading this certificate in English, a translation of the certificate.

MR. POMERANTZ. I now offer the certificate in evidence, if your Honor please, for two principal purposes:

First, under the law, which unfortunately I have not put before your Honor in the form of a memorandum, which I hoped to do—some of the cases I have right here—the law as I understand it, is this:

That where a man and a woman agree to live in any religious faith, be it Jewish, Protestant or Catholic, and if either spouse departs from the agreement, then under several decisions by, among others, Judge Panken——

THE COURT. I read Judge Panken's decision. That was a Domestic Relations Court decision in connection with support, where he speaks about holding a kosher table.

I do not think that case is applicable here.

I have read the dictum of Judge Panken in connection with an application for support but I do not think that is at all binding on this Court. Have you any other decisions?

MR. POMERANTZ. Yes, we have. They are in the memorandum which is in the process of being typewritten.

THE COURT. You want me to rule on something and you say you will supply the cases later on.

MR. POMERANTZ. I am sorry I do not have them for you now, but I want to give you my outline of the proof and my outline of argument, so that at least you will know what my conception of the relevancy is.

My feeling is that where the parties contract to live in any particular religious faith and either departs from that, that, per se, is ground for abandoning or leaving the home of the spouse who departs from the marital contract.

I think the law on that is pretty well established and for the time being, I am afraid, I do not have any authorities, but I will get them for you.

THE COURT. Now, you are making a lot of bold assertions there. You say the law on that is pretty well established, yet, for the time being, you have not got any cases.

Give me one case. I have read whatever cases there are on the subject and I cannot find a case in point. If counsel have one, I wish they would give it to me.

MR. ERDHEIM. There is no case in point. We have made a thorough research.

THE COURT. I have read the Martin case and from the opinion of the Appellate Division the only thing I can get is that the original Trial Court declined to grant an annulment on the ground that there was an antenuptial agreement to the effect that the children would be reared in the Catholic faith, which agreement was violated.

MR. POMERANTZ. I have three cases, but before citing them let me say that I agree with Mr. Erdheim that there is no case in the State of New York, or, so far as I have been able to find, in the United States of America, which holds squarely and pat that the change of religion by either spouse confers on the other the right to leave the marital home.

So that there will be no doubt about it, I want to say that clearly.

But there is a whole body of law ranging from the Domestic Relations Court to the Appellate Division, First Department, and I believe the Court of Appeals also, to this effect, your Honor, and that is why I am offering this substantive matter of law—never mind what the remedies are right now—whether it is for annulment, separation or custody—but as a substantive matter of law, children born into a religious faith and the offspring of their parents of a given religious faith are irrebutably presumed to be entitled to remain in that faith.

Judge Panken instances that rule with wholly different procedure on Domestic Relations enforcement.

The Appellate Division, First Department in In Re Santos, at 278 Appellate Division 373, instances it again in an adoption proceeding.

THE COURT. What does it say?

MR. POMERANTZ. In Re Santos, two girls, age seven and eight, had been neglected. They were placed with a Jewish organization which thought them to be Jews and reared them as such.

It was later learned that they were born and baptized as Catholics.

The law applicable to these custodial municipal agencies governing custody, that law reads that the agency which cares for such children should be of the children's faith "when practicable."

Although these children had no known faith but Judaism and had been instructed in the practice of that religion, the Court nevertheless transferred the children to Catholic auspices.

THE COURT. I drafted that law, Mr. Pomerantz, twenty years ago in the Legislature. How does that apply here?

MR. POMERANTZ. It shows, your Honor, that practically without exception, the religion at the time of the birth of the child——

THE COURT. Are we talking about custody? Are we talking about institutions? Or are we talking about justification for an abandonment?

MR. POMERANTZ. I am talking about the first and the last. Let me be more precise. I am offering this evidence for two reasons.

First, to show that the plaintiff here has no right to custody over children who were born in the Jewish faith, for the reasons, first, because of the marriage contract, and, second, because of the substantive law of the State of New York manifested in various kinds of regulations, all of which make one mosaic, that the children born into a faith must remain in that faith.

THE COURT. You want me to hold as a matter of law that a woman who enters into a Jewish orthodox ceremony by a rabbi and later changes her faith, that that warrants the justification of abandonment?

MR. POMERANTZ. I was only talking about the custody, to begin with.

Let me come to what you said right away. I say "Yes." I have no case in New York, and to that extent it is a case of novel impression, as Mr. Erdheim correctly states.

MR. ERDHEIM. I did not say that.

THE COURT. If this is being offered on the question of custody, I will take it. If this is being offered on the question of justification for an abandonment, I will take it subject to proof in connection that that may be the law in this State, about which I have my profound reservations at this particular moment.

BY MR. POMERANTZ

Q. Between the time that you set up your marital home and a time four or five years ago, whenever it was that you learned she had embraced Christian Science, I want to have a quick run through of the nature of your home as a Jewish home, and to that end I ask you these questions. Did your wife keep her home kosher? A. Yes, sir.

Q. Were there many Hebraic ceremonies performed in your home in connection with the Sabbath? A. Yes, sir. Friday night—we would have the children say a prayer or I would say a prayer and then the children would read from the Bible or I would read from the Bible. We had candles . . .

Q. Did your wife ever participate in those prayers? A. No, sir.

Q. Did you ever direct, as your wife put it in her testimony yesterday, did you ever direct your children to say prayers? A. No, sir.

Q. And by the way, are you a member of the synagogue in Mount Vernon? A. Yes, sir.

Q. Are you an official in the synagogue?

MR. ERDHEIM. Objected to as immaterial.

THE COURT. Objection sustained. It does not

mean anything. I am an official too, but it does not prove that I am a good Jew. I don't know what it means.

BY MR. POMERANTZ

Q. Did you, over the years that you were living at home, go to synagogue with your children? A. I did.

Q. And in the early years did your wife join you? A. Yes, she did.

Q. And did she in the later years? A. No, sir, she did not.

Q. There has been testimony here by your wife that she destroyed the Old Testament, or a Bible, in your home and she testified she did not know to whom that book belonged.

Who did own the Bible that was destroyed by your wife? A. Benjamin and Dee. I gave it to them.

Q. And was that Bible used by the children from time to time? A. Yes, sir, every Sabbath.

Q. Incidentally, was that destruction of the book the occasion for a violent episode with your wife? A. Yes, sir. We sat down to eat our Sabbath meal Friday night. I asked Ben to get the Bible. He went looking for it but he couldn't find it. I sent Dee, my daughter, to get the Bible. She went looking for it. She couldn't find it either. I then told them to ask their mother whether she had seen it or put it somewhere. They both came back to me stating that mother had thrown it away or done away with it.

I did not believe it. I got up from the table and went into the kitchen. I went over to my wife and I asked her what she had done with our Bible. She stated that she had thrown it away.

I then put my arm around her, picked her up, opened the door, put her outside and closed the door and told her she could not come back into the house.

Q. Did you throw her out? A. No, I did not. I picked her up bodily.

Q. In what position was she when you put her down outside the house? A. Standing up.

Q. What happened after that, Mr. Lesser? A. Either Dee or Ben brought a coat or sweater out to her. About half an hour later I told the children that she could come in and stay just for the night. They went out to tell her that. I guess she disregarded that part of the argument, stayed out, and took her car and left. I got a call about 8.30 or 9 o'clock from the Court, stating that my wife had sworn out a warrant, and I was about to explain to whoever called and they would not listen to me.

They said they were coming over to arrest me.

Q. Tell the Court what happened. A. I and my children were eating breakfast when the police came to the house and they said for me to get up and go with them.

Q. And is that one of the complaints that was later withdrawn by your wife? A. Yes, sir.

Q. From time to time over the past four or five years, Mr. Lesser, did your wife discuss Christian Science and Christian Science religion and dogma with you? A. As far as number of times, it might have been once a day or once every second day or once every third day, and as to time, there was no such thing. It might have been in the morning at 8 o'clock or it might have been 2 or 3 o'clock in the morning, when she woke me up and told me that God is talking to her and that she has to tell me something.

Q. In that connection I show you the paper which your wife has already testified was in her handwriting, and I ask you did you hear her testify yesterday that you got that paper by taking it out of one of her drawers or her pocketbook, or something that belonged to her? Did you hear that testimony? A. Yes, sir.

Q. Is that testimony true? A. No, sir.

Q. How did that piece of paper come to you? A. It was put down next to my bed on a night table. We have a lamp and a telephone. This was left for me when I got home to read, as many other notes were left.

Q. Was that night table in a room which was exclusively your bedroom during that period? A. Yes, sir.

BY THE COURT

Q. Do you know where these passages come from? A. I imagine they come from one of the books of Christian Science or Mary Baker Eddy.

Q. Maybe they come from some other place. A. Maybe the Bible, I don't know.

Q. Do you think they are addressed to you? A. I am positive of it. She has been preaching that thing to me, and the children have heard it, and in letters where she has always said God would punish me.

THE COURT. Mr. Pomerantz, where do you say it comes from?

MR. POMERANTZ. Christian Science. Look at the last paragraph of that and you won't find anywhere but in Christian Science a reference to "you people," meaning the Jews, "coming to some foul end."

MR. ERDHEIM. I move to strike it out.

MR. POMERANTZ. I object to that. I will prove that this is exactly an emanation of Christian Science.

I say there are anti-Semitic overtones in that, your Honor, and I offer it now. I submit its competence cannot be questioned. It is in her handwriting. The witness has said it arrived on his table in a room exclusively reserved for him.

THE COURT. I will strike out your interpretations.

MR. POMERANTZ. I respectfully except.

THE COURT. Your record is amply protected. You don't have to take exceptions to anything I do. You have your automatic exceptions under the Civil Practice Act. We have no jury here. I am not interested in the effect it had on his mind. I have read it. My determination as to what effect it could have on him is what controls. If I am wrong in my decision, the Appellate Division will correct me. I do not have to have it read, nor the witness' interpretation of what it contains, nor what effect it had on his mind.

MR. POMERANTZ. With all due deference, I have not put the question. Believe me, I mean no offense to your Honor. I would like to put the question so that at least I have a question before the witness and then if your Honor wants to sustain an objection, O.K.

THE COURT. Very well, put the question.

BY MR. POMERANTZ

Q. The question is: The phrase appearing in this letter, "The words the Lord hath spoken against you," was that the first time in your life with the plaintiff that such a phrase had been said or spoken to you?

MR. ERDHEIM. I object to the question.

THE COURT. Objection sustained.

MR. POMERANTZ. I note, your Honor, Professor Boaz Cohen has just arrived. May I have a few minutes' recess to confer with him?

THE COURT. Yes.

4.

BOAZ COHEN—FOR THE DEFENDANT

a. Direct Examination by Mr. Pomerantz

Q. Professor Cohen, you are an ordained rabbi? A. Yes, sir. I am Associate Professor of rabbinical literature at the Jewish Theological Seminary.

Q. Are you the author of any books and other literature on various subjects relating to Jewish laws, customs and traditions in particular with respect to matrimonial relations? A. Yes, sir, I have written on the law of dowry, betrothal, divorce, according to the Jewish law.

Q. When you say "law"—you don't mean the law of the State of New York? A. I mean the Jewish law.

Q. Now, Professor Cohen, I want to ask you this: In accordance with the Jewish traditions, customs, historical practices and law, would you state what are the duties and responsibilities of the parents of a Jewish marriage for their offspring?

MR. ERDHEIM. I object to that.

THE COURT. Does that vary from the duties of parents of any other nationality or religion?

MR. POMERANTZ. It may, your Honor. I would not know until I hear the answer, because it may very well be, and I could cite instances that there are varieties of experiences with regard to the duties of the parent, male or female, as the case may be, towards the religious education of the child, toward the maintenance of a kosher home——

THE COURT. Do the duties in accordance to Jewish tradition vary in any way from the duties of parents under the civil law of the State?

MR. POMERANTZ. I do not think you can equate the requirements of Jewish parents towards Jewish children with the common law or statutory requirements of parents towards children, or in different fields——

THE COURT. Is it your contention that when two Jewish people marry in the State of New York that their obligations and duties and rights vary from those of others?

MR. POMERANTZ. They very well might.

THE COURT. Is that what your contention is?

MR. POMERANTZ. Yes, your Honor, in these respects——

THE COURT. I don't know that this is the law in the State of New York, but I will permit this witness to answer.

BY THE COURT

Q. He wants to know what the duties of Jewish parents are to their offspring. A. Specifically, in addition to supporting them and taking care of them, it is the duty of Jewish parents to teach them Hebrew, to teach them the Jewish religion, to bring them up in the Jewish religion, to observe the Jewish ceremonies and in every way to obey the principles of the Jewish religion, and any deviation from that would be considered a serious infraction of the duties of the parent to the child. Sometimes things are not practiced, but a good Jew considers that one of the most important things is to give the child a Jewish education.

That was considered a more serious lack in the upbringing of a child than not preparing him for certain secular pursuits.

BY MR. POMERANTZ

Q. Now, again in accordance with Jewish customs and traditions and out of your experience and learning in the field, I ask you what can your experience bring to bear on the question of the change of faith by one of two spouses to a Jewish marriage?

MR. ERDHEIM Objected to.

THE COURT. Objection sustained.

BY MR. POMERANTZ

Q. Is there anything in Jewish customs, traditions or law with respect to the rights and duties of the husband in the event of the wife's change of faith after marriage?

MR. ERDHEIM. I object to that.

THE COURT. Do you contend, Mr. Pomerantz, that there was either an express or implied agreement between these parties, in the nuptial agreement, with respect to any permanency of their religious affiliations?

MR. POMERANTZ. Yes, your Honor, I do.

THE COURT. Well, you are putting the cart before the horse. There must be a foundation before you attempt to prove any of these things.

MR. POMERANTZ. There is already in evidence the testimony of Mr. Lesser that the rabbi who performed the ceremony at his wedding with his wife did pronounce these words, "And the said bride," meaning the plaintiff here, "has plighted her troth unto him in affection and sincerity and has thus taken upon herself the fulfillment of all the duties incumbent upon a Jewish wife."

And in response to that reading this plaintiff said "I do."

Now I submit to your Honor that it is perfectly in order for me to indicate what are the duties of a Jewish wife.

The Appellate Division and no other court will take no judicial notice of it, I submit.

The only way I can offer that is like offering evidence of foreign law—I have to call the expert in Jewish law and ask him, "What are the obligations in accordance with Jewish laws and traditions incumbent upon a Jewish wife?"

If, as already appears, the duties incumbent upon a Jewish wife embrace the positive affirmative duty to bring up her children as Jews and if she violated that duty, then, your Honor, I respectfully contend, and in all deference to your Honor, that that violation results, among other things, in this: That she cannot, switching the rules of the game or the rules of her contract, if you wish, insist that she, as she said in her direct testimony yesterday, has the right to subject the child to Christian Science, the same right, she implied as her husband has, to subject him to Judaism.

That was not the contract of the parties and for breach of that contract, among other results that flow is that the children are entitled to be brought up pursuant to the promise of the parties, whether they be Jews or Catholics or Protestants.

THE COURT. I will allow this testimony, but I may point out to you this: That so far as the plaintiff is concerned, it would be incumbent upon the defendant to show that she was a party to such a contract, that she understood the nature

and the details which you are now attempting to elaborate.

In other words, you cannot build up a man of straw and then proceed to knock him down.

If you are talking about the specific obligations which the professor has just attempted to enumerate, you must bring home to the witnesses that she was aware of the particular contract.

MR. POMERANTZ. Where a party subscribes to a contract——

THE COURT. It does not behoove a Judge to invoke his personal knowledge into these matters. It requires evidence to substantiate every contention. But the fact of the matter is that whenever two people contract to a marriage, and particularly where you are invoking a written document here which the witness says she never saw before and attempt to define it and read into this document folklore and tradition, I would say you have to bring it home to the contractual parties.

MR. POMERANTZ. It is not I who am reading it in. This plaintiff agreed, if you believe the testimony of the defendant, and it is on that premise and for this purpose that I am proceeding, that she would discharge duties incumbent upon a Jewish wife.

THE COURT. I will let the professor testify in answer to the question.

THE WITNESS. Yes. In case a wife changes her faith after marriage and persists in doing so, she does not want to go back to the Jewish religion, the law would even permit a termination of the marriage and the woman, the wife, would forfeit her property rights as a punishment for it, forfeit her dowry and so on.

b. Cross Examination by Mr. Erdheim

Q. Now, what law can you refer me to or can you refer this Court to which says that if a wife changes her faith after marriage, that law would permit a termination of the marriage and a forfeiture of dowry? A. Mishnah Ketubot, in Chapter 7.

THE COURT. I will accept Professor Cohen's testimony on that point.

MR. ERDHEIM. Nothing further.

5.

PERRY LESSER—DEFENDANT (cont'd.)

a. Direct Examination by Mr. Pomerantz

Q. What statements, if any, did your wife make concerning you from the time she embraced Christian Science up to the time of your separation from her in October or thereabouts of last year? A. She would consistently berate me and belittle me even in front of the children, both about my religion and also about my materialistic feeling, and she would say that we were a dead, decadent religion and that all the Jews were materialistic and that as far as our race, that we were something that is going to vanish, like the Indians, or something.

Q. Were any references made to your idealizing money? A. Consistently, but Mrs. Lesser always used it very well, buying everything that she needed, including a mink coat and a Cadillac.

Q. Did your wife give you any material to read with respect to Christian Science? A. Yes, sir.

Q. Please state briefly what she told you about her feelings about physicians and surgeons? A. She said that if a person believes, they do not need any surgeons or physicians because, firstly, they are breaking the Ten Commandments.

She explained to me, as a Christian Scientist, that the First Commandment is "Thou shalt have no other God before Me" and if you go to a physician or a surgeon you put him on a pedestal, as you put a God, because he is going to help you, and therefore that was the first thing always in her mind, as far as physicians go.

Q. Prior to Larry's tonsillectomy, was Larry complaining of suffering from colds? A. Not only was he complaining, but I know he had a drip, and at night, when he went to bed, it was very hard for him to breathe. The reason, the cause of his consistently getting colds, I took him to the doctor for that.

Q. And did she ever take Larry to the doctor? A. I don't remember that she ever took him to the doctor in the last three or four years.

Q. Did your doctor prescribe medicine for Larry? A. Yes, sir.

Q. And did you have any discussions with your wife concerning administering the medicine to the child? A. Yes. When I came home I would notice that the bottle was as full as when delivered or there was just a little missing.

I would have a discussion with her and she would say she did not think he needed medicine, so I would go to the maid and give her instructions or to my daughter, when she came home from school, to take care of the situation.

Q. Did you ever have quarrels with your wife concerning this business of medicine and doctors? A. Yes; many, many times.

MR. ERDHEIM. I object to the use of the word "quarrels."

THE COURT. Objection sustained, strike out the answer.

BY MR. POMERANTZ

Q. Did your wife, in connection with the tonsillectomy and about the time of the tonsillectomy

ever say to you that the child had a mucous condition which would make the operation dangerous or which would warrant the postponement of the operation? A. No, sir.

Q. And after your child had had his blood test taken and was being prepared for the operation, did you see your wife in a discussion with your son Larry? A. Yes, sir.

Q. And what, if anything, did she say to Larry or Larry to her? A. She told Larry that she was there to protect him and that she would not allow anything to happen to him. She was going to take care of him. Larry became a little frightened at all the things happening around him and he started to cry.

Q. Now, there is testimony in the record that on a certain night, I think it was in November 1955, at 2 o'clock in the morning, that you threw your wife out of or off the bed. Do you recall an episode involving your putting your wife off or out of bed? A. Yes, sir.

Q. Would you state to his Honor what happened with respect to that episode and prior to it, if it needs any prior preparation? A. I had come home late and I was tired and I went to my room and undressed and got into bed.

Q. Your wife has testified that November 1955 you left, never to return. Is that true? A. No, sir.

Q. Mr. Erdheim says it is September 1955 and I will accept his memory. A. I left and came back many times during the interval for a day or two days.

I also came home in March 1956 and stayed for March, April and May, for the full three months. I stayed there in the house.

Q. Without your wife? A. Yes, sir. I remember staying there up until about the middle of or rather, the end of May or the beginning of June.

Q. So you were at your wife's home for three months consecutively at least after your departure, as she testified to it? A. Yes, sir.

Q. Now, even after that time, did you again return to the home of your wife and your children after June of 1956? A. Yes. I returned on an average of once a week, but did not stay there overnight, maybe twice a week, maybe sometimes more.

Q. When is the last time you returned there? A. Saturday and Sunday.

Q. Of this past week? A. Yes, sir, of this past week.

MR. ERDHEIM. May we have the record clear as to whether he goes to visit there or to sleep there?

THE COURT. Was there a time when the defendant abandoned the Mount Vernon home?

MR. POMERANTZ. Let me rather put it this way, because "abandoned" is a legal term.

THE COURT. I am talking legally—was there a time that he left the home, not to live with her?

MR. POMERANTZ. In September of 1955 he left the home, not to live with her, that is right, sir.

In March, April and May he went back there and lived with her for three months.

THE COURT. As man and wife?

THE WITNESS. No, sir.

BY THE COURT

Q. You did not cohabit together? A. (No answer.)

Q. Did you understand my question? A. Yes, sir.

Q. Did you cohabit together? A. Yes, sir.

Q. Did you leave again after that? A. Yes, sir.

Q. When? A. Some time in June.

Q. And that was permanent? A. Yes, sir.

Q. You decided not to come back? A. Yes, sir.

BY MR. POMERANTZ

Q. Now, let's get back to the episode of 2 or 3 o'clock in the morning and your wife's testimony that you put her or pushed her out of bed at 2 o'clock in the morning. A. I undressed and I got into bed. I must have been in bed for about one hour when my wife came into the room, reached up and put the little bed light I had on and said she wanted to talk to me, that God was telling her to talk to me.

She had a book in her hand and she wanted to start preaching to me as she had done many, many times before.

I asked her to kindly leave the room. She paid no attention to me and went on doing exactly as she felt like.

I got out of bed and either pushed her out of the room or dragged her out of the room, I don't remember which.

Q. We were talking about the episode narrated by your wife, in which she said that about 14 years ago, while you were driving her and the newly born Benjamin back from the hospital, you put her or ordered her out of the automobile. Will you state to his Honor, please, keeping your voice up, your version of that happening? A. I went to the hospital to take my wife and a new born son home. I was sitting in the front. It was a 4-door sedan. I was sitting in the front. She got in the back and put the baby down on the back seat.

I did not notice that until I was driving for about five minutes. Then I turned around and I told her or asked her to kindly pick up the baby and hold him in her arms. I had been driving a car for quite some time and I have had experience where when you have to stop suddenly or make a short stop, anything that is not held or not in

the right position would roll over or fall down on the floor.

We got into quite an argument.

She would not do what I told her and we argued back and forth and then, after a heated discussion which took about five minutes, when we stopped, she said, "Well, you can take care of the baby," and she got out of the car and walked away.

Q. And you did not order her or put her out of the car? A. No, sir.

Q. Now, another episode or series of episodes testified to by your wife consisted of what she said was your refusal to eat with her at the same table and your relegating her to a separate table, separate from you and from your children.

Would you state to the Court whether it is a fact, to begin with, that you did refuse to eat at the same table with your wife during a certain period after your wife embraced Christian Science? A. Yes, sir. After a while, the constant bickerings and preachings got to be unbearable.

I suggested that if she wanted to eat with the children, that she eat with the children at the table; or when I would eat with the children at the table, that she do not eat with me.

Naturally, as far as Mrs. Lesser was concerned, she was always a stubborn character. She decided that that was not what she wanted, so if I would sit down with the children, she would sit down or try to sit down at the table. And when that happened, I would go away.

Q. Now, prior to these occasions when she and you did not join at the same table and during the period when you were eating at the same table, did she preach Christian Science to you and to your children? A. Yes, sir. Not only did she preach Christian Science, but she berated and belittled me and also talked about our religion, that hers was the best, and that as far as she was concerned, she was the spiritual one in the family, and that God was always talking to her and telling her to do things.

Q. And these discussions were at your dining table? A. Yes, sir.

Q. And it was after that that you determined to eat separate from her, is that right? A. Yes, sir.

Q. Did you in fact take the children to Bermuda, Mr. Lesser? A. Yes, sir. During the Easter holiday.

Q. And did you interrupt any of the children's schooling as your wife testified? A. I did not.

Q. Now, incidentally, I believe your wife testified that she did not know you were taking the children to Bermuda. Is that true or untrue? A. That is untrue, because my two children had to get some clothes to go to Bermuda and I am sure that she not only helped them to buy some of the clothes, but she helped them pack.

Q. Your wife further testified that at least fifteen or twenty times in the past few months, as she put it, you made trips to Florida.

Have you, within the past few months, taken an arbitrary period of six months, perhaps, have you made trips to Florida?   A. Yes, sir.

Q. Did you make as many as fifteen?   A. No, sir. Five or six, including the last.

Q. And was any trip a protracted trip—well, that calls for a conclusion—how long did these trips average?   A. About one week, with one exception, when I took my son and daughter to Florida, after the summer vacation, for about two weeks.

Q. Were these trips to Florida, with the one exception you have noted, pleasure or business trips?   A. Strictly business.

Q. Your wife testified that you told your children that they did not have to obey her because, she testified you said to them that she was insane. Did you ever say that, in words, or substance, or by suggestion?   A. No, sir.

Q. Did you ever tell the children or any of them that they did not need to obey your wife?   A. No, sir.

Q. Did you ever make any suggestion with regard to what happened should they become ill?   A. Yes, sir. I told my two older children, that is, Benjamin and Dee, that whenever they needed the services of a doctor or a dentist, not to go to mother and ask about it, but to go directly to the doctor, or to give me a buzz, and I will call a doctor to come to the house, as I knew I would get into difficulty by telling them to go to their mother, as she did not believe in any kind of physician or dentist, et cetera.

Q. Mr. Lesser, did you ever assault your wife?   A. No, sir.

Q. Did you ever get into violent altercations and quarrels with her?   A. Yes, sir, many, many times.

Q. Did you ever have any physical entanglements with her growing out of quarrels?   A. Yes, sir.

THE COURT. What does that mean, "physical entanglements"?

A. Well, many times we would have quarrels. She would get very violent and start throwing things or come at me, scratch me, throw her arms around.

I would try to get out of her way or I tried to push her out of the room, or tried to carry her out.

BY MR. POMERANTZ

Q. And these quarrels grew out of what, in each case, Mr. Lesser?   A. Out of her constant preaching and belittling me, berating me, practicing what she thought, that she should convert me to Christian Science.

Q. Now, finally, Mr. Lesser, would you have married your wife when you did marry her some 22 years ago if she were not Jewish?

MR. ERDHEIM. I object to that.

THE COURT. Objection sustained.

BY MR. POMERANTZ

Q. And if your wife had refused to assume the burdens incumbent upon her as a Jewish wife, as recited to her by Rabbi Bienenfeld on the occasion of the wedding ceremony, would you have married her?

MR. ERDHEIM. I object to that.

THE COURT. Objection sustained.

BY MR. POMERANTZ

Q. Your wife testified that prior to September 15, 1955, she had been getting from you an allowance of $209 a week. Is that true or untrue?   A. It is untrue. She was getting $125 a week. And then in September of 1956, she only received $100 a week.

Q. How long had she been getting $125 a week prior to September 1955?   A. The entire year. And in 1954 she was getting $200 a week. In 1953 she was getting $125 a week.

Q. And did you have any conversations with your wife concerning these ups and downs of her income?   A. Yes, sir. In 1955, the reason for the ups and downs of the income was that business was not good and I had taken a cut in my salary and I did likewise to hers.

Q. Your wife could not identify these documents as being in your home. You brought this pamphlet, "Youth Chooses," to my office?   A. Yes, sir.

Q. Where did you secure that pamphlet?   A. In my house.

MR. POMERANTZ. I offer it in evidence.

MR. ERDHEIM. I object to it.

MR. POMERANTZ. I am offering these not to show that she embraced the Christian Science, which is clear in the record by now, but to show in the aggregate three things.

First: That she has already testified that she subscribed to "Science and Health" which is typical of the rest.

Also, in her own language, she embraced the tenets propounded by "Science and Health".

I am offering it for the purpose of showing that "Science and Health" propagates and preaches a militant anti-Semitism, that it teaches a series of detracting things about the Jews which I do not want to burden the record with now, until your Honor rules on the admissibility.

And altogether it is for the purpose of showing that in view of the fact that she embraced not only Christian Science but the tenets in this book as she testified on cross-examination, that it is perfectly admissible, pre-eminently with regard to the issue of custody of the children; that those tenets of hatefulness towards the Jews, which is the marital religion of these people and their children, becomes at least relevant—its materiality I will take up at another time—to the issue of whether a woman who embraces a thesis which preaches a militant anti-Semitism is a fit custodian of her Jewish children, particularly in the light of the background in this case.

I submit in all humbleness to your Honor, that you take this and again I apologize for not having properly oriented the legal issues by a brief in a case of novel impression.

I ask your Honor to take it now and if when the briefs are submitted——

THE COURT. You don't have to go into this long dissertation to attempt to convince me of your particular proposition because I do not agree with it at the outset.

You are far afield from the whole subject entirely. While the subject is novel, it is certainly not germane to the issues in this case.

If you are attempting to persuade this Court that Christian Science as such teaches anti-Semitism and as a result a person of the Christian Science faith is unfit to bring up children, I disagree with you entirely.

If you are attempting to tell me that a person who was formerly a Jewish wife and has become a scientist should not be permitted to have the custody of Jewish children, that is another thing; but do not attempt to influence this Court—and it is repugnant to my finer senses—that because there is some statement in one of these books which you have, that all scientists are anti-Semitic.

MR. POMERANTZ. Your Honor, in all deference

———

THE COURT. I do not want to hear anything more about it. You have an exception on the record. The objection is sustained. The whole thing is very distasteful to me.

MR. POMERANTZ. It is no pleasure to me, your Honor.

b. Cross Examination by Mr. Erdheim

Q. On or about September 15, 1955, you did leave the house which your wife, your children and yourself were occupying up at Mount Vernon, New York, is that correct? A. Yes, sir.

Q. You did testify, did you not, that you did return to your home in the months of April, May and June of 1956, is that correct? A. I don't remember whether it was March or April.

Q. But when you did return, you returned to a different room: You did not occupy the same room as Mrs. Lesser? A. Yes, sir.

Q. Title to the house was in your name, is that correct? She could not stop you from getting into the house, could she?

MR. POMERANTZ. Objected to.

THE COURT. Objection sustained.

BY MR. ERDHEIM

Q. You testified you observed the Sabbath? A. Yes, sir.

Q. Did you ever work in your restaurants on Friday night? A. I don't recall that I ever did, in the last two or three years.

Q. You did go to your restaurant and work there on Saturday, you do, don't you? A. Once in a while.

Q. Now, you testified that your wife discarded or destroyed the book which belonged to Ben and Dee.

Did you ever destroy any of your wife's books or any of the testaments? A. I destroyed her pamphlets.

Q. And did you destroy two testaments? A. No, sir.

Q. Did you ever tear this book up, sir (handing witness book)? A. I tore out the New Testament and I left the Old Testament.

Q. Well, you tore it, didn't you? A. I tore it out. I did not destroy it.

MR. ERDHEIM. I offer this in evidence.

MR. POMERANTZ. I object to it. The witness has testified he tore out the New Testament and I do not know what further use can be gained by offering the Holy Bible in evidence. We certainly do not need it as proof of its contents.

THE COURT. Objection overruled.

BY MR. ERDHEIM

Q. I show you this book and I ask you, did you tear up this book? A. I answered that question, Mr. Erdheim, about tearing up a paper, a pamphlet, and a book. If that is one of them, I said I may have.

MR. ERDHEIM. I offer it in evidence.

MR. POMERANTZ. Same objection, in view of the fact that it is perfectly evident there is no dispute about the fact that this witness tore out certain New Testament pages from the Bible.

I object to burdening the record with the physical volume.

THE COURT. You are burdening the record with an awful lot of dissertation. Just object and I will rule.

BY MR. ERDHEIM

Q. Now, when you did return to the house and used another bed, in the early part of 1956, didn't your wife attempt to reconcile with you?

A. There is one statement. May I correct you, Mr. Erdheim?

Q. No. I am asking you a question.

BY THE COURT

Q. This is a trial, Mr. Witness. Do not dicker with the lawyer. If you cannot answer a question, say you cannot answer the question. If you can, answer it. A. May I have it read?

Q. Did your wife attempt to reconcile with you in the early part of 1956 when you returned? A. Yes and no.

BY MR. ERDHEIM

Q. Now, Mr. Lesser, your son Benjamin is living with you, is that correct? A. Yes, sir.

Q. Did your wife consent that he go to live with you? A. No, sir.

Q. And you go to business every day, do you not? A. No, sir.

Q. Well, how many days a week do you go to business? A. Approximately five days.

Q. And who do you leave the boy with when you go to business? A. In school.

Q. And what time of the day or night do you come home from business? A. Anywhere from 5 until about 6:30 or 7 o'clock.

Q. Now, don't you go home as late at 8:30 or 9 o'clock in the evening? A. I cannot recall that I did.

Q. Now, when you go to Florida, have you told the boy to go back to his mother? A. No, sir.

Q. As a matter of fact, you prohibited the boy from going back to his mother during your trips to Florida, isn't that right? A. No, sir.

Q. Who comes into your apartment? A. I have asked my sister and brother-in-law who are married and who have a child who has been married to come and live with my son and take care of him while I am gone.

Q. Didn't you testify that you came home in November of 1955 between 2 A.M. and 3 A.M. in the morning? A. I said I came home late. I remember that. I came home late and went to bed.

Q. How late was it? A. I went to bed and around 2:30 I was awakened—about 2 or 2:30 I was awakened by Mrs. Lesser putting the light on, but I did not say I had come home about 2:30, Mr. Erdheim.

Q. How long had you been home? A. A little over an hour or an hour and a half.

Q. When had you last slept in that room before this November of 1955? A. It might have been a week. It might have been two weeks.

Q. Did you make your presence known to Mrs. Lesser, that you had come in that morning? A. I cannot say that I did.

Q. You did drag her out of the room on that day, that night, isn't that correct? A. No. I pushed her out.

Q. Is it your testimony that after your baby was born in 1942, you and your wife were sitting in the back seat and you left the car and left the baby in the back seat? A. No, Mr. Erdheim, I cannot drive the car sitting in the back seat.

Q. You took the baby in the front, isn't that correct? A. After she left, yes, I had no alternative.

Q. Do you remember the police coming to your apartment that day? A. I remember my wife coming and knocking on the door with the policeman. When I opened the door, she was there as she always was, when she would go to the police when she thought something was wrong——

Q. What did the policeman say to you? Didn't the policeman tell you to let her into the house? A. I was not going to stop her.

Q. Didn't you have the door locked? A. Yes, sir.

Q. Wasn't your three-year-old child crying to let her mother into the apartment? A. I can't recall that she was there.

Q. In 1947, do you remember assaulting your wife? A. No, sir.

Q. You remember the occasions, do you not, when complaints were filed against you in the City Court of Mount Vernon for assaults which you perpetrated upon her, which she claims you perpetrated upon her in January, March and May of 1955?

Do you remember those assaults? A. No, sir.

Q. Do you deny ever assaulting her? A. Yes, sir.

BY THE COURT

Q. Do you remember the complaints? A. Yes, sir, but he said the assaults, your Honor.

BY MR. ERDHEIM

Q. You do admit that there have been violent altercations, is that correct?

MR. POMERANTZ. We not only admit it, we proclaim it.

THE COURT. Are you objecting to the question?

MR. POMERANTZ. I am, sir.

THE COURT. I will allow it.

BY MR. ERDHEIM

Q. How much did you give your wife for support for the house? A. I gave her a check for $125 a week.

Q. Now I ask you, before September 15, 1955, weren't you giving your wife a check drawn on one of your corporations in the sum of $209, each and every week? A. No, sir.

Q. Now, you are the sole stockholder, are you not, of two corporations? A. Yes, sir.

Q. Now, how many employees do you have?
A. About 75 to 80.

Q. A corporation in which you are the sole stockholder owns the building? A. Yes, sir.

Q. And how much rent does the food company in which you are the sole stockholder pay to the corporation which owns the building in which you are the sole stockholder?

MR. POMERANTZ. I object on the ground that this is no evidence whatever of value, what one pocket feeds the other.

THE COURT. I will allow it.

THE WITNESS. Somewhere in the neighborhood of—we pay about $23,000 yearly rent.

BY MR. ERDHEIM

Q. With respect to the building, you purchased that building, the corporation in which you are sole stockholder purchased that building in 1947? A. Yes, sir.

Q. Is not the property assessed at $250,000? A. I don't know.

Q. You have a first mortgage there on the building of a little less than $90,000? A. Something like that.

Q. Now, you own the building up in Mount Vernon, is that correct, this dwelling in which your wife and two children are living?

MR. POMERANTZ. I object. There is only one child living there.

THE COURT. I don't know whether this is a method to go about finding out his net worth, income and finances. What happened to this offer in connection with the stipulation as to finances? Has that been abandoned? Did you decline to accept it, Mr. Erdheim?

MR. ERDHEIM. No, sir. I asked Mr. Pomerantz if we could get the net worth figure of his assets, especially with respect to the value of the food company.

THE COURT. Are you attempting to prove now the net worth of the assets? Or do you want to attempt to work something out? I think you gentlemen should make an effort to determine what the net worth and income of the defendant are and then submit it to the Court.

MR. ERDHEIM. That is all for this witness.

c. Redirect Examination by Mr. Pomerantz

Q. You have admitted that you tore out certain pages constituting the New Testament portion of a book or books belonging to your wife in your home. Were those incidents before or after your wife destroyed the Bible of your children? A. They were after.

MR. POMERANTZ. That is all.

d. Recross Examination by Mr. Erdheim

Q. Did you at any time before your wife discarded the books which you gave to Ben and Dee destroy any papers or books? A. I did destroy pamphlets, books and papers, but not the Testament, before she did away with the Bibles.

MR. ERDHEIM. That is all.

MR. POMERANTZ. That is all.

BY THE COURT

Q. You lived together for 21 years? A. Yes, your Honor; yes, sir.

Q. And for 16 or 17 of these years, things were pretty peaceful? A. I should say as peaceful as with any married couple who have their quarrels.

Q. And then did you have some altercations? A. We did have quarrels, we did have misunderstandings, but there was not this consistent pressure and preaching that started when Mrs. Lesser went into Christian Science.

There was no berating, no belittling.

It was a quarrel, if I can just explain myself——

Q. I don't want a long speech. I just asked you a simple question, whether you had any quarrels before. A. I explained myself, your Honor.

Q. She told you she was going to become a Scientist? A. No, sir, she did not tell me. I acquired the knowledge when I found little booklets around and then somebody said to me that they saw my wife come out of church.

I asked her about it. At first she did not say anything, then she said, "I did it." This was around three or four years ago.

Q. What did you do then? A. I did the only thing I possibly could. I tried to convince her it was not the right thing to do, that I was a Jewish individual and I had my right to religion; our family was Jewish, we were brought up that way, there was a Jewish home life, a Jewish spirit.

Q. You could not persuade her? A. No, sir. In fact, she got more adamant; in fact, that is the time she started to explain to me that our religion was way down in the depths, that she would lift us up and make us something new, not old-fashioned.

Q. You resented it? A. Yes, sir.

Q. Spiritually and morally you resisted it? A. I resisted it, shall we say, because of my upbringing.

Q. You lived with her for five years after you found out she was a Scientist? A. Yes, sir.

Q. You lived together—— A. Not together.

Q. Didn't you live with her for four years? A. Yes, but I went nowhere with her for three and a half years. I never took her anywhere.

Q. You continued to sleep together? A. No. I meant to say that before, but I was not let, that for the past two or two and a half years I slept in my room and she slept in hers.

Q. But you cohabited together? A. On and off, but very seldom.

Q. Then on September 15th, 1955, you packed up and left? A. Yes, sir.

Q. You did not come back to live with her? A. No, sir.

Q. Then around March or April you came back and you did live in the house? A. I did come back every second week, as I stated before. I would sleep there overnight sometimes.

Q. In March, April and May, 1956, you came back? A. Yes, sir.

Q. And you cohabited with her? A. Very seldom. I lived in my room and I stayed in the house. Let me explain myself—I was in my own bedroom.

Q. Then you packed up and left again? A. Yes, sir.

Q. When was this? A. Around the end of May.

Q. What was the reason for that? A. I felt that my children were big enough to understand and that is the reason I tried to explain in the last five minutes to your Honor why I did leave before.

I felt my boy was fourteen and my girl was going to be eighteen and they understood what was happening and there was no use to try and cover up and live with this woman any more.

Q. So you packed up and left? A. Yes, sir.

6.

SADIE LESSER—REBUTTAL

a. Direct Examination by Mr. Erdheim

Q. Did you ever, Mrs. Lesser, offer to give up Christian Science? A. Yes, sir. About almost two years ago or a year and a half ago.

Q. Did you have a conversation with your husband with respect thereto? A. Yes, sir.

Q. Was that after some incident had taken place? Is that correct? A. We had reconciled.

MR. POMERANTZ. I ask that "reconciled" be stricken out as a conclusion.

THE COURT. Strike it out.

BY THE COURT

Q. Tell us the facts. A. Well, I thought that my husband would try to turn over a new leaf.

Of course it may have been my thought, but I always hoped for the best. We had reconciled many times before.

Q. What was it you said to him? A. I said that, "I am willing to give up Christian Science and stop going to church."

That was his main worry, that I was going to church.

Q. What did he say to that? A. I don't recall his answer. I guess he was agreeable to it.

BY MR. ERDHEIM

Q. Did something take place as the result of which there was a reconciliation? That is what I am trying to get at. A. I don't know what you mean.

BY THE COURT

Q. Well, did you give it up? A. No, sir, because he went off on a trip again and he refused to pay the fees of the attorney I had hired. I was forced to pay for it, and again he criticized my religion and persecuted me continually.

Q. Had you separated? A. Not legally.

Q. Well, did you live apart? A. Yes, sir.

Q. And you consulted an attorney? A. Yes, sir.

Q. And then you resumed living together again? A. Yes, sir, for a few weeks.

Q. For how long a period did the separation exist? A. It lasted about two weeks.

Q. Did he live in a different home from yours when you were separated? A. I believe he lived in the Downtown Apartments at the time.

Q. Were there any other occasions when he did not live in the same home or apartment as you did? A. Yes, sir, he did, about I think in 1942, before I gave birth to Benjamin, he moved out of the house, the apartment I lived at in the Bronx, and stayed at the hotel for about a month.

He said it was not convenient to travel to the Bronx from New York.

Q. You were not at that time in disagreement? A. No, sir, I was not in Science at that time.

Q. I don't mean that. You had agreed to live apart—he did that for convenience, you said? A. Yes, sir.

Q. Two years ago or eighteen months ago he lived at the Downtown Apartments and you lived in Mount Vernon? A. Yes, sir.

Q. How long did that last? A. A few months.

Q. And then did you agree to resume living together? A. Yes, sir.

Q. Did you have a talk about it? A. Not very much of a talk.

Q. He just came back and started to live at the Mount Vernon home again? A. Yes, sir.

Q. You did not talk it over? A. No, sir.

Q. This talk about your giving up Science eighteen months ago or two years ago, was this before he came back to live or afterwards? A. (No answer.)

Q. Do you follow me? A. Do you mean the conversation that we might have had?

Q. Yes. A. It was probably the same evening.

Q. When he came back or when he left? A. I don't remember the facts, that is, the dates.

THE COURT. Proceed.

BY MR. ERDHEIM

Q. There has been testimony by your husband,

Mrs. Lesser, that you constantly preached Christian Science to him as much as one day in the week, sometimes once every two days and sometimes once every three days. Is that a fact? A. No, sir.

Q. Did you ever preach Christian Science to him or to your children? A. No, sir.

Q. Did you at any time refuse to call a doctor for your children, as a mother? A. No, sir.

Q. If in your opinion a child or any of your children needed a doctor, did you call a doctor for the children? A. If I felt it was necessary, I did.

Q. And if you were awarded the custody of these children by the Court, will you preach Christian Science to these children? A. No, sir.

Q. Will you let them be their own judge with respect to what religion they desire to pursue? A. Yes, sir.

Q. You heard your husband testify that he was giving you $125 a week before September 15, 1955? A. Yes, sir.

Q. You testified on direct examination that you received $209 a week before September 15, 1955. A. Yes, sir.

Q. And for how long a period before September 1955 did you receive $209 a week? A. In the 40's, I think 1947 or 1946. I don't recall the year. It was mailed to me from my husband's office weekly. In the form of a check, signed by my husband.

BY THE COURT

Q. $209 a week for the past ten years? A. Approximately, yes, sir.

BY MR. ERDHEIM

Q. Your husband testified that you constantly berated him and belittled the Hebrew religion. Is that a fact? A. No, sir.

Q. Your husband testified that you constantly gave him Christian Science material, newspapers, magazines and books by Mary Baker Eddy. Is that a fact? A. No, sir.

Q. Did you at any time try to convert your husband into the Christian Science faith, Mrs. Lesser? A. No, sir.

Q. There has been some testimony by your husband that on November 12, 1955, you came into his room somewhere around 2:00 or 2:30 in the morning? A. No, sir, it is not true.

Q. What happened on that day? A. I was in my room reading, I believe, or asleep, and he stormed into the room and proceeded to beat me, on the bed until I fell off the bed. I tried to defend myself, but I did not accomplish very much.

Q. You heard your husband testify that there were violent altercations and during these violent altercations you attempted to attack him and scratch him. Did you at any time attempt to scratch him? A. Yes, sir, at one time. I began to resent the fact that he kept me from eating with the children at the table and I walked in there and I began to pummel him with words to the effect that it was not right.

Q. And for how long a period before that time had you been refused permission to sit at the same table with the children? A. Several months, I believe.

Q. Your husband has testified that he gave you the choice of either you sitting with the children or he sitting with the children down at dinner. A. He said that once to me many months after he had ordered me not to sit with them outside, that I could eat with them before he got home, but he was hardly ever home, so it was rather confusing as to whether I was to eat with them or not, and they were afraid of him.

Q. Your husband testified with respect to the incident which took place in September of 1942, that you left the baby on the back seat and told him, "You take care of the baby" and you walked out. Is that a fact? A. No, sir.

Q. You did call the police that day to get entrance into your apartment, is that right? A. Yes, sir. I also tried to make my entrance before I called the police.

Q. And would he permit you entrance? A. No, sir, but he did permit my three-year-old daughter to come out to me because she was crying "Mommy" through the door and I pleaded with him to let her come out, and she did, and we both strolled the streets looking for a policeman.

Q. Have you paid or promised to pay our office any moneys for the services rendered to you? A. No, sir.

Q. Have you paid any moneys on account of disbursements incurred? A. No, sir.

MR. ERDHEIM. That is all.

b. Cross Examination by Mr. Pomerantz

Q. Did you or did you not on occasion say to your husband words to the effect that the Jews would come to no good end, or no good would come to the Jews? A. I may have said it. Perhaps twice in the heat of argument, but he was constantly persecuting me.

Q. In response to your lawyer's question, you said that you never discussed Christian Science with your husband. Did I understand you correctly to say that? A. Yes, sir.

Q. But you did discuss the Lord, or God with your husband, did you not? A. I discussed the better things of life, the better way of living, inclusive of the Lord.

Q. Regardless of whether you discussed Christian Science as such or, as you once said "per se," the fact is you did often, did you not, take the initiative in discussing religion, the Lord, and other things? A. No, sir.

BY THE COURT

Q. How old are you now, Mrs. Lesser? A. Chronologically, about 43.

Q. Where were you born? A. In Newark, New Jersey.

Q. When did you meet your husband? A. In 1933.

Q. In 1933? A. Oh, no, sir. I am wrong. He was friendly with my brother many years before that. They were friends, but we did not keep steady company until 1933.

Q. Where did you go to school? A. In the Bronx.

Q. Your family moved to the Bronx? A. Yes, sir.

Q. And how far did you get? A. The third year high school. Then I took a summer position and I never went back to high school. I tried to go at night but I stopped going.

Q. What was the nature of your employment? A. I was a model, and I used to do some book-keeping, assistant bookkeeping, but I did not have too much schooling in that direction. That's about all.

Q. What was your father's business? A. He was a tinsmith at first and then he was in the auto-mobile repair line. He is retired now.

Q. Are there any other children in your family? A. Yes, sir, two sisters, and one brother.

Q. Is your father very orthodox? A. No, sir.

Q. Did you have a kosher home where you lived? A. No, sir. Mother does now, in recent years, but she did not then.

Q. Had you been to any synagogues or temples before you were married? A. Yes, sir, two or three times in my life.

Q. Did you ever attend Hebrew school? A. No, sir.

Q. Did you ever study anything about the history of the Jews? A. Yes, sir.

Q. You were not a very devoted Jew when you married your husband? A. No, sir.

Q. Before you were married, was there anything said between you concerning the nature of your home or about observing the religious tenets of Judaism? A. Not that I recall, I doubt it.

Q. When the ceremony was performed, you say there was some English used? A. I believe so. I believe they read and said "Do you take this man to be your lawful wedded husband?"

Q. Do you understand Hebrew? A. No, sir.

Q. Do you have a recollection of the rabbi say-ing to you, "Do you take upon yourself the ful-fillment of all the duties incumbent upon a Jewish wife?" Do you remember that language? A. We have heard it at other ceremonies but I do not recall whether I heard it at my own.

Q. Did you understand any of this ceremony to mean that you were obligated to perform all the duties of a Jewish wife? A. No, sir, I did not understand it that way then.

Q. Did you hear Professor Cohen testify as to the meaning of the words? A. Yes, sir.

Q. Did you understand when you got married that you agreed to have a kosher home and to bring up the children in the Jewish faith? A. No, sir, I did not understand that.

Q. Did you understand at the time that you got married that you agreed never to become a con-vert, and to observe nothing but the Jewish faith during your state of matrimony? A. No, sir. Does it say that in the marriage license?

Q. You said a little while ago that you were ready about two years ago to give up Science. A. Yes, sir.

Q. Being a member of the Christian Science faith, that requires real devotion to the Lord, as you see it? A. To the Lord, did you say?

Q. Yes. A. Yes, sir.

Q. And to the principles of the faith? A. Yes, sir.

Q. But you were ready to give up all that if he paid the lawyer—— A. And if I could get my family together, which seemed to be splitting up. I was not a member of the church at the time.

Q. When did you become a member? A. I have not. I am endeavoring to become one now. I am a student of Christian Science.

Q. When are you ordained? A. When the com-mittee of three agree that I am practicing Christian Science. They ask you about the Ten Commandments and so forth, things like that that we have to know. I know they would accept me any time I wanted to come in.

Q. Do you take an oath when you become a member? A. I don't know. I doubt it.

Q. Is there some ceremony, some religious cere-mony attached to your being accepted or ordained? A. Well, we take the inspired word of the Bible as our only guide and we work from the tenets thereof. It is difficult to explain.

Q. On this occasion when your daughter was ill, a year or so ago, you attempted to comfort her? A. Yes, sir.

Q. By asking her to have faith in the Lord? A. Well, we feel that the foundation of disease is fear. I was trying to alleviate her fear. And being a very fearful child and having been thoroughly poisoned by her father—I say that with reserva-tions—I feel that I could not say anything to her. Neither child would listen to what I had to say anyhow——

Q. The Christian Science Church as such, as I understand it, avoids having physicians or surgeons attend its members. It is their theory that God made them healthy and hale and if they believed in God, there would be no necessity for physicians or surgeons. Isn't that one of the tenets of the church? A. Yes, sir. We start from the foundation that there is no disease, that God made us in his image and likeness and we do not have to accept all the limitations that people seem to take upon themselves.

Q. You have practitioners who come and attempt to pray for the sick and in their manner heal them? A. Solely through prayer.

Q. Now, if you should become a Scientist would you feel dogmatically that you must accept that tenet of the church which provides that when you are ill you should call a practitioner and pray? A. If I were ill, I would.

Q. What about your child? A. If the Court order required it, I would call a doctor.

Q. You are in control, you are in your home alone with the child, you have sworn to uphold the tenets of your church? A. I have called doctors on many occasions.

Q. Now you have become a full fledged member of the Christian Science Church and your little boy is sick, he has a fever: Are you going to call a practitioner or are you going to call a doctor? A. Since the father believes in medicine, I would have to do what he would like as well. I now understand that which I did not understand two or three years ago.

Q. September 15th is the day you fixed in your complaint as the day when you say he packed up and left? A. Yes, sir.

Q. How long was he gone? A. I think four or five or six months.

Q. You didn't see him? A. Occasionally he would drop in without any prewarning.

Q. You did not sleep with him? A. Not during that time, no, sir.

Q. He said he came back in March, April and May and lived there for three months? A. Yes, sir.

Q. Did you resume relations as man and wife? A. Only when he insisted.

Q. And did you cohabit together during that period of time? A. Only when he insisted.

Q. Well, you acquiesced? A. Yes, sir.

Q. Then in June he packed up and left again? A. I suppose that is the date. I am not very good on dates.

Q. What did you do after he packed up and left? Did you do anything about it? A. No, sir.

Q. I am trying to find out from you when you first took action after September 15, 1955. By that I mean did you go to see your lawyer, any

lawyer? A. Mr. Erdheim must have the date; I am sorry. I do not.

THE COURT. Is there anything else?

MR. POMERANTZ. No questions.

c. Redirect Examination by Mr. Erdheim

Q. A Christian Scientist or one who practices Christian Science, a member of the Christian Science faith, such a person can be treated by a doctor, is that not a fact? A. Yes, sir.

Q. Now, when you responded to the Court, when the Court asked you whether or not you would call in a doctor if the child had a fever, and your answer was that if the Court ordered it you would do it, what did you mean by that?

MR. POMERANTZ. I submit the answer needs no clarification and I object to it.

THE COURT. Objection sustained.

MR. ERDHEIM. That is all. May I take the stand and testify with respect to the services rendered by me?

THE COURT. Yes.

7.

IRVING I. ERDHEIM, PLAINTIFF'S ATTORNEY—FOR HIMSELF

For the past seven or eight years I have specialized in the practice of matrimonial law.

In connection with the case of Lesser v. Lesser I have had approximately twenty-five telephonic conferences with Mr. Pomerantz, each one lasting somewheres between fifteen and twenty minutes, but as long as half an hour to forty minutes, all with an endeavor to ascertain whether or not a solution in this case could be worked out. This was after service of process.

I have had four or five personal conferences with Mr. Pomerantz, some lasting as long as several hours, one and maybe two conferences, but definitely one between the parties and the attorneys going way into almost midnight, all with a view to ascertaining whether this matter could be settled.

I have given this matter, exclusive of the Monday, Tuesday and today that I have been in court, approximately some 250 hours' worth of time on this case. I estimate that the reasonable value of my services is $35 an hour, and I estimate that the reasonable value of my services in this case, which includes the trial, is approximately $8,500.

That is all.

MR. POMERANTZ. No cross-examination.

MR. ERDHEIM. I will call Mr. Lesser as my witness.

8.

PERRY LESSER—REBUTTAL

a. Direct Examination by Mr. Erdheim

Q. You paid $39,000 for your house in Mount Vernon? A. About that. There is a $20,000 first mortgage.

Q. How much were you offered for the house? A. $42,000, less brokerage, which would make a net amount close to $39,500, which is what I paid for it.

Q. How much is the mortgage at the present time? A. About $15,790 or $15,750.

Q. You testified that you are the sole stockholder of the corporation? A. Yes, sir. I think its real estate was assessed at $225,000, but I am not sure. There was a first mortgage of approximately $90,000.

Q. How much rent does the company pay to the building corporation? A. Approximately $23,000.

Q. And you have tenants occupying the other floors? What is the income from that? A. It is about $15,000.

Q. And how much do you pay the manager of the company? A. One gets about $6,000 a year and one gets about $7,800 a year.

Q. The value of the fixtures and the equipment in the 54th Street store, is that worth about $80,000? A. No, sir.

MR. POMERANTZ. I object unless counsel defines whether he means sale value today, as fixtures, or whether he means sale as part of a going concern.

THE COURT. Objection sustained.

BY MR. POMERANTZ

Q. The question is, the value of the company, not the equipment. A. The value of the restaurant is only worth as much as the business or the amount of profit it takes in.

In the last two years we have shown from the company, as our income tax returns have been given to you, we have shown a loss in 1955 of $10,000; and this year, as far as my accountant showed me, up to September, we have a loss of $14,000.

BY MR. ERDHEIM

Q. Now, what was your salary for the year 1955? A. If you will look, you will see it there.

Q. Is that $15,600? A. Yes, sir.

Q. Now, in addition to the salary, did you draw any extra money from the corporations? A. No, sir, only as salary.

Q. You are the sole owner, the sole stockholder, of the corporation which operates the building in Manhattan, is that correct? A. Yes, sir.

Q. What did you pay for that building? A. $116,800.

Q. That was subject to a purchase money mortgage, was it not? A. Yes, sir. A first of $41,650 and a second of $45,637.

Q. You put in cash on that building of about $30,000, is that correct? A. Yes, sir.

Q. What is the income of that building? A. The net income? Around $2,870, and a gross about $11,000.

Q. And off that you took money to pay the first and second mortgages, is that correct? A. Yes, sir, and the taxes.

Q. And how much do you amortize the first and second mortgages, do you know? A. I think about 3 percent.

Q. $4,000 a year, is that so? A. No, sir. I think it is about 3 percent.

Q. Well, isn't the second mortgage almost paid off, the purchase money mortgage of $45,000? A. Oh, no, sir. In fact, two or three years ago we renewed both the first mortgage and the second mortgage.

Q. You just went into a venture in the State of Florida, is that correct? A. Yes, sir.

Q. Was that by yourself or with a group of individuals? A. With a group of individuals.

Q. What sort of a venture was that? A. It is a land development.

Q. And that is what kept you busy going back and forth to Florida for the last couple of months during which I think you said you went five or six times? A. Yes, sir.

Q. How much cash did you put into that venture? A. Either $57,000 or $58,000.

Q. Cash? A. Yes, sir.

Q. And where did you get that money from? A. From my account with the broker. I sold securities and took the money and put it down in Florida.

Q. As of October 31, 1956, you had securities of the value of approximately $550,000? A. I did not add it up.

Q. Would you say that my figure is in error when I say approximately—— A. I could add this, but I don't know.

MR. POMERANTZ. May we accept your figure, subject to my verification, and we will assume it is accurate, unless I otherwise communicate with you.

BY MR. ERDHEIM

Q. On account of this you owed money, is that correct? A. Yes, to various banks and brokerage firms.

Q. On account of this, from your figures, you owed approximately $372,000, is that correct? A. Yes, sir.

Q. How much of an equity did you have? A. $120,00 to $130,000.

Q. You hold how much life insurance—did you

tell me you had about $90,000? A. It is $90,000 to $95,000 insurance, mostly term insurance.

Q. With very little equity in the policies? A. That is right.

Q. Do you have any personal check accounts? A. Yes, sir; one.

Q. What is your cash balance? A. Somewhere around $5,000 or $6,000 at the present time.

Q. Do you have any other assets? A. Just a couple of very small savings accounts. As I showed you, there is about $110 in each.

Q. Any other properties to which I have not made a reference? A. No, sir.

MR. ERDHEIM. That's all.

b. Cross Examination by Mr. Pomerantz

Q. Mr. Erdheim made reference to a company which you had lost? A. Yes, sir.

Q. What was the capital loss, if any, in the opening and closing of that company during the period 1955 and 1956? A. Our capital loss was around $48,000.

Q. And that $48,000 loss was in addition to all of the other losses which you have just testified to, is that right? A. Yes, sir.

Q. Now, in connection with the fourth allegation, as to the alleged non-support, I ask you these questions:

Over the past few years did you buy your wife a mink coat? A. Yes, sir.

Q. And a Cadillac automobile? A. Yes, sir.

Q. Was there any solitary thing with reference to this claim of non-support that your wife ever asked you for, even after she embraced Christian Science, which you refused to give her?

MR. ERDHEIM. I object to that.

THE COURT. Objection overruled.

A. No, sir.

BY MR. POMERANTZ

Q. Did she ever complain to you about having insufficient money to buy her needs or necessities? A. No, sir.

Q. Now, as a matter of fact, you have heard your wife testify that she got not $125 a week, as you testified, pre-September 1955—that is, prior to September, 1955—but $209 a week.

Now, is it possible, by going back to your records, to get documentary proof as to whether yours or your wife's memory is more accurate in that regard? A. Yes, sir.

MR. POMERANTZ. Your Honor, would you permit us, if we can ascertain such documentation, to send it in to you informally, and, of course, a copy to Mr. Erdheim?

THE COURT. Yes.

BY MR. POMERANTZ

Q. And was there some delay in the payment of those bills in connection with the operation of the home because of all those transmittals from her to her attorney and then to me? A. Yes, sir.

Q. Now, there is one more line of questions and I am through.

Over and above the $125 a week which you paid and have been paying your wife since 1955 and in 1955, how much does it cost you to keep Dee in college? I mean by that, including her tuition, her board, her lodging and her other expenses incident to her being in college? A. Approximately $2,500 a year.

Q. And do you send and have you sent Dee and Ben and Larry to camp? A. Yes, sir.

Q. And can you give us a fair approximation over the past several years as to what the annual cost of that has been to you? A. Oh, anywhere from $1,500 to $2,000.

Q. And have you, over the past few years, paid and do you still pay the doctors, dentists, optometrists and opticians for their services to your children? A. Yes, sir. Around $600 or $700 a year.

Q. And do you pay the taxes on your home in Mount Vernon? A. Yes, sir. About $1,200.

Q. And do you pay interest and amortization on the mortgage on your Mount Vernon home? A. Yes, sir. It is about $900 a year.

Q. And do you pay for the repairs and the insurance on your Mount Vernon home? A. Yes, sir. I think the insurance is about $275 and the repairs are about $350 or $400.

Q. And the clothing for Ben or Benjamin and Larry, do you pay for that? A. Yes, sir. About $500 at least.

Q. And do you understand that in all my questions I mean you have continued to make these payments right up to now? A. Yes, sir.

Q. Now, do you pay your wife's automobile insurance? A. Yes, sir.

Q. And you still continue to do it? A. Yes, sir. About $250 a year.

Q. Now, over and above these items you maintain your own separate apartment, do you? A. Yes, sir.

Q. And in that apartment you presently support and maintain your son Benjamin? A. Yes, sir.

Q. And are you able to state—and if not you will tell me so—with some degree of accuracy about what the cost is, including in the cost his share of the apartment rental? A. It is about $2,500 a year.

Q. By the way, what rental do you pay for your apartment? A. I have a maid and the rental and gas and electricity is about $190 a month.

Q. And above that you have a maid, you say? A. Yes, sir.

Q. And then you have the food and the other

items of Benjamin's maintenance? A. Yes, sir.

Q. And the $2,500 estimate as to Benjamin represents, I take it, an allocation of the expenses of maintaining the home toward him? A. Yes, sir.

MR. POMERANTZ. That is all.

BY THE COURT

Q. You drew a salary of $4,800 and $15,600 and you spent $18,000 for these items about which you just testified and no doubt you spent several thousand dollars to maintain yourself? A. Yes, sir.

Q. Have you any other source of income? A. Yes, sir, from securities, about $7,000 to $12,000 a year.

Q. Do you contemplate selling this home in Mount Vernon? A. Yes, sir.

Q. That would eliminate a number of items amounting to $3,000 or $4,000? A. I suppose so, but my income won't be as great as it was last year either.

Q. You mean you anticipate you will draw less from the companies? A. I have drawn less. I get a monthly report. There is no use drawing money from my right side and pay for it on the left.

Q. Aside from the value of these two companies which you say are losing money today, my calculation is that you have a net worth of about $400,000. Is that approximately correct? A. I would say it is closer to $300,000 because of the intangible assets of the property.

We are in the property and it is only as good as the tenants, in there.

Q. What do you think it is worth? A. Well, I think the building is worth about $200,000. That would be a fair value I think.

Q. That would bring your equity down about $100,000? A. Yes, sir.

THE COURT. Is there anything else?

BY MR. POMERANTZ

Q. What interest do you pay, if you know the approximate dollars, on the moneys you have borrowed to finance your securities? A. Well, it is about 4 percent.

Q. And how much have you borrowed approximately? A. I think it is about $375,000—that is about $15,000 interest.

BY THE COURT

Q. That is not a recurring item, is it? A. It is as long as I keep the securities.

Q. You are in the market with both feet? A. Yes, sir.

THE COURT. Anything else?

MR. POMERANTZ. That is all.

MR. ERDHEIM. That is all.

THE COURT. Will you make these children available to me?

D.

The Judge Decides — In Favor of Wife

December 5, 1956

MR. JUSTICE STREIT:

This is an action by the plaintiff for a separation on the grounds that the defendant without justification abandoned her and the infant issue of the marriage; was guilty of cruel and inhuman treatment toward the plaintiff; that it has become unsafe and improper for her to cohabit with the defendant; and that the defendant has neglected and refused to provide for her.

The defendant admits that he has abandoned the plaintiff but contends that he was justified because of her misconduct.

The parties were married on March 24, 1935, in the City of New York. They have three infant children to wit, Dee, age 17, now a student at Cornell University; Benjamin, age 14, now a student at the Arnold Larabee Junior High School and residing with his father; and Larry, 6 years of age, who attends public school, and resides with

his mother at the family home owned by the defendant in the City of Mount Vernon, County of Westchester, New York.

To substantiate her charge of cruel and inhuman treatment, the plaintiff has testified to a series of acts of violence by the defendant, one during the year 1942, one during the year 1947, and five during the year 1955, wherein the defendant assaulted and inflicted bodily harm upon her. She also asserts that since she embraced the Christian Science religion, about five years ago, the defendant has ridiculed and embarrassed her, destroyed her bible and discredited her in the eyes of the children.

The defendant, in his testimony, denied that he ever assaulted his wife, and in justification of his abandonment, contends that prior to and at the time of the marriage the parties agreed that they would maintain their home and conduct their lives in accordance with the tenets of the Jewish faith, and that the children would be brought up in the

Jewish faith; that in violation of this agreement, and some time during the year 1950 or 1951, the plaintiff embraced the Christian Science religion, following which, said the defendant, the plaintiff has brought the preachings of Christian Science into the home, attempted to proselytize the children, humiliated the defendant, declined to give the children necessary medical attention, placed their lives in danger, and assaulted the defendant. In addition, said the defendant, she has upbraided and nagged him, caused Christian Science literature to be left about the house and discarded or destroyed the children's Bible (the Old Testament).

In my opinion, the evidence establishes that the plaintiff is entitled to a judgment of separation, both on the grounds of abandonment and cruel and inhuman treatment.

I find that the defendant unjustifiably abandoned the plaintiff during the early part of June, 1956.

I further find that the defendant unjustifiably assaulted the plaintiff in the face on January 15, 1955, breaking her glasses.

I find that he unjustifiably assaulted her on the evening of March 26, 1955, by lifting her bodily and throwing her out of the home; (as to that assaul a charge was filed against him in the City Court of Mount Vernon and later withdrawn).

I find that on June 1, 1955, he again unjustifiably struck and beat this plaintiff and threatened to kill her (following which the plaintiff complained to the police).

I find that during the early morning of November 12, 1955, this defendant unjustifiably again struck and beat the plaintiff at their home causing injuries as evidenced by Dr. William Reardon's certificate.

I find that there was bickering and quarreling concerning the religion of the defendant and the acquired creed of the plaintiff.

I find that there was petty, stupid, bigoted and nonsensical tearing and destruction of bibles and religious pamphlets by both parties.

I am of the opinion that there is no basis in fact or civil law for any conclusion that there was any prenuptial agreement concerning plaintiff's religion. I am also of the opinion that the defendant who now seeks some secular advantage because of his alleged religious devotion, lived and cohabited with this plaintiff for about five years before he "realized" or "discovered" that the teachings of Mary Baker Eddy were in conflict with the tenets and traditions of his forefathers or that the gospel of Christian Science conflicts with the Talmud.

The defendant has maintained throughout this trial that where two people of the Jewish religion are married by an orthodox rabbi, the change of religion by one of the spouses subsequent to the marriage constitutes a violation of their "agreement" and ipso facto justifies an abandonment by the other, and the divestiture of the children from the convert.

If the defendant contends that the facts in this case justify an inference that there was such an express contract between the parties, then I hold that the evidence is insufficient for such a factual determination.

If defendant contends that such a contract is implied then I hold that (with due deference to but) notwithstanding the Jewish or Hebraic or Mosaic law or tradition it is not the secular law in this or any other state in the union.

Counsel for the defendant's prolix brief does not fulfill his repeated assurances that he would supply this court with authority sustaining his novel position. However, my own research discloses a few principles that apply to the case at Bar.

It is settled law that it is not ground for divorce or separation that the spouses entertain different views on religion. (25 A.L.R. 2d 928; Smith v. Smith, 149 P. 2d 683; Trautman v. Krauss, 105 So. 376; Krauss v. Krauss, 163 La. 218; Hickman v. Hickman, 10 S.W. 2d 738.)

And it has been held that where a husband changed his religion after marriage and attempted to proselytize his wife and children this would not *alone* give the wife cause for a separation from bed and board (Trautman v. Krauss supra; Booke v. Booke, 207 Misc. 999.) However, religious convictions may induce a spouse to do things that would ordinarily constitute a ground for separation; *and in such a case the courts will be concerned primarily with the acts themselves and not with the motive behind them*. (Emphasis supplied.) (Smith v. Smith, supra; Bargrover v. Bargrover, 57 Cal. App. 43, 206 P. 461; Krauss v. Krauss [supra]; Robinson v. Robinson, 66 N.H. 600, 23A. 362.)

It has been said too that the law could not make diverse religious opinions a legal cause for separation because the fundamental law of the land guarantees freedom of religion. (Krauss v. Krauss, supra; Hausman v. Hausman, 285 App. Div. 1012.)

Applying the rule in the Krauss case "that the court will be concerned primarily with the acts themselves and not with the motive behind them," I find no such misconduct on the part of the plaintiff that could justify the defendant in abandoning her and the six-year-old infant.

*   *   *

E.

Appraising the Role and Function of Legislator, Court and Counsel

Before turning to the Lesser children and their participation in the proceedings, we present materials to illustrate some major problems in evaluating that part of the family law process most directly concerned with wife-husband relationships. In this section we use the religious conflict of the parties as a vehicle for identifying some fundamental questions which underlie the criteria and procedures for decision.

Possibly because of the emotional freight carried by the religious issue, Mr. Justice Streit and the attorneys may have been unable to take sufficient distance at the trial to focus the initial inquiry on the nature of the relationship between the Lessers as husband and wife. The confusion that characterizes the transcript seems to have been anticipated by Justice Streit, who early in the trial posed, but failed to act upon, these questions:

"Are we talking about custody? Are we talking about [religious] institutions? Or are we talking about justification for abandonment?"

We continue to search for the purposes of state intervention in the establishment, administration, and reorganization of adult family relationships—to determine the functions of separation, divorce and conciliation proceedings, the meanings and appropriateness of grounds for decision and their consequences, as well as the adequacy of the procedures and their personnel to elicit and recognize data relevant to decision.

1.

ON FINDING THE FACT OF "CRUELTY" AS A GROUND FOR STATE INTERVENTION

a. Conversion from the Marital Religion — A Relevant Factor?

ROBINSON v. ROBINSON
66 N.H. 600, 23 A. 362 (1891)

"LIBEL for divorce, filed February 24, 1890, charging extreme cruelty, treatment seriously injuring health, and treatment seriously endangering reason. . . . In 1884 the defendant became interested in the subject of Christian Science, and a believer in its doctrines. She attended lectures and courses of instruction in the science, and received the degree of 'Doctor of Christian Science.' In the fall and winter of 1884 she practised as a Christian Science doctor in Binghamton, N.Y., returning to Littleton about the first of January, 1885. For about a year after her return she refrained from practice at the request of her husband. About the first of January, 1886, she resumed practice in Littleton, and has continued to practice to the present time. The plaintiff did not believe in the doctrine, and had no sympathy with the defendant in her advocacy of it or in her practice under it. On the contrary, he regarded it as fanaticism and utter foolishness, and was

annoyed and irritated thereby. He did not object to her belief in the doctrine, but he was opposed to her practising as a doctor, which the defendant well knew, and he frequently requested her to give it up.

Twenty witnesses, including four physicians, called by the plaintiff, testified in regard to his health, bodily and mental, since his wife became a believer in Christian Science, as compared with his condition previously. For the two years next after their marriage they appeared to live as happily and contentedly as people in general. His health was good. He was sociable and jovial. They went into company together, and received visitors at their home. After she became interested in the subject of Christian Science, some of her most intimate female friends were women also interested in the doctrine. The plaintiff and the defendant appeared in public together, and mutual friends called upon them less frequently. He knew that unfavorable comments were made in regard to his wife's attempting to practice as a Christian Science doctor; that she was the subject of ridicule in this respect among some people; and that the physicians of Littleton entertained unkind feelings towards her for interfering, as they regarded it, with their practice. He also knew of rumors of malpractice in one case, and that a prosecution therefor was contemplated. His business, which was that of a druggist, suffered. The tendency of this state of things was gradually to alienate his affection for his wife. He was naturally proud, sensitive, and reasonably ambitious, besides being somewhat passionate and hasty. He became moody, morose, reticent, and to some extent inattentive to his business. He was troubled occasionally with insomnia and loss of appetite, and became generally despondent, discontented, and unhappy from brooding over his changed domestic relations. The plaintiff left his wife July 19, 1889. At the end of six weeks he went back to see whether their differences could be adjusted; if not, he intended to apply for a divorce. He wished her to give up practice: she refused. He called again: she declined to see him. He then sent a third person, who informed her that the plaintiff was willing to go back if she would give up practice—that he did not ask her to give up her belief in Christian Science: she replied that she did not believe it was her duty to give up practice, and sent word to the plaintiff that if he would come back it must be on the basis of Christian Science,—meaning that he should permit her to do what she deemed right— to go whenever and wherever she believed it right to go. No further attempt at reconciliation was made. The causes above mentioned operated upon the abnormally sensitive nature of the plaintiff, and have seriously injured his health. The defendant, in embracing and practicing Christian Science, intended no injury to her husband or to his business. She did not believe and ought not reasonably to have anticipated that her advocacy of the doctrine would seriously injure his health or seriously endanger his reason. She is sincere in her belief in the truthfulness of the doctrine. It was admitted on the trial that 'she treated her husband as well as a wife ought until she embraced Christian Science, barring the failings incident to humanity.' Testimony was introduced as to her character for kindness, tenderness, generosity, and peaceableness as woman, wife, mother, and neighbor: the evidence established that her character in these respects is good, and that she possesses all these qualities.

*   *   *

CARPENTER, J.

The act of February 17, 1791, declared that 'divorces may be decreed for the cause of extreme cruelty in either of the parties.' Laws (ed. 1830) 157. What constitutes extreme cruelty was left to be determined by the ecclesiastical common law. 'Mere austerity of temper, petulance of manners, rudeness of language, a want of civil attention and accommodation, even occasional sallies of passion, if they do not threaten bodily harm, do not amount to legal cruelty; they are high moral

offences in the marriage state undoubtedly, not innocent surely in any state of life, but still they are not that cruelty against which the law can relieve. Under such misconduct of either of the parties—for it may exist on the one side as well as on the other—the suffering party must bear in some degree the consequences of an injudicious connection; must subdue by decent resistance or by prudent conciliation; and if this cannot be done, both must suffer in silence. If it be complained that by this inactivity of the courts much injustice may be suffered and much misery produced, the answer is, that courts of justice do not pretend to furnish cures for all the miseries of human life; they redress or punish gross violations of duty, but they go no further: they cannot make men virtuous; and as the happiness of the world depends upon its virtue, there may be much unhappiness in it which human laws cannot undertake to remove.

'Still less is it cruelty when it wounds not the natural feelings, but the acquired feelings arising from particular rank and situation; for the court has no scale of sensibilities by which it can gauge the quantum of injury done and felt: and therefore, though the court will not absolutely exclude considerations of that sort where they are stated merely as matter of aggravation, yet they cannot constitute cruelty where it would not otherwise have existed. . . . In the older cases of this sort which I have had an opportunity of looking into, I have observed that the danger of life, limb, or health is usually inserted as the ground upon which the court has proceeded to a separation. This doctrine has been repeatedly applied by the court in the cases that have been mentioned; the court has never been driven off this ground; it has been always jealous of the inconvenience of departing from it; and I have heard no one case cited in which the court has granted a divorce without proof given of a reasonable apprehension of bodily hurt. I say an apprehension, because assuredly the court is not to wait till the hurt is actually done; but the apprehension must be reasonable; it must not be an apprehension arising merely from an exquisite and diseased sensibility of mind. Petty vexations applied to such a constitution of mind may certainly in time wear out the animal machine, but still they are not cases of legal relief; people must relieve themselves as well as they can by prudent resistance,—by calling in the succours of religion and the consolations of friends; but the aid of courts is not to be resorted to in such cases with any effect.' *Evans v. Evans*, 1 Hagg. Con. 35, 38-40 (decided in 1790). 'There must be something which renders cohabitation unsafe; for there may be much unhappiness from unkind treatment and from violent and abusive language;—but the court will not interfere—it must leave parties to the correction of their own judgment; they must bear as well as they can the consequences of their own choice. Words of menace are different: if they are likely to be carried into effect, the court is called on to prevent their being carried on to mischief.' *Harris v. Harris,* 2 Ph. Ecc. 111 (1813). . . . To constitute cruelty 'there must be either actual violence committed, attended with danger to life, limb, or health; or there must be a reasonable apprehension of such violence. This I apprehend to be the substance of the doctrine laid down in *Evans v. Evans.* . . .

* * *

To constitute extreme cruelty, direct bodily injury, actual or threatened, was essential. Threats of personal violence, unless of such a character as to create 'in a mind of ordinary firmness' a reasonable apprehension that they might be executed, were not legal cruelty. To the exceptionally sensitive and timid wife, put in actual and constant fear of limb or life by conduct not calculated to have that effect on a person of normal and ordinary sensibility, the law of divorce afforded no relief. The infliction of mere mental pain, however seriously it might injure health or endanger reason, was not legal cruelty. A husband might violate all the proprieties and decencies of social life; he might call 'his virtuous wife a strumpet, saying so not to herself alone, but before everybody,' although 'as far as suffering was concerned he had better kick her' (*Paterson v. Paterson,* 3 H. L. Ca. 308, 313); he might bring prostitutes into his family and seat them at his table,—make his house a brothel—and the law, if it would justify the wife in leaving him, afforded her no other remedy. For such conduct as that described in *W——— v. W———,* 141 Mass. 495, and the injury caused to 'her health by its effect upon her feelings,' the wife was then, in New Hampshire, as she is now in Massachusetts, remediless. Constant, innumerable, and nameless indignities of speech and action, each possibly petty and in itself, might cause mental anguish less endurable, more hurtful to physical well-being, and more likely to overturn reason, than any degree of pain produced by blows; they might make life intolerable and death welcome, yet they were not legal cruelty. The sufferer's only remedy was 'by prudent resistance,' and 'by calling in the succours of religion and the consolations of friends.'

In consideration of this state of the law, the legislature, in 1840, enacted that 'divorces . . . shall be decreed in favor of the innocent party . . . when either party shall so treat the other as

seriously to injure health or endanger reason.' . . . It was intended to provide for a divorce of the parties in cases of the character referred to, where the conduct complained of did not fall within the established definition of extreme cruelty.

* * *

. . . The purpose of the legislature was to make the remedy coextensive with the mischief. A malevolent motive in the party complained of need not be shown. Divorce is not punishment of the offender, but relief to the sufferer. Whether the behavior proved is sufficient ground of divorce depends on the question whether it has seriously injured health or endangered reason. This is the sole test. The question is, not whether the treatment reasonably ought, or could reasonably be expected, seriously to injure the health or endanger the reason of a person of ordinary intelligence and mental strength, but whether it has in fact had that effect upon the health or reason of the person complaining. A course of conduct which would drive one person crazy, might have no effect on, or might even be grateful to, another and perhaps more sensible or less sensitive person; but he or she whose reason is imperilled by it is not therefore to be compelled to endure the treatment. That the conduct complained of is in itself innocent, or even laudable, and is pursued from a sense of duty, does not afford a sufficient reason for requiring the party injured by it to submit to the destruction of health, reason, and life. The abstract reasonableness of the treatment, or its effect upon reasonable persons of ordinary firmness, does not enter into the question. If it did, the redress intended by the statute could not in many cases be obtained. The provision was designed for the benefit of the sensitive—not excepting the abnormally sensitive—and not for the insensible and apathetic, whom nothing but blows can effect. It was intended to reach and provide relief in a class of cases where extreme cruelty as defined by law cannot be established—cases, among others, of slow and continuous mental torture, destructive of health or reason, and caused by conduct not necessarily wrongful, possibly even praiseworthy, in itself, and made a cause of divorce only because of its effect upon an abnormally sensitive mind.

The injury, and in greater part the suffering, caused by acts tending to the destruction of health or reason may not depend upon the intention with which they are done. Whether they are done with or without malice, they may be in their effect equally hurtful and destructive. In the judgment of the legislature, it is better that the marital relation be dissolved, than that by its continuance the health or reason of either party be destroyed. Whether the legislation is wise or unwise is a question upon which opinions may differ; but with it the court has no concern. Its duty is to enforce the law as it is found to be. To hold that to warrant a divorce treatment seriously endangering health or reason must be wilful, malicious, or malevolent would repeal the statute.

It is found that the defendant's conduct has seriously injured the plaintiff's health, and the court cannot say that the finding is not warranted by the evidence. . . .

Divorce decreed.

NOTES

NOTE 1.

RAMON v. RAMON *
Domestic Relations Court of City of New York,
Family Court Division, Richmond County
34 N.Y.S. 2d 100 (1942)

O'BRIEN, JUSTICE.

In the Michigan Law Review, Vol. 14, page 177, Professor Roscoe Pound, in his article entitled "Individual Interests in the Domestic Relations," writes, "two elements must be taken into account in securing interests in domestic relations. On the one hand there is an individual spiritual existence * * * on the other hand, there is the individual economic existence. * * * These are interests of personality * * * peculiarly related to the mental and spiritual life of the individual."

Marriage is a natural right. It was not created by law. It existed before all law. Marriage is a right of personality. By the marriage ceremony these obligations became the vested rights of the personality of the respondent embraced in the law of the land, and defined as the rights of personality.

The reciprocal duties of husband and wife constitute property. "These reciprocal rights may be regarded as the property of the respective parties, in the broad sense of the word property, which includes things not tangible or visible, and applies to whatever is exclusively one's own." Jaynes v. Jaynes, 39 Hun 40, at page 41.

* * *

From Father Abraham to Pope Pius XII, from the dawn of Israel to modern Jewry a consistent and inflexible prohibition of "Mixed Marriages" is recorded upon the pages of Holy Writ, the history of Christendom and of Jewish history.

The book of Genesis records the command of Abraham to his favorite and trusted servant,

whom he sent out to seek a wife for his son Isaac: "And I will make thee swear by the Lord, the God of Heaven and the God of the earth, that thou shalt not take a wife unto my son of the daughters of the Canaanites among whom I dwell. But thou shalt go unto my country and to my kindred, and take a wife unto my son Isaac." Genesis Ch. XXIV, 3, 4.

* * *

And as frequent intermarriage threatened to disintegrate and even to destroy Israel, the alarmed Priest and Prophet Ezra denounced this practice:

"Now therefor give not your daughters unto their sons, neither take their daughters unto your sons." Ezra XI, 12, "And they entered * * * into an oath to walk in God's law * * * and that we would not give our daughters unto the people of the land, nor take their daughters for our sons." Nehem. X, 29, 30.

This sound principle has been recognized and maintained until this day and is clearly expressed in these words: "Intermarriage is not countenanced by modern Judaism * * * due * * * to a conviction that unity of religion is essential to the happiness of the home." Jewish Ency. Vol. 5, page 626.

The Roman Catholic Church likewise from the very inception of her existence forbade the marriage of Catholics to non-Catholics. At the Council of Elvira, A.D. 305, the early Christian Fathers adopted this Canon: "Haeretici si se transferre noluerint ad ecclesiam catholicam, nec ipsis catholicas dandas esse puellas." ("It has pleased us to decree that if heretics are unwilling to become members of the Catholic Church, Catholic girls need not be given them.")

* * *

NOTE 2.

KRAUSS v. KRAUSS
163 La. 218, 111 So. 683 (1927)

THOMPSON, J.
This is an appeal from a judgment granting the wife a separation from bed and board.

* * *

It is contended on behalf of the defendant that the religious differences between the spouses . . . furnished the only cause on which the suit for separation is founded.

* * *

If the plaintiff's evidence went no further than to show religious differences that would end the case.

The law has not designated and indeed could not make diverse religious opinions a legal cause

---

* This opinion as here published substitutes fictitious surnames in accordance with the spirit of Domestic Relations Court Act, Sec. 52.

for separation. The fundamental law of the land guarantees freedom of religion and the right to worship according to the dictates of one's own conscience.

The defendant had the legal and moral right to pursue and to practice his own religious faith, and no court could deny such right or even criticize adversely the proper exercise of that right.

But no law, divine or human, can be found to justify a husband in practicing his religious faith in such a manner as to reduce his wife and children to a state which would ultimately if continued, lead to extreme poverty. It is a warning of divine origin that he who does not provide for his own and especially for those of his own house, hath denied the faith and is worse than an infidel. Nor was the husband justified in so practicing his religious faith as to completely ostracize his wife from the public and to make of her a perfect recluse, to degrade her social status, and to humiliate her by forcing her to sever all associations and contact with her friends and the public in general except those of his own household of faith.

There cannot be found any religious tenets which would justify the husband in publicly declaring that his wife was leading a vain and empty life and was unfit to rear, educate, and train her children because forsooth she did not follow him in his religious convictions.

We said on the former hearing of this case, Trautman v. Krauss, 159 La. 371, 105 So. 376, that if the petition showed nothing more than that the defendant had changed his religion and was attempting to proselyte his wife and children, it would not disclose a cause of action for separation, but we did not hold, nor did we intend to hold, that the practice of religion, or one's religious conduct, may not be of such a nature and character as to constitute cruel treatment which would justify a separation.

We said, to the contrary, that:

"It is not impossible that such nagging as the plaintiff has charged against her husband could amount to cruel and intolerable treatment."

The courts will look, not so much to the originating cause of the cruel treatment, but to the nature and character of the treatment itself in determining the question as to whether it amounts to such cruelty as to warrant a separation.

* * *

[W]here the conduct of a spouse is calculated permanently to destroy the peace of mind and happiness of the other so as utterly to destroy the objects of matrimony, a divorce may be granted on the ground of cruelty.

We must hold therefore that any unjustifiable conduct on the part of either husband or wife which so grievously wounds the mental feelings of the other, or such as in any other manner utterly destroys the legitimate ends and objects of matrimony, constitutes cruelty, although no physical or personal violence may be inflicted or threatened.

As well said by some writer, if it be true that we are possessed of social, moral and intellectual notions, with wants to be supplied, with susceptibilities of pain and pleasure, if they can be wounded and healed, as well as the physical part, with accompanying suffering and delight, then we think that conduct which produces perpetual social sorrow may well be classed as cruelty and entitle the sufferer to relief.

There appears very little hope under a continuance of present conditions for reuniting the broken ties, and hence we do not feel justified in condemning the plaintiff to what appears to us to be a life of misery and suffering by rejecting her demand. We are therefore constrained to affirm the judgment. It is only for a separation, and the parties will have one year for reflection before the marriage ties can be finally dissolved.

* * *

NOTE 3.

FRANTZEN v. FRANTZEN
349 S.W. 2d 765 (Civ. App., Tex. 1961)

BARROW, JUSTICE.

The following statement of the nature and result of the suit, as well as the material allegations of plaintiff's petition, is copied from appellant's brief:

"This suit was filed in January, 1959, wherein Appellant sought a divorce and the custody of the children of the marriage—boys—one born on March 28, 1955, and the other August 28, 1957. Exceptions to husband's—Appellant's—Petition were sustained and the cause dismissed on January 14, 1961; to this Decree Appellant excepted in open court and gave Notice of Appeal * * *.

"The parties were married January 24, 1953, and up to the development of the controversy culminating in this suit, they lived in harmony and worked enthusiastically in their determination to provide security for the family and most especially to give the boys such education and training advantages as were calculated to develop them as moral, substantial and patriotic citizens. Accordingly, both parties joined the same Church, the Junior Chamber of Commerce, participated in political affairs, the Defendant becoming the Woman Chairman of the Women's County Republican Organization, and Plaintiff—especially with a view of impressing the sons with the importance of the organization—became a Boy Scout Leader. Thus, by both precept and example, the parties were engaged in doing their utmost to encourage the children to become intelligent, patriotic citizens, taking part in the affairs of Government and ever ready to defend the Nation from attack by those who would destroy it from within or without. * * *

"The first challenge to the aspirations of the family presented itself to Appellant on a night in April, 1958, when upon his return from a Scout Meeting, he found Appellee in company with—apparently engaged in a conference, known as a 'Study Session'—with three members of the local Jehovah Witness Organization. As soon as the parties to the cause were alone, Appellant expressed his apprehension to Appellee and requested her to desist in further studying with the group. Appellee refused, claiming Appellant's apprehension unfounded and insisted that Appellant meet with the Appellee and the local Jehovah Witness leader—'Pioneer'—so as to become informed of the true purposes of the Jehovah Witnesses. * * * In this meeting, the Appellant was informed by the Pioneer, Jehovah Witnesses believe, and advocate that: (a) 'All world governments are ruled by the devil', (b) for such reason Jehovah Witnesses refuse to take part in any governmental activities such as voting, offering for public office, service on juries, refuse to salute the Flag and to pledge allegiance to any Nation; (c) refuse to serve in the Armed Force, even to defend the Country against an aggressor who would enslave our people; (d) theirs, the religion of the Jehovah Witnesses, is the only true religion and only a select few are permitted to go to Heaven, (e) Jehovah Witnesses refuse to permit their children to join such character-building and patriotic organizations as Boy or Girl Scouts, Young Men's and Young Women's Christian Associations, (f) refuse to grant permission for the administration of blood transfusions even in case of severe illness involving the danger of loss of life; (g) and the Jehovah Witness beliefs and doctrines are so strong that unless both husband and wife are co-believers, divorce will as a general rule result.

"As a result of the discussion immediately following this meeting, the Appellee in the interest of the children agreed to remain away from the Study Sessions and the family continued to live happily together. * * *

"About the middle of August following—at the near-midnight return home—Appellee admitted that she had broken her promise, had been secretly attending the Study Sessions and stated she was a convert to the doctrines of the Jehovah Witnesses. Instantly, Appellant envisioned a wrecked home and the most terrible impositions which were going to be visited upon the helpless sons—subjecting them to embarrassment during their youth, and if, upon becoming devotees, to Appellee's teachings, being deprived of the opportunities available to normal American boys, and instead becoming absolutely useless to their community and valueless to the Nation which had made available to them the greatest opportunities afforded in any country in the world. The contemplation of these misfortunes for the sons caused Appellant to lose his self-control, and he appealed and begged Appellee over and over to change her course for the sake of the two sons. Appellee finally once more agreed to sever her relations with the 'Study Session Group'. And Appellant having full confidence in Appellee's promise, the family once more lived happily—Appellant being entirely confident of Appellee's good faith and that the family's ambitions for the two sons would be fulfilled. * * *

"On the following October 17th—being the day following a night when Appellee on leaving home had stated she was going to 'visit a mutual friend'—at the noon meal, the son Kurt announced, 'Mom and I went to class last night.' Being suddenly confronted with Appellee's apparent deliberate deception and her broken promise —under an immediate uncontrollable impulse— Appellant forcibly took both children from Appellee and carried them to her parents in San Antonio. Returning home with the children the next day, Appellant begged Appellee to return with him to her parents and her sister in the hope they might render effective assistance to Appellant. He also finally persuaded the Appellee to discuss the family situation with the Minister who had performed their wedding ceremony, with the Minister of their Church, with a 'Marriage Counselor', with the Family Doctor, and with several other mutual friends—all without avail—as equally was every other appeal by Appellant. * * *

"These efforts at persuading Appellee to change her course, were continued without success during the months of October, November and December. Appellee remained adamant in her position. All the time Appellant was constantly conscious of the certain impositions which would be visited upon the children if they were to remain under Appellee's influence, and the possibility of either or both unnecessarily losing their lives in case of severe illness because of Appellee's commitment to refuse to permit blood transfusions. As these thoughts were constantly with Appellant, he suffered loss of sleep, appetite and serious impairment of his health to the extent as to render the further living together with Appellee absolutely insupportable. His only remaining recourse for the children's protection was the law. He filed this suit."

The petition in this case alleged no overt acts of cruel, harsh, or unkind treatment that the law recognizes as being of such a nature as to render appellant's further living with appellee insupportable. It is apparent from the allegations that appellant's suffering is entirely mental and emotional and brought about by a difference of religious faith and belief. While we are unable to comprehend any religious faith that would regard allegiance and patriotic service to one's country as in any way repugnant to one's religious belief, nevertheless, the right to such religious belief is protected by the Constitution of the United States as well as this State, so long as the teachings and practice of such religious belief are neither immoral nor illegal. The Courts have no more power to enforce by decree a conformance to certain religious teachings and practices than does the Legislature to establish a national or state religion by law. . . . The Courts of this State have repeatedly and consistently held that differences of the spouses in religious faith, teaching and practice are not grounds for a divorce in this State. . . . Moreover, one's religious beliefs, teachings and practices are not grounds for depriving a parent of his or her children, so long as such teachings and practices are neither immoral nor illegal. Appellant has cited no authorities to the contrary, and we have found none. The trial court correctly sustained the exceptions to plaintiff's petition, and upon his refusal to amend properly dismissed the suit.

The judgment is affirmed.

NOTE 4.

JONES, ERNEST

The Psychology of Religion*

In the attempt to get as near as we can to the meaning of religion we are met at the outset by a very imperfect agreement about what is to be included under the term. Any psychological theory of religion, therefore, is open to the criticism that it does not comprehend this or that feature which is alleged to be essential. Some criticisms of this kind are merely factious and prove nothing more than that the theory in question is incomplete, which the author himself would in most cases admit: to seek to define religion exactly would be, like defining sexuality, a presumptuous undertaking in the present state of our knowledge and we must be content with the fact that after all we have a very good general idea of what is meant by the word. There is a wide agreement that any comprehensive theory must take into account at least the following aspects of the problem: (1) Other worldliness, the relation to the supernatural. This has been described as "the consciousness of our practical relation to an invisible spiritual order". The spiritual order is invested with the attributes of

_____

* Reprinted in Ernest Jones, *Essays in Applied Psychoanalysis*, London: The Hogarth Press Ltd, and The Institute of Psychoanalysis, 1926 (pp. 191-92) Reprinted with permission of the publisher and International Universities Press, New York.

power and sacredness. The emotional attitudes towards it vary, those of dependence, fear, love and reverence being the most characteristic; the first-named is perhaps the most constant. Propitiation is common, though not invariable. (2) The effort to cope with the various problems surrounding death, both emotionally and intellectually. (3) The pursuit and conservation of values, especially those felt to be the highest and most permanent. (4) A constant association with the ideals of ethics and morality. Religion is rarely found apart from these ideals, though they are often found, especially among civilized peoples, independently of religion. (5) The connection between religion and the sense of inadequacy in coping with the difficulties of life, whether these difficulties be external or, more characteristically, internal ones such as the conviction of sin and guilt.

NOTE 5.

ONDREJKA v. ONDREJKA
4 Wis. 2d 277, 90 N.W. 2d 615 (1958)

HALLOWS, JUSTICE.

*   *   *

The appellant's main argument is that as a matter of law membership in the Communist Party and different religious beliefs do not constitute grounds for divorce. The respondent contends this is not the issue but it is the activities and conduct of the appellant and its effect on him and on the marital relationship that constitutes cruel and inhuman treatment.

. . . Some of the issues of fact are that the plaintiff's activities in the Communist Party interfered with and destroyed the family life; her unexplained absences from the home; her association with persons abhorrent to the defendant; her interference with the defendant's associations with others; the violent arguments between the plaintiff and the defendant, and the plaintiff's statement that the Communist Party was her life, that it would always be her life and nothing could change it.

The originating cause of the cruel and inhuman treatment is not so important as the nature and character of the treatment itself in determining the question of whether the treatment by a spouse has been cruel and inhuman . . .

It is not ideas but the acts which constitute cruel and inhuman treatment. A person has the right to think freely in this country. But the nature of the overt acts and especially their effect on the spouse caused by or resulting from ideas and beliefs, but not the ideas and beliefs per se, are the important elements of cruel and inhuman treatment. The appellant relies on Donaldson v. Donaldson, 1951, . . . 231 P.2d 607, . . . and Braun v. Braun, 1948, . . . 197 P.2d 442. Both of these cases are to the effect that membership in the Communist Party would not constitute cruelty per se and be grounds in itself for divorce. These cases are not in point as the allegations in the counterclaim go beyond mere membership in the Communist Party and allege treatment of the respondent by the appellant which has its origin or reason in such membership. The same treatment of the respondent by the appellant, if proved, originating from any other source or reason would constitute, if proved, cruel and inhuman treatment. The question of whether membership in the Communist Party per se would constitute cruel and inhuman treatment is not before this court.

NOTE 6.

ONDREJKA v. ONDREJKA
Six Years Later

"The . . . case was remitted to the lower court for trial on the merits. The action had originally been commenced on November 15, 1954. The parties voluntarily separated immediately thereafter, the husband having moved to living quarters elsewhere.

The husband's activities in other areas had some bearing, although indirect, on the . . . divorce case. The husband had been a paid informer for the F.B.I. in Milwaukee since about 1949. These activities first came to light, and to his wife's attention, after she had served and filed her summons and complaint alleging cruel and inhuman treatment, but before the husband had served and filed his answer and counterclaim raising the political, i.e., Communist, issues. In early 1955, after the summons and complaint were served by the wife upon the husband, the husband publicly revealed himself as having been an informer for the F.B.I. He was active in that capacity until about the end of 1954.

At hearings subsequently conducted by the House Un-American Activities Committee in Milwaukee in early 1955, he testified as a chief witness against a number of Milwaukeeans, including his wife, regarding their alleged Communist party activities. His testimony before the Committee occurred after he had filed his answer and counterclaim, but embraced in a number of respects the same subject matter as appeared in his answer and counterclaim . . .

In both the hearings in Milwaukee of the House Un-American Activities Committee . . . Ondrejka testified that he had regularly filed reports with the F.B.I. on the alleged Communist activities of his wife.

On March 10, 1960, in *Lilly Ondrejka v. Michael John Ondrejka, Jr.,* Case No. 287-473, the wife commenced a new action for divorce in the Circuit Court of Milwaukee County on the ground of voluntary separation for a period of five years under Sec. 247.07(6) of the Wisconsin Statutes. The husband served and filed an answer which consisted in substance of a general denial. . . . The Circuit Court entered its decision on May 24, 1963, granting an absolute divorce to the plaintiff wife on the grounds of voluntary separation of the parties for five years." [Letter from M. Michael Essin, attorney for the wife, dated July 2, 1964.]

NOTE 7.

REIK, THEODOR
Of Love and Lust*

. . . The masochist uses all possible means at his disposal to induce his partner to create for him that discomfort which he needs for attaining his pleasure. He forces another person to force him . . .

* * *

. . . There are a great many "exasperated" masochists who torture their objects until they retaliate with the desired punishment or revenge. Till then the pressure will be increased. A peculiar spying on and watching of the object goes with this maneuver without the masochist being aware of it. In this behavior the masochist strongly resembles a naughty child who plagues his mother or nurse until he gets punished. Such a child too gets naughtier and naughtier all the while, nor is the watching and spying lacking. He seems to ask himself in the presence of the patient mother, "Will she now get angry? Not yet? Can she remain patient even now?" I once heard a little girl who was reprimanded by her mother in such a scene ask curiously, "But if I keep doing it, what will you do then?"

In the behavior described . . . the boundaries between masochistic and sadistic conduct are effaced for a short time. Aggressive and forceful means are used in order to attain punishment, scolding, humiliation. The pain addict becomes a tormentor. Roles appear to be reversed for this period. The masochist behaves like a sadist and his object, from whom he expects pain, suffering, and degradation, behaves like the victim of a sadist. This challenge, enticement, provocation to give the desired masochistic satisfaction goes on in a sadistic form . . .

* * *

If a masochist thus has succeeded in inducing his victim to injure him, it not seldom occurs that

---

* Reprinted from *Of Love and Lust* by Theodor Reik, pp. 248-49, 252, by permission of Farrar, Straus and Co., Inc. Copyright © 1941, 1957 by Theodor Reik.

he actually feels offended and hurt. This reaction, of course, is restricted to consciousness. But it does not exclude an unconscious satisfaction. A certain type of person who constantly feels slighted and offended is to be counted among the unconscious masochists who provoke their associates until at last they produce an insult or a humiliation. I believe that the score of those neglected by destiny includes a great number of such disguised masochists who claim to have been unjustly treated. The pertinacity and single-mindedness of the masochist nearly always succeeds in attaining his secret aim. As a reversed Shylock he insists on being injured although he consciously resists it with all his power. Of course his incessant and indefatigable efforts arouse all aggressive and vengeful tendencies of the partner who is tempted to give free rein to his own cruelty. In his unconscious search the masochist unfailingly finds his sadistic counterpart.

NOTE 8.

GOLDEN v. ARONS
36 N.J. Super. 371, 115 A. 2d 639 (1955)

NIMMO, J. C. C. (temporarily assigned).

* * *

The parties were married on May 12, 1950. One child, a girl, was born of the marriage, now four years of age.

Both parties were brought up in the Jewish faith. They were married by a magistrate and a month later were married by a rabbi. On June 15, 1951 defendant entered the armed service and went to Korea. Shortly before defendant left for Korea the child Linda was born. Until defendant's departure they lived as a normal Jewish couple, attending Jewish affairs and observing Jewish holy days and dietary laws. While in Korea defendant became friendly with a Roman Catholic chaplain and became interested in the Catholic faith. Upon defendant's return to the United States he told his wife of his conversion to Catholicism and charged her with being an unfit mother because she would not bring their child up in the faith he had embraced. Before he left for Korea he knew that he had what is termed a kosher home that observed all Jewish dietary laws. Upon his return he belittled all Jewish observances. On days recognized by Jewish people as holy days, he flaunted them. On the Day of Atonement he would turn on the radio in their home as loud as it would be possible and caused great unnecessary noise. He called plaintiff on many occasions in the presence of others a "lousy Jew" and an unfit mother. He became obsessed with his new-found religion and cut his wife off from all her Jewish friends and acquaintances. His discussion of re-

ligion became a daily occurrence. Defendant knew that all through their married life his wife was a religious, orthodox Jewess, and very active in Jewish social and charitable organizations, as he was himself until his conversion to Catholicism. Plaintiff is a college graduate of fine sensibilities. While his wife slept he would put a small chain about her neck with a medal in an effort to make her wear it. Observing the parties on the witness stand under examination and cross-examination it became apparent that defendant was determined to convert his wife to his way of thinking no matter what happened. He did state at one time that he would become a Jew again, but it did not appear sincere and further it was not his wife's wish that he return to his former religion but only leave her alone in the religion of her choice that had been his too. The plaintiff it was admitted did go with defendant to the church of his choice and attended Mass several times with him, in an attempt to appease him but that was not sufficient for him. It could be seen that defendant's conduct had greatly affected his wife when she testified. Her health became affected as the household was in a continual turmoil due to defendant's actions and talk.

This is an unusual case in that there does not appear to be any reported cases in New Jersey exactly in point. However, this court did hold in an unreported case, that where a husband of a devout Catholic wife would remove and destroy objects of the Catholic faith and ridicule such things, that it was extreme cruelty and the wife was accorded relief. There is no question that everyone has the freedom of choice of religious solace. It is a thing personal to them. When the religious faith of one is forced on another, courts will take cognizance of the matter. This defendant was and is at liberty to embrace such religion as to him seems best. The nub of this case is not that defendant changed his religion—that he had a perfect right to do—but he tried to force his religion upon his wife to the point where her life was wretched and miserable, that he cannot do. It is inescapable not to conclude that defendant did not absorb the true teaching of Christianity and Catholicism. He became a religious fanatic. There cannot be found any religious tenets which would justify a husband to declare that his wife was leading a vain life and unfit to rear her children because she did not follow him in his religious convictions. Where the conduct of a spouse is calculated to destroy the peace of mind and happiness of the other so as to utterly destroy the objects of matrimony, it amounts to extreme cruelty. The fundamental law of the land guarantees freedom of religion and the right to worship according to the dictates of one's own conscience.

As above stated, defendant has that freedom, but he denies it to his wife. Mere diverse religious opinions do not of themselves constitute a cause of action, it is only when, as we have here, a forcing of those opinions on another with the resultant effect on the plaintiff, that cause of action accrues.

People are sensitive concerning their religious beliefs. An irreligious person to whom religion means little or nothing, is beyond the pale of being hurt as would a devout adherent to the tenets of his or her religion. Relief for extreme cruelty can be stated as designed for the sensitive as well as the insensible and apathetic whom nothing but blows can affect.

Counsel urges that because defendant was and is under psychiatric care he might be excused for his acts. Yet, there is nothing to indicate that he did not know what he was doing and it bears out the conclusion of the court that he was fanatical in his treatment of his wife.

Judgment will be entered for plaintiff. . . .

NOTE 9.

GOLDEN v. ARONS
Six Years Later

Neither Ernest nor I have remarried.

Linda and I are living with my folks. She is nine years now and is being reared in the Jewish faith. She attended Sunday school from the age of 5 until this Fall when she 'graduated' into the Talmud Torah program. She goes to Talmud Torah Monday through Thursday for one hour each afternoon after school. On Saturday mornings she attends the 'Junior' Sabbath services. On Sunday mornings she goes to the synagogue to a club meeting of children her age. This is about the same religious training that I received at her age.

Ernest feels that she spends too much time among Jewish people but has done nothing to sway her toward any other religion. As to his religious convictions, I don't know how to answer. He does not attend church on Sunday mornings. I know this because he has frequently seen Linda the first thing on Sunday mornings. It is easy to say that he *is not* Jewish and that he would like Linda *not to be* Jewish. What he *is* and what he would like Linda *to be* is in the realm of the unknown as far as I can see.

As to a Jewish divorce, I did obtain one four years ago . . . I was able to get this without Ernest's knowledge or consent because provision is made for this in the Sacred Books. The case of a man converting is one of the rare instances when a woman may secure a divorce without her husband's consent. . . . I had questioned Ernest about granting a divorce to me. I did not then

know that I could get one without him. He refused to participate in any such action because he was not of the Jewish faith. Actually, he was just being ornery, because he did not have to participate in any ceremony, just state in front of a Rabbi that I was the woman to whom he had been married on the date of our marriage.

I surely think that it will take an Act of Congress to convince Ernest that he is truly divorced. Were I to remarry tomorrow he would call me a bigamist. He insists that a grave miscarriage of justice occurred when the divorce was granted. He also believes that I am an unfit mother and should not be responsible for Linda's unbringing (particularly religious training). Paradoxically, he believes he is still married to me and I should forget the nonsense and come back to him. Needless to add, I avoid any conversation with him except as regards Linda.

On the credit side of the ledger, he has been doing well vocationally, has been working steadily and maintains an apartment for himself in the same apartment house in which his parents live. My in-laws are as nice to me as they always were, cordial and appreciative that whenever I'm in the neighborhood I bring Linda up to see them. Linda sees her cousins on Ernest's side of the family regularly and her aunts too are kind to her, and gracious to me too, for that matter, whenever I happen to see them in my in-laws' home.

Ernest sees Linda once weekly at least and would like her to spend weekends with him which she has on three occasions and will again. Financially he lives up to the terms of the divorce ($20.) and probably would give more if pressed but I am in no great need of money for her—that is, more than that plus my earnings (above my own needs, I mean). He pays for her hospitalization and has an insurance policy of which she is the beneficiary so I would say that he meets his obligations. Since he is not a grasping person and neither am I we've never had any difficulties over money.

On the credit side of my ledger—after $4\frac{1}{2}$ years of teaching I made a big switch this October and started working in a movie picture advertising agency. It's small, exciting and I hope to grow along with it. Linda enjoyed day camp so much that it was obvious I would no longer have to spend the summers with her. So I just didn't go back after the summer and went back to work more diversified. (You may or may not recall that before I entered teaching, I worked for the producer of a summer theater and originally went into teaching so I could have the summers free). So vocationally my life is very stimulating, socially very busy, but romantically—or at least from the point of view of marriage—definitely on even keel . . . [Letter from plaintiff to her attorney—January 23, 1961].

b. Mental Illness—A Mitigating or Aggravating Factor?

WILLIAMS v. WILLIAMS
[1962] 3 All E.R. 441

WILLMER, L. J.: This is an appeal from a judgment of Mr. Commissioner GALLOP, Q.C., given on Feb. 8, 1962, whereby he dismissed a wife's petition for divorce on the ground of cruelty. The main question raised by the appeal is with regard to the application of the principles of the M'Naghten rules,[1] more particularly the second limb thereof, to a petition for cruelty where it is shown that during the material period the respondent was suffering from a disease of the mind. The so-called M'Naghten rules were contained in the advice tendered by the judges, following the decision in *M'Naughten's Case,* and provide as follows:

> ". . . it must be clearly proved that, at the time of the committing of the act, the party accused was labouring under such a defect of reason, from disease of the mind, as not to know the nature and quality of the act he was doing; or, if he did know it, that he did not know he was doing what was wrong."

I have not found the question which we have to decide at all easy of solution, and it has not been made any easier for me by the fact that the other two lords justices take divergent views. I confess that my own mind has fluctuated, both during the argument and since its conclusion. In the end, however, I have come to the conclusion that there is no reason to interfere with the decision arrived at by the commissioner. I am not satisfied, in all the circumstances of the case, that the husband has been proved to have treated the wife with cruelty.

The parties were married on Dec. 26, 1943, and there are four children of the marriage, a son and three daughters, born respectively in 1944, 1945, 1948 and 1949. They resided together in Pontypool. . . . The husband was a coal miner, though it appears to be the fact that from time to time he engaged in other occupations. Early in 1954 the husband began to display symptoms of mental disorder, and on Aug. 17 of that year he was admitted as a voluntary patient to the Abergavenny Mental Hospital. There he came under the care of Dr. Wales, now medical superintendent of the hospital, who has been responsible for his treatment ever since. Dr. Wales gave evidence at the trial, and said that the husband was suffering

from paranoid schizophrenia ; this caused him to believe that he was persecuted by people unknown, and he was harassed by auditory hallucinations. . . . He . . . remained in hospital for over four years. . . . During the whole of this period he was allowed to return home on leave on frequent occasions, and during these periods of leave he resumed cohabitation with his wife. On Mar. 21, 1959, the husband . . . discharged himself and once more returned to the matrimonial home. The wife, however, refused to have anything to do with him, and complained of his behaviour towards her, the principal complaint being that he persecuted her by constantly accusing her, without any justification, of misbehaviour with other men. On May 20, 1959, the wife presented her petition, alleging cruelty against the husband. At that time the husband was still living at the matrimonial home, and he continued to do so until Dec. 7, 1959, when he was re-admitted to hospital. As I understand it, he has been there ever since, and the prognosis is not favourable.

The wife's allegations of cruelty fall under three heads. The first ground of complaint, which relates to the period up to the husband's admission to hospital in 1954, is that throughout the whole of that period the husband repeatedly came home, especially on Saturday nights and Bank Holidays, in a disgustingly drunk condition, which usually resulted in his vomiting and urinating in the bed. . . . Thirdly—and this is the most important part of her case—the wife complained that since early 1954, in the period before he was admitted to hospital, during his frequent leaves, and in the period following his discharge in March 1959, the husband constantly accused her, to the point of persecution, of improper association with other men. She alleged that in consequence of the treatment that she received she suffered in health, and this was corroborated by the evidence of Dr. Jarman, the family doctor. The wife, it appears, suffered from asthma, and Dr. Jarman gave evidence to the effect that bouts of asthma were liable to be precipitated in a patient suffering from a nervous or anxiety state.

With regard to the first of these complaints, the learned commissioner found that the husband's drunken behaviour during the earlier part of the marriage did not amount to cruelty. He said:

> "The wife was demurring, no doubt, up to 1954, when the husband got drunk, but I think that she had taken it as the hard lot of a coal miner's wife. I do not think that it was made an issue in the sense that the marriage was being imperilled. The wife never said so or thought so. I accept the argument that . . .[i]f a man gets so drunk as to make the wife's life a misery, and jeopardise her health, that can be cruelty. I do

---

1. See *M'Naghten's Case* (1843), 10 Cl. & Fin. 200.

not feel justified in making a finding that the wife's health was thus jeopardised. I think she was disgusted and revolted but sufficiently resilient at that time to make the best of an extremely bad situation, and therefore that allegation is not established as cruelty."

* * *

With regard to the third and most important complaint, viz., that of constant accusations of adultery, the commissioner summarised the relevant facts as follows:

"A prominent feature of the husband's malady was auditory delusions. There were voices. He said at one stage the voices were three men and a woman. The voices were telling him his wife was committing adultery with numbers of men, and the voices generally told him that she had these men up in the loft of the house. Before going to hospital, and during his periodical leaves, and again during this period of nine months in 1959, the voices persisted, and the husband accused the wife of these innumerable adulteries. If she tried to get away from him he would follow her about the house for as long as ten minutes sometimes. Sometimes he would climb up into the loft to find the men. On the occasion, I think in 1958, he took a knife and went out to find the persons whose voices he was hearing, apparently in order to attack them. He had other delusions which must have been painful for him to bear; that a relative had been hanged, that a child of his had been murdered, are examples. I do not think that the wife spoke about them, but Dr. Wales told the court about them.

"The wife happened to have been an asthmatic since she was a girl. I hold that the condition was either aggravated or its amelioration impeded by this constant conduct of her husband. She tried to reason with him, but, as Dr. Wales explained, the patient is inaccessible. He is in a world apart. Irrespective of asthma, I am sure that it must eventually have injured her health. How can any sensitive wife, or any wife, be pursued, year after year, by accusations from her husband that she is committing adultery all the time without its jeopardising her health? Therefore, as Mr. Pitchford very helpfully acknowledged, there can be no answer to this case unless the second limb of the M'Naghten rules applies. Dr. Wales said in terms that when the husband made the accusations against the wife, he knew what he was doing. He certainly did not know that his accusations of adultery were wrong in any sense of the word. That was scarcely in dispute when the medical evidence had been heard."

The commissioner then considered a number of authorities to which he had been referred . . . in which the relevance of the M'Naghten rules to a petition for cruelty has been considered. [H]e came to the conclusion that . . . the second limb of the rules can apply. He accordingly gave effect to the view expressed by Dr. Wales, that the hus-

band, in making his accusations, did not know that what he was doing was wrong, and dismissed the wife's petition.

On this appeal three points have been taken. First, it is contended that the M'Naghten rules have no application whatsoever in a matrimonial case. Secondly, it is argued that, if the rules have any application, only the first limb is relevant ; if the husband knew what he was doing, the fact that he did not know it was wrong would, it is said, afford him no defence to his wife's charge of cruelty. Thirdly, we have been pressed to say that, even if the M'Naghten rules afford a defence to the charge in so far as it is based on the husband's repeated false accusations of adultery, his conduct during the earlier part of the marriage, particularly his persistent drunkenness, affords sufficient ground to justify a finding of cruelty against him.

I can deal briefly with the first and third of these points. As to the first, counsel for the wife himself recognised that so far as this court is concerned it is not open to him to contend that the M'Naghten rules have no application at all. For it was expressly decided in *Swan v. Swan*[7] that a spouse suffering from such a disease of the mind as not to know the nature and quality of the acts complained of could not be held guilty of cruelty. . . .

As to the third point, I can see no ground for interfering with the commissioner's conclusion that the husband's drunkenness during the earlier part of the marriage was not sufficient, in the circumstances of the case, to warrant a finding of cruelty based on that alone. . . . Here the commissioner had the advantage of seeing and hearing the wife, and was able to form his own view as to the impact on her of the conduct now complained of. We, who have not had that advantage, should not lightly interfere with his conclusion on such a matter. I can see no legitimate ground for complaint against the way in which the commissioner dealt with this charge.

* * *

The main dispute in the case has been with regard to the second point. . . . I see no reason to doubt the commissioner's findings of fact on this issue. I accordingly approach this question on the basis (a) that the husband's conduct in persisting in false charges against his wife was such as would in an ordinary case justify a finding of cruelty, but (b) that the husband, in persisting in such charges, did not know that he was doing anything wrong in any sense of the word. I have come to the conclusion, for three reasons, that the

---

7. [1953] 2 All E.R. 854; [1953] P. 258.

commissioner was right in holding that in such circumstances the husband had a good defence.

First of all, contrary to the view expressed by the commissioner himself, I think that we are bound, as he also was, by the authority of *Palmer v. Palmer*[8] to hold that both limbs of the M'Naghten rules apply in relation to a charge of cruelty in a matrimonial cause.

* * *

Thirdly, [i]t is true that the statute which we have to apply requires no more than proof that the respondent has "treated the petitioner with cruelty", which might be thought to imply that the questions whether the respondent knew what he was doing, or knew that he was doing wrong, were irrelevant. But it seems to me that, when the Matrimonial Causes Act, 1950, was enacted, Parliament must be taken to have intended that the language used should be interpreted in the light of previous judicial decisions. It must now be accepted, I think, that cruelty as understood in this context contains both a subjective and an objective element. . . .

Of what, then, does the subjective element in cruelty consist? The answer must be that it lies in the intention with which the conduct complained of is pursued. It is, I think, notorious that it is on this very point that the greatest difficulty is encountered in practice in deciding cases based on allegations of cruelty, particularly where the cruelty alleged is of the type conveniently described as mental cruelty, as opposed to physical cruelty. Where there is an actual intention to inflict pain on the other spouse, there is of course no difficulty. But it is now well settled that it is not necessary, in order to succeed, to prove an actual intention to hurt. The court is entitled to apply the maxim that a man may be presumed to intend the natural consequences of his acts, and to infer the necessary element of intention from the fact that the conduct complained of has been intentionally pursued. . . .

If, as I think is well established, the presence of intention, whether actual or presumed, is a necessary ingredient in cruelty, it must clearly be impossible to find such an intention to exist in the case of a man who does not know the nature and quality of his acts. But is it any more permissible, in a case of alleged mental cruelty such as the present, to infer such an intention in the case of a man who, though he knows what he is doing, is unable, through disease of the mind, to appreciate that what he is doing is wrong? It is not to be forgotten that cruelty is an "offence". . . . True, it is a matrimonial offence, and not a crimi-

8. [1954] 3 All E.R. 494; [1955] P. 4.

nal offence; none the less, it is an offence, and . . . it is in respect of standard of proof assimilated with a criminal offence. It seems to me to follow from what I have already said that, as with a criminal offence, so in the case of cruelty there must be an element of mens rea. It is only logical, therefore, that that which may be set up by way of defence to a criminal charge as going to show an absence of mens rea should also be admissible for the same purpose in relation to a matrimonial offence.

The principal difficulty which I have found is in the interpretation of the word "wrong" in the context of a matrimonial offence, and particularly in relation to an offence of mental cruelty such as we have here. In *R. v. Windle*[28] the Court of Criminal Appeal held that in relation to a criminal charge the word meant "contrary to law". Such a meaning is obviously inapt in relation to a matrimonial offence such as cruelty—though it could, I suppose, be more readily applied to more easily defined offences such as adultery and desertion. It is to be remarked that in *Stapleton v. R.*,[29] the High Court of Australia refused to follow *R. v. Windle* and assigned to the word "wrong" a much wider meaning. The test, it thought, was whether the accused had the capacity to distinguish right from wrong according to the standard adopted by reasonable men. . . . It is unnecessary for the purposes of this case to express any view as to which of these interpretations may be more appropriate in relation to criminal proceedings. But I think it is clear that, if the second limb of the M'Naghten rules is to be applied in relation to a charge of cruelty, some meaning must be assigned to the word "wrong" other than that held to be appropriate in *R. v. Windle*.

COLLINGWOOD, J., in *Sofaer v. Sofaer*,[32] expressed the view that "wrong" in this context was to be interpreted as equivalent to "culpable". I should, on the whole, be disposed to accept this meaning, if the second limb of the rules is to be applied at all, since it fits in with what I . . . define as the element of mens rea in the concept of cruelty when looked at from the subjective point of view of the party accused. Perhaps an even better word would be "inexcusable". . . .

The difficulty is that the question whether the conduct was inexcusable is the very question which the court has to determine in order to decide whether, from the subjective point of view of the party accused, the conduct complained of is capable of amounting to cruelty. Until this question has been determined by the court, it may be

28. [1952] 2 All E.R. 1; [1952] 2 Q.B. 826.
29. [1952], 86 C.L.R. 358.
32. [1960] 3 All E.R. 468.

said, no man could possibly know whether the conduct of which he is accused amounts to cruelty. Many a man who is charged with cruelty has pursued the course of conduct complained of in the firm and bona fide belief that this conduct, so far from being inexcusable, is in all the circumstances right and proper. This is particularly so, for instance, in the case of a party charged with nagging, who may well believe, and think he is justified in believing, that the constant complaints to which he gives expression are fully justified in all the circumstances. Such a man can well be said not to know that what he is doing is wrong. Yet that will not prevent the court from finding that he was guilty of cruelty if, in the view of the court, his conduct was in fact inexcusable in all the circumstances of the case. Why, it may be asked, should another man, who is in the same mental condition of bona fide believing that what he does is right, escape from being found guilty of cruelty merely because his mental condition is induced by disease of the mind? In either case the mental condition, or state of mind, is the same ; in both cases there is an absence of any sense that the conduct complained of is culpable, or inexcusable, or wrong.

The answer to this difficulty is, I think, that supplied by counsel for the husband in the course of his argument. In the case of a man suffering from a disease of the mind, the court must look at his conduct, as it were, through his eyes. He is entitled to be judged on the basis that his erroneous beliefs, being induced by delusions for which he is in no way responsible, are true. If on that basis it appears that his conduct would be excusable— i.e., if his conduct would not be unreasonable on the assumption that his deluded beliefs are true— then the court should not hold him guilty of cruelty ; for the necessary element of mens rea would be totally lacking. In the case of a man who is free from disease of the mind, however, the test is not the same. He must submit to the test of being judged by the standard of the reasonable man. If his conduct fails to satisfy that test, he may properly be held guilty of cruelty. For the court in his case is justified in applying the presumption that he intended the natural consequences of his conduct, and is entitled in effect to say to him "You ought to have known better". But this is the very thing that the court cannot say to the man whose erroneous beliefs are induced by disease of the mind.

In expressing this view, however, I think that it is necessary to utter a word of warning. What I have said is intended to apply in particular to cases in which the allegation is, as in the present case, one of mental cruelty. Such cases are in any case notoriously difficult to decide, and most of them can fairly be said to lie near the border-line between what amounts to cruelty and what does not. Where it is shown that the party accused is suffering from disease of the mind, which renders him incapable of appreciating that his conduct is in fact wrong—i.e., is inexcusable by ordinary standards—this circumstance must in my judgment be regarded as sufficient to tip the balance in his favour. Where, on the other hand, the conduct alleged is of a physical nature—e.g., where there have been violent assaults causing injury to the complaining spouse—a defence based on the second limb of the M'Naghten rules must be much more difficult to establish, especially where it is shown that the party charged in fact knew the nature and quality of his acts. It is one thing to say that conduct such as nagging, sulking, false accusations, and so forth, is to be excused on the basis of disease of the mind giving rise to deluded beliefs and rendering the party charged incapable of appreciating that his behaviour is wrong. It is quite another thing to justify behaviour of a violent nature on the basis of deluded beliefs, especially where there is no failure to appreciate the nature and quality of the acts. . . .

For these reasons, I should be disposed, on general principles and apart from authority, to come to the conclusion that in the case of matrimonial offences—at any rate, offences of the nature of that in question here—the party charged is entitled, as in the case of criminal offences, to invoke either limb of the M'Naghten rules.

*   *   *

DONOVAN, L. J.:

*   *   *

If Parliament had intended that the defence put forward in the present case should be a valid defence to a petition for divorce based on cruelty, it would have been simple so to provide, and I should have expected it to have been done in explicit terms. I cannot think that Parliament would have left it to be implied from the mere words "has treated the petitioner with cruelty". I can, if I may say so without presumption, well appreciate the view that the word "treated" carries with it the implication of intent ; so that a man who simply did not know what he was doing should not be regarded as having treated his wife with cruelty. But I do not think more is to be implied from this word. In particular, in the case of a man who intends to do something, and does it, knowing what he is doing, the word "treated" does not, in my opinion, imply that he must be able to form a sound judgment on the question whether his act is right or wrong. If one looks no further than the words of the statute, I think they afford this husband no defence. The word "cruelty" of itself does not assist in this respect. It connotes acts which give unnecessary pain to others, or which are savage or inhuman or merciless, but it certainly does not carry with it the implication that the doer is conscious that his acts are wrong. Otherwise such commonplace expressions as "a cruel fate" or "the cruel sea" would be meaningless.

The matter may be further tested by considering the results to which the husband's construction would lead. If one is to import consciousness of wrongdoing into the expression "treated . . . with cruelty", there would seem to be no valid reason for not importing it also into the expression in the same section "has committed adultery". Thus, a spouse who suffers from some disease of the mind may habitually commit adultery, knowing full well the nature and quality of his act, but because of his affliction not knowing that it is wrong. So that, however frequent these acts, and however many illegitimate children result, the other spouse can obtain no divorce while the mental disorder continues. Furthermore, if the second limb of the M'Naghten rules affords a defence, I cannot see how one can logically distinguish physical cruelty from mental cruelty.

* * *

In the present case it is, unfortunately, true that the husband may suffer, though he did not know that his acts were cruel or wrong. But I think that the law goes as far as it reasonably can in favour of a spouse of unsound mind by construing the word "treated" as implying an intention to do the acts complained of. To go further and to construe the statute in a way which enables the husband to go on being cruel, and disables the wife from obtaining the redress she here seeks, so long as the husband does not know he is doing wrong is, in my opinion, to read into the language of Parliament more than it contains, and thereby to whittle down still further the protection against cruelty which the Act confers. The same notion was more succinctly expressed by SHEARMAN, J.,[46] when he said that he did not doubt that the husband before him had been cruel unintentionally, but that his intentional acts were cruel.

* * *

NOTES

NOTE 1.

AVRUTIS v. AVRUTIS
140 N.Y.S. 2d 365 (Sup. Ct. 1955)

WALTER, JUSTICE.
Plaintiff wife sues for a separation on the

46. In *Hadden v. Hadden* (1919), "The Times," Dec. 5.

grounds of cruel and inhuman treatment, abandonment and nonsupport. Defendant husband counterclaims for a separation on the ground of cruel and inhuman treatment.

The parties were married in 1932 and lived together until 1953. There are no children of the marriage.

There apparently was no serious trouble for the first ten years or thereabouts, but during that time there were developing in plaintiff the habit of drink and the mental illness which later were to bring on great tragedy, and even within the first ten years there were incidents of plaintiff's locking defendant out of their apartment and one incident of plaintiff's breaking defendant's fishing rods into pieces [and striking him with a knife] because she thought he had defaced her piano.

* * *

On April 27, 1953, defendant caused plaintiff to be taken by ambulance to the psychiatric division of Bellevue Hospital. Defendant is a physician by profession and he secured the ambulance and plaintiff's admission to the hospital by means of his own certification, written by him on one of his prescription blanks, that plaintiff was mentally disturbed and should be under observation. It undoubtedly would have been far better if defendant had had some other doctor make that certification and had used more tact and courtesy in getting plaintiff into the ambulance and the hospital; but as plaintiff, after examination and hearing, was duly judicially found to be mentally ill and to be in need of institutional care and was in fact confined in institutions for the mentally ill until October 6, 1953, defendant's act in getting plaintiff into Bellevue cannot be denounced as either cruel or unnecessary.

* * *

Upon being . . . released, plaintiff did not return to the apartment where she and defendant had resided and where defendant then still resided, although, so far as appears, defendant would have received her if she had returned.

Plaintiff's charges of cruelty and abandonment hence are unsustained and her right to a judgment of separation must rest upon the admitted fact that since March 5, 1954, defendant has contributed nothing toward her support and maintenance; but unless defendant has established adequate justification for such admitted non-support, that is enough to entitle plaintiff to judgment.

For such justification defendant relies upon plaintiff's rages and tantrums, her wild and unfounded accusations against him, his relatives, his friends and associates, her listless lack of interest in life, her inattention to normal household duties, and upon the fact that she did not return to him when released from institutional custody on March 22, 1954; but the short and conclusive answer to all that is that those things were the acts of a mentally ill person.

The acts of a mentally ill wife sometimes may justify her husband in leaving the marital home and refusing to live with her; but they do not entitle him to a judgment of divorce or separation or relieve him of his obligation to support her. . . .

As was tersely stated in Goodale v. Lawrence, 88 N.Y. 513, 520: "An insane wife is incapable of abandoning her husband."

I conclude, therefore, that plaintiff is entitled to judgment dismissing defendant's counterclaim and awarding her a separation on the ground of non-support and alimony of $100 per week. I direct the entry of judgment accordingly. . . .

NOTE 2.

DIEMER v. DIEMER
8 N.Y. 2d 206, 168 N.E. 2d 654 (1960)

FULD, JUDGE.

The question on this appeal is whether a wife's repudiation of the validity of her marriage and her refusal to have sexual relations with her husband unless he submits to a remarriage in a church of her religious faith entitle the husband to a decree of separation.

Mr. and Mrs. Diemer were married in 1947. He was a Protestant, 41 years of age, she a Roman Catholic, a year younger. Having anticipated problems in accommodating their religious differences, they discussed this issue and reached an agreement concerning it. [I]t seems clear that Mr. Diemer's doubts about the success of their marriage had been allayed by the assurance of his bride-to-be that her "main ambition" was to be with him "in all things, for all times" and by her agreement that his faith would be her faith and his church, her church. It was in fulfillment of their agreement that the Diemers were married in the Church of the Garden, a church of Protestant persuasion, and a year and a half later Mrs. Diemer was admitted as a member of her husband's church.

In 1950, after three years of marriage, a daughter was born to the Diemers. Although it would not be accurate to say that marital discord was born with the infant, the unfortunate fact is that her baptism and subsequent religious training proved sources of contention, at first latent, but soon overt and bitter. The religious conflict which revolved about the child reached a climax and took a new form in 1954, shortly after Mrs. Diemer suffered an accident which induced in her a fear of death. She consulted a priest and, fol-

lowing her talks with him, issued an ultimatum to her husband. She told him that in the eyes of her Church she was not considered married to him and that, since this was so, she would not have any further sexual relations with him unless he submitted to a second ceremony in the Roman Catholic Church. In the six or seven months which followed, Mr. Diemer continued to live with his wife and made constant attempts to change her mind, but she persisted in her refusal to have sexual relations with him.

In October, 1954, realizing that his wife's decision was final and unalterable, he left home and instituted this suit. Alleging, in substance, the facts as they are set out above, Mr. Diemer characterized his wife's conduct as "cruel and inhuman" treatment, said that this conduct caused him suffering and seriously impaired his physical and mental well-being and sought relief in the form of a separation and custody of their child. Mrs. Diemer counterclaimed for separation, support and custody, but neither in her answer nor at the trial did she deny the essentials of her husband's story. In fact, on both occasions she reaffirmed that she did not consider herself married and unequivocally declared that she would not have any sexual relations with her husband until they were remarried before a Roman Catholic priest.

The trial court denied both husband and wife a separation and awarded custody of the child to the wife. On appeal by the husband—his wife sought no review—a divided Appellate Division affirmed the judgment. It was the view of both courts that the proof did not establish "cruel and inhuman treatment" on the part of the wife, apparently for two reason: first, that the wife had not "willfully and deliberately intended to inflict mental or physical suffering" upon the husband and, second, that he had not actually suffered any damage to his health. Although we are of the opinion that the criteria thus applied were too restrictive and that the essentials of cruelty were made out in this case . . . we prefer to place our decision of reversal and our award of a separation to the husband on the ground that the facts alleged and proved unquestionably establish the husband's right to a separation on the ground of abandonment (Civil Practice Act, § 1161, subd. 3).

* * *

. . . Marriage, of course, involves something far more fundamental than mere physical propinquity and, as a consequence, abandonment is not limited to mere "technical physical separation". . . . The essence of desertion or abandonment . . . is a refusal on the part of one spouse to fulfill "basic obligations springing from the marriage contract". . . . Obviously, not every denial of a marital right will be sufficient to support a charge of abandonment. The criterion is how fundamentally the denial strikes at the civil institution of marriage. Where primary rights and duties are involved, where the denial goes to one of the foundations of the marriage, it is the policy of our law to allow a separation from bed and board.

That a refusal to have marital sexual relations undermines the essential structure of marriage is a proposition basic to this court's decision . . . and as obvious as it is authoritative. Sexual relations between man and woman are given a socially and legally sanctioned status only when they take place in marriage and, in turn, marriage is itself distinguished from all other social relationships by the role sexual intercourse between the parties plays in it. This being so, it may not be doubted that a total and irrevocable negation of what is lawful in marriage and unlawful in every other relationship, of what unmistakably and uniquely characterizes marriage and no other relationship, constitutes abandonment in the eyes of the law. . . .

It is clear, therefore, that the plaintiff now before us is entitled to a separation on the ground of abandonment unless his wife had good legal cause to refuse to have sexual intercourse with him. And, as to that, it is equally clear that she had neither cause nor justification. Although it appears that she acted without malice and was activated by deep-felt and conscientious religious convictions, her motives were not sufficient in law to excuse the abandonment of her marital status. If, as a result of religious scruples, she considers her marriage invalid and non-existent and, on that account, neglects the fulfillment of a primary marital obligation, in fairness and in law her husband must likewise have the power to free himself of its obligations. While our law is not to be "unnecessarily construed in a manner which will be hostile to religion in family life or to any other of those principles of moral, ethical, and considerate conduct which ought to govern the marriage relationship", we may not forget that this State, "as a matter of long-continued policy, * * * has fixed the status of the marriage contract as a civil contract", governed by civil, not religious, law. It follows as a consequence of the civil nature of the marriage contract that a wife who disavows her marriage and repudiates a fundamental marital function out of deep-felt religious conviction has abandoned her husband just as effectively as one who has done so for base and illegitimate motives.

It is our conclusion, therefore, that on the evidence adduced the plaintiff is entitled to a separation on the ground of abandonment. . . .

NOTE 3.

Kentucky Revised Statutes—1953

403.020 [2117] . . . (1) A divorce may be granted to either party for the following causes:

(2) A divorce may be granted to the party not in fault for the following causes:

(f) Uniting with any religious society whose creed and rules require a renunciation of the marriage covenant, or forbid husband and wife from cohabiting.

NOTE 4.

STANTON v. STANTON
213 Ga. 545, 100 S.E. 2d 289 (1957)

MOBLEY, JUSTICE.

*　　*　　*

There is no merit in the defendant's contention that neither the petition for divorce nor the evidence sustained good ground of cruel treatment. The plaintiff alleged that the defendant had treated her in a cruel and inhumane manner, that such treatment was wilful, and was such as to reasonably justify apprehension of danger to her life, limb, or health. The specific acts of cruelty charged in the petition do not contradict the charge of cruel treatment as contended by the defendant, but support it. The defendant contends that there was no intentional or wilful infliction of cruel treatment by him, since in the acts charged he was only practicing and exercising his religious beliefs as a Catholic. "The law has not designated, and indeed could not make, diverse religious opinions a legal cause for separation. The fundamental law of the land guarantees freedom of religion and the right to worship according to the dictates of one's own conscience. The manner, however, in which one's spouse practices his or her religious belief, may constitute cruel treatment entitling the other to a separation or divorce. The facts that conduct which is actually cruel is motivated by an excess of religious zeal does not excuse it on any theory of a constitutional guaranty of religious freedom." 17 Am. Jur. 295, § 59. There was evidence that the husband not only tried to persuade the plaintiff to become a Catholic, but he continually nagged at her about it, laughed at her, accused her of being afraid to listen to him, became highly emotional, paced the floor, would go into rages with her, and would carry on in this way long into the night, causing her physical and nervous exhaustion, which resulted in her having to be hospitalized; that, after her return from the hospital, he continued such treatment, even though warned by her doctor that her health was being impaired, and she again had to be hospitalized. She testified to the following specific acts of cruelty: "He flew into a rage in the hall and took me by the shoulders and shook me like a rag doll. I don't know just what he was saying. He shook me with all the force he had, and I went through the door from the hall, down on the kitchen floor, and against the washing machine at the other end. He came in over me with a white face and clenched fists, swearing that he would strangle me"; and "All of a sudden he jerked off his glasses and threw them at me and stepped on the gas and started down the road about eighty miles an hour. He kept up that rate on the road all the way. I begged him to slow down, but he wouldn't. He said he was going down the road to hell, and nobody could stop him. It was about a four hour's drive to New Bedford, and when I got in I was just all out." On other occasions he falsely told her that her doctor had said that she was a pathological case, and on one occasion he called her a bitch. The evidence amply supported the charge of cruel treatment.

* * *

2.

ON FINDING WHAT FACTS— FOR WHAT PURPOSES?

a. Determining a Course of Action—The Decision to Seek Help

JOHNSON, NORA

A Marriage on the Rocks*

The moment when it first becomes apparent that one's marriage was a mistake is the beginning of probably the longest, darkest period in the human lifetime. It sets in motion the profound thinking that should have taken place during that easier and happier time, the engagement, when all the trouble really started, and it brings into the situation many more people—children, if there are any, funereal parents, doctors, lawyers, marriage counselors, psychiatrists, and well-meaning friends, each of whom makes it his personal business to rush in and try to save the marriage. Everyone is ready to moralize, grieve, and bend every effort to increase the burden of guilt on the two people who, in most cases, are already carrying an almost unbearable load. Keeping the marriage together is regarded as the desired goal no matter what the circumstances, even though the two people might well be on their way to destroying each other, and being tied together for the rest of their days might be, for them, a death sentence.

* *The Atlantic Monthly.* Vol. 210 (July, 1962), pp. 48-49, 50. Reprinted with permission of the author.

The exhaustive and completely personal search for what is right can be carried on in only one mind at a time, in an atmosphere of privacy, something hard to come by in a land where the virtuous voices of Main Street keep repeating themselves with the typically American predilection for noisy morality. Being such a nation of faith healers, we really think that we can solve others' problems from our own pedestals of perfection, and what we like to call an objective point of view. I doubt if there is one married person on earth who can be objective about divorce. It is always a threat, admittedly or not, and such a dire threat that it is almost a dirty word.

A whole bundle of our cherished tenets contributes to this situation. Marriages are made in heaven; togetherness is the answer to everything; if we cannot adjust, we might as well be taken out and shot. For a country with so many of the accouterments of sophistication, we remain astonishingly innocent about marriage. We believe in it with a faith that is almost touching, a boundless hopefulness that is rather like the way we feel about new presidents, new face creams, or anything new that promises to change our lives. With our uncritical enthusiasm for playing house, we are deeply and sincerely shocked by the continually rising divorce rate.

But because we are serious and self-analytical and hardworking, we see no reason to assume that emotional problems cannot be solved in the same way as business problems, by lining up all the facts and reaching a sensible solution. Marriage seems to have a certain corporate structure, and we proceed accordingly. Working hard for virtue is for us a foolproof method. A friend of mine, consulting a psychiatrist (not an analyst) about her marital problems, was given a lecture on what was wrong with her approach to her husband, and her attitude in general, which wound up with a brisk "Go home and work on your marriage." The psychiatrist, like most marriage counselors, made the mistake of thinking that he could really be of use to my friend in some way other than as a sounding board.

Admittedly, there must be forbearance on both sides when a marriage is under strain. But making a project out of marriage seldom works. It presupposes a failure of communications between the two people and suggests that they are simply running out, are not facing the problem, and are being generally irresponsible. It is also based on the fantastic but popular assumption, probably dreamed up by unhappily married people, that leaving is easier than staying. Of course, communications do fail, but what we are concerned with here are marriages like that of my friend, made between intelligent people in good faith ; and a communications failure is less likely to be the problem than a good many other things. What counts in this situation is the emotional truths, and the two people know those better than anyone else. A sounding board is useful to analyse the emotions and to articulate them, if only the sounding board would refrain from judging, from charging irresponsibility, from a virtuous urge to save the marriage, at all costs.

* * *

[W]hen the dissolution of a marriage seems possible, and the issues begin to take shape in their true gravity, panic frequently sets in. The two people revert to their old childhood devices as everything else around them fails. They fight ; they sulk ; they try to woo each other back ; they torture each other with minute knifelike thrusts that land in all the old wounds and weaknesses. They plead and weep and threaten and call each other names. Every good quality is turned into a vice. If things really get bad, the children are pulled into it and used as foils or bargaining material or pawns for creating more guilt. This can be torture for all.

It is at this point that the faith healers step in, in the form of marriage counselors, ministers, priests, or rabbis, moralistic psychiatrists, doctors, lawyers, parents, and friends. Most of the discussion centers on how to keep the marriage together, rather than on finding out if the marriage should be kept together—that is, if the benefits of the relationship seem to outweigh its disadvantages, if the disadvantages could be lessened at relatively little detriment to either person, and if the two people really want to stay together. But usually the faith healers pull social institutions into it, using them to make the guilty feel even guiltier: the church, the law, marriage, and motherhood ; or else the abstract values that are being violated: duty, maturity, obligation, responsibility. These are accompanied by the ancient admonitions: Think of the Children, Life Alone Is Lonely, Your Poor Mother, A Good Man Is Hard to Find, Where Will the Money Come From? and so forth, like a list of song titles. Now, of course, all of these things are important, but who is not aware of them to begin with? They are confusing because they obliterate the already fuzzy line between violation of conscience and the psychiatric false guilt, along with some appeals to expediency.

What may do some good, during this period . . . is an objective, nonjudging, minute dissection of the patient's emotions. In an age when the traditional values seem to shift and change and become meaningless before our eyes, our only

salvation is in ourselves and the things that *we* have found, usually the hard way, to be right. It is no easy job to find them. Some people were born knowing themselves, and some people learn by living, but a lot of us are not that strong, and we need some help.

b. Determining a Course of Action—The Initial Interview

[i]
By a Psychiatrist

GILL, MERTON ; NEWMAN, RICHARD ; and REDLICH, FREDRICK C.

The Initial Interview in Psychiatric Practice*

(*Therapist and patient enter interviewing room.*)

* * *

Q. What brings you here? (*Sits down.*)
A. (*Sighs.*) Everything's wrong I guess. Irritable, tense, depressed. (*Sighs.*) Jus' . . . just everything and everybody gets on my nerves.
Q. Nyeah.
A. I don't feel like talking right now.
Q. You don't? (*Short pause.*) Do you sometimes?

---

* New York: International Universities Press, 1954, pp. 134-200. Reprinted with permission of the publisher.

There are four major determinants of the interchange in an initial interview: . . .
First and foremost are the personality structures of the two participants. . . .

* * *

The second major determinant . . . is the socially defined roles of the two participants. Roles play an especially important part in the initial interview because the participants have not had an opportunity to know each other as individuals, and can therefore react to one another only in terms of how their individual personalities define their social roles. Even though the role of the psychiatrist will be relatively standardized by his training, his social position will influence his conception of his professional role. And his professional role may undergo subtle or even gross alterations when he deals with patients from various social positions. The roles which the patient assigns to himself and to the psychiatrist are likely to be more clearly and directly correlated with his social position. . . .

* * *

The third major factor which will play a role in the initial interview is its purpose. . . .

* * *

The fourth major determinant of what will go on in the initial interview is the technique which the interviewer employs, or . . . "the way in which the initial interview is handled." This technique will be in part an outgrowth of the interviewer's theories about personality functioning. These theories will also play a large role in determining the content of the initial interview . . . (*id.* at 65-74).

A. That's the trouble. I get too wound up. If I get started I'm all right.

Q. Nyeah? Well perhaps you will.

A. May I smoke?

Q. Sure. . . . What do you do?

A. (*Sighs; takes cigarettes out of pocketbook and lights one.*) I'm a nurse, but my husband won't let me work.

Q. How old are you.

A. Thirty-one this December.

Q. What do you mean "he won't let you work?"

A. Well . . . for instance I . . . ah . . . I'm supposed to do some relief duty two weeks (*Sighs.*) this month . . . next month, September, and he makes it so miserable for me that I'm in a constant stew. (*Sighs.*) And he says that my place is home with the children. I agree, but I wa . . . I need a rest. I need to get away from them. I need to be with . . . oh with people. I can't stay closeted up in the house all the time.

Q. How many kids are there?

A. Two.

Q. How old are they? (*Clears throat.*)

A. Three . . . five months.

Q. Mmmhnn.

A. (*Sighs.*) Oh it isn't only that. It's a million things.

Q. Tell me some of them.

A. (*Sighs.*) Well to begin with, there are a lot of things I didn't know about him before we got married that I should have known—at least I feel I should have.

Q. You've been married about four or five years?

A. Four years. . . .

Q. Mmm.

A. . . . in November. And (*Sighs.*) I think he's a chronic alcoholic. He drinks every day, and he just can't seem to let the stuff alone. He says he can, but he can't. . . .

Q. What does he do?

A. He's a truck driver.

* * *

Q. Is he away a good deal?

A. (*Sighs.*) He eats and he sleeps in the house, and that's all there is to it. And it's an insult to me naturally.

Q. Mmmhnn. (*Short pause.*)

A. (*Sighs.*) Once in a while he's decent. (*Pause; sighs.*) I keep thinking of divorce, but (*Half-sigh.*) that's another emotional death. And I don't want to do it with the kids right now. They're too young.

Q. Divorce is an emotional death?

A. (*Sighs.*) I think so.

Q. I don't quite understand what you mean.

(*Short pause.*)

A. (*Sighs.*) Well it's . . . I think it's a . . . worse than death. If he died I think I'd be happy. I honestly would. (*Tearful.*)

Q. Mmmhnn. I didn't understand . . .

A. (*Interrupting.*) And he won't get help. That's the trouble. He won't admit that it's any problem.

Q. I would like to hear more about that, but first I . . . I didn't quite understand that about divorce being an emotional death.

A. (*Wearily.*) I don't know whether I can explain it. (*Sighs.*) (*Short pause.*)

Q. Are you opposed to divorce . . . ah . . . generally or?

A. Yes, I am.

Q. On what grounds?

A. (*Interrupting.*) That's why I'm here. (*Smacks lips.*) Because I think a lot of marriages can be salvaged. (*Sighs; crying softly.*)

Q. Now, on what grounds are you generally opposed to divorce?

A. Well I think that the children . . .

Q. Mmmhnn.

A. . . . are the ones who suffer really. It's still a stigma to divorce in our family. It's very strong.

Q. Yes. What's your religious background?

A. (*Interrupting.*) Plus the children being taunted (*Sighs.*) about it.

Q. What's your religious background?

A. Protestant Episcopal.

Q. Mmmhnn.

A. (*Short pause.*) (*Sniffs and sighs.*) I just feel that if (*Half-sigh.*) I divorced him, I know it would be hard for me to readjust. It's hard enough now to keep my head above water.

Q. Yeah?

A. (*Sighs.*) I think it would be hard for the children. I know it would. And it would be hard for me to work and support 'em. You have to pay baby sitters so much that you're lucky if you have enough to eat on after the week's over. (*Sighs.*) All I can think is that (*Sniffs.*) if I can stand it a few more years. (*Half-sigh.*) And then I get to the point where I didn't think I could stand it a few more years. (*Sighs.*) And that's why I came here.

Q. Nya. What . . . what were you going to do if you could stand it a few more years?

A. (*Sighs.*) I'm going to school to get my B.S.

Q. You're going now?

A. Yes.

Q. Yes?

A. And then I just figured if things got too much I'd pack up my traps and leave if I had a good job where I wouldn't have to break my neck.

Q. You mean if the kids were a little older then you could make it?

A. Yes. Well if the kids were in school.

Q. If they were in school then you would consider a divorce?

A. Yes. And then I wouldn't . . . (Simultaneously with Q.) Then I would.

Q. I see.

A. But I'm still generally opposed to it . . .

Q. Yes.

A. . . . because I think that . . . that I can be straightened out.

Q. That you can be straightened out?

A. Yes.

Q. I didn't get the impression that you thought it was . . . ah . . . your problem.*

A. Well it's affecting me. It's making me unstable. I never used to be like this.

Q. Yes?

A. Things didn't used to bother me this way. I used to be depressed. Occasionally. Sure! Who isn't? But not the way I am now. Not so that I wanted to turn on gas and jump out of the window. (Tearful.)

Q. How long have you been feeling that way?

A. Ever since I've been married. And on the honeymoon (Voice breaks.) he drank every night. He didn't want to go anywhere. All he wanted to do was sit in and drink. And I couldn't see that.

Q. How long did you go with him before you married him?

A. (Sighs.) Four or five months.

Q. And he wasn't doing it then?

A. Well he was drinkin', but I was under the impression that it was social. I never had seen him drunk.

Q. Mmmhnn.

A. . . . Nobody told me that his father was a chronic alcoholic. His father went to——. (Sighs.) He was only there two weeks, but apparently they straightened him out. Something did because he hasn't had a drop to drink in twenty years. (Sniffs.) I think it's twenty. His father's disgusted with him. (Sighs.) He seeks older men for companions. He's down in the gin mill every night of the week. The only way I could have him stay with the kids at all is to force a showdown and have a temper tantrum like a kid.

Q. He doesn't care much for the children?

A. He apparently cares for them when he's with 'em, when he has to be with 'em. But that's all. He just doesn't seem to want to be bothered for any length of time. He comes home at night. He eats dinner. He reads his paper and he falls asleep. He doesn't want to be bothered with the kids when he's reading his paper. He might play with 'em a little while. Then he goes out and

---

* The therapist immediately seizes it—the contradiction— and presents it to the patient. But he does so rather sharply. . .

he drinks, and he comes home and he goes to bed. . . .

* * *

Q. . . . Where were you reared?

A. ——. Came from a very small community. I lived on an island.*

* * *

Q. How'd ja get in this neck of the woods?

A. Well I met my husband down home. My family had known him for about a year before I did.

Q. Yeah. Were you at home?

A. Yes.

Q. You trained out there?

A. No. There isn't any hospital there.

Q. Yeah. And . . .

A. Oh I . . . I guess I was just bored with everything and I wasn't really in love with him. I know that.

Q. You know it or you knew it?

A. I knew it then.

Q. You did?

A. I did.

Q. Then why did you marry him?

A. Well I figured if you lived with a man long enough you'd come to love him. I did love him. I still love him.

Q. You do? What do you mean by that?

A. I do. I love him, but he . . . at times I hate him. I know I love him, but he's so miserable that I can't love him sometimes. He's always trying to make me feel (Sighs.) . . . I dunno. I suppose he's trying to project his inferiority complex into me. (Half-sigh.) He's always telling me that I'm not any good as a nurse. He doesn't see why I want to go out and work. He doesn't know anything about my work in the first place. If I say anything when I know he's wrong, he said, "Oh, you're full of baloney. You think yuh know everything." Even though the statements I made were documented.

* * *

Q. Where are you going to school?

A. —— College.

Q. How much time do you spend there?

A. Well, I went for eight weeks this summer. I

---

* An abrupt change of topic. Is it because the therapist thinks that he has exhausted the topic they were on? Obviously the therapist is struggling with the problem of the patient's avoiding responsibility for her behavior (attributing responsibility to external situations). In the back of his mind, consciously or not, he feels he is going to have to confront the patient with her own role, and this question is a direct way of finding out more about her. It is a return to his earlier tactics: "If I can't force her to see the real situation now, I'll stop and collect more information to confront her with later on."

spent . . . ah . . . let me see, my first class was nine twenty-five until twelve-five, and then I go part time at night, two nights a week. And it's usually for about three hours at a time.

Q. You going to continue that through this school year?

A. If I can.

Q. They're night classes are they?

A. Yes.

Q. How long will it take you to get your degree?

A. Mmm, years. (*Sighs.*)

Q. How many?

A. Oh about three more years. (*Blows nose.*)

Q. And he fusses about your going to school?

A. He makes it miserable.

Q. So how do you get away with it?

A. Well, I started to hire baby sitters, and then that would bring him into the house 'cause he wouldn't trust anybody else with the kids at night. See, the house we live in is a . . . is very tense. The landlord was a . . . has been a mental patient. He was up at ——. I think he's paranoid schiz. We had a very rough time. His wife has been in the hospital twice. We don't know what's wrong with her. She just seems to be sort of moron I guess. She doesn't seem very bright. She's good-natured, but she's jittery, silly, giddy.

Q. You have . . . you have an apartment or what?

A. Yes. We have an apartment upstairs. Everytime he hears a noise he has to run up, "I heard a noise. What are yuh doing now? What are yuh doing to my house?" He gets . . . always running through the house and pulling stuff out of the cupboards and moving furniture and . . . (*Sighs.*)

Q. I didn't quite expect to hear you say that your husband was so concerned about the children that he wouldn't let anybody stay with them. Isn't that a little bit strange in view of what you've told me?*

A. Well at night . . . see he won't . . . in the daytime it's all right because then he can go out at night.

Q. Humm?

A. . . . It's perfectly all right with him if I go to school in the daytime because I can go . . . he can go out at night. It's staying in at night that he objects to. He wants to go out every night of the week.

Q. Yes. But what I mean is why is he not satisfied then for a baby sitter to be there?

A. I don't know.

Q. Well, you said he wouldn't trust the children with a baby sitter.

A. Yes. That's what he told me, but it was apparently all right for them to come during the day. He didn't want a baby sitter there at night.

Q. Why not?

A. Well, I don't know. I think because of the landlord, because he runs up in the house all the time. He doesn't want us to have any company or anything. In fact everything . . . way I . . . when my sister came down with her two kids he was up in the house three and four times a day to see what was going on. Well we're making too much noise ; we were using too much water—this is the landlord. Then my husband forbade me to have any company. He didn't want any of my family to come. He forbade my sister to come. And I had to write home and tell my mother that the plans had been changed, and she told me . . . wrote back and said that my husband would not be welcome there anymore, which I expected. That went on for months. I argued with him for two months before. I thought probably I could argue him into having her come down and take care of the kids for the summer, and bring her little boy. He didn't want her there. He was afraid she'd be out at night, goin' out on dates and so forth. And then the landlord came up and he said that I couldn't have anybody there, living there in the house, taking care of the kids. I would have to (*Sighs.*) . . . In fact, he said I couldn't have anybody, and I said, "Well I'm going to hire somebody to come up during the day and you can do what you want to about it." So I called the Rent Area Control Office, and they said that he had the last say, but to go ahead and do it anyway, that he probably wouldn't do anything about it. Well he didn't, except to walk up and ask the baby sitter what her name was and carry on as usual runnin' up and down around the house.*

---

* It is noteworthy how the therapist bides his time. He introduces what he has to say by saying that he didn't quite expect to hear this, instead of sailing into it. He is again working on his project of demonstrating that the trouble is not all external because he now goes on to question her about her unrelievedly critical picture of her husband.

* She has obviously missed the real point of the question or has deflected it. It is hard to understand her answer, although the implication finally seems to be that baby sitters are not permitted in the evening because the landlord objects to "company." There seems to be a contradiction—why is this not true in the daytime? Then she immediately goes on with further complaints about her husband. This passage shows clearly the real difficulty of entering into communication with the patient about this—her contradictions and the pressure that she is under to blame her husband. Another factor in the difficulty may be the pressure that the therapist is putting on her. Her aggression at this point against the landlord seems to be an indication to the interviewer that she would be unlikely to commit suicide—that she is able to direct hostility outwardly. It confirms the therapist's feelings that her complaints of "everything happens to me" are to be taken with a "pound of salt" because she demonstrated her capacity to take care of herself when crossed by the landlord.

Q. Does your husband come home drunk?

A. Occasionally.

Q. Has he ever physically abused you?

A. No. He made a pass at me once, but I got outa the way. I grabbed a knife and I guess he knew I'd use it. I was so mad.

Q. Does he get verbally abusive?

A. Yes. Very noisy. The whole neighborhood can hear it. (Sighs.)

Q. But why have you put up with all this?

A. Well frankly because, as I said before, if I had to go out and work and hire a baby sitter, I don't know how we'd live. I don't.*

Q. Mmmhnn.

A. It's very difficult. Baby sitters are expensive.

Q. Does that mean if you could manage it financially you'd leave him? †

A. (Sighs; moves around.) Then again I don't know. Sometimes I think I would. Other times I don't think I'd even be able to stay away from him. I know he'd come crawling back, and I'd probably take him back.

Q. Why?

A. I don't know. I had . . . I guess because I love him. (Tearful.)

Q. I'm not sure I understand exactly what you mean when you say that. Or do you mean that you'd sort of want him back under any circumstances?

A. No, not under any. I want to be treated decently.

Q. Yes. But the prospects for that don't look very bright, do they?

A. No, they don't. According to what our family doctor said, I should . . . well he didn't tell me to pack up and leave. He said that probably, eventually, I'd have to . . . to get myself ready to . . . to get a better job. He told me to go on with my school.

Q. Has anything happened recently that makes it . . . you feel that . . . ah . . . you're sort of coming to the end of your rope? I mean I wondered what led you . . .

A. (Interrupting.) It's nothing special. It's just everything in general.

Q. What led you to come to a . . .

A. (Interrupting.) It's just that I . . .

Q. . . . a psychiatrist just now?

A. Because I felt that the older girl was getting tense as a result of . . . of my being stewed up all the time.

Q. Mmmhnn.

A. Not having much patience with her.

Q. Mmmhnn. (Short pause.) Mmm. And how had you imagined that a psychiatrist could help with this? (Short pause.)

A. Mmm . . . maybe I could sort of get straightened out . . . straighten things out in my own mind. I'm confused. Sometimes I can't remember things that I've done, whether I've done 'em or not or whether they happened.

Q. What is it that you want to straighten out? (Pause.)

A. I think I seem mixed up.

Q. Yeah? You see that, it seems to me, is something that we really should talk about because . . . ah . . . from a certain point of view somebody might say, 'Well, now, it's all very simple. She's unhappy and disturbed because her husband is behaving this way, and unless something can be done about that how could she expect to feel any other way." But, instead of that, you come to the psychiatrist, and you say that you think there's something about you that needs straightening out. I don't quite get it. Can you explain that to me? (Short pause.)*

A. I sometimes wonder if I'm emotionally grown up.

Q. By which you mean what?

A. When you're married you should have one mate. You shouldn't go around and look at other men.

Q. You've been looking at other men?

A. I look at them, but that's all.

Q. Mmmhnn. What you mean . . . you mean a grown-up person should accept the marital situation whatever it happens to be?

A. That was the way I was brought up. Yes. (Sighs.)

Q. You think that would be a sign of emotional maturity?

A. No.

Q. No. So?

A. Well, if you rebel against the laws of society you have to take the consequences.

Q. Yes?

A. And it's just that I . . . I'm not willing to take the consequences. I . . . I don't think it's worth it.

---

* The therapist inquires as to why she submits to the aggression of others. He pursues his theme: "If the whole problem is external why don't you solve it by attacking the actual situation?" More sharply he implies: "I don't really believe you. Why do you put up with all of this if it's true?"

† The therapist continues to confront the patient with her behavior and is rewarded by her recognizing the contradiction between what she is saying and her feelings and behavior.

---

* Relentlessly following up "what is the trouble" and "what help do you really want," the therapist now summarizes the situation as he sees it, in a sympathetic manner which is easily understood; and he offers it to the patient for her scrutiny.

Q. Mmmhnn. So in the meantime then while you're in this very difficult situation, you find yourself reacting in a way that you don't like and that you think is . . . ah . . . damaging to your children and yourself? Now what can be done about that?

A. (*Sniffs; sighs.*) I dunno. That's why I came to see you.

Q. Yes. I was just wondering what you had in mind. Did you think a psychiatrist could . . . ah . . . help you face this kind of a situation calmly and easily and maturely? Is that it?

A. More or less. I need somebody to talk to who isn't emotionally involved with the family. I have a few friends, but I don't like to bore them. I don't think they should know . . . ah . . . all the intimate details of what goes on.

* * *

Q. . . . you find yourself in a situation and don't know how to cope with it really.

A. I don't.

Q. You'd like to be able to talk that through and come to understand it better and learn how to cope with it or deal with it in some way. Is that right?

A. I'd like to know how to deal with it more effectively.

Q. Yeah. Does that mean you feel convinced that the way you're dealing with it now . . .

A. There's something wrong of course.

Q. . . . something wrong with that. Mmmhnn.

A. There's something wrong with it.

Q. But then I'm not quite clear. Does that mean that you think that if you behaved in the . . . the right way or whatever way, that you could get your husband to change?

A. No, I don't think I could get him to change. But I think that I wouldn't be so nervous and upset myself.

* * *

Q. And you don't regard your husband as being the difficulty? You think it lies within yourself?

A. Oh he's a difficulty all right, but I figure that even . . . ah . . . had . . . if it had been other things that . . . that this probably—this state— would've come on me.

Q. Oh you do think so?

A. (*Sighs.*) I don't think he's the sole factor. No.

Q. And what are the factors within . . .

A. I mean . . .

Q. . . . yourself?

A. Oh it's probably remorse for the past, things I did.

Q. Like what? (*Pause.*) It's sumpin' hard to tell, hunh? (*Short pause.*)

* * *

Q. . . . What is this thing you had so much remorse about? (*Pause.*)

A. (*Sighs.*) It seems to me I'm going around in circles. (*Sniffs.*) In nineteen forty-six I met a man. He was married, but I loved him anyway. (*Sighs.*) I became pregnant. I left him first. Went to the ——— to get away. And then I came back, and I saw him once again. That's when it happened. (*Sighs.*) I was pregnant when I met my husband. He offered to marry me, and I said I didn't want to. And I didn't think it was fair to marry a man under these circumstances. At the end of the fourth month I lost the baby. Two months later I married him. (*Sighs.*) I always felt that he held that little bit of information above my head, that he'd blackmail me if he didn't get his way.

Q. Mmm.

A. And I guess that's why I married him.

Q. If he didn't get his way in what?

A. He wanted me to marry him, period. He just wanted a wife to be like the rest of the fellows. They all had wives.

Q. Yeah?

A. He wanted a home and he wanted kids. Just sort of like people want cars and television.

Q. Yeah. So you thought he'd hold this information over you?

A. I did. I still do.

Q. Mmm. How come it took you so long to tell me that?*

A. It's hard for me to talk about.

Q. Sure it is. I know. I'm real glad you did tell me. Got a lot of things on your chest you think you need to get off? (*Short pause.*) Yes. I think you should be talking to somebody. . . . And I'm sure that you can benefit with psychotherapy. . . .†

---

* This sounds a little punitive. Why was he punitive? It may be because she is complaining again.

† The therapist seems immediately to regret his previous remark and tries to make up for it. He now rewards the patient by telling her, after her telling him the whole hour that she wanted to talk to somebody, that he agrees with her that she should and that he will try to get her someone to talk to.

It seems in a way as if one could summarize the content of the session by saying that the patient came in with a statement that her husband was mistreating her and that she wanted to talk to somebody, When she finally admits that something is wrong with her the therapist says, "All right, you may talk to someone."

[ii]
By Lawyers

[ii-a]
GARRETT, W. WALTON

Summary of a First Interview in a Domestic Relations Case*

Mrs. M. called me for an appointment to discuss getting her a divorce on Thursday morning and came in that afternoon. I had not known her prior to that time. When she came in she introduced herself and told me she wanted to get a divorce from her husband and asked how quickly it could be obtained. I asked her why she wanted a divorce. She told me that her husband had threatened her again that morning and she wasn't going to take any more of it. I asked her for particulars and she said that about 3:30 Monday morning he woke her up talking and wanting her to fix his breakfast. He was a route delivery man for a dairy and had to be at work at 4:30 A.M. She told him she had been up late studying for her classes and had been up with the baby in the night and would he please be quiet and turn off the light so she could sleep. He told her it was a wife's job to get up and fix her husband's breakfast. She replied that with all her studying and looking after the baby she certainly was not getting up. When she refused to get up he started to push her out of bed; she started fussing, and climbed out of the bed. When she got up he boxed her ears, knocked her down on the bed and struck her several more times. This morning the thing had started over again and she had gone up to a neighbor's apartment to get away from him.

She stated that she had moved her clothes to her mother's home and wasn't going back. I asked her about the baby and she told me that they had an 18 months old child. I asked about the studying and she told me that she had gotten married when she was in her freshman year of college and that since the baby had come she was back in college working on her degree and teachers certificate. I asked her what her plans were if she obtained a divorce and she said she would live with her mother until she completed her degree in approximately one year. She said that her mother would be glad to have her during this time. We discussed the needs of a child for two parents and she agreed that this was important in the development of her child and that she was willing for her husband to have any visitation rights within reason but she wasn't going back to him. She

stated that he didn't approve of her going back to college and that she was going.

In our conversation I learned they had married when she was 18 and he was 20. The baby had come about a year later and this had made a great change in their way of life. He had dropped out of school shortly before their marriage and she . . . shortly after. She was not happy with his job as a milk truck driver. He was not happy with her plans to complete her education and teach. She told me they had no financial problems but when I added up the assets and liabilities I discovered their debts were considerable and monthly payments were . . . all their income could stand.

Mrs. M. wanted to know just what her rights would be with a divorce and what sort of custody decree and support for the child she could expect. I explained to her that she would have considerably greater rights without a divorce because as a wife she could compel support and that she could not hope to get alimony in the divorce action. She insisted this made no difference, that she didn't want support, she wanted freedom. I told her that she could expect around $40 to $50 per month child support and that the Judge would grant her husband one day of visitation per week because he believed the husband who paid support was entitled to see his children. She agreed that this was reasonable. She was not willing to discuss any attempt at reconciliation with her husband or with a family counselor. She said she had made up her mind that her child would be better off in a divided home than in the middle of a fight. Her parents were divorced; she thought she was better off for it, and thought her child would be also.

I wrote her husband a letter. The following day his attorney called me and informed me that the husband didn't want reconciliation either. The husband's offer of support was greater than the wife's demand; custody and visitation was agreeable and the case ended in a divorce.

[ii-b]
FORTAS, ABE

The Legal Interview*

* * *

The lawyer's task in the initial interview is exceedingly complex. He must ascertain the facts which are relevant to the problem, and frequently the most difficult part of this task is clearly to apprehend and particularize the problem—to separate the essential from the peripheral, the relevant from the unimportant. He must obtain the

---

* Paper submitted by the author, while a Graduate Student in the Yale Law School (1962). Printed with permission of the author, a member of the Alabama Bar, who retains all publication rights.

* *Psychiatry*, Vol. 15 (1952), pp. 91-93. Reprinted with permission of the publisher.

client's confidence, and he must assume control of the client's conduct with respect to the matter involved. He must be a therapist of a sort. If the client is unduly alarmed, he must moderate his fears. If the client is unduly aggressive, he must restrain him. And he must at least begin the task of preparing the client to perform as a witness— one of the most subtle and complex undertakings in the practice of the legal art.

It is a commonplace among trial lawyers that the real danger in litigation is not the adversary but the client. Upon the client's personality and statements, the trial lawyer builds an intricate strategy. His great hazard is that at the time of trial something happens that a lawyer characterizes by saying that his client let him down. This means that the lawyer built his presentation on a misapprehension of the facts or on an incorrect forecast of the form and manner in which the client would testify; in other words, he incorrectly appraised the client's personality for the purposes in hand, and partly because of this he incorrectly assayed the 'facts'.

In ascertaining the facts relevant to the problem at hand, the lawyer, like the psychiatrist, seldom has to be concerned about deliberate falsification, but he must always be concerned about the recollection of past events that is induced by a desire for vindication or success, or by anxiety or fear. Indeed a lawyer's observation may well lead him to conclude that there is no such thing as recollection, just as there is no such thing as history in the sense of past events recorded. There is only reconstruction. When a client recites a recalled experience, he may reveal less about the experience and more about himself. This phenomenon permits the lawyer to acquire a picture of his client's general attitudes and characteristics, but it also causes him some difficulty in ascertaining the 'facts.' With this in mind, the lawyer must realize that the most that he can hope for is a reconstruction of past events which is reasonably representative of those events and which will withstand attack by the opposition.

* * *

The lawyer . . . tries to do many complex things at once. He tries to discover the 'facts.' He tries to understand and appraise his client's personality to aid himself in evaluating the recital of the facts (the extent to which the recital is reliable, the extent to which there is withholding, and the extent to which a desire for vindication or sympathy has caused unfavorable recollections to be distorted—or indeed, the extent to which anxiety has caused nonexistent guilt to be confessed). The lawyer is also trying to understand and appraise the personality of the client in order

to determine strategy: How shall the person testify? What shall be his attitude and approach? Is he apt to be the sort of witness who should be instructed to reply briefly or fully? Should the tactics be defensive or aggressive? And so on.

The lawyer is also administering, in this legal-psychiatric interview, his own peculiar brand of therapy—if it may be called such. Usually, in these cases, this in part takes the form of a kind of transference. The client is no longer alone; he is no longer, so he feels, the chief actor; the responsibility is now the lawyer's; the client not only need not make decisions, he is discouraged from doing so and is thereby also relieved of the feeling of guilt that would otherwise attend the nonmaking of decisions. In general he has walked through the looking glass into a land ruled by magic. Not only is he no longer required to take action, but he is not even expected to form perceptions and to make judgments. All of this has been transferred to friendly, sympathetic hands.

Now in this process, the lawyer can and does do all sorts of things to his client—generally without realizing or understanding them. By the choice of words, by gestures, by attitudes, by intonation, he can instill or increase a sense of guilt, of anxiety, of outrage, of acceptance, of resignation, of fear, of martyrdom, or what not. He also influences his client by the words that he induces or permits his client to formulate or utter, because the words uttered by the client himself are important not merely as disclosures but in terms of the effect that their formulation and utterance have upon the client himself. To put it another way, the words—together with the complex apparatus of communication which accompanies them —that are exchanged in the interview profoundly affect the client's emotional attitudes and recollection, and his conduct, with respect to the matter in hand.

* * *

. . . There is generally no source to which the lawyer may refer for the purpose of ascertaining whether the client is vaguely recalling an occurrence or is merely responding to the suggestion . . . contained in the charges. In other words, is the statement made an indication that there is in fact a relevant and damaging story to be told; is this tentative admission the response of a person who is highly suggestible; is it the reaction of a person who is punishing himself because he feels that he must be guilty since a mysterious and awful power has accused him, or because he feels that he must be an inadequate person since he has been caught up in this nightmare? Or again, is the accused seeking the comfort that may be derived from inventing something tangible and specific to explain the terrible position in which he finds himself—and thereby to restore his belief that this is a world where nothing happens without predictable cause: a belief which to many people is rather necessary to sanity. . . .

* * *

[A]ny legal processes which shake the center of gravity of the persons involved, require of the lawyer that he employ extraordinary skill and sensitivity in the interviews with his client. His job of reconstructing past events is made difficult by their frequent remoteness in time and by the client's emotional difficulties in accurate recollection. His job of appraising the client's personality is even more hazardous because of the unusual and stressful moment in which he sees him. Most difficult of all is his job as therapist, that is, as the person required to help the client to function most adequately in the particular crisis and to emerge from the experience with as little personality damage as possible.

[ii-c]
DAILEY, ROBERT H.

The Catholic Attorney and the Moral Lawfulness of the Civil Divorce Case*

Catholic attorneys, aware of the sacredness of the valid marriage bond, are often in doubt about the moral lawfulness of accepting cases of clients seeking or defending themselves from actions for divorce, judicial separation, or annulment of marriage. . . . There are some cases which they may accept without offense to conscience, but there are others which they may not conscientiously undertake. . . .

* * *

[T]he attorney may represent his client in the domestic relations court whenever it is morally lawful for the client to approach the civil courts. This principle can be applied to the following kinds of cases.

1. *When the Marriage Has Been Celebrated Before a Priest*

If the plaintiff, Catholic or non-Catholic, seeks divorce or judicial separation because of adultery or any of the causes sufficient for temporary separation, he must have episcopal permission to approach the secular courts with moral impunity. For the attorney, therefore, the moral lawfulness or unlawfulness of representing the plaintiff depends upon whether the client has obtained permission for judicial action or not.

Sometimes marriages are declared null by the

* 38 U. Det. L. J. 255, 273-76 (1961).

ecclesiastical courts or dissolved by the Holy See as non-consummated or in favor of the faith. When this occurs the attorney can represent the plaintiff in seeking a divorce from a bond which has either never existed or has ceased to exist.

He may defend the respondent when his client is sued illegitimately for divorce or judicial separation. And in any case he can defend the respondent so as to assure the obtaining of his merely civil rights.

When permission is granted to seek a remedy in the courts, the Church prefers that judicial separation or separate maintenance be sought in order to remove the occasion for an adulterous second marriage and to leave the door open for a possible return to conjugal cohabitation. Frequently the Catholic petitioner is so instructed. Theoretically separate maintenance is a good solution but lawyers, at least in California, commonly protest that a suit for separate maintenance is often practically inadequate.[21]

In California, judges of the Superior Court, being non-Catholic for the most part and not sharing Catholic beliefs in the absolute indissolubility of Christian marriage, have a strong prejudice against issuing a decree of separate maintenance. That a wife can live apart from her husband while he is compelled to support her and to remain bound to her without enjoying the solace of married life constitutes a situation with which they are not in sympathy. This attitude is a fact and is one which must be taken into account.

Filing for separate maintenance, therefore, a wife often finds that she is at a disadvantage because the court is apt to avoid granting a decree if it can find a way to do so. The way out is at hand usually in the majority of cases because the husband immediately files a cross-complaint for divorce.

* * *

2. *When the Marriage Was Not Celebrated Before a Priest*

If one party to such a marriage is a Catholic, the marriage is invalid so that no real bond exists. It is morally lawful for the attorney to represent the plaintiff. He may also represent the respondent in order to assure his legitimate civil rights.

Doubts arise in situations in which both spouses are non-Catholics. The attorney must shoulder the serious responsibility of making a careful judgment about the lawfulness of his participation in

21. I am indebted for the remarks about separate maintenance in California to the Honorable Edwin J. Jones, Judge in the Superior Court of Santa Clara County. *Cf.* Weil v. Weil, 37 Cal. 2d 770, 236 P. 2d 159 (1951).

the case. Many of these marriages, being second and even third unions, are invalid because of a previous, unresolved matrimonial bond. But many are valid. Therefore the attorney has to know something about the canon law of marriage. . . .

*   *   *

A practical directive can be offered to the lawyer for marriages in which both parties are non-Catholics. He cannot cooperate in seeking divorce for his client, if the marriage is valid, when the divorce is sought for the purpose of remarriage. Circumstances, if such purpose exists, will usually enable him to make a prudent judgment so that he need not ask an explicit question. If such purpose does not exist he can accept the plaintiff's case when true, serious, and honestly provable statutory causes exist for divorce or judicial separation. He may also accept the defense of the respondent.

*   *   *

[iii]
By a Bar Association

WISCONSIN BAR ASSOCIATION
Interviewing Clients*

Most lawyers spend too much time in interviewing clients. This is very wasteful and costly to the lawyer. The use of time records will tend to regulate this difficulty. Also, the use of checklists in interviews will help to prevent drawn-out conferences with clients.

The following items will prove helpful in client interviews:

(1) Develop and use definite systems for keeping interview time at a minimum. For example, upon signal, the secretary can interrupt the interview with a message requiring the lawyer's attention. Mainly, however, limitation of interview time is a matter of sticking firmly to the matter at hand and not letting the interview wander to a point where the client is giving the advice and opinion rather than receiving it.

(2) Be affable and polite. Clients respond to friendly treatment and a smile.

(3) Get at the client's problem immediately and stick to it. Don't bother to explain the reasoning processes by which you arrive at your advice. The client expects you to be an expert. This not only prolongs the interview, but generally confuses the client. The client will feel better and more secure if told in simple straightforward language what to do and how to do it, without an explanation of *how* you reached your conclusions.

---

* R.M-11 (Sept. 11, 1959). Reprinted with permission of the publisher.

(4) Do something for your client, if possible. Perhaps a quick telephone call can be made or an on-the-spot letter dictated. A lawyer is trained in these matters and can do them easily. Many times a lawyer can do in minutes a job which would require hours of time and effort of the client.

(5) Take every opportunity to explain in simple language the functions of various courts and the basic rules of conduct and procedure in the courts. If the client understands that not all cases are matters for long, formal jury trials, he will approach the law with less fear and trembling. The client should know that most legal matters never result in trial and that most court procedures are rather informal in nature. It is natural for persons to be more at ease when dealing with matters with which they have some basic knowledge. Therefore, for the client's peace of mind, he should be made familiar with the basic workings of the court in which his matter is being handled and of his own role in the proceedings if he is required to make an appearance in court.

(6) Quit when you're ahead. When you have reached the conclusion of the conference, break it off clearly. Otherwise it will drag on as new themes and situations develop. Tactfully but clearly wind up the conference and usher the client out.

[iv]
By a Legislator

MR. LEO ABSE (Pontypool)
Matrimonial Causes and Reconciliation Bill*

. . . There can be no question but that sometimes when asked for advice by an estranged couple, the solicitor concerned advises one or other of the partners to break off all relations with the other side, and certainly not begin talking by discussing with the other the possibility of what is to happen if and when a divorce has taken place.

This is all wrong. When someone asks for advice, far from being told that it is dangerous or hazardous to talk about the future after the divorce, he should be encouraged to talk about it. Many of us have experience of what happens in a magistrates' court. Very often after the proceedings have commenced, after the court has heard the mutual recriminations on the part of both parties, a wise bench and understanding solicitors realize that there comes a point in the proceedings when it is best to ask for an adjournment and to suggest that the parties see the probation officer. It is as though at a certain point there has been a catharsis. It is as though they

---

* 671 H.C. DEB. (5th ser.) 813-14 (1963).

have poured out pent-up repressed aggressiveness which they have perhaps had for years and at that point it is possible to bring them together. This, in my experience, has happened dozens of times, and those who are magistrates know that often it is possible to break off the proceedings at a certain point and call in the probation officer.

I think that when people begin to talk, or if they can begin to talk, not about fantasies, but about the realities of what will happen if and when a divorce takes place, and talk specifically about how their matrimonial home will be divided up, how their children will find that they can see their father on only one occasion a week, when the actual reality of the loneliness is brought home to them—because they are bound to consider the real consequences of what they are attempting to do in breaking up the marriage—at that point there are still possibilities of bringing the couple together, and it is most unfortunate that the law of collusion as it stands inhibits the possibility of a reconciliation.

* * *

[v]
By a Sociologist

O'GORMAN, HUBERT J.

Lawyers and Matrimonial Cases*

. . . "As you see it, what is the lawyer's basic job when he represents a matrimonial client?" . . . The answers provided by seventy-three attorneys were classified into two major role definitions: one is labeled the Counselor's role; the other, the Advocate's role.

1. THE COUNSELOR As defined by forty-seven informants, the job of an attorney in a matrimonial case is primarily to ascertain the nature of the client's problem and then to work toward a solution that is fair to both spouses. This role definition emphasizes the active part played by a lawyer in his relationship with a client. The Counselor participates in three important ways. First, he attempts to clarify, to his own satisfaction, the content of his client's problem. He tends not to accept at face value the client's version of marital difficulties; instead, he looks for what he considers to be the underlying problem:

> You try and get a feeling for what's underneath. What's the real story? I don't put it to clients that way, but that's what I'm after.

The value of being able to identify the underlying problem, or "real story," is that it enables the

* Reprinted with permission of the publisher from *Lawyers and Matrimonial Cases* by Hubert J. O'Gorman, pp. 132-136. © 1963 by The Free Press of Glencoe, a Division of the Macmillan Company.

Counselor to arrive at an independent diagnosis of the client's case, which, in turn, permits him to distinguish between the client's opinion and his own professional judgment. As one informant explained: "Clients may come in here and tell you what they want when I know that is not what they need. . . . You keep listening and questioning until you feel that pang [sic], that pang that tells you what's underneath. . . . She may want a divorce but what she needs is a separation. You have to keep in mind the distinction between the two."

Second, the Counselor attempts to discover what, in his opinion, would be the most beneficial solution for the client. As our informants so often expressed it: "You try and figure out what is best for the client." This, too, requires an independent judgment in which the lawyer weighs his view against the client's. He asks himself, in the words of one attorney, "Will the action which the client contemplates help her?"

Finally, the Counselor participates in an effort to work out a solution to the problem that is also fair to the opposing spouse: "We try for the best solution for all concerned." This interest in a reasonably fair solution grows out of the lawyer's concern for his client who he feels is best served through reasonable negotiation and settlement. Unfair solutions, particularly where the opposing side is forced to yield excessively, may gratify his client, but the Counselor dislikes them because they eventually raise further problems that could be avoided. Here is one informant's explanation of this point:

> Suppose I get a huge alimony for a wife and I know that it is more than the man can afford in terms of spendable income. Well the wife thinks it's wonderful and I'm a great lawyer in her eyes. But in a few years he won't pay it any more; he can't afford it. He was anxious to get divorced and wasn't too cautious, but now it is impossible. Maybe he wants to re-marry. He's angry. He can't pay. The situation deteriorates. Why? Because the contract was not feasible to begin with. . . . I try for fairness in such situations, a settlement which can serve as a guide for my client for a long time.

The Counselor's goal of a fair solution is sustained by his disinclination to make extreme demands of the opposition. He wants his side to prevail but with qualifications: "I do the best job I can for my client within certain limits. The limits are these: If the husband is my client, I do not believe in cutting off the wife without a cent; if I represent the wife, I do not believe in taking the husband for every cent he's got. . . . Generally I try for a fair settlement, and within these limits I try and win the case."

2. THE ADVOCATE   As defined by twenty-six of our informants, the major task of a lawyer in a matrimonial case is to achieve the results desired by the client. This role definition emphasizes the relatively passive part played by a lawyer in his relationship with clients. As the next array of excerpts implies, the definition of the problem and its solution are made primarily by the client, not the lawyer:

> I try and accomplish the purpose that the client has in mind. The lawyer's job is to get the client the results they want. Whatever they want I get for them provided it's not illegal and can be done.
> My first job is to carry out their wishes.

If the Counselor takes the client's statement of intent as a point of departure for his own independent analysis, the Advocate takes it as a cue for action. The latter proceeds on the assumption that the client's plans are clear and certain: "I simply get them results. . . . They know what they want to do, so I simply carry out their desires. I work out the details." In centering his role definition around the client's will, the Advocate tends, correlatively, to give less weight to his own judgment. "Our job," observed one, "is to do what the client wants regardless of what we think or feel."

In performing his role the Advocate is guided by one general principle: within the limits of the law, he seeks maximum benefits for his client. He tries, as one attorney noted, "to do the most" and "get away with what you can for that client." Or, as another lawyer expressed it: "I tell you my job is to do the best thing for my client, that is, to get the best deal for my client."

The content of a "best deal" varies from case to case. However, the Advocate is apt to perceive it mainly as an economic issue; his specific goal then varies with the client's sex:

> In matrimonial cases clients are primarily interested in money. If you represent the wife, then your job is to get as much as possible for her. If you represent the husband, pay out as little as possible.

Success in a matrimonial action is defined by the Advocate as the triumph of his client over his opponent. In or out of court, he is oriented toward eventual victory. He is out "to win," to "beat the other fellow." Where he is able, in the name of the client, to defeat the opposing spouse decisively, he is apt to feel a strong sense of professional accomplishment. One informant described his recent achievements: "I might say that we have a small reputation for being pretty good at this stuff. We have recently had amazing success defending husbands. We had seven or eight

cases in a row where the woman got zero. You have to assume that the judge will lean over backwards to be fair to a woman, so when you win the way we do, it's quite a thing."

Furthermore, in striving to attain client-defined objectives, the Advocate tends to feel that he is demonstrating his ability to the client and that this is necessary. If the Counselor seems to take his professional skills for granted, the Advocate does not, as the next excerpt illustrates:

> What's fair support? . . . Let's say, on the basis of the man's income . . . the courts have been going along with something between twenty and thirty dollars a week for support. . . . Now the opposing lawyer tells me that the wife wants, or will settle for, twenty-five dollars a week for the children. Now my client can afford twenty-five dollars and probably would go along with it. But he figures that his wife will get part of that for herself, and, besides, he's going to buy clothes, toys, and take the children out. So he hedges a bit. Then he figures, *well, what have I, his lawyer, done for him?* He could have accepted that without a lawyer. So I tell him that legally that is a reasonable solution, but I'll see what I can do. I tell the other lawyer that my client wants to pay twenty dollars. So we dicker back and forth. Finally, we agree on twenty-two-fifty a week. I tell the husband and he agrees, and we end on that. *You have to show the client that you are doing something for him.*

[vi]
By a Bishop

PIKE, JAMES A.

Beyond the Law*

Paradoxically enough, it is before a man reaches the Court—right in the attorney's office—that the lawyer appears most fully in the role as an officer of the Court. . . . It is here that the lawyer is really acting as judge, as a deal is put together or as things are sorted out in connection with the decision to undertake, or to defend against, possible litigation.

In a measure any lawyer, with or without a conscious sense of overall vocation, exercises this role. It is much better if he exercises it consciously. It is in his office that he should regard the chair at his desk as a seat of justice. It is here that he should sit down each morning with a sense of solemnity (albeit without announcing "Oyez") as an officer of the Court, now viewing the phrase not merely as a restriction on his temptation to muck up the judicial process, but rather as a challenge to serve as a magistrate-in-the-first-

* From *Beyond the Law* by James A. Pike, pp. 35-38, 44-55. Copyright © 1963 by James A. Pike. Reprinted by permission of Doubleday & Company, Inc.

instance. . . . Once things get going, of course, the lawyer is an agent of his client. But it is important that there be a preliminary stage in which the lawyer is on a level removed from his client, sensitive to the latter's personal needs . . . yet judging the client's situation in the magisterial role.

Right here we must state that there are limits to this role. Unlike a judge, he cannot, in the last analysis, tell a client what or what not to do. In the first place, he *cannot,* because there are other lawyers available. The client need only go down the hall in the same building, or turn to the yellow pages of the phone book. But, second, he *ought* not to. He is not called upon to run the client's life. Yet there is an in-between role that is more than a judgment as to what might go in the courts, what might be a contract that will bind, what might be a deal that will hold together ; namely, an ethical judgment as to whether it will be a good thing. The degree to which the attorney can exercise the latter part of this role depends upon the sustained character of the relationship, the degree of trust the client has been able to place in him and, ultimately, what kind of person the lawyer himself is.

There is another aspect to the judicial role of the attorney in his office that is entirely in the attorney's hands, without appeal. [H]e will not take every case that comes in the office. He will not need to aid and abet everything proposed to him. Here I am not talking about those things he cannot do because of the prohibitions of the canons of legal ethics (ambulance chasing, double agency, etc.). We are now talking about the dimension beyond arrest or disbarment, namely, the effect on his choices that comes from his total perspective, his world view. The standard canons of legal ethics respect this privilege of choice on the part of the attorney. This provides there is nothing wrong in defending anybody or acting for anyone, but the canons also make clear that an attorney need take no case he doesn't want to take. Very similar is the canon law in my particular tradition. I can, as Bishop, with the aid of a matrimonial court, act as judge on the basis of a sheaf of papers and say to the given person that he may be remarried in the Church.[1] But any priest in my diocese who does not agree with my judgment or does not feel that the new marriage will be a sound one, need not marry the couple.[2] In short, the canons of legal ethics say that you can take any case, and then say that you need not take any case—whether because of preoccupation with other matters, laziness (the fishing may be good in your parts at this point), or moral discrimination.

This freedom of discrimination guaranteed, open then is the question, What kind of potential court case, or what kind of deal, will you be involved in? . . .

* * *

For the particular type of analysis we are now undertaking, divorce practice presents an especially difficult area. On the surface at least, it would seem to be considerably less difficult for an attorney who is a member of a religious body that sets down rules as to his role in such cases. For example, in the case of a Roman Catholic attorney with a Roman Catholic client, "if the client is seeking a divorce or separation illicitly [without permission of the Church], the attorney may not co-operate by taking the case unless there is a proportionately grave justifying reason for his co-operation."[6] In other words, what is normally expected is that the attorney will require that the client first seek permission from the Chancery of the diocese to proceed to a civil divorce. (Incidentally, the very existence of this procedure recognizes that there are circumstances in which, under episcopal authority, divorces are licit among Roman Catholics ; and since this permission is not limited to the single count of adultery, it is difficult to understand the ground of the steadfast opposition in the Roman Catholic Church in the State of New York to the extension of grounds for divorce beyond the one ground of adultery.) Further, "this grave reason on the part of the attorney must become more weighty as the unlawfulness of the petition of the client mounts in the scale of sinfulness." Monsignor Casey exemplifies this application of "the principle of material co-operation" : "If a client is seeking real dissolution of a valid marriage in order to remarry, the attorney cannot represent him unless there is a more serious justifying reason." What would constitute such a reason? The following answer is given : "Such a grave reason would be the necessity of giving up his profession or losing his means of livelihood if he refused to undertake the case. In practice such a justifying grave reason will never exist."

And non-Roman Catholic attorneys whose religious or ethical scruples have convinced them of the wrongness of divorce, in general or in particular types of situations, would be under a similar prohibition of conscience (even though the prohibition might not involve formal canon law,

---

1. Canons of the Episcopal Church, Canon 18, Sec. 2.
2. *Ibid.*, Canon 17, Sec. 4.

6. The Rt. Rev. Monsignor George J. Casey, "Canon Law on Civil Actions in Marriage Problems" (lecture before the Catholic Lawyers Guild of Chicago, 1944).

as in the case of the Roman Catholic Church) against aiding and abetting what they are convinced is sinful. Equally clear would be the answer in conscience of an attorney whose religeo-ethical system includes a positive endorsement of divorce as the best answer (that is, the least bad answer) if the marriage has really suffered a spiritual death, where there is no hope of reconciliation and where the continuance of the marriage relationship would appear to be positively damaging to the spouses and to the children. But for attorneys morally open to divorce, the case will not always seem this clear and it is these gray cases that raise the most difficult questions.

Behind all this is a more fundamental question. Should the religious or ethical attitudes of the attorney in regard to divorce, or his application of them to the particular case before him, bear on the question of his professional involvement at all? Is this not just a matter for the client's conscience? To answer yes is to simply paraphrase the lawyer . . . "He is supposed to do what he is paid for." It is too late in these lectures to endorse the "yes" answer. It would seem clear that the attorney, as informed by his own principles, does have a conscientious role here. At the minimum, if he does not assess the possibilities of reconciliation and if he does not fulfill in a measure at least the honorable role of *defensor vinculi,* he certainly has no right to the noble title, "Officer of the Court," since (as representing society) the courts have made clear their legitimate interest in the continuity of marriage. On the other hand, as is pointed out by Isabel Drummond, " . . . it is difficult to see what interest the State can have in coercing mismated couples to maintain to outward appearances a relation which actually does not exist."[7] Equally paradoxical is the interest of the Church in the continuity of marriage. Speaking generally, the interest is positive. But pastors in most traditions finding, after careful pastoral counseling, that a real relationship cannot be kept together will positively advise divorce, not as a good solution, but as the lesser of two evils. Even with the highest degree of conscientiousness with regard to the stability of marriage, the attorney may find himself precisely in the same situation. . . .

In order sharply to raise a second question, let us assume that the attorney has no moral problem in aiding in securing a divorce for his client, but that the methods required to be used are marginal. Let us take for example a situation in New York State, in which adultery is the only ground for divorce. It is not surprising that in seeking to broaden the channel of matrimonial dissolution the legal talent in the state has applied itself to fairly imaginative measures. So much so, that in support of a bill in the New York Legislature to revise the divorce laws, the Committee on Ways and Means reported:

> . . . that evidence exists of widespread fraud, collusion, perjury, and connivance which permeates matrimonial actions and proceedings of all types affecting the family unit and the marital status, instituted in the courts of this state; that the moral, social, economic and psychological well-being of the inhabitants of the state are affected thereby.[8]

It is true that if an important area of practice be permeated by dubious ways of achieving even legitimate ends, then public confidence in the whole legal system is threatened. Yet, as everywhere else, there are in the State of New York many unhappy marriages where adultery has not entered the picture, either as cause or effect. Suppose that with the highest moral discrimination, both the New York client and the New York attorney are convinced that marital dissolution should occur. Let's assume, too, to simplify the problem, that the other spouse and attorney agree. What should they do?

Several outs have been devised:

(1) *"Phony" residence.* Here it is discreetly arranged that one of the parties departs for one of the more lenient states—lenient both as to grounds of divorce and as to length of time to establish residence. (Generally it is the wife, since she usually has more free time, and because since somebody has to subsidize the expedition the breadwinner has to keep working.) Thus fraud is built into the arrangement, in one sense: there is no intent to change residence and to answer the standard question of the foreign court as to intention to settle there, there is a quick affirmation of that which in no way corresponds to the true situation. Yet, in another way, it is not fraud: nobody is fooled. It is certainly not fraud upon the court, since by virtue of the whole pattern, the court is actually part of the fraud. In short, no judge is deceived; no one intends to deceive anyone, and no one does. One difficulty with this solution is that it is expensive; not everyone can afford a six-week vacation in Reno, including the inevitable loss involved in playing the one-armed bandits.

(2) *Staged "adultery."* Actually, this experience is, from one perspective, the most non-immoral thing one could imagine. Nothing happens. Em-

---

7. *Getting a Divorce* (New York: Alfred A. Knopf, 1931), page 22.

8. Excerpt from Report of Committee on Ways and Means, New York State Assembly, 1955, on proposed Bill 1026.

ployed as part of a package fee the *dramatis personae* (the correspondent-elect, a photographer and an additional witness) arrive at a hotel, along with the putative defendant. The female lead dons a negligee ; the door of the selected room, conveniently left unlocked, is opened ; and the photographer takes his picture (perhaps he follows the usual pattern of his profession: "Just one more, please!"). The additional witness simply looks on. This neat "evidence" is brought before the referee, who, in effect, decides such matters ; and it is said that there is a "canned" list supplied the plaintiff in such cases as to what questions are to be asked in precisely such a situation. The fact is, as F. Benjamin McKinnon has pointed out, the real case of adultery is much more difficult to establish than the play-acting.[9] It is suspected that the referees prefer the latter type because it contributes better to the court record of cases handled per month.

(3) *"Where are you?"* Then there is the Enoch Arden law. Here the plaintiff avers that the other spouse has not been heard of for five years. When involved in a divorce by mutual consent, this ignorance as to whereabouts can be affirmed with relative safety by the plaintiff-spouse ; but an obvious difficulty with this particular device is that five years is sometimes a long time to clarify the status of a dead marriage.

(4) *The fake annulment.* As is found true in the ecclesiastical scene, when divorce is limited, annulment grows bigger. In New York State there are some one hundred and fifty types of fraud that have been claimed in annulment actions. A frequent and easy form of fraud (where there is mutual agreement to dissolve a marriage) is the pleading that there was no intent on the part of the husband and/or wife to have children (of course, this one doesn't stand up too well if, in fact, there are children).

At first blush, one is inclined flatly to condemn all this. But given the existential situation in New York, I am not so sure. Could there be in the development of one or more of these "ways round" simply the carrying on of the legal tradition of fictions? Suggestive here is the development of the common law action of ejectment. In order to establish a suit for determining the title of property there was at first a bit of playacting, the actors testifying in the court their choreography ; but it wasn't long before a play was not in fact performed, but simply recited in the plaintiff's pleading. By this time, it would have been thought gauche were the defendant (as in the story in which the child finally exclaims, "The

---

9. "Ethical Problems in Divorce Practice" (1957), unpublished essay.

King has no clothes") to defend on the ground that the show really never went on. It started like staged adultery: someone was hired to trespass on the property, while someone else was hired to chase him off, etc. ; and long after the events no longer were required to occur, the pleadings were required to affirm the "events." We can say that one or two or three of the above devices are fictions in a stage of development where obviously the development has not gone as far, for example, as in ejectment. Now something—not the real thing—simply has to happen "with pix" ; people still have to be hired. But it is beyond the realm of legitimate projecture to assume that in connection with this device there may occur the second and third phases in the development of suits to try title. The second stage: it really didn't have to happen, it only had to be pleaded. The third stage: when the Code procedure came in, the little tale didn't even have to appear in the pleadings.

Meanwhile, a lawyer seeking to achieve a marital dissolution (and we are still assuming that in the given case the idea is a sound one and he is in good conscience in the matter) has to raise this question with himself. Is this fiction or fraud and perjury? In his profession, he is accustomed to dealing with the former category, but he certainly doesn't want to get involved in the latter category. This is an example of Man in Transition. I must confess that personally—or perhaps because of my ecclesiastical role—I am somewhat put off by the staged adultery fiction/fraud ; yet, existentially speaking, what is the difference (except for its "sexy" connotation) between this and a long expensive trip to Reno? No less than a United States Supreme Court justice has expressed this kind of realism in at least one instance. The Virgin Islands tried to bid for what McKinnon calls "the tourist-divorce trade" and at the same time avoid the necessity of perjury involved in the usual migratory divorce. The Virgin Islands' law allowed the judge to eliminate any question about intention to remain (having gotten the tourist business out of the visitor they decided to let him depart in peace). The majority of the court blocked this attempt, but Mr. Justice Clark—joined by Mr. Justice Black and Mr. Justice Reed in his dissenting opinion—said:

> Divorce is an intensely practical matter, and if a husband and wife domiciled in any State want a divorce enough, we all know that they can secure it in several of our States. This being true, I see no sense in striking down the Islands' law. There is no virtue in a state of the law the only practical effect of which would be to make New Yorkers fly 2,400 miles over land to Reno instead of 1,450 miles over water to the Virgin Islands.

The only vice of the Virgin Islands statute, in an uncontested case like this, is that it makes unnecessary a choice between bigamy and perjury. I think the Court should not discourage this [the attempt to make such a choice unnecessary] and I would reverse.[10]

To return to such a fiction/fraud as staged adultery: in terms of the social outcome, is it better to require the long trip to Reno rather than simply to require them to take the shorter trip to a second-rate Manhattan hotel?

Speaking of the existential conditioning of law by sociology, it is interesting to note these phenomena:

1. New York is only one state out of fifty (though the most populous—temporarily, since my own state of California is soon to assume that place) and one third of all the annulments granted in the Nation emit from the New York courts.

2. Nevada is about the most relaxed state as to grounds of divorce, yet for the real residents of that state, there is one of the lowest divorce rates in the Nation.

The purpose here is not to solve the problem of marriage and divorce in this country. Time has been spent on this particular problem in order to illustrate the complexity of the decision-making of the lawyer in regard to field after field, should he take a conscientious view of what he will or will not involve himself in, and what means he will use to achieve given objectives. Earlier it was insisted there is a question; it is now evident that it is a tough one.

But by this time in the analysis, some are bound to rechallenge the fundamental presupposition. When we have reached this point in discussions on this subject in which I have participated, someone usually says: "All this confuses me. Wrestling with such ambiguous and paradoxical questions will interfere with business. And as to the cases I would take, it would keep me from wholeheartedly and effectively serving my clients. I would rather concentrate on serving the professed needs of my clients." Some put it more bluntly: "I may lose my clients if I am too stuffy about such matters."

The only answer to this is a question, What does the lawyer put first in life? Now no matter how nobly he would like to answer this, he has something to weigh out. He should know that there is nothing unworthy in keeping in the picture the question, What will this do to me? And this is particularly so where the lawyer is responsible for the support of others. The lawyer with even the most dedicated sense of his total calling cannot fail to take into account his chances of staying in the game in order to exercise that

calling; all this must be taken into account. Also to be considered is the continuing relationship with a given client. Perhaps he genuinely feels the relationship of trust he has been building up, enabling him to influence the client for good in his various decisions, and hence he may well hesitate to bolt the client whom he feels in a given instance to be pursuing an unworthy end.

[T]he lawyer will be less than a whole person if he does not at least raise these questions. If he is not disturbed and tormented by such things, then he is less than a whole person. And when what he has decided to do is in fact a shade of gray, at least he should realize that that is what he has done and not be under the illusion that he has chosen white. He will be deepened as a person by the very struggle of conscience through which he has arrived at his answer.

* * *

If the attorney will recognize the complexity of the decision-making process, and recognize his responsibility to make decisions beyond the requirements of the minimum, and in choosing the shade of gray recognize that he has not chosen the perfect good—thus protecting him from fanaticism and self-righteousness—he may well find that he is all the more successful. And, if it comes about that way, that's good, too. God is happy when we prosper. He wants us to be fully ourselves, and to have things turn out well for us.

NOTES

NOTE 1.

GOFFMAN, ERVING

The Presentation of Self in Everyday Life*

[W]hen an individual appears before others his actions will influence the definition of the situation which they come to have. Sometimes the individual will act in a thoroughly calculating manner, expressing himself in a given way solely in order to give the kind of impression to others that is likely to evoke from them a specific response he is concerned to obtain. Sometimes the individual will be calculating in his activity but be relatively unaware that this is the case. Sometimes he will intentionally and consciously express himself in a particular way, but chiefly because the tradition of his group or social status require this kind of expression and not because of any particular response (other than vague acceptance or approval) that is likely to be evoked from those impressed by the expression. Sometimes the traditions of an individual's role will

10. 349 U.S. 1, 28 (1954).

* From *The Presentation of Self in Everyday Life* by Erving Goffman, pp. 6-10. Copyright © 1961 by Erving Goffman. Reprinted by permission of Doubleday & Company, Inc.

lead him to give a well-designed impression of a particular kind and yet he may be neither consciously nor unconsciously disposed to create such an impression. The others, in their turn, may be suitably impressed by the individual's efforts to convey something, or may misunderstand the situation and come to conclusions that are warranted neither by the individual's intent nor by the facts. . . .

There is one aspect of the others' response that bears special comment here. Knowing that the individual is likely to present himself in a light that is favorable to him, the others may divide what they witness into two parts; a part that is relatively easy for the individual to manipulate at will, being chiefly his verbal assertions, and a part in regard to which he seems to have little concern or control, being chiefly derived from the expressions he gives off. The others may then use what are considered to be the ungovernable aspects of his expressive behavior as a check upon the validity of what is conveyed by the governable aspects. In this a fundamental asymmetry is demonstrated in the communication process, the individual presumably being aware of only one stream of his communication, the witnesses of this stream and one other. . . .

Now given the fact that others are likely to check up on the more controllable aspects of behavior by means of the less controllable, one can expect that sometimes the individual will try to exploit this very possibility, guiding the impression he makes through behavior felt to be reliably informing. For example, in gaining admission to a tight social circle, the participant observer may not only wear an accepting look while listening to an informant, but may also be careful to wear the same look when observing the informant talking to others; observers of the observer will then not as easily discover where he actually stands. A specific illustration may be cited from Shetland Isle. When a neighbor dropped in to have a cup of tea, he would ordinarily wear at least a hint of an expectant warm smile as he passed through the door into the cottage. Since lack of physical obstructions outside the cottage and lack of light within it usually made it possible to observe the visitor unobserved as he approached the house, islanders sometimes took pleasure in watching the visitor drop whatever expression he was manifesting and replace it with a sociable one just before reaching the door. However, some visitors, in appreciating that this examination was occurring, would blindly adopt a social face a long distance from the house, thus ensuring the projection of a constant image.

This kind of control upon the part of the individual reinstates the symmetry of the com-munication process, and sets the stage for a kind of information game—a potentially infinite cycle of concealment, discovery, false revelation, and rediscovery. . . . [I] would like only to add the suggestion that the arts of piercing an individual's effort at calculated unintentionality seem better developed than our capacity to manipulate our own behavior, so that regardless of how many steps have occurred in the information game, the witness is likely to have the advantage over the actor, and the initial asymmetry of the communication process is likely to be retained.

NOTE 2.

GILL, MERTON ; NEWMAN, RICHARD ; and REDLICH, FREDRICK C.

The Initial Interview in Psychiatric Practice*

The psychiatrist [formerly] saw himself as a medical practitioner who behaved as do practitioners in other specialties. He treated the patient as an object. From this object he elicited certain signs and symptoms and upon this object he performed certain manipulations. He carried out a mental examination which could be done according to a series of questions which could be asked in a relatively well-defined predetermined sequence. His ultimate goal was to carry out manipulations—whether somatic or psychological—on the diagnosed and assessed patient in order to bring about certain changes.

* * *

The revolutionary change—wrought by psycho-analysis—is that the psychiatrist has become aware of the fact that in his interaction with the patient he is a participant as well as an observer. It has become clear that all that takes place in the interview takes place within the therapist-patient relationship and can be understood only in terms of that relationship. The interview situation is one of communication. The freedom and character of the communication are determined by the relationship between the two participants. Another way of putting it is to say that the psychiatrist does not collect information from a static object. Instead he operates in the field of the interpersonal relationship. The data available will be a function of the field. All this is a drastic shift from the earlier attitude in which the psychiatrist dealt with his patient without any awareness of how their attitudes toward each other determined what took place between them. The doctor-patient relationship has now become the focal point of the interview. One of the most important things that the therapist has to learn about the

* New York: International Universities Press, 1954, pp. 76, 84-85. Reprinted with permission of the publisher.

patient is how he relates himself to the psychiatrist.

NOTE 3.

PILPEL, HARRIET F.

The Job the Lawyers Shirk*

. . . I was sitting in the anteroom of a lawyer whose secretary apologized for his lateness. He had been delayed, she said, by a warring married couple whom he was "reconciling" in his office. As I waited, I couldn't help overhearing the dialogue in the next room. Voices grew louder and louder. Finally the lawyer's rang out above the others:

"Now, damn it, shut up. I'm telling you—you love each other."

This was an intelligent attorney. And even though their tone might be more subdued, I suspect that a good many other lawyers would have no more refined technique of reconciliation at their command. Small wonder, then, that most of them wish their clients would take their wrecked marriages and family feuds elsewhere. Sometimes, if the client can afford it, the attorney can minimize the effect of his own ineptness by referring such problems to psychiatrists or other specialists. And certainly there are few marital cases which would not benefit from specialized professional guidance. But it takes insight—of a non-legal variety—on the lawyer's part to know how to persuade the client to accept such help and above all to realize when he is beyond his own depth in the troubled waters of human tensions and complexities.

For example, I recall one apparently hopeless case where the wife's lawyer and I, representing the husband, were asked on one day to work out details of a reconciliation and on the next to "throw the book" at each other's clients in a "lawsuit." There were children, which argued, of course, for keeping the couple together. On the other hand, the couple was at sword's point— the police had been called after the husband had pushed his wife downstairs. Even worse, the two children were caught in the conflict; the daughter sided with her father and refused to talk to her mother or to eat food she had cooked while the son was so terrified of his father that he once ran in front of a moving car to avoid having to talk to him.

This couple could afford a psychiatrist and agreed to consult one. After a series of psychological tests he reported that in his opinion and the opinion of the psychologist who had administered the tests the mother and father could never successfully bridge the gap between them—the man was highly intelligent but emotionally cold, untouched by feeling; the woman was intuitive, warm, with a low I.Q. Thus guided, their lawyers after so much fruitless persuasion abandoned further efforts at a reconciliation, which neither client really wanted, and instead worked out the best possible separation agreement.

But many couples can barely afford an attorney, let alone a psychiatrist or a psychologist. Then the lawyer must "cope," just as he did in the old days. This his casebook legal education rarely equips him to do, for few marital cases are clear-cut, black-and-white problems. For instance, a few months ago a couple came to my office who said they just wanted a divorce without any fuss. Would I please do the necessary? It would have been simple to proceed like a legal slot machine, for the required grounds for divorce in New York —adultery—were established. But somehow I felt my function involved something more. So I asked what they thought the basic trouble was.

The husband had a ready answer. "My wife and my father hate each other," he said "Since I have to choose between them, I've chosen my father because I've known him much longer and he's done and can do so much for me."

Obviously, this was only the top layer of deeper troubles that called for skilled psychological probing. But the couple refused to consult a marriage counselor or other expert on the grounds that they had neither the money nor the time. Besides, their minds were made up.

Thus, as happens in so many marriage and family difficulties, the lawyer became the only outside adviser who had anything to do with the case. And he does the best he can with whatever knowledge of human beings he has gleaned over the years. In most cases, if he stops to think about it at all, he wishes it had been more purposeful and scientific. For just about every time that a lawyer advises a client he is not merely practicing law; he is also, whether he knows it or not, practising psychology as well.

NOTE 4.

FREUD, SIGMUND

Fragment of an Analysis of a Case of Hysteria (1905)*

. . . I begin the treatment, indeed, by asking the patient to give me the whole story of his life and illness, but even so the information I receive is

---

* *Harper's*, Vol. 220 (1960), pp. 67, 68-69. Copyright 1960 by Harriet F. Pilpel. Reprinted with permission of the author.

* Reprinted from *The Standard Edition of the Complete Psychological Works of Sigmund Freud*. Vol. 7. London: The Hogarth Press, 1953 (pp. 16-18). Reprinted with permission of the publisher and of Basic Books, Inc., NewYork.

never enough to let me see my way about the case. This first account may be compared to an unnavigable river whose stream is at one moment choked by masses of rock and at another divided and lost among shallows and sandbanks. I cannot help wondering how it is that the authorities can produce such smooth and precise histories. . . . As a matter of fact the patients are incapable of giving such reports about themselves. They can, indeed, give the physician plenty of coherent information about this or that period of their lives; but it is sure to be followed by another period as to which their communications run dry, leaving gaps unfilled, and riddles unanswered; and then again will come yet another period which will remain totally obscure and unilluminated by even a single piece of serviceable information. The connections—even the ostensible ones—are for the most part incoherent, and the sequence of different events is uncertain. Even during the course of their story patients will repeatedly correct a particular or a date, and then perhaps, after wavering for some time, return to their first version. The patients' inability to give an ordered history of their life in so far as it coincides with the history of their illness is not merely characteristic of the neurosis. It also possesses great theoretical significance. For this inability has the following grounds. In the first place, patients consciously and intentionally keep back part of what they ought to tell—things that are perfectly well known to them—because they have not got over their feelings of timidity and shame (or discretion, where what they say concerns other people); this is the share taken by *conscious* disingenuousness. In the second place, part of the anamnestic knowledge, which the patients have at their disposal at other times, disappears while they are actually telling their story, but without their making any deliberate reservations: the share taken by *unconscious* disingenuousness. In the third place, there are invariably true amnesias—gaps in the memory into which not only old recollections but even quite recent ones have fallen—and paramnesias, formed secondarily so as to fill in those gaps. When the events themselves have been kept in mind, the purpose underlying the amnesias can be fulfilled just as surely by destroying a connection, and a connection is most surely broken by altering the chronological order of events. The latter always proves to be the most vulnerable element in the store of memory and the one which is most easily subject to repression. Again, we meet with many recollections that are in what might be described as the first stage of repression, and these we find surrounded with

doubts. At a later period the doubts would be replaced by a loss or a falsification of memory. . . . It is only towards the end of the treatment that we have before us an intelligible, consistent, and unbroken case history.

NOTE 5.

EHRLICH, STANTON L. and SPROGER, CHARLES E.
X-ray of Divorce—Recent Developments*

The client does not seek his lawyer for diagnosis of the extent or degree of his marital cancer; rather he announces his self-diagnosed condition and dictates the surgical remedy—divorce. Yet the same people, if suffering the pains of some physical ailment, would not tell the doctor to perform an appendectomy or any other type of surgery. They instead would ask for his diagnosis and would submit themselves to his treatment. If the physician, with the aid of x-ray, laboratory analysis and the like, can determine that surgery is unnecessary, he may be able to cure even a cancer with radiation therapy. However, that same person will try to dictate to the lawyer his course of legal action in the marital situation rather than ask advice and diagnostics in this regard.

It is not suggested that the lawyer be a therapist, act as a psychiatrist, or be other than what a lawyer should be—one who is to serve the client with his legal talents, his understanding of human nature, and his ability to advise the best course of action for the parties.

NOTE 6.

NIZER, LOUIS
My Life in Court†

A client, particularly in a matrimonial controversy, is so emotionally involved that he cannot be trusted to have cool judgment. His lawyer must be firm and in full control of the case, or he disserves his client. The lawyer must not be dependent on his client's favor either because of fees or even friendship. What a man in legal trouble needs is not merely a friend, but a counselor. If a client is strongly guided by skillful and loyal hands, he has received also the most significant expression of friendship. Sentiment alone will not do. When the lawyer, in order to please the client, permits him to have his way, he may incur his favor temporarily, but they are both likely to be in trouble at the end.

---

* 1962 U. ILL. L. F. 601, 607 (1962).
† From *My Life in Court* by Louis Nizer, p. 180. Copyright © 1961 by Louis Nizer. Reprinted by permission of Doubleday & Co., Inc.

Biases
Conscious or
unconscious

Tender yrs
Free wheeling sex
Homos
Lesbians
Class – Educ. + financial
moneys
Child rearing – permissive
or conventional

Race
Women's Lib
Political

~~Laws or~~ Administration +
interpretation of law is
made by human beings –
never purely logical but
by ratiocination

ntre, Massachusetts 02159   Telephone (617) 969-0100
Ext. 4372
4440
4373

c. Determining a Course of Action—The Judicial Selection of Facts

[i]

FRANK, JEROME

Law and the Modern Mind (1930)*

Now and again some judge, more clear-witted and outspoken than his fellows, describes (when off the bench) his methods . . . Judge Hutcheson essayed such an honest report of the judicial process. He tells us that after canvassing all the available material at his command and duly cogitating on it, he gives his imagination play,

> "and brooding over the cause, waits for the feeling, the hunch—that intuitive flash of understanding that makes the jump-spark connection between question and decision and at the point where the path is darkest for the judicial feet, sets its light along the way. . . . In feeling or 'hunching' out his decisions, the judge acts not differently from but precisely as the lawyers do in working on their cases, with only this exception, that the lawyer, in having a predetermined destination in view—to win the law-suit for his client—looks for and regards only those hunches which keep him in the path that he has chosen, while the judge, being merely on his way with a roving commission to find the just solution, will follow his hunch wherever it leads him. . . ."

And Judge Hutcheson adds:

> "I must premise that I speak now of the judgment or decision, the solution itself, as opposed to the apologia for that decision; the decree, as opposed to the logomachy, the effusion of the judge by which that decree is explained or excused. . . . The judge really decides by feeling and not by judgment, by hunching and not by ratiocination, such ratiocination appearing only in the opinion. The vital motivating impulse for the decision is an intuitive sense of what is right or wrong in the particular case; and the astute judge, having so decided, enlists his every faculty and belabors his laggard mind, not only to justify that intuition to himself, but to make it pass muster with his critics." Accordingly, he passes in review all of the rules, principles, legal categories, and concepts "which he may find useful, directly or by an analogy, so as to select from them those which in his opinion will justify his desired result."

We may accept this as an approximately correct description† of how all judges do their thinking. But see the consequences. If the law consists of

the decisions of the judges and if those decisions are based on the judge's hunches, then the way in which the judge gets his hunches is the key to the judicial process. Whatever produces the judge's hunches makes the law.

What, then, are the hunch-producers? What are the stimuli which make a judge feel that he should try to justify one conclusion rather than another?

The rules and principles of law are one class of such stimuli. But there are many others, concealed or unrevealed, not frequently considered in discussions of the character or nature of law. To the infrequent extent that these other stimuli have been considered at all, they have been usually referred to as "the political, economic and moral prejudices" of the judge. A moment's reflection would, indeed, induce any open-minded person to admit that factors of such character must be operating in the mind of the judge.

* * *

It is . . . a legal commonplace that a witness cannot mechanically reproduce the facts, but is reporting his judgment of the facts and may err in the making of this judgment.

Strangely enough, it has been little observed that, while the witness is in this sense a judge, *the judge, in a like sense, is a witness.* He is a witness of what is occurring in his court-room. He must determine what are the facts of the case from what he sees and hears; that is, from the words and gestures and other conduct of the witnesses. And like those who are testifying before him, the judge's determination of the facts is no mechanical act. If the witnesses are subject to lapses of memory or imaginative reconstruction of events, in the same manner the judge is subject to defects in his apprehension of the testimony; so that long before he has come to the point in the case where he must decide what is right or wrong, just or unjust, with reference to the facts of the case as a whole, the trial judge has been engaged in making numerous judgments or inferences as the testimony dribbles in. His beliefs as to what was said by the witnesses and with what truthfulness the witnesses said it, will determine what he believes to be the "facts of the case." If his final decision is based upon a hunch and that hunch is a function of the "facts," then of course what, as a fallible witness of what went on in his courtroom, he believes to be the "facts," will often be of controlling importance. So that the judge's innumerable unique traits, dispositions and habits often get in their work in shaping his decisions not only in his determination of what he thinks fair or just with reference to a given set of facts, but in the very processes by which he becomes convinced what those facts are.

---

* New York: Coward-McCann, Inc., 1930, pp. 103-105, 109-111. Copyright 1949 by Coward-McCann, Inc. Reprinted with permission of the publisher.
† . . . See Hutcheson, "The Judgment Intuitive: The Function of the 'Hunch' in Judicial Decisions," 14 Cornell Law Quarterly, 274.

The peculiar traits, disposition, biases and habits of the particular judge will, then, often determine what he decides to be the law. . . .

[ii]

WEIL v. WEIL
224 P. 2d 460 (Dist. Ct. App., Cal. 1950)

WILSON, JUSTICE.

*   *   *

Plaintiff commenced the action for a divorce from his wife on the ground of cruelty; she filed a cross-complaint charging cruelty and desertion on the part of plaintiff and seeking a decree of separate maintenance. [S]he amended her cross-complaint under conditions hereafter related so as to ask for a divorce.

Defendant assigns several grounds for reversal of the judgment, the principal one being the charge that the trial judge was guilty of misconduct and prejudicial error in coercing her against her will, as conditions to granting her any relief at all, (1) to amend her cross-complaint so as to pray for a divorce although she desired and had prayed for a decree of separate maintenance, and (2) to agree to accept as final any judgment which he might render.

Upon defendant's compliance with the requirements of the trial judge an interlocutory decree of divorce was granted in her favor providing that plaintiff should pay her $300 a month as support and maintenance commencing November 1, 1948, for a period of 30 months. . . .

The decree recited that findings of fact and conclusions of law had been waived by the parties and that defendant, in open court, had expressed her willingness to consent to and accept the decision and judgment as final; that plaintiff had treated defendant in an extremely cruel and inhuman manner, and wrongfully inflicted grievous mental suffering and pain upon her without any cause or reason therefor, all of which had caused her to become sick and ill in mind and body, specifically finding as true certain allegations of physical violence committed by plaintiff upon defendant.

After the entry of judgment defendant obtained a substitution of herself in propria persona in the place of her attorney who had represented her during the trial and in her own behalf filed a notice of motion for a new trial. [Thereafter her present counsel were employed and the motion for new trial was presented upon the affidavits of defendant, her former counsel, and one of counsel for plaintiff.] Defendant's affidavits relate the following: After the trial had progressed for several days the trial judge called both counsel to the bench and stated that he felt it was useless to prolong the trial and in the event defendant

would amend her cross-complaint and ask for a divorce he was "disposed to grant her a divorce and alimony for a short period" but he "didn't believe in separate maintenance for short marriages" and did not consider that separate maintenance should be granted in this case. The trial continued for two or three days and in further conferences in chambers between the judge and counsel for both parties defendant's attorney stated his client did not desire to amend her cross-complaint to ask for a divorce. The trial was thereupon resumed and near the close of the evidence the court said "there was enough evidence to justify him in granting a divorce to either party" but if defendant would amend her cross-complaint to pray for a divorce he would grant it together with a specified amount of alimony, but if she did not so amend her cross-complaint "he would not grant her separate maintenance but would grant a divorce to plaintiff" in which event she could not be given any alimony. On the last day of the trial there was another conference in chambers at which time the judge stated to defendant's counsel that he could tell his client that in the event she did not amend her cross-complaint as previously suggested and did not consent to accept the judgment of the trial judge as final he, the judge, intended to grant a divorce to plaintiff. Thereupon defendant's counsel told her of the conference and of the judge's ultimatum and advised her that if she wished to obtain a judgment . . . she would have to amend her cross-complaint to pray for a divorce and to state in open court that she accepted the judgment as final. Realizing that if she did not comply with the judge's requirement she would lose everything and get nothing, defendant authorised her counsel to amend her cross-complaint to ask for a divorce and she thereafter consented in open court to accept as final such judgment as the court might render.

*   *   *

The trial judge neither filed an affidavit nor made any statement from the bench denying any part of the affidavits filed on behalf of defendant.

The affidavit of plaintiff's attorney refers to statements made by the judge in chambers to the effect that in his opinion defendant had "embarked on a campaign" to obtain for herself an interest in trust funds to which plaintiff had "invasion rights,"[1] that "her continued pressure and intrigue" along those lines was a basic cause of the difficulties of the parties, and that the evidence

---

1. The term "invasion rights" refers to plaintiff's right to withdraw each year portions of the corpus of trusts from the income of which he received periodic payments.

introduced by plaintiff "was more than ample to justify a decree in his favor." The futility of plaintiff's argument based on such statements is found in the rule that whatever may have been in the judge's mind or expressed orally, or even in a formal opinion, cannot be employed to restrict, explain or override his decision embodied in the findings and judgment. . . . Despite the judge's aspersions he rendered judgment in favor of defendant.

In open court, after the last of the conferences in chambers had terminated, with the parties and their counsel present, defendant's attorney moved to amend her cross-complaint to pray for a divorce, which motion was granted by the court. Then the following occurrred:

"THE COURT: Now, Mrs. Weil, before I pass on this, I am going to inform you now that this judgment—if I give you judgment—I haven't made up my mind yet, because it has to depend on you, because I told your counsel that—and I say this to you: you are well represented by very competent counsel, who raised more fuss than I would have in his place, but as it is his business to make a row, he certainly does it—you understand that this judgment, if I give you one, is to be final. Do you understand that?

"MRS. WEIL: Yes, your Honor, I do.

"THE COURT: There are to be no more suits over this property or over your assets or over your liabilities, or over your welfare or his welfare.

"MRS. WEIL: I understand that and accept it.

"THE COURT: That will be final."

After a discussion relating to details of the judgment the court said:

". . . You heard your client stipulate that this is final in all respects in regard to this law suit or any other outcome of this law suit, that it is now terminated for good, once and for all. (Addressing Mrs. Weil): I want your counsel, who represented you, to know that he is in on that, and that takes care of that."

From the foregoing it is manifest that even after defendant's motion to amend her cross-complaint had been made as demanded by the judge and granted it was not certain that the decree would be in defendant's favor as evidenced by the judge's statement: "if I give you judgment—I haven't made up my mind yet." He did say that if he gave her judgment it was to be on condition that she agreed it should be final.

When it was suggested that the judge disqualify himself from hearing a subsequent motion in the case he said: "That lady had her choice, to choose one, and I gave her the divorce. I could have given it to the man just as well, but I did not desire to saddle this man with separate maintenance which has always been against my prin-ciples, on short marriages. Now, she could have refused to accept my suggestion, which she—sitting at this table—did accept, and she had advice of counsel as well, and competent counsel. She could have said, 'No, I don't want to do that,' and I could have given a divorce to the man, and then she could have appealed it."

When the motion for a new trial came on for hearing defendant's counsel cited authorities holding that it is error for the trial court to coerce a wife into changing her action from one of separate maintenance to one of divorce. The judge purported to distinguish such cases on the ground that the parties thereto had been married *"for a much longer time"* than the parties to the instant proceeding, again stating his opposition to separate maintenance "for short marriages." In giving his reasons for having coerced defendant to accept his judgment as final the judge said: "That was done because of the fact that she had changed lawyers, according to the record, five or six times and I wanted this litigation to cease." The fact is that defendant had changed attorneys only twice, not "five or six times." Moreover, the trial judge was without right or power to compel "litigation to cease" merely because he was of the opinion that it should terminate with the decree he was about to render or because he thought he had "made a very fair deal."

* * *

When allegations and proof of cruelty are made by both parties it is within the discretion of the trial court to award a decree to either. . . . If the evidence would have sustained a decree in favor of either plaintiff or defendant the court was without power to impose as conditions to a judgment for defendant that she (1) pray for a divorce when she did not want it, or (2) abandon her cause of action praying for what she did want, or (3) waive her statutory right of appeal in the event she was dissatisfied with the judgment.

In the judge's statement that the evidence was sufficient to justify the granting of a divorce to either party there is the implication that although defendant had proved her case he would render judgment in accord with plaintiff's evidence, would disbelieve that of defendant unless she amended her cross-complaint as demanded, and would believe her evidence only on condition that her pleading should be so amended.

It was the function of the trial court to evaluate the evidence and to determine the credibility of the witnesses but it is impossible to ascertain how this function could have been judicially performed if the evidence should be weighed and the credibility of the witnesses determined by defendant's acquiescence or her refusal to acquiesce in the court's demand that her pleading be amended to accord with its wishes. . . .

Notwithstanding several paragraphs of plaintiff's brief are devoted to the discussion of the duty of a trial judge in a domestic relations action to conciliate and to effect an adjustment, together with the citation of numerous court decisions and articles by legal and sociological writers, no part of the record is pointed out that indicates the trial judge made any effort to act as a conciliator or to bring about an adjustment of the differences existing between the parties. Instead of conciliating and adjusting he demanded that defendant change her cause of action and agree that such judgment as might be rendered should become final. As to the latter condition which was exacted by the court plaintiff himself correctly states in his brief: "He [the judge] must not coerce the parties into accepting his decision as final. The course is open to him to bind them against their will simply by entering judgment, leaving to them their statutory right of appeal. True conciliation leaves the parties free to accept or reject the judge's suggestions."

Each case should be tried according to the rules of law established by statute and by the decisions of the higher courts and not according to whimsical ideas and prejudices of the trial judge. "The trial of a case should not only be fair in fact, but it should also appear to be fair. And where the contrary appears it shocks the judicial instinct to allow the judgment to stand." Pratt v. Pratt, 141 Cal. 247, 252, 74 P. 742, 744.

It was judicial coercion to compel defendant to consent to a judgment in her favor for something she did not seek, something she did not desire, in a form objectionable to her, and to which she consented only because of the court's threat that she would not receive anything at all unless she consented to the court's demands hereinbefore related, including the surrender of her statutory right of appeal. The latter is a valuable right which a litigant should not be coerced or cajoled into relinquishing. Had the court in granting defendant a divorce awarded support money in an insignificant amount and for only a short period of time defendant would have had the right to appeal on the ground that the court had abused its discretion in that regard and she would have been entitled to a review of the judgment by the higher courts. Such right she was compelled to forego without any knowledge of what was in the judge's mind or what amount, if any, he intended to allow for her support.

* * *

It follows that the misconduct of the trial judge complained of constitutes prejudicial error by reason of which the judgment must be reversed.

NOTES

NOTE 1.

WEIL v. WEIL
37 Cal. 4770, 236 P. 2d 159 (1951

TRAYNOR, JUSTICE.

* * *

The judge's statement that he did not believe in separate maintenance for short marriages does not, in our opinion, evidence an unwillingness to try defendant's case according to law. A judge is not required to approve every statute or precedent by which his decision is governed. Like other citizens he is bound, not to believe in a particular law, but to obey it. Thus, he may doubt the wisdom of particular economic legislation but it is nevertheless his duty to enforce it in a proper case. The judge who disagrees with the policy of a statute is not necessarily disqualified from hearing a case in which that statute must be applied. In the present case, there has been no showing that the judge's opposition to separate maintenance for short marriages was anything more than a personal opinion concerning the wisdom of the legislation involved. According to the Pacht [plaintiff's attorney] affidavit, the judge stated that on this issue "his mind had not been made up and would be kept open." Whelan's affidavit [defendant's attorney] also shows that the judge's observation was qualified, for it quotes him as saying that he did not believe separate maintenance should be granted in this case "unless there was additional evidence that he hadn't heard." Had he regarded length of marriage as a controlling circumstance, "additional evidence" would have made no difference to him.

The judge was guilty of no misconduct in thus expressing to the parties what he believed the law should be. The Legislature itself has not infrequently heeded judicial comment suggesting modification of statutes. A judge may properly indicate to litigants the hardship that may result from a rigid insistence upon technical rights. Such suggestions are peculiarly appropriate in a court of equity, and all the more so when the task before the court involves the difficult social and legal adjustments that attend the tragedy of an unsuccessful marriage. Defendant had divorced her first husband before she met plaintiff, and she knew that plaintiff also had been divorced. Even after this suit was begun, settlement negotiations were had between the parties predicated upon the assumption that a divorce would be granted. It is apparent, therefore, that defendant's prayer for separate maintenance was not based upon conscientious or religious objections to divorce. In view of this fact, and in view of the seriousness and finality of the marital rupture, as disclosed by the evidence, it was not error for the judge to urge divorce as the more appropriate solution to their problems. "[P]ublic policy does not discourage divorce where the relations between husband and wife are such that the legitimate objects of matrimony have been utterly destroyed." Hill v. Hill, 23 Cal. 2d 82, 93, 142 P. 2d 417, 422.

It is clear from the record that the trial judge was anxious to spare the parties the spectacle of further embarrassing testimony; that he was tentatively persuaded that defendant's charges were exaggerated and her testimony unreliable and that plaintiff should be given a divorce; that, owing to defendant's possible need of an early operation, together with plaintiff's relatively favorable financial position and the absence of community property, he felt the desirability of temporary payments by plaintiff to enable defendant to reestablish herself economically; that in view of the merits of the respective cases as thus far presented, and particularly since this marriage had lasted less than five years, he was unwilling to decree separate maintenance as a means of effecting defendant's economic adjustment, for that could have deprived plaintiff of a divorce; and that he was willing to grant a divorce nominally to defendant in order that temporary alimony might be provided. There is no indication in either affidavit that he had prejudged the facts of the case—these were tentative views and expressly subject to modification in the event that later evidence should require it.

* * *

In . . . reviewing the record, we are not to be understood as having substituted our decision on the evidence for that of the trier of fact. . . .

There can be no doubt that the judge's suggestion that defendant amend her cross-complaint induced her to do so, but there must be more to a claim of coercion than mere causation. If the judge believed from the evidence that plaintiff was entitled to a divorce, and if he so stated to counsel, then his suggestion was not, *as to defendant,* improper. The judge's remarks would constitute prejudicial misconduct only if his announced intention to grant plaintiff a divorce were contrary to the facts of the case as he had decided them. Defendant has failed before this court to prove that fact. We have concluded, therefore, that defendant's amendment of her prayer and consent to the judgment were made to obtain alimony to which she would not otherwise have been entitled, and that she was persuaded to make that decision, not because of any prejudice or misconduct of the court, but because she had failed to establish her case.

Defendant relies upon the rule that an appellate court will not go behind the findings of fact in an effort to determine the trial court's true views on the evidence. Manifestly that rule can have no application to a situation where it is clear that the findings were entered solely to support what was in effect a consent judgment.

Defendant also points to the statement in the Whelan affidavit that the judge remarked that there was "enough evidence to justify him in granting a divorce to either party." This is a fair comment on the evidence from the standpoint of an attack by appeal, for the conflicting testimony of plaintiff and defendant made the decision on the facts depend largely upon the credibility of the witnesses. The judge's purpose in making this observation appears to have been to point out to counsel that if his suggestion were not followed and plaintiff were granted a divorce, defendant would probably be unsuccessful on appeal, but that if, by agreement, the divorce were given to defendant, it would have every appearance of evidentiary support. In our opinion this was an accurate description of the legal situation and was rendered with a view to assisting defendant in making her decision.

It is apparent from the proposal made by the trial judge, and from his other comments, that he believed a divorce was the only satisfactory solution to the problems presented in the marital tragedy that confronted him. His statement that "it was clear to him from all the evidence that he had heard and read in the case, that the legitimate objects of matrimony had been destroyed" is conclusively supported by the record. The evidence shows that the marriage of the parties began with mutual affection and happiness, but that arguments and misunderstandings, largely over financial matters, became increasingly frequent and acrimonious. The physical health of both parties has become seriously impaired. Family, social and even business relationships have been disrupted. No prospects of reconciliation remain—the final separation followed earnest efforts to overcome differences and live peacefully together. Since the filing of the complaint the activities of the parties have degenerated into a legal battle, characterized by extravagant and embittering charges, and in which the only remaining consideration of importance is money. We cannot ignore the important "social considerations which make it contrary to public policy to insist on the maintenance of a union which has utterly broken down." Blunt v. Blunt, [1943] A.C. 517, 525 (H.L.), 169 L.T.R. 33, 34; . . .

NOTE 2.

O'GORMAN, HUBERT J.
Lawyers and Matrimonial Cases*

[A] lawyer's attitude towards the probable accuracy of his client's story is influenced by a number of other considerations. For example, he is not obliged, legally or ethically, to represent only clients whose stories he believes to be true. Furthermore, he is not unaffected by the court's attitude. He is apt to believe . . . that judges grant decrees in matrimonial actions even though they may privately doubt the validity of the evidence presented. A lawyer may, therefore, reach the conclusion stated by one attorney: "If people meet the requirements of the statute, they are entitled to their divorce or annulment. Of course their stories look funny. . . . But you know the judges figure that these people are finished with each other; they want a divorce. So what difference does it make?" A lawyer may also find that it is extremely difficult to discover the truth about his client's marital conflict. Usually, he has only the testimony of the client and witnesses who, in most cases, are close friends and relatives of the client. . . .

[iii]

DEL RUTH v. DEL RUTH
75 Cal. App. 2d 638, 171 P. 2d 34 (1946)

SHINN, JUSTICE.

Appeal by plaintiff from a judgment which denied her separate maintenance and awarded defendant a divorce upon his cross-complaint. Plaintiff brought her action for separate maintenance, charging defendant with extreme cruelty. Defendant answered and filed a cross-complaint for divorce, charging plaintiff with extreme cruelty. The allegations of both parties were in general terms without specification of particular acts. The parties intermarried March 14, 1921, and have one child, a son, of the age of 21 years. They separated in July, 1944. Plaintiff is employed as a motion picture director at a salary of $1,750 per week. The parties were possessed of community property of substantial value. Defendant was called as a witness. . . . After he had been examined as to his property he was asked to state the particulars of the acts and conduct of plaintiff which were claimed to constitute her wrongful conduct. The court thereupon stated, "Not for 20 years, when did the marriage begin? * * * Well, I say there is no need to start out

* Reprinted with permission of the publisher from *Lawyers and Matrimonial Cases* by Hubert J. O'Gorman, p. 139. © 1963 by The Free Press of Glencoe, A Division of the Macmillan Company.

with the marriage and recite their squabbles for the past 24 years." Then occurred the following:

"MR. CRUMP [one of plaintiff's attorneys]: It seems to me, but if your Honor will indicate how far back we can go.
"THE COURT: Oh, two or three years.
"MR. CRUMP: I suppose that applies to both sides?
"THE COURT: Oh, yes.
"MR. CRUMP: Then we will start in say in 1941."

The record shows that although plaintiff's attorneys proceeded as the court directed, they declined to stipulate or consent to the ruling made shortly thereafter which excluded evidence of defendant's conduct prior to 1941. Defendant's counsel insisted that defendant should be allowed to prove plaintiff's conduct over a period of the last 12 to 15 years, his position being that there had been misconduct extending over that period, and the court stated: ". . . The Court wants to get this case in a place where we can try it in a reasonable time. There is no need of listening to acts of cruelty for twelve years on either side, all the detail of these things, we would be here for three weeks, and there are others waiting for the services of the Court. * * * I think we ought to get some pleadings." A plan was agreed upon for each side to specify the acts of cruelty relied upon, for in that manner, the court said, "We could work out some method by which we could take up some of the high lights and let the details be dissolved in the background." And later, "I want some allegations to which testimony may be directed." And further, "I need some statement of facts which you expect to prove. * * * A bill of particulars, just setting forth the particulars in which the cross-complainant complains, recite them, you can put it in as an amendment to your cross-complaint." The parties prepared specifications of the acts of cruelty which they proposed to prove. Plaintiff's specifications were fourteen in number. The court of its own motion selected five of these, as to which he would take evidence, and excluded the others, and likewise rejected about half of defendant's twenty-five specifications. The court further of its own motion made an order that all testimony relating to acts of cruelty on either side would be strictly limited to a period beginning January 1, 1941, and ending with the date of separation.

The five specifications of cruelty as to which plaintiff was allowed to offer evidence were that defendant called her vile names; that he spent his evenings away from home and when home shut himself in a room and refused to have anything to do with plaintiff; that many times he repulsed plaintiff when she went to his room and attempted to be affectionate with him, and that in 1941 or 1942, in the presence of plaintiff's mother, he spat in her face. Among the allegations excluded were those of an association between defendant and an actress in 1929 which, plaintiff alleged, caused comment among their friends, and which resulted in a suit by the husband of the actress against defendant, charging alienation of affections, which suit was the subject of newspaper articles and gossip which came to plaintiff's attention. Also excluded were allegations that defendant purchased large quantities of liquor for plaintiff, urged her to drink, urged her to go out socially with men as well as women, and at the same time was employing detectives for the purpose of entrapping her in misconduct; that at a time when plaintiff was pregnant defendant struck her a hard blow on the abdomen with his fist; that in 1933 he hit her in the eye with his fist, giving her a black eye, and in 1933 or 1934, in the home, threw a glassful of water in plaintiff's face; that in 1940, in the home, defendant, while angry, threw a glassful of water at a mirror, breaking the glass and shattering it over the floor. Among the specifications of cruelty charged by defendant, the court retained those charging plaintiff with great extravagance, with the purchase on charge accounts of some $800 worth of clothes on the date of separation, which defendant paid for, and with the purchase a few days later of $1,100 worth of merchandise, which had not been paid for; that plaintiff was possessed of a violent and ungovernable temper; that for nine years last past she had refused to maintain sexual relations with him; that for nine years and longer she had displayed no affection for him or interest in him; that she frequently addressed toward him vulgar and profane language; that she took telephone calls from his business associates and refused to give them to him, with the result that he had to rent an office where he could receive telephone calls and conduct his business; that she stayed in bed until late hours in the day, and at all times refused to do housework, even to making the beds when they could not be made by the servants; that she would habitually go shopping and not return for dinner until after defendant and his son had finished their dinner, and many times would not return for dinner at all; that she would not go to places of entertainment with defendant but would come home late at night, slam the doors, play the radio, turn on the lights, and that defendant was thereby compelled to take a separate bedroom, in which he had slept for the past nine or ten years; that plaintiff used intoxicating liquors to excess, criticized defendant's relatives, and that she cursed and abused defendant, and accused him of taking a picture of their son from

her dressing table, although it had been taken by the son without defendant's knowledge. Excluded were allegations of the cross-complaint that plaintiff, between the years 1931 and 1936, associated with a male acquaintance at hotels, night clubs, Catalina Island, and the beaches, appearing with him in public at all times of the day and night, leaving her car parked in front of his apartment house, and further allegations that defendant upon returning from Palm Springs one night in 1931, went into the apartment of plaintiff's male friend and found the two there completely undressed. There were also allegations of an automobile accident suffered by plaintiff when she had been at a party with the same man and was driving her automobile while intoxicated, as a result of which accident she was confined to the hospital for several months. There were also allegations concerning her difficulties with the nurses, her infatuation for her doctor, and her attacking a maid in their home for making a mistake, in which attack it was alleged she broke the maid's glasses, causing her to lose the sight of her eye, for which defendant paid $1,500 in settlement of the maid's claim for damages, which sum included his own attorney's fees. Other specifications of plaintiff's alleged misconduct which were rejected did not differ materially from those as to which evidence was received.

During the examination of defendant under section 2055, plaintiff's counsel produced a letter dated April 13, 1944, written to defendant by his niece. The letter said, in part: "Roy, I am so very happy over the grand news about you and ————. I am so anxious to meet her and I know I will love her, as she looks like such an understanding and gifted girl. She is what you should have had many years ago. I guess if we all could live our lives over again we sure would do differently, because that is the only way we can get a contrast, a little bitter with the sweet. I am looking forward to you, Mother and Dad and bring ———— with you some Sat. or Sunday for dinner," etc. The name in the letter was the same as that of the first name of the actress with whom defendant was alleged to have associated, as heretofore stated. Upon defendant's objection, the court excluded the letter from evidence upon the ground that it had a connection with the former association of defendant with the actress who had the same first name, and that evidence of such association and all matters connected with it had been excluded under the previous ruling. It was neither stated nor admitted that the woman named in the letter was the one who was involved in the earlier incidents. Plaintiff made an offer to prove that she found the letter in the mail box, opened it, placed it upon defendant's desk and questioned him about it, and that the incident was one that she could not get out of her mind; that it caused her grief and illness. The offer of proof was rejected by the court and no further evidence was received concerning the letter.

Evidence was received under the specifications of cruelty as limited by the court. The court made the following findings:

> "III. It is not true that the defendant and cross-complainant has treated the plaintiff and cross-defendant in a cruel or inhuman manner or that he caused her to suffer great or any humiliation or embarrassment or mental anguish or that he caused her health to become impaired.

> "IV. It is true and the Court finds that the cross-defendant Olive Del Ruth, has wrongfully inflicted upon the cross-complainant, Thomas Leroy Del Ruth, grievous mental suffering and because thereof, it is impossible for the parties to live together as husband and wife."

* * *

The findings which we have quoted are claimed to be insufficient because they fail to cover the specific allegations of cruelty which were added by means of the specifications made at the request of the court. . . . From the finding that plaintiff had been guilty of cruelty, it cannot be determined what alleged conduct on her part had been proved, and what had not been proved. Nor can it be determined from the finding that defendant has not treated plaintiff in a cruel or inhuman manner, whether he was found guiltless of the acts charged or whether the court believed that such acts, if proved, were not wrongful, or did not cause plaintiff physical or mental suffering. Although the evidence cannot be held insufficient to support a general finding if it was sufficient to prove any one of the charges of cruelty, in a contested case the findings as to alleged cruelty should be specific where the allegations of the pleadings are specific. If special findings are requested, it would be error for the court to refuse them, but if no special findings are requested and no objection is made to a proposed general finding, the only objection to such general finding which can be raised later is that it is insufficient to support the judgment. . . .

There were charges of serious misconduct on the part of defendant prior to January 1, 1941, and also charges of cruelty subsequent to that date, which were arbitrarily eliminated from the case by the rulings of the court. The implications in the letter from defendant's niece were calculated to seriously disturb plaintiff and to aggravate the dissension that already existed. They disclosed that defendant was contemplating divorcing plaintiff, which defendant in his testimony admit-

ted to be the fact. They called for an explanation by defendant. The letter should have been received in evidence, plaintiff should have been allowed to testify as to her conversations with defendant concerning it, and also as to whether the incident had occasioned her any mental distress. In explaining his ruling, the trial judge said: "The thought in the mind of the Court at the time and now is that by that method we eliminate any possibility of some other woman in the case, so far as the defendant is concerned, and to eliminate that part of the case which related to some alleged indiscretion on the part of the plaintiff when she was followed by a detective and found naked in a room with this man ———. I thought it was in the interest of good morals and possibly simplifying this procedure not to have that sort of thing taken up by either side of the case. This was one of the purposes that I felt we had accomplished, and it was a very fair proposition, equally fair to each side, to eliminate those things that might embarrass them or might embarrass their son. I believe in so many cases of domestic difficulty, divorce, or separate maintenance, innocent children are made to suffer for the sins of the parents, and I think that is one of the principal considerations we must have in mind in handling of these domestic problems." With due respect for the motives of the trial judge, we think he carried his sympathy and altruism too far for the good of the lawsuit. From a perusal of the record as to the domestic life of these parties, which was a matter of daily observation by the 21 year old son, who resided with them, we felt that any effort made at the time of the trial to spare the parties or their son embarrassment came far too late. It was the duty of the judge to try the lawsuit, and nothing which would have aided him materially in arriving at the facts of the case should have been omitted in order to save the feelings of the parties. They made no complaint of embarrassment. A trial of this sort is not an arbitration; it is an inquiry for the determination of matters of fact. However distressing and regrettable it may be to have to take evidence as to charges of infidelity, disloyalty, acts of physical violence, name calling, and the use of profane, obscene and disgusting language, it is not within the discretion of the court to arbitrarily refuse to receive competent, relevant and material evidence. Here the court selected the arbitrary date of January 1, 1941, and declined to hear evidence of alleged misconduct of either party prior to that date. This was apparently upon the theory that earlier acts had been condoned and forgiven; but condonation is conditional and is revoked and the original cause for divorce is revived, "1. When the condonee commits acts constituting a like or other cause of divorce; or, 2. When the condonee is guilty of great conjugal unkindness, not amounting to a cause of divorce, but sufficiently habitual and gross to show that the conditions of condonation had not been accepted in good faith, or not fulfilled." Sec. 121, Civil Code. The court could not know, without hearing evidence as to the conduct of the parties prior to January 1, 1941, that the ultimate conclusions as to the allegations of cruelty on either side would not have been materially influenced or controlled by such evidence. Furthermore, remoteness of the time of commission of acts of cruelty is not of itself a sufficient ground for excluding evidence of such acts where questions of condonation and the revocation thereof must be decided. Section 118 of the Civil Code provides: "Where the cause of divorce consists of a course of offensive conduct, or arises, in cases of cruelty, from excessive acts of ill-treatment which may, aggregately, constitute the offense, cohabitation, or passive endurance, or conjugal kindness, shall not be evidence of condonation of any of the acts constituting such cause, unless accompanied by an express agreement to condone." . . . The limitations imposed by the rulings of the court, which were not requested or suggested by either of the parties, were such as to force the conclusion that the case was not fully tried. If under the rulings each of the parties was excused from defending against serious charges made by the other, which the judge stated was fair to both, then each was thereby deprived of an opportunity to prove serious charges of misconduct against the other. It is a fact that contested divorce cases often make extreme demands upon the time of the court, but this situation cannot be obviated by admitting only a part of the material evidence in the case.

Plaintiff urged on motion for new trial, and urges here, that she was prevented from having a fair trial by irregularities occurring during the course of the trial. After the trial had been under way for two or three days, and before any evidence had been received in support of the charges of cruelty, the trial judge communicated to plaintiff at her home the fact that he wanted to talk to her about the case privately in chambers. The request became known to the attorneys in the case and, pursuant to the request, plaintiff attended upon the judge in chambers and the case was discussed without the hearing or presence of any other person.

Upon motion for new trial, affidavits were filed by plaintiff and by the judge, giving the substance of the discussion which took place at the meeting, as each remembered it. It is unnecessary to set out these affidavits, or to consider them at length.

From the affidavit of the judge it appears that he inquired of plaintiff whether a reconciliation were possible, was assured by her that it was not possible, and that he then stated to her that he did not look with favor upon separate maintenance and that he thought most of the judges felt the same way about it. He suggested that plaintiff amend her complaint to pray for divorce, stating that if the decree should be in her favor there could be an allowance of alimony, but that if a divorce were granted to the husband, he would not be required to pay alimony. Immediately after his interview with plaintiff the judge made his ruling that evidence would be received as to some of the acts of alleged cruelty, but not as to others, and that the evidence would be limited to occurrences since January 1, 1941. It does not appear that at that time the judge had consciously, or otherwise, made up his mind not to award plaintiff separate maintenance, but it cannot be denied that he would have been reluctant to grant her that relief. Plaintiff had to proceed under the handicap of a preconceived and declared disinclination of the judge to award her the only relief which she sought. It was therefore of vital importance that she make out the strongest possible case. She should have been afforded the fullest opportunity to convince the judge that she had a good case for separate maintenance. At the conclusion of the evidence, when plaintiff's counsel were still endeavoring to put in evidence the letter to defendant from his niece and to persuade the judge to hear the testimony of plaintiff as to the events which followed the discovery of the letter, the court, in sustaining the defendant's objection, stated: "Well, I think there is enough here on either side in the way of charges and counter charges, plenty of proof." But, although there was "plenty of proof" to establish the charges and counter charges, it developed that plaintiff's proof was not strong enough to convince the judge that she should have separate maintenance. In other words, she had not succeeded in overcoming the judge's reluctance to award separate maintenance. Considering the evidence of the judge's aversion to granting separate maintenance and his statement, in effect, that there was no insufficiency of evidence to warrant a judgment in favor of plaintiff, it is too clear for argument that the limitations placed upon her evidence constituted prejudicial error. We cannot speculate as to whether the result would have been the same if plaintiff had been permitted to present all her evidence. She was entitled to a full and fair trial, and under the circumstances was peculiarly in need of one.

The judgment is reversed.

NOTES

NOTE 1.

HESS, ROBERT D., and HANDEL, GERALD

Family Worlds*

Living together, the individuals in a family each develop an image of what the other members are like. This image comprises the emotional meaning and significance which the other has for the member holding it. The concept of image is a mediating concept. Its reference extends into the personality and out into the interpersonal relationship. Referring to one person's emotionalized conception of another, an image is shaped by the personality both of the holder and of the object. The image emerges from the holder's past and bears the imprint of his experience, delimiting what versions of others are possible for him. It says something about him as a person. But it is also a cast into the future, providing the holder with direction in relating to and interacting with the object. While it represents the holder's needs and wishes, it also represents the object as a source of fulfillment.

Each family member has some kind of image of every other member and of himself in relation to them. This image is compounded of realistic and idealized components in various proportions, and it may derive from the personalities of its holder and its object also in various proportions. It draws from cultural values, role expectations, and the residue of the parents' experiences in their families of origin. One's image of another is the product of one's direct experience with the other and of evaluations of the other by third parties. From this experience, from evaluations of it and elaborations on it in fantasy, a conception of another person is developed, a conception which serves to direct and shape one's action to the other and which becomes a defining element of the interpersonal relationship. *An image of a person is one's definition of him as an object of one's own action or potential action.*

In studying a family, then, it is necessary to investigate both the images which the members hold of one another and the ways in which these images are interrelated. It is necessary to understand how the interaction of the members derives from and contributes to this interrelation of images. The implication of this stance is that interaction cannot be fully understood in its own terms, that, instead, it must be viewed in the context of how the participants define one another as relevant objects.

* Reprinted from *Family Worlds* by Robert D. Hess and Gerald Handel, pp. 14-15, by permission of The University of Chicago Press. Copyright 1959 by The University of Chicago.

From his experience with other members of his family and from experiences outside the family, an individual comes to have another kind of image—an image of his family which expresses his mode of relationship to the unit and which defines the kind of impact the family has on him. A woman may gratifyingly conceive of her family as dependents who need and reward her, or she may see them primarily as the group that enslaves her and for whom she wears herself out. A man may feel proud of his family as a demonstration of his masculinity, or his image may be of a group of perplexing people with emotions and reactions he doesn't understand, or his family may mean to him primarily a welcome retreat from and contrast with his workaday world. For a child, too, the family may have diverse meanings. To one it is the group he is happy to belong to. For another it consists of those he lives with because he has no place else to go. A person's image of his family embodies what he expects from it and what he gives to it, how important it is and what kind of importance it has.

The images held of one member by the others diverge in varying ways from one another and from his image of himself. The intimate and constant exchange that characterizes the nuclear family makes such divergence far from a matter of indifference. The members of a family want to and have to deal with one another; from the beginning they are engaged in evolving and mutually adjusting their images of one another. This mutual adjustment takes place in interaction, and it is, in part, the aim of interaction. Since complete consensus is most improbable, life in a family—as elsewhere—is a process ongoing in a situation of actual or potential instability. Pattern is reached, but it can never be complete, since action is always unfolding and the status of the family members is undergoing change.

NOTE 2.

DOE v. ROE
143 New York L. J. 15 (1960)
Supreme Court

BECKINELLA, JUSTICE.

. . . Defendant insists that the real cause of the marital rift is plaintiff's habitual drunkenness. She says that when sober, plaintiff is a good father and considerate husband, but that under the influence of liquor his conduct becomes so irrational and violent as to make it unsafe for her to live with him. She cites many instances of this alleged conduct.

The plaintiff not only denies the truth of these allegations but also denies that he was ever intoxicated in his entire lifetime. How wholly irreconcilable their claims are, is best illustrated by putting side-by-side their versions as to one of the instances cited by the wife as having happened on September 19, 1959:

HER VERSION

"Q. Then what happened when this discussion started, as far as you were concerned? A. We were arguing, and my husband went to strike me, and Brian, my little boy, ran between us.

Q. Your little boy? Which one? A. The middle fellow, Brian.

Q. And the little 2½ year-old boy rushed over to his dad, and did what? A. He pushed him away from him.

Q. Tried to push his father away? A. Yes. My husband struck him in the eye. He punched him in the eye.

Q. Little Brian then was punched in the eye? A. Yes.

Q. What was the state of his sobriety at that time? A. He had a hangover.

Q. Your husband had a hangover; he tried to strike you, and the boy came between you, and as a result the boy was struck, where? A. In the eye.

Q. Now, Madam, are you saying that it was a deliberate striking on the part of your husband, as far as Brian is concerned? A. That was deliberate, your Honor. He was angry with the boy."

HIS VERSION

"Q. There was something said by your wife during the testimony that on one occasion when you attempted to strike her you were drunk, that you attempted to strike your wife and your son Brian got between you and your wife, and that you were so irritated by that that you deliberately struck your child? A. No, sir.

Q. Did that happen? A. No, sir.

Q. Did you strike your child by accident? A. No, sir. I know exactly what she was trying to tell you and what happened.

Q. We might as well get it. A. I was sitting down having dinner and my son Brian had a belt, a cowboy belt, and he was swinging it around in the air, and he was passing by me going from the kitchenette into the kitchen. It came down and struck him on the cheek. It didn't seem to bother him. He didn't cry. I asked him if it hurt, and he said it didn't hurt. My wife took the child then and started a commotion and went into the bedroom with him. Then the child came out crying. I asked the child, 'What happened? Did Mommy hit you?' Little Brian said to me, 'No, but mommy kept rubbing my face.' I looked at it and it was red. With that, my wife came out and said, 'I am going to take care of you now. I threatened to frame you up, and I am going to do it."

* * *

NOTE 3.

McMAHON v. McMAHON
167 Pa. Super. 51, 53, 74 A. 2d 718 (1950)

OPINION BY RENO, J.

. . . According to appellant's testimony his wife's conduct compelled him to leave the marital domicile. He testified "there was never a day when my life wasn't in turmoil." He complained that indignities commenced the day they were married. When he attempted to kiss her at the altar of the church she pulled away from him. He charged that she refused to have sexual relations with him during the first three months of their married life; ridiculed his lack of education; taunted him about her ex-boy friends; attended social functions several nights a week while he acted as baby sitter; accused him of infidelity; compelled him to sleep in a different room because she said he "wasn't fit to sleep with her any longer"; threw a loaf of bread in his face because he asked for catsup; terrified him by holding a long bladed butcher knife over him causing one side of his facial nerves to collapse; jabbed him with an umbrella while following him down street; pushed the newspaper in his face when he was reading; threw water on him while he was in bed; placed salt, knives, forks and spoons in his bed; and constantly nagged and embarrassed him in public.

Appellee testified the parties had no serious difficulties during their 17 years of married life. . . .

NOTE 4.

CARTER v. CARTER
191 Kan. 80, 379 P. 2d 311, 313 (1963)

WERTZ, JUSTICE.

* * *

Extreme cruelty as contemplated by the divorce statute is no longer regarded as being limited to acts of physical violence, nor need it connote viciousness but only conduct which is unusual, disapproved and not conducive to the normal acts in accepted society. It is now generally held that any unjustifiable and long-practiced course of conduct by one spouse toward the other which utterly destroys the legitimate ends and objects of matrimony constitutes extreme cruelty though no physical or personal violence may be inflicted or threatened. Under some circumstances it may not be necessary that such conduct should continue over a long period to constitute extreme cruelty. It is not necessary that the corroboration support plaintiff's allegations throughout the course of mistreatment or as to every detail of plaintiff's testimony. The principal reason for the requirement of corroboration has been, and is, for the prevention of collusion between the parties to a divorce.

It is not essential that it alone sustain the judgment or that it support the plaintiff's testimony as to all of the allegations. Such a strict requirement might tend to thwart justice owing to the privacy of the relations between the parties. . . .

NOTE 5.

KUBIE, LAWRENCE S.

Implications for Legal Procedure of the Fallibility of Human Memory*

Various aspects of legal procedure are based upon a tacit assumption that a "normal" man can tell the truth if he tries. By implication this assumes that the major sources of error will be either a mechanical failure of the brain to record and reproduce past events, or else a deliberate desire to deceive or a reluctance to tell all. It will be my thesis that these assumptions are invalid that in spite of every effort to be honest, the perceiving, recording, processing, reliving and reproducing of the events one observes and of the events in which one participates always are selectively colored; that these sources of error are ubiquitous; and that a relatively rare and minor role is played by those errors which are introduced by deliberate deceit, by mechanical limits of the brain as a recording apparatus or by organic brain damage. The disconcerting questions which these facts force upon us are (1) what role in legal testimony should be played by memory and by discrepancies among the memories of different men, and (2) how are courts of law to proceed, since all testimony depends upon memory?

* * *

In one seminar a young psychiatrist reported that in a previous session his patient had suddenly asked that the recording machine be turned off because he was about to divulge some material which was particularly painful. The seminar group discussed the possible reasons for this, basing the discussion on their knowledge of the patient gained in previous meetings. To check the accuracy of their speculations the group suggested that the five or ten minutes of the therapeutic interview just preceding and following the interruption of the recording be played back. To the blank astonishment of the young psychiatrist and of the group as a whole, they heard the psychiatrist himself make the suggestion to the patient that the recording be interrupted. Of this fact the psychiatrist had not the slightest recollection. Yet from the material that preceded the interrup-

---

* 108 U. PA. L. REV. 59-75 (1959). Copyright 1959 U. PA. L. REV.

tion it became clear that the psychiatrist's intuition had served him well. He had sensed the patient's mounting tension. He had realized the need for some gesture of special consideration and privacy. The patient had responded with relief and after a few minutes had apparently suggested that the recording be resumed. Nevertheless, the psychiatrist had felt anxious lest he be criticized for his action; out of this anxiety had come the unconscious reversal of his memory of events and of the roles which he and the patient had played.

* * *

What we call "memory" actually consists of several components, each of which is vulnerable to distortion.

Before there is anything to remember there must first have been a perceptual process. But even elementary perceptions are not simple acts of automatic registering. Perceptions themselves are selected under the influence of many processes of which the perceiver is unaware. Without realizing it we pick and choose among thousands of concurrent impressions. Moreover, in addition to the unaware selective influences which guide our perceptions we actually do a major amount of perceiving without awareness that we are perceiving at all. This is not an hypothesis. It is a fact that has been demonstrated repeatedly in experimental work, and which also is manifested daily in human life. . . .

* * *

The point is that the recording, storing and reproducing of experience (*i.e.*, recalling it to conscious memory) are only in small part mediated by conscious processing, but are under the constant influence of highly selective preconscious and unconscious influences. Such preconscious perceptions make up the major share of the daily life of every human being; in fact, only a small fragment of our life experiences are mediated by conscious processing.

Similar unconscious and preconscious mechanisms guide the storing and processing of experience. By this we mean the linking of one unit of experience to another, which in its primary steps depends upon the concurrence of more than one perceptual process in any unit of time. . . .

* * *

This processing and recombining of units of past experience make possible the re-experiencing or re-living of the past with varying degrees of vividness. The re-experiencing, again, may be broken down into a battery of interacting components. One may re-experience merely the sensory fragments of the past; a pain, an ache, a smell, a flavor, a color, a scene or a face may come vividly to mind almost as though it were present. . . .

* * *

This brings us to the usual re-experiencing of the past—as something which is represented largely by verbal symbolic clues. Actually this is the least vivid element in the total process of memory; it means remembering that something has happened to us, but almost as impersonally as though it had happened to someone else. Words here represent the past as from a safe distance, screening out all the more vivid sensory components of memory. Thus memory of this usual type actually involves a first step in dissociation and depersonalization. Yet it is to just this type that the word "memory" is usually restricted: namely, the memories which we represent by words. And these verbal clues to the past are themselves frequently experienced not accurately but with many unconscious distortions, as through the substitution of one memory for another or through the condensation of many similar experiences to represent them by one "memory."

* * *

NOTE 6.

HUNTER v. HUNTER
169 Pa. Super. 498, 83 A. 2d 401 (1951)

HIRT, JUDGE.

On a charge of indignities the lower court entered a decree of divorce. In spite of the fact that the master, from a patient analysis of volumes of testimony, recommended a decree, we find it necessary to reverse. The issue does not depend upon the credibility of witnesses but rather on the significance of undisputed facts established principally by plaintiff's own testimony which in our view reveal an injured but not an innocent husband. Under our divorce law . . . to obtain a divorce from the bond of matrimony, a complaining spouse must be *both* injured and innocent.
. . . The gravamen of his complaint goes to the defendant's excessive drinking . . . and his humiliation because of her conduct on occasions in public, especially among his friends and business associates. . . .

* * *

Plaintiff complained of frequent tirades he was subjected to by the defendant at night in their common bed chamber. The adjoining room was occupied by plaintiff's son, by a former marriage. Pursuant to prearrangement by plaintiff the son set up a microphone in the bedroom of the parties on the nights of April 7, 8 and 9th and the early morn-

ing of April 10th, 1949, and connected the device with a wire recording mechanism installed in his room. By this means he, with plaintiff's knowledge and consent, attempted to make a recording of what was said between the parties on the four occasions. This effort was not entirely successful but the recording, insofar as intelligible when reproduced, was read into the record over appellant's objection.

. . . The parties were not on an even footing. Plaintiff was conscious that a record was being made of what he said; the defendant had no reason to suspect this invasion of her privacy. The result was a self-serving record directed and for the most part controlled by plaintiff. During the course of the discussions not only did plaintiff urge the defendant to "speak up, I can't hear you" but he goaded her into making derogatory aspersions and he deliberately prolonged the discussions when she indicated that she wanted to go to sleep. Even if admissible the recordings could be given little weight under the circumstances. . . .

In making such recordings it is possible for a competent operator to shut out, or blur, parts of a conversation by use of the volume control and later pick it up again, thus eliminating unfavorable testimony. We do not charge the son with intentionally deleting parts of the conversations in this case. We will assume the unintelligible parts of the recordings are due to his lack of expertness in making them and not to design. But since parts of what was said by defendant, on all of the occasions are lacking, the recordings, on that ground alone, are not admissible against her. In general such conversations are admissible as a whole or not at all. In so holding however we do not intend in any way to qualify what we said in Com. v. Clark, 123 Pa. Super. 277, 285, 187, A. 237, 240, to this effect: "The phonograph, the dictaphone, the talking motion picture machine, and similar recording devices, with reproducing apparatus, are now in such common use that the verity of their recording and reproducing sounds, including those made by the human voice in conversation, is well established; and as advances in such matters of scientific research and discovery are made and generally adopted, the courts will be permitted to make use of them by way of presenting evidentiary facts * * * ." Admittedly, under proper circumstances, even in a divorce case, recorded conversations may be admissible provided that the rules governing privileged communications are not thereby violated.

Here, the recordings are inadmissible on the ground, also that as to the wife the communications were privileged. The relations between husband and wife are most intimate and many subjects are discussed by them in their bedroom only because of the cloak of absolute privacy there provided. In general it may be inferred that because of the confidence which the marital relation inspires, communications made by one spouse to the other "were made with the intent and in the confidence mentioned": Seitz v. Seitz, 170 Pa. 71, 32 A. 578. The rule at common law, reestablished by statute in Pennsylvania . . . is that confidential communications between husband and wife cannot be divulged by either without the consent of the other. That rule is based on public policy and with a view to preserve the harmony and the confidence of the relationship between husband and wife. Whether a particular communication between husband and wife is privileged depends upon its nature and character and the circumstances under which it was made. . . . Once a communication between husband and wife has been made in confidence its privileged character outlasts divorce and even death . . . and is in no way affected by the statutory provision . . . making husband and wife competent to testify against each other "to the facts" in a divorce action. . . . In our view the recordings in this case were of confidential utterances of the wife; the circumstances clearly so stamp them. There is nothing in this record indicating that defendant waived her privilege, . . . and plaintiff cannot do so for her.

Plaintiff under the circumstances cannot justify the admission of the recordings in evidence under the "eavesdropping rule". It is generally held that communications between husband and wife are no less confidential, inter se, because overheard although the eavesdropper in testifying to what he heard is absolutely unaffected by the rule of privilege. The spying or eavesdropping nature of an overheard conversation may affect its weight as evidence but not its admissibility. . . . But to admit the recordings of the defendant's voice in this case, made with the connivance of plaintiff, would enable plaintiff to utilize mechanical means of repeating her words, thus accomplishing indirectly what he could not do directly. Plaintiff was a party to their making and accordingly the recorded conversations when read into the record, in effect, became his testimony of privileged communications which the law holds inviolate.

NOTE 7.

POPPE v. POPPE
3 N.Y. 2d 312, 144 N.E. 2d 72 (1957)

FULD, J.:

Mr. and Mrs. Poppe, married in 1922, lived together until 1949. In that year, the husband left home and, six years later, Mrs. Poppe, alleging that her husband had abandoned her, brought this action for separation. The husband denied the allegations of the complaint and interposed an affirmative defense that his wife's cruelty induced and justified his leaving her.

In the ensuing trial, held by the court without a jury, husband and wife were the only witnesses. Mrs. Poppe testified that her husband had abandoned her and had refused to support her. He acknowledged leaving home, but offered evidence to establish that conduct on the part of his wife justified his action. Thus, in the course of his testimony, he stated, over objection, that in 1949 his wife had told him that she had had illicit relations "a number of times" with another man and that they "thought" that they "would elope and go away together." Not long after this conversation, he went on to testify, his wife rented the room previously used as their bedroom, moved his own bed into the dining room and took up her quarters on the porch. It was immediately after this that he left to live elsewhere.

At the conclusion of the case, the court found that "defendant was justified in living separate and apart from plaintiff" and dismissed the complaint. In a short opinion, the judge reaffirmed his belief as to the propriety of the husband's testimony of what his wife had told him "to prove cruel and inhuman treatment." . . .

*   *   *

. . . The disclosure related, it is evident, not to the confession of a penitent wife confiding to her husband the story of her wrongdoing, but to a defiant declaration of misconduct and of an intention to persist therein and go away with the other man. No considerations of domestic peace or of conjugal loyalty, no considerations of the sanctity of the marital relation, prohibit disclosure of such a communication. The wife's statement in the present case, particularly when coupled with her subsequent conduct, not only negated any inference that the statement was induced by any confidence or trust between the parties, but actually demonstrated its absence.

*   *   *

It would be anomalous if it were to be decided that a privilege designed to encourage the marital relation operates to permit one spouse to be cruel to the other as long as the hurt-provoking words are spoken in private. The cloak of secrecy placed about confidential communications between husband and wife could never have been, and was not, designed to force the victim to put up with such conduct. It could never have been, and was not, intended to seal his lips and prevent him from relying upon such behavior as evidence of cruelty in a separation suit. . . .

The judgment should be affirmed.

VAN VOORHIS, J. (dissenting).

. . . An admission by a wife to her husband that she has engaged in sexual relations with another man during marriage is a confidential communication within this section.

The testimony in the instant case is: "She said she was going out with this man and had relations together, for a number of times, and they also thought they would elope and go away together." Afterwards she asked her husband to return to live with her, but he refused. There is nothing in this testimony indicating that this communication was made to injure the husband or for any ulterior purpose. For anything that appears to the contrary, it was a simple, unembellished statement of how things stood with her at the time when she was speaking. This is an example of the full and free communication between married people which the law encourages. . . .

Exclusion in separation actions of communications between husband and wife which have been induced by the marriage relation, has a salutary effect upon the use of such actions as a form of legalized blackmail, which is a practice that is occasionally followed by an unscrupulous spouse to bring a more upright marriage partner to heel.

The judgment appealed from should be reversed. . . .

NOTE 8.

The Administration of Divorce: A Philadelphia Study*

* * *

The story of divorce administration in Philadelphia is essentially the story of the mastership system. The extent to which masters comply with and enforce the statute is more significant than appellate court decisions in terms of the actual conditions under which the vast majority of divorces are granted.

Year	Number of Divorces Granted In Philadelphia	Number of Appeals to Superior Court From Philadelphia Divorce Proceedings	Number of Appeals to Supreme Court From Philadelphia Divorce Proceedings
1938	1713	9	0
1944	2933	8	0
1948	3866	7	0

If the testimony in divorce cases is to be effectively scrutinized at all, the master's hearing would seem to be the place to do it, since the master has the opportunity to see and hear the witnesses and observe their demeanor. In fact, the master has not only the means, but the affirmative duty to scrutinize the testimony offered. If the

* 101 U. PA. L. REV. 1204, 1222-1225 (1953). Copyright 1953 U. PA. L. REV.

state has an interest in preventing indiscriminate divorces, it is up to the master to protect that interest in the typical uncontested case where there is no adversary serving as a check on the plaintiff.

It is apparent that many masters seriously misapprehend their statutory function. Many lawyers conceive the function of the master to be merely to decide whether a case has been made out ; even judges are sometimes inclined to consider it sufficient that the interests of both parties have been protected, overlooking the state's interest in the matter. Some lawyers even feel that the master should aid the plaintiff in the presentation of his case and the occasional master who diligently probes the plaintiff's allegations is likely to find himself the object of other lawyers' criticism for treating the plaintiff "like a defendant in a criminal trial."

Many aspects of the mastership procedure . . . raise serious doubts as to the effectiveness of the search for facts. . . . Typically, the substantive facts come chiefly from the plaintiff, who may be led by his attorney or by the master if he is slow or ineffective in making a case. If there are corroborating witnesses they are generally supplied by the plaintiff and will first hear the plaintiff's story before being called to bolster it. The master's questioning tends to be perfunctory, with the master eyeing technical requirements or a particular judge's demands rather than attempting to make the most of his first hand opportunity to learn all the facts of the case. Rarely does a master exercise his power to call a witness on his own motion. A misplaced emphasis on jurisdictional requirements is often present. The purpose of jurisdictional requirements is to prevent migratory divorce, but statistics indicate that migratory divorce is a problem in only a small percentage of cases. Perjury and collusion are at least suspected in a majority of cases, yet the kind of searching inquiry which might disclose perjury or collusion is seldom resorted to. All too often general charges and accusations play an important part in the testimony.

In addition to representing the state as investigator, the master is expected to be an impartial judge. That it may sometimes be unrealistic to expect an absolutely impartial judicial performance is illustrated by an episode related by one of the official court stenographers. Two masters' meetings were scheduled in a single day. After the first one was over the plaintiff's lawyer and the master had lunch, came back, changed places at the table, and the master in the prior case became counsel for a different plaintiff. The plaintiff's lawyer in the prior case happened to have been appointed master in the second case. While this may not happen very often, the master, if he does any amount of divorce work at all, knows that he is likely to appear before the plaintiff's lawyer who may be appointed master in a subsequent case.

Another factor in the decisions which may not be apparent in the review of the record is the attitude of the masters toward the divorce law. Many feel that the statute is either too stringent or too lax and as a result either unconsciously or consciously tend to conduct and decide the case in accordance with their own ideas. Much of the difficulty in the administration of the divorce law seems to stem from the fact that in all cases an adversary procedure is prescribed, whereas in the overwhelming majority of cases there is actually no adversary interest present. One authority [Alexander, *The Follies of Divorce: A Therapeutic Approach to the Problem*, 36 A.B.A.J. 105, 107-08 (1950).] described the situation thus:

". . . although in some 90 per cent of cases the defendant stays carefully away, the plaintiff must, nevertheless, put on an exhibition of shadow-boxing and give the shadow a knockout to the satisfaction of the law. Whoever originated the forms and procedures for divorce litigation little realized that he was setting the stage for a sham battle against the little man who isn't there. Yet to this day all our forms and procedures remain those designed for adversary litigation."

* * *

NOTE 9.

RAINEY v. RAINEY
38 So. 2d 60 (Fla. 1948)

TERRELL, JUSTICE.

Appellant sued appellee for divorce alleging extreme cruelty. Appellee countered with an answer and counterclaim in which he denied the material allegations of the bill and prayed to be divorced from appellant, that she be required to return $3,000 which he contributed to the marital venture and to pay him $10 per day for services rendered on her property during the time they cohabited. Testimony was taken and on final hearing the chancellor awarded defendant a divorce, required the plaintiff to return the $3,000 and pay the Special Master a fee of $1,500. All other relief was denied. This appeal is from that part of the final decree ordering return of the $3,000 and requiring the plaintiff to pay the Special Master's fee.

* * *

The challenge to the fee awarded the Special Master is a delicate question to treat . . .

* * *

Every law course ought to be fortified with sufficient lessons in noblesse oblige to point the spiritual responsibility that membership in the bar imposes. It will save us jabs in the professional slats to remind us that as lawyers we are trustees of the public, clothed with a responsibility that we dare not neglect or fail in, lest we suffer the consequences. All this talk about the recession of the bar in the confidence of the public is due to lag in sensitiveness to its spiritual responsibility. Abuse of or failure in spiritual responsibility always incurs dire consequences. Jonah attempted to dodge his spiritual responsibility and we are told that he drew a free ride around the ocean in a whale's belly.

This is a run of the mill divorce suit that presents no unusual questions. In truth, the only real controversy revolved around the return of the $3,000. Both parties were clamoring for a divorce and were pleased with that phase of the final decree. The Special Master's fee in a litigated matter like this is of secondary importance to the attorney's fee. If the litigant is required to pay one-half the amount involved in the litigation for a Master's fee, an attorney's fee in proportion, and costs of courts in addition to all this, he will be required to resort to other resources to pay for the luxury of having his name connected with a lawsuit. Such a result is contrary to every canon of noblesse oblige and will justly shower undue criticism on the administration of justice.

You cannot convince the litigant or the public in a thousand years that there is justice in such a proceeding. Any system for administering justice that tends to liquidate the litigant or to absorb the fruit of the victory in costs is a misnomer, it will discredit the means provided and precipitate a popular demand for other agencies to accomplish that purpose which may not be near so thorough and efficient . . .

* * *

[W]e think the fee awarded the Special Master was exorbitant and without support in the record. The case was not complicated and no extraordinary skill or means were required to negotiate the judgment. The taking of folio after folio of evidence that sometimes runs into reams is tedious but requires no special skill. The statute, Section 62.07, Florida Statutes of 1941, F.S.A., prescribes the compensation for Special Masters and ordinarily this should not be departed from. It may be modified or enlarged on a showing that the case required the expenditure of extraordinary skill or means not contemplated by the state. We find no reason to vary from the compensation allowed by the statute in this case. . . .

d. Determining a Course of Action—The Meaning and Need of Awareness of Factors Æffecting the Selection of Facts

In examining the material in this section consider the extent to which the following information about Justice Streit, presiding judge in the Lesser case, is relevant to understanding and evaluating these proceedings:

Born in Vienna on May 5, 1897, Saul Streit was brought to the United States at the age of 3. His father was an Orthodox rabbi. The son went through public schools here and was graduated in 1921 with highest honors from New York University Law School. He became an Assistant District Attorney in 1925 and was elected the following year to the state Legislature from the old Seventh Assembly District on the middle West Side.

A loyal Tammany worker in election campaigns, Mr. Streit was given the Democratic organization's designation for General Sessions judge in 1936 against Judge Jonah J. Goldstein, who was serving an interim appointment made by Gov. Herbert H. Lehman. Mr. Streit beat Judge Goldstein in a primary fight and was elected in November to the bench.

When, in 1954, Judge Streit aspired to the Supreme Court bench, he was nominated by the Democratic, Republican and Liberal parties.

* * *

Justice Streit manages to attend art classes in the Metropolitan Museum of Art every two weeks and to take a weekly lesson from a French tutor. His wife—the former Jean F. McBride—shares both courses with him.

The Streits were married in 1950, when he was a General Sessions judge and she was a television actress appearing in the daytime serial "Love of Life."

Justice Streit is soft-spoken and has an urbane manner in the courtroom. He rarely displays strong feelings except when he dubs an approach on the golf course.

The stream of college students implicated in the widespread basketball fix scandal of 1951-52 stirred Judge Streit deeply. An avid reader, especially of the law, he began studying anything he could find on the subject of college sports and their ramifications.

Almost a year of research went into the preparation of a judicial report in which he denounced commercialism and corruption in intercollegiate sports as a national shame.

Despite his many years on the bench in General Sessions, during which he presided at trials involving many types of crime, the case he found most difficult was one in which he was called upon to impose a mandatory death sentence.

A colleague recalled that on that occasion, the judge's voice seemed to "quaver with emotion as he read the statement sending a defendant to the chair."*

These materials are addressed to the problem of determining why, when and under what circumstances, if at all, counsel or judge should disqualify himself or be disqualified from a case involving a matrimonial dispute.

[i]

UNITED STATES v. GILBOY
162 F. Supp. 384 (M.D.Pa. 1958)

JOHN W. MURPHY, CHIEF JUDGE.

Defendant, William J. Green, Jr., charged with conspiracy to defraud the United States, 18 U.S.C. § 371, purporting to comply with 28 U.S.C. § 144,[2] made and filed an affidavit asserting his belief that the judge before whom the matter is pending is "personally prejudiced against" him. . . . Defendant moves that the judge proceed no further herein; that another judge be assigned to hear such proceeding.

* * *

The bias or prejudice must be personal—possessed by the judge and specifically applicable to and against the affiant or in favor of an adverse party. . . . "Personal", the significant word of the statute, is in contrast with "judicial". It character-

---

* *The New York Times*, June 14, 1962 (p. 22 c. 4). © 1962 by The New York Times Company, Inc. Reprinted by permission.

2. "Whenever a *party to any proceeding* in a district court makes and files a *timely and sufficient affidavit* that the judge before whom the matter is *pending* has a *personal bias or prejudice either against him* or in favor of any *adverse party*, such judge shall *proceed no further therein*, but another judge shall be assigned *to hear such proceeding*.

"*The affidavit shall state the facts and the reasons for the belief that bias or prejudice exists*, . . . (Italics supplied).

izes an attitude of extra judicial origin.[14] . . . Disqualification does not arise solely on the basis of a bias or state of mind against wrongdoers acquired from evidence presented in the trial, . . . nor from the possession of definite views on the law, . . . nor was it directed against an impersonal prejudice which goes to the judge's background and associations or experiences rather than an appraisal of the defendant personally. . . .

"The statute relates only to adverse opinion or leaning towards an individual and has no application to the appraisement of a class * * *", Berger v. United States, 255 U.S. at page 42, 41 S. Ct. at page 236. "Intense dislike of a class does not render the judge incapable of administering complete justice to one of its members." . . . The converse is true. . . .

* * *

. . . West Virginia State Board of Education v. Barnette, 1943, 319 U.S. 624, at pages 638, 640, 641, [642] . . . "If there is any fixed star in our constitutional constellation, it is that no official, high or petty, can prescribe what shall be orthodox in politics, nationalism, religion or other matters of opinion * * *". And see Frankfurter J., 319 U.S. at pages 646, 647, . . . "* * * as judges we are neither Jew nor Gentile, neither Catholic nor Agnostic. We owe equal attachment to the Constitution and are equally bound by our judicial obligations whether we derive our citizenship from the earliest or the latest immigrants to these shores."[24]

* * *

Judges are not assumed to be flabby creatures. They may have an underlying philosophy in approaching a case. They are assumed to be men of conscience and intellectual discipline capable of judging a particular controversy fairly on the basis of its own circumstances.[25]

. . . "No judge fit to be one is likely to be influenced consciously except by what he sees and hears in court and by what is judicially appropriate for his deliberations." Frankfurter J. in

Pennekamp v. State of Florida . . . 328 U.S. at page 357. . . .

If conscientious, able and independent men are put on the bench, you cannot predict their course as judges by reference either to partisan motives or to personal or party loyalties. If you could get further down to the bedrock of conviction as to what are conceived to be fundamental principles of government and social relations, you might be able to get closer to accurate prophecy. But you cannot expect to have judges worthy of the office who are without convictions and the question from that point of view is not as to the qualifications of judges but whether you will have a court of this character and function." Hughes, "The Supreme Court of the United States", p. 49 . . .

As to a judge having convictions and "value judgments", see In re J. P. Linahan, Inc., 2 Cir., 1943, 138 F. 2d. 650, 652 ; United States v. Valenti, 120 F. Supp. at page 86. "A judge * * * is human, and, like every other man, must have his likes and dislikes, * * *. In so far as he is not swayed by these natural emotions to do any man an injustice, the fact that he has them in common with his brother man does not disqualify him from trying a case." May v. May, 1912 . . . 150 S.W. 685, 686. . . .

"He must have neighbors, friends and acquaintances, business and social relations, and be a part of his day and generation. * * * [T]he ordinary results of such associations and the impressions they create in the mind of the judge are not the 'personal bias or prejudice' to which the statute refers. The impressions, whether favorable or unfavorable, of men, which a judge receives, or his convictions about them growing out of his contact or acquaintance with them in the ordinary walks of life, cannot fall within the evil the statute designs to suppress, unless they are so strong that they result in personal bias or prejudice as to individual suitors, dominating the judge to such an extent that they beget a mental or moral condition which makes the judge willing to do wrong although he sees the right, regarding the justiciable matters brought before him, or else, though the judge's intentions be good, render him incapable of rightly seeing the justice of the cause, or impartially enforcing the right involved as between the parties to the suit." Ex Parte N. K. Fairbank Co., supra, 194 F. at pages 989, 990.

---

14. "Every * * * judge, when he hears a case or writes an opinion must form an opinion on the merits and oft times no doubt an opinion relative to the parties involved." Tucker v. Kerner, supra, 186 F. 2d at page 84. . . .

24. And see comment Maxey C. J. in O'Donnell v. Philadelphia Record Co., 1947, . . . 51 A. 2d 775, at page 793, "This is the first time the writer ever heard of any attorney injecting into a case the religious affiliations of either a litigant or a witness * * *. So careful is our law to keep religion out of the trial of a case that . . . 28 P.S. Sec. 312, forbids the questioning of any witness in any judicial proceeding, 'concerning his religious belief'. If a witness' religious belief cannot properly be injected into a judicial proceeding, a litigant's religious belief * * * cannot be * * *."

25. "To practice the requisite detachment and to achieve

sufficient objectivity * * * demands of judges the habit of self-discipline and self-criticism, incertitude that one's own views are incontestable and alert tolerance toward views not shared * * * these are precisely the presuppositions of our judicial process. * * * [Q]ualities society has a right to expect from those entrusted with the ultimate judicial power." Rochin v. People of State of California, 1952, 342 U.S. 165, 171, 172, ...

NOTES

NOTE 1.

FORER, LOIS G.

Psychiatric Evidence in the Recusation of Judges*

. . . The Congressman [defendant Green in United States v. Gilboy] filed an affidavit of prejudice and a motion for change of judge, alleging that he believed that the trial judge was "personally prejudiced against me by reason of the many favors I have done for him and the obligation he owes me and that by reason of his desire to prove his integrity, he will be unable to afford me a fair and impartial trial." The affidavit contained supporting factual allegations. Appended to the motion was the opinion of a psychiatrist indicating that gratitude for favors done under the circumstances alleged would result in subconscious bias and prejudice on the part of the judge against the defendant.[3]

NOTE 2.

GREEN v. MURPHY
259 F. 2d 591 (3d Cir. 1958)

KALODNER, CIRCUIT JUDGE (dissenting).

I would grant forthwith the writ directing Judge Murphy's withdrawal from participation in the Green case.

A judge should not preside at the criminal trial of one (1) whose sponsorship he sought and received in obtaining his judicial appointment and confirmation; (2) whose aid he importuned to procure a lucrative State office for a lifetime friend; (3) with whom he had enjoyed a close personal and political relationship beginning with their service as members of Congress; and (4) whose co-defendant (Herbert W. McGlinchey) is allegedly an intimate friend of the judge who gave material assistance in obtaining his judicial appointment, and as to whom the judge is alleged to be "prejudiced in favor of".

* * *

---

* 73 HARV. L. REV. 1325 (1960). Copyright © 1960 by The Harvard Law Review Association.

3. The hypothetical question asked of the psychiatrist was as follows:

> Assuming the judge and the defendant are of the same racial and religious background; that they are members of the same political party; that they have served together in the United States Congress; that they have been close friends and political associates; that, while he was a member of Congress, the judge requested petitioner to assist him in obtaining an appointment to the bench; that since his elevation to the bench, the judge has requested personal and political favors from petitioner, who has performed such favors for the judge; and that defendant is accused of an offense arising out of his office as a Congressman; under these

The sum of Green's "leaning backward" contention is that Judge Murphy, because of their long-standing prior friendship and association, will consciously or subconsciously, through the trial, be affected by its existence.

As Green put it in his brief here:

> "If a motion for judgment of acquittal were to be made before the respondent judge, could he pass upon that issue without considering, consciously or subconsciously, whether he would be accused of doing a favor in return for his friend? * * *
>
> "If the judge should grant a motion for acquittal, will the public think he is favoring an old friend? Must the judge deny a proper motion to forestall such criticism? Is the defendant, under the Constitution, required to take this risk? * * *
>
> "Obviously, the facts of the relationship between the defendant and the respondent, and the relationship between the respondent and co-defendant McGlinchey, present ample facts from which any mind might properly draw an inference of bias or prejudice."

The nub of Green's contention was well-stated by the concurring judges as follows:

> "The sole complaint is that the judge may overcompensate for his inclination toward the accused by leaning backward."

I think such complaint merits consideration.

Certainly it cannot be gainsaid that the detachment which is an indispensable ingredient of the judicial attitude does not exist where a judge presides at the trial of one who has been his long-time friend and benefactor.

As was stated in 48 C.J.S. Judges S 72, p. 1039:

> "The underlying principle of rules for disqualification of judges is that no judge should preside in a case in which he is not *wholly free*, disinterested, impartial, and independent." (Emphasis supplied.)

Can it be said that the trial judge here is "wholly free"?

Judges are human beings and not mechanical machines dispensing undistilled justice on a push-button basis. They are not judicial Univacs or mechanized "brains".

---

circumstances, will the judge be biased and prejudiced against the defendant?

The answer given by the psychiatrist was: "There will be a tendency for any action to be made more difficult and more inappropriate in relation to a fair trial on the issues resulting from psychological prejudice."

An attached chart explained that the relations between judge and defendant would result in an over-identification with the defendant upon the part of the judge and both a subconscious sense of hostility and a feeling of gratitude for past favors. Since reciprocity for such favors would violate the judicial oath, there would be a subconscious over-compensation resulting in prejudice.

As was so well said by Mr. Justice Frankfurter in his concurring opinion in Pennekamp v. State of Florida, 1946, 328 U.S. 331 at page 357 . . .:

> " * * * judges are also human, and we know better than did our forbears how powerful is the pull of the unconscious and how treacherous the rational process."

Mr. Justice Cardozo, in speaking of "The Subconscious Element in the Judicial Process"[18] said

> "I have spoken of the forces which judges avowedly avail to shape the form and content of their judgments. Even these forces are seldom fully in consciousness. They lie so near the surface, however, that their existence and influence are not likely to be disclaimed * * * *Deep below consciousness are other forces, the likes and the dislikes, the predilections and the prejudices, the complex of instincts and emotions and habits and convictions, which make the man, whether he be litigant or judge.* . . . The great tides and currents which engulf the rest of men, do not turn aside in their course and pass the judges by." (Emphasis supplied.)

To say more would be "to gild refined gold".[19]

I would grant the writ.

NOTE 3.

BOARD OF EDUCATION v. BARNETTE
319 U.S. 624, 646-47 (1942)

MR. JUSTICE FRANKFURTER, dissenting:

[A]s judges we are neither Jew nor Gentile, neither Catholic nor agnostic. We owe equal attachment to the Constitution and are equally bound by our judicial obligations whether we derive our citizenship from the earliest or the latest immigrants to these shores. As a member of this Court I am not justified in writing my private notions of policy into the Constitution, no matter how deeply I may cherish them or how mischievous I may deem their disregard. The duty of a judge who must decide which of two claims before the Court shall prevail, that of a State to enact and enforce laws within its general competence or that of an individual to refuse obedience because of the demands of his conscience, is not that of the ordinary person. It can never be emphasized too much that one's own opinion about the wisdom or evil of a law should be excluded altogether when one is doing one's duty on the bench. . . .

---

18. Cardozo's "Nature of Judicial Process," pp. 168-69; Hall's Selected Writings of Benjamin Nathan Cardozo," p. 178.

19. Sallust, Catilina, Ch. li, sec. 1: "All men who deliberate upon difficult questions should be free from hatred and friendship, anger and pity."

Lord Chesterfield, Letters, 13 April, 1752: "Our prejudices are our mistresses; reason is at best our wife, very often heard indeed, but seldom minded."

NOTE 4.

PHILLIPS, HARLAN B.
Felix Frankfurter Reminisces*

. . . There was one office, Hornblower, Byrne, Miller & Potter, that was one of the best offices at the time. Lots of Harvard people were in there. I'd heard that they had never taken a Jew and wouldn't take a Jew. I decided that that was the office I wanted to get into not for any reason of truculence, but I was very early infused with, had inculcated in me, a very profoundly wise attitude toward the whole fact that I was a Jew, the essence of which is that you should be a biped and walk on the two legs that man has. To me as a philosophy of action, as an attitude, it's as simple as saying you should neither be truculent nor subservient. You should just be a biped. You should take that ultimate fact that you were born of these parents instead of some other parents as much for granted as the fact that you've got green-brown eyes instead of blue eyes.

An uncle of mine said to me when I was a boy, "You'll encounter a great deal of anti-Semitism in your life, but don't go around sniffing anti-Semitism."

Some of the lads at the Harvard Law School occasionally—a Jewish lad who failed and then thought there might be reasons for that—were soon made to realize that I was not a Jewish professor at the Harvard Law School, but I was a Harvard Law School professor who happened to be a Jew. In fact, I know that I exacted higher standards from Jews than from other people, and perhaps that was on the whole a good thing for Jews who have any capacity.

NOTE 5.

ANTONOVSKY, AARON
Like Everyone Else, Only More So: Identity, Anxiety, and the Jew†

* * *

On June 19, 1953, Julius and Ethel Rosenberg were executed. They had been indicted in August, 1950, and found guilty on a charge of conspiring as espionage agents. Their death sentences were carried out after almost three years of legal maneuvering. Their codefendant, Morton Sobell, was sentenced to a prison term of thirty years. The Rosenbergs, Sobell, Irving Kaufmann (the trial

---

* New York; Reynal and Co., 1960, p. 37. Copyright © 1960 by Harlan B. Phillips. Reprinted with permission of the publisher.

† Reprinted from M. R. Stein, A. J. Vidich, & D. M. White (eds.), *Identity and Anxiety*. New York: The Free Press of Glencoe, 1960, pp. 429-434. Reprinted with permission of the publisher.

judge), Saypol (the prosecutor), Bloch (the defense attorney), Greenglass and Gold (the self-confessed agents turned state's witnesses)—anyone sensitive to ethnic characteristics could not but have been aware that these were all Jews.

*   *   *

It was during the spring and summer of 1953 that the interviews which provide the basis of this paper were conducted. . . .

The respondents were few—58 in all—and the community was a middle-sized Eastern city whose 22,000 Jews constituted 10 per cent of the strongly Catholic population. These fifty-eight, all married men, made up a small random sample of second generation Jews of eastern European descent living in this community. . . .

*   *   *

. . . First, there is the question of Judge Kaufman's Jewishness and the death sentence. The respondents were all aware of the former and not opposed to the latter. A substantial majority, discussing Kaufmann's predicament, raised the question of the human elements of sympathetic identification, of empathy, and understanding . . . raised it in order to point out its complete absence. Indeed, Judge Kaufmann, *precisely because he was Jewish,* had no alternative but to impose the death sentence! A Gentile judge might or might not have done so; certainly the law permitted it, and the crime might have warranted it. But a Jew could only have acted in one way. Thus ran the thinking of the respondents.

Two mutually reinforcing factors are seen as the basis for the inevitability of Kaufmann's decision. On the one hand, there was the belief that a sentence short of death, imposed by a Jew, would have aroused a substantial degree of anti-Semitism. No responsible Jew could have avoided imposing the maximum sentence. The second motive ascribed to Kaufmann is even more revealing. As a Jew, it is posited that he could only feel violent hatred for the Jewish Rosenbergs. This phenomenon is, of course, well-known: what greater hatred is there than that of the "loyal" (to whatever cause or group) to the ex-loyal, the "formerly one of us" turned "traitor"? The respondents' sentiments are projected onto Kaufmann.

It is at this point in the interviews that the strongest language emerges. At first, there is a vigorous denial that the Rosenbergs were Jewish: they were atheistic Communists, belonged to no Jewish organizations, etc. However, the very vigor of the denial reveals, and the respondents quickly acknowledge, that this is not the case: in the final summing up they said, in essence, 'once a Jew, always a Jew.' But they go beyond this: whether we see the Rosenbergs as Jewish or not is beside the point; all of America knows that they are Jewish.

*   *   *

The meaning given by American Jews to the Rosenberg case, . . . occurs on an unconserious level, and can be fully understood only when associated with another attitude which I call the sense of collective accountability. This is to be distinguished from a sense of mutual responsibility, the notion that "all Jews are brothers." The former is passive, the latter, active. In most of Jewish history, the two attitudes coexist. But in a democratic society, in which integration with the majority is a desired possibility, mutual responsibility declines in intensity. Collective accountability, on the other hand, the attitude that "they" —the majority which can accept or reject "us"— hold all of "us" responsible for what one of "us" does, continues in full force just so long as there is a sense of incomplete integration.

NOTE 6.

GROUP FOR THE ADVANCEMENT OF PSYCHIATRY

Psychiatry and Religion*

[M]atters of religious faith and practice contribute to and reflect the formation and maintenance of attitudes, thinking and behavior of men, and . . . emotional factors ordinarily beyond our ken are influential in all aspects of behavior and thought. Consequently, it behooves the psychiatrist to have optimal awareness of the way his own emotional life and development interdigitate with his position concerning religion. He should, when it is indicated, be prepared to scrutinize further or again the psychological significance of his own beliefs and practices, or his disbeliefs, whenever this seems relevant in work with particular patients.

Such self-examination would include recognition that there can be blurring of those distinctions that must be made between sanctity and sanctimoniousness, righteousness and self-righteousness, or neutrality and apathy—when these apply either to himself or to his evaluation of his patient. A somewhat subtler aspect of his own attitude has to do with skepticism. Skepticism defined as "suspension of judgment" is second nature to him as a practitioner and researcher. This he should not confuse with skepticism as a philosophical viewpoint, which holds that all knowledge is uncertain. Such confusion might lead a psychiatrist to attempt to impose philo-

* *Psychiatry and Religion*, Report No. 48, (1960), Group for the Advancement of Psychiatry, Inc., pp. 330-331. Reprinted with permission of the publisher.

sophic skepticism on his patient. *Neither this nor any other philosophical viewpoint should be imposed on any patient. . . .*

The psychiatrist strives constantly to reduce even inadvertent influences on his patient to a minimum. On the other hand, these admonitions are not to be construed as discouraging him from confronting his patient with inconsistencies in religious belief or behavior, even at the risk of a change in the patient's beliefs. It is to be noted that the same principles hold in connection with political, civic, filial, parental, marital, financial, or any other highly charged grouping of attitudes and behavior.

Here is a place where clarity is desirable within the psychiatrist's mind as to what he includes for himself under the rubric of "religion". . . . If a psychiatrist is going to deal temperately and objectively with the beliefs of his patient, he should know at least when or where he is himself unsettled, just as he should in regard to other areas of life.

[*ii*]

In re J. P. LINAHAN, INC.
138 F. 2d 650 (2d Cir. 1943)

FRANK, CIRCUIT JUDGE.

* * *

Democracy must, indeed, fail unless our courts try cases fairly, and there can be no fair trial before a judge lacking in impartiality and disinterestedness. If, however, "bias" and "partiality" be defined to mean the total absence of preconceptions in the mind of the judge, then no one has ever had a fair trial and no one ever will. The human mind, even at infancy, is no blank piece of paper. We are born with predispositions; and the process of education, formal and informal, creates attitudes in all men which affect them in judging situations, attitudes which precede reasoning in particular instances and which, therefore, by definition, are pre-judices. Without acquired "slants," pre-conceptions, life could not go on. Every habit constitutes a pre-judgment; were those pre-judgments which we call habits absent in any person, were he obliged to treat every event as an unprecedented crisis presenting a wholly new problem he would go mad. Interests, points of view, preferences, are the essence of living. Only death yields complete dispassionateness, for such dispassionateness signifies utter indifference. "To live is to have a vocation, and to have a vocation is to have an ethics or scheme of values, and to have a scheme of values is to have a point of view, and to have a point of view is to have a prejudice or bias * * *"[4] An "open mind," in the

sense of a mind containing no preconceptions whatever, would be a mind incapable of learning anything, would be that of an utterly emotionless human being, corresponding roughly to the psychiatrist's descriptions of the feebleminded. More directly to the point, every human society has a multitude of established attitudes, unquestioned postulates. Cosmically, they may seem parochial prejudices, but many of them represent the community's most cherished values and ideals. Such social pre-conceptions, the "value judgments" which members of any given society take for granted and use as the unspoken axioms of thinking, find their way into that society's legal system, become what has been termed "the valuation system of the law." The judge in our society owes a duty to act in accordance with those basic predilections inhering in our legal system (although, of course, he has the right, at times, to urge that some of them be modified or abandoned). The standard of dispassionateness obviously does not require the judge to rid himself of the unconscious influence of such social attitudes.

In addition to those acquired social value judgments, every judge, however, unavoidable has many idiosyncratic "learnings of the mind," uniquely personal prejudices, which may interfere with his fairness at a trial. He may be stimulated by unconscious sympathies for, or antipathies to, some of the witnesses, lawyers or parties in a case before him. As Josiah Royce observed, "Oddities of feature or of complexion, slight physical variations from the customary, a strange dress, a scar, a too-steady look, a limp, a loud or deep voice, any of these peculiarities * * * may be, to one, an object of fascinated curiosity; to another * * *, an intense irritation, an object of violent antipathy."[9] In Ex parte Chase, 43 Ala. 303, Judge Peters said he had "known a popular judicial officer grow quite angry with a suitor in his court, and threaten him with imprisonment, for no ostensible reason, save the fact, that he wore an overcoat made of wolf skins," and spoke of "prejudice which may be swayed and controlled by the merest trifles—such as the toothache, the rheumatism, the gout, or a fit of indigestion, or even through the very means by which indigestion is frequently sought to be avoided." "Trifles," he added, "however ridiculous, cease to be trifles when they may interfere with a safe administration of the law." Frankly to recognize the existence of such prejudices is the part of wisdom. The conscientious judge will, as far as possible, make himself aware of his biases of this character,

---

4. Kenneth Burke, *Permanence and Change* (1936), 329.

9. Royce, *Race Questions, Provincialism and Other American Problems* (1908), 47-52.

and, by that very self-knowledge, nullify their effect.[10] Much harm is done by the myth that, merely by putting on a black robe and taking the oath of office as a judge, a man ceases to be human and strips himself of all predilections, becomes a passionless thinking machine.[11] The concealment of the human element in the judicial process allows that element to operate in an exaggerated manner; the sunlight of awareness has an antiseptic effect on prejudices. Freely avowing that he is a human being, the judge can and should, through self-scrutiny, prevent the operation of this class of biases.[13] This self-knowledge is needed in a judge because he is peculiarly exposed to emotional influences; the "court room is a place of surging emotions * * *; the parties are keyed up to the contest, often in open defiance; and the topics at issue are often calculated to stir up the sympathy, prejudice, or ridicule of the tribunal." The judge's decision turns, often, on what he believes to be the facts of the case. As a fact-finder, he is himself a witness—a witness of the witnesses; he should, therefore, learn to avoid the errors which, because of prejudice, often affect those witnesses.[16]

But, just because his fact-finding is based on his estimates of the witnesses, of their reliability as reporters of what they saw and heard, it is his duty, while listening to and watching them, to form attitudes towards them. He must do his best to ascertain their motives, their biases, their dominating passions and interests, for only so can he judge of the accuracy of their narrations. He must also shrewdly observe the strategems of the opposing lawyers, perceive their efforts to sway him by appeals to his predilections. He must cannily penetrate through the surface of their remarks to their real purposes and motives. He has an official obligation to become prejudiced in that sense. Impartiality is not gullibility. Disinterestedness does

not mean child-like innocence. If the judge did not form judgments of the actors in those court-house dramas called trials, he could never render decisions.

His findings of fact may be erroneous, for, being human, he is not infallible; indeed, a judge who purports to be superhuman is likely to be dominated by improper prejudices. When upper court judges on an appeal decide that the findings of a trial judge are at fault because they—correctly or incorrectly—think those findings insufficiently supported by relevant and competent evidence, that appellate decision does not brand him as partial and unfair. When, his decision reversed because of errors in his findings of fact or conclusions of law, the case comes back to his court for a further hearing, he will not, if he is the kind of person entitled to hold office as a judge, permit his previous decision in the case to control him.

*   *   *

NOTES

NOTE 1.

OFFUTT v. UNITED STATES
348 U.S. 11 (1954)

MR. JUSTICE FRANKFURTER . . .

Of course personal attacks or innuendos by a lawyer against a judge, with a view to provoking him, only aggravate what may be an obstruction to the trial. The vital point is that in sitting in judgment on such a misbehaving lawyer the judge should not himself give vent to personal spleen or respond to a personal grievance. These are subtle matters, for they concern the ingredients of what constitutes justice. Therefore, justice must satisfy the appearance of justice.

*   *   *

. . . Plainly, the Court of Appeals thought that in the trial court's disposition of the misconduct

---

10. One of the subtlest tendencies which a conscientious judge must learn to overcome is that of "leaning over backwards" in favor of persons against whom his prejudices incline him. Pascal wrote of some men who have been unjust in their efforts to exclude bias: "The sure way of losing a just cause is to get it recommended to these men by their near relatives." Pascal, *Pensees*, No. 82.

11. The judicial mind is subject to the laws of psychology like any other mind. When the judge assumes the ermine he does not divest himself of humanity. He has sworn to do justice to all men without fear or favour, but the impartiality which is the noble hallmark of our Bench does not imply that the judge's mind has become a mere machine to turn out decrees; the judge's mind remains a human instrument working as do other minds, though no doubt on specialized lines and often characterised by individual traits of personality, engaging or the reverse." Lord Macmillan, *Law and Other Things* (1937), 202.

13. There would have been no disqualification of the trial judge in Berger v. United States, 255 U.S. 22, 41 S. Ct. 230, 65 L. Ed. 481, if he had said, not that he was virtually

incapable of being fair to German American citizens during World War I, but that he was aware of his prejudice against them and could therefore discount it.

The unrecognized, unspoken, bias is dangerous. Darwin said that he found it so easy to pass over cases opposed to his favorite generalizations that he made it a habit to jot down every exception which he observed or thought of, as otherwise he would be almost sure to forget it. It is difficult to agree with Rohrlich (17 Am. Bar Assn. J. 481) that it is wise for judges to suppress the expression of certain factors in the process of decision-making, that such suppression tends "to reduce the influence of those factors."

16. The judge, if he is not careful, will carry "over into his finding more * * * of himself than he has discovered from the facts;" he will reshape "the real facts by utilizing his own attitude towards * * * life." Wurzel, loc. cit., 398. Wurzel says that there is a constant interaction between the "facts" and legal principles: "There is no sharply defined boundary between the principles applied by" the judge "and the facts to which he applies them"; a "transition zone" lies "between rules and facts." *Loc. cit.*, 390, 396-399. . . .

of the petitioner [attorney for the defendant] there was an infusion of personal animosity. . . . That court spoke of "the excessive injection of trial judge into the examination of witnesses, his numerous comments to defense counsel, indicating at times hostility, though under provocation," which it concluded "demonstrated a bias and lack of impartiality." *Peckham v. United States, supra,* 93 U.S. App. D.C., at 145, 210 F. 2d, at 702.

It bears repeating that the whole record amply supports this characterization of the trial judge by the Court of Appeals.

[For our purposes it will be sufficient to quote two specific instances:

"THE COURT: Motion denied. Proceed.

"MR. OFFUTT: I object to Your Honor yelling at me and raising your voice like that.

"THE COURT: Just a moment. If you say another word I will have the Marshal stick a gag in your mouth." (R. 215.)

"THE COURT: Don't argue with the Court.

"MR. OFFUTT: I am not arguing with the Court, Your Honor.

"THE COURT: Don't answer back to the Court, either.

"MR. OFFUTT: Oh, I thought Your Honor—I am merely trying to present my point.

"THE COURT: Proceed with the next question.

"MR. OFFUTT: Thank you, Your Honor.

"Your Honor, I object to your raising your voice like that and shouting at me, and I urge Your Honor not to do it.

"THE COURT: Well, you are misbehaving, Mr. Offutt.

"MR. OFFUTT: And I have a right—

"THE COURT: And it is my function to hold the reins tight and preserve order and decorum in the courtroom.

"MR. OFFUTT: But not to yell at me, Your Honor.

"And I submit I am entitled, and my duty is to make objections and to state for the record, and I am putting my objections on the record.

"THE COURT: You have forfeited your right to be treated with the courtesy that this Court extends to all members of the Bar." (R. 250.)]

And his feeling toward the lawyer on whom he had to pass sentence is revealed by his statement to the jury in discharging them.

["I also realize that you had a difficult and a disagreeable task in this case. You have been compelled to sit through a disgraceful and disreputable performance on the part of a lawyer who is unworthy of being a member of the profession; and I, as a member of the legal profession, blush that we should have such a specimen in our midst." (R. 260.)]

The question with which we are concerned is not the reprehensibility of petitioner's conduct and the consequences which he should suffer. Our concern is with the fair administration of justice. The record discloses not a rare flare-up, not a show of evanescent irritation—a modicum of quick temper that must be allowed even judges. The record is persuasive that instead of representing the impersonal authority of law, the trial judge permitted himself to become personally embroiled with the petitioner [attorney for the defendant]. There was an intermittently continuous wrangle on an unedifying level between the two. For one reason or another the judge failed to impose his moral authority upon the proceedings. His behavior precluded that atmosphere of austerity which should especially dominate a . . . trial and which is indispensable for an appropriate sense of responsibility on the part of court, counsel and jury. . . .

NOTE 2.

LASSWELL, HAROLD D.

Psychopathology and Politics*

. . . On one occasion the judge began to enumerate the three principal alternatives which lay before him in deciding a pending case. He remembered two of them but hesitated several seconds before the third came into his mind. This led him to remember that he had often casually noticed that this third possibility seemed to elude him, although on reflection he felt that it deserved as much attention as the other two. He began spontaneously to relax and report everything that crossed his mind, and produced a long string of catch phrases from law and politics like "freedom of contract," "life, liberty, and pursuit of happiness," "freedom of speech and assembly." He presently noted that a picture was forming of one of his old law-school classrooms. He felt that someone was just about to speak to him, and had to resist the temptation to turn around. Then there came across his mind a long series of incidents in which one of his law professors was the principal figure. This teacher was reputed to possess a mastermind and a caustic tongue; and the judge, though he had always wanted to make a great impression on him, had met with no particular success. The professor had a habit of using his most ironic tone of voice when he spoke of "this freedom of contract." Now it happened that the attorney who was arguing for alternative No. 3 before the court pronounced the word "freedom" with unction. This aroused in the judge's mind the ironic tone of the old professor's voice, and this in turn brought back the rather humiliating failure he had been in his efforts to impress the professor. He now exhibited a tendency to repress everything

---

* New York: The Free Press of Glencoe, 1960, pp. 35-36. Reprinted with permission of the publisher.

connected with the episode, including the attorney's argument.

The world about us is much richer in meanings than we consciously see. These meanings are continually cutting across our ostensible criteria of judgment, and compulsively distorting the operations of the mind whose quest for an objective view of reality is consciously quite sincere. Good intentions are not enough to widen the sphere of self-mastery. There must be a special technique for the sake of exposing the hidden meanings which operate to bind and cripple the processes of logical thought. With practice one may wield the tool of free-fantasy with such ruthless honesty that relevant material comes very quickly to the focus of attention which we call "waking consciousness."

NOTE 3.

Lord Denning's Report*

On Monday, 24th June, 1963, I started work. On Tuesday, 25th June, 1963, I started hearing witnesses and the hearings continued for forty-nine days. There were about one hundred and sixty witnesses in all. . . . Some of the witnesses did not wish their identity to be disclosed. I have not, therefore, appended a list of them. But they covered a wide range: The Prime Minister, eight Cabinet Ministers, four other Ministers, as well as three of the Law Officers, five Members of the House of Lords, 15 Members of the House of Commons, several Civil Servants, including the Official Head of the Civil Service, the Secretary of the Cabinet, the Permanent Under-Secretary of State for the Home Department; and the Principal Private Secretary to the Prime Minister; the Commissioner of the Metropolitan Police and several officers of the force; the Director-General of the Security Service, his Deputy and several members of his staff (I also visited twice the Headquarters of the Security Service); 25 members of the newspaper profession, including newspaper proprietors, editors, reporters and other journalists; six girls and nine men who knew Stephen Ward well; and several members of the general public who volunteered information. I received also numerous written memoranda. After hearing evidence, I have devoted four weeks to the preparation of this report. . . .

* * *

[This inquiry] has the advantage that there can be no dissent, but it has two great disadvantages: first, being in secret, it has not the appearance of justice; second, in carrying out the inquiry, I

---

* London: H.M.'s Stationery Office. Cmnd. 2152., 1963, pp. 1-2. Reprinted by permission of the Controller of Her Britannic Majesty's Stationery Office.

have had to be detective, inquisitor, advocate and judge, and it has been difficult to combine them. But I have come to see that it has three considerable advantages. First, inasmuch as it has been held in private and in strict confidence, the witnesses were, I am sure, much more frank than they would otherwise have been. Secondly, I was able to check the evidence of one witness against that of another more freely. Thirdly, and most important, aspersions cast by witnesses against others (who are not able to defend themselves) do not achieve the publicity which is inevitable in a Court of Law or Tribunal of Inquiry.

. . . I have been told as much truth without an oath as if it were on oath. It was not the lack of powers which handicapped me. It was the very nature of the inquiry with which I was entrusted.

At every stage of this inquiry I have been faced with this great anxiety: How far should I go into matters which seem to show that someone or other has been guilty of a criminal offence, or of professional misconduct, or moral turpitude, or even incompetence? My inquiry is not a suitable body to determine guilt or innocence. . . .

. . . I have come to the conclusion that all I can do is this:

> When the facts are clear beyond controversy, I will state them as objectively as I can, irrespective of the consequences to the individuals: and I will draw any inference that is manifest from those facts. But when the facts are in issue, I must always remember the cardinal principle of justice—that no man is to be condemned on suspicion. There must be evidence which proves his guilt before he is pronounced to be so. I will therefore take the facts in his favour rather than do an injustice which is without remedy. For from my findings there is no appeal.

To those who in consequence will reproach me for "white-washing", I would make this answer: While the public interest demands that the facts should be ascertained as completely as possible, there is a yet higher public interest to be considered, namely, the interest of justice to the individual which overrides all other. At any rate, speaking as a Judge, I put justice first.

NOTE 4.

HARTMANN, HEINZ

Psychoanalysis and Moral Values*

In dealing with "moral values" in the analytic situation, there are three aspects the analyst has to keep separate. We consider, first of all, the genesis, the dynamics, the economics of the patients' imperatives and ideals, and the structure

---

* New York: International Universities Press, 1960, pp. 54-57. Reprinted by permission of the publisher.

of his moral codes. Secondly we meet the problem of the confrontation of his attitudes with the codes of his family and, more generally, of the culture he lives in. There are, third, the personal moral valuations of the analyst with respect to the material presented in analysis. One cannot deny the actuality of the third factor—it is, above all, the natural outcome of the analyst's having his own value system, a "given" in the same sense as is his intellect, his interest and so on. It may, in a secondary way, get involved with counter-transference. But technical knowledge will teach us that this third factor is best kept in the background in contacts with the patient; also, that in order to achieve this the analyst must be clearly aware of his own valuations and must know how to distinguish them from statements of fact. It has been doubted whether such reserve is really possible. Experience decides that it is, at least to a very considerable degree. Thus it can become part of the transference reactions of every patient that he attributes moral value judgments to the analyst which are far from being the analyst's own.

However, in the therapeutic situation something appears that we can account for only if we decide to make a distinction between the therapist's general moral codes and the one he is guided by in his therapeutic work, which could be called his "professional code." In his therapeutic work he will keep other values in abeyance and concentrate on the realization of one category of values only: health values. These are given special consideration in his work; they are taken for granted; and every therapist will, in his therapeutic work, consider their realization in his patients as his immediate and overriding concern. Is this an exception to the technical rule I just referred to, that the psychoanalyst should, in the analytic situation, try to keep his personal system of values in the background? I do not think so. It would be quite erroneous to assume that outside his professional activities the same therapist considers health values as the "highest." It is even very likely that there exists no human being for whom, in his authentic morality, health values actually do represent the highest form of values altogether. It is helpful for the analyst to keep himself aware of the difference between his general moral and his professional codes. A compartmentalization of codes in which one imperative, in our case the therapeutic imperative, takes over is not infrequent. For some, as you will know, it is evident that, so far as their work is concerned, every avenue which could lead to an increase of our knowledge deserves to be followed, regardless of the consequences. This is the professional code, or rather one of the professional codes, we find in men of science.

NOTE 5.

KNIGHT, ROBERT P.
A Critique of the Present Status of the Psychotherapies*

Freud . . . had the objectivity to observe and analyze his own reactions to patients, and concluded that all psychotherapists would have their own particular tendencies to react inappropriately (that is, inappropriately from the standpoint of correct therapeutic technique) to the material, or behavior, or persons of their patients. He called such reactions and reaction tendencies "counter-transference," and bade all analysts to be acutely observant of themselves in this regard so that they might analyze and dissipate these counter-transference reactions without letting themselves be unwittingly influenced by them to the detriment of the therapeutic efforts. Again, such countertransference reactions are not confined to psychiatrists, psychoanalysts, or psychotherapists, but are present in all physicians toward their patients, albeit with considerably less significance, for the most part, in therapy other than psychotherapy. Once more, then, we see the importance for the psychotherapist of those personal qualities of integrity, objectivity, sincerity, and relative freedom from emotional blind spots.

NOTE 6.

GANTNER v. GANTNER
39 Cal. 2d 272, 246 P. 2d 923, 929 (1952)

TRAYNOR, JUSTICE.

Vallejo [the husband] suggests that the trial judge's "own domestic difficulties affected or confused his thinking on the subject" and alleges that the trial judge was divorced in 1950. There is nothing in the record to indicate that the personal life of the trial judge led him to be biased against Vallejo.

3.

ON CONCILIATION AS AN OBJECTIVE OF STATE INTERVENTION—WHY?

a. Court Responses to "Reconciliation" Efforts

[i]

STAHL v. STAHL
221 N.Y.S. 2d 931 (Sup. Ct. 1961)
Modified 16 App. Div. 2d 467, 228 N.Y.S. 2d 724 (1962)

HARRY B. FRANK, JUSTICE.

This action is brought by plaintiff wife for a decree of separation on the grounds of abandonment and cruel and inhuman treatment. In addi-

---

* 25 BULL. N.Y. ACAD. MED. 100-114 (1949). Reprinted with permission of the publisher and the author.

tion, she seeks to set aside an agreement entered into by the parties on February 8, 1960, on the grounds that it is void as against public policy and that it was obtained through the fraud, duress and overreaching of the defendant husband.

As an affirmative defense, the defendant husband pleads the provisions of the agreement of February 8, 1960, which provide in detail for the maintenance and support of the plaintiff and infant child of the marriage in the event of a separation of the parties, as a bar to the bringing of the separate action.

Since a valid and subsisting provision for support and maintenance in a separation agreement bars the maintenance of a separation action, if the agreement relied upon by the defendant is in fact a valid existing separation agreement between the parties then plaintiff is bound by its terms and defendant's affirmative defense is well taken. . . .

* * *

At the outset, the agreement recites that it is entered into between the husband and wife both residing at 935 Park Avenue, New York City. Summarizing the introductory preliminary recitals, which are painfully detailed and repetitive, they set forth that the parties are husband and wife having been married on June 26, 1958, who have one child, and that the parties were in the process of separating and had arranged to live separate and apart but could not mutually agree upon the terms of support and custody and that the wife would have to commence an action for separation "upon those grounds which gave rise to their marital differences", and that the parties now "desire to reconcile their marital differences and forego their contemplated separation", the wife desiring to forbear the commencement of an action for legal separation and the husband desiring to forego his defense to such an action, and that the parties "have agreed to resume their Husband-and-Wife relationship and remain together in the apartment premises which they now occupy". This is followed by a lengthy recital to the effect that the parties now desire to "amicably adjust, compromise and settle their respective present and their future marital rights and obligations", including support, custody and visitation rights, and their respective rights in and to the property of the other by virtue of the marital relation, and that it is the express intention that the mutual waivers of the husband's and wife's every right to share in the estate and property of the other, pursuant to section 18 of the Decedent Estate Law, and the present amount, manner and measure of the maintenance and support of the wife, child and household, shall take effect immediately upon the signing of this agreement. And substantially

the same amount, manner and measure of the separate maintenance and support of the wife, child and household shall prevail upon the occurrence, if ever, of certain contingencies, and that the provisions relating to separate maintenance, custody, and visitation rights, shall be incorporated in any judgment of separation or decree of divorce which may be obtained by either of the parties.

This is followed by a lengthy recital wherein the parties mutually agree that the agreement is entered into for "the specific purpose of reconciling their marital differences, and for the restoration, resumption, continuance, maintenance and promotion of their marital relationship", and that it is not intended to contravene public policy or any laws of the State, the intention being, the agreement states, "to make proper provision, in the nature of an agreed allowance, for the present and future maintenance and support of the Wife," child and household, and "for the purpose of obviating the necessity of any future differences, disputes, negotiations, wrangling, and/or legal resort to the Courts about the amount, manner and measure of the separate maintenance and support of the Wife, the infant child of the marriage, and the household, by the Husband and/or his estate, upon the happening" of any of the contingencies.

There are also detailed recitals declaring full disclosure by each to the other as to financial condition, assets, . . . and that each was fully . . . advised of their respective legal rights by counsel of their own choice.

The operative clauses, which follow a standard clause setting forth consideration, repeat much of the foregoing and are summarized as follows:

FIRST: The parties "mutually reconcile their every marital difference and dispute ; forego and forbear each of their legal and marital right and remedy" and agree to restore and resume their marital relationship and live together harmoniously as husband and wife.

SECOND: The husband undertakes and agrees to provide for the full maintenance and support of the family unit and household in same manner and measure as he has been doing from the date of the marriage, commensurate with his earnings and income.

"THIRD: The Husband and Wife, in a mutual desire to obviate and avoid the embarrassment and emotional strain attendant upon any future differences, disputes, negotiations, wrangling and/or legal resort to the Courts, respecting the Husband's obligation for the amount, manner and measure of the separate maintenance and support of the Wife, the infant child of the marriage, and the running household, upon the happening of any one of the following eventualities, if ever:

(a) The parties shall separate and cease living together as Husband and Wife;

(b) The Husband shall desert the Wife and/or otherwise refuse to support her;

(c) The Wife shall, for any reason whatsoever, desert the Husband;

(d) Either of the parties shall commence an action for separation or divorce against the other, in any Court of competent jurisdiction of this State, or of any other State, territory or dependency of the United States, or of any foreign country;

(e) Either the Husband or the Wife shall die,

mutually undertake and agree that the Husband shall pay unto the Wife, and the Wife shall accept from the Husband, for her complete separate maintenance and support and that of the infant child of the marriage and the running household, for the period hereinafter stated, and for the maintenance, support and education of GREGORY, the infant child of the parties, until he shall have reached the age of 21 years, married, or become otherwise emancipated, whichever shall first occur, the following monies, property and increments, which, it is agreed, is substantially the same amount, manner and measure of the present cost to maintain the entire family unit:"

1. Provides for the net sum, after deduction by the husband from a larger gross sum of enumerated taxes, of $175 a week (tax free), allocated: $125 a week for the wife and $50 a week for the child—commencing on the date of the happening of any one of the eventualities set forth in Subdivisions "(a)" to "(e)" and "to continue weekly thereafter until the death of either of the parties hereto, or the remarriage of the Wife (after divorce), whichever shall first occur;"

This is followed by 8 additional subdivisions covering, in detail, items such as cessation of support upon remarriage of the wife, additional financial benefits for the child, insurance obligations to be assumed by the husband, division of household goods, moving expenses, legal fees, and other such matters.

FOURTH: Sets forth, in minute detail custody and visitation rights concerning the infant child in the event any of the contingencies should occur.

FIFTH: Provides that the separate maintenance, support, and custody provisions are to be incorporated into, and form a part of any judgment of separation or decree of divorce which may be obtained by either of the parties.

SIXTH: Sets forth in great detail mutual waivers of all right . . . which each has or might have in the estate of the other. . . .

SEVENTH: Each warrants and represents that they have no present intention to separate, nor do they contemplate future separation and that the

within agreement is "mutually and voluntarily entered into between them for the promotion of their marital relationship and for the more peaceful and harmonious continuance thereof." There is a reiteration of the intention of the parties "to make proper provision for both the present, as well as the future, maintenance and support of the Wife, the infant child of the marriage and that of the household; custody and visitation and estate, so that in the event an unforeseen catastrophe results in the interruption or termination of the marital state between the parties, the Husband and Wife, * * * for the purpose of obviating the possibility of even greater differences, more disputes, further negotiations, bitter wrangling, and/or legal resort to the Courts, upon the happening of such an unforeseeable catastrophe, do hereby voluntarily and mutually subscribe to all the terms * * * hereof."

EIGHTH: Mutual warranties that each has fully informed and disclosed to the other their true financial condition; the nature and amount of their respective assets, estate, holdings, and property; and that each has for himself personally investigated the same and in addition sought and obtained the advice and guidance of others.

NINTH: Contains warranties and representations that "each has been separately and independently advised of their respective legal rights", by counsel of their own choice, and there is a particularization of certain considerations by each of the parties, and the conclusion that each believes the agreement adequate, fair, just and reasonable, and that each signs voluntarily without coercion or duress by either of them against the other.

The TWELFTH paragraph provides that the agreement shall not be merged as the result of incorporation into any separation judgment or divorce decree but shall survive any of the same.

The provisions in the agreement relating to support and separate maintenance are similar to like provisions to be found in any ordinary separation agreement. Irrespective of the recitals indicating that the parties were living together . . . if this agreement were made after a separation of the parties had in fact taken place, or in prospect of their immediate separation which in fact occurred, or if it were followed by an immediate separation of the parties, then we would have a true separation agreement, apparently valid on its face, and these provisions for support and maintenance would be a bar to the plaintiff's action for separation and support, unless the agreement were otherwise impeached. . . .

However, it has long been the policy of this State that an agreement between husband and wife to separate in the future, or which has for its object the future separation of the parties or provides for a possible separation in the future, or a separation contingent upon the happening of a future event, is void as against public policy. . . .

The repugnance with which agreements to separate in the future are viewed is a logical extension of the favored position accorded to marriage as a matter of public policy under the law. "Our modern society is built about the home. Its perpetuation is essential to the welfare of the community". . . . And the law looks with disfavor upon contracts whereby parties agree to separate in the future, because such agreements produce a destruction of the home and tend to dissolve or alter the marriage relation. . . . The more tolerant attitude extended toward separation agreements made while the parties are living apart, or in prospect of immediate separation, is conditioned upon a recognition that in such cases public policy is not offended because the contract does not bring about the separation nor promote the marital discord. And once faced with the realities of the separation as an accomplished fact, our courts recognize the advisability of voluntary accommodations and uphold agreements where the parties themselves delineate the measure of the obligation of support and, indeed, encourage such agreements where possible, in preference to litigation. . . .

In this case, the pleadings, the recitals in the agreement itself, and the testimony of the parties, establish beyond doubt that at the time the agreement was entered into, the parties were not separated but were living together in the same household. And, further, the agreement was not made in contemplation of an immediate separation, but on the contrary it was the intention of the parties to reconcile their differences and to continue to live together as husband and wife in every sense, which they did for almost two months thereafter. The provisions relating to separate maintenance and support were to take effect only upon the occurrence of a possible future separation of the parties. Thus, if this agreement is to be evaluated solely as a separation agreement, it is clearly in violation of public policy since it is predicated upon a possible future separation of the parties.

It is the unusual nature of this agreement, and the injection of the concept that the agreement was not intended to be a separation agreement at all, but rather a "reconciliation agreement" with the purpose of keeping the parties together and delineating all of their present and future marital obligations, which requires additional examination.

Defendant has properly recognized that the law encourages the resumption of marital relations . . . and agreements which bring about such reconciliations will be upheld. . . . The issues before this court are whether the agreement of February 8th is in fact a true "reconciliation agreement", and whether the terms of such an agreement may be used as a bar to the maintenance of a subsequent action for separation. . . .

* * *

. . . When the present agreement was executed, the parties were not separated and no matrimonial action had been brought by either of them. At most, it could be found that relations between them were not ideal and that by reason of their differences there had been possible contemplation of legal steps, but there is no question that from the date of their marriage up to the date of the agreement they continuously lived together. This agreement did nothing *to bring* them together. The reconciliation cases . . . make clear that public policy was served because the parties were in fact living separate and apart for cause, with a matrimonial action actually pending, and it was the agreement in each case that directly operated to erase these impediments and bring the parties back together. These cases go no further than to hold that the discontinuance of a pending matrimonial action by a wife separated from her husband with good cause, is good consideration to uphold an agreement wherein she is to receive a financial reward for so doing. That the existence of a separation with good cause is a vital factor can best be illustrated by the language in the Rodgers case (229 N.Y. 255, pp. 258-259, 128 N.E. 2d, p. 118), wherein the court stated:

> "The wife condoned the alleged adultery of the husband. That was a detriment to her. She surrendered a right. * * * The performance of marital duty should not be made the subject of bargain and sale, but it does not appear that reconcilement was plaintiff's duty in this case. Rather it was her right to refuse to condone an offense against the marriage relation and to insist on a divorce, with separate support and maintenance. *The husband was not hiring a discontented wife, separated from him without good cause, to return to him.* She was to be paid to give up her *right* to live apart from him." (Emphasis supplied.)

* * *

Under the circumstances here present, where the parties were living together and were not separated for good cause, there was no legal basis on which they could enter into a valid and enforcible "reconciliation" agreement.

Even more decisive, however, is an evaluation of defendant's contention that the provisions for support and maintenance should be upheld because they are an essential factor in promoting the "reconciliation" of the parties. As already indicated, in each of the reconciliation cases, the financial consideration from the husband in no way related to the immediate, or future, maintenance and support of the wife. On the contrary, in each case it served as a monetary inducement, separate and distinct from the support obligation, which directly functioned, to bring the separated parties back together. It was the quid pro quo for which the matrimonial actions were discontinued and the reconciliation effected. It became operative only by reason of a reconciliation of the parties. In the instant agreement, the financial payments in no way operate to bring, or keep, the parties together in the marital relation, but have precisely the opposite effect. These payments are to commence only in the event of a future separation of the parties, irrespective of the reasons for such separation, and irrespective of fault. Thus, even if the wife should engage in the most flagrant violations of the marital code, or leave her husband capriciously and completely without cause, under the terms of this agreement she would be assured of receiving a substantial weekly sum for her support. Likewise, if the husband should at any time abandon his wife and home for any reason whatsoever, he could do so secure in the knowledge that his obligation for support would be limited and certain, irrespective of how prosperous he be at the time. Certainly such provisions are not promotive of domestic tranquility. Indeed, their very existence is an open invitation to the ripening of normal and commonplace domestic quarrels and differences into open breach and separation. Reconciliation agreements have been upheld because they resulted in bringing husband and wife together. The effect of the instant agreement would be to foster and promote marital discord and disharmony between husband and wife and to facilitate a formal separation of the parties. Contracts supported by consideration or inducements which tend to encourage divorce or separation are against public policy and may not be enforced. . . .

The agreement recites that the provisions for future support and maintenance are included in a mutual desire to obviate and avoid the embarrassment and emotional strain attendant upon future differences, negotiations, wrangling or legal resort to the courts in the event of a separation. But it is precisely the spectre of such distasteful proceedings which ofttimes deters hasty separations and which tends to induce a married couple to ameliorate their differences and continue with their marriage.

* * *

It would be particularly inequitable in this case to attempt to sever any particular provision from the rest of the agreement. The agreement is a unified whole. . . . Each provision is inexorably intertwined with the rest. . . .

. . . Where . . . the agreement is void, as in this case, because it is in violation of the prohibition against contracts to alter or dissolve the marriage relation, the entire agreement must fall. . . .

Moreover, the evidence presented at the trial indicates that the entire agreement must fall, in any event, because it does not meet the standards of good faith and fair dealing required in such transactions.

The relation of husband and wife is of a highly confidential nature, and transactions between them are closely examined. In such cases, a court of equity does not limit its inquiry to whether the transaction, as between other persons, would have constituted a binding contract. It further investigates whether the agreement was just and fair and equitably ought to be enforced. . . .

By reason of the relationship of husband and wife, and in order to prevent undue advantage from the close and confidential relations created thereby, the law requires a course of conduct of the utmost degree of good faith in all transactions between the parties. Any contract for the separate maintenance of the wife must be made under circumstances wherein all the material facts are disclosed. She should know her husband's circumstances and any other facts which might affect the terms of the contract. The wife, when she finally binds herself and waives her statutory remedies, should be regarded as having done so only when she is in possession of every material fact affecting her act and, furthermore, it is the duty of the husband, he being in a position of trust, to disclose such facts and his actual circumstances. The burden rests upon the husband to prove that the agreement was not procured by fraud, undue influence, unfair dealing or coercion, and the court is entitled to have evidence presented relevant to the question of whether the wife executed the agreement with full knowledge of all material facts, or on the part of the husband whether his conduct fulfilled the test of open dealing and good faith required by the law. . . .

In view of the fiduciary relations of the parties, a separation agreement may be set aside at the wife's instance on grounds which would be insufficient to set aside an ordinary contract. . . .

In the instant case, the evidence conclusively establishes that there was no disclosure by the defendant as to the full extent of his financial worth. On the contrary, he refused to discuss this issue at all with either his wife or her counsel, and this fact is substantiated by the testimony of defendant's own counsel. The only disclosure made by him was the production of a tax return for the year 1958 showing his income to be under $10,000, which was highly misleading and not indicative of his true financial position. . . .

Defendant's reticence in revealing his economic background continued throughout the trial, making it impossible to determine with complete accuracy the full extent of his financial condition. . . .

. . . When she signed this agreement she did not have in her possession the necessary material facts regarding his true financial condition. Not only did the defendant fail to fulfill the duty upon him to disclose such facts, but he, in addition, sought to conceal and misrepresent his financial worth. Such information was particularly relevant in connection with the waiver of her rights to the defendant's estate, as well as to the maintenance provisions.

Although the plaintiff had consulted counsel in connection with this agreement, this in no way abrogated the confidential relations existing between the parties which required the exercise of the utmost good faith and frankness on the part of the defendant. . . . This is not a situation where they had long been living apart and were dealing at arms length. . . . Here the parties were living together with no severance of communication between them, and it appears that plaintiff was to a great extent under the influence of the defendant during this period. She acquiesced in his direction not to consult particular attorneys, and while the defendant and his attorney insisted that she obtain counsel, this was done only after preliminary discussions had been held wherein the substantive provisions to be included in the agreement were decided upon. Plaintiff participated in these important preliminary discussions without counsel, and her attorneys took no part in the negotiation of the various provisions. It is evident from the record, and it is substantially admitted, that plaintiff was to obtain counsel primarily for the purpose of lending an air of regularity to the execution of the agreement. He was, in effect, to be a rubber stamp to an agreement, the terms of which had already been determined. Furthermore, plaintiff's counsel was frustrated in the discharge of his duties to his client by the adamant refusal of the defendant to disclose or discuss his financial background, and by the arbitrary limitations imposed upon his examination and exploration of the agreement, which was a most unusual one.

While I cannot find that the plaintiff did not fully comprehend the nature of the proceedings, or that she was forced to sign it under physical duress or mistreatment, I do believe that her assent to this agreement was prompted by her intense desire to continue with the marriage relationship, and the defendant's insistence upon the execution of this agreement, coupled with his threats to leave her if she did not sign, were a form of moral coercion. While such conduct would not be of moment in an action to set aside an ordinary agreement, it is not insignificant in a case such as this involving an agreement between husband and wife enjoying confidential relations. . . .

NOTES

NOTE 1.

THEODOROPOULAS v. THEODOROPOULAS
[1963] 2 All E.R. 772

SIR JOCELYN SIMON, P., stated that the case had *caused him anxiety* because he found himself unable to accept the unsupported evidence of either the husband or the wife and had to rely on probabilities supported by some evidence of independent witnesses, and continued: . . . I must refer to . . . evidence which was tendered and which I ruled inadmissible, reserving my reasons. It relates to two alleged conversations. The first took place when a Mrs. Gray had a discussion with the wife after she had left the husband; this approach was made at the request of the husband with a view to reconciliation. Counsel for the husband sought to cross-examine the wife as to what was said between her and Mrs. Gray and to call Mrs. Gray as a witness. The second conversation was said to have taken place in the following circumstances. It was sought on behalf of the husband to allege that after the petition was filed the wife called on the husband, emphasised that the visit was without the knowledge of her solicitor and that he should be kept in ignorance of it, and then discussed financial terms on which she might consider returning home. Counsel wished to cross-examine the wife as to the approach which was said to have taken place, to ask the husband questions about it, and to call a Mr. Brewer, who was said to have been present during part of the conversation. Counsel outlined at my request the nature of the evidence and also its purpose, namely, that the wife in making overtures herself for a reconciliation, showed that she was not terrified of her husband, as she suggested in evidence that she was, and that her motives both in leaving and in offering terms on which she might come back were of a purely mercenary nature.

Counsel for the husband accepted that statements made to a probation officer whose services have been enlisted with a view to reconciliation are privileged, if one of the parties objects to their disclosure. . . . He argued, however, that the rule does not extend to a private individual whose services are enlisted towards the parties' reconciliation; certainly not to conversations between the parties themselves; and least of all to a witness fortuitously present and overhearing part of any such communication. I think that it is, therefore, important to ascertain the object of the privilege which has been conceded in the authorities. In *McTaggart v. McTaggart* [1948] 2 All E.R. at p. 756 ; DENNING, L.J., said:

> "The law favours reconciliation, and the court will not take on itself a course which would be so prejudicial to its success."

That is to say, will not take on itself to insist on statements made in the course of an attempt at reconciliation being disclosed.

* * *

It seems to me that the reasoning . . . applies with equal force to a private individual's attempts at reconciliation as to those of an official person.

* * *

. . . No doubt, when a probation officer . . . or a clergyman is approached, the law will readily infer that the parties have gone to him with a view to reconciliation and on the tacit understanding that nothing said should afterwards be used against them ; but, equally, where it is proved that any private individual is enlisted specifically as a conciliator, in my view the law will aid his or her efforts by guaranteeing that any admissions or disclosures by the parties are privileged in subsequent matrimonial litigation. It was, therefore, quite clear that evidence of the conversation between the wife and Mrs. Gray was inadmissible.

Moreover, it seems to me that the principle . . . is just as applicable to communications between the parties themselves with a view to reconciliation as to those conducted through intermediaries. In the case of "without prejudice" communications with a view to settlement of actual or pending litigation, the privilege equally attaches whether the communication is directly between the parties, or through an intermediary such as a solicitor. . . .

* * *

It follows . . . that privilege attaches to communications between the spouses themselves when made with a view to reconciliation. It also extends to excluding the evidence of an independent witness who was fortuitously present when those communications were made and who overheard or read them. I therefore ruled that all the evidence tendered, whether by way of cross-examination of the wife, or in chief from the husband or by calling Mr. Brewer, was inadmissible.

[HIS LORDSHIP then reviewed the evidence, found that each party had been guilty of cruelty to the other party, the husband being the more blameworthy, and in the exercise of the court's discretion granted a decree nisi of divorce to both parties.]

NOTE 2.

COLE v. COLE
30 N.J. Super. 276, 104 A. 2d 76 (1954)

MCLEAN, J. S. C.

This application is for an order requiring defendant husband to pay to plaintiff wife's attorney a proper and reasonable amount as and for counsel fees for legal services performed by said attorney in prosecuting plaintiff's separate maintenance action and defending plaintiff on the counterclaim for divorce brought by defendant husband.

* * *

That plaintiff wife's counsel shall be permitted a counsel fee . . . where the parties have become reconciled is well established under the laws of New Jersey. The court, in Morrison v. Morrison, . . . 193 A. 908, 909 (Ch. 1937), set down the basis for such a recovery and stated:

> "In the case at bar the wife's solicitor in good faith instituted and pressed the suit in her behalf. She has not, and never has had, the means to compensate him. He has acted from the first upon the knowledge that his compensation must come from the husband. As solicitor for the wife he has done his work well. He has gone further and has aided in bringing about a reconciliation. In this respect he has acted in the interest of society and the public policy. Is he to be penalized for doing so by being denied a fee honestly earned? In matrimonial cases we regard the wife as the favored suitor, and call upon the husband to pay her suit moneys; otherwise, in many cases the wife would be powerless to assert her legal rights against him. We encourage reputable counsel to represent wives in meritorious cases, upon the implied assurance that they will be compensated for the reasonable value of their services through orders against the husband. We also applaud and encourage their efforts, as officers of the court, to effect reconciliations where possible. Unless all this is mere platitude, how can we penalize them for doing what we preach to them is their duty? If we do so, how can we expect counsel to be willing to undertake a destitute wife's case against her husband, no matter how meritorious? Public policy requires that lack of means shall not deprive the wife of the services of a competent solicitor, and it follows that it is contrary to public policy to deny reasonable compensation to such solicitor in proper cases to be paid by the husband; a fortiori, where the suit has abated by reconciliation due to efforts of the wife's solicitor. It is true that the cause of action no longer exists and that as between the parties the only order which can properly be entered is an order dismissing the suit, but the wife's solicitor has acquired a separate interest of his own, which cannot be divested by act of the parties without his consent, and which it is the duty of this court to protect."

Counsel for defendant argues that in case of reconciliation no allowance for counsel fee should be made. . . . In the instant case a considerable amount of time was given and a considerable amount of work was done by counsel and substantial results were attained over defendant's opposition, and plaintiff was called upon to prepare her defense to defendant's counterclaim. Fairness to counsel justifies the consideration of the application under the philosophy of the Morrison case. . . .

NOTE 3.

O'GORMAN, HUBERT J.

Lawyers and Matrimonial Cases*

Several different points of view have been expressed by members of the legal profession about the problem of reconciliation in matrimonial cases. . . .

We discussed the problem of reconciliation with our informants. Though most of them did not include it in their role definitions, a majority—three out of five—said that a lawyer should explore the possibility of reconciliation before proceeding with a matrimonial action. However, while Counselors were more disposed than Advocates to take this position, both were equally pessimistic about a lawyer's chances for success. . . .

These findings suggest that for most of our informants, the problem of reconciliation involves a question of professional norm priority. The norms that define the Counselor and Advocate roles are, in general, given higher priority than the norm of reconciliation. This differential in norm priority grows out of the cross-pressures of law practice, pressures that both motivate and inhibit attempts at reconciliation. Six such pressures were identified in reviewing the interview protocols.

1. THE ACCEPTANCE OF THE NORM . . . When most of our informants identify themselves as lawyers, they believe they have an obligation to examine reconciliation as a possible solution in matrimonial cases.

> I always try and see if reconciliation is possible before going ahead. I believe it is an important part of my job. I feel that *it is part of a lawyer's job.*
>
> *A lawyer should try.* I always try. . . . Sometimes it works . . . not generally.
>
> A lawyer is not likely to succeed in most cases. But *he should try* and *I think most of us do.*

* Reprinted with permission of the publisher from *Lawyers and Matrimonial Cases*, by Hubert J. O'Gorman, pp. 145-151. © 1963 by The Free Press of Glencoe, A Division of the Macmillan Company.

Certainly, he ought not to let the idea of a fee deter him.

As these excerpts make plain, the norm is perceived as applying to the professional's status. It is more than a personal inclination; not just "my job," but "part of a lawyer's job." And it is believed that the norm is conformed to throughout the profession: "Most of us do." Furthermore, the norm is complied with despite the recognition of obstacles—"A lawyer is not likely to succeed"—and countervailing pressures—"He ought not to let the idea of a fee deter him."

2. LAWYERS' PERSONAL SENTIMENTS As husbands and fathers, as sons and brothers, attorneys share with clients many significant cultural norms about marriage and family life. Hence, they often react to matrimonial clients not only as professionals but as individuals with similar social ties and with potentially similar problems. Given their own familial commitments, they are not insensitive to the consequences of matrimonial actions. "As a human being," said one informant, "you hate to see a marriage break up." Because they share important values with matrimonial clients, lawyers can derive a deep gratification from their participation in reconciliation. This may prompt attorneys to make strong efforts to reunite estranged spouses. Here is one lawyer's description of what he called "the most satisfying thing that ever happened to me in practice":

> A couple had been married for thirty years and were going to break up. . . . I kept after both of them, and it finally worked out. . . . I'd run into them on the street, walking to a movie arm in arm and I'd have a real glow, a tremendous sense of satisfaction. I didn't get a penny for it. He wanted to pay something, but how can you put a price on a thing like that?

3. THE PRAGMATICS OF PRACTICE Even should a lawyer reject the norm of reconciliation on the ground that it is not part of his role, or what it represents at best a futile gesture, he may be forced into examining the problem simply to protect his own interests. When there is any likelihood that his client may be reconciled with the spouse, he may be reluctant to devote his time to the case. He may therefore comply with the norm in order to be sure that the marriage will be dissolved:

> We search the matter of reconciliation out as a possibility but really don't expect anything to come of it. It's much too late by then. *But the important thing is that I don't want to go ahead and work on a matter if it isn't going through. I don't want to work for nothing.*
>
> The first thing I do is to look into the possibility that a reconciliation may occur. I do this not because I'm a marriage counselor. *I just*

don't want to waste my time if they are not certain.

The attitude expressed here need not mean that a lawyer will engage in merely perfunctory efforts at reconciliation. His concern with his own schedule of work elicits a genuine interest in knowing what the client plans to do.

4. THE EXPERIENCE OF FAILURE   Very few informants believed that a lawyer actually could successfully reconcile estranged spouses. "My job should be to try and reconcile them," remarked one lawyer, "and I always see if it is possible, but there's no chance as a rule." His judgment was shared by most of the informants whose experience with reconciliation attempts was largely one of failure:

* * *

The experience of failure would seem to be a strong pressure undermining the norm of reconciliation; and the reason why lawyers define their roles without including the norm is clear: men are not likely to give high saliency to a norm so far out of line with experience.

5. THE CLIENT: SYMBOL OF A DEAD MARRIAGE Another pressure subverting the norm of reconciliation is the belief that identifies the presence of the marital client with the termination of his marriage. Slightly more than one out of five informants spontaneously asserted that if an individual sees a lawyer about his marital conflict, it is only a matter of time before the marriage is dissolved: "People don't come to a lawyer to be reconciled. Generally reconciliation is out or they don't see a lawyer." This belief, mentioned equally by Counselors and Advocates, is based on the assumption that people first go through some kind of formal or informal institutional machinery in order to renew their marriages, and that only then, do they come to an attorney:

> The spouses probably tried reconciliation themselves. After all, no one wants to admit failure in such a situation. It isn't easy to break up a marriage relationship. Then you'll find that the family and friends of the couple have tried because they hate to see the break-up.

> By the time these people get to a lawyer, they have seen psychiatrists, they've talked to friends, counselors, rabbis, priests. Once they decide to see a lawyer, it's over.

. . . There is . . . the possibility that, in an unknown proportion of cases, lawyers, by believing that their clients' marriages are beyond rehabilitation, may be contributing to the dissolution of those marriages. This is the familiar process of a "self-fulfilling prophecy": "A false definition of the situation" evokes "behavior which makes the originally false conception come true." If the active intervention of a court can save some marriages after spouses have hired their attorneys, then the belief that a marital client symbolizes an irreconcilable marriage warrants careful study.

6. THE LACK OF COMPETENCY   An attorney's attitude toward reconciliation is apt to be influenced by his sense of competency. There was no doubt in the minds of some informants that lawyers lack the necessary professional preparation: "No lawyer is trained or equipped to decide who should live together and who should not."

NOTE 4.

PILPEL, HARRIET F.

Discussion of Marriage Counseling in a Legal Setting*

[C]an anyone seriously imagine suggesting that a marriage counselor be made a part of the regular staff of any law office that handles a considerable number of marital cases[?] The protests if such a suggestion were made would, I am sure, ring out from coast to coast.

True—law offices often have accountants in attendance on the premises; but even this has created minor hullabaloos from time to time in terms of questions, such as, "Are the accountants practicing law?" "What happens to the confidential relationship between lawyer and client?" and so forth. But a marriage counselor! I simply cannot imagine such a solution to the handling of marital problems in a law office being regarded . . . as "obvious." In fact, I do not think it would even be regarded as possible.

However, since lawyers as a profession are intimately involved in family problems, whether they wish to be or not, some solution must be found to make it possible for them to do a better job than their present training, experience, and professional points of view ordinarily permit. . . .

* * *

. . . If lawyers in private offices cannot practically put marriage counselors on their staffs, and if referring to outside marriage counselors often does not work, and if legal cases involving marriage problems call for some degree of counseling skill and understanding of human relations—what is left?

* * *

If other disciplines can be taught the rudiments of marriage and other counseling, and of psychodynamics—social workers, for example, and

* *Marriage and Family Living*, Vol. 22 (1960), pp. 216-217. Reprinted with permission of the publisher, the National Council on Family Relations, and the author.

clergymen—why can't lawyers too? I am not suggesting they become counselors rather than lawyers, but I am suggesting they become sufficiently aware of the factors involved in most of the cases they handle so that they can exercise human wisdom as well as technical skill.

* * *

NOTE 5.

O'GORMAN, HUBERT J.
Lawyers and Matrimonial Cases*

However personal a matrimonial case may be, it is still, after all, a legal problem. Why, then, is it characterized by some attorneys as nonlegal? The informants who reported this . . . were not denying the presence of legal issues in matrimonial actions; rather, they judged such issues to be incidental to the "real" problem, which was variously identified as "psychological," "social," and "medical."

This nonlegal orientation appears to be a product of the extremely personal quality of marital conflict, a quality that almost precludes its perception in legal terms. "Matrimonials," remarked one attorney, "involve the personal problems of people and really isn't a legal problem." In these cases, insisted another, "you're just wrapped up in the personal and emotional problems of people. It isn't really law." But why should a personal problem be perceived as not "really" law? . . .

NOTE 6.

WISCONSIN BAR ASSOCIATION
"Preventive Law"†

Most clients do not engage a lawyer on a regular retainer basis. The concept of a "family lawyer" has never developed to the same extent as the concept of "family physician." Now, with the aid and encouragement of the organized bar, greater stress is being placed on "preventive law." Periodic legal check-ups are proving advantageous for both lawyer and client. In a well managed law office attention can be directed to the interrelated nature of the problems of an individual client. Frequently, when a client comes in for one task, the lawyer will best serve the client's interests if he reviews or points out possible related problems or needs for legal help. . . .

Lawyers should stress the "preventive" aspects of the law and make periodic legal check-ups with clients. Such a check-up might include:

(1) A review of the client's will in light of the current situation as to family, property and the law.

(2) A review of the desirability of the manner in which title to real estate and personal property is being held.

(3) A review of the adequacy of the client's insurance coverage, not only as to dollar amount, but also as to the risks being covered by public liability insurance.

(4) A review of newly accruing rights of the client, with emphasis on the proper time and manner for exercising or protecting these rights.

(5) A review of the obligations of the client; how they are being met; whether the client has secondary obligations or liabilities where the primary obligation is open and enforceable.

NOTE 7.

"Checkup on Marriage" Urged by Psychiatrist*

An "annual checkup on marriage," similar to a yearly medical checkup, is advocated by Dr. Lena Levine, a psychiatrist and family counselor. Dr. Levine considers an annual re-evaluation beneficial to both new and old marriages.

. . . Dr. Levine said, "The newest wrinkle in marriage is happiness. Previously the important ingredient in marriage was stability. However, stability did not necessarily insure happiness."

The big question now is whether the desire for personal happiness must lead to increasingly widespread instability, separation and divorce.

To check up on their marriage, a couple might re-evaluate it once a year, perhaps on their wedding anniversary. They might suggest to each other important changes that would make their partnership an even happier one in the coming year.

To be happy, this counselor believes, the marriage partners must accept each other's differences, including differences in emotional expression and feelings. It is a mistake, she believes, to think that one's partner can be made over.

Learning to understand another person, to get along with him or her is not instinctive, Dr. Levine emphasized. It must be taught.

[ii]

PASHKO v. PASHKO
45 O. O. 498, 101 N.E.2d 804 (1951)

KOVACHY, JUDGE.
In this matter the plaintiff filed an alimony action against her husband, James Pashko, and in her prayer, in addition to asking for the usual relief asks "that during the pendency" of this

* Reprinted with permission of the publisher from *Lawyers and Matrimonial Cases*, by Hubert J. O'Gorman, pp. 107-108. © 1963 by The Free Press of Glencoe, A Division of The Macmillan Company.
† RM-10 (Sept. 11, 1959). Reprinted with permission of the Wisconsin Bar Association.

* *The New York Times*, Feb. 6, 1960, p. 22, col. 2. © 1960 by The New York Times Company. Reprinted by permission.

action the defendant, Florence Haas, be restrained from visiting, conversing socially, associating or meeting and being with the defendant, James Pashko; that she be restrained from interfering with the marriage relationship; * * * that the defendant, James Pashko, be temporarily * * * restrained from visiting, conversing socially, associating, or meeting and being with the defendant, Florence Haas * * *."

In her amended petition with respect of Florence Haas she claims that the defendant, Florence Haas, "has enticed him (her husband) by using various designs and wiles to have the defendant leave her and in trying to induce her husband to transfer his affections to her" and "that the defendant (her husband) and said Florence Haas openly, notoriously and brazenly have been seen in each other's company and have made no pretense of their relationship and friendship for each other and have flagrantly displayed their affections for each other in public places where they could easily be seen by the general public and by others who are acquainted with both plaintiff and the defendant". Further "that said defendant, Florence Haas, maliciously and wrongfully used her design upon the plaintiff's husband for the purpose of destroying the love and affection that her husband had for her and for the purpose of bringing about the separation of the plaintiff from her husband."

With respect of her husband the plaintiff "alleges that prior to the new defendant, Florence Haas, interfering with their lives that she and her husband enjoyed happiness, peace and contentment and that her husband treated her with great kindness, affection and tenderness during the greater portion of the time they lived together" and "that until such time as the defendant, Florence Haas, enticed her husband by various means and methods, that she and the defendant were a normal, happy husband and wife, living a normal life in the community, and they enjoyed the respect and companionship of their friends and relatives, but ever since the defendant, Florence Haas, has interfered with their marriage and has by undue influence and various wiles and means enticed her husband, he has been dissatisfied with his marriage and has left her and engaged in the activities that have hereinbefore been related."

The plaintiff filed a written "Motion For a Temporary Restraining Order" with notice of a hearing upon the same at a time and court certain and obtained personal service upon each defendant. At an oral hearing upon the same each defendant demurred to the granting of a temporary restraining order on the ground,——

1. That the amended petition does not state a cause of action for same and,——

2. That the Court has no equitable jurisdiction to grant the relief prayed for.

* * *

. . . To evaluate the efficacy and propriety of the request made herein it is necessary to understand the basic philosophy of the law in divorce and alimony matters.

1. Marriage is a civil contract between husband and wife considered by law a status in which the state has an interest and over which it should exercise watchful vigilance to safeguard its sanctity and to prevent its disruption, if possible. . . .

2. The historic purpose of the divorce and alimony laws is to serve the best interests of society by protecting and maintaining the family. . . .

3. The state is a party to every divorce and alimony proceeding and in Ohio where no provision by law is made for actual representation, the court represents the state. . . .

4. It is the duty of the court to use every proper means to reconcile parties seeking divorce or separation. . . .

5. The six-week waiting period before a divorce or alimony action can be heard in Ohio is intended as a cooling-off period for the parties and the time for affecting reconciliation if possible. Ohio General Code § 8003-10.

6. A wife by law is entitled to the affection, society, cooperation and aid of her husband in all conjugal relations.

* * *

The court in this case has complete jurisdiction over the marital status of the husband and wife involved. It has a duty to safeguard and preserve such status if possible during the pendency of the action in order to allow all forces working toward a reconciliation to operate with the view of maintaining the family relation.

According to the plaintiff, one Florence Haas is wrongfully and maliciously bent on disrupting her conjugal relations with her husband. She is asking this court to restrain Miss Haas from so doing during the pendency of her action. Now it is obvious that if Florence Haas has her way that the plaintiff will suffer irreparable injury in her relationship with her husband. It is also manifest that if Florence Haas is permitted to pursue her designs unhampered the chances for a reconciliation of this couple is greatly lessened and the beneficial purpose of a waiting period between the filing and hearing of the cause most probably thwarted. The matter therefore resolves itself into the following question: Does a Common Pleas

Court acting in domestic relations have the power which it should exercise to halt a brazen and designing third person from wrongfully, maliciously and notoriously interfering with the marital rights of the plaintiff during the pendency of her alimony action or must it proclaim its impotence to control such a situation and supinely permit the flagrant violation of substantial rights to continue unabated?

* * *

From a consideration of the authorities and the duties devolving upon a court of domestic relation with respect to marriage and the family this court believes that if the facts set forth in the amended petition be true, that this is then an appropriate case in which to exercise its equity powers to restrain the third party pendente lite from continuing her deliberate depredation upon the marriage of the plaintiff.

Defendants claim that such an order in a matter relating to domestic affairs would be violative of the right of free speech and of normal social relations. The court believes that under the circumstances herein depicted it would be no more of an infringement of the mentioned rights than the enforcement of the law of careless driving in a proper case is an abridgement of the right of citizens to operate their automobiles upon the highway.

* * *

They also say that human passion is involved in this matter which is not amenable to regulation by law. That, of course, is not sound thinking because it is only through the exercise of discipline with respect to human passion that man has evolved above the level of brute force and laws in many instances merely reflect such discipline. The killing of another in the "heat of passion," for instance, is manslaughter.

They further maintain that the order if made would be difficult to enforce since its disobedience in the main would only involve the defendants themselves. The answer to that assertion is the fact that this court issues hundreds of orders in domestic relation matters as a matter of routine all of which are enforcible through contempt proceedings and no insurmountable difficulties have been encountered with respect to their enforcement.

Divorces are at a scandalously high level in the United States today. Courts should use whatever powers they have to stem the tide. A restraining order against the third party in this case will be notice to others deliberately intent upon breaking up a family to take heed and desist from their course. The court is convinced that it will deter others from similar action and become a shield in protecting the integrity and the sanctity of family life in our community.

With respect to the demurrer of the defendant, James Pashko, it appears to this court that if an order is entered against defendant, Florence Haas, it will become necessary to stay the hand of said James Pashko as well in order to prevent any possible circumvention of the court's order in respect of their relation.

The demurrers of both defendants are therefore overruled and exceptions noted.

The defendants herein at the hearing on the motion for a temporary restraining order stated that through their respective demurrers they raise the question of law permitting the order sought in this case and if the law should prove against them that they do not care to present any evidence to controvert the allegations of the amended petition and concede that an order should issue.

A temporary restraining order pendente lite is therefore granted and a bond of $100 set as to each defendant.

NOTES

NOTE 1.

PASHKO v. PASHKO
Ten Years Later

(a) As far as we can determine from our files, Florence Haas did not violate the Court Order, and therefore there were no contempt proceedings instituted against her. No other sanctions were applied to uphold the Court Order, since our client was unable to ascertain whether or not Mr. Pashko and Miss Haas violated the temporary restraining order. [Letter dated Dec. 22, 1960, from Jack A. Feingold, attorney for the plaintiff.]

(b) Mr. & Mrs. Pashko were divorced several weeks after the Court entered the restraining order. Florence Haas did not violate the order. There were no sanctions.

A word of comment about this case. Ohio follows the general rule that equity courts will not attempt to regulate the personal social conduct of individuals. The Pashko case simply ignored this rule on the theory that the court was only granting a temporary restraining order. The judges here have refused to follow the Pashko case for the excellent reason that enforcement is nearly impossible.

In Ohio temporary restraining orders are not considered "final orders" and are not appealable. If the Pashko rule ever reaches the Appellate Court in some fashion, I doubt that it would be followed. [Letter dated Dec. 23, 1960 from Myron D. Malitz, attorney for the defendant.]

NOTE 2.

[ANONYMOUS]
Padlocks and Girdles of Chastity*

You may see, if you will, the origin of padlocks of chastity in that peculiar knot, called the Herculean knot, which used to fasten the woolen sash of the Grecian maiden, and which the husband alone was to unite [sic] on his wedding night. Solidify this knot, apply it to iron bars, and you have almost the padlock. But the Greeks do not appear to have been acquainted with this safety-apparatus. . . .

. . . We see in the pseudo-Meursius's Aloysia, that elegant picture of the morals of the 16th century, with what arguments a husband, who has good grounds for being on his guard, persuades his wife to put one on; it is herself, Tullia, who relates the incident to her friend Ottavia: "Truly," said he, "I am fully persuaded that thou art exceedingly honest and chaste; yet I fear for thy virtue unless we both come to its aid—" "What act, what fault have I committed to put such an idea into thy head, my heart?" I asked; "what opinion hast thou formed of me? Withal, I do not wish to depreciate any scheme thou mayst have fostered."—"I want," said he, "to put a girdle of chastity on thee; if thou art chaste, thou wilt not be annoyed at it; why, if not, it is thy business to see how right I am in doing what I propose."—"I will put on me whatever thou choosest," I replied; "be it what it may, I shall gladly wear it. as I was born to be thine: I shall heartily be a wife for only thee and live isolated from the rest of men, whom I despise and detest. I shall neither speak to Lampridio nor look at him."—"Don't act thus," said he; "on the contrary, I wish thee to act friendly and decently with him, so that neither he nor I may have any reason to complain of thee: he, in case thou didst treat him too rudely, and I, shouldst thou make too free with him. But the girdle of chastity will permit thee to live at greater liberty with him, whilst offering me full security on the side of Lampridio." Then with a silk ribbon which he placed round my body above the hips, he measured the size the girdle should be round the thick part of my body; with another ribbon, he took the measure of the space from my groins to my hips. This done: "Even in this matter," said he. "I shall try and let thee see how greatly I esteem thee. The little chains, which are to be overlaid with velveting, will be of gold; the portcullis will be of gold, the gold opening will be studded over with precious stones. The most famous goldsmith of our town will, as he is under

---

* Publisher and date of publication not given. A copy may be found in the Yale University Library. Pp. 9-12.

great obligations to me, set to work at it that it may be a master-piece of his art. I shall be but conferring an honor upon thee, while seeming to be doing thee wrong."

NOTE 3.

FOSTER v. WITHROW
20 Ga. 260, 39 S.E. 2d 466 (1946)

Mrs. Beatric Withrow filed a petition for habeas corpus, alleging that she was being illegally restrained . . . in the common jail. . . . She alleged that the pretense of her restraint was by virtue of a peace warrant issued on the affidavit of her husband, John O. Withrow; . . . that she was unable to give a $500 bond, and was therefore confined. . . .

HEAD, JUSTICE

The particular question presented by this case, whether or not a husband can institute a peace-warrant proceeding against his wife, have never been decided in this State. Section 76-201 of the Code, in regard to peace-warrant proceedings, reads as follows: "Upon the information of any person, under oath, that he is in fear of bodily harm to himself or his family, *from another,* or of violent injury to his property, any judicial officer authorized to hold a court of inquiry may issue his warrant against such other person, requiring his arrest; and if, upon the return thereof, the court is satisfied, upon hearing the evidence of both parties, that probable cause for such fear exists, he may require the accused to give bond, with good security, to keep the peace as against the person, family, and property of the affiant, and, on failure to give the bond, shall commit him to jail." (Italics ours.) It will be noted that this section does not exclude by its terms the right of the husband to institute such proceedings against his wife.

*   *   *

It has always been the policy of our law that husband and wife are criminally liable for crimes committed against each other, and it is well recognized that a wife would be criminally responsible for crimes committed against her husband, such as murder, manslaughter, assault with intent to murder and assault and battery. "The requirement of surety of the peace is preventive justice and consists in obliging those persons of whom there is a probable ground to suspect future misbehavior, to stipulate with, and to give full assurance to, the public that such offense as is apprehended shall not happen, by finding pledges or securities for keeping the peace." . . . The primary purpose of the peace-warrant proceeding is not to award the person seeking its protection money damages for injuries which he may receive; the primary purpose is to prevent violence, and keep the peace. If the magistrate hearing the proceeding determines that the person instituting it has probable cause for his fears, then the one against whom the proceeding is brought must find persons willing to be securities on a bond covenanting that he or she will keep the peace, or be committed to jail. "Preventive justice, on every principle of reason, of humanity, and of sound policy, is preferable to punitive justice, the execution of which is always attended with harsh circumstances * * *. As a restraint on the commission of crime in the nature of a breach of the peace or other misdemeanor, courts in this country generally have power to bind a person in a penal bond to the State, conditioned that such person will keep the peace of the State as to all of its citizens, and especially as to the one at whom the threatened breach of the peace appears to have been pointed." 8 Am. Jur. 842, § 19. Since the husband is competent to give evidence in any criminal proceeding against his wife on her trial for a criminal offense committed or attempted to have been committed against him (Code, § 38-1604), then we see no reason why he should not be allowed to make an oath that he is in fear of bodily harm from his wife, and thereby institute proceedings to restrain his wife from committing a crime or misdemeanor against him.

. . . It is, of course, the duty of the justice of the peace hearing the case to ascertain, to the greatest degree of certainty possible, whether the applicant for the peace bond has actual fears, or whether the proceeding is instituted only for the purpose of annoying or harassing the person against whom it is brought. The fact that a husband might bring such a proceeding against his wife because he was angry with her or tired of her, cannot affect our ruling here. The law must presume that the justice of the peace will perform his duty in hearing evidence from both sides and making a legal and just decision.

. . . It is common knowledge, however, that through the period from 1862 to the present time the status of married women in this State has undergone a complete transformation. At the time peace-warrant proceedings appeared in the Code of 1862, the relation of the wife to her husband was more nearly in accord with the Biblical statement made to Eve, concerning Adam, "He shall rule over thee." Gen. 3 : 16. While the codifiers of that Code could envision a situation where a wife might need the law's protection to keep her husband from harming, or threatening to harm her, it is probable that it did not occur to them that the wife would become a menace to the husband's peace. In our present generation, the wife has equal rights with the husband in all things necessary to her protection, and the law gives her

several safeguards which the husband does not have. The theory of the law that the husband is the head of the family and the wife is subject to him has become in most instances merely a legal theory. However, while our customs have changed, and women have become almost completely emancipated from the laws and customs that once bound them, subsequent codifiers and legislatures have not changed the provision of law now found in the Code, § 76-205. In fact, no substantial changes have been made in peace-warrant proceedings since the Code of 1862. We do not think, however, that the fact that the law has not been changed would prevent the husband from requiring the peace bond to be made by his wife, since under the provisions of the peace-warrant law he is not excluded. Rather it may be said that the change in the status of married women by law and custom since the time when § 76-205 was originally placed in the Code has rendered such section superfluous.

In our judgment it would violate no principle or policy of our law for the husband to be allowed to institute a peace-warrant proceeding against his wife to require her to keep the peace as against him ; and since the plaintiff in error, as sheriff, held Mrs. Withrow under a valid commitment of the justice of the peace issued because she did not make bond in the peace-warrant proceeding against her, the court erred in discharging her on the hearing of the writ of habeas corpus.

Judgment reversed.

* * *

NOTE 4.

RAPAPORT, DAVID

The Theory of Ego Autonomy: A Generalization*

. . . When a man pulls up stakes and moves far away where his past is not known, he is subject to temptations: in the course of his sea voyage, the mutt he left behind may grow into a Saint Bernard, or the painting by a local amateur which he owned may turn into a Rembrandt. The superego is a persistent structure, but its conscious parts seem to require stimulus-nutriment. In the lack of nutriment it becomes prone to compromise and corruption, and the greater their extent, the more mercilessly does the unconscious superego exact its pound of flesh: the unconscious sense of guilt. The maintenance of conscience seems to require the continuous input of the nourishment readily provided by a stable, traditional environment in which the individual is born, grows up, and ends

* Reprinted with permission from the *Bulletin of the Menninger Clinic*, Vol. 22, p. 13. Copyright 1958 by The Menninger Foundation.

his life; that is, the stimulus of the presence, opinions, and memories of the "others" who have always known him and always will. We seem to choose the social bonds of marriage, friendship, etc., to secure that familiar (paternal, maternal) pattern of stimulation which we need as nutriment for our various superego and ego structures (for example, those which underlie our values and ideologies).

[iii]

PEOPLE v. CONNELL
9 Ill. 2d 390, 137 N.E. 2d 849 (1956)

HERSHEY, JUSTICE.

This case involves the constitutionality of a 1955 amendment to the Divorce Act, which provides that actions for divorce "shall be commenced by filing a praecipe for summons" and which prohibits the filing of the complaint and entry of the decree for a period of 60 days from the day the summons is served or the last day of publication of notice, unless leave of court is obtained in the manner outlined. . . .

The circuit court of Cook County refused appellant's request for *mandamus* to compel the clerk of that court to receive and file her complaint for divorce despite her refusal to commence the suit by filing a *praecipe* for summons as required by said statute. . . .

In asserting constitutional objections, the appellant relies mainly upon People ex rel. Christiansen v. Connell, 2 Ill. 2d 332, 118 N.E. 2d 262, 264, which invalidated a 1953 amendment to the Divorce Act containing somewhat similar provisions. However, the appellee contends that this legislation does not have the features condemned in the Christiansen case and that the decision is actually an authority in support of the present act.

The 1953 statute considered in the Christiansen case contained three significant provisions (none of which is included in the 1955 act) modifying the practice and procedure in divorce, separate maintenance and annulment. First, it required, as a condition precedent to the commencement of an action for divorce, separate maintenance or annulment, that the plaintiff file a "statement of intention" to institute the action. Second, it provided for a mandatory waiting period after the filing of the statement of intention of 60 days before suit could be instituted, summons issued, and jurisdiction obtained over the person of the defendant. Third, it provided for a voluntary informal conference during the 60-day waiting period, directed to reconciliation of the parties and to be participated in by the court and one or both of such parties.

We held the legislation unconstitutional on two grounds: (1) The 60-day prejurisdictional waiting period denied to the plaintiff a right of access to

the courts in violation of section 19 of article II of the Illinois constitution. S.H.A. (2) The voluntary reconciliation conference imposed nonjudicial duties upon judges in violation of the separation of powers provisions of article III of the Illinois constitution.

In an obvious effort to cure these defects, the legislature omitted from the present act all mention of reconciliation conferences and provided for immediate commencement of the suit by the filing of a *praecipe* for summons, with the consequent prompt obtaining of jurisdiction of the subject matter and the parties.

In holding the 1953 act invalid we pointed out that it differed from so-called "cooling off period" statutes in force in other States in that the latter provided for periods of delay *subsequent* to the institution of the action for divorce or the service of process, and prior to hearing or the entry of a decree. With reference to these statutes of other jurisdictions requiring the lapse of giving periods of time after the filing of suit or service of process, we declared that "Such legislation applies uniformly to all litigants and does not involve any delay of access to the courts." People ex rel. Christiansen v. Connell, . . . 118 N.E. 2d 262, 268.

Likewise, the instant statute provides immediate access to the courts by a procedural means applicable alike to all litigants, with no delay being interposed before jurisdiction is obtained. The commencement of a suit by the filing of a *praecipe* for summons, a practice familiar to most Illinois lawyers, was in effect in this State for over a hundred years preceding the enactment of the Civil Practice Act of 1933 . . . and still prevails in the municipal court of Chicago . . . and in municipal courts organized under the general Municipal Court Act. . . .

Therefore, the statute in question does not fall under the constitutional inhibition elaborated in the Christiansen case. However, it does retain a form of "cooling off period;" and while post-jurisdictional delays of this type were approved inferentially in the Christiansen case, the question warrants further consideration and discussion.

The parties agree there was no right of divorce in the common law, and the legislature could abolish the statutory remedy altogether. Moreover, "an action for divorce involves interests other than those of the parties litigant. The State, as the sovereign, has an interest in maintaining the integrity and permanency of the marriage relation." Ollman v. Ollman, . . . 71 N.E. 2d 50, 52. . . . It follows that the legislature, as an exercise of its police power and to promote the public welfare, may adopt any reasonable rules regulating divorce that do not conflict with the Illinois and Federal constitutions.

The "60-day cooling off period" provision is designed to effectuate a legislative policy directed toward affording an opportunity for reconciliation of the parties prior to hearing and decree. This court in previous decisions has recognized the laudable purposes which are sought to be achieved by legislation of this type. . . .

* * *

The Nebraska statute, which provides for a six-month delay after service of summons and before hearing, was upheld in Garrett v. State, . . . 224 N.W. 860. The Nebraska constitution contains a provision equivalent to article II, section 19, of our constitution. In discussing the policy to be implemented the court said, . . . 224 N.W. at page 863: "[The legislation] was undoubtedly to give parties time to recover from anger, to recall affection, to remember benefits, to reflect on the well-being of offspring, and to consider from the standpoint of personal duty and responsibility. Immediate trial and preparation for trial are inherently such as to keep alive resentment and develop new animosity, hence the waiting time prescribed by the lawmaker in order that the relation in which the state is so vitally interested may not be terminated too easily and too speedily." Cf. Berghean v. Berghean, . . . 48 N.E. 2d 1001 ; . . .

The appellant's challenge is not to the statutory objective, but to the means or procedures adapted to that end. Immediate access to the courts being assured, the procedures are to be judged by the same rule of reasonableness applicable to other legislative acts establishing special limiting, regulatory and restrictive procedures. . . .

The issue of due process of law is to be determined by judging whether the particular statute is reasonable in the light of the legislative objectives. . . . So judged, we cannot say that a post-jurisdictional delay of 60 days is unreasonable. . . . The legislature, mindful of the State's interest in maintaining the integrity and permanency of the marriage relation and taking account of the high divorce rate and its effects, cannot be said to have acted arbitrarily or unreasonably in requiring, as a means of fostering reconciliation, that a divorce complainant wait at least 60 days before making the charges a matter of public record and having a hearing thereon. "With the growth and development of the State the police power necessarily develops, within reasonable bounds, to meet the changing conditions." Clarke v. Storchak, . . . 52 N.E. 2d 229, 236.

It is, of course, not for us to say whether the particular law before us is desirable from the standpoint of legislative policy, since the wisdom of legislation is a matter committed exclusively to a coordinate branch of our government, the General Assembly. It is sufficient to show that it is not unreasonable in the light of legislative objectives and was within the province of legislative power.

Under certain conditions the 60-day waiting period may be waived, the law providing as follows: "The court in its discretion, may upon written motion supported by affidavit setting forth facts showing that immediate relief is warranted or required to protect the interests of any party or persons who might be affected by a final decree or order in the proceedings, grant leave to file or order the filing of a complaint before the expiration of the 60-day period." (Ill. Rev. Stat. 1955, chap. 40, par. 7c). The appellant contends that this provision is so vague, indefinite and uncertain as to amount to a deprivation of due process ; that it violates section 29 of article VI of the Illinois constitution, which requires that all laws relating to courts be "general, and of uniform operation ;" and that it contravenes section 22 of article IV which prohibits local or special laws in the granting of divorces.

* * *

It is true that individual judges may differ as to what state of facts necessitates waiver of the 60-day waiting requirement "to protect the interests of any party or persons who might be affected by a final decree or order in the proceedings," but this does not render the law invalid. The same is true in many cases, including that of an injunction which may be issued if it appears to the court "that the rights of the plaintiff will be unduly prejudiced." (Ill. Rev. Stat. 1955, chap. 69, par. 3.) It would manifestly be impossible for the legislature to foresee and provide explicitly for every possible exigency which might be considered sufficient to call for an immediate filing of a divorce complaint. Accordingly, the course followed by the present statute of conferring discretion upon the courts, coupled with a declaration of legislative policy, is a reasonable method of operation. In effect, the legislature has done no more than confer upon the courts the necessary discretion to regulate proceedings pending before them, similar to that exercised in a wide variety of situations.

We conclude that this authority of the court to exercise judicial discretion in determining whether the immediate filing of the complaint is warranted or necessary satisfies due process of law, and since all divorce litigants are subject to its provisions, it is not special legislation violative of section 22 of article IV or section 29 of article VI of the Illinois constitution.

* * *

The judgment of the circuit court of Cook County is affirmed.

NOTES

NOTE 1.

WEBER v. WEBER
257 Wisc. 613, 44 N.W. 2d 571 (1950)

FAIRCHILD, JUSTICE.

An action for an absolute divorce differs decidedly from one in which a party is seeking a partial suspension of the marriage relation and providing for a legal separation, that is, a divorce from bed and board. The reason for a judgment providing for the latter arrangement is that it leaves hope for a reconciliation. . . .

The action brought by the wife in which judgment was entered on the 8th day of March 1948 was for divorce from bed and board. The judgment entered was not an interlocutory judgment. This legal separation which is provided for in the judgment has not been disturbed by any subsequent conduct on the part of either party. There has been evidently a change of mind, the appellant here now desiring absolute divorce. Because the judgment entered in her first action and on her particular complaint is a final judgment passing upon the very facts which are now presented as a new cause of action, her complaint must be dismissed as decided by the trial court.

* * *

Under section 247.07(7), Wis. Stats. 1947,

"A divorce from the bond of matrimony may be adjudged * * * :

* * *

"(7) Whenever the husband and wife shall have voluntarily lived entirely separate for the space of five years next preceding the commencement of the action, the same may be granted at the suit of either party. And such living apart for five years or more, pursuant to a decree of divorce from bed and board, without request during that period by either party to the other in good faith for a reconciliation and revocation of said judgment, shall not be any bar to an absolute divorce upon this ground at the suit of either party. . . . "

This provision for separation has been incorporated into our divorce law and recognizes that the marriage relation under a divorce from bed and board is merely suspended as to certain marital rights. They are not annulled. They are regulated by the terms of the decree. But property rights and interests remain undisturbed. It appears that in the case of the death of either party the survivor is the widow or widower, as the case may be, but when "such living apart for five years or more, pursuant to a decree of divorce from bed and board, without request during that period by

either party to the other in good faith for a reconciliation and revocation of said judgment, shall not be any bar to an absolute divorce upon this ground at the suit of either party * * *." Section 247.07(7), Wis. Stats.

Judgment affirmed.

GEHL, JUSTICE (dissenting).

This appeal presents a question of first impression in this state. It has been considered, however, by the courts of other jurisdictions, and . . . a majority of those courts have held that a decree for a limited divorce does not bar a subsequent action by the same plaintiff for an absolute divorce founded upon the same acts which were offered as grounds for the first decree. . . .

* * *

They persuade me . . . and therefore I must respectfully dissent. It would be presumptuous for me to attempt to elaborate upon what the courts have said with respect to the question or to attempt to improve upon the language used by them in expressing reasons for their conclusions. Therefore, I content myself with quoting their language.

A wife had obtained a decree of limited divorce on the ground of adultery and subsequently brought an action in a Scottish Court for an absolute divorce founded upon the same acts of adultery. The husband's defense was that the first decree was a bar to the second action, and the court said: "* * * the two remedies are collateral—they are directed to distinct objects and have totally different effects ; and, therefore, the circumstances of this lady (plaintiff) pursuing a remedy for the purpose of obtaining protection against being compelled to cohabit with her husband, either during a given time or an indefinite time, is quite consistent with the proceedings which she afterwards instituted to dissolve the marriage * * *."

Geils v. Geils, 1 Macqu, H.L. Cas. 255. "The practice of granting to married people a decree of separation from bed and board forever, while authorized by our statute, is an anachronism. . . . It breaks up the home, deprives the parties of the benefits of the marriage relation, yet subjects them to its restrictions. During the continuance of the operation of such a decree both the parties are married and yet separated. They may not lawfully remarry and they may not lawfully cohabit together. As a temporary expedient calculated to bring the parties together again, such a decree of separation may be useful. As a method of penalizing an erring husband, it may be justified. But as the establishment of a status to continue 'forever,' it has little to commend it as a matter of public policy . . . and the court should hesitate long to hold that such a degree once entered is immutable, unless the mandate of the law to that effect is unequivocal. We think there is no such mandate in our statute. The decree may be granted only at the suit of the wife. G.S. 1913, § 7134. It is a mere suspension of the marriage relation as to certain rights and relations. The purpose is to afford protection to the wife and to hold the marriage status, and, with it, the prospect of eventual reconciliation. The statute was not intended to abridge the law on the subject of absolute divorce nor to restrict its operation and a decree of separation is not a bar to a suit for divorce on grounds subsequently accruing". . . . Kunze v. Kunze, 153 Minn. 5, 189 N.W. 447, 448.

Nor is there any such mandate as the Minnesota Court refers to in our statutes which makes a decree for a limited divorce immutable.

The majority looks to sec. 247.07(7) as support for its conclusion, and reads out of its provisions a legislative declaration that in a situation such as we have here the first decree is a bar to the second except under the circumstances in the statute set forth, that is, that only where the separation has continued for five years pursuant to a decree for limited divorce and there has been no good faith request during that period by one of the parties to the other for a reconciliation may absolute divorce be granted. I cannot agree that the statute may be so construed.

The relief there provided adds to the grounds upon which an absolute divorce may be had, but does not provide that only upon the grounds there stated may an absolute divorce be granted following a decree a mensa et thoro.

NOTE 2.

ALLEN v. ALLEN
132 Kan. 468, 295 P. 705 (1931)

JOHNSTON, C. J.

This action was brought by J. Fred Allen to obtain a divorce from his wife, Margaret Allen. . . . The defendant appeals and assigns numerous errors and rulings on motions directed at the pleadings, the denial of a motion for a change of venue or a change of judges, adverse rulings in the admission of evidence, insufficiency of the evidence to sustain the judgment, and prejudice on the part of the judge in giving consideration to testimony obtained elsewhere than in the evidence produced in court, and some other statements, rulings, and acts which, it is claimed, established prejudice as well as the refusal of the court to grant a new trial.

* * *

After the evidence had been produced, and be-

fore the argument was commenced, the court, it appears, announced that the contending parties should come to his chambers, as he wished to meet them alone there. The affidavit of defendant presented on the motion for a new trial relating to the private interview with the plaintiff and defendant states in effect, that:

"Counsel for defendant, then addressed the court and stated in substance that he guessed he did not understand the court, that surely the court did not mean to ask the plaintiff and defendant to meet him in conference after all the proceedings and at that juncture. The court again assured Mr. Richardson that such was his wish. The judge retired to his chambers, followed by plaintiff and defendant. The defendant asked the judge if they were not to have the reporter and the judge said 'No, this is to be man to man, without reporters, lawyers, or anyone else'."

Among other things, the affiant stated in effect that the judge urged the parties to attempt a reconciliation, and, if that was not effected, to agree upon a compromise and settlement of their property interests. He discussed with them features of the evidence relating to charges made by the defendant against her husband and also indicating a weakness of plaintiff's case as a reason for a settlement and the avoidance of further litigation by way of an appeal. Affiant said that these and other matters urged upon her by the judge for a considerable time caused her great humiliation and distress.

* * *

There is a dispute as to what transpired in the private hearing in the chambers of the court, but it is evident that the court did not intend that counsel should be present or that a record of what transpired in the chambers should be made by the reporter. It would seem that the court was transformed into a sort of conciliation tribunal, and at a time when the parties were in a belligerent attitude, and had been during a trial which had lasted about a week and down to the conclusion of the evidence. There may have been a time when a reconciliation might have been desirable and practicable. It was quite manifest that the proceedings had reached a stage where concord between the parties could hardly be brought about even through the efforts of one with the prestige and power of a trial judge. The interview or hearing, although called by the judge at the trial, and to be held "without reporters, lawyers, or anyone else," cannot be regarded as a judicial hearing and the facts learned in this secret manner used in the determination of the issues of the case. The proceeding being announced in the court at the trial could not well be resisted by the defendant, and, being in a sense forced on her at that time and place, a compliance with the judge's order is easily understood. Efforts to bring about a reconciliation of matrimonial clashes is not to be condemned or discouraged, if undertaken at opportune times and by friendly intervention of one in whom both parties have confidence, and to whom they are willing to listen. Uninvited and compulsory intervention is more likely to create discord than it is to bring a cessation of strife, and it appears that the defendant at least did not welcome the non-judicial interference of the judge, taken, as it was, during the pendency of the trial.

* * *

. . . We conclude that there was cause for the complaint of defendant, and that the case should be tried again in the ordinary judicial way by a judge free from the objections which have been mentioned.

* * *

NOTE 3.

PEOPLE v. BICEK
405 Ill. 510, 91 N.E. 2d 588 (1950)

PER CURIAM.
The People of the State on the relation of Max Bernat, a resident and taxpayer of the city of Chicago and the county of Cook, filed a petition for *mandamus* in this court . . . to expunge from the public records a resolution adopted by the judges on September 19, 1949, creating a Divorce Division for the judicial circuit of Cook County. . . .

* * *

Petitioner contends that section 12 violates constitutional guaranties by authorizing the master in chancery of a Divorce Division to ascertain the possibility of effecting a reconciliation of the parties, and, where deemed feasible, invite the assistance of representatives of the religious denominations to which the parties litigant belong. The first amendment to the Federal constitution and section 3 of article II of our constitution are invoked. Violations of due-process guaranties are also charged. Section 12 admits of the construction, as petitioner urges, that a master, in his sole discretion, may invite the representatives of religious denominations to any hearing without the acquiescence of the parties. It may well be that a person seeking a divorce does not desire attempts at reconciliation. Indeed, a party may, for reasons sufficient to himself or herself, oppose such an effort. Section 12 does not require, as a prerequisite, the consent of the parties to an attempt to effect a reconciliation. There is no statutory restraint as to the number of persons who may be called in by the master in his attempt

to reconcile the parties. Reconciliation attempts could easily develop into inquisitions. In any event, during the period, which may well be an extended one, the party would be deprived of his right to a hearing upon the complaint for divorce or separate maintenance and would, necessarily, be denied due process of law, within the contemplation of constitutional safeguards.

* * *

The Domestic Relations Act of 1949 and its companion acts, Senate bills Nos. 308 and 309, are void. Accordingly, the writ of *mandamus* is awarded.

Writ awarded.

b. Implementing a Legislative Decision to Provide Conciliation Courts—The California System

[i]

CALIFORNIA SUPERIOR COURT (LOS ANGELES COUNTY)
A Personal Message to Parents (1960)

TO THOSE WITH MARRIAGE PROBLEMS:
The two minutes you take to read this may change the course of your life.

What is said here is not to criticize or blame you for having marital difficulties. These are common to many marriages. This letter suggests a solution which thousands have followed successfully. It is one that is open to you. It costs nothing. It requires only good will, some effort, and a sincere desire to do what is best for your children.

The failure of a marriage is tragic where only husband and wife are involved. It becomes a social and economic calamity where there are children. You, like most parents, love your children and we assume you are deeply concerned over their future welfare. Children are too often the forgotten third parties to a divorce action.

In the heat of anger and injured pride divorce-bound couples do not take time to look ahead to the lonely and grim future which faces them,—a future where both parents and children commence to live on the "ragged edge of nothing," because two households must be supported out of income usually barely ample to support one. . . .

Remarriage is not only difficult, but the problems a person runs away from in one marriage haunt him in the next. Other complications are added; for example, . . . [resentment, quarrels, and accusations] . . . [nagging and jealousy]. . . .

The percentage of second-marriage failures where children are involved is high. . . .

Failure is not a popular American word, yet every divorce statistic means two people have failed in life's most noble and important relationship,—failed themselves, failed each other, failed their children, failed their Creator, and failed society.

Because our experience proves that most unhappy marriages are merely sick and can be made healthy and happy again, we don't want your marriage to be just another failure.

We ask that you seek the help of the Family Relations Division Conciliation Service. . . . You are assured that you and your children will benefit from such a move whether or not a reconciliation is effective.

* * *

If the reconciliation conference fails, you will have the satisfaction at least of knowing in your heart that you tried to save your marriage—if it is successful you will be one of the most fortunate and we predict one of the most grateful individuals. . . .

* * *

We sincerely urge you to avail yourself of these conciliation services right away—and perhaps avoid becoming just another divorce statistic.

[ii]

BURKE, L. H.

The Conciliation Court of Los Angeles County*

* * *

It has been the policy of the [California] court to require an affidavit setting forth general information concerning the parties involved and their background. This affidavit includes a check list of marital difficulties. Our experience indicates that this list has greatly aided our Counselors in getting to the heart of the trouble.

In the event that temporary restraining orders are needed (for example, against disposal of money or property, removal of children, etc.), then the parties are required to state in the affidavit the facts upon which such relief is requested. These allegations are reviewed by the Court, and if they are sufficient the Court may in its discretion issue a temporary restraining order.

* * *

The hearing is conducted informally in an office by one of the Counselors. The Counselor talks to the attorneys first, if attorneys are involved and present at the hearing. Then the Counselor talks briefly to the parties together. The Counselor advises the parties of the purposes of the Conciliation Court and tells them that he is there to talk over with them the problems of their marriage in an effort to see if a reconciliation can be effected

---

* 40 CHI. BAR REC. 255 (1959).

[sic?] The fact is stressed that the Court will not force them to do anything that they do not wish to do, but that it is available to help them if they desire. They are then told that the Counselor will confer with each one separately and then with both together. Whichever one wishes to speak first remains with the Counselor. The other party is asked to go into the outer office, and while waiting is given a copy of a typical Reconciliation Agreement to read. * * * After conferring with each party, the Counselor brings both into the conference. If either, or both, refuses to give further consideration to a reconciliation, the proceedings are terminated and the attorneys, if any, are notified.

* * *

Experience has demonstrated that the terms and conditions upon which persons agree to reconcile should be reduced to writing for several reasons:

(1) Memory may be short concerning the promises that one may make to bring about a reconciliation.

(2) Having brought their troubles to the Court the parties' promises to one another should be dignified by a formal court order requiring them to comply fully with such promises under penalty of being found in contempt of court for any willful violation.

(3) Having in mind that it is only by the mutual consent of the parties that the 30-day limitation upon the duration of orders of the Conciliation Court may be extended, a Reconciliation Agreement in writing serves as the means of securing the consent of the parties that the orders of the Court shall remain in full force and effect until further order of the Court. The 1955 amendments to the law authorize Reconciliation Agreements to be made in writing and further authorize the issuance of court orders requiring compliance with them. (C.C.P. Sec. 1769.)

A copy of the form of court order requiring compliance with the Agreement is attached to the Agreement and served on the parties in the event an agreement is reached.

It became evident early in the study that any agreement arrived at between the parties should be assembled with a minimum of effort and, if possible, right at the time when the parties have come to an understanding with each other. It also appeared important that the parties should be able to take with them from the hearing a copy of their agreement and of the court order for future reference. This necessity led to the preparation of the forms of typical paragraphs covering most phases of domestic problems so that the agreements can be assembled quickly.

Judge Pfaff has inaugurated the practice of having the Counselors bring the couples which they have reconciled into his chambers so that he may congratulate them. Meeting the judge in charge of the Court is meaningful to them and adds further dignity and solemnity to the occasion.

. . . Third parties—paramours, in-laws, or other persons whose conduct may be interfering with the marriage—are named as respondents and brought into the proceedings.

Where a domestic triangle exists and the husband and wife agree that they want to forgive and forget and start over again, upon the condition that the erring spouse will not consort further with the third party, then the Court may make its order prohibiting such consorting. . . .

. . . The fact that the erring spouse is willing to back up his assurance that the affair is ended with a promise which, if violated, may land him in jail, is often sufficient to convince his spouse of his sincerity.

Our experience has demonstrated that quite often the third person, having been brought into the proceedings much against his or her will, is only too pleased to join in a consent to an order not to consort with the penitent spouse in the future. One such instance, where all three parties joined in the consent to the order, resulted in a subsequent contempt proceeding which did place the erring spouse and the third party in the county jail for contempt of court. This one occurrence had a salutary effect in making the parties think twice before they consent to a court order. It is interesting to note that bringing in the parties to a triangle for a conference with a representative of the Court often has resulted in breaking up what may have been considered by one or more of the parties to have been a "harmless" affair, and in time to save the marriage. The examination of the respective interests of all parties concerned in the broad light of day, including the rights of children, has had a beneficial result in many instances.

* * *

Approximately one month after the holding of a Conciliation Court hearing the Judge reviews the file of the case and sends a letter to parties who have reconciled. This letter is meant to accomplish several things:

(a) Extend congratulations to the reconciled couple, if for any reason the Judge was not able to do so personally, and encourage them to continue their efforts to comply with the promises which they have made to one another.

(b) Advise them that in the event that either of them should become convinced that they cannot continue to live together under the Agreement, then such person should call the Clerk of the Court and ask for a further conference. After such conference, if the party decides that he can no longer remain reconciled, then at his request or at the request of both parties the Agreement and court order will be terminated.

(c) In the event that the parties have agreed to arrange for follow-up counseling, to remind them of that fact and to urge them to comply with their agreement in this respect. If no reference was made in the Agreement to further counseling, then the Court advises the parties in the follow-up letter that should they feel that they can benefit from additional counseling, there are private family service agencies which they can contact for help. Should such need arise and should the parties desire to avail themselves of such help, it is suggested that they contact their Counselor in the Conciliation Court for help in locating such a service in the community.

(d) In some instances reconciliations are brought about merely through the filing of the petition and the notice to the parties of the hearing which is to take place. This sometimes has the salutary effect of having the parties talk out their troubles with one another, with the result that they arrive at a satisfactory solution; whereupon the hearing date is cancelled by them. The form letter which is sent out in this instance contains the suggestion that it is often helpful to talk over serious domestic troubles with a trained and neutral third party and that should such difficulties arise again the parties are free to call the Court and to arrange to restore the matter to the Court's calendar.

* * *

The question has been asked as to how we insure the revival of an action filed by a person who has consented to go back to an errant spouse if the contractual provisions in our reconciliation agreements are subsequently violated by the spouses; also whether or not we have encountered considerable resistance to the program by spouses who do not desire to risk the loss of their grounds for divorce through condonation which would be the legal effect of an unqualified and complete reconciliation. This has been a problem, and when we have encountered it we have met it by inserting in the reconciliation agreement a paragraph entitled "Trial Reconciliation" which indicates clearly that it is not the intention of the parties to condone or forgive the offences which each has committed against the other and that neither the entering into of the agreement nor the resumption of cohabitation shall be construed as a condonation or as a reconciliation of the parties. On the contrary, the parties express their intention that it is to be a trial reconciliation upon the terms and conditions expressed in the agreement. Further, that in the event that each of the parties complies with his or her obligations for the full term of the reconciliation period, then at the expiration of such term the parties agree to reach a conclusion as to whether or not they shall become reconciled in the full sense of the word and forgive and condone the offenses previously committed against one another.

*   *   *

The Judge has the over-all responsibility for all the operations of the Court. His supervision, interest, and participation in its functions must be active and direct. It is his responsibility to evaluate and interpret the work of the Court to his fellow Judges.

The Judge *does not* hold the conciliation conferences except in rare instances where, in a case previously screened by a Counselor, it is felt that the aid of the Judge might be helpful. . . . Marital counseling is now recognized as a professional field for which special college training in the social sciences and in psychology should be required. Preferably, Counselors should possess a master's degree in social work or the equivalent in years of actual training and experience.

The Judge supervises the staff of the Court. It has been found helpful for him to hold weekly conferences with the Counselors at which difficult or unusual cases are reviewed and where practices, proceedings, and policies are discussed. These conferences serve to keep him abreast of the problems of the Court and also, through the exchange of information, enable the Counselors to aid one another.

The Judge reviews Reconciliation Agreements and signs all court orders requiring compliance with the Agreements.

[iii]
CONCILIATION COURT OF LOS ANGELES COUNTY
Case of Mr. and Mrs. T*

Husband's age 45, wife's age 30; number of

* From the files of the Conciliation Court of Los Angeles County, 1961.

children 2, ages 3 and 5; married for 7 years. No divorce pending at the time husband filed a petition for conciliation.

CONFERENCE WITH WIFE

Mrs. T is an attractive woman who indicated that she had no complaints and that in her opinion the marriage was a stable one. The only source of conflict between her and her husband was the fact that he was objecting strenuously to her working as well as to her going to school. Mrs. T indicated that she has full-time employment as a typist and while working is also going to college to complete her requirements for teaching. She has always aspired to be a teacher. The children are in a qualified nursery school and in her opinion were being well taken care of while she is working during the day. She felt that if she could not follow through on her goal to be a teacher, she would be forever frustrated and resentful and that this might interfere with the relationship she had with her husband. She did not feel that she was neglecting the children even though her husband was trying to give her this impression at this time, and as she spoke it became apparent that this woman was sensitive to the needs of her children and had the capacity to very adequately fulfill the role of a wife and mother.

CONFERENCE WITH HUSBAND

Mr. T expressed a great deal of fear and anxiety about the effects of his wife's working and going to school upon the children. The Counselor helped Mr. T to realistically appraise the effects of Mrs. T's schedule on the children. The Counselor pointed out that a nursery school experience is a good one for young children and that even if women are not working, they usually want to expose their children to a nursery school experience as a preparation for elementary school and in general to help the children learn at an early age how to get along with others. The Counselor also pointed out that it is not the number of hours that a wife spends with her children but rather the things she does and the attention she gives the children, as well as love, in the time that she does spend with them which determines whether or not the children's needs are being met. Mr. T replied that he had not looked at it in this way and agreed with the Counselor.

The Counselor commented that if Mrs. T did not complete her schooling she might be left with too many frustrations to enable her to be a happy person, in which case her relationship with her husband and children might suffer. The Counselor also added that if Mrs. T did reach her goal to become a teacher and in so doing would fulfill herself as an individual, the whole family could benefit from this. The Counselor also appraised with Mr. T the type of nursery school the children were in and was able to help Mr. T accept the fact that the nursery school was a good one and that their children's needs were being met while his wife was at work. Mr. T's reaction to the Counselor's comments was that he felt better and that it was important for him to hear what had been said from a trained third party so that he could know whether he was right or wrong in the way he felt and thought. He stated that he felt like a tremendous load had been lifted from his shoulders.

CONFERENCE WITH HUSBAND AND WIFE

Mr. T. told his wife that he was better able to see her need to become a teacher and that he was now prepared to help her all the way in reaching her goal. The interview was used by the husband and wife to work out a plan which would enable Mrs. T to get her degree at the earliest possible time. Mrs. T indicated that if she returned to school full time and did not work, she could get her degree in six months. Mr. T agreed to this. The Counselor told both parties that it would take a lot of patience and understanding on both sides while Mrs. T was completing her degree inasmuch as they would not be able to spend as much time together as they ordinarily might. Mr. T indicated that he could understand this and would try to take a long range perspective.

Basically we have a couple here in which the marriage is a stable one. Had the parties not come in to the Conciliation Court, there is a strong possibility that they would not have reached an agreement, and the resentments and conflict would have become seriously aggravated. The one interview was of help to Mr. T in enabling him to see that his fears were unrealistic ones which in turn helped him to accept his wife's need to finish her schooling so that she could go into the teaching profession.

NOTES

NOTE 1.

HOLLINGSHEAD, AUGUST B., and REDLICH, FREDRICK C.

Social Class and Mental Illness*

[This] directive approach [as opposed to the psychoanalytic approach] consists of changing attitudes, opinions, and behavior of the patient by means of directive and supportive methods such as assertion, suggestion, reassurance, advice, manipulation, and even coercion. It is usually not based on analytic insight but on the therapist's

judgment and what is called clinical experience and evaluation of the patient's problems and situation. Depending on the therapist and the patient, the therapist may try to buck up the patient's low esteem, convert him to the therapist's own philosophy of life, give him a stern lecture, friendly advice, tell him to go to a resort, to take it easy or work harder, to treat his wife kindly or get a divorce. The success of any of these maneuvers, and they can be quite successful, depends on the wisdom and strength of the therapist rather than on his technical knowledge and also on the suggestibility and the ego strength of the patient. The directive approach requires, besides clinical experience, and even more urgently than technical knowledge, broad human experience and a willingness to assume authority.

NOTE 2.

BURKE, LOUIS H.

The Conciliation Court of Los Angeles County*

. . . The Court Counselors are neutral parties who do not take sides and they are trained in family counseling. Four out of five have their Masters Degrees and all have had more than ten years' experience in counseling. Since the files are sealed and communications to Counselors are privileged by law, there is everything to gain and nothing to lose in having a lawyer recommend that his clients go through the conciliation process. Even if the conciliation efforts fail, the process very often results in a better understanding between the parties with respect to their continuing obligations to their children and in a lessening of ill will and hostility.

NOTE 3.

BURKE, LOUIS H.

An Instrument of Peace: The Conciliation Court of Los Angeles†

Family counseling at the court level is work which demands a tremendous amount of patience, self-restraint, ability to listen, and natural sympathy for the problems and welfare of others. In this connection, our court has been exceedingly fortunate in the degree of devotion and ability of its staff. In my limited experience, I have found that it takes a heavy toll on the nervous system of the official who conducts such conferences all day long. On the other hand, there is little to equal the satisfaction one feels when one is successful in aiding a deserving couple to surmount misunderstandings, forgive transgressions, and go

---

* Reprinted with permission from August B. Hollingshead and Fredrick C. Redlich, *Social Class and Mental Illness*, 1958, p. 156, John Wiley & Sons, Inc.

* 40 CHI. BAR REC. 255 (1959).
† 42 A.B.A.J. 621, 691 (1956).

back together determined to look to the future with love, hope and trust. What a grand feeling it is to aid in restoring to the security of a home and to the love of both parents the bewildered and helpless children of such a home.

NOTE 4.

FOSTER, ROBERT G.
Critical Phases in Marital Counseling*

The first critical phase in dealing with any marital situation must be evaluated in terms of the motivation with which the individual or the couple comes for help.

Although there is usually ambivalence with reference to their getting a divorce or their ability to work out their marital difficulties, there may be divided feelings in which one party is anxious to get a divorce and the other is exceedingly resistant to the idea.

Even though a couple comes with considerable motivation and tries to work out whatever their marital difficulties may be, they always come with certain questions in their minds, such as: "I wonder if counseling will really help? Will they be able to talk about their difficulties? Will the counselor understand them, and especially important, will he take the part of one spouse over and against the other?"

It is important in this phase of counseling to make it clear to the couple how counseling works, what is expected of them, and particularly that it takes time and sacrifice on the part of both individuals if they are sincerely interested in trying to work out whatever differences may have arisen between them over the course of their married life, which may range anywhere from two months to twenty years or more.

This beginning phase is a particularly sensitive one in view of the fact that after one or more interviews people often feel either that it is hopeless to try to resolve their differences or now that some of their feelings are relieved they feel it is no longer necessary to continue with any kind of professional help.

The role of the counselor in this first phase is to try to imply by his accepting, non-judgmental understanding attitudes, although mostly unverbalized, that he appreciates the difficulty of expressing feelings, that they have some fears about entering into counseling, that they wonder how the counselor will react, and particularly to convey to the couple by questions, by attentiveness and by warmth and empathy that he is trying to understand each person and the problems involved in their relationships. Whether or not this couple

continues counseling depends largely upon the rapport established and the understanding that abatement of symptoms is not the whole answer to their problem.

A second phase should result in an increase in understanding between the couple and the counselor, the couple always having some question or some doubts as to whether this whole process is going to be helpful.

Some of the questions that come to the mind of the client are: "This counselor seems to be interested in what I tell him, but I wonder if he is really sincere in his interest? I am not really sure that I want to go on with counseling because this might involve my discussing things of which I would be ashamed or which would be painful to me. As a matter of fact I wonder if I should have said as much as I have said—yet I feel I ought to discuss everything related to my problems if I am going to get help! If only I could be certain that this process which is painful would help, I would feel more comfortable in continuing."

The role of the counselor in this phase is somewhat similar to Phase One but requires greater patience and skill in helping the individuals continue to ventilate their feelings and clarify their differences. The clients should come to feel safe in doing so as a result of the counselor's attitude of empathy and acceptance.

In the third phase the clients begin to show more confidence in the counselor, less resistance in talking about basic problems that bother them and an evidence of more desire to look into their own roles with reference to the conflicts and difficulties which have been confronting them. It is as if each spouse were saying to himself, "I know I have not been able to talk about some of the things that are bothering me because I was afraid to do so. In other words, I was afraid of what I would see about myself. The counselor sometimes makes me angry especially when he confronts me about certain details or amplification of something I may have mentioned. I wonder if he knows how really angry I am? There are times when I think that the counselor is very stupid and I say to myself, but not to the counselor, that I will never go back for another appointment but somehow or other I always go."

If and when this stage in counseling has been reached, the counselor feels more confident that now there is a possibility of working through to some kind of compromise or some way of life for this couple who are now able to begin to see themselves and how each has contributed to their relationship in a negative way.

The fourth and most difficult phase is coming to

---

* Unpublished Manuscript, 1963. Printed with permission of the author.

grips with the basic problems confronting the couple.

This involves the final recognition on their part that the solution to their problems depends largely upon them. They come to recognize that the role of the counselor is to help them accept this and is not to offer them ready-made solutions or prescriptions.

The spouses may be angered at the fact that the counselor does not help them more directly at times. They often have mixed feelings in that they want to arrive at the best possible decision and solution much faster than is possible. This phase should bring the couple to the point of saying to themselves, "We have talked a great deal about our problems and conflicts. We have gotten some insight into ourselves and now we would like to find out how each of us has contributed to our difficulties."

They should also reach the point of realizing that they have some strengths and that the problems which brought them to counseling sessions are only a part of their total life picture.

When projection decreases and introspection and clarification begin, they may both have some feeling of anxiety about assuming responsibility for doing something about their behavior and attitudes and feelings, but they also have a sense of strength and well being as they realize that conflicts are only part of the picture. They are now ready to explore in greater detail, if necessary, the next phase which has to do with a trial of tentative solutions.

In this fifth phase, as each spouse feels a new sense of courage in facing himself and the situations which have been confronting them, he may in many situations see the insignificance as well as the significance of the matters over which there has been conflict. If the counseling process is a successful one, the couple comes to realize that the counselor's role now is to help them clarify their thinking; to help them put their decisions into practice; to give them support with patience and understanding in the trial and error process of working out a new pattern of relationships with each other and many times with other family members and their children.

The final phase, that of termination, which I am not sure is a good term, is a critical one in that often one or •both spouses, although they have increased in strength as far as dealing with their problems is concerned, are not entirely certain that they can get along without the support of the counselor.

It is my belief that all cases should end on an open door basis, namely, that if either or both spouses should wish to come back at any time for a consultation or further counseling, they should feel free to do so.

* * *

[iv]

Excerpts from a Typical Reconciliation Agreement*

Forgetting the Past: We agree that the most important job ahead of us is the carrying out of our responsibility to raise our children in a proper home. We realize, however, that this cannot be done if we do not bury the past. We agree that we will not accuse, blame or nag each other about things which have happened in the past. Each agrees to start afresh and to do his very best to carry out the promises he makes in this agreement.

We realize that love deepens just because it has survived a crisis in which it might possibly have perished. Having survived such a crisis our marriage is stronger than before.

Division of Responsibility: We know that in maintaining a home there must be a division of responsibility between us.

The Home: Generally speaking, the care of the inside of the home, the preparation of meals, the care of the physical needs of the children and the family clothing are the responsibility, mainly, of the wife.

Support of the Family: The financial support of the family and the care of the outside of the home are the responsibility, mainly, of the husband.

Welfare of the Children: The supervision of the children is the joint responsibility of the parents in which each must support the other.

Where Wife Works Outside the Home: Where the wife works on the outside then the husband must share to a larger extent in the work of the home.

If the above or other provisions of this agreement which apply to families generally do not fit our particular needs or abilities, we agree to speak up now so that as finally written and signed by us the agreement will fit our own individual case.

We agree to the above division of responsibilities, with whatever changes we have inserted. Where the main responsibility is something that belongs to one of us, the other agrees not to interfere with it or to belittle that one's efforts, but, on the contrary, agrees to help the other in any reasonable way.

Husband's Role in the Family: As individuals, men and women have been endowed by God with an equality in dignity and potential. They do not,

---

* 30 CAL. S. B. J. 207-215 (1955).

however, have the same functions to perform in society. In marriage they are joined together to attain a common goal, and it is then that one must be able to depend on the other. Sometimes men forfeit this right of having their loved ones depend upon them by active brutality or passive weakness, and, upon the happening of either event, women refuse to accept a dependent role. In either case women are robbed of their full dignity.

It will always be true in marriage that the greatest giving will be required on the part of the wife. Through pregnancy and child-raising she loses the independence which the man continues to retain. When today we find a woman who is reluctant to face the loss of such independence, it is generally because she does not trust the man to be loving, confident and considerate, particularly at the times when she must, of necessity, depend solely upon him. Generally speaking, a good woman is happy to go through a great amount of sacrifice for her husband and family, as long as his step is firm, his love tender and his faith in her and in himself is strong.

The husband agrees to do everything in his power to merit his wife's confidence in him. The wife agrees to respect her husband and to encourage him in his efforts. . . .

A Normal Married Life: Many people who feel aggrieved at the state of their marriage lament the fact that they do not have a "normal" married life. In determining the cause of this unhappy state, these people should first ask themselves, "what do I put into the marriage?"; "does the word 'love', as I live it, require 'sacrifice' on my part?" If it does not, then it generally means that such a person gets little out of the marriage because that's exactly what he puts into it.

Falling Out of Love: When people say they are "falling out of love" they usually mean out of romantic or passionate love. Often it is just the beginning of real love. . . .

The French philosopher Jean Guitton states that the "process of love consists in the gift of oneself to another. . . ." But that there "is no real gift without a sacrifice of self. . . . The loftiest act of love is therefore not in receiving, but in giving. Here, moreover, lies the difference between love and passion; the latter is nothing but love without sacrifice and consequently without gift. It is the essence of love to be reciprocal."

Work, Hobbies, Etc.: Each party should make a deliberate effort to become interested in the work, hobbies and activities which the mate enjoys. Usually, this requires some "giving and taking" on the part of each. Married people should resolve to spend at least one-half of their leisure

time together, but still allow each other some freedom.

Successful marriages are those in which husband and wife plan together, work, play and laugh together, and suffer, sacrifice and pray together.

Mutual Friends: When a man marries he must cease to be one of "the boys." His interests and responsibilities are no longer the same as theirs. Likewise, the married woman soon finds that she lives in her own little world; one entirely different than that of her single friends. . . .

Association by high-minded and essentially good people with persons of intemperate habits, of doubtful morals, or of vulgar or obscene speech can lead, little by little, to the dulling of fine sensibilities and to serious trouble.

We agree to strengthen our marriage through the making of mutual friends, new ones, if necessary, among happily married couples with responsibilities and problems akin to our own.

Fighting: Neither party shall strike, slap, molest, harass, or threaten the other in any manner.

The parties acknowledge that it takes at least two to make a fight and that when one is obviously angry, or "out of sorts," it is agreed that the other shall refrain from any action which may aggravate such condition.

Sarcastic, Belittling Remarks: _____Wife_____ admits using sarcastic, cutting and belittling remarks to spouse and agrees to make every effort to avoid doing so in the future.

Silent Treatment: Each party agrees not to give the other the "silent treatment" by refusing to engage in normal conversation with the other for extended periods of time.

Third Persons: _____Husband_____ agrees not to visit, consort with, contact or correspond with _____Nellie Roe_____

Late Hours: _____Husband_____ agrees not to maintain late and unusual hours or to stay away from home without advising the other of the necessity therefor in advance and of the place where such party may be reached in the event of emergencies.

Social Activities: _____Husband_____ agrees to take out the wife for dinner, entertainment, for a drive or outing, or for other social activities within the financial means of the famiiy at least once a week.

Nagging: "Nagging" is persistently annoying or fault finding. It is a tremendous contributor to marital discord and unhappiness.

The mere fact that the fault finding may be

done for some justifiable reason does not excuse it. A nagging wife or husband is a most difficult person to live with. As a rule, nagging accomplishes nothing constructive; if anything, it merely gives the person being nagged an excuse for a very negative attitude.

_____*Wife*_____ admits having "nagged" spouse and agrees to make every effort to avoid doing so in the future. In return, spouse agrees to listen to the suggestions of the other and to discuss matters calmly, thereby doing away with any excuse for nagging.

Mealtimes: Mealtimes should be times of great peace and calmness. They should never be the times for fault finding or the occasions for unloading upon one another the unhappy events that have transpired during the day. Bickering and quarreling between children or children and parents should not be permitted at mealtimes.

Some people with a background of religious training have found that the pausing of the family at the start of each meal for the invoking of God's blessing serves as a great deterrent to discord at mealtimes and as a reminder that with God's blessing each meal can be a time of peace and contentment.

Sometimes one or the other of the parties requires a brief pause to relax before commencement of the evening meal. In such instances the children should be fed and the mealtime for the husband and wife deferred until both are ready in order that the mealtime may be a time of leisure and contentment for both.

Control of Temper: _____*Husband*_____ has a quick temper. It has been a contributing cause of unrest in the home. If the members of the family are to assist in minimizing the effects of a difficult temper, they must first understand its nature. Generally speaking, a good temper or a bad temper is something we are born with. Like the color of our skin, hair, or eyes, or whether or not we have a talent for music, these are things beyond the control of the individual. It is not one's fault that one has no ear for music, or is color blind, or has a bad temper. These things are handicaps that one starts out with. One is not to be blamed for them.

Bad temper, therefore, is a handicap. The person having it is a handicapped person and merits the understanding and assistance of his loved ones in coping with it.

What we have said here does not excuse the person with the bad temper from doing his very best to control his temper.

The main responsibility for the control of a bad temper lies with the person himself. But others can be of great assistance by avoiding things which aggravate such persons and by withdrawing from any scenes or arguments, when it is apparent that such person has lost, or is about to lose, his temper. The parties to this agreement agree to cooperate fully to help control this problem.

Children: Children bring life to a marriage. There are no dull moments in parenthood. With children a "house" becomes a "home"; the "married couple" becomes "a family". Each parent takes on a new dignity and new responsibility. Teamwork between the parents becomes a necessity.

The coming of children must not be permitted to disturb the warm relationship between husband and wife. One must not neglect the other.

When parents hold their newly-born for the first time—they must ask themselves—Is it possible that we, alone, are responsible for this perfect little bundle of humanity? The answer is obvious to most.

They see in the child the handwork of God!

God entrusts in the parents a new life, a body and soul. The child is His child and theirs. They become God's agents in the upbringing of the child. And what an awesome responsibility it is! It is estimated that 80 per cent of what a child is, or turns out to be, is attributable directly to his parents, or to those in whom his upbringing is entrusted.

We realize that a child is the outgrowth of the love of its parents and just as his conception required their joint act so will each step in his training and development require the love, attention and self-sacrifice of each parent. We agree that neither of us can do the job alone.

Sexual Intercourse: Sexual intercourse provides a safe and healthy outlet for passion and preserves each party from temptations to infidelity, or to self-abuse. Moderation and considerateness should be observed in their sexual relations. Moderation is simply the ability to manage one's self wisely, not allowing oneself to be carried away with passion; whether for food, drink, sex, or other pleasures.

The amount of sexual activity that constitutes moderation differs with persons, just as the amount of food they require likewise differs. To show selfishness in sexual matters brings on the offender the punishment of forfeiting respect and love. Love and consideration for the other partner will operate to find the right balance.

The parties have agreed that it should not be necessary for one to urge or insist that the other shall indulge in an act of sexual intercourse; because the other does not have the right to refuse, except for serious reasons. They further agree that it would be quite selfish and unjust for one to manufacture excuses or put difficulties in the way of granting the other's request. Mere inconvenience or disinclination are not sufficient reasons for refusing. The attitude of continual unwillingness or of reluctant and uncooperative acquiescence is a common cause of marital unhappiness. On the contrary, to anticipate the other's wishes—while sparing the other the embarrassment of having to insist—is proof of a love that is thoughtful, as well as genuine.

The Importance of Lovemaking: The importance of "lovemaking" in the first stages of intercourse must not be ignored. Unfortunately, this occurs quite often between husband and wife after a few years of marriage. "Lovemaking," consisting of all those tender and gentle acts which are utilized to show affection . . . should not be rushed. The attentions given, however, must be such as to be agreeable and welcome—else they would repress desire, instead of arousing it.

"Lovemaking" as a prelude to sexual intercourse takes into account the difference in the nature of love in man and woman. In man, the physical or passion side is generally quickly and strongly aroused. In woman, it is the emotional and mental side that is most in evidence ; for her love is meaningless unless it be manifested in a profusion of loving attentions. Consequently, her passion side is slow to make its appearance, generally speaking ; nor will it become strongly enough aroused except after an abundance of appropriate lovemaking.

If a husband and wife have quarreled, the husband will often suggest or even demand an act of sexual intercourse as a part of "making-up". Many husbands feel that this is the one big way to make up. This ignores the importance of a woman's mental attitude upon her participation in sexual union. It takes time for the wife to forget and forgive and to get herself mentally in hand so that she feels kindly and lovingly disposed toward her husband. The suggestion of intercourse, until this mental attitude has been adjusted, is generally objectionable to her.

Repeated acts of intercourse which do not result in satisfaction for the wife become unpleasant. Under such conditions the evident satisfaction of the husband and his repeated requests must inevitably give the wife the impression of male selfishness. All the while, the ill-advised husband will come to blame her for not being interested in him —he will complain bitterly of her reluctance and her refusals—never realizing that he is himself responsible because of his own ineptness. . . .

In the event that any phase of intercourse is a cause of pain or discomfort to either one, the parties agree to jointly discuss the matter with a competent physician ; rather than to allow such a condition to continue until it becomes a real threat to the success of the marriage.

Personal Appearance: During the years when persons are courting one another, and generally speaking for a few years thereafter, each is very careful about his own personal appearance. However, as time goes on, husband and wife tend to take each other for granted and to assume that the love of one for the other is permanent. As a result, quite often one or the other allows his personal appearance to take a very secondary place to the other cares and responsibilities of married life.

Sometimes one or the other will give gentle hints that something should be done to rectify the situation, but these hints are usually not taken very seriously until real trouble has developed. Such things as uncleanliness, overweight, vulgarity, or carelessness in dress, can become so offensive to the other party as to lead to the breakup of the home.

The parties recognize that the passing years carry with them a definite toll, and that some things result over which the parties have no control—such as baldness, wrinkles, denture difficulties, arthritis, the physical results of all types of illnesses, etc.—and that it would be sinful for one to blame the other for such failings. However, this does not apply to many conditions which are simply the result of carelessness or of a lack of real effort to remedy.

Earnings: The parties agree to deposit all earnings in a joint bank account and to pay as many of their household and other expenses by check as possible.

Community Funds: The parties recognize that under the law irrespective of who earns the money, the husband or wife, or both, such earnings are community property and belong to the husband and wife jointly, share and share alike.

Pocket Money: Parties further agree that there is to be deducted from each weekly check the sum of . . . as "pocket money" for the husband and . . . as "pin money" for the wife. Out of these sums the parties are to bear their own expenses for the following enumerated items as well as for the general purpose implied by the terms of "pocket money" and "pin money." . . .

Charge Accounts: Neither party shall open any charge account for any purpose whatsoever. Joint charge accounts may be opened only by the written consent of both parties, and in such written consent the parties agree that they will enumerate the types of items of expense which may be charged against any such account. The parties agree that any existing charge accounts shall be utilized solely for the purposes hereinafter enumerated under the description of the particular charge account: . . .

An End to the Day's Problems: Married people should acquire the habit of ending each day by calling a definite halt (as definite as the factory whistle) on the day's work and problems. Perhaps that halt might be when they close the door of their room at night. Once this time has been reached, they must resolutely keep out everything unpleasant (for their retirement hour is no place for such things). From then until sleep overtakes them, they should gladly give to each other the comfort, encouragement and loving solace they daily need, so that with strengthened hearts they can both face cheerfully the tasks and troubles of the morrow. The daily measure of mutual interest, support and love, is just as neccesary for their happiness and welfare as their food and drink ; and given this daily portion, they will be much less likely to forget and wound each other.

Such love, between husband and wife, is so strong a force for developing all that is good in human nature, that wise couples will not suffer their mutual attachment to become casual and commonplace under the spell of monotony, or to languish with neglect, or to degenerate into mere selfish passion ; for they will realize that in this life they possess nature's most valued treasure— the loyal love of a human heart.

We promise that we will do our utmost to give

each other the daily measure of interest, support and love required for a happy marriage and for a happy home for our children.

NOTE

PFAFF, ROGER A.

The Conciliation Court of Los Angeles County*

We in the Conciliation Court know that the Husband-Wife Agreement is a practical and workable tool in ensuring the permanence of a reconciliation. Countless replies we receive, in response to the questionnaires we send out one year after the parties are reconciled, praise it and relate how the parties have read and reread it many times, and how much it has meant to them.

We term the Husband-Wife Agreement "unique," and do so deliberately. This document is more than simply expressing in writing the important relationship between two parties to a marriage. It is a blueprint for successful living.

It is like the script of a play in which the leading man and woman, by faithfully portraying their dramatic and romantic roles, can bring the story to a happy ending.

This common sense and practical document used in the conciliation process is not only psychologically sound but in the opinion of an eminent psychiatrist utilizes a technique entirely in keeping with the most advanced thinking in the psychiatric field.

* P. 8 (July 15, 1960). Reprinted with permission of the author.

c. A Court Appraises its Role in Conciliation—The New Jersey Experiment

Assume that the state seeks to implement its policy of promoting "stable" and "meaningful" family relationships not only be providing opportunities for marriage, divorce and remarriage, but also by providing opportunities for conciliation:

1. By what criteria would you, as legislator or as a member of a committee of judges, evaluate the procedure and administration of a conciliation service?

2. In light of the state's basic policy, would statistics on the frequency of reconciliation and divorce be relevant to an evaluation of a conciliation service?

3. Should a goal of a conciliation service be to help the parties discover that either divorce or reconciliation may be the most satisfactory solution?

4. What would you set forth in a *purposes* section of a conciliation statute to guide its administrators?

[i]

New Jersey Supreme Court's Committee on Reconciliation—1956*

The appointment of this committee is a mark

* Report (Feb. 14, 1956).

of the continued awareness of the Supreme Court of the problem of divorce and its eroding effect upon the institution of marriage and the unity of the family. Although it is fair to say that conditions in New Jersey are not as appalling as in many of our sister states where the practices of the supermarket have been introduced into divorce legislation, still the difference between a big cancer and a little one is a matter of degree. Eventually, unless the little one is checked or excised before it metastasizes, the end result is the same—destruction.

Our 1950 precursor made a substantial general study of divorce and custody. . . .

. . . There was universal agreement as to the need for methods of preserving apparently failing marriages but a specific *modus operandi* could not be reached. The principle that the preservation of the marriage tie represents the highest interest of our society is the spark which has moved the Court to this renewed effort.

*   *   *

Sixty years ago there were 3 divorces for every 1,000 marriages. By the end of 1946 it was said that there was one divorce for every 2.6 marriages. But a more significant feature in the search for basic causes was the statement in a popular weekly magazine that at about that time 25% of all divorced couples ended their marriage during the first two years; 50% by the end of five years. The influence of the war is reflected in those figures and, of course, there has been a decline in the incidence of divorce, but the situation is still most serious.

Professor Tappan reported that the rate of marital dissolutions in the United States was 0.3 per 1,000 population immediately after the Civil War; 1.0 per 1,000 at the beginning of World War I; in 1946 the rate was 4.5 and by 1948 it had dropped to 2.9. It was estimated that there were 450,000 divorces in the country in 1947; more than 300,000 children were affected by them. In 1953 there were 1,546,000 marriages and 390,000 divorces, involving 330,000 children.

*   *   *

The report of Mr. McNeil's subcommittee estimated that in 1950 there were 55,000 divorced persons in New Jersey, more than twice the 1940 figure. It noted also the disturbing statistic that in this state there were approximately 175,000 persons in the category designated "married—spouse absent". Some of these absences were said to have resulted from military service, institutionalization, etc., but most of them resulted from separations not fomalized by court action.

In 1950, 54% of the divorce actions in New Jersey involved minor children and 78% of those children were under 15 years of age. And the estimated number of minor children of the divorced and separated parents was 175,000, or 12% of all the children in the state. But the real tragedy of this situation is that 29% of all the delinquent children came from this group.

More than this, there is evidence that the effects of broken homes do not wear off with the passage of years. The 1951 statement of Florence Crittenden Home in Newark, New Jersey, indicated that 108 children of unwed mothers were born there during the year; 80 of the mothers came from broken homes. And, according to newspaper accounts, of the original 23 service men who announced that they preferred to remain with the Russians at the close of the Korean conflict, the great majority came from homes where the parents' marriage had failed or where one or both parents had been lost by death.

Some people say that statistics are dull but these are loaded with poignancy.

Beyond question these figures, particularly those relating to the early termination of marriage, demonstrate that enough serious thinking about marriage is not engaged in before the status is assumed. Real awareness is lacking of its duties and obligations, of the adjustments that two persons must make to each other and particularly of the fact that the state is intended to be for life. If such understanding existed and intending spouses realized the need for subordinating some individual desires and habits and traits to the common good of the union, there would be fewer signs of disintegration in those perilous early years. This has to be so, since the plain tendency to impermanence markedly lessens after the first 5 years.

*   *   *

The State has always regarded itself as an interested third party in every marriage and an interested third party in every divorce action. It has been declared many times by the courts that this vital connection of the State requires that every defense to an action for dissolution of the status should be made or compelled. Thus the State is in at the birth of the marriage and in at the death. Between those two terminal points no provision is made to keep it viable. This is patently inconsistent with the professed belief that family life is a vital organism in our society.

The judicial as well as the legislative and executive branches of government should concern themselves with the problem. The courts (especially now in New Jersey) with their rule making power must recognize the utility of and need for the preventive approach. Manifestly they do not have the means or the facilities, or even the authority to undertake the task in its full proportions. But they should do what they can within the ambit of their powers and because of their affinity with the subject, suggest and perhaps sponsor remedial procedures. If the courts and the lawyers remain inactive, the *laissez faire* attitude of other groups cannot be expected to change.

Intervention cannot wait until the marriage has been hopelessly wrecked. The forces of prevention must be available and put in motion, if possible, at the earliest signs of breakdown. Churches, social agencies and, to some extent, probation departments, have recognized this and endeavored to provide sympathetic guidance whenever possible.

Although much benefit has been derived from such activities, no system, no organized approach has been established. Maximum efficiency cannot be brought about that way. Some permanent organization composed of persons with specialized training must be created and so well publicized that everyone will be aware of its existence and its objectives—with a title such as Family Counselling Service. And its services should be available for both premarital and postmarital guidance.

It was the thought of the Lord Chancellor's Committee* that such an organization should be permitted and encouraged to evolve from the existing social agencies and church groups and that it should be sponsored by the state but should not be a state institution. But "grant-aid" should be given by the state so that the service would not have to depend upon voluntary contributions. The opinion seemed to be that such an independent agency would retain more of the voluntary and personal elements which are necessary factors in the confidential relationship between it and the parties involved.

The tremendous study and effort by that committee is worthy of the utmost consideration. However, the experience gained and the accomplishment of our probation departments cannot be overlooked. They speak and augur well for an agency—Family Counselling Service—established and maintained by the state; it must be an adjunct of the probation departments, in the sense of being under the jurisdiction of Chief Probation Officer (whose title might well undergo a change to remove the implications of "probation") but from the public standpoint its identity should appear separate. Moreover, as a state instituted project undoubtedly it would be put into operation more quickly and standard qualifications for personnel would be required. The agency would bear the indicia of permanency and reap the advantages of experience which would come about as the result.

In the operation of a Family Counselling Service, the most favorable conditions for effective

---

* Final Report of the Committee on Procedure in Matrimonial Causes, presented to Parliament February, 1947.

reconciliation must be recognized. They are:

(1) The prospects of reconciliation are much more favorable in the early stage of marital disharmony than in the later stage;

(2) The prospects of reconciliation are much more favorable when the parties have children than when they have none;

(3) One at least of the parties should seek help of his own free will, probably under guidance (compulsion being avoided, if possible, except in the court situations adverted to later);

(4) Each party must have absolute confidence that nothing he says will be disclosed without his permission;

(5) Reconciliation demands the help of a person of wide sympathy and understanding who is able to win the confidence of those with whom he deals.

We hold the view unanimously that, if possible, an agency should be established and maintained by the State, to be designated Family Counselling Service, for the purpose of providing for the public premarital counselling and postmarital conciliation and reconciliation services. Its creation and the giving of wide publicity to its existence and the nature of its functions, we feel will result in a tremendous advance towards the objective of protecting and preserving the institution of the family in our State.

Aside from considerations of the general utility of such a service, it may be noted that, in many instances, the first contact between the courts and warring spouses is at the municipal level and in the Domestic Relations Court. Usually involved are threats, beatings, intoxication and nonsupport. Here experience has shown that the magistrates not only seek to dispose of the immediate problem but they endeavor to reach and to discuss root causes of the difficulties.

These sporadic meetings cannot be expected to accomplish the real work of conciliation. Probation at the order of the court is of some help but psychologically the attitude of the subject spouse is frequently antagonism at the restraint. The proposed Family Counselling Service, as a state instituted agency, with its personnel skilled in marital conciliation and able to establish regular contact with the troubled mates, is bound to be more effective.

Assuming the existence of such a service, the preliminary efforts of the judge and his staff should be to persuade the husband and wife to seek its assistance (or that of the Conciliation Division of the Superior Court, hereafter discussed). But refusal should be met with an order requiring submission to the agency, particularly where minor children are involved.

There can be no doubt that the voluntary seeking of reconciliation services in the church, social agency or Family Counselling Service represents the ideal. Compulsion in so personal a matter, it has been suggested, may provoke resentment and tend to frustrate efforts to bring the parties together. But where neither spouse has sought conciliation before seeking to dissolve the marriage by court action, should it be assumed that the situation is hopeless and allow the litigation to proceed in ordinary course? Or should an attempt be made by mandate as a condition to institution of the suit?

* * *

Of course, if a court mandate for a reconciliation conference is going to receive lip service, the practice might better be abandoned. However, everyone recognizes that emotions run high in marital disputes. Frequently both parties, rigid in their anger and in the righteousness of their position, spurn the idea of the voluntary measure. But if they have no choice but to meet *vis à vis* in the presence of a sympathetic counsellor who assures them that their statements have a privilege comparable to that of the confessional, they may begin in heat with their recriminations and end in the light of tolerance and understanding, or if not in such a complete metamorphosis, at least in a willingness to try again.

The admission must be made that the possibility of success at this stage is not as favorable as when the symptoms of breakdown first appear. The choice is to give up entirely then or to make a last sincere effort. Progress is not always made on the path of least resistance.

Statistics regarding the results of mandatory reconciliation are completely inadequate. . . .

* * *

The conclusion is inescapable that sentiment is on the upsurge in many states and in England for conciliation and reconciliation procedures to save marriages and impede the flow of divorces. Agreement is almost universal that conciliation before differences crystalize into the hostility that brings people to court, is better and more effective than reconciliation attempts afterward. But when court action is imminent, such agreement does not warrant rejection of efforts at voluntary or mandatory reconciliation conferences, at least where children are to be affected, as a final gesture to preserve the marriage. And the favorable experience in California in the instances where divorce actions were actually pending, points to definite advantages to be gained from mandatory conferences before suit.

We are unanimously of the view that efforts to bring about a resumption of connubial relations, especially where minor children are involved, should not cease as one party approaches the court for divorce, or separate maintenance. Mandatory reconciliation conferences were favored in 1950; the further study and the experience gained since then fortify the conclusion that they are advisable. Some members of the bar being of the opinion that the recommendation carried an implication that they did not try to bring the parties together upon being consulted about a divorce or separation action, opposed the suggested rule. But the rule was not considered a criticism of their efforts but rather an assumption that their very best had been engaged in unsuccessfully.

NOTE

KUBIE, LAWRENCE S.

Psychoanalysis and Marriage*

Before going further, let me dispel one basic misconception: People think that the disruption rate of marriages is increasing. This is not true. In fact, quite on the contrary, it may be decreasing. According to the most accurate available statistics, from 1890 to 1940 there was a drop in the rate of disruptions from about thirty-three disruptions per one thousand marriages to thirty. In that same period, however, the cause of disruption changed. In 1890 about thirty disruptions per one thousand occurred because of death, and less than three per one thousand were caused by divorce. In 1940, marital disruptions by death had dropped from thirty to twenty-one per one thousand, whereas disruptions by divorce had risen from three to nine per one thousand. This is a drop of nine against an increase of six. Thus the rising tide of divorces has not been large enough to offset the decrease in family disruption due to the decline in the death rate. The surprising net result shows that more families were holding together in 1940 than in 1890.

The difference remains, however, that divorce today is accomplishing some of the reshuffling of marriages which only a few years ago occurred through death. Fifty years ago death was the rule during the age period between twenty and fifty. The divorce rate has increased largely because of the increased life expectancy in the middle years. Apparently, longevity has now exposed for study the fact that the human race never has been mature enough for enduring marriages, a fact which used to be obscured by early deaths.

Just as the statistics for cancer and heart dis-

* Reprinted from Eisenstein, V. W.: *Neurotic Interaction in Marriage.* New York: Basic Books, Inc. 1956, pp. 11-12. Reprinted with permission of the publisher.

ease have risen as we survive into the age period for these illnesses, so our divorce statistics are up because we live longer. This increase in divorce in the middle years accounts for some increase in divorce in the early years of marriage as an imitative phenomenon. It might be expected that young people who are brought up in an atmosphere in which divorce is accepted as a deplorable but not disreputable event, would be likely to turn to divorce more quickly than are young people who are brought up in a more rigid atmosphere. Available statistics are inadequate for the precise measurement of this tendency; but those that are available seem to indicate that divorce by unhappy example is not frequent enough to make a significant difference in the statistics.

[ii]
New Jersey Practice—1957*

§ 1010.1 *General Principles.* With the promulgation of R.R. 4:94A by the Supreme Court, New Jersey has entered into an experiment in the reconciliation of matrimonial disputes and difficulties. . . .

* * *

The basic provisions of the new procedure may be found in the following Rule:

(a) This rule shall govern any actions brought for separate maintenance or divorce, or for nullity of marriage . . . where

(1) there are unemancipated minor children of the marriage; or

(2) there are no unemancipated minor children but in the demand for relief the plaintiff [or defendant] requests that a reconciliation conference be held; . . .

* * *

§1010.2 *Complaint.* Under these Rules, the original complaint filed by the plaintiff must not specify the facts constituting the marital wrong or the ground for annulment. There may be merely a reference to the statute pertaining to the ground or the wrong. . . .

* * *

§1010.9. *Standing Masters.* Standing masters, known as reconciliation masters, are appointed by the Supreme Court to hold and conduct the reconciliation conferences. . . .

. . . Such persons need not be members of the bar but shall be trained and experienced in family and marriage counselling. They shall devote their full time to such service and while in office shall not engage in any other gainful pursuit. . . .

* * *

* 33.5 § 1010.1—§ 1011 (1957) (Pocket Supp. 1960).

§ 1010.10 *Proceedings at Conference*

* * *

(a) *Conferences.* The master shall promptly set one or more conference dates for each matter, and by a suitable form of notice or letter he shall request each of the parties to attend such a conference or conferences for the discussion of reconciliation, support and related matters.

Whenever a defendant has not been served personally within the State of New Jersey and has not voluntarily appeared in the action, the master shall (if the address is known) invite him or her to attend the conference with the assurance that he or she shall be immune from the service of process while coming to, attending and leaving the conference.

(b) *Powers of Master.* The reconciliation master, by such means as may be appropriate to the case, including the utilization of the facilities of probation offices, public or privately supported social service agencies, or of any religious group, shall seek to effectuate a voluntary reconciliation of the parties to the marriage, and to provide advice and guidance with respect to the social and personal adjustments required to avoid further marital discord. The master may procure the attendance of the parties or witnesses by the issuance and service of subpoena . . . whenever in his discretion the purposes of this rule will be served thereby.

Such conferences shall be subject to the general supervision of the appropriate judges assigned to the vicinage. In exceptional cases and for good cause such judges may, on their own motion or on request of the reconciliation master, conduct the conference. Any judge who does so shall not sit thereafter in the trial of the action or on any motion pertaining thereto.

(c) *Conferences Privileged.* Reconciliation conferences shall be entirely privileged. At the conclusion of the conference, whether terminated by reconciliation or otherwise, all papers, notes, correspondence in anywise relating to the matter (except the complaint, summons, notice of appearance or acknowledgment of service, orders, agreements, and master's abstract of proceedings) . . . shall be destroyed. Before destroying such papers, notes and correspondence, the master may record any factual data (exclusive of names, addresses or other identifying matter) for statistical and study purposes.

(d) *Agreements.* Whenever reconciliation is effected at such conference, with the consent of the parties the master may in his discretion prepare written agreements embodying any particular understanding arrived at by the parties. The written agreements with the consent of the parties may be included in orders to be executed by a judge assigned to the vicinage for the hearing of matrimonial causes; such orders may be temporary in character and may be renewed by consent.

§1010.11 *Notice of Reconciliation.* Should the conference prove successful, a notice of reconciliation is filed, whereupon the matrimonial action becomes inactive for a period of 6 months after which time it is dismissed without prejudice. The Rule reads as follows with regard to the notice of reconciliation:

> . . . An action transferred to inactive status pursuant to this rule may be reactivated by the plaintiff not less than 90 days after the filing of the notice of reconciliation, by the filing and service of an amended complaint and notice to answer . . . The action shall then proceed in the regular course prescribed for matrimonial actions. . . .

* * *

§ 1010.13 *Termination.* The reconciliation proceedings may be terminated at any time by the master or by the order of the court.

* * *

§ 1010.19 *Pendente Lite Relief.* Reconciliation proceedings do not bar the granting of pendente lite relief. . . .

* * *

The intent of this rule is that wherever possible such proceedings (except to the extent that they may be accomplished by agreement of the parties) shall await the reconciliation conference.

* * *

§ 1011. *Authority to Grant Allowance*

* * *

(a) In a matrimonial action . . . including those resulting in reconciliation . . . the court in its discretion may make an allowance [for counsel fees] to be paid by any of the parties to the action, charging, if deemed to be just, any party successful in the action . . .

[iii]
New Jersey Supreme Court's Committee on Reconciliation—1960*

[Rule 4:94A] adopted by the Supreme Court to be effective at the commencement of the court year in September, 1957 . . . established the present reconciliation program on a three year experimental basis in two of the matrimonial vicinages. . . .

* * *

The duty of the Master is to make every effort

---

* Report (April 14, 1960).

to work out a reconciliation between the parties . . . .

Recognizing that the type of marriage counselling required for . . . reconciliation conferences called for a person specially trained for and experienced in such work, rather than a person of legal training and background, the Supreme Court appointed as Masters two qualified marriage counsellors. Mr. Gerald A. Tracey was assigned as Master for Bergen, Passaic and Sussex counties, with offices in Paterson, and Dr. Charles F. Marden was appointed as Master to serve the remaining seven counties, with offices in Trenton. Each Master was furnished with a secretarial assistant.

During the period from September 1, 1957 through February 29, 1960 a total of 2293 cases were referred to the two Masters. By the latter date they had held a total of 4821 conferences, an average of 4 each working day, and had closed a total of 2075 cases. Of the cases closed 287 were terminated without any conference having been held, 1731 were restored to the trial calendar after reconciliation conferences proved fruitless, and 57 cases (2.7% of the total) were placed on an inactive status by reasons of the reconciliation of the parties. A follow-up in these 57 cases reveals that as of February 29, 1960 the parties were still living together in all but five instances.

The fact that reconciliations were effected in less than 3% of the cases handled by the Masters, while perhaps somewhat disappointing, is not at all surprising. From the very beginning everyone, including the Supreme Court and the Committee, was well aware of the fact that the number of reconciliations was apt to be very low.

In establishing the present program wholly by rule of court it was not possible to take advantage of all these favorable conditions [noted in the 1956 report] . . . since the jurisdiction of the courts is not involved until an action for divorce, nullity or separate maintenance is filed. This meant that the efforts at reconciliation would in all likelihood come too late to be effective in any but a few instances. It also meant that participation in the reconciliation proceedings must in most cases be mandatory and compulsory rather than voluntary. It meant, too, that the plaintiff in the matrimonial action would generally be quite skeptical of any overtures towards reconciliation because of a feeling, however unjustified, that he or she might thereby prejudice the very cause of action for divorce or other relief for which purpose the jurisdiction of the court was originally invoked. Ever since the present program was first suggested it has been criticized, and not without justification, as offering "too little and too late."

In the opinion of the Committee, however, the success or failure of the program as an experiment is not to be measured solely in terms of the percentage of cases resulting in reconciliations. There are other factors which must be considered in making a fair evaluation of the program.

An analysis of the first 1398 cases in which the Masters held reconciliation conferences indicated that the possibilities of reconciliation vary widely depending upon the nature of the complaint. This is well illustrated by the following table:

Nature of Complaint	Number of Cases	Number of Reconciliations	Percentage of Reconciliations
1. Annulment	10	0	0
2. Desertion	715	1	0
3. Adultery	204	8	3.8
4. Separate Maint.	137	11	8
5. Extreme Cruelty	332	29	8.7
Total all cases	1,398	49	3.5
Total 3, 4 & 5 above	673	48	7.1

Thus the record of reconciliations in separate maintenance and extreme cruelty cases is in sharp contrast to that in annulment and desertion cases where reconciliation efforts proved almost completely fruitless. In the opinion of the Masters the lack of success in the desertion cases is not attributable to the grounds for divorce *per se,* but rather to the time factor. In desertion cases the reconciliation conferences generally come three or more years after the parties have actually separated. Almost invariably they have made their adjustments to living apart and are not the least interested in making the effort to start life together all over again. In cases brought on other grounds, the fact that the parties come before the Masters at an earlier date accounts for the better reconciliation results.

The attitude of the parties toward reconciliation has also proved to be most important. In 77% of the first 1398 cases in which conferences were held, both parties initially indicated no willingness to explore the possibilities of reconciliation and out of this group only one reconciliation resulted. On the other hand, in the other 23% of the cases, where at least one party indicated a willingness to consider the possibility of reconciliation, 48 reconciliations were effected.

The creditable results, even after the institution of an action for divorce or separate maintenance, in those cases where the reconciliation efforts come reasonably early after the parties were separated and in those cases where one party still is interested in reconciliation indicate the likelihood of very substantial success for a program which would permit or require parties to avail themselves of competent counselling services at the very first sign of marital discord.

It is to be noted that the present procedures have been operative in counties of widely varying characteristics and the results obtained by the Master in serving in Bergen, Passaic and Sussex counties were considerably better than those obtained by the Master serving the seven counties in the central part of the State. Several factors might account for the difference in the reconciliation rate between the two vicinages.

(1) It might be attributable to a difference in the skill and effectiveness of the two Masters. The members of the Committee (excluding the two Masters) do not believe this to be a significant factor. They believe that both Masters are equally skilled, able and effective. Both are extremely well qualified for this type of work, both have worked diligently and conscientiously, and both have carried out their duties with a firm belief in the importance of their task and in the objectives of the program. At the end of the first year of operation a confidential questionnaire was sent out to attorneys whose clients had participated in reconciliation conferences, asking, among other things, what their and their clients' opinions were of the Masters. The response in both vicinages was overwhelmingly favorable. After two and a half years of operation a further questionnaire was sent to a sizeable sample of attorneys and parties who had been involved with the program. The attorneys reported that the large majority of their clients were favorably impressed by the manner in which the Masters conducted the conferences and this was confirmed by the responses of the litigants themselves. There was no significant difference in the questionnaire returns from the two vicinages. Thus the opinion of the members of the Committee as to the capabilities of both Masters is supported by that of the attorneys and parties who had occasion to participate in the program.

(2) The difference in results between the two vicinages might also be influenced by differences in the characteristics of the cases and parties coming to the attention of the Masters in the two areas. However, a comparison of the detailed information compiled by the Masters reveals a marked similarity between the two vicinages, except for certain differences in race and religion. There is no evidence, however, to indicate that these differences had any substantial effect upon the chances of reconciliation.

(3) There is a considerable difference in the geographical characteristics of the two areas served by the Masters, the northern vicinage being more compact and the Master there more readily accessible to the parties. The Master having the larger territory to cover experienced considerable reluctance upon the part of the litigants to return for a second conference because of the distances

and inconvenience involved. The Committee is inclined to believe that the size of the area served by a Master is of considerable significance and that a Master, to be of maximum effectiveness, should not be called upon to cover too large an area.

(4) The number of cases referred to the Master having the larger vicinage has been about 20% greater than that in the smaller vicinage. This has resulted both in some delay in the scheduling of conferences and in reducing the number of conferences that could be scheduled in any one case. The Committee is of the view that this may well have been a factor contributing to the difference in results between the two vicinages.

In addition to bringing about reconciliation in 57 cases up to February 29, 1960, the present reconciliation procedures have had several other incidental, but nonetheless important beneficial results.

(1) In a considerable number of cases the Masters report that although no progress was made toward reconciling the parties, the conferences were instrumental in bringing about a better understanding between the parties concerning the needs of their children and in resolving conflicts with respect to such matters as custody and support.

(2) The very existence of the program apparently stimulated the interest of attorneys and others in the possibilities of reconciliation. The Masters report that they have received over 200 inquiries from attorneys, clergymen and persons with marital troubles with respect to the availability of reconciliation services and that in many instances they were able to make appropriate referrals. Moreover, some of the social agencies have indicated that since the inauguration of the program they have noticed an increase in referrals from attorneys who have been able to convince their clients to assume the initiative in seeking professional help in the resolving of their marital problems. This increased awareness on the part of attorneys of the possibilities of reconciliation is further evidenced by a report from Judge William A. Hegarty, who throughout most of the period during which the program has been in effect handled the matrimonial calendar in Bergen and Passaic counties, to the effect that reconciliations brought about by attorneys in these two counties increased from 7 in the year before the reconciliation program went into effect, to an average of over 2 a month thereafter.

(3) While the data is inconclusive, . . . there is some indication that the reconciliation procedures may have resulted in a reduction in the number of divorce actions instituted, in the length of trials, and in the percentage of contested cases in the countries where such procedures were operative.

(4) The attempt on the part of the judiciary to take some concrete and positive action in an effort to alleviate the problem of the broken home has elicited a favorable reaction from the public generally. In this regard it is to be noted that whatever their views as to the merits of the present program, the overwhelming majority of attorneys questioned by the Committee were of the opinion that it is desirable to have a publicly supported conciliation service and the overwhelming majority of the parties involved in cases coming under the program were of the opinion that the courts should make some effort to reconcile parties in divorce cases. In short, the Committee is of the opinion that the reconciliation program has been good public relations for the courts.

Considering both its direct and ancillary beneficial results and taking into account the helpful information obtained as to the potential of a properly constituted reconciliation program, the Committee is unanimously of the view that this experiment in the field of reconciliation has been most worthwhile. The Committee considers that this experiment has amply demonstrated that a well designed program, organized on a permanent and continuing basis, would be a valuable asset to both the courts and the people of this State.

* * *

Appendix I

MEMORANDUM [from Charles F. Marden, Reconciliation Master]
TO: Committee on Reconciliation

* * *

[D]esertion cases are substantially a waste of time so far as reconciliation itself is concerned. Another approach to the same point can be seen in terms of the posture assumed toward reconciliation in the initial interviews. The following table relates initial reconciliation posture to the number of reconciliations.

Reconciliation Posture	% Holding	No. of Reconciliations
Both parties "No"	72	1
Plaintiff "No", Defendant "Yes"	20	3
Plaintiff "Yes", Defendant "No"	5	1
Both parties "Yes"	3	11

While no Reconciliation Master will easily take "No" without further probing, when both parties take this position (72%) with reasonable firmness, it is difficult to justify a second interview unless a serious visitation or custody conflict can be used as a handle.

The next most common situation (20%) is

where the defendant wants to reconcile but the plaintiff takes a firm "No". The typical case is the long-suffering wife who indicates a husband with some combination of the following traits: irresponsibility, selfishness, physical abusiveness, excessive drinking, philandering, whom she has left before—often several times—and returned on his promise to reform. This time she is not willing to accept previous promises again, or to wait, as I suggest until it can be seen if he will undertake intensive counselling, psychiatric, or otherwise. The other most typical case is that of the philandering wife who would go back to her husband but he feels he cannot ever trust her again. Of the 16 reconciliations, there were three instances where, despite a firm "No" from the plaintiff, the plaintiff did reconcile.

Less common (5%) were cases where the plaintiff posed as wanting reconciliation while defendant did not. In a few of the cases the plaintiff brought the complaint in the hope that proceeding legally against the spouse would actually lead to a reconciliation. One of my reconciliations fits this pattern. Also here fall the cases (referred to above) where the plaintiff still wants to reconcile the marriage but is "suing her husband for divorce as a favor."

It would, of course, be expected that there would be few cases where each spouse would indicate some willingness to consider reconciliation. Actually, there in 3% of the cases the initial interview revealed some open-mindedness by both parties. It was from this group that 11 of the 16 reconciliations were finally obtained. It is, of course, understandable that in more instances here, lack of faith in the capacity of willingness of the other party to make the adjustments one or the other wanted, caused ultimate failures to reconcile.

While I have not had time to check this in statistical terms, I feel sure that in a good three-fourths of the cases at least, the process of deterioration in the marriage antedates the filing of a complaint by a considerable time. A frequent statement is, "I have known this was coming a long time but I have not had the courage or been in a situation where I could make the break, until now." Having come to a painful conclusion after long deliberation, the party is now in no mood to "re-think and re-feel" the question.

In addition to the foregoing, there are other lesser factors operating against reconciliation in the situations after a formal complaint has been filed. Most strikingly, the legal requirements for divorce work against reconciliation. Once having filed, plaintiffs are often instructed by their attorneys to have as little to do with defendant spouses as possible so that efforts by a contrite spouse to "talk things over with his wife" are blocked. The difficulty here is not primarily with the attorney but with the law itself.

This Master has found the fear that reconciliation under the program would invalidate the complaint and the so-called "conditional condonation" part of the law might not be ignored, a serious deterrent to a trial reconciliation. I have no knowledge of whether this has been actually tested or not. I held six interviews each with one couple where the wife had spent a lot of money obtaining evidence of adultery. While there was a mutual interest in reconciliation here, I could not overcome her feeling that conditional condonation might not be honored in case she wanted to reactivate her case.

* * *

There are indications that the very existence of the reconciliation rule has been effective in curbing the incidence of divorce complaints. Judge Hegarty's data indicating the greater number of voluntary withdrawals and the Administrative Office data on the greater drop in complaints in the reconciliation areas have been supplied the committee members. To this I should like to quote a statement forwarded by the head of a family agency in my area.

> "The repercussions of the current plan have touched our Agency in only one perceptible way. We noted an increase in referrals from lawyers, usually involving clients who were initiating a divorce petition. When these clients came in, they would indicate that their lawyer had informed them that they would have to submit to counselling within the court before they could bring their divorce action into court anyway, so wouldn't they prefer going to a family agency now."

Measuring the full possible reconciliatory value by the actual number of official reconciliation agreements signed is indeed a strict measurement. Some official reconciliations were "lost" to me by the parties reconciling following initial conference, but where they did not want to sign official reconciliation forms and so voluntarily withdrew the case. This was sometimes because the parties did not want to place the case "inactive for three months", they wanted it dismissed completely.

There were only 18 childless cases referred at request of either party in the first 750 cases closed with conference. This is a disappointing number. None of these was reconciled. Still further, six of these cases were in a sense spurious, that is to say the requesting party had not really wanted a reconciliation, but apparently felt, or the attorney did, that a formal request would somehow help his case when brought to trial.

On [the] question [of permanence of reconciliation] I have taken the 13 reconciliations signed prior to September 1, 1958. None has been reactivated within the six months permissible. However, one case was filed over again after six months; went through reconciliation proceedings a second time and was then terminated. I have learned that in one other reconciled case brought on grounds of cruelty, the couple are again separated and now waiting for two years of "desertion" to elapse. The best information I have is that the remaining 11 are still living together.

* * *

Appendix II

MEMORANDUM [from Gerald A. Tracey, Reconciliation Master]

TO: Committee on Reconciliation

* * *

[T]he following recommendations are made for a continuing reconciliation program:

(a) Deletion of mandatory requirements for reconciliation efforts on all matrimonial cases wherein there are minor children;

(b) Referral of matrimonial cases where there are minor children and where either spouse (plaintiff or defendant) requests this service (referral of cases without minor children to be accepted only if time available by Master);

(c) Permitting the filing of a petition or request for this service by any spouse who considers his or her marriage to be in jeopardy—and where there are minor children involved, without the need for a formal complaint initiating a matrimonial action in court;

(d) In all such referrals on petition or request in lieu of formal complaint, granting the Master the same powers as in formal suits, particularly the power to require the presence of the other spouse and any essentially involved others (e.g. the adulterous partner in an extra-marital affair) by issuance of subpoena if necessary.

* * *

NOTES

NOTE 1.

BODENHEIMER, BRIGITTE M.

The Utah Marriage Counseling Experiment: An Account of Changes in Divorce Law and Procedure*

[T]he Chairman of the Judges Advisory Committee on Marriage Counseling Services, Judge Aldon J. Anderson, testified before the [Utah] State Legislative Council. He stated that judges

---

* 7 UTAH L. REV. 443, 465-66 (1961).

vary in their opinion . . . but that they have one area of agreement: that psychological therapy has no place in a court setting. Counselors, he said, place little stock in what he termed "directional counseling" but prefer methods which are lengthy and costly to the State. For the courts to administer a mental health program, Judge Anderson stated, does not make economic sense or philosophical sense.

The judges had come to the conclusion that there was a basic philosophical gulf between them and the counselors which could not be bridged. They believed that some married couples on the verge of divorce could benefit from being "directed" what to do, from being educated to the obligations of marriage, and from efforts "to bring out their moral strength," as Judge Anderson expressed it. This approach to counseling, the judges felt, was completely rejected by the counselors who preferred a more permissive, long-term method of counseling. It is true that most counselors saw little good in the more authoritative approach of the judges, but they now say that their methods were not as unbending or one-sided as the judges assumed; that they were quite direct at times, depending on the case; and that a different approach to court cases might, perhaps, have been worked out. Unfortunately this basic conflict did not come out into the open until the 1961 Legislature was about to convene, and it was too late then to "reconcile" the counselors and the judges.

NOTE 2.

New York Report of the Joint Legislative Committee on Matrimonial and Family Laws*

The failure to enact legislation creating the family court system is, in great part, the result of suspicion and opposition from within the legal profession. Lawyers and judges guard most jealously prerogatives, and seem to believe that social workers, psychiatrists, marriage counselors, and the like would have a dubious influence upon litigants. The disciplines with which we are here concerned, are not a part of ordinary legal training and experience. As evidence of this fact, we have obtained, through the courtesy of Professor Joseph Laufer of the University of Buffalo School of Law, a treatise by Dr. Quintin Johnstone which best sums up the attitudes in the various jurisdictions in the following manner:

"The hesitancy that legislators and judges have shown to creating family courts is due to many factors in addition to the disregard of orthodox fault concepts in the family court idea. An important factor in this hesitancy has been

---

* P. 79 (1958).

suspicion and opposition from within the legal profession. Many lawyers and judges believe that social workers, psychiatrists and marriage counselors are a dubious or even evil influence on our society and that they certainly have no proper place in the judicial system. Generally such beliefs are based on uninformed prejudices, as these other disciplines are outside the ordinary lawyer's and judge's realm of training and experience. In addition, most lawyers consider the advocate system an essential element of the judicial process and react unfavorably to proposals that will eliminate or reduce its significance. Where this is accompanied by a possible decrease in the role of lawyers in profitable areas of practice such as divorce and child custody, opposition is heightened. Another obstacle to adoption of family courts is the shortage of competent investigators, probation officers and counselors. This is largely a problem of appropriations. If local and state governments were willing to pay adequate salaries, such personnel would become available. But the prospects of this are discouraging. The lack of competent personnel is related to another major family court obstacle—cost. An adequately staffed family court staff is expensive. Demands for increased local and state government services of all kinds are great, resistance to increased local and state taxation is tremendous, and the chances of federal grants-in-aid for family courts are slight. Inflationary wage scales and pressures for better schools, roads, police protection, mental hospitals and public assistance care make it extremely difficult to finance new government services such as family courts. And if the government does increase its efforts to improve marriage stability, there are institutions other than the courts that contribute to marriage stability and are in need of added funds. It is arguable that if government resources for aiding marriage stability are limited, more will be achieved by channeling these resources into school and college instruction in marriage and the family, pre-marital counseling, and child guidance than allocating them to the courts. Still another family court obstacle is the questionable constitutionality of some family court procedures, including required submission to marriage counseling, use by the courts of investigators' reports in deciding family law cases, weakening of the advocate system, and extended discretion of judges. Appellate judges often come from that segment of the legal profession with the least experience in family law administration and the greatest suspicion of family court innovations. Lastly, an obstacle to creation of family courts is the lack of proof that family courts can be established that would be an improvement over presently prevailing methods of dealing with family law cases. Its superiority can be convincingly proven only by more intensive experimentation with the family court idea.

Family courts offer so much promise that they merit' wide adoption in the United States, at least on an experimental basis, and greater efforts should be made to overcome obstacles to their adoption. . . ."

NOTE 3.

Matrimonial Causes Bill—Australia, 1959*

Sir GARFIELD BARWICK (Parramatta-Attorney-General)—by leave—I move—

[T]he paramount endeavour of this bill, as contrasted with the existing laws of the States, is that it seeks to maintain marriage and to protect the family.

Let me sketch the provisions of the bill designed to this end. The first step to promote sound and strong marriage is the support the bill promises to marriage guidance organizations. I am very conscious—and in this connexion I have taken counsel of those who have so much more first-hand experience than I could possibly have—very conscious of the fact that many marriages go "on the rocks" and founder for want of somebody to assist the parties to overcome their difficulties, to assist the one to understand and to adjust to the other. I have been most impressed . . . by the efforts in this direction of the marriage guidance organizations. I am sure they have already in this country saved many marriages from breaking down. I think they should be supported. The Government has decided that these voluntary and independent organizations should be encouraged and subsidized. Consequently, in this bill provision is made to approve marriage guidance organizations and to subsidize them, exercising for that purpose some limited supervision of their activities. Naturally, I think, there is no further function for government in this sphere.

Let me read clause 9 of the bill, which provides——

> The Attorney-General may, from time to time, out of moneys appropriated by the Parliament . . ., grant to an approved marriage guidance organization, upon such conditions as he thinks fit, such sums by way of financial assistance as he determines.

Mr. Speaker, I do not hold with the view that this work can be done satisfactorily by people who make it no more than a means of livelihood. The work will best be done by those who, as well as being trained, have a sense of vocation and who, to a large extent, volunteer their good offices in this very skilfull and sympathetic task. Consequently, the subsidy is not intended to institutionalize these organizations, but rather is confined to giving them that financial support which

---

* Australia, H. Parl. Deb. of R. 23 (new series) 2222, 2225-27 (8 Eliz. II, 1959).

will assist them in their administration, and enable them to do their work adequately and to train those who are to perform it.

So that consultation with marriage guidance counselors can be attended by the utmost frankness and with a sense of security, the bill requires marriage guidance counselors to take an oath of secrecy, and disqualifies them from giving in any proceedings evidence of what is said in the course of their consultations. . . . In making provision for the support of the work of marriage guidance organizations I have been thinking largely, though, of course, not exclusively, of the stage in a marriage before any open breach has occurred or before a breach has widened to the point where one of the parties has commenced judicial process to put an end to the marriage.

Mr. Speaker, I am conscious that in the early days of married life, particularly amongst younger people, the two personalities which had theretofore no need to consider any one's interest or comfort but their own, must make many adjustments in accommodation each to the other in married life. I would expect that, in this period, marriage guidance organizations, if they earn acceptance can be most useful. I have felt that if, in this period, it was not easy for either party to commence judicial proceedings to end the marriage there would be a much greater prospect of a more earnest endeavour to make a success of the marriage ; and there may be added scope for the services of the marriage guidance organizations. Accordingly . . . this bill provides that, with certain exceptions, no proceedings for dissolution or judicial separation may be commenced within three years of marriage, except by leave of a court. The exceptions relate to conduct which would mostly, if not universally, preclude reconciliation. Leave to commence proceedings under three years may be given only in exceptional circumstances where to refuse would create exceptional hardship on the moving party or where the case is one of exceptional depravity on the part of the defaulting party. The bill expressly provides . . . that in considering whether or not to grant leave in these exceptional cases the court shall have regard to the interests of the children and to the possibility of a reconciliation of the parties. . . .

[T]he provisions of the bill which relate principally to the effort to maintain marriage before proceedings for dissolution are commenced . . . constitute a signal advance and the Government would hope that their use would be attended with much success. However, Mr. Speaker, it would be unrealistic not to recognize the fact that, notwithstanding these beneficial provisions and their use, there will still be many cases reaching the courts.

I know there is a considerable body of opinion which considers that the training of the lawyer is not apt to qualify him for the administration of laws relating to matrimonial causes. This is not the place to debate such a matter. Lawyers, Mr. Speaker, like members of this House, are often condemned by those who know nothing of them and have had no experience of what they do and how they do it. The bill, like the legislation of every State in Australia, leaves the administration of the law with the judges and the legal profession, and for myself, I am not afraid of the result.

Nevertheless, Mr. Speaker, I am conscious of the fact that a judge not unnaturally feels reticent about intruding into the human relationships of those who come before him. He is aware that he does not necessarily know everything about the matter before him, because, apart from the confining effects of the rules of evidence, the parties themselves so often enter into a conspiracy of silence where their innermost secrets are concerned. The Government feels that however proper this aloofness is in matters of mere legal right, the judge in a matrimonial cause must enter more nearly into the human problems which bring the parties before him. Consequently, Mr. Speaker, this bill contains provisions designed to impress upon the legal profession that, in the administration of this law with respect to matrimonial causes, they must not lose sight of the human relationships and human values with which they are dealing. . . .

[iv]

Letter from John J. Francis, Justice of the Supreme Court of New Jersey—1962*

. . . I was the chairman of the Supreme Court Committee on Reconciliation which recommended the establishment of a mandatory reconciliation conference in divorce, separate maintenance and certain annulment suits. The court installed the procedure on a trial basis for a period of three years. At the end of that time the project was abandoned because of lack of funds in the judicial budget and because we were not able to persuade the legislature to give sufficient statutory authority to enable us to do the work on a proper scale.

*   *   *

[v]

New Jersey Supreme Court's Committee on Conciliation and Reconciliation Report—1963†

The Supreme Court's continuing concern in developing a workable reconciliation program in

---

* November 21, 1962.

† February 18, 1963 (pp. 1 and 6).

New Jersey led to the formation of the Committee on Conciliation and Reconciliation on August 1, 1960.

The committee's charge was "to continue efforts for the establishment, with legislative support, of a conciliation and reconciliation service which would be available to people of the State at the first sign of marital discord, without the necessity of first instituting" a matrimonial action.

* * *

[The] committee has arrived at the following conclusions:

(1) Any approach restricted solely to marital conciliation and reconciliation represents only a partial approach to a much larger problem;

(2) Any program of family preservation must not only include marital counseling but deal with all related family problems;

(3) An integrated, broad-based service to families in trouble may properly become a part of a court setting;

(4) Our existing court structure should be organized in such fashion as to establish a single court—the Family Court—geared to deal with the problem of preserving the family;

(5) The Family Court should be a part or division of the Superior Court; and

(6) The Family Court should be established on a state-wide basis.

d. A Legislative Committee Examines the Problem of Policing Those Who Counsel in Marital Affairs.

HEARINGS BEFORE THE
JOINT LEGISLATIVE COMMITTEE ON
MATRIMONIAL AND FAMILY LAWS
OF THE STATE OF NEW YORK
August 28, 1963

[i]

Opening Statement by Senator Henry Curran, Chairman

Good morning, ladies and gentlemen. I'm sorry we got off to a late start. This is a hearing of the Joint Legislative Committee on Matrimonial and Family Law. We have convened this hearing to take testimony relative to marriage counselling in New York State. . . . This Committee has received indications that a considerable amount of harm is being done to the public in the State of New York by individuals posing as qualified to help solve marital problems. As we all know, these are very delicate problems and, in addition to the quacks that are found in this particular field, there is a serious question as to even people highly

qualified in their own speciality are competent enough to go outside their field and into the field of marriage or family counselling unless they have taken suitable training in such work. Marriage is a very sacred relationship. Any individual who presumes to hold himself up as an expert in this sensitive area of personal relationship can cause damage that might wreck a family, particularly when children are involved. The problem, therefore, is a serious one. There apparently is no university or college that we know of which gives a degree in Marriage Counselling. We do train physicians, lawyers, clergymen, social workers, psychiatrists and psychologists, and part of their training may include marriage counselling. As of this time we do not license marriage counsellors in New York State. We feel that in marriage counselling there are many emotional factors involved, and that one should be conversant with the many facets of behavior in order to properly advise our citizens in this field. The problem of defining a specific field of practice and of deciding the qualifications of those permitted to function in various areas of human relationship is a difficult one. We realize that it is hard to draft a definition of the functions of a marriage counselor, and when we talk about marriage counselling it is also difficult to segregate family relationship and individual counselling. We know that there are many physicians, attorneys, responsible clergymen, psychiatrists and psychologists and social workers doing an excellent job in such counselling. In many cases they apparently refer a person from one to another for specific help in a particular field. Many of these professions are, of course, already licensed in this State, and there have been certain recommendations made that this Committee may possibly exempt those professions which are already covered by registration or licensing programs. We do know, however, that there are many other groups which do some marriage counselling and who have backgrounds which prepare them for this. I might mention sociologists, legitimate family service groups, clergymen of recognized or legitimate religious groups, with proper training in this and other areas. In the Conciliation Courts of Los Angeles, of the State of California, I am told, they have marriage counselors who must have a master's degree in the behavioral sciences, plus at least five years' prior counselling experience. I am also informed that most of them have over ten years of such experience, and it is believed that this background is responsible for their record of reconciling 65 out of every 100 couples who solicit their service. They also state that three out of four couples are still together a year later. Today we are informed that one in every four marriages end in divorce, affecting over 3,300,000 innocent children each year. There are approximately 400,000 divorce decrees granted each year in the United States. That's more than 1,000 per day. In teen-age marriages the situation is even more tragic. One out of every two of these marriages fail. If the home and family unit are the bulwark of civilization, then widespread and contagious divorce is more dangerous than a foreign conspiracy which would undermine our free way of life. It's been said that in over 90 per cent. of all divorce cases, the divorce is neither necessary nor justified, and with proper counselling the family unit could have been saved. In addition we have the "poor man's divorce," namely, desertion. The Director of the National Desertion Bureau has stated that there are nearly 2,000,000 wives with children deserted by husbands and receiving no support, which figure undoubtedly exceeds the number of divorces granted. Nor should we overlook the disastrous by-products of divorce. It is estimated that 75 per cent. of all the young people in our juvenile courts are the product of broken homes, and two-thirds of the people in our psychiatric courts have a background of marital discord or broken homes. Over one-half of prison inmates have similar family backgrounds. It was recently revealed that 20 out of the 23 American soldiers who defected to the Chinese Communists were the product of broken homes. In many cases these divorced or deserted wives and minor children become public charges. Now, we realize that competent marriage counselling is probably the best means at our disposal to help troubled individuals and families, but we must be sure that the counselling that is given is competent. We must be careful as to who is declared qualified to counsel in such cases, and who is not. If we are to legislate in this field, we must help and not hinder the qualified person. On the other hand, we must drive out those not qualified, and get the quacks, if any are found, out of this highly sensitive and specialized field. In addition, today we expect to hear from a number of witnesses who are experts in the field of marriage counselling, as well as others who represent various departments of our State government . . . . At this time I would like to ask Mr. D'Auria to read into the record the pertinent facts of some statements that have been submitted to this Committee by people who could not appear. . . .

[ii]

Statement on Communication by Mr. Michael D'Auria, Counsel to Committee

Mr. Chairman, we have received many statements, some of which I will read for the pertinent information contained therein. . . . In answer to our investigations and communications with the New York Telephone Company legal department, we are advised . . . that they do not have any minimum standards, and that any person with any background whatsoever, without any investigation on the part of the telephone company, can be listed in the telephone directory under any listing they desire in the field of marriage counselling, marriage brokerage, etc., except for the field of psychology. . . .

[iii]

Testimony of Richard D. Rogers, Executive Director of the Family Service Association of Nassau County

BY SENATOR CURRAN

Thank you, very much. At this time I would like to call our first witness, Mr. Richard B. Rogers, Executive Director of the Family Service Association of Nassau County. Mr. Rogers, would you please come forward and take your seat right there? (Witness complies.)

* * *

A. . . . I feel I can be most helpful by providing a general picture of how social workers fit into the field of marital counselling, and some of the problems which must be considered in taking any remedial action in this area. By and large, marital counselling is done by two groups of social workers—the case worker in a family agency, be it non-sectarian or sectarian, and social workers in private practice. Marriage counselling within a family agency today is fairly well standardized. Without exception all of the case workers have master's degrees from an accredited school of social work; they are members or eligible for membership in the National Association of Social Workers, and the majority are certified by the Academy of Certified Social Workers as a result of meeting the requirements prescribed by the National Association of Social Workers. Marriage counselling constitutes a large volume of the work of the family service agency. Recent national studies have shown that the clientele coming to the family service agency is generally a reflection of the total population within the community they serve. As a result of serving a wide cross-section of the community, the upper income as well as the lower, and a preponderance of the middle-income, the problems expressed by the clientele are fairly reflective of the problems of social adjustment within the community. . . .

When couples come to a family agency for marital counselling, we recognize a number of things: (1) the presenting problem is very often not the real problem, (2) adjustment in personality problems are so interwoven a diagnostic process is essential to focusing the basic problem. We recognize that to change is often a very painful experience and requires a relationship between the client and therapist that is intensive but subject to many controls. The objectivity of the therapist requires a high degree of knowledge about himself, his own problems and procedures. The intricate helping process, which we call case work, takes in the fears, anxieties, motivations and pathology common to human behavior. There is a recognition of the conscious and unconscious factors that motivate behavior and that come into play in the counselling relationship. A family case worker must have knowledge of the potential as well as the limitations of his own discipline and training. He must have the ability to determine how and in what ways the psychiatrist and psychologist can be used to provide optimum service to the client. Within the family agency graduate training for case workers is mandatory. Case work process is utilized in determining what the problems are and the treatment program needed. On top of this is a basic supervisory level and process which serves to guide and be a resource for the case worker. In addition, psychologists are available for testing purposes and psychiatrists for consultation. Seminars are held regularly, enabling the family case worker to refine and increase the quality of service rendered. A major problem facing the typical family service agency in New York State is that of a long waiting list for service, often involving couples with marital problems. . . .

While most of us in the field feel that legal regulation is essential if the public is to be protected, agencies—and most of them do—follow the National Association of Social Workers' standards for desirable minimum qualifications for the private practice of social work with marital and other problems. They are as follows: Graduation from a school of social work accredited by the Council on Social Work Education; membership in the National Association of Social Workers; membership in the Academy of Certified Social Workers of the National Association of Social Workers; lastly, five years of acceptable full-time practice in agencies providing supervision by professionally trained social workers, of which two years were consecutively held in one agency, using the method or methods to be used in private practice. These are minimal standards, for it is felt that most case workers in agency practice need six years to develop minimum confidence and ten years for consistently skilled performance. . . . In conclusion, I would like to make two specific recommendations: . . . the sponsoring of legislation enabling the public to identify

the professionally competent social worker. . . . The second recommendation which I would make is that the family agency as a basic community counselling agency be included as a service eligible for supplementary financing through New York State mental health funds. . . .

[iv]

Testimony of Mrs. Jane Ranzoni, Research Associate at Vassar College

BY SENATOR CURRAN

* * *

At this time, we'd like to call Mrs. Jane Ranzoni, Research Associate at Vassar College. Mrs. Ranzoni. It's nice to have you here, Mrs. Ranzoni.

* * *

A. . . . I would like to see the State of New York attempt to pioneer in the certification of function, as opposed to the certification of licensing. We have spoken . . . of "title licensing," but the psychologists—and I am one of them— have title licensing in this State, and I would like to call to the Committee's attention the fact that the listings in metropolitan telephone books throughout the country, when the title of "psychologist" was prohibited for use, the listings under "psychologist" dropped remarkably. And correspondingly, the listings under "marriage counselor," under "counselor," under "hypnotherapist," under "psycho-therapist," which titles are not prohibited by law, increased correspondingly. And I think it would be terribly wasteful of the time of the legislators of the State of New York to license marriage counselors, and then find out that the quacks and the unscrupulous were now calling themselves "counselors," or then to license counselors and then find they're calling themselves "therapists." And this is the plea: In no state, to my knowledge, has any legislature tried—and it would be a very difficult job—in no legislature have they tried to determine function. It would be time-consuming. It would involve talking to members of various groups that are involved in psychological counselling— the psychiatrists, the lawyers, the clergymen, the social workers and the psychologists should all be consulted on this basis. . . .

BY MR. D'AURIA

Q. . . . Mrs. Ranzoni, you have given testimony at other times to other groups concerning this matter . . . you had one case in which I was particularly interested in California. I wonder if you would tell the Committee about that case.

A. The case of the ex-convict who set up in California as a marriage counselor. He was listed in the telephone book as a marriage counselor.

And it turned out on investigation when people complained that he was not only an ex-convict, but he had all of a seventh grade education and his fees were $50 an hour, and his treatment, which was the area in which the State was particularly concerned at that time before the licensing, was—his treatment of marital difficulties of all kinds—was to recommend extra-marital sex relationships, and particularly offering himself and his wife as "cooperates," I guess you could call them, in this particular project. And they had quite a good deal of difficulty prosecuting him for the simple reason that people under these circumstances were extremely reluctant to testify as to what had been going on in his offices.

Q. You would agree, therefore, with the statements made by the District Attorneys and others, that people have been subjected to this treatment in many cases but are very reluctant to tell anyone about it.

* * *

Q. Being aware of the present licensing statute for psychologists in New York State, do you believe that if a marriage counselling statute were enacted in this State that you would automatically exclude licensed psychologists, any person who was licensed? Would you be in favor of excluding them?

A. Yes, I would be in favor of excluding them. But if you define this in terms of function, some psychologists would qualify and some wouldn't.

Q. Then we couldn't exclude them as a body. . . .

A. Yes. We have, for example, extremely competent people in the field of experimental psychology, or learning psychology, who are marvelous in their own field, but who have had no experience whatsoever in the field of counselling. I would hate to see them, as a licensed psychologist, go into the business of family advising because they have had no training in this particular field.

Q. Then it would be possible for a licensed psychologist to give as bad advice, possibly, as this convict then? A. Well, it would be difficult to give as bad advice, very hard. . . .

Q. Well, the point is, you wouldn't necessarily say just because they're licensed psychologists that they should be allowed to practice marriage counselling, whatever the definition might be? A. Precisely.

* * *

[v]

Testimony of Milton Gershenson, Professor of Law

BY SENATOR CURRAN

Thank you very, very much, Mrs. Ranzoni. We appreciate your coming here. Our next witness is Professor Milton Gershenson, Professor of Law at Brooklyn School of Law.

BY PROFESSOR GERSHENSON

. . . Having been in the field of family law for over 25 years, I'd like to make a few observations on the legalistics of any regulation of family counselling. First of all, let us see what the evil is. Probably the primary evil deals with the metropolitan area and the practitioner who seeks profit. The hard core of any regulation would have to be draped around those who engage in the vocation of marriage counselling for a profit. That immediately brings us into the exemptions. Certain categories traditionally are turned to by those in need for help. Perhaps the most prominent would be the clergyman, followed secondly by the family doctor, and then third, possibly, by the family lawyer. To rule these three groups out and require that they obtain licenses would be a futility. I doubt whether the average lawyer would be interested in qualifying. The same for the average doctor. But for any legislation to be meaningful, it must be workable. There is nothing more stultifying than a statute which expresses lofty ideals and accomplishes nothing. Perhaps the most feasible way of handling the three traditional groups—the clergyman, the doctor, the lawyer—would be to do something similar to what happens now in New York for lawyers who do real estate brokerage—to talk of a more mundane activity. A lawyer may handle a real estate transaction and collect a brokerage fee if it is incidental to his lawyer's activity. However, if he engages separately in the vocation of real estate brokerage, he must obtain a license. Therefore, it would seem to be that any legislation with reference to these three traditional groups ought to be along the lines that incidental counselling done by clergymen, doctors, lawyers, may be done without licensing, but that if they engage in the vocation of marriage counselling for profit, the two factors being full-time activity plus profit, then they must qualify and obtain a license. With reference to the scope of a statute, it is obvious that title protection is meaningless. . . . I admit that functional licensing is difficult. It will be difficult to define, and will involve the interplay of the many disciplines that come into the marriage counselling field. But I think that we must face up to it and perhaps over a period of years, if necessary, evolve a workable standard. That has been the progress of the law . . . —as loopholes develop, plug them up. . . . Further in scope I would be reluctant to stop with the word "marriage." I would include the marriage counselor, the family counselor, the child counselor. Certainly the three primary units that we are concerned with are just semantics and ought to be all-embracing. . . . There is presently in the law, sponsored by this Committee some years ago, authority for the Appellate Divisions within the State of New York to set up conciliation procedures within the matrimonial parts of the court. However, there has been little implementation of this. To my knowledge, it has been implemented only in New York County. There are two ladies who are engaged by the court to assist in what is called a "Family Counselling Service," a Mrs. Golumb and a Miss Petlicka. I am informed that they are not drawn on too heavily, that they are used primarily in custody disputes where family discord has already reached the court, and the judge is concerned with the social factors in making a proper custody disposition of the minors of the broken marriage. It would seem to me that this Committee should return to the conciliation field and perhaps look more closely into the California system where, prior to filing for a divorce, there is compulsory conciliation, including a rather successful idea under which if one spouse requests the other to return there is a mandatory minimum period of thirty day reconciliation prior to any legal proceedings. Certainly we ought to attack the problem of the broken family from its many aspects, and not confine ourselves solely to the regulation of marriage counselling. . . .

BY SENATOR CURRAN

Q. Could you give me a legal definition of marriage counselor? A. I examined with care the minutes of the public hearing in California, and whenever any of the so-called experts was asked this question he made the reply which I am about to make, which is, I would like more time to think about that.

BY MR. D'AURIA

Q. Professor Gershenson, I have here before me the wording of an ordinance of the City of San Diego which was at one time the only law or ordinance in this entire country on marriage counselling. And they define it as a person conducting or carrying on a business, occupation or profession of psychologist or other, who counsels people with mental, emotional or marital problems. Does that seem like a good definition to you? A. Well, I think they've gone to the other extreme by trying to define it as inclusive of most anything.

Q. You think it would be very difficult to make a definition of a counsellor? A. I do not think so. I think it requires application and participation of the several disciplines involved, but there are very few things in this life that we can't get across to one another by the written word. And then, of course, the amendment practice is always open to the Legislature.

* * *

BY SENATOR CURRAN

I think you might be interested in what Senator Rosenblatt just said to me. He said his barber gives more counselling on more matters than any one person he knows. Are there any more questions?

BY MR. D'AURIA

Q. Professor, are you familiar with the statute itself, as it was enacted in California? A. Yes, I have recently got a copy of the California statute which became law on July 19th of this year. There is a weak effort in that statute to control function. I say "weak" because they fail to define the function. But they did say anyone who holds himself out as marriage, family or child counselor, who performs or offers to perform or holds himself out as able to perform such service must be licensed or be subject to criminal prosecution. Notice, then, that there is some functional language in there—if he does marriage counselling. It is not strictly a title statute which would say, "You cannot use the word marriage counselor unless you're licensed." But they fail to define it.

Q. Professor, would you care, in your capacity, to make any recommendation to the Committee as to whether or not a separate agency would have to police this, or an existing department of the State of New York would police it? A. I think the manifold activities of the State Department of Education are thoroughly available for taking on the licensing problem. I believe they already license the psychologist, psychiatrist, doctors, lawyers, what-have-you.

* * *

[vi]

Testimony of Jeremiah B. McKenna, Assistant District Attorney of the City of New York

BY SENATOR CURRAN

. . . I would like to call as our first witness this afternoon Mr. Jeremiah B. McKenna, the Assistant District Attorney of the City of New York. Mr. McKenna.

* * *

A. . . . I am . . . assigned to the Rackets Bureau of the District Attorney's Office. On August 14th of this year your Committee inquired of the District Attorney, Frank Hogan, whether his office had any information in the form of complaints addressed to the District Attorney, or case histories which would assist your Committee in measuring the magnitude of the problem it is presently investigating, that of marriage counselling. Mr. Hogan, in turn, directed me to relate to you the subject under investigation conducted by our office in the years 1959 to 1961. By way of a precedent I might repeat a paragraph contained in your letter to our office, and I quote: "Information received by this Committee indicates that many unqualified and unscrupulous persons are operating in this field, and their activities have frequently resulted in great mental anguish to those seeking assistance, and in many cases have caused the breaking up of family units." This is almost an understatement when measured against the activities of the group that was the subject of our investigation. I might also add that, as an Assistant District Attorney, we are accustomed to prosecuting lawbreakers with visible and tangible injuries to the victims. We can introduce medical testimony in a trial as to the nature and seriousness of a wound or trauma. However, in the area that you are investigating, the wound inflicted by the unscrupulous and incompetent practitioner upon the unsuspecting client-victim is invisible and almost beyond objective description, but no less serious and traumatic. And like the physical injury which heals and may deface, the psychological injury remains even worse and can be far more dangerous to the total well-being of the victim, as you will see from the case I am about to relate.

In early 1959 a young married couple came to our office to make a complaint. I was the assistant assigned to interview them and record the complaint. The husband was highly intelligent and the wife was intelligent as well as very attractive. They related how they had been having trouble with their marriage and they were recommended by a friend to go to the group. I shall refer to this organization hereinafter as "the group," which, considering the subject under discussion I think is an appropriate appellation. From the group the wife expected to receive some marriage counselling. In a short time the wife was instructed to bring her husband in for therapy and counselling as well. At this point I had a little difficulty in describing the nature of the treatment that was going on. The group referred to themselves as psycho-therapists, which I later discovered was deliberately designed to avoid the licensing law that had just recently been passed in the field of psychology. . . . The diagnosis made of their marital problem was that the husband was a latent homosexual, unsatisfied in sexual relations with his wife. She, in turn, was sexually inhibited and unable to fully satisfy her husband. The rec-

ommended therapy for the wife was passionate kissing and petting between her therapist-counselor and herself, designed, of course, to reduce her inhibitions. Also recommended were sexual relations outside the marriage which were intended to deepen her sexual experience, which experience would then, in turn, be brought to the marriage bed. Of course, the partners in it all were the other therapists in the group as well as her own therapist or the clients of the group which had similar problems. Of course, they would all solve their problems together. For example, she was informed that she needed sexual experience and that a fellow who had problems relating to women was available, and if these two could get together and have sexual relations he, of course, would solve his problems and she would solve hers. As for any moral objections by this young lady, and she had several, she was instructed to forget her childish notions of morality. Her therapist would tell her what was right or wrong. The only standard was what was good for her. From the very first it became apparent, as I interviewed other patients, that this was a consciously designed attempt to break down the entire moral code of their patients. Morality was thrown out of the window; the group was now the arbiter of morality. The married couple came to their senses one night in the course of an argument where they revealed to each other the nature of their therapy. They had both been instructed not to confide in each other what was occurring at their therapy sessions. They realized they had been cruelly deceived and had been maliciously misinformed as to each other's views of what was wrong with the marriage. She was told what her husband was allegedly saying to his therapist, and he was told what his wife was allegedly saying to her therapist. They realized that the group was consciously trying to destroy their marriage. What they were being told was not the fact; it was not what they were telling their therapists; and it appeared that this was a conscious attempt by the group to destroy their marriage, to break it up. Because the wife was very attractive and could be very useful to the group in their later activities. On the day they came to our office they fortuitously met a therapist of the group who had broken with the group and wanted to expose the group for the charlatans they were. It's one of those chances that so often make an investigation. They directed him to see me, and he, in turn, gave me an inside general view of what the group was like, which, of course, this married couple could not give me from their viewpoint as patients. This young man had gone to the group as a patient seeking their help and by remaining there long enough and undergoing enough of their guidance, he was promoted to the rank of therapist and allowed to counsel new patients, and this became the pattern. Every therapist in the group had started out as a patient, and over a period of years had been brought along and, in fact, then transferred into the role of therapist and given his own patients to counsel. You can imagine the result, with all these mentally sick people who had gone there for help, undergoing therapy which was quackery and then transferring into therapists to practice their quackery upon other patients who were brought into the group. He had lately come to his senses, this young therapist, and realized the cruel fraud the group was, and was able to give us an inside picture. He informed us that the advice given this young couple was given, without exception, to all young couples having marital problems, no matter what the nature of the particular problem or its complexion. The group was bigger than first imagined. It occupied several floors of a Manhattan office building and had anywhere from ten to fifteen therapists, all of whom were former patients, and had almost 150 patients.

. . . I did consult a psychiatrist at Bellevue and a practicing psychologist on the licensing board of the State Department of Education. I asked whether this sort of advice could be considered legitimate, though unorthodox. Both said no. This was occasioned by an attorney coming to me, representing a member of the group, who was an active subject of the investigation. This attorney informed me that he could prove that these practices were orthodox. He was willing to put psychiatrists on the stand. I checked, and the reply was, no. There is a vast difference between counselling a patient who is having an extra-marital affair and recommending it, arranging it, and providing the partner and place of assignation. For example, in one instance, after a female patient had been advised to have extra-marital relations, she was asked which of the other male patients caught her eye, or she was asked to assist her therapist with a male patient who had a sexual problem and couldn't relate to women. Thus, they could solve their problems together. And another patient would supply the apartment to insure their complete privacy. . . .

I will close with the most recent complaint that came to our office. A young and quite attractive mother had come under the influence of this group. She was mentally ill and her marriage was in dissolution. In the fumbling attempts by the group to assist her she became pregnant and was aborted. She, of course, denied it. Her divorce became final. Much of her alimony was dissipated in payments to her therapist in the group, and she was reduced to living in meager circumstances.

Her mental illness grew worse under the pressure of it all. Finally last year she was committed to Manhattan State Hospital and the children returned to their father. I communicated with the authorities in the hospital and informed them of the background of the case. I suggested they could learn from her the nature of her past therapy, and she could become a classic case history of the damage done by quackery. Unfortunately, she was too severely psychotic for anything to be done. It's hard to believe that such a thing goes on in the City of New York. But consider the window dressing of the group. They had very nice offices. The head of the group had published —vanity press, but he had published, and if asked for his qualifications he could point to the books that had been written. As a matter of fact, he was on the faculty of a well-known city university, and other members of the group were being infiltrated into this same faculty. And all the patients in the group were instructed to go to this same university and take courses there in the field of psychology or education. As a matter of fact, when I subpoenaed their records I discovered that they were up for a foundation grant of almost a million dollars. Therapists in the group were well placed in strategic locations throughout the city where they would come in contact with people who were seeking legitimate counselling. For example, in vocational counselling for the Y.M.C.A. Another was a social worker with Bellevue Hospital. Some worked in various functions as counsellors in the field of speech therapy, which could be related to mental disorders. Others had connections with city hospitals. And from all these sources patients would be routed and brought into the group, and then the group would take over. I hope my case history will be of assistance to you in writing the law. It's a difficult problem. We feel that something should be done.

*   *   *

BY SENATOR CURRAN

*   *   *

Q. Do you know, or could you estimate as to how long this group was organized and how long they were operating? A. I understand it was operating since World War II.

Q. And this was in 1959, was it, that you said— this was going on from '46, approximately? A. Some of these investigations are still going on.

BY SENATOR ROSENBLATT

Q. The investigation is still going, or the practice? A. The group is still in existence.

*   *   *

BY MR. D'AURIA

Q. And there is no law that you can use to stop this? A. Three or four of our assistants have worked on this thing for two to three years trying to find a law upon which we can base prosecution. We just cannot.

Q. Even though these people, in effect, are referring people to abortionists and prostitution and everything, and you can't do anything about this? A. The abortions are out of state, unfortunately. We couldn't prosecute within this State. They were very careful how they manipulated their patients in this respect. As far as prostitution is concerned, it's moral prostitution, but not criminal prostitution. . . .

[vii]

Testimony of Dr. Jack Herman, Psychologist

BY SENATOR CURRAN

I'd like to call as our next witness . . . Dr. Herman . . . a psychologist and past president of the Nassau County Psychological Association. . . .

BY DOCTOR HERMAN

. . . The problem, as I see it, in relation to licensing, is basically a problem of definition. That is, that marriage counselling is not a specific body of definable techniques. There is no specific body of definable techniques that one can label as marriage counselling. If one reviews the psychological and psychiatric literature now, that is, scientific papers written by recognized professional people, we find that the field of marital counselling is in its infancy, but that there is just a beginning of defining just what marital counselling is and what marital counselors do. And we feel—at least, I would feel—that we are a long way from being able to define with any kind of exactitude just what marital counselling is. Because, after all, marital counselling can include anything from telling a person to take up a hobby to saying that they need prolonged psychoanalysis for six years. A bartender can give marital counselling for a profit. So that the problem becomes one of definition and of control. Marriage involves the most basic and central of human relationships in our society. It involves the intimate relation between two personalities. As a psychologist, my contention would be that if two people are unable to make a more or less satisfactory adjustment in their marriage, this is an indication of some kind of psychological disorder, or some kind of psychological disturbance, some kind of psychological distress within and between the two marital partners. Very often people come for marital counselling in order to have the other partner change. "You change her, and everything will be fine." And she says, "You change him, and everything will be fine." Most of the time it has been our experience in human relationships that it takes two to tango. But if two people are having marital difficulty, they are both contributing to it. The problem becomes one, then, in trying to help them, of change—of changing them as people ; of changing their personalities so that they can live together in some kind of mutuality and in a better frame of mind. In order to change a person, some kind of psychotherapeutic process is required. We do not change people. It has been the experience of psychologists, working in the field of psychotherapy, we do not change people by advice. You don't change a person by telling him to do such and such, or stop doing such and such. If a person is more or less mentally competent, their common sense can frequently guide them toward the right thing to do. The problem is that many people cannot use their common sense, and the question becomes of helping them to see what is obvious to someone else, but that they can't see or are unable to follow through even if they could see. The problem, then, is one of trying to help a person change—change his philosophy of life, his outlook, his feelings about other people, his feelings about himself, his feelings about his marital partner, his attitude toward them. This is a very, very complicated, long-term process which is not always successful, and which is not the answer to all kinds of problems in our society. . . . It would be my contention . . . that in order to help a couple in marital distress, one would need psychological training. This training can be gotten in the field of social work ; it can be gotten in the field of psychiatry ; and it can be gotten in the field of psychology. This does not necessarily mean that every psychologist is competent to do marital counselling, nor every psychiatrist nor every social worker. Marital counselling is some kind of sub-speciality within the mental health field which is not very well defined at this point. This is the basic problem. . . .

* * *

. . . And one of the problems is that patients, or prospective patients, frequently seek the kind of therapist that they want in the first place. There are many people who are quite intelligent enough, simply on the basis of intelligence, to seek a properly qualified person, but for reasons of their own, as part of their emotional disorder, they may very well seek an incompetent person, at some level dimly recognizing that such a person is not competent.

BY SENATOR CURRAN

Q. When I asked that question about the intelligence, it was brought out. As a psychologist, what you say, then, is that regardless of the intelligence of the person if anyone desires to go to somebody, whether they're qualified or not . . . A. They're looking for trouble.

Q. They're seeking for what they want. And this could possibly still happen, regardless of any legislation too? A. Yes. But certainly I think legislation would tend at least to minimize these things. . . .

BY SENATOR ROSENBLATT

Q. Doctor, I just want to make sure I understood some of your remarks. Did you say that you cannot define marital counselling? A. No. There in no specific definable body of techniques.

Q. . . . [W]hat do you mean by that? A. Well, for example, a marital counsellor could use persuasion, he could use inspiration. A clergyman can appeal to a person's faith. He can use autocratic means and command a patient to do something or not to do something. He can plead with a person. These are all different kinds of techniques that we use in dealing with other people.

Q. But they are considered appropriate and correct. A. They may or may not be. We don't know. At this point in the game we don't know enough to say what is good marital counselling and what isn't, except in the most grossest kinds of deviations. But there is a broad range within which one can perform as a marital counselor, do all kinds of things within a broad range. He can give advice; he cannot give advice; and he can say to a person, "I don't know the answer to your problem at the moment. We may have to wait and see. I want to learn more about you and to understand you better, your background and so on." And begin to work with them in this manner, rather than immediately giving them a prescription for solving their problem.

Q. Well, how could we frame legislation to say that you are eligible to be licensed as a marriage counselor? A. You're the legislator. This is the problem that I'm raising. Essentially I am saying, in my opinion there is definitely a need for legislative regulation and control in this field. The critical problem, however, is defining what it is that you're trying to control.

* * *

[viii]

Testimony of Sanford W. Sherman, Executive Director of Jewish Family Service

BY SENATOR CURRAN

Doctor, I don't have any further questions. I want to thank you. . . . Is Mr. Sherman here?

BY MR. SHERMAN

. . . I think I would generally agree with the major purport of his comments. I think I would put it slightly differently, and say that marriage counselling is an area, or a part of human relations that many professions counsel in relation to marriage, many non-professionals counsel in relation to marriage, so it's such a vague, ill-defined it or entity that it would be hard to see how there could be any legislation about such an amorphous it. Rather, the answer would seem to be in confining the use of that area of counselling to recognized counselling professions or professionals, whether pastoral, legal, any of the mental health professions. . . .

BY SENATOR CURRAN

Q. Doctor, you are the Executive Director of the Jewish Family Service. Now in this capacity your organization probably has people working there that do give counselling that are not psychiatrists or psychologists. Isn't this true? As with practically all family service organizations. A. We have three professional groups—psychiatrists, psychologists, social workers. We have found that each of the professional backgrounds qualifies that person, whether social work, psychiatry or psychology, qualifies that person for further orientation and training in marriage counselling. That is, you might say, post-academic training. It is inservice training within the agency. None of the professions really prepares people for marriage counselling, as such.

* * *

Q. And can you give me a little background as to the organization and what they do. . . . A. Well, the Jewish Family Service is a family counselling agency. It is a member of the Family Service Association of America which is a national kind of trade association in this field. The Jewish Family Service, along with the Community Service Society, which is a counterpart in the non-sectarian area here in the City, is the largest or the two largest family counselling agencies in the country, and probably quantitatively—I won't speak about its qualitative job for a moment—quantitatively, probably these two agencies do more marriage counselling than any other groups or agencies.

* * *

BY SENATOR ROSENBLATT

Q. On the question of marriage counselling, could you tell us how many people come to you before they get married? A. You mean in terms of a pre-marital problem?

Q. Before they get married, do any people come to you to discuss whether they should get married or not? Do they have problems in that field? A. Right, they do.

Q. So that not only married people come to you,

but those who are unmarried, who have not yet been married. A. That's right. May I make an addition—allude to something you said earlier, Mr. Curran? Increasingly, in any kind of counselling or treatments—that is, you refer to the treatment of a child problem—if it's to be an effective treatment will usually include a definable marriage counselling as part of the total approach, or assault, on the problem. So that most mental health practitioners, certainly within the recognized agencies and institutions who don't confine themselves to single patient or in-patient, do some kind of marriage counselling, of course, even of treating the behavior problem of a child.

*   *   *

Q. Is it possible to require people to take a competitive examination in order to be eligible to achieve a title or a license as a marriage counselor? A. At this point I don't think you would find agreement on what the content of that examination would be. I think we would have some ideas on what the content should be, but I think you would find other groups that would have very different ideas. I frankly don't see how that would be possible at this point since it is not a definable profession.

Q. That's what I'm trying to get clear. A. You see, a parallel would be if we said that geriatric counselling, that is, the counselling of aged persons, was a profession, which we know it is not. Or counselling adolescents. That is not a distinct profession. It has certain distinctive features, problems, technical aspects—and depending upon the profession whence someone comes, there is a different approach, a different slice of that problem that that person would be qualified to deal with.

*   *   *

BY SENATOR CURRAN

Q. Mr. Sherman, you stated once or twice in your testimony here that your group did more family counselling than marriage counselling. Would you please state to me what do you mean by family counselling as opposed to marriage counselling? A. I'd be glad to, because I think that's an important question. We, and I think certain other segments of the field, believe that marriage counselling in a family situation is often an artificially delineated segment of the troubled spot. That is, usually if there is enough marital friction or difficulty between two people as marital partners it is not confined to their roles as marriage partners, but is confined also to their roles as parents. And if you look hard enough— sometimes it's dug under the rug somewhere— you find that there's a disturbance in their relations with their children or in their children's

adjustment. Therefore, we prefer to think of it as family counselling. We prefer, even if the couple comes to us and says, "We believe that our problem lies between us two," we would not deny they may partially be right, but we suggest that we take a look at what is going on in the whole family. And we find that this approach usually—often, I would put it—uncovers the fact that there are perhaps even more alarming problems in the children's adjustment or in their relations with their children. Their children are forgotten, scapegoated, put into the closet as a skeleton, and it has been well for us to assume that the family is not so separable in compartments. That usually there is a kind of contagion. The germ sort of seems to spread in the family from marital friction to other relations within the family. Now, we even sometimes want to see "Grandma" and the in-laws, because we find that some of the strong tentacles of the problem processes of disturbance go that far.

Q. That is all counselling, no matter what way you call it, and you feel that only people qualified should be giving it, regardless of that? A. That's right.

*   *   *

BY SENATOR CURRAN

Thank you very, very much. . . .

. . . I now declare this meeting and hearing adjourned.

NOTE

SCHAFER, ROY

On the Nature of the Therapeutic Relationship*

I would like to mention that many of the issues to be touched on concern the practice of psychotherapy in general as well as psychoanalysis in particular; however, in the interest of conciseness I will restrict my remarks almost entirely to psychoanalysis.

Psychoanalysts have long recognized that the nature of their work exposes them to emotional stimulation of every variety and intensity—from the patient's irritation to his fury, from trepidation to terror, from liking to sexual passion, from moodiness to profound despair, from the maudlin to sheer tragedy, and from the excitement of discovery to the distress of sheer confusion. And so forth. Accordingly, it is not always easy for the analyst to maintain sufficient neutrality to be consistently able to help the patient understand what he is experiencing, why he is experiencing

_____

* Unpublished manuscript (1963). Printed with permission of the author, who retains all publication rights.

it and what its consequences are. He may then become defensive. It is his responsibility, however, to maintain *that* sufficient degree of neutrality and he does the best he can. It is his work ideal to do so. Without that neutrality—which should not be confused with cold aloofness and indifference—he cannot do his job well. If he gets swept up in the patient's emotional currents, he cannot maintain that balance of patience, curiosity, empathy, tolerance, perspective and mobility of thinking that he needs in order to be a help rather than a hindrance to his patient.

What helps the analyst maintain an adequate degree of neutrality and balance? I do not pretend to offer a complete answer to this question but mention only a handful of salient factors. There is his intelligence and especially his common sense about people that enable him to appreciate the complexity of human experience and to keep his bearings in the face of it. There is his capacity for sublimated interest in the emotional lives of other persons. There is his belief in the unconscious which enables him to take strong emotions as partial and often direct expressions of processes going on beneath the surface. There is his personal analysis which increases his understanding of himself and fortifies his emotional stability so that he is not vulnerable to every passing reaction to him and not itching to form transferences of his own. Then there is the factor of his leading a personal life of his own that is sufficiently satisfying that he is not dependent on his patients for direct, non-professional gratifications. Also, his experience with patients teaches him that much of the time the feelings they have about him have little objective foundation and may change drastically even from one moment to the next. His formal training is another help, for he learns from it, among other things, how to recognize, investigate and understand emotions directed at his person or behavior as analyst. Finally there are his ethical sense and his ideals which are expressed in his respecting his patient and his keeping a watchful eye on his own frailties and self-indulgent tendencies.

My piling up of these characteristics may give the effect of portraying the analyst as a paragon of mental-health virtues, but if you were to review the list you would find that this is not so. Or it may seem to present an ideal of emotional indifference and non-participation, and this too is not implied for it is well-established in psychoanalysis, as in psychotherapy generally, that the analyst's empathy is an essential ingredient of the treatment process—and there can be no empathy without subjective participation in the patient's emotional experience. Any properly accredited graduate analyst more or less approximates the description I have given, and, with the exception of the factors specific to psychoanalytic training, so does any competent practitioner of dynamic psychotherapy.

My understanding of transference and its analysis are as follows—and I am confident that in its essentials it is the prevalent understanding in Freudian psychoanalysis. In the course of analysis, the patient has thoughts and feelings about his analyst. Some of these thoughts and feelings refer to observable characteristics of the analyst and how he goes about analyzing; some refer to information or misinformation about the analyst picked up outside the analysis; and some, as the patient himself may spontaneously recognize, center around pure fantasy. With the exception of countertransference, the analyst is not primarily concerned with whether the patient's thoughts and feelings refer to something real or not, though he does, of course, take account of that difference. Primarily, he is concerned with *what* the patient selects to say and feel about him, *when* and *how* the patient brings it up, *which* expressive or defensive function his bringing it up is meant to serve, *what* the background is in the patient's present life situation and past history that would predispose him to be concerned with this matter and to be concerned with it in the way that he is, and *which* unconscious and archaic fantasy systems concerning basic drives, body functions and personal relations lie behind the immediate reaction. In other words, in the interest of helping the patient define, understand and master his own experience, the analyst uses the thoughts and feelings concerning himself as an opening into the patient's unconscious conflicts.

What is essential is that the behavior relative to the analyst has a long and individually characteristic history in the patient's previous experience with significant persons in his life, especially his experience during his early formative years and thus especially with respect to his parents. And considering the scope and power of infantile fantasy, even the child's early experiences with his parents may have striking unreal elements.

Suppose, for example, that the psychoanalyst is actually somewhat stiff in his behavior. His patients will react to this trait soon enough. But one patient may find it forbiddingly aloof, the next reassuringly controlled, and a third an indication of anxious suppression of sexual excitement. Further, even in the instance of one patient, he may move from one of these reactions to the other and back again many times in the course of the analysis. These interpersonal and intrapersonal variations are matters to be investigated. The reality of the analyst's behavior does not explain them; it simply provides an occasion for the patient's unconscious wishes and defenses to express themselves. It may be harder to analyze transference when it is hung on a peg in reality but in principle the reality peg does not preclude or contradict such analysis.

And this is the way it is in analyzing the patient's relations with persons other than the analyst. For example, a husband is, in fact, a husband but unconsciously he may also be a father, a mother, a son, or some combination of these. The patient, even, is himself, of course, but unconsciously may be, through identification his spouse or parent or long-lost love. It is with transference within reality that we deal in such instances, the degree of transference varying from one relation to the next and often from one time to the next.

PART THREE

ADMINISTERING AND REORGANIZING PARENT-CHILD RELATIONSHIPS—ON THE SELECTION OF CUSTODIANS FOR WHAT PURPOSES

A.

Legislative Decision—Custody with or without Separation

NEW YORK DOMESTIC RELATIONS LAW

Sec. 1170. *Custody and maintenance of children . . . in action for divorce or separation.* Where an action for divorce or separation is brought by either husband or wife, the court . . . must give . . . such directions as justice requires, between the parties, for the custody, care, education, and maintenance of any of the children of the marriage. . . . The court, by order, upon the application of either party to the action, or any other person or party having the care, custody and control of said child or children pursuant to said final judgment or order, after due notice to the other, . . . may annul, vary or modify such directions, or in case no such direction or directions shall have been made, amend it by inserting such direction or directions as justice requires. . . .

B.

Informing the Judge for Decision—Lesser v. Lesser, Trial I (Continued)—1956, 1957

Before:

Mr. Justice Saul S. Streit

November 28, 1956

BY THE COURT. We now come to the question of custody for the children. I would like to talk with the youngest son in Chambers.

1.

LARRY LESSER IN CHAMBERS

BY THE COURT

[after some preliminary questions, not included in the record]:

Q. What is your full name, it is Larry what? A. Larry J. Lesser. Everybody I see asks me what my name is and I tell them my name and they ask me what the "J" stands for and I tell them I don't know, because I don't know what it stands for.

Q. Do you know who I am? Do you know me? A. No, sir.

Q. Do you know where I am? A. In New York City.

Q. Do you know what this building is about? A. No, sir.

Q. You don't? A. No, sir.

Q. Whom did you come down with? A. My mother.

Q. And whom do you live with? A. I know who I live with but——

Q. Who lives home with your mother, you? A. Yes, sir.

Q. Anybody else? A. My sister, but my sister is not home, because she is at college.

Q. How about your brother? A. No, sir.

Q. You have a brother, haven't you? A. Yes sir, I have a brother.

Q. What is his name? A. Ben.

Q. Ben, you said? A. Yes, sir.

Q. When did you see him last? A. I see him a few times—not all the time—I don't know why.

Q. When is the last time you saw him? A. I have seen him a few times. I don't remember the last time I saw him. I don't remember, but I see him.

Q. Does your father live with you? A. No, sir.

Q. When did you see him last? A. I see him a few times, too, at the same time with my brother. I don't get it. The only way my brother can get to my house is with my daddy, unless he takes the bus or something.

Q. Where does your brother live? A. I forget.

Q. Where do you live? A. In Mount Vernon.

Q. Do you live in the apartment or do you have your own house? A. I have my own house.

Q. Do you have a garden in the back? A. Yes, but it's not so good now, because we don't have any flowers left.

Q. Is there a playground near by? A. No, sir, we don't have one, but my friend has one.

Q. Do you have a bicycle? A. Yes, sir.

Q. Is it a two-wheeler or a three-wheeler? A. It's a four-wheeler. You see, my friend doesn't know how to ride a two-wheeler. My daddy won't take my two wheels off. I don't know how to take them off.

Q. Do you go to school? A. Yes, sir.

Q. Where is your school? A. Down in Westhill.

Q. How far is that away from your home? A. I don't know.

Q. Do you ride to school? A. Yes, sir, in a taxi.

Q. By taxi? A. Yes, sir. You see, we have a taxi man, and his name is Jackson and he always picks up a lot of children.

Q. Is it a school bus? A. No, sir, it's in a car.

Q. What is the name of the school? A. The Rochester School.

Q. What is that? A. The Rochester School.

Q. Is that a public school or a private school? A. I don't know. I think I heard my mama say it was a private school. What did you say.

Q. I asked you, is it a public school or a private school? A. I think it's a public school. I think I heard my mommy say that in the car, when we were coming here, but I'm not sure I heard her say that.

Q. What grade are you in ? A. The first grade.

Q. And how old are you? A. I was six on April 30th.

Q. Did you have a birthday party? A. Yes, sir.

Q. Were there many children at the party? A. Not too many, but I think when I will be seven I think I will have more people, I think I will have more children than when I was going to be six.

Q. I hope so. A. But I know what my daddy is going to get me for Christmas.

Q. What's he going to get you? A. A train.

Q. When did he tell you that? A. You see, I went out with daddy and Ben once and we saw an electric train, so he said on Christmas he would get me one, which he is going to get me, I think.

Q. What time do you usually finish school? A. I really don't know. I should know, but I don't.

Q. Well, you said you only went for half a day today. A. I went a whole day, but I had to come to New York, so I didn't go all day.

Q. Who brought you down here? A. My mommy.

Q. By car? A. No, sir, by train.

Q. Oh, by train? A. Yes, sir.

Q. Did you take a taxi down here or did you take the subway? A. We took a taxi down here.

Q. Did anybody else come down with you from Mount Vernon? A. No, sir.

Q. Do you like your daddy? A. Yes, sir.

Q. Do you like your mommy? A. Yes, sir.

Q. Do you miss your brother? A. No, I don't miss my brother because he is not kind, but my sister is.

Q. Do you miss her? A. Yes. I would like her to come back. She is coming home tomorrow to play a game with mommy and Flora the maid. They're going to play a game of scrabble. She stays home two days and then she goes back again.

Q. Does she stay at your house when she comes from college? A. Yes, sir. She stays home two days and she goes back to college again and comes back for two days and she stays home at Christmas and she goes back after Christmas over again.

Q. What about Thanksgiving? A. She came home.

Q. Do you know how many months there are in a year, Larry? A. No, sir.

Q. Do you know how many days there are in a week? A. No, sir, I never count, or anything. I count numbers but I don't know how many days or anything yet like that.

Q. Or how many weeks there are in a month? A. No, sir.

Q. Did you ever go to Sunday School? A. No, sir, but I think I'll go to one. My mother is trying to let me go.

Q. To which school? A. I don't know, but she's trying to get me to go to Sunday School when I want to go.

Q. Do you feel like you want to go to a Sunday School? A. Yes, sir.

Q. But you don't know which Sunday School it is? A. No, sir, but I think I might go to one.

Q. Did your mommy tell you why you are coming down here this afternoon? A. She said I was coming down here to talk to you, I think.

Q. Talk to whom? A. (No answer.)

Q. Who am I supposed to be? A. I don't know.

Q. Well, do you know what a Judge is? A. Yes, sir, I know what a Judge is, I think.

Q. You think you know what a Judge is? A. Yes, sir.

Q. What does a Judge do? A. I don't know.

Q. Do you know why I want to talk to you? A. Do I know why? Why do you?

Q. Well, did your mother tell you why I want to talk to you? A. Oh, yes.

Q. Why? A. I forget.

Q. You forget? A. Yes, sir.

Q. Well, I want to see what kind of a fellow you are. I want to see if you are the kind of a fellow that gets along with other fellows. Do you get along with other boys pretty good? A. Yes, sir.

Q. Do you like to play with other boys? A. Yes, sir. I don't have too many friends, but I have a few of them, not too many.

Q. Do you enjoy living with your mother? A. Yes, sir. I always have a lot of fun.

Q. What about your dad? He has not been around lately, has he? A. Sometimes he comes to the house.

Q. Well, do you miss him very much? A. No, sir.

Q. No? A. No, sir.

Q. How would you feel if you moved into an apartment instead of living in a big house like you do now? A. I don't know, but I just wouldn't want to move into an apartment.

Q. You wouldn't? A. No, sir. I would like a nice big house. If I moved into an apartment I would not be able to go and play with my friends.

Q. Have you got a room of your own now? A. Yes, sir, and my mommy just got me a new toy today.

Q. What did she get you? A. A horse and an Indian, but I'm not playing with him.

Q. Let me see it. A. Sure—oh, it's in the wrong pocket—here they are. They're rubber.

Q. What is it? A. Here's a cowboy. Here's an Indian there on the horse.

Q. What do they teach you at school? A. They teach me how to read. I know a few words already. I don't know how many, but I know a few already.

Q. Do they teach you how to write? A. To write? Yes, sir.

Q. Do they teach you anything about playing games? Do they teach you how to play games? A. Yes, sir, but do you know what I did today? We have gym. So today we put our sneakers on and went down to the gym room. We were climbing ropes. There was a boy in our class, he was really climbing high, and I can't hardly get up an inch, I can't climb good.

Q. Are you a good boy, Larry? A. Yes, sir.

Q. Do you do what your mother tells you to? A. Yes, sir.

Q. Do you do what your father tells you to do?

A. Yes, sir.

Q. Do you do what everybody tells you to do? A. Not my friends, I don't. Big children and big, like big men and big ladies, and things like that, I listen to them, but if I don't know them, I can't.

Q. Well, Larry it is very nice to have you here and I am glad you came down. A. I would like to stay here.

Q. What's that? A. I'd like to stay here for a little while.

Q. I know, but you want to go back to Mount Vernon, don't you? A. Yes, but not this minute, though.

Q. Well, that's up to your mother. I will turn you back to your mother and I thank you for a very pleasant visit, for coming down here to visit me. A. All right.

Q. Good-bye, Larry (shaking hands). A. Good-bye.

2.

BENJAMIN LESSER IN CHAMBERS

BY THE COURT

[after some preliminary questions, not included in the record]:

Q. Do you know me? A. No, sir, I don't believe so.

Q. Do you know who I am? A. No, sir, I cannot say that I do.

Q. Whom did you come down with? A. My father.

Q. Did he tell you whom you were going to see? A. Oh, I mean I thought you had reference to whether I had met you before. I have heard of you.

Q. Where did you hear about me? A. Through my father. He told me your name.

Q. But you know now who I am? A. Yes, sir.

Q. Do you know who this gentleman is (indicating the reporter)? A. He is the recorder.

Q. Yes, we call him a recorder, or reporter or stenographer. A. Yes, I know.

Q. Now, do you know who this other gentleman is (indicating)? A. No, sir.

Q. That is my secretary. A. Well, I am not very versed about these things, although we are doing an occupation unit on law, and I was hoping I would get a chance to talk to someone in that particular field.

Q. Where do you live now, Benjamin? A. I don't know whether you are familiar with Mount Vernon, but it is near the Diana Yates Junior High School.

Q. How far is that from where your mother is living? A. Oh, I would say two and a half to three miles.

Q. With whom are you living? A. My father.

Q. Has he taken an apartment in Mount Vernon? A. Yes, sir.

Q. Did he once live at the Downtown Apartments, at the Downtown Hotel? A. Yes, sir.

Q. Until recently? A. No, sir, not until recently, within a year I would say or approximately more.

Q. How old are you, Benjamin? A. Fourteen, as of August.

Q. When were you fourteen? A. August 30th.

Q. And you were born where, in the Bronx? A. Yes, sir, at the Prospect Park Hospital, I believe the name was.

Q. Did you go to school in the Bronx? A. No, sir. We moved a number of times but I don't remember—the first I remember where I started my schooling was at 320 Central Park West and I attended the first four primary grades and on January 15, 1952, I moved to Mount Vernon High where I am now attending in my final year.

Q. Are you perfectly relaxed? A. Yes, sir.

Q. Are you O.K.? A. Yes, sir.

Q. Have you started at high school? A. No, sir. Technically I am in high school, the Arnold Larabee Junior High School, but I really start next year in high school.

Q. Where is that? A. In Mount Vernon.

Q. Did you go to any private school? A. No, sir. My sister did. She attended the Leonard Private School in New York.

Q. Not in Mount Vernon? A. She went to private school through I think it was the fourth or the sixth grade in New York City, at Leonard Private School. I cannot give you the address. I don't remember it.

Q. And how long have you been attending this school in Mount Vernon? A. I started in the Mount Vernon school system in the middle of my fourth term. Right now I am on my ninth.

Q. That is the final term? A. Yes, sir.

Q. Are you enjoying your school there? A. Not particularly, because the school was built for 800 and it now holds close to 1500 so you can see how cramped we are. Also, there is a certain element of people such as don't particularly appeal to me, such as pickpockets and other people.

Q. It's getting kind of rough there, is that it? A. I was hoping that if my marks were good enough my dad would send me to Horace Mann or Lincoln next year, but he seemed to think in the negative.

Q. Are you crowded there? A. Yes, sir.

Q. Do you get marked by percentages? A. No, sir, it's usually A, B, C, D, E, and F.

Q. How are your marks? A. They are pretty good.

Q. Are you among the first or the top 20 per cent? A. I imagine so. My principal told me I was among the top 2 percent in the school. I haven't gotten to figuring out the percentages. I am just going by what he said.

Q. Do you expect to major in any particular subject? A. Political science and law.

Q. Do you want to become a lawyer? A. I don't know. It seems to me that a lawyer has a great deal of responsiblity, as does the Judge, but, I don't know, because if you become a lawyer you are liable to get cases like my mother and father's.

Q. And that would be distasteful to you, is that it? A. Yes, sir.

Q. Do you engage in any sports? A. Yes, sir, football, basketball and so on.

Q. Are you good in any sports? A. Oh, I do pretty well.

Q. Do you have intra-mural sports among the classes? A. Yes, sir, in the physical ed. class, I have it twice a week.

Q. Do you participate in any of them? A. Oh, yes, sir. It is compulsory. The State requires that you attend.

Q. Are there any school teams there? A. Yes, sir. As a matter of fact, the intra-mural program consists of boys in the school and their teams. In other words, at the end of the year, the ninth grade plays the Diana Yates Junior High School team.

Q. Are you a member of any of the teams? A. Yes, sir, the basketball team.

Q. Do you like basketball? A. Not particularly.

Q. Did you ever hear about me in connection with basketball? A. No, sir, I don't believe I have.

Q. Do you know what is going on between you and your mother? A. You mean between my mother and my father.

Q. Yes. A. Oh, most definitely. I have lived with it for a good many years, so it's nothing new.

Q. Did you form some opinion about it? A. Oh, well, you mean as to who is wrong and who is right, is that what you mean?

Q. Yes. A. Oh, well, I don't know. I feel that in a sense they are both wrong.

For example, religion is not to be taken lightly. You are born, for example, as my mother was born, Jewish. After 20 years you don't switch. But then again, if you feel that some religion offers you solace and yours does not offer you anything that you consider worthwhile and you do switch to another religion as my mother has,

I feel that possibly my father should be a little more forgiving, you might say, or a little more sympathetic, so honestly I think they are both in the wrong and I feel that with some sort of compromise they should have worked this out.

Q. Have you talked it over with your father? A. Oh, I have talked it over with both of them a good many times.

Q. Without much success? A. Well, it was evident to me in the last year or so that it was futile. I mean, there was nothing to discuss there. Their viewpoints differed. My mother feels, for example, that whenever anybody gets a cold or she gets a cold, she doesn't have a cold at all. She doesn't believe in doctors. My brother is told to wear eyeglasses and my mother doesn't feel it is necessary, so these little things started friction. Then there were many common interests that my parents had a few years ago and they don't have them any more.

Q. Do you do much reading? A. Quite a bit.

Q. Do you read any particular authors? A. Yes, sir, I do.

Q. Which ones? A. Hemingway, Marx and Nietzsche.

Q. Are you a prolific reader? A. I try to be.

Q. Are you at the head of any of your classes in school? A. Well, I am Chairman of the Law and Political Science Conference which we are having. We are getting two out-of-town lawyers to speak at our school on these different subjects.

Q. Do you live in an apartment now? A. Yes, sir.

Q. How large is the apartment? A. It has four and a half rooms.

Q. Are you comfortable? A. Oh, sure.

Q. Not as comfortable as you were in the old home? A. Well, I imagine you might say that, yes. Of course, there is more room there in the home, but I get along quite well.

Q. What do you do in the afternoon when you get home from school? A. Some days I play football or basketball with my friends. Some days —I have a Hi-Fi set—so I enjoy playing that. Of course my homework has to be done and I usually do it in the afternoon.

Q. Does anybody else live with your father? A. No, a maid comes in from three to seven, and she cleans up.

Q. What about your dinner? A. She usually gives me dinner.

Q. When does your father come home? A. 6:30 or so. Sometimes he has business engagements and can't make it.

Q. You are by yourself most of the time? A. I don't look at it that way. I feel my father is doing quite a job, trying as far as possible to make a home for me.

As a matter of fact, a few years ago he was never home at that time because he had many business engagements.

Now he has made it a point to be home and I feel he has done quite a good job.

Q. How often do you see your mother? A. Oh, three or four times a week. As a matter of fact, this last week I think I saw her mostly every day.

Q. Does she come to you or do you go there? A. Well, it's a compromise, you might say.

Q. Are you on friendly terms with your mother? A. Yes, oh, surely.

Q. Do you still love her? A. Naturally.

Q. Well, don't you miss the companionship of your mother and your sister and your brother at home? A. Well, in a case like this, I made up my mind a year or two ago that you can't have the both of them and that you had to make yourself somewhat aloof from one, so that it's not so hard when the final break comes or a head is reached.

Do you understand?

Q. Are these your own views? Or are they the views of your father? Or someone else? A. Oh, no, sir. These are strictly my own. Of course, in the last few years you might say each gave me their doctrine and then I toss it up and come up with my own conclusion.

Q. Have there been many altercations between them in your presence? A. Oh, there are so many I don't think I could enumerate.

Q. And do you favor one side or the other in connection with these altercations? A. Well, sometimes. For example, I might tell you about one. These are not the nicest things in the world to talk about but they happen and I imagine they have to be told.

About a year and a half ago—it was a Friday night, which we try to observe to the best of our ability by lighting candles and saying prayers over the wine and the candles.

At any rate, my father looked through the house—we have a few Bibles—one was given me as a Bar Mitzvah present. My father has one— we came to look for them and couldn't find them.

Then my mother very casually said she had thrown them out and it was quite a shock to me because we just don't go throwing Bibles out.

I could understand if she was of another religion, but not to the extent of throwing Bibles out.

Then my father became enraged and threw her out of the house literally.

Q. Have you had much religious training? A. Oh, yes, sir. I have attended Hebrew instruction for six years. I try to attend Sabbath services whenever possible.

Q. You feel that you enjoy attending Friday night services? A. I don't go Friday night. I go Saturday morning .

Q. You go to the synagogue on Saturday morning? A. I would say about twice a month, possibly more.

Q. You do? A. Yes, sir.

Q. Do you speak Hebrew? A. No, sir, not too fluently.

I must say that when I did attend Hebrew school, it was not too much of an advantage to me as far as learning. I was not too serious, you might say. I kidded around a lot.

Q. Do you still take Hebrew instruction? A. No, sir. I was graduated last year.

Q. Do you have non-Jewish friends? A. Oh, absolutely.

Q. Do you mix with non-Jews? A. I should say so. As a matter of fact, I mix with them as much as with Jewish people. I don't know whether you read the article in Look Magazine by William Atwood on the Jews in America ; but he said the Jews were quite a clannish group as far as associating with gentiles and I don't believe that's the truth in some cases. I feel just as much at home with gentiles as with anyone.

Q. Don't you think they keep to themselves quite a bit and are afraid to mingle? A. It depends. Some people have a stumbling block, a mental block. They feel that because they are Jewish that they don't have their place in the sun which they are looking for ; and some people change their name and they marry a gentile woman and have a family name that is gentile, as Atwood said, but the rabbi came to this gentleman and asked for a contribution to a new synagogue and it more or less pricked his conscience, because he felt he was a Jew.

Q. Do you find comfort in the association of non-Jewish boys? A. Oh, sure, because I think this parochial idea or the parochial schools which many Catholics and Christians do attend—I feel that the idea of hating the Jews or that they are Christ killers, that that sort of thing has gone out ; to a certain extent I believe there will always be some anti-Semitism but I don't think it is as great as it once was. You never hear mention of it.

Q. Do you feel your mother is anti-Semitic? A. Well, I've done quite a bit of reading on Christian Science and since my mother became a Christian Scientist——

Q. From your recent associations and living with your mother, do you think she is anti-Semitic? A. To a certain degree I feel that she is a Christian Scientist now and that anti-Semitism—she is a little in that direction because she feels that Judaism is a dead religion, as she says, and she has no respect for it.

Q. She has no respect for what?   A. The Jewish religion, in some sense, as I told you. She says it is a dead religion and that we should accept Christ as the Saviour and that the Jewish religion will eventually completely vanish from the earth, something in that direction.

Q. Notwithstanding that you still love her?   A. Oh, well, I imagine so.

Q. Tell me, Benjamin, and in this respect you could help me. If I had to make a decision as to who should have custody of you, have you got any preference?   A. I imagine that would be my own decision. Wouldn't it?

Q. No, it is my decision.   A. Oh, is it?

Q. Yes. I will listen to what you have in mind but in the final analysis it is entirely my decision.   A. Because I heard differently. That is why I was in doubt.

Q. The law is that it is up to the Court. It is up to the Judge. It is up to me to listen to the boy or the girl and their wishes may or may not have some influence or effect upon me.   A. In other words, for argument's sake, let us say this is another case and the boy, for example, chose his mother and yet the Judge thought the custody should be with his father. Now, couldn't there be some sort of appeal from that decision by the Judge, or something like that?

Q. Yes, but the Judge must decide what is best for the welfare of the boy.   A. Even though he is not happy with the decision?

Q. The boy, sometimes in his youth or in his zeal may favor one parent or the other and the Court must weigh all of the considerations, including the ideas and the thoughts of the boy, and then decide. The boy does not make the decision. You are a ward of the Court.   A. I see.

Q. This is a Court in Chancery and you are a ward of the Court and the Court decides what is best for you. Do you see?   A. Yes, sir.

Q. You don't make the decision.   A. I see.

Q. I make the decision as to where you should go, but, as I said before, you might help me in making up my mind by telling me whether or not you favor one or the other.   A. Well, let me put it this way, Judge. I don't think I would be as happy with my mother as with my father. One implication of that is the reason we both moved out of my mother's house, because we felt that the Jewish life which we had known was not being kept and that my mother was a completely changed woman.

I remember when we first moved out of the house—she doesn't believe in medicine—not that it is such a big thing, but all her actions and thoughts are different.

I know many a time I will come home and she is never there. She is out preaching to people about Christian Science, and I did not feel I would have so much of a home with her.

Q. You haven't got any woman in the house now, have you?   A. No, but at least with my mother, you see, in years gone by at least she would be home. I know many of the maids who have come to our house, she has always tried to preach Christian Science to them. Life with her would be a continual mention of Christian Science, Christ, Christian Science, Christ, all day long, it's God, God, God.

Now, I feel there is a place for religion but I don't feel it is every second of the day.

If she is trying to remind me that there is a God around—well, I think I am well aware of it, and those are my feelings in the matter.

Q. You feel very strongly that if you had a choice, you would rather be with your father?   A. Yes, sir.

Q. Do you feel any bitterness towards your mother?   A. No, sir, I think she is a very nice woman and everything.

Q. Do you think I ought to throw her out without giving her any support at all?   A. I don't understand you.

Q. Do you think I ought to decide in favor of your father and just throw her out on the street and say she is not any good and not worthwhile and not give her any support?   A. Well, there is such a thing as alimony, or a daily allowance, or whatever it is, and I imagine she would always have a roof over her head. I think my father is pretty just there. I know that my father's opposing attorney told me that he thought my mother should receive more money. I think what she gets is a fair amount because she does not have five people in the house. She has just two.

Q. Who told you that?   A. My father said that the opposing attorney thought she should have more money.

Q. How do you know that about the attorney?   A. Oh, he just mentioned it to me when he came home.

Q. Your father did?   A. Yes, sir.

Q. Have you spoken to your father's lawyer?   A. No, sir.

Q. Well, it is very nice seeing you, Benjamin. You are a very intelligent young man and good luck to you.   A. O.K., thank you.

Q. Good-bye (shaking hands).   A. Good-bye.

(Testimony of Dee Lesser impounded by the Court and will be released upon Court order.)

C.

The Judge Decides—Custody for Each Parent

1.

INITIAL JUDGMENT—DECEMBER 5, 1956

MR. JUSTICE STREIT:

We now come to the question of custody of the children. Both sides ask the court for the custody of all three infants. Of course, the supreme issue here is the interest and welfare of the children. (People ex rel. Spreckles v. De Ryter, 150 Misc. 323.)

The character of the parents, their ability to care for and protect the children, the advantages the children will obtain from control being given to one parent as against the other, the sex and age of the children, the wishes of the children if they are of sufficient age to use discretion in choosing, are all factors to be taken into consideration by the court. (Israel v. Israel, 38 Misc. 335.)

I have examined all three children. Dee, seventeen years of age and a college student, is an intelligent, dignified little lady with a perfect understanding of the many discordant home factors. At present her domicile is with her mother. Benjamin, the fourteen-year-old, is a very precocious young gentleman of superior intelligence. He has expressed a desire to live with his father. Larry, the six-year-old, is an alert, intelligent child. Here are three excellent mannered children who have been well trained and of whom any parent may well be proud. [They are] the real victims of this marital rift. Any charge that the plaintiff is unfit to rear or be the custodian of these children is belied by the breeding of these children. Both parents are refined and cultured and seem to possess a more than average education. Both seem devoted to the children.

The intense nature of the case has engendered rancor if not vindictiveness and there has been the usual exchange of excoriations.

Dee has asked me to defer making a decision as to her custody until after the first of the year and her wish will be granted.

Benjamin, whose mind is way past his fourteen years, feels very strongly about living with his father who is hereby granted custody of said Benjamin.

And the welfare and interests of Larry, in my opinion, would be best served in the custody of his mother, the plaintiff.

If the parties cannot agree as to the terms of visitation as to Benjamin and Larry, I will conduct a hearing and fix the times and places.

As to counsel fees, alimony, support, maintenance and education of the children, I would suggest that counsel agree but if that be not possible, I will determine the necessary and proper amounts.

Submit your findings and judgment.

(Discussion off the record between Court and counsel.)

THE COURT. This is a note primarily for the plaintiff with respect to her custody of Larry: In view of the fact that the Penal Law provides that the parent or guardian who is in custody of an infant, and I think it applies up until sixteen years of age, *must provide the child with the necessary care and medical attention.* She is hereby directed, notwithstanding any religious beliefs she may have had, to see to it that Larry is examined at least once a month by a physician or family physician or pediatrician and be guided solely by the doctor's advice as to what treatment to give him in connection with his physical needs. In the event that the oculist prescribes glasses, that she is to see to it that he obtains the necessary glasses for his eyes. And you instruct her accordingly.

MR. ERDHEIM. I certainly will.

THE COURT. The defendant has asked for a thirty-day stay of execution in connection with the payment of counsel fees. Counsel for plaintiff acquiesces in the stay and under the circumstances he is granted a thirty-day stay of execution.

2.

AMENDED JUDGMENT— FEBRUARY 9, 1957

MR. JUSTICE STREIT:

Examination of the infant, Dee Lynn Lesser with respect to her custody, maintenance and education has been completed. The infant does not desire to indicate a preference. Under all the circumstances, her custody is awarded to the plaintiff. With respect to visitation, defendant shall have such rights thereto as the parties may agree, bearing in mind that the infant expressly desires to share her vacations and spare time equally with both parents. Provision for the support for Dee Lynn's maintenance and education has been held in abeyance pending my determination as to her custody. The defendant is presently paying for her board and tuition at the university, but neither the infant nor her mother is receiving any allowance for this infant's clothing and other necessities. My original award to the plaintiff is therefore modified to the extent that the defendant is directed to pay the plaintiff the sum of $200 per week as and for her support and maintenance as well as that of the infants, Larry and Dee Lynn. Settle amended judgment in accordance with the foregoing.

—Order signed directing the sealing of transcript of the interrogation of infant.

3.
AMENDED JUDGMENT OF SEPARATION— FEBRUARY 17, 1957

Hon. Saul S. Streit, Justice. Now, on motion of Erdheim & Armstrong, attorneys for the plaintiff, it is

ORDERED, ADJUDGED AND DECREED, (1) that Sadie Lesser, be and hereby is separated from the defendant Perry Lesser, his bed and board forever, upon the ground[s] of cruel and inhuman treatment and of abandonment;

(2) that Sadie Lesser, have the care and custody of Dee and Larry, subject however, to the reasonable right of visitation by Perry Lesser;

(3) that Sadie Lesser, is directed, that notwithstanding any religious beliefs that she may have, to cause Larry, to be examined at least once a month by a medical doctor, and that she be guided solely by the doctor's advice in connection with any medical treatment;

(4) that Perry Lesser have the care and custody of Benjamin, subject however to the reasonable right of visitation by Sadie Lesser, who is at no time to remove [him] from within the jurisdiction of this Court;

(5) that commencing with December 5th, 1956, the defendant pay to the plaintiff, during her life, the sum of Two Hundred ($200.00) Dollars per week, each and every week, as and for the support and maintenance of herself, Dee Lesser and Larry Lesser;

(6) that in addition to the allowance of support and maintenance Perry Lesser, permits and allows the plaintiff Sadie Lesser and Larry the exclusive use and occupancy of the home, free of rent, and that in addition, he pay all of its expenses and upkeep, including but not limited to the taxes, mortgage interest and amortization, as he has heretofore paid;

(7) that Perry Lesser, is directed to pay to the university, all board and tuition fees for and on behalf of Dee;

(8) that Perry Lesser, is directed to pay to Erdheim & Armstrong, the attorneys for the plaintiff, for their services rendered to date, a counsel fee in the sum of $5,000.00, said payments to be made as follows: $2,500.00 on or before December 15th, 1956, and the balance of $2,500.00 on or before January 3rd, 1957;

(9) that the plaintiff recover the costs and disbursements of this action, amounting to $192.10;

(10) that the plaintiff and the defendant have leave to apply at the foot of this decree, for such other and further relief as to this Court may seem just and proper in the premises.

D.
Decisions of the Parties, their Attorneys, and the Court to Appeal

1.
THE FATHER SEEKS REVIEW AND THE MOTHER DEMANDS FUNDS TO OPPOSE HIM

a. Notice of Appeal

On April 4, 1957 Mr. Lesser filed a *notice of appeal* "from the whole and each and every part" of the order dated Feb. 17, 1957. Subsequently Mrs. Lesser filed a *notice of motion* for counsel fees and printing costs to defend the appeal. Her notice was accompanied by the following *affidavit in support:*

A reading of the Court's decision readily discloses that the facts in this case are quite novel and unique. That considerable time will have to be expended in a research of the legal authorities in other jurisdictions. That the record on appeal, consisting of some 430 pages of testimony and many exhibits, will be so voluminous that a great deal of time will be required to digest the contents thereof. It is apparent also, that this appeal taken by the defendant, will be vigorously prosecuted by him. In view thereof, it is respectfully submitted that a reasonable fee be awarded to me to defend the said appeal.

I have no monies whatsover to pay my attorneys for their many services to be rendered on this appeal, nor for the costs and disbursements to be incurred by them, in the printing of my brief.

b. Affidavit in Opposition—Counsel Fees

Attorney Pomerantz then signed and filed an *affidavit in opposition*, saying:

The plaintiff has already been awarded $5,000. for counsel fees. Mr. Erdheim, her attorney, testified at the trial:

> "I have given this matter, exclusive of the Monday, Tuesday and today that I have been in court, approximately some 250 hours worth of time on the case."

These hours for which he was compensated included, by his own statement, research into the "novel and unique" aspects of the case. The plaintiff ought not be awarded counsel fees twice for the same legal service.

The "many exhibits" in the "voluminous" record on appeal consist of a dozen documents, all of which can be read and absorbed in 20 minutes.

Just as plaintiff inflates the extent of the record, so she exaggerates and twists defendant's alleged wealth.

It is apposite to point out that on his request for counsel fees for the work involved below, the plaintiff's attorney chose to wait until the trial itself when he was better able to report accurately as to the time and effort he expended. The counsel fee already awarded is being appealed. It is impossible to determine the value of the services to be rendered on Appeal until the value of the services already rendered are finally established.

Plaintiff's professed indigence (and her claimed inability to pay her lawyer) would seem to be more relative than absolute. On the eve of the trial, by her own admission, she bought a new and expensive automobile out of her own funds (accumulated out of her allowance).

Neither the plaintiff nor her attorney allege that they will be harmed or prejudiced in any way if the matter of counsel fees awaits a fuller determination of the facts upon which such a fee is based.

WHEREFORE, I respectfully pray that the plaintiff's application for counsel fees be in all respects denied, with leave to renew the application upon the conclusion of the appeal.

c. Affidavit in Opposition—Custody and Repossession of Home

While the motion on counsel fees was still pending Mrs. Lesser filed an *affidavit in opposition* to Mr. Lesser's motions to reargue the custody of Dee and for exclusive occupancy of the house:

With respect to the defendant's motion to reargue the award of the custody of Dee to me, I submit the following: Heretofore, and on the $100.00 per week that I have been receiving from the defendant, I have given Dee some spending money for herself. I have had extreme difficulty in meeting my obligations because the defendant failed to comply with the judgment of this Court. Whatever I have had left from the $100.00 received by me, after paying the bills for necessaries, I have given Dee. In addition thereto, I have previously had some of her clothes made, as I am presently doing, with my limited income.

The defendant, in his moving affidavit set forth a schedule of monies which he has allegedly given to Dee. Most of these monies were given by the defendant before the decree of separation, the exception being one payment of $125.00 made on February 1st, 1957. I respectfully submit to this Court that if the defendant had paid the monies to me which he had been directed to pay, the payment by him of $125.00 for spending money for Dee, would have been obviated. The actions of the defendant in being so obstinate, and giving Dee spending money, is so characteristic of him; not only that, but I feel sure, his conduct in giving this spending money to Dee is intended solely for the purpose of currying favor with her, so that she might become partial to him.

The urgings by this defendant that the award of $50.00 per week for Dee, by Justice Streit, "is based on a wholly inaccurate factual basis", is likewise typical of him. There was nothing inaccurate in the decision of Justice Streit, when he gave me $50.00 per week for Dee's "clothing and other necessities" exclusive of her educational costs.

With respect to Dee's custody, Justice Streit in awarding her to me, exercised the right and duty imposed upon him by law, to make an award of an infant. The defendant argues in support of his motion for re-argument, that in view of the fact that Dee "does not desire to indicate a preference" between the defendant and myself, that no award of custody should therefore be made. Such argument is fallacious and as I have been advised by my attorneys, the cases and law are academic on that point. In view thereof, it is respectfully submitted that the defendant's motion for re-argument of the award of the custody of Dee to me, should be denied.

One further thought on the subject of custody. The defendant has recently acquired new business interests in the State of Florida, which keep him there. As a result of these new ventures, the defendant leaves our 14 year old boy, Benjamin, in the custody of his sister. I believe he has a lot of temerity and nerve to ask this Court, to do like-wise with my daughter Dee.

With respect to the defendant's motion which seeks an order amending the judgment of separation, by granting to him the exclusive use and occupancy of the premises which our two children and myself occupy, I submit the following:

On December 20th, 1956, and only 5 days after the entry of the judgment of separation in my favor, the defendant's attorney caused to be dispatched a letter to my attorneys, in which they stated in part "our client, Mr. Perry Lesser, is anxious to resume possession of his home presently occupied by his wife". In view of the defendant's demand, I immediately and up to the present time, have looked everywhere for premises similar to that which we occupy. All of my efforts to date, have been to no avail.

It might interest this Court, in order to show the defendant's persistent viciousness towards myself and my children, that on January 21st, 1957, he commenced an action against me in ejectment. That action, although issue has been joined, has not been placed upon the calendar for trial by my husband.

If the Court feels that my husband is entitled to the property in question, notwithstanding the present suit in question, I submit that I should be allowed 6 months to find suitable and comparable living quarters for my children and myself.

If however, this Court feels that notwithstanding the defendant's present suit against me in ejectment, that it should give the defendant possession of those premises, then alternative relief that my cross motion to increase my weekly allowance from $200.00 per week to $400.00 per week, be granted, and that I be allowed a counsel fee of $1,500.00 for my attorneys for their services rendered herein.

(Sworn to February 28, 1957.)

d. Supplemental Affidavit—Repossession of Home

In response to this affidavit and to supplement Mr. Lesser's motions, Attorney Pomerantz filed the following affidavit:

The defendant seeks to avail himself of the alternative given him by Mr. Justice Streit by regaining his house. The plaintiff labels this "persistent viciousness". I insert here a copy of my letter to plaintiff's attorney, dated December 20, 1956, which shows the considerate manner in which the defendant sought to exercise the right given him by Mr. Justice Streit:

"December 20, 1956.

My dear Mr. Erdheim:

You asked me to put the subject matter of our telephone conversation in writing and I am glad to do so.

As I explained to you, our client, Mr. Perry Lesser, is anxious to resume possession of his home presently occupied by his wife. We are both in agreement that there is no doubt whatever as to his right to demand possession of that house. I have also made it clear to you that Perry Lesser is anxious to be altogether fair and reasonable in allowing his wife sufficient time to find a new abode. However, there is a point where reasonableness ends and excessiveness begins. I have therefore invited you to suggest a period of time which would be fair within which your client would have to vacate the premises. You have told me that you would prefer to discuss this matter with your client after your return during the first days of January from a trip. I have told you that that would be wholly satisfactory to me.

Sincerely,

A. L. Pomerantz (sgd)"

A month passed; we never received either the courtesy of acknowledgment or reply. It was only after plaintiff completely ignored our request that we brought a suit in ejectment.

The plaintiff asserts that she is looking for "comparable quarters", i.e., an eleven room apartment or home. Nowhere does she say why such a spacious home is required for herself and her six year old son. Her daughter, who lives in an out-of-town university, is seldom home. It would seem obvious that the marital home which housed plaintiff, defendant and their three children is a little oversized for plaintiff and Larry. The idea that "reasonable" means $200 a week or about $900 a month, is just further evidence that plaintiff is asking to punish defendant, not to fairly take care of herself. Plaintiff's statement that it costs $700 per month ($8,400 per year) to maintain the house is further evidence of her punitive and reckless approach to this situation.

With relation to plaintiff's conception of her needs, it is to be noted that defendant presently occupies, with his son Benjamin, in the City of Mount Vernon, a two bedroom apartment for which his monthly rental is $160. The apartment is adequate to house defendant and his son. A somewhat similar apartment would be adequate for plaintiff and Larry. Additional apartments at the same rate or rental are available.

The plaintiff declares that she needs six months in which to find a new home. She says that she has been looking since December. While the plaintiff is entitled to a reasonable time, she ought not be permitted to use the excuse of searching for an apartment to frustrate the defendant's right to possession. Since the plaintiff has been searching since December, it is suggested that April 15,

1957 be set as the date the defendant may re-occupy his house.

The custody and support of Dee

The plaintiff's remark that the defendant is giving money to Dee in order to curry her favor is a crass statement. The defendant pays, and at all times has paid, all the expenses of his daughter, Dee, which were conceded to be $2,500 a year. And the defendant shall continue to support Dee and all his children to the best of his abilities.

2.
THE TRIAL JUDGE DECIDES

On March 1, 1957, Mr. Justice Streit rendered his *decision* on Mrs. Lesser's motion for counsel fees:

Plaintiff is awarded the sum of $1,250 as and for counsel fees and, in addition, such sums as may necessarily be incurred for printing the record and briefs. The defendant is directed to pay the counsel fee within ten days after service upon him of the order, and upon presentation to him by plaintiff of the bills for printing, is directed to pay such bills within five days thereafter.

And on March 14, 1957, Mr. Justice Streit decided:

The motions are disposed of as follows: Defendant is awarded exclusive use and occupancy of the aforesaid premises with possession stayed to July 15, 1957. Plaintiff's alimony is increased in

the sum of $300 per month, said increase to take effect upon plaintiff's removal from the premises, and payable on or before the first day of each and every month. Plaintiff is further awarded the sum of $200 as and for a counsel fee.

3.
THE HUSBAND MOVES TO REARGUE THE ALIMONY AWARD—DENIED

On March 30, 1957 Attorney Pomerantz included the following letter in his affidavit in support of the motion to reargue the $50 increase in alimony awarded (supplemental decision of Feb. 9) to Mrs. Lesser for the care of Dee:

"March 15, 1957

Dear Dad:

At your request I am writing to tell you that I received no monies whatsoever for my support from my mother. However, mother does send me an occasional food package. Whatever my financial needs are, you are taking care of them adequately. I have no use for any additional money.

Love,

Dee."

On April 6, 1957 Mr. Justice Streit denied the motion.

E.
The Appellate Court Instructs the Trial Judge to Reconsider Larry's Custody

1.
THE APPELLATE DECISION
July 5, 1957

By PECK, P.J.; BRIETEL, BOTEIN, RABIN and COX, JJ.

Lesser plf-res-ap. v. Lesser, def-ap-res—Special Term, in granting a decree of separation to plaintiff wife, awarded her custody of the parties' six-year-old son. It is this provision only that causes the court concern. Despite the careful and admirable conduct of the trial of the action and of the post-trial procedures by Special Term, it is most difficult to determine the relative qualifications of

these bitterly opposed parents from the record alone. It is likely that a thorough investigation and report by a trained social worker may help resolve some of the doubts that evidently troubled Special Term, and that trouble this court. The services of such a skilled person are available in the recently established Special Term, Part XII (Family Part). Accordingly, the amended judgment of February 17, 1957, is unanimously modified to the extent only of remitting same to the justice who tried the action for the purpose of utilizing the services aforementioned as an aid in deciding the custody of the six-year-old son of the parties, and is otherwise affirmed.

2.

THE TRIAL JUDGE APPOINTS
SOCIAL WORKER

August 2, 1957

JUSTICE STREIT:

Ordered, that Frieda E. Moshowitz, a Social Worker be appointed to investigate and to make a report with respect to the custody of Larry Lesser.

3.

FATHER SEEKS CUSTODY OF LARRY

On October 17, 1957, Mr. Lesser filed with his motion to be granted custody of Larry the following affidavit:

Plaintiff's persistence in refusing my youngest son Larry the necessary medical attention and even prescribed medicine, has not altered since the trial of the action. Instead, she continues to teach Larry the philosophy of "Healing". Typically:

On September 15, when I last saw Larry, he was sneezing and coughing. His rectal temperature showed 100-$\frac{1}{2}$ (Dr. Reardon, the physician to whom my wife takes Larry for his prescribed monthly check-ups was out of town.) My daughter Dee took Larry to Dr. Foreman. After examination, Dr. Foreman diagnosed the condition as mucous in the lungs and a slight touch of asthma. He prescribed medicine which Dee secured from the pharmacist. He stated that Larry needed continued medical attention. Larry was given his first spoonful of medicine and was returned to his mother. Dee explained to her mother about Dr. Foreman's diagnosis and suggested that her mother keep up with the medicine. That evening, at about 8:45, I telephoned plaintiff and asked whether she was giving Larry the prescribed medicine. Plaintiff stated that there was nothing wrong with Larry, Dr. Foreman to the contrary notwithstanding, and that she would not give Larry the medicine.

Dee later and thereafter called plaintiff in my hearing to urge her to give the medicine, but to no avail.

Since I did not insist that Larry be treated by a physician of my choosing, and I was anxious about Larry getting medical surveillance, I suggested to my physician, Dr. Foreman, that he telephone Mrs. Lesser's physician Dr. Reardon. I am told that Dr. Foreman did so. He explained to Dr. Reardon the condition which he observed and suggested that perhaps Dr. Reardon, apparently enjoying plaintiff's confidence, arrange for a visit to his office. Whether Dr. Reardon did or did not call plaintiff, I do not know, but I do know from Dr. Reardon that plaintiff never returned to his office after Dr. Foreman's call to Dr. Reardon on September 17. I also know from communicating with the school authorities that Larry has been out of school for several days.

Fearing that my child might be very ill, I have attempted to make contact with him, and in any case to see him. To that end I telephoned plaintiff on September 19, 21, 22, 23, 24, 25, 26, 27 and October 8. Plaintiff consistently refused to permit me to speak to my child or to see him. Likewise, when my son Benjamin attempted to speak to Larry, plaintiff refused him permission. On October 8, the last time I called, I was told by plaintiff that she would not let me speak to Larry. However, at 4:45 P.M. of that day, plaintiff apparently changed her mind, or at least her tactic. Larry called me back and said that he would be happy to see me and that I could meet him the next day at 4 o'clock and that we could have dinner together. There followed a pause and then Larry stated, "Mom says she won't let me come." I thereupon got on the wire with plaintiff and I said to her, "What's the idea?" Plaintiff stated "I am guardian." And that was the end of that conversation.

Coming back to my visit with Larry on September 15 (when Dee took him to Dr. Foreman), Larry manifested considerable resistance to going to a physician. He mentioned that all he needed was "Healing". He referred to the fact that he picked up something in the fire and that it "did not hurt". He has learned well his new therapy.

At the moment of making this affidavit I am gravely anxious that my child may be critically ill. His absences from school increase my fear. Any thought that plaintiff may have mended her ways, as she implied during the trial, is negatived by the occurrences I have just narrated.

Should there be any issue of fact about the statements which I make herein, I respectfully request a hearing so that we can arrive at the truth through the crucible of cross-examination rather than by affidavit assertions and affidavit negations.

I respectfully submit that the alimony order should be modified as suggested and that, to prevent a threat to his very existence, the custody of Larry should be awarded to me, with reasonable rights of visitation in plaintiff.

Perry Lesser.

F.

Informing the Judge for Decision—Lesser v. Lesser, Trial II—1957

Transcript of Hearings Held Pursuant to Remand Concerning Custody; Motion to Modify Amended Judgment of Separation; and Motion for Contempt of Court

NEW YORK SUPREME COURT

October 22 and 26, 1957.

Before:

Hon. Saul S. Streit,

Justice.

THE COURT. I have called this hearing following a report I received from the social worker for redetermination of the custody of the child, Larry, and for a further consideration of the maintenance provisions of the judgment.

* * *

THE COURT. And the Social worker has interviewed you a few times? MRS. LESSER: Yes.

THE COURT: And now I have called a hearing in connection with that report, and also to satisfy myself as to certain facts about which I am about to make inquiry. You know now what this hearing is about?

MRS. LESSER. Yes, sir.

THE COURT. Do you, Mr. Lesser? Do you understand the purpose of this hearing?

MR. LESSER. Yes, I do, yes.

THE COURT. Now I am going to ask you, Mrs. Lesser, first a few questions under oath.

1.

SADIE LESSER

a. Direct Examination by the Court

Q. Subsequent to my awarding of a decree of separation in your favor, you continued to remain at the home in Mount Vernon for a few months? A. Yes.

Q. And during that time, did you receive any money from your husband? A. $100 a week.

Q. And after my decree, did you receive any money February, March, April, May? A. To my best recollection, yes. A hundred dollars a week.

Q. He didn't give you the amount that I awarded you? A. No, sir.

Q. How much are you receiving now? A. I'm not getting anything.

Q. For how long past? A. Well, I would say about three weeks, maybe more—four.

Q. Now then there was an application for permission to sell the home. And how long did you stay in the home? A. Until the 15th of July.

Q. And where do you live now? A. I live with a friend in Mount Vernon.

Q. And who is this friend? A. Well, just a friend—Mrs. Weinfeld.

Q. Is she married? A. Yes.

Q. Does she have a family? A. She has two children.

Q. And how many rooms in the home? A. About six.

Q. And you have made your home with her? A. Well, I had lived there all summer, and when I moved out July 15th, I moved into her home because she and her children went to Europe with her husband for the summer.

Q. Is she back now? A. She's back a few weeks and I stayed well after she came back. I went to the Manor Inn in Larchmont, but I found it was too expensive and as I wasn't getting any money, I thought I better find another way, so I have a room with her.

Q. And does your son stay in the room with you? A. Yes.

Q. There was some reference to an apartment. A. Well, I wanted to sign a lease for an apartment but I didn't know how large an apartment to take or whether I would get the money.

Q. Well, I directed that you get $300 a month for an apartment and you didn't receive any part of that? A. It wasn't forthcoming, no.

Q. And what about the furniture in the house? A. Well, I left it there thinking I might get half or some part of it at a future date when I had an apartment.

Q. What happened during the summer, did the boy stay with you all during the summer? A. Yes. I took him to the pool for swimming and so forth, on outings.

Q. Did he attend any summer school or summer camp? A. No, sir, I couldn't spend the money and I asked the father for it but he wouldn't.

Q. You still have your car? A. Yes, sir.

Q. Now during the summer months, what was the boy's schedule? What did he do? How was his time occupied? A. Well, there was a boy who moved into the same street, a little Catholic boy that he played with about his age, and I think there are eight or nine other boys that would congregate on that street and they played, and right next door was a little girl he played with her; she's a little bit older but he nevertheless played, and I would have my friend's two boys over to play with him, or I would take him there. I have quite a number of friends with sons.

Q. What about his meals? A. Oh, I prepared those.

Q. You prepared all his meals, all three meals? A. No, sometimes we would eat out.

Q. But if there was any cooking to do, you would do the cooking? A. No, I had a maid; I had my woman there.

Q. Whose maid? A. Well, that's the maid I had for many years who came.

Q. Is she still with you? A. No. I don't have a maid.

Q. Do you do the cooking? A. No, Mrs. Weinfeld is going to do the cooking. And I will assist her.

Q. I see. And his clothes, what about his clothes, did you buy him any clothes? A. Well, I did buy him some blue jeans and some things about two weeks ago which he absolutely needed, but he does need outer things, heavy clothes.

Q. What school does he go to? A. Rochester School, a public school.

Q. Does he have a separate bed in the room where you are in? A. Yes.

Q. And he sleeps in a separate bed? A. Yes.

Q. Now on Saturdays and Sundays, how does he spend his time? A. Well, it's all different. Last Saturday I went up to Bedford Hills with my friend and her son; we had lunch at the hotel, and then we went out. Well, it's always something different to do; sometimes a movie occasionally.

Q And has Mr. Lesser had occasion to visit with him during all this time since February? Have you made any arrangements or have the lawyers made any arrangements for his visiting with the boy or seeing him? A. I don't suppose the lawyers have. They couldn't seem to, and I haven't been——

Q. There haven't been any arrangements that you are aware of? A. No.

Q. What about Benjamin, have you seen him during all this time? A. I haven't seen Benjamin, I think it's over two months.

Q. Have you been invited over to the home to see him? A. No, sir.

Q. And when you saw him last, where did you see him? A. He called me on the telephone at the hotel, but I don't recall when I saw him prior to that. Must have been a few weeks before, but I moved into the hotel about five or six weeks ago, and he called me. I informed Mr. Lesser that I was staying there so that he could send my check there, and the boy became aware of this evidently and he called me, and I spoke to him on the telephone but that was the last thing.

Q. And Dee, have you seen much of her? A.

Well, during the summer not too much, no. She's at college.

Q. She will be coming on November 20th? A. Yes, Thanksgiving, and I do get mail; I have a letter here from her which is——

Q. I directed that you have custody of Dee, and I also increased the allowance to you because of that. She hasn't been with you very much? A. No.

Q. And you haven't spent any money on her—— A. Not too much.

Q. Tell me, how is Larry's health? A. Perfect.

Q. I have a note here both from the social worker, and some papers here from your husband which speaks about an incident concerning Dr. Foreman and a cold and some asthma, and Dr. Foreman gave him some medicine. Are you familiar with that incident? A. That was the Jewish Day of Atonement. The child was visiting with his father because he asked to have him so he could go—be with him that day, and around— I don't remember the time, but I picked the boy up—well, my daughter brought him to my house —I don't recall—and he brought a bottle of medicine with him and I says, "What is this?" and he said, "Daddy asked Dee to take me to the doctor," and I says, "Well, are you going to take the medicine?" He said, "I promised Daddy." He took the medicine twice. The evening the father called and asked me if I had given the child the medicine and I said no, because I hadn't.

Q. And how did he get custody of him that day on September 21st? A. I think I drove him there.

Q. And you left him at the home? A. Yes, because if I'm not mistaken, Benjamin had a cold then and I wanted—I think my older son had a cold at the time and I was very anxious to see how he was getting on.

Q. Did you go upstairs to the apartment? What floor is the apartment on? A. This is a private house.

Q. I was under the impression that Mr. Lesser was living in an apartment. Am I wrong about that?

MR. POMERANTZ. He was at one time in an apartment.

THE COURT. And now he is living at the home?

MR. POMERANTZ. That's right, you were quite correct. At one time he was living in an apartment.

THE COURT. And this house is the original home?

MR. POMERANTZ. Is the original home.

THE COURT. It has not been sold?

MR. POMERANTZ. No, it has not.

THE COURT. The application to me was for the sale of the home and the reason you wanted her to vacate it is so you could sell it.

MR. POMERANTZ. I don't quite recall it that way.

My recollection, your Honor, is that he wanted to repossess the home and——

THE COURT. No, the papers before me indicated that he wanted to sell the home and that he fixed a price that he was offering for the home. I think there was conversation, or there were papers, affidavits, motion papers before me that you prepared.

MR. POMERANTZ. I say my recollection of those papers, your Honor, is that he wanted to be free to sell the home. I don't recall myself at this point whether he reserved the right to occupy the home or to sell it. That is my recollection. He wanted to be free to do either thing.

BY THE COURT

Q. Anyhow, you brought Larry home? A. Yes.

Q. And when you delivered him that morning, was he well? Was he coughing or was he sick? A. He was well.

Q. And at any rate he came back and he had this bottle of medicine? A. Yes, sir.

Q. And you didn't know what it was about? A. Yes.

Q. Thereafter, did you talk to Dr. Reardon about the boy? A. I haven't spoken to Dr. Reardon in many months.

Q. In how long? A. Well, since August 17th when I had the child last examined.

Q. And what about having him examined in September? A. Well, doctor—the other doctor examined him in September, Dr. Pearlman. I changed doctors.

Q. Now I asked you some very pointed questions, about your views concerning medicine and doctors. And this is a problem which might be a ticklish problem and you might feel very sensitive about it, but it's an important problem and it's a practical problem and your answers are important. Do you follow me? A. Yes, sir.

Q. All right. Now, you remember we discussed some small phase of Christian Science at the time of the trial and I asked you, and you pointed out to me that Science as such does not believe in physicians or surgeons? If I am wrong about that, you correct me. A. Yes.

Q. At any rate, the principle and the theory and the doctrine of Science is that if a person has something the matter with him, complete faith and devotion would be a great healer, and if need be you call a practitioner as it is known in Science, is that correct? A. No, sir.

Q. No? Well, tell me what it is. A. Well, we don't heal through faith alone. We must have an understanding of what God is and his relationship to man.

Q. Having that understanding, and having complete faith, you believe that God will do the healing? A. Yes, sir.

Q. All right. And we discussed questions of whether, in the event that in our secular world as distinguished from your religious world—do you follow me? A. Yes, sir.

Q. If the boy needed a physician as the non-Science people understand, that you would call a physician, is that correct? A. I'm sorry, I don't quite get your question.

Q. All right; I will put it a little more clearly and more simply. The law of the State of New York recognizes the fact that children, minors, must be treated by doctors and surgeons whenever it is necessary, and are not to be treated by Science or faith. That is the law in the State of New York. A. Well, I thought there was an amendment.

Q. The amendment which was enacted in 1945, in no way changes the Penal Law. The law is superior to any religious faith or religious doctrine, and the law provides that the parent who is in custody of a child is responsible civilly and criminally responsible, for giving that child medical and surgical attention. Do we understand each other? A. Yes, sir.

Q. Now I am telling you that is the law, and that is my understanding of the law, and that is a ruling, and I was under the impression that I made that clear to you at the trial, and I asked you if in case of emergency, you would call a doctor; you said you would. Do you remember that? A. Yes, sir.

Q. Have you changed your mind about that? A. Whether I would call a doctor in an emergency?

Q. Yes. If the boy had a fever, would you call a doctor? A. I'm willing to obey all the laws of the land.

Q. That is not what I am asking you, Mrs. Lesser. I am asking you as I did at the trial then, that if the boy had a fever or in case of an emergency, would you give the boy medicine and would you call a doctor; have you any doubts about that? Is there any hesitancy about that? A. No, sir.

Q. Now I don't want lip service on this, and I don't want you to give these answers to please me, or in order to obtain a decision favorable to yourself, because I pointed out in my opinion that I thought that you were a very honest, upright woman; I still feel that way. I still feel that you are a very conscientious person, and I don't think you would lie to me. Now I am going to ask you the question again, very pointedly and bluntly.

Would you accept the principle of law in this state that you will in letter and in spirit, regardless of your devotion to Christian Science, which we all respect, but regardless of your devotion to Christian Science, will you respect and comply with the law in spirit and in letter and not merely give lip service to it, and give this boy medical and surgical treatment? A. I want to keep my child, your Honor, and I will do whatever the mandate of the Court says.

Q. Well, now, I will repeat it once more. The law requires that a parent or guardian who is in custody of a child, must—and I will read you the law so that there be no misunderstanding about it. A. Well, I was misinformed.

Q. Well, I am informing you and you must take my word for what the law is and the section which you have learned and thought of, which is 495 and was enacted in 1945, in no way conflicts with this law, and I will read it to you, and I don't care who informed you concerning Section 495. Now, 495 may have been enacted at the instance of the Christian Science church, and this one you are talking about which you have in mind, which says that "This article shall not be construed to deny the right of a parent or guardian or custodian, to treat or provide treatment for an ill minor in accordance with the religious tenets of any churches authorized by other statute of this state provided."

Now this means that if you are in control or in custody of a child, it may naturally follow that you could teach that child a religion which is not obnoxious or abhorrent—any religion, and Christian Science is not obnoxious or abhorrent. You may teach to a child such religious doctrines as in your opinion you believe in. But it does not conflict with this section which I am about to read to you, so that there be no misunderstanding on your part.

Q. Now let me read this to you, which I tell you is the law of this state: "A person who wilfully omits to furnish food, clothing, shelter or medical or surgical attendance to a minor, is guilty of a misdemeanor." Do you understand that language? A. Yes, sir.

Q. All right. Now I am going to repeat my question to you and I want a very direct, honest answer from you.

Will you both in spirit and in the letter of the law comply with this section and give this boy the medical and surgical attendance that is required? A. I cannot say in spirit. I would happily do so but in the letter of the law I will comply.

Q. All right.

THE COURT. Do you wish to ask this witness any questions?

MR. POMERANTZ. Thank you, sir. I would.

b. Cross Examination by Mr. Pomerantz

Q. You referred to an episode earlier when you delivered Larry to your husband's home, and when on his return to you, Larry had a bottle of medicine with him. A. Yes.

Q. And do you recall on that occasion that Dee informed you that she, Dee, had taken your boy to a doctor for an examination, and that the doctor had prescribed the medicine which Larry held in his hand? A. I can't recall the fact that she said anything about it or whether Larry told me about it.

Q. Now, no matter from what source you may have learned it, did you or did you not learn of the fact that Larry had been to a doctor in the course of that day? A. Yes, Larry told me.

Q. And did he tell you or did anyone tell you that the doctor had prescribed medicine? A. Well, I assume it was the doctor because it had the label on the bottle.

Q. Now, did you give Larry any of that medicine? A. No, sir.

Q. Did anyone telephone you or communicate with you asking you to do so? A. Yes, sir, Mr. Lesser.

Q. And did he ask whether you had given the medicine? A. Yes, sir. I said no, I hadn't, and I did not intend to.

Q. And did your daughter Dee also call at or about that time? A. Yes, immediately after that call she called me, and she informed me, that she had taken the child to the doctor, and that the doctor had said that he had a claim of bronchial something or other, and that the doctor had given the medicine to be taken at such and such a time, as nearly as I recall the conversation.

Q. And did you learn that Larry had a fever? A. No, sir, I didn't think he had a fever. She told me he had 100 something—a hundred point something, and I never did consider that fever, so I couldn't take her word for it.

Q. Did you thereupon take the temperature of Larry yourself? A. I didn't think the child was sick.

Q. Well, my question is, did you take his temperature? A. No.

Q. And you were satisfied from your own observation that the doctor was wrong? A. Well, I can't say.

MR. ERDHEIM. I object to the form of the question.

THE COURT. Sustained.

Q. You were also informed by your daughter, were you not, that a medical doctor said your child was sick, is that right? A. Well, she said he had a touch of bronchial asthma, that was her words as nearly as I recall.

Q. Well, that to you would indicate an illness, would it not, whether it be a touch or more than a touch? A. Well, if I admitted the reality of illness I would think that I could be ill, too.

Q. So that in the last analysis, your real feeling is that since you don't admit reality of illness, Larry couldn't have been ill, is that right?

MR. ERDHEIM. I object to that. A. That's right.

MR. ERDHEIM. I object to that, your Honor.

THE COURT. Sustained.

MR. ERDHEIM. I move to strike out the answer.

MR. POMERANTZ. I except to the answer being stricken out.

Q. Now, did you then or about that period of time take Larry to any physician for the purpose of ascertaining whether the doctor's judgment was correct or whether your judgment was correct? A. Well, I don't know why I should doubt a physician's opinion by taking the child to another physician.

Q. Did you then accept the doctor's opinion that Larry had what you referred to as a touch of bronchial something or other? A. No, sir.

Q. So that there was no point to take him to any other doctor, was there? A. No.

Q. Because if the other doctor had confirmed that opinion you wouldn't have believed that either, would you? A. I wouldn't have taken him to another doctor or any doctor in the first place; I didn't think the child needed a doctor.

Q. Even though some other physician told you the child was ill, right? A. He didn't tell me anything; I hadn't spoken to this——

Q. Well, you are correct and I am wrong. You were informed by your daughter, Dee, that some physician diagnosed your child as being ill? A. Well, he didn't diagnose him as being ill. He said he had a touch of bronchial asthma and I know many children who are whooping and coughing for many years and nothing comes of it. They are treated temporarily through materia medicine and they can't do nothing for them either.

Q. And do you know of many, or do you have any experience with other children who whoop and cough and die as a result of whooping and coughing?

MR. ERDHEIM. I object to that.

THE COURT. Sustained.

MR. POMERANTZ. I submit, your Honor, I am trying to explore this witness's state of mind.

Q. Who was the last physician to whom you took Larry? A. Dr. Stanley Pearlman.

Q. Did you inform Dr. Pearlman about some other doctor having said that Larry had a touch of bronchial asthma? A. No, sir. I don't see any reason that I should tell a doctor what another doctor's opinion is.

Q. Now, did Dr. Pearlman discuss with you Larry's condition after his examination of Larry? A. No, sir, he didn't find any condition; he found him well.

Q. That is all he said to you, that he found him well? A. Yes, sir.

Q. No abnormality whatever? A. I don't know what he wrote there.

Q. No, I am asking you what he said to you, Mrs. Lesser, and not what he wrote. A. What he said to me?

Q. Yes. A. I'm not very good at remembering conversations.

Q. Well, let me put it more sharply. Did Dr. Pearlman suggest to you that perhaps there was some condition of Larry that might warrant some kind of treatment or medication? A. Treatment, no. I don't remember.

Q. Is there any hesitation at all in your answer that perhaps Dr. Pearlman did suggest treatment, that there were certain conditions— A. You have the affidavit.

Q. No, thank you, I don't have it to begin with and I am not asking you about it. I am asking you about what Dr. Pearlman said to you; I am asking you whether it's not true that Dr. Pearlman stated to you that it might be a good idea for you—— A. Are you doubting Dr. Pearlman's integrity?

MR. ERDHEIM. Answer the question.

THE COURT. Did he say anything to you that there were any shortcomings or that the boy required any particular treatment or any particular observation?

THE WITNESS. No, sir, I don't remember.

THE COURT. All right; go to something else.

Q. Did he say anything to you about medication for the boy? A. No, sir.

Q. You are sure of that now? A. I'm pretty sure of that. If he found nothing wrong, why would he give him medication?

Q. I'm asking you the questions. A. I'm sorry.

Q. Did you ever discuss with Larry the art of healing with a capital "H"?

THE COURT. We are not going to go into that. She answered my questions; she said she would comply with the letter of the law but not with the spirit of the law and I do know what that means.

MR. POMERANTZ. I want to even impugn that premise, your Honor, by showing that she will not comply with the letter of the law, and that her work has been antagonistic to that.

THE COURT. We are not going to retry this case now, Mr. Pomerantz; I am just holding a hearing, in an amplification of the investigator's report, and that is all, and on that particular score——

MR. POMERANTZ. May I ask——

THE COURT. That is all that the higher court is concerned about. As to the question of the religion of the child, I hold as a matter of law that the parent has a right to teach a child—a parent who has custody of the child—the religion of the parent. Now with respect to medical and surgical treatment, after exploring that phase of it we will curtail your cross-examination. We are not going to go into the religious beliefs of this woman any further than Section 482 of the Penal Law which is the only phase of it that concerns me.

MR. POMERANTZ. Is that report going to be available to counsel, your Honor?

THE COURT. No, it isn't. It is a confidential report to the Court only.

MR. POMERANTZ. I have no alternative but to abide by your Honor's judgment. I want to show and go into the question of healing insofar as a word of art in Christian Science terminology, for the purpose of showing that Mrs. Lesser is affirmatively teaching this child to abhor and to reject all medical attention.

THE COURT. The thing has been passed upon by the Court of Appeals, and I can tell you exactly what the Court of Appeals said. People against Pierson, 176 N.Y. 201, construing Section 482 of the Penal Law. Now this was an instance of a parent who did not furnish medical attendance for his daughter who was suffering from catarrhal pneumonia, and the parent was prosecuted, and he believed in the Christian Catholic Church and its creed with respect to medical treatment was similar to the Christian Science church as we know it today, and he believed that—he said he did not believe in physicians and his religious faith led him to believe that the child would get well by prayer. He believed in disease; he believed that the religion was a cure of disease. Now he was convicted in the lower court. The Appellate Division reversed but the Court of Appeals said, and I quote: "But sitting as a court of law for the purpose of construing and determining the meaning of statutes, we have nothing to do with these variances in religious beliefs, and have no power to determine which is correct. We place no limitation upon the power of the mind over the body, the power of faith to dispel disease, or the power of the Supreme Being to heal the sick. We merely declare the law as given us by the legislature. We have considered the legal proposition raised by the record, and have found no error on the part of the trial court that called for a reversal." And the trial court found that the defendant had failed to furnish medical attendance for his daughter who was suffering from catarrhal pneumonia.

Now it is my view that people of all faiths must comply with the law. The law draws no distinction. And that is what the Court of Appeals said. We are not going to go into the tenets of the faith; we are not going to go into the distinc-

tions; we are just going to consider the law as it is written by the Legislature.

MR. POMERANTZ. Just a few more questions on another track, your Honor.

THE COURT. All right.

BY MR. POMERANTZ

Q. I believe you said, Mrs. Lesser, in response to the Judge Streit's question, that all you had been getting up to a few weeks ago when you ceased getting anything—but up to that time you had been getting only a hundred dollars a week, is that correct? A. May I amend that? I don't know whether Mr.——

Q. Well, you did say it, and will you please amend it to make it correct? A. Well, I got two monthly checks for rent. Did I say that to you, Judge?

THE COURT. You didn't tell me about that.

A. (Continuing) $175. each, two months, July and August.

Q. After September 15th, if that is the date when this episode of your son's examination by a doctor occurred—after that date, did your husband in fact telephone you and attempt to make arrangements to see your son? A. Yes, sir. One occasion.

Q. When your husband called and asked to see your son Larry—

THE COURT. Mr Pomerantz, if I decide that she is entitled to custody which is the only issue before me, this all falls by the wayside, because we will determine visitation rights for both sides, so I think we are just wasting a lot of time on that point. We are not going to retry the case. That issue has been decided. It's just a question of custody, and if she is entitled to custody, we will fix the visitorial rights for both sides. There are only two questions sent down here by the Appellate Division, and one is a question of custody, reconsideration of the question of custody, and the other one to determine the amount of alimony, that's all.

MR. POMERANTZ. The only thing I did want to bring out in that connection, your Honor, was that in response to her statement or testimony that she hadn't received any alimony over the past three weeks. I think the testimony was, and I want to point out that during that period she has withheld Larry from his father.

THE COURT. Well, I have a view with respect to that, and it's up to counsel to enforce that view, and that is that up to this point, she is entitled to all the money that she has been awarded.

MR. POMERANTZ. Well, may I state for the record, your Honor, that we have posted a surety company bond.

THE COURT. So we don't have to discuss that phase of it at all.

MR. POMERANTZ. All right, on that question, but I think it may be important in view of the connotation perhaps that Mr. Lesser may have been contumacious in not making these payments in the last few weeks.

THE COURT. I am not going into that and I am not trying the case all over again. I am not going to penalize him. There has been an award and there is a bond. She will be entitled to collect it.

MR. POMERANTZ. Now would your Honor hear any questioning with regard to Dee's custody?

THE COURT. Just a moment. Do you want to ask a few questions?

MR. ERDHEIM. Yes, your Honor.

c. Cross Examination by Mr. Erdheim

Q. Have you, Mrs. Lesser, since the judgment of this Court, taken Larry to a doctor for a physical examination every month? A. Yes, sir.

Q. And in addition thereto, did you take the child to a dentist? A. Yes, sir.

Q. And what has Larry's health been throughout, from February to date? A. Perfect.

Q. And do you intend, Mrs. Lesser, if the Court continues the custody of Larry in you, do you intend to carry out and comply with the order of this Court with respect to taking the child to a doctor? A. If that is the order of the Court, it isn't something I would like to do, but if I would have to do it I would do it.

Q. But notwithstanding the conflict between your religious belief and the order of the Court, which would you follow? A. Well, the law.

Q. Is there any question or hesitancy in your mind as to which you would choose, the law or your religion? A. I have always followed the law in every way.

THE COURT. Wait a minute, wait a minute.

BY THE COURT

Q. Now when you were interviewed by this Miss Moshowitz, she discussed this phase with you a couple of times, didn't she? A. Yes, sir.

Q. Did you indicate to her some resentment of my order to take the child to a doctor once a month to have him examined? A. I don't think it was resentment. I may have indicated that—if you pardon my saying so—that I thought perhaps the father would do better to take the child once a month at the time instead of my going with the child.

Q. Now let's see. Supposing I provided, if I gave you custody of the child, supposing I provided that the father has a right to see the child, say at least one day a week all day Saturday or Sunday—to have the child all day Sunday or all day Saturday, and the father takes the child to his own doctor and he provides the necessary medical treatment required and takes the child

to his own doctor and then that doctor gives you a list of requirements and directions to treat this child with respect to such treatment as in the opinion of the physician or dentist is necessary. Will you faithfully comply with those provisions that his doctor and his dentist directs you to do? A. If that is a mandate of the Court, I will.

Q. Well, I say to you now, the doctor gives you a prescription and he says you have got to give this boy a spoonful of this medicine once a day, will you do it? A. You know my answer, your Honor.

Q. What? A. I wouldn't do it willingly, but I will do it, if that's your order.

Q. Would you do it? I understand your faith, but I am asking you whether you would do it? A. Yes, sir.

Q. Well, can I trust you that you wouldn't take the medicine and throw it in the garbage can? A. Well, I think I do have a certain amount of integrity. If I say I will do something, even though it's against my religion, and it's your order, the law of the land, I will do it.

Q. Supposing the doctor says to you, "I want you to take this boy's temperature every day," or "every other day" if the occasion should arise, "and I want you to go to the drugstore and get a thermometer and take his temperature and let me know what it is," will you do it? A. Yes, sir.

Q. With a little hesitation? A. No, sir. Not willingly, but without hesitation.

Q. But you would do it? A. Yes, sir.

THE COURT. Anything further?

MR. ERDHEIM. I have nothing further, your Honor.

MR. POMERANTZ. Just one more question that has been opened up.

BY MR. POMERANTZ

Q. Would you regard a stomach ache as an illness? A. No, sir.

MR. POMERANTZ. That's all.

BY MR. ERDHEIM

Q. Did you take the boy and have polio shots given him this summer? A. Yes, sir.

Q. Incidentally, Mrs. Lesser, you did talk with me sometime ago about a lease for an apartment, is that correct? A. Yes, sir.

Q. And did I advise you against leasing an apartment at this time? A. Yes, sir.

Q. Did you have any money to pay down for the security for the lease required? A. Yes, I sold my engagement ring.

Q. Now, in a letter which you received the other day, Mrs. Lesser, from Dee——
Did Dee have any plans with respect to staying with you?

BY THE COURT

Q. Have you had a talk with Dee about who

she wants to stay with? A. Yes, sir.

Q. What did she say? What did she tell you? A. Well, during the summer she said she was tired of packing and moving around so much and she felt she would stay in her room because she did feel happy there. Her father had redecorated it for her, and she wanted to stay in that house.

Q. Well, she is old enough to decide where she wants to stay, and we are going to let her decide for herself. If she wants to stay there, there isn't anything that you or I could do about it. A. Well, she wants to stay with me. She just wrote me the other day that she would like to stay with me over Thanksgiving. I don't know whether she assumes it would be for the future.

Q. Well, she has a right to stay where she wants to stay. But she can't dilly-dally around and keep equivocating. She is old enough to know what she wants to do.

2.

PERRY LESSER

a. Direct Examination by the Court

Q. I believe you are back in the home? A. That's right, your Honor.

Q. And Benjamin is living with you? A. That's right, your Honor.

Q. And Dee has a room in the home? A. Yes, she asked and demanded a room, that is why I'm back there.

Q. She asked to live with you? A. That's right.

Q. And do you have any maid in the house now? A. Yes, full time.

Q. And any other help besides the maid? A. Whenever it's needed.

Q. Like what? A. Gardener or heavy work or anything like that.

Q. Benjamin goes to school? A. Yes, every day.

Q. And you go to business? A. Yes, I do.

Q. What time do you leave for business? A. Oh, it varies. Any time between 7:30 to 9:30.

Q. What time do you get back? A. Well, that varies too. I may get back 5 o'clock; I may get back 6 o'clock; I may get back 8 o'clock.

Q. And what happens with Benjamin while you are away at business; who takes care of him in the afternoon? A. Benjamin is not a child, he goes to school, he gets out of school and he has his friends to play with. He sometimes comes home after I do. If I come home at 5, he comes home at 5:30 and if he wants to stay out, he usually calls up the house when he leaves the school about 3:30, somewhere around that, and if he wants to play or go to extra-curricular activities—he's in the choir, he is in a service

organization in his school, and he has various things that a boy his age does, but he has rules and regulations which he has to abide by, and if he wants to stay out till 5 or 5:30, he's got to call up when he gets out of school and let us know where he is. He has dinner at home, and it's a cooked dinner.

Q. Do you go away on any business trips? A. Yes, I do when I have to. Once a month or once in two months, for three days—five days.

Q. And who keeps the boy company while you are gone? A. The maid is in the house. My sister comes in. If he wants her there she stays there for a couple of days. My brother-in-law. He has his friends in the house. Last time he slept over his friend's house for one day and he had one of his friends over the house with him. He's not a child.

Q. He does pretty much as he pleases all day long? A. Oh, he does not; he does not, your Honor.

Q. No? What does he do? A. He has more supervision now than he had before.

Q. Who supervises him when he comes home? The maid? A. No, the maid don't have to supervise him, he's 15 years old.

Q. Where is the supervision? A. When he comes home he relates to me what's he's done and what he hasn't done.

Q. Does anybody direct his activities after he comes home? A. Yes, I do. I do more so now than before. In fact, he even made a remark to me the other day I was much stricter than I was a year ago.

Q. Has he seen his mother? A. Benjamin hasn't seen his mother for about three weeks, and that's due to her own negligence. He's called her up. The last time I was around there he called her up and this was about two weeks ago, and he asked to talk to Larry. This is the second or third time in three weeks, and if your Honor doubts me you can pick the phone up and call him at school to verify every word I've just said. He called her up and asked to speak to his brother Larry and his mother said he couldn't. His mother asked what did he want to talk to Larry about, so he said, "I want to talk to my brother."

Q. You weren't on the phone then, were you? A. No, I was in the room. We had about five phones over the house. I happened to be downstairs while he was calling, and then he got into another argument over the phone and he slammed the phone down and he said he wasn't calling her any more.

b. Cross Examination by Mr. Erdheim

Q. Did you notify your wife prior to the time that you went to Florida that you were taking your son and daughter away? A. She knew about it.

Q. Did you notify her? A. I don't remember whether I did or my son did or my daughter did, but she specifically knew about it because I remember, she tried to talk Dee out of going and Dee come back to me one night and said to me mother didn't want her to go. I says, "It's up to yourself; you're a big girl now. If you don't want to go you can stay home."

Q. And when you are in Florida, the maid takes care of Benjamin, is that correct? A. The maid doesn't have to take care of Benjamin.

MR. ERDHEIM. That is all.

c. Cross Examination by Mr. Pomerantz

Q. In response to Mr. Erdheim's question, you made some statement about Larry coughing while in your home if I understood you correctly. Did you hear him cough? A. He coughed and sneezed. I suggested to Dee that if he didn't get any better, she should take him to the doctor; that is how it came about.

MR. POMERANTZ. That's all.

THE COURT. All right. If you will all excuse me, I want to have a few minutes with Larry.

(Whereupon all parties left and Larry Lesser was brought into the room.)

3.
LARRY LESSER IN CHAMBERS

BY THE COURT

Q. Did you ever see me before? A. I seen you but I can't remember you.

Q. Well, didn't we have a talk once before? A. Yes.

Q. You remember downtown? A. Yes.

Q. And I asked you some questions? A. Yes.

Q. You know where you are, what this room is? A. No.

Q. Well, this is my office; it's my chambers. And do you know who I am? A. No.

Q. Well, I am a judge. You know what a judge is? A. Yes.

Q. What? A. I forget what you call it.

Q. All right. Where are you living? A. In Mount Vernon.

Q. You go to school? A. Yes.

Q. How far away is that from your house? A. I don't know.

Q. You don't know. And how do you get to school in the morning? A. She drives me.

Q. And how do you get home, does she call for you? A. No. Well, I have——

Q. Who takes you home? A. My mother.

Q. And how about breakfast in the morning. Who makes breakfast for you? A. Mrs. Weinfeld.

Q. And how about dinner, who makes dinner for you? A. She does too.

Q. Is the food any good? A. Yes.

Q. Where did you get that suit that you got on? A. Well, my brother got it and I have a few holes in it.

Q. Let me see where the holes are. A. I don't know where it is but I'll have to look for it.

Q. How long have you had it? A. I don't know. It happened with a little puppy dog.

Q. How long ago was this? A. I don't know.

Q. Do you have any more suits? Do you have any other suits? A. No, this is my only one.

Q. Haven't you got any other suit? A. Oh, yes, I have one more but I gave it away for poor children because it's too small on me.

Q. How do you feel? A. Fine.

Q. Stand up a minute, let me shake your hand. Give me a real hard handshake. Hard.

Q. Do you play with the boys? A. Yes.

Q. What kind of games do you play? A. We really don't have any games.

Q. You don't? A. No.

Q. I see. How old are you now? A. Seven and a half.

Q. And what grade are you in in school? A. Second grade.

Q. What is your teacher's name? A. Mr. Hoffman.

Q. Do you like him? A. Yes, he's all right, but we have three arithmetic books and we have to do them every day.

Q. That's pretty rough, isn't it? A. Yes, and he makes us do a lot of that stuff.

Q. Do you go to the doctor's office? A. No, not often, but I go.

Q. Do you like to go? A. No.

Q. Why not? A. I don't know. I don't like to.

Q. I see. Did you just see your father here? A. Yes.

Q. And you and your father are good friends? A. Yes.

Q. How often do you see him? A. I don't know.

Q. How about Benjamin, do you ever see him? A. Yes.

Q. How often? You don't know how often you see him either, do you? A. No.

Q. What about Dee, when do you see her? A. Well, I can't see her until she's out of college.

Q. When does she come back? A. I don't know. Am I supposed to know? I don't know when she comes back from college.

Q. Larry, I'm glad to see you again.

(Whereupon Larry left the room, and the attorneys, Mr. Pomerantz, Mr. Erdheim and Mr. Leman, entered the room.)

4.

ATTORNEYS IN CHAMBERS

MR. ERDHEIM. I have a cross-motion, sir, for counsel fees, since July, although we haven't been paid the original award made by your Honor, nor any of the other awards, outside of the fee for the payment of $1200. to defend the appeal; we have rendered services for this woman since July 25th up to today, and we are asking your honor for fees.

(*Discussion off the record.*)

THE COURT. You have a right of visitation. What day do you want?

MR. POMERANTZ. Sunday.

MR. ERDHEIM. We would like the same of Benjamin.

MR. POMERANTZ. Yes, of course.

THE COURT. Yes; all right. Reciprocal rights for each temporarily for the time being, of visitation of the child who is in each other's custody. Have the parents come in.

5.

PARENTS IN CHAMBERS

THE COURT (to Mr. Lesser). Now, what day do you want to visit? You have a full day. What day do you want to visit with Larry, Saturday or Sunday?

MR. LESSER. I would like—is it possible to have him Friday nights and go home Saturday night, so it will be just——

THE COURT. Well, for the time being I would rather you made it during the day, or took him in the morning and brought him back at night. In other words, you can have Saturdays or Sunday, whichever you wish.

MR. LESSER. I think Saturday would be better.

THE COURT (to Mrs. Lesser). What do you want as far as Benjamin is concerned?

MRS. LESSER. Well, I guess they'd be together, the two brothers. It would be better to have them together at each home.

MR. ERDHEIM. You want them Sunday?

MRS. LESSER. I think that would be the best way.

THE COURT. Sunday; all right.

6.

DEE LESSER IN CHAMBERS

October 26, 1957.

BY THE COURT

Q. Did you just come down from college? A. Yes, I got down yesterday.

Q. Tell me now, you are still a freshman or are you now a sophomore? A. I'm now a sophomore.

Q. Are you enjoying college? A. Yes.

Q. Do you contemplate finishing your course? A. Well, I contemplate finishing, but I don't know about the school. I might switch.

Q. You may want to change your school? A. Yes.

Q. But you are pretty sure you enjoy college and you would like to finish? A. Yes.

Q. You remember the talk we had about seven or eight months ago? A. Yes.

Q. And at that time you were undecided whether you wanted to be in the custody of your father or in the custody of your mother. You remember that? A. Yes, I remember.

Q. And then I made the decision for you. And I think you said something about wanting to spend your time equally between them during the summer? A. Yes.

Q. And how did you spend the summer? A. I wouldn't say it was divided equally, but I remember I stayed most of it with my father though.

Q. Well, let's see. At that time when you got back, your mother still was occupying the house? A. Yes.

Q. And was there a room set aside for you there? A. That's right. I had my own room.

Q. And did you continue to stay on at the house? A. No. Well, I asked my father if he was going to give up the apartment.

Q. This was in June? A. No, in July.

Q. When she indicated that she was going to leave? A. Yes.

Q. And he said he was going to move back into the house? A. No, I asked him if he would.

Q. What did he say? A. He said he would.

Q. And you decided to stay at the house? A. Yes.

Q. From then on, how did you spend the summer? A. I stayed in the house.

Q. And would it be fair to say that you stayed with your father during the summer? A. Well, most of the summer, yes.

Q. Your mother didn't have any apartment of any consequence, did she? She didn't have a room for you wherever she was? A. She was staying in somebody else's house.

Q. Did she have a room for you there? A. There were three bedrooms, so there would have been a room for me.

Q. Did you ever stay over there? A. I never slept there.

Q. Well, you just stayed on at the house. Did you make a choice then as to whose custody you wanted to be in, or was it just the fact that you stayed on at the house? A. No, I just wanted to stay in the house. I told him that—at first my mother told me that she didn't know what was going to happen with the decision, and I didn't— she was telling me she'd have to stay some time at a hotel, and then when the friends of hers moved out of their house to go to Europe, she would move in there, and I'm moving all along, and I told her I was sick of moving and I knew no other home except for that home at least I knew that room is mine, and if I lived in a house I'd have to—it's like living in a hotel.

Q. Well, did you make a choice then as to——
A. No.

Q. And you are still not making any choice? A. No.

Q. Who has been buying your clothing? A. My father.

Q. And has he been giving you all your expense money? A. Yes.

Q. And he has been paying your tuition? A. Yes.

Q. And your mother hasn't furnished you with any—— A. No.

Q. I understand you say you still have no choice? A. I still have no choice.

Q. Whoever has the house, that is whom you stay with? A. No. I stayed there because my mother has no place for me now. If she had— if she had an apartment in the summer which was her own, I would have stayed with her. I probably would have split it up about evenly. But actually she had no room in that house that was mine. I would have had to do quite a bit— it would be just a matter you know, starting to call up all my friends and tell them I can't be gotten at the other apartment again.

Q. Well, let me ask you this, Dee. And on what you tell me may depend the amount of alimony that I am to award your mother. I awarded your mother an additional $50 per week so as to take care of your clothes and your expenses. That is in view of the fact that I awarded custody to her. I thought at that time, that your father was not justified in leaving the house at the time, and so I decided in her favor, and you weren't able to make up your mind, so I awarded, so far as it has any effect at all, your custody to her. Now, if you have a preference to stay with your father, the amount of alimony which she will get will be less, because I will not make provision for you under those circumstances. Do you prefer to stay with your father? A. I don't have any preference, but last year, I'd say 99 per cent of my money came from my father.

Q. It all comes from your father; it doesn't make any difference. A. Yes. I asked from him because my mother wasn't getting what she was supposed to, and I didn't want to ask her because

everything I asked her for I knew that she had to substitute in some other means. So I have no preference, and if you—I don't know—I just don't have any preference.

Q. But you would rather stay at the house? A. I always think of it as my home, but if my mother is living there I'd still rather stay there.

Q. If your mother were living there you would rather stay there? A. Yes. I mean, it doesn't matter who lives there, it's just the only home I have, so I like it, but I imagine if my mother has some kind of home or apartment where— someplace I know is mine, I'd stay there just as much also.

Q. Supposing your mother had, say, a five room apartment with two baths. Would you stay with your mother all the time? Most of the time? A. I would still try to divide it evenly. I would try to divide it evenly. The only reason I didn't divide it evenly this summer is because she had no place for me, which was wrong anyway; I shouldn't spend more time there, just that I was selfish, I didn't want to keep moving all the time.

Q. All right Dee, thank you for coming.

7.

SADIE LESSER— MOTION TO HOLD PERRY IN CONTEMPT

Sadie Lesser, being duly sworn, deposes and says:

I submit this affidavit in support of an application which seeks an order.

(1) adjudicating the defendant in contempt of Court because of his failure to return the custody of Larry Lesser to me pursuant to the judgment of this Court dated the 16th day of February, 1957;

(2) directing the defendant to pay to my attorneys the fees for bringing on this proceeding.

On Saturday, November 3rd, 1957, the defendant exercised his right of visitation of Larry. At 7:00 P.M., the same day, the defendant called me and told me that the child was ill with a fever and he could not return the child to me. I called the defendant's physician, a Dr. Charles Foreman, who told me that I could take the child home. After an exchange of telephone calls, between Dr. Foreman, the defendant, and myself, I still was refused the child.

I called my attorney, Irving I. Erdheim, that evening and related the events to him that led up to the defendant's refusal to return my child. Mr. Erdheim called Abraham Pomerantz, Esq., the attorney for the defendant, and not finding him at home, left a message to call my attorney back that night or Sunday morning. Needless to say, Mr. Pomerantz did not call my attorney back.

On Sunday, November 4th, 1957, I went to see Larry at the defendant's home. The defendant had stated to me over the telephone prior thereto, that he would allow me a one-half hour visit and that I was to come alone. That if I violated his direction, I would be forbidden that right to see Larry. On my arrival, I saw my son on the floor playing with trains. My visit, brief as it was, was interrupted by the defendant with a direction that I leave.

On Monday, November 5th, 1957, I again visited my son, who opened the door for me. The defendant was not at home, the child being attended by a Sophie Sternberg, the defendant's sister. I remained some two hours, during which time I was advised that for lunch, Larry had a salami sandwich. I requested the return of my son before departure, but this was refused.

On Tuesday, November 6th, 1957, I again visited my son. Once again, the defendant was not at home. On this occasion, the child's guardian was the defendant's brother-in-law. I again requested the return of the child, but I was advised that the defendant forbade the same.

On Wednesday, November 7th, 1957, fully realizing that the defendant intended to flout the Court's order, I once again asked my attorney to call Mr. Pomerantz, defendant's counsel. This he did, but Mr. Erdheim was unable to speak to Mr. Pomerantz. A message was left with his secretary for Mr. Pomerantz to call back, but as of this writing, Mr. Pomerantz has not had the courtesy or decency to do so.

In addition to violating the order of this Court, the defendant has wilfully harmed the child's education, by keeping him out of school. It is apparent that the conduct of the defendant was calculated to and actually did defeat, impair, impede and prejudice my rights, that he should be adjudicated in contempt for failure to return Larry and that he should be required to pay the expenses for bringing on this proceeding.

Wherefore, I most respectfully pray that the annexed order to show cause be signed, and that my application be granted for which no previous application has been made.

Sadie Lesser.

(Sworn to November 8, 1957.)

8.

PERRY LESSER

November 13, 1957.

Before: Hon. Saul S. Streit, *Justice.*

THE COURT. Mr. Pomerantz, you have read these papers, I assume. I take it you are familiar with what has transpired.

MR. POMERANTZ. Generally; I would say yes. I am familiar with the fact that Mr. Lesser has refused to return the child to the plaintiff.

THE COURT. Is this on your advice?

MR. POMERANTZ. No, it isn't sir.

THE COURT. Is this with your approval?

MR. POMERANTZ. I would rather not go into what I advised Mr. Lesser.

THE COURT. I beg your pardon?

MR. POMERANTZ. I say I would rather not go into what I advised Mr. Lesser to do. That's a confidential communication between attorney and client.

THE COURT. I see. Well, on what theory does Mr. Lesser withhold the child from the mother?

MR. POMERANTZ. In that connection I would like to make this statement to the Court. This child is a sick child. I have a doctor prepared to testify —and I respectfully request your Honor to permit him to testify—here or in open court as to the sickness of the child—on the ground that the doctor has prescribed that the child take certain medicine, on the ground that the mother, as you well know, has refused to give the child and continues to refuse to give the child this medicine.

THE COURT. Why don't you answer my question, Mr. Pomerantz?

MR. POMERANTZ. I have, sir.

THE COURT. On what theory does the defendant withhold the child from the mother?

MR. POMERANTZ. I have answered your question the best way I know how, sir.

THE COURT. Now you are directed to produce the defendant and the child here this afternoon at four-thirty.

MR. POMERANTZ. I will do as you direct. Now may I ask your Honor whether I may at the same time produce the doctor.

THE COURT. I will take that up at the proper time.

MR. POMERANTZ. Dr. Foreman of Mount Vernon will be here at that time prepared to testify as to the child's condition.

a. Direct Examination by the Court

(The matter was resumed at 4:30 P.M. in the Court's chambers, both the plaintiff and the defendant being present as well as their counsel.)

THE COURT. Mr. Lesser, you recall the hearing we had in the Bronx on October 22, 1957?

MR. LESSER. I do.

THE COURT. On that occasion I directed that Mrs. Lesser continue to have the custody of

Larry until after I write my decision in this case and that you have visitation rights on Saturdays. Do you remember that?

MR. LESSER. I do.

THE COURT. The following Saturday did she deliver the child to you?

MR. LESSER. Yes.

THE COURT. Was it our understanding that you were to deliver the child back to her after dinner, which would be about seven o'clock? Do you recall that?

MR. LESSER. Yes.

THE COURT. You didn't bring the child back at seven o'clock?

MR. LESSER. No.

THE COURT. Was there some special reason for that?

MR. LESSER. Very special.

THE COURT. What was the reason?

MR. LESSER. When the child was delivered to me Saturday he was sick. He was coughing and sneezing. In fact, he was sick Thursday and Friday of that week.

After he was there about a half hour I took him over to the doctor. The doctor examined him and told me he had bronchial asthma. He gave me a medicine and he told me to put him to bed, to give him medication, and to take care of him. I did exactly as the doctor told me to.

THE COURT. You didn't take the child back.

MR. LESSER. I did not, your Honor.

THE COURT. Did you tell the mother what the situation was?

MR. LESSER. I called up the mother about seven o'clock.

MR. POMERANTZ. Which day?

MR. LESSER. The same day, Saturday, and told the mother that the boy was sick; he needed medication, observation, and that I was going to keep him in the house until the doctor said he could leave—until he was able to leave.

THE COURT. And since that time has the doctor told you that the child was able to leave?

MR. LESSER. The doctor was over to see him last night. He examined him and he told me he can go to school. I took him to school this morning. And the doctor said that he wanted to take an X-ray; he wanted to take some tests and he wanted to do a blood test on him today or tomorrow.

THE COURT. Do you wish to ask Mr. Lesser, Mr. Pomerantz?

MR. POMERANTZ. I do.

THE COURT. I will swear you.

b. Direct Examination by Mr. Pomerantz

Q. Do you know whether Larry attended school the two days preceding his visit to you? A. He did not attend school. He was absent Thursday and Friday.

Q. When this child arrived at your home Saturday morning, that would be a week ago Saturday, whatever the date is, will you describe to Mr. Justice Streit, so far as you could observe and hear, the condition of your child? A. After the child was around the house for about ten or fifteen minutes he started to cough; he started to sneeze. I then went over to him. I felt his head, and he felt warm. So I picked up the phone and called Dr. Foreman and I went over to him immediately.

Q. Between a week ago Saturday and today how many times did Dr. Foreman see the child? A. He made approximately four or five visits.

Q. Will you state what Dr. Foreman did by way of medication or therapy? Whatever you saw or whatever the doctor said to you. A. I was instructed by the doctor to give him the medicine four times daily. After three or four days the doctor instructed me to give him the medicine three times a day. I then was instructed by the doctor to give him a spray. The doctor brought an electric spray and I sprayed Larry's throat in the morning and at night. I sprayed it up until last night, when the doctor saw him and told me that I didn't have to spray his throat any more and we would see how he would get along.

Q. When was the last time you saw the doctor? A. Last night.

Q. Now, Mr. Lesser, has your child been told to wear eyeglasses? A. Yes, he has.

Q. When the child arrived at your home a week ago Saturday morning, was he wearing eyeglasses? A. No, he was not. I asked Larry about his eyeglasses and he said he didn't have them. I asked him where they were, and he said he didn't know; that he had brought them home from school Wednesday, but he hasn't worn them since. I then went out, called up the eye doctor, and I got him to make a pair of glasses as fast as humanly possible.

Q. Did Larry thereupon wear those glasses while in your home? A. In the home and at school.

Q. How many pairs of eyeglasses have you had occasion to buy Larry in the recent past? A. In the last six months this is the third pair of glasses.

MR. POMERANTZ. I think the record should show that obedient to your Honor's direction Larry is available. I don't know whether he is in this room at the moment, but he is certainly here or outside.

Q. In connection with your wife's visits to your home while Larry was under your roof, would you state to Mr. Justice Streit, if you are able to, the frequency of your wife's visits to see Larry while he was confined to your house? A. My wife came over Sunday to visit him——

Q. Would that be a week ago Sunday? A. A week ago Sunday she came over to visit him. She had gone upstairs—his bedroom is upstairs on the second floor—she had gone in the room and closed the door, and she was trying to tell Larry —getting him all upset and excited and she wanted Larry to go over to me and say to me that he doesn't want to stay in the house.

I told her that I didn't think it was fair to take the child and do this to him ; that she didn't have to leave it up to the child, she could leave it up to me. And I told her that if she didn't stop doing these things I would have to order her out of the house.

Larry sat there. He was very much excited. He didn't say a word. And she started all over again, and I told her that she would have to leave the house.

Q. On any occasion did you deny your wife access to your home for the purpose of seeing her son Larry? A. Yes. On two occasions when I was home I wouldn't allow her to see Larry because of what had transpired. She didn't really come to see Larry. She came to the house with the intention of——

MR. ERDHEIM. I move to strike out everything after "on two occasions."

THE COURT. Motion granted.

Q. Why did you deny your wife access to your house on the two occasions you refer to?

MR. ERDHEIM. I object to that. It calls for the operation of the witness' mind.

MR. POMERANTZ. Well, this man is sought to be held in contempt.

THE COURT. I will allow it.

A. I objected to my wife coming to the house to get my child excited, riled up, and my sister and brother-in-law threatened by her. I didn't think that was a thing she should do.

MR. ERDHEIM. I move to strike out the answer.

THE COURT. Strike it out.

c. Cross Examination by Mr. Erdheim

Q. Wasn't the sum and substance of the conversation between yourself and Dr. Foreman to the effect that the child could leave your home and go back to Mrs. Lesser's home? A. No. That's exactly what the doctor said I shouldn't do, but keep him in the house. Dr. Foreman told me I should keep him in the house. So how could he tell me to take the child out.

Q. Did you forbid Mrs. Lesser from coming to your home the following day, on Sunday, with any person other than herself? A. Yes, I did.

Q. Now, Mr. Lesser, did you not also tell Mrs.

Lesser Saturday that she could see the child alone on Sunday, alone by herself, but only for a half hour ; is that correct? A. I don't recall. I might have.

Q. On the following day, Monday, you went to business, did you not? A. That's right ; I went to business.

Q. And you left the child with your sister, is that correct? A. I left the child with my sister and the girl in the house, right.

Q. Do you know what the child had for lunch that day? A. No.

Q. Do you know whether the child had a salami sandwich for lunch?

MR. POMERANTZ. I don't know whether counsel means to be frivolous, your Honor.

MR. ERDHEIM. I am not frivolous, your Honor.

MR. POMERANTZ. But if the suggestion is made that a salami sandwich is inconsistent with bronchial asthma I suggest the question is frivolous.

THE COURT. I will allow it—if he knows.

A. No.

Q. Is it not a fact that on Wednesday, November 7th, when Mrs. Lesser came again she was not permitted to see the child? A. She was permitted to see him Tuesday, then. I can't recall. One of the days I did leave instructions not to let Mrs. Lesser in the house because, as I stated before, she got my son upset and she threatened my sister and my brother-in-law, as I stated before.

Q. You mean when she asked for the return of the child you construed that as a threat to your sister and brother-in-law? A. I did not say that she asked for the return of the child. I said that she threatened them.

Q. Did you tell anyone that you intended to flout the orders of this court with respect to the custody of Larry and that you would rather go to jail than return Larry's custody to his mother? Did you ever say that? A. I said I would take care of my son, if I had to, when he was sick in reference to a doctor or medicine or anything like that.

Q. Mr. Lesser, did you ever say to your wife or to anyone else that you would never obey the order of the court and that you would never return Larry to your wife? A. I can't recall it.

9.

SADIE LESSER

a. Direct Examination by the Court

Q. On that Saturday morning, November 3rd, did you deliver the child to anybody in particular? A. No. He was standing outside with the housekeeper, at the garage door, and I watched the child go into the driveway, and I drove away.

Q. The previous day was the child home from school? A. Yes, sir. He had coughed during the night and I thought it wise to keep him home.

Q. Saturday he was all right? A. He had a slight cough, but I thought it was permissible for him to go out.

Q. How about the prior Thursday? A. The same thing. He coughed during the night. I kept him home.

Q. Notwithstanding the fact that he had a cough on Thursday and Friday you took him, pursuant to my order home? A. Yes, sir.

Q. That night did you receive a telephone call? Did you await the arrival of your son? A. Yes, sir.

Q. And he wasn't forthcoming? A. No, sir.

Q. And what did you do about it? A. Well I called my attorney and he directed me to write some things down here, which I wrote.

Q. Did you receive a telephone call from your husband? A. Yes, sir. He said the child was ill; that he had had the doctor, and that he was not bringing him home.

Q. Then you spoke to your lawyer? A. Yes, sir.

Q. Then what did you do? Did you call Dr. Foreman? A. Yes, he said that the child—he didn't tell me what his findings were, as I recall, but that the child had 100.6 temperature.

I said, "Do you consider that a temperature?" He said, "Yes."

I said, "Well, would it be permissible for the child to be taken home nevertheless?"

He said, "Well, I would permit it," or words to that effect. I don't recall his exact words. I believe he said there was no reason that the child could not go home.

Q. What happened the next day? A. I asked the doctor would he call—that was the same evening—would he call Mr. Lesser and inform him of those facts, which he said he would do. And I called him back. He said Mr. Lesser had hung up on him without giving him any answer. That was the conversation of that day.

Q. What happened the next day? A. Mr. Lesser called me and said I could visit the child for a half hour providing I brought no one with me—which I did. I believe I called Mr. Erdheim and informed him and asked him whether I should go there, and he said, "Yes, you should go to see the child," and I went there.

I found the child playing on the floor with trains with his brother and father, and I left after a half hour. I did sit and talk to the child for a while, and he asked me when could he come home, and I said to be patient and wait. I know I didn't make any trouble there. That I am sure of.

Q. What about the next day? A. I stayed two hours that day. The father was not at home nor the housekeeper. The sister was taking care of the boy. When I arrived the boy himself answered the doorbell, and he was watching television. We played checkers and other things, and I was told by the sister that the boy had a salami sandwich for lunch, which Mr. Erdheim stated. The child again asked me when he could go home.

Q. And Tuesday, November 6th? A. The 6th I came and found that Larry had a friend in the house playing with him, a little boy from next door, and the brother-in-law was watching the child. I asked him—the phone rang or he called the father, and there was a conversation. I said to him did the father say when I could take the child home, and he said no. I said, "Would you please ask him?"—which he did. And evidently the father became angry with him, because he told him to mind his own business and not to consort with me. He didn't use the word "consort." He said to mind his own business. That was that day.

THE COURT. You may examine the witness.

b. Cross Examination by Mr. Pomerantz

Q. You say, Mrs. Lesser, that on the Thursday and Friday prior to your bringing Larry to your husband you kept him away from school because he was wheezing or coughing? Are those your words? A. I said he was coughing.

Q. Did you on either of those two days bring the child to see a doctor? A. No, sir.

Q. Did you on either of those two days give the child any medication? A. I didn't think he needed any.

Q. Is it or is it not true that you were informed, and had been informed prior to that occasion, that Dr. Foreman had diagnosed your son's condition, and specifically his cough, as being a symptom of bronchial asthma? A. Well, my daughter mentioned something about it when she brought me some medicine one time, but I don't know whether—I mean, I don't recall too well.

Q. I don't want to put words in your mouth. You tell Mr. Justice Streit what your daughter said to you about what Dr. Foreman said to her concerning Larry's condition. A. I couldn't possibly remember because there was no condition.

Q. No; my question is were you aware at all, did anybody in the world tell you, your daughter, Dr. Foreman, or anybody else, prior to this Thursday and Friday that you have testified to, that Dr. Foreman diagnosed your son's condition as bronchial asthma or, perhaps, to prod your memory, a touch of bronchial asthma? A. Well someone told me. I don't recall whether it was Mr.

Lesser, my daughter or my son, because all three spoke to me that day.

Q. Told you what? A. I don't recall the conversation, Mr. Pomerantz. I am sorry.

Q. Well, did they tell you that Dr. Foreman felt that your child was ill? A. No, sir.

Q. You don't recall that? A. No, sir. I don't recall their even using the word "ill."

Q. I am not fencing with words; ill or sick or in need of medicine, shall we say? Did you know that Dr. Foreman had prescribed medication for your child? A. Yes, sir. A red bottle of medicine.

Q. Tell us what knowledge you had about his medicine and who brought the information to you. A. The child brought it into the house, and he said, "I promised Daddy that I would take this medicine," and he did so. I did not object.

Q. How many times did the child take the medicine? A. Two times.

Q. Did you ever give the child the medicine? A. No, sir. I haven't made the promise; the child had.

Q. And you were aware of the fact that the medicine had been prescribed by a medical doctor? A. Yes, sir.

Q. And nevertheless you decided not to give it to your child, is that right? A. It wasn't within my jurisdiction to.

Q. I don't want to argue law with you. I am asking you a simple question. I say in spite of the fact that you knew that a medical doctor had prescribed the medicine you determined not to give the child the medicine; is that right?

MR. ERDHEIM. I object to that, your Honor. There is no proof that the child needed it.

THE COURT. Sustained.

Q. Well, now, when your child began coughing on this Thursday and Friday, which I think now is November 1st and 2nd, in the light of what you had understood about Dr. Foreman's prescribed medication, did it occur to you that perhaps in the light of Mr. Justice Streit's instructions to you in the Bronx a few weeks ago, did it run through your mind at all that perhaps you ought to take this child to a doctor for an examination? A. Yes, sir. But this diagnosis was made many, many weeks ago, and I didn't feel it had to hold true forever.

Q. Well, you thought your child was sick enough to keep him out of school, Mrs. Lesser, for two days. A. I kept him out because I thought it was wisdom to do so.

Q. Why do you think it was wisdom? A. Because the world would look upon it as taking proper care of a child, and that's what I proposed to do.

Q. You were anxious, in other words, to give a proper aspect to the appearance of things to the world; is that correct? A. To the child himself. I am not thinking of the world. I am just thinking of the child.

Q. Well, now, if the child were sick enough to be kept out of school don't you think he was sick enough to see a doctor? A. No, sir.

Q. How long has this occasional coughing of your son's been going on? Six months? A year? Less or more? A. Well, he coughed about two weeks ago slightly during the night, and the next day he was fine, he didn't cough at all, and I sent him to school. Now, if it's the same cough—which I doubt—he coughed again Thursday and Friday while asleep. It is my opinion that it is probably a drip through the back of his nose. But I am not a physician.

Q. Let me ask you this: When your child was going through this coughing and at any time that he was going through this coughing business did you administer to him faith healing in accordance with the Christian Science therapy?

MR. ERDHEIM. I object to that.

A. We don't heal by faith——

THE COURT. Hold it. Sustained.

Q. Did you give your child any treatment——

MR. POMERANTZ. Withdrawn.

Q. You once used the phrase during the trial of this action——

THE COURT. We are not going into that, Mr. Pomerantz.

MR. POMERANTZ. I am trying——

THE COURT. We are not going into that, Mr. Pomerantz.

MR. POMERANTZ. May I make the offer of proving that the treatment this child may have been given by this mother is not the treatment of materia medica, as she called it, but the treatment of the "Book." That's all I was trying to prove by my question.

THE COURT. We are not going into it. Do you have anything further?

BY MR. POMERANTZ

Q. When did Larry last lose his eyeglasses? A. He came home the Wednesday prior to the Saturday he stayed at his father's and the child claims he brought the glasses home; but I did not see them in the house. I searched thoroughly, and so did the child. So I sent a note with Larry to Mr. Lesser stating that he had lost his glasses and would he kindly replace them, which Mr. Lesser did. Now, I did send a note so that Mr. Lesser would know that I was aware that the child needed his glasses and that he had lost them, and I believe the child will testify to that. If he gave him the note, I don't know.

Q. Isn't it true that the reason the child doesn't wear eyeglasses is because you don't believe in eyeglasses? A. No, sir. I wear them myself.

Q. In response to questions asked by His Honor you have looked at a diary to refresh your recollection; isn't that right? A. Yes. As to this last incident my attorney advised me to make notes of my visit, and so forth.

Q. May I see your diary? I am only interested in the period involved and I will look at no other points. The period involved is from November 1st. (*The witness handed a book to Mr. Pomerantz.*)

Q. Mrs. Lesser, would you be good enough to point out to me—I don't want to pry into any earlier period—whether you have a notation there for November 1st and if not what is the first date after November 1st for which you have a notation. A. I wrote down that the father kept the child——

Q. I am not asking you to read it. I am asking you to point out anything to me.

MR. ERDHEIM. It starts Saturday, November 3rd.

A. There is something here on October 27th. I brought the child to the father at ten a.m. and he was not returned until eight-thirty. That was the week prior.

Q. I wasn't asking about that, although I don't object to your putting it in the record.

MR. POMERANTZ. Your Honor, I wonder whether rather than to detain you at this late hour, there seems to be considerable writing at the period in question—I assume we will have the testimony of the doctor soon, I hope tomorrow—may I read this without detaining you?

THE COURT. Read what?

MR. POMERANTZ. These diary entries.

THE COURT. You mean you want to take it with you to read?

MR. POMERANTZ. No, I would read it here, but without detaining your Honor. Then I could examine her tomorrow on the basis of it if there should be anything inconsistent. I don't suggest there is. I just don't know. I could do it now, but there is a good deal of writing and it is not easy to read.

THE COURT. We will defer that for the time being.

MR. POMERANTZ. May I see it after our formal session?

MR. ERDHEIM. You certainly may.

THE WITNESS. May I say something, your Honor?

THE COURT. Yes.

THE WITNESS. The father bought the child a television set and some new clothing, and I called him one evening. He was not at home and he called me the following morning. I wanted to bring out that he would not give me sufficient to buy the child anything but he bought the child these things. Also when I spoke to him about returning the child he said, "This child is in my home right now." That was his reply when I asked him when he was returning the child.

BY MR. POMERANTZ.

Q. Mrs. Lesser, his Honor suggested or commanded you, whichever it is, to take your child to a doctor at least once a month. Isn't that true? A. Yes, sir.

Q. When was the last time you took Larry to a physician?

THE COURT. I have a letter from the doctor here to the effect that he has examined him nine times.

MR. POMERANTZ. My last information is about seven weeks back, and I was wondering if there was anything in the interval.

THE COURT. This was prior to Dr. Pearlman.

MR. POMERANTZ. Dr. Reardon.

THE COURT. Dr. Reardon sent me a letter as a result of the social worker's investigation and inquiry, and in this letter he says that he has examined him nine times in nine successive months and that he found him well, and that in his opinion the mother would come to him in case of an emergency. This letter come on October 30th. This is nine times since January 1957.

MR. POMERANTZ. I am afraid this doesn't answer the question. Let me ask Mrs. Lesser the fact.

BY MR. POMERANTZ

Q. Have you within the past seven weeks. Mrs. Lesser, taken Larry to a doctor? A. I don't remember the date, but I took him to Dr. Pearlman last and then the hearing came. I don't know what Judge Streit has ordered me to do.

BY THE COURT

Q. October 22nd was the hearing. Had you gone to Dr. Pearlman before the hearing? A. Yes.

Q. And how long before the hearing did he examine him? A. There is a medical report. I don't remember the date. I don't think it was much before that.

Q. Haven't you taken him to a doctor since September 22nd? A. Dr. Pearlman was the last doctor I went to, and then I had to move to a hotel and move back again, and I am afraid I wasn't reminded.

(The plaintiff and the defendant were excused, left the room, and the boy, Larry Lesser, was brought in.)

10.

LARRY LESSER IN CHAMBERS

BY THE COURT

Q. Larry, do you remember me? A. Yes.

Q. Who am I? A. I don't know.

Q. Do you remember seeing me? A. I remember seeing you, but I don't remember you.

Q. Do you remember what we talked about? A. No.

Q. Do you remember telling me about your suit? It was the only suit you had? A. Yes.

Q. Did you get any new clothes since? A. Yes; a new winter coat.

Q. What else did you get? A. A new shirt, a new pair of pants and two pairs of socks.

Q. Where did you get those? A. My father got them for me.

Q. Where are you living now? A. With my father—now.

Q. When did you see your mother last? A. I don't know.

Q. How do you feel? A. Fine.

Q. Have you got any cough? A. No.

Q. Have you got any sneeze? A. No.

Q. Have you seen a doctor? A. Yes.

Q. What did he say? A. He said I had a cold.

Q. Did he put you to bed? A. I went to bed.

Q. And how long did you stay in bed? A. I would say a week.

Q. Did you get out at all? A. No. But since this week I got dressed; and then last week I was in bed.

Q. Did you go to school? A. Not those days.

Q. Did you go to school today? A. Yes; but I came out of school early.

Q. Why? A. Because I was supposed to come to New York.

Q. Who brought you from school? A. My brother went in and got me, and then my maid drove me to the station. He went down to get a haircut and we got on a train and came here.

Q. Do you feel a little bit tired now that you came all the way down here? A. No, I don't feel tired.

Q. Where would you like to go from here? A. It doesn't matter.

Q. Would you like me to send you home with your mother or would you like me to send you home with your father? A. I don't know.

Q. Which one would you like to go home with? What do you want me to do? A. I would like to go home with my mother.

Q. What happens if you get a cough? How are we going to take care of that? A. I don't know. I will probably go to the doctor in the end.

Q. Does the doctor give you any medicine? A. Yes. I just finished it.

Q. Finished what? A. My medicine, last week.

Q. Let me see your glasses. A. (After handing glasses to the Court) They are new because I lost my other pair.

Q. What are you, near-sighted or far-sighted? A. I don't know the difference.

Q. You don't know the difference? A. No.

Q. Let's see. Do you see that man over there? A. Way back there?

Q. Yes. A. Yes.

Q. What color suit does he have on? A. Blue.

Q. That's the fellow you think is a policeman? A. Yes.

Q. Do you see his badge? A. Yes, I can see it.

Q. Can you see how many buttons he has got? A. Yes; three.

Q. What's the color of the buttons? Are they gold or silver or what? A. I think it's gold.

Q. Can you see the initials on his lapel over there? A. Yes; S.C.—unless I made it backwards and it's C.S.

Q. You can see better than I can. Do these glasses help you? A. Yes; they make it closer.

Q. Do you like to wear them? A. It doesn't matter.

THE COURT. Bring the parents in.

(The boy left the room and the plaintiff and defendant returned.)

11.
PARENTS IN CHAMBERS

THE COURT. It is my opinion that there may be instances where under emergencies one parent who only has visitation rights may retain custody of a child for a limited period of time. Whether such an emergency existed at this particular time I am not prepared to say without further testimony. However, unless there is such an emergency no man or woman under such circumstances can take the law into his own hands.

However, the child will now be returned to the mother with the direction that she forthwith take him to a doctor, Dr. Pearlman or any other doctor, and that he be examined thoroughly, his nose, throat and lungs be examined for allergy, X-rays taken, and I want to see a copy of that report.

Following the receipt of this report I will hold another hearing, at which time I will hear the doctor who made the report as well as Dr. Foreman, and if necessary I will refer the matter to another physician designated by the Court.

In the meantime, and until final decision as to custody, the plaintiff is directed to have the child examined every two weeks, filing a copy of the report with me as well as counsel for the defendant.

Visitation periods at this time will be limited to the defendant's, the child at the home of the plaintiff for a period of two hours each Sunday afternoon in the presence of someone designated by the plaintiff, that is, until my final decision as to custody.

The child will be turned over now to the mother.

MR. POMERANTZ. Will your Honor permit me to make a very brief statement in connection with your opinion?

THE COURT. Yes.

MR. POMERANTZ. I just want to state for the record, your Honor, that this is probably the eighth or ninth admonition of record to Mrs. Lesser to take her child to a doctor when ill, in spite of which—your Honor has heard just a half hour ago the testimony of this woman—in spite of these repeated admonitions—and the record will speak for itself as to her attitude with respect to them—this woman has nevertheless defied these rulings by appointing herself the threshold judge or diagnostician as to whether the child is sick enough to require the services of a doctor. And I submit in all earnestness, your Honor, that this ninth or tenth admonition must be assumed to carry the same weight as all the other prior ones—and it will be disregarded. I know from Dr. Foreman that this child can become dangerously and acutely and mortally ill as a result of this lack of attention, and if I say this with some vigor, your Honor, it's because I feel a professional responsibility to the Court to communicate this information to you, and I am prepared to-morrow morning to have you hear that directly from someone more technically skilled than I am to make that diagnosis and prognosis.

THE COURT. I do not share the same alarm at this particular time as you do, nor do I place the weight to your remarks that you do, nor do I think that this plaintiff will defy the orders of this Court. In the very near future I will render my opinion in connection with the question of custody. I will bear your remarks in mind and will consider them in connection with my decision. In the meantime the custody is returned to the plaintiff. My final decision as to the custody will be rendered as soon after I have heard these physicians as is feasible.

November 26, 1957.

(A discussion was had at the bench off the record.)

MR. FISHER. If your Honor please, my name is Mitchell Salem Fisher. I am the attorney for the New York Board of Rabbis and, in addition, I am a member of the New York Board of Rabbis. The New York Board of Rabbis is a board consisting of approximately 700 rabbis, orthodox, conservative and reform.

THE COURT. Tell me what you have in mind.

MR. FISHER. Judge, I am advising your Honor that I have come into this matter at the request of the New York Board of Rabbis, and I am now going to act with the consent and approval of the New York Board of Rabbis and with the consent and approval of Mr. Lesser.

THE COURT. The Board of Rabbis has no standing in this case.

MR. FISHER. It is precisely because of that that by appropriate arrangement with Mr. Perry Lesser, the defendant in this case, I am now going to appear as trial counsel and as special counsel for him. Mr. Pomerantz, for the time being at least, is remaining as attorney of record, but I am appearing today, technically, as attorney for Mr. Lesser.

MR. ERDHEIM. I move at this time, your Honor, that all the statements by Mr. Fisher with respect to his association with the New York Board of Rabbis be physically expunged from the record. Mr. Lesser has the right to choose his own counsel or special counsel or trial counsel, but I submit the New York Board of Rabbis are no part of this case and any statement made by Mr. Fisher with respect thereto should be stricken from the record.

THE COURT. Your motion is denied. The statement stays in. Let's proceed with the hearing. We adjourned the hearing for the purpose of taking testimony with respect to the physical condition of the child.

12.

DR. REARDON FOR SADIE LESSER

a. Direct Examination by Mr. Erdheim

Q. You are duly licensed to practice medicine in the State of New York? A. Yes.

Q. And, doctor, you have had occasion to examine young Larry Lesser for some months prior to this date? A. Yes.

Q. From the time in December of '56, your first examination, up to November 14, 1957, your most recent examination, what did your examinations of Larry reveal with respect to his general health? A. All examinations revealed that he was in good general condition.

b. Cross Examination by Mr. Fisher

Q. Doctor, do you have the notes of your examination on November 14th? A. No, I do not.

Q. Did you make any notes of that examination? A. I did.

Q. And did you know that you were going to come here today to be examined with respect to this child? A. Yes.

Q. Did you take his temperature on November 14th, doctor?   A. No.

Q. Did you weigh him, doctor?   A. I think I did.

Q. Well now, you think you did. I am not interested in your thoughts. Did you weigh him?   A. I would have to refer to my records to give you that answer. If I weighed him the record will show it.

Q. Well, do you recall that he was weighed?   A. No, I don't.

Q. Did you measure his height?   A. I think I did, yes.

Q. Doctor, you say you think you did. Did you measure his height?   A. I couldn't tell you without referring to my records.

Q. Is there some particular reason why you haven't brought your records today, doctor? You have testified before, haven't you?   A. I have.

Q. Doctor, may I ask you this question: Prior to November 14, 1957 when was the last time that you had examined the child?   A. I don't think I had examined him for two or three months prior to that.

Q. Do you recall whether she communicated with you with respect to the child at any time in October, 1956?   A. I don't recall, no.

Q. Doctor, are you aware of the fact that sometime toward, I think it was, the beginning of November of this year on, I think, a Thursday and Friday immediately prior to November 3, 1957, this child did not go to public school?   A. No.

Q. You don't know that, do you?   A. Mrs. Lesser just informed me this morning that the child was sick during the last two weeks. That's the extent of my knowledge.

Q. And that's the first information that you had with respect to any sickness of the child?   A. Correct.

MR. FISHER. I have no further questions.

BY THE COURT

Q. If a child has 100 or a 100.5 temperature is it necessary to call a doctor?   A. Ordinarily I would say no. It depends on a lot of the circumstances.

Q. Did you find any asthmatic condition in this child?   A. I did notice on the last visit that with deep breathing he did have one or two wheezes, yes.

Q. What does that mean?   A. It means he probably had a little congestion in there.

Q. Did you prescribe for that? What is there to be done for that?   A. Well, as I told Mrs. Lesser at the time, it's something that should be watched.

Q. Is there any treatment for it?   A. If it gets worse. I didn't feel it was severe enough to start the child on a course of treatment.

Q. I have a letter from you that I received subsequent to the time that this social worker visited you in which you said: "Observing the attitude and reactions of Mrs. Lesser I feel she would seek medical aid if the boy were seriously ill." Do you still feel that way?   A. I do.

Q. That if anything of a serious physical nature happened to this child she would call you?   A. Yes, I do.

BY MR. FISHER

Q. Did Mrs. Lesser tell you the nature of the sickness that the child had when the child was kept home from school?   A. No, she did not. Do you mean just now, this morning?

Q. When she took the child to you on November 14th.   A. She said he had a cold the last one or two days; yes.

Q. And did she tell you anything else?   A. No.

Q. You relied on that statement that she made?   A. Yes.

Q. And, in general, you have relied on these statements that she has made to you; is that right, doctor?   A. Yes.

Q. And that is what has led you to form your opinion that she would seek medical aid and guidance?   A. If the child were sick, yes.

MR. FISHER. That's all.

13.

DR. FOREMAN FOR PERRY LESSER

a. Direct Examination by Mr. Fisher

Q. Doctor, on November 3, 1957, did you receive a telephone call from Mr. Perry Lesser?   A. I did.

Q. After you had that conversation with Mr. Lesser did he come to your office?   A. He did. I examined Larry. I took his temperature. He had a fever. He was wheezing. He was out of breath. In other words, he was sick.

MR. ERDHEIM. I move to strike out "in other words, he was sick."

THE COURT. I will allow it.

Q. You speak of the child wheezing, doctor. Can you tell us what you observed with respect to the character or the nature or the intensity or the frequency of the wheezing?   A. Well, he was wheezing almost continually. If you got right near him you could hear the wheezing in his chest. He was out of breath. When I asked him to climb up on the table he started to breathe with a little bit of difficulty. When I listened to his chest there were the rales, sibilant, sonorous rales, and some crepitant rales, throughout the chest. The child was coughing two or three times every three or four minutes.

Q. What was your diagnosis? A. My diagnosis was bronchial asthma and possibly pneumonia.

Q. As far as the child was concerned, was the child in comfort or discomfort? A. The child was in discomfort.

Q. And did you give instructions to the father with respect to the child? A. I did. I told him that the child had the clinical findings of bronchial asthma and possibly pneumonia. If he had had a temperature of 103 or 104 I would probably be more certain of the diagnosis of pneumonia, or if I had a chest X-ray to find these things. You can run a little bit of fever with some bronchial asthma, but in bronchial asthma you do not hear crepitant rales. On the basis of this I decided that this child probably had pneumonia. I decided to treat him as though he had pneumonia. I told Mr. Lesser to take the child home, to put him to bed, to give him this medicine that I prescribed, and that I would see him daily as long as necessary, and I told Mr. Lesser, "You had better take the child home to your house."

Q. What did Mr. Lesser say to you? A. Well, he said he is supposed to see Larry once a week. I said, "Look, that is your problem. All I know is that if this really develops into a full-blown pneumonia, where you don't need X-rays any more, in twenty-four hours this child can be critically ill." And I told Mr. Lesser, "I am sure you are dealing with reasonable people. The child is sick. Take him home. Do what I told you to." But he pointed out to me, as I said, that Larry was supposed to go back to the mother that day; he is only supposed to see him one day a week. I told him the child was going to be sick for more than a few days and he had better take him home. He isn't going to get medicine with Mrs. Lesser, and he needs it.

THE COURT. You said that?

THE WITNESS. Yes, sir.

Q. On what did you base that statement, doctor?

MR. ERDHEIM. I object to that.

THE COURT. Sustained.

Q. Did you, as a physician, advise him not to take the child to Mrs. Lesser's home? A. Yes.

Q. And was it because of your interest in the health and welfare of this child that you gave him those instructions, doctor? A. Yes.

Q. What medicine did you prescribe? A. Trisulfanil. I decided to treat him for pneumonia.

Q. Doctor, did you prescribe any diet? A. I said that he may eat anything he likes to eat.

Q. Doctor, what was the temperature of the child at the time of your examination? A. At the time I examined him he had orally a temperature of 99.6. This temperature to me had significance.

Q. On what do you base your view? A. Well, 98.6 is the average, normal temperature of a human being. Over 99 by mouth I consider abnormal.

Q. Was it, then, the temperature together with the other things that you observed, the wheezing and the coughing, that led you to make your diagnosis? A. No; the temperature alone was abnormal.

Q. On September 15, 1957, doctor, which, to my recollection, was the Day of Atonement, had you examined the child? A. Yes. That day I have written down—you see, I wasn't quite definite about the diagnosis—he had no fever. He had some rales in his chest and I wrote down, "Either bronchial asthma or bronchitis."

Q. Doctor, that evening did you receive any communication from Mrs. Lesser? A. Yes.

Q. Will you now state what she said to you and what you said to her. A. Well she called me and said that her husband has Larry in his house and she wants him back, and she asked me is there any reason why she shouldn't have him. I said, "Larry is sick. He has bronchial asthma. Possibly he has pneumonia. He needs the medicine that I prescribed for him and you won't give it to him. So I told Perry to take the baby, put him to bed and give him the medicine."

Q. What did she say? A. Well, she asked me if I would call Perry and say that she wants to have the boy in her house. I said, "All right; I will call Perry and tell him you want the boy in your house."

BY THE COURT

Q. Did you tell her that there was no reason why the child couldn't go home to her? A. No.

Q. You never said that to her? A. No.

Q. Did you later tell her that you called Mr. Lesser and that he hung up on you? A. No.

Q. You never said that? A. No.

BY MR. FISHER

Q. When next did you see the child, doctor? A. I saw the child the next day. I advised that they continue the medicine that I gave him. He was at rest; so that he wasn't so much out of breath. He was still wheezing; he was still running some fever. I said he is to remain in bed and I will see him each day and see how things progress.

Q. And on those days what was the condition of the child? A. The child appeared to be improving. On the 6th he no longer had fever. You couldn't hear the wheezing any more unless you actually put the stethoscope to his chest. He was so much improved, without any fever, without any distress at all, that I said, "It isn't necessary for me to see the child any more. When the child is ready to go back to school you call me and I will examine him again."

Q. Is bronchial asthma a serious matter with respect to a child? A. Bronchial asthma is a serious matter with respect to a child.

BY THE COURT.

Q. You have an opinion that the condition existed prior to November 3rd? A. I am certain that it did.

Q. What are the possibilities in the event medical treatment is not given? A. If medical treatment is not given to a case of asthma that is frequently recurrent, as it was in this child, in a large percentage of these cases in five, ten, twenty years they become what I define as respiratory cripples. There is actual damage to the lung done.

BY MR. FISHER

Q. Will you tell us the reasons in your opinion why this child had developed bronchial asthma? A. Well, in this particular case I feel that the bronchial asthma is to a large degree, to the greatest degree, a psychosomatic manifestation of conflicts within the child itself.

Q. Is it also possibly due to outside influences in connection with allergy? A. Both. Usually the outside influences, like pollens and dust, are the trigger that brings out or brings on an attack of asthma.

Q. Assuming, doctor, as you have told us, that bronchial asthma has psychosomatic aspects, when it finally exists in a child does the child require actual medical treatment of the normal character that physicians give to children? A. That's what I advise, not only medical treatment. This child in particular requires both medical and psychiatric treatment.

Q. Doctor, I am quite certain that all of us are interested in the emotional and physical health of this child. What is your advice, if any, with respect to this child and its future treatment?

THE COURT. Are you objecting to the question?

MR. ERDHEIM. I object to it.

THE COURT. Sustained.

BY MR. FISHER

Q. Doctor, in your view is a psychological and psychiatric examination of both parents required?

MR. ERDHEIM. I object to that.

THE COURT. Sustained.

MR. ERDHEIM. Your Honor, my recollection is that in the examination of the prior physician your Honor in cross-examination, or in your Honor's examination of the doctor I believe your Honor read something from Miss Moshowitz' report.

THE COURT. No, I did not. I read from the doctor's report. There was a report of the doctor subsequent to Miss Moshowitz' interview with the doctor.

MR. FISHER. Your Honor, I respectfully request the right to examine Miss Moshowitz' report.

THE COURT. The application is denied. It is confidential to the Court as an aid to the Court.

MR. FISHER. Your Honor, I offer the Moshowitz report in evidence.

THE COURT. Your application is denied.

MR. FISHER. I respectfully except. Your Honor, I respectfully request that, since we are concerned with the custody of the child and the welfare of the child, I trust that your Honor is considering this testimony in this contempt hearing in connection with the general question of custody.

THE COURT. I certainly am.

MR. FISHER. I am appreciative of that, your Honor.

I have no further questions.

b. Cross Examination by Mr. Erdheim

Q. Do you know Dr. Reardon, doctor? A. Yes.

Q. You don't specialize in pediatrics, do you? A. No.

Q. And you have testified with respect to pediatrics, have you not? A. Yes.

Q. Now, doctor, this child, when you examined the child on November 3rd, had a low-grade temperature; isn't that so? A. Yes.

Q. In your opinion, doctor, the child was cured on November 6th? A. No.

Q. Well, wasn't that the date you said there was no wheezing? A. I said this particular attack had improved to the point where I could let the child go.

Q. Without any further medication? A. That's right. I didn't say it was cured. Bronchial asthma doesn't get cured like that.

Q. There was no reason why Perry Lesser should hold the child as late as November 10th or 11th? A. I told him to.

Q. Notwithstanding the fact that as of November 6th he needed no further medication? A. I didn't say that.

Q. Didn't you say the child had no wheezing, was all better? A. That's right.

MR. FISHER. When?

Q. On November 6th? A. Very little, if any.

Q. Did you prescribe for the child to eat anything? A. Yes.

Q. Even salami sandwiches? A. Yes, if he liked it.

Q. You have made no diagnosis here on your

report with respect to pneumonia, have you? A. No.

Q. Well, in settling for the diagnosis, if there is a possibility of pneumonia, don't you set that forth in your report? A. This isn't the regular report. These are my notes.

Q. Where is your regular report? You don't have it here? A. I don't have a regular report. Nobody asked me to make a regular report. These are notes that I scribble in my office. They mean things to me. It is sort of a shorthand.

Q. You know the child was out in the street? Didn't you know that? A. Around the house.

Q. In front of the house, in the street? A. That's right. I told him to do it.

Q. Doctor, on the 12th of November, when you saw the child, did you tell Mr. Lesser to have the child's chest X-rayed? A. I told him before the 12th. I told him what I would do—if you will look at my notes there——

Q. Was it done? A. Mr. Lesser asked me if I would see that these things were done. I said that I was interested at the moment in treating this child so that he would be better, get over this attack—the child was going to get more attacks— but if Mr. Lesser wasn't going to have the child there would be no point to it.

Q. You felt that the child was not going to be in Mr. Lesser's custody and for that reason you weren't going to do that? A. That's right.

Q. Yet you knew Mr. Lesser had the child until November 13th, did you not? A. Well, that was another problem. I knew that he was not supposed to have it. He asked me what does he have to do to make the child better. So I said, "There are two things. There is a long-range treatment and there is a treatment now." I said, "I will treat him now if you keep the child."

Q. Did Mrs. Lesser ever say to you that she would not give the child medicine? A. Yes, she said that.

Q. When did she say that to you? A. When I was her doctor and the child's doctor—years ago.

Q. Did she say that to you recently? A. I didn't have the opportunity to speak to her recently except for that telephone conversation.

Q. Excuse me, sir. After Mrs. Lesser called you the first time did you then call Mr. Lesser? A. I did.

Q. What was your purpose in calling Mr. Lesser after Mrs. Lesser called you the first time? A. Well, you see, Doctors do a lot of strange things. She asked me to; and I don't want to fight with anybody. I said, "You want me to call Perry, I will call Perry."

Q. What was said? A. She asked me to call Perry to tell him that she wants the child back. She didn't ask me how ill the baby was. She

never asked me how ill the baby was. She tells me that the baby is not sick.

Q. What did you say to Mr. Lesser? A. I said, "Mrs. L. says I should call you. I am doing as I am told. Mrs. L. asks me to call you and tell you she wants the baby back."

Q. And what did Mr. Lesser say to you? A. He said, "All right. So you called me."

Q. Then Mrs. Lesser called you back? A. That's right.

Q. And what did you then say? A. I said, "Perry doesn't want to give you the baby back because I told him to keep the baby."

MR. ERDHEIM. That's all.

THE COURT. Mrs. Lesser, I have just one question.

14.
SADIE LESSER

a. Direct Examination by the Court

Q. Tell me again what happened when you called Dr. Foreman, what you said to him and what he said to you. A. I called Mr. Leman, my attorney. I told him that Mr. Lesser had just called me and said he had the child; that the child was ill and that he was going to keep him. Mr. Leman said to call the doctor and find out how sick the child was, which I did. I asked him what was wrong with the child, and he said he had a touch of bronchial asthma.

I said, "Does he have a temperature?"

He said, "100.4."

I said, "Well, is it possible for him to be taken out to come home this evening?"

He said, "I don't see any reason why he can't go home."

So I said, "Well, will you please call Mr. Lesser and inform him of the fact and I will pick up the child and I will call you back."

Which I did. I called him back, and he said that Mr. Lesser had not answered him or hung up on him. I just don't recall exactly.

b. Cross Examination by Mr. Fisher

Q. When you refer to "Mr. Leman" to whom do you refer? A. Herbert Spencer Leman.

Q. And is he the attorney for the Christian Science Church?

MR. ERDHEIM. I object to that, your Honor.

MR. FISHER. I know a Mr. Leman has been here previously and I would like the record to indicate the capacity of Mr. Leman in this matter.

THE COURT. Mr. Fisher, you are not—much as you may like to—going to relegate this case into a quarrel or fight or contest between the Christian

Science Church and the Board of Rabbis. That is not in this case. Please understand that.

MR. FISHER. I so understand.

THE COURT. The objection is sustained.

MR. FISHER. Now, Judge, previously there was some reference——

THE COURT. The hearing is closed.

MR. FISHER. I object to the closing of the hearing and I wish to offer testimony with regard to the emotional behavior of this child and with respect to the desirability of a psychological and psychiatric examination both of the child and of both parents, and particularly of the mother.

THE COURT. Motion denied.

MR. FISHER. If your Honor please, I believe that your Honor has received a letter from the daughter, Dee Lesser.

THE COURT. Yes, I have.

MR. FISHER. And I do not know whether that is part of the record. I offer it in evidence. I offer a duplicate original of that letter in evidence.

MR. ERDHEIM. I object to that, your Honor. That is not within the purview of the order of the Appellate Division remanding the case back to your Honor.

MR. FISHER. We are interested to the very last moment in the custody of these children, and I do believe that unless we have an inquiry here showing very definitely what is the prognosis——

THE COURT. You needn't raise your voice, counsellor. These are my private chambers. There is no jury here.

MR. FISHER. I apologize for raising my voice. My zeal occasionally leads me to emphasize——

THE COURT. I have the letter. You don't have to offer a copy. I have the letter from Dee.

MR. FISHER. Will the original be deemed part of the record?

THE COURT. I have the letter; that's enough.

MR. FISHER. I ask will it be part of the official record of these proceedings.

THE COURT. It's unnecessary.

MR. FISHER. I offer in evidence, then, this duplicate original. Will your Honor please rule upon my offer?

THE COURT. Is there any objection?

MR. ERDHEIM. There is an objection.

THE COURT. Sustained.

MR. FISHER. I ask that it be marked for identification.

MR. FISHER. I ask that the Moshowitz report be marked for identification.

MR. ERDHEIM. Objection.

THE COURT. Application denied.

MR. FISHER. I except.

MR. FISHER. Judge, I believe that it is in the interests of a determination of the custody of this child that evidence be submitted to the Court by such psychoanalyst or psychiatrist or psychologist as your Honor may direct and appoint so that we can consider what effect the shift, among other things, of the religious life of this child will have upon the child's future.

I believe that this record will be woefully incomplete unless there is such a psychiatric examination of the mother—and of the father, also. My understanding is that the father, pursuant to the recommendation of the psychiatric case worker, did go to a psychologist or psychoanalyst and that the other refused to do so. And I believe that the record will be incomplete unless this is done.

THE COURT. Are you making an application?

MR. FISHER. I so apply.

MR. ERDHEIM. I object to it.

THE COURT. Application denied.

MR. POMERANTZ. In your previous interrogation of Mrs. Lesser you did refer to the Moshowitz report to the extent of asking Mrs. Lesser whether she did or did not make a certain declaration assigned to her by the Moshowitz report—according to the pitch of your question. Under the circumstances we respectfully beg leave that at least so much of the report as was postulated in your question to Mrs. Lesser be made available to counsel.

THE COURT. So that there will be no misunderstanding about my ruling with respect to reports of social workers or anybody else who is not an employee or an officer of this Court, they are an aid to the Court. They are not public documents. The witness is not subject to cross-examination. They are confidential to the Court only. They pose problems for the Court to pursue and inquiries for the Court to be made on the record, for the record, under oath. That is all. Everything else is hearsay.

MR. POMERANTZ. I except to your Honor's ruling.

G.

The Judge Decides

1.

TO GRANT MOTION FOR CONTEMPT

December 10, 1957

Mr. Justice Streit.

Motion to punish defendant for contempt is granted. I am of the opinion that the defendant has deliberately and unjustifiably withheld the custody of this child from its mother from November 3 to November 13 and that he has been contemptuous of the order of this court. In view of my decision this day as to the custody of Larry J., I see no need at this time of inflicting any punishment upon the defendant. Plaintiff, however, is awarded the additional counsel fee in connection with this contempt proceeding in the sum of $150 to be paid within five days of service of a copy of the order to be entered herein. Settle order.

2.

TO GRANT MOTHER CUSTODY OF LARRY

December 11, 1957

Mr. Justice Streit.

Pursuant to the remittitur, this court designated a social worker, recommended by the Association of the Bar of the City of New York, to make an investigation and report. After receipt of the report, the court conducted hearings, in which counsel participated, at which the parties and witnesses were examined, and, in addition, the court interviewed Dee, the daughter, and Larry, the (now) seven-year-old boy, whose custody is to be determined. The report consists of a series of interviews with the parents, the children, and others. It is only "an aid" to the court and cannot become part of the record or form the basis for a decree (cf. People ex rel. Kessles v. Cotter, 285 App. Div., 206; Handler v. Handler, 282 App. Div., 694). The social worker is not an officer of the court. It would not be feasible to have her sworn or subjected to cross-examination. Even if this were done, most of her testimony would constitute hearsay, consisting of her version of what others said to her. Although the investigator's reactions and views are entitled to the court's consideration for the purpose of assisting the court in arriving at its determination, the ultimate decision must be made by the court itself, not by the unofficial investigator. Otherwise the court would be abdicating its legal duty as an officer of the state judicial system. The report of the social worker was, however, given careful study and consideration by the court, and its contents formed the basis of questions put by the court to witnesses at the hearings held after the filing of the report.

Were it not for the fact that the plaintiff is a member of the Christian Science Church and the bearing such membership has upon the possibility that Larry may not receive necessary medical attention and care if his custody is entrusted to plaintiff, there would be no question, in the court's opinion, but that she should be awarded the boy's custody. Larry is only seven years old. In the absence of exceptional circumstances, the mother, if she is a proper person able to discharge her duty to the child, is entitled to the custody of an infant of that age (People ex rel. Sinclair v. Sinclair, 91 App. Div., 325; Application of Mac-Alpine, 50 N.Y.S. 2d 232 [Mr. Justice Shientag]). This is all the more true in view of the fact that the plaintiff was the innocent party to the breakup of the marriage, the decree of separation having been granted to her because of repeated assaults upon her by defendant and the latter's unjustified abandonment of her. As the Court of Appeals said in Harrington v. Harrington (290 N.Y., 126, page 130): "Apportionment between the parents of the blame for the broken marriage may not be the decisive factor in the determination (of custody) (People ex. rel. Herzog v. Morgan, 287 N.Y., 317). Nonetheless the past conduct of the parents, the unwillingness of one or both to carry out their marriage obligations are factors which may not be disregarded in determining which parent will provide the better home."

If the custody of Larry were given to his father, he would see very little of that parent and would enjoy the companionship and parental guidance of his mother only on days of visitation. The defendant leaves home for business at varying times between 7:30 A.M. and 9:30 A.M. and returns at varying times between 5 P.M. and 8 P.M. In addition, the defendant makes frequent trips which absent him from home for periods of three to five days. During his absences, both on business days and on said trips, the only adult companionship and guidance Larry would receive would be that of the maid and, occasionally, that of defendant's sister and brother-in-law. On the other hand, were Larry intrusted to the custody of the plaintiff, he would enjoy the companionship, care and *parental* guidance normally received by a child of his age. Although the present home of plaintiff is not all that it might be from a physical standpoint, this situation is only temporary and is due entirely to defendant's willful failure to pay plaintiff the amount required by the decree of this court. The boy himself told the court that he enjoyed living with his mother and always had "a lot of fun" with her and that he did not miss his father much and prefers to live with his mother. The plaintiff is a refined and cultured person and appears to be devoted to Larry.

Under the circumstances it seems clear that the only doubt to the suitability of the plaintiff to be intrusted with the custody of Larry is created by the fact that she is a member of the Christian Science Church and, as a believer in its doctrines, might fail to furnish necessary medical or surgical care to Larry in the event of his illness. This is what the Appellate Division appears to have had in mind when it referred, in its opinion, to "the doubts that evidently troubled Special Term, and that trouble this court." The court, at the trial, had interrogated plaintiff as to whether she would call a doctor if her child were ill and had directed, in the decree of separation, that she cause Larry to be examined at least once a month by a physician and that she be guided solely by the latter's advice as to medical treatment that might be required.

Before taking up the question of the plaintiff's attitude toward healing by medicine or surgery, it might be well to point out that the mere fact that plaintiff's religion is Christian Science does not ipso facto disqualify her from the right to custody of her infant child. If mere membership in that church were a ground of disqualification, the Appellate Division could, and presumably would have so decided without remitting the question of custody for further investigation. Nor does the fact that awarding custody to the plaintiff may result in the child's being educated according to the tenets of the Christian Science Church affect the right which she would otherwise have to its custody. In Weinberger v. Van Hessen (260 N.Y., 294), the court said (p. 298): "While the court will not take the question of a child's religious education into its own hands short of circumstances amounting to unfitness of the custodian, it must on occasion decree partial custody, including the right of religious education, according to the views of the custodian." In Matter of Kamanack (272 App. Div., 783), it was held that (p. 784) "the court will not take the question of the child's religious education into its own hands short of circumstances amounting to unfitness of the custodian (Weinberger v. Van Hessen, supra) and in a dispute relating to custody

religious views afford no ground for depriving a parent who otherwise is qualified (Denton v. James, 107 Kan. 729.)" (See also Harvard Law Review, vol. 29, p. 485, where, referring to the English law that the father had the right to choose in what religion his child should be educated unless by his acts he forfeited, abandoned or waived that right, the statement is made [p. 497] that "In the United States the constitutional limitations against any established religion have fortunately suggested a different judicial approach to religious" education, and [p. 499] that "as between father and mother any question respecting the child's religion should be settled by the award of the right of custody.") Indeed, if the Appellate Division had been of the opinion that an award of custody should not be made to the plaintiff because of the fact that it might result in the child's education according to the tenets of the mother's religion, there would have been no necessity for a remission to this court for further investigation. The possibility that Larry might be educated according to the doctrines of the Christian Science Church was not one of "the doubts that evidently troubled Special Term and that trouble this court," for there is nothing in the record on appeal that indicates that the Special Term was troubled by the possibility that Larry might be educated as a Christian Scientist.

We therefore turn to the question which troubled both this court and the Appellate Division, the solution of which is determinative of the custody issue, viz., will an award of custody to the plaintiff subject Larry to a substantial risk that his mother may fail or neglect to furnish him medical care and treatment if he should become ill and need it, because of her views, as a Christian Scientist, toward healing by faith rather than by medicine? At the trial, the plaintiff testified that if the court order required her to call a doctor if her child were ill, she would do so * * *. She added that "I have called doctors on many occasions" * * *. Since the making of the decree, dated December 15, 1956, which required plaintiff to cause Larry to be examined at least once a month by a physician, plaintiff has submitted him to a physician for such examination at least once a month, except that no examination was had between September 22, 1957, and the time of the hearing of November 13, 1957. The hearings commenced on October 22, 1957, and plaintiff's failure, after nine successive months of compliance, to submit the child for medical examination between October 22 (one month from the date of the last examination) and November 13 appears to have been inadvertent and due to the holding of the hearings as to the question of custody. During this period the plaintiff also took

Larry to a dentist and an oculist for examination and treatment. At the hearing of October 22, 1957, the court, after instructing plaintiff that the law required her to give her boy necessary medical and surgical care, if she had custody of him, asked her whether she would comply with the law. She swore that she would do so, although she did not like to do it because of her religious beliefs. *"Q. But notwithstanding the conflict between your religious beliefs and the order of the Court which would you follow? A. Well, the law."* * * *.

An attempt has been made by defendant to establish that plaintiff has failed and refused, on several occasions when Larry was ill, to furnish him with medical care. A similar charge had been made at the trial by Doctor Foreman ("the family physician"; * * *), but this court discredited his testimony and found "that the plaintiff herein has not imperiled the health and lives of the children of the parties hereto and she has not failed and refused to secure needed medical attention for the children from licensed physicians and surgeons" * * *.

Two instances of alleged failure to give medical attention to Larry were claimed by defendant to have occurred since the trial. The date of the first was September 15, 1957, the Day of Atonement. The defendant had asked to have the boy that day. Defendant claimed that when he arrived home about 3 P.M. from the synagogue, he heard Larry cough and sneeze and that he had his daughter take him to defendant's "family physician," Dr. Foreman. The latter prescribed some medicine. When the boy was returned to the plaintiff, he brought with him a bottle of the medicine. Plaintiff allowed the child to take the medicine, which he did twice, but she herself did not give him any of the medicine to take. The defendant swore that the child had a fever, but Dr. Foreman admitted that Larry had had no fever at the time he examined him and that he was not definite about the diagnosis. He testified that the boy had some rales in his chest and that he had written down "either bronchial asthma or bronchitis." Plaintiff, on the other hand, testified that the boy was well when she took him to defendant's home; that he had no fever; that she had him examined by Dr. Pearlman on September 22, only a week later, and the report of Dr. Pearlman showed that he found nothing wrong with the child. The evidence relating to the incident of September 15 fails utterly to persuade the court that plaintiff would deny Larry medical care if his condition required it.

The other incident took place on Saturday, November 3, 1957. The defendant's claim that Larry was ill on November 3 and required medical care and attention has come into the record as defendant's defense to plaintiff's motion to punish him for contempt for failure to return Larry to her at the end of that visitation day. (The court has found defendant to have been guilty of said contempt—see opinion filed on companion motion, decided simultaneously herewith.) On the morning of November 3, plaintiff, in compliance with a previous order of the court left Larry at defendant's home. She had kept him home from school on November 1 and November 2 because he had a cold. Defendant testified that when the boy arrived, he was coughing and sneezing; that he took him to Dr. Foreman who said he had bronchial asthma, prescribed some medicine, and told defendant to put Larry to bed. Defendant testified that he did so and, because of the boy's illness, refused to return him to plaintiff that evening as required by the court's order. Dr. Foreman testified that Larry, at the time he examined him, had fever and was wheezing and out of breath. He claimed that when he listened to his chest he had sibilant, sonorous, and some crepitant rales. His diagnosis was bronchial asthma and possibly pneumonia. He decided to treat him "as though he had pneumonia" and he prescribed trisulfanil. Dr. Foreman admitted that the boy's mouth temperature was 99.6, only 6/10 of a degree above normal, and 100.4 rectally, only 4/10 of a degree above normal. He further testified that by November 6 the temperature had disappeared and he told defendant that it was unnecessary for him to see the child any more. Although the doctor had not seen the boy until November 3, and therefore could not have known whether he had any fever on November 1 or November 2, he testified that, in his opinion, the boy required medical attention on those days. On cross-examination, the doctor admitted that he had not fluoroscoped or X-rayed the child's chest; that his notes failed to mention the possibility of pneumonia, and that he had permitted the child to be out in the street prior to November 12. Plaintiff admitted that Larry had a slight cough on the morning of November 3, after she had kept him home for two days, but she testified that she thought it was permissible for him to go out. She testified that she called Dr. Foreman that Saturday night, November 3, and said to him: "Does he have a temperature" to which he replied "100.4". She asked: "Well, is it possible for him to be taken out to come home this evening?" and he said: "I don't see any reason why he can't go home." Plaintiff went on: "So I said, 'well, will you please call Mr. Lesser and inform him of the fact and I will pick up the child and I will call you back' which I did. I called him back and he said that Mr. Lesser had not answered him, or hung up on him" * * *. Dr. Foreman categorically denied that he told plaintiff that he did not see why the child could not go home, or that he told her that Mr. Lesser had hung up on him.

On November 14, 1957, Dr. Reardon examined Larry and found him in good health. Even if Dr. Foreman's testimony and diagnosis are accepted as true, there is nothing in the record to indicate that plaintiff could or should have known, prior to the time she brought Larry to defendant's home on November 3, that he had any fever or that he was ill. Nor does her request that the boy be returned to her indicate that she would not have given him proper medical care if he required it. Admittedly the boy's temperature was only a trivial amount above normal, a frequent occurrence in well persons, particularly children. It is also undisputed that on Saturday evening, November 3, the defendant told Mrs. Lesser that she would be permitted to visit with the child the following day *alone* for half an hour.

Plaintiff testified that when she visited the boy at the defendant's home on November 4, the day after Dr. Foreman's examination, she found him playing on the floor with his father and brother. This testimony, too, is undenied. The court is satisfied that Dr. Foreman's testimony as to the boy's rales and as to the proper diagnosis was, to say the least, grossly exaggerated, and where his testimony was in conflict with that of the plaintiff, it is my opinion from an observation of these two witnesses that the plaintiff was telling the truth.

Dr. Reardon testified that his examination of the boy on November 14, 1957, only eleven days later, showed his general condition to be good and that X-rays of his chest on November 16 were negative. He noticed a slight congestion which he felt was not severe enough to require treatment. He also testified that if a child has a temperature of 100 or 100.5, it ordinarily is unecessary to call a doctor. Dr. Reardon testified further that it still was his opinion that after *"observing the attitude and reaction of Mrs. Lesser I feel she would seek medical aid if the child were seriously ill"* * * *.

The testimony relating to the incident of November 3 fails to establish in the slightest that the plaintiff, if granted custody of Larry, would fail to submit him to medical or surgical treatment in the event of an illness requiring such treatment. Even parents who are not Christian Scientists do not rush their children to doctors whenever they cough or have a fraction of a degree of temperature. From the evidence before me I am convinced that the plaintiff has and will faithfully continue to comply with the orders of the court.

On the other hand I find that the defendant has failed to pay the plaintiff the amounts ordered by this court for support and maintenance, has attempted to rewrite the decisions of this court, has imposed economic sanctions on the plaintiff and has contemptuously deprived plaintiff of the custody of the infant for a period of ten days.

On the present record, to deny to this plaintiff the custody of the seven-year-old boy would be practically tantamount to a holding that a parent who is a Christian Scientist is unfit as a matter of law to be the legal custodian of her own child.

I am satisfied: 1. That the plaintiff, notwithstanding her religious beliefs, will provide Larry with the necessary medical and surgical care. 2. That she has admirably nurtured and reared this infant. 3. That she is fit and qualified to have permanent care and custody of this child. 4. That the welfare and interests of Larry J. would best be served in the custody of his mother.

I am also of the opinion that the defendant has neither the time nor the ability to care for or nurture this young child.

Custody is therefore granted to the plaintiff with the proviso that she continue to have the child examined by a physician each month and continue generally to provide the child with necessary medical and surgical care. The defendant shall have the right to visit the infant each Sunday from 1 P.M. to 5 P.M. at the home of the plaintiff.

With respect to the order of remission by the Appellate Division of the support and maintenance provisions to be made for the plaintiff and the infant son, they are to remain the same, namely, $150. per week plus $300. per month in lieu of the use and occupancy of the home.

Settle order.

H.
The Appellate Court Affirms

Per Curiam. . . . The decision on the matter of the custody of Larry, youngest of three children to the marriage, is . . . unimpeachable here. The evidence tending to establish the mother's devotion and fitness as a custodian, even when considered with the disadvantages consequent upon the difference between the mother's chosen religion and that to which the child had earlier been exposed, provided a reasonable basis for the trial court's exercise of discretion. That matter, therefore, creates no issue of law . . . .

The judgment of the Appellate Division should be affirmed, without costs.

I.

Appraising the Role and Function of Legislator, Court and Counsel

The underlying problem for decision at both Lesser trials is how to dispose of their children. Phrased in terms of the generally prevailing "guide" the question is: "What custodial arrangements will serve each child's best interests?" The materials in this section have been selected to illustrate some of the major questions essential to evaluating the family-law process directly concerned with the parent-child relationship, which is the subject of a more detailed analysis in Chapter III.

In continuing the search for the meanings of "in the best interest of the child," we seek to evaluate its appropriateness as a guide for determining the disposition of children in a variety of settings and to assess the adequacy of procedures and personnel for eliciting and recognizing data relevant to these decisions.

1.

FAMILY DISPUTES ABOUT CHILDREN AND "RELIGION" — DETERMINING THE AMBIT OF STATE INTERVENTION

a. PEOPLE ex. rel. SISSON v. SISSON
156 Misc. 236, 281 N.Y.S. 559 (1935)

PERSONIUS, JUSTICE

This proceeding involves the custody, care, and control of Beverly Jane Sisson, hereinafter, for convenience, referred to as Beverly, an infant now nine years of age. She is the daughter of the relator and respondent, and resides with them in their home at Sherburne, Chenango county, N.Y . . . .

The relator urges, among other things, that the respondent, a Megiddo, aided and abetted by other Megiddo adherents, places so much emphasis on the study and practice of the Megiddo teachings that Beverly is kept from home to an unreasonable extent, alienated in some respects from her mother, thereby destroying the natural relationship which should exist between them and tending to make her peculiar and perhaps fanatical, rather than normal.

In our view of the case, the Megiddo beliefs are not very material. However, brief reference thereto may be helpful. The word "Megiddo" is a Hebrew word signifying, "God is in this place with a band of soldiers," or "a true soldier of God." The church or cult was founded in 1880 by the Reverend L. T. Nichols. It first carried

on its work in a steamer on the Mississippi river; later, its adherents acquired a site near Rochester where they now maintain their mission. Maud Hembree, one of the original members, is the present pastor. She is sincere, devout, and appears well educated. There is nothing immoral in their teachings, practices, or conduct. They accept the bible and practice its teachings, as they construe them, very literally. We think they may be fairly characterized as ultra religious and strict. This has led to certain beliefs and practices which are, at least, unusual. They seem to believe that the present "age," about 6,000 years, will end at the second coming of Christ. Then a "few," some 144,000, will be accepted and "chosen" to start another age. In the meantime, marriage, though not forbidden, is frowned upon, celibacy is advocated and propagation not favored, even among married members. Though not anarchistic, they refrain from participation in government, either by voting or holding public office. Originally, attendance at public schools was not favored, because the schools were a part of the government. At present, attendance at the Megiddo school is preferred, if practical. All frivolity is disapproved, only seriousness and much Bible study is held to be profitable.

We are not here concerned with the Megiddo church and its beliefs, except indirectly. We are concerned only with the question of what is for the best interests of Beverly; the question of her welfare. . . .

Mr. and Mrs. Sisson, married in 1920, have

but the one child now aged nine. They reside in a good modern house in the suburbs of Sherburne. Mr. Sisson is forty years of age, a graduate of Cornell University, and a successful produce dealer. Mrs. Sisson is about the same age, of keen intellect, capable and well informed. She suffers, however, from acute arthritis and has been bed-ridden for about six years. Both were adherents of and attendants at the Baptist Church. Mr. Sisson was a trustee. Both apparently read Megiddo literature; Mrs. Sisson stating that since she had been confined to her bed she had read most everything available, including Christian Science literature. She denies that she ever became particularly interested, although Megiddo people called upon her and made tiresome visits. She tried to be polite to them, but finally asked them not to come to her room. Mrs. Sisson read the literature without being carried away. Mr. Sisson became not only interested but obsessed, not to say fanatical.

The relator and respondent are legally entitled to joint guardianship and joint control of Beverly. The relator, being an invalid and unable to go out or even about the house except on rare occasions, has very limited opportunity to exercise any control. The respondent, on the other hand, has every opportunity and persistently imposes his influence and control. Does Beverly's welfare require the interference of the court? This question should, we think, be determined in the light of present-day generally accepted standards and thought.

Neither her comfort, education, nor health are being neglected or impaired, except that her frequent journeys and absences from home to some degree cause fatigue and injury to health and school-work. But are these the only elements to be considered as bearing on her welfare? We think not. A child is entitled to develop and mature normally; to enjoy childhood's normal playtime, recreation, and relaxation; to grow up rationally, unwarped, without narrowness, and evenly balanced mentally. Too much serious application may be as injurious as too little. Above all, a girl should enjoy the love, companionship, and unrestricted comradeship of a worthy mother.

We firmly believe in the study of the Bible and religious subjects to a reasonable extent. We think there is here over-emphasis in this respect. Beverly is absent from home each school day from 8:30 in the morning until late afternoon. At least every other week end from Friday after school until Sunday night, and sometimes Monday morning, she is taken by respondent to Rochester, staying there with a Megiddo family, comparative strangers to her mother, and in exclusive asssociation with Megiddos. On occasions she remains there without her father. Fifty days or parts of days out of 200 were spent there. These trips are made when she is not too well; once with a fractured arm. At home each morning, sometimes before arising, and each evening, she engages in Bible study with her father and sometimes a Megiddo visitor or employee who resides at the home. She has committed about 500 Bible verses, is urged to repeat them at odd times, for instance, while waiting for the school bus, and has attended Megiddo meetings held by her father and others at a shack in the field. A letter written by Mr. Sisson to Beverly is largely devoted to sermonizing, as is a three-page letter written to her by Brother Simmons.

On the other hand, normal activity and the innocent pleasures of childhood are limited. The celebration of Christmas on December 25 is strenuously opposed. It is claimed that the date is erroneous, as though that was vital. Christmas is not a date, it is an event. Children's parties are discouraged and have been given up. One planned by Mrs. Sisson in her room was practically broken up by Mr. Sisson who presented bible verses, had them read and committed to memory by the children, and then gave a test to see which child had best learned the lesson. Paper party costumes and valentine parties are objected to, as is the wearing of play suits, ordinary bathing suits, pajamas, and the like. Long dresses with long sleeves, made of velvet or woolen, are advocated, and the light sleeveless dresses ordinarily worn disapproved. Only "useful" and "instructive" toys are approved. . . . There is an absence of dolls, toy automobiles, fire engines, etc., although the adults have their band and orchestra, enjoy fishing and hunting trips and hot dog roasts. Mottoes (verses) are substituted for the usual pictures on the wall. No fiction is read. Listening to the radio and viewing the motion picture is disapproved. . . . This illustrates the atmosphere and influence with which Beverly is surrounded. While this situation concerns only Mr. and Mrs. Sisson and Beverly, the Megiddos have been much interested in extending their influence over Beverly. She enjoys the trips to Rochester. Why not? Coming practically from the country, she is taken to new surroundings, to the parks, shown the flowers, the animals, the zoo; to the lake shore, to a mountain camp and entertained and made much of. She goes swimming, but apparently with a dress on.

. . . Megiddo visitors are frequent at the Sisson home; Megiddo employees live there. Both participate with Mr. Sisson in Beverly's instructions; this in the absence of her mother.

If we understand Christianity and its teachings, it would seek to draw this family together, rather than apart, even at the expense of yielding some, not too important, tenets. Here Megiddo adherents have sought to impress their doctrines upon this family at whatever cost. In the name of their form of Christianity we see a family torn asunder; the sacred relationship between this mother and her infant daughter interfered with; a crippled and bedridden woman who should be humored by her family and friends inflicted with a cruelty more refined perhaps, but not less torturing, than physical pain.

The respondent avers that he has never insisted that Beverly refrain from participating in Christmas, children's parties, and other amusements, and that he has never insisted upon her participating in Megiddo practices. Perhaps not expressly, but he dominates by his persistent attitude and influence as effectively as he could by direct command. The influence of his fellow Megiddos strengthens the domination. Notwithstanding his letters to Beverly's school teacher, he insists that he has never prevented Beverly from participating in Christmas exercises. This, he says, he left for Beverly to decide. In other words, this child at seven, eight, and nine years is called upon to decide whether December 25, or some other date, is the true date of the birth of Christ. In view of the attitude of her father and his friends, it approaches mockery to say that she is left to her free choice.

Is Beverly developing and maturing normally? At the age of eight she thinks it is "babyish" to play with dolls and would rather say verses. She has and attends no children's parties. In place of a prayer in which she mentioned her father and mother, a prayer has been substituted which does not mention individuals but only the "family" which is understood to mean the Megiddo family. She asks her mother if the latter "were her real mother," saying she "thought the person that first taught me the Megiddo religion was my mother."

Beverly, a bright attractive child, is undoubtedly loved dearly by both parents. Yet it seems impossible to paint a true word picture of her life. Reading the entire record fails to do so, without reading between the lines. It is quite intolerable. We do not think it is for her best interests to mature in this atmosphere, counseled one way and then another, bewildered, called upon in her immaturity to determine questions beyond most adults, her pleasures and recreations circumscribed, developing not in normal ways but quite the contrary.

The court may take one of three courses: (1) Continue the joint guardianship and control; (2) award exclusive control to the respondent; (3) award exclusive control to the relator. We hesitate to interfere with the joint control. No reason appears for the taking it from the relator. However, the respondent has exercised his joint control to the practical exclusion of the mother in some very vital respects. To give him exclusive control would only aggravate the situation. We think the relator can be trusted to reasonably exercise exclusive control. When the respondent first began to exercise his influence in favor of Megiddoism to the exclusion of all others, she tried to tolerate it. She endeavored to satisfy the respondent relative to Beverly's clothes by remodeling them. At a conference between the relator, respondent, and their respective fathers, she submitted certain, compromise propositions, among them the suggestion that Beverly should not be taken to the Megiddo Mission until she was old enough to know her own mind, or that she spend as much time in an orthodox church as at the Megiddo church, or that she be taught no particular religion, but left free to choose. To all these the respondent objected. He objects to Beverly's visiting her maternal grandparents in his absence; and insists upon enforcing his own beliefs on Beverly's immature mind.

We feel impelled to award the control of this child to one parent or the other. We award it to the relator relying upon her to exercise her control reasonably and with that fairness which she has already displayed.

NOTES

NOTE 1.

PEOPLE ex rel. SISSON v. SISSON
271 N.Y. 285, 2 N.E. 2d 660 (1936)

PER CURIAM.

* * *

In proceedings for the custody of children, the courts have reiterated that their sole point of view is the welfare of the child. The parents of this child are obviously interested only in her welfare. When they realize that for the good of the child it is necessary for them to repress to some extent the natural desire of each to have the child educated solely according to his or her point of view, the remaining sources of difficulty doubtless will disappear.

The court cannot regulate by its processes the internal affairs of the home. Dispute between parents when it does not involve anything immoral or harmful to the welfare of the child is beyond the reach of the law. The vast majority of matters concerning the upbringing of children must be left to the conscience, patience, and self-restraint of father and mother. No end of difficulties would arise should judges try to tell parents how to bring up their children. Only when moral, mental, and physical conditions are so bad as seriously to affect the health or morals of children should the courts be called upon to act.

* * *

The order of the Appellate Division and that of the Special Term should be reversed . . .

NOTE 2.

KILGROW v. KILGROW
268 Ala. 763, 107 So. 2d 885 (1958)

GOODWYN, JUSTICE.

* * *

It would be anomalous to hold that a court of equity may sit in constant supervision over a household and see that either parent's will and determination in the up-bringing of a child is obeyed, even though the parents' dispute might involve what is best for the child. Every difference of opinion between parents concerning their child's upbringing necessarily involves the question of the child's best interest.

* * *

It may well be suggested that a court of equity ought to interfere to prevent such a direful consequence as divorce or separation, rather than await the disruption of the marital relationship. Our answer to this is that intervention, rather than preventing or healing a disruption, would quite likely serve as the spark to a smoldering fire. A mandatory court decree supporting the position of one parent against the other would hardly be a composing situation for the unsuccessful parent to be confronted with daily. One spouse could scarcely be expected to entertain a tender, affectionate regard for the other spouse who brings him or her under restraint. The judicial mind and conscience is repelled by the thought of disruption of the sacred marital relationship, and usually voices the hope that the breach may somehow be healed by mutual understanding between the parents themselves.

* * *

In view of what we have said it is unnecessary to decide whether the decree, in effect ordering that the child attend a school of a particular religious denomination which, according to the evidence, involves mandatory teaching of the religious doctrines of that denomination, would be giving preference by law to a particular religious sect contrary to the First and Fourteenth Amendments of the Constitution of the United States and § 3 of Article 1, Alabama Constitution of 1901.

The decree appealed from is due to be reversed and one rendered here dismissing the petition. It is so ordered.

NOTE 3.

KILGROW v. KILGROW
Three Years Later

[T]he daughter continues to attend Loretto School and the parents continue to live together. In answer to your question as to whether the law suit helped to settle the argument, I am not in a position to say. However, since the parents have continued to live together I feel that the litigation did impress both parties with the necessity of settling family disagreements within the home rather than in the court. [Letter from Sol. E. Brinsfield, Jr., attorney for the mother, dated May 19, 1961.]

NOTE 4.

UNITED NATIONS
Principles Relating to Discrimination in Respect of Right to Freedom of Thought, Conscience and Religion*

Part 1

1. Everyone shall be free to adhere, or not to adhere, to a religion or belief, in accordance with the dictates of his conscience.

2. Parents or, when applicable, legal guardians, shall have the prior right to decide upon the religion or belief in which their child should be brought up. In the case of a child who has been deprived of its parents, their expressed or presumed wish should be duly taken into account, the best interests of the child being the guiding principle.

3. No one shall be subjected to material or moral coercion likely to impair his freedom to maintain or to change his religion or belief.

4. Anyone professing any religious or non-religious belief shall be free to do so openly without suffering any discrimination on account of his religion or belief.

* * *

8. (a) Everyone shall be free to teach or to disseminate his religion or belief, either in public or in private.

(b) No one shall be compelled to receive religious or atheistic instruction, contrary to his convictions or, in the case of children, contrary to the wishes of their parents and, when applicable, legal guardians.

* * *

12. In countries where exemptions from participation in certain or all public ceremonies are

---

* *United Nations Review*, Vol. 6 (Feb. 1960), p. 29.

granted to individuals who object to such participation on the ground that it is contrary to their
conscience, such exemptions shall be granted in
such a manner that no adverse distinction based
upon religion or belief may result.

Part IV

Public authorities shall refrain from making
any adverse distinctions against, or giving undue
preference to, individuals or groups of individuals
with respect to the right to freedom of thought,
conscience and religion ; and shall endeavour to
prevent any individual or group of individuals
from doing so. In particular:

1. In the event of a conflict between the demands of two or more religions or beliefs, public
authorities shall endeavour to find a solution
reconciling these demands in a manner such as
to ensure the greatest measure of freedom to
society as a whole ;

2. In the granting of subsidies or exemptions
from taxation, no adverse distinction shall be
made between, and no undue preference shall be
given to any religion or belief or its followers ;
. . . .

NOTE 5.

ABINGTON SCHOOL DIST. v. SCHEMPP
374 U.S. 203 (1963)

MR. JUSTICE CLARK.

* * *

The place of religion in our society is an
exalted one, achieved through a long tradition of
reliance on the home, the church and the inviolable citadel of the individual heart and mind. We
have come to recognize through bitter experience
that it is not within the power of government to
invade that citadel, whether its purpose or effect
be to aid or oppose, to advance or retard. In the
relationship between man and religion, the State
is firmly committed to a position of neutrality.
Though the application of that rule requires
interpretation of a delicate sort, the rule itself is
clearly and concisely stated in the words of the
First Amendment . . . .

NOTE 6.

ODELL v. LUTZ
78 Cal. App. 2d 104, 177 P. 2d 628 (1947)

WOOD, J.

This is an action in declaratory relief to determine whether plaintiff has the right to visit her
eight-year-old granddaughter at reasonable times.
Judgment was in favor of defendants (the parents
and the minor child), and the plaintiff appeals
therefrom.

Plaintiff's daughter, the mother of the child, is

deceased. The child's father remarried, and his
wife adopted the child. There is no dispute between the father and his wife as to the custody
of the child, or any dispute at all between them,
and it was stipulated at the trial that they are fit
and proper persons to have custody of the child.
It was also stipulated that the grandmother is a fit
and proper person. No question of custody is
involved. The only question is whether the grandmother is entitled to an order compelling the
parents to permit her to visit the child at reasonable times.

The child is the only living descendant of the
plaintiff. . . .

* * *

Adoptive parents occupy the same position as
the natural parents, with all the rights and duties
of that relationship. (Civ. Code, § 228.) One of
the natural rights incident to parenthood, a right
supported by law and sound public policy, is the
right to the care and custody of a minor child.
. . . Although the rights of parenthood are not
absolute, but subject to the superior right of the
state to intervene and protect the child against
abuse of parental authority, the state may not
constitutionally interfere with the natural liberty
of parents to direct the upbringing of their
children. . . . The supremacy of the mother and
father in their own home in regard to the control
of their children is generally recognized. "It is said
that the natural rights of a father . . . are greater
than those which any guardian can have. . . .
The legal obligations of parenthood include the
duties of support, of care and protection, and of
education. As compensation therefor, the law
recognizes certain rights in the parent. . . . So
fundamental are the rights of parenthood that
infringements thereof have been held to constitute
an encroachment on the personal liberty of the
parent forbidden by the Constitution. . . ." (39
Am. Jur., 593, 594.)

In the case of Robertson v. Robertson, . . . the
court stated, 72 Cal. App. 2d at page 137, 164
P. 2d at page 57: "Their [grandparents] right, if
it can be called that, is no different from that of
any third person or stranger." The same rule
would apply to the right of visitation by a grandparent where the parents have custody, and there
is no question as to their fitness or ability to care
for the child. There is nothing in the record which
would indicate that the association of the plaintiff and her grandchild would be anything but
beneficial to the child. However, the court does
not have the power to compel the parents to allow
the grandmother the right of visitation merely
because the relationship is that of grandparent.

* * *

b.   LIDZ, THEODORE ; FLECK, STEPHEN ;
CORNELISON, ALICE ; and TERRY, DOROTHY

The Intrafamilial Environment of the
Schizophrenic Patient:
Parental Personalities and Family Interaction*

We have selected the Grau family for presentation because the pathology was not too extreme and because the parents came from sufficiently divergent backgrounds to illustrate some areas of interest with reasonable clarity. It is an upper middle class suburban family, relatively aloof from kin. The family, when the study was started four years ago, consisted of the father, 56 ; the mother, 52 ; Nancy, a 22-year-old schizophrenic daughter ; and Ellen, a college girl of 19. The marriage was troubled from the start because both parents were strange, showing many psychotic features both in our contact with them and on projective tests.

Let us first look at the persons who married 27 years ago. At 29, Mr. Grau had never dated a girl before meeting his wife. He was a shy chemist who even then viewed the world with a jaundiced eye, and was given to depressive moods. He came from a northwestern farm family of German Evangelican origin. His father, a relatively wealthy man, must have been rigid and somewhat paranoid ; we know, for example, that his wife was not permitted to leave the farm to shop in town more than once or twice a year, Born in Germany, she was better educated than most farm wives of her generation. Our patient's father had little use for his numerous siblings, except for one sister Ellen, and retained little contact with his married sisters and one bachelor brother, all of whom settled on farms near the family home. Mr. Grau had always been aloof and without close friends. He felt an outsider in high school because most of the others came from Scandinavian families, and in college because he was a "hick" even though it was a state college. He had difficulty finding himself after high school, and was permitted to go to college by his father only when he promised not to study agriculture, as his father had set prejudices against scientific farmers. After completing a year of graduate school, Mr. Grau accepted a position with a large chemical firm in upper New York state, and remained with it. Just how and why he married his wife remains obscure, because he talked as if he had been an unwary country boy who had been trapped. We know he could have escaped since she agreed to

* 28 AM. J. ORTHOPSYCHIATRY 762-776 (1958). Copyright 1958, American Orthopsychiatric Association, Inc, Reproduced by permission.

marry only after he had willingly given his written promise to raise their children as Catholics.

Mrs. Grau's father was a German Catholic and her mother a devout Irish Catholic. The father was a strict man, cruel to his wife and sons, but he favored his only daughter. According to Mr. Grau he was a tavern keeper, while Mrs. Grau said he was a restaurant owner. At any rate he ran a speak-easy at the time of the marriage. Mrs. Grau's mother managed to get along with her difficult husband. The bond between mother and daughter was very close. Mrs. Grau had an adequate social life before marriage, and had just completed two years at a junior college. She had set ideas of right and wrong and adhered strictly to her Catholicism. For many years before our study started, at least, she had been vague and scattered in her talk, conveying the impression of being childish and feebleminded, but it soon became clear that her intelligence was not defective. Though perhaps attracted by a scientist from a well-to-do family, she certainly married a man who resembled her father in being stubborn, German and set in his beliefs.

Trouble started almost immediately. Mr. Grau, insecure as a man, followed his father's pattern and expected his wife to obey, and to mother him. He deeply resented her attachment to her church as an infidelity to him. He claimed that he had known few Catholics, and had not understood that Catholicism was a way of life as well as a religion. He was suspicious of his wife's fidelity without provocation, and he trailed her on occasion. He developed great contempt for her "stupidity." The arguments soon focused on religion, because Mr. Grau decided not to have children as a way out of his pledge to raise them as Catholics. Evidence indicates, however, that he could not tolerate having rivals for his wife's attention.

When Mrs. Grau became pregnant three years after they were married, Mr. Grau felt that his wife had trapped him, following her mother's advice to have a child to preserve the tottering marriage, although he had assumed responsibility for the contraception. Fighting raged constantly, and Mr. Grau struck his pregnant wife in the abdomen, a fact which she never forgot. Thereafter, the marriage became a hostile encounter, focusing on the daughter's religion. Mr. Grau refused to allow her to be baptized Catholic. Mrs. Grau felt betrayed and attacked by his assault on her religion. She considered leaving him but was advised by her priest to stay for the sake of the child. Mrs. Grau could not accept a situation that left her child living in sin. Her insecurities in raising the child were heightened because she could not rear her in the tradition in which she felt secure. In any event, she was very rigid

[handwritten margin note: Mother Catholic class ?]

with Nancy, following to the letter the strict schedules taught in her book, and she was apprehensive of any initiative the girl showed. Nancy became a docile, conforming child who never stood up for herself with her mother or playmates when small. Her birth had clearly separated the parents, rather than bringing them closer together. Three and a half years later Ellen was born— also unwanted by her father but welcomed by the mother. The birth did not arouse such violence but the discord continued. The father, having gained his way with Nancy, expected his wife to follow his orders with Ellen. However, hopeless about ever gaining his consent, Mrs. Grau secretly had both children baptized, justifying herself because of her husband's broken promise. When, at some later date, Mr. Grau learned of her action, he became infuriated and grew increasingly distrustful of her.

Mrs. Grau, however, was much less restrictive in raising Ellen, having learned that raising a child required more than providing for physical needs according to schedule. Ellen soon showed herself to be more aggressive and less compliant than her sister.

Several attitudinal patterns were permanently established in this family. The father constantly displayed a peculiar paranoid attitude about Catholicism, blaming his troubles and many of the troubles of the world on the way Catholics raised children. He could not tolerate the acceptance of a belief which conflicted with his own cynical suspiciousness of people's motives. He constantly deprecated his wife as a Catholic, contemptuously calling her a fisheater and still less complimentary terms, and never missed an opportunity to call attention to Catholic miscreants he read about in the newspaper. He had fixed ideas about education, derogating anyone without a college degree, and considered his wife in particular stupid, and her views worthless because she had attended only junior college. Mrs. Grau received no emotional support from her husband in raising the children. He constantly deprecated her to the children and she responded in kind. The family had almost no social life: the mother saw a few women friends, and the father stayed home in what seems to have been a disinterested and almost apathetic state. Communication had descended into irritable fights over trivia, always turning into conflicts over religion. Under stress, the mother became even more scattered than usual. As Nancy grew older, the father wooed her to gain her to his side of the conflict.

This couple, who had hoped their needs would be met in the marriage, floundered in a hapless situation. Mr. Grau, whose insecure narcissism needed constant support through admiration, became jealous of the attention his wife gave the children and attacked her and her way of life. Mrs. Grau, who had been her father's favorite, married a man like her father, but found no fatherly support but only criticism from a husband who favored the children and rejected her. Mr. Grau, who tried, like his father, to insist upon his pseudomasculine dominance, only provoked defiance. They were enemies but could not get along without one another. They could not avoid fights because Mr. Grau could not forego cynical comments, and Mrs. Grau, with remarkable tactlessness, did not know when to keep quiet. Afraid of her husband, she often pretended to agree but then did as she wished, further infuriating him. Talk of separation became common, but they stayed "because of the children."

When Nancy was 9, the situation deteriorated further when Mr. Grau developed a chronic disease which incapacitated him for long periods, and forced dependence upon his wife. He was an irritable patient with a violent temper at home, and apparently preferred the hospital. When Nancy was 14 and Ellen 10, Mr. Grau became completely invalided for three years because he refused an operation which would improve his condition. Mrs. Grau worked, and with liberal help from both grandfathers, the family managed without notable change in economic status. Mr. Grau could not take the pressing needs of the family into account and undergo the operation for their sake. Eventually he had to accept the operation, after which he was able to return to work though he continued to suffer considerable pain at times.

When, during her father's invalidism, Nancy entered adolescence, she changed markedly. Mrs. Grau had continued to be distrustful and extremely intrusive, wanting to know exactly what Nancy did whenever she was away from home. Nancy began to fight back, and unable to retain some privacy by maintaining silence, because her mother would nag and insist that she tell, she learned to talk but reveal nothing. She purposefully became vague and confusing—in a sense all she had to do was to copy her mother's confused talk and her father's evasiveness. Her father would not permit her to date until she was 16—but then Nancy focussed her attention on boys, dressing in a dramatic and inappropriate fashion that infuriated her mother and made her suspicious. If Nancy went out with a Catholic boy, her father was infuriated; if with a non-Catholic, her mother hounded her. Aside from his concern about the boy's religion and education, Mr. Grau showed a peculiar neglect concerning whom she dated, as if in collusion with Nancy to aggravate and worry her mother. Nancy went with some rather questionable characters, and Mrs. Grau would chase her about the house, insisting on hearing every detail of the evening, and slapped her if she would not tell. Fights between Nancy and Ellen would soon turn into fights between Nancy and her mother, with Mr. Grau on the sidelines making no effort to head off the battle.

Entering upon the genesis of Nancy's illness would require too much detail for this presentation. We wish only to note that by the time Nancy entered college she clearly sided with her father, insisting that her mother had deceived him in having her baptized and that she was a Lutheran. She considered her father to be the perfect man, a judgment which made the hospital staff shudder, for he was a bitter, cynical and verbally sadistic person who consciously sought to make his daughter cynical and suspicious. Nancy felt that completing college was essential, as her father could not respect her unless she gained her degree. She wished to become an interpreter, a meaningful and necessary occupation in this family. Hating her mother and seeking love from her father, she sought to become totally different from her mother.

Whereas Nancy always got caught between her parents and became the focus of their hostility to one another, Ellen managed differently. There had been notable differences in the way the two girls had been raised. Ellen had not been a source of conflict, nor a substitute conflict for the parents, nor had her mother restricted or nagged her as much as Nancy. Her father had become seriously incapacitated when Ellen was only four or five.

Ellen considered that she had profited greatly from seeing how her sister got into trouble, and sought to avoid repeating her errors. She patterned herself to be different from Nancy. She managed to pick the strengths of each parent, and warily and diplomatically placated both of them. She sought to gain their trust by being the type of daughter each wanted. Even when permitted to go out with boys at 16, she disclaimed any interest in boys, and concentrated on studies and athletics. Above all she gained her mother's approval and confidence by letting her know that she espoused Catholicism, a fact which through silent collusion they hid from Mr. Grau. As a Catholic she was not so restricted by her mother, and since she did not go out on dates, she avoided the Catholic boy vs. non-Catholic boy controversies. To all except the father it was clear that the family was divided into two camps: mother and Ellen as against father and Nancy. How well Ellen concealed her loyalty to her mother became apparent when Mr. Grau and Ellen were interviewed together, Mr. Grau acting as if Ellen were on his side and shared his contempt for her mother. Ellen considered such concealment essential, for if her father knew for instance that she had joined a Catholic society at college, he would hate her as much as he hated her mother. Ellen saw her mother's shortcomings, and considered that she had handled Nancy very badly; but she had few misconceptions about her father.

When Ellen went away to college she joined the Catholic society and started dating Catholic boys. Ellen chose strength, for Catholicism was her mother's strength and the only consistent guiding principle in the family. She also chose to study science, for her father's strength lay in his profession, and she also thus bought his interest and approval. Her father had sent her to a western college to lessen the chances of her meeting Catholics, but he could not observe what she did away from home. There are many such details, but the essence of her ways was shown in her choice of a husband. He was Catholic, and a chemical engineer. Her father's violent objections to this religion were dissipated in his interest in finding that his prospective son-in-law shared his professional interests. In a sense, Ellen was correcting the error her mother had made 27 years before in marrying a non-Catholic, as if this had been the source of her unhappiness. Although Ellen was reasonably well adjusted, in fact, a master at tightrope walking, she paid a price, for both interviews and projective tests clearly indicated that this highly intelligent girl was seriously constricted, deprived of imagination and inner stimuli.

In leaving the description of the family at this point, we wish to comment that attention to these family problems proved rewarding therapeutically. Mrs. Grau came to believe that the constant conflict over religion was largely responsible for Nancy's illness. Knowing that her husband would never give in, she did. She encouraged Nancy to become a Lutheran, and her father to take her to church. Perhaps this shift was made possible because she now knew that she had been victorious with Ellen. Mr. Grau, pleased by his Pyrrhic victory with Nancy, managed to restrain himself in his quarrels with his wife to some extent.

We have examined this 27 years of family interaction, abstracted briefly here, according to a number of systems of reference which have contributed to the understanding of the problems involved. Sociologic approaches which pay minimal attention to the individuals concerned and their personal assets, idiosyncrasies and problems do not meet our needs. Still, consideration of family dynamics must include the value systems and cultural usages that fuse along with the parents to form the new family unit. We cannot understand the functioning of a family, its assets and liabilities, without grasp of its structure in relation to the society in which it exists.

* * *

2.

DETERMINING PARENTAL RIGHTS AND RIGHTS OF CHILDREN TO PARENTS— RELIGIOUS AFFILIATION AND NEED FOR CONTINUITY OF WHAT AS A FACET OF "IN THE CHILD'S BEST INTEREST"

a. In Support Proceedings

RAMON* v. RAMON*
Domestic Relations Court of City of New York
34 N.Y.S. 2d 100 (1942)

O'BRIEN, JUSTICE.

This is a proceeding wherein the petitioner-wife seeks from the respondent-husband support for herself and the child of the parties.

Respondent admits his liability for the support, but asserts that the child of the parties is not being reared and educated in the Catholic religion, all in violation of an ante-nuptial contract and agreement made between the parties. The petitioner is a Protestant. The respondent is a Roman Catholic.

The child now eight years of age is baptized a Roman Catholic. Up to recently the child attended a Roman Catholic Parochial school and had been brought up in the Catholic religion.

Differences having recently arisen between the parties, the petitioner left the home of the respondent and went to live with her mother. Simultaneously she removed the child from the Catholic school, entered her in a public school and sent her to a Protestant Church, which she attended at the time of this hearing and also to the Sunday school connected with it.

* * *

The petitioner concedes that the petitioner and respondent prior to their marriage and in the presence of witnesses signed a written agreement, in conformity with the rule and the Canon Law of the Roman Catholic Church, the substance of which agreement was as follows: "All children of either sex born of the proposed marriage would be baptized and educated in the Catholic religion," and that she, the petitioner, "would not hinder nor obstruct in any manner whatsover the respondent in the exercise of his religion."

Upon this agreement the respondent married the petitioner with a Catholic ceremony performed by a Catholic priest. Under the Canon Law of the Catholic Church no priest, in the absence of such an agreement, can officiate at a marriage between a Catholic and a non-Catholic. Canon 2319-2375.

Subsequent to the birth of the child, the petitioner consented to its Catholic baptism. Accordingly, the child was prepared, godparents were selected, and with the knowledge and consent of the petitioner the child was taken to the Catholic Church where the baptismal ceremony was performed.

The godparents, in accordance with the Canon Law of the Catholic Church, assumed the obligation and personally pledged themselves to see to it that their godchild would be instructed in the Catholic religion and that they would take an interest in the spiritual welfare of the child "in perpetua", and that they would see to it that during its whole life the child would live up to the principles of the Catholic faith. Canon 769.

* * *

The question now before the Court is whether this pre-nuptial agreement contains all the elements of an enforceable valid contract.

* * *

Section 81 of the Domestic Relations Law gives both parents equal powers, rights and duties. . . .

* * *

In the case of People ex rel. Rich v. Lackey, 139 Misc. 42, 248 N.Y.S. 561, 577, the Court declared that the Catholic education of children at the wish of their Catholic parents was not a sectarian view *but a matter of sound public policy.* In that case two children were placed in the care and custody of a third person of good character, who, inadvertently, failed to continue their Catholic education. The Court said: " * * * It is important that the spiritual education of children of such an impressionable age should be properly safeguarded. It is conceded that the wishes of their parents to have them brought up in the religion of their ancestors must be respected. And this is also the view which the law takes. It does so, not as a matter of sentiment or out of deference to narrow sectarian views, *but as a matter of sound public policy.*" (Italics those of the Court.)

"The family is the institutional unit in which infants, in co-operation between the home, the school, and the Church or other spiritual agency, can best be prepared as members of society and as good citizens. Even though the infant be *physically separate from the family, it is still constructively a part of it,*" declared the Court, "and entitled to be brought up in the religious faith professed by its parents. These principles are entirely consistent with the American view of

---

* This opinion as here published substitutes fictitious surnames in accordance with the spirit of Domestic Relations Court Act, Sec. 52.

religious liberty." People ex rel. Rich v. Lackey, 139 Misc. 42, 248 N.Y.S. 561, 577. (Italics those of the Court.)

*   *   *

In the Matter of De Marcellin, 24 Hun 207, at page 209, the Appellate Division unanimously upheld the ruling of the Surrogate of Kings County, and affirmed the rule that mere material well being of a child in a non-Catholic home cannot offset, counterbalance or destroy the right of the child to be brought up in the religion, associations and background of its Catholic parents. In that case a nine year old orphan girl came before the Surrogate upon an application of a stepmother for guardianship of the infant. The child's paternal aunt challenged the appointment on the ground that she was in better circumstances than the stepmother, owned some property and could give the child a better home, surroundings and education. The father a day or two before his death, and when he was beyond recovery, wrote these words upon a piece of paper and handed it to his wife: "Keep the children. Be a good Catholic, live a good Catholic and die a good Catholic, and pray, pray for me when I am dead." In denying the application of the non-Catholic aunt the Court said: "It is quite true that in the ordinary view it seems more desirable that the child should reside with the aunt and enjoy the comforts of a home in her family, but this consideration cannot overcome the dying wishes of her father. His declared will in relation to the custody and religious education of his child should be followed * * *. He had the power to dispose of the custody of this child if he had exercised it in a legal manner, and * * * his * * * wishes should now control and be carried out, and that the surrogate exercised his discretion well."

*   *   *

The recognition by our American courts of the right of the Catholic party as a matter of sound public policy to determine the religious upbringing of the children, with or without an antenuptial agreement, may arise from an instinctive and tacit recognition of three fundamental concepts, to wit: (1) Ante-nuptial agreements providing for the religious education of children, are exclusively a Catholic rule. (2) The Roman Catholic Church is the only Christian Church which holds marriage, and has always held it to be indissoluble and a Sacrament. . . . (3) The procreation of off-spring under the natural law being the object of marriage, its permanency is the foundation of the social order.

Indissolubility of marriage and prohibition of "mixed marriages" are not mere sectarian rules but are deeply rooted in the consciousness and history of mankind. Indeed, it would be a challenging omission in this memorandum if reference were not made to their age old historic origin and enforcement.

*   *   *

"Agreements between parents relating to the religious training of their children are generally upheld." Williston on Contracts, Sec. 1744a, note, page 4939 . . . .

The respondent had the legal, equitable and constitutional right to protect, to preserve and to maintain inviolate his membership in the Roman Catholic Church. He had the undoubted right to enter into any agreement which would insure to him the continued enjoyment of its privileges and its protection, the religious and moral inspiration and the spiritual tranquility which he felt it inspired.

He had the right to determine that in his married life he would continue as formerly to abide by its rules, obligations and discipline. He had the right to seek to preserve this advantage for his children, the issue of the marriage, the same privileges, contacts and inspiration which he as a father considered essential to his and to their happiness and well being. . . .

He had the right to choose for a spouse one who, though not a Catholic, would at least agree not to interfere in the exercise by him of his solemn religious duties, the most important of which would be to *see that his children were brought up in the Catholic faith,* and to see that they would attend Mass, to partake of the Sacraments, and to faithfully undertake and discharge all of the Catholic duties, inseparable in a Catholic home. For it is important to note that *it was only by a concurrence with these obligations, that the respondent's membership in the Catholic Church* would be insured and continued. Canon 2316-2319. "A Practical Commentary on the Code of the Canon Law," . . . .

Relying on this solemn promise by which the petitioner agreed to protect and preserve this right, respondent married the petitioner and irrevocably and for life changed his status from the single to the married state.

Not only was the status of the respondent changed, but the godparents, under the provisions of the Canon Law, assumed also a new and irrevocable spiritual status and impediments, the details of which need not be outlined here. Canon 768.

The law favors ante-nuptial agreements and they will be enforced in equity according to the intention of the parties. . . .

*   *   *

Section 53 of the Domestic Relations Law provides, " a contract made between persons in contemplation of marriage, remains in full force after the marriage takes place."

* * *

From a consideration of the case, and the decisions . . . these rules of law are clearly established: (a) An ante-nuptial agreement providing for the Catholic faith and education of the children of the parties, in reliance upon which a Catholic has thereby irrevocably changed the status of the Catholic party, is an enforceable contract having a valid consideration; (b) the Court will take judicial notice of the religious and moral obligations of the parties; (c) the spiritual and Catholic training of a child amid religious persons or institutions of its own faith is paramount over any material considerations; (d) a holding that religious training of children may be dispensed with until they reach maturity upon the theory that they then may adopt any or no religion as they deem fit, is repugnant to our American background and traditions; (e) a court and especially the Domestic Relations Court is bound to approve the demand of a Catholic parent that its child be given a Catholic education and a Catholic upbringing in a Catholic home or institution, Domestic Relations Court Act, Art. 3, Sec. 88; (f) the Court will take judicial notice that the Roman Catholic Church is the only church whose members are bound by its laws even to the penalty of ex-communication of the Catholic party who permits non-Catholic training and education of their children; (g) the fact that a child, in violation of the ante-nuptial contract, has for a period of time been brought up in some other religion than that fixed in the ante-nuptial agreement, is not sufficient ground to deprive the respondent of his rights to have the child educated in the religion fixed by the ante-nuptial contract.

It is clear that the respondent is enitled to have the child brought up in the religion agreed upon in the ante-nuptial contract. It is equally apparent that the child being baptized Catholic is entitled to and must receive the training and education of that faith.

The Court is informed that since the beginning of this proceeding the parties have placed the child in a Catholic boarding school and the respondent has assumed the obligation of paying for the child's maintenance and tuition therein. This arrangement of the petitioner and respondent is submitted to this Court for approval.

Accordingly, the said arrangement is hereby approved and the respondent is ordered and directed to pay the child's board, tuition and maintenance at the said Catholic boarding school as aforesaid. Judgment accordingly.

b. In Separation Proceedings

[i]

DOE v. ROE
143 N.Y.L.J. 15 (Sup. Ct. 1960)

BECKINELLA, JUSTICE.

In this action the plaintiff (husband) sues defendant (wife) for separation in her favor. Both parties base their actions on cruel and inhuman treatment. Plaintiff is a Roman Catholic; defendant a Baptist. Both seek custody of the three young male children, the issue of the marriage, whose ages range from one to four years.

The parties were married on January 23, 1950. The facts that led up to the marriage are briefly these: Plaintiff and defendant began going "steady" while in their early teens. For about two years prior to their marriage they began to indulge in sexual intercourse. In the fall of 1949 defendant discovered she was pregnant. She discussed this with plaintiff who told her that he would marry her but only in a ceremony performed in the Roman Catholic church. Following this conversation she went to her husband's parish church and spoke to one of the priests. When she told him that she was a non-Catholic he informed her that it was necessary to get a dispensation from the bishop, which dispensation would only be granted on certain conditions, among which were that she agree in writing to rear the children as Catholics. She so agreed and placed her signature on the following document: "Diocese of Brooklyn. In consideration of the promises herein made in contemplation of marriage of each to the other, we, the undersigned, agree as follows: Form of Promises for Non-Catholic. I, the undersigned non-Catholic, desiring to contract marriage with the Catholic named in this petition before a Catholic priest, hereby promise in the presence of the undersigned witnesses: (1) That all children of either sex born of this marriage will be baptized and educated in the Catholic religion alone, even if the Catholic party should be unable so to provide because of death or for any other reason. (2) That I will not in any manner whatsoever prevent the Catholic party from practising faithfully the Catholic religion. (3) That in the solemnization of the marriage there will be only the Catholic ceremony. 'Mary Roe' (signature of non-Catholic). Form of Promises for Catholic. I, the undersigned Catholic, hereby promise in the presence of the undersigned witnesses: (1) That all children of either sex born of this marriage will be baptized and educated in the Catholic religion alone. (2) That in the solemnization of the marriage there will be only the Catholic ceremony. (3) That I shall endeavor in all prudence by prayer and by good example to lead the non-Catholic to the one true Faith. 'John Doe' (Signature of Catholic). I, the undersigned Roman Catholic priest, do hereby declare that I am morally certain that the promises made by both the Catholic and the non-Catholic party will be fulfilled. Martin J. Donlon (Signature of Priest). Marie Huguensi (Signature of Witness). Jan. 23, 1950 (Date).''

As to the signing of this document defendant claims two things: First, that she was forced to sign it under duress of her pregnancy, and second, that she had a private understanding with plaintiff that he would never hold her to the agreement, but insisted on the Catholic ceremony merely to appease his parents. Plaintiff categorically denies this private understanding.

In addition to the sharp questions of fact involved concerning the religious issue, there is equal divergence concerning the allegations in the counterclaim. . . . Defendant insists that the real cause of the marital rift is plaintiff's habitual drunkenness. . . .

*   *   *

My feeling is that the issue of plaintiff's alleged drunkenness was calculatingly injected by defendant to obviate the effect of the antenuptial agreement. Defendant apparently reasoned that if a separation were granted in her favor, the children would be awarded to her and she could then raise them in her religion. This, I believe, she feels is the most important mission in her life. . . .

On the evidence, defendant's counterclaim is dismissed as not proven, and a separation is awarded in plaintiff's favor on the ground of cruel and inhuman treatment as evidenced by defendant's unjustified refusal to live and cohabit with him, in excluding plaintiff from his own home, and in bringing groundless criminal charges against him.

It now becomes necessary to determine the question of the custody of the children and their religious education and, of course closely connected with this is the question of the validity of the antenuptial agreement. In the March, 1916, Harvard Law Review, Leo M. Friedman wrote as follows: "Our courts have been remarkably free from litigation over the religious education of children. It is only in very recent years that it is beginning to make its appearance. Most of the states—even a state so important as New York— are still without any decisions on the subject from a court of last resort. Such litigation as has arisen has either been decided by side-stepping the religious aspects of the controversy altogether, and resting the decision on some other grounds entitling one or the other party to custody of the infants, or too often in more or less slipshod fashion, the courts have treated the matter as if it were a novel issue to be decided as law of the first impression or has fallen into an undiscriminating citation of an English Authority to justify some particular disposition of the case under consideration" (The Parental Right to Control the Religious Education of a Child, 29 Harv. L. Rev. 485).

Since that was written, two decisions, Ramon v. Ramon (34 N.Y.S. 2d 100 [1942]) and Shearer v. Shearer (73 N.Y.S. 2d 337 [1947]), neither reported officially, have thoroughly explored the subject and leave no doubt that in New York State an agreement such as the one involved herein is valid. . . . In the case at bar it cannot be said that the religious issue is merely an internal affair, because it has actually wrecked the home and undoubtedly is doing violence to the children's sense of security and subjects them to great psychological tensions.

Nor does the defendant's course of conduct commend her to equity. Quite the contrary. She shamelessly deceived the Catholic priest into performing the marriage ceremony when, had he the slightest inkling of her insincerity, he would have refused. She duped the plaintiff into marrying her by appearing to agree to the terms imposed by him. Her claim that he acquiesced in the sham, I reject entirely. He has been too steadfast in his insistence that the tenets of his religion be followed in regard to his children to leave room for acceptance of her story; and were it necessary to choose between her word and his, the long course of deceit practiced by her upon her own mother makes the choice a foregone conclusion. Moreover, this case does not present a picture of a young girl seduced by a promise of marriage. According to her own testimony she was perfectly willing to have continued the out-of-wedlock sexual intercourse had it not resulted in her pregnancy, perhaps up to the present time. Only when she found that she was pregnant did marriage then become of frantic importance to her. When the priest on their first interview (there were three before the one in which the marriage ceremony was performed) learned of her reason for wanting to marry, namely, to extricate herself from her awkward fix, he told her it was "not a good way to start a marriage" and "I cannot marry you under those conditions." He considered her motive for marrying so unworthy from a religious point of view that he told her that under the circumstances he would not perform the ceremony even if she were a Catholic.

That there was ample consideration for the agreement there can be no question. Plaintiff was under no legal compulsion to marry defendant. Accordingly, I find the antenuptial agreement to be valid and enforcible.

In view of the fact that in New York by statute (Domestic Relations Law, sec. 81) mother and father are deemed to have equal rights in the control of their offspring, an interesting question is posed here as to what disposition should be made irrespective of the validity of the agreement. The statute, in effect, creates two heads of family. This is fine when they are in agreement, but where, as here, the family is torn asunder by an irreconcilable conflict over the question of the children's religious upbringing, it is worse than a family with no head. The children in the instant case cannot be left to decide for themselves, as in the Martin case, for they are too young. They cannot be taken from either parent on the basis of moral unfitness for this is not claimed, nor can it be said that their best interests would be better served with one or the other. As a matter of fact, I cannot see that disaster would befall them if they were brought up in either parent's religion. However, they cannot be brought up in both and it would be wrong to bring them up in neither. Thus, a choice between the conflicting wishes of the parents must be made. What was said, therefore, in Matter of Jacquet (40 Misc. 575), which was decided in 1903 when a statute similar to the present section 81 of the Domestic Relations Law was in effect, is noteworthy: "While the ancient doctrine of patria potestas is only now an historical fact, and the common-law merger of the existence of the wife into that of her husband has ceased, while the wife is now in most respects the legal equal of her husband, yet the headship of the husband in the family is something more than mere sentiment. It is his name which is perpetuated, and his character should shape the conduct, and his ability achieve the success, of the household. In the nature of things it must still remain true that the father, though not in a tyrannical or opprobrious way, should be the head of the family."

Here, in addition to the antenuptial agreement, the infants by baptism have been initiated into the Catholic faith. They should be permitted to continue in that faith without interference until such time as they are old enough to make a choice of their own. . . .

There is another complicating factor with regard to awarding custody of the children. Ordinarily, with children of the tender years as these, and where, as here, the mother is not charged with unfitness on moral or other grounds, she would be awarded their custody with a direction or mandate that she raise them in accordance with the Catholic faith. But here the defendant is so uncompromising on the religious question that such a course would be ineffectual. Under oath she testified that under no circumstances would she bring the children up as Catholics, not even if the court directed her to do so. Her lawyer, in his brief, referring to this says: "Mrs. 'Roe' cannot be forced by government, courts or man to desist from upbringing her children in her faith. She has said she will die rather than yield."

Moreover, not only has the defendant excluded the plaintiff from his home since September 1959 but has stated that under no circumstances will she consent to live with him again. She gives as her reason for this her opinion that he is an incurable, unredeemable drunkard. He, on the other hand, is perfectly willing to resume family life and asks only that the children be raised as Catholics in accordance with the agreement.

Under the circumstances, the court has no recourse except to award the custody of the children to the plaintiff, with visitation rights to the defendant as the parties may agree, and, in the event they are unable to agree, the court will fix same upon application.

Settle judgment on notice in accordance with this decision.

NOTES

NOTE 1.

BEGLEY v. BEGLEY
reversing DOE v. ROE
13 App. Div. 2d 961, 216 N.Y.S. 2d 417 (1961)
aff'd. 185 N.E. 2d 912, 12 N.Y. 2d 691 (1962)

MEMORANDUM BY THE COURT.

Basically, this is a contest between the parties for the custody of their three very young children, who at the time of the trial ranged in age from one to four years. There is no charge concerning the mother's fitness. The learned Justice at Special Term granted custody of these infants to the father because the mother refuses to fulfill her antenuptial promise to rear the children in the Catholic religion. The court's inquiry must be directed toward determining what is best for the children. In our opinion, the welfare of such very young children will be better served by allowing them to remain with their mother.

In reaching this decision we do not pass upon the enforcibility of the prenuptial agreement. That question may be presented at a later time when the children shall have reached an age which makes them less dependent upon mother-care and which gives them sufficient maturity to receive religious instruction.

* * *

NOTE 2.

MARTIN v. MARTIN
308 N.Y. 136, 123 N.E. 2d 812 (1954)

PER CURIAM.

After a fairly extensive hearing, at which the boy, then twelve, now fourteen, years old, testified, the Referee, appointed to hear and determine the matter, decided that the "boy's welfare" called for modification of the decree in the respects requested, and the Appellate Division affirmed. 283 App. Div. 721, 127 N.Y.S. 2d 851. There being ample evidence to support both the finding that the youngster was old enough to testify intelligently and the conclusion that the modification was for his best interests and welfare, the order appealed from should be affirmed, with costs.

DESMOND, JUDGE (dissenting).

* * *

There is no finding and no testimony that enforcement of the religious training provision of the 1949 judgment (and of the 1938 agreement which it confirmed) would damage, or has damaged, the boy, mentally, physically or in any other way. All statements as to his becoming "unhappy" or "mentally disturbed" or ill-adjusted" are taken from the mother's ex parte affidavit which is a mere pleading, not proof. Neither the mother, nor the boy nor anyone else gave any testimony as to any such mental hurt or disturbance. The Referee's decision makes no such finding. The Referee amended the decree solely because, so he found, this twelve-year-old boy "has a mind of his own", because failure to amend the decree "would strip him of his independent judgment in matters of this kind", and because (so held the Referee) "neither the mother's wishes nor the father's wishes should control what is here to be done". True, at the end of the decision, the Referee said he was doing what "is best for the boy" but it is impossible to read the decision as based on anything except the boy's own wishes and his supposedly mature and considered choice of a religion for himself. That was not within the Referee's competency in the face of a Supreme Court judgment as to the place and nature of his religious training, based on a solemn prenuptial agreement.

The idea that a child of twelve is competent to make a choice binding on the Supreme Court and on his parents in such a matter, is not only contrary to our decisions . . . and contrary to all human experience, but is directly opposed to the *parens patriae* public policy of New York. . . .

NOTE 3.

Cushing Would Ease Marriage Restrictions*

Richard Cardinal Cushing of Boston suggests lifting many of the Roman Catholic Church's restrictions on religiously mixed marriages.

Specifically, he wants to do away with the requirement that a non-Catholic who marries a Catholic promise that their children will be raised in the Catholic faith and not interfere with the Catholic partner's religion.

Cardinal Cushing . . . says the promises are "an irritant to many."

And "it is clear from what happens subsequently," he says, that some non-Catholics "make the promises in bad faith."

One of the requirements for a dispensation to allow such mixed marriages is the moral certainty that the promises will be fulfilled.

* * *

Cardinal Cushing's statements followed by a month the official stand taken by the Church of Scotland, a Protestant body, in objecting to Catholic mixed marriage rules on grounds they were a cause of broken homes and a stumbling block to Christian unity.

* * *

By eliminating the required marital promises, Cardinal Cushing said, "we would not be changing any dogma of the church."

"After all," he said, " . . . the laws of the past that were put on the books to take care of the problems of the past may not be of much help to a later generation.

"In fact, they can sometimes be a hindrance in the care of souls. . . . "

[ii]

FREUD, SIGMUND

The Future of an Illusion (1927)†

[R]eligious ideas, in spite of their incontrovertible lack of authentication, have exercised the strongest possible influence on mankind. This is a fresh psychological problem. We must ask where the inner force of those doctrines lies and to what it is that they owe their efficacy, independent as it is of recognition by reason.

. . . It will be found if we turn our attention to the psychical origin of religious ideas. These,

---

* Reprinted with permission from *America*, June 15, 1963, The National Catholic Weekly Review, 920 Broadway, New York, New York.

† In 21 *The Standard Edit. of Complete Psychol. Works*, London: The Hogarth Press, 1961 (pp. 15-20, 29-56). Reprinted with permission of the publisher and The Liveright Publishing Company, New York.

which are given out as teachings, are not precipitates of experience or end-results of thinking: they are illusions, fulfilments of the oldest, strongest and most urgent wishes of mankind. The secret of their strength lies in the strength of those wishes. As we already know, the terrifying impression of helplessness in childhood aroused the need for protection—for protection through love —which was provided by the father; and the recognition that this helplessness lasts throughout life made it necessary to cling to the existence of a father, but this time a more powerful one. Thus the benevolent rule of a divine Providence allays our fear of the dangers of life; the establishment of a moral world-order ensures the fulfilment of the demands of justice, which have so often remained unfulfilled in human civilization; and the prolongation of earthly existence in a future life provides the local and temporal framework in which these wish-fulfilments shall take place. Answers to the riddles that tempt the curiosity of man, such as how the universe began or what the relation is between body and mind, are developed in conformity with the underlying assumptions of this system. It is an enormous relief to the individual psyche if the conflicts of its childhood arising from the father-complex—conflicts which it has never wholly overcome—are removed from it and brought to a solution which is universally accepted.

When I say that these things are all illusions, I must define the meaning of the word. An illusion is not the same thing as an error; nor is it necessarily an error. . . . What is characteristic of illusions is that they are derived from human wishes. In this respect they come near to psychiatric delusions. But they differ from them, too, apart from the more complicated structure of delusions. In the case of delusions, we emphasize as essential their being in contradiction with reality. Illusions need not necessarily be false—that is to say, unrealizable or in contradiction to reality. For instance, a middle-class girl may have the illusion that a prince will come and marry her. This is possible; and a few such cases have occurred. That the Messiah will come and found a golden age is much less likely. Whether one classifies this belief as an illusion or as something analogous to a delusion will depend on one's personal attitude. Examples of illusions which have proved true are not easy to find, but the illusion of the alchemists that all metals can be turned into gold might be one of them. The wish to have a great deal of gold, as much gold as possible, has, it is true, been a good deal damped by our present-day knowledge of the determinants of wealth, but chemistry no longer regards the transmutation of metals into gold as impossible. Thus we call a

belief an illusion when a wish-fulfilment is a prominent factor in its motivation, and in doing so we disregard its relations to reality, just as the illusion itself sets no store by verification.

Having thus taken our bearings, let us return once more to the question of religious doctrines. We can now repeat that all of them are illusions and insusceptible of proof. No one can be compelled to think them true, to believe in them. Some of them are so improbable, so incompatible with everything we have laboriously discovered about the reality of the world, that we may compare them—if we pay proper regard to the psychological differences—to delusions. Of the reality value of most of them we cannot judge; just as they cannot be proved, so they cannot be refuted. We still know too little to make a critical approach to them. The riddles of the universe reveal themselves only slowly to our investigation; there are many questions to which science today can give no answer. But scientific work is the only road which can lead us to a knowledge of reality outside ourselves. It is once again merely an illusion to expect anything from intuition and introspection; they can give us nothing but particulars about our own mental life, which are hard to interpret, never any information about the questions which religious doctrine finds it so easy to answer. It would be insolent to let one's own arbitrary will step into the breach and, according to one's personal estimate, declare this or that part of the religious system to be less or more acceptable. Such questions are too momentous for that; they might be called too sacred.

*   *   *

To assess the truth-value of religious doctrines does not lie within the scope of the present enquiry. It is enough for us that we have recognized them as being, in their psychological nature, illusions. . . .

Having recognized religious doctrines as illusions, we are at once faced by a further question: may not other cultural assets of which we hold a high opinion and by which we let our lives be ruled be of a similar nature? Must not the assumptions that determine our political regulations be called illusions as well? And is it not the case that in our civilization the relations between the sexes are disturbed by an erotic illusion or a number of such illusions? And once our suspicion has been aroused, we shall not shrink from asking too whether our conviction that we can learn something about external reality through the use of observation and reasoning in scientific work— whether this conviction has any better foundation. Nothing ought to keep up from directing our observation to our own selves or from applying our thought to criticism of itself. . . .

*   *   *

. . . Religion has clearly performed great services for human civilization. It has contributed much towards the taming of the asocial instincts. But not enough. It has ruled human society for many thousands of years and has had time to show what it can achieve. If it had succeeded in making the majority of mankind happy, in comforting them, in reconciling them to life and in making them into vehicles of civilization, no one would dream of attempting to alter the existing conditions. But what do we see instead? We see that an appallingly large number of people are dissatisfied with civilization and unhappy in it, and feel it as a yoke which must be shaken off ; and that these people either do everything in their power to change that civilization, or else go so far in their hostility to it that they will have nothing to do with civilization or with a restriction of instinct. . . .

It is doubtful whether men were in general happier at a time when religious doctrines held unrestricted sway ; more moral they certainly were not. They have always known how to externalize the precepts of religion and thus to nullify their intentions. . . . If the achievements of religion in respect to man's happiness, susceptibility to culture and moral control are no better than this, the question cannot but arise whether we are not over-rating its necessity for mankind, and whether we do wisely in basing our cultural demands upon it.

*   *   *

When civilization laid down the commandment that a man shall not kill the neighbour whom he hates or who is in his way or whose property he covets, this was clearly done in the interest of man's communal existence, which would not otherwise be practicable. . . . Insecurity of life, which is an equal danger for everyone, . . . unites men into a society which prohibits the individual from killing and reserves to itself the right to communal killing of anyone who violates the prohibition. Here, then, we have justice and punishment.

*   *   *

[I]f we were to leave God out altogether and honestly admit the purely human origin of all the regulations and precepts of civilization . . . these commandments and laws would lose their rigidity and unchangeableness as well. People would understand that they are made, not so much to rule them as, on the contrary, to serve their interests ; and they would adopt a more friendly attitude to

them, and instead of aiming at their abolition, would aim only at their improvement. This would be an important advance along the road which leads to becoming reconciled to the burden of civilization.

*   *   *

. . . We know that a human child cannot successfully complete its development to the civilized stage without passing through a phase of neurosis sometimes of greater and sometimes of less distinctness. This is because so many instinctual demands which will later be unserviceable cannot be suppressed by the rational operation of the child's intellect but have to be tamed by acts of repression, behind which, as a rule, lies the motive of anxiety. Most of these infantile neuroses are overcome spontaneously in the course of growing up, and this is especially true of the obsessional neuroses of childhood. The remainder can be cleared up later still by psychoanalytic treatment. In just the same way, one might assume, humanity as a whole, in its development through the ages, fell into states analogous to the neuroses, and for the same reasons—namely because in the times of its ignorance and intellectual weakness the instinctual renunciations indispensable for man's communal existence had only been achieved by it by means of purely affective forces. The precipitates of these processes resembling repression which took place in prehistoric times still remained attached to civilization for long periods. Religion would thus be the universal obsessional neurosis of humanity ; like the obsessional neurosis of children, it arose out of the Oedipus complex, out of the relation to the father. If this view is right, it is to be supposed that a turning-away from religion is bound to occur with the fatal inevitability of a process of growth, and that we find ourselves at this very juncture in the middle of that phase of development. Our behaviour should therefore be modelled on that of a sensible teacher who does not oppose an impending new development but seeks to ease its path and mitigate the violence of its irruption. Our analogy does not, to be sure, exhaust the essential nature of religion. If, on the one hand, religion brings with it obsessional restrictions, exactly as an individual obsessional neurosis does, on the other hand it comprises a system of wishful illusions together with a disavowal of reality. . . .

It has been repeatedly pointed out . . . in how great detail the analogy between religion and obsessional neurosis can be followed out, and how many of the peculiarities and vicissitudes in the formation of religion can be understood in that light. And it tallies well with this that devout believers are safeguarded in a high degree against the risk of certain neurotic illnesses; their acceptance of the universal neurosis spares them the task of constructing a personal one.

* * *

. . . Since men are so little accessible to reasonable arguments and are so entirely governed by their instinctual wishes, why should one set out to deprive them of an instinctual satisfaction and replace it by reasonable arguments? It is true that men are like this; but have you asked yourself whether they *must* be like this, whether their innermost nature ncessitates it? . . . Think of the depressing contrast between the radiant intelligence of a healthy child and the feeble intellectual powers of the average adult. Can we be quite certain that it is not precisely religious education which bears a large share of the blame for this relative atrophy? I think it would be a very long time before a child who was not influenced began to trouble himself about God and things in another world. Perhaps his thoughts on these matters would then take the same paths as they did with his forefathers. But we do not wait for such a development; we introduce him to the doctrines of religion at an age when he is neither interested in them nor capable of grasping their import. Is it not true that the two main points in the programme for the education of children to-day are retardation of sexual development and premature religious influence? Thus by the time the child's intellect awakens, the doctrines of religion have already become unassailable. But are you of opinion that it is very conducive to the strengthening of the intellectual function that so important a field should be closed against it by the threat of Hell-fire? When a man has once brought himself to accept uncritically all the absurdities that religious doctrines put before him and even to overlook the contradictions between them, we need not be greatly surprised at the weakness of his intellect. But we have no other means of controlling our instinctual nature but our intelligence. How can we expect people who are under the dominance of prohibitions of thought to attain the psychological ideal, the primacy of the intelligence? . . .

NOTES

NOTE 1.

BOWERS, SWITHUN

The Child's Heritage
From a Catholic Point of View*

Religion is that which binds man to his Creator.

* Reprinted from *A Study of Adoption Practice*, Vol. II, New York: The Child Welfare League of America, 1955, pp. 130-33. Reprinted with permission of the Child Welfare League of America, Inc.

More explicitly, it is the acknowledgment by man of his complete dependence upon God. The extent to which the individual human being in the living of his life acknowledges this dependence is the measure by which his practice of religion may be evaluated.

Worship is one aspect of religion. The private worship of the individual as a person and the public worship which he renders as a social being are explicit acknowledgments of this dependence. The dependent relationship of man to God implies far more than this formal and explicit acknowledgement by religious worship. If man is dependent upon God, and to deny this is to deny the nature of one's own being, then man must recognize and fulfill the law of God, whether it be the rule and order pertaining to and inhering in the very nature God has given no man, natural law, or the rule and order specifically revealed to him, positive law. To do otherwise is to assert that man is a law unto himself, that God is not God, that man depends on no one but himself. The practice of religion requires, therefore, that man in the living of his life be governed by moral values implicit in the law of God. It is only thus that the practice of religion has ultimate meaning.

Such is the Catholic concept of religion. This means that we do not look at religion merely in terms of the values that it may hold for this or that individual, but as a basic and fundamental obligation that falls upon man as a created being, upon every man. Religion is a duty incumbent upon man as man, irrespective of the values that may accrue to him from it. As we consider the role of religion in the life of the child and its importance in evaluating adoption homes, it will be essential to remember that from the Catholic viewpoint religion is something more than a value to the child. It is also an obligation basic to his very nature.

If there is to be a wholesome and desirable religious atmosphere, religion must have meaning in the life and activties of the family. This will be connected with the two major aspects of religion—worship and life. . . .

For religion to have meaning, moral values must be given due authority within the family, since life cannot be divorced from the application of these ultimate standards. So that there be no dichotomy between values inculcated through home training and those taught, explicitly or implicitly, in the school, we are concerned with the type of education provided the child. We believe that no educational system, even so-called neutralism, can separate itself from moral and religious values, and that the validity of these values is a matter of prime import.

Sometimes we encounter adoptive applicants

who fulfill satisfactorily the external obligations of worship but who flagrantly and willfully ignore moral values in some aspect of life. One Catholic adoption agency received an application from a couple who were quite influential people in the community and who were regular churchgoers. The husband, owner of a small business, had frequently asserted that "there will never be a union among my employees; I'll close up the business first." This was discussed with him by the priest-director of the agency and he quite readily acknowledged that his stand was in direct contradiction to the social teaching of the Church as set forth in various Papal Encyclicals. The authority of papal pronouncements was explained to him, but he remained adamant. The application was refused on the ground that the agency would not place a child in a family where he would be taught, directly or indirectly, that there was an area of life, business, in which moral values, emanating from the natural law and enunciated through the teaching authority of the Church, did not bind. This may be an unusual illustration, but we are constantly confronted with the necessity of making decisions, sometimes equally difficult decisions, about the degree to which this or that individual lives his religion.

*   *   *

Good balance in religious factors should be looked for in adoption home studies. There are Catholics who are more Catholic than the Church. Some of these would impose upon a child a most undesirable religious atmosphere in which unwarranted rigidity, compulsions and excessive demands would be gravely detrimental to both the religious and the psychosocial development of the child. Some of these are often ranked as pillars of a parish, and frequently can exert a great deal of pressure on agencies when they apply to adopt a child. If we are to fulfill our responsibilities toward children, such pressures must be withstood. Persons of this type will prove as unsuitable adoptive parents as they have so often proved themselves to be unsatisfactory natural parents. A neurotic can be a saint, but we could not deliberately place a child in that person's home. The child is most likely to grow up into a neurotic who is a very long way removed from sanctity.

*   *   *

Beyond the minimum, the religious values in a home must be related to and weighed with the other factors evaluated—economic situation, health, age, the social and emotional climate. Final decision will be made in terms of our assessment of a factor profile and the over-all balance. There will be instances where applicants will be rejected despite a high rating in religious factors,

because of deficiencies in inter-personal relationships, or in motivation, or because of age. Sometimes there will be applicants approved despite a rather low religious rating, so long as the minimum is present, but where other factors rate highly. In other cases, where the religious atmosphere is minimal and other factors are below average, the home will be rejected.

Religion is an obligation and a duty related to the ultimate purpose of enabling man to obtain the highest of values within his grasp—his eternal salvation. Since all human values are related to the supreme value in some way, religion will have value in life and in adjustment to life. These temporal values for the child will usually be conditioned by the use made of religion within a family. Parents and others, in their dealing with a child, may use religion, or rather abuse it, in a punitive and destructive way so that it becomes an instrument wherewith to instill fear. Other parents will use it to convey to the child its heart of love.

We all know how vital to the child, or to the adult, is that sense of belonging which is tied in with the need we all have to establish and preserve a sense of personal worth. Religion can give this sense of belonging even when all else fails so to do. Religion insists on the dignity of the individual as a child of God, and an heir to Heaven. Religion emphasizes God's concern for the lowliest of his children. Here lies the highest sense of belonging, the most fundamental feeling of personal worth, knowable to man.

NOTE 2.

ERIKSON, ERIK H.

Growth and Crises of the "Healthy" Personality*

As a psychologist it is not my job to decide whether religion (or, for that matter, tradition) should or should not exist, or whether it should or should not be confessed and practiced in particular words and rituals. The psychological observer must ask whether or not in the area under observation religion and tradition are living psychological forces creating the kind of faith and conviction which permeates a parent's personality and thus reinforces the child's basic trust in the world's trustworthiness. The psychopathologist cannot avoid observing that there are millions of people who cannot really afford to be without religion, and whose pride in not having it is that much whistling in the dark. On the other hand, there are millions who derive faith from other

---

* Reprinted from Kluckhohn, C., et al.: Personality in Nature, Society and Culture, New York: Alfred A. Knopf, 1955, (pp. 196-197). Reprinted with permission of the Josiah Macy, Jr. Foundation.

than religious dogmas, that is, from sources of fellowship, of work completion, of social action, of scientific pursuit, and of artistic creation. And again, there are millions who profess faith, yet in practice mistrust both life and man. With all of these in mind, it seems worth while to speculate on the fact that religion through the centuries has served to restore a sense of trust at regular intervals in the form of faith while giving tangible form to a sense of evil which it promises to ban. All religions have in common the periodical childlike surrender to a Provider or providers who dispense earthly fortune as well as spiritual health; the demonstration of one's smallness and dependence through the medium of reduced posture and humble gesture; the admission in prayer and song of misdeeds, of misthoughts, and of evil intentions; the admission of inner division and the consequent appeal for inner unification by divine guidance; the need for clearer self-delineation and self-restriction; and finally, the insight that individual trust must become a common faith, individual mistrust a commonly formulated evil, while the individual's need for restoration must become part of the ritual practice of many, and must become a sign of trustworthiness in the community.

NOTE 3.

FLUEGEL, J. C.

The Psycho-Analytic Study of the Family*

[T]he future progress of human culture will demand a very considerable modification and purification of most existing religious forms. The study of the psychology of religion is showing that these forms are, for the most part, based on crude unconscious motives which have to be outgrown and superseded if civilisation is to prosper and advance. In retaining and fostering these forms we are in many cases playing into the hands, not of the higher, but of the baser and more primitive aspects of our nature, aspects which, at our present level of development, it is necessary indeed to understand, but not to venerate or even to approve. Even in so far as the forms of religion give expression not so much to the direct promptings of these baser aspects as to the reactions we have formed against them, it must be remembered that true moral advance lies in sublimation rather than in repression and that so long as the human mind confines itself to the purely negative task of opposing its own primitive

* London: The Hogarth Press and The Institute of Psychoanalysis, 1950, pp. 154-55, Reprinted with permission of the publisher and The Humanities Press, Inc.

tendencies, it will never achieve either true emancipation or true progress.

c. In Divorce Proceedings

[i]

TAYLOR v. TAYLOR
32 Ill. App. 2d 45, 176 N.E. 2d 640 (1961)

BRYANT, JUSTICE.

This is an appeal from an order modifying a divorce decree. The decree for divorce was entered on January 21, 1957. That decree adopted verbatim the entire agreement of the parties, wherein the parties declared that they considered it to their best interests to settle between themselves their respective rights and obligations. Each party had the advice, investigation and recommendations with reference to the subject matter of the agreement.

The dispute arises over the provision giving the plaintiff the right "to determine the religion in which each child shall be raised" and the defendant the right "to determine the education which each child is to have and the schools which each child shall attend."

Mr. Taylor, the defendant, is a Protestant; Mrs. Taylor, the plaintiff, is a Catholic. The parties have two children; Jacqueline, ten years old at the time of the divorce decree and Hunt Marshall, who was then eight.

Hunt Taylor, the younger child, has been attending Chicago Latin, a private, nondenominational institution and is not involved in these proceedings. Jacqueline, the daughter, was attending a grade school maintained by the parish of Our Lady of Mount Carmel. In the spring of 1958, the defendant made arrangements to have Jacqueline attend the Ferry Hall School for Girls, a boarding school in Lake Forest, Illinois. Jacqueline visited the school at that time and returned in the fall of 1958 to take her entrance examinations and other tests. Upon receiving notice that his daughter passed these entrance examinations, the defendant made a financial commitment in excess of $2,000 to cover the expenses involved in matriculating her at Ferry Hall.

Plaintiff objected to the defendant's choice of school on the ground that Ferry Hall was not a Catholic institution and thereafter, in the fall of 1959, contrary to the terms of the divorce decree, enrolled Jacqueline at Immaculata, a Catholic day school. The defendant sought relief from the court to enforce his rights as to the selection of the proper school for his daughter.

The proceedings were held and upon the conclusion of the testimony, the Chancellor ordered that the petitioner's right to determine the education of his children, which had been incorporated in the divorce decree, be stricken; he further ordered the defendant to pay for the cost of the Catholic education and to pay the plaintiff's attorney $350 for their expenses in changing the original decree.

The Chancellor was evidently motivated by the lack of judgment in dividing the responsibility for religion and education between the parties. In his words: "It is my considered opinion that this decree is going to cause trouble of all kinds. I am going to modify it. It is my opinion, gentlemen, that the line between education and religion is so thin, it is so easy to step over this line either way * * *".

The Chancellor did not base his opinion on any change in the circumstances since the entry of the decree, although he did recognize that the conflict between the parents over the question of the child's schooling was affecting the child academically since her enrollment at Immaculata. He did not regard the decree as being inherently defective.

It is well settled in Illinois that a decree for divorce cannot be modified or amended unless there has been a material change of circumstances since the entry thereof. . . .

Nothing has occurred in the instant case which would warrant the court in modifying the divorce decree. There were no changes of circumstances, other than those which resulted from the plaintiff's violation of the decree. The plaintiff cannot treat this violation, the enrollment of the daughter in a Catholic School, as a *fait accompli,* and use that as a basis for her contention that it would be in the best interest of the child to remain in the Catholic School.

* * *

It is important to stress the fact that the defendant does not object to the provision in the decree granting the plaintiff the right to determine the religion of the children. Although Mr. Taylor is a Protestant, he is willing to have the children raised as Roman Catholics. His choice of Ferry Hall was in no way designed to obstruct this understanding.

Ferry Hall School for Girls enjoys a very high academic standing as a college preparatory school. It is nondenominational and non-sectarian. There is no religious proselyting. There are numerous students and faculty members of the plaintiff's religious persuasion presently attending and teaching there. Each student is encouraged to practice her own faith and is required to attend her own church on Sundays. A local parish priest attends to the spiritual needs of the Catholic students and

visits the school at least once a week to give instructions in that faith.

The plaintiff objects to the fact that Ferry Hall has morning services and a Sunday vesper service; however, these services are non-denominational, and at any rate, it is understood that Jacqueline would be excused from attendance.

* * *

. . . The implication of the plaintiff's argument that secular education cannot be isolated from religious teaching is contrary to the basic tenets of our public school system and it is a well known fact that millions of American Catholics send their children to public schools without any apparent violation of their religious precepts.

The real question here is whether both of the provisions of the decree should be enforced. In the absence of changed circumstances, both provisions in the decree should be enforced and, given good will on the part of the plaintiff, they can be. Surely it is to Jacqueline's best interest that she be enrolled in a boarding school with an excellent academic rating, where she can be given individual attention, rather than continue in her present surroundings in a large day school. With many of the students and several of the faculty at Ferry Hall practising the Catholic religion, provisions for weekly religious instructions of the Catholic students by a Catholic priest, and the requirement that each student attend her own church every Sunday, Jacqueline will be given a helpful environment in which to practise the religion which the plaintiff has chosen for her.

Accordingly, we hold that the Chancellor erred in divesting the defendant-petitioner of his right to select his daughter's school and education and that order is reversed and the cause is remanded with directions to reinstate the provisions of the divorce decree relative to the education of the children.

* * *

BURKE, JUSTICE (dissenting).

Jacqueline, now 15 years of age, is finishing her sophomore year at Immaculata High School in Chicago. She lives with her mother and brother in their home nearby. Immaculata is an excellent school. Many of her schoolmates in grammar school are with her in high school. She is an average student. She likes Immaculata and wishes to continue her studies there. Ferry Hall is also an excellent high school. Jacqueline visited that school. Nevertheless she desires to remain a student at Immaculata High School. Her feelings should be considered.

The agreement between the parents should not be the sole criterion in determining the welfare of their daughter. She should be consulted. She is not a chattel to be shunted around. She has rights independent of the parents. We should be reluctant to interfere with the decision of the chancellor. He saw the parties. He talked to Jacqueline. She has a home and is now in a good school with friends. The majority opinion would wrench her from this environment and send her among strangers away from home.

* * *

NOTES

NOTE 1.

LYNCH v. UHLENHOPP
248 Iowa 68, 78 N.W. 2d 491 (1956)

THOMPSON, CHIEF JUSTICE.

* * *

It may seem at first impression that the decree tells the petitioner sufficiently what she must do. But this impression, if indeed it be held at all, will not bear analysis. What constitutes "rearing" a child in the religion or cultus of this church, or of any church? Must he be taken to church once a week, or once in two weeks, on Sunday? If midweek services are held, must he be taken to them? Is it required that he attend catechism class? Must he attend a parochial school if the particular denomination in question maintains such schools? What fast days must be observed, what Lenten observances followed? Would it be sufficient if the child be required to conform to a part of these things, and if so which part? Or are all of them required? The difficulty would be the same, no matter what church might be named in such a decree as the one now before us.

Further, small boys are not usually sent to church services unaccompanied. Not being highly trained, as a rule, in the social graces and amenities, they need some adult control. Is it required that the petitioner, although not a communicant of this church, attend its services regularly with her son? The decree gives no answer.

Again, the matter of rearing a child in any religion is commonly, and we believe properly, thought to be a matter of cooperation between church and home. In order to avoid a conviction for contempt here, must the petitioner endeavor to supplement the teachings of the church, of which she is not a member, in her home? Without this cooperation, church attendance might well result in lip service only, to the faith taught there.

* * *

. . . It must be noted that the part of the decree with which we are concerned here is not merely a prohibition against doing a certain act. It is affirmative, or mandatory, requiring the performance of unspecified acts. . . .

If the court meant to pronounce its original decree which would be so clear and definite that all parties could understand what was meant by it and what they must do to comply, it should have spelled out an interpretation of what it would consider sufficient to show a "rearing in the Roman Catholic religion"; whether this imposed a duty upon the petitioner to take the boy to church regularly, or to other ceremonies and forms of observance and instruction in that church, or to parochial school, or to several or all of them; and whether or not she was under any duty to instruct and encourage the child in the adoption of this faith in their home. These questions can be answered only by the uncertainties of opinion and conclusion evidence. The petitioner, left without any real guide, is now being punished for violation of a judgment so indefinite and uncertain, in the respect in question, that it must be held to be wholly void.

* * *

While probably not decisive of the case, it may be well to point out the unfortunate effect upon the child of an attempt to enforce the vague and uncertain provisions of any decree ordering religious training. The able trial court was disturbed by this aspect of the case. It said: "There is a matter of separating church and state; the possibility of inharmony with the mother going to one church and the child to another; the difficulty of policing this part of the decree; the cumbersome nature of court processes compared with the sensitive nature of this subject; and so on. Surely these are good reasons for parties not placing a provision on religion in a default decree * * *". Our court is committed to the rule that the welfare of the child is generally the governing purpose in all proceedings involving custody, care and training. Chiefly for this reason, the courts have generally refused to enforce agreements between the father and mother concerning the religious training of children, but have held that the parent having custody is not bound by a previous contract. . . .

* * *

[E]nforcement . . . would do much harm, no matter what the denomination involved. The child is already the unfortunate victim of a broken home. He is only seven years of age. Controversies between his father and mother, arising from the uncertain provisions of the divorce decree as to his training will certainly subject him to many harmful problems. With constant bickering of his parents concerning compliance or noncompliance with the decree, the real sufferer would be the child. Courts should be slow to place provisions controlling religious beliefs in decrees, even granting certainty and constitutionality and the consent of the parties.

*   *   *

NOTE 2.

HACKETT v. HACKETT
40 Ohio 2d 245, 146 N.E. 2d 477 (1957)

ALEXANDER, JUDGE.

[W]e are constrained to hold that the court does not have the right or the power to enforce the contract the mother has repudiated or the order of which she appears to be in contempt, either by imprisoning her until she sends the child back to the Catholic school or by any other means. Our study of the question has convinced us that the violated portion of the contracts and hence the order embracing same are really void. "Void" means "empty, having no legal force, ineffectual, unenforceable." It is not the court's function to pronounce a value judgment upon the contracts, i.e., to decide whether good or evil, right or wrong, wise or unwise, proper or improper.

The Constitution of Ohio, Art. 1, Sec. 7 reads as follows: "All men have a natural and indefeasible right to worship Almighty God according to the dictates of their own conscience. No person shall be compelled to attend, erect, or support any place of worship, or maintain any form of worship against his consent; and no preference shall be given, by law, to any religious society; nor shall any interference with the rights of conscience be permitted. * * *"

*   *   *

Regardless of what the mother assented to or solemnly promised, if the court were to *compel* her now, *vi et armis* or otherwise, to keep her promise, that would appear to be compelling her to support or maintain a certain "form of worship, against her consent." . . .

*   *   *

The Catholic father would be well within his rights were he to place preservation of his faith above preservation of his family. Unfortunately for him, while the former may take precedence over the latter in an ecclesiastical tribunal, no faith or religious dogma may ever take precedence over a state constitution in a state court.

Plaintiff-mother is therefore found not guilty of contempt of court. . . .

[ii]

SMITH v. SMITH
90 Ariz. 190, 367 P. 2d 230 (1961)

STRUCKMEYER, CHIEF JUSTICE.

This is an appeal from an order of the superior court changing the custody of a minor child based on these significant facts. On September 13th, 1957, appellant, Betty Jean Smith, was granted a divorce from appellee, John Paul Smith and given the care, custody and control of their child, Mark, with reasonable visitorial rights in appellee. The same year the minor child being then six years old was enrolled in the first grade in the public schools in Phoenix. On August 4th, 1958, appellee petitioned the superior court for a change of custody alleging inter alia that the child was not receiving proper care, teaching and education. Following a hearing, an order was entered changing the custody from appellant to appellee during the school year. Review of that order is here sought.

*   *   *

Appellant is a member of a religious group known as Jehovah's Witnesses. Apparently she became affiliated with this religious group some time prior to her divorce since the counter-claim in the divorce action alleged such affiliation. Pursuant to their beliefs appellant instructed the minor child not to salute the flag of the United States of America and not to participate in school activities where allegiance is pledged, and kept the child home on the day of the Christmas play. Appellant's testimony is illustrative of her attitude:

"Q. All right, do you object to the child saluting the flag? A. Yes.

"Q. Do you object to the child pledging allegiance to the flag? A. Yes.

"Q. Do you object to the child observing or participating in Christmas plays in school? A. Yes.

Q. Even though all the rest of the children or most of them, participate? A. Yes."

The Jehovah's Witnesses teach that the obligation imposed by Law of God is superior to laws enacted by governments. As one of their religious beliefs they consider that the flag is an image within the literal version of the Bible, Exodus, Chapter 20, Verse 4—"Thou shalt not make unto thee any graven image," and that the pledge of allegiance to the flag is a form of worship violating God's commandment against idolatry.

The lower court stated during the course of the trial:

"* * * unless the court is satisfied that Mrs. Smith is willing to forego those beliefs as far as her child is concerned, I certainly feel that there is some justification for a change of custody in this case."

and in pronouncing judgment:

"It is the judgment of the court, Mrs. Smith, that your attitude in that respect tends to bring ridicule upon your son. It tends to implant into his mind intolerance for his father's beliefs; and as long as that attitude prevails, I feel in all fairness you are not a fit and proper person to have his care and custody."

and thereafter:

"You don't love him enough, Mrs. Smith—although the court has repeatedly put this question to you—to forego your religious beliefs to the extent of letting him acquire some of the religious beliefs and the normal activities that children enjoy and participate in in the public schools."

* * *

Since the decision in West Virginia State Board of Education v. Barnette, [319 U.S. 624] supra, it has been the uniform judgment of every court reaching the question that if a teaching does not conflict with the fundamental law of the land a parent may not be deprived of the custody of a child because of the court's disagreement with such parent as to religious beliefs. . . . A parent who teaches a child doctrines at variance with majority views does not give rise to grounds sufficient to support a change of custody.

Appellee argues that there is no religious issue in this case because the hearing in the lower court was to determine the fitness of appellant as a parent. Patently, the determination of fitness was predicated on appellant's religious beliefs, for in the end the court put appellant to the compulsion of foregoing her beliefs or suffering the loss of her child. We can but reflect that if government through its courts can lawfully place the individual in the extreme of choosing between the active practice of a religious belief or suffering a burdensome loss, whether liberty, property or a child's association and companionship, what profit the people of this nation from thousands of years of bigotry and intolerance?

The First Amendment of the Constitution of the United States provides in part that "Congress shall make no law respecting an establishment of religion, or prohibiting the free exercise thereof." By the Fourteenth Amendment the fundamental concepts embodied therein embrace the liberties guaranteed by the First Amendment. . . . Were the Constitution in need of justification, we would need only point to the language of the Supreme Court of the United States in Barnette.

"Those who begin coercive elimination of dissent soon find themselves exterminating dissenters. Compulsory unification of opinion achieves only the unanimity of the graveyard. * * * But freedom to differ is not limited to things that do not matter much. That would be a mere shadow of freedom. The test of its substance is the right to differ as to things that touch the heart of the existing order." 319 U.S. 624, 641-642, 63 S. Ct. 1178, 1187.

The foregoing should be dispositive of the appeal, however, there is a suggestion that the practices by appellant of her beliefs were injurious to the child. Appellee points to the language of the trial court:

"* * * and I think I must recognize that any deviation from the normal school routine brings a certain amount of ridicule and criticism to the child which is, of course, the basis of implanting neuroses in the child."

We are not unaware that deviation from the normal often brings ridicule and criticism. We reject, however, the notion that it is necessarily the basis for implanting neuroses. Criticism is the crucible in which character is tested. Conformity stifles the intellect fathering decadency. New ideas are the rungs upon which mankind supports itself in the long climb to perfection. It is sufficient to say until then, man's personality is not to be warped into a universal mold. A judgment supported only by the tenuous threads of a possible neuroses derived from deviation in normal activities will not withstand the thrust of constitutional guarantees.

The order of the court below is reversed.

NOTE

LOWREY, LAWSON G.

Emotional Factors in Family Instability*

. . . It is imperative in rearing children to strive for these things: emotional security, an inner feeling of adequacy such that they can be comfortably self-assertive without having to be hostile; an inner feeling of being valued, and especially being valued within the family. It is essential to rear children to have independence, and to help them to be able to use it; to rear individuals who will have adequacy in social relationships, ability to face reality and to deal with the people with whom they come in contact; children who will have respect for authority but not be slavishly obedient, and have what should go with respect for authority, namely, a correlated sense of responsibility.

d. In Adoption Proceedings

In re MAXWELL'S ADOPTION
4 N.Y. 2d 429, 151 N.E. 2d 848 (1958)

FULD, JUDGE.

Shortly after his birth in 1953, the infant Maxwell was turned over to the respondents with the

---

* Reprinted in New York County Lawyers' Association, *Law, Medicine and the Unstable Family*, 1949, p. 125. Reprinted by permission of the New York County Lawyers' Association.

consent of the appellant, his natural mother, and since that time the respondents have had his care and custody. Sometime in 1954, they petitioned to acquire his permanent custody by adoption. After a hearing, at which the appellant appeared in opposition, the County Court of Erie County made an order, dated July 20, 1956, approving and granting the adoption. . . .

This is not a case where the mother surrendered the baby after birth on the spur of the moment or without having given thought to the matter. On the contrary, what she did was planned, the product of deliberate consideration. Separated from her husband since 1950, she had, while living with him, six children. Of these six children, only one, a young daughter, was living with her in Canada in 1953. The others, apparently taken from her by the Canadian authorities, were being cared for either by private families or in public institutions. In 1953, the appellant engaged in an adulterous course of conduct with a man by the name of Jones. The child here involved is the fruit of that illicit relationship. The appellant was most intent on keeping her pregnancy, and her wrongdoing, a secret lest, if it became known, the daughter still with her would also be taken away. In order to conceal the situation, she went from her home in Canada in July of 1953 to Buffalo, where she selected an obstetrician to attend her upon the delivery of the child. She told him in no uncertain terms that she "did not want" the baby and expressly asked him whether he would be able to "place it any place." He indicated that he would make the necessary arrangements, and had her return for periodic monthly examinations on four occasions. A boy baby was born on November 15, 1953 in the Buffalo General Hospital and five days later the appellant's paramour came to the hospital and accompanied her back to Canada.

The matter of having the baby adopted was discussed by the appellant, who had given a false name and a false address, not only with the physician but also with the nurse who had attended her at the hospital. And, several hours after the baby was born, she signed an affidavit, prepared by the attorney for the respondents, in which she stated that she consented that the infant be adopted by the respondents. In addition, she declared that she "does not at the present time embrace any religious faith." Her assertion at the trial that she told the doctor and the lawyer that she was a Catholic was denied by each of them, and the nurse testified that the appellant stated that "she went to no church at this time", although the nurse went on to say, she understood from her conversation that the appellant had been "brought up a Catholic."

After leaving the hospital and her baby, the appellant . . . returned to Canada with Jones and not a word was heard from her until the attorney for the respondents communicated with her, asking her to appear in the adoption proceedings. The child was then almost a year old.

It is the appellant's claim that she is of Catholic faith and that she had not known that the persons to whom the baby had been given were Protestants. However, when about a year after the infant's birth, she saw the attorney for the respondents and was informed that the child was not in a Catholic home, she told him in so many words that she had no objection to that. Some time later, though, she stated, and repeated in court, that she wanted the child returned to her and that, in any event, she desired him to be brought up in the Catholic faith. Regarding the affidavit in which she declared that she did not then embrace any religious faith, she testified that she had not read that document and did not know its contents.

The trial judge disbelieved her. He found not only that she had deliberately abandoned the child, but that her affidavit was her free and voluntary act and that she knew full well what she was signing. He granted the order of adoption, giving custody of the child to the respondents, who agreed to have him baptized in the Catholic faith and educated in a Catholic elementary and high school, and the Appellate Division unanimously affirmed.

* * *

Subdivision 3 of section 373 of the Social Welfare Law . . . provides that, "in granting orders of adoption * * * the court shall, *when practicable,* * * * give custody * * * only to * * * persons of the same religious faith as that of the child." The words "when practicable" are significant and may not be construed or read out of the statute.

It is, of course, the settled policy of this state to insist upon adoption by persons of the same religious faith as that of the child. But this policy does not require a court to deny custody to adoptive parents where a child has been accepted by them following a declaration or representation by the mother, which may or may not be true, that she *does not embrace any religious faith.* See Matter of Krenkel, 278 App. Div. 573, 102 N.Y.S. 2d 456, adoption to persons of different religious persuasion approved, where mother falsely stated her own religious faith to be that of the foster parents. If the rule were otherwise, the foster parents would ever run the risk of not being able to adopt the child, and the child ever subjected to the danger of having attachments formed painfully severed, for how may it be known that the natural mother has not lied about her religious affiliation?

Section 373 of the Social Welfare Law contains no absolute requirement that the faith of the foster parents be that of the child. The statute calls upon the court to give custody to persons of the same religious faith as that of the child "when practicable." That term is of broad content, necessarily designed to accord the trial judge a discretion to approve as adoptive parents persons of a faith different from the child's in exceptional situations. Had the legislature intended that in every case the child be adopted by persons of its own religious faith, it obviously would have made its design known by langauge far different from that which it used. The presence in the statue of the words "when practicable" was to enable the court to relax the requirement in the unusual case such as the one before us.

The statute may not be employed as a means of wiping out a relationship between foster parents and child which originated in good faith and has continued for the entire four and a half years of the youngster's life. To upset the determination of both the Trial Court and the Appellate Division, to tear the child from the love and care of these petitioners, the only mother and father he has ever known, and send him instead to an institution until other parents are found, would be inordinately cruel and harsh. No law requires consequences so distressing.

The order appealed from should be affirmed, without costs.

* * *

DESMOND, JUDGE (dissenting).

This adoption order was invalid. [I]t violated section 373 of the Social Welfare Law and section 113 of the Domestic Relations Law, each of which requires that in making any order of adoption the court must "when practicable" give custody "only to * * * persons of the same religious faith as that of the" child. . . .

Adoptions in this State are strictly controlled by statutes. . . . The statutes protecting an adopted child's religion are so fundamental that the People of this State voted them into the State Constitution itself (art. VI, § 18). Much is said here about the hardship of taking this four-year-old boy from his adopted parents but hard cases make no exception to the constitutional mandate or to our own duty to enforce it. And let it be remembered that the boy was not four years old but four hours old when, although all concerned knew the facts as to his religion, the completely illegal adoption consent was signed in the hospital. He was less than two years old when the true facts as to religion were testified to in County Court,

some months after the adopted parents had falsely testified that he "was born in the Presbyterian faith". That the mother at an earlier time and before court proceedings were taken had made a false statement as to her religious affiliation could not lessen the court's duty to protect the child's religious rights when the court learned the truth. The passing of time could not make right what was wrong from the beginning.

* * *

. . . Significantly, identity of religion is, other than age of adopting parents (Domestic Relations Law, § 110), the only substantive test in our comprehensive adoption laws of the eligibility of proposed adoptive parents. . . . The only possible uncertainty as to meaning comes from the use of the qualifying phrase "when practicable". . . . In subdivision 5 of section 88 we find what amounts to a legislative definition of "when practicable" since that subdivision says that the phrase shall be of no force or effect if there is available "a proper or suitable person of the same religious faith or persuasion as that of the child".

* * *

Apart from more fundamental reasons for such a rule of law, the rule was and is consistent with good social work practice (Lockridge, Adopting a Child [1947], p. 27; Cady, How to Adopt a Child [1956], p. 24 ; Glickman, Child Placement [1957], p. 7). In social work theory the religious requirement is part of the "matching" process to decide which children and parents are best suited to each other . . . . And in legal principle it is an application of the fundamental right of a parent to control the upbringing of a child. . . .

* * *

. . . In the present case no effort was made to find adoptive parents of the same faith as that of the child and at the first hearing they stated the child's religion to be Protestant. As to whether an adoption to Catholic parents was practicable, there is no proof . . . but it is inconceivable that in the city of Buffalo such persons could not be found. We conclude that this adoption was in direct violation of the statutory and constitutional mandate and was beyond the power of the court to order.

* * *

We realize that the effect of a reversal here would be to take this four-and-a-half-year-old child from the people who have cared for him since birth. It would be a sad experience for them. However, when the baby was only a year and some months old, the court was informed of the religion of the mother and her husband and the child's putative father and the different religion of the petitioners and informed that the mother's consent was withdrawn. Under the statutes the proceeding should have been dismissed forthwith.

These uncertainties and frustrations are always possible in so-called "private" adoptions. We point out that, on the contrary, when a parent "has surrendered the child to an authorized agency for the purpose of adoption" the parent's consent is not required (Domestic Relations Law, § 111). Only through such surrenders, made voluntarily, freely and finally, can the purpose be achieved of protecting adopting parents "from later disturbance of their relationship to the child by natural parents whose legal rights have not been given due consideration" (see Essentials of Adoption Law and Procedure, U.S. Children's Bureau, Publication No. 331 [1949], p. 2, supra).

The order should be reversed, without costs, and the proceeding dismissed.

NOTES

NOTE 1.

WICKLEIN, JOHN

Religious Rule on Adoption Bars Many Couples in State*

A childless couple must profess to have a religion if they want to adopt a baby in New York State. If they are atheists or agnostics and say so, their application will be rejected. It will be turned down whether it is made to a court or to an adoption agency, sectarian or nonsectarian.

This is because state law requires the couple to promise to raise the adoptive child within a specific religion.

If the husband and wife are of mixed faiths, they have little chance of getting a child through the routine channels of adoption. Only if they are of the same faith, and have documents to prove it, can they have a reasonably strong hope that an agency will find a child for them.

Even then the chances aren't good. The number of childless couples of the same faith who want to adopt children exceeds the number of babies available . . . .

* * *

"From the Jewish point of view," said one mother . . . "we have a very half-hearted attitude about trying to adopt, because there are so few so-called 'Jewish' babies and no agency that will place a baby in a home of another religion."

More and more, she said, childless Jewish couples are turning away from the agencies and to private adoption.

Private adoption, in which a physician, lawyer,

clergyman or relative arranges for the transfer of a child, is legal in this state provided that no money is paid for the child. If money is paid, then the transaction is considered "black-market" and is forbidden by law.

The committee has found, in polling its 500 adoptive parents, that judges or surrogates handling private adoption cases are more willing than are the agencies to approve the placement of children across religious lines and with couples of mixed faiths.

The parents believe adoption agencies are much more interested in preserving the religious status quo of children than are the adoptive parents and possibly even the natural parents.

* * *

Only in the case of Negro children are religious lines crossed with any regularity.

The placing of Negro children outside their designated religion is, understandably, almost standard practice in cases where the designation is Jewish.

The problem arises when a foundling designated as Jewish in the rotational system happens to be a Negro, and when a dark-skinned child is born out of wedlock to a Jewish woman and a Negro man.

Such births have been increasing steadily in the city, and six years ago the Louise Wise Services, a Jewish agency, set up an interracial placement program to meet the situation.

Mrs. Florence G. Brown, the director, said the service had first looked into the possibility of placing these babies with childless parents in the small Negro Jewish community in New York. But, she said, almost no adoptive homes could be found in this group.

"We feel that any child who can't be cared for by its own family is entitled to an adoptive home," Mrs. Brown said. "So we decided that we were going to make adoption possible for these children by crossing religious lines."

Since then, the agency has placed 150 children of Negro or mixed racial background in the homes of Negroes who were Protestants or Catholics. If the child appeared white, and a white couple could be found who wanted a child of mixed background, she said, then the child was placed as Jewish.

NOTE 2.

AMERICAN ETHICAL UNION

Religion in Adoption*

. . . We accept as the primary purpose of adoption the promotion of the welfare of the depen-

* The New York Times, Oct. 11, 1959 (pp. 1, 82). © 1959 by The New York Times Company. Reprinted by permission.

* Pamphlet distributed by National Women's Conference of the American Ethical Union, December, 1958. Reprinted by permission of the publisher.

dent child. However, a secondary factor not to be lightly ignored is that prospective adoptive parents who meet the necessary standards shall have equal opportunity to adopt. It is our contention that religious reasons should not bar the way to an otherwise satisfactory adoption. . . .

* * *

At the National Conference on Adoption held in January 1955 under the auspices of the Child Welfare League of America, three papers were presented on "The Religious Component in Adoption" by representatives of the Protestant, Catholic and Jewish faiths. Dr. Abraham Duker, in discussing Jewish attitudes to Child Adoption, said:

"The proposal has been made that children be given for adoption to families affiliated with religious bodies or which practice the religious rites and life as prescribed by the individual denominations. I know quite a few highly moral and ethical persons who are not religiously affiliated, for all kinds of reasons, some because they cannot accept belief in the supernatural, others because they do not approve of religious institutionalism. . . . I am convinced that such persons can be good adoptive parents and that they will attempt to raise their children as decent human beings and good citizens. . . . Who are we to decide that persons who cannot become parents by an act of God should be deprived of the joy of adoptive paternity because of religious requirements or should be forced to lie or pretend that they will become religious in order to obtain the child? . . . Granted that American society is basically a religious society. However, should it be the province of social workers to enforce religious beliefs and practices under the threat of deprivation of paternity? What about the public agency? Would not such an involvement be tantamount to the interference of the church in the area of the state?"

In regard to the question raised in the foregoing quoted remarks on the matter of church-state separation, Judge Justine Wise Polier states:

"Any attempt by the state, through overzealous employees in our courts, public departments, or hospitals to infringe on the parent's religious freedom or right to choose adherence or nonadherence to any faith violates the Constitution and its guaranty of freedom of conscience and freedom of religion . . . In terms of moral law and human compassion it would also seem that no voluntary agency, whether sectarian or not, should exact as the price for its services adherence to a particular faith or commitment to religious adherence by mother or child, except as it is freely given. . . . To the extent that children can be placed in the homes of the same faith as that of their parents, this practice should be followed, except in the cases in which the parent or parents freely choose to have the child placed in a home of another faith."

* * *

. . . The spokesman for the Protestant point of view . . . found evidence of a definitely secular trend in the field of adoption and stated that many ministers share the opinion that social work has become so secular as to relegate religious components to the background, if not to ignore them completely. There is extensive agreement among Protestant ministers in the belief that religion is an indispensable factor, inasmuch as they feel that homes which maintain meaningful connections with the religious resources of a community are more likely to provide the spiritual climate needed by the child. He added, "It would seem in the child's best interest, except in certain notable exceptions, to bring him up in the faith of his natural parents." . . .

The ministers interviewed . . . were one in their belief that among the significant contributions of religion to life are the preservation of values and their transmission to succeeding generations. "Granted the foregoing, this means then, that the parents have indirectly the right to decide in which religion the child is to be raised. By inference, this suggests that child-rearing agencies and the government have a duty to see to it that the religious interests of parents and children are honored." . . . We come now to a consideration of the issue from a Catholic point of view, which was presented by Rev. Swithun Bowers, C.M.I., Director School of Social Welfare, St. Patrick's College, Ottawa. [See Note 1, p. 232 *supra*.]

NOTE 3.

In re G. (AN INFANT)
[1962] 2 W.L.R. 1010

WILLMER L. J. . . . Of course, it hardly needs to be said that in a great many cases the matter of religious faith may be a most important consideration; certainly, it must be a consideration of vital importance in any case where the infant proposed to be adopted is sufficiently old to appreciate and have some understanding of the change involved. But in this case no such situation arises. Even now the infant is still under one year of age, and can have no possible understanding.

NOTE 4.

PETITIONS OF GOLDMAN
331 Mass. 647, 121 N.E. 2d 843 (1954)
Cert. den 348 U.S. 942 (1955)

QUA, C. J. . . .
General Laws (Ter. Ed.) c. 210, §5B, inserted by St. 1950, c. 737, §3, is as follows: "In making orders for adoption, the judge when practicable

must give custody only to persons of the same religious faith as that of the child. In the event that there is a dispute as to the religion of said child, its religion shall be deemed to be that of its mother. . . .

* * *

The judge also found that "there are in and about the city of Lynn [which is near the residence of the petitioners] many Catholic couples of fine family life and excellent reputation who have filed applications with the Catholic Charities Bureau for the purpose of adopting Catholic children of the type of the twins, and are able to provide the twins with a material status equivalent to or better than that of the petitioners, and with whom the twins could be placed immediately." This finding was in effect a finding that it was "practicable," within the meaning of that word in §5B, to "give custody only to persons" of the Catholic faith. . . .

* * *

It is contended that §5B is unconstitutional as a law "respecting an establishment of religion, or prohibiting the free exercise thereof," contrary to the First Amendment to the Constitution of the United States, and as in some manner contrary to art. 2 of our Declaration of Rights and to art. 11 and art. 46, §1, of the Amendments to the Constitution of this Commonwealth. With this we cannot agree. All religions are treated alike. There is no "subordination" of one sect to another. No burden is placed upon anyone for maintenance of any religion. No exercise of religion is required, prevented, or hampered. It is argued that there is interference with the mother's right to determine the religion of her offspring, and that in these cases she has determined it shall be Jewish. Passing the point that so far as concerns religion she seems to have consented rather than commanded and seems to have been "interested only that the babies were in a good home," there is clearly no interference with any wish of hers as long as she retains her status as a parent. . . .

* * *

We do not attempt to discuss the philosophy underlying the concept that a child too young to understand any religion, even imperfectly, nevertheless may have a religion. We have no doubt that the statute was intended to apply to such children, and that in such instances the words "religious faith . . . of the child" mean the religious faith of the parents, or in case of "dispute" the faith of the mother. There is nothing new in this idea. . . .

e. In Neglected-Child Placement Proceedings

In re GLAVAS
203 Misc. 590, 121 N.Y.S. 2d 12 (1953)

PANKEN, JUSTICE.

This matter came on before the Children's Court Division of the Domestic Relations Court of the City of New York, first, on the 14th of January 1953, on a petition charging the father with neglecting the child. After a hearing, the child was found to have been neglected by his father.

It may be beside the point to here inquire into the bases for the establishment of children's courts ; yet it must always be borne in mind when the rights and interests and the protection of a child are to be considered, to remember that the children's courts were instituted for that purpose. The rights, interests and protection of children are always paramount. They are superior to the rights of parents when they are in conflict with what is best for the child. Children's courts were established in this State, as elsewhere throughout our nation, to serve definite purposes. . . . The intent and purpose always is to protect children against neglect by their parents or others ; to protect children against themselves because of delinquency . . . .

Children's courts are often confronted with insoluble problems, problems which are difficult to meet and to dispose of ; sometimes it is because of the insistence on the part of one parent or the other upon what the religious affiliation of their child should be, and so difficulties creep in regardless of the harmful consequences which may flow to the child. It is not easy to pass upon, indeed, it is quite difficult, as to what the religion of a child is ; as in this case, when the child is only four years old, and there is a sharp difference between father and mother on that question. I should think that the welfare of and the future for the child should be controlling ; and the religious affiliation of the youngster might very well be held in abeyance until he, himself, is in the position to determine what religion he desires to follow providing, always, that ethical concepts and life in response to such concepts are inculcated and instilled in the child.

Under our law, when a child is neglected and it is so found, or even if it be a baby, or a child is found to be delinquent, the religion of the child is to be established to make possible its placement either on remand or commitment to an agency or foster home, when the child cannot be returned to the bosom of his family. . . .

In its wisdom, the Legislature provided that, "placement or parole must, when practicable, be with or in the custody of a person or persons of the same religious faith or persuasion as that of the child." . . . Parenthetically, sometimes I question whether a child under the age of four or six or seven has a distinctive religious faith or has any particular religious persuasion. Children who are non sui juris, or who have not as yet reached the age of reason, cannot be converted from one religion to another. A Catholic, Protestant, or Jewish child may not be converted to another religion or faith if he is under the age of seven since the child has not yet reached the age of reason. Conversion, when effected, if effected, is accomplished by the parents.

While parents are endowed with the right and a duty to guide the steps of their children in the formative years in life, as well as towards a religious faith of the child, when the steps mapped out are harmful, either because of inadequacies or unfitness or neglect by the parent, the right of such parent may be limited, curtailed. The religion of a child, however, is not a matter in which the Court may interfere except when it becomes an issue of fact to be determined in providing protection and proper care for the child.

Children's courts have come into existence, undoubtedly, in response to a greater understanding of the forces and influences necessary in the upbringing and protection of our childlife to the end that ultimately the citizenry of any community which, in a full measure, may respond to the duties which cooperative and communal life calls for and imposes. The law is a living organism; it must be stable. It must not, however, be permitted to remain or become static. The philosophy of the law and the changes in the philosophy of the law and in the law itself occurs in response to changed conditions and changes in the mentality, psychology and culture, due to political, economic and social changes which at one time or another prevail in the group.

* * *

The question to be decided here is whether the boy concerned in this proceeding is Jewish or Roman Catholic. It is asserted and testimony submitted that this child had been circumcised according to Jewish rites early in the year of 1948 and therefore he is of Jewish faith. Circumcision, of itself, does not mean that a child is of Jewish faith. Much medical authority believes that it is also a health measure. However, when a child is circumcised within the tenets and rules prescribed by the Jewish religion, the circumcision establishes and completes the Jewishness of the child as to his religion. Usually circumcision takes place eight days after birth or as soon as his health permits.

Some four years or more after the circumcision, in October 1952, the father of this child had him baptized by a priest of the Roman Catholic Church, and he claims that the child is now a Roman Catholic. It would appear that by circumcision according to Jewish rules and rites and by baptism according to the Roman Catholic Church, the child has two religions and has been accepted in both religions. The question to be solved and answered, here, is, has the baptism in October 1952 superseded the circumcision in 1948; and has a father without the consent of the mother the right to change the religion of his child? That is a matter of law.

It is my understanding in conversion from any religion to any other religion the person must know and understand the tenets of the church and accept its standards. The Catholic Church will test very carefully the sincerity of one seeking to be converted to Roman Catholicism though he had taken instruction for a shorter or longer period of time. If a Jew seeks conversion to Catholicism he must aver, and beyond that, with all sincerity that he understands and accepts the tenets, the rules and the theology of Roman Catholicism. Does it apply to a child four years of age? The child at that age has not yet, under the most favorable conditions, reached the age of reason.

It is the father's view in this case that he had the right to convert the child from the Jewish religion to the Roman Catholic Church and so had him baptized as a Roman Catholic. . . . It was while the mother was in the hospital that the father had, without her knowledge and consent, baptized the child . . . .

* * *

It is significant that the father is not a Roman Catholic. He testified that he was and still is of the Greek Catholic persuasion, not the Greek Catholic Church according to Roman rites. He did, from time to time, he said, visit or attend Roman Catholic Churches. . . . Religion cannot be changed for a person just because of association with others of a different religious faith. Associating with Jews does not make one a Jew, nor does associating with Catholics make one a Catholic. Something more than that is prescribed by all faiths in connection with a conversion. For Catholic, Jew, Protestant, I believe Mohammedan, as well, an affirmative act must be performed before one is accepted into any church. Baptism by a priest or minister into any church, or circumcision according to Jewish rites is required. I am not sure what the Mohammedans would require.

. . . The faith of a person changing the religion of his child should be considered. It should be considered as to whether since the child is non sui juris the act of the father was in response to a conviction, an honest belief, a change of faith or persuasion, or desire to change religious affiliation or principle, or was it merely in response to a momentary whim or some other factor. The father did not impress me as being deeply concerned as to what denomination or religion his child should follow.

* * *

It has been held quite uniformly that parents have the right to select the religion of their children. It is questionable in my mind whether the courts would go the distance in preserving the rights of parents to include therein the right to repeatedly change the religion of a child after it had been baptized or circumcised. If that were so, parents might change the religion of a child periodically and even do so in all sincerity without any regard as to the impact that the changes will have upon the child. . . . That, it seems to me, is not contemplated either by natural law or the law as it stands or public policy, or the needs of the child.

A most important factor in the evolution of character in children is a sense of security. Without security the child might develop an inferiority complex. A child's future is deeply affected either by a sense of security or insecurity in the formative period during his upbringing. Change of religion in children of tender age may well do violence to a sense of security.

To determine the rights of the parents, the Court must always bear in mind the needs and the rights of the child, too. One cannot supersede the other. The former cannot supersede the latter.

To provide a child with love of his parents so that he might obey the commandment which requires him to honor his father and mother, they must agree upon the religion of the child, and if they cannot agree, harm is in store for the child. Disagreement on religion, as other disagreements in the family unit, and particularly in religion, reacts detrimentally to the welfare of the child and to the serenity of the home of which the father and mother should be a part.

* * *

The questions to be determined by me are, (1) has the child been circumcised according to the Jewish rites before he had been baptized according to the Roman Catholic Church precepts? I find as a matter of fact that the testimony is abundant on that question as to whether the child was initiated into the Jewish religion and circumcised according to the rules and tenets prescribed for the performance of that ceremony. (2) The question to be decided is, does the baptism of this child, four years old, and four years after he had been initiated into the Jewish religion in compliance with prescribed tenets and rules supersede

his admission to the Jewish religion, and deem him converted to Roman Catholicism? The evidence on that score seems to me to be quite clear, that the father, who is a Greek Catholic, not of Roman rites, for unexplained reason, without the consent of the mother, whatever his purpose was, caused the child to be baptized by a Roman Catholic priest, and not having the consent of the mother, not even having apprised her of that; the baptism does not supersede the circumcision. (3) The question to be decided by me is, can a father without the consent of the mother change the religion of his child? There was statutory law until this year that even the changing of the name of a child may not be accomplished by one parent without the consent of the other. The question of religion is much more important than a change of name, and hence, I find as a matter of law that a change in the religion of a child cannot be effected unless both parents consent thereto.

. . . Parents may change their own religion. They are adult. They presumably act on conviction. It is not fair, however, to expose a child . . . to possible trauma which changes in religion and culture may cause.

I find as a matter of fact that the child is Jewish; that the baptism did not change the boy's religion. My finding here does not preclude the possibility of a change in religion of the child if both parents agree thereto. I should, however, advise serious thought on the part of both parents as to whether the child should embrace a religion other than the religion of either of the parents. That, certainly, would do harm to the child. The father is a Greek Catholic, the mother Jewish, and the child in some other religion. He will find himself rather at sea.

3.

HEALTH AS A FACET OF "IN THE CHILD'S BEST INTEREST" IN DETERMINING CUSTODY—CONFLICTS BETWEEN MEDICAL AND RELIGIOUS BELIEFS

a.   HOENER v. BERTINATO
          67 N.J.Super. 517, 171 A. 2d 140 (1961)

KOLE, J. The defendants, husband and wife, are members of a religious sect known as Jehovah's Witnesses. The defendant Gloria Bertinato is pregnant by Louis Bertinato with her fourth child and is expected to give birth to the baby within the next few days. Gloria Bertinato has a blood condition known as RH negative. The undisputed medical evidence of both physicians who testified at the hearing in this matter established, beyond a reasonable doubt, that, as a result of this blood condition of the mother, unless a blood transfusion was given the child soon after birth, the child would die, or even if there were the remote possibility of its surviving, it would be born physically or mentally deformed for life.

The testimony of the physicians is supported by the history of Gloria Bertinato's former pregnancies. Her first child was born without the necessity of blood transfusions and is a normal child. This accords with the medical testimony at the hearing that the mother's RH blood condition adversely affects the second and subsequent children but rarely is harmful to the first-born.

Gloria Bertinato's second child, born in 1955, required a blood transfusion immediately after birth. Both defendants then refused on religious grounds to consent to the transfusion after the child was born. Concern by defendants' then physicians for the child's welfare prompted the filing of a complaint at that time in this court under N.J.S.A. 9:2-9 to 9:2-11, inclusive. According to the affidavits of the physicians attached to the complaint in that cause, even a day's delay in performing the transfusion could be fatal to the new infant. An emergent night hearing, therefore, was held before this court, after which an order was entered granting custody to the Bergen County Child Welfare Department for the purpose of having the necessary transfusions effected. Upon the subsequent certification to the court by the physicians that the transfusions had been performed and that the child was in good health, custody of the child was then returned to its parents—the present defendants. At the hearing in the instant proceeding, both defendants admitted that the child has been and presently is normal and in good health.

Gloria Bertinato's third pregnancy resulted in a baby who admittedly also needed a blood transfusion to save its life. But defendants again refused to permit this on religious grounds. No legal proceedings were instituted to compel the transfusion. The infant died.

It is the welfare of the child which will be born within the next few days that is the subject of the present proceeding. It was initiated by a complaint of the Bergen County Child Welfare Department, under N.J.S.A. 9:2-9 to 9:2-11, inclusive. The complaint seeks an order awarding that Department custody of the child, when it is born, for the purpose of having the necessary blood transfusions made. It charges that the defendants, by their refusal to authorize the transfusions, are endangering the life of the unborn child and are, therefore, neglecting to provide it with proper protection . . . . An order to show cause why

the relief prayed for should not be granted was duly served on defendants. . . .

* * *

Both defendants testified. They did not dispute the medical opinion as to the absolute need for the transfusions; nor did they object on the ground that the transfusions might be physically harmful to the baby. Their sole objection was on religious grounds, which I find they genuinely believe in. They testified that, as Jehovah's Witnesses, if they consented, they would be breaking the commands of their faith which prohibit any taking or injection of blood, and that the strength of their belief was such that, even if it meant that the baby could not survive without the transfusions, they would, and could, not consent thereto. They stated, however, that, if the transfusions were ordered by the court—a matter beyond their control and against their wishes—, they would nevertheless accept the child into their home as their child. . . .

There is no doubt of the defendants' good faith as to their religious principles; nor is there any doubt as to their being good and devoted parents, except in their refusal to consent to the transfusions.

Nevertheless, I have no difficulty in finding that, by their refusal to consent to the blood transfusions, defendants are neglecting to provide the child to be born with proper protection within the meaning of N.J.S.A. 9:2-9.

* * *

This court's authority to intervene in this case to protect the child's welfare . . . is further buttressed by the Juvenile Court Act itself, which grants this court express power to act, on behalf of the State, as *parens patriae* with respect to children within its jurisdiction and protect them from neglect or injury. . . . Thus, N.J.S. 2A:4-2, provides:

"It is hereby declared to be a principle governing the law of this state that children under the jurisdiction of said court are wards of the state, * * * entitled to the protection of the state, which may intervene to safeguard them from neglect or injury * * *."

N.J.S. 2A:4-34, provides:

"Children under 18 years of age who appear before the juvenile and domestic relations court in any capacity shall be deemed to be wards of the court, and protected accordingly."

"This *parens patriae* jurisdiction is a right of sovereignty and *imposes a duty* on the sovereignty to protect the public interest and to protect such persons with disabilities who have no rightful protector." *Johnson v. State* . . . 18 N.J. at p. 430, 114 A. 2d at p. 5. (Emphasis added.)

Since the blood transfusions are required in order for the child to live, the defendants' refusal to consent thereto constitutes "neglect to provide the child with proper protection" under the statute. . . . The parents' constitutional freedom of religion, although accorded the greatest possible respect, must bend to the paramount interest of the State to act in order to protect the welfare of a child and its right to survive. Cf. *Greenspan v. Slate,* . . . where our Supreme Court said, 12 N.J. at p. 140, 97 A. 2d at p. 397:

> "There is a law of natural humanity as extensive as our race, which impels parents * * * to protect and support their helpless children."

Laws are made for the government of actions. While they cannot constitutionally interfere with mere religious beliefs and opinions, they may interfere with religious practices inconsistent with the peace and safety of the state—here, the protection of the lives and health of its children. . . .

As the United States Supreme Court stated in Prince v. Commonwealth of Massachusetts, 321 U.S. 158, at pp. 166, 170, 64 S. Ct. 438, at p. 442, 88 L. Ed. 645 (1944):

> "The right to practice religion freely does not include liberty to expose the community or the child to communicable disease or the latter to ill health or death * * * Parents may be free to become martyrs themselves. But it does not follow they are free, in identical circumstances, to make martyrs of their children before they have reached the age of full and legal discretion when they can make that choice for themselves."

> * * *

. . . Does the fact that the child has not yet been born mean that N.J.S.A. 9:2-9 is inapplicable and the court is without jurisdiction? I think not.

> * * *

[T]here is nothing in any of these provisions which would preclude their application to an unborn child. Even the provision that the purpose of the complaint is to have the child brought before the court is satisfied by having the mother brought before the court. Moreover, the child—even if born—may be "brought before the court" for the purpose of a hearing . . . without it physically being present.

Additionally, it is now settled that an unborn child's right to life and health is entitled to legal protection, even if it is not viable. . . . As our Supreme Court stated in [Smith v. Brennan,] 31 N.J. at pp. 363, 364, 367, 157 A. 2d at p. 502:

> "Our criminal law regards an unborn child as a separate entity. . . . And our law of property

and decedents' estates considers him in being for purposes beneficial to his interests. . . . Under our Workmen's Compensation Act it has been held that a posthumous child may recover as a dependent of his deceased father, on the ground that the infant is both a 'child *in esse*' at the time of his father's death and, when born, a 'posthumous child,' . . . . And it has been widely held that an infant may bring a statutory action for wrongful death of its father occurring before its birth.

> * * *

From the foregoing it is clear that medical authorities recognize that before birth an infant is a distinct entity, and that the law recognizes that rights which he will enjoy when born can be violated before his birth.

> * * *

And regardless of analogies to other areas of the law, justice requires that the principle be recognized that a child has a legal right to begin life with a sound mind and body. . . .

Finally, the history of the mother's former pregnancies makes it evident that the relief sought should be granted prior to the baby's birth. An interpretation of the statute which would require an emergency court hearing after birth in every case—as was held in connection with the second baby in 1955—does not comport with good sense.

> * * *

An order will be entered granting to the Bergen County Child Welfare Department custody of the child, when born, with authority to consent to the necessary blood transfusions. If and when the child's health and circumstances warrant, in view of the defendants' expressed desire to receive the child in their home, and their other good qualities as parents, a further order may be entered terminating such custody and returning the child to the custody of defendants.

b.

PEOPLE v. PIERSON
176 N.Y. 201, 68 N.E. 243 (1903)

HAIGHT, J. The indictment accused the defendant of the crime of violating section 288 of the Penal Code in that he "did willfully, maliciously, and unlawfully omit without lawful excuse, to perform a duty imposed upon him by law, to furnish medical attendance for his said (J. Luther Pierson's) female minor child, under the age of two years, the said minor being then and there ill and suffering from catarrhal pneumonia, and he, the said J. Luther Pierson, then and there willfully, maliciously, and unlawfully neglecting and refusing to allow said minor to be attended and prescribed for by a regularly licensed and practicing physician and surgeon, contrary to the form of the statute in such case made and provided."

The facts disclosed upon the trial are without substantial dispute, and are in substance as follows: The defendant and his wife lived at Valhalla, near White Plains, New York, with an infant girl sixteen and a half months old, whom they had adopted. In January, 1901, the child contracted whooping cough, which continued to afflict her until about the 20th day of February, at which time catarrhal pneumonia developed, resulting in death on the 23rd of February, 1901.

The defendant testified that for about 48 hours before the child died he observed that her symptoms were of a dangerous character, and yet he did not send for or call a physician to treat her, although he was able financially to do so. His reason for not calling a physician was that he believed in Divine healing, which could be accomplished by prayer. He stated that he belonged to the Christian Catholic church of Chicago ; that he did not believe in physicians, and his religious faith led him to believe that the child would get well by prayer. He believed in disease, but believed that religion was a cure of disease.

In submitting the case to the jury the trial court charged, in substance, that before the jurors could convict the defendant they must find that he knew the child was ill, and deliberately and intentionally failed or refused to call a physician, or to give the child such medicines as the science of the age would say would be proper that a child in its condition should have ; that if at the time he refused to call a physician he knew the child to be dangerously ill, his belief constitutes no defense whatever to the charge made. In other words, no man can be permitted to set up his religious belief as a defense to the commission of an act which is in plain violation of the law of the state. The jury rendered a verdict of guilty of the crime as charged. The Appellate Division has reversed, but, as we have seen, has examined the facts and found no error therein, but rests its reversal upon what it considers to be errors of law. The majority of the court appears to have entertained the view that the indictment failed to charge a criminal offense, for the reason that it did not contain an allegation that the case was one in which a regularly licensed and practicing physician ought to have been called.

Section 288 of the Penal Code, so far as is material upon the question under consideration, provides as follows: "A person who 1. Willfully omits, without lawful excuse, to perform a duty, by law imposed upon him, to furnish food, clothing, shelter, or medical attendance to a minor, * * * or 4. Neglects, refuses or omits to comply with any provisions of this section, * * * is guilty of a misdemeanor." It would seem that the legislative intent in adopting this provision of the Code is reasonably clear, although possibly more precise language could have been employed. It contemplates that there are persons upon whom the law casts a duty of caring for minors, but it does not specify the persons. They are, however, those upon whom the duty is "by law imposed." They are designated in the statutes and in the common law as the parents, guardians, or those who by adoption or otherwise have assumed the relation in loco parentis. The duty of such a person is specified by the provisions of the section. It is "to furnish food, clothing, shelter, or medical attendance." Giving the statute a reasonable construction by applying the rule of necessity, it is apparent that it means the necessary food, clothing, shelter, or medical attendance required for the preservation of the health and life of the child. We quite agree that the Code does not contemplate the necessity of calling a physician for every trifling complaint with which the child may be afflicted, which in most instances may be overcome by the ordinary household nursing by members of the family ; that a reasonable amount of discretion is vested in parents, charged with the duty of maintaining and bringing up infant children ; and that the standard is at what time would an ordinarily prudent person, solicitous for the welfare of his child and anxious to promote its recovery, deem it necessary to call in the services of a physician. . . .

It is now contended that section 288 of the Penal Code does not in terms, or in effect, make it the duty of any one to furnish medical attendance to a minor child, and that under the common law it is not part of the duty of parents to provide medical attendance for their children . . . Under this . . . statute, the duty of parents to furnish medical attendance for their children is expressly provided for, and is made obligatory upon them, even if they were exempt from such duty under the common law. * * *

We are thus brought to a consideration of what is meant by the term "medical attendance." Does it mean a regularly licensed physician, or may some other person render "medical attendance"? The foundation of medical science was laid by Hippocrates in Greece 500 years before the Christian era. His discoveries, experiences, and observations were further developed and taught in the schools of Alexandria and Salerno, and have come down to us through all the intervening centuries, yet medicine as a science made but little advance in northern Europe for many years thereafter, practically none until the dawn of the eighteenth century. After the adoption of Christianity by Rome, and the conversion of the greater part of Europe, there commenced a growth of legends of miracles connected with the lives of great men who became benefactors of humanity. Some of these have been canonized by the church, and are today looked upon by a large portion of the Christian world as saints who had miraculous power. The great majority of miracles recorded had reference to the healing of the sick through Divine intervention, and so extensively was this belief rooted in the minds of the people that for a thousand years or more it was considered dishonorable to practice physic or surgery. At the Lateran Council of the church, held at the beginning of the thirteenth century, physicians were forbidden, under pain of expulsion from the church, to undertake medical treatment without calling in a priest ; and as late as 250 years thereafter Pope Pius V renewed the command of Pope Innocent by enforcing the penalties. The curing by miracles, or by interposition of Divine power, continued throughout Christian Europe during the entire period of the Middle Ages, and was the mode of treating sickness recognized by the church. This power to heal was not confined to the Catholics alone, but was also in later years invoked by Protestants and by rulers. We are told that Henry VIII, Queen Elizabeth, the Stuarts, James I, and Charles I, all possessed the power to cure epilepsy, scrofula, and other diseases known as the king's evil ; and there is incontrovertible evidence that Charles II, the most thorough debauchee who ever sat on the English throne, possessed this miraculous gift in a marked degree, and that for the purpose of effecting cures he touched nearly a hundred thousand persons.

With the commencement of the eighteenth century a number of important discoveries were made in medicine and surgery which effected a great change in public sentiment, and these have been followed by numerous discoveries of specifics in drugs and compounds. These discoveries have resulted in the establishment of schools for experiments and colleges throughout the civilized world for the special education of those who have chosen the practice of medicine for their profession. These schools and colleges have gone a long way in establishing medicine as a science, and such it has come to be recognized in the law of our land. By the middle of the eighteenth century the custom of calling upon practitioners of medicine in case of serious illness had become quite general in England, France, and Germany, and, indeed, to a considerable extent, throughout Europe and in this country. From that time on, the practice among the people of engaging physicians has continued to increase, until it has come to be regarded as a duty, devolving upon persons having the care of others, to call upon medical assistance in case

of serious illness. . . . In England the first statute upon the subject to which our attention has been called, was that of 31 & 32 Vict. c. 122, § 37, which made it the duty of persons having the care of infants to provide them with "medical aid". This statute was amended in 1894 by 57 & 58 Vict. c. 41, so as to read substantially the same as section 289 of our Penal Code, to which we have referred. . . .

*   *   *

It will be observed that the provision of the Penal Code under consideration was first adopted in 1881, following the statute of 1880 prohibiting the practice of medicine by other than physicians duly qualified in accordance with the provisions of the act. This, we think, is significant. The legislature first limits the right to practice medicine to those who have been licensed and registered, or have received a diploma from some incorporated college, conferring upon them the degree of doctor of medicine ; and then the following year it enacts the provision of the Penal Code under consideration, in which it requires the procurement of medical attendance under the circumstances to which we have called attention. We think, therefore, that the medical attendance required by the Code is the authorized medical attendance prescribed by the statute, and this view is strengthened from the fact that the third subdivision of this section of the Code requires nurses to report certain conditions of infants under two weeks of age "to a legally qualified practitioner of medicine of the city, town or place where such child is being cared for," thus particularly specifying the kind of practitioner recognized by the statute as a medical attendant.

The remaining question which we deem it necessary to consider is the claim that the provisions of the Code are violative of the provisions of the Constitution, art. 1, § 3, which provides that "the free exercise and enjoyment of religious profession and worship, without discrimination or preference, shall forever be allowed in this state to all mankind ; and no person shall be rendered incompetent to be a witness on account of his opinions on matters of religious belief ; but the liberty of conscience hereby secured shall not be so construed as to excuse acts of licentiousness, or justify practices inconsistent with the peace or safety of this state." The peace and safety of the state involve the protection of the lives and health of its children, as well as the obedience to its laws. Full and free enjoyment of religious profession and worship is guaranteed, but acts which are not worship are not. A person cannot, under the guise of religious belief, practice polygamy, and still be protected from our statutes constituting the crime of bigamy. He cannot, under the belief or profession of belief that he should be relieved from the care of children, be excused from punishment for slaying those who have been born to him. Children, when born into the world, are utterly helpless, having neither the power to care for, protect, or maintain themselves. They are exposed to all the ills to which flesh is heir, and require careful nursing, and at times, when danger is present, the help of an experienced physician. But the law of nature, as well as the common law, devolves upon the parents the duty of caring for their young in sickness and in health, and of doing whatever may be necessary for their care, maintenance, and preservation, including medical attendance, if necessary ; and an omission to do this is a public wrong, which the state, under its police powers, may prevent. The legislature is the sovereign power of the state. It may enact laws for the maintenance of order by prescribing a punishment for those who transgress. . . .

We are aware that there are people who believe that the Divine power may be invoked to heal the sick, and that faith is all that is required. There are others who believe that the Creator has supplied the earth, nature's storehouse, with everything that man may want for his support and maintenance, including the restoration and preservation of his health, and that he is left to work out his own salvation, under fixed natural laws. There are still others who believe that Christianity and science go hand in hand, both proceeding from the Creator ; that science is but the agent of the Almighty through which He accomplishes results, and that both science and Divine power may be invoked together to restore diseased and suffering humanity. But sitting as a court of law for the purpose of construing and determining the meaning of statutes, we have nothing to do with these variances in religious beliefs, and have no power to determine which is correct. We place no limitations upon the power of the mind over the body, the power of faith to dispel disease, or the power of the Supreme Being to heal the sick. We merely declare the law as given us by the legislature. We have considered the legal proposition raised by the record, and have found no error on the part of the trial court that called for a reversal.
. . .

The judgment of conviction of the trial court affirmed.

CULLEN, J.   I concur in the opinion of Judge HAIGHT. The State, as *parens patriae*, is authorized to legislate for the protection of children. As to an adult (except possibly in the case of a contagious disease which would affect the health of others), I think there is no power to prescribe what medical treatment he shall receive, and that he is entitled to follow his own election, whether that election be dictated by religious belief or other consideration.

NOTES

NOTE 1.

TRESCHER, ROBERT L., and O'NEILL, THOMAS N., JR.

Medical Care for Dependent Children: Manslaughter Liability of the Christian Scientist*

The question of whether religious belief is a defense to a manslaughter prosecution based on failure to provide medical attention for a dependent child recently has been raised again after a lapse of several decades. In 1956 Mr. and Mrs. Edward Cornelius were indicted for involuntary manslaughter in Pennsylvania following the death of their infant son from diabetes. Both parents were Christian Scientists and, interpreting the teachings of the Bible as conferring the power and duty to rely solely on spiritual means for healing, believed that healing takes place by the action and power of God and that all sickness, however serious, can be healed by spiritual means alone.

* * *

Between 1915 and 1956, when the *Cornelius* indictment was returned, no cases involving the question of religious belief in spiritual means of healing arose in Pennsylvania. Meanwhile, judicial decisions were handed down granting charters to Christian Science churches, sanatoriums, and nursing services ; and statutes were passed indicating legislative approval of spiritual means of healing. . . .

The Non-Profit Corporation Law of Pennsylvania provides that a nonprofit corporation may be founded under the provisions of the act "for any purpose or purposes which are lawful and not injurious to the community."[59] . . . More important, both the sanatorium in which the Cornelius child was placed and an organization known as the Philadelphia Nursing Service for Christian Scientists had received charters based on such decrees, indicating that not only the form of worship but also the precise form of healing treatment prescribed by Christian Science had been judicially declared "lawful and not injurious to the community." These decrees are a natural

---

* 109 U. PA. L. REV. 203, 204, 213-217 (1960). Copyright 1960 U. PA. L. REV.

59. Pa. Stat. Ann. tit. 15, Sec. 2851-201 (1958).

concomitant of the broad principle of law that the right of conscience " 'is simply a right to worship the Supreme Being according to the dictates of the heart; to adopt any creed or hold any opinion whatever, or to support any religion; and to do, or forbear to do, any act for conscience sake, the doing or forbearing of which is not prejudicial to the public weal.' " [64]

The granting of charters to Christian Science churches, sanatoriums, and nursing services indicates judicial acceptance of the purposes of such institutions and, impliedly, the right of the individual to utilize such services, at least for himself. Not so clearly implied is public acceptance and approval of the right of a parent to choose spiritual means of healing for his child. A greater indication of the acceptance of such doctrines in the latter area is found in legislative action. At the time of the *Cornelius* indictment, the legislature had prescribed a program of required medical and dental examinations for school age children. The act further provided that recommendations as to medical, surgical, or dental care should be forwarded by the school authorities to the family physician or dentist and to the parent or guardian of the child, who was then obligated to notify the school of the action taken with respect to the recommendations. However, a specific exemption was made to these comprehensive requirements where the parent objected to examinations or treatment on religious grounds, provided that the objection did not create a "present substantial menace" to the health of others.

In the law governing adoption the Pennsylvania legislature has further indicated its approval and acceptance of spiritual means of healing. The adoption law prescribes the procedures and conditions for the adoption of children and provides that "whenever possible, the petitioners shall be of the same religious faith as the natural parents of the child to be adopted. *No person shall be denied the benefits of this act because of a religious belief in the use of spiritual means or prayer for healing . . . .*" [68] The only reasonable implication of this language is that parents of an adopted child may practice spiritual means for healing their child. And if adoptive parents may employ spiritual means or prayer for the treatment of their adoptive child, it seems clear that natural parents have the same right.

The Disease Prevention and Control Law of 1955 authorizes the issuance of a marriage license without the medical examination and laboratory tests normally required, if the examination and tests "are contrary to the tenets or practices of the religious creed of which the applicant is an adherent, and . . . the public health and welfare will not be injuriously affected thereby." [69] Pursuant to a similar predecessor provision, Pennsylvania courts have waived the premarital examination for members of the Christian Science faith.

Still further indications of the legislature's approval of spiritual means of healing as a healing art are found in the statutes governing the practice of medicine and the nursing profession. The Medical Practice Act, while defining "healing art" as "the science of diagnosis and treatment *in any manner whatsover* of disease," specifically exempts healing by spiritual means from the regulations governing the licensed practice of medicine and surgery. Likewise, the Chiropractic Registration Act does not apply "to any person who, as an adherent of a well recognized religion which uses spiritual means of prayer for healing, practices the healing art in accordance with its teachings." [73] And the Professional Nursing Law specifies that it does not prohibit "care of the sick, with or without compensation or personal profit, when done in connection with the practice of the religious tenets of any church by adherents thereof." [74] Thus, under the least permissive reading of these statutes, healing by spiritual means is certainly recognized and not prohibited.

Not only the legislature but also various private groups have accepted Christian Science as a permissible means of healing. Numerous accident and health insurance companies in the United States, Canada, and other countries now recognize Christian Science care and treatment by paying the expenses incurred for the service afforded by Christian Science practitioners and nursing homes. Furthermore, money paid for the services of Christian Science practitioners and nursing care stands on an equal footing with medical expenses so far as deductibility under the federal income tax laws is concerned.

As a result of the judicial, legislative, and public recognition and acceptance of Christian Science and its healing methods, it is unlikely that a conviction could have been had in the *Cornelius* case and doubt was cast even upon the desirability of continuing the prosecution. These doubts evidently were persuasive in the mind of the prosecutor. Citing the "present day legislative acts" recognizing healing by spiritual means and noting that "the disease of diabetes, did not subject the public to any danger," he moved to *nolle prosequi*

---

64. Specht v. Commonwealth, Sec. Pa. 312, 322 (1848) . . . .

68. Pa. Stat. Ann. tit. 1, Sec. 1(d) (Supp. 1959). (Emphasis added).

69. Pa. Stat. Ann. tit. 35, Sec. 521, 12(e) (Supp. 1959).

73. Pa. Stat. Ann. tit. 63, Sec. 623 (1959).

74. 3 CCH 1943 Stand. Fed. Tax Rep. para. 6175.

the indictment. The court, also persuaded, granted the prosecutor's motion.[76]

As a result of the disposition of the *Cornelius* case, the legality of a parent's exclusive reliance upon spiritual means for the healing of his child seems to be confirmed. . . . With the possible exception of cases involving contagious diseases, a parent's decision to forego medical remedies and to employ spiritual means of healing—where that decision is based on a sincere belief in a religious tenet of a denomination whose beliefs and practices have been determined both legislatively and judicially to be lawful and not injurious to the community—will no longer subject him to criminal penalty if the healing be unsuccessful.

NOTE 2.

EDDY, MARY B.

Science and Health with Key to the Scriptures*

Nine years ago my only child was hovering between life and death. Some of the best physicians in Boston had pronounced his case incurable, saying that if he lived he would always be an invalid and a cripple. One of the diseases was gastric catarrh. He was allowed to eat but very few things, and even after taking every precaution, he suffered to the extent that he would lie in spasms for half a day. He also had rickets; physicians saying that there was not a natural bone in his body.

It was while he was in what seemed to be his greatest agony, and when I was in the darkest despair, that I first heard of Christian Science. The bearer of the joyful tidings could only tell me to come and hear of the wonderful things that Christian Science was doing. I accepted the invitation, for I was willing to try anything to save my child, and the following Friday evening I attended my first meeting, which was in The Mother Church of Christ, Scientist. Long before the service began every seat was filled, which was amazing to me, being an ordinary weekly meeting, and that night I realized from the testimonies given that Christian Science was the religion for which I had been searching for years. The next

day I went to find a practitioner, but was unable to get the one who had been recommended, he being too busy. On my way home I thought of some of the testimonies which I had heard the night before,—of people being healed by simply reading Science and Health. I resolved at once to borrow a copy, and not dreaming of the sacrifice that my friend would make by conferring such a favor, I went and asked her for a loan of Science and Health. I never saw any one part so reluctantly with a book as my friend did with her copy of the textbook.

I read it silently and audibly, day and night, in my home, and although I could not seem to understand it, yet the healing commenced to take place at once. The little mouth which had been twisted by spasms grew natural and the child was soon able to be up, playing and romping about the house as any child should. About this time we decided to move to the far West.

I was young in Science at the time, and my husband greatly feared that the journey would cause a relapse for the child, but instead, he continued to improve. I constantly read the Bible, Science and Health, and Miscellaneous Writings, the two weeks we travelled, and we were the only ones in our car who, throughout the journey, did not get train sick. The child's limbs grew perfectly straight, he ate anything he wanted, and for years he has been a natural, healthy child in every way. He has passed through some of the worst forms of contagion untouched and unharmed.

I had been reading Science and Health several months, before I gave any thought to myself and my numerous complaints. I had never been very strong, and some of my ailments were supposed to be hereditary and chronic, hence I dragged through many tedious years with a belief in medical laws and hereditary laws resting upon me. Just before I commenced reading Science and Health I spent a half day in having my eyes examined by one of the leading oculists in Boston. His verdict was that my eyes were in a dreadful condition, and that I would always need to wear glasses. In the meantime I commenced to read Science and Health, and when I thought of my eyes, I had no need for glasses. The years that I have been in Science I have used my eyes incessantly, night as well as day, doing all kinds of trying work and without requiring the aid of glasses. I was healed of all my complaints whilst seeking the truth for my child, and many of them have never returned. Those that appeared simply came to the surface to be destroyed. Teeth have been restored and facial blemishes removed, unconsciously, simply by reading Science and Health. All of this is, however, nothing to compare with the spiritual uplifting which I have received, and

---

76. Commonwealth v. Cornelius, No. 105, April Sessions, 1956, Philadelphia County (Pa.) Quar. Sess., Nov. 5, 1958. "[W]hile a conviction of involuntary manslaughter may, under some circumstances be predicated upon death attributable to the failure to provide medical care, the character of the ailment, the good faith of the parent is of supreme importance. If the failure to provide medical care is the result of religious tenet or a sincere belief in the inefficacy of medical treatment there may be no criminal responsibility under the law." Verbal opinion of Reimel, J.

* Boston: Trustees under the Will of Mary Baker G. Eddy, 1934 (pp. 612-614). Reprinted with permission of the publishers.

I have everything to be thankful for.—M.T.W., Los Angeles, Cal.

NOTE 3.

EGGLESTON v. LANDRUM
210 Miss. 645, 50 So. 2d 364 (1951)

LEE, JUSTICE.

After hearing the cause, the court found that the petitioners "are fit, suitable and proper persons to be the adopted parents of said minor, except that they are believers in the doctrine and teaching of the Church of Christ Scientists, and the court finds that by reason of their belief in such faith, and solely for that reason, they are not proper persons to be the adopted parents of said minor, and that, therefore, the petition should be denied."

From the decree entered, the Egglestons have appealed here.

* * *

Keeping in mind the several contentions, pro and con, the decision of the case must turn on the question of the extent, if any, to which the religious creed of adoptive parents may warrant the State in withholding the privilege of adoption. The answer to the immediate question necessitates a consideration of the facts.

. . . Mrs. Eggleston . . . and her husband have been married fifteen years, but have no children. They . . . own a home in a desirable residential section, and other property. Mr. Eggleston is regularly employed at a substantial salary, and has additional income from rents. The record indicates that they are substantial people of high character. The child has been with them most of the time since June 1948. They have already started an educational fund for him. They have formed a strong love and deep affection for the child, and wish to adopt him and bestow upon him all rights which he would have as their own son.

The Egglestons are not members of, but they attend, the First Church of Christ Scientists in the city. However, since the child has been in their custody, they have procured medical care for his circumcision, smallpox vaccination, and shots or preventives against diphtheria, whooping cough, and typhoid fever. When he had measles, Mrs. Eggleston contacted her sister-in-law, a registered nurse, who advised that, since the disease was broken out, it would not be necessary to call a doctor. The Egglestons affirmed that they had provided medical care and attention whenever it was necessary, and that they would continue to do so in the future.

There can be no doubt, under the doctrine of *parens patriae,* that the State has the sovereign power of guardianship over persons under disability, and it alone has the right and power to determine the recipient of the privilege to adopt one of its wards. To insure the best interest of a child, the power of the State transcends the rights of natural parents; and if they are unfit to have the custody, their children may be taken from them. . . .

Likewise, there is no absolute right of adoption. It is the extension of a privilege. . . .

It is not necessary, in the decision of this case, to declare that our public policy forbids the adoption of a ward of this State by one, who, on account of religious beliefs, is opposed to medical treatment. However, necessary surgical and medical care falls into the same category as necessary subsistence; and a child, who is not supplied with such care, becomes "neglected" within the meaning of our law; and penalties may be imposed against parents who omit the performance of their duty in such respect. . . .

* * *

Appellants are not members of the Christian Science church, though they are students of that creed. There was no proof that they are opposed to medical treatment. It is not safe to brand the member of a religious sect as a believer in all of the dogma of his sect. Oftentimes, members accept creeds with reservations, and do not profess to be orthodox in all of the tenets. These appellants maintained that they had provided all necessary medical and surgical care for this child ever since he had been in their custody. Besides, they solemnly declared to the court, under oath, that they have no objection or conscientious scruples against having a physician or surgeon, or both, attend the child, if such services are necessary; and that they will provide medical care and attention when and if the same becomes necessary. While the boy attends the Sunday School of that faith, even though he may desire to embrace that form of religion, according to the proof, he may not do so until he is twenty years old.

* * *

. . . Whatever may be their religious views, the child has incurred no ill effects on that account. On the contrary, he has been the recipient of all necessary medical attention, as well as tender and loving care, in a good home and environment. Consequently, this is not a case of reversing a chancellor on his finding of fact, where the evidence is in dispute. It is a case without dispute as to the facts, in which the chancellor withheld from the appellants the privilege of adopting this little boy on the idea that the religious beliefs of the appellants would not be for the best interest of the boy. On this appeal, in review, we sit as chancellors; and we are of the opinion that the appellants were entitled to the privilege of adopting this child, and that the prayer for adoption, with all of the proferred benefits, should have been granted.

* * *

NOTE 4.

SPOCK, BENJAMIN

Illness and Injury—A Child's Attitude Reflects His Parents'*

In the early years of our marriage my wife Jane and I found that the most difficult adjustment we had to make was to our different attitudes toward illness. When she was sick occasionally with acute sinusitis, she admitted she was sick and stayed home from work. If she had fever, she went to bed and expected to have a doctor take care of her. She wanted the appropriate medicine or other treatment. When I had an illness, I ignored it unless the symptoms were truly alarming. I kept on working, though this was a disservice to my patients and colleagues as well as to myself. I would take medicine if ordered to by a doctor, but if he gave me a choice I would brush it aside. I'd rather take the pain of tooth filling than take Novocaine.

But it wasn't just that I reacted in this way to my own illness. It made me uncomfortable to see Jane doing what I called "giving in" to her symptoms. I ostentatiously ignored them and I made it clear that I thought she should change her attitude and ignore them too. Needless to say, she felt that I was an inconsiderate husband—in this respect, anyway—and I was. To make matters worse, I was spending all my working hours taking care of other people's diseases.

Differences like these are, of course, built up during childhood by family attitudes. But even in the same family the influences on a boy are apt to be different from those on a girl. Boys are usually taught not to cry, not to run to their mother when hurt (or insulted), to work things out for themselves—not only by words but by their father's example. Most girls are permitted to have feelings and to show them, to admit the need for help, to put themselves in the care of another person when the occasion demands it.

* * *

[P]arents who make a great fuss about illness will, in general bring up children who act the same way. And stoical parents will raise little

---

* Reprinted from *Problems of Parents*, Boston: Houghton Mifflin Company, 1962, pp. 107-112. Reprinted with permission of the publisher.

stoics. It seems to me sensible to avoid either extreme. The child who grows up too easily alarmed about bodily ailments is apt to be generally worrisome. He'll always be a hindrance in emergencies. Furthermore, his friends and associates, in the American scene, will consider his anxiety undignified and boring. And the person who has to ignore any infirmity in himself constantly jeopardizes his own and other people's health. Because he also can't stand having his family admit their diseases, he creates tensions in all of them.

The issue is first apt to present itself dramatically in the three and four-year-old period. This is the age when children are unusually sensitive to ideas of injury, illness and death. They readily become worried about the physical differences between boys and girls. Partly this is because they are intensely curious, and interested in cause and effect. Partly it's because they identify with other people and can imagine what it would feel like to have the afflictions they see. So they are easily frightened by pains, cuts, blood. (The reassuring concept of making things get well has great appeal, too; at times they search their bodies for scratches to cover with bandages.) So they have to depend on their parents for their cues in how to take injuries and illness. Only the parents have the experience, the knowledge, the stability to set the tone realistically. If a mother goes all to pieces over a small accident, the young child has to assume that he is in desperate danger. If the father sternly insists that a hurt doesn't hurt, the child has to learn to deny his feelings in order to keep his father's respect and his own.

* * *

There is considerable variation throughout the world in beliefs about what causes illness and injuries. In the uneducated regions they are most often considered the work of displeased gods or mischievous demons or malevolent neighbors. But right in our own country there is a wide range too. There are people who always see a significant connection between their disease and one that occurred long ago in a relative, no matter how dissimilar these may be from a medical point of view. There are millions of Americans who hold superstitious belief about certain ills; for example, that the umbilical cord becomes wrapped around the unborn baby's neck when the pregnant woman reaches for an object on a high shelf. Others tie every symptom to some indiscretion in diet. There are people who assume that all their afflictions are intended by God as just punishment.

These attitudes of adults are not essentially different from those that small children develop.
. . .

Since it's preferable to keep children from becoming excessively guilty people, and from being guilty about the wrong things, I think it's preferable not to accuse them of having harmed themselves and, particularly, of having harmed others, when there is no proof of bad intention. Even when a child has hurt another deliberately or in anger, but is a generally considerate character, it may be wise to reassure him that he didn't mean to hurt him that badly. If the child is definitely mean, he (and his parents) needs professional help rather than more and more reproaches that are doing no good.

When a member of the family has a serious disease, it's good to remember that a child may well be harboring a completely unrealistic conviction that he's partly to blame. A parent should at least explain in simple terms the cause of ill health in a close relative and then listen to a child's questions and comments, to see how he understands it or misunderstands it. If the parent gets a hint that the child feels guilt, it's wise to get it out in the open so that he can be reassured. "Maybe you think you made Susie sick because you were mean to her that day. But that didn't make her sick. It was a germ she caught."

NOTE 5.

WESSEL, MORRIS A.

The Role of the Pediatrician in the Lesser Case*

. . . There is little evidence from a medical point of view in the Lesser trial transcript to support the concept that Larry was critically ill. Although he undoubtedly did have upper respiratory infections on repeated occasions, and with associated episodes of bronchial asthma, his continued physical activity suggests that at no time was the condition critical or severe. Even if he did have small areas of pneumonia, which might have been noted on X-ray examination, it was in a mild form, and relatively of no serious consequence. Whether he would have gotten worse— or even better—without any medical treatment is an unanswered question. From a life and death point of view, one cannot see that a physician needed to see the child at all. The reported fever elevations are really of no consequence, since, particularly in childhood, due to the immaturity of the neuro-physiological control of body temperature, there can be a rapid change from 97 degrees to 105 degrees within a few hours. The important clinical observations which help to determine the

seriousness of an illness are the patient's behavior, appearance, respiratory rate, restlessness, and in particular his ability—or lack of ability—to carry on his normal activity. The data presented indicates that Larry was able to play, be up and around; and in fact he limited his activity in practically no way whatsoever.

However, the major function of a physician . . . is to make a patient feel better. All patients feel better, when *their* doctor, or even *a* doctor, comes to see them when they are ill. The physician brings to the patient a psychological force (some call it the art of medicine), built upon the trust of the patient's past experiences with idealized parents, parent figures, other doctors, and this particular doctor. In addition, the physician's scientific training, his skills, his body of knowledge, his tools, his examination procedures, all combine with this trust which exists between patient and doctor, to bring to sick human beings a force which supports the patient's ego and helps him to maintain physiological equilibrium and tolerate the anxiety which accompanies pain, fever, malaise, and an inability to function normally.

In the Lesser case, it was very difficult for any physician to function in a way which facilitates this professional role. Even if the doctor did see the child when physical or psychological malaise indicated, it was only with the grudging reluctance of the mother. There was no promise that medications would be given as recommended by the doctor.

This point raises the question as to whether a physician should allow himself to be caught in such a situation. Unless he is free to prescribe medications, and know that the patient will get them, he might do better to refuse to assume any responsibility at all.

The court's suggestion that the child be examined at monthly intervals is untenable for the family's physician. If the court wants to hire a physician to act as an observer to evaluate what is occurring, that is another question. A physician, in a therapeutic relationship to a patient, must be free to see, or not see, a patient according to the patient's needs, or the professional standards in his community. A court order interferes with the normal process by which a patient or the parents, and the doctor, establish frequency of contact. As the patient improves, the family and doctor must be free to reduce the frequency of contact, as evidence that the patient is getting better. Under the court ordered medical visits on a monthly basis, the therapeutic effect of timing visits at less frequent intervals as an evidence of cure is lost. In fact, the maintenance of medically unnecessary contacts might well prolong the illness, or at least,

---

* Printed with permission of the author, who retains all publication rights (1962).

the patient's feelings about his illness, even though in actuality the condition might be improving.

NOTE 6.

KANNER, LEO
Child Psychiatry*

[I]t has been observed that an attack caused by pollen during a visit to a certain place may produce "reflex asthma" when the same place is revisited, even at a time when the pollen is not in season. Hurst named "expectation" as one of the most common exciting causes of an attack, giving second rank to annoyance, excitement, and anxiety. Thus a state may be reached when attacks, no longer dependent on allergic catalysts, may be brought on by an emotional "trigger" alone. The frequent observation, first reported by Rogerson, that asthmatic children placed in convalescent homes enjoy freedom from attacks and resume them promptly upon their return to a difficult home situation, testifies to the significance of emotional factors in determining the occurrence of asthmatic incidents.

NOTE 7.

ZWEIG, STEFAN
Mental Healers†

The gods are responsible for illness; the gods alone have power to cure: this conviction is an invariable prelude to the rise of the art of healing. Primitive man was ignorant of his own powers; in face of sickness he was helpless, alone, weak; he knew of no other way than to turn to his gods for succour and beseech them not to forsake him in his need. The only curative art known to him was an appeal to magic, to prayer, to the sacrificial knife. He was defenceless against the all-powerful one who dwelt in the realm of the shades and against whom it was vain to struggle. It behoved a man, therefore, to be humble, to ask forgiveness, to pray, to beseech, in order that the pain might be removed. But how was the invisible deity to be reached? How was he to be addressed, seeing that none knew his abiding place? How prove to him one's penitence, one's subjection, one's willingness to make the expected sacrifice, one's desire to take a pledge of future good behaviour; how discover a means of communication? In its childhood days, humanity could give no answer to these questionings. God does not reveal himself to the ignorant, he does not note the everyday doings of poor

---

* Springfield, Ill.: Charles C Thomas, 2d ed. 1950, p. 389. Reprinted with permission of the publisher.

† London: Cassell & Co. 1933, pp. x-xi. Reprinted with permission of the publisher and The Viking Press, Inc.

dumb mortals, does not deign to answer, does not incline his ear. Man in his distress had to seek a brother man to act as mediator between himself and god, a man wiser than himself, one with wider experience, who knew the words that would open the magic doors, that would conciliate the powers of darkness and would assuage the wrath of the unseen ruler. In primitive times the only mediator between man and god was the priest.

The fight against disease was, then, not a fight against a particular illness, but a hand-to-hand struggle to find god. All medical art, at the outset, takes a theological cast, becomes a cult, a ritual, a form of magic, a spiritual combat of man against divine chastening. . . .

4.

ON PROVIDING DATA FOR FINDING THE FACT OF "IN THE CHILD'S BEST INTEREST" IN DECIDING CUSTODY

a. Determining a Course of Action—The Relevance of a Child's "Preference"

SMITH v. SMITH
15 Utah 2d 36, 386 P. 2d 900 (1963)

WADE, JUSTICE.

Joseph Thurston Smith commenced a divorce action against his wife, Alyce M. Smith. The divorce was granted to the wife upon her counterclaim. He appeals only from that portion of the decree granting her the custody of their minor children. All but one of the six minor children were 10 years of age or over, and these five children expressed a preference to remain with the father, the appellant herein.

Under Section 30-3-5, U.C.A. 1953, in divorce proceedings, where neither party is found to be an immoral or unfit person to have the custody of the children, must the children more than 10 years of age be awarded to the custody of the parent which is chosen by such child? In cases where the child is not entitled to make such choice and child custody cases generally, we have emphasized that the best interest of the child is controlling. Judges often disagree on what will be for the best interest of a child and the child's reaction to the award and many other factors may have a bearing on that question.

The above section provides "* * * that if any of the children have attained the age of ten years and are of sound mind, such children shall have the privilege of selecting the parent to which they will attach themselves." In Dorsey v. Dorsey, speaking of this provision, we said: "[I]n case the parent the child selects is found to be an immoral or unfit person to have the care and custody of the child, and the court finds it to be for the best

Also see 206 NE2d 720 57 Ill. App. 2d 286 (1965) strickler case, holds change in child's preference alone does not constitute a

interests of the child, that the court may, nevertheless, determine the child's custody otherwise." We have found no case to the contrary, and we think this is a correct statement of the law. This requires a finding that the parent selected be an immoral or unfit person; otherwise, the child must be awarded to the parent chosen. It is unthinkable that a court would award a child to the custody of an immoral or unfit parent even though the statute does not expressly provide such an exception. However, a finding that the best interest of the child requires that it be placed in other custody is not sufficient to justify the court in placing the child elsewhere.

Case reversed with directions that the children be awarded to the father . . . .

CROCKETT, JUSTICE (dissenting).

The main opinion reverses the decree granting custody of the children to their mother, the defendant, on the ground that the statute gives the children over 10 the absolute choice of parental custody, which supersedes the finding of the court that their best interest and welfare would be served by being with their mother and confers upon the father the incontestable right to their custody, so that the court is powerless to do other than to award the children to him. Because I am alone in my taking the opposite view, I acknowledge some degree of deference to the opinion of my colleagues. Nevertheless, because of the firmness of my conviction, I desire to set forth as clearly as possible the reasons for my conclusion.

In the first place, I am unable to reconcile the ruling of the majority with the more fundamental rules which have always been recognized as applicable to questions of child custody: that the welfare of the children is the paramount consideration, which overrides all others; that the trial court has broad discretion in making that determination; and that it will not upset unless there is plain abuse.

Secondly, it seems to me that the court's decision reaches its result by placing unwarranted literal emphasis upon only one clause of the statute, whereas I believe that if the entire statute and the background and purpose of the law are all given due consideration together, as they should be, the contrary conclusion will result.

Due to the position taken by my colleagues that the statute is controlling anyway, I assume that no matter how praiseworthy the qualities of the defendant mother may be, nor however to the contrary with respect to the plaintiff father, nor however meritorious the case may seem for the mother having the children's custody, because of the children's choice, the award must, nevertheless, be to the father, unless he is completely unfit.

This being the majority view, there would be no useful purpose in laboring in detail the question of the relative fitness of these parents. But I think it not amiss to observe in summary that if we look at the matter in the light most favorable to the finding of the trial court, as we should do, there is ample basis to justify the conclusion that it is in the best interest of these children to be awarded to their mother. Yet, it is only fair to state that to characterize her as a completely blameless and long-suffering wife, and the plaintiff as a villain, would be naive and unrealistic. There obviously is here, as there always is, some fault on both sides. But the trial court, from its advantaged position, and with its acknowledged prerogatives, has chosen to believe her version of the evidence; found the issues in her favor; granted her the divorce, and has found that it would be for the best interest and welfare of the children to be in her custody.

To give the plaintiff his due, in spite of his faults, a good case can be made that he has a sincere desire to be a good father to his children; that he disciplines and manages them quite well; and that they love and respect him. However, beyond this, it also appears from the evidence that in all likelihood the plaintiff as a doctor and a psychiatrist assumes to himself an air of superiority; that he has tended to overshadow his wife; and is somewhat aggressive and domineering. There are some aspects of his conduct which, from a detached perspective, seem a bit irrational, the epitome of which is exemplified by a telephone call to the defendant, during the emotional throes of their trouble, in which he clung on to the conversation continuously for nine hours.

Plaintiff's aggressiveness and tenacity is manifest in this proceeding itself. He initiated the divorce action against his wife, bent upon disgracing her and taking the children away from her. But as to the hypothesis upon which he proposed to do so, that she was immoral and unfit, he failed in his proof, and the trial court found the other way. He nevertheless stubbornly insists that he is right, and that the court itself has no power to decide the issue against him. It is obvious that the economic leverage he has is at least one of the important factors influencing the choice of the older children. Under the circumstances shown, it strikes me as an egregious miscarriage of justice to thus regard his aggressiveness and intransigence.

Further, and more important than the result in this case, is the fact that the holding with respect to this statute seems to me to completely distort its true purpose and reaches a high point in forebearance of the judicial prerogative, if not an outright abdication of judicial duty. If the mere fact that a child has become 10 years old endows him with power to make a choice of his parental custodian, which must be honored in any event, and whether his reasons are good or bad, or in fact whether he has any reasons at all, so that his choice is absolute and not subject to control or review by anyone, even by the court, he could be empowered to make a decision of the gravest possible consequence to himself, his family, and society, under circumstances where, because of his immaturity, and the usual emotional stress, there is little assurance that his judgment would be sound. It would be one of the most arbitrary and far-reaching prerogatives known to the law. This is plainly nonsensical and impractical.

Fortunately for society and the individuals in it, the law does not function by singling out and placing all of the emphasis on one clause in a statute. Throughout the long and prideful history of our common law system, its principal merit has been that instead of casting aside reason and clinging slavishly to unintended literalness, its usefulness and its durability have been served by applying the rule of reason to adapt it to the practical exigencies of life. The cardinal principle has constantly been adhered to that when the course of justice is clear, it is the purpose of the law and the duty of the courts to fashion it out of the materials available.

A study of the decisions will show that it has invariably been considered that in basic structure our law is of more profound character than a mere catalog of words or rules to be applied to the affairs of life in more than mechanical routine fashion ; and that it has always been regarded as a proper judicial function to give it a reasonable and sensible application to avoid unjust or absurd results. Correlated to this is an appreciation that in the multifariousness of legislation it is inevitable that there will at times be conflicts between provisions of the law ; and that it is difficult for statutes, which necessarily must be in general language, to apply to the variety of life with absolute clarity and precision in all instances. Consequently, where by inept wording, lack of certainty, or simply through error or inadvertence, the statute is such that too literal an interpretation would produce absurd results, the courts have wisely looked beyond such frailties or superficialities to the background of the statute to find the true intent and purpose sought to be accomplished ; and similarly, where there appears to be conflict, a provision of law which is paramount in the public interest will prevail over one which is less important . . . .

. . . There is no more vital precept than that no man, however high or low his station, nor whatever the right he claims, nor even the law itself, should be above the rule of reason. This comes to us from antiquity and has persisted as the transcendent force in the law . . . This step was taken early in the 17th century when Lord Coke said in his famous dictum in Bonham's Case:

"'And it appears in our books, that in many cases, the common law will control acts of parliament, and sometimes adjudge them to be utterly void; for when an act of parliament is against common right and reason, or repugnant, or impossible to be performed, the common law will control it, and adjudge such act to be void.'"

* * *

In accordance with the foregoing . . . in divining the meaning of the statute here in question, it should be considered in the light of the historical role courts have played in divorce proceedings and of the entire act treating the subject in a manner to harmonize with the purpose sought to be accomplished. Anciently, and without variation to the present day, such proceedings, and especially, the phase dealing with child custody have been considered equitable in a high degree, over which the court, because of the interest the public has in the family and the children, has exercised plenary powers. In earlier times the courts actually assumed the role of guardians of children in families broken by divorce ; and have always regarded the custody of children as of the most vital importance. Acceptance of the rule proposed by the plaintiff would greatly limit the court's ability to perform this important duty. The incongruity is pointed up by the fact that this decision does not affect the custody of Naniloa, age 7, nor can it take into account the desirability that she be with her brothers and sisters.

It is submitted that if the whole structure of the divorce law is looked at in the correct light it will be seen that the clear purpose of the legislature was to grant to the court discretion to do what it has always done, i.e., whatever justice and equity require in regard to the parties, the children and the property rights, and that there are a number of reasons why it is unthinkable that the legislature intended a 10-year-old child to have any such absolute and incontestable power.

Under such a rule, parents already too deeply immersed in woes because the family is breaking up would have them added to by having to compete with each other for the children's choice. Without elaborating thereon it is easy to see the hazards to them and to the child this would create. Such a battle might well go to the more unscrupulous parent, who may not be above poisoning the child's mind against the other ; or resorting to coercion ; or showering him with ill-advised gifts or favors. Even more damaging would be the subjecting of a child to such pressures and making him a pawn in the contest of the spouses for his custody. It is extremely doubtful that under such circumstances a child of that age would have the stability and judgment to see through the maze of troubles and make a wise choice. In some instances it would be cruel to subject him to it and wholly unrealistic to regard his choice as absolute.

Because of the foregoing, the court should be reluctant indeed to place this responsibility upon a small child, forcing him to face and cope with difficulties which the parents themselves have found insurmountable. This is especially so when a further effect is to rob the court itself of the role the law obviously intends it to play as arbiter and conciliator of troubles which have proved too much for the family to deal with.

It also must be remembered that any award of custody made by the court must necessarily be an integral part of the overall adjustment of the family situation. The provision by way of support money or property settlement, and the values to be found in children being together, are considered by the court in judging what is best for the welfare of the entire family. This could all be lost if the choice were dependent entirely upon the whim or caprice of a 10-year-old child.

There is another reason why I think it is indisputably clear that it was not intended to invest the child with any such absolute power. The provision upon which the decision rests that the children 10 years old, "* * * shall have the privilege of selecting the parent to which they will attach themselves" presents just two alternatives: it either means that the child has the choice and that it is absolute and incontestable; or that the choice is subject to veto by the court under some circumstances. If the former, then his choice would be absolute whatever the conditions. If the latter, then his choice is not absolute but is subject to review by the court and to veto under proper circumstances. That the latter is the case is inescapable. Everyone, even the plaintiff's counsel, concede that if the child chooses a parent who is physically or mentally unfit, or so morally depraved as to be totally unsuited to be his custodian, the court does not have to honor such a choice. . . . [T]he general supervisory power of the court over the welfare of the children supersedes the choice of the child . . . That view is in harmony with the traditional policy of the courts of maintaining the keenest interest and surveillance over the interest and welfare of children, which, of course, involves vital concern over their proper custody.

. . . Inasmuch as the court can veto the child's choice on the ground of fitness, there is no logical escape from the conclusion that the court must then have the prerogative of determining the degree of fitness or unfitness of the parents. This is so as a practical matter because the question of being fit or unfit is something which is rarely seen as either all black or all white. Seldom would one parent be either completely insane, immoral, an utter drunkard, or otherwise so entirely lacking in parental qualities as to be totally unfit, as contrasted to a spouse who is a paragon of all of the virtues. Human personalities are so variegated that the question of fitness or unfitness is practically always a comparative one, and of necessity the court is both empowered and obliged to take the responsibility of determining on a comparative basis which parent is the one "fit" to have custody for the best interest and welfare of the child.

Returning to the wording of the statute in question, with the foregoing discussion in mind, I fail to see in the language itself any justification for such an absolute and rigid application as the plaintiff insists upon. . . .

* * *

. . . The question arises as to what reason in law or logic could there be in interpreting the statute as meaning that at the time of the divorce the child had the absolute right of choice, and that "subsequently," which could be immediately, the court has plenary powers to make any order with respect to the children as it shall deem proper. To see this necessary and proper power in the court certainly does not require any disregarding nor distorting this statute. It only requires looking at the whole statute together in such a way that all of its parts harmonize with each other and with the background structure of the entire law on the subject, as contrasted with considering in isolation and placing an unwarranted literal emphasis on one clause to the exclusion of all of the rest. . . .

I would affirm the trial court. . . .

HENRIOD, CHIEF JUSTICE (concurring).

* * *

Considerable stress is laid by the dissent on the judgment of a 10-year-old. What about the judgment of the $17\frac{1}{2}$ year-old girl and the other three children ranging in ages between those extremes? At 18 the girl could marry. At 18 a boy goes to war. Under the statutes a 14-year-old boy is held responsible for his criminal acts. The legislature obviously thought that all things being equal, and both parents being fit, one 10 years old, or older, had enough sense and judgment to live with one or the other of his natural parents, according to his choice. It seems safer, so far as the humanities are concerned, to let the elected representatives of the people set the age of discretion in such case, than to leave the decision arbitrarily to one man, a judge, who might personally prefer one over the other of two spouses. I am of the opinion that more than once a 10-year-old has proven himself more capable of determining his best interests in the area of filial feeling and domestic relations than has a judge, who, in the last analysis, has not popped corn in the kitchen or helped to trim a Christmas tree with such youngster.

* * *

. . . Kids 10 years and older generally have pretty good sense, including a sense of greater devotion to one or the other of their parents. If their parents do not have sense enough to bring these kids to full fruition because of fractured domestic relations why give one judge the awful power to force five kids to live with one of the recalcitrants against their expressed wishes, where the two homebreakers nonetheless are found to be equally fit to raise their children according to the latter's choice of parents.

The dissent talks about children becoming pawns on the occasion of a divorce. *They always are* and invariably suffer more than the parents who brought them here without any choice on the offsprings' parts. Perhaps the legislature was not so unwise after all in letting the kids reverse the situation, have a genuine choice as to their future, make pawns, for a change, out of their parents and say that although there be a plague on both your houses, I want to live in the one in which I want to love. . . .

NOTES

NOTE 1.

COLEMAN, ROSE W. ; KRIS, ERNST ; *and*
PROVENCE, SALLY

The Study of Variations of Early Parental Attitudes. A Preliminary Report*

Parental attitudes to the child are continuously influenced by the child's growth and development. With the changing needs and demands of the child different reactions of the parents are stimulated, since changing demands tend to mobilize different unconscious material in the parent (Kris, 1944). [On Psychoanalysis and Education. Am. J. Orthopsychiatry] In principle this is equally true of both parents. The interaction between the child's development and the unconscious material which it

mobilizes in the parent suggests that "fixed" and "static" designation of parental attitudes . . . are unsatisfactory or incomplete. Parental attitudes are subject to variations in accordance with the varying needs and demands of the child. The mother who genuinely delights or can tolerate all of the infant's demands may react with irritation when the child becomes "independent", when early in his second year he can move away and at the same time may develop an intolerance against separation upon bedtime. And again the reverse occurs: the child that has become independent may gain admiration from a mother who did not gain satisfaction from her care of the infant.* In the later course of development bowel training, the first manifestations of negativism or the first sign of phallic and oedipal strivings may elicit previously dormant reactions in the parent. The most frequent and probably best known intolerance concerns the parental reaction against the child who shows sibling rivalry. Therefore, no study of parental attitudes seems to us complete which neglects the variations arising in the course of those changing characteristics of infant and child.

NOTE 2.

COMMONWEALTH v. LOTZ
188 Pa. Super. 241, 146 A. 2d 362 (1959)

WOODSIDE, JUDGE.

. . . The girl is now thirteen years of age and has been the subject of continual litigation since March of 1948. The conduct of both parties in regard to the various orders for visitation which have been entered throughout the years has been less than admirable.

The last time that the child visited her father was February 23, 1957. During the evening of that visit, a disagreement occurred between them in which it can be determined from the varying stories of the occurrence that the father struck the child and that the child kicked her father and threw newspapers and davenport pillows onto the floor. Thereafter, Elizabeth Ann refused to visit her father at the times ordered for visitation by the court.

The court below properly concluded that "Even though we should accept the child's version of the events of February 23, 1957, it is not of such a serious nature that it should work a permanent estrangement between the child and her father."

The mother contends, however, that the testimony shows that Elizabeth Ann "has a strong

---

* *The Psychoanalytic Study of the Child*, Vol. 8 (1953), p. 25. Reprinted with permission of the publisher, International Universities Press, New York.

---

* Much of this has become general knowledge. Child placement agencies are accustomed to take into account that certain foster mothers do better with infants, others with toddlers or older children of a specific age group.

fear of appellee and is so emotionally disturbed at the prospect of visiting him that it would be a rash gamble with her future to compel her to make the periodic visits required by Judge Curran." The lower court did not so find, and it is in a far better position to evaluate the evidence and judge the parties than we are.

*   *   *

A thorough review of the record in this case does not reveal sufficient evidence to warrant the termination of appellee's visitation rights. It is against public policy to destroy or limit the relation of parent or child. . . .

A parent has seldom been denied the right of visitation. The cases in which visitation rights of a parent have been limited or denied have been those in which severe mental or moral deficiencies of the parent have constituted a real and grave threat to the welfare of the child. . . . The courts have granted visitation rights to parents even in those circumstances where the parent has ignored the children for a long period of time. . . .

*   *   *

In the present case, a reversal of the order of the court below can only lead to a permanent estrangement between Elizabeth Ann Lotz and her father. The court below was in a position to appraise the attitude of the child and to determine the effect of the order upon the girl. It was Judge Curran's conclusion that the best interests of the child would be advanced by effecting a reconciliation with her father. We cannot render the court below powerless to effectuate its decision. Minor children, being wards of the state, may be taken from their parents when their welfare so requires. . . . Certainly if the court can remove a child from the custody of its parents, it can, for the welfare of the child, conversely order custody or visitation with a parent.

. . . Were we to reverse the order of the court below, we would provide an easy method for any person who has obtained the custody of a child to nullify the visitation rights granted by the court. A court which has awarded custody of a child can require the person to whom such custody has been awarded to exert reasonable authority over such child to require it to obey the lawful orders of a court.

The order is affirmed.

WRIGHT, JUDGE dissenting.

I cannot go along with the majority in ordering this mother to force her thirteen year old daughter to visit her father. The record discloses that the girl refused to make the visits voluntarily because the father has inflicted serious physical injuries upon her, and she fears and dislikes him. While I fully agree that it is against public policy to destroy or limit the relationship of parent and child, and that a parent should not be denied the right of visitation, the instant order does not provide for visitation of the child by the father. On the contrary, it requires the mother to compel visitation of the father by the child. . . . .

NOTE 3.

ISRAELI DRAFT FAMILY CODE **(Section 101)** 1956*

Consent of the Adopted Child

The Court shall not make an adoption order unless it is satisfied

(1) that the child has been with the adoptive parent for six months before the order was made;

(2) that the child, being capable of understanding the matter, desires to be adopted by this particular adoptive parent.

Comments

The child's wishes have been given prominence in many laws. We propose a two-fold test: If the child has reached the age in which he is "capable of understanding the matter," he must be asked (Clause (2); in any event, it must be ascertained whether the child and the adopting parent are in fact suited to each other; this will be determined in the light of experience (Clause (1). A similar provision is contained in Sec. 2 of the English Act of 1950 where the trial period is three months.

b. Determining a Course of Action—The Judicial Selection of Facts—The Problem of Interviewing Children

FREUD, ANNA

On the Difficulties of Communicating with Children—The Lesser Children in Chambers†

When Mr. Justice Streit summons Larry, Benjamin, and Dee Lesser to his chambers to inform himself about their preferences regarding future custody, he is lucky to be spared almost all the major difficulties which usually arise when adults in authority try to communicate with children. None of the three meet his questions with the blank wall of silence or the contradictory statements which are often the child's automatic defence when a delicate or dangerous situation is investigated. None of them intentionally hides

* Cambridge: Harvard Law School–Brandeis University, Cooperative Research for Israel's Legal Development, Draft Family Code for the State of Israel, 1956 (p. 128).

† Unpublished manuscript printed with permission of the author, who retains all publication rights (1964).

his thoughts, opinions, and feelings, as children do whenever they suspect possible criticism, reproach, or ridicule. They make no attempt to confuse or distort the truth, since he succeeds in being neither feared not distrusted by them. If nevertheless their statements, especially Larry's, are not as informative as the Judge might wish, this is not due to lack of frankness or cooperation on their part. What each has to contribute to the picture is limited inevitably to what they know about themselves. To face up to one's real emotions and to probe into one's real motives is not a capacity which we expect to find in children. On the contrary, children of all ages have a natural tendency to deceive themselves about their motivations, to rationalize their actions, and to shy back from full awareness of their feelings, especially where conflicts of loyalty come into question. To pierce through these defenses demands more than usual skill from the investigator. Verbal and nonverbal communications (attitudes, behavior) have to be scrutinized, assessed, and translated into their underlying meaning; openings offered by the child, all unknowingly, have to be pursued and utilized. In short, an entry has to be found into the child's inner world of emotions, phantasies, and judgments, irrespective of the fact whether this is hidden only from the interviewer or also from the child himself. The ability to make such contacts is demanded from psychiatric diagnosticians or child analysts as part of their professional equipment. In a legal investigation such as in the Lesser case, it also becomes the Judge's task.

Where Larry is concerned, it is true of course, that no six-year-old can feel at ease when interviewed by a stranger and that such a situation produces invariably a wary and respectful blandness which proves rather unrevealing. Nevertheless, Larry as informant is not completely unproductive, even when questioned by an adult in authority. Almost immediately, even if involuntarily, he reveals the main measure which he has adopted to defend himself against the pressures and upsets of his broken family life. He does not attempt to master what happens by understanding it, as his six-year-old intellect might well be able to do, but on the contrary proclaims an attitude of "not knowing," a turn of speech which is repeated over and over in his conversations with the Judge. Spontaneously and immediately he begins by informing the Judge that he "does not know" what his middle initial stands for and proceeds from there to all the other things he "does not know," such as the purpose of the building he is in; the person and the function of the Judge; the type of visits by brother and father 'which he "does not get"; his place of

living; the type of school he attends; the time when school breaks up; the days in the week or the months in the year; the number of words he can read, etc. Expressions such as "I should know but I don't," return repeatedly. Obviously, he behaves like somebody who complains that "no one tells me anything," and this plea for knowledge is the opening offered to the adult interviewer. If the examination had been a clinical-diagnostic and not a judicial one, the psychiatrist would have been blamed at this point for not recognizing and making better use of the offered opportunity. There is little doubt that a frank explanation and discussion of the family situation would not only have gratified and relieved this bewildered child, but also would have opened up a path to his confidences and, probably, brought forth a flood of further complaints and information. The psychiatrist needs to say no more to the child on such an occasion than a sympathetic "Isn't it awful how they never explain things to you, as if you were a stupid little boy!", establishing himself thereby firmly as an ally of the child against the nonunderstanding and enigmatic adult world.

In clinical experience, Larry's attitude of "not knowing anything" is found not infrequently in children who live in an atmosphere of parental quarrel or who try to close their eyes and ears to the recognition of sexual irregularities in father or mother. Even though this defense protects the child from insights which he is not ready to digest, it can become a serious handicap if it spreads from the home situation to the world at large, to school, and to the learning process in general. There is already a hint in this direction in Larry's diffidence about his reading ability, although in his case the unsatisfied wish to know is still more obvious than the determined fight against knowledge which may take its place later with many other children.

For whatever they may be worth to the Court as relevant information, there are also some hints given by Larry how much he misses his father. Although they are veiled and indirect, as information given by children often is, they are probably more reliable than the perfunctory "Yes, Sir" to the Judge's standard question "Do you love your father?" or "Do you do what your father tells you?" One is that the father is the powerful dispenser of electric trains, an item which Larry brings in spontaneously, not in answer to a question; obviously according to the child's mind, he can give what the mother cannot give. Secondly, he can do things which have to be left undone in his absence, such as taking the extra wheels off the bicycle, a statement which betrays some of the helplessness felt by the child when fatherless. The third indication is contained in the boy's behavior at the end of the interview when he is reluctant to leave the judge's presence. In analytic language we would call this a piece of "transference" and understand it as a quick attachment of a "fatherless" boy to the big man who has given him some time and shown some interest in him, and whom the child does not want to give up again, even though his questions have remained unanswered and his curiosity is unsatisfied. If it is our intention to learn more about Larry's conflicting loyalties to mother or father, here is again an opening offered which would make it possible to verbalize and ventilate the question.

Finally, Larry's "all right," when leaving the Judge against his inclination, can be taken as an instructive demonstration of the boy's habitual, rather passive acquiescence and compliance when faced with unsatisfied wishes and with frustrating situations not under his control.

The transition from six-year-old Larry to fourteen-year-old Benjamin demands a complete readjustment in the questioner's approach. Where Larry is diffident, befogged, and betrays his attitudes involuntarily rather than revealing them intentionally, Benjamin makes the Judge's task easy by being highly verbal and open in his communications. He does not lose any time in setting the tone of the interview himself by stating that he was hoping he "would get the chance to talk to someone in that particular field" (of law). Although overtly the remark refers to his own position as "Chairman of the Law and Political Science Conference" in school, it contains also the hidden hint to the Judge that he cannot be talked down to, that no opening gambit of routine questions is necessary for him and that, so far as he is concerned, the problem of his parents should be approached in a man-to-man atmosphere of intelligent detachment, tolerance, and understanding for the weaknesses of human nature. Altogether, he does not hesitate to provide the information which is sought as a guide for the Court's decision, namely that his preference is for living with his father, that this is his own "decision," influenced by neither parent, and that he is quite ready to pursue what he takes as his rights even if it had to be through "some sort of appeal from that decision by the Judge."

It is interesting to note that in spite of their frank interchange of opinion, Benjamin and the Judge also occasionally block each other's lines of approach. The boy ignores the offering to talk about basketball and the Judge's role in it and insists on keeping the interview on more adult ground. The Judge on his side does not enter into Benjamin's interest in the Law and his school

functions with regard to it, trying to keep the interview to the personal matters in hand. Momentarily they tangle both on the power question, each affirming their right to decide the final issue.

Although Benjamin's preferences are not in doubt and this is all the information needed by the Court, it may be instructive also to pursue the matter further and to get a glimpse of the happenings in Benjamin's mind behind the outward veneer of intellectual mastery. Obviously, there is more feeling here than the boy likes and cares to admit to himself. He denies in so many words that there is "bitterness" in him, he praises his father for doing "a good job" in providing a home for him, while he is "surely" on very good terms with his mother and "naturally" still loves her. But he also reveals how this apparent impartiality is achieved, namely by becoming "somewhat aloof" from both so that it is "not so hard when the final break comes." We see here an adolescent who has escaped from his feelings to his intellect because, in reality, he has lived with the parents' quarrelling "a good many years," with "so many" that he cannot "enumerate," that he feels "that in a sense they are both wrong" and that the only way to manage is to live on compromise. That, behind this open disillusionment, there is even deeper distaste and even fear of the task of judging them is borne out by his double attitude to the legal profession. In spite of his marked interest in the law, there is an equally marked disinclination to become a judge or lawyer. Attraction to and turning away from the necessity of designating father or mother as the guilty party here fight openly against each other. Perhaps the Judge is right here if he remains cautiously on the outward fringe of this hidden conflict of loyalties and avoids opening up a depth of feeling with which the boy manages to cope with his own efforts, by means of an intelligence which is admittedly beyond his years.

There is less information about the nature of the interviews with Dee, but still sufficient evidence to show how she has tried to cope within the situation. Unlike Benjamin, who "tosses it up and comes up with his own conclusions," she much prefers to leave the decision of this most private concern to an impartial Judge, thereby escaping the responsibility of hurting either her father's or her mother's feelings. One wonders whether Mr. Justice Streit guesses what device has enabled her to take this attitude. In her testimony she reveals unmistakably that she has managed to transfer the meaning of "home" from the disturbed image of the person of the parents to the safe picture of the "house" itself, with the result that she holds on to living in the house as other girls would hold on to either father or mother. The house has become for Dee a symbol of the home base to which one belongs (probably a symbol of the parents when they were still united), and in a way it has ceased to matter who of the two quarreling parents is in actual occupancy.

Whether the Judge has understood Dee's not quite usual way of solving her problem or not seems immaterial here. He has a right to expect that she will settle down to any decision so long as she did not have to inflict it on her parents by herself.

In this manner each of them finds his own escape from judging the parents harshly: Larry by confusion, Benjamin by intellectualization, Dee by displacement of her feelings.

NOTES

NOTE 1.

SCHAFER, ROY

Generative Empathy in the Treatment Situation*

. . . Aichhorn had just seen the father and had familiarized himself with the life situation of the delinquent boy he was about to see. The boy, until recently a good boy, had misappropriated some money, had disappeared for a week, and had since become shiftless, obdurate, and defiant in manner and behavior. Severity and kindness were tried alternately several times, but the boy only acted worse. 'I talked', says Aichhorn, 'to the boy alone. He was a very thin young man who looked somewhat older than his seventeen years.'

'Do you know where you are?'
'No.'
'In the child guidance clinic of the Juvenile Court.'
'Oh yes. My father wants to put me in a reform school.'
'Your father has told me what has happened and I'd like to help you.'
'It's no use.' He shrugged his shoulders and turned away.
'Certainly it's no use if you don't want help.'
'You can't help me.'
'I know you don't have much confidence in me; we don't know each other yet.'
'Not that, but anyway it's no use.' He showed the same hopeless, uncooperative air.
'Are you willing to talk to me?'
'Why not?'
'I must ask you various questions and I'll make you a proposition.'
'What?' The tone betrayed expectation.

* 28 *Psychoanalytic Quart.* 362-367 (1959). Reprinted with permission of the publisher.

'That you don't answer any question you don't like.'
'How do you mean?' He was astonished and incredulous.
'The questions you don't like you need not answer or you may tell me it's none of my business.'
'Why do you say that?'
'Because I'm not a detective nor a policeman and I don't need to know everything. Anyway you wouldn't tell me the truth if I asked questions you didn't like.'
'How do you know that?'
'Because that is what everybody does and you are no exception. I wouldn't tell everything either to someone whom I'd met for the first time.'
'But if I talk and tell you lies, will you know that too?'
'No, but that would be too bad. And anyway it isn't necessary because I don't want to force you to answer me.'
'At home they always said if I'd talk, nothing bad would happen to me, but when I did it was always much worse. So I quit talking.'
'But here it's a little different. I'll be satisfied with what you are willing to tell. But I'd like to be sure you are telling me the truth.'
'Good.'
'You agree?' I offered him my hand which he took eagerly.
'Agreed.'

What does Aichhorn convey in his few masterful remarks to the discouraged, sullen adolescent? To begin with he explicitly establishes where the boy is, emphasizing thereby that the boy is in trouble. He also makes it explicit that they are not in court but in a child guidance clinic attached to the court, thereby differentiating himself from law enforcement. The boy rejects this differentiation, and at the same time excludes Aichhorn from individual consideration when he says, 'My father wants to put me in reform school.' Aichhorn now begins an active approach: 'Your father has told me what has happened and I'd like to help you.' He says thereby that he does not feel repelled or accusing by what he has heard. What he has heard has led him to conclude that the boy needs help rather than manipulation, and, moreover, has encouraged him to offer it. But note too that he neither says, 'I am going to help', which would be uninvited intrusion and manipulation and would attempt to take away autonomy from the boy, nor 'I am sorry for you' or 'You've had some tough breaks', which would be pitying. . . .

When the boy replies, 'It's no use', he does not flatly repudiate Aichhorn's offer to help. By not rejecting the idea of help or the need for help, he leaves a little, though not much, opening for further approach. Aichhorn's rejoinder, 'Certainly it is no use if you don't want help' again supports the boy's autonomy by admitting at once that he is helpless without the boy's collaboration, but he does so without renouncing his own role as helper in the situation. By saying 'If you don't want help', he implies that the boy does or might want help. Aichhorn knew that this had been a good boy before the current difficulties developed and apparently he is counting on utilizing the boy's conflict. Aichhorn is not calling a bluff; he is helping the boy to talk about needing help without insisting that the boy express the need for help first and then feel too vulnerable to being abused and too ashamed of unmanliness. Aichhorn does not allow the boy to present himself as a helpless victim, for he confronts him with an assertion that he, the boy, has control—a challenge but also a reassurance. The boy's response, 'You can't help me', implies a bit more definitely that he does want help—and still he has not had to ask for it openly. The boy's attention is now focused on Aichhorn and on his ability to help. He departs from his position of futility and engages—and challenges—Aichhorn. Aichhorn does not become defensively self-confident, nor does he alienate the boy by reproval for challenging him. Instead he offers a clarification that trust or confidence in personal relationships is a mutual achievement and is not to be produced on order and quickly. He is self-assured but not so demanding or insensitive as to say, 'Of course I can help'. He says simply, 'I know you don't have much confidence in me; we don't know each other yet'.

The boy seems to start to elaborate his problem when he replies, 'It's not that'. He then relapses by adding, 'But anyway it's no use'. At this point he might well be beginning to test Aichhorn. 'Not that' is a dangling invitation to continue. Aichhorn thereupon takes a new tack, apparently sensing that explicit talk of help will get no further results. He asks, 'Are you willing to talk to me?' The boy's 'Why not?' is noncommittal, cautious, but still not a definite refusal. Aichhorn's 'I must ask you various questions and I will make you a proposition' grants the boy a choice without surrendering his own function of helpful investigator. Responding to the boy's increased interest and expectation, Aichhorn then explicitly gives control of the answers to his questions to the boy: ' . . . don't answer any question you don't like . . . tell me it's none of my business . . . I'm not a detective or a policeman. . . .' It would have been quite different and less effective if he had first attempted to encourage the boy to confide in him by abruptly saying he was not a policeman. 'I don't need to know all these things' expresses again the absence of an anxious or resentful sense

of surrender; his own autonomy and workmanship will not be violated in this deal. He then anticipates the boy's temptation to lie by stating it explicitly.

'I wouldn't tell everything either to someone whom I'd met for the first time' clinches the initial differentiation of himself from the social and legal authorities. This comes closest to what we consider an example of empathic communication, but everything he has said before has built up to it and is part of it. Aichhorn rejects the arbitrary social line between good and bad; he himself is trying to be 'good' now but makes no false pretense that under certain stress he would not be 'bad' as the boy is. By his candor, he says in effect that he is not cowed by social anxiety or by a harsh superego; he can admit without trepidation that he can be 'corrupt' too. He demonstrates in action here that he really knows how it is when you feel 'up against it', that he can be remote from conventional oversimplifications of morality, that he can be an honest ally. When he goes on to say, simply and tolerantly, that it would be too bad if the boy did lie, he expresses regret based on partial identification; he does not mistrustfully reprove the boy in advance by exhortation to be honest. By now, the initial negative transference to Aichhorn has been dissipated and, as symbolized in the handshake, a therapeutic alliance with the boy has begun to be established.

In this interchange Aichhorn steadily respects the boy's need for trust, autonomy, and initiative. He conveys this respect with no overtones of having sacrificed his own confidence, autonomy, initiative, or sense of workmanship, and no hint of feeling threatened in his own ego identity and his strivings toward intimacy. He encourages an alliance through the 'manly' deal he offers the boy and through indicating that he has a relationship to his own superego and to society such as the boy might hope for. This relationship is candid without being exhibitionistic, tolerant without being seductive, benevolent without being excessively altruistic. He conveys that one can be good without being indulgent or submissive, one can be active without being rapacious, one can be aware of one's own limits and even corruptibility without undue anxiety, guilt, shame, and passive retaliation, and one can acknowledge one's part in bringing about a hopeless situation in which one is apparently passively victimized. He provides a model for identification and ego identity formation that is a way out for an adolescent boy caught in vacillations between extremes of behavior on the part of his parents. . . . There can be little doubt that Aichhorn's flair emanates from a history rich in crises of contact, communication, and collaboration in his work with delinquents—and himself.

* * *

NOTE 2.

AICHHORN, AUGUST

Wayward Youth*

After a while [at the close of the interview discussed by Dr. Schafer in Note 1] I asked him if he thought it was possible for him and his father to come to some understanding. I offered to help. He was sceptical, but not so reluctant as at first. He said, "Oh I've talked to my father time and again. It's no use." I tried to make him see that his father could not understand him as long as he did not know what he was really thinking. He might let me try to explain to the father. He released me from my promise to say nothing.

NOTE 3.

BOERGER v. BOERGER
26 N.J. Super. 90, 97 A. 2d 419 (1953)

GOLDMANN, J.S.C.

* * *

The court privately examined Dianne, now going on ten, in chambers with the consent of counsel, and reported the interview to them in writing. Such practice is well established. The object of such an examination is to determine, if possible, the predilection of the child. Such predilection, when ascertained, is a factor that will be considered by the trial court. The preference of a young child has a place in the determination, but not a conclusive place. . . . The limitations of such an interview are almost self-evident, as are its dangers, among them that of influenced judgment. . . . Age and the capacity to form a rational judgment are the important considerations. . . .

As reported to counsel, Dianne is a bright girl, far above average in intelligence and insight. She discussed her home life, parents, and particularly Sunday School and church. She appears to have been little influenced against going to church with her father, or against the Church itself, although the mother did at one time object to her being taught catechism. Dianne is happy in Sunday School, likes her teacher and enjoys the company of her young friends. She says that she does not understand the language of her father's church and has no opportunity to sing there. She feels she should not have to go to church with her father after Sunday School, but should be allowed

---

* New York: The Viking Press, 1951, p 100. Reprinted with permission of the publisher.

to play, as do her girl friends. She remembers parochial school ; she liked the sisters there but they were strict. She "loves" public school and her teacher, but recognizes that the work there is necessarily different from what she did in parochial kindergarten. She loves her father, but didn't think it was nice of him to make her learn answers to questions (catechism) when she could have been playing. She prefers to go to Sunday School and her mother's church.

Obviously, the child cannot, because of her immaturity, have any real capacity for forming an intelligent opinion on so complex a subject as the relative content and values of Lutheranism and Catholicism. Her reaction is to externalities. The most that can be said is that she is happier when she is in her mother's church, and that she finds her experience there personally more meaningful for the time being.

* * *

NOTE 4.

KREUTZER v. KREUTZER
226 Ore. 158, 359 P. 2d 536 (1961)

LUSK, JUSTICE.

This is a proceeding for modification of a decree of divorce in which there was an award of custody of the minor children of the parties. . . . On January 11, 1960, the court held a hearing at the conclusion of which the following occurred:

* * *

"Mr. Slack (Attorney for defendant): Prior to the time of trial this morning, Mr. Bedingfield (Attorney for plaintiff) and I stipulated that the Court might talk to these children in the privacy of your office.

* * *

"The Court: The Court doesn't desire to drag the children into these proceedings at all, I don't see any reason for it, I don't think the children should be put ·to that test, I am not going to call them in and ask them what they think of one parent or the other, or anything of the kind.
"Mr. Slack: I would like to put the children on the stand, then.
"The Court: That request will be denied, and you can appeal to the Supreme Court if you want to. You won't be allowed to, I will not allow children of that age to be called to testify in a matter like this . . . ."

An order denying the motion was thereupon entered and defendant has appealed, assigning as error, inter alia, the court's refusal to permit the children to testify.

So far as appears, the children were competent witnesses. Neither was under ten years of age, . . . nor in any other respect shown or claimed to be incompetent. See ORS 44.020, 44.030.[1] Nor is there any claim or basis for a claim that the court acted pursuant to ORS 45.530 which authorizes the court to "stop the production of further evidence, upon any particular point, when the evidence upon it is already so full as to preclude reasonable doubt."

Consequently, the right of the defendant to call the children to the stand and to elicit testimony from them material to the issues was precisely the same as it would have been in the case of any other competent witness. This is, of course, a fundamental right. . . . In divorce cases, it seems to be uniformly held that the court has no authority to exclude the testimony of children of the parties of tender years if they are otherwise competent witnesses. . . . There is no reason for a different rule in a proceeding for modification of a provision in a divorce decree granting the custody of children, for the parties to such a controversy have the same right to present evidence in open court as in any other case. . . .

* * *

We have examined the record for the purpose of determining if it is possible to hold that the exclusion of the children from the witness stand was not reversible error, but, in view of the fact that there was conflict in the testimony on the issue of changed conditions and that the children were in a position to testify concerning some of these matters, we have no alternative other than to reverse the decree and remand the cause for further proceedings.

We are reluctant to do this, for we share the view of the circuit judge that in a case of this kind, young children of the parties should not be forced to become witnesses and, perhaps, to take sides in open court against one or the other of their parents. . . .

---

1. ORS 44.030: "The following persons are not competent witnesses:

"(1) Those of unsound mind at the time of their production for examination.

"(2) Children under 10 years of age who appear incapable of receiving just impressions of the facts respecting which they are examined, or of relating them truly. Whenever a child under the age of 10 years is produced as a witness, the court shall, by an examination made by itself, publicly or separate and apart with counsel present, ascertain to its own satisfaction whether the child has sufficient intelligence and sense of obligation to tell the truth to be safely admitted to testify."

NOTE 5.

ERIKSON, ERIK H.
Childhood and Society*

Maybe a word should be said here about the thoroughly difficult situation which ensues when a mother brings a child for observation. The child has not chosen to come. He often does not feel sick at all in the sense that he has a symptom which he wishes to get rid of. On the contrary, all he knows is that certain things and, most of all, certain people make him feel uncomfortable and he wishes that we would do something about these things and people—not about him. Often he feels that something is wrong with his parents, and mostly he is right. But he has no words for this and, even if he did have, he has no reason to trust us with such weighty information. On the other hand, he does not know what the parents have told us about him—while God only knows what they have told the child about us. . . .

* * *

Ann, a girl of four, enters the office, half gently pulled, half firmly pushed by her worried mother. While she does not resist or object, her face is pale and sullen, her eyes have a blank and inward look, and she sucks vigorously on her thumb.

Once inside the office the child lets go of the mother's hand and walks into my room with the automatic obedience of a prisoner who no longer has a will of his own. In my playroom she stands in a corner, sucking tensely on her thumb and paying only a very reserved kind of attention to me.

* * *

The child indicates clearly that I will not get anything out of her. To her growing surprise and relief, however, I do not ask her any questions; I do not even tell her that I am her friend and that she should trust me. Instead I start to build a simple block house on the floor. There is a living room; a kitchen; a bedroom with a little girl in a bed and a woman standing close by her; a bathroom with the door open; and a garage with a man standing next to a car. This arrangement suggests, of course, the regular morning hour when the mother tries to pick the little girl up "on time," while the father gets ready to leave the house.

Our patient, increasingly fascinated with this wordless statement of a problem, suddenly goes into action. She relinquishes her thumb to make

---

* Reprinted from *Childhood and Society* by Erik H. Erikson, pp. 224, 48-52, by permission of W. W. Norton & Company, Inc. and the Hogarth Press, London. Copyright 1950, © 1963 by W. W. Norton & Company, Inc.

space for a broad and toothy grin. Her face flushes and she runs over to the toy scene. With a mighty kick she disposes of the woman doll; she bangs the bathroom door shut, and she hurries to the toy shelf to get three shiny cars, which she puts into the garage beside the man. She has answered my "question": she, indeed, does not wish the toy girl to give to her mother what is her mother's, and she is eager to give to her father more than he could ask for.

I am still pondering over the power of her aggressive exuberance when she, in turn, seems suddenly overpowered by an entirely different set of emotions. She bursts into tears and into a desperate whimper, "Where is my mummy?" In panicky haste she takes a handful of pencils from my desk and runs out into the waiting room. Pressing the pencils into her mother's hand, she sits down close to her. The thumb goes back into the mouth, the child's face becomes uncommunicative, and I can see the game is over. The mother wants to give the pencils back to me, but I indicate that I do not need them today. Mother and child leave.

Half an hour later the telephone rings. They have hardly reached home when the little girl asks her mother whether she may see me again that same day. Tomorrow is not early enough. She insists with signs of despair that the mother call me immediately for an appointment the same day so that she may return the pencils. I must assure the child over the phone that I appreciate her intentions but that she is quite welcome to keep the pencils until the next day.

* * *

The little girl had not come of her own free will. She had merely let herself be brought by the very mother against whom, as everything indicated, her sullenness was directed. Once in my room, my quiet play apparently had made her forget for a moment that her mother was outside. What she would not have been able to say in words in many hours she could express in a few minutes of non-verbal communication: she "hated" her mother and she "loved" her father. Having expressed this, however, she must have experienced what Adam did when he heard God's voice: "Adam, where art thou?" She was compelled to atone for her deed, for she loved her mother too and needed her. In her very panic, however, she did compulsively what ambivalent people always do: in turning to make amends to one person they "inadvertently" do harm to another. So she took my pencils to appease the mother, and then wanted to force the mother to help her make restitution.

The next day her eagerness to conciliate me is paralyzed. I think I had become the tempter who makes children confess in unguarded moments what nobody should know or say. Children often have such a reaction after an initial admission of secret thoughts. What if I told her mother? What if her mother refused to bring her back to me so that she could modify and qualify her unguarded acts? So she refused to act altogether, and let her symptom speak.

c. Determining a Course of Action— Accessibility of Data to Whom and for What Purpose—The Problem of Confidentiality

[i]

KESSELER v. KESSELER
10 N.Y. 2d 445, 180 N.E. 2d 402 (1962)

VAN VOORHIS, JUDGE.

The decision involves the modification of a separation decree by granting custody to the father of a girl who was six years old at the time of the trial at Special Term and is ten years old today . . . .

* * *

The order directing the change in custody is challenged in this court mainly on the ground that Special Term erred as matter of law in considering the reports of a psychiatrist and of a psychologist concerning their examinations of the parties and their child, and in the refusal of Special Term to allow the parties or their counsel to see these reports or the report of the investigation made by the family counsellor of the court. The latter officer, named Mrs. Sylvia L. Golomb, belongs to the Family Counselling Unit, an advisory arm of . . . the Family Part of the Supreme Court, New York County, and was authorized by a written stipulation of the parties to make any relevant investigation and inquiry which the court might deem appropriate, including interviewing the parties and their child without further authorization from the attorneys, and this stipulation further provided: "That the Family Counsellor is authorized to report to the Court concerning the investigation and inquiry conducted pursuant hereto."

As originally drawn, this stipulation contained a clause authorizing the use of psychiatrists and psychologists, but by agreement of the attorneys it was deleted from the stipulation. This clause which was thus eliminated provided: "That said Family Counsellor may use psychological, psychiatric and other medical assistance in her inquiry and may require the parties and the child of the parties to be examined by psychologists, psychiatrists or other professional medical personnel, without the further authorization of the attorneys for the parties."

Under this stipulation, Mrs. Sylvia L. Golomb, the family counsellor of the court, was directed by the justice presiding at Special Term to make an impartial, out-of-court evaluation of the factors bearing on the custody of Heidi. She interviewed many persons having some knowledge of the living conditions of these people whose hearsay declarations are recorded in her report. In addition, as stated in the opinion by Special Term written at the conclusion of the custodial hearing (11 Misc. 2d 607, 608-609, 178 N.Y.S. 2d 160, 161): "In an endeavor to ascertain the best scientific and psychiatric information possible, this court availed itself of the services of a noted psychiatrist, a prominent psychologist and the court's family counsellor. Careful investigation, study and interviews with all the principals, including the infant Heidi were initiated in the Spring of 1957. By agreement of counsel (May 23, 1957) and in accord with the underlying necessity therefor, such reports have been held confidential. They are available to the appellate courts in a review of the instant decision. These reports are, however, in complete agreement and strongly urge that the welfare of the infant Heidi demands her removal from the household of the mother and that she be placed in an appropriate school for disturbed children."

In considering this independent investigation by means of a psychiatrist and a psychologist, the Special Term Justice went beyond what had been agreed upon in the stipulation which, wisely or not, declined to consent to psychological or psychiatric examinations and reports. The stress which was placed by Special Term on all of these reports appears from its opinion of April 2, 1958, adhering after reargument to its earlier interim order directing the placement of Heidi in an institution for disturbed children known as St. Christopher's School at Dobbs Ferry, New York. In that opinion (N.Y.L.J., April 4, 1958, p. 5, col. 3) it was stated: "The ample reports of the psychiatrists and the court's family counsellor together with counsel's stipulation rendered wholly unnecessary oral testimony. These confidential reports will be available to the Appellate Division on its review of the proceedings. The record should include the papers on this motion for reargument and this determination thereof. Permanent custody is not changed, but the infant's welfare commands that the present school arrangements be carried out. Order signed."

*   *   *

[W]e consider that it lay within the power of the parties to stipulate that such reports could be made confidentially to the court, and that they did so in this instance respecting the investigation and report of the family counsellor, Mrs. Golomb. It is true that the stipulation does not state in so many words that the report of the family counsellor need not be disclosed to the parties or their counsel, but that appears to be the effect of their consent that the family counsellor report to the court concerning her investigation and inquiry. In trying and deciding questions concerning the custody of young children, the parties frequently stipulate that the Trial Justice may interview the child in chambers, and obtain whatever impressions or information the child may give privately to him. What is said by the child to the Justice under such circumstances is necessarily secret unless the Justice chooses to disclose it, nor do we think that he is obliged to spread upon the record whatever the child has said as was held to be necessary where a zoning board views the *locus in quo* and makes a determination on the basis of its own independent investigation. . . . If parties to matrimonial disputes are competent to stipulate that there may be confidential interviews between the Justice and the child without disclosure of what is said by the child, there is little further difficulty in arriving at the conclusion that the parties can stipulate that the probation officer or the family counsellor attached to the court or other qualified and impartial persons may make investigations and report to the court with similar confidentiality . . . .

. . . In disposing of the custody of children, courts are not so "limited that they may not depart from strict adversary concepts" in certain respects. . . . Custodial questions have sociological implications, and we are confronted here by a situation where common-law adversary proceedings and social jurisprudence are not entirely harmonious and where some reconciliation between them is necessary.

The parties did not have to stipulate that the report of the family counsellor, Mrs. Golomb, should be made to the court. The court could have directed Mrs. Golomb to make an investigation, to be sure, and then could have left her testimony to the parties to deal with under common-law rules in the absence of their consent. Even without their consent the report might have been used to furnish leads for the introduction of common-law evidence. . . . Nor is there any reason which would prevent the court in the proper exercise of a judicial discretion from calling upon qualified and impartial psychiatrists, psychologists or other professional medical personnel, preferably under the auspices of the probation officer or family counselling unit connected with the court, to examine the infant or to examine the parents also if they will submit to such examination. In such case the psychologists, psychiatrists or other medical personnel could not report to the court in the absence of stipulation by the parties but would be available to be called as witnesses by either party subject to cross-examination by the other party under common-law evidence rules. No question is before this court concerning how such professional aid should be compensated, nor is it indicated that in the absence of consent the parties could be compelled to pay for their services. The following statement was made in the case of Rea v. Rea by the Supreme Court of Oregon (. . . 245 P. 2d 884, 895 . . .): "The trial court cannot delegate to anyone the power to decide questions of child custody. All parties to the controversy have a right to present competent evidence in open court. When the court, in the absence of any stipulation, and in the face of timely objection, makes an independent investigation concerning child custody, it commits error. Its action, however, is not void for want of jurisdiction. The better-reasoned modern cases tend to support the view that when an independent investigation is made by the court, or a private conversation is had with an infant whose custody is in issue, or when investigation is authorized and made by a member of the staff of the court, such action being pursuant to stipulation of the parties or being acquiesced in by the parties, the consideration by the court of such investigation will not constitute reversible error even though the report is not incorporated in the record."

* * *

Where, as here, a stipulation was made regarding the report of the family counsellor attached to the court, but not regarding the psychiatrist or psychologist, we consider, . . . that the court was authorized under the stipulation to consider the report of the family counsellor, even though the attorneys for the parties did not see it, just as it would have been competent for both sides to have stipulated that the Special Term Justice might interview the child in chambers and obtain whatever impressions or information might be imparted from such an interview. We believe that to have been the purport of the stipulation that the family counsellor should report to the court concerning the investigation and inquiry consented to be conducted by her without further authorization of the attorneys. . . . The natural purport of such stipulations, unless they state otherwise, is that the common-law rules of evidence are suspended *pro tanto* in adapting to the social nature of the problem to be solved. In a case like the present, where this matrimonial dispute and custodial question were widely publicized in the newspapers, it may well be that the parties preferred a procedure of that sort to curtail some-

what the publicization of the intimacies of their lives.

The situation is otherwise, however, respecting the reports by the psychiatrist and psychologist. . . . The parties refused to stipulate that [the family counselor] might use psychological, psychiatric and other medical assistance in her inquiry. Under our interpretation of the law, that did not prevent the Trial Justice from ordering a psychological and psychiatric inquiry (provided that arrangements were made concerning the expense) but, after they had been made, the reports of the psychiatrist and of the psychologist had to be dealt with under common-law rules since they were not covered by the stipulation. Either party could have called those expert witnesses, in that event, whose views regarding the parties and the custody of Heidi would then have become known immediately to the opposite side with opportunity of cross-examination. We do not go so far as to hold that the parties *could not* stipulate that such reports could be made confidentially to the court, but the fact is here that they did not so stipulate and expressly refused to do so. Therefore, the Special Term Justice erred in keeping confidential the reports of the psychiatrist and psychologist, and in considering them at all.

It may well be that the determination of a special term justice based on confidential reports under stipulation cannot, under certain circumstances, be reviewed on appeal. . . . The right to appeal is not part of due process, as the Supreme Court of Oregon said; parties to litigations can stipulate to waive the right to appeal, and we find no obstacle to giving effect to such stipulations notwithstanding that they may in some instances limit the right of appeal.

These views vary somewhat from the expression in this case by the Appellate Division's memorandum, where it was said: "In commenting upon the use of such reports we said in People ex rel. Fields v. Kaufmann, 9 A.D. 2d 375, 378, 193 N.Y.S. 2d 789, 792: ' * * * reports of experts are * * * aids to the court in custody matters * * *. What must be borne in mind, however, is that they are only aids and, if not woven into the fabric of the record, should not form a base for the decision. . . . If such reports should be taken into consideration by the trial court, of course, they must be made available to counsel. In this case it appears, however, that extended hearings were conducted herein and the court's decision is based, in the major part, upon the testimony and documentary evidence there adduced. Disregarding the confidential reports of the experts as the court below should have done inasmuch as they were not made part of the record, we still find in the record ample evidence to sustain the determination awarding custody of the child to the respondent with limited privilege of visitation to the appellant. . . ."

This statement is erroneous in several respects. First, as has been said, if the parties so stipulated (as they did here in regard to Mrs. Golomb's report) there is no more reason why they had to be disclosed to counsel for the parties than would be necessary if they stipulated that the Trial Justice might interview the child in chambers, or in the case of a probation report which need not be submitted to the defendant's counsel when sentence is imposed in a criminal case. Even the right of a public trial may be waived under some circumstances. . . . Neither do we think that the report needs to be part of the record where such a stipulation has been made. . . . If stipulation were not entered into, it could not be admitted into evidence or examined by the court without consent of the parties.

The Appellate Division could hardly disregard these reports "as the court below should have done" and proceed to decide the case on the basis of different factors from those which the trial court had before it. Concerning that the Oregon Supreme Court observed pointedly in Rea v. Rea (. . . 245 P. 2d 888): "This general principle appears to be applicable here. Technically, the 'evidence' received in court appears in the record. Actually the record does not disclose the factual basis of the trial court's decision. For this court to retry the case on the 'evidence' alone would be to try a different case from that decided by the trial court. This we are not required to do."

Expressed somewhat differently, it was the trial court that saw and heard the witnesses, the parties and the child and was deeply versed in the reports of the family counsellor, the psychiatrist and the psychologist. These last were sufficient, in the Trial Justice's own words, without oral evidence, to warrant taking away the child from the mother and placing her at St. Christopher's institution at Dobbs Ferry. It was impossible for the Trial Justice later to eradicate from his mind the important factors supplied by these reports. Moreover, not only did he state in his opinion after deciding the question of custody following the hearing . . . that he had considered them, but he observed that they would be available to the appellate courts in a review of his decision . . . .

The orders of the Appellate Division should be reversed, we think, and the matter remanded to Special Term for a hearing de novo, at which the facts may be considered as of the present time after the child has been with the father about three years. One of the orders under review, it will be recalled, asked for a trial of custody de novo at the instance of the mother, and this was de-

nied . . . mainly on the basis of a letter written to the justice presiding by an associate of Dr. Kesseler on the staff of the Lenox Hill Hospital, which was not exhibited to counsel for the wife nor its existence disclosed until after the decision. This is a two and one-half page, single-spaced typewritten letter, stating that Heidi had been under intensive psychiatric treatment by the author of the letter, that she is a seriously disturbed girl whose treatment has been made more difficult by her mother's attitude, and concludes that the mother's visitation should be limited to once per month so that her bad effect on Heidi can be minimized. No stipulation had been entered into concerning this letter. It was not brought to the attention of plaintiff or her counsel until they read about it in the Special Term opinion. The author of it was not even an appointee or attache of the court, but was a colleague of Dr. Kesseler's on the staff at the Lenox Hill Hospital. It is quite clear that it should not have been received nor have entered into the decision.

The conclusion of this analysis is that the stipulation was broad enough to render the report of Mrs. Golomb, the family unit counsellor attached to the court, confidential to the court so that its disclosure to counsel was not required by due process, that the circumstance that it was used by the trial court does not vitiate its decision but that the reports of the psychiatrist and psychologist did not come within the stipulation and it was, therefore, error for him to have considered them. In fact, without any stipulation, either party was free to raise the question of their examination by the court. In this instance, review on appeal is not precluded on account of the confidential report of the family counsellor, or the reports of the psychiatrist and psychologist, inasmuch as they have been identified and are before the appellate courts and may be considered in conjunction with the evidence. The Appellate Division erred, we think, in excluding from its consideration all of these reports, and by doing so decided a different case, in important respects, from that which was before the Trial Justice. . . . It is appropriate that there should be a hearing de novo both in view of the circumstance that three years have elapsed while Heidi has been in the custody of her father, and that the fact mentioned by the Special Term Justice did not come to pass that Dr. Kesseler's mother and aunt would be living with him and caring for Heidi. Instead he purported to marry again after obtaining a Mexican divorce from Mrs. Kesseler, and the child is now living with Dr. Kesseler and his new consort who are cohabiting as husband and wife. We do not intimate that this should necessarily preclude the awarding of custody to Dr. Kesseler, but it is a factor which has occurred since the decisions appealed from and goes counter to their rationale in certain respects.

It is pertinent to observe that the record indicates that the Trial Justice was clearly endeavoring to decide this question of custody according to what he considered to be for the best interest of Heidi. Nevertheless, in the context in which the case comes to our court, we are persuaded that the orders cannot be affirmed for the reasons stated.

* * *

DESMOND, CHIEF JUDGE (dissenting).

I see no reason for a retrial. In and out of the courts for six years, this sordid family squabble is now to be fought over again, not because of any doubt as to the essential rightness of the decision below, but because of a supposed error which was undoubtedly waived by appellant (if error it was) and which related to reports which, as both courts below assure us, did not affect the decision at all. All six of the Justices below agree (and I agree with them) that, with or without these psychiatric and psychological reports, the record is completely convincing that plaintiff should not have the child. Earnestly I ask: what right of a party or what rule of law or justice is vindicated by another lengthy, harrowing trial?

* * *

NOTES

NOTE 1.

KESSELER v. KESSELER
236 N.Y.S. 2d 472 (Sup. Ct. 1963)

THOMAS A. AURELIO, JUSTICE.

* * *

On consent of the parties, I had a private chat with Heidi in Chambers, lasting half an hour, in the absence of the parties and their attorneys, but which some time later was read to them. I do not think it necessary to set forth in detail in this opinion what she said. Suffice it to say that she is happy, pleased and content to be in her father's home where she is receiving love and affection with her spiritual, moral and educational needs attended to. Heidi wants to stay there and gave reasons therefor.

I am satisfied from the evidence adduced before me that Heidi was a disturbed child in June, 1958 and for considerable time prior thereto, and that some action was required to be taken by the Court for the safety and welfare of the child. Mr. Justice Epstein resolved the problem by making the order of June 2, 1958, awarding custody to the father. Since then Heidi has done well and the record indicates the need for further care and

attention such as she is receiving in her present surroundings.

Since it satisfactorily appears that the union of Dr. Kesseler and Sally DiGiovanni is a happy one and that they are living in peace and harmony in a well established home and in view of the foregoing pronouncement of the Court of Appeals, that defendant's marriage to Sally DiGiovanni after obtaining a Mexican divorce from plaintiff and now cohabiting as husband and wife and the child living with them, does not necessarily preclude the award of custody to Dr. Kesseler, I find and decide that Dr. Kesseler is a fit and proper person to have the care and custody of his daughter.

In the circumstances here involved, there is no merit to plaintiff's claim that defendant is not a fit father to have the child's custody because he is living with a woman not his legal wife in New York State. Moreover, to uproot Heidi from a wholesome home and pleasant surroundings where she has been for close to five years and where she is happy and wants to be would, in my opinion, based upon all the evidence adduced before me, have a most disastrous impact upon her. To disrupt a continuity of steady and healthy progress and contentment in a comfortable household of her liking and where she is living peacefully, would not be beneficial to her future well-being in the light of this little girl's troubled past . . . .

NOTE 2.

REA v. REA
195 Ore. 252, 257, 245 P. 2d 884, 886 (1952)

BRAND, CHIEF JUSTICE.

. . . The existence of a back door to the court room, and thus, to the judge's private ear, is abhorrent to our ideas of justice. On the other hand, in recent years we have witnessed great changes in the attitude of society and of public officials in dealing with the thousands of children of broken homes who are wards of the state. Throughout the nation, men and women are being trained in the social sciences, and prepared for work in public employment and in fields authorized by statute, to the end that the state, as parens patriae may better perform the difficult task of determining what is for the best interest of the unfortunate child. . . . It appears to have become common practice for judges in custody cases to make use of these modern facilities in a highly informal way, quite inconsistent with the procedure in strictly judicial inquiries on other matters. We know also of the practice of many judges who, for sound reasons, are reluctant to require an infant to testify in open court for or against one parent in a divorce case. With the consent of both parties, expressed in open court, judges have invited the child into chambers and in quiet conversations have secured valuable insight into the child's attitude, whether of fear or of affection, toward a parent. It must be conceded that such informal procedure is likely to shed more light upon the issue than would result from subjecting the child to examination and cross-examination (perhaps after coaching) in open court. If such action is illegal, then many trial judges, some of them now on this court, have erred. The problem is not a simple one and is distinguishable from all other judicial procedures. Although, in form, the issue is raised between plaintiff and defendant as adversaries, we have frequently pointed out that the claims of the divorced husband and wife are subordinate to the welfare of the child who is the subject of the controversy and is neither plaintiff or defendant. In view of the fine service being impartially performed by child welfare agencies and of the benefits which are sometimes derived by personal interviews by a judge with a ward of his court, we should be very sure before we brand all such service as illegal. This much, however, is fundamental. Any person who desires to stand upon his strict legal rights, and to preserve his right of appeal to this court, may insist that no fact should be brought to the attention of the trial court and that no influence should be exerted upon it, except in the manner of the common law, by testimony and argument in open court, with the right accorded to both parties to testify, to produce witnesses, and to confront, cross-examine or contradict adverse witnesses. . . .

NOTE 3.

CALLEN v. GILL
7 N.J. 312, 81 A. 2d 495, 497-9 (1951)

CASE, J.

Appellant's . . . point is that . . . the testimony by Mr. Barrow [plaintiff's lawyer] of conversations with the child were inadmissible. . . . Mr. Barrow's testimony was concerning his observation of the child and the reaction of the child to his surroundings. Such few remarks attributed to the child as were given in the testimony did not go to contested facts but to the child's emotional reactions. The rules of evidence are somewhat relaxed in trials having to do with a determination of custody of an infant where it is necessary to learn of the child's psychology and preferences. Therefore it is sometimes pertinent to bring to the court's knowledge the temperament, disposition and reactions of the child by testimony that borders upon hearsay in that it embraces a recital of the child's remarks. Such testimony, however, is not strictly hearsay because the objective and the result are to look into the child's mind and not to establish the truth or falsity of other matters set up as facts; and instances of it in the present case were few and unimportant. We find no reversible error under the point.

It is next said on behalf of the appellant that the court below erred in refusing to make known to counsel the boy's statements given to the judge in private. This presents a delicate and, in view of the record, a confused question. The authority of the judge to conduct a private examination of a child in order to discover its wishes as to custody is well established . . . and the ages beneath which the child shall not be examined at all . . . and above which the examination shall be public are largely within the discretion of the court. But the object of a private examination is to ascertain the predilection of the child, and that predilection, when ascertained, should be openly stated. It is a factor which will be considered by the trial court and an appellate court as well. . . . Manifestly, however, it would not be just to elicit from the child a statement of the facts upon which that predilection rests, as that the father was cruel or that the mother did not supply nourishing food, and for the court to accept and act upon such a statement as proof of facts bearing upon the determination, without making disclosure to the parties and upon the record. . . . The preference of a young child has a place, although not a conclusive place . . . , in the determination and the preference ascertained by the judge in private, if that be the procedure, should be stated openly as the end result of the examination. But no assertion of fact by the child should be permitted by the judge to influence his decision unless he makes the same known. Parties must have an opportunity to be heard upon the facts, . . . else due process is not had, and a reviewing court must be put in possession of the proofs which lead to the decision, else it may do an injustice.

NOTE 4.

KRIEGER v. KRIEGER
59 Id. 301, 305, 81 P. 2d 1081, 1083 (1938)

AILSHIE, JUSTICE.

Claire Krieger, whose custody is sought by appellant, was placed on the witness stand and testified that she lived with her daddy; and that he came home every night; that Mrs. Altmaier took care of her and she liked her, liked her teacher and got along fine in school. She said she liked her daddy and mama both but when asked the following question: "Do you care who you live with, Claire, whether it is your daddy or your mama?", she replied: "I would like to live with my daddy better, I think." It should be observed just here that this kind of examination of an eight-year-old child, in the presence of its parents, is hardly fair to the child. If such an examination is thought proper at all, it should take place out of the presence and hearing of the parents so as to save the child the embarrassment and possible fear of expressing a preference between the father and mother. . . .

NOTE 5.

BOARD OF JUSTICES OF THE DOMESTIC RELATIONS
COURT OF THE CITY OF NEW YORK

Brief on the Proposed Family Court Act*

In Sections 347 (b), 625 (b), 746 (b) and 834 (b) the proposed Family Court Act provides that reports prepared by the probation service for use by the Court at any time prior to the making of an order of disposition shall be deemed confidential information furnished to the Court "and to the parties in interest." Furnishing probation reports to the parties in interest will completely destroy the confidentiality of information given by many social agencies, interested parties and others, who often refuse to speak frankly unless the confidentiality of their information can be maintained.

To make probation reports the subject of examination and cross-examination by parties and their counsel at dispositional hearings and to make these reports then the subject of records on appeal is carrying due process far beyond any present requirements of the law or the decisions of the courts. The mischief this will do in drying up important sources of background information now available to the probation service and through it to the Court, far outweighs any possible benefits to the parties in the disposition of their cases. Even if the information should continue to be available, this adversarial opening of old wounds will not heal family centered problems involving families and children.

The Court most strongly urges that the confidentiality of probation reports be maintained by striking from Sections 347 (b), 625 (b), 746 (b) and 834 (b) the following words:

> " and to the parties in interest, but the Court may withhold from the parties in interest medical data and any psychiatric diagnosis contained in a report."

[*ii*]

OFFICIAL SOLICITOR v. K. AND ANOTHER
[1963] 3 All E.R. 191

LORD EVERSHED: . . . Your lordships are asked to answer what is posed as "a pure question of law"

with no knowledge of the facts save in the barest outline ; and to do so in circumstances in which the question ultimately for the court's decision is the welfare and upbringing of two young children born respectively in June, 1952, and July, 1953, both of them wards of court. They were made wards of court in October, 1960, over two and a half years ago, on the issue in the Chancery Division of an originating summons . . . their mother, Mrs. K. (who is a respondent . . . and to whom I shall refer as "the mother") asking that her children be made wards of court and that their care and custody should be committed to her. The summons was served on Mr. K., the applicant's husband, who has also been a respondent before your lordships (and to whom I shall refer as "the father"). The children were themselves (incorrectly) made parties originally to the summons but by order of the master in the Chancery Division the summons was not served on them.

The marriage of the father and the mother has unfortunately come to grief, the mother having in February, 1960, left the father, taking the two children with her. After the issue of the summons a considerable amount of evidence was put in by both the mother and the father. Your lordships were given to understand that such evidence demonstrates a state of acute hostility now unhappily subsisting between husband and wife. Your lordships, however, have seen none of it. It was in these circumstances—and due no doubt to the sharpness of the conflict between their parents—that the master on July 27, 1961 (ten months after the issue of the summons) felt obliged to order and ordered that the Official Solicitor should be appointed to act as guardian ad litem of the children . . . On October 23, 1961, the Official Solicitor put in a brief statement of facts, stating no more than that he had been appointed guardian ad litem of the children and that since his appointment he had perused the "voluminous evidence" and personally interviewed the two infants and their parents. He asked, in order to assist him in making a recommendation to the court, that the mother be directed to take the infants to see Dr. Newton, the Medical Director of the Child Guidance Clinic at the St. Marylebone Hospital for Psychiatry and Child Guidance: and an order to that effect was made. The mother then attended on Dr. Newton with her two children on December 13, 1961, and thereafter Dr. Newton saw separately both the father (on January 4, 1962), and the mother (on January 31, 1962). The next step was the submission by the Official Solicitor of another statement of facts dated February 7, 1962, reciting the attendances above mentioned on Dr. Newton and "as a result

---

* Memorandum 1962 (pp. 5-6).

of his investigations" submitting that the care and custody of the two infants be committed to the mother on condition that she should take them to see Dr. Newton at six-monthly intervals and that the father should be allowed to have access to the children at the intervals suggested in the statement.

So far the case seems indeed straightforward enough . . . It is, however, also the fact that on each of the occasions when the Official Solicitor submitted his statements he presented also to the court (in accordance with what your lordships were informed is not infrequently done by the Official Solicitor in such cases) reports described as confidential. These reports were seen by the learned judge, UNGOED-THOMAS, J., but were not disclosed to either of the parents of the children and (if I may add and emphasise) they likewise have not been seen either by the Court of Appeal or by your lordships. It was the view of the learned judge, and the view also (as your lordships were informed) of the Official Solicitor himself and his learned counsel, that disclosures of these reports would be seriously harmful to the children though it appears also that the learned judge was proposing to take some account of them in arriving at his decision.

No decision has however been made; for at this stage in the proceedings the mother took the point that she was, as a matter of right, entitled to see the reports on the general ground that, in accordance with the principles on which cases are determined by the judges in English courts including the principles of natural justice, it was wholly wrong to withhold from a party to the proceedings any statement or information made which reflected or might reflect on that party or on his or her qualities or character without giving to him or her an opportunity of challenging or correcting them. It was also said with some force by counsel on behalf of the mother that, if she were given the care and custody of the infants on the condition of their seeing Dr. Newton at six-monthly intervals, she was at least as a "self-respecting parent" entitled to know what it was in the condition of the infants which called for these repeated medical interviews—and that in the absence of such knowledge it would be very difficult for her properly to perform her parental duties and, therefore, would be to the disadvantage of the children themselves. But apart from, and indeed overriding, this point was counsel for the mother's submission that on the principles of justice she must, as a party to the proceedings, be entitled to see (and if necessary to challenge) all the material on which the judge would be acting. In so contending it is plain that the mother feels that the reports in some degree reflect on her character or condition.

Whether they in fact do is, of course, wholly unknown to your lordships . . . Counsel who appeared before your lordships on behalf of the father, supported the argument of counsel for the Official Solicitor, but reserved the right, if your lordships' decision were adverse to the appellent, to contend before the judge in the Chancery Division when the matter came again before him, that in the circumstances of the case care and custody of the children ought not to be committed to their mother. When the matter was before UNGOED-THOMAS, J., the suggestion was made that the learned judge should disclose to the parties' legal advisers the contents of the confidential reports provided that they were not disclosed to the parties personally; and the judge was indeed ready and willing so to do. As UPJOHN, L.J., observed in the Court of Appeal ([1962] 3 All E.R. 1003) "this is an excellent and common-sense practice and until this case I have never known any objection to it". But unfortunately when the judge suggested it in the present case the mother instructed her counsel that he should not receive any information derived from the confidential reports unless such information were also made available to her. The learned judge went on to observe that

> "this attitude of [the mother] might seem surprising having regard to the disclosed recommendation of the Official Solicitor in his second statement of facts to the effect that the mother should have the care and control of the children."

But there unfortunately there it is: and as I have said the learned judge was then invited without making any decision on the substance of the originating summons to decide whether the mother had in truth any such right as she claimed and alleged.

UNGOED-THOMAS, J. concluded the question in the Official Solicitor's favour. In his lordship's view the jurisdiction of the Chancery Court regarding wards of court being derived from the prerogative of the Crown as parens patriae was not to be treated as subject to the rules applicable to any ordinary lis between parties but partook "of an administrative character". In his view:

> "Where, however, the paramount purpose is the welfare of the infant, the procedure and rules of evidence should serve and certainly not thwart that purpose."

*   *   *

. . . I cannot think, because this jurisdiction is essentially judicial in its exercise, that since there may arise a conflict between the paramount interest of the infant which the court is concerned to promote on the one hand and the rights on the other hand which according to proper principles of justice generally belong to other persons properly parties to the proceedings, and since therefore . . . there has to be a "balancing" of these considerations, the process is one which, if no escape can be found, must inevitably be concluded by choosing the course thought likely to be harmful to the infant. My lords, I think it not enough to say that the proceeding is a judicial proceeding. It is necessary to define or to have in mind what is the true character of this judicial proceeding and what is its end or purpose. . . . TUCKER, L.J., in the case of *Russell v. Duke of Norfolk* ([1949] 1 All E.R. 118) said:

> "There are in my view no words which are of universal application to every kind of inquiry and every kind of domestic tribunal. The requirements of natural justice must depend on the circumstances of the case, the nature of the inquiry, the rules under which the tribunal is acting, the subject-matter that is being dealt with and so forth."

My lords, I would adopt TUCKER, L.J.'s language and apply it to the present case. It is not in doubt that a judicial inquiry concerning the proper steps to be taken for the care and maintenance of a ward of court is subject—and necessarily subject because of the nature and purpose of the inquiry—to a procedure in many respects quite special. The case is normally heard in private and it is conceded that the judge may properly see—that it may be his duty to see—the infant (and perhaps one or other or both parents) in private ; and it is important to have in mind that in ordinary circumstances no final order is ever made. I venture to repeat and to emphasise that the aim and purpose of the judicial inquiry is the welfare of the infant, and for such purpose to make a decision about his or her immediate future upbringing or control. For such purpose also the infant is in relation to the court in a special position distinct from that of other parties—for he or she is a ward of the court, a "child-in-law" of the court exercising the ancient prerogative and parental jurisdiction. If this be so, then it cannot, as it seems to me, be right that the court is always compelled in circumstances such as have arisen in the present case, to choose the lesser of two evils, to do that which in the court's view will be against the infant's interest and to console itself in so doing by regarding the result as a distressing consequence of a broken home. If the court is compelled so to act, then it is surely disqualifying and disabling itself from exercising the judicial function with which it is invested.

My lords, I should indeed be sorry to think that this ancient and most useful function of the Chancery judges should be so disabled. The jurisdiction is not only ancient, but it is surely also very special, and being very special the extent and application of the rules of natural justice must be applied and qualified accordingly. The judge must in exercising this jurisdiction act judicially ; but the means whereby he reaches his conclusion must not be more important than the end. The procedure and rules, in the language of UNGOED-THOMAS, J., should serve and not thwart the purpose.

It follows, therefore, in my opinion, that there cannot be in circumstances such as exist or as are suggested in the present case, an absolute right on the mother's part to see the report of the Official Solicitor. On the other hand I have equally no doubt that the judge must give very great weight indeed to the principle that he should not base a conclusion adverse to a proper party to the proceedings (and particularly a parent) on information which that party has not seen and has had no opportunity of challenging or contesting. When a situation arises such as has in the present case arisen, there may well indeed have to be, in the language of RUSSELL, L.J., a "balancing" of the generally accepted right of a properly interested party, particularly a parent, to disclosure of information submitted to the judge on which he proposes in some measure to base his conclusion (on the one hand) and the paramount interest of the ward of court (on the other hand). It may, however, be that, in such a situation, the latter consideration on the balance should outweigh the former. But in reaching such a conclusion the judge must in the first place be well satisfied that the confidential information to which he proposes to pay regard is in truth reliable. When, therefore, the information is derived from some statement attributed to the ward, he should (I should say) see the ward himself. And I add that in cases such as the present where (it may be) the information is derived from Dr. Newton, the judge will bear in mind that on many matters medical opinion is apt to differ. In the second place the judge must plainly have in mind that if (as in the present case) information is withheld from a parent, he or she will or may go from the court with a sense of grievance which may well be to the real disadvantage of the infant. It must, therefore, follow that a judge should not reach such a conclusion without the relevant disclosure to the party or parent save in rare cases and where he is fully satisfied judicially that real harm to the infant must otherwise ensue.

My lords, I am well aware that this statement of my view will be regarded as extremely imprecise, though I hope in the end of all in this case it may not be unhelpful. But for my part I find it impossible to arrive at any greater definition and therefore prefer not to accept the amended

olding must be imperative or necessary

formulation of his case by counsel for the appellant to the effect that the withholding of information by the judge must depend on his view that it is "imperative or necessary" so to do in order inevitably to avoid causing grave mental or physical harm to the ward. I am concerned only to express my view that, though the judge must indeed attach very great weight to the principle which I have stated, yet there can be no unqualified right on the part of a parent or other proper party to disclosure of information supplied by the judge, unless the judge wholly rejects such information in arriving at his conclusion. I accept entirely the view of UPJOHN, L.J., that

> "the rights, claims or wishes (however one likes to describe them) of the parents or other proper parties must be . . . given such weight as the judge may consider proper in forming his final view."

But I cannot deduce from that premise the conclusion that, if the conflict arises, the "right" of the parent to disclosure must inevitably override what the judge regards as the best interest of the ward. The interest of the infant is the paramount interest and purpose of the jurisdiction. Disclosure or no disclosure therefore must in the end remain a matter for the judge's discretion; but being such, its exercise will be subject to the right of the party who has been or thinks he has been adversely affected to challenge the exercise of the discretion in the Court of Appeal; and it will then be for the Court of Appeal, seeing the information, to review the judge's exercise of his discretion on it. It is at this point that I must emphasise the misfortune in the present case of the matter coming before your lordships, as it has done, on what is said to be a "pure question of law" but in truth as an academic question—almost, I should say, as an academic mystery. I venture to remind your lordships that we are on the appeal still exercising as regards the two infant wards of court the special jurisdiction derived from the royal prerogative as parens patriae and that we cannot escape the duty, in answering "the pure question of law" posed before us, of treating the interests of the wards as the paramount consideration. I note also that during the period of more than $2\frac{1}{2}$ years since the infants became wards of court they have continued to be in the care and custody of their mother, and that it is now eighteen months since they saw Dr. Newton. Yet your lordships were informed by counsel for the appellant that the Official Solicitor, as their guardian ad litem, was satisfied with their condition and with the way in which they have been looked after.

It follows, therefore, in my view that your lordships should allow the appeal and refer the matter back to the Chancery Division. In all the circumstances of the case it has on the whole seemed to me that the best course in the interests of all the parties concerned and, most of all, of the wards of court, will be that the case should be heard by some judge of the Chancery Division other than UNGOED-THOMAS, J. In so saying it will be understood that I am not in any way whatever criticising or casting the slightest reflection on the learned judge whom I have named and with whose decision I am indeed in accord. But I am aware that in these cases feelings are apt to run somewhat high. The mother of the wards, whose assertion of a right to disclosure I would reject, but to whose care and custody the Official Solicitor has proposed that the wards be committed, may still entertain strong feelings in the matter. It has, therefore, seemed to me that with advantage to all concerned the case should be remitted to some other judge of the Chancery Division whose duty it will be to consider all the material available, including the confidential reports of the Official Solicitor, and to reach a conclusion on the question raised in the originating summons. In so doing the judge must in the exercise of his discretion determine to what extent, if at all, he will regard it as proper, on the principles which I have endeavoured to state, not to disclose to either parent anything in the reports which he will regard as material in reaching his conclusion. I express the earnest hope that, if and so far as he may regard it as his duty not to disclose material in the reports relevant to his decision, he will be able to avail himself successfully of the practice . . . of disclosure to the learned counsel concerned. I find it difficult to believe that if their mother and father have the interests of these children truly at heart they will not permit their counsel at least to co-operate with the judge to this extent. . . .

Holding

It remains for me to express my view on certain other matters raised in the argument before your lordships. In the first place I agree with the learned members of the Court of Appeal in expressing some dissatisfaction with what your lordships were told was the general practice of the Official Solicitor when acting as guardian ad litem to submit confidential reports. I am fully conscious of the responsibility and difficulty cast on the Official Solicitor when required to act as guardian ad litem of wards of court in cases of this kind; and I have no doubt at all of the great service that has been rendered to wards of court by the Official Solicitor in that capacity. But your lordships have been informed that the practice of submitting confidential reports is peculiar to the Official Solicitor and is not followed by other persons when acting as guardians ad litem and further, that such practice cannot be traced further back than about the year 1928. Again I appreciate that the position of the Official Solicitor is in material respects special—he is a complete stranger to the wards and to their family. Nevertheless the arguments in the present case have satisfied me that the submitting of confidential reports as a general practice is not to be recommended. I do not doubt that occasions may sometimes arise (having regard again to his peculiar position) when the Official Solicitor may strongly feel that information which he has obtained should be submitted confidentially to the court; and in such cases he will be entitled so to do. But in my opinion the "right" should be very carefully and strictly exercised—exercised, that is to say, only when in the Official Solicitor's view the information must in the interest of the ward be submitted to the judge, but yet in his opinion should not without the judge's authority be communicated to the other parties to the proceedings; and in such cases the Official Solicitor should, in my view, state to the judge the reasons that have persuaded him to take such a course.

* * *

LORD JENKINS: . . .

If the mother is to be entitled as of right to disclosure of the two reports with which the present application is concerned, I do not see why, by parity of reasoning, she should not equally be entitled to insist on like disclosure of information from other sources however damaging to the ward such disclosure might be. I appreciate that the welfare of the infant is the paramount consideration, but surely this requirement can only be complied with if the judge, or the master on his behalf, is given a wide discretion to determine whether the disclosure sought by the parents in the particular case is in the best interests of the ward.

It is objected that the use by the court of undisclosed documents or information in wardship cases is objectionable as offending against the fundamental principle of justice to the effect that anyone against whom a charge is made must be given a fair opportunity of knowing and understanding what the charge is and on what evidence it is based. The question whether in a particular case compliance with that principle should be accorded greater or less importance than the probability, whatever it may be, of damage (if any) to the infant ensuing from such compliance, depends on the facts of that particular case; and any attempt to formulate general pronouncements applicable in all cases will be likely to create more difficulties than it solves.

In conclusion I will content myself by saying that in my belief the time-honoured Chancery jurisdiction in regard to wards of court has in the main worked well and that, speaking for myself, I would deprecate the introduction of major alterations merely for the sake of providing for cases which in actual practice are relatively rare.

NOTES

NOTE 1.

Re G. (T.J.) (AN INFANT)
[1963] 1 All. E.R. 20

ORMEROD, L.J.:

The boy was born on August 10, 1950. The mother at the time of the birth of the boy was sixteen and the father twenty-one. The boy was born in wedlock. On August 7, 1953, the mother, having left the father, got a separation order from the magistrates on the ground of the father's desertion. At that time the boy was living with his paternal grandparents, and continued to do so until the summer of 1954. . . . In the summer of 1954 the applicant joined the father in the flat in which he was then living, and the boy came to live with them. There were later divorce proceedings between the father and the mother, and a decree granted on the ground of the father's adultery with the applicant, who married the father on April 28, 1956. In the year 1959 the father was lost in a yachting accident, and probate of his will, in which he had appointed the applicant the testamentary guardian of the boy, was granted to her on October 12, 1961. Since the boy went to live with the applicant and his father, she has looked after him, and, indeed, since the father was lost at sea, she has been solely in charge of him, and the boy did not know that she was not his mother until about twelve months before the hearing. He has been at a boarding school since he was seven years old; first at a preparatory school and now at a school in the south of England. It was hoped that he would go to a well-known public school, but this has not proved possible for financial reasons.

There was an application for an adoption order on January 21, 1961, into which was incorporated a request to dispense with the consent of the mother as she had refused to give it. The judge refused to dispense with the consent of the mother, and, in consequence, no order for adoption was made, and this appeal follows from the judge's decision.

* * *

[R]ules have been made for proceedings in the county court and they are known as the Adoption (County Court) Rules, 1959, and are to be found in the COUNTY COURT PRACTICE, 1962, at

p. 1220 onwards. Rule 9 reads as follows:

"(1) With a view to safeguarding the interest of the infant before the court the guardian ad litem shall, so far as is reasonably practicable— (a) investigate all circumstances relevant to the proposed adoption, including the matters alleged in the originating application and those specified in sch. 2 to these rules; and (b) perform such other duties as are specified in the said schedule or as the court may direct.

"(2) On completing his investigations the guardian ad litem shall make a confidential report in writing to the court.

"(3) With a view to obtaining the directions of the court on any particular matter, the guardian ad litem may at any time make such interim report to the court as appears to him to be necsssary".

It seems therefore that if the guardian ad litem is appointed, and the rule provides that one shall be so appointed so far as is reasonably practicable, then he will prepare a report, described as "confidential" . . . . It is contended on behalf of the applicant that, in the circumstances of this case, the learned county court judge had no regard for the wishes of the boy ; that he paid no attention to them, and came to his conclusion without seeing the boy or requiring him to attend before him. It is to be noted . . . that a judge shall not make an adoption order or an interim order unless the infant has attended personally before him. In this case no order was made, and it would appear therefore that there has been no breach of that rule. But it is contended that there was a breach by the learned judge of s. 7(2), as it would be impossible to give due consideration to the wishes of the infant without first ascertaining what those wishes were, and the only satisfactory way of ascertaining those wishes would be by the attendance of the infant. The learned judge in his judgment has said specifically that neither the applicant nor either objecting party requested him to interview the boy, and he decided in the circumstances that there were special circumstances which justified him in not interviewing him. I doubt whether the circumstances set out by the learned judge amounted to special circumstances. He was anxious that nothing should be thought by any party to be the result of something said by the boy which might cause trouble at a later time. There was, however, before the learned judge the report of the guardian ad litem. There were as a matter of fact two reports, a final report and an interim report. The date of the final report was immediately before the date of the hearing. It was suggested in the course of the argument . . . that it was important to assess the wishes of the infant at the time of the hearing and not at some date long before the hearing. That question

did not arise as the date of the report was so very close to the date of the hearing. The learned judge disclosed a small portion only of the report of the guardian ad litem. The question arose whether the judge had given "due consideration to the wishes of the infant" in pursuance of s. 7(2). It was submitted that the judge could not act on information not in the possession of the parties. That position has been discussed at length in a recent decision of this court— Re K. (infants) [(1962) 3 All E.R. 1000]. The situation was different there, however. The question arose in wardship proceedings, and the confidential report submitted by the Official Solicitor was not authorised by statute or by rule. In adoption proceedings the rules provide that the guardian ad litem should make a confidential report in writing to the court. . . . It appears from the judgment of the learned judge that he read the report. In any event, as it was his duty to read it, we should assume that he did so. I think, too, that we could assume that the report contained information as to the wishes of the boy, as para. 3 of sch. 2 to the Adoption (County Court) Rules, 1959, provides that the guardian ad litem is required to ascertain, as soon as is reasonably practicable, whether the infant is able to understand the nature of an adoption order and, if so, to inform the court and ascertain whether the infant wishes to be adopted by the applicant.

It transpired, however, that the parties were willing that the guardian's report and interim report should be before the court, and by agreement the reports were read. It was stated in the report that the nature of an adoption order was explained to the boy, who said he would like to be adopted. In these circumstances, although it is true that the judge did not accede to the boy's wishes, it would in my judgment be difficult to find that he failed to have due regard to them. The Act of Parliament does not prescribe that the judge should see the infant. It may be that this may often seem to be the most satisfactory way of finding out the wishes of the infant and of deciding whether and how far to accede to them, but there is no statutory obligation on the judge to do this and in some cases, and this may well be one, the judge may prefer to rely on the skill of a trained and experienced welfare officer.

* * *

PEARSON, L.J. . . .

. . . The peculiarity of the procedure arises solely from the use of the word "confidential" . . . . That word must impose some restriction on disclosure of the report, and must, I think, have at least this effect, that the parties to a contested application are not automatically as of right entitled to see the report or to be informed of its contents. . . . In the sphere of administration it is usual and natural for the minister or other authority to come to a decision with the aid of confidential reports or minutes or memoranda, which the parties interested in the decision would not expect or be allowed to see. In the sphere of judicial procedure there is a very well-established and vitally important principle that all the information which is available to the court should also be available to the parties, so that they may have an opportunity of commenting, cross-examining and calling rebutting or explanatory evidence. . . .

* * *

. . . Questions may arise as to the use which the judge ought or ought not to make of the report in this or that class of cases, and the extent, if any, to which, and the circumstances in which, and the conditions on which, disclosure of the report to the parties may or should be given, and whether the maker of the report should be consulted as to any disclosure of it. The rules afford no guidance except by using the word "confidential". . . .

NOTE 2.

BOTEIN, BERNARD, and GORDON, MURRAY A.
The Trial of the Future: Challenge to the Law*

Juvenile and family courts—and civil and criminal courts to the extent that they affect children or the family unit—are fast taking on the coloration of social problem courts rather than courts of law. Children, and often youths and their parents, are assisted and not prosecuted, treated and not punished by such courts. As one writer puts it, the search is for "redemption, not retaliation." To this end the trend is quickened toward the use of highly specialized tribunals— children's courts, family courts, domestic relations courts—with their attendant personnel of social workers and psychologists. This body of experts will develop increasingly the data bearing upon issues of fault, or, more accurately, "cause" ; and relief, or, more precisely, "therapy"—a function which is, of course, performed in the field and not in the courtroom. Fact-finding is thus shifted from the courtroom with its adversary process and rules of evidence, to the home, office, and neighborhood, with the nonjudicial mode of inquiry employed by the social sciences. In many jurisdictions today, important aspects of custody, adoption, guardianship and support proceedings, to-

gether with sentencing and juvenile procedures, involve the use of investigations and reports by probation officers and other social workers. The extensive use by courts of extrajudicial investigative reports reflects the tendency toward the "individualization" of treatment of litigants whose problems evoke consideration of social values.

* * *

In the main . . . the techniques of . . . family courts have gone unchallenged and, when challenged, have been judicially approved. Judge Paul W. Alexander of the Toledo, Ohio, Division of Domestic Relations writes that in over forty thousand domestic relations and children's cases ranging over twenty years in his court, not a single attorney objected to the use of extrajudicial investigation reports: "In less than one case in hundreds does the lawyer bother to exercise his right to cross-examine the court worker." Thus, the extrajudicial investigations conducted by our family . . . courts often invade the private lives of children and adults in a fashion that would never be tolerated in a court handling litigation of a purely adversary nature. And indications confirm the future widening of the breaches already made in the walls of the juvenile and family courtroom through which evidence packaged outside is delivered and accepted in a form that would stamp it as contraband in conventional courtrooms.

Our canvass of the extent to which disputes in American society are no longer litigated in courts or by traditional judicial processes is not intended to be critical. The changes we have noted are principally for the better, and King Canute long ago demonstrated the futility of trying to shout down history. But it is timely to see and to state how far reality deviates from the American myth that a prescribed mode of trial, with all the protections of the Bill of Rights, is available when controversy remains unresolved or when government threatens personal freedom. It is no less timely to ask whether the inevitable continuance of the discernible trend away from the courts and their complement of judges, juries, lawyers, advocacy and rules of evidence and procedure will not just as inevitably erode the integrity of the trial process as we know it today.

What is involved is not only the future migration of still more business from the court's domains, but the contagion of indifference, at times approaching disdain, for the forms of the judicial trial. How long will the guarantees of the trial process remain vital if other processes, dealing with comparable problems, demonstrate the dispensability of those guarantees? If arbitration can do very well without lawyers, and ad-

* New York: Simon and Schuster, 1963, pp. 93-95, 98-99. Copyright 1963 by Bernard Botein and Murray A. Gordon Reprinted with permission of the publisher.

ministrative adjudication can function effectively while receiving hearsay, how long can the judicial trial continue to be unaffected by such experience?

NOTE 3.

In re CHANDLER
230 Ore. 452, 457, 370 P. 2d 626, 627 (1962)

SLOAN, J.

*   *   *

In this case the state had intervened in a family to take a child from the custody of its parent. It was placed in the custody of the Welfare Department. The conduct of the case workers who were supervising the child and the relationship of these people to the child and to the parent and stepmother was directly in issue. During the trial, counsel sought to elicit certain information from this file and was unable to satisfactorily obtain it. He then moved to put the entire file in evidence. This was denied. However, the real question presented here is, should counsel have been permitted reasonable access to the file in order to use that part of it that was relevant to the issues being presented to the court? We think the court should have permitted such an examination. No one asked to take the file away from the immediate custody of the court. The court could have required such safeguards as he may have felt necessary in respect to the examination of the file, but complete denial of access to the file was wrong.

It would be unthinkable to say that an agency of the state may seize a person's child and then be the sole judge of how much of the evidence in respect to the agency's conduct it will refuse to divulge. It could not be contended that the statutes mentioned were intended to deny to the proper court the right to control these files, evidence, reports and the like that are material to the exercise of the court's jurisdiction and functions. . . . ORS 419.500(2) makes it clear that this material can only be used by the court, if it is not otherwise competent or admissible, when the court is deciding the disposition to be made of the child. When deciding the basic question if the child should be made a ward of the court which was the issue in this case, such material cannot be considered by the court unless it is competent, relevant and admissible. ORS 419.500(1).

We see little to distinguish this case from Jencks v. United States, 1957, 353 U.S. 657 . . . . There a majority of the court decided that counsel for a person charged with crime should have access to F.B.I. records in order to impeach government witnesses. The case is limited to criminal cases. Certainly the case before us is not a criminal case. But the rights being challenged are equally fundamental, and probably more ancient, than the right to liberty itself. We think the procedure

urged in the concurring opinion of Justice Burton in the Jencks case is the proper one to be adopted in these proceedings. He held that the trial court should first examine the file and delete any irrelevant material and any material inimical to the security of the government. The latter type of evidence would not, of course, be in question in a juvenile case. Any relevant material should be made available to counsel. In this case, the record does not show whether the court examined the entire file or not. It only appears that some of the material contained in the file may have been relevant and helpful to have had in evidence. An opportunity to put it in evidence should have been allowed.

*   *   *

d. **Determining a Course of Action—Assuring Presentation of Data from Child's Point of View—The Problem of Party Status for Children**

[i]

DESPERT, J. LOUISE

Children of Divorce*

Parents often seek the aid of a psychiatrist in reopening a custody case, but . . . too often they are seeking better terms not so much for the children as for themselves. Too often, also, the law plays into the hands of parents whose emotions distort, for themselves no less than for the court, the question of the children's welfare. On the surface the child appears to be the focus of everyone's concern. We have only to scratch the surface and we find that the child is being tragically ignored.

Sometimes we have access to the truth behind the story that is told in court, as in the case of Evelyn.

Evelyn was six when her mother came to the court in the Midwestern city where they lived with the mother's parents. Three years earlier this young mother had left her husband taking the child with her. In her youthful inexperience, she explained, she had agreed that her husband should have the child for Christmas and Easter and the long summer vacation. Now she asked the court for full custody of the child, with the father's visitation privileges either cut to a minimum or withdrawn altogether.

In brief this was her story: While in college and against her parents' wishes she had married a man in his late forties, a successful businessman in a small city adjacent to the college town. He had never been married before. He had taken his bride to the family mansion, where he lived with an aged housekeeper who had been there since his mother's day. After four years of what she described as virtual imprisonment in this grim and gloomy home isolated on a large estate, she had fled with her child to her own parents' home.

It was in this dark setting, with a morbid old man and an ancient crone to look after her, that Evelyn was forced to spend three or four months of the year. This was the picture Evelyn's mother drew, of a child crying for her mother, held against her will in a home which belonged in a Brontë novel, omitting only the mad relative caged in the attic. There was even a suggestion that the father was so excessively demonstrative in his affection as to be a potential danger to the child's sexual development; the idea of incest was implanted in the court's mind, though the word was not mentioned. The young mother impressed the court as genuinely despairing over the damage being caused to the child.

When the father came to the witness stand the contrast confirmed the mother's story. A man of dignified and distant manners, he was old enough to be his own child's grandfather. His face was dour and cold, and only monosyllables escaped his rigid lips. He seemed in the grip of violent emotion severely controlled, and it took not much imagination to suppose that the emotion was rage that his wife might succeed in freeing the child from his clammy grasp.

His own lawyer could draw nothing from him which would soften his wife's picture. To his wife's counsel he admitted, yes, the child did sometimes cry for her mother, and yes, he had once or twice taken the little girl into his own bed; alleviation of her fears was his justification. He sent the child little dresses; did she ever wear them? No, he could not say that he had ever seen her wear one of them. He sent the child toys; did she ever play with them? No, he had never actually seen her playing with one of those toys.

If the judge had any remaining doubts, he had only to glance from Evelyn's stony-visaged father to her mother, glowing with bright vitality, and to the kindly, gray-haired grandparents who sat close to their daughter as if to protect her. This pretty young mother would surely marry again and provide Evelyn with a suitable father. Meanwhile the grandparents could not be other than a bulwark of love and security.

So Evelyn was entrusted to her mother's care. Her father could see her occasionally, by appointment at her mother's home, a thousand miles or more from his own home and business; this con-

cession, an impractical privilege at best, the judge made only because the man had no actual blot on his character which would abrogate even so slender a claim as was left him.

Evelyn's father went home a brokenhearted man, deprived of the one object of love and tenderness in his whole life. And Evelyn was parted from a father whom, despite the court evidence, she truly loved and needed.

We know this because some months before she took her case to court Evelyn's mother had consulted a psychiatrist in her city. He undertook the case with the understanding that his findings might or might not support her claim to full custody. He might come to the opinion that the child's emotional needs were better served by continuing the relationship with her father.

"Why, of course," Evelyn's mother blandly agreed, and added, unaware that she was revealing her motives, "If your opinion won't help me I won't use it in court, that's all."

The psychiatrist also interviewed Evelyn's father. He spent several sessions with Evelyn. He spent enough time with Evelyn's mother to observe, as the court could not, that she was determined to get the child completely away from her husband, that she had bided her time since the divorce until she could build a psychological case against him.

At the time of her divorce she could not have done this, having left him without any provocation which would make him the guilty party in court. He still loved her and would have contested the divorce. She had agreed to the liberal visitation privileges in return for an uncontested divorce. Now she felt strong enough to go back on the bargain.

The psychiatrist delved into the motives which prompted her marriage to this man, and he saw— as the court could never have seen—that she had married to escape a neurotic attachment to her father, that her choice of an older man was part of the same neurotic pattern, and her rejection of him after a few years of marriage was a further expression of it. He saw behind the kindly grandmother's facade a dominating woman who had thwarted her daughter's emotional development and was already at work on her granddaughter, putting confusion into the child's love for her father, breaking a natural and wholesome link in the child's emotional growth.

In the father the psychiatrist found a man who had lived an austere, high-principled life until his marriage to the beautiful young girl released all his capacity for tenderness. True, he was repressed and inhibited, and he had his sexual difficulties; but in his expression of love, first toward his wife and then toward his daughter, he had been able to give a great deal of himself. To this the little girl had responded, and the relationship was rewarding to both father and child.

During the marriage he had made a practice of shortening his business hours to spend more time with Evelyn. He had taken over many of the chores of baby care to spare his young wife, and because he loved the baby. Since the divorce he and his housekeeper had rearranged the house considerably to enlarge the child's play space and make her visits there happier. He described with strict factualness the rambling house, in which he had been born and lived all his life; he had prepared a sunny nursery for Evelyn, facing on the garden, with bright curtains and Mother Goose wallpaper.

Despite his rigidity, the father was responsive to suggestion. He had taken the little girl into his bed at night because she was afraid of the dark and he did not know how else to comfort her. When the psychiatrist pointed out that such physical nearness to her father might be disturbing to a little girl, he spontaneously admitted that he could learn new ways. He would, as the doctor suggested, leave her door open at night and a light in her room; he would sit by her bed and read or talk to her until she was ready for sleep. The psychiatrist was impressed with the man's dependability and, in contrast to the mother, with the genuineness of his concern for what was best for the child.

From the grandmother and the mother the psychiatrist elicited the information that it was not the little girl who rejected her father's presents. "Those dresses, such horrors!" the chic mother exclaimed, telling why she gave them away. And the toys the child brought home from her father's house or which he sent her were quickly replaced with "much nicer ones" by the grandmother.

Also, while it was true that Evelyn sometimes cried for her mother when she was with her father, when she was at home she begged to call up her father and ask him to visit them. This is a familiar response in children divided by two loyalties.

How different from the gloomy abode described in court does this father's house seem now, a warm and friendly home for a little girl, with a motherly old woman—the housekeeper—and a father who wanted only to be allowed to continue loving her. How different, too, is the young mother from the impression she made in court.

The psychiatrist not being amenable to the mother's purpose, his testimony was of course not called for in court. The father, an unworldly man, baffled by his wife's sophisticated lawyers, never realized that expert testimony was buried somewhere which might have been of help to him.

[*ii*]

ESHELMAN v. ESHELMAN
133 Cal. App. 2d 376, 284 P. 2d 103 (1955)

MCCOMB, JUSTICE.

An interlocutory decree of divorce was granted plaintiff from defendant on February 6, 1950. Such order awarded the custody of the two minor children of the parties to plaintiff. On October 13, 1954, the trial judge modified the previous order relative to the custody of the children and awarded them to defendant. From this latter order, plaintiff appeals.

Facts: Plaintiff on December 23, 1953, filed an order to show cause for modification of the order permitting defendant to visit his children. On April 20, 1954, defendant filed an application for a modification of the order awarding the custody of the children to plaintiff. These matters came on for hearing June 17, 1954. At that time the court directed an investigator to examine the physical, spiritual and psychological environment of the two minor children and the matter was continued until October 8, 1954. On such date evidence was introduced on behalf of defendant, at the termination of which the following colloquy occurred between the court and plaintiff's counsel:

"THE COURT: * * * I will give consideration to any school or schools that Dr. Eshelman and his former wife, Mollyanne Eshelman, will recommend, and to the end that we determine what school these boys are going to be placed in, I am going to continue the matter until Wednesday, the 13th of October, at 9:00 o'clock.

"Right now, I am going to make an order that on that day both of these boys are going to be packed up and taken to some school and we will make further disposition of the question of visitation by both parents thereafter.

"For all other issues involved in this case, we have agreed upon the date of November 8, at which time the Court will endeavor to conclude all phases of this most unhappy litigation.

"MR. PINNICK: Your Honor, I apologize before I make this statement, but it is my opinion that I haven't been given an opportunity to present evidence combatting this order or combatting the proposition that these boys should go to a military school. I would like to have that order read, not that the Court will now order that they be ready to go to military school, but will take evidence on the advisability of placing them in school on Wednesday, and make the order at that time that they shall go to school.

"THE COURT: Well, Mr. Pinnick, I will be indulgent to you to the extent that you may be heard, provided it will not interfere with the resumption of a trial that is going on on that day. It is a trial that was continued over from last Thursday. I have a trial pending in this court at this time. I will hear you, but it will have to be limited to that time.

"Now, understand counsel, that this matter has been considered by the Superior Court in this County for several years and understand that we have already had evidence at the previous hearings in this matter regarding what is best for the welfare of those boys. While I appreciate the fact that you are newly substituted in here and have lacked the opportunity to experience what has preceded this proceedings here this morning, and while I want to be perfectly reasonable with you and give you every opportunity to be heard, I can't, for the interests of these children, vacate the order that I have made unless you show me good cause next Wednesday morning. These orders are always subject to alteration.

"MR. PINNICK: Yes, sir. I thought perhaps that some qualified opinions should be allowed to be expressed on whether the boys should go to a military school.

"THE COURT: Mr. Pinnick, I will be very glad to hear from you Wednesday [October 13] morning."

Thereupon the matter was continued until Wednesday, October 13. When court convened on October 13, 1954, after the court had recited some previous facts pertaining to the litigation between the parties, the following occurred between the court and plaintiff's counsel:

"THE COURT: * * * Let the record also show that the Court has had the advantage of discussing this matter with Mr. Warren Benton. Mr Warren Benton is, in one sense, a court attache and doing a high minded work with his associates in investigating home conditions and environments and the fitness of parents who have the custody of children of tender years. Mr. Benton has made numerous reports to this court covering many back hearings. I have talked to Mr. Benton as late as this morning. I have told him that it was my opinion that at the present time there is quite a crisis with reference to the welfare of these two little fellows, and that I think that something should be done in order to give them a new atmosphere and a new opportunity to forge out into the status of development that has long since been retarded. He agreed with me wholeheartedly and he said that he felt that that is precisely what he would like to have done himself.

"Now when I speak of Mr. Benton, I am speaking of advice and observations of an expert. I don't claim to be an expert, but I am trying to deal with these problems with a heart. It isn't like taking these children away from mother and father; they will have many opportunities to visit with their children and we will cooperate in every way we can with the school authorities to the end that the children are made happy and that the parents will have an opportunity to live normal lives, seeing the children whenever they can.

"Now, do you desire to protest that, Mr. Pinnick?

"MR. PINNICK: Your Honor, did you make a finding as to who now has legal custody?

"THE COURT: No, I am not disturbing that order. This case is continued until the 8th of November for further decisions to be made, and as far as the physical custody of the children are concerned, when they are in that school they are of course going to be in the custody of the school authorities. Otherwise the school wouldn't be able to do anything for them.

"MR. PINNICK: Well, Your Honor, there are cases that show that the law presumes that the person are [sic] fit and I would like to remind the Court that we haven't been allowed to put any evidence on behalf of the plaintiff's side, as to her fitness.

"THE COURT: Well, you may be reminded, counsel, that you and Mrs. Austin have come into this case very lately. Mrs. Austin is as late as this morning and you are as late as last week, and there have been quite a number of hearings up here and the Court has heard a considerable amount of testimony in connection with the claims and counterclaims of both parents in this case.

"MR. PINNICK: Yes, Your Honor, I am relying upon my client's advice that she hasn't been able to present on the witness stand testimony in support of her fitness.

"THE COURT: Well let us bravely cooperate on this thing. It has, after all, developed into an age old tug of war and is a rope that you are using around the life of these two children. You are using the life of the older one and that will break soon, and soon you will come into the life of the other one. Let's not ruin the lives of these children. It isn't a contest where you will win or they will win or the lady on one hand and the father on the other will win. Let's win for these children ; let's do something for them.

"MR. PINNICK: Yes, Your Honor, that is the way I feel about it, only I feel the children will win, as you put it, with the mother. I respectfully submit that they are better off with the mother. I can't help my opinions on this thing. I wouldn't submit the notice I am going to submit without feeling that way, and then I would like also to call your Honor's attention to [Roche v. Roche]

25 Cal. 2d 141 [152 P. 2d 999], which says the artifices of giving bare legal custody to the parents and putting the actual physical custody in strangers cannot be used to deprive a parent of custody unless there is a clear finding of unfitness of that parent.

"THE COURT: I thought I had found that.

"MR. PINNICK: Yes, you did your Honor.

"THE COURT: Counsel, I respect you sincerely and I am not trying to be short with you. It seems I have been having more than my share of heartaches up here for the last two weeks and that is not enough. I will see you all on November 8.

* * *

"MR. PINNICK: Might I call your Honor's attention to the case of [Luck v. Luck] 83 Cal. 574 [23 P. 1035], which says that an appeal may be taken from this order and that such an appeal suspends and stays the jurisdiction of the Court to enforce the modification. I believe I am within my rights to say that the children shall not go to school pending that appeal.

"THE COURT: I don't agree with you and I think you had better be very careful about thwarting the Court's order on this.

"MR. PINNICK: I am, your Honor. I researched this point carefully and I can give you the citations, if you wish.

"THE COURT: Well, November 8 will roll around soon. Meanwhile I hope those children are in that school.

"MR. KAUFMAN: Your Honor, will you also include in the order that the father has the right at 7:00 or 8:00 o'clock tonight to pick up the children for the purpose of bringing them immediately to that school.

"THE COURT: Is that the arrangement that you have made, Dr. Eshelman?

"THE DEFENDANT: Your Honor, I have made arrangements to put the children in as soon as I can get them in my possession to take them there or furnish the transportation. I can furnish the transportation this evening and have them in the school tonight or tomorrow morning.

"THE COURT: Do I understand you counsel for the mother of these children, that you are not going to permit that?

"MR. PINNICK: *I think it is our legal right to say that this appeal suspends the order of the court.*

"THE COURT: *There is no appeal pending.*

"MR. PINNICK: *I have just filed a notice of appeal, your Honor, and that is the institution of the appeal from this specific order, and under the law the situation——*

"THE COURT: Well, apparently you don't want us to.

"MR. KAUFMAN: Will you also include in the order, your Honor, that the father has the right to pick up the children at 7:00 o'clock tonight.

"THE COURT: Yes, that is in the order. If you want to thwart it, you will suffer the consequences. What is the name of the school?

"MR. KAUFMAN: The Ramsey Military Academy, Santa Monica.

"Your Honor, one point further on the question of custody. Shall we, in view of the attitude of counsel and plaintiff in this particular action— will your Honor make an order granting the custody of these children so we may have a right to pick up the children?

"THE COURT: Yes. Let the previous order of this Court awarding custody to the mother, be vacated and set aside, and from now on the custody of these children for the purpose of effectuating the order of this Court is now in the father. He is awarded the legal custody of these children."

Questions: First: *Was plaintiff deprived of her day in Court?*

Yes. It is a cardinal principle of our jurisprudence that a party shall not be bound or concluded by a judgment unless he has had his day in court. This means that a party must be duly cited to appear and afforded an opportunity to be heard and at such hearing to offer evidence in support of his contentions. His right to a hearing does not depend upon the will, caprice or discretion of the trial judge who is to make a decision upon the issue. Judgment without such an opportunity is lacking in all of the attributes of a judicial determination. . . .

* * *

Clearly plaintiff was deprived of her day in court by not being permitted to present the testimony she desired. . . .

Second: *Did the trial court exceed its jurisdiction in refusing to stay enforcement of its order modifying the custody of the children after the notice of appeal from such order had been filed?*

Yes. An appeal from a custody order deprives a trial court of jurisdiction to change the custody status which exists at the time of the appeal . . . In view of the foregoing rule the trial court erred in making an order changing the custody of the children pending the appeal from his previous order.

Reversed.

[iii]
Report of the New York Joint Legislative Committee on Matrimonial and Family Laws*

While the court may have difficulty enough deciding the rights of the adult parties in a matrimonial action, its task becomes infinitely more complex where children are involved. More than one Supreme Court Justice has been confronted with the mental agony involved in this phase of the matter. The nature of the contest pertaining to the custody question may call for different considerations. There comes into operation an exercise of social or other philosophy of the court which is not related to the legal questions. The legal power of the court is not questioned; how that power should be exercised for the welfare of the children is the problem.

One of the main concerns of the Committee is with the care, custody, control, support, maintenance and education of children involved in family disputes. The disposition of children is one of the major features of separation agreements when there are children of the parties. While the father is primarily responsible for the support and care of his children, the mother may also become responsible for them. Both parents appear to have equal natural rights of custody. . . . Since therefore the responsibility for the children is evenly divided (all other factors being equal) between the parents, each is in the position to assert the right for bargaining purposes. The children become of prime importance, either as a shield or as a weapon.

Since the separation agreement is most frequently drawn up in the privacy of a lawyer's office, only the parties present can take care of the rights and needs of the children. Often the same lawyer represents both parties, and therefore he is not in a position to represent vigorously either party. It must be said in this connection, however, that competent and ethical lawyers do not remain in this position if it appears that the views of one or the other of the parties will cause a conflict in which he cannot give unbiased advice and counsel. Until the irreconcilable conflict appears, however, he necessarily acts as a referee, calling to the attention of the parties their rights and duties, as well as the rights and needs of the children concerned. Many times the children become pawns in a game between battling parents.

In this situation the children are used by one or the other of the parents to pry better terms of agreement out of the other, and in the process, the children may suffer. This is particularly true where one of the parents is especially attached to the children: in such event this parent will give up a great deal to which he or she might equitably be entitled to retain custody of the children, but it is also obvious that with the exception of the lawyer no one is present at the conference to see that the children get what they are entitled to and need. In this situation the children may lose by the agreement finally made.

Mr. Milton Grossman has graphically outlined what happens in court in many cases.

> "Another factor of the utmost importance and one which has received comparatively little attention, is that of the welfare of the children of parties to a matrimonial action. The litigating parties to the defended action generally are well protected by their counsel and the interests of the innocent children, if their custody is in issue, receives adequate attention from the court. The evidence adduced permits the court to decide wisely upon the questions of custody and maintenance.

> But . . . contested actions are the exception. In the non-defended case the question of the children becomes merely a minor theme in the major dissonance. They, the most seriously affected persons, are without any unbiased and objective champion. It is asking too much to expect the harassed court to probe deeply and conscientiously into questions concerning the children, having before it only the bare facts of name, age, present custodian, etc. The court, in the person of an all too-human judge cannot be expected to raise issues which apparently have been settled amicably between the parties, particularly where the only information in the court's possession comes from the plaintiff and there is no one present to dispute it. The cursory direct examination of the plaintiff regarding the allegations of the complaint obviously does not disclose information sufficient to arouse interest on the part of the court. Only those judges, either with long experience or a mature curiosity and deep-rooted concern over the welfare of the children, can detect overtones in the testimony requiring further probing. This curiosity then competes, in the mind of the court, with the pressure of terminating each case so as to have time to hear all the others waiting their turn. The latter contender is too often the victor."

Thus we note that the agreement made may work to the disadvantage or positive harm of the children in many ways.

When children are young, most separation agreements give their custody to the mother. It therefore becomes important on the question of support not only how much is paid for the

---

* State of New York: Leg. Doc. No. 32, 1957 (pp.31-33, 85-88).

children but also how much is paid for the mother. The money received by the mother for the children is in effect a trust fund for them, and she cannot legitimately or morally take that money for her own use. Legal questions are raised where there is no breakdown of payments between mother and children. The agreement which makes a generous provision for the children but a meager provision for the mother, may very well mean that the mother must go to work to provide the deficiency for herself, and in this process her young children may lack proper guardianship. Until a court proceeding of some nature is begun, the wife and the children are forced to get along on what the agreement gives, even assuming the father furnishes it, and during this period the mother and the children suffer. The wife is bound by the bargain she made, within certain limits, and the burden of the children, if she has them, not only reduces her freedom to work but also adds to the distress. That the wife is to be bound by the bargain she made may be justifiable, but its repercussions on the children are not justifiable. And when the bargain the mother has made for herself and her children becomes untenable, she is normally reluctant to commence any court proceeding. Having made a "package" deal with her husband involving a number of personal and property rights and duties she feels hesitant to upset it and perhaps open up the whole matter for a new and perhaps more distressing argument. The children, originally unrepresented and used as bargaining points, now are squeezed by the various forces that played upon the agreement.

*   *   *

February 19, 1957

*   *   *

AN ACT *to amend the civil practice act and the domestic relations law, in relation to the appointment of infant guardians in matrimonial actions*

*   *   *

§ 207-a. Guardian of infant in matrimonial actions. 1. In an action to annul a marriage, or to declare the nullity of a void marriage, or for divorce or separation, the court may, in its discretion appoint a guardian ad litem or special guardian of any minor children of the marriage for the proper protection of the rights and interests of such children, and shall fix the fees and compensation of such guardian, which shall be payable as costs of the action from the interest of the children therein, or by either or both of the parents, as the court shall direct.

2. The guardian so appointed shall be known to

the court to possess the experience necessary fully to protect the interests of the child, and shall be, whenever practicable, a member of the same religious faith as that of the child.

3. The guardian so appointed and any such child who has attained age fourteen, shall have notice of all proceedings and shall have copies of all pleadings, orders, motions and other papers served upon him by the parties to the action, and such guardian shall have power to subpoena witnesses and take testimony with respect to custody, support and maintenance, education, both academic and religious, and legitimacy, if such issue be raised, and shall file a written report thereon with the court.

4. Rules shall be made governing the appointment, qualification, security, powers and duties of such guardian.

*   *   *

MEMORANDUM ON

AN ACT in relation to the appointment of infant guardians in matrimonial actions. . . .

*   *   *

The bill seeks to accomplish without the erection of an expensive court staff what other states are accomplishing by means of a so-called "proctor" or "friend of the court." . . .

Michigan has the "friend of the court" arrangement where a paid court staff member takes on the investigative job and reports to the court. But the magnitude of this system, with its cost, can be guessed from the fact that there are at least 100 of these "friends of the court" in the City of Detroit alone. The cost of such a program appears prohibitive for New York State at this time. . . .

NOTES

NOTE 1.

DEWEY, THOMAS E.
Memorandum*

"AN ACT to amend the civil practice act and the domestic relations law, in relation to the appointment of infant guardians in matrimonial actions"

*   *   *

Concerning the bill the Committee on State Legislation of the Association of the Bar of the City of New York has written as follows:

"In disapproving the bill, we want to make clear that we are not opposed to the appointment of a special court officer or guardian, if properly skilled and qualified, in many of the situations

---

* April 17, 1954

covered by the present bill. It is undoubtedly true that frequently neither the parties nor the Court gives adequate attention to the interests of the minor children concerned, and we believe that a skilled official or guardian, trained in the particular field involved, could give great aid to those instances.

But the bill as drawn has, we believe, several serious defects which warrant its disapproval, as follows:

1. *The Bill is Too Broad.* The present provisions of Section 207 of the Civil Practice Act do not, by their terms, restrict the court in the appointment of a guardian ad litem to cases where the infant is a party to the action or proceeding. Accordingly, guardians ad litem have upon occasion been appointed where possible property rights of an infant are involved . . . or in matrimonial actions where the legitimacy is in issue. . . .

The advisability of the appointment of guardians in the above situations would seem clear. The proposed bill goes far beyond this, however, in *requiring* the appointment of such a guardian in *every* defined case where there are infant children of the parties, although in many of these cases the guardian would serve no useful function.

Under the terms of the bill the guardian is to make an examination and report on matters of custody, support, maintenance and education. Yet, these matters would usually present no problems where a child is 18, married, or emancipated. In many other cases, particularly contested ones, the financial resources of the parents will be fully explored in connection with alimony or claims for separate maintenance, and the services of the guardian ad litem in soliciting such information would be largely superfluous. . . .

The unnecessary appointment of guardians that would be required by the mandatory provisions of the bill would not merely waste time. The bill is not entirely clear as to the source from which the guardian's fee is to be paid, particularly with respect to the meaning of 'the interest of the children therein', out of which the court may direct the cost to be paid as an alternative to payment by 'either or both of the parents'. But in most cases, however the term is defined, the source would be the husband's pocketbook. To burden the husband with this additional obligation, when he is already obligated to his own attorney and possibly may have to pay the wife's attorney, will usually diminish the funds available for the very infants whom the bill is designed to protect. And it is to be noted that wealthy litigants in New York matrimonial actions are in the great minority; the majority are wage-earners of modest or little means, often young and married only a short time. . . .

2. *The Bill is Wrong in Approach.* Under the proposed bill the judge would be free to appoint anyone as guardian ad litem, regardless of experience. While most appointments would no

doubt be proper, the temptation to make patronage appointments may be strong, particularly because in many instances the practical function of the guardian would be obscure. . . .

3. *The Bill May Prevent the Use of a Guardian Ad Litem on the Issue of Legitimacy.* As has been indicated, one of the few cases where appointment of the guardian ad litem may be desirable is that where legitimacy is in issue. Curiously enough, however, the bill makes no mention of the issue of legitimacy as one of those questions to be examined and reported on by the guardian ad litem. . . .

4. *The Bill Contains No Provision for Making the Court's Decree Binding on the Infant.* Although the husband or wife would usually be subjected to additional expense by the appointment of a guardian ad litem, the bill fails to make any provision that would give the parents the protection of a decree that would be binding on the child. There is serious doubt under present law whether the infant could properly be made a party to matrimonial proceedings . . . and the bill makes no attempt to change the law in this respect. It provides for service of papers only on the guardian ad litem, which would not result in jurisdiction being obtained over the child. . . . Because of this failure to confer jurisdiction over the child, moreover, it is doubtful whether either the guardian ad litem or the infant could take an appeal from any judgment or order. Civil Practice Act § 557. . . ."

The bill is disapproved.

(Signed) THOMAS E. DEWEY

NOTE 2.

BOTEIN, BERNARD
Trial Judge*

It is not entirely fair to criticize overworked judges and referees for not challenging most uncontested requests for custody of children—especially when there is nothing in the record to excite misgivings. No court of general jurisdiction that I know of is equipped to probe thousands of such situations a year, to investigate homes, reputations, and environments, and to secure a psychiatric examination of every proposed custodian of a child. There have been proposals that a unit of trained social investigators and psychiatrists be attached to every court which has the power directly to chart the lives of children. Another proposal is that in any instance where the custody of a child is sought, whether by out-of-court arrangement or contested or uncontested action, the court appoint a special guardian to protect the best interests of the child.

---

* New York: Simon and Schuster, 1952, pp. 271-273. Copyright 1952 by Bernard Botein. Reprinted with permission of the publisher.

I do not believe these proposals go far enough. Certainly competent inquiry should be made to place the child where its welfare and happiness will be promoted, and to put an end to the prevailing practice which generally gives the child to the successful party, as a sort of prize of war.

But I believe that anybody who seeks and accepts the custody of a child should do so subject to periodic check and supervision by the court, over a long probation period. A person may impress a judge as a responsible and well-meaning guardian at the time of appointment. But children are complicated little creatures—particularly those who are the frightened, insecure products of broken homes. The best-intentioned person may unwittingly do them irreparable harm. A timely visit from a social worker with trained insights may result in remedial guidance for the guardian. And if he or she cannot or will not follow professional instructions, the child should be taken away and the custody award vacated.

NOTE 3.

DIAMOND, BERNARD L.

The Fallacy of the Impartial Expert*

The crude charge is sometimes asserted that under the adversary system the expert witness sells his opinion. Because he is paid by one or the other side, he is accused of prostituting his medical knowledge in providing untruthful testimony in return for the money he is paid. This charge is too base to defend by more than just a simple statement: I do not believe that this happens.

Undoubtedly what does happen is that the expert witness, through his close operational identification with one side of the conflict, does become an advocate. Because his testimony does in fact support one side of the legal battle, he, if he is at all human, must necessarily identify himself with his own opinion, and subjectively desire that "his side" win. This can vary all the way from the deliberate, conscious participation in the planning of the legal strategy with the lawyers who call upon him for expert advice and opinion, to a more aloof, detached facsimile of impartiality that masks his secret hope for victory of his own opinion. Such a detached witness may be totally unconscious of the innumerable subtle distortions and biases in his testimony that spring from this wish to triumph.

This is well recognized by our courts of law. It is the duty of the counsel for the opposing side to cross examine the witness, revealing these dis-

tortions and biases, attempting to impeach his testimony. It is wholly legitimate to impeach the testimony through an attack upon the witness himself. That is, by eliciting evidence to show that the witness is not the expert he proclaims himself to be, that the clinical facts upon which the expert bases his opinions are not complete or may not even be true, that the skill and knowledge of the expert in his professional field are deficient, and that his expert opinions are faulty and unwarranted. Under such cross examination or through redirect examination by the counsel who engaged him, the expert is expected to defend his expert status, his clinical facts, his professional knowledge, and to justify his opinions. It is absurd to pretend that the psychiatric expert remains neutral under such a legal procedure. For the sake of his own ego integrity, he must identify himself with his own opinions and become the advocate of those opinions. But in proportion as those opinions favor one side or the other, the witness loses his hypothetical impartiality.

Because both the impartial, court-appointed, independent witness as well as the adversary witness are required to submit to cross examination and defend their opinions, it is here asserted that there is no such thing as a truly impartial expert; that all witnesses, regardless of who engaged them, identify closely with their own opinions, and unintentionally introduce, as a result, a certain degree of bias and deviation from their oath to tell the truth, the whole truth, and nothing but the truth.

NOTE 4.

BANK OF CALIFORNIA NAT. ASS'N
v.
SUPERIOR COURT
16 Cal. 2d 516, 106 P. 2d 879 (1940)

GIBSON, C. J.

This is a petition for a writ of prohibition, to restrain the respondent superior court from proceeding with the trial of an action without bringing in certain parties alleged to be "necessary and indispensable."

Sara M. Boyd . . . died testate in June, 1937, leaving an estate valued at about $225,000. On July 8, 1937, in the superior court in San Francisco, her will was admitted to probate, and petitioner, Bank of California, was appointed executor. The will left individual legacies and bequests amounting to $60,000 to a large number of legatees, including charitable institutions and individuals, some residing in other states and in foreign countries. Petitioner, St Luke's Hospital, was named residuary legatee and devisee, and thereby received the bulk of the estate.

On October 14, 1937, Bertha M. Smedley, a

---

* *Archives of Criminal Psychodynamics*, III (1959), pp. 221-226, 234-236. Reprinted with permission of the publisher.

niece and legatee, brought an action to enforce the provisions of an alleged contract by which decedent agreed to leave her entire estate to the plaintiff. . . .

* * *

In support of their application, petitioners point out that the complaint challenges the right of every legatee and devisee to share in the estate, and prays for an award of the entire property to plaintiff. It is contended that a trial and judgment without the absent defendants would adversely affect the rights of such parties, would result in a multiplicity of suits, and would subject the petitioning executor to inconvenience, expense and the burden of future litigation.

To test the theory of petitioners, it will be necessary to examine briefly the origin and nature of the rules on required or compulsory joinder of parties. We may eliminate, at the outset, the field of permissive joinder of "proper parties", for there is no doubt that the absent defendants are interested in the issues and subject of the action, and could properly be joined. For the same reason, these legatees, if they had not been named as defendants, could no doubt have intervened in the action. These propositions are conceded by all parties, and the precise issue is thus made clear, whether the absent defendants are not only proper parties but "indispensable parties" in the sense that service upon them or their appearance is essential to the jurisdiction of the court to proceed in the action. . . .

At common law, joinder of plaintiffs was compulsory where the parties, under the substantive law, were possessed of joint rights. Joint promisees under a contract, partners, and joint tenants were familiar examples. Equity courts developed another theory of compulsory joinder, to carry out the policy of avoiding piecemeal litigation and multiplicity of suits. Those persons necessary to a complete settlement of the controversy were usually required to be joined, in order that the entire matter might be concluded by a single suit. Obviously, this theory of joinder covered many situations where the substantive rights were not joint, and accordingly joinder would not have been required in an action at law. See Clark, Code Pleading, pp. 241, 242, 245. Generally speaking, the modern rule under the codes carries out the established equity doctrine. Thus, section 389 of the Code of Civil Procedure states: "The court may determine any controversy between parties before it, when it can be done without prejudice to the rights of others, or, by saving their rights; but when a complete determination of the controversy cannot be had without the presence of other parties, the court must then order them to be brought in. . . ." Such statutes have been interpreted as declaratory of the equity rule and practice. . . .

But the equity doctrine as developed by the courts is loose and ambiguous in its expression and uncertain in its application. Sometimes it is stated as a mandatory rule, and at other times as a matter of discretion, designed to reach an equitable result if it is practicable to do so. . . . Bearing in mind the fundamental purpose of the doctrine, we should, in dealing with "necessary" and "indispensable" parties, be careful to avoid converting a discretionary power or a rule of fairness in procedure into an arbitrary and burdensome requirement which may thwart rather than accomplish justice. These two terms have frequently been coupled together as if they have the same meaning; but there appears to be a sound distinction, both in theory and practice, between parties deemed "indispensable" and those considered merely "necessary". As Professor Clark has remarked: "It has been objected that the terms 'necessary' and 'indispensable' convey the same idea. . . . But a distinction has been drawn. While necessary parties are so interested in the controversy that they should normally be made parties in order to enable the court to do complete justice, yet if their interests are separable from the rest and particularly where their presence in the suit cannot be obtained, they are not indispensable parties. The latter are those without whom the court cannot proceed." (Clark Code Pleading, p. 245, note 21.) . . .

First, then, what parties are indispensable? There may be some persons whose interests, rights, or duties will inevitably be affected by any decree which can be rendered in the action. Typical are the situations where a number of persons have undetermined interests in the same property . . . and one of them seeks, in an action, to recover the whole, to fix his share, or to recover a portion claimed by him. The other persons with similar interests are indispensable parties. The reason is that a judgment in favor of one claimant for part of the property or fund would necessarily determine the amount or extent which remains available to the others. Hence, any judgment in the action would inevitably affect their rights. Thus, in an action by one creditor against assignees for the benefit of creditors, seeking an accounting and payment of his share of the assets, the other creditors were held indispensable. . . .

* * *

The other classification includes persons who are interested in the sense that they might possibly be affected by the decision, or whose interests in the subject matter or transaction are such that it cannot be finally and completely settled without them ; but nevertheless their interests are so separable that a decree may be rendered between the parties before the court without affecting those others. These latter may perhaps be "necessary" parties to a complete settlement of the entire controversy or transaction, but are not "indispensable" to any valid judgment in the particular case. They should normally be joined, and the court, following the equity rule, will usually require them to be joined, in order to carry out the policy of complete determination and avoidance of multiplicity of suits. . . .

NOTE 5.

HENLEY v. FOSTER
220 Ala. 420, 125 So. 662 (1930)

BOULDIN, J.

. . . Has a child a standing in a court of equity to challenge a decree fixing the marriage status of his or her parents because of collusion and fraud on their part?

* * *

Broadly speaking, no third person is entitled to intervene in divorce suits ; even children, vitally affected as the necessary result of the breaking up of the family, cannot interfere in such proceedings between their parents. A court of equity, exercising a guardianship over infants within its jurisdiction, is charged with the duty of making such provision as it may for their custody and support upon granting a divorce ; but divorce cannot be refused upon proven statutory grounds because children may be involved. . . .

* * *

Assuming that a child may not intervene or become a party either in divorce or annulment proceedings, the question recurs whether a child, bastardized by a fraudulent and collusive decree of annulment on the part of the parents, may avoid such decree in so far as it affects the legal rights of such child?

Speaking generally of the right of third persons, not permitted to take part in divorce proceedings, to avoid the same for fraud by collateral attack, Mr. Bishop says: "And the doctrine is settled that in some way, hence necessarily in this way, any third person against whom a fraudulent divorce sentence is produced may avoid it by showing the fraud ; since fraud in these causes, as in all others, vitiates every judgment into which it enters." 2 Bishop on Marriage, Divorce and Separation, § 1567, p. 596.

* * *

No case is found in this country applying the doctrine to a child situated as in this case. Naturally such a case would rarely arise.

In England, however, it is declared as of course that the child may in equity avoid a decree of this class for fraud and collusion on the part of the parents. . . .

We can see no good reason why the child may not have relief as other third persons not permitted a hearing in the original proceeding. The child has personal as well as property rights involved. Legitimacy is favored in the law. Infants are the special objects of the care of courts of equity.

Just as in other cases avoiding transactions for fraud, the decree need not and should not disturb the marriage status as between the parents, parties to the decree, nor disturb any rights of others growing out of such decreed status, save as they stand in the way of doing equity to the defrauded complainant. Such was the decree rendered here. We approve the well chosen words of the trial court in his opinion: "* * * It appears to the Court that natural justice and equity of the matter would dictate a holding that no child should be deprived of his birthright and rendered illegitimate by . . . collusive actions of its parents. A status of legitimacy is a right of value and should have the same protection as property rights against fraud and collusion of others."

Affirmed.

[iv]
In re CLARK
21 O.O. 2d 86, 90 O.L.A. 21 (1962)

ALEXANDER, J. On September 6, 1962 the court received from officials of Mercy Hospital an application for authority to administer blood transfusions to one Kenneth Clark, aged 3 years. . . .

It was made to appear that the child was suffering second and third degree burns over forty percent of his body ; . . . that the child's blood condition was deteriorating, and it might become necessary at any time to administer blood transfusions ; that the child's parents refused to authorize same because the religious sect to which they belong (Jehovah's Witnesses) forbids it as violating certain Biblical injunctions ; that the hospital and attending surgeon could not adequately or safely treat the patient without the authority sought.

Ohio's Juvenile Code empowers the Juvenile Court to protect the rights of a child in this condition:

"§ 2151.33, Revised Code. * * * Upon the certificate of one or more reputable practicing physicians, the court may summarily provide for emergency medical and surgical treatment which appears to be immediately necessary for any child concerning whom a complaint or an application for care has been filed, pending the service of a citation upon its parents, guardian, or custodian. * * *"

Even without this specfic authorization we believe the court would have had ample power to act summarily under its broad equitable jurisdiction. We accordingly made the following docket entry:

"9-6-62: It appearing to the Court that an emergency exists . . . and in order to save his life a blood transfusion will become necessary, and it further appearing that . . . Kenneth Clark is a child whose condition is such as to warrant the State in the interest of the child in assuming his guardianship, authorization is hereby given to Dr. James G. Sullivan or other competent member of the medical staff of Mercy Hospital, to administer any and all blood transfusions necessary in the premises, any objection to the contrary notwithstanding. It is further ordered that such child be not removed from said Mercy Hospital without the consent of Dr. James G. Sullivan."

Counsel for the parents promptly protested verbally to the court, and demanded to be heard and to cross-examine the doctors. Accordingly, a hearing was scheduled at an early date and the parents, hospital authorities and attending surgeon were cited.

Now, we have long noted in the reported cases dealing with children's rights, a tendency to identify them with parental rights, i.e., to regard them as identical. This is quite understandable, but not always correct. One doesn't have to work in a family court very long to learn that in countless circumstances a juvenile's rights and interests at many points are at sharp variance with those of his parents. This case clearly promised to be one such, so we entered the following on the court docket:

"9-10-62. It appearing that a conflict of interest may develop between parents and child, John M. Mahoney, Esq. is hereby assigned as legal counsel for the child, Kenneth Clark."

The parents attacked the order . . . authorizing blood transfusions, moving to vacate it on these major grounds:

1. No emergency existed in fact.
2. The order is void because made before the parents were cited to appear.
3. The statute under which it was made is unconstitutional and violates the due process clause of the Fourteenth Amendment.
4. Blood transfusions are dangerous and contrary to good medical practice.
5. Blood transfusions are forbidden by Holy Scripture.

To take up these points in order:

1. The evidence showed that at the moment of the order the child was not at death's door, but that his blood condition had been steadily deteriorating, and if he were allowed to continue without a blood transfusion he might die. The witness James G. Sullivan, M. D., the attending surgeon, testified that he did not then know how long the child could live without a transfusion, but that he "did not propose to find out." Out of consideration for the parents' feelings he postponed giving one until a week after he received authorization, and from that time the deterioration ceased and the child's condition showed steady improvement.

The witness made it clear that whether or not the situation was emergent at the time he sought the court authorization, nevertheless it was pregnant with emergency in that the need for blood might become imperative at any moment, and for the child's sake the attending surgeon did not dare cast himself in the role of a foolish virgin.

This evidence was uncontroverted and therefore the Court finds that an emergency did exist. . . .

3. The complaint that the parents were deprived of "due process" can only mean that they were deprived of life, liberty or property without due process. This imports an unpleasant consideration, to say the least.

There was no syllable of suggestion, much less evidence, that they were deprived of their life or of their liberty. This leaves only their property. What the parents were deprived of was their *claimed* right to deny their child certain treatment which medical science deemed necessary. Would this be a property right? Do the parents *own* their child's body? Is he their *chattel*? (Emphasis added by the court.)

It is true that parents exercise a dominion over their child so mighty and yet so minute as to be sometimes frightening. For example, they determine whether and whom the child may marry . . . ; whether and where he goes to school or college; which, if any, religious faith he may espouse; where he shall live; whether and where he may work, find his recreation, and so on; even whether he wears his rubbers, his pink tie, or she has her hair bobbed. Parents may, within bounds, deprive their child of his liberty and his property.

But there are well-defined limitations upon this appalling power of parent over child. . . . The New York State Children's Bill of Rights lists eleven natural and moral rights with which every child is endowed, and which no person would willingly deny.

No longer can parents virtually exercise the power of life or death over their children. No longer can they put their child of tender years out to work and collect his earnings. They may not abuse their child or contribute to his dependency, neglect, or delinquency. Nor may they abandon him, deny him proper parental care, neglect or refuse to provide him with proper or necessary subsistence, education, medical or surgical care, or other care necessary for his health, morals, or well-being; or neglect or refuse to provide the special care made necessary by his mental condition; or permit him to visit disreputable places or places prohibited by law, or associate with vagrant, vicious, criminal, notorious or immoral persons; or permit him to engage in an occupation prohibited by law or one dangerous to life or limb or injurious to his health or morals. . . . And while they may, under certain circumstances, deprive him of his liberty or his property, under no circumstances, with or without due process, with or without religious sanction, may they deprive him of his *life*!

The evidence was undisputed that blood transfusion was necessary and the best available medical opinion held that to deprive the child of it would have been to risk his life. We hold the parents had no right to subject their child to such a risk, and there could have been no violation of the 14th Amendment; and that Section 2151.33, of the Revised Code, is not unconstitutional, counsel's many citations having no application here.

* * *

. . . Religious doctrines and dogmas, be they obviously sound or curiously dubious, may not control. The parents in this case have a perfect right to worship as they please and believe what they please. They enjoy complete freedom of religion. The parents also have the right to use all lawful means to vindicate this right (and in the present instance they appear to have done their full duty by their religion.)

But this right of theirs ends where somebody else's right begins. Their child is a human being in his own right, with a soul and body of his own. He has rights of his own—the right to live and to grow up without disfigurement.

The child is a citizen of the State. While he "belongs" to his parents, he belongs also to his State. Their rights in him entail many duties. Likewise the fact the child belongs to the State imposes upon the State many duties. Chief among them is the duty to protect his right to live and to grow up with a sound mind in a sound body, and to brook no interference with that right by any person or organization.

When a religious doctrine espoused by the parents threatens to defeat or curtail such a right of their child, the State's duty to step in and preserve the child's right is immediately operative.

To put it another way, when a child's right to live and his parents' religious belief collide, the former is paramount, and the religious doctrine must give way.

The motion to vacate is overruled; the subsisting order may stand until further order. . . .

NOTES

NOTE 1.

STATE v. PERRICONE
37 N.J. 463, 480, 181 A. 2d 751, 761 (1962), *cert. den.*, 371 U.S. 890

SCHETTINO, J.

The question arose at oral argument as to why the trial court felt it necessary to appoint a special guardian for the limited purpose of ordering a blood transfusion rather than directly ordering a transfusion. Probably the trial court was motivated by considerations suggested in *Labrenz*, [411 Ill. 618, 104 N.E.2d 769 (1952)]. There, the chief probation officer of the trial court was appointed and directed to consent to the transfusions. The court retained jurisdiction in case further orders were found necessary. On May 4, 1951 the guardian reported to the court that a transfusion had been administered on April 18, 1951, and that the child's health had greatly improved. The court then ordered the child released from the hospital and returned to her parents. However, it refused to discharge the guardian at that time because it felt that periodic medical examinations might be necessary to determine the need for additional transfusions (and if so the guardian could order them without instituting another suit). We think the court here acted properly in appointing a guardian under the facts presented.

In passing we note that the appointment of a special guardian was not intended to reflect adversely upon appellants' general standing and conduct as parents.

NOTE 2.

Vasectomy or Salpingectomy upon Person under Twenty-one
Code of Virginia § 32-424 (Cum. Supp. 1962)

Any . . . physician or surgeon may perform a vasectomy or salpingectomy upon any person under the age of twenty-one years, provided that the . . . court . . . wherein such minor resides, . . . shall determine that the operation is in the best interest of such minor and society; and further that said infant is afflicted with any hereditary form of mental illness that is recurrent, mental deficiency or epilepsy, and shall enter an order authorizing the physician or surgeon to perform such operation. In any such proceeding, the infant shall be made a party defendant and served with process, a discreet and competent attorney at law shall be appointed as guardian ad litem for such infant to faithfully represent and protect its interest. . . .

[v]

DRINIAN, ROBERT F.

The Rights of Children Whose Parents Are Divorced*

A Massachusetts statute confers on a validly divorced spouse the right to remarry "as if the other (spouse) were dead." Some forgotten legal draftsman a century ago inserted into the law this dramatic phrase suggestive of the revolutionary ideas of free divorce which, for reasons that are still all too obscure, invaded the field of family law in America during the last half of the nineteenth century.

* * *

. . . The law does not say that the children have all the rights they would have if one of the spouses "were dead." On the contrary, the law seeks as its objective the creation and maintenance of those rights for the children of divorced parents which the children would have if no divorce had occurred. In other words, the ex-spouse is to his or her former spouse "dead," but to the children of the marriage neither spouse is, theoretically at least, permitted to be less of a parent than if the marriage had never been dissolved.

. . . Very little settled law can be discovered with respect to the rights of children whose parents have been granted a divorce and the right to remarry. Appellate courts have done little to develop the concept that the child of a broken home must logically be assigned a juridical status with rights of a firm and fixed nature. Beyond the actually useless adage that the interests of the child are paramount, it is difficult to discover in judicial opinions or elsewhere any developed theory on the nature and extent of the rights of children who are left as "half-orphans" by divorce rather than death.

* * *

It may be that divorce, like the death and disabling of fathers, is such a permanent phenomenon of American life that law and society have some obligation to provide by some type of "divorce insurance" for those millions of children who, with seeming inevitability, will be disadvantaged by the divorce of their parents.

The moment, however, that the law admits the inevitability of divorce as well as the impossibility of guaranteeing the rights of children whose fathers are given permission to remarry, new and serious dilemmas emerge. Would the establishment of a tax-supported system to equalize the advantages of the children of divorced parents with those of other children tend to promote even more divorces on the part of spouses who knew

that, upon their divorce, they could rely on some state assistance in connection with the children of the marriage which they desire to dissolve? Furthermore, would recognition by the state that a man should be granted permission to have a second set of children, while being, by the nature of things, excused in part from the support and education of his first set of children, cause a further weakening of the hitherto "absolute" principle that the natural father of children is morally and legally liable for all the expenditures which are necessary for their well-being?

The basic assumption (and fundamental contradiction) of family law in America has been that a father can give substantially equal opportunities to the children of his first marriage while simultaneously extending equal benefits to the offspring of his second (or third) marriage. To state the assumption is to reveal the basic problems it conceals. . . .

* * *

If marriage is a contract, albeit a unique one, can the children of a marriage be said to be its third-party beneficiaries, whose rights are vested and should be protected if a termination of the contract is to be permitted? Probably no one would seriously object to this line of reasoning until some of its consequences become clear. Some of these consequences might be the following:

(1) If a child can be described as a third-party beneficiary of a marriage contract, should the state by means of a guardian or friend of the court, or, as in England, by the King's proctor, represent the interests of the child at the time of a divorce? Such a representative of the child would seek not merely to identify and protect the rights of the child but would secure the fulfillment of these rights by every available means. To guarantee the fulfillment of these rights presupposes that they have priority over the rights of other individuals which arise at a subsequent time. Such priority, however, must be claimed and inserted into a court order if it is to be granted judicial recognition.

(2) If the priority granted to the rights of children whose parents have been granted a divorce is to be given a solid legal foundation, is it not reasonable and logical to establish a financial arrangement which would guarantee the fulfillment of these rights regardless of any and all foreseeable and unforeseeable contingencies? The priority to be granted to these rights could be compared with the lien which the federal government has in certain types of bankruptcy or tax cases; in such cases the claim of the federal government has preference by law over all other claims.

Would it be reasonable therefore for legal

---

* 1962 U. Ill. L. F. 618-19, 624-28 (1962).

machinery to be instituted by which a designated amount or a fixed per cent of a father's income would be assigned by operation of law for the support of his children after their home has been broken by a divorce? Pursuing this same line of reasoning, would it be unreasonable for an attorney representing the children, whose home is about to be broken by divorce, to insist that insurance policies calculated to cover the costs of major medical, dental, and higher educational expenses be underwritten by the father?

In other words, if law and society are convinced and sincere about the existence, validity, and importance of the rights of children, then all children during the time when their parents are negotiating for a divorce deserve to have their case stated and heard by the court which will issue decrees affecting the future of the children's rights in overwhelmingly significant ways. Basic due process means that the rights which are vested in a child by his birth, by the type and quality of the family into which he is born, and by a thousand other factors cannot in justice be disregarded because of the mistakes, selfishness, or even by the exercise of the best judgment of one or both of his parents. If the concept of pre-existing rights means anything, it means that there are certain fixed moral and legal relationships which give rise to inherent expectations, the frustration of which is shocking to everyone's sense of justice.

(3) If the rights of the children of divorce to economic security and to equality of educational opportunity are to be respected, is it unreasonable to suggest that a form of payment from their father be guaranteed to these children by means of a system comparable to the method used in the military to provide for wives a periodic allotment of the salary of their husbands? Although one could question the necessity for such a system in child-support matters, the fact is that the recent adoption by all 50 states of the Uniform Reciprocal Support Act in the unprecedented period of about 10 years still does not prevent thousands of divorced fathers from neglecting their duty to pay for the support of their children by a previous marriage.

*   *   *

If the element of tort is an inherent part of the cause of action for a divorce, can it be reasoned that the children whose parents are separated by the tortious conduct of one of them have some claim to recover as the injured third party hurt in a manner foreseeable to the wrongdoer? Proximate causation is clearly present and no problem about foreseeability exists. The only question is: What is the basis on which to assess the damages?

Several serious difficulties and objections can be advanced to this line of reasoning. In the first place, no father or mother seeking a divorce would concede that his or her "tort" towards a marital partner has even unintentional consequences for the children of the marriage. Indeed, many spouses about to be divorced would claim that it would be an injury to the child *not* to seek or permit a divorce.

However, despite the difficulties in this "tort" theory of marital dissolution, it is undeniable that the law grants a divorce only for the most serious personal injury inflicted by one spouse against another. If such injury gives rise to a cause of action in the adversely affected spouse, can it be denied completely that the children of these spouses would seem to have some derivative right to recover damages on account of the tortious conduct which has terminated for the children an advantageous relational interest?

Drawing out some of the implications of the tort theory of divorce leads to some interesting speculations. Could the child of a marriage be considered to have the status and the rights of an invitee? And, if the child does have this status, is it one which continues after the dissolution of the marriage? Would the presence of such a status bring to the child the right to recover for tortious acts committed long after the divorce by the child's father against the child's mother? Such tortious conduct could quite reasonably be said to injure the child inasmuch as he is not merely the "invitee" of his mother, but a "captive" in the home of the spouse to whom he has been assigned by law.

Admittedly all these hypotheses are doctrines in search of decisional authorities. Concededly some of them may sound novel and not easily deduced from the commonplace phenomenon of a home broken by divorce. But the necessity for some inherent logic with regard to the juridical status and basic rights of the children of divorce may lead appellate courts to develop a line of reasoning based on the notion that divorce action is predicated on a cause of action arising from tortious conduct. . . .

NOTES

NOTE 1.

LEMKIN, RAPHAEL

Orphans of Living Parents: A Comparative Legal and Sociological View*

The integrity of the family being a problem of major public concern, the legislators of various

* Reprinted from a symposium, *Children of Divorced Parents*, Vol. 10, No. 5, pp. 834-54 (Summer 1944), by permission from *Law and Contemporary Problems*, published by the Duke University School of Law, Durham, North Carolina Copyright 1944 by Duke University Press.

countries have taken the attitude that divorce proceedings should not be left to the discretion of the judge and parties alone. The public interest in such matters is believed to call for the participation in such proceedings of the representatives of public or of appropriate private organizations and persons interested in family problems and in the welfare of the children.

In most of the European, and in many of the Latin-American countries, the public prosecutor is a participant in divorce proceedings. He makes recommendations to the judge especially in cases where children are involved. In Austria the court used to appoint for every divorce case a special "protector of the marriage ties" (Eheverbandverteidiger). In England a registrar may direct that separate counsel for children be appointed. In Alberta (Canada) the mayor of the municipality where the child resides, or the Superintendent of Child Welfare can apply summarily to the judge for a maintenance order.

The participation of a public prosecutor is especially effective in some countries in the post-divorce period when the enforcement of the maintenance and custody orders is involved. . . .

The success of the persons representing public interest in the divorce proceedings depends on how much real authority they possess and in particular whether the judge has to listen to their recommendations by fiat of law or as a matter of grace ; and also, whether the judge must treat them as equals or as subordinates. . . .

The position of the child in a family crisis needs to be improved not only through a more efficient system of protection of its economic rights (enforcement of maintenance orders), but also by taking care of its moral right to live in a peaceful family, and to have this family preserved in its unity (conciliation). If, however, a divorce seems to be inevitable then the rights of the child should be most efficiently protected in the court.

[T]o achieve this purpose, some of the existing institutions should be strengthened and some new institutions created.

Specifically, attention is directed to: A family adviser, conciliation procedures, a conciliation council, the family court and a family jury.

The crisis of the family in modern society with all its complexities, conflicts and tensions calls for the creation in every community, and especially in those communities where family courts are located, of an office of a specially trained family adviser. Indeed the problem of the family is too important to leave to persons who would handle it is a part-time job, or who would not have the appropriate knowledge and authority to exercise enough influence upon the family and within the community. The services of the family adviser should be available not only during a period when an actual and grave crisis arises in family life, so as to threaten its disruption by divorce. But he should be ready to act as an adviser and friend of the family, whenever the interested parties call for advice and assistance in marital difficulties. Moreover, he should assist the interested parties in carrying out and enforcing maintenance and custody orders. Especially important would be his role as conciliator in order to prevent divorce.

When the case is actually brought before the family court for divorce the family adviser should act before the judge as representative of the public interest. . . . As representative of the State for the purpose of preserving the unity of the family and the welfare of the children, the family adviser should make his recommendations to the judge. The judge should be obliged to evaluate such recommendations in his decision ; and, if he disagrees with them, the reasons of such disagreement should be given. The brief of the family adviser should be handled by the judge with the same legal consequences as the brief of the counsel of every party.

The family adviser should be an official appointed by the State from among the best trained social workers, with security of tenure. In order to lend more authority to his recommendations he should be made independent from the judge in the same way as the public prosecutor is independent. The family adviser should have a deputy and a staff of assistants including doctors, psychiatrists and experts in sexual hygiene. For practical reasons the services of local clinics may be invoked. As family difficulties necessarily concern both sexes either the family adviser or his deputy should be a woman.

. . . One should not overlook the well-established fact that real progress in law is effectuated not so much by general principles established in substantive law as by the creation of appropriate procedural machinery.

. . . If the parents are in irreconcilable conflict, if they are neglecting the children, if the father deserts the family and leaves it without support, it means that something is wrong in the moral structure of the given family. These problems seem to be mutually interrelated. It is only reasonable to urge that they should be treated in one and the same court which would be called "Family Court." Such a court should also try cases of adoption, because that too is a typical problem connected with the life of the family. By centralizing different family cases in one court it is possible to obtain a higher degree of technical specialization on the part of the judge and also on the part of the court.

NOTE 2.

KUBIE, LAWRENCE S.

Memo on Provisions for Care of Children of Divorced Parents*

I have been giving much thought to the difficult problem which confronts us in trying to make flexible and wise provisions for the care of the children of parents who are separating. The question which confronts us is how to provide for the children's welfare, not just for a week or a month, but over the years, until one by one each comes of age.

The usual legal device is either to award blanket custody to one parent or to the other, or alternating custody, or else to specify shared custody with provisions for visits to the home, or for a part of the year spent in one home and part of the year in another. All such stipulations are rigid and since no one can foresee the future, can have only accidental relationship to the changing emotional needs of children and adolescents as they develop. I wish to suggest a much better device. I am not a lawyer, and my only right to say that this is feasible rests on the fact that it has been used in a large number of separation agreements which have been drawn up by several eminent law firms in this city.

The goal of this plan is to achieve flexibility and to put a premium on the efforts of the parents always to try to reach mutual agreement about anything of importance which has to do with each child's welfare, while at the same time creating a committee to make decisions about any issue on which the parents are unable to agree. This committee is more than an advisory or arbitrating agency. It has the power to act in the event that the parents are deadlocked in a disagreement which they cannot resolve.

The plan is described in a few paragraphs which are incorporated into any separation agreement and subsequently in the divorce papers.

These paragraphs contain several statements: (1) That since the separating parties are unable to maintain an harmonious home, they declare that *they have no rights in the children,* that it is the *children* who have all rights. Each specifically disavows all rights of exclusive custody. (2) They specify further that they agree to attempt to decide together by mutual consultation and conference, either in person or in writing, every question that has a bearing on the welfare of each child (e.g. where the child shall live, and with whom, and for how long, where the child shall go to school, the kind of school, what kind of medical and psychological help the child may have if needed, what kind of vacations to spend, and

where and with whom.) (3) It provides that each child shall have one trusted adult ally, outside of the immediate family, with whom the child can talk in strict confidence. Thus there will always be someone who is in a position to explore the child's reactions to parents, home, and school, for the guidance of any advisors. (4) The parents must specify further that if and whenever they cannot agree, they pledge themselves to accept unconditionally the advice of a committee which they themselves create when they enter into this agreement. They specify the make-up of this committee, secure from the individuals involved their consent to serve, and also give to the members of the committee the right to replace anyone who becomes ill or dies with the consent, preferably not of the two principles but of their legal advisors. It is usual to have such a committee consist of a pediatrician, child psychiatrist, and an educator, impartial lawyer or enlightened clergyman. This committee has nothing to do with the financial guardianship of the children, but only with their spiritual, educational, and psychological welfare and general health. One can be quite detailed in drawing up the list of issues over which the committee will have final say, or one can be very general.

In my experience, only rarely has such a committee had to be called into action. The mere fact that such a committee exists in the background exerts a strong pressure on the two parents to reach agreement between themselves. I have seen parents who have squabbled like fish-wives for years, behave with restraint and generosity under the civilizing influence of this externalized Conscience, which the committee which they have chosen represents. Moreover, once it is called into action, I have never once known its decisions to be rejected by either party.

Lawyers usually ask at this point whether such an agreement would stand up in court. I cannot answer this question because to the best of my knowledge it has never been tested. However, such an agreement is eminently fair and wise, and is concerned not with the vanity, pride or egotism of the parents but with the welfare of the children. Consequently once such an agreement has been entered into, if either party should reject the decisions of a committee which he has created and chosen, he would go into court with a case strongly weighted against him.

NOTE 3.

HILL v. HILL
199 Misc. 1035, 104 N.Y.S. 2d 755 (1951)

VALENTE, JUSTICE.

This is a motion pursuant to Section 1450, Civil Practice Act, to compel arbitration. The petitioner

---

* Unpublished Manuscript, 1959. Printed with permission of the author, who reserves all publication rights.

and the respondent are wife and husband respectively and the parents of the minor children whose custody is the subject matter of the proposed arbitration.

In December 1950, the parents were engaged in a separation action brought by the wife in this court. Incidental to the adjustment and discontinuance of that action the parties entered into a separation agreement which, among other things, provides in paragraph 15: "In the event that either party shall move, or notify the other party of his intention to move, out of the City or State of New York, then upon the failure of the parties to agree between themselves as to the necessity or desirability, or the extent, if any, of resettlement of custody or visitation rights, same shall be arbitrated in accordance with the arbitration agreement hereinafter set forth."

Pursuant to this provision the petitioner notified the respondent of her intention to move to Florida, taking the children with her, and requested the respondent to advise her as to the extent, if any, of resettlement of the custody and visitation provisions of the agreement which he felt to be necessary or proper in view of her contemplated move to Florida. Not being advised of the respondent's feelings in the matter, she served a demand that the question of the necessity or advisability and the extent, if any, of resettlement of custody and visitation rights to be enjoyed by each parent be arbitrated in accordance with the agreement.

The result of such demand may be interpreted reasonably as a refusal by the petitioner to abide by the present custody and visitation provisions of the agreement upon her removal to Florida. She has failed, however, to indicate in what respects she proposed changes to be made.

It will be noted that the parties state expressly in their agreement (par. 10) that "the welfare and interests of the minor children of the parties hereto will best be served by the arrangements herein set forth." It is idle, therefore, for either disputant to argue that a change in such arrangements does not affect the welfare and best interests of these minor children.

Obviously the undertaking of the parties expressed in the agreement is not binding upon this court.

* * *

There may be an ever widening field of usefulness for arbitration in commercial controversies and it may be a practical, efficient and expeditious way to settle a multitude of disputes and disagreements, but as was so aptly stated by the late Mr. Justice McLaughlin in withholding approval from an arbitration award: "* * * Such matters as the custody of a child and the right of visitation are not properly the subject of arbitration, depending for their determination upon a judicial finding as to the best interests of the child." (Waltman v. Waltman, N.Y.L.J.[1] Jan. 15, 1940, p. 22.)

* * *

The petitioner's attorneys concede that any award of the arbitrators would be in no way binding upon the court. Their suggestion that if the respondent were dissatisfied with the award he might then properly avail himself of a petition in equity seems all too flimsy a reason upon which to predicate an order to arbitrate.

* * *

NOTE 4.

AMERICAN ARBITRATION ASSOCIATION
Marital Disputes Arbitration*

The American Arbitration Association is a nonprofit organization which since 1926 has provided orderly and impartial administration of commercial, accident claims and labor disputes, and now handles almost 9000 cases each year. This brief memorandum describes the arbitration of socalled marital disputes which arise between two persons who have been married and who now live apart under a separation agreement. These controversies usually concern some provision in that agreement, and often concern the interests and welfare of their children.

In order to better handle the arbitration of such disputes, now a small but growing part of the AAA case load, the panel of arbitrators capable and qualified to determine such matters is being expanded and improved. This panel contains prominent lawyers, clergymen and other professionals in the field of social service.

Furthermore, the Association is designing streamlined procedures to provide a prompt and private hearing at reasonable cost, as well as an award which is legally valid. The parties are assured of dignified and responsible administration.

A matter may be brought to the AAA either under an arbitration clause in a separation agreement naming the AAA as administrator or by an agreement to submit an existing dispute to arbitration . . . The AAA will appoint a mutually acceptable arbitrator, or a panel of three arbitrators if the parties so desire. If the parties can't agree, the AAA selects an arbitrator from other members of the panel.

. . . The arbitrator fixes the time of the hearing

---

1. No opinion for publication.

* Memorandum Nov. 1963. Reprinted with permission of the American Arbitration Association.

at the convenience of the parties. The arbitrator may grant adjournments but may proceed if a party is deliberately absent. The parties may offer such evidence as they desire and will provide such further evidence as the arbitrator may require. The arbitrator determines the relevancy of testimony. All evidence is taken in the presence of both parties. Under AAA Rules, there may be no communication between the parties and the arbitrator other than at the oral hearing, all communications being directed through the AAA. If the parties wish to compensate the arbitrator, arrangements must be made through the AAA. Many arbitrators are willing to contribute their services.

The administrative cost of providing this service is paid by the parties. Fees are based upon the amount in issue. If the dispute concerns less than $1700, the fee under AAA Rules is $50. Since the AAA is a public service organization, the fee will be reduced in the case of hardship. . . .

The arbitrator must render his award promptly and his award is final. After the arbitrator renders his award, he has no further contact with the parties.

*　　*　　*

NOTE 5.

ROSS v. ROSS
4 Misc. 2d 399, 149 N.Y.S. 2d 585 (1956)

MONTESANO, JUSTICE.

If the parties cannot agree on custody and incidental rights within ten days from the date of this decision, I shall award complete custody to the father subject to visitation rights to the mother starting Friday of each week after dismissal from school and ending the following Sunday evening, and for six weeks during the usual summer school vacation period. . . .

ADMINISTERING REORGANIZED FAMILY RELATIONSHIPS—THE PROBLEM OF BRINGING LITIGATION TO A CLOSE AND ESTABLISHING A MODUS VIVENDI

SPIEGEL, JOHN P.

Homeostatic Mechanisms within the Family

". . . We need to know how to understand the family as a whole, the principles on which it is organized, the bases upon which it maintains its equilibrium, maintains its intactness. Just as the individual has certain processes both at the somatic level and the psychological level whereby he maintains his integrity and his intactness, so, too, the family has processes at work within it which maintain it as a whole, which serve to govern and control conflict, which serve to keep it from falling apart, and which in certain circumstances may also serve to produce disturbance or illness in one member of the family in order to preserve the health or the intactness of the inclusive family. We have found that quite frequently the individual is sacrificed for the sake of the over-all integration of the family. Conversely some individuals are able to establish adequate adjustment only at the expense of some other member or members of the family. We have frequently observed that when a maladjusted family member is helped through medical procedures, some other individual, some other family member, falls ill, as if the process of integration within the family requires that *somebody* be sick. This transmissibility of pathology in the family from one member to another is quite fascinating and needs extensive investigation. It can only be brought into focus if we study the family as a whole. . . ."*

We return to the Lesser "family as a whole" to examine and evaluate the work of the law and lawyers in bringing litigation to a close and establishing a new equilibrium for the family.

---

* Reprinted in Galdston, I., Ed.: *The Family in Contemporary Society*. New York: International Universities Press, 1958 (pp. 74-75). Used with permission of the publisher.

A.

Absolute Divorce—A Final Judgment?

1.

THE LESSERS DECIDE—AN AGREEMENT TO DISAGREE

New York, January 23, 1960

THIS AGREEMENT made between Perry Lesser, residing in the State of New York, hereinafter called "Perry" and sometimes the "Father", and Sadie Lesser, residing in the State of New York, hereinafter called "Sadie" and sometimes the "Mother".

WITNESSETH:

The parties were married on or about the 24th day of March 1934, in the City and State of New York. There has been issue of the marriage, to wit, Dee, twenty (20) years of age, Benjamin, seventeen (17) years of age, and Larry, nine years of age. Heretofore, an action was instituted by Sadie against Perry in the Supreme Court of the State of New York, New York County, which resulted in a judgment of separation in favor of Sadie dated December 15, 1956, which said judgment was thereafter amended on February 16, 1957; further amended on April 5, 1957 and further amended on January 9, 1958. In consequence of the prior disputes and irreconcilable differences and the judgment of separation, the parties have heretofore separated and are now and have for some time been living apart. In view of their intention to live apart, the rest of their lives, and with a view to settling all the differences and litigation between the parties and of settling their property rights and agreeing upon terms for the support of Sadie and the support, education, custody and visitation with respect to Larry, the parties make this agreement intending to settle all differences.

NOW, THEREFORE, in consideration of the promises and the mutual undertakings herein contained, the parties agree as follows:

FIRST: The parties may and shall continue to live apart for the rest of their lives. Each shall be free from interference, direct or indirect, by the other as fully as though unmarried. Each may, for his or her separate benefit, engage in any employment, business or profession he or she may choose.

SECOND: The parties shall not molest or interfere with each other, nor shall either attempt to compel the other to cohabit or dwell with him or her by any means whatsoever.

THIRD: Perry shall pay, during the joint lives of the parties, to Sadie for her support and maintenance, so long as she does not remarry, as follows:

(A) The sum of One Hundred ($100.00) Dollars per week, payable in advance on the first day of each week, commencing with January 1, 1960.

(B) The sum of One Hundred Fifty ($150.00) Dollars per month, on the first day of each month, commencing with January 1, 1960. Such sum of One Hundred Fifty ($150.00) Dollars shall be increased to One Hundred Eighty ($180.00) Dollars per month, beginning at such times as Sadie shall move to a two-bedroom apartment or purchase a one-family dwelling house in which Larry resides with her.

(C) Simultaneously with the execution of this agreement Perry shall pay to Sadie the sum of Three Thousand Five Hundred ($3,500.00) Dollars by certified check, receipt of which is hereby acknowledged. Such payment is in no wise to be considered payment on account of support and maintenance for Sadie or Larry.

FOURTH: The custody of the children is determined as follows:

(A) The Father shall have custody of Dee and Benjamin, subject to the following:
The Mother shall have the right to visit Dee and Benjamin at their place of residence, but the Mother agrees to telephone in advance when she is to visit, and the Mother shall have the right to have them visit and stay overnight at her residence.

(B) The Mother shall have custody of Larry, subject to the following:

(1) The Father shall have full charge of the religious education of Larry and may bring him up in the Orthodox Jewish faith, notwithstanding any different religion which the Mother may have. The Mother agrees that she will not obstruct any such religious education and will not teach the child, directly or indirectly, any other religion.

(2) The Father will, at his own cost and expense, provide the religious education, including school and transportation to and from any school for religious training. The religious training shall be such as is provided by an Orthodox Hebrew School serving the community in which Larry resides.

(3) The Father shall have the right to have Larry with him at his home every third weekend, beginning with the date of the making of this agreement. Such weekends shall begin at sundown on Friday evening and end at sundown on Sunday evening.

(4) The Father shall have the right to have Larry with him on Saturday or Sunday of each week that Larry is not spending the weekend with him. The day shall be determined in the following manner: If Larry receives religious instructions on either Saturday or Sunday, then the balance of such day on which he receives religious instruction shall be spent with the Father. For example, if Larry attends Hebrew School on Sunday, then the Father's visitation rights shall continue for the balance of that Sunday. As a further example, if Larry receives religious instruction on Saturday, then the Father's visitation rights shall continue for the balance of that Saturday. The visitation rights provided for in this subparagraph shall not run two days consecutively. The Father shall have the right to take Larry to the Father's home at any and all times that the Father has visitation rights.

(5) The Father agrees that Larry will be called for and then returned to the home of the Mother at the end of any visitation period.

(6) The Father shall have the right to have Larry on all religious Holy Days required for observance by the Orthodox Jewish faith. For these Holy Days, the Father shall have the right to have Larry visit at the Father's home and stay over for any nights that may be involved. The Holy Days include New Years (two days), Day of Atonement (one day), Feast of Tabernacles (first two days and seventh and eighth days), Passover (first two days and seventh and eighth days) and the Feast of Weeks (two days).

(7) The summer vacations of Larry shall be determined as follows: The Father and Mother shall mutually agree on whether Larry shall go to camp during any or all summers. If Larry does go to camp, then the balance of any summer vacation that Larry may have shall be divided equally between the Father and Mother. If Larry does not go to camp, then his entire summer vacation shall be divided equally between Father and Mother. The determination of whether Larry shall go to camp and the selection of the camp shall be mutually determined, but the cost and expenses incidental thereo shall be paid solely by the Father. Christmas vacation shall be divided equally between the Father and Mother, the Mother having the first half and the Father the second half.

(8) The Father agrees that he will not at any time take Larry for any weekends or overnight stays if the Father is out of town during the period of such visitation right, unless some adult member of the Father's family is present during such period. Dee shall not be considered an adult until she reaches the age of twenty-one (21) years. The parties will agree on other visitation rights in place of any visitation completely missed under this provision.

(9) The Father agrees that at no time will he permit Larry to be transported in an automobile operated by Benjamin during the minority of Benjamin.

(10) Perry agrees that he will at no time enter into the residence of Sadie unannounced, and without telephoning in advance.

(C) The Father shall have complete charge of any medical, dental, surgical or optometric needs or requirements of Larry at his own cost and expense. The Mother agrees that she will follow, at the sole cost and expense of the Father, any medical, dental, surgical or optometric regimen or treatment that may be prescribed by a medical doctor for Larry, and that she will promptly advise the Father of any situation which ordinarily might require any such professional attention or treatment, and that at such times the Father may visit Larry at the Mother's home.

(D) In order that the rights of the parties with respect to visitation as set forth in this agreement may not be impaired, both parties agree that neither Larry nor Benjamin will be taken out of the jurisdiction of the State of New York by either party without the consent of the other, except that Benjamin and Larry may attend any college and that the parties may take the children out of the state for short vacations of not more than one week, but this shall not enlarge the visitation rights of either party.

(E) Both parties agree that they will confer with each other on all important matters pertaining to the children's welfare, health, education and upbringing with a view to arriving at a harmonious policy calculated to promote the childrens' best interest. Each party shall promptly notify the other in case of a child's serious illness while in his or her custody or control.

(F) The Mother agrees that the Father may have Larry confirmed in the Orthodox Jewish faith when he is thirteen (13) years of age, and the Mother agrees that she will not interfere in any manner with such confirmation or the instruction, or ceremonies attendant thereon.

FIFTH: The Father agrees that, until Larry reaches the age of twenty-one (21) years, and is in the legal custody of the Mother, he will pay to the Mother, for the support and maintenance of Larry, the sum of Fifty ($50.00) Dollars per week, payable in advance on the first day of each week, commencing with January 1, 1960, except that, at any time or times during the winter or summer vacations of Larry, that Larry may be at a sleep-away camp or otherwise not at home with the Mother or if he does not go to camp, then during whatever time he spends with the Father, the Father will pay to the Mother the sum of Twenty-five ($25.00) Dollars per week. Such reduction shall only apply to full weeks and not to fractions thereof.

The Father and Mother agree to discuss between themselves and with Larry the desirability of Larry having instruction in cultural or athletic activities (e.g. music, dancing, swimming, horseback riding, etc.) and provided both Father and Mother are in agreement, the Father will pay such costs in addition to the aforesaid support and maintenance. Father and Mother agree that they will discuss between themselves and with Larry the desirability of Larry having college and/or vocational education and they will agree on the choice of any such college and/or vocational education.

During the time Larry is a college or vocational school student, and living and boarding at such college or school, the Father shall be relieved of the obligation to pay the Mother the aforesaid sum of Fifty ($50.00) Dollars per week for the support and maintenance of Larry and instead the parties agree that the support and maintenance of Larry shall be paid as follows:

(A) While Larry lives and boards at such college or vocational school, the Father will pay the tuition, board and lodging, books and all incidental living expenses of Larry.

(B) At such times as Larry shall be with the Mother during winter and summer vacations, or in the event that Larry shall attend a local college or vocational school and shall not live and board at such a college or school and be at home with his Mother, the Father will pay the Mother Fifty ($50.00) Dollars per week.

SIXTH: Perry agrees that he will cause to be delivered to Sadie Two Hundred (200) shares of the common stock of Philip Morris, Ltd. free and clear of all encumbrances.

SEVENTH: Sadie acknowledges that the provisions herein made for her support and maintenance and for the support and maintenance and secular education of Larry and the provisions with respect to supervision of the religious education and medical and other similar needs of Larry, are fair, adequate, reasonable and satisfactory to her. Accordingly, she acknowledges the same in lieu of and in full and final settlement and satisfaction of any and all claims and rights that she may now or hereafter have against Perry for her support and maintenance and for the support, maintenance and education of the children, including Larry, except as may be herein contained.

EIGHTH: The parties agree that a decree shall be submitted to the Supreme Court of the State of New York, embodying the pertinent terms and provisions of this agreement, and that the said decree at the time of submission to the Court for signature and entry shall be accompanied by a stipulation executed by the parties and their respective attorneys, consenting to the entry of said decree without further notice to either party. The decree to be submitted shall be in the form approved and initialed by the parties simultaneously with the execution of this agreement.

NINTH: Except as herein otherwise provided, each party releases the other from any and all claims and demands, up to the date of the execution hereof. It is the intention of the parties that henceforth there shall be as between them only such rights and obligations as are specifically provided in this agreement.

TENTH: Each party hereby waives and releases any and all rights of every kind, nature and description, that he or she may acquire as the surviving spouse of the other in his or her estate, upon his or her death, including (but not by way of limitation) any right to act as Executor or Administrator of the estate of the other, or to participate in the administration thereof; any and all rights in intestacy; any share in the estate of the other upon the death of the other; and any and all rights of election to take against the other's Last Will and Testament under Section 18 of the Decedent's Estate Law of the State of New York, any law amendatory thereof or supplementary or similar thereto, or the same or similar law of any jurisdiction. This provision is intended to and shall serve as a waiver and release of each party's right of election in accordance with the requirements of Section 18 of the Decedent's Estate Law of the State of New York.

ELEVENTH: The parties agree, for the purposes of this agreement, that any ceremony of marriage shall be considered a remarriage, even though any such remarriage may be annulled or otherwise be rendered or declared invalid.

TWELFTH: (A) None of the provisions of this agreement shall be affected by the institution or prosecution by either party of an action for divorce.

(B) The parties consent that this agreement may be incorporated in any decree of divorce, but notwithstanding that any of the provisions of this agreement may hereafter become a part of any decree of divorce, this agreement and all of its terms, shall survive and continue in full force and effect, it being the intention of the parties hereto that this agreement or any of the terms, covenants and conditions hereof, being absolute, unconditional, irrevocable and legally binding upon them and shall not merge in said decree. Neither party shall apply to the Court for a modification of the decree with respect to any of the terms, covenants and conditions of this agreement incorporated in said decree or judgment.

THIRTEENTH: In the event either party shall have obtained an absolute divorce, then Sadie agrees that, following such divorce, she will promptly institute and prosecute, at her own cost and expense, a proceeding for a change of her surname, or will resume her own maiden name or such other name as may be legal for her to use. Sadie agrees that upon the completion of such change of name proceeding or beginning with three (3) months after the date of a final decree of divorce, she will no longer use Perry's name.

FOURTEENTH: Sadie has been represented by counsel in all negotiations in connection with this agreement and the preparation thereof. The counsel fees of Sadie amounting to Two Thousand Five Hundred ($2,500.00) Dollars have been paid simultaneously herewith by Perry to Sadie's attorney. Perry has been similarly represented by counsel.

FIFTEENTH: Each party shall, at any time and from time to time, hereafter take any and all steps and execute, acknowledge and deliver to the other party any and all further instruments and assurances that the other party may reasonably require for the purpose of giving full force and effect to the provisions of this agreement.

SIXTEENTH: No modification or waiver of any of the terms of this agreement shall be valid unless such modification or waiver is in writing and signed by the party against whom enforcement of the change or modification is sought. This agreement cannot be changed orally. No waiver of any breach hereof or default hereunder shall be deemed a waiver of any subsequent breach or default of the same or similar nature.

SEVENTEENTH: Any and all notices given hereunder shall be in writing and shall be sent by registered mail, return receipt requested, as follows:

(a) To Perry Lesser . . .
(b) To Sadie Lesser (or such other name as she may be known by). . . .

EIGHTEENTH: All matters affecting the interpretation of this agreement and the rights of the parties hereto shall be governed by the laws of the State of New York.

NINETEENTH: This agreement constitutes the entire understanding of the parties. It supersedes any and all prior agreements between them. There are no representations or warranties other than those expressly herein set forth.

IN WITNESS WHEREOF, the parties have set their hands and seals this 23 day of January, 1960, in the City of New York, State of New York.

Perry Lesser (L.S.)
Sadie Lesser (L.S.)

2.
THE COURT OF CHIHUAHUA, MEXICO, DECIDES—JANUARY 29, 1960

Poder Judicial del Estado de Chihuahua Copia Certificada de Sentencia de Divorcio

ACTA No. 38428

EL CIUDADANO RODOLFO SILVA, SECRETARIO DEL JUZGADO PRIMERO DE LO CIVIL DEL DISTRITO BRAVOS, ESTADO DE CHIHUAHUA, REPUB-

LICA MEXICANA,—C E R T I F I C A :—Que en el juicio de divorcio necesario promovido por la senora *SADIE LESSER* en contra del senor *PERRY LESSER* obra una resolucion del tenor literal siguiente : — — — —

JUDGMENT.—City of Juarez, Chihuahua, the 24th of January, 1960.

WHEREAS there comes for final judgment the action for absolute divorce instituted by Mrs. SADIE LESSER against Mr. PERRY LESSER (Docket 203 /960) and I T A P-P E A R I N G :— By petition dated in this City today, Mrs. SADIE LESSER, expressly submitting herself to the jurisdiction of this Court, instituted an action for absolute divorce against her husband, Mr. PERRY LESSER, alleging as cause the abandonment from the conjugal domicile for more than three months without justifiable cause on the part of the defendant and the incompatability of characters that exists between both, and showing in addition : That the marriage was contracted the 24th day of March, 1934 in the City and State of New York, United States of North America, as is shown by the testimonial information that was offered ; that of the said marriage there were born three children, DEE, who was born in the year 1938, BENJAMIN, who was born in the year 1942, and LARRY, who was born in the year 1949, of which the minors, DEE and BEN-JAMIN shall remain under the custody of the defendant, the father, and LARRY under the custody of the plaintiff, with the right to the defendant, her husband, and she to visit them, all in accordance with the provisions of paragraph 4, sub-divisions a and b, and sub-paragraphs 1, 2, 3, 4, 5, 6, 7, 8, 9 and 10, and paragraphs c. d. and e. of the separation agreement executed between the parties the 23rd day of January of the current year 1960, and in accordance with paragraph 3, subdivisions a. and b. of the said agreement, the defendant husband shall pay to the plaintiff the sum of $100.00 each week, commencing on the 1st of January, 1960, for her support, plus $150.00 monthly for rent, and the sum of $50.00 each week for the support of the minor son, Larry. She attached a copy of the said separation agreement and prayed that it be approved in all of its parts and provisions, and be incorporated in this judgment by reference, and it be declared that it shall survive it. THE COMPLAINT WAS ADMITTED, ordering that the defendant be notified, and the plaintiff, Mrs. SADIE LESSER, having personally appeared in the Court, accompanied by her attorney, Lic. Luis A. Trias, before the presence of the C. Judge, said : That expressly submitting herself to the jurisdiction of this Court and to the Tribunals of the Mexican Republic, she ratified in each and everyone of its parts her complaint for divorce, and exhibited the certificate of her registration of residence in the Municipal Presidency of this City, thus complying with the order of articles 22, 23 and 24 of the Law of Divorce, and by petition dated today, senor Licenciado Fernando Flores appeared as the duly appointed attorney in fact of the defendant, Mr. PERRY LESSER, and answered the complaint entered against him in his name, admitting it in each and everyone of its parts, alleging that he expressly submitted him to the jurisdiction of this Court and praying for the judgment that is pronounced today, all of the legal requisites having been satisfied. By virtue of the foregoing and based further on articles 1, 2, 10, 21, 37, 43, 44 and 45 of the Law of Divorce stated, let it be decreed: *FIRST*.—There is declared dissolved with all of its legal consequences the marriage contracted by PERRY LESSER with SADIE LESSER the 24th day of March, 1934 in the City and State of New York, United States of North America, leaving both parties in a legal capacity to contract new marriages. *SECOND*.—The minor children of the marriage named DEE, BENJAMIN and LARRY, shall remain in accordance with the provision in the separation agreement executed between the parties the 23rd day of January of the current year 1960, which agreement is approved in all of its parts and provisions and is incorporated in this judgment by reference, and it is declared that it shall survive it. *THIRD*.—There is restored to the plaintiff the name which is: *SADIE GANS*. *FOURTH*.—Let the present judgment be registered, published, and let there be issued to the interested parties the certified copies that they request, and in due time let the record be filed. Thus definitively adjudging the judgment and signature of C. Licenciado Ignacio Martinez Aguayo, Judge of the Court of the First Civil Instance of the District of Bravos.—Attest.—Ignacio Martinez A.—R. Silva.—Signatures. ⸻

IN COMPLIANCE WITH THE ORDER CONTAINED IN THE FOURTH PARAGRAPH OF THE JUDGMENT, THIS COPY IS ISSUED FAITHFUL AND EXACT WITH ITS ORIGINAL, ON THIS USED PAGE FOR THE PLAINTIFF, AND ITS COMPARISON WAS DULY AUTHORIZED AND SIGNED IN THE CITY OF JUAREZ, CHIHUAHUA, MEXICO, THE

TWENTY-NINTH DAY OF THE MONTH OF JANUARY, ONE THOUSAND NINE HUNDRED SIXTY. — ATTEST.

————

THE SECRETARY
/s/ Rodolfo Silva
RODOLFO SILVA

3.

THE NEW YORK COURT DECIDES—

JANUARY 30, 1960

Hon. Samuel M. Gold, Justice: Upon the annexed stipulation dated January 23, 1960, duly signed and acknowledged by the parties hereto and their respective attorneys and upon the agreement dated January 23, 1960, duly signed and acknowledged by the parties hereto, and upon all the proceedings had herein . . . it is

ORDERED, ADJUDGED AND DECREED, that the Judgment of separation dated December 15, 1956 and amended on February 16, 1957, April 7, 1957 and January 9, 1958, all entered and filed herein be further amended and modified so as to include all of the terms and provisions of the Agreement between the parties hereto, dated and acknowledged January 23, 1960, which said Agreement is attached hereto and made part hereof, and it is further

ORDERED, ADJUDGED AND DECREED, that if the terms and conditions of the said Agreement conflict with the Judgment and amendments thereof as heretofore entered herein, the terms and conditions of said Agreement shall prevail.

B.

Appraising the Role and Function of Legislator, Court and Counsel — Two Problems of Divided Loyalty

1.

CONFLICT OF LAWS BETWEEN STATES AND FAMILIES—FULL FAITH AND CREDIT?—A PROBLEM OF PARTY STATUS FOR THE STATE

a. WILLIAMS v. NORTH CAROLINA
325 U.S. 226 (1945)

MR. JUSTICE FRANKFURTER delivered the opinion of the Court.

This case is here to review judgments of the Supreme Court of North Carolina, affirming convictions for bigamous cohabitation, assailed on the ground that full faith and credit, as required by the Constitution of the United States, was not accorded divorces decreed by one of the courts of Nevada. *Williams* v. *North Carolina,* 317 U.S. 287, decided an earlier aspect of the controversy. It was there held that a divorce granted by Nevada, on a finding that one spouse was domiciled in Nevada, must be respected in North Carolina, where Nevada's finding of domicil was not questioned, though the other spouse had neither appeared nor been served with process in Nevada and though recognition of such a divorce offended the policy of North Carolina. The record then before us did not present the question whether North Carolina had the power "to refuse full faith and credit to Nevada divorce decrees be-cause, contrary to the findings of the Nevada court, North Carolina finds that no *bona fide* domicil was acquired in Nevada." *Williams* v. *North Carolina, supra,* at 302. This is the precise issue which has emerged after retrial of the cause following our reversal. . . .

* * *

Under our system of law, judicial power to grant a divorce—jurisdiction, strictly speaking—is founded on domicil. . . . The framers of the Constitution were familiar with this jurisdictional prerequisite, and since 1789 neither this Court nor any other court in the English-speaking world has questioned it. Domicil implies a nexus between person and place of such permanence as to control the creation of legal relations and responsibilities of the utmost significance. The domicil of one spouse within a State gives power to that State, we have held, to dissolve a marriage wheresoever contracted. . . . Divorce, like marriage, is of concern not merely to the immediate parties. It affects personal rights of the deepest significance. It also touches basic interests of society. Since divorce, like marriage, creates a new status, every consideration of policy makes it desirable that the effect should be the same wherever the question arises.

It is one thing to reopen an issue that has been settled after appropriate opportunity to present their contentions has been afforded to all who had an interest in its adjudication. This applies also to jurisdictional questions. After a contest these cannot be relitigated as between the parties. . . . But those not parties to a litigation ought not to be foreclosed by the interested actions of others; especially not a State which is concerned with the vindication of its own social policy and has no means, certainly no effective means, to protect that interest against the selfish action of those outside its borders. The State of domiciliary origin should not be bound by an unfounded, even if not collusive, recital in the record of a court of another State. As to the truth or existence of a fact, like that of domicil, upon which depends the power to exert judicial authority, a State not a party to the exertion of such judicial authority in another State but seriously affected by it has a right, when asserting its own unquestioned authority, to ascertain the truth or existence of that crucial fact.

These considerations of policy are equally applicable whether power was assumed by the court of the first State or claimed after inquiry. This may lead, no doubt, to conflicting determinations of what judicial power is founded upon. Such conflict is inherent in the practical application of the concept of domicil in the context of our federal system. . . .

Although it is now settled that a suit for divorce is not an ordinary adversary proceeding, it does not promote analysis . . . to label divorce proceedings as actions *in rem.* . . . But insofar as a divorce decree partakes of some of the characteristics of a decree *in rem,* it is misleading to say that all the world is party to a proceeding *in rem.* . . . All the world is not party to a divorce proceeding. What is true is that all the world need not be present before a court granting the decree and yet it must be respected by the other forty-seven States provided—and it is a big proviso—the conditions for the exercise of power by the divorce-decreeing court are validly established whenever that judgment is elsewhere called into question. In short, the decree of divorce is a conclusive adjudication of everything except the jurisdictional facts upon which it is founded, and domicil is a jurisdictional fact. To permit the necessary finding of domicil by one State to foreclose all States in the protection of their social institutions would be intolerable.

But to endow each State with controlling authority to nullify the power of a sister State to grant a divorce based upon a finding that one spouse had acquired a new domicil within the divorcing State would, in the proper functioning of our federal system, be equally indefensible. No State court can assume comprehensive attention to the various and potentially conflicting interests that several States may have in the institutional aspects of marriage. The necessary accommodation between the right of one State to safeguard its interest in the family relation of its own people and the power of another State to grant divorces can be left to neither State.

The problem is to reconcile the reciprocal respect to be accorded by the members of the Union to their adjudications with due regard for another most important aspect of our federalism whereby "the domestic relations of husband and wife . . . were matters reserved to the States," . . . and do not belong to the United States. . . . The rights that belong to all the States and the obligations which membership in the Union imposes upon all, are made effective because this Court is open to consider claims, such as this case presents, that the courts of one State have not given the full faith and credit to the judgment of a sister State that is required by Art. IV, § 1 of the Constitution.

But the discharge of this duty does not make of this Court a court of probate and divorce. Neither a rational system of law nor hard practicality calls for our independent determination, in reviewing the judgment of a State court, of that rather elusive relation between person and place which establishes domicil. "It is not for us to retry the facts," . . . The challenged judgment must, however, satisfy our scrutiny that the reciprocal duty of respect owed by the States to one another's adjudications has been fairly discharged, and has not been evaded under the guise of finding an absence of domicil and therefore a want of power in the court rendering the judgment.

What is immediately before us is the judgment of the Supreme Court of North Carolina. We have authority to upset it only if there is want of foundation for the conclusion that that Court reached. The conclusion it reached turns on its finding that the spouses who obtained the Nevada decrees were not domiciled there. The fact that the Nevada court found that they were domiciled there is entitled to respect, and more. The burden of undermining the verity which the Nevada decrees import rests heavily upon the assailant. But simply because the Nevada court found that it had power to award a divorce decree cannot, we have seen, foreclose reexamination by another State. . . .

. . . The judgments of conviction now under review bring before us a record which may be fairly summarized by saying that the petitioners left North Carolina for the purpose of getting divorces from their respective spouses in Nevada and as soon as each had done so and married one another they left Nevada and returned to North Carolina to live there together as man and wife.

Against the charge of bigamous cohabitation under § 14-183 of the North Carolina General Statutes, petitioners stood on their Nevada divorces and offered exemplified copies of the Nevada proceedings. The trial judge charged that the State had the burden of proving beyond a reasonable doubt that (1) each petitioner was lawfully married to one person; (2) thereafter each petitioner contracted a second marriage with another person outside North Carolina; (3) the spouses of petitioners were living at the time of this second marriage; (4) petitioners cohabited with one another in North Carolina after the second marriage. The burden, it was charged, then devolved upon petitioners "to satisfy the trial jury, not beyond a reasonable doubt nor by the greater weight of the evidence, but simply to satisfy" the jury from all the evidence, that petitioners were domiciled in Nevada at the time they obtained their divorces. The court further charged that "the recitation" of *bona fide* domicil in the Nevada decree was "prima facie evidence" sufficient to warrant a finding of domicil in Nevada but not compelling "such an inference." If the jury found, as they were told, that petitioners had domicils in North Carolina and went to Nevada "simply and solely for the purpose of obtaining" divorces, intending to return to North Carolina on obtaining them, they never lost their North Carolina domicils nor acquired new domicils in Nevada. Domicil, the jury was instructed, was that place where a person "has voluntarily fixed his abode . . . not for a mere special or temporary purpose, but with a present intention of making it his home, either permanently or for an indefinite or unlimited length of time."

The scales of justice must not be unfairly weighted by a State when full faith and credit is claimed for a sister-State judgment. But North Carolina has not so dealt with the Nevada decrees. She has not raised unfair barriers to their recognition. North Carolina did not fail in appreciation or application of federal standards of full faith and credit. Appropriate weight was given to the finding of domicil in the Nevada decrees, and that finding was allowed to be overturned only by relevant standards of proof. There is nothing to suggest that the issue was not fairly submitted to the jury and that it was not fairly assessed on cogent evidence.

* * *

If a State cannot foreclose . . . all the other States by its finding that one spouse is domiciled within its bounds, persons may, no doubt, place themselves in situations that create unhappy consequences for them. This is merely one of those untoward results inevitable in a federal system in which regulation of domestic relations has been left with the States and not given to the national authority. But the occasional disregard by any one State of the reciprocal obligations of the forty-eight States to respect the constitutional power of each to deal with domestic relations of those domiciled within its borders is hardly an argument for allowing one State to deprive the other forty-seven States of their constitutional rights. Relevant statistics happily do not justify lurid forebodings that parents without number will disregard the fate of their offspring by being unmindful of the status of dignity to which they are entitled. But, in any event, to the extent that some one State may, for considerations of its own, improperly intrude into domestic relations subject to the authority of the other States, it suffices to suggest that any such indifference by a State to the bond of the Union should be discouraged, not encouraged.

In seeking a decree of divorce outside the State in which he has theretofore maintained his marriage, a person is necessarily involved in the legal situation created by our federal system whereby one State can grant a divorce of validity in other States only if the applicant has a *bona fide* domicil in the State of the court purporting to dissolve a prior legal marriage. The petitioners therefore assumed the risk that this Court would find that North Carolina justifiably concluded that they had not been domiciled in Nevada. Since the divorces which they sought and received in Nevada had no legal validity in North Carolina and their North Carolina spouses were still alive, they subjected themselves to prosecution for bigamous cohabitation under North Carolina law. The legitimate finding of the North Carolina Supreme Court that the petitioners were not in truth domiciled in Nevada was not a contingency against which the petitioners were protected by anything in the Constitution of the United States. A man's fate often depends . . . on far greater risks that he will estimate "rightly, that is, as the jury subsequently estimates it, some matter of degree. If his judgment is wrong, not only may he incur a fine or a short imprisonment, as here; he may incur the penalty of death." *Nash* v. *United States,* 229 U.S. 373, 377. The objection that punishment of a person for an act as a crime when ignorant of the facts making it so, involves a denial of due process of law has more than once been overruled. . . .

Affirmed.

* * *

MR. JUSTICE MURPHY, concurring.

While I join in the opinion of the Court, certain considerations compel me to state more fully my views on the important issues raised by this case.

The State of Nevada has unquestioned authority, consistent with procedural due process, to grant divorces on whatever basis it sees fit to all who meet its statutory requirements. It is entitled, moreover, to give to its divorce decrees absolute and binding finality within the confines of its borders.

But if Nevada's divorce decrees are to be accorded full faith and credit in the courts of her sister states it is essential that Nevada have proper jurisdiction over the divorce proceedings. This means that at least one of the parties to each ex parte proceeding must have a bona fide domicil within Nevada for whatever length of time Nevada may prescribe.

* * *

MR. JUSTICE RUTLEDGE, dissenting.

Once again the ghost of "unitary domicil" returns on its perpetual round, in the guise of "jurisdictional fact," to upset judgments, marriages, divorces, undermine the relations founded upon them, and make this Court the unwilling and uncertain arbiter between the concededly valid laws and decrees of sister states. From *Bell* and *Andrews* to *Davis* to *Haddock* to *Williams* and now back to *Haddock* and *Davis* through *Williams* again—is the maze the Court has travelled in a domiciliary wilderness, only to come out with no settled constitutional policy where one is needed most.

* * *

I agree it is not the Court's business to determine policies of divorce. But precisely its function is to lay the jurisdictional foundations upon which the states' determinations can be made effective, within and without their borders. For in the one case due process, in the other full faith and credit, commands of equal compulsion upon the states and upon us, impose that duty.

I do not think we perform it, we rather abdicate, when we confide the ultimate decision to the states or to their juries. This we do when, for every case that matters, we make their judgment conclusive. It is so in effect when the crucial concept is as variable and amorphous as "domicil," is always a conclusion of "ultimate fact," and can be established only by proof from which, as experience shows, contradictory inferences may be made as strikes the local trier's fancy. The abdication only becomes more obviously explicit when we avowedly confess that the faith and credit due may be determined either way, wherever "it cannot reasonably be claimed that one set of inferences rather than another" could not be drawn concerning the very matter determined by the judgment; and the final choice upon such a balance is left with the local jury.

No more unstable foundation, for state policies or marital relations, could be formulated or applied. In no region of adjudication or legislation is stability more essential for jurisdictional foundations. Beyond abnegating our function, we make instability itself the constitutional policy when the crux is so conceived and pivoted.

* * *

MR. JUSTICE BLACK, dissenting.

Anglo-American law has, until today, steadfastly maintained the principle that before an accused can be convicted of crime, he must be proven guilty beyond a reasonable doubt. These petitioners have been sentenced to prison because they were unable to prove their innocence to the satisfaction of the State of North Carolina. They have been convicted under a statute so uncertain in its application that not even the most learned member of the bar could have advised them in advance as to whether their conduct would violate the law. In reality the petitioners are being deprived of their freedom because the State of Nevada, through its legislature and courts, follows a liberal policy in granting divorces. They had Nevada divorce decrees which authorized them to remarry. Without charge or proof of fraud in obtaining these decrees, and without holding the decrees invalid under Nevada law, this Court affirms a conviction of petitioners, for living together as husband and wife. I cannot reconcile this with the Full Faith and Credit Clause and with Congressional legislation passed pursuant to it.

* * *

Implicit in the majority of the opinions rendered by this and other courts, which, whether designedly or not, have set up obstacles to the procurement of divorces, is the assumption that divorces are an unmitigated evil, and that the law can and should force unwilling persons to live with each other. Others approach the problem as one which can best be met by moral, ethical and religious teachings. Which viewpoint is correct is not our concern. I am confident, however, that today's decision will no more aid in the solution of the problem than the *Dred Scott* decision aided in settling controversies over slavery. This decision, I think, takes the wrong road. Federal courts should have less, not more, to do with divorces. Only when one state refuses to give that faith and credit to a divorce decree which Congress and the Constitution command, should we enter this field.

* * *

NOTES

NOTE 1.

SHERRER v. SHERRER
334 U.S. 343, 344, 349-52, 356, 361 (1947)

MR. CHIEF JUSTICE VINSON delivered the opinion of the Court.

* * *

That the jurisdiction of the Florida court to enter a valid decree of divorce was dependent upon petitioner's domicile in that State is not disputed. This requirement was recognized by the Florida court which rendered the divorce decree, and the principle has been given frequent application in decisions of the State Supreme Court. But whether or not petitioner was domiciled in Florida at the time the divorce was granted was a matter to be resolved by judicial determination. Here, unlike the situation presented in *Williams* v. *North Carolina*, 325 U.S. 226 (1945), the finding of the requisite jurisdictional facts was made in proceedings in which the defendant appeared and participated. The question with which we are confronted, therefore, is whether such a finding made under the circumstances presented by this case may, consistent with the requirements of full faith and credit, be subjected to collateral attack in the courts of a sister State in a suit brought by the defendant in the original proceedings.

* * *

[T]he requirements of full faith and credit bar a defendant from collaterally attacking a divorce decree on jurisdictional grounds in the courts of a sister State where there has been participation by the defendant in the divorce proceedings, where the defendant has been accorded full opportunity to contest the jurisdictional issues, and where the decree is not susceptible to such collateral attack in the courts of the State which rendered the decree.

Applying these principles to this case, we hold that the Massachusetts courts erred in permitting the Florida divorce decree to be subjected to attack on the ground that petitioner was not domiciled in Florida at the time the decree was entered. Respondent participated in the Florida proceedings by entering a general appearance, filing pleadings placing in issue the very matters he sought subsequently to contest in the Massachusetts courts, personally appearing before the Florida court and giving testimony in the case, and by retaining attorneys who represented him throughout the entire proceedings. It has not been contended that respondent was given less than a full opportunity to contest the issue of petitioner's domicile or any other issue relevant to the litigation. . . .

* * *

MR. JUSTICE FRANKFURTER, with whom MR. JUSTICE MURPHY concurs, dissenting.

* * *

Massachusetts says through this statute that a person who enjoys its other institutions but is irked by its laws concerning the severance of the marriage tie, must either move his home to some other State with more congenial laws, or remain and abide by the laws of Massachusetts. He cannot play duck and drakes with the State, by leaving it just long enough to take advantage of a proceeding elsewhere, devised in the interests of a quick divorce, intending all the time to retain Massachusetts as his home, and then return there, resume taking advantage of such of its institutions as he finds congenial but assert his freedom from the restraints of its policies concerning severance of the marriage tie. Massachusetts has a right to define the terms on which it will grant divorces, and to refuse to recognize divorces granted by other States to parties who at the time are still Massachusetts domiciliaries. Has it not also the right to frustrate evasion of its policies by those of its permanent residents who leave the State to change their spouses rather than to change their homes, merely because they go through a lukewarm or feigned contest over jurisdiction?

* * *

NOTE 2.

Uniform Divorce Recognition Act (1948)*

§ 1. . . . A divorce from the bonds of matrimony obtained in another jurisdiction shall be of no force or effect in this state, if both parties to the marriage were domiciled in this state at the time the proceeding for the divorce was commenced.

Comment

[A]n . . . effect upon the existing law "in action" is that the legislative declaration of policy specifically denying recognition to "tourist divorces" may cause seekers after freedom to consider seriously whether they can acquire a valid divorce before setting out on their journey. Certainly, it will prevent any respectable lawyer from advising that they invoke the jurisdiction of an extra-state court without change of domicil.

NOTE

b.   ROSENSTIEL v. ROSENSTIEL
               151 N.Y.L.J. 15 (May 20, 1964)

MR. JUSTICE GREENBERG:

Plaintiff Lewis E. Rosenstiel has invoked the authority of this court to annul the marriage which he entered into on November 30, 1956, in the city and state of New York, with the defendant Susan L. Rosenstiel. This marriage, plaintiff contends, cannot be afforded the legal

---

* 9A U.L.A., pp. 278, 283. Printed with the express permission of the Edward Thompson Company, Brooklyn, New York.

aegis of validity, as a purported Mexican divorce dissolving defendant's prior marriage to one Felix E. Kaufmann must be rejected as a nullity under the laws of New York. . . .

The issue, in essence, therefore, is the effect to be accorded the divorce decree of the Mexican court. The resolution of this issue, in its effect on the fortunes of the defendant and its likely application to others similarly situated, requires the court to approach the disposition with caution, and yet with due regard to its duty and the recognition it must give to the public policy of this state. The unfortunate result in relation to the individual defendant must yield to the law of this jurisdiction. . . .

* * *

. . . In mid-1954 the defendant and her first husband *agreed* in New York, where both had been domiciled since their marriage in 1945, to divorce each other. A New York attorney was engaged. (The defendant in this case claims that the attorney was engaged by her then husband, Kaufmann; Kaufmann in his deposition says that his then wife engaged the attorney; and the Mexican attorney, Mr. de la Torre, called to the stand by defendant, testified that he was retained by the New York attorney acting on behalf of the defendant in this case, the present Mrs. Rosenstiel.) Mr. de la Torre testified, without contradiction, that he was retained to effectuate the planned dissolution of the Kaufmann marriage; he, in turn, selected two resident State of Chihuahua attorneys, one of whom had been recommended by the other, to represent Mrs. Kaufmann and forwarded the necessary documents, including a power of attorney executed by Mrs. Kaufman, to them. Financial compensation for the services was provided by Mr. de la Torre, for both Mexican attorneys resident in Mexico, who had received an all-inclusive fee from the New York attorney.

* * *

Mr. Kaufmann, who planned a trip to the western part of the United States, agreed to be present in Ciudad Juarez in order to obtain the divorce. As he had departed prior to the completion of all arrangements for the divorce, instructions informing him that a Mr. Trias in Ciudad Juarez had been retained as his attorney and that he was to appear at Mr. Trias' office on the morning of October 1, 1954, were forwarded to him by mail. Immediately prior to the fixed date Mr. Kaufmann traveled to El Paso, Texas, and registered at the Del Camino Motel.

On the morning of October 1, 1954, Mr. Kaufman drove by taxi to the International Bridge leading to Ciudad Juarez, walked across the bridge, and then proceeded to his appointment with Mr. Trias. Without any delay, Mr. Trias guided Mr. Kaufmann to what the latter has identified in his testimony as the courthouse. There Mr. Kaufmann was instructed and did sign "some kind of register." Pursuant to further directions, he swore to the accuracy of some document (the complaint), written in Spanish, and signed it, although, in fact, he was not aware of its contents. All of the discussions and transactions were conducted in Spanish, a language with which Mr. Kaufmann professed no familiarity. Within approximately one hour from his arrival in Mexico, Mr. Kaufmann returned to El Paso, Texas. Except for this one-hour presence to transact the foregoing, Mr. Kaufmann had never been in Ciudad Juarez, Mexico, nor has he returned at any subsequent time.

Of critical significance, and defendant does not deny this, at no time in his life did Mr. Kaufmann become a domiciliary of any part of Mexico.

On the following day, the Mexican lawyer, Heber Lopez, appeared on behalf of Mrs. Kaufmann, expressly submitted to the jurisdiction of the court, renounced all other jurisdictions, confessed to the allegations of the complaint and, too, requested the divorce decree. The decree was granted on October 2, 1954, and it is valid in Mexico.

Jurisdiction of the court rendering the decree constitutes the ultimate touchstone for the adoption or rejection of the foreign judgment as a part of the law of New York. "Under our system of law, judicial power to grant a divorce—jurisdiction, strictly speaking—is founded on domicile [citing cases]. . . .

. . . Judgments of . . . foreign countries, we said in Martens v. Martens, 284 N.Y. 363, 365, 31 N.E. 2d 489, 490, 'differ from judgments of course of our Sister States to which, by constitutional mandate, full faith and credit must be given. They must not contravene our public policy.' *Thus, under comity—as contrasted with full faith and credit—our courts have power to deny even prima facie validity to the judgments of foreign countries for policy reasons, despite whatever allegations of jurisdiction may appear on the face of such foreign judgments.* (Emphasis ours.) * * * It is therefore clear that the recognition of a foreign country judgment is far less certain, the judgment itself is far more assailable and vulnerable, than sister State judgments, and is subject to a test of policy. There is thus no significant basis for treating sister State and foreign country divorce judgments as identical in legal effect within this State" (Rosenbaum v. Rosenbaum, supra).

Decisional precedents thus mandate a determination by this court of whether the Mexican court which rendered the Kaufmann divorce decree possessed jurisdiction over the marital res based on domicile.

The decree itself recites in relevant part that, "* * * This court (Mexican) has jurisdiction to decide the present case according to article 22 and 24 of the Law of Divorce, because the plaintiff proved that he is registered in the municipal registry of this city in accordance with the law at the time that he started this suit, and in accordance with article 23 of the same law, because both parties submitted expressly to the jurisdiction of the undersigned judge."

The jurisdictional recital in the decree refers to the three articles of the Divorce Law of the State of Chihuahua which provide: "Article 22. The judge competent to take cognizance of a contested divorce is the one of the place of residence of the plaintiff; and to take cognizance of the one by mutual consent, the one of the residence of either of the spouses. Article 23. Competence may also be fixed by express or tacit submission. Express submission exists when the parties concerned renounce clearly and conclusively that forum which the law accords to them, and designate wtih all precision the judge to whom they submit. Tacit submission exists by the fact that the plaintiff files his complaint, or by the fact that the defendant, after having been summoned in proper form, does not timely raise the lack of competence, or, after having raised it, desists therefrom. Article 24. Residence for purposes of article 22 of the present law shall be proved by the respective certificates of the municipal register of the place."

In arriving at an understanding of the foregoing specific provisions of the Divorce Law of the State of Chihuahua, within the context of the fundamental concepts of the law of that state and of Mexico, this court is indebted to the expert witnesses from that country.

Contrary to our concept of the marital res and jurisdiction predicated upon domicile, submission of the parties to the power of the court constituted the essence and the source of jurisdiction to grant a divorce in the State of Chihuahua. Domicile is superfluous. A marriage may be dissolved by mutual consent, in which case a single petition is presented to the court, or by a "contested" divorce, which later classification comprehends a divorce in which the defendant admits the allegations of the complaint and requests that the decree be granted. The domiciliary state's interest in the marital res upon which our law is based represents an alien concept to the law of the State of Chihuahua. The Divorce Law does not distinguish between "inhabitants" and "tran-

sients." Instead, any "requirement of residence" in the law more closely approaches our doctrine of venue and can be waived by "express" or "tacit submission." Consonant with the Divorce Law of the State of Chihuahua, it cannot be gainsaid that the Kaufmann divorce decree rests upon a jurisdictional recital which *need not* comprehend domicile; consonant with the undisputed facts of the Kaufmann divorce and the uncontroverted conclusions arising therefrom, it cannot be gainsaid that the Kaufmann divorce decree rests upon a jurisdictional recital which *does not* comprehend domicile.

Precedent and policy mandate the rejection of the Kaufmann decree in the State of New York. . . . The Kaufmann divorce decree can be accorded no higher legal status. Nor was the jurisdictional infirmity in the Kaufmann decree cured by the patently collusive arrangement to submit to the power of the State of Chihuahua and to renounce the authority of the state of the marital res, i.e., New York. The defendant and Mr. Kaufmann violated the express interdiction of section 51 of the Domestic Relations Law of New York which forbids any agreement between a husband and wife "to alter or dissolve a marriage". "They violated our statute embodying our public policy * * * Their collusive agreement and conduct may not be the foundation for the creation of any rights. . . .

* * *

The testimony of this case has established that the obtaining of a certificate of residence is a mere formality with no prerequisite that the party be in Mexico for any length of time or state any intention to become a resident. By the standards of Chihuahua the question of domicile was completely irrelevant and therefore the crucial issue is now before this court for decision. It was not adjudicated in the Mexican court and has no binding effect on this jurisdiction.

The situation is aptly summed up, to quote again from Mr. Justice Coleman's decision in the Wood case[*]: "We do not question the power of the court (in Mexico) to take that position with regard to its own citizens and perhaps with respect to those whom it considers as being domiciled there. We do question the power when it concerns our citizens who either by mail or by personal appearance of one party in lieu of mail and by mail by the other party, asked to be treated as though they were citizens or domiciliaries of the foreign country and to have their marital status determined upon request alone. . . ."

[*] 245 N.Y.S. 2d 800.

The conclusion here is irresistible that the Mexican decree in Kaufmann v. Kaufmann has no validity in this jurisdiction and will therefore not be recognized.

. . . The defendant urged upon the court's consideration the argument that by attacking the validity of his purported marriage to the defendant the plaintiff bears the burden of "proving the negatives." . . .

The cases cited by the defendant dealing with negatives are not here pertinent and do not demonstrate an inadequacy in plaintiff's proof with respect to the situation as it existed before, during, and after the Kaufmann marriage. Unfortunately, counsel for the defendant quoted extensively from Surrogate Hildreth's opinion in Matter of Newin's Will (213 N.Y.S. 2d 255) [Suffolk County]); that case was cited as the authority which required plaintiff herein to prove every possible and conceivable fact imaginable before a court of law will declare a marriage null and void. The court was astounded to find that that case, upon which so much reliance was placed by defendant's counsel, was reversed by the Appellate Division (16 App. Div. 2d 436) on the point in question, and this reversal was affirmed by the Court of Appeals (12 N.Y. 2d 824). In fact, the Appellate Division in commenting upon the Surrogate's theory of the presumptions of validity of a marriage and legitimacy of issue adopted the words of Justice Cardozo to the effect that this theory of such presumption is a presumption "gone mad." . . . Accordingly, the court directs judgment in favor of the plaintiff for the relief demanded in the complaint. Settle judgment which shall provide for a hearing with respect to alimony and counsel fee, which the court decrees in its discretion under the circumstances of this case that defendant is entitled to recover.

NOTES

NOTE 1.

ROSENSTIEL v. ROSENSTIEL
152 N.Y.L.J. (Oct. 23, 1964)

BOTEIN, P. J.

[New York policy] was summed up in Matter of Rhinelander (290 N.Y. 31, 36, 37) thus: "It is no part of the public policy of this state to refuse recognition to divorce decrees of foreign states when rendered on the appearance of both parties, even when the parties go from this state to the foreign state for the purpose of obtaining the decree and do obtain it on grounds not recognized here." Since it is common knowledge that the parties, with rare exceptions, return here, the quotation indicates rather plainly New York's indifference, in the juridicial sense, as to whether they achieved

domiciliary status in the foreign state, if both appeared there.

Accordingly, domicile, as distinguished from a visit, has been held to be a jurisdictional requisite where but one spouse enters the foreign country and proceeds ex parte. . . .

The decisions . . . rendered at various times during the past quarter-century . . . reflect impressive and reiterated judicial opinion that recognition of the decree with which this case is concerned would be consistent with New York's public policy. No change in public policy has been identified for us, and it is significant that despite the continuing awareness of those decisions in the field of law and in the community, the Legislature has never sought to limit their doctrine. . . .

The trial court also indicated that Kaufmann and defendant had been guilty of collusion . . . but in our opinion the evidence does not sustain such a finding. . . .

The annulment should be vacated and the injunction action reinstated. . . .

VALENTINE, J. (concurring).

[B]efore the parties went to the license bureau plaintiff arranged to have defendant bring the Mexican divorce decree to his attorney for examination and opinion. Moreover, the parties had the corporation counsel's office approve their respective divorce decrees before a marriage license was issued. After having been married for five and one-half years, plaintiff commenced this action in April, 1962, for an annulment. To grant an annulment herein would, in effect, import into the law a species of marriage terminable at the will of one spouse by the simple expedient of changing his attorney.

*   *   *

I would hold that one who knowingly accepts the benefits of a bilateral-appearance Mexican divorce decree, with awareness of the legal doubts with respect to it, even though not a party to the divorce proceeding, should not thereafter be permitted to change his position and challenge that decree before a court of equity. . . .

NOTE 2.

ROSENBAUM v. ROSENBAUM
309 N.Y. 371, 130 N.E. 2d 902 (1955)

FROESSEL, J.

The issue . . . raised is, simply, whether the drastic remedy of injunction may be employed to restrain the prosecution of a concededly invalid divorce action in a foreign country, namely, Mexico. . . .

The rationale upon which such injunctions have been allowed is as follows: Since the Supreme

Court of the United States, in 1942, decided *Williams* v. *North Carolina* (317 U.S. 287; see, also, 325 U.S. 226), and there overruled *Haddock* v. *Haddock* (76 App. Div. 620, affd. 178 N.Y. 557, affd. 201 U.S. 562), such *sister State* divorces granted to plaintiffs domiciled in such States— provided "the requirements of procedural due process" are met (317 U.S. 303)—are entitled to a presumption of validity under the "full faith and credit" provision of the Federal Constitution (art. IV, § 1). . . .

However, we have never held that any such presumptive legality and validity must be accorded Mexican divorces—which are, of course, beyond the scope of "full faith and credit." [U]nder comity—as contrasted with full faith and credit— our courts have power to deny even prima facie validity to the judgments of foreign countries for policy reasons, despite whatever allegations of jurisdiction may appear on the face of such foreign judgments.

Our Legislature has expressly declined . . . to declare the "effect" of a judgment of a foreign country beyond authorizing our courts to receive such judgment as "evidence" . . . obviously because it recognized that the full faith and credit clause of our Federal Constitution was inapplicable to such judgments. It is therefore clear that the recognition of a foreign country judgment is far less certain, the judgment itself is far more assailable and vulnerable, than sister State judgments, and is subject to a test of policy. There is thus no significant basis for treating sister State and foreign country divorce judgments as identical in legal effect within this State.

In our opinion, the question as to whether an injunction may issue to restrain defendant from prosecuting this Mexican divorce action—a clear legal nullity under the allegations of plaintiff's complaint, and of no more validity than a so-called mail-order divorce, from which we said "no rights of any kind may spring" . . .—is controlled by valid precedent in our court. . . .

* * *

Plaintiff need not go to any foreign jurisdiction. If, in fact, defendant obtains a Mexican divorce and thereupon enters into a subsequent marriage, plaintiff need have no fear for her property rights and marital status under New York law. . . . A simple action for declaratory judgment, when all the facts may be fully developed, is at all times available to her . . . the expenses of which may be assessed against defendant (Civ. Prac. Act, § 1169-a) . . . Since plaintiff thus has an adequate remedy under section 473 of the Civil Practice Act, equity should refrain from granting the drastic relief of injunction.

The orders of the Appellate Division should be reversed. . . .

CONWAY, CH. J. (dissenting). . . .

The relief prayed for is that defendant and his agents and attorneys be permanently and perpetually enjoined from prosecuting the Mexican action for divorce and that he be similarly enjoined *pendente lite*.

It is said that no injunction may issue, that plaintiff need have no fear for her property rights and marital status under New York law, that a simple action for declaratory judgment is at all times available to her and that, under the circumstances, it is an adequate remedy. While we agree that plaintiff may institute a suit for a declaratory judgment should defendant obtain a Mexican divorce, we disagree with the conclusion that it is an adequate remedy or one which excludes the necessity for injunctive relief.

In *Garvin* v. *Garvin* (302 N.Y. 96), this court held that an injunction may be obtained in this State to restrain the prosecution of a divorce action in a sister State, or in a United States possession or territory. The theory of the case is that the spouse who remains in New York should not be required to wait until the foreign court has rendered a decree of divorce and then have to bear the burden of overcoming, in a subsequent declaratory judgment action, the *prima facie effect* of the foreign court's finding of residence by the spouse who appeared in such jurisdiction. . . .

What we intended to point out in the *Garvin* case (*supra*), when we spoke of the prima facie validity of the sister State decree, was the fact that a sister State divorce decree is entitled to a presumption of validity and, once it is procured, the wife "to save her rights as wife, will have to bring a new suit to set aside the foreign decree" . . . Until such time as the wife successfully maintains a collateral attack on the sister State decree by way of a declaratory judgment action, such decree is, for all practical intents and purposes, valid and the procuring spouse may use it to jeopardize the rights of the other spouse.

By permitting the aggrieved spouse to apply for injunctive relief in this State, we also spare her the physical and financial hardship of making a journey to a foreign jurisdiction to present her defense.

We fail to perceive why we should not with more justification afford the same relief to a spouse who is aggrieved as a result of her spouse's going into a *foreign country* to seek a decree of divorce in such country. That will affect her in a greater degree both physically and financially.

. . . We cannot say, therefore, that a Mexican decree of divorce founded upon the domicil of one of the spouses is invalid for lack of jurisdiction. Until a sister State divorce decree is proved to have been rendered by a court lacking jurisdiction it can have an injurious effect on the rights of the nonappearing spouse. It is a voidable decree, i.e., one which is valid until declared invalid. The same must be said of a Mexican decree which recites residence (. . . where there was no claim of residence).

* * *

The grounds . . . for overturning a foreign judgment are the same as those for overturning the judgment of a sister State with the additional qualification that a foreign judgment will not be recognized if it contravenes our public policy. If there is jurisdiction in the foreign court and the judgment does not contravene our public policy such a judgment will be accorded recognition. The burden of proving that such a judgment does contravene our public policy, like the burden of proving lack of jurisdiction, is on the plaintiff, of course. . . .

c.   HARTIGAN v. HARTIGAN
                    272 Ala. 67, 128 So. 2d 725 (1961)

MERRILL, JUSTICE.

Appellant seeks a review of an order vacating an original divorce decree rendered in 1954, which was made by the trial court in 1960 in a proceeding to modify alimony payments included in the original decree. . . .

On July 28, 1954, Helen Hartigan filed a bill for divorce in the circuit court charging her husband, John Hartigan, with voluntary abandonment. She alleged in the complaint that she was a bona fide resident citizen of Birmingham, Jefferson County, Alabama, and had been for more than one year next preceding the filing of the bill, and that the respondent was a resident of Jefferson County, Alabama.

The respondent, appellant in this proceeding, filed an answer and waiver in which he admitted the jurisdictional facts but denied the other material allegations of complainant, and agreed that the case "may be carried forward to its final determination and decree of divorce issued without other notice to respondent." He signed the answer and waiver in the presence of a witness.

An agreement between complainant and respondent, purported to have been signed by both parties on July 28, 1954, was filed with the complaint and answer, under the terms of which, respondent agreed to pay the complainant alimony of $60 per week and retain her as beneficiary of a $5,000 life insurance policy on his life, both conditioned on her remarriage. The complainant prayed that the agreement be incorporated in the divorce decree.

In her deposition, the complainant swore that she was a bona fide resident of Birmingham and had been for more than a year ; . . . A decree of divorce incorporating the property settlement was entered on July 28, 1954.

On June 17, 1960, Hartigan filed a petition in the Circuit Court of Jefferson County praying for a modification of the 1954 divorce decree so as to eliminate the requirement that he pay Mrs. Hartigan alimony of $60 per week. He averred certain financial grounds as changed circumstances.

* * *

The cause was heard before Judge Bailes on July 14, 1960. Both parties were represented by local counsel and, in addition, Mrs. Hartigan was represented by a New York attorney. We quote from Judge Bailes' answer to the petition for mandamus :

"* * * Considerable discussion between the parties took place 'off the record' during the forenoon of July 14th. During the course of this informal conference it became evident to Circuit Judge that neither of the Hartigans had ever been a bona fide resident citizen of Alabama, either before, at the time of, or subsequent to the rendition of the 1954 decree of divorce. At this stage of the off-the-record discussions Mrs. Hartigan's local counsel withdrew from the case. . . ."

* * *

The following facts were then established without objection :

Mrs. Hartigan came to Birmingham by plane from New York on July 28, 1954. She had been driven to the New York airport by Hartigan, who had provided plane tickets for her trip to Birmingham and return. When she arrived in Birmingham, she went to the office of a Birmingham attorney, now deceased, who had been chosen by Hartigan and he was Hartigan's attorney. She signed the complaint, the property settlement agreement and her deposition. After a period of some four or five .hours, she returned to New York by plane. She received a copy of the divorce decree some days later.

Mrs. Hartigan testified that she had never resided in Alabama and had never been in Alabama before July 28, 1954 ; . . . that Hartigan had never lived in Alabama or in the western part of Birmingham ; that her trip to Alabama had been agreed upon between her and her husband in New York ; that she came to Alabama to get the divorce, and that she had been represented by counsel in New York City, who had approved the plans for the Alabama divorce.

On the following day, July 15, 1960, Judge Bailes on his own motion entered a decree setting aside the 1954 final decree of divorce on the ground that it was procured by fraud on the court, was illegal, null and void, and dismissed the petitions of both parties. . . .

* * *

[H]ere, both parties to the divorce action are guilty of fraud. They concocted the fraudulent scheme and perpetrated it on the court together. Then after over five years, they both appear voluntarily, seeking modification or enforcement of the decree which the court had no authority to render in 1954.

Suits for divorce are not ordinary contract cases. Such suits are of a tripartite character, wherein the public occupies in effect the position of a third party, and the court is bound to act for the public in such cases, though the rights of the parties themselves must be fully respected. . . .

* * *

The specific question here presented is whether the Circuit Court of Jefferson County, in Equity, has the power to vacate, of its own motion, the divorce decree rendered by the court in 1954, not void on its face, when in 1960, it is shown in an adversary proceeding between the same parties to modify the decree, and both parties are physically before the court, that the 1954 decree was void because the court did not have jurisdiction of the subject matter.

[J]udicial power to grant a divorce is founded on domicile under our system of law. This is so because domicile in the state gives the court jurisdiction of the marital status or the res or subject matter which the court must have before it in order to act. Jurisdiction of the res is essential because the object of a divorce action is to sever the bonds of matrimony, and unless the marital status is before the court, the court cannot act on that status. Thus, where both parties to a divorce action do not reside within this state, the marriage relation is without the state and jurisdiction cannot be acquired by courts of this state even by consent of the parties. . . .

In Gee v. Gee, 252 Ala. 103, 39 So. 2d 406, 408, it was said . . .: "Therefore, we held that the proviso did not authorize the court in this State to grant a divorce. The parties cannot by consent confer such jurisdiction, nor can the legislature do so by an act, when the res is not within the power of State authorities." . . .

* * *

. . . It has long been recognized that where a judgment or decree is void on its face, the court rendering it has inherent power to vacate it at any time, and such power is not dependent on statute. . . .

But the 1954 decree in the instant case admittedly was not void on its face. . . .

* * *

. . . The parties . . . voluntarily reappeared before the court and made the supervening invalidity apparent on the face of the record.

Under such circumstances, the court correctly vacated the original decree. . . .

We think the court was authorized to vacate the 1954 decree in order to protect the integrity of its judicial proceedings.

Here, the fraud was not perpetrated against the other party, it was solely against the court. Both spouses came from New York, and by joint collusion and fraud obtained a decree of divorce from our court; and then they both had the temerity—after the running of the statute of limitations against perjury—to ask the same court, in the same case, to modify some of the objectionable results of their joint fraud, but to remain blind to the fact that the court never had jurisdiction in the first place.

. . . The public welfare demands that the agencies of public justice be not so impotent that they must always be mute and helpless victims of deception and fraud. . . .

Appellant argues that Mrs. Hartigan has no standing before the court to have set aside a decree of divorce rendered in her favor through her own fraud on the court. . . . Those cases hold that she would be estopped by her own fraudulent conduct. But the principle is inapplicable here. The action complained of here was not the act of Mrs. Hartigan, it was the act of Judge Bailes. . . .

* * *

We come now to the most difficult aspect of this case. While the record proper does not so show, the briefs before us are in agreement that at the present time Mr. Hartigan has remarried and probably has a child by that marriage. This and other states have recognized that a question of public policy is involved. We said in Davis v., Davis, 255 Ala. 488, 51 So. 2d 876, 878:

"As preliminary to the discussion, however, we should like to first refer to the general principle that the humane instincts of civilized society are against supercritical legal technicalities which would bastardize children and when a decree of divorce is rendered, another marriage contracted and children born, it is against public policy to vacate the decree if such an order would render innocent parties guilty of bigamy and their children illegitimate. . . . We therefore must approach a decision of the question with this declared public policy in mind and if the record is susceptible of two interpretations, the burden being on the appellee to establish the invalidity of the prior divorce, as well as the nullity of his own marriage, we will accept the interpretation which would sustain that public policy and the validity of the subsequent marriage, if at all plausible from the recorded proof."

Here, neither of the parties was seeking to establish the invalidity of the prior divorce. The facts showed conclusively that it was void for the want of jurisdiction. And if Hartigan did remarry, and by that marriage does have a child, he had ample opportunity to show it at the hearing or in his application for rehearing. However, as already noted, the setting aside of the original decree was brought about by the action of Hartigan in seeking a modification of the decree.

It is almost universally held that the remarriage of a party to a divorce does not deprive a court of the power to set aside the decree or that, as it is often said, the remarriage is not itself a sufficient reason for refusing to vacate or set aside the decree. . . .

*   *   *

Not only is it conclusive that the 1954 divorce decree was void for want of jurisdiction of the subject matter in Alabama, but it is not entitled to full faith and credit in other jurisdictions.

*   *   *

Affirmed.

NOTES

NOTE 1.

EDITORIAL
New York Divorce Law*

After being a legal resident of New York for more than thirty years, the Governor's wife will become a "resident" of Nevada for six weeks. This legal fiction is mandated by the unrealistic, antiquated New York divorce law, unchanged in its exclusion of all causes save one—adultery—since enactment in 1787. Repeated efforts over the last twenty years to liberalize this law have come to naught; the Legislature refuses even to authorize a commission to study grounds of divorce.

No other state is so blindly restrictive. The result is a general admission, as a grand jury found in 1948, that "widespread fraud, perjury, collusion and connivance" pervade divorce and annulment court actions brought in New York State. This leads to public contempt for all law, for the courts, and casts a reflection on both bench and bar. How much longer will New York allow this iniquitous absurdity to persist?

NOTE 2.

NEW YORK GRAND JURY
Presentment—Fraudulent Matrimonial Actions†

This Grand Jury returned indictments growing out of fraudulent matrimonial actions. These in-

---

* *The New York Times*, 3 Feb. 1962 (p. 20, c. 1). © 1962 by The New York Times Company. Reprinted by permission.
† N.Y. County Court of General Sessions, Mar. 6, 1951.

dictments resulted in the convictions of a number of professional witnesses and the disbarment of two attorneys. Immediately after the first arrests, in November 1948, there was a marked drop in the number of matrimonial actions filed in New York County.

*   *   *

The investigation confirmed what had long been suspected: widespread fraud, perjury, collusion and connivance pervade matrimonial actions of every type. In short, the Grand Jury is of the opinion that the present practices exude a stench and perpetuate a scandal involving the courts and the community.

Moreover, examination of the records of the Supreme Court leads to the conclusion that those charged with the administration of justice in this type of litigation could not have been unaware of these conditions.

The manner in which uncontested matrimonial actions are conducted encourages laxity and the other evils disclosed by this investigation. Cases go through on an assembly line basis, with no consideration of the family problems involved. Much more attention is given to meeting the formal requirements of the law than there is to the social desirability of preserving or of terminating the marriage.

*   *   *

NOTE 3.

ALTON v. ALTON
207 F. 2d 667, 678 (3rd Cir. 1953)
[Judgment vacated, case dismissed as moot, 347 U.S. 610]

HASTIE, CIRCUIT JUDGE (dissenting).

[T]he legislative authority of the Virgin Islands in 1953 amended the divorce statute . . . in two ways. First, proof that the plaintiff in a divorce action has been continuously present in the Virgin Islands for six weeks is now made *prima facie* evidence of that party's domicil in the territory. Second, where personal jurisdiction has been obtained over both spouses the divorce power may be exercised in favor of a complaining spouse who has resided in the territory for six weeks, regardless of domicil. The result of this legislation is to establish alternative bases of divorce jurisdiction, the one predicated upon domicil without regard to personal jurisdiction over the defendant, and the other predicated upon personal jurisdiction over both spouses without regard to domicil. . . .

*   *   *

Here the question is whether an indivdual has acquired a new domicil of choice. Ordinarily to establish the affirmative of that issue it would be necessary to show that the individual in question had come to the place of alleged new domicil and that his presence there was coupled with an intention to make that place his home for an indefinite period. . . .

* * *

. . . English and American judges in recent times have refrained, in the absence of statute, from exercising their divorce power except in cases involving local domiciliaries. But what is it that raises this judicial rule of self-restraint to the status of an invariable Constitutional principle? What makes any legislative effort to establish an alternative basis upon which state power may be exercised in divorce cases a violation of due process of law?

I can find nothing in the history of the present judge-made rule which entitles it to Constitutional sanction. . . .

The common law courts in England had no divorce jurisdiction at the time of the American Revolution and I know of none which was exercised by the courts in the North American British colonies. The English ecclesiastical courts could grant a form of relief analogous to our present separation from bed and board. And Parliament could legislate an absolute divorce, presumably for any subject of the King wherever he might make his home. But it was not until 1857 that the common law courts in England were for the first time given authority to entertain divorce causes. . . .

In the United States our Constitutional scheme placed this power among those relegated to the several states. They began exercising it through their courts in the early days of the nation. A contemporary scholar has suggested, and I have seen no contrary evidence or suggestion, that it was Story, in the 1834 publication of the first edition of his Commentaries on the Conflict of Laws, who first gave currency to and soon won rather general judicial acceptance for the theory that matters of divorce should be left to the place where the spouses made their home. . . . Perhaps this is an oversimplification of history. However, it does seem clear that the rule that divorce jurisdiction will be exercised only by the courts of a state which has a domiciliary connection with the spouses is a creation of nineteenth century American judges. [W]e seem to have the curious chronology of the American courts adopting a rule of practice in the first half of the nineteenth century under the influence of the creative scholarship of a distinguished writer, the British courts adopting this doctrine in the latter half of the nineteenth century, and now in mid-twentieth century, American judges saying that the doctrine is one of those fundamental ideas which must be read into the original provisions of our Constitution. My conclusion is that, on such evidence, as is at hand, the limitation of the divorce power to the domiciliary state has no such ancient roots or impressive history as to suggest its entitlement to perpetuation as a Constitutional requirement.

I do not mean to suggest that pre-revolutionary existence is essential to Constitutional protection of a doctrine. But it does seem to me that when a rule is one of self-limitation which judges have imposed upon themselves in relatively recent times we should not treat it as a Constitutional requirement unless it is very plain that a proposed legislative change would result in a fundamentally arbitrary and unfair way of dealing with men in modern society. Accordingly, I think our real question on this phase of the case is whether it is clearly arbitrary or unfair for a legislature to adopt an alternative for domicil as an appropriate foundation for divorce power.

* * *

I think the soundness of this view is but emphasized if one contests the majority's position on the ground of its own choosing. The court reasons this way: "Because it [marriage] is a matter of public concern, the public, through the state, has an interest both in its formation and in its dissolution, and the state which has that interest is the state of domicile, because that is where the party 'dwelleth and hath its home' ". Accordingly, the court concludes "that adherence to the domiciliary requirement is necessary if our states are really to have control over the domestic relations of their citizens",[*] and that any departure from the domiciliary rule would be a denial of procedural due process. This statement of social justification of a legal rule presupposes a stable and intimate attachment of both spouses to a single community which in fact and alone has a genuine interest in their relationship. But this picture is no longer characteristic of our society or of the conduct of estranged spouses in it. In their activities and their careers men are increasingly mobile. Community attachments tend to be less intimate and less lasting than heretofore. And when the unsettling factor of domestic estrangement is added there is considerable likelihood that the spouses will go their separate ways in different communities. One need not approve these patterns of behavior to recognize what doubt they cast upon the essentiality of a legal rule which must be justified by premising a single community which alone

---

[*] The court continued: "The instant case would be typical. In the Virgin Islands incompatibility of temperament constitutes grounds for divorce. In Connecticut it does not. We take it that it is all very well for the Virgin Islands to provide for whatever matrimonial regime it pleases for people who live there. But the same privilege should be afforded to those who control affairs in Connecticut." *Id.* at 676-77.

and intimately is concerned with each unsuccessful marriage.

Actually, the concept of domicil as a basis of jurisdiction is in practice elusive and very unsatisfactory for several reasons. It is a highly technical concept depending upon the proof of the mental attitude of a person toward a place. Whether in taxation or in divorce, the use of domicil as a jurisdictional base gives trouble when it is applied to people who really have no "home feeling" toward any place or, at the other end of the scale, to those who have more than one home. And, . . . in the divorce field difficulties are multiplied because the estranged spouses so often establish separate homes. Thus, when a court is asked to grant a divorce it very often finds that not one domicil but at least two—potentially more through refinements of the "marital domicil" concept—may be interested in the parties and their relationship. In these all too familiar situations of divided domicil, the jurisdictional requirement which the majority regards as so essential to fairness that it can not be changed is a troublemaker and a potential source of injustice.

d.   MAY v. ANDERSON
                      345 U.S. 528 (1953)

MR. JUSTICE BURTON delivered the opinion of the Court.

The question presented is whether, in a habeas corpus proceeding attacking the right of a mother to retain possession of her minor children, an Ohio court must give full faith and credit to a Wisconsin decree awarding custody of the children to their father when that decree is obtained by the father in an *ex parte* divorce action in a Wisconsin court which had no personal jurisdiction over the mother. For the reasons hereafter stated, our answer is no.

*   *   *

The parties were married in Wisconsin and, until 1947, both were domiciled there. After marital troubles developed, they agreed in December, 1946, that appellant should take their children to Lisbon, Columbiana County, Ohio, and there think over her future course. By New Year's Day, she had decided not to return to Wisconsin and, by telephone, she informed her husband of that decision.

Within a few days he filed suit in Wisconsin, seeking both an absolute divorce and custody of the children. The only service of process upon appellant consisted of the delivery to her personally, in Ohio, of a copy of the Wisconsin summons and petition. Such service is authorized by a Wisconsin statute for use in an action for a divorce

but that statute makes no mention of its availability in a proceeding for the custody of children. Appellant entered no appearance and took no part in this Wisconsin proceeding which produced not only a decree divorcing the parties from the bonds of matrimony but a decree purporting to award the custody of the children to their father, subject to a right of their mother to visit them at reasonable times. Appellant contests only the validity of the decree as to custody. See *Estin* v. *Estin,* 334 U.S. 541, . . . recognizing the divisibility of decrees of divorce from those for payment of alimony.

Armed with a copy of the decree and accompanied by a local police officer, appellee, in Lisbon, Ohio, demanded and obtained the children from their mother. The record does not disclose what took place between 1947 and 1951, except that the children remained with their father in Wisconsin until July 1, 1951, He then brought them back to Lisbon and permitted them to visit their mother. This time, when he demanded their return, she refused to surrender them.

Relying upon the Wisconsin decree, he promptly filed in the Probate Court of Columbiana County, Ohio, the petition for a writ of habeas corpus now before us. Under Ohio procedure that writ tests only the immediate right to possession of the children. It does not open the door for the modification of any prior award of custody on a showing of changed circumstances. Nor is it available as a procedure for settling the future custody of children in the first instance.

*   *   *

Separated as our issue is from that of the future interests of the children, we have before us the elemental question whether a court of a state, where a mother is neither domiciled, resident nor present, may cut off her immediate right to the care, custody, management and companionship of her minor children without having jurisdiction over her *in personam*. Rights far more precious to appellant than property rights will be cut off if she is to be bound by the Wisconsin award of custody.

> [I]t is now too well settled to be open to further dispute that the 'full faith and credit' clause and the act of Congress passed pursuant to it do not entitle a judgment *in personam* to extra-territorial effect if it be made to appear that it was rendered without jurisdiction over the person sought to be bound." *Baker* v. *Baker, Eccles & Co.,* 242 U.S. 394, 401. . . .

In *Estin* v. *Estin* . . . and *Kreiger* v. *Kreiger* . . . this Court upheld the validity of a Nevada divorce obtained *ex parte* by a husband, resident in Nevada, insofar as it dissolved the bonds of matrimony. At the same time, we held Nevada powerless to cut off, in that proceeding, a spouse's right to financial support under the prior decree of another state. In the instant case, we recognize that a mother's right to custody of her children is a personal right entitled to at least as much protection as her right to alimony.

In the instant case, the Ohio courts gave weight to appellee's contention that the Wisconsin award of custody binds appellant because, at the time it was issued, her children had a technical domicile in Wisconsin, although they were neither resident nor present there. We find it unnecessary to determine the children's legal domicile because, even if it be with their father, that does not give Wisconsin, certainly as against Ohio, the personal jurisdiction that it must have in order to deprive their mother of her personal right to their immediate possession.

*   *   *

Reversed and remanded.

MR. JUSTICE FRANKFURTER, concurring.

*   *   *

What is decided—the only thing the Court decides—is that the Full Faith and Credit Clause does not require Ohio, in disposing of the custody of children in Ohio, to accept, in the circumstances before us, the disposition made by Wisconsin. The Ohio Supreme Court felt itself so bound. This Court does not decide that Ohio would be precluded from recognizing, as a matter of local law, the disposition made by the Wisconsin court. For Ohio to give respect to the Wisconsin decree would not offend the Due Process Clause. Ohio is no more precluded from doing so than a court of Ontario or Manitoba would be, were the mother to bring the children into one of these provinces.

Property, personal claims, and even the marriage status . . . generally give rise to interests different from those relevant to the discharge of a State's continuing responsibility to children within her borders. Children have a very special place in life which law should reflect. Legal theories and their phrasing in other cases readily lead to fallacious reasoning if uncritically transferred to determination of a State's duty towards children. There are, of course, adjudications other than those pertaining to children, as for instance decrees of alimony, which may not be definitive even in the decreeing State, let alone binding under the Full Faith and Credit Clause. Interests of a State other than its duty towards children may also prevail over the interest of national unity that underlies the Full Faith and Credit Clause. But the child's welfare in a custody case has such a claim upon the State that its responsibility is obviously not to be foreclosed by a prior adjudication reflecting

another State's discharge of its responsibility at another time. Reliance on opinions regarding out-of-State adjudications of property rights, personal claims or the marital status is bound to confuse analysis when a claim to the custody of children before the courts of one State is based on an award previously made by another State. Whatever light may be had from such opinions, they cannot give conclusive answers.

MR. JUSTICE JACKSON, whom MR. JUSTICE REED joins, dissenting.

The Court apparently is holding that the Federal Constitution prohibits Ohio from recognizing the validity of this Wisconsin divorce decree insofar as it settles custody of the couple's children. In the light of settled and unchallenged precedents of this Court, such a decision can only rest upon the proposition that Wisconsin's courts had no jurisdiction to make such a degree binding upon appellant. . . .

A conclusion that a state must not recognize a judgment of a sister commonwealth involves very different considerations than a conclusion that it must do so. If Wisconsin has rendered a valid judgment, the Constitution not only requires every state to give it full faith and credit, but 28 U.S.C. § 1738, referring to such judicial proceedings, commands that they "shall have the same full faith and credit in every court within the United States and its Territories and Possessions as they have by law or usage in the courts of such State, Territory or Possession from which they are taken." The only escape from obedience lies in a holding that the judgment rendered in Wisconsin, at least as to custody, is void, and entitled to no standing even in Wisconsin. It is void only if it denies due process of law.

The Ohio courts reasoned that although personal jurisdiction over the wife was lacking, domicile of the children in Wisconsin was a sufficient jurisdictional basis to enable Wisconsin to bind all parties interested in their custody. This determination that the children were domiciled in Wisconsin has not been contested either at our bar or below. Therefore, under our precedents, it is conclusive. . . .

*   *   *

I am quite aware that in recent times this Court has been chipping away at the concept of domicile as a connecting factor between the state and the individual to determine rights and obligations. . . .

The Court's decision holds that the state in which a child and one parent are domiciled and which is primarily concerned about his welfare cannot constitutionally adjudicate controversies as to his guardianship. The state's power here is defeated by the absence of the other parent for a period of two months. The convenience of a leave-taking parent is placed above the welfare of the child, but neither party is greatly aided in obtaining a decision. The Wisconsin courts cannot bind the mother, and the Ohio courts cannot bind the father. A state of the law such as this, where possession apparently is not merely nine points of the law but all of them and self-help the ultimate authority, has little to commend it in legal logic or as a principle of order in a federal system.

* * *

The difference between a proceeding involving the status, custody and support of children and one involving adjudication of property rights is too apparent to require elaboration. In the former, courts are no longer concerned primarily with the proprietary claims of the contestants for the *"res"* before the court, but with the welfare of the *"res"* itself. Custody is viewed not with the idea of adjudicating rights *in* the children, as if they were chattels, but rather with the idea of making the best disposition possible for the welfare of the children. To speak of a court's "cutting off" a mother's right to custody of her children, as if it raised problems similar to those involved in "cutting off" her rights in a plot of ground, is to obliterate these obvious distinctions. Personal jurisdiction of all parties to be affected by a proceeding is highly desirable, to make certain that they have had valid notice and opportunity to be heard. But the assumption that it overrides all other considerations and in its absence a state is constitutionally impotent to resolve questions of custody flies in the face of our own cases. The wife's marital ties may be dissolved without personal jurisdiction over her by a state where the husband has a genuine domicile because the concern of that state with the welfare and marital status of its domiciliary is felt to be sufficiently urgent. Certainly the claim of the domiciled parent to relief for himself from the leave-taking parent does not exhaust the power of the state. The claim of children as well as the home-keeping parent to have their status determined with reasonable certainty, and to be free from an incessant tug of war between squabbling parents, is equally urgent.

NOTES

NOTE 1.

SAMPSELL v. SUPERIOR COURT
32 Cal. 2d 763, 197 P. 2d 739 (1948)

TRAYNOR, J. . . .

Several theories have been advanced with respect to the correct basis for jurisdiction over the subject matter of a child custody proceeding. According to one theory jurisdiction over children's custody is based on *in personam* jurisdiction over the children's parents. . . . Another theory regards the question of custody as simply one of status and as such subject to the control of the courts of the state where the child is domiciled. . . . A third theory requires the child to be physically present within the state, on the ground that the basic problem before the court is to determine what the best interest of the child is, and the court most qualified to do so is the one having access to the child. . . .

There is, of course, no question that the courts of a particular state have jurisdiction to determine the child's custody if the court has jurisdiction *in personam* over both parents, and the child is both physically present and domiciled within the state. The court then has a substantial basis for determining not only the rights of the parents but what the best interest of the child is. All the basic elements in each of the foregoing theories are present. Difficulties have been encountered, however, when one or more of these elements are lacking.

It is apparent that each of the foregoing theories, if regarded as exclusive tests of jurisdiction, ignores important considerations underlying the other theories. It would, however, be no solution of the problem to require all these elements to be present before a court could acquire jurisdiction. Unfortunately cases will arise where one or two elements are lacking, and some court must have jurisdiction in the interest of the child to make proper provision for its custody. The principal difficulty with each of the theories as exclusive tests of jurisdiction is the difficulty inherent in any attempt to apply hard and fast rules of res judicata and conflict of laws to the problem of child custody. The principal cases and most of the secondary authorities have been concerned less with the question whether a court has jurisdiction than with the question whether the courts of other states are bound by the particular decision, when that jurisdiction has been exercised. The respective theories are based on the assumption that in order to achieve finality in this matter one court at one given time must have an exclusive right to determine the issue. "From a standpoint of expendiency and of achieving socially desirable ends, there seems to be only one argument in favor of confining jurisdiction to a single state; that it will produce stability and discourage the crossing of state lines to avoid the effect of unpalatable custody decrees." (Stansbury, Custody and Maintenance Law Across State Lines 10 Law and Contemp. Prob. 819, 830.) It is doubtful, however, whether the best interest of the child, the paramount consideration in custody proceedings, is served thereby.

There is authority for the proposition that

courts of two or more states may have concurrent jurisdiction over the custody of a child. . . . In the interest of the child, there is no reason why the state where the child is actually living may not have jurisdiction to act to protect the child's welfare, and there is likewise no reason why other states should not also have jurisdiction. As stated by Justice Cardozo in *Finlay* v. *Finlay,* 240 N.Y. 429, 431 [148 N.E. 624, 40 A.L.R. 937], "The jurisdiction of a State to regulate the custody of infants found within its territory does not depend upon the domicile of the parents. It has its origin in the protection that is due to the incompetent or help- less. . . . For this, the residence of the child suf- fices though the domicile be elsewhere. . . . But the limits of the jurisdiction are suggested by its origin. The residence of the child may not be used as a pretence for the adjudication of the status of parents whose domicile is elsewhere, nor for the definition of parental rights dependent upon status. . . . Parents so situated must settle their controversies at home. Our courts will hold aloof when intervention is unnecessary for the welfare of the child."

Thus, if the child is living in one state but is domiciled in another, the courts of both states may have jurisdiction over the question of its cus- tody. It does not follow, however, that the courts of both states will exercise that jurisdiction and reach conflicting results. The courts of one state may determine that the other state has a more substantial interest in the child and leave the mat- ter to be settled there. On the other hand, if the jurisdiction of one state has been exercised over the child, there is no reason why, if the welfare of the particular child is a matter of real concern to the courts of another state, those courts may not also have jurisdiction, which might be exercised in the interest of the child "with respectful consideration to the prior determination of other courts simi- larly situated." (Stansbury, 10 Law and Contemp. Problems, *supra,* at pp. 830-831. . . .) In any event, there is no reason why courts of one state should not be able to "assume with confidence that the courts of the other jurisdiction will act with wisdom and sincerity in all matters pertaining to the welfare of this child." (*Miller* v. *Schneider,* (Tex. Civ. App.) 170 S.W. 2d 301, 303.)

The problem is not one of rendering custody decrees for the courts of other states to regard as final and conclusive determinations. Indeed such decrees are not given conclusive effect in our own courts, for under Civil Code, section 138, the court granting the decree "may at any time modify or vacate the same." In order to avoid interminable and vexatious litigation it is generally required that before modification or vacation of such a decree "there must be a change of circumstances

arising after the original decree is entered, or at least a showing that facts were unknown to the party urging them at the time of the prior order . . ." (*Olson* v. *Olson,* 95 Cal. App. 594, 597. . . .) Whatever proof may be required for a modification or vacation of a custody decree, it is not a final judgment. . . . As a matter of comity the courts of this state treat valid custody decrees of the courts of sister states with the same respect as custody decrees of California courts. . . . No more or less respect for California decrees is ex- pected from the courts of other states. If the de- crees of California courts with respect to child custody are subject to modification or annulment in this state, they are likewise subject to modifica- tion or annulment in any state having jurisdiction over the subject matter, for such a decree "has no constitutional claim to more conclusive or final effect in the State of the forum than it has in the State where rendered." (*New York* v. *Halvey,* 330 U.S. 610 . . .; see Harper, *Conflict of Laws,* 47 Col. L. Rev. 883, 907-909.)

Since the courts of this state do not finally and conclusively determine custody in a divorce pro- ceeding, there is no reason to attempt to arrive at some basis for jurisdiction that should be ac- cepted as final and conclusive in all states. It is a sufficient basis for jurisdiction that the state "has a substantial interest in the welfare of the child or in the preservation of the family unit of which he is a part . . . and this jurisdiction may exist in two or more states at the same time." (Stansbury, 10 Law and Contemp. Prob. *supra* at 831.)

Since this is a proceeding in mandamus to deter- mine only the question of whether the respondent court has jurisdiction over the subject matter of the custody proceeding, we are not concerned at this time with the question of how the jurisdiction of the respondent court should be exercised or whether under the facts of this case, as they may be determined by the trial court, it would be proper for the trial court to refuse to determine the custody of the minor child in the pending pro- ceeding. It is sufficient that the respondent court has jurisdiction to hear petitioner's application for a custody award. It is likewise immaterial to the determination of this case whether defendant has been awarded custody of the child by a Nevada court. It may be assumed for the purposes of this decision that the temporary presence of the child in Nevada provided a sufficient basis for a custody award and that the decree of the Nevada court was valid to the extent that it determined the child's custody. . . . Such a decree does not de- prive the California courts of jurisdiction over the child . . . for the state of domicile, where the child has lived most of its life, clearly has as substantial an interest in the child's welfare as a state in which the child's presence was merely temporary.

The fact that the child is now living in Utah, where it was taken by defendant sometime after the commencement of the present action, likewise does not deprive the respondent court of jurisdiction over the child's custody. The respondent court acquired jurisdiction over the subject matter of the custody of the child while the child was clearly domiciled within this state. Any subsequent change in the child's abode is relevant only to the determination of how the court's jurisdiction should be exercised with due regard for the welfare and best interest of the child. . . .

NOTE 2.

FORD v. FORD
371 U.S. 187 (1962)

MR. JUSTICE BLACK delivered the opinion of the Court.

* * *

. . . The Full Faith and Credit Clause, if applicable to a custody decree, would require South Carolina to recognize the Virginia order as binding only if a Virginia court would be bound by it. Recognizing this, the South Carolina Supreme Court's opinion was largely devoted to a review of Virginia cases to determine the effect in Virginia of the order of dismissal. The cases relied on by the South Carolina court do hold that the parties to some actions may agree to a dismissal and that in such cases a "dismissed agreed" order is *res judicata* between the parties. All of the Virginia cases discussed by the South Carolina court, however, involved purely private controversies which private litigants can settle, and none involved the custody of children where the public interest is strong. In each case the Virginia dismissals were the result of agreements between the parties equivalent to a compromise intended to settle a cause of action. Whatever the effect given such dismissals where only private interests of parties are involved, cases involving custody of children raise very different considerations. We are of the opinion that Virginia law, which does not treat a contract between the parents as a bar to the court's jurisdiction in custody cases, would similarly not treat as *res judicata* the dismissal in this case.

The Virginia court held no hearings as to the custody of the children. In entering its order of dismissal, the court neither examined the terms of the parents' agreement nor exercised its own judgment of what was best for the children. The court's order meant no more than that the parents had made an agreement between themselves. Virginia law, like that of probably every State in the Union, requires the court to put the child's interest first. . . .

* * *

Unfortunately, experience has shown that the question of custody, so vital to a child's happiness and well-being, frequently cannot be left to the discretion of parents. This is particularly true where, as here, the estrangement of husband and wife beclouds parental judgment with emotion and prejudice. In Virginia, the parents cannot make agreements which will bind courts to decide a custody case one way or the other. . . .

* * *

We hold that the courts of South Carolina were not precluded by the Full Faith and Credit Clause from determining the best interest of these children and entering a decree accordingly. . . .

2.

VISITATION RIGHTS OF PARENTS AND CHILDREN—FULL FAITH AND CREDIT?— A PROBLEM IN THE ADMINISTRATION OF CUSTODY

a.   ANGEL v. ANGEL
      2 Ohio App. 2d 136, 140 N.E. 2d 86 (1956)

BAYNES, JUDGE.

This matter came on to be heard on plaintiff's motion to change visitation rights, each week, from noon Saturday, until Sunday 6 p.m. to Friday when school is dismissed until Saturday 6 p.m., during the school year, and from Friday noon to Saturday 6 p.m., during summer vacation. No contra motion was filed. Plaintiff and defendant offered testimony for and against the motion.

Plaintiff's sole reason for the motion is that he desires the child to be brought up in the Catholic Church. Defendant desires him to be brought up as a Protestant. The child has been attending Sunday School at a Protestant Church and the London Public Schools.

Plaintiff contends that since this court in January 1955 ordered custody to him from defendant, who had been awarded custody in the original decree in April 1950, which custody was reaffirmed during the present term of this Court contra defendant's motion, he has the sole right to decide what religious affiliation the child shall have.

Neither counsel cited any authority for their respective contentions nor alluded to the Ohio Statutes relating to care, custody and control of minor children. This imposes an unfair burden on the Court.

* * *

. . . Four sections of the Revised Code are to be considered in pari materia, establishing the legislative policy and the basis of decison for Courts in cases involving custody and visitation rights. Section 3109.03, R.C., provides:

"When a husband and wife are living separate and apart from each other, or are divorced, . . . they shall stand upon an equality as to the care, custody, and control of such offspring, so far as parenthood is involved."

Section 3105.21, R.C., provides:

". . . the court . . . shall make such order for the disposition, care, and maintenance of the children of the marriage, as is just, and in accordance with section 3109.04. . . ."

The applicable part of Section 3109.04, R.C., provides:

". . . the court shall decide which of them shall have the care, custody, and control of the offspring, taking into account that which would be for their best interest * * *."

The applicable part of Section 3109.05, R.C., provides:

"The court may . . . make any just and reasonable order or decree permitting the parent who is deprived of the care, custody, and control of the children to visit them at such time and under such conditions as the court may direct * * *."

It will be noted that the statutes in each section continuously use the word parent. In legal contemplation "parenthood" is the state or relation of a parent. "Parent", in legal contemplation, is not only the father and mother, that is the male and female who generated the child, but is the one or both of them who still possesses some right to the custody or control of a child, which he, she or they can relinquish.

* * *

[O]ur courts have no authority to direct either the person having custody or the visitation rights . . . to direct or prevent any particular unobjectionable form of worship or lack of worship, Christian or otherwise. On the other hand courts recognize that there is more to religion than the teaching of a moral code of conduct, which, of course, is inherent in all Christian denominations, and perhaps as well in others.

* * *

When it is made to appear that a conflict between divorced parents as to religious instruction is affecting the welfare of their children, a court should always act in accordance with what is best for the happiness and welfare of the child. In legal contemplation the court recognizes no difference in object between religious or other conflicts. As between Christian religions denominational differences are irrelevant and cannot be the basis of decision by the court.

* * *

In the instant case we have twice decided that it was for the welfare of the child that his father have legal custody. On the other hand the welfare of the child also required that his mother have most liberal visitation rights not inconsistent with that welfare.

This in effect designates the domicile of the child to be that of his father who has the primary, but not the exclusive right, especially in the interval that the mother has the child, to determine what is proper for the welfare of the child.

In these adverse circumstances of a "split relationship" the power of the Court is directed solely to making the condition, as it affects the welfare of the child, as harmonious as can be. Harmony is not only the strength and support of all institutions but the strength and support of the individual human being.

Nothing in the record of this case shows that the nine year old boy has been or will be affected by the kind of religious training he has received in the past or will receive in the future. Whether the form of training is single or dual is not of present, or should it be of, concern.

Therefore on the basis of the testimony adduced on this motion the court is of the opinion that visitation rights are to be changed as follows:

1. Defendant shall have visitation rights out of the home of plaintiff each week end from 4 p.m. Friday to 6 p.m. Sunday, except the second week end of the month. December 7th to the 9th is to be taken as the first such week end.

2. During the summer school vacation period defendant is to have the child for two weeks as plaintiff and defendant may arrange.

* * *

b.   LUSTMAN, SEYMOUR L.

Split Custody—A Clinical Evaluation*

Mr. and Mrs. S. approached me for consultation with reference to their twelve-and-a-half year old son, named John. Mrs. S. is a very attractive young woman, who is now married for the second time to Mr. S.—and John is the only child of the first marriage. The history appears to be that of a very unhappy marriage between the boy's real father and mother. Although they were quite interested in each other, they had a marked sexual incompatibility which led to a divorce when the boy was two years of age. Both the mother and the father were quite immature and immediately returned to

---
* Unpublished report printed with permission of the author, who retains reprint rights (1962).

the homes of their own parents, following the divorce.

According to the real parents, the trial judge first made an effort at reconciliation, stressing the importance of the marriage to the child. However, when this failed, he apparently told both parents that he found them individually "quite pleasant people and that it was important for the child to have both a mother and a father." In view of their apparent ease of communication with each other at the time—and quite likely predicated on this spurious or pseudo-maturity—the trial judge granted these parents the split custody of John.

Throughout the early part of this child's life there was a great deal of contact between his now divorced parents. The father made numerous efforts to recement the marriage, which with time became increasingly coercive and threatening to the mother. He made numerous manipulative efforts involving her family, all of which were of increasing distress to the mother. She also felt that the custody of the boy was at stake and lived with some threat (real or imagined) that the father was trying to "get her on a morals charge" and thereby obtain complete custody of the child. It would thus seem quite clear that the interaction—primarily pathological—continued between this man and woman but increasingly used the custody of the child as the arena.

The father finally tired of his attempts to "make a marriage" out of his first marriage and remarried when the boy was six. He moved to another town and now has three children in his second marriage. The mother's mother and father were extremely protective of her and of their grandchild, which persisted up until the age of eight, when she very precipitously married her present husband.

Throughout the period prior to the remarriages, the boy spent one-half of his time with the mother and one-half of his time with the father and their respective parents. The present Mr. S. is a very passive person, who is quite confused and ambivalent about John and about his responsibilities to John. He made one abortive attempt to raise the issue of adoption of John. This went to the same court for discussion.

The judge gave John the choice of saying whether he wanted to be adopted or not. John was then nine years old, was very resentful of this "new daddy" and flatly refused to be adopted by him. He told the judge he preferred things the way they were with one-half of his time going to his mother and one-half of his time to his father. Varying techniques were used around the boy's problem of going to school, including at one time the thought of sending him to a boarding school so that neither parent would have him more than

the other. However, the father relinquished the major portion of time so that the boy spent his academic year with the mother and the remainder with the father.

In spite of their deeply invested manipulations of each other, which continue to date, both mother and father pretend to give John a choice in picking for himself. The mother has the firm belief that as he grows older he will begin to realize what a "despicable person" his father is and side with her. The father has the same belief about the mother. It is important to note around the issue of the judge giving the boy the choice about adoption with the second father, that there was an unusual degree of closeness between the mother and the child prior to her marriage. He slept with her in her bed until the second marriage. It was quite striking to hear this mother, in the presence of her second husband, say that "no one in the world can give me as much pleasure or as much grief as John." The second husband's passivity is blatantly revealed in joint interviews and it is quite obvious that the second husband was viewed as an intruder by the boy. Furthermore, the boy was able to use his real father as a threat against Mr. S.

Around my interviews with Mrs. S., she revealed herself as a person who had a great deal of awareness of her involvement in the problems and a considerable amount of guilt. It became quite clear to her, as well as to myself, that the vividness of her feelings and the resurgance of what she felt were "dead issues" about her former husband were a very great problem to her. In addition, there was a contemptuous attitude toward the present husband. Around this it was possible to make a referral for her for psychiatric treatment.

Briefly, the attempted resolution of the boy's difficulties was the establishment of two warring families—who constantly struggled and manipulated for control of him and his feelings—with very superficial attempts at maintaining non-prejudicial attitudes toward each other. The boy had thus two of everything, and his divided loyalties were astonishing. He also seemed to have been caught up in a very competitive "give away" in which both sets of grandparents vied with each other to gain his favor and thereby to demonstrate to him the inadequacy of the other family.

The child, in this atmosphere of pampering, ambivalence, and confusion, developed a number of "smart alecky" and grasping, selfish attitudes. These were equally disturbing to both households and both blamed on the other. He was enuretic until two years prior to consultation.

Although it is quite clear that the mother was seeking help for herself, she had very real concerns for the child which motivated her seeking consultation. She and Mr. S. have three children of their own—the last having been born six months ago. The mother had then to return to the hospital for a hemorrhoidectomy. In her absence, the boy on four separate occasions, took her automobile and drove it around the city. On several of these occasions he took other children with him and was caught when he drove the car into a ditch. There were several quite interesting features in this behavior—one being that the characteristic way the mother has of dealing with excessive tension is to "throw her hands up," leave the house and go for a drive. The other is that this boy, only twelve-and-a-half, learned to drive some years ago when he visited his real father in another state. This father has repeatedly promised the boy that he would give him a car for his birthday.

There are other incidents in his recent play of a disturbing nature to his parents. His sexual curiosity has increased with adolescence and he has taken to enticing several girls (one his age, one ten) into the house and has either stripped them or played doctor with them. This is particularly disturbing to the mother who was irately informed of this over the phone by the parents of the children involved.

The issue of his split custody is by now part of the boy's manipulation. For example, he flatly refused to see me, saying that he didn't have to do what his mother said unless his father agreed. It was only after his real father agreed to consultation that he permitted himself to be brought in against his will.

He was a very attractive, somewhat pampered looking child, who flatly refused to come up from the waiting room and who refused to talk with me. He attempted a bravado and an aura of strength, defying me to try to make him leave the waiting room. It was impossible to talk with him in the waiting room and I finally told him that it was easier for him to look like he was angry, but that he was one of the most frightened boys I had ever seen. This seemed to startle him and after this he agreed to come to my office but saying he would never come back again.

While upstairs, I reviewed his problems with him, trying to let him know that I knew he was in trouble and finally at the end of the hour I told him I thought he was old enough to decide for himself whether he wanted to see me or not but that I was going to give him an appointment because I wanted to see him and I knew he was in enough trouble to need help. I subsequently learned that shortly before this second appointment he went to his mother and said he thought he should come to see me. The evaluation consisted of four interviews and in each of these he presented his major conflict as being one of

divided loyalties and confusions toward the two family situation in which he finds himself. Since he was a baseball fan, I interpreted to him as if he was a boy who rooted for the Yankees in the American League and the Dodgers in the National League and then suddenly found they were playing each other in the World Series. He seemed to understand this very well and then quite clearly defined his problem of overwhelming inability to cope with the demands of these two families. The straw that broke the camel's back appeared to be the planning around his "bar-mitzvah" celebration. Both parents and both sets of grandparents were heavily invested in attempting to insist that this celebration take place in their own homes and in their own synagogues. Once again each parent, while vying for the child's presence, gave him the impression that he had a choice in this. This manipulating went on during the course of the evaluation and the increased tension was evident in another incident at home. The second youngest infant of Mrs. S. apparently swallowed or was fed some paint thinner and John is reputed to have saved his life by calling the mother. The baby had to be taken to the hospital, have his stomach pumped out, and then developed a chemical pneumonitis which required hospitalization. I subsequently learned from the mother that this might have been John's fault and that she held a suspicion of his having done this to the baby. Around this he was able to tell me about his tremendous confusion with all the half brothers and half sisters he has and how this is obviously fed into by the two conflicting households. It seems apparent that even the children are involved in this competitive relationship and John's rivalry with his half siblings is one of incredible intensity.

The situation became much worse at home with the approaching date of the decision about the birthday party and with the boy relying more and more on the manipulative aspects of pitting one family against the other. The reality result of this was fostered by the parents in the sense that they were in constant communication with each other via telephone, superficially attempting to make decisions about the boy.

The primary result of the consultation was that the boy accepted and became quite deeply invested in longing for help and was thus referred for treatment. The mother also was referred for treatment.

This case seems to illustrate several psychological problems involving the law. One was the entire issue of split custody; two, the inability of the judge either during the divorce or subsequently around the question of adoption, to evaluate the interview he had with the child or the information he had about the child; three, the needs of the child differ with his development; and four, the fact that decisions made at one time—while they may be adequate for that period—by remaining unalterable during the time that every other aspect of the situation alters, become untenable.

NOTES

NOTE 1.

FRAZIER, BRENDA
My Debut—A Horror*

How could my mother possibly succeed. . . ? Her marriage to my father failed after two years and was ended by divorce after three more years. After that I had two homes, in theory; in fact, I had none. My mother and father fought over my custody, but I never felt that either of them really wanted me except as a symbol of victory. I felt rejected on all sides, unloved, alone in a frightening world. To add to my young confusion, I learned in my father's home that his family would not even speak to my mother; and in my mother's home I was told that my father was a cad who got drunk when I was born and disappeared for two days, even though my mother nearly died in childbirth. My parents could not even agree on what to call me. My full name was Brenda Diana Duff Frazier, but in my mother's house I was called Brenda, and in my father's house I was called Diana.

When I was 9, I had to go to court to testify, in most carefully rehearsed words, that I wanted to live with my mother; and after that I saw my father only occasionally at the apartment in which he lived in New York City. The visits, on which my governesses reluctantly and somewhat indignantly took me, were stiff and awkward. When my father sent me toys as presents, my mother assured me that I really didn't like them. When he sent me clothing, it was put away as unsuitable for a girl my age. At times when I felt affectionate toward him, I felt guilty toward my mother. When I clung to my mother, I felt guilty toward my father. I had two parents, in two different homes, yet psychologically I was an orphan.

NOTE 2.

HEHMAN v. HEHMAN
13 Misc. 2d 318, 178 N.Y.S. 2d 328 (1958)

J. IRWIN SHAPIRO, Acting Supreme Court Justice.

This is a motion by the defendant husband to punish the plaintiff wife "as and for contempt of court for her failure to permit the defendant the right to visit with the infant John Henry Hehman on each and every Sunday for the purpose of

* *Life*, Vol. 55, No. 23 (December 6, 1963), pp. 136-137. Reprinted with permission of the author.

attending to the religious education of said infant."

* * *

Defendant avers that plaintiff has surreptitiously been taking their son John to the St. Gerard Roman Catholic Church and . . . that this conduct of plaintiff is in violation of a pre-nuptial understanding that their elder son Kenneth was to be raised in the Catholic Church and that John was to be raised in the Lutheran Church.

* * *

[T]his court, mindful of the interest of the infant John, must bear in mind the day-to-day realities of his existence. He is in constant contact with his brother and sister; they live in the same home. They are Catholic; he is not. They are presumably engrossed, to the extent that children can be, with the teachings and worship of their creed; so is he, or at least has been, with similar facets of Lutheranism. But in this tiny society of three siblings, he is outnumbered. In addition, their mother is Catholic. This court does not say that numbers, any more than might, make right, nor does it hold that God is on the side of the mightiest legions. "In my Father's house are many mansions," says the Gospel of St. John, but we must be realistic and recognize that diversity of religious outlook and practice is frequently an abrasive factor among adults, *who certainly should know better.* How much more then can it be so among children? This is truly visiting the sins of the fathers upon the children. If each religion may claim validity in the development of one's personality, the achieving of a sense of responsibility to society, and the formulation of a satisfying, uplifting and inspiring conception of Almighty God, then reason dictates little difference whether these three children were *originally* brought up as Catholics or Lutherans—*except that two are now Catholic. From this point of view, this should no longer be a home divided against itself, and John should clasp hands with his mother and brother and sister before the same altar.*

There remains, however, one consideration: John may not wish to become a Catholic. To require him to adopt that creed may seem logical, under the circumstances of this case, but since the welfare of the court's ward is paramount, John cannot be *forced* to enter a religion against his wishes. John may wish to *remain* in the religion of his father despite his mother, brother and sister. That would be his right as an inhabitant of this country. . . . He has been made acquainted with both credal points of view and forms of worship, and with the heart of a child he may speed directly to what is truth for him more quickly and accurately than we adults whose lives and actions, like Hamlet, are "sicklied o'er with the pale cast of thought."

* * *

It is the court's decision that the choice of John Henry Hehman's religion should be left to him and that such choice should be ascertained under circumstances and safeguards that will make certain that it is his wish, and not alone that of either parent, that the court is carrying out.

Submit order.

NOTE 3.

POPE v. POPE
267 S.W. 2d 340 (Mo. App. 1954)

HOUSER, COMMISSIONER.

Motion to modify the custody provisions of a divorce decree. The original decree entered in October, 1950 granted the wife a divorce and awarded her the custody of the two children, a girl then aged 7 weeks and a boy 7 years old, together with the right to remove the children to Butte, Montana, reserving to the father the right to see and visit the children at reasonable times and to have the boy for a period not exceeding two months in the summer. In April, 1953 the mother filed a motion to modify so as to secure the custody of the boy from 9 o'clock a.m. to 1 o'clock p.m. on each Sunday during the two-month period, on the ground of changed conditions in that she has moved back to St. Louis; that the religious faiths of the parents differ and that during the two-month period the father has been taking the boy to the father's church and refusing to allow the boy to attend the church of the mother's faith; that the boy is upset by the conflict and that it is to the best interest of the child that he attend one church, the church of the mother's faith, throughout the entire year. Upon a hearing the circuit court made the order of modification as prayed, and the father has appealed.

* * *

[D]uring the last seven years of their marriage defendant did not attend church at all. The parties could not agree on the church to which their son should be sent. Plaintiff refused to permit the boy to attend the father's church although plaintiff testified that defendant never suggested that he be sent to his church. The boy was baptized in the faith of the mother, but the father would not permit him to attend that church. The child apparently was the innocent victim of the strong conviction on the part of each of the contending parents that the child should not be reared in the church of the other parent, each of them seemingly preferring that the child have no religious contacts than to be raised in any church other

than his very own. As a result of the disagreement the boy did not attend any church. . . .

Following the divorce plaintiff sent her son to her own church regularly. . . . In May, 1952 defendant remarried, joined the church attended by his new wife, and commenced taking an active part in the work of that church. At the beginning of his 1952 visit with his father the boy stated that his mother had asked him to talk to his father about the church he was to attend. Father and son had a rather lengthy discussion on the subject. According to the father, the boy expressed the view that at present he was unable to decide to which church he wished to belong during his adult life; that he wished to suspend judgment on that subject until he got a little older and that he was quite willing to go with his father to the church the father and his then wife were attending. That was the only occasion the boy discussed the subject of religious instruction with his father.

It was plaintiff's opinion that it would be for the best welfare for the boy to attend the same church all the time. . . . Defendant testified that he was not willing to send the boy to the church of the mother's faith while he had custody in the summer although he was not objecting to the boy's attending her church at other times, but that if the boy had asked to be taken to her church he would have taken him. He stated that the boy did not request to be taken to any church nor did he object to the church to which his father took him. Plaintiff testified that she wanted the custody of the boy during the Sunday morning hours "because it is church hours at that particular time." She conceded that there was no real reason why the boy could not go to church without her "if he were shown where to go, and were given advantage."

* * *

Upon the record presented plaintiff failed to show any change of condition affecting the child's best interest and welfare warranting the modification which was made.

* * *

. . . The problem is not a new factor in the relationship of the parties . . . and we find no change of conditions which makes it any more of a problem now than it was then. . . . Conceivably a parental dispute over religion might be waged in such a manner as to create in the mind of the innocent victim a deep-seated religious conflict which eventually would affect, or threaten to affect, the child's mental health. In such an event the court should intervene for the protection of the child's health. But that is not the situation here, so far as this record discloses. Plaintiff gave brief testimony, in seven words, that "There is a conflict in his mind." She did not explain or enlarge on this bare statement except to give her opinion that the question becomes increasingly important as the child grows older. She did not testify to any facts from which it might be inferred that it is a serious conflict, or that his welfare has been adversely affected thereby. She gave no testimony whatever that his general demeanor, attitude, school work, appetite, health or outlook has been affected one iota by the so-called conflict in his mind. Her testimony was wholly uncorroborated. No church, school, medical or psychiatric authorities, nor any of the boy's associates, in or out of school, appeared in support of this charge. Plaintiff's opinion was nullified by her further testimony that the child is a "fine, big, healthy boy—a nice boy—who weighs about eighty pounds and is almost five feet tall," ten years of age and apparently "a thinking, rather precocious child, with a good understanding."

NOTE 4.

FREUD, ANNA

Introduction to Psychoanalysis for Teachers*

. . . When the parents are separated and each parent tries to win over the child to his or her side and to represent the other as the guilty party, then the entire emotional development of the child suffers. His confiidence is shattered by his critical powers being too early awakened. I will quote to you here the judgment of an eight-year-old boy who made vain efforts to bring his parents together again. He said: "If my father does not love my mother, then my mother does not love my father, then they can't like me. Then I don't want them. And then the whole family is no good." The consequences which such a child deduces from the position of affairs are generally serious. He acts like an employee in a bankrupt firm who has lost all confidence in his principals and no longer therefore feels any pleasure in his work. Thus the child in such circumstances stops work—that is, his normal development is checked and he reacts to the abnormal conditions in some abnormal way.

NOTE 5.

TIGHE v. MOORE
151 So. 2d 910 (Miss. 1961)
Cert. den. 375 U.S. 921 (1963)

KYLE, JUSTICE.

* * *

On July 2, 1962, the appellee, Mrs. Lou Frissell (Tighe) Moore, the mother of the two children,

---

* London: George Allen and Unwin, 1949 (pp. 35-36). Reprinted by permission of the publisher.

filed her petition in the chancery court, in Cause No. 55,727, asking that the court modify the decree of December 28, 1960, relating to the visitation rights of the appellant. In her petition the petitioner alleged that there had been a material change in circumstances of the parties since the rendition of the agreed decree of December 28, 1960; that soon after the decree was entered she realized that the visitation arrangement established by the terms of the decree was harmful and injurious to the children, and that after waiting eighteen months she realized that the visitation arrangement set forth in the agreed decree was impracticable and unworkable. The petitioner alleged that the children during the last eighteen months had made many and lasting friends in their neighborhood; that the children had arrived at the age when they could visit in the homes of their little friends during the week ends and have their little friends visit in their homes; and it was not to the best interest of the children that they should be required to leave their home and friends practically every week end during the school year.

The petitioner further alleged that, because of the unreasonable and impracticable visitation schedule set out in the decree, the children did not have a sense of permanency in their home and had not been able to enjoy their association with their mother during the week ends, thus depriving them of the pleasure and enjoyment of having a mother to do with them and for them the little things that they would treasure for the rest of their lives; and that because of the confusion created by the visitation provided for in the decree, the children had become uncertain and emotionally unstable. The petitioner further alleged that the material changes in circumstances mentioned above were due in part to the fact that the children were older, and that it was for the best interest of the children that the former decree be modified. . . .

The respondent . . . denied that there had been a material change in the circumstances of the parties since the rendition of the decree [and] averred that the decree had been agreed to and signed by the petitioner and her attorney after every provision therein had been submitted to and discussed with her . . . .

. . . The chancellor found that there had been a material change in the circumstances . . . and that the best interest of the children and the parties would be served, if the decree . . . were modified.

* * *

We think there is no merit in the appellant's contention that he was denied a fair and impartial hearing on the petition for modification of the agreed decree of December 28, 1960. It is true that the court, at the beginning of the hearing, expressed disapproval of the schedule of visitation set forth in the agreed decree, which the court described as "the most complicated and the most intricate system of visitation that I have ever seen," and "not for the best interest of these children," and that the court also said: "I don't intend to hear much testimony on this in defense of this agreed decree by virtue of the fact that it was agreed to." But, notwithstanding the remarks made by the court, it appears from the record that we have before us that the court granted a full hearing to the parties on the issues presented by the pleadings. The hearing consumed several hours, and the testimony of the appellant and the appellant's witnesses cover more than one hundred pages of the 236-page transcript of testimony that we have before us. The chancellor was not disqualified from hearing the case. No request was made by the appellant's attorney that the chancellor recuse himself, or that the case be transferred to another division and be heard by another chancellor. The record does not reflect any personal bias of the trial court toward the appellant.

* * *

. . . The question which the chancellor was called upon to decide was whether or not the circumstances and surroundings of the children at the time of the hearing on the petition to modify the agreed decree were such as to require a change in the schedule of visitation established by that decree.

The evidence shows that at the time of the rendition of the agreed decree Lynn Adelaide was seven years of age and that Bowman Stirling was 5½ years of age. During much of the time since the separation of their parents in April 1959 the children had been deprived of the benefits of a fixed place of residence and a stable family life. For a period of ten months next preceding the date of the agreed decree the children had lived with their mother in the home of their mother's parents in Little Rock, Arkansas. After their mother's second marriage they returned to Jackson and moved into a new home. Both of the children had reached school age and during the next succeeding eighteen months the children made new friends among the school children of their own ages and other children in the neighborhood; and at the time of the hearing of the petition for modification of the agreed decree the children had become accustomed to a stable family life and a friendly association with other children at home and on the play grounds. The testimony was conflicting on the issue as to whether the children were upset by the enforced observance of the

terms of the agreed decree, and whether the visitation arrangement provided for was detrimental to the best interests of the children. . . .

From the testimony as a whole we think the chancellor had a right to conclude that the children had reached the age when it was not to their best interest that their custody be shifted from one home to another during each week and through the school year. . . .

The fact that the decree of December 28, 1960, was agreed to by the appellant and the appellee at the time the decree was entered did not preclude the court from subsequently modifying the decree when at a later date, after a hearing, it appeared to the court to be detrimental to the welfare of the children. . . .

* * *

We find no reversible error. . . .

NOTE 6.

DAVIS v. DAVIS
255 Ala. 488, 51 So. 2d 876 (1951)

SIMPSON, JUSTICE.

. . . The trial court thought that alternating the custody from one to the other each week would be proper. But to our minds this method would be very deleterious to the stability of the child's home surroundings. We think an award on a more permanent basis would be better. As stated, the child is of tender years (two) and the presumption is that she would fare better in the care of her mother and in her mother's home. . . .

NOTE 7.

RADFORD v. MATCZUK
223 Md. 679, 164 A.2d 904 (1960)

HORNEY, JUDGE.

* * *

In essence, the mother relies on five factors which she contends indicate that the best interests of the child requires that the father be barred from further access to the child. These are (1) that the father was the "guilty" party in the original divorce; (2) that the father was convicted of a serious criminal offense; (3) that the child has declared a desire not to see or know his father; (4) that the father did not attempt to enforce his visitation rights until adoption by the stepfather was contemplated; and (5) that the father has in effect abandoned his right to visit the child because of his complete lack of interest in either visiting him or contributing in any way to his support.

The first part of the mother's contention is clearly without merit. . . .

The second part of the contention is like unto

the first in that there is nothing in the record to even indicate that the father continued to live a life of crime after his conviction more than a decade ago for stealing.

The third circumstance in the contention—the desire of the child—even if it has merit, is not controlling. It is true, of course, that the desire of an intelligent child, who has reached the age of discretion, should be given some consideration in determining custody, but even in a custody case the wish is not controlling. . . . In this visitation rights case, where the father has asked only that he be allowed to see his son at reasonable times, and where the child has not seen or known his father nor had an opportunity to make an independent choice based on something more than what had been imparted to him by others, we think the wishes of the child should be given slight, if any, consideration. A choice based on emotions inspired by one parent is no choice at all and need not be honored by a court. . . .

The fourth element of the contention—the long delay in seeking further access—besides being devoid of substantial merit, may be susceptible of another explanation than the one seemingly attributed to it by the mother. Instead of being motivated by spite or some manner of obstructionism, as she seems to believe, it may well be that the request to consent to adoption shocked the father into a realization that he was in danger of losing his visitation rights unless he did something about it. In any event, there is nothing in the record to suggest that his motives were improper.

The fifth and final factor of the contention—that the father has abandoned his right to see the child—is the antithesis of the second contention of the father that his failure to assert sooner his rights of visitation does not bar him now unless he is presently unfit to associate with the child.

* * *

. . . We fully appreciate the efforts of the mother and her present husband to build a secure future for the child, and we can understand their misgivings over the results the visits of the father may engender. We think it is clear, however under the law and on the record, that the father cannot be deprived of the right to see his son.

We hold that the provisions allowing the father to visit his son should not have been stricken from the divorce decree. For that reason we must reverse the order . . . and remand the case for the entry of an order allowing the father reasonable access to the child upon such terms as the chancellor may prescribe. In so doing, he can decide whether the visits should take place in the homes of the relatives of the father or in the home of the mother and stepfather of the child as well as the frequency and duration of such visits.

NOTE 8.

COMMONWEALTH v. BRADLEY
171 Pa. Super. 587, 91 A. 2d 379 (1952)

RHODES, PRESIDENT JUDGE.

. . . When respondent was asked during the hearing why she objected to permitting relator to have the children over night, she stated: "Several reasons. I thought they were too young * * * I felt, staying away would be harmful to their physical and mental health, and * * * since Mr. Bachman admitted his homosexual tendencies to me, I always had that feeling that they would be exposed to his associates."

While relator denied respondent's statement, it is difficult to reconcile such a denial with his own testimony: "I told Mrs. Bradley, that I was as much homo-erotic as I was hetero-erotic. * * * I told her I was bi-erotic; that I was as much attracted to male friendships as I was to female friendships, * * *" There is much evidence in the record which would warrant the conclusion that relator's propensities were abnormal and his conduct immoral. A convicted sodomist, formerly in relator's employ, testified that he had relations with him on four occasions. There is also testimony of indecent assaults made by relator on three different persons, the last in 1948. Relator went on frequent business and pleasure trips, and letters written by and to him indicate that he made numerous casual acquaintances. The uninhibited tenor of these letters, which were introduced in evidence, suggests illicit relations with those of his own sex and affairs with the opposite sex; they reveal a decidedly erotic engrossment. However, there is no evidence that he allowed his propensities to be known to his children.

* * *

Custody of children is not a property right of a parent, and an agreement as to the custody of a child is voidable and may be set aside in the best interest of the child. . . . As we have so frequently said, in cases of this type, the prime consideration is the best interest and welfare of the child, including his physical, intellectual, moral and spiritual well-being, . . . and that minor children, being wards of the state, may be taken from their parents when their welfare so requires. . . .

. . . Therefore, the custody of the children shall be committed to the respondent, and she may grant the relator such limited visitation as she deems to be in the best interest of the children.

NOTE 9.

JONES, EVE
The Intelligent Parent's Guide to Raising Children*

. . . A divorce means that for some time your family has been the center of discord violent enough to make you believe there is no longer any good basis for a continued marriage. Your child probably has suffered, no matter what his age. He has felt confused and unsure of himself, unable to feel a firm tie to each of his parents. After the divorce, he may feel even more unsure. It's that situation of divided and unsure loyalties which causes most of the emotional disturbance in a child after a divorce.

No child can grow up healthily without having the opportunity to form a solid identification with close adults of each sex. So if your divorce results in your child's being stranded away from the possibility of having a continuing relationship with his father (I'm taking the most common situation following divorce), you need to alter this situation.

Whatever the arguments between you and your husband might have been, unless he has been judged criminally unfit to associate with the child, you need to promote visits between him and his child. This calls for a lot of determination on your part, as well as for an agreement with your husband. You may never use your child as a sop to your ego, haranguing him about the faults of your former husband, ridiculing him for his feelings of loyalty to his father, jealously questioning him about what he's done on his visits with his father, etc. These sorts of activities force him to divide his loyalties; they make him repudiate his identification with his father. They lead him to feel guilty about himself.

If, instead, you have agreed on frequent visits —every other weekend, for example—and you then cooperate willingly and without comment, permitting your child his privacy to form his relationship to his father, many of the most disastrous effects of divorce can be ameliorated.

I'm firmly convinced that every woman who has divorced should consult a psychotherapist, for her feelings about herself absolutely must have been disturbed by the failure of her marriage. These emotions, projected onto the child, cause him a lot more difficulty than does the absence of his father for 12 days out of every 14. Once you have acknowledged to yourself all the experience which has led to the failure of your marriage, if you have accepted your own confusions, have sorted them out—in short, if you truly have learned from

your experience—then your child will be in no worse position than the child of a traveling salesman who only gets home twice a month. And such sorting out of self is easier if a trained worker is helping you.

* * *

If your divorce has not been the result of some neurotic impulse, if your husband really is as unnice as you believe him to be, your child needs to learn this himself. Obviously, if the facts are so damaging that your child is prevented, by court order, from knowing his father, the situation is different. But if the real truth is that your husband just has different values, ones which society at large doesn't condemn, it won't hurt your child to learn about them. He'll be hurt only if you try to make him keep from experiencing and judging these values for himself. That's why the cardinal rule is "hands off" from any critical or evaluative comments about his visits and his father. If you are honest and consistent about this, you'll be learning something about tolerance at the same time that you're permitting your child to make the best of a bad bargain.

NOTE 10.

R. v. R. and I.
[1961] 3 All E.R. 461

In this case the husband sought an injunction to restrain the wife from allowing a letter written by her and dated July 4th, 1961, to be handed to R., their son.

The parties were married in 1944 and in 1948 the husband obtained a decree absolute of divorce on the ground of the wife's adultery. The husband was granted the custody of the child, R., who was then about three years of age. R. was brought up by the husband and his second wife. . . .

SCARMAN, J. . . .

In my judgment, the court has jurisdiction to intervene for the simple reason that this application arises out of the matters of custody of and access to this child of the family. It cannot be doubted that, should the court think fit, it can deny a parent access to its child, and it cannot be doubted in my judgment that in a suitable case, and in support of that denial of access, it can enjoin a parent from writing to her child. Here there is no difficulty in enforcing the court's order because of the steps very properly taken by the wife's solicitors; and, in my judgment, there is no difficulty in the matter of jurisdiction because the court is being asked to act in a matter which arises out of the problems of custody of, and access to, a child over whom the court has jurisdiction.

I take the view, therefore, that the court has

---

* New York: The Free Press of Glencoe, 1959, pp. 217-219. Reprinted by permission of the publisher.

jurisdiction to interfere if it thinks it just or convenient so to do . . . As to the justice of the matter, I have read the letter and I think it a most disturbing and unhappy letter to send to a boy of his age and antecedents. I have every sympathy with the wife in desiring to put her point of view forcefully to the boy and it is plain that the boy is probably already of an age, or certainly will soon be of an age, at which he can receive the strong meat of a parent's forcefully put point of view. This letter, however, goes beyond anything which could reasonably in the circumstances be addressed to this boy by his mother at this juncture.

I, therefore, think that this is a case in which the order of the court should go addressed to the mother and in the terms in which it is sought—namely, enjoining her from allowing her letter of July 4 to be handed to the boy. . . .

NOTE 11.

THURMAN v. THURMAN
73 Id. 122, 245 P. 2d 810 (1952)

THOMAS, JUSTICE

The best welfare of minor children is promoted by having such children respect and love both parents. This is natural and every effort should be directed to the end that such respect and affection will not be destroyed and alienated; any other course is not in the interest of and for the best welfare of such minor children. Since the rendition of the decree modifying the original decree and giving custody to the father, the evidence shows beyond doubt and without question that circumstances have arisen since such date and within the short period of three weeks and became more intense and pronounced thereafter, in which the affections of the children for their mother had been almost completely alienated; this change affects the welfare of these children of tender years.

The acts and conduct of the custodial parent, resulting in the alienation of the love and affection which children naturally have for the other parent, is a vital and very serious detriment to the welfare of such children and is grounds for modification of the decree with respect to such custody. . . .

NOTE 12.

COLEMAN v. COLEMAN
386 P. 2d 811 (Ore. 1963)

ROSSMAN, JUSTICE.

The trial judge who gave careful consideration to the evidence, at its conclusion rendered his decision orally. He stated in part:

"* * * The next question, of course, the most far-reaching and the most important question here, and it concerns the custody of the children. The plaintiff has admitted, of course, that the defendant is a fit and proper mother for the children. The plaintiff has conceded the fact that the mother should have the custody of the 17-month-old-daughter. And I think rightly so. So I do grant to the defendant the sole care, custody, and control of her 17-month-old daughter. It is an extremely difficult decision to reach concerning the [3-year-old] son. It does appear that the son has been with his father for some months. That there is a great deal of affection toward the son by the father, and also, I might add, a great deal of a mother's affection toward her son, also, by the defendant. But it does appear that the father is a fit and proper person to have the custody of the son and I want it clearly understood that I am not finding the mother unfit, in any way, to have the custody of the son. She is also a fit and proper person. But I do feel that the father, at the present time, is better able to offer his son a home. He's going to have the son out on the ranch working with him. The testimony was that his father is a top ranch hand, drawing top pay, and he can teach his son the ranching trade. So I am going to grant to the plaintiff the sole care, custody, and control of this minor son. Now, there has been a prayer here in the Complaint concerning splitting custody during the Summer months. I am not going to do that at the present time. Both of you parties are adults and, certainly, you should be able to work out between yourselves the visitation rights that your children should have with the other party. And there is no reason why this Court should step into that matter of visitation rights nor of how many months the daughter should be with the father during the summertime or the son should be with the mother in the summertime. You two should be able to work that out. * * * I did very seriously consider the advisability of keeping the brother and the sister together in the same home. Of course, it did appear to the court that the 17-month-old daughter would have the benefit of her two half-sisters in the home. It did seem that the brother would be better off with the father. Now, I will grant to the defendant the sum of $50.00 per month as assistance in the supporting of her minor daughter. That will be paid, of course, by the father. * * *"

Gonyea v. Gonyea, 232 Or. 367, 375 P2d 808, declared, as have many other decisions, that in situations such as this the welfare of the children is of paramount importance. In determining that issue this court has access, generally, to nothing concerning the parties except the silent, unspeaking record. The record displays no warmth or feeling. None of its words has more color than any other. When judged solely by her testimony, the shrew may be a better wife than a sainted mother and make a good husband appear to be a failure. The record rarely reveals anything of the parties except the words they employ while testifying. A moment in the courtroom such as the trial judge experienced is a superior index to the truth than the transcript of what the witnesses said. We do not know even so unimportant a fact as the age of either the plaintiff or the defendant. Each has been married before. The defendant is the mother of two other children—each being born in a different marriage. The plaintiff also had a previous venture in matrimony. His employer, as a witness, spoke in terms of high commendation of the plaintiff as an employee and as a man. The employer's wife will take care of the boy, Ronnie, while the plaintiff is at work. The employer's wife is the mother of a little daughter and is a former school teacher. That arrangement appears to be very suitable.

In instances such as this where people have married, become parents, and then have entered the divorce court it is rarely possible for a court to do justice for the parties and their children.

*   *   *

NOTE 13.

JONES v. JONES
67 N.M. 414; 356 P. 2d 231, 235 (1960)

MOISE, JUSTICE.

[T]he complaint is to the effect that the court has indirectly made it impossible for plaintiff to leave Chama, a small town where she can't find employment, on pain of forfeiting her custody of the children. . . .

It is apparent from the court's remarks at the close of the hearing that his order concerning joint custody, and requiring that the children remain in Chama, was to permit them to have their father's care and direction as well as their mother's and that the children's welfare was uppermost in his mind. This was the primary concern of the trial court, as it should be . . . . Also, although, to our minds placing restraints upon a person's free movement is a questionable practice generally, nevertheless where a court in its discretion and in the best interests of the children concludes, that they should be reared where guidance can be had from the father while living with the mother, we can not reverse unless the conclusion is a manifest abuse of discretion under the evidence in the case. . . .

PART FIVE

IN SEARCH OF FUNCTIONAL
DEFINITIONS OF FAMILY

T his Part portrays the "family" as perceived by decisionmakers from many different vantage points and by observers from many disciplines.

Before returning to an examination and evaluation of the impact of past and subsequent decisions on the growth and development of the Lesser family, we pause to search for definitions of the family in functional terms and to identify the values in issue for decisionmakers in the family law process. There are many definitions of family. Each depends upon individual and societal values and goals. To settle on a single, constant, and authoritative definition would arbitrarily restrict the inquiry, for it would obscure reasons which might have been crucial in determining whether and to what extent the state should have a role in establishing, administering, and reorganizing family relationships. But "family" must be explicitly defined in each decision and commentary, for we must always know and force ourselves to ask: "Family for what purpose and from whose vantage point?"

In integrating, yet in separating the concepts of "family" as viewed by specialists from many specialties, we are responding to the observation that lawyers be "specialists . . . in being unspecialized."[1] And we join Karl Mannheim in asking: "To what degree and at what later stage of the investigation is the reality which has been divided up for purposes of specialization, recombined and re-integrated?"[2] We are guided by his view that "(m)odern specialization in scientific work follows two lines. First that of subject-matter, and secondly that of method. Specialization of subject is a self-evident necessity. A single investigator cannot occupy himself with every possible phase of social life. In this sense we must give our assent when one investigator concerns himself with the family, or, specializing still further, with the family at given

---

1. Llewellyn, K. N. "The Common Law Tradition: Deciding Appeals," 1960 (p. 263).
2. Mannheim, Karl, *Man and Society*. London: Routledge & Kegan Paul Ltd., 1946 (p. 171). Reprinted with permission of Routledge & Kegan Paul Ltd. and Harcourt, Brace & World, Inc.

period or of a given social class; another with constitutions, and so on. This specialization will not do any harm as long as one remembers that one is dealing with fragments of a larger context.

". . . We do not examine every fragmentary aspect of the situation which confronts us; we consider the situation according to abstract principles, which when logically carried out, lead to the creation of the so-called 'pure spheres'. One studies, for instance, the family in its different manifestations from a political, [a legal,] an economic, an educational, a biological, or a psychological point of view and on the basis of this abstraction, homogeneous fields are set up in which only political, [legal] economic, educational, biological, or psychological aspects emerge. This type of specialization does not so much deal with fragments as cross-sections of the whole and it is clear cut and consistent when it carries through its abstractions with unambiguously defined concepts. This way of cutting out a cross-section of the total context which arises from the necessities of the division of labour, is admissible and highly fruitful as long as it is not forgotten that we are dealing only with fragments, cross-sections, and spheres of reality."[3]

A.

An Introduction to the Family as a Subject for Analysis — From the Past and into the Present

1.

THE NINETEEN-THIRTIES

OGBURN, WILLIAM F., with the assistance of
TIBBITTS, CLARK

The Family and Its Functions*

Two outstanding conclusions are indicated by data on changes in family life. One is the decline of the institutional functions of the family as for example its economic functions. Thus the family now produces less food and clothing than it did formerly. The teaching functions of the family also have been largely shifted to another institution, the school. Industry and the state have both grown at the family's expense. The significance of this diminution in the activities of the family as a group is far reaching.

The other outstanding conclusion is the resulting predominant importance of the personality functions of the family—that is, those which provide for the mutual adjustments among husbands, wives, parents and children and for the adaptation of each member of the family to the outside world. The family has always been responsible

3. *Id.* at 171-172.

* From *Recent Social Trends in the United States—The Family and Its Function*, by William F. Ogburn. Report of the President's Research Committee on Social Trends. New York: McGraw-Hill Book Company, 1933 pp. 661-708. Copyright 1933, 1961. Used by permission.

to a large degree for the formation of character. It has furnished social contacts and group life. With the decline of its institutional functions these personality functions have come to be its most important contribution to society. The chief concern over the family nowadays is not how strong it may be as an economic organization but how well it performs services for the personalities of its members.

In colonial times in America the family was a very important economic organization. Not infrequently it produced substantially all that it consumed, with the exception of such things as metal tools, utensils, salt and certain luxuries. The home was, in short, a factory. Civilization was based on a domestic system of production of which the family was the center.

The economic power of the family produced certain corresponding social conditions. In marrying, a man sought not only a mate and companion but a business partner. Husband and wife each had specialized skills and contributed definite services to the partnership. Children were regarded, as the laws of the time showed, not only as objects of affection but as productive agents. The age of marriage, the birth rate and the attitude toward divorce were all affected by the fact that the home was an economic institution. Divorce or separation not only broke a personal relationship but a business one as well.

Other institutional functions of the family were at the same time strongly developed. It furnished protection to its own members, with less aid from the community than is expected today; it might even, as in the case of feuds, carry on private wars. The authority of the father and husband was sufficient to settle within the family many of the problems of conduct. Religious instruction and ritual were a part of family life. For a successful marriage it was considered important that couples should hold the same faith. In general the home was the gathering place for play activities though there were some community festivities. Educationally, the farm and home duties constituted a larger part of learning than did formal instruction in schools. Farm life furnished what we now call manual training, physical education, domestic science instruction and vocational guidance. The individual spent much of the daily cycle in the family setting, occupied in ways set by the family pattern. Kinship was part of the structure and family status meant much.

Such was the family in colonial days and with slight variations such it has been during much of our history. But changes set in as manufacturing technique evolved, as economic division of labor progressed and as trade developed. More people lived in towns, where they produced less of the food they consumed. Manufacturing first became specialized in the urban household, but with the introduction of steam power and the growth of mechanical invention it went into the factory. Markets and railroads stimulated the growth of cities. The making of furniture, thread, cloth, medicines and leather early left the household. At varying intervals other productive operations have been similarly transferred wholly or in part. This loss of economic functions has been a factor in many social questions, including the position of women in society, the stability of the family and the birth rate.

The family has been losing other functions as well. The government is assuming a larger protective role with its policing forces, its enormously expanded schools, its courts and its social legislation. Religious observances within the home are said to be declining. Opportunities for recreation can be sold for a profit and the existence of theaters, dance halls and ball parks indicates that members of families find more recreation than formerly outside the home. A child or adult is regarded more as an individual and less as a bearer of the family name.

These historical changes in family functions have not been accomplished without corresponding changes in structure. The household of today is about a quarter smaller than that of the colonial family. Marriage occurs probably somewhat later in life now than in earlier times, especially for women. There are many more families without children. The American home is broken much more frequently by separation and divorce than in colonial times. Children are an economic burden for a longer time and an economic asset for a shorter time, although in this respect there is still a difference between the city and the country. Wives, except when they work outside the home for pay, contribute proportionately less to the family support. The organization of the family is becoming diversified. The rural family differs from the city family, and the family in the village from both. Families in cities vary according to economic level, cultural status and occupation.

The personality functions of the family have suffered somewhat by the decline in the number of children in the average family and by the increase in the relative number of families with no children at all; by the growing demands of the schools; and perhaps also by the fact that the modern city makes possible a wider range of contacts beyond the limits of the family circle. Men in particular seem less dependent on the family for social contacts than was formerly the case.

Nevertheless, it may be said that the affectional function is still centered in the family circle and that no evidence is recorded of any extensive transfer elsewhere. The evidence of increased separations and divorces does not prove that husbands and wives now find marriage less agreeable than their ancestors did. It may mean only that certain functions and traditions which once operated to hold even an inharmonious family together have now weakened or disappeared.

If the personality functions have undergone a slight positive decline they have risen in relative importance because of the much greater decline of the institutional functions. To express it differently, the family is thought of much less as an economic institution than as an organization for rearing children and providing happiness. There is thus a greater individualization of the members of the family.

The changes in the family outlined in the preceeding paragraphs have taken place over a long period of time. [I]t is essential to bear in mind the long time trends. For example, in interpreting data on the recent growth in the number of restaurants and delicatessens it is important to know whether such a development indicates a continuation at a slower or faster rate of a long time trend in the transfer of economic functions from the home. In other words, is cooking about to follow manufacturing out of the home? Or will the departure of economic functions from the home be retarded by the increased use of electrical appliances and other mechanical aids? These questions and others relating to the shift in emphasis in the functions of the family will be discussed. . . .

THE FAMILY AS AN ECONOMIC INSTITUTION

[T]rends will be shown by considering one at a time some of the economic functions of the household that appear to be in transition.

Household Economic Activities.—The production of bread has already been transferred in large part from the home to the bakery. In a sample study of over 1,000 homes in 1930 it was found that two-thirds of the farm households used baker's bread only. . . .

. . . The per capita production of bakery goods made outside the home increased 27 percent from 1919 to 1929, whereas the per capita consumption of wheat flour both inside and outside the home decreased about 10 percent.

Since 1929, however, this transfer of baking from the home may have been somewhat retarded, for during the depression years there is scattered evidence of a slight revival of some of the earlier economic activities of the household. As to the future, it is difficult to predict whether or not the village and rural homes will become as dependent upon the outside bakery as the city home is now.

The evidence indicates also that canning is leaving the home. Certainly during the decade 1919-1929 it has developed rapidly outside of the sphere of the household. The per capita quantity of vegetables, fruits and soups canned outside the home approximately doubled during the decade. . . . The growth of canning and preserving outside the home is so rapid that a continuance may be expected in the future with a consequent lessening to time required in the household preparation of food.

Laundering has not left the household to the extent that baking has. In the special study referred to in presenting evidence on baking, the data show that 88 percent of farm homes and 33 percent of the city homes have no laundry done outside. Only 3 percent of the urban families sent all of their laundry out. . . .

* * *

As to sewing, the making of men's clothing seems to have left the home in earlier decades. . . . With regard to the clothing of women and children, the evidence indicates a possible increase in per capita production, although perhaps not much more, save in the case of dresses, than might be explained by a not unlikely change in the standard of living or a decline in seamstresses not in the employ of manufacturers. . . .

Losses in the Occupation of Women at Home.—

These shifts of occupation from the home to the factory must obviously reduce the economic importance of the woman in the home. The tendency is, therefore, for her to seek outside employment or activities. . . .

* * *

The family dwelling tells something as to the economic functions carried on within. Thus the heating in the multi-family dwelling is often attended to by a janitor who is, of course, outside the family circle, and many other services are handled by outsiders. In addition, the individual family usually has less space to care for. [S]ince the war the number of homes provided for in multi-family dwellings in cities has increased, until in recent years about 50 percent of the new homes were in apartment buildings and only about one-third in one-family houses. . . .

* * *

The Protective Functions.—Throughout history the family has afforded protection to its members. The marriage contract that comes down from earlier times carries the promise to protect. The family has traditionally guarded its members against bodily harm from enemies and against economic insecurity in infancy, illness and old age.

In recent times, the state has assumed important duties in protecting health. The budgets for public health and sanitation in cities of 30,000 and over have increased about twice as fast as urban families since 1903. The care for health has also passed in part to the hospitals, many of which are non-governmental. The number of beds in hospitals increased 115 percent in the 20 years from 1909 to 1929. Nearly one-third of all babies are born outside the home. . . .

The protection of the very old members of the family was formerly rendered almost exclusively by their offspring. With smaller families and greater mobility of the population they are less often so protected. In some countries, the care of the aged has been assumed in part by the state today. Within the decade preceding 1932, 17 states of the United States have legalized or adopted some form of old age insurance, either enabling counties to pass enactments, or being mandatory. . . . The number of endowment insurance policies, largely a protection against old age, increased 800 percent from 1899 to 1929. But equally rapid has been the growth of other forms of life insurance which may be viewed as a protection for the family through the aid of an outside institution. Many relatives are cared for by the family and in so far as the family does not do so, there is a tendency for this duty to fall to philanthropy or to the state.

The care of the feeble minded and the insane in

public institutions is an assumption by the state of protective functions formerly belonging to the family and still exercised by many families, particularly outside the cities. Patients in state hospitals for mental disease increased 110 percent from 1904 to 1929, while the number of families increased 67 percent. . . .

The extent to which the family is delegating the protection of life and property, or at least the extent to which such protection is growing up outside the family, is suggested by the fact that the total number of policemen, guards, watchmen, detectives, probation officers, sheriffs, marshalls and firemen increased 40 percent from 1920 to 1930, while the number of families increased only 23 percent. . . . Of course the property to be protected has increased also and much of it lies outside the family habitation.

Some of the protective functions recently assumed by the state are designed to safeguard the family as a unit rather than as individuals. The state steps in to arrest what might otherwise be a process of disintegration. Thus provision for mothers' aid out of public funds, spreading rapidly over most of the states since 1911, enables mothers, though the allowances are small, to stay at home with their children. Child labor legislation and juvenile courts . . . illustrate protective functions developed by the state to care for interests that were formerly thought of as family matters. Compulsory education, truancy laws and the provision for visiting teachers also represent an assumption of family functions by government agencies. If the provision and control of income is thought of as protective activity, however, the family, at least in the United States, is still the primary guardian of its members' interests.

* * *

Recreational Functions.—The great growth in commercialized amusements and the recreational programs of industry, church and state show that much recreation is provided by other institutions than the family. But this growth is not due solely to a transfer of function. Recreation has itself grown in institutions outside the home, thus affecting the relative position of the home in comparison with outside agencies. The reduction of 15 percent in hours of labor between 1890 and 1926 has made possible more leisure for recreation.

* * *

In the study of the home activities of parents and children previously referred to, it was found that reading aloud was practiced in the families of 33 percent of the American born white children in the rural samples, but of only 13 percent of the children in the large city. The family played games together in about half the cases in the country and in about 40 percent of the cases in the city. The same percentages held true for singing or playing music together. Attendance of the family together at the moving picture was about twice as great in the city (65 percent) as in the country. Family visits were as numerous in the city as in the country ; and walking together was twice as frequent among the city families.

* * *

Educational Functions.—The school teacher may be viewed as a substitute parent in regard to the function of training the child. The teacher is reaching into the home earlier and taking the child at a younger age for part of the day. . . .

That the teacher is a competitor of the parent (without a feeling of rivalry, of course) for influence over the child is not readily recognized, for the teacher aids both child and parent and is in this sense a cooperator also. Yet the school performs many services which were once the function of the home. . . .

* * *

Family Status.—Another function which the family performs is to confer upon its members a social status which as individuals they might not possess. In binding them together in a group it enables them to deal as they otherwise could not with other groups and agencies. . . . In many countries marriages are often primarily arrangements between families rather than between the young couples on the basis of a love impulse, although even under such conditions the desires of the young may be more often respected than the traditions of romantic fiction would lead a casual reader to believe. The family name, at any rate, tends to overshadow the individual. Family *espirit de corps* and the family impulse toward mutual protection extend to all the members. A break between two members of different families often means a break between all the members of the two families and difficulties are frequently settled by the families rather than by the courts. The family feeling extends to relatives, between whom there is felt to exist an altogether special tie which implies hospitality and financial aid. To be born into or to marry into a particular family is all important in giving prestige to an individual. Such is the concept of family status.

That this family function of determining status is changing is obvious, though it is impossible to find data that can be presented in brief compass to establish a trend. The evidence is largely to be found in analyses of social conditions and in case histories of individuals. Certain theories of the factors causing such changes may, however, be briefly presented. Property holdings in land are very likely to help to fix family status, especially in small communities where everybody knows everybody else. Permanence of tenure also seems to be a supporting factor. Clearly it is difficult to maintain family status in a high degree when there is much mobility of population. The growth of large cities, in which the effectiveness of gossip and other forms of non-legal social control is diminished, tends also to diminish family prestige. With few exceptions the personality of the individual family is lost in the crowd. The very phenomenon of rapid change makes the difference between generations appear greater than the differences between families.

For these reasons it is thought that family status as such has been declining in importance, though to what degree in recent years can only be inferred. Loyalty to the club, the school, the city, the team, the state, competes with loyalty to the family, yet no one of these groups absorbs the individual as fully as the family did historically. As the forces determining family status weaken, therefore, the individualization of the members of the family is accentuated. The knowledge and application of the facts of heredity might conceivably aid in restoring family status at some future time, but this development can not be anticipated in any predictable future.

The individualization of the members of the family finds recognition in changes in the law, particularly with regard to the wife. In very early times the law barely admitted the individuality of the wife. The common law held that "the legal existence of the woman is suspended during marriage." By marriage she lost the right to control her property; as a married woman she could not sue or be sued in her own name; and she could not make a will. Her earnings and the earnings of the children went to the husband as symbol of family authority. These and other laws illustrate the submergence of the personalities of the wife and children in that of the family, though in practice there was undoubtedly much freedom.

The laws, however, have undergone fundamental changes. Before 1900, all states had given married women the right to make a will. Eight states of the southwest and far west did not follow the ancient common law but adopted the system of "community property" rights. But while the property acquired after marriage belongs to both husband and wife, the husband still controls it. The other states before the close of the last century modified the common law by permitting married women to own property separately....

The question of domicile becomes more important in an age when people move about freely. The recognition of separate domicile of the wife, largely for purposes of voting, holding office, or serving on juries, has been accorded by laws passed in eight states since the World War.

In other family laws there are still some states which do not accord the same rights to a married woman that they do to a single woman. Though in general married women can make contracts, in perhaps half of the states there are some restrictions, however slight, on this right. In one state a wife's earnings are her own only if she is living apart from her husband; and in one state the father can will away from the mother the custody of the child. There are still other evidences of the fact that the individualization of the married woman is not complete under the law.

* * *

THE PERSONALITY FUNCTIONS

. . . The functions of the family may be viewed not as institutional, but rather as personality functions. The economic functions and the protective functions, for instance, not only produce goods and services, but they may also affect the personality. But in the main, the personality functions are those that affect the personality relationships of parents and children and of husbands and wives, and quite generally by procedures not emphasized very much in the discussion of the institutional functions. To what extent have these personality functions of the family been lost or transferred to other institutions? What changes have been taking place in recent years that affect these personal relationships?

Parents and Children.—In the section on the educational function it was seen that the content of much of the subject matter that children learn is being given by the schools. To some extent the schools help also to develop personality. But the fundamental personalities of children are pretty well formed by the time they go to school. Between birth and the age of six, the year when the child is generally first exposed to the influence of formal education, he comes in contact chiefly with the other members of the family group and is permanently affected by them. They are the stimuli to which he responds, many times each day and every day in the year. Such a repetition and limitation of stimuli cannot but leave on the infant's plastic nature a reaction pattern involving affection, fear and rage, the development of the ego, the quickness of response, feelings of inferiority, inhibitions, etc. The influence of the mother, who has repeated and frequent contacts with her offspring, is probably greater than that of any other member of the family, with that of the child's brothers and sisters, if there are any, coming next.

The importance of the influence of the parents and of the early home life is easier to demonstrate than to analyze and measure. Nor is there any concise factual evidence as to the changes in the intrafamily relations during recent years. . . .

It is clear, in the first place, that the diminution in the size of the family must affect family relationships in regard to children. . . .

It may be that the size of the family has not decreased sufficiently to produce a measurable psychological effect. In the case of the one-child family the statistics give no help at all with this problem, for, strange to say, the percentage of one-child homes has neither increased nor diminished since 1900, remaining around 25 percent during the whole period for the sample study of families.

The broken family also affects the parent-child relationship, but . . . the percentage of broken families has not changed during the thirty-year period studied. Marital discord in families undoubtedly has an unfortunate influence on the life of the child, although accurate evidence as to the precise nature of this influence cannot be cited. Though the percentage of divorced families has increased there are no data which will aid us to determine whether or not marital discord is increasing in families still technically unbroken.

The employment of nursemaids for children must affect the parent-child relationship by its introduction of an additional person with no ties of kinship into the limited social circle of the child. The percentage of families with nursemaids is, however, too small for this factor to affect the general trend. Relatives in the household are another factor of importance, but though 33 relatives are found with each 100 families in the sample family study there has been no appreciable change in the number over the period under survey.

Another change which may affect the parent-child relationship is the increase in the number of urban families, and in particular the increase in the number of those living in apartment houses. The absence of play space around the home and the limited space within the apartment itself may mean closer contacts between parents and children. On the other hand the clustering of homes in the city would seem to provide more playmates than would be available in the country, and thus the monopolistic home contacts of the child would be subject to more interference. . . . Among city families there has been in recent years a marked increase in the percentage of married women who work outside the home. For those of them who have young children the parent-child relationship is affected by the fact that during their absence they must leave the child in a day nursery or a kindergarten, or under the care of a nurse, neighbor or relative. Even when the mother remains at home the child, after he reaches school age, may divide his allegiance among play groups, gangs and clubs outside the home. The city streets are believed to provide many opportunities for children at later ages to escape family supervision.

Another factor . . . in the parent-child relationship is the widening of the gap between the generations by education and by social changes. In the case of immigrant families and their adolescent children this effect is especially noticeable. Such differences, joined with the growing individualization of the members of the family, and the complexity of the new urban environment, reduce the conscious control of the parents over their children. While psychiatrists speak of the problem of the "over-protected" child there are many families where there exists the problem of the under-protected child, especially during the adolescent years.

The foregoing fragments of evidence indicate some loss of the family's personality function in so far as it relates to children, together with some changes in its nature. To counteract in part the trend away from the home there are some indications that the function of child rearing is being relinquished by institutions and re-assumed by the home. The general opinion in child-placing organizations is that the demand by families for children to be adopted is growing and that the drift is away from the care of children in orphanages. . . .

Husbands and Wives.—The personality functions affecting the relationship of husbands and wives would appear to be inherent in the family and non-transferable. Yet husbands and wives may have close friendships with others outside the family circle and the opportunities for such friendships may increase with improved transportation facilities and the growth of cities. These outside relations may extend to sexual intimacies. But there are no reliable statistics on prostitution, much less on more informal liaisons. The bans against segregated districts for prostitutes, against street solicitation and against organized houses of prostitution have become more effective since pre-war years and may indicate a weakening of this ancient institution.

The changes in . . . occupations . . . suggest a number of ideas as to possible influences on the personality relations. Thus the increased travel incident to business tends to separate the members of the family for varying lengths of time. Night work is an influence for deviation. Work on transportation lines as railroads and buses cuts across family association. For many migratory or casual laborers family life is impossible. . . . The occupational developments also probably make desertion easier. . . .

*   *   *

The facts as to trends in marital harmony are meager and a search for changes in the factors producing disharmony are even less satisfactory. . . .

The relationships of husbands and wives are not encompassed wholly under the word affection. Older persons, for instance, sometimes marry to extend aid and comfort to one another. But such needs of family life may be lessened with the declining economic importance of the household and with increased contacts and services outside the home.

EFFORTS TO DEAL WITH FAMILY PROBLEMS
* * *

Problems of the Family as a Social Institution.— . . . Society gives much more attention at present to preventing the breaking of families than it does to safeguarding their formation. Something, however, has been done to prevent the marriage of children, a problem thought of as usually involving girls rather than boys. . . . The other side of the picture is that though some women marry too young others do not marry at all. About one woman in 10 reaches the age of 45 without marrying, and few marry for the first time after 45 years is reached. But though society may take steps to prevent premature marriages it does nothing to prevent delayed marriages or failure to marry at all. This problem is still left to the individual.

* * *

Child Rearing in the Home.— . . . In earlier times, when life was much the same from generation to generation, rules for bringing up children were developed in detail and readily disseminated. But the new and changing perplexities of modern life require education for parenthood. Three hundred married alumnae were asked in what subjects they felt themselves least prepared for their family life. Three-quarters replied, "In child training."

* * *

Society's Concern with Marital Problems.—The problems of husbands and wives reach their crises in separation or divorce and maintenance of strict divorce laws represents society's major effort to deal with them. The more fundamental problem for the future stability of the family is to ward off the disharmony which leads to separation. . . .

There is a growing need not only for more knowledge in this field but for agencies to disseminate such knowledge. To some extent such agencies, largely unorganized, already exist. Advice on marital problems is furnished by some of the professions—ministers, doctors, teachers and lawyers. The extent of their services is unknown. . . . A number of family clinics dealing with a variety of marital and sex factors have been planned during the past decade, but so far as can be learned, only three have been established. . . .

* * *

The relationship of husband and wife is clearly at the center of the problem of the modern family, since most families have children with them for only a part of married life or not at all and since so many other functions of the family have declined. The stability of the future family is not clearly seen. . . .

2.

THE NINETEEN-SIXTIES

BELL, NORMAN W., and VOGEL, EZRA F.

Introductory Essay: Toward a Framework for Functional Analysis of Family Behavior*

Terms and Terms of Reference

The family is a popular but not well-organized field of special interest. Many reasons, rational and nonrational, could be adduced to account for this state of affairs: the difficulties in investigating the intimate details of what is regarded as a private, sometimes almost sacred, part of life; the push felt (especially by the adolescent) in an individualistic society to leave the parental family behind; the great variety of interests in the family, with the resulting inability of one profession to lay claim to it as its own area, and so on. Another significant reason is the lack of a clear and consistent referent for the word "family." This common word, with its many emotional overlays, means many things to different people. If the word is to be used as a concept in scientific discourse, it must be given a stable and precise meaning.

[W]e shall regard the family as a structural unit composed, as an ideal type, of a man and woman joined in a socially recognized union and their children. Normally, the children are the biological offspring of the spouses, but, as in the case of adopted children in our society, they need not necessarily be biologically related. This social unit we shall call the *nuclear family* or simply the *family*. This unit is familiar and easily identifiable in American society, and it is the expected household unit. In accordance with current usage, we shall use *family of orientation* to designate the nuclear family in which a person has, or has had, the status of a child, and *family of procreation* in which a person has, or has had, the status of parent. *Extended family* is used to refer to any grouping, related by descent, marriage, or adoption, that is broader than the nuclear family.

* * *

Starting with the nuclear family as a stable point of reference, we attempt to spell out the patterned relationships and processes in those "structures" existing within the family, between the family and broader social units, and between the family and personality. Our approach will be a structural-functional one, producing a conceptual framework that may allow a theory to be built. . . .

Another concept basic to our approach is that of the *social system*. A system, as *Webster's Unabridged Dictionary* defines it, is " . . . an organization or assemblage of objects united in some form of regular interaction or interdependence. . . ." A social system is such an aggregation—of persons, or for some purposes, of roles. The family as a social system is not a closed system, existing in isolation. Rather, it is an open system which sustains relationships with other systems in the total transactional field. What is treated as a system is a heuristic matter. For some purposes, the nuclear family may be treated as an undifferentiated system; for other purposes, one might want to view it as a system composed of several subsystems—such as the husband-wife subsystem, the parent-child subsystem, the sibling subsystem, etc. For still other purposes, each of these subsystems might be treated as a system in its own right. The nuclear family may also be treated as a subsystem of some larger system, e.g., an extended-kinship system. If analysis is to be careful, it is essential to be explicit about what system is being referred to.

Analysis cannot rest with identifying systems and describing the structure of their relationships. This would result in a static picture which had form without content, anatomy without flesh. We will attempt to add the dynamics by identifying the *interchanges* that take place between and within systems. . . .

* * *

Functions of the Nuclear Family

There has been much confusion as to whether "the functions of the family" refer to functions the family performs for other social institutions, the wider society, the individual personality, or simply to activities* performed within the family. The family has functions which relate to each of these other systems, and it is important to be clear about which functions pertain to which system. With regard to the total society, the family may serve such general functions as replacing members, primary socialization, and maintaining motivation for participation within the society. There

* We shall use the term "activities" to refer to specific behavioral acts or sequences and patterns of acts, and "function" to refer to the more general consequences of activities.

are, also, specific functions which the family performs for each of the other social systems. For instance, the family discharges basic personality-formation, status-conferral, and tension-management functions for an individual member. Moreover, since functional interchanges seldom operate in one direction only, it is necessary to ask what functions are performed for the family by each other system in return.

Any general analysis of family functions is complicated by the many variations in concrete family functions within different societies, and by further variations among families in a given society. Frequently, however, the variation, or the change over time in a given society, is grossly exaggerated because the reference point is not clear and constant. For instance, it is often said that the "functions" of the family are being lost in modern society, but it is not clear whether the nuclear family or the extended family is the unit under consideration. In some primitive and agrarian societies, the family is said to have (or have had) major economic, political, religious, and educational duties, but in many cases these are (or were) functions of the extended family, not the nuclear family. In more complex societies, these functions are performed not by the extended family, but by specialized institutions organized on other bases than kinship; the nuclear family's relationship with these institutions has become more important, while the relationship with the extended family has become less important. Although the nuclear family seldom operates as a unit of direct economic production in contemporary industrial societies, the same is true for the nuclear family in many other societies. Moreover, certain activities and functions performed by the nuclear family in industrial societies have increased in recent decades. For example, the care of infants, household maintenance, and individual tension management, formerly performed in large part by the extended family or the community, are now almost exclusively the province of the nuclear family.

Failure to distinguish the extended family from the nuclear family has confused other issues—for example, that of authority. The "patriarchal family" vested strong authority in one person, but the authority often was over the extended family and was restricted to certain specialized activities. The persons in any one nuclear family were subject to the authority of the patriarch for some purposes, but in other respects they might have had considerable freedom. Often, the father who did have this patriarchal authority in the extended group did not have much authority over his own nuclear family. Even the patriarch's authority frequently had little relationship to many specific household activities. Just as the extended family's functions may be taken over by specialized institutions, so the authority formerly in the hands of the patriarch is now in the hands of specialized institutions. This may mean considerable change in the locus of authority outside the nuclear family, but does not necessarily mean drastic change within the nuclear family.

* * *

[T]he following analysis will focus on certain common characteristics of the functional relations between the nuclear family and external social systems.

THE NUCLEAR FAMILY AND OTHER SOCIAL SYSTEMS

The nuclear family's internal activities and the functions they serve are always intimately related to the position of the family in society. Hence, before taking up the activities internal to the nuclear family, it is necessary to examine the relationship between the nuclear family and other social systems.

This relationship can be conceived of as a series of functional interchanges. Some sort of balance is achieved in this interchange, between those contributions made by the family and those received by the family, even though the balance is not necessarily stable or perfect, particularly in the short run. The interchanges need not consist of concrete goods, but may consist of behavior and behavior response. For example, a nuclear family may live up to the standards of family life regarded as proper by the surrounding community. Because the family is respectable, the community rewards it with a certain status and prestige. This can be considered an interchange, just as the exchange of money income for labor services by family members is an interchange. . . .

In these interchanges, the external systems regard the nuclear family to some extent as a corporate, separate unit, and all other persons or units are regarded, at least from a certain point of view, as outsiders. The individual family member then is viewed as a representative of his nuclear family, and the actual interchanges between the family and the external systems may take place either as a family acting as a unit or as an individual acting as a representative of his family.

There are certain functional problems which any social system must solve concerned with the adaptation, goal gratification, integration, and pattern maintenance of the system; functional subsystems to meet these problems can be identified for any society. These subsystems may be termed respectively the economy, the polity, the community, and the value system. The same kind of functional problems arise within the family, but

again it is important to be clear about the reference points, since there is no one-to-one relationship between fulfilling a function for society and fulfilling the analogous function for the nuclear family. For example, what the nuclear family receives as a contribution from the polity may help solve not only goal gratification problems within the nuclear family, but adaptive, integrative, and pattern-maintenance functions as well. This section is concerned with the functional subsystems of a society in relation to the nuclear family. The functional subsystems should not be thought of as having concrete structural referents. A given functional subsystem may consist of different types of structural units. For example, in some societies the economy may consist of such concrete groups as business firms and governmental agencies. In other societies, the economy may consist of such concrete groups as the extended family or the community. . . .

a. *The Nuclear Family and the Economy.*— The economy may be defined as that part of a society which is concerned with the creation and distribution of valued goods and services. One interchange between the nuclear family and the economy is the contribution of labor by the nuclear family in exchange for rewards for services. The family of orientation must have provided the individual with a certain minimum of basic skills before he can enter into the labor market, a minimum which has been rising, at least insofar as opportunities for education are concerned. The individual must have a certain degree of emotional integration and control sufficient to allow him to operate adequately, and he must have certain basic information about, and attitudes toward, work that are essential to the performance of his tasks in the economy. In addition to providing the individual with this basic motivation and the basic skills, the family must then allocate certain of the performance capacities of its members to the economy.

* * *

In this interchange of labor for wages, various adjustments are made by the nuclear family, by the firms involved, and by the economy in general. In this way, the terms of the interchange, not only concerning the amount of wages and services but also the "conditions of employment," are established. Even in relatively impersonal industrial societies, the wages are determined not only by the laws of supply and demand, but in part by the needs and demands of the family. Some of these considerations are institutionalized in laws or union contracts regulating minimum wages, working hours and conditions, the dismissal rights of employers, etc. In some societies, family needs are explicitly recognized in policies of differential remuneration for workers depending on family responsibilities. In the United States, differential exemptions from income taxes serve the same ends. In addition, the business firm ordinarily has certain other responsibilities to the worker and his family. For example, a firm ordinarily provides special considerations of time and money when family problems or important family activities occur, such as marriage, birth, funerals, and the like, and it may offer help in arranging housing, meal, and even recreational facilities. Because large formal organizations have much greater power than the individual worker, special organizations such as labor unions develop to insure that these various demands of the worker and his family are being met by large firms. . . .

Similarly, there are certain adjustments which the nuclear family must make to the demands of the firm, in regard to when and where labor services shall be rendered. Principally, this means that the family must give encouragement and the necessary facilities to the wage earner, so that he can continue his participation in the economy. . . . It may . . . mean that even internal family activities will tend to be modeled on and adapted to the economic roles in the society. . . .

b. *The Nuclear Family and the Polity.*—Every social system has some type of administration of its activities to attain the system goals. The sub-system which fulfills these functions for the society may be termed the polity; in contemporary societies, this approximates roughly what is referred to as government. It is not coterminous with government since a government may perform other functions (as, for example, economic), and other institutions such as a clan or lineage may serve polity functions for the society. Ordinarily, the family acts as a unit in relation to the polity, as is suggested, for example, by the fact that husbands and wives and even . . . youth tend to vote for the same party, and by the solidarity of the family in relation to the totalitarian societies . . . . While a family may decide to have the wage earner change jobs if his employment situation is not satisfactory, and is able to shop around for consumer goods and services, it does not have the same option in relation to the polity. Since governing bodies typically are given a mandate to remain in power for one or more years, and since they (if elected) are elected by a large number of constitutents with many different interests, the burden of adjustment may be on the family. In the first interchange with the polity, the family contributes loyalty in exchange for leadership. At a very minimum, the members of the nuclear family recognize the legitimacy of the political

order and signify a loyalty to the regime sufficient for its policies to be carried out. In return for this, the society provides a variety of advantages to the family through its leadership—legal protection and regulation, legitimacy, and the like.

In the typical case, the family's loyalty goes far beyond recognizing the legitimacy of the regime and includes active commitment to the polity. . . . The austerity programs or military service in war times are indications of the extent of the family's loyalty to the polity in times of emergency. Even though this exchange is usually a relatively inactive one, compared to the interchange between family and economy most of the time, it is expected that the leadership will work to provide optimum conditions for the society, which in turn will provide direct and indirect benefits for the nuclear family.

To some extent, there is always a gap between the interests of the family and the interests of the state. In general, the time perspective of a single nuclear family is much shorter than the time span of the state. For example, state expansion, austerity programs for basic state development, military programs, and the like, frequently require sacrifices from the nuclear family for which there is little immediate motivation. Perhaps the ideal is that the family will be sufficiently motivated to provide the loyalty without fear of coercion by the state. . . .

On the second level of interchanges between the polity and the family, the family supplies compliance in exchange for decisions made by the polity. . . .

In individualistically oriented western societies, we are accustomed to thinking of the person as relating to the polity as a separate individual. It is clear that in many ways the individual is the significant unit in the eyes of the polity. Appearances may be deceptive, however. In fact, there is probably a good deal more homogeneity and solidarity among the members of a family than we commonly assume. There are too, other solidarity units which relate to the polity—peer groups, ethnic groups, political clubs, and so on. Such groups may mediate the relations of the family and the polity, but the family is always operative in some way. Because the family is stable, compared to many other concrete units, and because family sentiments tend to become associated with attitudes towards the polity, the family is always a unit of importance. This is most evident at the symbolic level, with leaders striving to present themselves as "solid family men (or women)," and to gather support by favoring the "family farm" or the values of strong family life. But the polity's orientation to the family is also evident in its decisions and policies, which protect the privacy of the home, refuse to compel spouses to testify against each other, distribute welfare benefits in relation to the family's condition, and . . . act in various ways to inhibit the dissolution of marriages.

c. *The Nuclear Family and the Community.*— All social systems face the problem of integrating various parts and activities of the system ; this problem is solved by institutionalizing patterns of behavior and by using mechanisms of social control to motivate members to conform to these patterns. The subsystem of society concerned with this problem may be termed the community, defined not as a single concrete group, such as a village or neighborhood, but as diffuse affective relationships of varying extensiveness, including . . . various social networks. . . . In primitive societies, the community usually consists of a very small number of concrete groups such as a village or kin group ; in modern industrial societies, instead of such close-knit groups, there are many different "communities" based on such criteria as common participation in an industrial firm or religious group, common interests, physical proximity, or previous membership in other social systems.

Even in simpler societies where a single group or a few overlapping groups constitute the community and the polity, there is often a functional differentiation between the community and the polity. For example, a patrilineal lineage may serve as a political unit, and the kin group as the community. Whether one single group serves as both the polity and the community, or whether there is a variety of different "communities," the diffuse affective bond to the community serves to integrate the family into the society.

As one of the functional interchanges, the nuclear family participates in community activities in exchange for the support of the community. Daily interaction, gifts, special kindnesses, and the like, come to symbolize the solidarity of the bonds among families. These favors imply an obligation of the receiver to the giver, and to the community in general. Often these reciprocal obligations between the family and the community are relatively latent and come to have real significance only in times of difficulties or crises.

Ordinarily, the community reinforces the bonds of solidarity within the nuclear family, but it may also prohibit the family from such intensive involvement in its own internal processes that it withdraws from participation in community affairs. Thus, from the viewpoint of the community, both strains and involvements within the family must be kept below a certain level, so as not to interfere with community activities. However, ordinarily there is a wide range of permissiveness for the nuclear family which does not participate in community activities ; because of the nature of the close affective bonds, there is usually room for subtle adjustments and permissions on the part of the community not possible on the part of the economy or polity. For example, not only is the family exempt from participation in community activities at times of birth, marriage, death, and serious internal family problems, but the community offers social support to the family, just as society gives special exemptions and therapy to the "sick" person.

In the other functional interchange, the community gives the nuclear family an identity in exchange for adherence to community patterns. At a minimum, the family is recognized as a legitimate part of the society, and usually the community provides the family with a specific status position, along with appropriate standards of behavior and rewards for behavior which accord with these norms. The identity provided by this membership and a specific position within the group gives the family a feeling of belonging and prevents anomie.[*] When the society is relatively stable and the "community" is a relatively closed network, identity may not be a serious problem.

[*] "Mr. [Robert] MERTON: . . .

" . . . If you are enough of an alien in a group, you are experiencing *anomie.* . . . You are in conflict; you don't know the expected behavior and may at first not know that the behavior you are acting out is of the wrong sort. If you face diverse expectations, differing cultural norms, and it is the same with the other fellow, how can you count on him? When that becomes reciprocated, you have an acute kind of social *anomie.* . . .

"One implication . . . is a decline in the predictability of the environment, in the predictability of the behavior of others, and this reacts on the individual. It is important to be able to know what the other fellow is going to do, whether or not he is going to be friendly or hostile in response to your behavior. Another implication is relative lack of group support. This support will not be provided by those who live by other standards."

*   *   *

"Miss [Ruth] KOTINSKY: 'Normlessness' is a translation of *anomie.* In translating into a more common word, we are losing some of the meaning of the original concept—perhaps in part because we don't understand the full meaning of *anomie.*"

*   *   *

"Mr. MERTON:

" . . . The term *anomie* has historically referred to the progressive breakdown of norms. It then becomes important to ask: given a state of relative breakdown in the shared standards of a group (the cultural or normative aspect), what is the impact on further social relations between the members of the group who are experiencing this normative breakdown? Do social relations become charged with mutual distrust? Or does one observe progressive social isolation as a phase response to normlessness? . . ."

[Reprinted from: Witmer, H. L. and Kotinsky, R. "New Perspectives for Research On Juvenile Delinquency" Children's Bureau Publication Number 356-1956 (pp. 62, 67, 54, 39).]

However, in a very mobile, highly industrialized society, with a variety of concrete "communities" wherein there is no clear, stable identity, there may be a considerable problem in maintaining an identity consistent with multiple and changing group memberships.

In exchange for identity, the nuclear family adheres to and makes concrete the community patterns. While various members of the nuclear family have differential commitment to various segments of a "community" or to different "communities," at a minimum the nuclear family gives tacit permission to its members to behave in accord with these various standards. In many cases, the family may actively encourage or even require adherence to such standards. If the family's ties to the community are very strong, this adherence to group standards is not regarded by the family as a duty or obligation, but simply as a natural expression of the family's solidarity and of its solidarity with the community. [T]his attachment to the group strengthens adherence to the norms. Through its participation in community activities and through the support it receives from the community, a family is motivated to adhere to the norms of the community, including norms regarding its own stability. Just as a family's identity consists not only of membership in a given community but of a certain status within this community, so the nuclear family adheres to standards appropriate to this particular position.

The relationship between the nuclear family and the community also has many implications for the family's relationships with the rest of the society, i.e., the community becomes a reference group for the family and its relationship with other social institutions. For example, the style of life supported by the community becomes an important basis for the pattern of relationships between a family and the economy. The political attitudes of the community similarly become an important basis for the relationship between the family and the polity. The community also is the reference group for relationships with the basic value standards of the society.

d. *The Nuclear Family and the Value System.*—No society, however simple, can persist in an orderly fashion without general orienting principles. These principles are at a higher level than the concrete patterns for governing specific behavior, and they constitute a reference point and *raison d'etre* for the more concrete patterns of behavior. From basic alternatives facing any society, such as what is the nature of man, and how should man relate to fellow man, each society must select certain solutions which serve as guides for behavior. Value patterns do not simply influence family behavior, but there is an active interchange between the family and the value system, and problems arising from attempting to live up to values may lead to modifications and changes in the basic value patterns.

While it is true that some societies have more flexible values permitting adaptability to contemporary situations, as a whole, the ultimate values have considerable stability over time. Even the phenomena of shame or "other-directedness" signify the variety, not the absence, of internalized values. A society may have value conflict, but there is usually some fundamental agreement about the hierarchy of values underlying even the conflict. . . . Despite the existence of value conflicts, the value system works toward achieving a certain amount of order between the various value elements in a society.

* * *

An exchange between the nuclear family and the value system takes place in that the value system specifies standards and the nuclear family accepts them—at a more general level than the community's specification of norms and the family's adherence to them. The value system defines what behavior is legitimate and desirable. . . . Ordinarily, children internalize these values through relationships in the family, and the nuclear family thus aids in the preservation of these values.

A second interchange between the nuclear family and the value system occurs when the value system gives approval and the nuclear family supplies conformity. Not only do the representatives of the value system specify what the values are, but they offer approval for conformity to these values. Ordinarily, this approval or disapproval is internalized within the personality at an early age, and the internal sanction operates to select and reject, to approve or disapprove of alternative behaviors. . . . This internalization is reinforced by the community, which operates to see that the nuclear family conforms, at least to some measure, with the more specific norms derived from basic values.

Because the nuclear family is concerned with approval, both internal and external, it strives to maintain a satisfactory relationship with the societal value system. Typically, this means conformity to the basic values. If there is not strict conformity then there is, ordinarily, an attempt to establish a relationship with the value system through modification of the basic values. Because the basic value system changes very slowly, the attempts at modification have relatively little success in the short run, and various rationalizations develop to define the behavior so that it seems really to be conforming with the basic values. Often, there is some cleavage between the ideal value system of the society and the specific concrete norms enforced by the community. In this case, the nuclear family may conform to the basic value system of the society, but be considered a nonconformist or a superconformist by the community ; or the family may violate basic values in exchange for community acceptance. The nuclear family is also considered responsible, to some extent, for the conformity of the family members. In the case of young children this responsibility may be stated and enforced very explicitly. Aside from the responsibility of socializing new members, the nuclear family is ordinarily considered at least partially responsible, by other groups in society, for maintaining the conformity of its members.

INTERNAL FAMILY ACTIVITIES

In order to participate in these interchanges with external social systems, certain activities must be performed within the nuclear family. The nuclear family must carry on internal activities related to these external exchanges, and it must perform other internal activities directly for its own benefit. Most activities carried on in the family have functional significance for the family itself *and* external systems, and the various functions fulfilled can be separated only analytically. Similarly, activities of external systems have implications for the family, but external-system activities are not sufficient in themselves to guarantee stability and smooth operation. The two approaches are, therefore, complementary, neither standing by itself.

The general functional problems facing the family are analogous to those facing the society as a whole, and those facing any other social system. In the case of the nuclear family, the functional problems may be termed task performance, family leadership, integration and solidarity, and pattern-maintenance. In examining these internal activities, it should be kept in mind that meeting a function within a family does not necessarily lead to the fulfillment of the analogous function for the society. Moreover, any given interchange between the economy and the family, such as the granting of wages in return for the performance of services by family members, may involve internal activities such as family leadership, integration and solidarity, and pattern-maintenance, as well as task performance. Similarly, the goods received from the external systems may have implications for all the subsystems in the family.

a. *Task Performance.*—Task performance within the nuclear family always occurs in the context of the family's relationships with external systems. The internal activity is governed in part by the requirements of the external interchanges and in part by the amount of goods obtained in the external interchanges. In addition, internal task performance is related to internal family characteristics, such as the standard of living and the solidarity and integration of relationships within the family. These tasks cannot be performed except as they are made consistent with the existing patterns of interpersonal relationships within the family. This is partly a problem of obtaining the motivational commitment of the family members for the performance of the tasks, and this can only be done as they are related to other family goals.

The goods obtained from the external systems are never completely ready for consumption when they come into the nuclear family, and some must be cared for if they are to continue to be used by the family. . . .

If there are dependent members of the family, then other members are expected to perform various tasks in connection with their welfare. The family is, at least to some extent, responsible for the technical problems of childcare as well as socialization. In many cases, it is responsible for the care of other dependents such as the sick or aged, although . . . various changes have taken place in the urban family which make it more difficult for the family to carry out these tasks itself.

To some extent, the relationships within the family develop as a result of the nature of task activity. For example, if productive activities performed within the family require close interaction between family members, then one would expect family bonds to be very strong, particularly if there is considerable interdependence between members in the performance of these tasks. . . .

If there are major task activities performed within a family, the nature of the task may also require that appropriate standards exist between family members to regulate their activities. . . .

In addition to the problem of the influence of tasks on the norms governing family relationships, there is the problem of distributing tasks within the family. To some extent, this distribution appears to be based on certain biological factors. The biological nature of the mother-child bond ordinarily leads the mother to perform tasks connected with the child, particularly when it is small, and the father to perform (frequently away from the home) activities that, directly or indirectly, will produce the needed goods and services. This division of labor is . . . evidently universal, and a fundamental principle of family life the world over. It usually means that the mother is more economically dependent upon the father than vice versa. The availability of the mother in the home ordinarily leads to her performing other incidental tasks in the home. . . .

* * *

b. *Family Leadership.*—Because the family is a stable group with the same membership over a relatively long period of time, its division of leadership is ordinarily rather clearly structured. For example, parents have clear-cut leadership over children. However, because of the complex nature of the family and the wide variety of activities within it, many subtle considerations are involved in its leadership, depending on such things as the particular activity pursued, the present family situation, the needs of family members, and the willing (though not necessarily conscious) turning over of leadership in certain affairs to other members.

If a minor problem develops, disturbing the usual pattern of relationships, the individual concerned may simply assume the leadership required for solving the problem. Other problems involve more than one person, and certain major issues, such as family size, life-plans for children, and inheritance, clearly involve several or all family members. These problems require leadership of the entire family, either by some member of the family or by someone acting for the family.

It is usual to think of the solution to these problems as a result of conscious decision-making processes. While family members may be conscious of their problems and various possible solutions, often . . . solutions are reached without a conscious decision-making process and may be in conflict with consciously desired goals. An equilibrium may be restored as a result of manipulations analogous to those in power-politics. One party may attempt to induce another to behave in the desired way by a variety of techniques, such as exploiting the coalition patterns within the family. The familiar case of the child who forms an alliance with the favored parent, when the other refuses his wishes, is one example; many other manipulations and coalition patterns are used to reinforce one's position in the family or to achieve the desired pattern of relationships.

Even if decision-making is conscious, it is not a simple matter of obtaining the desired number of votes before action can be taken. Because of the long period of intimate relationships between the family members, various subtle considerations enter into the process. . . .

* * *

c. *Integration and Solidarity.*—For a group to maintain close relationships between members over a long period of time requires some commitment and feeling of solidarity. For example, one of the functions of romance, especially early in marriage, can be to provide a feeling of solidarity even when economic interdependence of the spouses and external social systems do not exert strong sanctions for the continuance of the family. In turn . . . solidarity gives members the motivation to abide by the norms. If there is little solidarity within the family, the obligations imposed by the group may seem oppressive, but if there is a great deal of solidarity, the obligations may be accepted as natural and not even felt as obligations. In addition, feelings of solidarity are very important in dealing with individual tensions and personality problems.

To some extent, the mere process of interaction, even when frustrating to the individuals involved, is related to solidarity; over a long period of time, the meeting of expectations leads to a feeling of faithfulness which adds to solidarity. Furthermore, there are certain activities particularly significant for family solidarity. . . . The performance of certain specific routines at mealtime, in which the family unites as a whole, gives the family a feeling of solidarity; special family holidays, such as birthdays and special occasions, also serve to give the family a feeling of solidarity. . . .

While the importance of ritual activities for family solidarity has long been recognized, there are many other family symbols of family solidarity. For example, family photographs or photograph albums, family vacation experiences, favorite jokes and stories, family secrets, family history, endurance of hard economic times, and the like are remembered and treasured, in large part because of their significance for family unity and solidarity. It has long been recognized that family furnishings are symbols of social-class membership; it has been less common to note the extent to which certain family possessions, hope chests, heirlooms, and even the family house or car can serve as concrete symbols of family solidarity. These possessions unite the family by presenting a common pattern of taste and symbolizing the unity of the particular family. Experience of affect and sexual relationships also operate to give greater solidarity to relationships within the family. Aside from the purely physical aspects of sex, the sexual relationship serves to express and reinforce certain ties within the family. Other expressions of affection, such as physical contact, politeness, and "consideration," also help to express and maintain ties of family solidarity.

Both as a result of, and to promote these feelings of solidarity, the family attempts to preserve the motivational commitment of its members. If a family member is losing interest in family activities in ways considered inappropriate, the family will apply various sanctions, either positive or negative, to renew the individual's participation. Any lack of motivation is always a potential threat to the entire group, and the family cannot let deviance from family norms occur, without attempting to supply motivation to correct this deviance or at least making clear that such behavior is unacceptable. . . .

* * *

Because of the strength of family ties, there are very strong pressures operating to prevent group disintegration, as noted in studies of family responses to stress. The family appears to have a certain level of tension tolerance. When tensions become so severe as to threaten the group with disintegration, there is often a sudden rallying of forces to unite the family by dealing with the threat to the family's solidarity. These family "coping mechanisms" operate in ways very similar to individual personality mechanisms.

* * *

Not only are these pressures for solidarity expressed directly within the family, they are reflected in attitudes about families in general. Part of the negative reaction toward prostitution and divorce springs from the threat to family solidarity which they constitute. If divorce and separation were to be freely and easily permitted for others, this would involve a potential threat to one's own family solidarity. The continued negative attitude towards divorce and separation serves to reinforce the stability of one's own family and to insure that the threat does not come "too close to home." . . .

d. *The Family Value System.*—Through their relationships with each other, family members come to have certain expectations about how other members should behave; these expectations are associated with feelings of rightness or wrongness. Specific expectations are related to more general standards, and together they constitute a system of values for organizing and giving direction to various family activities. This value system provides a hierarchy of goals and a body of rules for their attainment. These are valued far beyond their mere utility in solving specific problems. The family attempts to maintain this value system, because it gives meaning and purpose to specific family activities.

While the societal value orientations are more general and govern all of society's basic values, the family value system is more specific and governs only behavior among family members and how they, as family representatives, should relate to outsiders. For example, while a society may have certain dominant and variant values, the family's values may be related only to the variant values of society. It is also possible for children and their parents to have different general values, but if the family is to continue to exist, there must be some agreement about the values which serve as a basis for and regulate family activities. The values of a family are not entirely, or even necessarily, conscious, except when there is conflict or when they are made explicit in the socialization process. . . .

. . . The leadership, task performance, solidarity, and division of labor . . . all take place within the context of the family's over-all value system. . . .

FAMILY AND PERSONALITY

. . . If a social system is to operate successfully, the members must have, to a considerable extent, similar orientations to the group and activities within it, to themselves, and to each other member, and they must have motivational commitments sufficient to maintain the system and to meet its functional requirements. On the other side of the coin, it has been suggested that personality develops not entirely, but to a considerable extent, within the matrix of the family system and is maintained by the family. Now, personality can be conceived of as a system of activities, orientations, motivations, etc., which has some internal cohesion, as well as a tendency to have and maintain boundaries. In this section, a very tentative formulation of some relationships between personality, as a system, and the family, as a system, will be offered.

At this level of analysis, the problem of keeping clear one's point of reference is especially acute. On the one hand, in many interchanges the family is but a mediator between the personality and broader systems outside of the family; on the other hand, some interchanges are not primarily with the whole family but with sub-systems, for example the mother-child subsystem, within it. Another problem . . . is that many interchanges of the family and personality tend to remain unconscious as long as the process operates smoothly; when problems arise the relationships reveal themselves much more readily. [P]ersonality has been investigated in most detail by another discipline, which has developed a conceptual system different from that employed here . . . . In psychoanalytic and psychiatric literature, attention has been focused mainly upon the relationships of one personality to another, in particular mother and child, with relatively little attention to the relationship of the family as a system and personality. . . .

[P]ersonality will be treated as an undifferentiated system having interchanges within the various functional subsystems of the family, just as, in the first section, the family was treated as a unitary system having interchanges with the functional subsystems superordinate to it.

a. *Task Performance.*—Task activities in the family have to do with adapting to the instrumental requirements of living—providing and utilizing food, shelter, other possessions, etc., organizing the activities of various members to carry out such tasks, and organizing motivation and trained performance capacities to insure that they are carried out. . . . The family, if it is to develop its members' personalities adequate for them to advance into the "outside world," must then give individuals the opportunity for graded involvement in, or identification with, task activities, and insure that learning takes place. This assignment of tasks must be appropriate to, and not above or below, the intellectual, physical, and attitudinal capacities of the individual. . . .

The personality does not acquire the structures appropriate to task performance solely through actual experience. A wide range of activities, from being read fairy tales, to playing with father on his day off, or observing him bid goodbye to mother on workdays, contribute to the formation of the appropriate attitudes, etc. Still, the assignment of tasks within the family, and the sanctions experienced by carrying them out (or failing to do so) do play an important part in the personality development. . . .

The significance of the family's adaptive functional subsystem is not by any means restricted to the developing personality. Even the most mature adult personalities require some support and recognition, if they are to preserve the proper orientations to work and maintain the appropriate flow of motivational energy. Of course, this support comes not solely from the family, but consistent lack of support and validation can affect the personality, . . . also shows in relation to the unemployed man. Nor is this a one-way process. Personality structure, along with family values and varying conditions, affects the organization of tasks in the family. Severe personality problems in one spouse may require the wife to become the wage-earner, or may lead the husband to perform most maternal activities. Even in less dramatic situations, personality affects the structure of task activities; family activities may have to be restructured to accommodate to the personality of a member, averting internal strain and maintaining motivational commitment.

b. *Family Leadership.*—The modes of meeting the leadership problems of co-ordination and authority which the family develops similarly have wide-ranging effects upon the developing and the developed personality. Psychoanalytic theory holds that attitudes and orientations to authority figures are laid down early in life and are basic elements of the whole personality. [G]enerally, it would be expected that the person or persons with greatest authority would have greater ability to establish patterns of family activities suited to their personality needs. There are, of course, limits to this freedom, set by the support requirements of, and alienative potentials in, the personalities of other members.

Since personality is acquired through the process of accepting roles assigned by parents, the child is particularly susceptible to deviant development when parents express their conflicts by assigning inappropriate roles in implicit ways. The process of assigning roles is an important part of the leadership functions in a family; when there is a coincidence of impulses of the parents at a covert level, so that there is both implicit stimulation for certain behavior and implicit permission of it, the results can be very traumatic for the child's personality. . . .

c. *Family Integration and Solidarity.*—The need of the family to maintain some integration of the activities and sentiments of its members also plays upon the individual personality and, in turn, is affected by it. It can be asserted with justification that minimum integration is essential if socialization is to take place. Without quite intense bonds among members, the motivational leverage necessary to encourage children to give up dependency strivings, for instance, would not exist; in any event, all persons forever bear the mark of how their families handled problems of integration and solidarity. The Oedipal conflict is a good illustration of how deeply into personality structure the nature of each person's integration into the family runs.

There is probably a fairly wide range of degrees of integration which can be produced and tolerated by stable personalities. . . . The intense solidarity that may be effective when the child is a dependent infant may be incapacitating when the child is old enough to be breaking away from the family and forming emotional ties to outsiders. In a society in which social and geographic mobility are valued characteristics, the family needs to be flexible and capable of finding alternate modes of preserving its solidarity.

*   *   *

d. *Family Value System.*—From the family value system, the individual derives direction and the standards which become internalized as part of his personality. When there is consistency of values and consistent affirmation of them, the individual develops a consistent superego . . . .

Much of the process of acquiring values goes on unconsciously, and thus there tends to be a good deal of continuity from one generation to the next. This continuity includes conflicts as well as conflict-free areas of values. . . . There is not, however, inevitable replication; modification can and does occur. Influences, from peer groups, other reference groups, and situational factors, have some impact on personality structure, independently of the family value system, though usually such influences can be expected to be mediated by the family. Variation, and even innovation, may also occur through the selective transmission of values to different children. . . .

Concluding Remarks

This essay has attempted to provide the broad outlines of a conceptual model which can be applied to various levels of family phenomena. This schema is not yet a systematic "theory," from which emerges testable hypotheses. Rather, it is a way of systematically relating phenomena often left disconnected, and of giving a more acute awareness of the many layers and levels of the context within which specific problems are embedded. As such, the test of its utility will be in application to empirical problems.

B.

The Family as Perceived in Law — Problems in the Administration of Family Relationships

The state's perception of family and its functions may be pieced together from many decisions in law which make special provision for members of a family—*qua* members of family. A mosaic of the state's image of the "family" emerges from areas of decision not directly concerned with the establishment or reorganization of family relationships—such as evidence, crimes, torts, contracts, property, debtor's and creditor's rights, workmen's compensation, taxation, aid to dependent children, immigration, and education. Do the functions of family operative in these areas, though traditionally not conceptionalized as part of family law, serve or undermine the values sought to be preferred in decisions more directly associated with the family-law process? More precisely: "Are the left hands of law administering family relationships aware of what the right hands are working to achieve directly in establishing and reorganizing these relationships?"

1.

IN EVIDENCE—THE FAMILY AS AN ENCLOSURE FOR SECURITY AND SPONTANEITY IN COMMUNICATION

a.   HAWKINS v. UNITED STATES
358 U.S. 74 (1958)

MR. JUSTICE BLACK delivered the opinion of the Court.

Petitioner was convicted and sentenced to five years imprisonment by a United States District Court . . . on a charge that he violated the Mann Act, 18 U.S.C. § 2421, by transporting a girl from Arkansas to Oklahoma for immoral purposes. Over petitioner's objection the District Court permitted the Government to use his wife as a witness against him.[1] . . .

The common-law rule, accepted at an early date as controlling in this country, was that husband and wife were incompetent as witnesses for or against each other. The rule rested mainly on a desire to foster peace in the family and on a general unwillingness to use testimony of witnesses tempted by strong self-interest to testify falsely. Since a defendant was barred as a witness in his own behalf because of interest, it was quite natural to bar his spouse in view of the prevailing legal fiction that husband and wife were one person. . . . The rule yielded to exceptions in certain types of cases, however. Thus, this Court in *Stein*

---

1. While the wife had been placed under bond to appear in District Court, she offered no objection in court to testifying against her husband.

v. Bowman, 13 Pet. 209, while recognizing the "general rule that neither a husband nor wife can be a witness for or against the other," noted that the rule does not apply "where the husband commits an offence against the person of his wife." 13 Pet., at 221. But the Court emphasized that no exception left spouses free to testify for or against each other merely because they so desired. . . .

Aside from slight variations in application, and despite many critical comments, the rule stated in *Stein v. Bowman* was followed by this and other federal courts until 1933 when this Court decided *Funk* v. *United States,* 290 U.S. 371. That case rejected the phase of the common-law rule which excluded testimony by spouses *for* each other. The Court recognized that the basic reason underlying this exclusion of evidence had been the practice of disqualifying witnesses with a personal interest in the outcome of a case. Widespread disqualifications because of interest, however, had long since been abolished both in this country and in England in accordance with the modern trend which permitted interested witnesses to testify and left it for the jury to assess their credibility. Certainly, since defendants were uniformly allowed to testify in their own behalf, there was no longer a good reason to prevent them from using their spouses as witnesses. With the original reason for barring favorable testimony of spouses gone the Court concluded that this aspect of the old rule should go too.

The *Funk* case, however, did not criticize the phase of the common-law rule which allowed either spouse to exclude adverse testimony by the other, but left this question open to further scrutiny. . . . The Government does not here suggest that authority, reason or experience requires us wholly to reject the old rule forbidding one spouse to testify against the other. It does ask that we modify the rule so that while a husband or wife will not be compelled to testify against the other, either will be free to do so voluntarily. Nothing in this Court's cases supports such a distinction between compelled and voluntary testimony. . . . Consequently, if we are to modify the rule as the Government urges, we must look to experience and reason, not to authority.

While the rule forbidding testimony of one spouse *for* the other was supported by reasons which time and changing legal practices had undermined, we are not prepared to say the same about the rule barring testimony of one spouse *against* the other. The basic reason the law has refused to pit wife against husband or husband against wife in a trial where life or liberty is at stake was a belief that such a policy was necessary to foster family peace, not only for the benefit of the husband, wife and children, but for the benefit of the public as well. Such a belief has never been unreasonable and is not now. Moreover, it is difficult to see how family harmony is less disturbed by a wife's voluntary testimony against her husband than by her compelled testimony. In truth, it seems probable that much more bitterness would be engendered by voluntary testimony than by that which is compelled. But the Government argues that the fact a husband or wife testifies against the other voluntarily is strong indication that the marriage is already gone. Doubtless this is often true. But not all marital flare-ups in which one spouse wants to hurt the other are permanent. The widespread success achieved by courts throughout the country in conciliating family differences is a real indication that some apparently broken homes can be saved provided no unforgivable act is done by either party. Adverse testimony given in criminal proceedings would, we think, be likely to destroy almost any marriage.

Of course, cases can be pointed out in which this exclusionary rule has worked apparent injustice. But Congress or this Court, by decision or under its rule-making power, 18 U.S.C. §3771, can change or modify the rule where circumstances or further experience dictates. In fact, specific changes have been made from time to time. Over the years the rule has evolved from the common-law absolute disqualification to a rule which bars the testimony of one spouse against the other unless both consent. . . . In 1887 Congress enabled either spouse to testify in prosecutions against the other for bigamy, polygamy or unlawful cohabitation. 24 Stat. 635. . . . Similarly, in 1917, and again in 1952, Congress made wives and husbands competent to testify against each other in prosecutions for importing aliens for immoral purposes. . . .

[T]here is still a widespread belief, grounded on present conditions, that the law should not force or encourage testimony which might alienate husband and wife, or further inflame existing domestic differences. Under these circumstances we are unable to subscribe to the idea that an exclusionary rule based on the persistent instincts of several centuries should now be abandoned. As we have already indicated, however, this decision does not foreclose whatever changes in the rule may eventually be dictated by "reason and experience."

. . . The prosecutrix testified that petitioner agreed to take her to Tulsa where she could earn money by working as a prostitute with a woman called "Jane Wilson." . . . The Government placed "Jane Wilson" on the stand. In response to questions by the Assistant United States Attorney she swore that she was petitioner's wife and that she was a prostitute at the time petitioner took the prosecutrix to Tulsa. Not wholly satisfied with this testimony the prosecutor brought out for the first time on redirect examination that "Jane Wilson" had been a prostitute before she married petitioner. The mere presence of a wife as a witness against her husband in a case of this kind would most likely impress jurors adversely. When to this there is added her sworn testimony that she was a prostitute both before and after marriage we cannot be sure that her evidence, though in part cumulative, did not tip the scales against petitioner on the close and vital issue of whether his prime motivation in making the interstate trip was immoral. . . . At least, use of the wife's testimony was a strong suggestion to the jury that petitioner was probably the kind of man to whom such a purpose would have been perfectly natural.

Reversed.

MR. JUSTICE STEWART, concurring.

The rule of evidence we are here asked to re-examine has been called a "sentimental relic." It was born of two concepts long since rejected: that a criminal defendant was incompetent to testify in his own case, and that in law husband and wife were one. What thus began as a disqualification of either spouse from testifying at all yielded gradually to the policy of admitting all relevant evidence, until it has now become simply a privilege of the criminal defendant to prevent his spouse from testifying against him. . . .[2]

Any rule that impedes the discovery of truth in a court of law impedes as well the doing of justice. When such a rule is the product of a conceptualism long ago discarded, is universally criticized by scholars, and has been qualified or abandoned in many jurisdictions, it should receive the most careful scrutiny. Surely "reason and experience" require that we do more than indulge in mere assumptions, perhaps naive assumptions, as to the importance of this ancient rule to the interests of domestic tranquillity.[4]

In the present case, however, the Government does not argue that this testimonial privilege should be wholly withdrawn. We are asked only

to hold that the privilege is that of the witness and not the accused. Under such a rule the defendant in a criminal case could not prevent his wife from testifying against him, but she could not be compelled to do so.

A primary difficulty with the Government's contention is that this is hardly the case in which to advance it. A supplemental record filed subsequent to the oral argument shows that before "Jane Wilson" testified she had been imprisoned as a material witness and released under $3,000 bond conditioned upon her appearance in court as a witness for the United States. These circumstances are hardly consistent with the theory that her testimony was voluntary. Moreover, they serve to emphasize that the rule advanced by the Government would not, as it argues, create "a standard which has the great advantage of simplicity." On the contrary, such a rule would be difficult to administer and easy to abuse. Seldom would it be a simple matter to determine whether the spouses's testimony were really voluntary, since there would often be ways to compel such testimony more subtle than the simple issuance of a subpoena, but just as cogent. Upon the present record, and as the issues have been presented to us, I therefore concur in the Court's decision.

NOTES

NOTE 1.

PEOPLE v. DAGHITA
299 N.Y. 194, 199, 86 N.E. 2d 172 (1949)

CONWAY, J. . . .

Certainly, the wife's knowledge gained by observance of defendant's conduct in bringing home stolen property in the early morning hours and storing it in different parts of the house and more particularly under his bed was the result of confidential communication on his part. It cannot be supposed that the defendant would have so conducted himself except in reliance upon the free and unrestrained privacy of the marital relation and the socially desirable confidence which exists, and should exist, between husband and wife. The record makes plain that defendant made no effort

---

2. We are not dealing here with the quite different aspect of the marital privilege covering confidential communications between husband and wife. See *Wolfle v. United States*, 291 U.S. 7.

4. The facts in the present case illustrate how unrealistic the Court's basic assumption may be. At the time of the acts complained of the petitioner's wife was living apart from him under an assumed name. At the time she testified they were also living apart. In his testimony the petitioner referred to her as his "ex-wife," explaining when his counsel corrected him that he and his wife had never lived together very much.

Before assuming that a change in the present rule would work such a wholesale disruption of domestic felicity as the Court's opinion implies, it would be helpful to know the

experience in those jurisdictions where the rule has been abandoned or modified. It would be helpful also to have the benefit of the views of those in the federal system most qualified by actual experience with the operation of the present rule—the district judges and members of the practicing bar. The Judicial Conferences of the several Circuits would provide appropriate forums for imparting that kind of experience. 28 U.S.C. Sec. 333.

It is obvious, however, that all the data necessary for an intelligent formulation "in the light of reason and experience" could never be provided in a single litigated case. This points to the wisdom of establishing a continuing body to study and recommend uniform rules of evidence for the federal courts, as proposed by at least two of the Circuit Judicial Conferences....

to conceal or disguise his conduct at his home from his wife. He was, in a word, confiding in her the information disclosed by his conduct. . . .

. . . After Mrs. Daghita had been compelled to disclose the confidential communication made to her by her husband and outlined above, a verdict of guilt was assured to the prosecution which had called her as a witness.

The judgments of conviction should be reversed and a new trial ordered.

NOTE 2.

NIETZSCHE, FRIEDRICH

Human, All-Too-Human (1878)*

Marriage as a long conversation. When marrying, one should ask oneself this question: Do you believe that you will be able to converse well with this woman into your old age? Everything else in marriage is transitory, but the most time during the association belongs to conversation.

NOTE 3.

STATE v. KOLLENBORN
304 S.W. 2d 855, 864 (Mo. 1957)

EAGER, JUDGE.

[W]e hold that the wife testifying voluntarily, is a competent witness against her husband in a prosecution for acts constituting a crime of personal violence against her child. The exact scope of the common law exception has been somewhat nebulous and confused; we need not attempt at this time to define further its precise limits and boundaries. The present offense can well be classed as one against the marital status, within the authorities using that test as a guide. We hold that every reason of public policy and true necessity which permits the wife to so testify in the event of a personal injury to herself, applies equally here. . . .

NOTE 4.

DURGALA, MILAN M.

Husband and Wife Privilege—Effect of Third Person's Knowledge†

Communications made in the presence of children present special problems. Two New York cases, involving children of the parties, denied the existence of the privilege. However, the children in both cases were adults and actually participated in the conversations. Other jurisdictions consider as factors age, intelligence, and participation of the children. A West Virginia court held that a communication made in front of a 13-year-old

daughter is not confidential unless the child is "totally incapable of comprehending what is being said." Concerning the presence of a nine-year-old child, a Massachusetts court stated, "It was for the judge to determine whether [the child] was of sufficient intelligence at the time to pay attention and to understand what was being said." The same court in an earlier case viewed a conversation in the presence of young children as confidential where the children were not shown to have taken any part in or paid any attention to what was said.

NOTE 5.

ESCALONA, SIBYLLE

Children and the Threat of Nuclear War*

How Much Do Children Know?

Apparently children know a great deal more than we sometimes give them credit for. Children seem so absorbed with their games, their friends, their life at school, that it is hard to believe they pay much attention to grownup problems. Yet even a young child nearly always seems to know when something really matters to his elders. As soon as American families became concerned over issues of fallout, testing and shelter building, children also knew about these issues. Signs of their awareness turned up in the questions they asked and even in the games they played.

For example: at times of particularly tense Soviet-American relations, preschool children went right on playing their usual war games. But often the "bad guys" became Russians, and were endowed with all the powers of evil the children could imagine. Again, in October 1961, when renewed nuclear testing aroused worldwide concern, fourth- and fifth-graders in a New York City school were given a routine assignment. Asked to write one question each about themselves, their school and the world, ninety-eight percent of these ten- and eleven-year-olds mentioned war or bombs or the possibility that there might not *be* a world.

In short, American children four years old and up are aware of a danger to life. With greater or lesser understanding, they connect this danger with the language of nuclear war: fallout, Russia, radiation, H-bomb are all part of their vocabulary.

NOTE 6.

Privileged Communications during Engagement

To what extent and why should communications between engaged persons be privileged?

---

* Reprinted in Kaufmann, W., *The Portable Nietzsche,* New York: The Viking Press, 1954, p. 59. Used with permission of the publisher.

† 13 SYR. L. R. 454, 456-7 (1962).

---

* New York: Child Study Association of America, Inc., 9 East 89th Street, 1962, pp. 5-6. Reprinted with permission of the publisher.

Should it make a difference whether marriage follows? What procedure, if any, would be necessary to establish the status of being engaged—for such purposes?

b.   COMMONWEALTH v. O'BRIEN
        390 Pa. 551, 136 A. 2d 451 (1957)

COHEN, JUSTICE.

We have allowed this appeal from a judgment of the Superior Court in order that we might determine whether, in an action for the support of a minor child, born during wedlock, a husband may obtain compulsory blood grouping tests in order to exclude himself from being the father of the child.

The present proceedings were instituted by the relatrix in 1954 in order to increase the amount of a support order entered in favor of herself and a daughter, and to include therein a son born before her divorce. At the hearing before the Domestic Relations Division of the Municipal Court of Philadelphia, the former husband moved for compulsory blood grouping tests of his wife, the son, and himself under the Act of 1951, providing, *inter alia*:

> "In any proceeding to establish paternity, the court, on motion of the defendant, shall order the mother, her child and the defendant to submit to one or more blood grouping tests . . . to determine whether or not the defendant can be excluded as being the father of the child . . ." Act of May 24, 1951, P.L. 402, §1, 28 P.S. §306 (Supp).

* * *

The sole question before us is whether in an action for support a husband may obtain, as a statutory right, compulsory blood grouping tests of the mother and her child born during wedlock.

At the outset we note that the legislature placed two qualifications upon the right to compulsory blood grouping tests which substantially limit the scope and application of the act:

1. Only a male defendant who is the putative father may move to have the blood grouping tests taken.
2. Such tests are permitted only in "proceedings to establish paternity."

These qualifications render the statutory procedure unavailable, among others, to the following parties who might seek blood grouping tests to negate paternity: husbands bringing an action for divorce on the ground of adultery, or an action for annulment because of fraudulent representations as to parenthood; mothers seeking custody of children; parties seeking a determination that they are the parents of a child of whom another claims to be the father; parties disputing the claim of a child to share in an estate; parties attempting to prove non-citizenship of a child; or to defendants in prosecutions for rape in which the prosecuting witness testified that as a consequence of the rape she became pregnant and gave birth to a child.

On the other hand, the act does apply to at least two classes of cases—prosecutions for fornication and bastardy . . . and actions for neglect to support a bastard . . . Thus, apparently the act was designed to aid the man who is accused by an unwed mother of being the father of her illegitimate child. Except for protestations of innocence, a blameless defendant is often helpless to refute such a charge lodged against him, and consequently is convicted of the crime. In addition to being compelled to support a child which he has not fathered, the defendant also receives the condemnation of the community. The legislature apparently believed that the occasions of injustice in these two classes of cases were so numerous as to overcome any reluctance to compel a complaining witness to submit her body to blood tests at the option of a defendant, and therefore provided this procedure whereby a defendant might successfully assert his innocence.

The husband herein, however, contends that this action for support of a child born during wedlock is also a "proceeding to establish paternity" within the meaning of the act's second qualification.

We cannot agree. It is true that the present proceeding is one in which paternity is *relevant* or one in which paternity has been *controverted,* or one in which paternity is an *issue,* but it is not a proceeding brought to *establish* paternity. In support actions brought by a wife against a husband for support of a minor child born during wedlock, paternity has already been established in the eyes of the law by operation of the presumption of the legitimacy of children born during wedlock . . . The presumption of legitimacy is invoked at the very moment of birth and no further proceedings are required to establish the paternity of the child. This presumption is essential in any society in which the family is the fundamental unit.

* * *

We hold, therefore, that the present proceeding is not a "proceeding to establish paternity" within the intendment of the Act of May 24, 1951, and that the defendant herein was not entitled to have compulsory blood grouping tests taken of his former wife and their child.

Judgment affirmed.

CHIDSEY, JUSTICE (dissenting).

The majority opinion makes it quite clear that it is not concerned with the question of "the admissibility of, or the probative weight to be accorded to, blood grouping tests offered in evidence."
. . .

By virtually limiting the Act of 1951 to prosecutions for fornication and bastardy and to actions for neglect to support a bastard, the majority does not eliminate the use of blood grouping tests in actions such as the instant one, but simply restricts the ability of a defendant to have a court order the taking of such tests, admittedly relevant if the results are otherwise obtained. Thus the ultimate effect of the majority opinion in the instant class of cases is to prohibit the taking of blood grouping tests under the impartial direction and scrutiny of a trial court, but to permit the admission of such test results should the defendant be fortunate enough to have secured the necessary blood types from tests made under other circumstances. This anomalous result is one which I submit the Legislature never intended when it enacted a statute clearly designed to aid defendants and expand the judicial use of conclusive scientific evidence by requiring a trial court to order blood grouping tests upon motion of the defendant "In *any* proceeding to establish paternity. . . ."

From a policy viewpoint, . . . [t]o hold that a "presumption" *establishes* a fact "in the eyes of the law" is not only to look upon justice as blindfolded, but to blind her by the law's own hand. The very nature of a "presumption" is to permit it to be rebutted by clear evidence to the contrary, and no evidence known to the judicial process is more lucid and scientifically certain than the blood grouping test when used to negative paternity.

*　*　*

The test for rebutting the presumption of legitimacy . . . is that the evidence be "clear, direct, convincing and unanswerable". It is to be reiterated that no test known to the law more adequately meets these requirements than the blood grouping tests with which this case is concerned. Testimony by witnesses as to access is always subject to close scrutiny because of the witness's interest and the fallibility of human observation. Even medical testimony as to impotency is often a matter of medical opinion; learned, but nonetheless opinion. These tests (and the Act provides for one or more, in case there is any question as to the validity of the results) are impartial, perfected to the limits of modern science, and unquestionable when used to prove nonpaternity.

The ultimate vice of the majority opinion is not merely the improper use of a "presumption" as a substitute for fact, but the use of the presumption at all in regard to the question at bar. Were admissibility in issue, then the social considerations inherent in the presumption of legitimacy, such as the sanctity of the family relationship and the social consequences of bastardization, might come into play.[2] . . .

The blood grouping tests used in paternity cases are based on the scientific principle, nowhere seriously disputed today, that certain components of the blood may be transmitted to an offspring only from its parents. Thus if a child's blood contains a particular blood characteristic not contained in the mother's blood, then either the purported father must have the blood characteristic being tested for in his bloodstream, or he could not possibly have fathered the child. Since maternity is rarely in issue, the blood grouping test has been found of inestimable value in excluding purported fathers from the liabilities of unwarranted legal parenthood. The tests have not been found of probative value to affirmatively show paternity because of the large class of possible fathers in each blood group. Their use in paternity cases, therefore, has been largely confined to negativing paternity, and the Act before us conforms to the prevailing usage in this regard. Thus if a defendant is unjustly accused of being the father of a child, he has a reasonably good chance of clearing himself via these blood tests, and as science increases the number of reliable tests, so will the defendant's chances of thereby proving nonpaternity. It is undisputed that, if the tests are properly administered, a defendant who is excluded thereby could not possibly have been the father of the offspring in question.

*　*　*

. . . Strictly speaking there is no "proceeding" in this Commonwealth "to *establish* paternity", unless it may be said that a declaratory judgment or an adoption proceeding might have this effect. Paternity is "established" by a physical act according to the laws of nature, not by a judicial "proceeding" under the laws of this Commonwealth. There are many proceedings in which it is important to prove that one is in fact the father of a child, or that one is the child of a certain father, and for the purposes of that particular suit it may be found that the fact of paternity is "established", but these are actions for support, criminal prosecu-

---

2. It may be observed that the sanctity of the family relationship has inevitably been destroyed prior to the institution of suit where the husband-defendant has denied paternity. Whatever social consequences arise out of bastardy and infidelity have been visited upon the family involved long before the courtroom issue of admissibility of evidence arises.

tions, will contests, etc., not "proceedings to establish paternity". The action for neglect to support a bastard child makes parentage pertinent to the inquiry in these words: "Whoever, being a parent, wilfully neglects or refuses . . . to . . . support . . .". The action for desertion and nonsupport says: "If any . . . father . . . separates himself . . . or neglects to maintain. . . ." In either case a man must be shown to be the father of the child before liability for its support will attach. In both cases "paternity is *relevant*", and where *"controverted"*, it is an *"issue"* to be determined at trial. . . .

* * *

The undisputed facts in the case at bar illustrate better than any hypothetical case the manifest unfairness of the result reached by the majority. Robert J. and Adele O'Brien were married on October 24, 1938, and a daughter, Barbara, was born to them on June 25, 1939. In 1942 the husband and wife separated and have since lived apart. In 1946 a support order was entered against the husband for support of his wife and the daughter, Barbara. On February 11, 1947, five years after the husband and wife began living apart, a boy, Richard, was born to Adele O'Brien. Three years later, on February 27, 1950, Adele and Robert O'Brien were divorced, and on March 6, 1950, the support order was modified so as to exclude the now-divorced wife and to increase the support for the daughter, Barbara. No mention was made in this order of the boy, Richard, although he was three years old at the time. Similarly, pending the divorce action, the wife filed a petition for alimony pendente lite in which she noted that ". . . the defendant is endeavoring to support herself and their minor daughter, but said sum is grossly inadequate for that purpose."— no mention was made of the boy, Richard. Indeed it was not until October 28, 1954, four years after her divorce, seven and a half years after Richard was born, and twelve years after Adele stopped living with Robert J. O'Brien, that Adele O'Brien first moved to make the appellant, Robert J. O'Brien, liable for the support of the boy. The inference is inescapable that neither relatrix nor the appellant had hitherto considered Richard to be the son of Robert J. O'Brien. It was during the hearing in February, 1955 on this petition to include a then eight-year-old boy in a support order for the first time, that the appellant moved that a blood grouping test be taken. It appears patent that this appellant is trying to do just that which the law, in my opinion, allows him to do, namely, gather what evidence he can to enable him to escape liability for support of a child he believes he has not fathered.

The facts raise one further question: What possible reason is there for not requiring relatrix to submit to the blood grouping test here in question? If the defendant is in fact the father of the child, or in the class of those who could be the father of the child, the results of the tests are inadmissible and of no effect. If the defendant is excluded by the test results, then the cause of justice has been advanced though the aid of modern science. No possible harm can come to the relatrix mother if indeed her claim is well founded.

* * *

NOTE

THE BUREAU OF PUBLIC ASSISTANCE
Illegitimacy*

Many of the State laws still reflect the terminology and thinking of the old bastardy laws. The principle of punishing the man responsible for the birth of a child is found in many of the laws. Paternity must be proved against him and criminal procedure must be used to bring him before the court. By requiring criminal procedure, with all its implications for mother, child, and father, the requirement may, in some degree, account for the reluctance of many a woman to identify the father of her child and, as a result, for her willingness to do without essential financial help for herself and her baby. Moreover, the experience of some courts and social agencies has shown that many men, when approached in an understanding, helpful way, will acknowledge paternity and will often provide some support for their children.

* * *

c.   SACKLER v. SACKLER
        16 App. Div. 423, 229 N.Y.S. 2d 61 (1962)

BELDOCK, P. J.— On April 5, 1961, in the Supreme Court, Kings County, the defendant wife obtained a judgment of separation from the plaintiff husband and thereafter moved into her own apartment. Some four months later, on August 20, 1961, at about 3:30 A.M., plaintiff and other members of a raiding party (none of whom was a police officer) entered defendant's apartment without her consent and without a search warrant, and allegedly obtained evidence of her adultery.

In this action for divorce, defendant moved to suppress and exclude the evidence so gathered. Special Term granted the motion on the grounds:

_____

* Washington D.C.: U.S. Department of Health Education and Welfare, 1960 (p. 23).

(a) that although the federal and state constitutional protection against unreasonable search applies only to official acts, the New York State statutory protection against unreasonable search, which is contained in section 8 of the Civil Rights Law, applies both to private and official persons; (b) that evidence gathered by private persons in violation of section 8 of the Civil Rights Law is inadmissible in civil suits; (c) that the search by plaintiff and his raiding party was unreasonable because it was the result of uninvited entry; and (d) that the exclusion of the evidence is not contrary to public policy because it will protect the innocent spouse from nightly visitation even at the risk of protection of the adulteress.

In our opinion, the order of Special Term was erroneous because the exclusionary rule does not apply (a) to evidence gathered by private persons, or (b) to civil causes.

The Fourth Amendment of the Constitution of the United States protects against "unreasonable *governmental* intrusion" into the privacy of a person's home . . . ; and any evidence discovered as a result of such governmental intrusion is now constitutionally tainted and inadmissible in a State court criminal trial. . . . The similar provisions of the constitution of New York State (N.Y. Const., Art I sec. 12) also relate solely to the sovereign authority and to its agencies. . . .

HOPKINS, J.—I dissent . . . .

It is anomalous to enforce opposite rules concerning evidence blighted by the same pollution. The unlawful search violates the identical privacy, whether its fruits are used to convict in a criminal prosecution, or to forfeit a personal right in a divorce action. Other states do not find the distinction. If the defendant were prosecuted for the crime of adultery . . . the evidence would be excluded. Her right to defend herself and her home against the unlawful intrusion . . ., an act in itself a crime . . ., has precisely the same vigor and effectiveness whether exercised against a public officer or the plaintiff. . . . Her personal liberty, and the security of her home, are fundamental rights woven into the fabric of the Federal and State Constitutions. . . . "The common law has always recognized a man's house as his castle, impregnable, often, even to its own officers engaged in the execution of its commands. Shall the courts thus close the front entrance to constituted authority, and open wide the back door to idle or prurient curiosity?" (Warren & Brandeis, The Right to Privacy, 4 Harv. L. Rev. 193, 220.) If that question be answered in the negative, then the same constitutional considerations and policy require exclusion of the evidence obtained by violence in an early morning divorce raid using the

constitutionally prohibited device of an unlawful search and seizure.

* * *

NOTES

NOTE 1.

STATE v. EVANS
45 Ha. 662, 372 P. 2d 365 (1962)

LEWIS, JUSTICE.

* * *

Defendant contends:

"*First,* a wife cannot, during her husband's absence and without his authority, waive his constitutional rights. . . .

* * *

In some cases it is reasoned that a wife has an equal right in the premises occupied by husband and wife, and her consent suffices to legalize the search and seizure by reason of this equal right. This is to be compared with the theory—followed by some of the courts but denied by others— that a wife being in charge of the premises in the absence of the husband has authority to consent to the search and seizure made. . . . Humes v. Taber, 1 R.I. 464, 473 . . . held incorrect a charge to the jury to the effect that the law implied an authority in the wife, in the absence of the husband, to license a search of his house for stolen goods. The court said:

> "* * * The law implies no such authority. Undoubtedly, the wife's authority extends to the rendering the ordinary civilities of life. If she invites a neighbor, friend, or even stranger, to enter the house in the way of hospitality, such invitation would, under ordinary circumstances, be a valid license so to do.
> " . . . An artful man might impose on the wife in the absence of the husband, and thus, for malicious and unlawful purposes, obtain from her a license to search the desks and private papers of her husband. . . ."

In Illinois the cases proceed on the theory that joint occupancy of the premises by the wife with the husband enables her to give consent to a search, and in such case the evidence disclosed may be used against either. . . .

* * *

Clearly, one in joint control of the premises, at least when no objection is made by the other occupant, may admit police officers to the house, and the question of coercion aside it also is clear that no illegal search is involved as to what is in plain sight when the police officers are so admitted. . . . We are not prepared to say how much further the officers may proceed. . . .

We are of the view that the wife's right as joint occupant of the premises is the starting point for consideration of the lawfulness of a search made with her consent, that one of the circumstances to be considered is the husband's presence or absence, that assuming for present purposes but not deciding that the wife has implied authority to permit a search in the absence of her husband, nevertheless the search and seizure here made were not within the scope of that authority. When the officers searched the husband's personal effects to discover jewelry hidden in a cuff link case in a bedroom bureau drawer they went beyond the bounds of any possible justification. As stated in **People v. Carter, 48 Cal. 2d 737, 746, 312 P. 2d 665, 670:**

> ". . . When the usual amicable relations exist between husband and wife . . . *and the property seized is of a kind over which the wife normally exercises as much control as the husband,* it is reasonable to conclude that she is in a position to consent to a search and seizure of property in their home. * * *" (Italics added.)

* * *

NOTE 2.

CHIPP v. MURRAY
191 Kan. 73, 379 P. 2d 297 (1963)

SCHROEDER, JUSTICE.

This is an action by a private detective against a divorced man for services performed under a contract independently made by the man's wife prior to the divorce. . . .

* * *

No allegation is made in the petition herein that the wife was left destitute, or that the detective's services were necessary to obtain necessities to support the wife or children. This is not the theory of the appellant's case, and we do not, therefore, pass upon this point.

* * *

The appellant states few husbands would be willing to furnish money to a wife for detective fees to his own personal detriment. He then argues:

"* * * Without the credit of her husband, Mrs. Murray could not have obtained the advantages of the appellant's investigative services, no more than she could have obtained the services and derived the advantages of competent counsel. Both the attorney and the private detective have a role in the preparation and conduct of a lawsuit. Perry Mason and Paul Drake seem in point. Although neither is a party to the suit, the attorney as an officer of the court and drafter of pleadings and conductor of the course of litigation can secure, and commonly does, fee allowances in the case. The detective is relegated

to compensation by the husband, appellee, in a separate action or to payment by the divorced wife. If payment is not forthcoming from the wife then his course is solely against the husband, appellee herein."

The appellant contends that a progressive, realistic interpretation of G.S. 1949, 60-1507, warrants the inclusion of detective fees for services rendered a wife in a divorce suit on the ground that detective fees are as much a "necessity" as attorney fees.

* * *

. . . Generally, it may be said necessaries include those things needed and suitable to the rank and condition of the spouses and the style of life they have adopted. What necessaries are in kind and amount is to be determined in each case by the means, ability, social position and circumstances of both husband and wife.

The implied authority of the wife, where it exists, to pledge the credit of her husband seems to arise from the marriage relation itself, if not as an incident essential to its preservation, certainly as a consequence of its continual existence, and not as a power reserved for its destruction.

We hold in the eyes of the law the services of a detective to unearth the reputation, character, assets and activities of a husband at the instance of the wife is not a necessity for which the husband will be presumed to have pledged his credit by reason of the marriage relationship.

* * *

NOTE 3.

YOUNG v. KNIGHT
329 S.W. 2d 195 (Ky. 1959)

STANLEY, COMMISSIONER.

This is an action seeking an order prohibiting Honorable Thomas J. Knight, a Judge of the Criminal Branch . . . from enforcing a rule of contempt against the petitioner, Alma Young, for refusing to answer questions asked her in a grand jury investigation. Judge Knight has suspended his order adjudging the petitioner in contempt and ordering her committed to jail until the present action is decided.

* * *

The sequence which led to the proceeding is that the petitioner's father, Seavy Young, stands charged with the murder of John Charles Kirchner. Young had waived examining trial. The grand jury was in course of determining whether an indictment against him or anyone else should be returned. The petitioner is seventeen years old.

A transcript of evidence heard by the grand jury was filed with the circuit judge. A detective had testified at length as to his detections and as to particular circumstances of the homicide. In brief, his testimony was that the deceased, nineteen years old, had been the escort of Alma Young on the evening of May 17, 1959, and they had come home about half past one o'clock in the morning. Her father was waiting for them and after upbraiding the young couple, got in the rear seat of the boy's automobile and shot him while he and his daugher were on the front seat. The detective learned this and other circumstances from the daughter's statements to officers and newspaper reporters.

The petitioner went before the grand jury in obedience to a subpoena. She testified to some particulars which the detective had described. But she declined, upon advice of counsel, to answer several questions on the ground that her answers "may tend to incriminate me." The witness was taken before Judge Knight, and a hearing was had on the witness's refusal to answer these two questions: (1) "Were you in the car that night with your father and this young man who was killed at the time he was killed?" (2) "If your answer to the question now before the Court is in the affirmative, state to the grand jury who it was that shot John Kirchner."

Judge Knight ruled that the witness was not privileged from answering the questions as he did not believe the answers would incriminate her. The court directed the witness be returned to the grand jury room and advised her that she should answer the questions, warning her that if she still refused, he would hold her to be in contempt of court. Thereupon, it was stipulated by the attorneys representing the witness and her father that she would persist in her refusal. The court then adjudged the witness to be in contempt.

* * *

Juvenile courts are established as special tribunals with particular and limited jurisdiction. Their function in its application to public offenses is to administer justice in accordance with the progressive and humanitarian treatment of delinquent children charged with violating the criminal law. The proceedings are corrective and preventive—to prevent delinquency, to discipline and to check a criminal tendency in its inception—rather than punitive.

We construe the juvenile court statute as not depriving any other court of the inherent and essential right and power to consider and dispose of direct contempt.

* * *

The constitutional provision against self-incrimination is a shield and protection, available to all persons summoned as witnesses, whether or not they have been accused of crime, including those called up to testify at a grand jury inquiry.

However disagreeable it may have been to require this young girl, the petitioner herein, to testify to facts that may incriminate her father in the murder of which he stands accused, it is to be borne in mind that the constitutional immunity is for the protection of the witness and not for the protection of other persons. So, sympathy or a compassionate appeal cannot deprive the state of evidence to which it is entitled.

* * *

The conclusion of the whole matter is that an order prohibiting the respondent from proceeding to enforce his rule of contempt should be, as it is,

Denied.

d. HUTCHINS, ROBERT M., and SLESINGER, DONALD
Some Observations on the Law of Evidence: Family Relations*

[The] conception of the home as a unit, with all the members dwelling in sacrosanct confidence and harmony was never, apparently extended beyond the husband and wife. A son might testify against his father, and a brother might cast grave doubts on his sister's paternity. Even in days when some remote financial interest in the result of the action would disqualify, the most intimate blood relationship would not. Children might quarrel; they might attack their parents on the stand; their parents might appear for or against them in the most bitterly contested litigation; the domestic peace remained undisturbed.

In contrast with the legal conception of the family as indicated by the rules described . . . let us examine the actual situation of the family at the present time. Before the industrial revolution a family unit was a function of several forces all working in the same direction. Individual members of families were tied by sexual and affectional bonds. If these bonds were frequently ambivalent, disharmony was prevented by economic necessity and social pressure. It was important to keep the family together because it was a producing unit, and economic disaster might very well follow a breakup. These sexual and economic forces found formal expression in the law, but one may seriously doubt that the law of evidence had any formative effect on family life in general. Too few people get into court, and the adjective law is little known outside of it. Family unity there was, be-

---

* 13 MINN. L. Rev. 675, 677-680, 682-86 (1929).

yond reasonable doubt. But evidence was merely parallel to it.

The industrial revolution wrought profound changes in family life. It gradually altered family economy, by emphasizing the family as a consuming, not a producing unit. Means of support grew up outside the home, freeing the children and the women from economic family domination. It increased mobility and destroyed the physical unity of the home. In many cases it forced disunity on unwilling families by introducing competition between parents and children, husbands and wives, or by creating widely separated labor markets that had to be tapped if individuals were to live. That male heads of families were able to find satisfactory employment in coal mines, for instance, was no guarantee that the same locality would also absorb the energies of wife and children. Economically it was no longer necessary, or even desirable, for the family to remain a unit ; indeed, in the early days of child labor the dormitory system made such unity impossible.

As a result of the removal of economic pressure negative attitudes more easily find expression in family disorganization. . . .

* * *

If economic life is disorganizing to the family, so are many other modern developments. The breakdown of religion, the diversified recreation made possible by the automobile and the movie, have destroyed the religious and recreational unity of the family, and laid emphasis on dispersion. It is literally true in many modern families that the right hand knows not what the left hand doeth. All the social and economic forces of society then are acting centrifugally, tending to break up the old family relationship. The only remaining binding ties are sexual and affectional. This realignment of forces makes a new family adjustment inevitable.

In the face of all this we find the law of evidence making a rather ineffectual effort in a restricted field to stem the tide. No wonder the disqualifying rule has been swept away in civil cases. In this period of readjustment, we can see no reason for sacrificing individual justice (as it has demonstrably been sacrificed in several cases) to a mythical family unity.

It may be argued that even though the disqualification is removed the rule protecting confidential communications should be retained ; that with everything breaking up the home, and only affection and intimacy holding it together, these qualities should be fostered as much as possible. At the present time the chief protection of the homes of those who succeed in keeping out of the criminal courts is this privilege. The theory of the privilege is clear ; it is intended to promote confidence between husband and wife by assuring them that their confidences will never be revealed without their consent. Hence death, divorce, and annulment do not remove the bar. Although in the particular case the home has gone to pieces, other people whose homes are still intact must be assured that their confidences will remain secret should their homes ever go to pieces, too.

* * *

. . . People in personal difficulties are tending more and more to disclose secrets of their personal lives to psychiatrists. Where scientific truth is desired innumerable people, many with no personal problems, are not unwilling to betray marital confidences. A number of recent studies substantiate this view, and the subjects of them have not become demonstrably unhappy as a result. Individual justice is as important as social science or personal difficulties and has clearly as much to gain by compulsory waiver of privilege where, in the discretion of the trial judge, important evidence might be obtained in that way, and no other. Spouses have a perfect right to protection from publicity (all social science studies guarantee that absolutely) ; but this protection can be obtained in other ways than that of silence.

It seems clear, then, that family relationships should not disqualify witnesses, nor render important evidence inadmissible through privilege. If the evidence is admitted, then, should not the relationship be offered in order to aid the tribunal in evaluating it? Should not one be able to impeach a witness by pointing to relationship and deducing therefrom bias which would discredit the testimony offered?

Unlike the rules on competency and privilege, the rules on impeachment by showing bias extend to other relationships than that of husband and wife. A communication between parent and child or sister and brother is never privileged because of relationship. But any relationship may be used to show the possibility that the witness is lying because of it. The rule extends to illicit love affairs, which are protected by no privilege, and to all family situations. It is supposed that the jury should have an opportunity to appraise the testimony in the light of the witnesses' relations to the parties by blood, marriage, affection, or interest.

* * *

We find, on the whole, then, that there is a decided lag in the judicial attitude towards the family, at least as far as the rules of evidence are concerned. The courts are trying to maintain a family organization that is being superseded by a new one. There seems to be no special reason for maintaining a moribund family concept, for the modern one is demonstrably better suited to our economic structure, and according to any observers, is better for the independent development of children. Furthermore, even if it were desirable to emphasize the mediaeval family, it seems that the law of evidence is a peculiarly ineffectual branch of jurisprudence to foster it, because it is the most technical, and least known field as far as the general public is concerned. Thus the courts, in some cases at least, are sacrificing justice to a questionable and, by this means, unenforceable ideal. Therefore it would not be unsafe to extend the attitude in civil cases to cover the whole family field. Disqualification thus would be removed. Privilege might well be restricted, with the understanding that it is automatically waived wherever crucial evidence can be obtained in no other way. When family bias is shown in order to impeach a witness, it should be rebuttable by detailed individual histories, whenever the evidence offered is important enough to have great weight with the tribunal.

2.

IN CRIME—THE FAMILY AS AN ENCLOSURE FOR COLLABORATION, AGGRESSION, PROTECTION, DISCIPLINE AND SEXUALITY

a. In Conspiracy

UNITED STATES v. DEGE
364 U.S. 51 (1960)

MR. JUSTICE FRANKFURTER delivered the opinion of the Court.

This is an indictment charging husband and wife with conspiring to commit an offense against the United States . . . in that they sought illicitly to bring goods into the United States with intent to defraud it. . . .

[T]he District Court dismissed the indictment on the ground that it did not state an offense, to wit, a husband and wife are legally incapable of conspiring. . . .

The question raised . . . is clearcut and uncomplicated. The claim that husband and wife are outside the scope of an enactment of Congress in 1948, making it an offense for two persons to conspire, must be given short shrift once we heed the admonition of this Court that "we free our minds from the notion that criminal statutes must be construed by some artificial and conventional rule," *United States v. Union Supply Co.,* 215 U.S. 50, 55, and therefore do not allow ourselves to be obfuscated by medieval views regarding the legal status of woman and the common law's reflection of them. Considering that legitimate business enterprises between husband and wife have long been commonplace in our time, it would enthrone an unreality into a rule of law to suggest that man and wife are legally incapable of engaging in illicit enterprises and therefore, forsooth, do not engage in them.

None of the considerations of policy touching the law's encouragement or discouragement of domestic felicities on the basis of which this Court determined appropriate rules for testimonial compulsion as between spouses, *Hawkins v. United States,* 358 U.S. 74, and *Wyatt v. United States,* 362 U.S. 525, are relevant to yielding to the claim that an unqualified interdiction by Congress against a conspiracy between two persons precludes a husband and wife from being two persons. Such an immunity to husband and wife as a pair of conspirators would have to attribute to Congress one of two assumptions: either that responsibility of husband and wife for joint participation in a criminal enterprise would make for marital disharmony, or that a wife must be presumed to act under the coercive influence of her husband and, therefore, cannot be a willing participant. The former assumption is unnourished by sense; the latter implies a view of American womanhood offensive to the ethos of our society.

The fact of the matter is that we are asked to write into law a doctrine that parrot-like has been repeated in decisions and texts from what was given its authoritative expression by Hawkins early in the eighteenth century. . . .

For this Court now to act on Hawkins's formulation of the medieval view that husband and wife "are esteemed but as one Person in Law, and are presumed to have but one Will" would indeed be "blind imitation of the past." It would require us to disregard the vast changes in the status of woman—the extension of her rights and correlative duties—whereby a wife's legal submission to her husband has been wholly wiped out, not only in the English-speaking world generally but emphatically so in this country.

How far removed we were even nearly a century ago when Congress passed the original statute against criminal conspiracy, the Act of March 2, 1867, 14 Stat. 484, from the legal and social climate of eighteenth century common law regarding the status of woman is pithily illustrated by recalling the self-deluding romanticism of Blackstone, whereby he could conscientiously maintain that "even the disabilities, which the wife lies under, are for the most part intended for her protection and benefit. So great a favourite is the female sex of the laws of England." Blackstone, Commentaries on the Laws of England (1765), Bk. I, ch. 15, p. 433. It would be an idle parade of learning to document the statement that these common-law disabilities were extensively swept away in our different state of society, both by legislation and adjudication, long before the originating conspiracy Act of 1867 was passed. Suffice it to say that we cannot infuse into the conspiracy statute a fictitious attribution to Congress of regard for the medieval notion of woman's submissiveness to the benevolent coercive powers of a husband in order to relieve her of her obligation of obedience to an unqualifiedly expressed Act of Congress by regarding her as a person whose legal personality is merged in that of her husband making the two one.

Reversed.

MR. CHIEF JUSTICE WARREN with whom MR. JUSTICE BLACK and MR. JUSTICE WHITTAKER join, dissenting.

* * *

It is not necessary to be wedded to fictions to approve the husband-wife conspiracy doctrine, for one of the dangers which that doctrine averts is the prosecution and conviction of persons for "conspiracies" which Congress never meant to be included within the statute. A wife, simply by virtue of the intimate life she shares with her husband, might easily perform acts that would technically be sufficient to involve her in a criminal conspiracy with him, but which might be far removed from the arm's-length agreement typical of that crime. It is not a medieval mental quirk or an attitude "unnourished by sense" to believe that husbands and wives should not be subjected to such a risk, or that such a possibility should not be permitted to endanger the confidentiality of the marriage relationship. While it is easy enough to ridicule Hawkins' pronouncement in Pleas of the Crown from a metaphysical point of view, the concept of the "oneness" of a married couple may reflect an abiding belief that the communion between husband and wife is such that their actions are not always to be regarded by the criminal law as if there were no marriage.

By making inroads in the name of law enforcement into the protection which Congress has afforded to the marriage relationship, the Court today continues in the path charted by the recent decision in *Wyatt v. United States,* 362 U.S. 525, where the Court held that, under the circumstances of that case, a wife could be compelled to testify against her husband over her objection. One need not waver in his belief in virile law enforcement to insist that there are other things in American life which are also of great importance, and to which even law enforcement must accommodate itself. One of these is the solidarity and the confidential relationship of marriage. The Court's opinion dogmatically asserts that the hus-

band-wife conspiracy doctrine does not in fact protect this relationship, and that hence the doctrine "enthrone[s] an unreality into a rule of law." I am not easily persuaded that a rule accepted by so many people for so many centuries can be so lightly dismissed. But in any event, I submit that the power to depose belongs to Congress, not to this Court. I dissent.

NOTES

NOTE 1.

LUTWAK v. UNITED STATES
344 U.S. 604 (1952)

MR. JUSTICE MINTON delivered the opinion of the Court.

The petitioners, Marcel Max Lutwak, Munio Knoll, and Regina Treitler, together with Leopold Knoll and Grace Klemtner, were indicted on six counts in the Northern District of Illinois, Eastern Division. The first count charged conspiracy . . . "to defraud the United States of and concerning its governmental function and right of administering" the immigration laws and the Immigration and Naturalization Service, by obtaining the illegal entry into this country of three aliens as spouses of honorably discharged veterans. . . .

* * *

The first count of the indictment charged that the petitioners conspired to have three honorably discharged veterans journey to Paris and go through marriage ceremonies with Munio, Leopold and Maria. The brothers and Maria would then accompany their new spouses to the United States and secure entry into this country by representing themselves as alien spouses of World War II veterans. It was further a part of the plan that the marriages were to be in form only, solely for the purpose of enabling Munio, Leopold and Maria to enter the United States. The parties to the marriages were not to live together as husband and wife, and thereafter would take whatever legal steps were necessary to sever the legal ties. It was finally alleged that the petitioners conspired to conceal these acts in order to prevent disclosure of the conspiracy to the immigration authorities.

* * *

When the good faith of the marital relation is pertinent and it is made to appear to the trial court, as it was here, that the relationship was entered into with no intention of the parties to live together as husband and wife but only for the purpose of using the marriage ceremony in a scheme to defraud, the ostensible spouses are competent to testify against each other. Here again, we are not concerned with the validity or invalidity of these so-called marriages. We are concerned only with the application of a common-law principle of evidence to the circumstances of this case. In interpreting the common law in this instance, we are to determine whether "in the light of reason and experience" we should interpret the common law so as to make these ostensible wives competent to testify against their ostensible husbands. The reason for the rule at common law disqualifying the wife is to protect the sanctity and tranquility of the marital relationship. It is hollow mockery for the petitioners in arguing for the policy of the rule to invoke the reason for the rule and to say to us "the husband and wife have grown closer together as an emotional, social, and cultural unit" and to speak of "the close emotional ties between husband and wife" and of "the special protection society affords to the marriage relationship." In a sham, phony, empty ceremony such as the parties went through in this case, the reason for the rule disqualifying a spouse from giving testimony disappears, and with it the rule.

* * *

MR. JUSTICE JACKSON, whom MR. JUSTICE BLACK and MR. JUSTICE FRANKFURTER join, dissenting.

Whenever a court has a case where behavior that obviously is sordid can be proved to be criminal only with great difficulty, the effort to bridge the gap is apt to produce bad law. We are concerned about the effect of this decision in three respects.

1. We are not convinced that any crime has been proved, even on the assumption that all evidence in the record was admissible. These marriages were formally contracted in France, and there is no contention that they were forbidden or illegal there for any reason. It is admitted that some judicial procedure is necessary if the parties wish to be relieved of their obligations. Whether by reason of the reservations with which the parties entered into the marriages they could be annulled may be a nice question of French law, in view of the fact that no one of them deceived the other. We should expect it to be an even nicer question whether a third party, such as the state in a criminal process, could simply ignore the ceremony and its consequences, as the Government does here.

We start with marriages that either are valid or at least have not been proved to be invalid in their inception. The Court brushes this question aside as immaterial, but we think it goes to the very existence of an offense. If the parties are validly married, even though the marriage is a sordid one, we should suppose that would end the case. On the other hand, if the marriage ceremonies were for some reason utterly void and held for naught, as if they never had happened, the Government could well claim that entry into the United States as married persons was fraud. But between these two extremes is the more likely case—marriages that are not void but perhaps voidable. In one of these cases, the parties (on the trial) expressed their desire to stay married, and they were acquitted; and no one contends that their marriage is void. Certainly if these marriages were merely voidable and had not been adjudged void at the time of the entry into this country, it was not a fraud to represent them as subsisting. We should think that the parties to them might have been prosecuted with as much reason if they had represented themselves to be single. Marriages of convenience are not uncommon and it cannot be that we would hold it a fraud for one who has contracted a marriage not forbidden by law to represent himself as wedded, even if there were grounds for annulment or divorce and proceedings to that end were contemplated.

* * *

2. . . . The Court's position seems to be that privileged testimony may be received to destroy its own privilege. We think this is not allowable, for the same reason that one cannot lift himself by his own bootstraps.

* * *

NOTE 2.

BLACKSTONE, WILLIAM

Commentaries on the Laws of England of Public Wrongs*

. . . In treason . . . (the highest crime which a member of society can, as such, be guilty of), no plea of coverture shall excuse the wife; no presumption of the husband's coercion shall extenuate her guilt: as well because of the odiousness and dangerous consequence of the crime itself, as because the husband, having broken through the most sacred tie of social community by rebellion against the state, has no right to that obedience from a wife, which he himself as a subject has forgotten to pay. In inferior misdemeanors also, we may remark another exception; that a wife may be indicted *with* her husband, for keeping a brothel; for this is an offence touching the domestic economy or government of the house, in which the wife has a principal share; and is also such an offence as the law presumes to be generally conducted by the intrigues of the

---

* Boston: Beacon Press, 1962, p. 27.

female sex.[1] And in all cases where the wife offends alone, without the company or coercion of her husband, she is responsible for her offence as much as any feme-sole.

NOTE 3.

EISENHOWER, DWIGHT D.
The White House Years: Mandate for Change 1953-1956*

On my desk, when I took office, lay a document which was to lead to much controversy throughout the spring of 1953. Submitted to the Department of Justice but not acted upon in the final weeks of the Truman administration, it was an appeal for executive clemency in the case of Julius and Ethel Rosenberg who, convicted of espionage against the United States, were under sentence of death.

* * *

. . . On May 25, however, the Supreme Court delivered its decision: it again refused to hear the appeal. On June 15 it denied a plea to stay the execution.

The next day, because this problem was very much on my mind, I wrote to my son, John, then serving in Korea, about one aspect of the case:

To address myself more specifically to the Rosenberg case for a minute, I must say that it goes against the grain to avoid interfering in the case where a woman is to receive capital punishment. Over against this, however, must be placed one or two facts that have greater significance. The first of these is that in this instance it is the woman who is the strong and recalcitrant character, the man is the weak one. She has obviously been the leader in everything they did in the spy ring. The second thing is that if there would be any commuting of the woman's sentence without the man's then from here on the Soviets would simply recruit their spies from among women.

1. 'Mr. Christian says that' in all misdemeanors the wife may be found guilty with the husband; and that the reason why she was excused in burglary, larceny, &c., was because she could not tell what property the husband might claim in the goods. (10 Mod. 63 & 335.) But the better reason seems to be, that as by the ancient law the husband had the benefit of clergy, if he could read, while in no case could women have that benefit; and as it would, when clergy was prayed, have been an odious proceeding to have executed the wife, and dismissed the husband with a slight punishment, it was thought better that in such cases she should be altogether acquitted. This reason is stated also not to apply to misdemeanors; 'but see on this point R. v. Price, 8 Car. & P. 19, 541.'

* From *The White House Years: Mandate for Change 1953-1956* by Dwight D. Eisenhower. Copyright © 1963 by Dwight D. Eisenhower. Reprinted by permission of Doubleday & Company, Inc. and William Heinemann, Ltd., publishers.

b. In Traffic Violations

PEOPLE v. STATLEY
91 Cal. App. 2d 943, 206 P. 2d 76 (1949)

BISHOP, JUDGE.

Convicted on a charge that she had failed to yield the right of way to a pedestrian in a crosswalk, the defendant contends that the judgment of conviction should be reversed because the trial court failed to give her requested instruction that "under the laws of this State, a married woman is not capable of committing a misdemeanor while acting under threats, command or coercion of her husband." In support of her contention the defendant advances three arguments: (a) the instruction embodies a correct principle of law; (b) it was called for in this case by direct evidence that she was acting under her husband's command; (c) it was made pertinent by the common law presumption that a misdemeanor committed by a married woman in her husband's presence is done under his coercion. We have reached the conclusion that the instruction should have been given. It was a correct statement of the law, and the evidence before the jurors made it applicable. We cannot, however, square the ancient presumption with the facts of modern life. We are not ready to put our stamp of approval on the statement that, when a married woman who is operating a motor vehicle in which her husband is a passenger, neglects to make a boulevard stop, fails to signal before she turns, or commits any other violation of the traffic laws, the probability is that she did so because he made her do so.

There can be no doubt that the requested instruction is a correct statement of the law, for we find in section 26, Penal Code: "All persons are capable of committing crimes except: * * * Seven. Married women (except for felonies) acting under the threats, command, or coercion of their husbands." . . . The possibility that this code provision has become anachronistic does not justify the courts in disregarding it. A legislative enactment is not repealed by time or changed conditions, but only by further legislation. . . .

* * *

. . . In Smith v. Meyers, 1898, 54 Neb. 1, 74 N.W. 277, 278, we [said] " . . . A wife is no longer a marionette, moved at will by the husband, either in fact or in law; and, with the legal recognition of a separate and responsible existence, she must assume some of the burdens of life,—among others, that of testifying to the truth, under the customary penalties."

* * *

We conclude, then, that the reign of the thousand year old presumption has come to an end.

In our society, where almost no bride promises to obey her husband, and where it is not accepted as the usual that a wife does what her husband wishes by way of yielding obedience to a dominant will, the basis for the presumption has disappeared. A presumption that has lost its reason must be confined to a museum; it has no place in the administration of justice. If, therefore, a wife is to escape the consequences of her disobedience of a statute on the ground that she was acting in obedience to her husband, the fact is not established by the mere circumstance that her husband was present when she offended. . . .

c. In Murder

HOLMES v. DIRECTOR OF PUBLIC PROSECUTION
[1946] A.C. 588, 596-600

VISCOUNT SIMON.

My Lords, the point of law in this appeal is whether Charles J. was right in telling the jury that, on the evidence at the trial, and having regard to the law, it was not open to the jury to find a verdict of manslaughter, and that the statement by the accused's wife to him that she had been unfaithful to him was not such provocation as could justify a verdict of manslaughter instead of murder. . . .

. . . The whole doctrine relating to provocation depends on the fact that it causes, or may cause, a sudden and temporary loss of self-control whereby malice, which is the formation of an intention to kill or to inflict grievous bodily harm, is negatived. Consequently, where the provocation inspires an actual intention to kill (such as Holmes admitted in the present case), or to inflict grievous bodily harm, the doctrine that provocation may reduce murder to manslaughter seldom applies. Only one very special exception has been recognized, viz., the actual finding of a spouse in the act of adultery. This has always been treated as an exception to the general rule. . . . Blackstone (Commentaries) (Book IV, p. 190) justifies the exception on the ground that "there could not be a greater provocation." But it has been rightly laid down that the exception cannot be extended. . . . Even if Iago's insinuations against Desdemona's virtue had been true, Othello's crime was murder and nothing else.

Necessary self-defence, or action taken in the necessary defence, for example, of wife or child from outrage or maltreatment, stand apart, as in such cases there is no crime at all committed.

This brings me to the question which, as I understand, was the actual reason why the Law Officer's certificate was given in this case: viz. whether "mere words" can ever be regarded as so provocative to a reasonable man as to reduce to manslaughter felonious homicide committed upon the speaker in consequence of such verbal provocation. . . . There is . . . a . . . sense which may sometimes attach to the meaning of "mere words," for they may be used, not as an expression of abuse, but as a means of conveying information of a fact, or of what is alleged to be a fact. This must be the sense in which Blackburn J. spoke in *Reg.* v. *Rothwell,* 12 Cox. C.C. 145, 147, when, in the course of summing up to a jury in the case of a man charged with murdering his wife, he went so far as to say: "As a general rule of law, no provocation of words will reduce the crime of murder to that of manslaughter, but under special circumstances there may be such a provocation of words as will have that effect; for instance, if a husband suddenly hearing from his wife that she had committed adultery, and he having had no idea of such a thing before, were thereupon to kill his wife, it might be manslaughter." It is to be noted that Blackburn J. said "might," and not "would," and the illustration had no resemblance to the facts of the case he was trying. Blackburn J.'s dictum was applied in the accused's favour in *R.* v. *Jones,* 72 J.P. 215, and was not dissented from in *R.* v. *Palmer,* [1913] 2 K.B. 29, when, however, the Court of Criminal Appeal refused to extend the suggested exception to cover the case of a man engaged to be married to a young woman whom he killed when she confessed to illicit intercourse with someone else. . . . In my view, however, a sudden confession of adultery without more can never constitute provocation of a sort which might reduce murder to manslaughter. . . . The rule, whatever it is, must apply to either spouse alike, for we have left behind us the age when the wife's subjection to her husband was regarded by the law as the basis of the marital relation, when, as Bracton said [Pollock and Maitland's History of English Law vol. II., p. 406.], she was "sub virga viri sui" and when the remedies of the Divorce Court did not exist. Parliament has now conferred on the aggrieved wife the same right to divorce her husband for unfaithfulness alone as he holds against her, and, neither, on hearing an admission of adultery from the other, can use physical violence against the other which results in death and then urge that the provocation received reduces the crime to mere manslaughter. It is not necessary in this appeal to decide whether there are any conceivable circumstances accompanying the use of words without actual violence, which would justify the leaving to a jury of the issue of manslaughter as against murder. It is enough to say that the duty of the judge at the trial, in relevant cases, is to tell the jury that a confession of adultery without more is never sufficient to reduce an offence which would otherwise be murder to manslaughter. . . .

NOTES
NOTE 1.

MORRIS v. UNITED STATES
217 F. Supp. 220 (N.D. Tex. 1963)

BREWSTER, DISTRICT JUDGE.

[T]here existed in the ranch country of Texas what was known as the "unwritten law". Every young man understood it just as well as he knew what the meat course was going to be at ranch headquarters while calves were being "worked" during a roundup. The effect of the "unwritten law" was to make a bad insurance risk out of a man who broke up another man's home and deprived him of the daily association of his wife and children. He usually died suddenly out of lead poisonin'. That was a disease contracted the first time the outraged husband and father came in gunshot range of the homebreaker. The husband himself was never plagued with the disease, but he was an almost certain carrier of it. He was usually equipped to give six doses of lead in rapid succession if necessary to produce fatal results. In some cases, the husband was not even indicted; but he was usually brought to trial so that his justification could be made public. . . . It made no difference in the outcome of the case if it developed that the deceased was unarmed. During their deliberations, the juries usually found that the law given them in the charge was inadequate to do what they thought was equity. To supply that deficiency, they resorted to the "unwritten law" for the purpose not only of acquitting the husband, but also of endorsing his conduct, of recognizing that it was open season on homebreakers, and of serving notice on each one of them, actual or potential, to stay in his own back yard.

*   *   *

NOTE 2.

PEOPLE v. TOMLINS
213 N.Y. 240, 107 N.E. 496 (1914)

CARDOZO, J.

The defendant shot and killed his son, a young man of 22. The shooting took place on August 26, 1913, in the little cottage in Stony Point where the son had been born and reared. On the trial, the father maintained that . . . he had acted justifiably, in lawful self-defense. . . . We have . . . only to inquire whether there was material error in the court's statement of the law. The jury were properly instructed that homicide in self-defense is not justifiable unless there is reasonable ground to apprehend a design on the part of the person slain to commit a felony, or to do some great personal injury to the slayer, and unless also there is reasonable ground to apprehend that the danger is imminent.

These instructions were coupled, however, with a statement that it was the defendant's duty, if possible, to retreat and escape. "A man," said the court, "has no right to resort to force and violence against another, even where the danger is imminent, even where he has reasonable cause to believe that he is in danger, unless he has no reasonably safe means of escape and retreat."

We think that these instructions are erroneous as applied to the case at bar. The homicide occurred in the defendant's dwelling. It is not now and never has been the law that a man assailed in his own dwelling is bound to retreat. If assailed there, he may stand his ground and resist the attack. He is under no duty to take to the fields and the highways, a fugitive from his own home. More than 200 years ago it was said by Lord Chief Justice Hale (1 Hale's Pleas of the Crown, 486): In case a man "is assailed in his own house he need not flee as far as he can, as in other cases of se defendendo, for he hath the protection of his house to excuse him from flying, as that would be to give up the protection of his house to his adversary by flight." Flight is for sanctuary and shelter, and shelter, if not sanctuary, is in the home. [T]here is, in such a situation, no duty to retreat . . . . The rule is the same whether the attack proceeds from some other occupant or from an intruder. . . .

We think that if the situation justified the defendant, as a reasonable man, in believing that he was about to be murderously attacked, he had the right to stand his ground.

*   *   *

. . . The defendant admitted, on cross-examination, that it was possible for him to run away from the house and escape the danger. The charge that it was his duty to escape, if he could, was therefore equivalent to an instruction to the jury that the defendant had failed to justify the homicide on the ground of self-defense. It was thus a direction to find the defendant guilty, at least, of some degree of crime. . . . The situation is the same in effect as if the issue of self-defense had not been submitted to the jury at all. It was submitted in form, but not in substance, for the submission was coupled with instructions that predetermined the answer. . . .

NOTE 3.

MITCHELL v. STATE
43 Fla. 188, 30 So. 803 (1901)

MABRY, J. . . .

The fourth assignment . . . imputes to the court error in refusing . . . to have the jury instructed that, if they believed . . . that, at the time defendant Mitchell fired the fatal shot that killed the deceased, Waterman Joiner, the latter . . . was in the act of striking at the sister of defendant with an open knife in an angry manner. . . . The avowed object of this request was to place defendant Mitchell in a position to avail himself of the defense of justifiable homicide embraced in . . . section 2378, Rev. St., to the effect that a homicide is justifiable when committed . . . in defense of his or her husband, wife, parent, child, master, mistress, or servant. . . . In the specific enumeration of the persons in the statute the legislature has employed no terms under which the courts are authorized to include other persons of similar relation, and, until the statute is amended, brother and sister cannot be included. . . .

NOTE 4.

COMMONWEALTH v. HALL
322 Mass. 523, 78 N.E. 2d 644 (1948)

SPALDING, JUSTICE.

The defendant was convicted of the murder in the second degree of her daughter Jane Doe Hall. . . .

There was evidence tending to show the following: The defendant, who was twenty-four years of age and unmarried, lived with her father, and brother in Woburn. She was the mother of two illegitimate children, a son, David, aged 2, and a daughter born on August 18, 1946, to whom no name was given. The children lived with the defendant. . . . Two days after the birth of the daughter the defendant left the hospital and returned home. Two or three days later one Linscott, the chairman of the board of health and charities of the city of Woburn, and Gorman, an agent of the board, called on the defendant to see what was to be done with her child who was still at the hospital. The defendant was asked whether she was married and she stated that she was. She refused, however, to divulge the name of the child's father or to furnish any information as to his whereabouts. When told by representatives of the board that it was customary to approach the father to see what he was going to do toward bringing up the child she replied, "What is the matter with the city of Woburn bringing it up? What do we pay taxes for?" Linscott then said to the defendant, "If you want us to do something about it you will have to work along with us." He suggested that she think the matter over and if she changed her mind to get in touch with them and they would do what they could. Linscott never heard from her again.

Ten days after its birth the baby was discharged from the hospital and was entrusted to the care of the defendant. At birth the child was normal and weighed nine pounds and four ounces. While it was at the hospital it "progressed normally" and at the time it was discharged it was in good health. At that time the defendant was given a formula for feeding the baby by the doctor who had delivered the child and had cared for it since birth.

*　*　*

On Thursday, October 24, 1946, shortly after 11:00 A.M., one Reil, a police officer of the city of Woburn, accompanied by Miss Reynolds, a nurse of the board of public welfare, went to the house where the defendant lived. The defendant, who answered the door, said to the officer, "Now, who is complaining of me?" The officer informed the defendant that he had a warrant to take the two children to the city infirmary by reason of a complaint charging neglect. The defendant told the officer that he could take the baby but not the boy. . . . [T]he defendant told the officer that the baby was up in the attic. In reply to a question whether the baby was alive or dead the defendant stated that she did not know. She stated that she had put the child in the attic Tuesday morning and had not gone to see it since that time. . . .

The nurse and the officer then proceeded to the attic where they found the dead body of the baby lying on the floor wrapped in blankets; it appeared to be "very, very thin," and "bones were showing through the body."

Later that day (October 24) the defendant made a statement to a State detective which included the following . . . The baby was losing weight and was starving to death because it was not getting the proper food. The formula called for some syrup, but she had run out of it and was unable to get any money from her brother or father to buy more. The cost of the syrup was about 69 cents. Groceries for the house were purchased by her at the grocery store and were paid for by her father. They also received four quarts of milk a day which were paid for by her father. The baby was last fed by her at 1 A.M. Tuesday. On Tuesday afternoon the defendant heard the baby crying but did not go up to see it. On that same afternoon the defendant with her son David went to the stores to do some shopping. She had $5 or $6 which her father had given her to buy some clothing for David. Failing to find what she wanted, she purchased some curtain rods. She did not purchase syrup for the baby because "she didn't think of it." She was getting so many complaints from her brother and father about the noise the baby was making that "she was sick and tired of it all." Asked whether she had put the baby in the attic for the purpose of having it die, the defendant replied, "I guess so."

*　*　*

The judge rightly denied the defendant's motion for a "directed verdict of not guilty of murder in the second degree. . . ." While the precise question seems never to have been decided in this Commonwealth, we have no doubt that such conduct in the circumstances obtaining here would constitute murder at common law. In Regina v. Hughes, 7 Cox C.C. 301, page 302, Lord Campbell, C.J., said, "But it has never been doubted that if death is the directed consequence of the malicious omission of the performance of a duty (as of a mother to nourish her infant child) this is a case of murder. If the omission was not malicious and arose from negligence only, it is a case of manslaughter". . . .

By the law of this Commonwealth the defendant was under a duty to provide for the support and maintenance of her child notwithstanding its illegitimacy. It was said by Parsons, C.J., in Wright v. Wright, 2 Mass. 109, 110, "In legal contemplation, a bastard is generally considered as the relative of no one. But, to provide for his support and education, the mother has a right to the custody and control of him, and is bound to maintain him, as his natural guardian." . . .

To render criminal the defendant's omission to discharge the duty owed to the child she must have had the capacity and means of performing it. . . . There was evidence which would have warranted the jury in finding that the defendant's physical condition was such, despite her testimony to the contrary, that she was able to take care of the child after she returned from the hospital. . . .

NOTE 5.

ROYAL COMMISSION REPORT ON CAPITAL PUNISHMENT*

Fifty Cases of Murder in England and Scotland, 1931-1951

1. A coloured seaman stabbed a woman who had bigamously married him. He had stabbed her and her daughter on a previous occasion and was then sentenced to 11 months' imprisonment. The woman took him back to live with her on his release from prison, but later, because of his brutal treatment of her, gave herself up to the police for bigamy. She was released on bail. While she was on bail he killed her in revenge for her action in confessing to bigamy. No recommendation to mercy. Executed.

*   *   *

* Cmd. 8932 (Sept. 1953), pp. 320-323. Reprinted by permission of the Controller of Her Brittannic Majesty's Stationery Office.

8. A man struck his brother in the groin with a knife after an altercation about payment for drinks. They had been drinking but were not drunk, and had previously been close friends. The prisoner immediately made frantic efforts to obtain help for the wounded man. Strong recommendation to mercy. Reprieved.

*   *   *

17. A man killed his fiancee, because she persisted in going out with another man on the two evenings each week when she did not go out with him. He was a man of good character and was said to be of even temper and quiet disposition. Strongly recommended to mercy. Reprieved.

*   *   *

23. A chauffeur-handyman, aged 18½, had become the lover of his elderly employer's wife, who was 39. He and his mistress stayed for four days together at a London hotel, and two days after their return he killed her husband with a mallet in a nervous outburst of jealousy because the husband and wife were preparing to go out together. The woman was also charged with murder, but was acquitted and three days later committed suicide. Recommended to mercy. Reprieved.

*   *   *

25. A woman poisoned her husband with strychnine. For a long time the pair had lived in a state of unhappiness, but, although she maintained that he was a drunkard and that she and their son lived in terror of him, he had the reputation locally of being respectable and well-liked man. Strongly recommended to mercy. Executed.

*   *   *

30. A boy of 19 sided with his father in a quarrel with his mother, and afterwards packed a suitcase and went to his fiancee's house, intending to stay there; but late that night he returned to "make it up". The doors were bolted and, entering through a window, he found a soldier with his mother in circumstances pointing to misconduct. The soldier escaped and a violent quarrel ensued. Later the soldier returned to ask for his clothes, whereupon the youth chased him and stabbed him in the back. Strongly recommended to mercy. Reprieved.

31. A youth of 18 inflicted fatal injuries with a chopper on his step-father, who was abusing and insulting his mother. He had arrived home to find his mother in a very distressed condition because of her husband's treatment, and had been told by his sister that she feared their mother would com-

mit suicide. Strongly recommended to mercy. Reprieved.

* * *

36. Two Jewish refugees, mother and daughter, who had come to this country from Germany, had become depressed and worried by German successes in the war and by the thought of what might happen to them in the event of invasion. Finally they decided to die together and both took overdoses of veronal. The mother died, and the daughter was convicted of murder as the survivor of a suicide pact. Strongly recommended to mercy. Reprieved.

* * *

38. A man and his wife were convicted of murdering their three eldest children by asphyxiating them with coal gas and attempting to murder their two other children by the same method. The family was very respectable and the parents appeared to have been very much upset on discovering that their eldest daughter (aged 15) was pregnant. The whole family was discovered gassed in the kitchen of their house, but the parents and the two youngest children recovered, probably because they were on the floor, where the concentration of gas was lower, while the elder children were on a bed. Reprieved.

39. A woman gassed her son, aged 30, a hopeless imbecile, who had to be attended to like a baby. She had been told that she must enter a hospital immediately to undergo an operation. She at first said that she could not have the operation because there was no one to look after her son, but it was made clear to her that she could not live for more than six months unless the operation was performed. Strongly recommended to mercy. Reprieved immediately.

d. In Manslaughter and Assault

[i]

STATE v. ENGLAND
220 Ore. 395, 349 P. 2d 668 (1960)

PERRY, JUSTICE.

The grand jury returned an indictment against the defendant David C. England seeking to charge him with the crime of involuntary manslaughter. The charging part of the indictment is as follows:

"* * * then and there being, did then and there unlawfully, feloniously and in the commission of a lawful act, to-wit: while disciplining his son Charles Edwin England, age 12, act without due caution and circumspection in that said defendant then and there having a duty to use reasonable force in said disciplining, did strike said Charles Edwin England about the head and face with defendant's hand with force and violence thereby inflicting injuries upon the said

Charles Edwin England, and did thereby . . . produce the death of him . . . on the 8th day of February, 1959."

The trial court sustained the defendant's demurrer thereto on the grounds that the indictment failed to state facts sufficient to constitute a crime and the state has appealed.

ORS 163.040(2) defines the crime of involuntary manslaughter as follows:

"Any person who, in the commission of any unlawful act, or a lawful act without due caution or circumspection, involuntarily kills another, is guilty of manslaughter. . . ."

Under certain circumstances the law recognizes a homicide as excusable:

ORS 163.110(1): "The killing of a human being is excusable when committed:

"(1) By accident or misfortune in lawfully correcting a child, or servant, or in doing any other lawful act, by lawful means, with usual and ordinary caution and without any unlawful intent."

The parties agree that these statutes are in pari materia and must be construed together. . . .

It is the contention of the state that, having alleged the doing of a lawful act in a negligent manner which resulted in a homicide, the indictment fully and sufficiently charges the defendant with the crime of involuntary manslaughter. The difficulty, however, lies in the fact that the indictment alleges that the homicide was the result of a parent lawfully correcting his child "without due caution or circumspection,"—in other words, in a negligent manner.

Since time immemorial organized society has recognized that the duty of training children while under parental care rests with the parents and thus the law recognizes that parents have the right to "chastise their refractory and disobedient children." The law also requires, for the safety of the child, that the chastisement must not exceed the bounds of due moderation or the law will imply malice, thus making the parent criminally liable. . . .

Criminal malice or intent is not an element of the crime of involuntary manslaughter. In fact, it is this lack of intent that distinguishes manslaughter from murder. . . .

The parties are agreed, and we agree with them, that ORS 163.110 deals with two distinct situations. The first portion deals with the correction of children and servants, the second portion with human relationships in general. The first portion of this act, which deals solely with the right of a parent to correct a child, or a master his servant, excuses a homicide through accident or misfortune. The second portion, which deals with all other human relationships, excuses a homicide where the act is lawful and performed not in a negligent manner. Had it been the intention of the legislature not to excuse the negligent homicide of a child while being lawfully corrected by a parent the legislature would have included in the first portion, the same as in the last, the words "with usual and ordinary caution." In excluding these words from the parent-child relationship the maxim of "expressio unius est exclusio alterius" is applicable in that, having applied the rule of due care in general to all homicides arising from human relationships, the legislative intent is clearly expressed to exclude the crime of involuntary manslaughter committed through negligence while lawfully correcting a child or servant.

Since the indictment in this case charges only that the defendant as a parent while lawfully correcting his child did so negligently and as a result of his negligence the child died, it states no criminal offense under the laws of this state and the trial court correctly sustained the demurrer to the indictment.

Affirmed.

[ii]

PEOPLE v. GREEN
155 Mich. 524, 119 N.W. 1087 (1909)

BROOKE, J.

The respondent was convicted of assault and battery in the recorder's court for the city of Detroit, and brings his case before this court on exceptions before sentence.

The material facts seem to be as follows: The respondent at the time of the commission of the alleged offense was 30 years of age. . . . Up to the happening of the occurrence under consideration he had borne a good reputation. He was a married man, but without children of his own. About $2\frac{1}{2}$ years prior to the alleged assault and battery, he adopted the complaining witness, Mabel Green, as his child, and she continued to live with him and his wife as their child from the time of adoption to the 16th day of August, 1907, when the assault with which he is charged occurred. Mabel, at the time of the alleged assault, was between 12 and 13 years of age. The respondent's treatment of the complaining witness during the $2\frac{1}{2}$ years she occupied his home as his daughter seems to have been in the main kindly. He had corrected her on more than one occasion for alleged offenses; once because she had signed his name to an excuse for absence from school, and again for failing to report to him money which she had received for the sale of some eggs. On the day in question, the 16th day of August, respondent missed a 50-cent piece, and charged the complaining witness with its theft.

With reference to the alleged assault, the respondent testified as follows:

"There is no doubt I gave this child a whipping on Friday, the 16th of August. I used the whip in court here. I could not say as to the number of times. I do not know the number of times I hit her, but it was not 70. My purpose in whipping her was not to wring a confession from her. * * * I tied her hands to prevent her leaving the room and ending the punishment of her own volition. * * * I whipped her when she was naked. She was standing before me nude when I applied that whip to her body. * * * What I was trying to get her to say from Friday afternoon to Sunday morning was that she was going to try to do better and to refrain from habits of dishonesty. I could not limit the number of times I struck her. It was not a great number. * * * As I have had a chance to look over the past two years and a half, I am satisfied that some other method might have been used with the child to better advantage. It is hard for a man to decide those questions on the spot."

. . . We think that the respondent by his own testimony as to the assault in question practically admitted his guilt of the offense as charged, provided, only, that it should be determined by this court that the punishment inflicted went beyond the legitimate exercise of parental authority. . . .

* * *

. . . It was the respondent's claim that in order to render him criminally liable the punishment must be such as to cause permanent injury, and that correction, however severe, which produces temporary pain only and no permanent injury, involves no such liability. The people urge that a proper construction of the law is that, whether or not the particular punishment under consideration is or is not reasonable is a question of fact for the jury, to be determined by all the circumstances surrounding the case, and that a punishment may be held to be unreasonable which does not involve permanent injury, disfigurement, or disability.

* * *

We think the law is correctly stated in *State* v. *Koonse,* 123 Mo. App. 655 . . .

"The parent is the sole judge of the necessity for the exercise of disciplinary right and of the nature of the correction to be given, and the mere fact that a castigation he gives his child may appear to others to be unnecessarily harsh or severe does not make of his conduct a subject of judicial cognizance. As long as he acts in good faith, honestly thinking that what he does is for the benefit of the child, he is within his prerogative, and the law will not interfere. Courts do not and should not constitute themselves the arbiters of the household. There the authority of the parents, within the limits we shall presently define, is supreme, and from their judgment there is no appeal; but those domestic tribunals have limits to their jurisdiction, beyond which they may not go with impunity. The welfare of the child is the principal ground on which the parental right to chastise him is founded, and where the punishment inflicted is so excessive and cruel as to show beyond a reasonable doubt that the parent was not acting in good faith for the benefit of the child, but to satisfy his own evil passion, he no longer is to be considered as a judge administering the law of the household, but as a malefactor guilty of an unlawful assault on a helpless person intrusted to his care and protection. Thus to maim the child or endanger his life or health, or to severely beat him with an improper and dangerous instrument, though no permanent injury be given, or to subject him to unusual forms of physical torture, or to whip him with such excessive severity as implies the absence of a due appreciation of parental duty, are acts which in themselves bespeak evil intent; and a parent guilty of such excess will not be heard to say that he thought he was acting for the benefit of the child."

* * *

[I]t is not necessary, to sustain a conviction, to show that the punishment inflicted by the parent was such as to cause permanent injury or disfigurement to the child. It is sufficient to show that the punishment was cruel and unreasonably severe, and such as in its very nature would negative the idea of good faith on the part of the parent. The uncontradicted evidence of the people's witnesses in the case, supplemented by the testimony of the respondent himself, disclosed such a state of facts as in the opinion of the court fully warranted and demanded the respondent's conviction. We think one of the most serious elements of the respondent's offense is the conceded fact that he compelled the complaining witness, a female between 12 and 13 years of age, to stand before him nude and receive the castigation. This act tended to shock her modesty, to break down her sense of decency and the inviolability of her person, which is the most valuable possession of a young girl. It is not the intention of the court to in any wise weaken parental authority On the contrary, we hold that it is the unquestionable right of parents and those in loco parentis to administer such reasonable and timely punishment as may be necessary to correct growing faults in young children; but this right can never be used as a cloak for the exercise of malevolence or the exhibition of unbridled passion on the part of a parent.

* * *

The conviction is affirmed.

NOTES

NOTE 1.

STATE v. STRAIGHT
136 Mont. 255, 347 P. 2d 482 (1959)

CASTLES, JUSTICE.

* * *

A parent, teacher, baby-sitter or anyone else standing *in loco parentis* is not given [assault] unlimited discretion in the mode or degree of chatisement under our statute. Some cases in other jurisdictions go so far as to say that one standing *in loco parentis* acts in a quasi judicial capacity and has almost unlimited discretion regarding the punishment of the child entrusted to his care. This court expressly disapproves of this view. . . .

* * *

In determining whether the manner is reasonable and the degree moderate, the jury should consider all the facts and circumstances surrounding the punishment. They should especially consider: (1) The age of the child and whether he is old enough to understand the cause of the punishment and benefit by it; (2) The nature and degree of seriousness of the act which motivated the punishment; (3) The instrument used to inflict the punishment; and (4) The resulting injuries whether permanent or temporary and their degree of severity. We do not mean to suggest that these should be the only factors which the jury should consider. Each case should be decided on its own peculiar facts and circumstances. The factors mentioned above should be considered along with all the other evidence in the case in order that the jury may determine whether the manner is reasonable and the degree moderate.

* * *

The judgment is affirmed.

NOTE 2.

ROLLER v. ROLLER
37 Wash. 242, 246, 79 P. 788 (1905)

DUNBAR, J.

. . . *Hewlett v. George*, 68 Miss. 703, 9 South. 885, 13 L.R.A. 682, . . . held that a parent is not civilly liable to a child for personal injuries, inflicted during minority, and where the relation of parent and child with its mutual obligations exist. This was an action by the daughter against the mother for wrongful incarceration in an insane asylum, and was brought after the marriage of the daughter who, at the time of the alleged injuries, was separated and living away from her husband . . . . The court, in refusing the remedy, said:

"The peace of society, and of the families composing society, and a sound public policy, designed to subserve the repose of families and the best interests of society, forbid to the minor child a right to appear in court in the assertion of a claim to civil redress for personal injuries suffered at the hands of the parent. The state, through its criminal laws, will give the minor child protection from parental violence and wrongdoing, and this is all the child can be heard to demand."

NOTE 3.

ERIKSON, ERIK H.

Growth and Crises of the "Healthy Personality"*

[T]he psychiatrists, obstetricians, pediatricians, and anthropologists, to whom the writer feels closest, today would agree that *the firm establishment of enduring patterns for the balance of basic trust over basic mistrust* is the first task of the budding personality and therefore first of all a task for maternal care. But it must be said that the *amount of trust* derived from earliest infantile experience does not seem to depend on absolute *quantities of food or demonstrations of love* but rather on the *quality* of the maternal relationship. Mothers create a sense of trust in their children by that kind of administration which in its quality combines sensitive care of the baby's individual needs and a firm sense of personal trustworthiness within the trusted framework of their community's life style. (This forms the basis in the child for a sense of identity which will later combine a sense of being "all right," of being oneself, and of becoming what other people trust one will become.) Parents must not only have certain ways of guiding by prohibition and permission; they must also be able to represent to the child a deep, an almost somatic conviction that there is a meaning to what they are doing. In this sense a traditional system of child care can be said to be a factor making for trust, even where certain items of that tradition, taken singly, may seem unnecessarily cruel. Here much depends on whether such items are inflicted on the child by the parent in the firm traditional belief that this is the only way to do things or whether the parent misuses his administration of the baby and the child in order to work off anger, alleviate fear, or win an argument, with the child or with somebody else (her mother, her husband, her doctor, or her priest). This latter kind of situation we shall refer to as the parental *exploitation of the inequality* between adult and child.

---

* Reprinted in Kluckhohn, C. *et al.*: *Personality in Nature, Society and Culture*, 1955, pp. 185-225. New York: Alfred A. Knopf. Reprinted with permission of the Josiah Macy, Jr. Foundation.

e. In Theft

A.L.I. Model Penal Code 206.13*

(1) *Theft by Spouse.* Where the property involved is that of the actor's spouse, no prosecution for theft may be maintained unless:

(a) the parties had ceased living together as man and wife prior to the alleged theft; or

(b) the alleged theft was committed when the actor was leaving or deserting or about to leave or desert his spouse; or

(c) the actor entered into the marriage within 6 months prior to the alleged theft with the purpose of committing theft; or

(d) the property involved exceeded $500 in value exclusive of household belongings.

(2) *Theft by Other Relatives Living in a Common Household.* [No prosecution for theft may be maintained against any member of the household where the property involved consists of household belongings.]

[Theft of household belongings by a member of the household other than a spouse constitutes no more than a misdemeanor even where the amount involved may exceed $500.]

(3) *Petty Misapplication by Servant.* No prosecution for theft may be maintained against a household servant when the property involved consists of household belongings, in the amount of $50 or less, which the actor applied or disposed of for the benefit of a member of the household or of the household generally.

(4) *Necessity of Prompt Complaint.* No prosecution for theft may be maintained against a spouse or member of the household, or against a household servant in relation to household belongings, unless the victim or someone acting on his behalf complains to public authority within six months after learning of the offense and the probable identity of the offender.

(5) *Definitions.* Member of the household means a relative who regularly lives in the household of the victim. Household belongings means furniture, personal effects, vehicles, money or equivalent in amounts customarily used for household purposes, and other property usually found in and about the common dwelling and accessible to its occupants. A person shall be deemed a spouse or relative for the purpose of this section, regardless of the legal invalidity of any marriage, adoption, or legitimation involved, where the

---

* (Tent. Draft §4 1955). Copyright 1955. Reprinted with permission of the American Law Institute.

parties live in the same household and are generally reputed to be married or related.

NOTE
EWELL v. STATE
207 Md. 288, 114 A. 2d 66 (1955)

HAMMOND, JUDGE.

* * *

Statutes have been passed in almost all of the States which have made failure of the husband to perform his duty of support, unless adequately excused, a crime. The statutes fall generally into two classes, those which require the wife to be in destitute and necessitous circumstances before the husband's failure to support her is a crime, and those which merely state, as does the Maryland statute, Code 1951, Art. 27, Sec. 96, that it is a crime for one without just cause to "* * * wilfully neglect to provide for the support and maintenance of his wife * * *." Even in the statutes which require destitution as a prerequisite, the courts have refused generally to interpret the statutes literally. They have carried over into the testing of the criminal offense the same standards applied at common law to necessaries and what constituted them.

* * *

The state's attorney is given broad discretion as to the cases he will prosecute. As was said in Brack v. Wells, . . . 40 A. 2d 319, 321, . . . : "He must be trusted with broad official discretion to institute and prosecute criminal causes, subject generally to judicial control. The office is one not purely ministerial, but involves the exercise of learning and discretion." We think that the practice of the state's attorney of Baltimore in not prosecuting cases of non-support in which the wife has funds, if such practice had been proven, would amount to no more than the exercise of his discretion on a general basis and could not be considered as an administrative practice intended to, or having the effect of, interpreting the statute. As was pointed out in the Brack case, if the state's attorney does not act, the prosecuting witness may seek directly the aid of the Grand Jury.

* * *

f. In the Use of Contraceptives
POE v. ULLMAN
367 U.S. 497, 522, 523, 545-553 (1961)

MR. JUSTICE HARLAN, dissenting.

I am compelled, with all respect, to dissent from the dismissal of these appeals. . . .

Between them these suits seek declaratory relief against the threatened enforcement of Connecticut's antibirth-control laws making criminal the use of contraceptives, insofar as such laws relate to the use of contraceptives by married persons and the giving of advice to married persons in their use. . . .

* * *

Appellants contend that the Connecticut statute deprives them, as it unquestionably does, of a substantial measure of liberty in carrying on the most intimate of all personal relationships, and that it does so arbitrarily and without any rational, justifying purpose. The State, on the other hand, asserts that it is acting to protect the moral welfare of its citizenry, both directly, in that it considers the practice of contraception immoral in itself, and instrumentally, in that the availability of contraceptive material tends to minimize "the disastrous consequence of dissolute action," that is fornication and adultery.

* * *

[T]he very inclusion of the category of morality among state concerns indicates that society is not limited in its objects only to the physical well-being of the community, but has traditionally concerned itself with the moral soundness of its people as well. Indeed to attempt a line between public behavior and that which is purely consensual or solitary would be to withdraw from community concern a range of subjects with which every society in civilized times has found it necessary to deal. The laws regarding marriage which provide both when the sexual powers may be used and the legal and societal context in which children are born and brought up, as well as laws forbidding adultery, fornication and homosexual practices which express the negative of the proposition, confining sexuality to lawful marriage, form a pattern so deeply pressed into the substance of our social life that any Constitutional doctrine in this area must build upon that basis.
. . .

It is in this area of sexual morality, which contains many proscriptions of consensual behavior having little or no direct impact on others, that the State of Connecticut has expressed its moral judgment that all use of contraceptives is improper. Appellants cite an impressive list of authorities who, from a great variety of points of view, commend the considered use of contraceptives by married couples. What they do not emphasize is that not too long ago the current of opinion was very probably quite the opposite, and that even today the issue is not free of controversy. Certainly, Connecticut's judgment is no more demonstrably correct or incorrect than are the varieties of judgment, expressed in law, on marriage and divorce, on adult consensual homosexuality, abortion, and sterilization, or euthanasia and suicide. If we had a case before us which required us to decide simply, and in abstraction, whether the moral judgment implicit in the application of the present statute to married couples was a sound one. The very controversial nature of these questions would, I think, require us to hesitate long before concluding that the Constitution precluded Connecticut from choosing as it has among these various views. . . .

But, as might be expected, we are not presented simply with this moral judgment to be passed on as an abstract proposition. The secular state is not an examiner of consciences: it must operate in the realm of behavior, of overt actions, and where it does so operate, not only the underlying, moral purpose of its operations, but also the *choice of means* becomes relevant to any Constitutional judgment on what is done. The moral presupposition on which appellants ask us to pass judgment could form the basis of a variety of legal rules and administrative choices, each presenting a different issue for adjudication. For example, one practical expression of the moral view propounded here might be the rule that a marriage in which only contraceptive relations had taken place had never been consummated and could be annulled. . . . Again, the use of contraceptives might be made a ground for divorce, or perhaps tax benefits and subsidies could be provided for large families. Other examples also readily suggest themselves.

Precisely what is involved here is this: the State is asserting the right to enforce its moral judgment by intruding upon the most intimate details of the marital relation with the full power of the criminal law. Potentially, this could allow the deployment of all the incidental machinery of the criminal law, arrests, searches and seizures; inevitably, it must mean at the very least the lodging of criminal charges, a public trial, and testimony as to the *corpus delicti*. Nor could any imaginable elaboration of presumptions, testimonial privileges, or other safeguards, alleviate the necessity for testimony as to the mode and manner of the married couples' sexual relations, or at least the opportunity for the accused to make denial of the charges. In sum, the statute allows the State to enquire into, prove and punish married people for the private use of their marital intimacy.

This, then, is the precise character of the enactment whose Constitutional measure we must take. The statute must pass a more rigorous Constitutional test than that going merely to the plausibility of its underlying rationale. . . . This enactment involves what, by common understanding through-

out the English-speaking world, must be granted to be a most fundamental aspect of "liberty," the privacy of the home in its most basic sense, and it is this which requires that the statute be subjected to "strict scrutiny." . . .

That aspect of liberty which embraces the concept of the privacy of the home receives explicit Constitutional protection at two places only. These are the Third Amendment, relating to the quartering of soldiers, and the Fourth Amendment, prohibiting unreasonable searches and seizures. While these Amendments reach only the Federal Government, this Court has held in the strongest terms, and today again confirms, that the concept of "privacy" embodied in the Fourth Amendment is part of the "ordered liberty" assured against state action by the Fourteenth Amendment. . . .

It is clear, of course, that this Connecticut statute does not invade the privacy of the home in the usual sense, since the invasion involved here may, and doubtless usually would, be accomplished without any physical intrusion whatever into the home. What the statute undertakes to do, however, is to create a crime which is grossly offensive to this privacy, while the Constitution refers only to methods of ferreting out substantive wrongs, and the procedure it requires presupposes that substantive offenses may be committed and sought out in the privacy of the home. But such an analysis forecloses any claim to Constitutional protection against this form of deprivation of privacy, only if due process in this respect is limited to what is explicitly provided in the Constitution, divorced from the rational purposes, historical roots, and subsequent developments of the relevant provisions.

*   *   *

. . . Certainly the safeguarding of the home does not follow merely from the sanctity of property rights. The home derives its pre-eminence as the seat of family life. And the integrity of that life is something so fundamental that it has been found to draw to its protection the principles of more than one explicitly granted Constitutional right. Thus, Mr. Justice Brandeis, writing of a statute which made "it punishable to teach [pacifism] in any place [to] a single person . . . no matter what the relation of the parties may be," found such a "statute invades the privacy and freedom of the home. Father and mother may not follow the promptings of religious belief, of conscience or of conviction, and teach son or daughter the doctrine of pacifism. If they do any police officer may summarily arrest them." *Gilbert v. Minnesota,* 254 U.S. 325, 335-336 (dissenting opinion). . . . These decisions, as was said in *Prince* v. *Massachusetts,* 321 U.S. 158, at 166, "have respected the private realm of family life which the state cannot enter."

Of this whole "private realm of family life" it is difficult to imagine what is more private or more intimate than a husband and wife's marital relations. We would indeed be straining at a gnat and swallowing a camel were we to show concern for the niceties of property law involved in our recent decision, under the Fourth Amendment, in *Chapman* v. *United States,* 365 U.S. 610, and yet fail at least to see any substantial claim here.

Of course, just as the requirement of a warrant is not inflexible in carrying out searches and seizures, . . . so there are countervailing considerations at this more fundamental aspect of the right involved. "[T]he family . . . is not beyond regulation," *Prince* v. *Massachusetts, supra,* and it would be an absurdity to suggest either that offenses may not be committed in the bosom of the family or that the home can be made a sanctuary for crime. The right of privacy most manifestly is not an absolute. Thus, I would not suggest that adultery, homosexuality, fornication and incest are immune from criminal enquiry, however privately practiced. So much has been explicitly recognized in acknowledging the State's rightful concern for its people's moral welfare. . . . But not to discriminate between what is involved in this case and either the traditional offenses against good morals or crimes which, though they may be committed anywhere, happen to have been committed or concealed in the home, would entirely misconceive the argument that is being made.

Adultery, homosexuality and the like are sexual intimacies which the State forbids altogether, but the intimacy of husband and wife is necessarily an essential and accepted feature of the institution of marriage, an institution which the State not only must allow, but which always and in every age it has fostered and protected. It is one thing when the State exerts its power either to forbid extra-marital sexuality altogether, or to say who may marry, but it is quite another when, having acknowledged a marriage and the intimacies inherent in it, it undertakes to regulate by means of the criminal law the details of that intimacy.

In sum, even though the State has determined that the use of contraceptives is as iniquitous as any act of extra-marital sexual immorality, the intrusion of the whole machinery of the criminal law into the very heart of marital privacy, requiring husband and wife to render account before a criminal tribunal of their uses of that intimacy, is surely a very different thing indeed from punishing those who establish intimacies which the law has always forbidden and which can have no claim to social protection.

* * *

NOTES

NOTE 1.

REDLICH, NORMAN

Are There "Certain Rights . . . Retained by the People"?*

If we are unable to draw upon any portion of the Bill of Rights to meet problems such as those raised by the Connecticut birth control law, and other possible similar statutes, limitations on federal action in this area appear quite uncertain. . . .

But the Bill of Rights contains two additional amendments—the Ninth and Tenth, whose history suggests that they might be peculiarly suited to meet the unique and important problems suggested by the Connecticut birth control law case.

The Ninth Amendment provides: "The Enumeration in the Constitution of certain rights, shall not be construed to deny or disparage others retained by the people." The Tenth Amendment, better-known because it has been invoked more often in litigation, provides: "The powers not delegated to the United States by the Constitution, nor prohibited by it to the States, are reserved to the States respectively, or to the people."

These two Amendments have frequently been linked together and, particularly in recent years, written off as redundancies adding "nothing to the rest of the Constitution." A careful reading of the words and history of the two Amendments, however, indicates that they were intended to play a role in our constitutional scheme and ought not to be so lightly dismissed.

The Ninth Amendment was drafted by Madison to cope with the problem created by the enumeration of specific rights in a Bill of Rights. Fearing that the enumeration of these rights would imperil others not enumerated, Madison said:

> It has been objected also against a bill of rights, that, by enumerating particular exceptions to the grant of power, it would disparage those rights which were not placed in that enumeration; and it might follow, by implication, that those rights which were not singled out, were intended to be assigned into the hands of the General Government, and were consequently insecure, This is one of the most plausible arguments I have ever heard urged against the admission of a bill of rights unto this system; but, I conceive, that it may be guarded against. I have attempted it, as gentlemen may see by turning to the last clause of the fourth resolution.[85]

* * *

The Tenth Amendment, it will be recalled,

---

* 37 N. Y. L. Rev. 787, 804-809 (1962).

85. I Annals of Cong. 456 (1834).

speaks not of "rights retained by the people" but of "powers" which are "reserved to the States respectively, or to the people." Were it not for the last four words, the Tenth Amendment could easily be dismissed as a redundancy in a constitution establishing a government of limited powers.

* * *

. . . The Amendment would not be a truism, however, if the last four words are viewed as delineating powers possessed by neither the federal government nor the states. Since, as we have indicated, the Amendment was not intended to restrict the states, the last four words have meaning only if they were intended to impose additional restrictions on the federal government. The pieces start to fall into place when the Tenth Amendment is considered in conjunction with the Ninth Amendment.

Once "certain rights . . . retained by the people" had been removed from the scope of federal power, it would have been inconsistent to provide that all powers resided either in the federal government or the states. The last four words of the Tenth Amendment must have been added to conform its meaning to the Ninth Amendment and to carry out the intent of both—that as to the federal government there were rights, not enumerated in the Constitution, which were "retained . . . by the people," and that because the people possessed such rights there were *powers* which neither the federal government nor the states possessed.

. . . The adoption of the Fourteenth Amendment in 1868 provides the constitutional basis for judicial enforcement of both Amendments against the states.

* * *

The Connecticut statute would provide a particularly appropriate vehicle for giving life to these dormant constitutional provisions. A birth control law is totally unlike the regulatory laws of the 1920's and 1930's whose invalidation spurred an entire generation of Justices to keep hands off legislative experimentation in this area. The birth control law invades the privacy of the marital relationship by preventing a married couple from limiting the size of its family. Whether the decision not to have children is based on economic factors, health, simple personal preference, or a multitude of other possible reasons, no government in this country should force a husband and wife to choose between abandoning this most basic of human choices and either breaking the law or abstaining from sexual relations. In Justice Harlan's words, "In sum, the statute allows the State to enquire into, prove and punish married people for the private use of their marital intimacy."

The Court could hold that the Ninth and Tenth Amendments reserve to a married couple the right to maintain the intimacy of the marital relationship without government interference. . . .

NOTE 2.

TALCOTT v. REED
217 F. 2d 360, 363 (9th Cir. 1954)

STEPHENS, CIRCUIT JUDGE.

. . . Respondent . . . cites General Hershey's Operation Bulletin No. 57, issued to the local boards, in his brief as follows:

> "* * * that pregnancy is a status over which the registrant does have control, and it is therefore not a claim which can be classified under 'hardship' such as sickness, death, or any extreme emergency beyond the registrant's control."

We think the contents of the bulletin are morally and legally wrong. It invades the most sacred precinct of family life at a time when there should be the most complete mutuality between the spouses and in the face of nature's most demanding and significant urge in nature's scheme for propagating the species. It obliquely charges the youth of the land with corrupting the family relation into a way of avoiding service for cowards.

g. In Adultery

STATE v. ASTIN
106 Wash. 336, 180 P. 394 (1919)

MACKINTOSH, J.

Chapter 98, p. 341, Laws 1917, provides that no prosecution for adultery shall be commenced except on complaint of the husband or wife injured. Such a complaint having been filed and the prosecution thus begun, can the husband or wife discontinue and terminate that prosecution by moving to have it dismissed, or in any way interfere in the conduct of the case by the prosecuting attorney? The purpose of the act is . . . to put the commencement of the prosecution in the exclusive control of the injured spouse, in order that reconciliation might take place free from publicity and notoriety; but this reason no longer exists when the publicity and notoriety have occurred by the filing of the complaint or information, which is necessarily of record. . . .

* * *

The case, after the complaint is filed, is no longer a matter of private concern, but has partaken of all the attributes of a public offense, and the injured spouse should have no more right to control the further disposition of the case than should the complaining witness in any other criminal action. To hold otherwise would be to open the door of a treasure room for a horde of blackmailers. . . . In no other case of litigation is the opportunity for blackmail already so great, and to increase it by putting into the power of the complaining witness, not only the institution, but the entire destiny, of the prosecution, is to close our eyes to a grievous situation and add to its immense possibilties for the evilly disposed. If the complaining witness can dismiss the action at his pleasure, he may enjoy that right until final judgment; before, during, or after trial at his whim the defendant may be discharged. What becomes, then, of the argument that the right to control the action rests with the complaining witness for the purpose of protecting innocent persons from the publicity attached to such actions? To allow such a result, especially in a class of crime where the making of complaint is so subject to abuse, is abhorrent to the fundamental principles of law and morals. . . .

The lower court was in error in dismissing the information in this case, and its action in so doing is reversed.

CHADWICK, C. J. (Dissenting) . . .

Adultery is not a crime against the state. It is an offense against the unoffending spouse, and it is wisely provided, as was consistent with the ancient law, that no grand jury can indict, no person can make charge, and no prosecuting attorney can present by information, a defendant upon a charge of adultery unless such prosecution is commenced upon the complaint of the husband or wife, and then only upon complaint before a committing magistrate, or by the filing of an affidavit with the prosecuting attorney within a time limited to one year. . . . [I]n State v. La Bounty, 64 Wash. 415, 116 Pac. 1073 . . . the court said . . . that it was "the evident intention of the Legislature which incorporated the proviso in the law" to regard adultery "as a crime against the husband or wife personally rather than as a crime against society, leaving the husband or wife * * * to condone the offense if he or she desired to do so, unembarrassed by the publicity incident to a prosecution instituted by the officers of the state." The court used the word prosecution advisedly. It used it in the sense of a trial, rather than in the sense of filing a complaint with a magistrate or an affidavit with a prosecuting attorney.

The complaining witness filed an affidavit in which he says:

"That the said Laura B. Wilcox is the wife of affiant. That he was persuaded to file the said charge against the said parties at a time when he was worried over his domestic troubles and not in a normal condition, and was over-persuaded to make said charge against his own feelings and wishes, and that, if he had had an opportunity to think the matter over without the influence of third parties, he would not have preferred said charge.

"That since said time * * * affiant * * * has condoned the offense of his said wife and Joe H. Austin, and a reconciliation with his said wife, Laura B. Wilcox, has been effected by affiant.That the said Laura B. Wilcox and affiant are the parents of one child of the age of six years. That, in order to effect a complete harmony between said Laura B. Wilcox and affiant, affiant desires that the above-entitled action as to Joe H. Austin be dismissed and no further prosecution be had in the above cause. That Laura B. Wilcox's parents are living, and in ignorance of the pending suit. That she and affiant have a number of relatives and a great number of friends that will obtain knowledge of said suit if it is brought to trial, and will cause them considerable notoriety and painful publicity, and will destroy the domestic happiness of affiant and bring disgrace and ridicule upon them and upon their minor child, if said cause is further prosecuted, and affiant believes that his future domestic happiness and the welfare of their child depends upon the discontinuance of said action."

* * *

. . . The court misconceived the purpose of the statute, and perhaps unconsciously departed from the reason and the spirit of the law, and, in seeming anxiety to find a beaten path, switched the case upon the main track of the criminal law. To say that a law designed for the protection of the home may be nullified by resort to the rules of criminal procedure is to stand upon the letter of the statute . . . this law, being grounded in a public policy, should have the sanction of its spirit rather than be shackled by its letter.

* * *

NOTES

NOTE 1.

DAVIS v. BEASON
133 U.S. 333 (1890)

FIELD, J.

. . . Bigamy and polygamy are crimes by the laws of all civilized and Christian countries. They are crimes by the laws of the United States, and they are crimes by the laws of Idaho. They tend to destroy the purity of the marriage relation, to disturb the peace of families, to degrade woman and to debase man. Few crimes are more pernicious to the best interests of society and receive more general or more deserved punishment. To extend exemption from punishment for such crimes would be to shock the moral judgment of the community. To call their advocacy a tenet of religion is to offend the common sense of mankind. . . .

* * *

[If] those who make polygamy a part of their religion are excepted from the operation of the statute . . . then those who do not make polygamy a part of their religious belief may be found guilty and punished, while those who do must be acquitted and go free. This would be introducing a new element into criminal law. Laws are made for the government of actions, and while they cannot interfere with mere religious belief and opinions, they may with practices. Suppose one believed that human sacrifices were a necessary part of religious worship, would it be seriously contended that the civil government under which he lived could not interfere to prevent a sacrifice? Or, if a wife religiously believed it was her duty to burn herself upon the funeral pile of her dead husband, would it be beyond the power of the civil government to prevent her carrying her belief into practice? So here, as a law of the organization of society under the exclusive dominion of the United States, it is provided that plural marriages shall not be allowed. Can a man excuse his practices to the contrary because of his religious belief? To permit this would be to make the professed doctrines of religious belief superior to the law of the land, and in effect to permit every citizen to become a law unto himself. . . .

NOTE 2.

STATE v. HUNTSMAN
155 Utah 283, 204 P. 2d 448 (1949)

WADE, JUSTICE.

Defendant appeals from a conviction of carnal knowledge. The act shown to have been accomplished with a married female just a few days under 18 years of age. . . .

* * *

[T]he question posed [is] whether by marriage a female under the age of 18 years becomes capable of consenting to illicit sexual intercourse, and is a bar to a prosecution of the male participant in such act under our carnal knowledge statute. The fact that a female under that age is capable of consenting to marriage does not indicate that she can consent to illicit sexual intercourse, nor does the fact that by marriage she is capable of consenting to intercourse with her husband indicate that she is capable of consenting to illicit intercourse with another person. The purpose of the statutes establishing the age of consent is to protect young girls from the illicit acts of the opposite sex, but what a woman does by agreeing to marry, and by indulging in intercourse with her husband after marriage, is not either illegal or

considered immoral, and is not the kind of sexual acts that the statutes establishing the age of consent is intended to avoid. But such a married woman still is immature and still needs the protection of this kind of law. Had the legislature intended to exclude her from the protection of this statute it could have very easily so provided. Since it did not, we do not feel justified in reading such a provision into the statute. . . . We conclude that illicit sexual intercourse with a female between the ages of 13 and 18 years constitutes the crime of carnal knowledge even though the female is a married woman.

Finally, defendant argues that since the female was a married woman, if defendant committed the act charged he was guilty of adultery under Sec. 103-51-3, U.C.A. 1943, and therefore he is not guilty of carnal knowledge because the legislature did not intend to make him guilty of two offenses by one and the same act. It is possible for the same act to constitute many offenses under our penal code, each of which require a different element and therefore none of them would be included offenses but all of the elements of the different offenses might be present in one act. Thus if an unmarried man by force had sexual intercourse with his married daughter who was between the ages of 13 and 18 years, that act would satisfy the requirements of adultery, incest, fornication, rape and carnal knowledge, and all would be accomplished by one and the same act. . . .

NOTE 3.

R. v. CLARKE
2 All E.R. 448 [1949]

BYRNE, J.:

As a general proposition it can be stated that a husband cannot be guilty of a rape on his wife. No doubt, the reason for that is that on marriage the wife consents to the husband's exercising the marital right of intercourse during such times as the ordinary relations created by the marriage contract subsist between them. The marital right of the husband in such circumstances exists by virtue of the consent given by the wife at the time of the marriage and not by virtue of a consent given at the time of each act of intercourse as in the case of unmarried persons. Thus, the intercourse is not by virtue of any special consent, but is based on an obligation imposed on the wife by reason of the marriage. In HALE'S PLEAS OF THE CROWN, vol. 1, p. 629, the learned author states the law in this way:

> ". . . by their mutual matrimonial consent and contract the wife hath given up herself in this kind unto her husband, which she cannot retract."

NOTE 4.

PROPOSED ILLINOIS REVISED CRIMINAL CODE (1961)
Committee Comments*
ARTICLE 11. SEX OFFENSES

The broad scope of personal, family, community, social and religious interests which can be affected by sexual activities renders more difficult the problem of drafting legislation proscribing specific acts of sexual conduct. The Committee approached the problem from several basic premises: (1) protection of the individual against forcible acts; (2) protection of the young and immature from the sexual advances of older and more mature individuals; (3) protection of the public from open and notorious conduct which disturbs the peace, tends to promote breaches of the peace, or openly flouts accepted standards of morality in the community; and, (4) protection of the institution of marriage and normal family relationships from sexual conduct which tends to destroy them. It will be noted that the key interests sought to be protected are freedom from force for everyone, freedom from the unfair exploitation of youth before they are mature enough to make valid individual judgments, freedom of the public from "open and notorious" acts, and the community's interest in preserving the monogamous marriage and family institution which is the current basis of our social and moral structure. The Committee considers the protection of these interests sufficiently vital to warrant criminal sanctions for their violation.

The Article is not intended to proscribe any sexual conduct between consenting adults unless such conduct adversely affects one of the key interests sought to be protected.

§11-10. *Aggravated Incest.*

(a) Any male person who shall perform any of the following acts with a person he knows is his daughter commits aggravated incest:

(1) Has sexual intercourse; or
(2) An act of deviate sexual conduct.

(b) "Daughter" for the purposes of this Section means a blood daughter regardless of legitimacy or age; and also means a step daughter or an adopted daughter under the age of eighteen.

(c) Penalty.

A person convicted of aggravated incest shall be imprisoned in the penitentiary from one to twenty years.

COMMITTEE COMMENTS

. . . The limitations placed on the meaning of daughter follow from the rationale that underlies this and the following section, viz., that *criminal*

* By permission of Illinois and Chicago Bar Associations.

concern for incest should be limited generally to situations involving either (1) abuse of family authority; or (2) the possibility of biological risk of genetically defective offspring. (See comments to Section 11-11, *infra*). Where a female is not the blood daughter of the accused, there is no particular biological risk involved if conception were to result. Thus, criminal penalties are limited in the case of adoptive and step-daughters to those situations where parental authority may be abused in taking advantage of a young and dependent child. By the time a female has arrived at age 18, it is felt that she is ordinarily sufficiently mature and autonomous to be free from undue parental pressure to submit to sexual advances. However, where blood daughters are involved, whatever biological risk may exist remains present irrespective of the age of the daughter—and thus though the daughter may be sufficiently adult to be free from paternal pressures in such matters, the biological risk remains and intercourse ought to be discouraged.

§11-11. *Incest.*

(a) Any person who has sexual intercourse or performs an act of deviate sexual conduct with another to whom he knows he is related as follows commits incest:

(1) Mother or son; or
(2) Brother or sister, either of the whole blood or the half blood.

(b) Penalty.

A person convicted of incest shall be imprisoned in the penitentiary from one to ten years.

COMMITTEE COMMENTS

Section 11-11 is aimed at supplanting the existing incest section affecting sexual intercourse between relatives other than fathers and daughters. . . . The section . . . abandons the idea that criminal incest provisions must be identical in scope to similar marriage prohibitions. Denying the right to marry may justly be responsive to influences which are not so compelling when the scope of criminal laws are seriously reviewed. . . . Historically, incest has been principally a matter of spiritual concern. It was never a common law crime . . . and save for a brief period during Cromwell's Puritan reign in England (circa 1650) when incest was a statutory offense, England recognized no crime of incest until 1908. . . . And in Illinois, too, marriage was prohibited because of kinship between the parties for several decades before criminal penalties were provided. . . . The general scope of incest laws in the United States has been one of increasing breadth as the nation developed westward and new states were admitted to the Union. . . . The result is that there is no fixed and uniform pattern of kinship that may be called incestuous throughout the United States beyond the very closest members of the family. . . . Since an overhaul of marital restrictions based on incest is clearly beyond the scope of this Code, the problem of incest restrictions was considered only within the confines of the criminal law. Taking this approach, two alternatives were considered by the Committee. First, a defense of valid marriage could be allowed against a charge of incest. This possibility was seriously considered but abandoned since it would, in effect, unjustly discriminate against Illinois residents. . . .

Second, criminal incest could be limited to relationships which pose the "biological risk" and which would not create any serious problems in relation to marriage contracted outside the state.

The second alternative was considered to present the more practical solution. Thus, criminal restrictions on incest have been limited to a very narrow scope: parent-child and brother sister. This may be said to be the area of greatest "biological risk" and clearly it presents no problems in relation to the recognition of foreign marriages. The "biological risk" rationale for incest prohibitions is probably most overrated. Reviewing current scientific data, the commentators of the Model Penal Code have explained:

> First—an unusual risk of defective offspring occurs only when the blood line carries a "relatively rare, recessive, unfavorable gene." If the gene is not relatively rare, the probabilities of defective offspring is not substantially enhanced by marriage within the blood line. If the gene is not recessive, it is not necessary that both parents carry it in order to affect the offspring.
>
> Second—more importantly, marriage outside the blood line spreads the unfavorable genes more widely in the population, so that in the long run, there is a greater risk of genetically defective offspring resulting from the mating of unrelated persons. (Model Penal Code, Tent. Draft No. 4, commentaries, pp. 231-33).

Thus, it appears that genetics does not provide a very convincing scientific rationalization for broad ranging prohibitions against intra-family matings. . . . There is, however, an enhanced possibility of genetically defective offspring in the first succeeding generation where the relationship is very close. And cultural traditions afford a basis for concern in the criminal law.

h. In Miscegenation

STATE v. BROWN
236 La. 562; 108 So. 2d 233 (1959)

HAWTHORNE, JUSTICE.

Defendants James Brown and Lucille Aymond were charged in a bill of indictment with the crime of miscegenation "in that they did habitually cohabit with each other, he being of the Negro race and she being of the White race, they having knowledge of their difference in race". They were tried jointly, convicted, and sentenced to serve one year in the state penitentiary. Both have appealed.

The statute under which appellants were charged, Article 79 of the Louisiana Criminal Code, provides:

> "Miscegenation is the marriage or habitual cohabitation with knowledge of their difference in race, between a person of the Caucasian or white race and a person of the colored or negro race."

The statute then provides that whoever commits the crime miscegenation shall be imprisoned, with or without hard labor, for not more than five years.

Appellants filed a motion to quash the indictment on the ground that the statute under which they were being prosecuted was unconstitutional because it violates the Equal Protection and the Due Process provisions of the Louisiana and United States Constitutions, in that it makes a particular course of conduct a crime when committed by persons of certain races only. The motion to quash was overruled, and Bill of Exception No. 1 was reserved.

As we view the matter, marriage is a status controlled by the states, and statutes prohibiting intermarriage or cohabitation between persons of different races in no way violate the Equal Protection clauses of the state and federal Constitutions. See 16A C.J.S. Constitutional Law §§541, 543, pp. 474, 479-480. A state statute which prohibits intermarriage or cohabitation between members of different races we think falls squarely within the police power of the state, which has an interest in maintaining the purity of the races and in preventing the propagation of half-breed children. Such children have difficulty in being accepted by society, and there is no doubt that children in such a situation are burdened, as has been said in another connection, with "a feeling of inferiority as to their status in the community that may affect their hearts and minds in a way unlikely ever to be undone."[1]

The United States Supreme Court had occasion to consider the identical question presented here in Pace v. State of Alabama, 106 U.S. 583, 1 S. Ct. 637, 27 L.Ed. 207. In that case a Negro man and a white woman were indicted under a provision of the Code of Alabama for living together in a state of adultery or fornication. The Supreme Court, in considering whether the Alabama statute

---

1. This quotation is from Brown v. Board of Education of Topeka, 347 U.S. 483, 74 S.Ct. 686, 691, 98 L.Ed. 387.

violated the Equal Protection clause of the Constitution and in holding that it did not, stated that the punishment of each offending person whether white or black is the same. This is true of the Louisiana statute here involved.

The next bill which we shall consider has merit and in our view entitles the appellants to a new trial. According to the bill the trial judge in charging the jury defined the term "cohabitation" as "access for the purpose of sexual intercourse", and defined "habitual cohabitation" as "access for the purpose of sexual intercourse as a matter of habit". . . .

* * *

Article 79 is found under that subpart of the Code dealing with "sex offenses affecting family". The preceding article in that same subpart, Article 78, provides that incest is the marriage to, or cohabitation with, any ascedant or descendant, brother or sister, uncle or niece, aunt or nephew, with knowledge of their relationship. This court as far back as 1906 in the case of State v. Freddy, 117 La. 121, 41 So. 436, 437, had occasion to consider the word "cohabit" as used in the incest statute then in effect, and concluded in a well reasoned opinion that the meaning of the word "cohabit" was "simply that of sexual intercourse". The word "cohabitation" in the present incest statute has the same meaning, and we are convinced that its meaning in Article 79 is also the same.

In the miscegenation statute, Article 79, the word "cohabitation" is preceded by the adjective "habitual", and the crime denounced is the "habitual cohabitation with knowledge", etc. Webster's Dictionary defines "habitual" thus: "Of the nature of a habit; according to habit; established by, or repeated by force of, habit; customary; as, the *habitual practice* of sin; *habitual* drunkenness." As we see the matter, the words "habitual cohabitation" as used in Article 79 simply mean customary or repeated acts of sexual intercourse, and not merely an isolated case of intercourse.

Obviously, when the trial judge charged the jury that "habitual cohabitation" meant "access for the purpose of sexual intercourse as a matter of habit", he committed reversible error, for under this charge an accused could be convicted of the crime of miscegenation without any evidence that sexual intercourse had ever occurred. Such is not the law.

* * *

The convictions and sentences of the appellants are reversed and set aside, and the case is remanded to the district court for a new trial.

NOTES

NOTE 1.

STATE v. BROWN
Two Years Later

There was no second trial and hence no sentence; James Brown still resides in Bunkie, Louisiana, the situs of the alleged crime; Mrs. Aymond left Bunkie and now lives in Alexandria, Louisiana, about 30 miles north of Bunkie.

After reversal of the conviction by the Louisiana Supreme Court, both defendants were rearraigned and both again entered pleas of not guilty; however, they were not brought to trial a second time. The district attorney advised me privately that he would not bring the case up for a second trial because the evidence did not establish a corpus delecti sufficient to support a conviction. . . [Letter dated Jan. 21, 1961 from Harold J. Brouillette, appointed counsel for defendant James Brown.]

NOTE 2.

McLAUGHLIN v. STATE
153 So. 2d 1 (Fla. 1963)

CALDWELL, JUSTICE.

This cause is here on appeal from the Criminal Court of Record of Dade County. The trial court directly passed upon the validity of a State statute and we, therefore, have jurisdiction.

Defendants are charged with having violated Fla. Stat. § 798.05, F.S.A. in that "the said Dewey McLaughlin, being a negro man, and the said Connie Hoffman, being a white woman, who were not married to each other did habitually live in and occupy in the nighttime the same room." The defendants moved to quash the information on the ground that the aforesaid statute was in violation of the Federal and State Constitutions. The motions were denied. Defendants were then arraigned and entered pleas of not guilty. The jury trial terminated in a verdict of guilty, a sentence of thirty days in the county jail and a fine of $150 for each defendant.

The defendants contend they were denied equal protection of the laws because "Firstly, the law provides a special criminal prohibition on cohabitation solely for persons who are of different races; or, secondly, if this special statute is equated with the general fornication statute, the higher penalties are imposed on the person whose races differ than would be applicable to persons of the same race who commit the same acts."

* * *

The appellants seek adjudication of their right to engage in integrated illicit cohabitation upon the same terms as are imposed upon the segregated laws. But, as was admitted by counsel in argument, this appeal is a mere way station on the route to the United States Supreme Court where defendants hope that, in the light of supposed social and political advances, they may find legal endorsement of their ambitions.

[I]f the new-found concept of "social justice" has out-dated "the law of the land" . . . and, by way of consequence, some new law is necessary, it must be enacted by legislative process or some other court must write it.

Affirmed.

i. In a Draft Penal Code

PROPOSED NEW YORK PENAL LAW*

Title O. Offenses Against Marriage, the Family, and the Welfare of Children and Incompetents

Article 260: Offenses Affecting the Marital Relationship.

§260.00 *Unlawfully solemnizing a marriage.* A person is guilty of unlawfully solemnizing a marriage when:

1. Knowing that he is not authorized by the laws of this state to do so, he performs a marriage ceremony or presumes to solemnize a marriage with intent to deceive some person; or

2. Being authorized by the laws of this state to perform marriage ceremonies and to solemnize marriages, he performs a marriage ceremony or solemnizes a marriage knowing that a legal impediment to such marriage exists.

Unlawfully solemnizing a marriage is a class A misdemeanor.†

§260.05 *Unlawfully issuing a dissolution decree.* A person is guilty of unlawfully issuing a dissolution decree when, not being a judicial officer authorized to grant judgments or to issue decrees of divorce or annulment, he issues a written instrument reciting or certifying that he or some other purportedly but not actually authorized person has granted a valid decree of civil divorce, annulment or other dissolution of a marriage.

Unlawfully issuing a dissolution decree is a class A misdemeanor.

---

§260.10 *Unlawfully procuring a marriage license.* A person is guilty of unlawfully procuring a marriage license when he procures a license to marry another person and when:

1. He has a living spouse at the time; or

2. The other person has a living spouse at the time.

Unlawfully procuring a marriage license is a class A misdemeanor.

§260.15 *Bigamy.* A person is guilty of bigamy when:

1. Having a living spouse, he contracts or purports to contract a marriage with another person; or

2. He contracts or purports to contract a marriage with a person who has a living spouse.

Bigamy is a class E felony.*

§260.20 *Unlawfully procuring a marriage license, bigamy; defenses.* It is an affirmative defense to a prosecution for unlawfully procuring a marriage license or bigamy that the defendant acted under a reasonable belief that he or, as the case may be, the other party to the marriage or prospective marriage was unmarried or legally eligible to remarry.

§260.25 *Incest.* A person is guilty of incest when he marries or engages in sexual intercourse with a person whom he knows to be related to him, either legitimately or illegitimately, as an ancestor, descendant, brother or sister of either the whole or the half blood, uncle, aunt, niece or nephew.

Incest is a class E felony.

§260.30 *Incest; corroboration.* A person shall not be convicted of incest or of an attempt to commit incest upon the uncorroborated testimony of the person with whom the offence is alleged to have been committeed.

Article 265: Offenses Relating to Children and Incompetents.

§265.00 *Abandonment of a child.* A person is guilty of abandonment of a child when, being a parent, guardian or other person legally charged with the care or custody of a child less than

---

fourteen years old, he deserts such child in any place with intent to wholly abandon it.

Abandonment of a child is a class E felony.

§265.05 *Non-support of a child.* A person is guilty of non-support of a child when, being a parent, guardian or other person legally charged with the care or custody of a child less than sixteeen years old, he fails or refuses without lawful excuse to provide support for such child when he is able to do so.

Non-support of a child is a class A misdemeanor.

§265.10 *Endangering the welfare of a child.* A person is guilty of endangering the welfare of a child when:

1. He knowingly acts in a manner likely to be injurious to the physical, mental or moral welfare of a child less than sixteen years old; or

2. Being a parent, guardian or other person who has care or custody of a male child less than sixteen years old or of a female child less than eighteen years old, he fails or refuses to exercise reasonable diligence in the control of such child to prevent him from becoming a "neglected child," a "juvenile delinquent" or a "person in need of supervision" as those terms are defined in articles three and seven of the family court act.

Endangering the welfare of a child is a class A misdemeanor.

§265.15 *Unlawfully dealing with a child.* A person is guilty of unlawfully dealing with a child when:

1. Being an owner, lessee, manager or employee of a place of entertainment or amusement or of a place where alcoholic beverages are sold or given away, he permits a child less than sixteen years old to enter or remain in such place unless:

(a) the child is accompanied by its parent, guardian or an adult authorized by a parent or guardian, or

(b) the entertainment or amusement is given for the benefit or under the auspices of a non-profit school, church or other educational or religious institution, or

(c) otherwise permitted by law to do so; or

2. He knowingly permits a child less than eighteen years old to enter or remain in a place where illicit sexual or illegal narcotics activity is maintained or conducted; or

3. He marks the body of a child less than eighteen years old with indelible ink or pigments by means of tattooing; or

4. He sells or causes to be sold any alcoholic beverage, as defined by section three of the alcoholic beverage control law, to a child less than eighteen years old; or

5. He sells or causes to be sold tobacco in any form to a child less than eighteen years old.

It is no defense to a prosecution pursuant to subdivision four or five of this section that the child acted as the agent or representative of another or that the defendant dealt with the child as such.

Unlawfully dealing with a child is a class B misdemeanor.

§265.20 *Endangering the welfare of an incompetent person.* A person is guilty of endangering the welfare of an incompetent person when he knowingly acts in a manner likely to be injurious to the physical, mental or moral welfare of a person who is unable to care for himself because of mental disease or defect.

Endangering the welfare of an incompetent person is a class A misdemeanor.

COMMMISSION STAFF NOTES

Article 260: Offenses Affecting the Marital Relationship.

This Article collects a number of crimes scattered through the existing Penal Law all of which deal with marriage. However, one such crime in the existing law, "Adultery" (P.L. §§ 100-103), is omitted from the revision. A majority of the Commission is of the opinion that the basic problem is one of private rather than public morals, and that its inclusion in a criminal code neither protects the public nor acts as a deterrent. In fact, it may well be said that proscribing conduct which is almost universally overlooked by law enforcement agencies tends to weaken the fabric of the whole penal law.

* * *

Article 265: Offenses Relating to Children and Incompetents.

Existing Penal Law Article 44, "Children," contains twenty-five sections, some of which are archaic or otherwise unnecessary and some of which properly belong in other bodies of law (see Table II following text of proposed law, for disposition of individual sections.) Since this revision groups offenses by subject matter, existing Penal Law §§ 483-a and 483-b, dealing with carnal abuse of children, are treated in proposed Article 130, "Sex Offenses"; and existing Penal Law §§ 484-e through 484-h, on comic books and pornography, are included in proposed Article 240, "Obscenity and Related Offenses." The balance of existing Article 44 has been condensed into four sections (proposed §§ 265.00 through 265.15).

* * *

265.05 *Non-support of a child.* Ideally, the problems of abandonment and non-support of children should not be in a penal code at all. The primary objective of legislation in this area should be to compel recalcitrant parents and guardians to recognize and fulfill their legal and moral obligations of care and support. Since this is difficult to achieve by imprisoning offenders, the optimum solution is a judicial and administrative framework such as is found in the Family Court Act. However, practical experience has shown that penal sanctions serve a necessary function in this area as a deterrent and, occasionally, are the only effective means of dealing with the situation.

* * *

NOTE

THE SECRETARY OF STATE FOR THE
HOME DEPARTMENT AND LORD PRIVY SEAL

Debate on the Queen's Speech*

MR. R. A. BUTLER:

* * *

What is the scope of the Government action? Except in totalitarian countries, Governments are not omnicompetent and nowhere this side of heaven are they omnipotent. A society's laws should be such as to encourage and protect virtue, but a moral basis of conduct can no more be imparted by the Government than can a religious belief. The roots of crime lie deep in society and the sources from which they are nourished are almost wholly beyond the Government's reach. Belief in moral obligations, pride in integrity and respect for the rights of others can and should be instilled by the family. . . .

It is not for me to say what is the duty of the Churches. I think they understand what is so often described by the religious leaders as the challenge before them. But I think there is an immense task to be done by the schools, and, in so far as in my time I have been responsible for encouraging education, my one disappointment is that in comparison with the immense amount of time and money spent by us and the local authorities on education we have had considerable disappointment in this one respect.

I would add only this. While we must continue to spend much of our time on the problems of buildings, administration and conditions, let us remember that it was partly to deal with this problem that we introduced religious education into the Education Act, and that it was partly to deal with this problem that we wished to see the influence of the teachers in the schools exercised to produce among their pupils moral behaviour and the life of a good citizen.

There is, therefore, a great responsibility on the schools and teachers, the Churches, the family

---

* 594 H.C. DEB 495, 500-501 (31 Oct. 1958).

and others to help us out, and anything that Her Majesty's Ministers can do—I feel sure that I am speaking for leaders of the Opposition as well—to meet these representatives of our society and help them through this problem we should do, with all modesty. . . .

* * *

Reverting to the Government's position, what can a Government do? A Government must first ensure that the forces of law and order are adequate, and that has been referred to by hon. Members who have spoken in the debate. Secondly, we must see that the courts are armed with sanctions sufficient to enforce the law, and I shall say a word in reply to the right hon. Gentleman about the courts. Thirdly, it should promote a study of the causes of crime and the most effective methods of dealing with it, and, lastly, do everything possible to ensure that the offenders who come into our charge leave it less likely to offend than when they came in.

* * *

3.

IN TORTS—THE FAMILY AS AN ENCLOSURE FOR AFFECTION, SERVICE, INCOME, CONFLICT, COLLABORATION AND GUIDANCE

a. Disputes between Members of the Family and Outsiders

[i]

Injury to Parent as Damage to Child

MODE v. BARNETT
361 S.W. 2d 525 (Ark. 1962)

HARRIS, CHIEF JUSTICE.

This litigation stems from the killing of D. L. Russell by Lee Mode, appellant herein. Suit was instituted by Clida Russell Barnett . . . as Guardian and next friend of Jerry Russell, Don Russell, Ferrell Russell and Darrell Russell, minor sons of the deceased. Count I of the complaint alleged that Russell and his wife, Mildred Sellars Russell, lived happily together as man and wife for more than 15 years until the fall of 1957, at which time appellant, Lee Mode, commenced making clandestine visits to Mrs. Russell, showering his affections and attentions upon her in an effort to entice her favor; that Mode did willfully and wickedly steal and alienate her affections, and about the 18th day of April, 1958, lured her away from her children and her husband, causing her to desert and abandon the children and to separate from their father; that since said date, Mode and Mrs. Russell had been living together, and that the children had been injured and damaged by being deprived of the comfort, companionship, love, affection and society of their mother. Actual damages were sought on this count in the sum of $100,000, together with punitive damages in the sum of $50,000.

Under Count II, it was alleged that Mode, after learning that D. L. Russell was attempting to effect a reconciliation with his wife, and after deliberation and premeditation, killed Russell on October 13, 1958, by shooting the latter on the streets of Conway; that the children had been deprived of their father's support, contributions, and future earnings, and as a result of his wrongful death, had suffered extensive grief, mental pain and anguish; that they had been deprived of the companionship, love and affection of their father and had been damaged in the sum of $100,000. $100,000 in damages was sought as actual damages to the estate, together with $50,000 punitive damages. . . . Mode filed an answer himself, stating: "I deny every statement (sic) and every thing the plaintiff says and deny that they are entitled to anything from me and ask that the court dismiss their suit and deny them anything." . . . After the conclusion of the evidence, judgment was entered against appellant in the total amount of $90,102.75, broken down as follows:

For disruption of the family ties, depriving the children of the parental care, affection, and instruction of their mother:

1. Jerry Russell	$2,000.00
2. Don Russell	3,000.00
3. Ferrell Russell	3,000.00
4. Darrell Russell	3,000.00

For loss of their father's contribution and support:

1. Jerry Russell	$2,181.40
2. Don Russell	3,116.28
3. Ferrell Russell	4,051.16
4. Darrell Russell	4,051.16

For the use and benefit of the children by reason of the loss of decedent's parental care, instruction, love and affection:

1. Jerry Russell	$2,500.00
2. Don Russell	5,000.00
3. Ferrell Russell	5,000.00
4. Darrell Russell	5,000.00

For the use and benefit of the children as damages for their grief and mental anguish:

1. Jerry Russell	None
2. Don Russell	$7,500.00
3. Ferrell Russell	7,500.00
4. Darrell Russell	7,500.00

Under Count II of the complaint, the court granted punitive damages in the sum of $25,000 for the use and benefit of the four children. From the judgment so entered, appellant brings this appeal. . . .

* * *

[T]he weight of authority holds that minor children cannot recover for disruption of family ties, and some of the reasons (in addition to lack of statutory authority) are pointed out in cases from other jurisdictions. In Henson v. Thomas, . . . 56 S.E. 2d 432, . . . the Supreme Court of North Carolina said,

> "To hold otherwise would mean that every time a person persuades or induces a mother to engage in other activities to such an extent as to cause her to neglect her children, he commits a tort for which he may be compelled to respond in damages. The only difference lies in the gravity of the wrong and the extent of the damage.
>
> "The problem here, in its last analysis, is sociological rather than legal. No one would question the fact that a child has an interest in all the benefits of the family circle. Nor may it be denied that the legislative branch of the government may give this interest such legal sanction as would make the invasion or destruction thereof a legal wrong. So far, it has not deemed it wise to do so."

In Whitcomb v. Huffington, 304 P. 2d 405, the Supreme Court of Kansas stated:

> "No one will deny the fact that under such circumstances a child is the innocent victim and, in most instances, suffers damage—emotional, financial, and otherwise. But, that is not the question. The question is whether, under such circumstances, the child is to be permitted to bring the action.
>
> "If we were to answer the question in the affirmative the ramifications and far-reaching results of our decision would readily be apparent to anyone giving much thought to the matter. In practical effect we would be opening up a new field of litigation, heretofore entirely unknown, between minor children and their grandparents, for instance, or between minor children and business or social companions or acquaintances of their parents, when, perchance, some incident, or line of conduct on the part of those persons occurs which might be said to have contributed to the eventual breakup of the family home and circle. We recognize fully that merely because the asserted cause of action was unknown to the common law and has no statutory sanction in this state, such fact does not present a conclusive reason for the denial of the existence of such right. Nevertheless, we are of the firm conviction that from the standpoint of sound public policy the creation of new rights of action in the field of alienation of affections is a question for the consideration and determination of the legislature, and is a function which this court should not usurp."

It follows that the court erred in rendering judgment against appellant under Count One of the complaint for $11,000, and that item is disallowed, set aside, and stricken from the judgment.

*   *   *

It is contended that some of the awards were excessive. It is first asserted that the sum of $13,400 awarded for contributions and support is not justified by the evidence. Russell's income, at the time of his death, was $45.00 per week, which would amount to $2,340 per year. Jerry Russell was 14 years of age; Don Russell was 11 years of age; the twins, Ferrell and Darrell, were 8 years of age. It is true that the record does not disclose just what amount the father contributed for the support of these children, but it is certain that he took care of them, i.e., fed them, clothed them, and apparently provided them with whatever sums of money they used for recreation. Considering that the two youngest boys were 13 years away from attaining their majority, and Don and Jerry were respectively 10 and 7 years away from that period, we cannot agree that the total amount is excessive.

It is likewise asserted that the awards for cedent's parental care, instruction, and love and affection, in the total amount of $17,500, are excessive. No contention is made in appellant's brief that this last was not a proper element of damage, but it might be mentioned that we find no wrongful death case from this state that uses the term "love and affection"; in fact, in Railway Co. v. Maddry, . . . 21 S.W. 472, this court held that the happiness found by the child in the love and companionship of the decedent father should never be considered. Subsequently, however, in several cases, we used language which indicated this to be a proper award. For instance in St. Louis & N.A. Rd. Co. v. Mathis, . . . 91 S.W. 763, it was said,

> "So, in a case of this kind, no amount of money can fully compensate children for the distress of mind suffered by them in the violent and painful death of the father, and in *the loss of his affectionate care*[5] and attention, but the court must ascertain some just amount to allow a fair compensation for the injury."

*   *   *

It would, therefore, appear that the terms used in the cases cited, and others of similar import, are, to a degree, synonymous with the term "love and affection". Appellant states there is no evidence in the record that Russell did other than take his sons fishing and swimming; also, occasional visits to the old homeplace in order for the boys to see their friends. It is also contended that the award for "grief and mental anguish", in the amount of $22,500 is not sustained by the evidence.[6]

We are not familiar with any rule by which the explicit pecuniary value of parental care, instruction, and affection, can be determined, but the children were definitely entitled to such an award. It would certainly appear from the record that these benefits to the children were mainly furnished by the decedent, for the mother voluntarily left her home—and these children. According to the record, the children had seen their mother but few times after she left the home; in fact, two of the boys testified that they had not seen her at all subsequent to their father's funeral.

In Strahan v. Webb, . . . 330 S.W. 2d 291, in discussing mental anguish, we said:

> "Who can say how much mental anguish is worth? * * * Unquestionably, the anguish and total loss of companionship will be felt far more in some cases than in others. There are individuals who really never completely reconcile themselves to the loss of a loved one, while, on the other hand, there are those who adjust themselves within a reasonable period of time, and are pretty well able to continue along in the usual pattern."

In the instant case, we have three small boys who had been in close association with their father, probably a closer relationship than in the average family, due to the fact that there was no mother present to share in the companionship. Suddenly the one remaining parent was taken away from them—and in a violent manner. According to the evidence of Cecil Barnett, husband of Mrs. Clida Barnett, the boys' grandmother, the younger boys cried many nights, and on several occasions awakened the Barnetts in the middle of the night, "There's been a many of nights that me and my wife would go to bed, pick them up and take them in and love them and talk to them." The witness stated that Ferrell, one of the twins, had been under a doctor's care due to extreme nervousness. The boys testified that their father was good to them, and would take them fishing, swimming, and to the picture show. Mrs. Barnett stated, "He took the boys everywhere he went when he wasn't working, and they were not in school. It he went anywhere, they were with him, because he didn't leave them behind. And he worshiped those boys." She also testified that their father's death affected their school work: "They were able to continue in school but they had to stay in that same grade that year. They had to stay in that grade two years."

___
5. Emphasis supplied.

___
6. No award for mental anguish was made for the oldest boy, Jerry, who did not testify in the case.

As stated, there is no way to measure mental anguish. Who can determine the grief of a small boy over the sudden death of his father—a father with whom he had been closely associated—and who had been the lone source of parental advice and encouragement? The adult child who loses a parent is generally better able to withstand the blow than a minor child whose close and constant association with the parent in the home creates considerably more of a binding tie. It need not be added that the manner of the death of a loved one contributes to mental anguish, and the facts of Russell's death were well known by the children.

The $25,000 award for punitive damages is not specifically attacked, but, even so, the record supports the award made.

We are unable to say that any of the awards were excessive.

NOTES

NOTE 1.

DAILY v. PARKER
152 F. 2d 174 (7th Cir. 1945)

EVANS, CIRCUIT JUDGE.

The instant appeal raises this question: Have children, living in Pennsylvania, a cause of action for damages against a woman living in Illinois who caused their father to leave them, their mother, and their home and go to Chicago and live with her and to refuse to further contribute to their maintenance and support? The District Court answered the question in the negative and dismissed the complaint.

* * *

Our approach to the question must be based on a study of the rights and obligations of *all* who are parties to a *family*. The father, the mother, and the children ordinarily constitute the family. Each is entitled to the society and the companionship of the others. Within the limits of the others' abilities, each is entitled to the financial aid and support of the others, although generally speaking the children in their tender years can contribute nothing, and the wife, in view of her place in the home, may make but small financial contribution to the family exchequer. The children are entitled to shelter, food, clothing, and schooling and to the social, the moral support, guidance, and protection of their father, though in turn they can contribute only companionship and the inspiration which comes from their association in the family circle.

Is the family relationship and the rights of the different members therein, arising therefrom, sufficient to support a cause of action in each, the father, mother, or children, against one who breaks it up and destroys rights of the said individual members?

Appellee concedes that such a cause of action exists in favor of the father and within certain limits and certain jurisdictions, also in favor of the wife. She denies that such a cause of action, however, exists in favor of the children.

The history of the development of the family and the family relations and the duties and obligations of the members of the family is a long one, covering centuries. Its development was slow, due to society's acceptance of the relative positions of the parties in the family and its reluctance to change such status. The husband was lord and master, and the rights of all of the members of the family were merged in him. He ruled. He spoke in the first person singular in all matters. He spoke authoritatively for all. Through the centuries, however, there came slowly a change. The father is still the master, it may be said, but the duties of the master have changed. Where it was said to be his duty to rule, he now serves. He recognizes rights of the others and his obligation to meet them.

Perhaps he is still the titular head of the family. If so, his position merely carries with it greater duties and obligations. The duties of each member of the family are measured (at least in theory and in legal conception) by the position, the role, each takes in the family. Thus we see the wife, the breadwinner, and speaking for the family when the husband becomes incapacitated through sickness or invalidism. And children of tender years take on the family fiancial burdens when father is incapacitated and mother must attend him or or for other reasons is unable to contribute to the fiancial support of the family. Relativity of rights and duties marks the rights and the obligations of the group and relativity is determined in each case by the situation of the family. But relativity does not eliminate or destroy the rights of any member.

It is this conception of the family which must constitute our approach to the question at hand.

Another factor deserving consideration is the division which we must make of the rights of children. For the purpose of considering redress of such rights, we divide them into two groups. (a) The right to recover for injuries which arise from their right to support and maintenance from their parent. These rights are financial in character. (b) The right to recover for injuries to feelings and damages which arise from their rights to the comfort, the protection and the society of the father.

Defendant argues that such rights as here asserted have never been, and should not now be, recognized by any court until and unless legislation has been enacted creating such right. . . .

Plaintiffs, on the other hand, rely upon the maxim, Ubi Jus Ibi Remedium. . . .

Instead of holding that there is no remedy, because there is no precedent, they argue for what they assert to be the better rule, and what Dean Pound calls judicial empiricism. In other words, the common law has been and is sufficiently elastic to meet changing conditions. We quote from Dean Pound's book, "The Spirit of the Common Law," 183:

"Anglo-American law is fortunate indeed in entering upon a new period of growth with a well-established doctrine of law-making by judicial decision. * * * Undoubtedly * * * judicial empiricism was proceeding over-cautiously at the end of the last century. * * * If the last century insisted over-much upon predetermined premises, and a fixed technique, it did not lose to our law the method of applying the judicial experience of the past to the judicial questions of the present."

* * *

Our conclusion, without going further into the matter, is that a child today has a right enforceable in a court of law, against one who has invaded and taken from said child the support and maintenance of its father, as well as damages for the destruction of other rights which arise out of the family relationship and which have been destroyed or defeated by a wrongdoing third party.

* * *

There is, we must confess, weight to the argument that no loss was suffered when the children were deprived of the society of a father who deserted them to run away with a married woman and who left his wife and children to struggle as best they could with the task of making a livelihood. In other words, before there can be a loss measured in damages, there must be something to lose. And a father should have at least a shadow of character before his loss can be said to create a claim for damages in his children. This question of the amount of damages is, however, for the jury and the loss of financial support conceding there was nothing lost in the way of society when the father left his family, is still present.

NOTE 2.

BOWLBY, JOHN

Child Care and the Growth of Love*

. . . The services which mothers and fathers habitually render their children are so taken for granted that their greatness is forgotten. In no other relationship do human beings place themselves so unreservedly and so continuously at the disposal of others. This holds true even of bad parents—a fact far too easily forgotten by their critics, especially critics who have never had the care of children of their own. It must never be forgotten that even the bad parent who neglects her child is nonetheless providing much for him. Except in the worst cases, she is giving him food and shelter, comforting him in distress, teaching him simple skills, and above all is providing him that continuity of human care on which his sense of security rests. He may be ill-fed and ill-sheltered, he may be very dirty and suffering from disease, he may be ill-treated, but, unless his parents have wholly rejected him, he is secure in the knowledge that there is someone to whom he is of value and who will strive, even though inadequately, to provide for him until such time as he can fend for himself.

[ii]
Injury to One Spouse as Damage to the Other
MONTGOMERY v. STEPHEN
359 Mich. 33, 101 N.W. 2d 227 (1960)

SMITH, JUSTICE.

The action before us is brought by a wife. She tells us that the defendant was driving his car in a reckless manner and in so doing struck her husband's car at a time when her husband, driving with care and caution, was almost completely across an intersection. As a result of such impact her husband's car was driven against a tree, embedding the bark thereof in his head. He suffered brain concussion which may develop into epilepsy, he lost the voluntary functioning of his kidneys, he sustained 4 fractures of the pelvis, a puncture of the abdomen, and other severe injuries. We could go on for some time but need not. Some of the injuries may be repaired, at least after a fashion, and others may not.

She is suing for damages for none of these. Her cause of action involves a hurt directly to her, equally obvious, she says, equally disastrous, and equally deserving of the protection of the law. She says in effect, that the negligence of the defendant has reduced her husband to a physical and psychological wreck, a mere shell of manhood, unable to sleep, unable to work effectively, in constant pain, scared, worried constantly, physically weak, and unable to enjoy even normal social life. She asserts that she has been deprived of her husband's society and comfort, of his aid and companionship, and of normal conjugal affection.

The legal term for her asserted loss is that of "consortium." It has been variously defined, sometimes in terms enormously complex as the judges followed the habit of lawyers of never

---

* Harmondsworth, England: Penguin Books, Ltd., 1953 (p. 76). Reprinted with permission of the publisher.

using one word where two may be employed. One of the most careful of the studies of consortium, in fact, attributes to the redundancies of common law pleading much of the confusion and injustice prevalent in this field. Actually, all that consortium means is conjugal fellowship. But the pleader at the common law (following his practice in deeds, wills, contracts, and what-not) alleged the loss of love, companionship, affection, society, comfort, sexual relations, services, solace, and on and on until his dictionary ran dry. It does, indeed, (since it is fellowship between man and wife), embrace all of these things, and more. But the verbosities of common law pleading should not lead the court to absurdities, such as the conclusion, for instance, that consortium has an economic side, for loss of which one may recover, and a sentimental side, for loss of which no recovery may be had. What of the spiritual side? The parental side? The carnal side? It would be a reckless semanticist who would assert that he was able, justifiably to place each of the various elements of conjugal fellowship in one or the other of the suggested pigeonholes, just as it would be a bold artist who would assert that he could categorize all of the hues of the spectrum into 2 pigeonholes, one marked "light," the other marked "dark." Such efforts may be amusing as mental exercises but when judges seriously put them forward as grounds for decision, absurdities will result and injustice is bound to be done.

The wife before us, then, seeks recovery for her loss of consortium. To this the trial court replied that, legally speaking, she had not suffered a loss. So it is that she comes to us. The precedents do, indeed, deny her recovery. The husband, it is usually said, may recover for loss of consortium, but not the wife. This is nothing short of ridiculous. If one of the marriage partners may recover for loss of consortium, why may not the other? If the family larder is empty, does only one hunger? They stood together at the altar and jointly they entered into their conjugal relationship. They assumed commensurate rights, duties, and responsibilities. Where, along the line, did it all become one-sided, so that the law will grant recompense to one, on the theory that he has suffered a loss, but not to the other?

These precedents are venerable. Their chains may be moss-encrusted and rusty but only a few courts have held that they no longer control or confine. Thus again we reach the conflict that divides us, for the law, as Dean Pound put it, must be stable, and yet it cannot stand still. Were we to rule upon precedent alone, were stability the only reason for our being, we would have no trouble with this case. We would simply tell the woman to be gone, and to take her shattered hus-

band with her, that we need no longer be affronted by a sight so repulsive. In so doing we would have vast support from the dusty books. But dust the decision would remain in our mouths through the years ahead, a reproach to law and conscience alike. Our oath is to do justice, not to perpetuate error.

Is the holding that recovery be denied, in truth the demand of the common law? If so, and the vast amount of authority so saying bears witness thereof, there must, one day, have been reasons for the rule, for, as Holmes tells us, the common law has grown by an historical process.[6]

The reasons then, we seek in the period of time in which the monstrous doctrine had its origin. The status of the wife and mother at this time is made clear in the periodical rulings of the time. She was part chattel, part servant. As we observed in a concurring opinion in an earlier case, Sovereign v. Sovereign, 354 Mich. 65, 73, 74, 92 N.W. 2d 585, 590:

> "The picture we receive, sketchy as it is, of late 16th and early 17th century women is, by today's standards, a depressing one. She was regarded as a creature (the choice of words is not our own) of limited intellectual attainments or possibilities. Education was largely denied her. There were few schools for even the girls of the wealthier families and the training given in those was limited to that of a 'polishing nature, music and the arts.' There was almost no opportunity for the rigorous intellectual discipline given to young men. They were married young, pawns in their father's hands for the attainment of title or prestige. They could not possibly hope to reach, in fact, they were not 'meant' to reach, intellectual equality with their husbands. Their existence, socially and economically, pivoted around that of a dominant husband, authoritarian and paternalistic."

With respect to the children of the marriage the husband's so-called rights were near absolute. Although we find no case paralleling the early Roman law, under which the *pater familias* had the power to sell his child in the open market, or put it to death, it was clear that the English father might effectively prevent the mother's access to

---

6. Holmes, The Common Law 5:
    "The customs, beliefs, or needs of a primitive time establish a rule or a formula. In the course of centuries the customs, belief, or necessity disappear, but the rule remains. The reason which gave rise to the rule has been forgotten, and ingenious minds set themselves to inquire how it is to be accounted for. Some ground of policy is thought of, which seems to explain it and to reconcile it with the present state of things; and then the rule adapts itself to the new reasons which have been found for it, and centers on a new career. The old form receives a new content, and in time even the form modifies itself to fit the meaning which it has received."

her child during his life, and even after his death maintain the bar with statutory sanction.

Such being the mother's "rights" with respect to her children it follows, with the relentless logic of the common law, that her rights respecting her property and her person are no more generous. She was his chattel. What was hers was his. The wife says Bracton, "has nothing which is not her husband's." They were one, and, as one opinion put it, he was that one. All of her personal property, money, goods, and chattels of every description, became his upon marriage. Since she was "under the power of her husband," it followed that she had "no will of her own" and having no will of her own could not enter into a contract. Of course, he was entitled to her services in the home as he would be to those of any servant in his employ. Should he lose them through the acts of another that other must respond in damages. But should the husband be injured, and she thus lose his protection and solace, might she, equally with him, maintain a like suit for her loss? In light of what has been said the question is nonsensical. To have a lawsuit we must have to start with, some one capable of suing another. She, however, could not bring any action in her own name, for she was a legal nonentity. But this was not all. What if she were so injured by another as to be incapable of performing her wifely duties? Has the husband suffered a legally recognizable loss, so that he might cause that other to respond in damages? The answer is clear from the common law, as is the theory upon which it was based. He had. It was an actionable trespass for one to interfere with the services of another's servant. This menial in the house, this chattel, responding to the term "wife," also rendered services. It would follow, and it did follow, that the husband had a right of action for injury to her, grounded upon the theory that she was his servant. But could she sue a wrongdoer for injury to him? A servant sue for the loss of services of the master? Clearly not.

Any attempt to pursue the manifold reasons offered by modern courts for their refusals to permit the wife a recovery for her loss of consortium takes us on a tour similar to that of Minos in labyrinth of Daedalus. Each path leads to a dead end of reasoning and logic. Thus it is said that the injury suffered by the wife is too remote a consequence of defendant's act to be made the subject of an action. . . . It is said, moreover, that there is danger of double recovery, since the husband recovers for his diminished ability to support, and he is under a duty to support his wife. This merely sidesteps the issue. The wife is suing for damages to her interest. She does not seek recovery for loss of support.

Her effort is to recover for loss of companionship and of society. Moreover, here again we see the paradox before noted, the peculiar reasoning that sets up (as insuperable obstacles to the action of the wife) objections deemed completely immaterial when the husband sues for damage to the same interest. We have just noted it with respect to the problems of remoteness. Here we see it with respect to double recovery, for the husband has consistently been permitted to recover for loss of consortium. Yet, insofar as material services are included within the concept of consortium (and there is no doubt they form a part of the whole), it cannot be denied that there is a danger of allowing him a double recovery. This danger, however, has never been thought sufficiently real to bar the husband's action for loss of his consortium, in addition to all other elements of damage. The solution is not difficult and was noted in Hitaffer v. Argonne Co. [87 U.S. App. D.C. 57, 183 F. 2d. 819.] "it is a simple matter to determine the damages to the wife's consortium in exactly the same way as those of the husband are measured in a similar action and subtract therefrom the value of any impairment of his duty of support."

To a large degree, the objection in the cases to allowing the wife recovery for loss of consortium turns directly or indirectly upon the aspect of consortium just mentioned, that of material services. It is often said that the wife's cause of action for loss of consortium must include an allegation of her loss thereof, for without it, we are told she cannot maintain her action. It is then concluded that since she cannot make this allegation (who ever heard of a servant suing her master for loss of services?) her case must fall. If she replies that the element of service is not the gist of the concept of consortium she is told that without it nothing remains but sentiment and the law does not permit recovery for injuries to sentiment alone.

The argument thus made involves two fundamental errors. The first is that the concept of consortium, of conjugal fellowship, is capable of dismemberment into material services and sentimental services. Is the well kept home or the carefully prepared meal a manifestation of affection (i.e., a sentimental service) or of the skilled performance of menial chore (i.e., a material service)? Does the well-trained child know anything of sentimental services? Of material services? Of both? Are they different? Which is which? The fact of the matter is that the effort to break down consortium into its component parts is no more than a theoretician's boast, the modern counterpart to the medieval resolution of the number of angels able to dance on the head of a pin. It requires a wisdom, and an effrontery, far greater than ours to make differentiations so subtle, if, indeed, they are within the realm of human competence.

The second fundamental error in the objection made is that (assuming we can and do make the theoretical differentiation described) the law does not permit recovery for the sentimental aspect alone of consortium. We need only to glance about us to see that the law actually is otherwise. The actions for criminal conversation and alienation of affections are in point. It is law well-established, not even worth a counter struggle, that the gist of such actions is not the loss of services but the loss of conjugal rights. Such actions are, consequently, maintainable by the husband, for such injury even though he was no longer living with his wife at the time the injury occurred, and it is significant to note that in one of the earliest cases in this field, Guy v. Livesey (1619) Cro. Jac. 501 (79 Eng. Rep. 428), the loss suffered by the husband, for which action lay, was not a loss of services at all but a loss of company. The fact of the matter is that there is no predominant element in the concept of consortium, that consortium is not capable of subdivision, and that it is not necessary that there be an allegation of the loss of any particular "element" thereof.

Finally, it is urged by some that the Married Women's Acts, designed to remove from them their degrading and demeaning common law disabilities, and (in some cases) to implement their constitutional guaranties, not only did not aid the wife's cause of action for loss of consortium, but eliminated the husband's as well. Since we do not here consider the husband's action we will not pay our respects to the curious theory that we remedy the wrongful denial of a cause of action to one by denying it also to the other. This solution of the problem will appeal only to those enamored by symmetry. For the purposes of the case before us we cannot conclude that an act designed to shield women from the imposition of inequitable and sometimes degrading disabilities shall, rather, be employed as a sword to strike down her cause of action for the loss of an interest at the very heart and core of her married existence, the love, companionship, and society of her husband. . . .

*   *   *

We are remitted, then, to a matter of sound judicial policy, a decision to be reached in the light of today's society and the current common law solution of comparable problems. Discussion of the issue in those terms may not result in unanimity but at least it will be conducted upon a rational, understandable, basis, not in the metaphysical realm of fictions. We come, then, . . . to a balancing of interests. On the one hand we have a wife deprived of the affection of her husband,

his companionship, his society, possibly deprived even of her opportunity to bear sons and daughters. On the other, we have a defendant, whose liability because of his act must involve the violation of a duty of care with respect to it, and, furthermore, whose liabilities as a result of his negligent act must have some reasonable limitation. So analyzed, we see the problem not as a unique and peculiar historical anomaly but as a part of a much larger pattern, as a part of a clearly discernible movement in the law. We have long since passed by the time when the function of the law "was to keep the peace by regulating or preventing private war [which] only required it to deal with personal violence and with disputes over possession of property." We now recognize that "the law protects interests of personality, as well as the physical integrity of the person." Stewart v. Rudner, 349 Mich. 559, 467, 84 N.W. 2d 816, 817 . . . .

*   *   *

Relief is extended the wife in the intentional cases, . . . for one basic reason, the interest of society in the protection of the family as the social unit upon which, at least in this country, society rests. Our concern is not with the family of the middle ages, with its tyrannies and abuses, but with the family of today. If this is the interest to be protected, and we conclude that it is, the law's protection should extend as well to the negligent as to the intentional injury. In each case the loss is equally severe and the importance to our society of the welfare of the family unit outweighs the importance of the defendant's claims to immunity.

The gist of the matter is that in today's society the wife's position is analogous to that of a partner, neither kitchen slattern nor upstairs maid. Her duties and responsibilities in respect of the family unit complement those of the husband, extending only to another sphere. In the good times she lights the hearth with her own inimitable glow. But when tragedy strikes it is a part of her unique glory that, forsaking the shelter, the comfort, the warmth of the home, she puts her arm and shoulder to the plow. We are now at the heart of the issue. In such circumstances, when her husband's love is denied her, his strength sapped and his protection destroyed, in short, when she has been forced by the defendant to exchange a heart for a husk, we are urged to rule that she has suffered no loss compensable at the law. But let some scoundrel dent a dishpan in the family kitchen and the law, in all its majesty, will convene the court, will march with measured tread to the halls of justice, and will there suffer a jury of her peers to assess the damages. Why are we asked, then, in the case before us, to look the other way? Is this what is meant when it is said that justice is blind?

. . . The precedents of the older cases are not valid precedents. They are violative of women's statutory rights and constitutional safeguards. They are out of harmony with the conditions of modern society. They do violence to our convictions and our principles. We reject their applicaability. The reasons for the old rule no longer obtaining, the rule falls with it. The obstacles to the wife's action were judge-invented and they are herewith judge-destroyed. We conclude that the wife before us has pleaded a cause of action.

*   *   *

CARR, JUSTICE (dissenting).

[T]he legislature of the State . . . abolished all civil causes of action for criminal conversation, seduction, and also for alienation of affections unless the defendant is a designated close relative of the plaintiff's spouse. In other words, actions for direct invasion by affirmative means of rights of consortium, formerly recognized, do not now exist under the statute cited. The thought naturally suggests itself that for this Court to decree that such an action may be brought, based on negligent conduct resulting in impairment of rights of consortium, would be inconsistent with the legislative action. The obvious fact is that questions of public policy are involved, and in accordance with basic principles of government the determination thereof should be left to legislative action.

*   *   *

Involved also in a consideration of the problem from its various angles is the Workmen's Compensation Law of the State. Assuming that the situation arises, as it has in cases in other States, where the negligence of an employer has resulted in injury to an employee and compensation has been awarded and paid in accordance with the statute, may the other spouse be permitted to maintain an action for damages for loss of consortium? In some instances . . . specific provisions may be construed as barring such cause of action. . . . If not, we would have clearly involved in a plaintiff's right to recover, if sustained in this case, a matter for legislative regulation and adjustment of legal rights.

*   *   *

NOTES

NOTE 1.

TINKER v. COLWELL
193 U.S. 473 (1903)

PECKHAM, JUSTICE.

The assault *vi et armis* is a fiction of the law, assumed at first, in early times, to give jurisdiction of the cause of action as a trespass, to the courts, which then proceeded to permit the recovery of damages by the husband for his wounded feelings and honor, the defilement of the marriage bed, and for the doubt thrown upon the legitimacy of children.

Subsequently the action of trespass on the case was sustained for the consequent damage, and either form of action was thereafter held proper.

Blackstone, in referring to the rights of the husband, says (3 Bl. Com., edited by Wendell, page 139):

"Injuries that may be offered to a person, considered as a *husband,* are principally three: *abduction,* or taking away a man's wife; *adultery,* or criminal conversation . . . with a man's wife, though it is, as a public crime, left by our laws to the coercion of the spiritual courts; yet, considered as a civil injury (and surely there can be no greater), the law gives a satifaction to the husband for it by action of trespass *vi et armis* against the adulterer, wherein the damages recovered are usually very large and exemplary."

*   *   *

. . . It is also said that the husband has, so to speak, a property in the body and a right to the personal enjoyment of his wife. For the invasion of this right the law permits him to sue as husband.

For the purpose of maintaining the action, it is regarded as an actual trespass upon the marital rights of the husband, although the consequent injury is really to the husband on account of the corruption of the body and mind of the wife, and it is in this view (that it is a trespass upon the rights of the husband) that it is held that the consent of the wife makes no difference; that she is incapable of giving a consent to an injury to the husband. . . .

*   *   *

Many of the cases hold that the essential injury to the husband consists in the defilement of the marriage bed, in the invasion of his exclusive right to marital intercourse with his wife and to beget his own children. This is a right of the highest kind, upon the thorough maintenance of which the whole social order rests, and in order to the maintenance of the action it may properly be described as a property right.

NOTE 2.

McFARLAND v. ILLINOIS CENTRAL RAILROAD CO.
122 So. 2d 845, 860 (La., 1960)

LANORY, JUDGE AD HOC.

[The] elements of damages which must be determined on behalf of the surviving widow is the loss of the love, companionship and affection of decedent. In this connection the testimony of plaintiff is unrefuted to the effect decedent was a devoted husband and father who loved, and, in return, was loved by his wife and children. We believe that all attending circumstances considered, an award to plaintiff widow in the sum of $7,500 will amply compensate her in this regard.

*   *   *

The evidence discloses that plaintiff widow remarried December 18, 1959. Her marriage, however, can have no effect upon her right of recovery herein and is not to be considered in mitigation or reduction of the damages otherwise due. . . .

[iii]
"Family Membership?" in Denying or Granting Damages

KOPLIK v. C. P. TRUCKING CORP.
27 N.J. 1, 141 A. 2d 34 (1958)

FRANCIS, J.

Plaintiff Rosemarie Koplik was injured in a motor vehicle collision on June 17, 1955, in the State of New York. The defendant Frederick Patrizio was the driver of one of the vehicles involved and plaintiff was riding in it as an invited passenger. At that time both parties resided in New Jersey and they have continued to do so. On January 11, 1956, Miss Koplik instituted this action against Patrizio to recover damages on account of her injuries. Thereafter, on June 2, 1956, she married him. . . . The issue here is simply whether the subsequent marriage before judgment extinguishes the right to prosecute the action.

It is universally acknowledged that at common law a tort such as this one could not be redressed between wife and husband by action at law or in equity. . . . This immunity has been diluted in the various states and in England by "married persons" statutes. The extent of the refinement brought about by these acts has been the source of much conflict among the courts throughout the country. But . . . such legislation does not sanction suits between spouses for personal torts. . . . If the enactment expressly or by clear implication preserves the interspousal exemption and the ancient barrier against actions between husband and wife for injuries negligently inflicted by one on the other, whatever may be the personal predilections of the particular court in such matters, they must give way to the legislative will. Thus, we are brought to an examination of the Married Persons Act of this State.

Over a period of more than 100 years, a succession of New Jersey Legislatures have narrowed the scope of the disability of the husband and wife in their jural relations with each other and with third persons. Out of the numerous enactments has evolved the body of law appearing in *N.J.S.A.* 37:2-1 *et seq.* . . . The important factor to be noted is that despite the changes thus made in the common law, and the decisions construing the statutory language by which they were accomplished, *N.J.S.A.* 37:2-5 still contains the following wordage which is comparatively more pervasive than that of the original enactment in the *Revision of 1877,* p. 639; § 14:

> "Nothing in this chapter contained shall enable a husband or wife to contract with or to sue each other, except as heretofore, and except as authorized by this chapter."

It is not suggested that personal injury tort actions between husband and wife based upon negligence were maintainable prior to 1877, or that this enactment authorized them.

As far back as 1880, the clarity of that language was the subject of judicial comment. In *Woodruff v. Clark & Apgar,* 42 *N.J.L.* 198 (*Sup. Ct.* 1880), Chief Justice Beasley, speaking of the disability to contract, said:

> . . . The clause is virtually a legislative declaration that, as heretofore, they may enter, *inter sese,* into equitable agreements, but not into legal agreements.

*   *   *

> At all events, the will of the legislature is expressed in an unequivocal manner, to leave unaltered the *status* of married persons in relation to this subject, and the consequence is the contract in question cannot be carried into effect in a court of law."

And as late as 1949, this court adopted Chief Justice Beasley's view of the unambiguous character of the provision and applied it with unabated vigor as a bar to enforcement of alleged workmen's compensation rights arising out of interspousal employment contracts. *Bendler v. Bendler,* [3 N.J. 161 (1949)]. Continuance of the "disablement of husband and wife * * * to sue each other * * * 'except as heretofore, and except as authorized' " by the Legislature, was recognized and the acceptance of the rule was accompanied by the statement:

> " * * * The integrity of the marriage relation is of primary concern to society. That is the principle of the statutory provision that continues the common-law mutual disability of a husband and wife to contract *inter se* and to sue each other. * * *"

*   *   *

[I]n this State the common law interspousal negligence tort immunity has been perpetuated, and . . . it has been made a part of our statutory law as well. . . .

. . . There is no doubt that the parties are now husband and wife. The statute establishes no qualifications on the general prohibition against a suit between them. It is of no material consequence whether the action was instituted before or after the marriage. The word "sue" in its ordinary connotation, and patently in the sense used by the Legislature, means to commence or to continue legal proceedings to their proper and usual termination . . . So the crucial criterion is simply whether the litigants are husband and wife. If so, the public policy of the State, as reflected in the statute, bans the action. . . . And the right to sue, that is, to prosecute the cause of action, must be considered as having been extirpated by the voluntary assumption of the marital status. For manifestly our statute simply disables or incapacitates the spouse possessing the cause of action from suing the tortfeasor mate. . . . The principle with which we are concerned does not look to the relation of the parties when the cause of the action accrued or when the case was commenced but to their status at the time when their rights are judicially determined. . . .

* * *

. . . The policy issue is clear and if a legislature wishes to abrogate the immunity, it ought to say so clearly and unequivocally. . . .

NOTES

NOTE 1.

GORDON v. POLLARD
207 Tenn. 45, 336 S.W. 2d 25 (1960)

PREWITT, CHIEF JUSTICE.

* * *

We think that the annulment of a voidable marriage may well restore certain existing property and statutory rights to a spouse, but does not create in a spouse, husband or wife, a right to maintain an action against the other for a tort which occurred . . . during the period the status of the parties was that of husband and wife.

Upon the solemnization and consummation of the marriage of the plaintiff and defendant, each was subject to all of the privileges and all of the disabilities of coverture, and these privileges and disabilities continued until the marriage was avoid by the plaintiff.

May these actualities be obliterated retroactively by an annulment decree?

To give an annulment decree such an effect would be to substitute legal theory for practicality. The retroactive effect of annulment is not without limits, prescribed by policy and justice. . . .

* * *

The Supreme Court of the State of Massachusetts held that . . . .

* * *

"While it doubtless is true that a decree of nullity ordinarily has the effect of making a marriage, even one which is voidable, void ab initio, this is a legal fiction which ought not to be pressed too far. To say that for all purposes the marriage never existed is unrealistic. Logic must yield to realities. Public policy requires that there must be some limits to the retroactive effects of a decree of annulment. * * *

"On the day after the accident if the plaintiff had brought suit against the defendant it could not have been maintained, for the marriage at that time had not been declared invalid. The situation was unaffected by the subsequent decree of annulment."

* * *

We think the reasoning in the Massachusetts case is sound and we are of the opinion that the trial judge was correct in dismissing the suit.

NOTE 2.

BIEKER v. OWENS
350 S.W. 2d 522 (Ark. 1961)

BOHLINGER, JUSTICE.

The appellant, plaintiff . . . filed . . . his complaint against Milton Owens, Carroll L. Owens, Bill Griffin and M. N. Griffin, alleging . . . . That Milton Owens was a minor who resided with his father, Carroll . . . ; that Bill Griffin was a minor residing with his father, M. N. . . . ; that on or about August 26, 1960, the defendants, Bill Griffin and Milton Owens, driving an automobile which was the property of Carroll Owens, pursued and overtook the plaintiff, Johnnie Bieker, and by driving directly in front of the automobile driven by Johnnie Bieker, forced him to stop and that the defendants, Griffin and Owens, forcibly, deliberately, maliciously, willfully and intentionally dragged the Bieker boy from his automobile and physically assaulted him by striking, beating and kicking the plaintiff and so injuring him that he was hospitalized for contusions of the face, lacerations, broken nose and mild concussion with other injuries. That the defendants, Carroll Owens and M. N. Griffin, knew that their sons, Milton and

Bill, had dangerous tendencies and propensities of a willful and malicious nature and that by their lack of parental discipline and authority they had permitted, or failed to correct, the acts of their sons in the striking, beating and abusing other younger men less physically endowed than themselves and thus knowing of the propensities of these minors, the defendant parents failed and neglected to exercise needed restraint and authority over them and that due to such negligence the appellant alleges he was injured.

To this complaint Carroll L. Owens, appellee, interposed a general demurrer and the court, on February 20, 1961, sustained the demurrer and dismissed the complaint. From that action of the court comes this appeal.

> "The general common law rule is that a parent is not liable for the minor child's torts unless there is some element of participation," Bonner v. Surman, 215 Ark. 301, 220 S.W. 2d 431, 433.

[T]his court has recognized the rule that the negeligence of a child cannot be imputed to the parent merely because of the parental relationship. . . .

But here we are not concerned with the negligence of a child but with the negligence of the parent in permitting, either actively or passively, a minor willfully or negligently to commit such acts which could reasonably be expected to cause injury to another.

It is within reason and good logic to say that the parent has a responsibility to control minor children while they are in their formative years. For while they are not in the custody of the parents, absent any official action to the contrary, no other source of control may be found. Of course minors above a certain age are subject to criminal and civil sanctions but these sanctions are remedial rather than preventative. There is a question whether the civil sanctions are of any consequence since judgments against minors are of little practical effect. The old adage "an ounce of prevention is worth a pound of cure," could be applied in these situations if the responsibility for the prevention is placed on the parents.

Since each human mind and personality is exclusively that of the individual possessing it, it would be unreasonable to place an absolute responsibility for the acts of another on any person. But where the parent (1) has the opportunity and ability to control a minor, and (2) has knowledge of the tendency or proclivity of the minor to commit acts which could normally be expected to cause injury to others, and (3) after having such opportunity, ability and knowledge has failed to exercise reasonable means of controlling the minor or appreciably reduce the likelihood of injury to

others because of the minor's acts, the parent should be made to respond to those who have been injured by such acts of the minor.

* * *

The question before us is, does the complaint state a cause of action? We think that it does. . . .

HARRIS, CHIEF JUSTICE (concurring).

I thoroughly agree with everything that is said in the majority opinion but, due to my long interest in matters relating to parental discipline, cannot refrain from making special comment in this case. I feel that this is one of the most important decisions that has been handed down by this Court, and truly "strikes a blow" for home discipline. I fervently trust that it will be effective in bringing to the attention of parents their responsibility for the actions of their minor children. Too many, though aware of the tendencies of the child to engage in improper or unlawful conduct, are unwilling to take the time, or make the effort, to curb such propensities, but rather, surrender this duty to the general public. Of course, I recognise that in some instances, children are incorrigible,[1] but these instances are rare when considered in relation to the overall problem. In such event, proper discipline would seem to preclude the use of the family automobile. I am proud to have a part in handing down this opinion . . . .

b. Disputes between Members of the Family

[i]
Injury by Parent as Damage to Child
HASTINGS v. HASTINGS
33 N.J. 247, 163 A. 2d 147 (1960)

HALL, J.

This appeal presents the single clear-cut question whether an unemancipated minor child may maintain a cause of action against her father for personal injuries caused by his simple negligence in the driving of an automobile in which she was a passenger when he was insured by a policy of liability insurance obligating his insurer to pay all sums for which he was legally obligated as damages because of injury to others arising out of the ownership, maintenance and use of the car.

The child was four years of age at the time of the mishap and had lived with her parents since birth. Her father was her sole support. The suit, prosecuted by her mother as guardian *ad litem* . . . alleged that injuries to face and head resulted from the father's operation of the car in a

---

1. As defined by Webster: "Incapable of being corrected; not reformable; unmanageable, delinquent."

careless manner so that he ran into the rear of a vehicle in front of him, and specifically set forth the insurance coverage. The insurer was not made a party. There is no suggestion the car was being driven for business rather than family purposes.

The trial judge granted defendant's motion for summary judgment . . . .

There is no doubt that the ruling below is strictly in accord with the present law in this State . . . .

Plaintiff's position is that we should now overturn the rule, and sole reliance in support of the contention is placed on expressions of theoretical opinion by text writers and authors of law review articles and notes during the past 30 years. While this court has not been hesitant or backward in overruling judge-made principles and concepts that have become outmoded in the light of modern thought, knowledge and conditions . . . we have done so only when we have been thoroughly convinced that there is no longer any sound reason to retain the old rule and that essential justice compels a change. . . .

The question is not one of the absence of a duty of reasonable care owed by the father to his child, but rather of immunity from suit thereon. Matters of immunity must be determined, in the absence of specific legislation, on the basis of policy or, perhaps more accurately, on the weighing of competing policies. Here we think the weight of a combination of policies dictates the result. . . .

A succinct expression of the policies which have led other courts to reach the result we adhere to in this case is found in a recent opinion of the Pennsylvania Supreme Court where it was called upon to decide the precise question for the first time. The case is *Parks v. Parks, 390, Pa. 287, 135 A. 2d 65 (Sup. Ct. 1957)*, where it was said:

"It is a rule based on the sound principle of public policy to promote family unity and avoid family discord and disturbance, it prevents possible collusive action between parent and child in situations where the liability of either parent or child is covered by insurance and it is in line with the great weight of judicial authority represented by practically every court of every state in this country." (135 A. 2d at p. 71).

It will be recalled that we are dealing with a situation where parents and children living together under the ordinary conditions of family life and the charge is one of mere negligence. Such a claim is a very thin thing. It implies no intentional or even thoughtless disregard of intra-family responsibilities and benefits, which in the last analysis rest not on cold rules of law but on mutual love and affection. Legalistically speaking,

under these circumstances simple negligence amounts to no more than a very slight breach of a parental duty, and the well established rule of law is that a parent should not ordinarily be accountable to the child in money damages in such a situation. . . . It appears quite unseemly, to say the least, to suggest that a mere act or omission within the family circle amounting to no more than carelessness, which the one to blame would do almost anything to avoid, should require the payment of money by one member of the group to another. We believe that true family life, so important to our civilization, should not include among its foundation stones the concept of recompensable fault between parents and unemancipated children. The idea seems utterly foreign, whether a family member or some third party is compelled to produce the money. And it should not be overlooked that the principle plaintiff asks us to establish would be applicable to injuries suffered in the home as well as in the family car and that an injured parent would also have to be permitted to sue his child for the latter's negligence.

If the negligent parent were uninsured, so that judicial process in a real adversary proceeding would compel him to pay personally the child's recompense, which would necessarily have to come from the family estate and exchequer created and intended for the benefit of all members, the likelihood of the disruption of family unity and discipline is obvious. Of course, the injured child knows nothing of legal duties and remedies and would have no idea of suing his parent. That decision has to be made for him by someone else, which in the usual situation is the other parent, the spouse of the one to be sued and to pay after a public litigation arraying the family members against each other.

But we all know that realistically such actions are never thought of, let alone commenced, unless there is an insurance policy, automobile or comprehensive personal liability (which ordinarily indemnifies against the legal consequences of acts or omissions of all members of the family), on the basis of which money can be sought to be obtained. Such contracts are not commitments to pay in all events, such as are policies providing for medical payments and weekly indemnity in case of accident or hospitalization and medical and surgical treatment, now so commonly held by families or individual members, but depend for their operative effect on the insured being found legally at fault. Again, practically speaking, an action is not going to be commenced unless the family member to be sued is in effect prepared to say that he was negligent. The decision for the child to sue will be determined within the family circle and obviously the proposed defendant is going to participate in making it, quite an unorthodox situation under our basic concept of adversary litigation, to say the least. The risk of collusion is indeed a very great and human one, when the insured's own flesh and blood and the family pocketbook are concerned. It is unlikely in most instances that the insurance carrier, whose interests are the only ones really at stake, can adequately defend itself. The defendent under the insurance contract has the obligation to cooperate with the insurer, an obligation which, unless there is absolutely no question of his sole or concurrent and proximate negligence (a somewhat rare situation in everyday life), he will find it difficult to fulfill and at the same time further the successful outcome of the suit for the benefit of the child (and incidentally his own), which in reality is what he wishes to accomplish. The possibility of collusion, and the corollary of breakdown of most desirable individual integrity within the family frequently involving children as well, is so great in so many cases of the kind before us that we feel constrained to conclude, in conjunction with the other considerations previously mentioned, that sound public policy precludes their prosecution. It may be urged that the possibility of similar fraud also exists in other situations where our law permits suits, as in actions by guest against host, but we are convinced that the danger is not so great and the matter of integrity within the family is not involved.

* * *

JACOBS, J. (dissenting).

The just progress of the law is needlessly retarted by the failure of judges to deal with modern-day realities as they find them. In today's society, practically every man with any sense of responsibility carries suitable insurance coverage on the automobile he owns and operates. He does this not only to protect himself against the consequences of the neglectful operation of his automobile, but also because he wants to make certain that anyone injured by the neglect is fairly compensated for his injury. His insurance policy is in broad terms and covers injuries to others, including his passengers who may be close friends and relatives and their wives and children. So long as the wives and children are those of his friends and relatives the insurance is effective, but under the majority's holding here . . . it becomes meaningless when his own wife and children are the injured. It seems to me that this result lacks the support of any sound reason or policy. . . .

Nothing in the English common law precluded an action by a minor who had been wronged by his parent. . . . And until the decision of the Mississippi Supreme Court in *Hewlett v. George,* 68 *Miss. 703, 9 So. 885, 13 L.R.A. 682 (Sup. Ct. 1891),* there was no case in the United States which precluded such an action. In *Hewlett* the court refused to allow an unemancipated daughter to sue her mother for damages resulting from the alleged malicious imprisonment of the daughter in an insane asylum. It cited no authority for its holding but took the position that in the interests of the peace and tranquility of the family, a minor child should, as a matter of public policy, be prohibited from suing his parent for personal injuries. . . . [I]n *Lusk v. Lusk* . . . the court distinguished the ordinary parental immunity rule, saying:

> "But a different situation arises where the parent is protected by insurance in his vocational capacity. [A]s was said in the case of *Dunlap v. Dunlap,* 84 *N.H.* 352, 150 *A.* 905, 910, 71 *A.L.R.* 1055, 'The law does not make fetishes of ideas,' and we must not exalt this rule above ordinary common sense. A maxim of the common law (and of the ages for that matter) is when the reason for a rule ceases the rule itself ceases (*cessante ratione legis cassat ipsa lex*). There is no reason for applying the rule in the instant case. This action is not unfriendly as between the daughter and the father. A recovery by her is no loss to him. In fact, their interests unite in favor of her recovery, but without hint of 'domestic fraud and collusion' (charged in some cases). There is no filial recrimination and no pitting of the daughter against the father in this case. No strained family relations will follow. On the contrary, the daughter must honor the father for attempting to provide compensation against' her misfortune. Family harmony is assured instead of disrupted. A wrong is righted instead of 'privileged.'" 166 *S.E.,* at *pp.* 538-539.

* * *

Those who still oppose personal injury actions by children against their fully insured parents generally recognize the total inapplicability of any policy based on the preservation of the family relationship, but urge instead the danger of fraud and collusion. [T]here is opportunity for fraud and collusion in many legal proceedings, but our system of courts and juries is well designed to seek them out and the opportunity for fraud and collusion clearly furnishes no just or moral basis for precluding honest and meritorious actions. Furthermore, as parents who seek to instill decent principles of integrity and ethics in their offspring will readily realize, there would be greater restraint and less danger of fraud and collusion between the minor child and his parent than there would be between the parent and his adult friends and relatives who admittedly may maintain actions when injured by the parent's negligent operation of his automobile. In *Rozell v. Rozell, supra,* the Court of Appeals of New York rejected an attack on the right of a 12-year-old child to bring an action against his 16-year-old sister who injured him while driving an automobile covered by liability insurance ; in the course of his opinion for the court Judge Rippey said:

> "But I am unwilling to admit that sanction to the maintenance of such an action between brother and sister is any more of an incentive to fraud than when a similar action was sanctioned between husband and wife, between an emancipated son and his father, between grandmother and grandchild, between owner and guest, or between intimate friends. No warrant is found for any prediction that brothers and sisters will flock into the courts on fictitious claims through mere judicial recognition of the right of one to sue the other in personal injury cases. Common honesty inherent in the family unit presents an effective barrier. If it should appear that there is any foundation for the suggestion, a means of protection may be found in diligence on the part of the insurance carriers to ferret out and expose the fictitious claims and reliance may be placed on our courts and juries to detect and prevent a fraud." 22 *N.E. 2d,* at *p.* 257.

* * *

The only other argument advanced against the child's action worthy of mention here . . . is that it may undermine parental authority and discipline. Whatever force this argument may have on other types of action, it clearly has no bearing on the type of action instituted in the instant matter. In *Borst v. Borst, supra,* 251 *P. 2d* at *p.* 153, *the* Washington Supreme Court, in upholding an action by a minor child against his father for personal injuries sustained when the child was run over by his father's automobile which was being operated for business purposes, had this to say:

> " . . . The field of parental control and discipline covers such matters as the maintenance of the home, chastisement, and no doubt other activities which need not here be delineated. But when the parental activity whereby the child was injured has nothing to do with parental control and discipline, a suit involving such activity cannot be said to undermine those sinews of family life. And even if such a suit should tend to impair family discipline in some degree, that would not seem to call for application of the immunity rule any more than in cases where the child sues to enforce a property right." 251 *P. 2d,* at *pp.* 153-154.

* * *

Outmoded legal doctrines are rarely overturned abruptly for courts seem to prefer to erode them gradually by differentiation, exception and ultimately extinction. . . . All this court is now called upon to hold is that a father who carelessly and negligently injures his passenger child while driving his fully insured automobile is not immune from a legal action on the child's behalf. It seems to me that fair and just application of the fundamental common law duty of due care, with tort liability for its breach . . . clearly calls for such a holding ; accordingly, I would reverse and remand the matter for trial.

NOTES

NOTE 1.

SELDIN, JOSEPH J.
The Golden Fleece*

. . . The advertising community says its job is to sell the world, not to save it ; the saving it leaves to education and religion. And the selling job is so important to the continuation of the nation's prosperity that it invests the advertising community with a special license to indulge in small and medium-sized built-in selling deceptions. Regrettable as it is to have to proceed by these somewhat shabby methods, it is considered a small price indeed for the citizenry to pay for their material well-being.

* * *

[S]ince an ad runs until conclusively proved false, all too many advertisers promote deceptive campaigns and rely on administrative remedies to block FTC action until the campaigns have run their course. Frequently, before the FTC gets to the point where it issues a cease and desist order, the campaign is over and the advertiser is off on a new one. The chase then begins anew. Given the power to issue an interlocutory cease and desist order on the basis of a prima facie showing, however, the FTC could freeze the campaign indefinitely while the cumbersome process of taking evidence and reaching a decision unfolds. The public would gain the full measure of benefit.

* * *

. . . Marketable competition being what it is, there . . . was a perceptible movement to retailers' shelves around the nation of larger packages with the same content, and less content in the same sized packages. With rare exceptions, advertisers

---

* New York: The Macmillan Co., 1963, pp. 286-288, 159-160. Reprinted with permission of the publisher.

scrupulously adhered to the law by specifying the number of ounces on the label, but only house-wives blessed with 20/20 vision and a mind for detail could read the minuscule type and know how many ounces were in the package. What added palpably to the confusion in the super-market was the handiwork of the designers who created packages that optically looked larger than they really were.

Hence few housewives were probably aware of the shift in the early fifties of can sizes in which fruits and vegetables were packed. The trend was away from the No. 2 can (19.7 fluid ounces) to the No. 303 can (16.2 ounces), without any general reduction in price. In 1955, citing figures by the National Canners Association, *Printers' Ink* traced the movement of green beans, corn, peas, apricots, and peaches into the smaller can. Whereas in 1947, for instance, 74 percent of the green beans were packed in the No. 2 can, by 1953 some 65 percent were ensconced in the No. 303 can. Without plac-ing the two cans side by side, the difference in size was practically undetectable.

*   *   *

The Food and Drug Administration sent out the word to every advertiser who would listen that it had uncovered far too many packages with im-proper weights. An FDA survey of 32,225 pack-ages had found short weights in 39 percent of them. Most of the short weights were less than 2 percent, but ½ of 1 percent came out short by 5 percent or more. Some spaghetti shortages were as much as 17 percent. Offenders ran the range of corn meal, butter, sugar, oleomargarine, farina, oatmeal, macaroni, frozen fish, vegetable shorten-ing, liquid salad dressing, and rice.

NOTE 2.

BRENNECKE v. KILPATRICK
336 S.W. 2d 68 (Mo. 1960)

ELMO B. HUNTER, SPECIAL JUDGE.

*   *   *

It is our view that where an unemancipated minor child by next friend is suing the representa-tive of his deceased parent's estate for his negli-gently inflicted personal injury by that parent, public policy does not prohibit such suit and recovery. The doctrine of intra-family immunity from such suits, expires upon the death of the person protected and does not extend to the decedent's estate for the reason that death terminates the family relationship and there is no longer in existence a relationship within the reasonable contemplation of the doctrine. . . .

EAGER, JUDGE (dissenting).

. . . The immunity springs from a disability imposed by reason of public policy, the underlying reason for which is a desire to protect the family relationship and interest, social and economic. The reason for the rule may extend beyond the death of a wife, or a mother, or a father. In this case a father and at least one child survive; the father proceeds to sue the mother's estate for him-self and for a six-year-old child. We shall not elaborate here upon the possible effects of such litigation in a family (disregarding insurance for the moment), the bitterness engendered, the estates destroyed, the relationships disrupted. The evils may depend, in some measure, upon which mem-bers of the family remain. The reasons for the rule may often outlive a death.

*   *   *

NOTE 3.

BURDICK v. NAWROCKI
21 Conn. Supp. 272, 154 A. 2d 242 (1959)

TROLAND, J.

This is an action to recover damages for per-sonal injuries caused to Raymond Burdick, an unemancipated minor, brought on his behalf by his mother and next friend against his stepfather, Mitchell Nawrocki, the defendant Thompson.

The plaintiff was a passenger in the tractor trailer of Nawrocki which was being operated by the defendant Thompson on the business of Nawrocki. . . . As a result of collision . . . the plaintiff received serious personal injuries. . . .

At the time of the accident resulting in his injuries, the plaintiff was sixteen years of age. His father was dead; his mother had remarried. He was residing at home with the family consisting of his mother, his stepfather and himself. The plaintiff was unemployed. He took his meals at home, received his spending money from time to time from his mother and occasionally from his stepfather. He helped his mother with household chores and from time to time, when at his step-father's place of business, "helped out" without compensation.

The defendant has set up as a special defense that the plaintiff, being a stepson of the defendant Mitchell Nawrocki and being an unemancipated minor, is barred by law from bringing an action against his stepfather.

. . . It is well established in Connecticut that an unemancipated minor may not maintain an action against his parents. . . .

The public policy . . . emphasizes the main-tenance of harmony in the family and the avoid-ance of unseemly family discord as reasons for the rule against an unemancipated minor maintaining an action against his parents. This policy seems to support defendant's claim. However, the stepfather, although he presently voluntarily stands in loco parentis, is not under legal obligation to care for, guide and control the child. Since the death of his father, the above obligations have fallen to plantiff's mother alone. It is she alone who has the power to emancipate her son before he reaches the age of twenty-one. The son's legal reciprocal obligations are to the mother.

The court therefore holds that it is not warranted in extending the provisions of the rule . . . to include one standing in loco parentis in a limited sense, such as a stepfather.

* * *

NOTE 4.

EMERY v. EMERY
289 P. 2d 218 (Cal. 1955)

TRAYNOR, JUSTICE

. . . Since the law imposes on the parent a duty to rear and discipline his child and confers the right to prescribe a course of reasonable conduct for its development, the parent has a wide discretion in the performance of his parental functions, but that discretion does not include the right wilfully to inflict personal injuries beyond the limits of reasonable parental discipline. No sound public policy would be subserved by extending it beyond those limits. While it may seem repugant to allow a minor to sue his parent, we think it more repugnant to leave a minor child without redress for the damage he has suffered by reason of his parent's wilful or malicious misconduct. A child, like every other individual, has a right to freedom from such injury. Accordingly, we conclude that an unemancipated minor may sue his parent for a wilful or malicious tort . . . .

NOTE 5.

GOLLER v. WHITE
20 Wisc. 2d 402, 122 N.W. 2d 193, 198 (1963)

CURRIE, JUSTICE.

After a careful review of the arguments for and against the parental-immunity rule in negligence cases, we are of the opinion that it ought to be abrogated except in these two situations: (1) where the alleged negligent act involves an exercise of parental authority over the child; and (2) where the alleged negligent act involves an exercise of ordinary parental discretion with respect to the provision of food, clothing, housing, medical and dental services, and other care. Accordingly the rule is abolished in personal injury actions subject to these noted exceptions. . . .

NOTE 6.

FREUD, SIGMUND
Introductory Lectures on Psychoanalysis (1915)*

. . . A small child does not necessarily love his brothers and sisters ; often he obviously does not. There is no doubt that he hates them as his competitors, and it is a familiar fact that this attitude often persists for long years, till maturity is reached or even later, without interruption. Quite often, it is true, it is succeeded, or let us rather say overlaid, by a more affectionate attitude ; but the hostile one seems very generally to be the earlier. This hostile attitude can be observed most easily in children between two and a half and four or five, when a new baby brother or sister appears. It usually meets with a very unfrienedly reception. Such remarks as 'I don't like him ; the stork can take him away again !' are quite common. After this, every opportunity is taken of disparaging the new arrival and attempts to injure him and even murderous assaults are not unknown. If the difference in age is less, by the time the child's mental activity has awakened to some degree of intensity he finds his competitor already there and adjusts himself to him. If the difference is greater, the new baby may from the first arouse a certain sympathy as an interesting object, a sort of live doll ; and where the difference in age is of eight or more years, solicitous, maternal impulses may already come into play, especially in girls. But, honestly speaking, if one comes upon a wish for the death of a brother or sister behind a dream, there is seldom need to find it puzzling and one can trace its prototype without any trouble in early childhood and often enough in later years of companionship as well.

There is probably no nursery without violent conflicts between its inmates. The motives for these are rivalry for parental love, for common possessions, for living space. The hostile impulses are directed against older as well as against younger members of the family. It was, I believe, Bernard Shaw who remarked: 'As a rule there is only one person an English girl hates more than she hates her mother ; and that's her eldest sister.' But there is something in this remark that strikes us as strange. We might at a pinch find hatred and competition with brothers and sisters intelligible. But how can we suppose that feelings of hatred can make their way into the relation be-

---

* Reprinted from 15 *The Standard Edition of the Complete Psychological Works of Sigmund Freud.* London: The Hogarth Press, 1963 (pp. 204-206). Reprinted with permission of the publisher. Also from *A General Introduction to Psychoanalysis* by Sigmund Freud. By permission of Liveright, Publishers, N.Y. Copyright © R, 1963 by Joan Riviere.

tween daughter and mother, between parents and children?

This relation is undoubtedly a more favourable one, from the children's point of view as well. That is what our expectations demand; we find an absence of love far more repellent between parents and children than between brothers and sisters. In the former case we have, as it were, made something sacred which in the latter we have left profane. Yet daily observation can show us how frequently the emotional relations between parents and their grown-up children fall behind the ideal set up by society, how much hostility is ready to hand and would be expressed if it were not held back by admixtures of filial piety and affectionate impulses. The motives for this hostility are generally known and their tendency is to divide those of the same sex—the daughter from the mother and the father from the son. The daughter finds in her mother the authority which restricts her will and which is entrusted with the task of imposing on her the renunciation of sexual freedom which society demands; in a few instances she even finds in her a competitor who struggles against being supplanted. The same thing is repeated between the son and his father still more glaringly. In the son's eyes his father embodies every unwillingly tolerated social restrain; his father prevents him from exercising his will, from early sexual pleasure and, where there is common property in the family, from enjoying it. In the case of an heir to the throne this waiting for a father's death reaches an almost tragic height. There seems less danger to the relation between father and daughter or mother and son. The last provides the purest examples of an unchangeable affection, unimpaired by any egoistic considerations.

Why am I speaking of these things, which are after all commonplaces and universally known? Because there is an unmistakable inclination to disavow their importance in life and to make out that the ideal demanded by society is fulfilled far more often than it really is. . . .

[ii]
Injury by a Spouse as Damage to the Other

LEACH v. LEACH
227 Ark. 599, 300 S.W. 2d 15 (1957)

GEORGE ROSE SMITH, JUSTICE.

This case presents a question that is novel in this state and very nearly so in the United States: Can a husband maintain a suit against his wife for damages due to her negligence? The appellant's complaint, as supplemented by a stipulation, alleges that on August 9, 1956, he was the owner of a pick-up truck and a Ford sedan. As Leach was driving the truck on a country road he collided with his wife, who was driving the

sedan in the opposite direction. It is asserted that Mrs. Leach was driving on the wrong side of the road and at an excessive speed. The trial court sustained a demurrer to the complaint and dismissed the action.

At common law neither spouse could maintain a tort action against the other. . . . Prosser's criticism of the majority rule typifies the position generally taken by legal writers: "The chief reason relied upon by all these courts, however, is that personal tort actions between husband and wife would disrupt and destroy the peace and harmony of the home, which is against the policy of the law. This is on the bald theory that after a husband has beaten his wife there is a state of peace and harmony left to be disturbed; and that if she is sufficiently injured or angry to sue him for it, she will be soothed and deterred from reprisals by denying her the legal remedy—and this even though she has left him or divorced him for that very ground, and though the same courts refuse to find any disruption of domestic tranquillity if she sues him for a tort to her property, or brings a criminal prosecution against him. If this reasoning appeals to the reader, let him by all means adopt it." Prosser, *loc cit.*

This reasoning has never appealed to us . . . .

. . . Our emancipation act is far more sweeping in its language than are most statutes on the subject: "Every married woman and every woman who may in the future become married, shall have all the rights to contract and be contracted with, to sue and be sued, and in law and equity shall enjoy all rights and be subjected to all the laws of this State, as though she were a femme sole; provided, it is expressly declared to be the the intention of this act [section] to remove all statutory disabilities of married women as well as common law disabilities, such as the disability to act as executrix or administratrix as provided by § 6 of Kirby's Digest [§ 62-205], and all other statutory disabilities." Ark. Stats. 1947, § 55-401.

We do not perceive that the explicit language of the statute leaves any doubt about the legislative intention. The appellee's suggestion that the act was meant only to broaden the rights of married women, and not to curtail the protection afforded them at common law, is rebutted by the unquivocal and unrestricted declaration that married women may "sue and be sued." This clause was the basis for our holding that a wife may sue her husband in tort. There can be no sound basis for a different conclusion when the shoe is on the other foot, for in the same breath the legislature abolished her disability to sue and her immunity from being sued.

*   *   *

Reversed, the demurrer to be overruled.

HARRIS, CHIEF JUSTICE (dissenting).

In dissenting to the ruling of the majority, I desire to make it clear that my dissent is not based upon the fact that the common law did not grant either spouse the right to maintain tort action against the other; nor am I concerned because we are the first state to allow the husband the right to sue his wife for tort. I fully agree that if the wife has the right to sue the husband in tort, the converse should likewise be true, but I am persuaded that to allow either spouse to sue the other for *unintentional* tort is against public policy.[1] . . .

* * *

The theory of the law . . . is that permitting suits between spouses would adversely affect harmony in the home. The majority, in this current Opinion, quote Prosser. . . . I have no quarrel with [his] language; in fact, I quite agree that the harmony of the home is already disrupted when either spouse commits an *intentional* tort against the other. The same language does not apply to an *unintentional* tort.

Let us take a hypothetical case. The wife, after finishing her housecleaning, neglects to return the vacum cleaner to the closet where it usually is placed, and negligently leaves same in the middle of the hall. The husband, returning home that night from a business trip, after the wife has retired, stumbles over same, and receives injuries. Under the view of the majority, he is entitled to sue the wife. Of course, if she is without means, he would not bring a suit; if, on the other hand, she is gainfully employed, or financially independent in her own right, and he goes to court to recover from her for the injury, no imagination is needed for one to know that harmony in that home would be completely disrupted, and connubial bliss abruptly terminated. The marriage relationship, which might have been happy enough, would totally disintegrate. But, on the other hand, let us say that this particular family has comprehensive personal liability coverage, and suit is brought. In such event, I concede that domestic harmony would not be destroyed, but it could not be logically argued that such a suit between spouses would be justified simply because the insurance company, after all, would be the one to pay. This brings me to one of the worst features involved in permitting this type of suit.

Using my same example, let us say that the husband fell and injured himself in the home, not because of his wife's negligence but because of his own carelessness. There will be medical expenses and loss of time from work, with perhaps a resulting loss of income. Under this set of facts, the husband would have to stand this loss himself, which would also directly affect the welfare of the wife. Now, if this man and wife are without morals and conscience, what is to prevent the husband from instituting suit against his wife, alleging that his injury occurred in the manner first stated. (Wherein she left the cleaner in the hall.) She does not deny it, and how can it be proved that it did not happen in that manner? There are no other witnesses to establish that injury was sustained by the husband because of his own negligence rather than that of his wife. Unfortunately, I fear that there might be a few husbands and wives who would welcome the opportunity to make a joint raid upon an insurance company. This certainly should not be permissible. Either set of facts presents an intolerable situation, not in the interest of the public, and one which the law should not countenance. While I hope that it will not so result, the holding of the majority, in my opinion, opens the door to fraudulent claims against insurance carriers.

Be that as it may, litigation between man and wife for an unintentional tort committed by one against the other is not salutary, and actually is repugnant, to the marriage vows. The bulwark of our community and national strength is the home, and we should not adopt a policy that might well, in individual cases, rupture marital happiness.

Solely because I consider such holding to be *against public policy,* I respectfully dissent.

NOTE

FENICHEL, OTTO

Concerning Unconscious Communication*

The patient, who came into analysis on account of characterological difficulties, had a relationship with a widow who was considerably older than he; he had made her acquaintance by "rescuing" her from financial difficulties. Consciously, he felt contempt for her, but could not break with her; and he came into the analysis with, among other things, the wish to be freed of this tie. That this widow represented his mother had not yet come up in the analysis. The woman herself was in her climacteric and obviously knew full well that were

---

1. Bouvier's Law Dictionary defines Public Policy as: "That principle of the law which holds that no subject can lawfully do that which has a tendency to be injurious to the public or against the public good." It has been designated by Burroughs, J., as "an unruly horse pursuing us, and when once you get astride of it you never know where it will carry you."

* Reprinted from *The Collected Papers of Otto Fenichel*, First Series, pp. 94-96, by permission of Routledge & Kegan Paul Ltd, and W.W. Norton & Company, Inc. Copyright 1953 by W.W. Norton & Company, Inc.

she to lose her lover, she would spend the rest of her life without gratification; she held onto him with all her might and occasionally made scenes of jealousy, but in general she anxiously over-looked—as far as was possible—all the indications he gave of his intention to break with her. She was a simple woman from whom neither subtlety nor lies could be expected. She lived in a suburb and rarely came to town, and my patient used to visit her in her home.

One morning, after lengthy internal struggles, the patient picked up a girl on the street, went walking with her, sat down in a small park—of the existence of which he had not known before—chatted and smoked some cigarettes with her, and then took her to a restaurant. After that, they agreed on a date and he went about his business In the evening, as he was undressing, he saw that he had lost one of his cuff links. He remembered that while walking with the girl, he had noticed that a cuff link had come open, and he was angry with himself for not having put it to rights at once. The next day he visited his old friend. In her dining-room, on the table, there was a tray for visiting cards. As he entered the room, he saw a cuff link lying on the tray, as though it had been put there especially for him to notice. He picked it up and saw that it was a link of the same kind as his own and matched the one he was still wear-ing. He became very frightened; it at once occur-red to him that the link was there to convict him of his yesterday's adventure. He gave up this idea immediately, because he knew that his friend was unable to pretend and would already have made a scene if she had known anything. He asked her: "What is this cuff link?" "I found it yesterday." "Why is it here?" "It occurred to me that one might need a cuff link like that on some occasion, so I brought it home and put it down there for the time being." "Where did you find it?" "In such-and-such a park." "How did you come to be there?" "Usually enough, I had to buy something in that neighborhood yesterday; I rested in the park, whose existence I did not know of before, and there was the cuff link under the bench." "About what time?" "About one o'clock." This was the time when he himself had sat there. It was thus certain that she had sat down on the bench immediately after he had gone, found the link he had lost there, and taken it home.

Two circumstances give one pause, one on the side of the patient, the other on that of the woman. Throughout the time he spent in the park, the patient had a bad conscience about his un-faithfulness, and thought of what his friend would say if she saw him there; his whole psychological situation was such as to lend itself to an uncons-cious self-betrayal. Furthermore, just before he sat

down on the bench he had noticed the open cuff link, and had thus offered his unconscious, as it were, a convenient occasion for a self-betrayal. As for the woman, it is striking, first that she should pick up the link and take it home, and then that she should put it down in an unusual place so that her friend would see it on entering and would be reminded of his misdemeanor. If she had seen him with the girl and wanted to confront him with a *corpus delicti,* she could not have done better. These circumstances admit of only one explana-tion. The only part which chance played in the business was that both of them had come at the same time to the park which was unknown to them before. All the rest was unconscious, pur-posive action at lightning speed. The man sitting on the bench saw the woman nearing; without being in the least aware of it, he was overcome by a storm of feeling in his doubt whether or not he should reveal himself; he decided not to, and left the bench quickly with his companion, but not without fulfilling his self-betraying tendency by shaking his arm so that the loose cuff link dropped down. The woman must also have seen and recognized the man. But she did not *want* to see anything; she did not go after him but sat down on the bench on which he had sat just before. She found the link, took it home, and put it on the tray. Perhaps she did not recognize the man for sure, and put him to the test with the link. It should be stressed once more that she certainly did not lie, and even after my patient told her the story truthfully, she insisted that she had not seen him and had not recognized the link, and that she had brought it home and put it down without any intentions—and that, indeed, it did not even cross her mind that he could have been in that part of town.

The patient was at first very much astonished by this interpretation; but then a detail occurred to him which substantiated it beyond any doubt. He and the girl had wanted to go away five minutes earlier, but had then decided to stay for one more cigarette. Now he remembered that very suddenly, in the middle of the cigarette he had wanted to finish, he had jumped up, and said impatiently to his companion: "Now we really must go!" and made off with her as fast as he could. This must have been the instant at which he unconsciously caught sight of his woman friend.

Thus not only did the two parties, as though by agreement, immediately repress their having seen each other, since that would have been un-pleasant for both; the woman also immediately understood the meaning of the loss of the cuff link and reacted accordingly. Indeed, she did exactly what the behavior of the man secretly challenged her to do. When he jumped up and ran away, but lost his link in so doing, he was saying to her: "You are not to *notice* that I have sat here with a girl; but you are to *know* it!" And that is what she did.

4.

IN CONTRACTS AND PROPERTY—THE FAMILY AS AN ENCLOSURE FOR AFFECTION, OWNERSHIP, PROCREATION, HEALTH, AND WELL-BEING

a. PHILLIPS v. FREDERICK
257 Ala. 283, 58 So. 2d 584 (1951)

LIVINGSTON, CHIEF JUSTICE.

This appeal is from a¹ decree of the Circuit Court, in Equity . . . allowing a claim for $7,000.00, filed against the estate of John W. Phillips, deceased, by Paul Frederick, a minor, by his next friend, Ola Gregory, who is the maternal grandmother of the minor.

John W. Phillips . . . departed this life intestate on or about January 26, 1950. . . .

*   *   *

The basis of the claim of Paul Frederick against the estate of John W. Phillips is, in substance, an oral agreement made by Alene Frederick, the mother of Paul Frederick, with the said John W. Phillips, whereby Phillips was to have the care, custody and control of the minor during his, Phillips' lifetime, and, in consideration whereof, Phillips agreed to care for, feed, clothe and educate, including a college education, the minor, and that in the event Phillips died before the minor received his education, the minor was to receive $7,000.00 for that purpose.

Claimant's evidence tended to prove the following facts:

. . . John W. Phillips was about 68 years of age when he died. Mrs. Ola Gregory was his housekeeper at the time of his death, and had been for some 18 or 20 years. Mrs. Gregory was the maternal grandmother of Paul Frederick. Douglas Frederick and Alene Frederick are the parents of Paul Frederick. During the month of July, 1945, Douglas, Alene and Paul Frederick visited Ola Gregory for some time in the home of John W. Phillips, deceased. Paul Frederick was then some 13 or 14 months old. The deceased became attached to the child and on several occasions asked that he be allowed to adopt him. The mother refused. The deceased then proposed

that he be allowed to keep the baby as long as he, Phillips, lived and he would give him a complete education, including four years of college, which he could do, "with careful handling, for seven thousand dollars." The deceased also told Alene Frederick that "regardless of what happens to me, it will be fixed whether I live or die." Alene Frederick agreed to the proposal of the deceased and left the infant, Paul Frederick, with the deceased when she returned to her home, and the infant remained with Phillips as long as Phillips lived.

Claimant's evidence further tended to show that Phillips loved the child; that he kept the child with him as much as he could, considering the child's age; that the child slept with Phillips, and that Phillips was good and kind to him as long as he lived.

*   *   *

The Hooks case, 111 Tex. 122, 229 S.W. 1114, 1118, . . . declares a contract, similar to the one here under review, contrary to public policy. The Supreme Court of Texas there said:

". . . A parent has no property interest in his child and should not be permitted to deal with his child as property. . . . The law should not encourage the relinquishment by parents of their children and the renunciation of a sacred relation imposed by nature merely for the children's enrichment by placing the seal of validity upon a contract in which a parent in effect barters his child away for a property return. It is more concerned in fostering and maintaining that relation and guarding its valuable and wholesome influences than in promoting the child's financial prosperity. Let it be once held that a parent's contract of this kind is valid and may be enforced, and every parent will be free to transfer his children to any one willing to pay them well for the bargain. We are unwilling to subscribe to such a doctrine. It tends to the destruction of one of the finest relations of human life, to the subversion of the family tie, and to the reversal of an ordering of nature which is essential to human happiness and the security of society. It reduces parental duty and the child's welfare to the sordid level of financial profit, and would license the easy surrender of that duty for merely the child's financial advantage. The custody of a child is not a subject matter of contract and therefore can constitute no consideration for a contract. The attempted agreement here was therefore not a contract.

*   *   *

[On the other hand in] Godine v. Kidd, 64 Hun. 585, 19 N.Y.S. 335, 338, it was said:

"The enforcement of the contract here will not result in injustice to any third persons, nor is it against public policy; but, in view of the literal way in which it has been performed upon the part of the defendant's parents and her own, it would be an extreme hardship, and both inequitable and unjust, if she were now prevented, after all these years of performance on her part and that of her parents, from enforcing it. Even though we should assume, therefore, that none of the arrangements between the parties was of original binding obligation upon the defendant's parents, yet the subsequent performance and fulfillment thereof by defendant and her parents, so that thereby the Knapps actually got all they bargained for, would furnish a sufficient consideration to support their promises as effectually as if the agreement had been of original binding obligation. What the Knapps bargained for was, at the very least, forbearance by and on the part of defendant's parents of some of their rights, and was an adequate and sufficient consideration for their promises and undertakings. It has frequently been held that the consideration for a contract or promise need not be adequate in point of value. If there be any consideration, the court will not weigh the extent of it. It has no means of scrutinizing the varied hidden motives and reasons that may have influenced the parties, and induced them to enter into the contract, nor can it determine upon the prudence or propriety of the transaction. Where an offer is accepted by the party doing the act which forms the consideration, and when the promisor has had the benefit of the consideration for which he bargained, it is no answer, in an action brought for a performance of the agreement, to say that the promisee was not bound by the contract. It is enough if the promisee did it on the faith of the undertakings of the promisor, and upon showing that the latter got the benefit of it."

* * *

Appellant also argues that there is a lack of mutuality between the parties and for that reason the contract is unenforcible.

On this point the Supreme Court of Missouri in the case of Healey v. Simpson, 113 Mo. 340, 20 S.W. 881, 883, said:

"The surrender by the mother of all control of the child, and the services and companionship of the latter, constituted valuable considerations for the promise of Brewster and his wife that she should 'have and inherit from the estate of said parties * * * in the same manner and to the same extent that a child born of their union would inherit.' The influences of a child of tender years in the home circle are too sacred and holy to be estimated in dollars and cents. And when the mother sent her child to dwell in another family, in a distant state, she yielded much of

affection and love, and Brewster, by the same act gained the companionship of one who added much, no doubt, to his enjoyment of life. The sundering of natural ties and the formation of artificial ones for the enjoyment and gratification of the party at whose instance this is done, is held, and ought to be held, to be such a consideration as the courts will recognize as valuable where the other party has in good faith acted on and carried out the agreement on his part. This is upon the principle that the parties cannot be put in statu quo. In the very nature of things, nine years in the life of a child so change conditions that it is out of the power of an earthly tribunal to restore the parties to their original situation and environment, and the courts therefore compel them to stand upon and abide by the record they have made."

* * *

In the instant case the agreement was fully performed by the parent and child. Phillips, the deceased received all that he bargained for. Although a contract by a parent to surrender the custody of a child to another in consideration of his promise to care for, rear, and educate it may not be binding when made because of the peculiar character of the duty and rights of the parent in respect to the child, and where the welfare of the child demands it, it is binding on the other party after the parents and child have, as here, fully executed their part. Its enforcement has no element of immorality or illegality, and so far as we can see, is not violative of public policy.

NOTE

In re SHIRK'S ESTATE
186 Kan. 311, 350 P. 2d 1 (1960)

FATZER, JUSTICE.

[A] contract of a parent by which he bargains away for his pecuniary gain the custody of his child to a stranger and attempts to relieve himself from all parental obligation, placing the burden on another who assumes it, without natural affection or moral obligation, but only because of the bargain, is void as against public policy. Such a contract would be the mere sale of the child for money. But the instant case involves a family compact. The proposal for adoption upon which the contract was based came from the grandmother. It was not prompted by self-seeking on the part of the mother. Implicit in it is the favorable inference that the controlling consideration was the welfare of the two-year-old child. That fact permeates all the circumstances alleged. While the mother received the promise of the grandmother that she would receive one-third of her estate we cannot say that, under all the circumstances alleged and the favorable inferences to which they are entitled, the mother's consent to the adoption falls within the rule that a parent may not transfer his parental rights and duties to another in an attempt to sell or barter his child for his own finanical gain.

In the first place, the mother could not do for the child what she would like to have done. She was having difficulty in supporting herself and the child and was required to be away from time to time. As a result, the welfare of the helpless child was in peril. The grandmother, conscious of this and being of ample fortune and believing that her only grandchild was receiving inadequate care, came to Topeka and took the child to her home in McPherson. She wanted to be personally assured the child would receive the best care possible. Her pride centered around the child as her only hope of posterity. It was there the grandmother proposed the adoption. The mother, cognizant of the welfare of the child, agreed. The effect of the contract was to permit the grandmother to take the child, care for and support it as her own daughter for a limited period —until the mother remarried and established a happy home at which time she could reclaim its custody by readoption. Both parties desired to give the child the best home possible and they realized that the child would be better cared for with the grandmother until such time as the mother could provide such a home. What was done for Carmen was highly commendable and her interests were best served by the family agreement.

*   *   *

b.   LAMONT BLDG. CO. v. COURT
          147 Ohio 183, 70 N.E. 2d 447 (1946)

On February 19, 1945, the plaintiff, the appellant herein, rented to defendant, on a month to month basis, an apartment in an apartment building in the city of Cleveland. At the time, defendant was advised that the occupancy was to be confined exclusively to adult persons. On the first month's rent receipt given defendant was the notation, "Specific rental rule—No pets—adults only."

Defendant and his wife moved into the apartment. The wife was then pregnant, which fact was not known to the plaintiff. In the course of a few months a child was born to the defendant's wife and came to live in the apartment with its parents.

Thereafter, plaintiff gave written notice to the defendant that he must arrange for the occupancy of the apartment by adults only or vacate. Defendant did not comply with the notice and an action in forcible entry and detainer was brought in the Municipal Court of the city of Cleveland. Trial before the court and a jury resulted in a verdict for the defendant, upon which judgment was entered.

Plaintiff thereupon took its appeal to the Court of Appeals on questions of law. That court affirmed the judgment below on the ground, as appears from its opinion, that plaintiff's rule against permitting children to occupy its premises was against public policy and void.

ZIMMERMAN, JUDGE.

As succinctly stated in 12 American Jurisprudence, 641, Section 149:

> "It is the inherent and inalienable right of every man freely to deal or refuse to deal with his fellow men. Competent persons ordinarily have the utmost liberty of contracting, and their agreements voluntarily and fairly made will be held valid and enforced in the courts. Parties may incorporate in their agreements any provisions that are not illegal or violative of public policy."

Ordinarily, the owner of real property may surround its occupation and use by others with such reasonable restrictions as he may deem fit and proper. Here, plaintiff was in the control of the apartment building. Defendant rented an apartment and moved into it with knowledge of the condition that its occupancy was to be solely by adults. In bringing a child to dwell in the apartment against plaintiff's stipulation to the contrary, the defendant breached a material part of the agreement.

We know of no constitutional provision, statutory enactment or decision by this court denying plaintiff the privilege of imposing a condition of the kind involved here. Nor can we conceive that such a condition may be classed as injurious to the public or in contravention of any established interest of society. Although we are aware that a temporary housing shortage exists in this state, the argument that plaintiff's rule against permitting children to live in its property would encourage race suicide is hardly tenable.

At best, "public policy" is an uncertain and indefinite term. When judges come to apply the doctrine, they must take care not to infringe on the rights of parties to make contracts which are not clearly opposed to some principles or policy of the law. Notwithstanding we may be sympathetic toward the defendant and his problem of securing living accommodations for himself and his family, we cannot allow that sympathy to prevail over plaintiff's legal rights.

Plaintiff did not say to the defendant, "You cannot have children"; it said, merely, "If you do have children, they may not occupy my premises."

*   *   *

Consequently, the judgment of the Court of Appeals is reversed and final judgment is entered for the plaintiff.

NOTES

NOTE 1.

LAMONT BLDG. CO. v. COURT
45 Ohio 250, 66 N.E. 2d 552, 554 (1946)

MORGAN, JUDGE.

*   *   *

After weighing this matter carefully, a majority of this court are of the opinion that the condition and obligation, "adults only" is against public policy and void when applied to the case of a child born to the defendant and his wife while they are occupants of the premises. In the present extreme housing shortage such a provision in a lease of an apartment, if valid, could not but act as a deterrent to tenants holding the lease from having children. The danger of race suicide is often spoken of in these modern days, and it is not wholly an imaginary danger. The power and influence of the law should be exerted in the direction of encouraging and not discouraging married couples to have offspring.

*   *   *

If the fact that the wife was pregnant when the lease was made would influence the court to hold that the occupancy of such premises by such child when born would not be permitted, and would call for an eviction such a holding would be an inducement for the parents by unnatural means to avoid and to prevent the birth of the child.

It is quite true that in a great majority of cases parents would resist such a temptation even at the risk of being evicted from the premises. However, we know that there are many abortions committed for even slighter reasons, and the law should be on its guard not to hold forth the least inducement to married couples not to have children.

*   *   *

NOTE 2.

39 McKinney's Consolidated Laws of New York § 2041-42 (1944 and 1961 Supp.)

§ 2041. Discrimination against children in dwelling houses

Any person, firm or corporation in any city owning or having in charge any apartment house, tenement house, or other building used for dwelling purposes who shall refuse to rent any or part of any such building to any person or family solely on the ground that such person or family has or have a child or children shall be guilty of a misdemeanor and on conviction thereof shall be punished by a fine of not less than fifty nor more than one hundred dollars for each offense. Added L. 1921, c. 298, eff. April 21, 1921.

§ 2042. Discrimination in leases with respect to bearing of children

Any person, firm or corporation in any city owning or having in charge any apartment house, tenement house or other building used for dwelling purposes who shall, in any lease of any or part of any such building, have a clause therein providing that during the term thereof the tenants shall remain childless or shall not bear children, shall be guilty of a misdemeanor. Added L. 1946, c. 846, eff. April 17, 1946.

NOTE 3.

TAUSIK v. TAUSIK
21 Misc. 2d 599, 200 N.Y.S. 2d 543 (1960)

HOFSTADTER, JUSTICE (dissenting) . . . .

The question is whether a husband may evict his wife by *summary proceedings* from a matrimonial domicile, when there is no decree of divorce or separation, nor a formal, binding separation agreement. The only reported cases hold in the negative. . . .

My brethren disregard these holdings because of the letter the respondent wife wrote, and the effect they accord it under the 1951 amendment to section 1411 of the Civil Practice Act, as a license to the wife to occupy the apartment. In this letter she said:

> "Since I have decided to live apart from you, I appreciate your allowing me to remain in this apartment until I find a permanent place in which to move. I shall try to accomplish this as quickly as possible and in any case, I shall not stay any longer than two months."

*   *   *

Strained relations between husband and wife need not invariably end in the break-up of the union; rifts, even though serious, may be and often are healed and bridged. It is the settled policy of the state to preserve the marriage relation and to encourage every measure towards that end. A summary proceeding for the removal of a spouse from the family home, before there has been a legal separation, flies in the face of that policy. Instead of arresting, it hastens and encourages the final sundering of the marriage tie. It tends to obstruct rather than to open the path to reconciliation. The law cannot countenance such an easy method of destroying marriage and family.

When the wife wrote the letter claimed to constitute the "license" under which she thereafter occupied it, she was living in the apartment by virtue of her status as the petitioner's wife. It is far from clear that the letter was intended to transform her status to that of a licensee, no longer occupying her home as of right, but only on sufferance of her husband. Even if, however, this was the intent, for the reasons stated, it may not be effectuated through *summary proceedings*.

* * *

NOTE 4.

BERMAN v. BERMAN
277 App. Div. 560, 101 N.Y.S. 2d 206 (1950)

PER CURIAM.

Plaintiff has been awarded a judgment of separation on findings of cruel and inhuman treatment and such conduct on the part of defendant as renders it unsafe and improper for plaintiff to live with him. . . . Our difficulty is with the fact that plaintiff has not left the apartment in which both parties reside, and that during all the time of her complaints and even at the time of trial and since the trial plaintiff continued to reside in the same apartment with defendant. . . .

We think it is contrary to the policy of the law and incongruous to separate parties judicially who have not separated themselves. . . .

VAN VOORHIS, JUSTICE (dissenting).

[I]t appears to be erroneous to establish a rule of law that a judgment of separation can never be granted if the parties are living under the same roof. It is difficult, even for persons of independent means, to find housing accommodations in New York City at the present time. It is impossible for a middle-aged married woman without near relatives, funds or employment if her husband is intransigent, to leave his abode and find support and maintenance except with the gravest difficulty. Where, as here, the husband has been adjudged guilty of severe mental cruelty as well as of physical violence, and has refused to pay for the wife's necessary medical or hospital expenses, and their married life of 18 years' duration has been terminated in all other respects, it seems unwarranted to deny her a limited divorce as a matter of law. . . . It is especially difficult to justify a condition precedent that estranged couples must be under separate roofs in a state where continued refusal of sexual intercourse,

without excuse, is held to be by itself a sufficient ground for a separation decree. . . . Are we to say that such a state of facts cannot be considered except where the parties are living at different addresses? . . .

NOTE 5.

BERMAN v. BERMAN
Eleven Years Later

Following the reversal by the Appellate Division, First Department, New York, the parties obtained a divorce. [Letter dated May 16, 1961 from Benson H. Begun, attorney for the wife.]

c.

LIONSHEAD LAKE
v.
WAYNE TP., PASSAIC COUNTY
13 N.J. Super. 490, 80 A. 2d 650 (1951)

DAVIDSON, J. S. C.

This proceeding in lieu of prerogative writ seeks to set aside the provisions of the zoning ordinance of the Township of Wayne with respect to the minimum size requirements of dwellings, plaintiff charging that the ordinance is unreasonable and constitutes an invalid exercise of the police power of the municipality.

* * *

The New Jersey Code of Minimum Construction Requirements for One- and Two-Family Dwellings provides that:

> "Living rooms shall have an area not less than 150 square feet, or not less than 160 square feet when dining space is included and not less than 220 square feet when dining and cooking space is included, provided that this area shall be not less than 210 square feet when located in a dwelling unit having two bedrooms.
>
> "The area of kitchens shall be not less than 60 square feet, or not less than 90 square feet when dining space is included, provided that the area of the kitchen shall not be less than 50 square feet when located in a dwelling unit having less than two bedrooms.
>
> "The area of at least one bedroom in each dwelling unit shall be not less than 100 square feet.
>
> "The area of any other bedroom in the same unit shall be not less than 70 square feet."

[W]hile our Legislature has unquestionably given municipalities the right to pass ordinances "to regulate and restrict the height, number of stories, and sizes of buildings," such ordinances to be valid must be designed to promote public health, safety, and general welfare. . . . The mere power to enact an ordinance such as the one here involved does not carry with it the right arbitrarily or capriciously to deprive a person of the legitimate use of his property. . . .

* * *

[I]t is beyond dispute that regardless of personal interest or potential financial loss, every landowner is subject to the control of his property for the public good. . . .

Defendant, recognizing the legal situation, contends that the reasonableness of the control now questioned, specifically the minimum square foot dwelling requirement throughout the entire municipality, is based on the relation of the regulation to the health or the general welfare of the community, and with this contention, after resolving the factual question, I cannot agree.

While defendant produced an outstanding and nationally known public health expert, his testimony, in my judgment, materially substantiated plaintiff's position, for he based his observations, not upon physical health in the ordinary and generally accepted sense of the words, but upon what he termed "emotional health," a sense of inferiority due to living in a sub-standard home. He fixed a minimum requirement essential to healthful living of 400 sq. ft. for one person, 750 sq. ft. for two persons, 1,000 sq. ft. for three persons, 1,150 sq. ft. for four persons, 1,400 sq. ft. for five persons, and 1,550 sq. ft. for six persons, stating that these were not suggested as legal standards, but goals at which to aim. He freely acknowledged that physiological and emotional needs were the essentials considered, that 750 sq. ft. (slightly below the ordinance requirement) was adequate for two persons, and that the federal space requirements were about 20% less than his figures. As the average family is comprised of 3.6 persons, defendant rather uniquely theorizes that all dwellings should be constructed for such occupancy. This would seem to require no comment.

* * *

Here the factual situation, in my opinion, amply demonstrates that the minimum size requirement for one story dwellings is not reasonably related to the public health or general welfare of the community, but is arbitrary and unreasonable and not within the domain of the police powers of the defendant municipality.

* * *

NOTES

NOTE 1.

LIONSHEAD LAKE v. WAYNE TP.
10 N.J. 165, 89 A. 2d 693 (1952)

VANDERBILT, C.J.

* * *

[I]f some such requirements were not imposed there would be grave danger in certain parts of the township, particularly around the lakes which attract summer visitors, of the erection of shanties which would deteriorate land values generally to the great detriment of the increasing number of people who live in Wayne Township the year round. The minimum floor area requirements imposed by the ordinance are not large for a family of normal size. Without some such restrictions there is always the danger that after some homes have been erected, giving a character to a neighborhood, others might follow which would fail to live up to the standards thus voluntarily set. This has been the experience in many communities and it is against this that the township has sought to safeguard itself within limits which seem to us to be altogether reasonable.

* * *

The judgment . . . is reversed.

* * *

OLIPHANT, J. (dissenting).

* * *

It should be borne in mind that the threat to the general welfare and health of the community usually springs from the type of home that is maintained within the house rather than the house itself. Certain wellbehaved families will be barred from these communities, not because of any acts they do or conditions they create, but simply because the income of the family will not permit them to build a house at the cost testified to in this case. They will be relegated to living in the large cities or in multiple-family dwellings even though it be against what they consider the welfare of their immediate families.

* * *

NOTE 2.

KUBIE, LAWRENCE S.

The Disintegrating Impact of "Modern" Life on the Family in America and its Explosive Repercussions*

[T]here used to be several adults of assorted ages in each rambling home: an uncle and an aunt or so, an older cousin, 1 or more grandparents. There is no room for these any more. Few older siblings or parental surrogates live together under one gabled roof, to divide up the parental functions or to provide a special ally to buffer the situation for the child who is passing through an unhappy phase. The built-in baby sitter is gone. Moreover, nurses and servants, these other parental substitutes, are a vanishing breed

* Reprinted from Liebman, S.: *Emotional Forces in the Family*, Philadelphia: J. B. Lippincott Company, 1959, pp. 140-143. Used with permission of the publisher.

except for the numerically insignificant top economic layer. This means that there is no one other than the beleagured parent to help a child. A remarkable intensification and sharpening of domestic rivalries results. One further paradoxical consequence is that within this conical microcosm of the family the more dedicated and devoted the parents are the more bitter becomes the rivalry among the children. This is a situation which by its very nature breeds hostility and illness.

The home is a stage-set on which the drama of human life evolves, and there are few things more destructive to this drama than overcrowding, no matter what the economic level or how pretentious the address. Yet families are living in ever smaller, more cramped and transitory quarters. Lack of space means lack of privacy, making it impossible for any member of the family to live with freedom or dignity, forcing an inescapable proximity on both child and adult, allowing no peace to eye or ear.

This is an assault on human dignity and human values. In our cities space has become a major health problem, as important as the control of poliomyelitis today or of typhoid fever and smallpox in previous generations. To allow real estate interests to pile more and more hapless human beings on a pinpoint of land for the sake of skyrocketting real estate values is literally criminal negligence. . . .

NOTE 3.

LE CORBUSIER

Concerning Town Planning*

A society seeking to defend an equilibrium which it has already lost, looks for means of tying down the nomadic elements of a society which is in need of a new and harmonious organization of its life. By what means can it then hope to arrest the advance of time? By the attraction of the little houses of garden cities, promising family security and arbitrarily entitled: family house. This so-called family house will never merit its title, but will drag society into the universal waste land of garden cities. Universal, for the crisis is world-wide.

It does not merit its title because the family melts in the course of twenty years: it marries, brings up children, and sees them leave the house . . . it must be recognized that this family house has no duration. And soon afterwards it constitutes a formidable urban or interurban residue.

The garden city makes suburbs; these suburbs become the tentacles of the town. The tentacled towns provoke a great squandering of "utilities";

the laying and provision of water, gas, electricity, telephone, the crushing budget of roads and suburban railways; a fabulous host of vehicles: tramways, trains, cars, buses, etc. A gigantic expense in equipment, and a gigantic annual expenditure on maintenance. And the result of this lavish outlay? 2, 3, 4 hours of daily work exacted from everyone throughout the years of their life in order to pay for all this confusion and equipment which add nothing to their lives but a disturbance! Fever, the daily chaos, loss of freedom. The modern form of slavery.

Garden cities make business and building estates, philanthropic discourses and a forced social equilibrium (by attaching people daily to the extremities of suburban railways) and permit the triumph of a famous social manoeuvre by the obstructive elements of society by means of a snare baited with the mirage of nature: if it is a question of living with nature then the answer is: not to live in slums; and the aim: to live intensely and harmoniously.

The garden-city is a will-o'-the-wisp. Nature melts under the invasion of roads and houses and the promised seclusion becomes a crowded settlement. I spoke above of the "horizontal garden-city" (so-called family houses). But the solution will be found in the "vertical garden-city," the fruit of modern techniques adapted to the conditions of modern life.

NOTE 4.

PERKINS, G. HOLMES

The Regional City*

The new town fitting into the complex of the metropolitan region might take any one of many forms. Any thoughtful examination of its future shape must start from the needs of the smaller social units. As a basic premise I would assume that one of our most urgent tasks is to strengthen family ties, to bring harmony and happiness to each individual within the family, and to allow each one the chance to make friends readily. Now families differ radically in size, in age, in income, and in tastes and this calls for a wide variety of houses and apartments. We need not be overly concerned here with the details of arrangement within the apartment or the home. Our attention instead must focus on the relation of homes to one another and to those community spaces whose arrangement may well have a decisive effect upon the formation of social habits and patterns.

* New Haven: Yale University Press, 1948, pp. 67-68. Reprinted with permission of the publisher.

* Reprinted from *The Future of Cities and Urban Redevelopment* by Coleman Woodbury, 1953, pp. 30-36, by permission of The University of Chicago Press. Copyright 1953 by The University of Chicago.

Seen through the eyes of the preschool child the city hardly exists beyond the few blocks nearest home. A few key points such as the movie, perhaps his brother's school, the neighborhood shops, a playground if he is fortunate, are known. To this young explorer the rest is *terra incognita*. His world is that of his friends and neighbors whom he can visit on foot. This small world of the pedestrian is, as sociologists are finding, an extremely real one that is not confined to the youngest members of the family.

Walking distances and the patterns followed in the daily routine play an important and sometimes decisive role in molding the social intercourse of families. Here contacts are most easily made and friendships cultivated. How different the cordial behavior of one pedestrian to another from that of the speeding motorist. How quickly there develops a pride of place; how warmly one defends his neighbors once they are met and understood. Yet how sadly most cities provide for youngsters or their mothers. This civic neglect seems particularly tragic since so many of the activities of the family, perhaps a majority of their collective time, are carried on within walking distance of the home. Surveys of the habits of individuals and families from different income, occupational or regional groups are becoming plentiful enough to make us fully aware how vital the physical layout of a neighborhood is in making friends. Proximity is perhaps the dominant factor but is modified by the actual arrangement of the homes and particularly the habits of preschool age children. For the latter the irresistible appeal of pavements where bicycles can be raced has upset many of the best-laid plans of architects who visualized the children romping carefree on the lawn and among the trees behind the houses. In rental or in sales projects alike the smoothly paved cul-de-sac with its dozen to sixteen houses tightly grouped around it proves invariably the meeting place for children and, of course, the mothers, while the large, safe, attractive (apparently to adults only) park areas remain deserted.

The future city must recognize clearly the function of these small groupings of families as part of the social organization of the larger neighborhood. There is a crying need for units intermediate in size between the family and the large group needed to support an elementary school. . . .

* * *

The small social groupings of fifteen to thirty families around the green have been almost universally neglected in our plans, yet they are essential elements of the community. As we achieve through our designs some measure of success in making it easy for children and their parents to meet without effort, we may find the problems of the larger neighborhood simplified and clarified. But especially here we need an even clearer statement of our objectives for the concept of the neighborhood has gained such classic currency that it is almost immune to criticism. The idea that it should be safe and easy to walk to school, to local shops, the clinic, library, and the park can hardly be refuted. No less convincing is its corollary of grouping these facilities so that they may reinforce each other by making their use easier and the daily contact of their patrons more frequent and we may hope thereby more friendly. Yet there are difficulties in this concept.

* * *

[T]here appear to emerge four criteria by which the quality of design of these smaller social units may be measured. The first is that the social values to the individual and to the community shall, in case of conflict, outweigh any temporary financial advantage. And to my mind enough variety in homes, jobs, and play to give a freedom of choice to all persons regardless of age, temperament, or purse is an essential ingredient of every design. Secondly, the plan must foster family life with widely diverse opportunities for wholesome outdoor as well as indoor social activities. But gregariousness also breeds a demand for privacy. The plan that fails to give asylum to the individual who wishes at times to escape the most friendly crowd is guilty of as grievous a shortcoming as that which neglects the public parks and playgrounds.

The third of the criteria is the effectiveness of the scheme in promoting friendliness among neighbors. This involves an ability to recognize or to create those physical arrangements which bring preschool-age children and their mothers together almost daily in natural and informal play and talk. Doubtless these same greens may also, if properly designed, become the rallying point for groups of older children and their parents after work or school is over. On a larger scale the neighborhood park, the playground, school, the clinic, library, and shops by their mutual support may act as catalysts in promoting a community sense of participation among the larger group. . . . Adult programs must become an inherent part of every school and not something added on and tolerated with reluctance by the staff. Nor must the school be a nine-month affair where, as in so many cities, the doors are locked throughout the summer and even playgrounds forbidden the children because of inadequate staff to keep them safely open. To some extent our failure to achieve the utmost with our resources stems from that creeping disease of overspecialization that even divides responsibility for schools, recreation, public clinics, and libraries between departments with little knowledge and less curiosity about each other's objectives and ambitions. Even in the relatively simple problems of site selection there rarely appears any sincere attempt at co-operation.

The fourth criterion is the recognition of the rightful dominance of the pedestrian within the social unit centering on the smaller elementary school. This does not mean exclusion of the automobile since it has become second nature for the American to expect door-to-door transportation in his daily activities and he is happiest when this ideal is most closely approached. . . .

5.

IN DEBTORS' AND CREDITORS' RIGHTS—THE FAMILY AS AN ENCLOSURE FOR SUPPORT AND SECURITY

a.   SOLOMON v. DAVIS
          100 So. 2d 177 (Fla. 1958)

DREW, JUSTICE.

The appellant Solomon, plaintiff in the court below, instituted a proceeding under Section 222.10, Florida Statutes, F.S.A., to attack the homestead character of property owned by the appellee, Mary Davis, and claimed by her to be exempt from levy pursuant to Art. X, Sec. 1, Florida Constitution F.S.A. Following trial before the chancellor a final decree was entered for appellee, finding her to be the head of a family residing upon the property in question and adjudicating the lot upon which the dwelling house was located to be her homestead under the constitutional provision cited, and exempt from levy of execution to satisfy the lien of the appellant, a judgment creditor.

. . . The appellee acquired and made her home upon the subject property in 1925. She then married her present husband, Tom Davis, and since their marriage they have lived together in the home. Both have been continuously employed, earning approximately equal salaries. For most of the past twelve years the appellee's minor grandniece and nephew have been members of the household. According to the testimony, their care and control was undertaken by appellee alone, and, although she has never formally adopted them, she has assumed the whole burden of their support, maintenance and control. Her entire income together with accrued savings is alleged to have been expended for this purpose and for her own necessities, her husband using his money only

to purchase and operate an automobile, pay the household telephone bill, acquire properties, and otherwise support himself.

From these facts the court concluded that appellee "is the matriarch of the household * * *. Her household would exist as a family unit, regardless of her marital status, and regardless of the presence or absence of a husband in the home. * * * The equities of the case justify a liberal application of the principle involved * * * from the viewpoint of the public purpose to be served by a recognition of the existence of a family relationship with headship in the really dominant leader of the family group, even though such recognition is at variance with the preconceived traditions of headship in the male of the species."

A homestead claim can, of course, be based upon headship of a family in fact as well as a family in law. . . . The difficulty in the present case, however, lies in determining which of the two basic alternative tests shall receive emphasis in defining the particular family relationship, "(1) the legal duty to maintain arising out of the family relationship at law, and (2) continuing communal living by at least two individuals under such circumstances that one is recognized as the person in charge." Crosby and Miller, Our Legal Chameleon.

The court below recognized at the outset a presumption that where married people live together in a common home, the husband is the head of the family. . . . In view of the widespread applicability of this principle throughout our law, there would be little doubt that in the circumstances of the case at bar the appellee's husband would have been deemed the head of the family when he and appellee assumed the normal marital relationship in spite of the fact that she continued to work and they lived upon her separate property. . . . It is settled that factual dependency is not the sole test of family headship. . . . Further, the parties' vigorous assertions that the husband did not in fact "support" the wife, because he spent his money for items other than her necessities, has little weight particularly where the evidence indicates that many of his expenditures benefitted her either directly or indirectly. And such testimony, when subjected to careful analysis, might logically be brought within the rule that the parties cannot stipulate as to family headship. . . .

Perhaps for the latter reason the rule of "personal authority and responsibility" has been used largely to determine family headship where a family in law does not exist. . . . "When the natural relation of husband and wife or parent and child * * * does not exist, the relation should be one in which an established and continuing personal authority, responsibility, and obligation actually rests upon one as 'the head of a family' for the welfare of the others who, in law, should, or in fact, do, recognize and observe a family relation to the one as 'head of a family'." Dania Bank v. Wilson & Toomer Fertilizer Co., 127 Fla. 45, 172 So. 476, 479 ; . . . Johns v. Bowden, 68 Fla. 32, 66 So. 155.

The last cited decision makes it equally clear, as recognized in the opinion of the court in this case, that for purposes of acquiring homestead privileges there cannot be two heads of a single family. "To constitute a 'head of a family' there must be at least two persons who live together in the relation of one family, and *one* of them must be 'the head' of that 'family'." . . . The appellee's position, then, would have been untenable prior to the addition of her two minor relatives to the household. The question now presented is whether her assumption of their care and maintenance in the home which was her separate property, in the face of her husband's avowed intent to have no share in such care, could eliminate her primary legal family relationship with her husband, with whom she continued to live amicably. It was the opinion of the chancellor that "Except for the anomaly of declaring a married woman with a self-supporting husband to be the head of a family of which he is a part, no legal impediment exists which would inhibit the Court in sustaining her position." But we find no basis in the record for any contention that the husband in this case did in fact "recognize and observe a * * * relation to [his wife] as 'the head of a family'" of which he was a member. Dania Bank v. Wilson & Toomer Fertilizer Co., supra. It is apparent that he is then left in a truly anomalous position.

While a wife can certainly be the head of a family for purposes of acquiring homestead privileges and exemptions if the facts substantiate her claim . . . we find no case in which an able-bodied, continuously employed husband has been found to have abdicated his presumptive position as head of the family, where the primary family relationship of husband and wife remains intact with all the attendant duties and obligations thereby imposed upon him under our law. . . .

The equities of the cause are indeed moving in any situation where a home will in fact be disrupted by forced sale, but there are limitations inherent in the simple language of the constitutional provision itself: "A homestead * * * owned by the head of a family residing in this state * * * shall be exempt from forced sale * * *" Art. X, Sec. 1, Florida Constitution. Plainly, family headship and ownership of the home property must coincide in one person, and where property is sub-

jected to obvious homestead use but family headship rests in one who has no beneficial interest in such property and consequently cannot claim homestead immunity, then the legal duties and obligations imposed upon the head of a family in law would seem to take the place of the benefits denied such a family under the constitutional provision relating to homesteads. The application of the plain language of the provision does not, of course, need any such rationale by a reviewing court, but it serves to illustrate the point that equities alone cannot control the disposition of a homestead claim.

The judgment is reversed and the cause remanded for the entry of a decree for appellant.

b.   DIAMOND v. BENT
           157 Cal. App. 2d 210, 320 P. 2d 621 (1957)

WAGLER, PRESIDING JUDGE.

The plaintiff recovered judgment against the defendant, a doctor of medicine, upon a promissory note executed by the latter in payment of office rent. Thereafter, pursuant to the provisions of C.C.P. § 710, plaintiff levied upon wages due the defendant from both the City of Oakland and the County of Contra Costa.

The defendant moved to vacate this levy upon the ground that the entire amount . . . being "for the common necessaries of life" was exempt from execution. . . . The trial court ruled that the defendant's entire earnings were exempt under C.C.P. § 690.11. The plaintiff has appealed.

* * *

The agreed statement recites the following facts:

> The defendant is the mother of three daughters, age 21, 20, and 18; they all attend the University of California, and she is their sole support; she is divorced from their father who, although under Court order to support the two who are minors, does not do so.
>
> The defendant's average monthly net take-home pay is $637.57 and the necessary monthly expenses of the defendant and her three daughters are $706.

Under the above facts all of the debtor's earnings received for her personal services rendered at any time within 30 days next preceding the levy are exempt, *provided* all of such earnings are necessary for the use of the debtor's family residing in this State and supported in whole or in part by such debtor.

The term "necessary for the use of the debtor's family," however, does not embrace just any use. It is incumbent upon the debtor claiming the exemption to show that the wages are necessary for the purchase of the necessaries of life. Appellant contends that money expended for a college education is not expended for "a necessary of life."

Just what are "necessaries" as that term is used in Section 690.11 depends upon the circumstances surrounding each individual case. It is a relative term to be restricted or enlarged in scope depending upon the condition of the parties. That which is a necessary under one set of circumstances might be a luxury under others. . . .

The learned trial judge impliedly found that expenses on behalf of defendant's daughters incidental to attendance at the University were for necessaries. Since the duty of parents to "support, maintain and educate" their children existed at common law and has been enacted as a part of the statutory law of this State, this Court cannot say, as a matter of law, that under the circumstances of this case the trial court was in error.

We cannot agree, however, with the further implied finding of the trial court that an adult child under the circumstances disclosed by the record in this case is a member of the "debtor's family" within the meaning of that term as used in Section 690.11.

The legal obligation of a parent to support his child terminates when the child reaches the age of 21 years, unless such child is a "poor person who is unable to maintain himself by work." Civil Code, § 206.

There being nothing in the record to indicate that defendant's eldest daughter is such a person, we hold that she is not a member of the debtor's family within the meaning of that term as used in C.C.P. § 690.11.

*   *   *

. . . The trial court should therefore ascertain the sum expended monthly by the defendant for the support and education of her adult daughter and subtract said sum from the sum of $706 (the defendant's claimed expenses). The resulting sum will represent the defendant's monthly exemption.

NOTES

NOTE 1.

CALIFORNIA CIVIL PROCEDURE

§ 690 (1955 AND 1960 SUPP.)

Exemptions

The property mentioned in Sections 690.1 to 690.25, inclusive, this code, is exempt from execution or attachment, except as therein otherwise specially provided, when claim for exemption is made to the same by the judgment debtor or defendant as hereinafter in Section 690.26 provided. . . .

§ 690.1 Chairs, tables, desks and books, to the value of two hundred dollars belonging to the judgment debtor. . . .

§ 690.2 Necessary household, table, and kitchen furniture belonging to the judgment debtor, including one refrigerator, washing machine, sewing machine, stove, stovepipes and furniture ; wearing apparel, beds, bedding and bedsteads, hanging pictures, oil paintings and drawings drawn or painted by any member of the family, and family portraits and their necessary frames, provisions and fuel actually provided for individual or family use, sufficient for three months, and three cows and their suckling calves, four hogs and their suckling pigs, and food for such cows and hogs for one month ; also one radio, one television receiver, one piano, one shotgun and one rifle. . . .

§ 690.3 The farming utensils or implements of husbandry of the judgment debtor, not exceeding in value the sum of four thousand dollars ($4,000) ; also two horses or two mules and their harness, including saddles, and two wagons, and food for such horses or mules, for one month ; also all seed grain or vegetables actually provided, reserved or on hand for the purpose of planting or sowing at any time within the ensuing six months, not exceeding in value the sum of one thousand dollars ($1,000) ; and 75 beehives. . . .

§ 690.4 The tools or implements of a mechanic or artisan, necessary to carry on his trade ; the wardrobe of an entertainer ; the uniforms of a waitress or waiter ; the tools or implements of a cook necessary to carry on his trade ; the notarial seal, records and office furniture of a notary public ; the tools and instruments of an optometrist, chiropodist or chiropractor ; the instruments and chest of a surgeon, physician, surveyor or dentist, necessary to the exercise of their profession, with their professional libraries and necessary office furniture ; the professional libraries of attorneys, judges, ministers of the gospel, editors, school teachers and music teachers, and their necessary office furniture ; including one safe and one typewriter ; also musical instruments of a musician that are used by him in earning a livelihood and the musical instruments of music teachers actually used by them in giving instructions, and all the indexes, abstracts, books, papers, maps and office furniture of a searcher of records necessary to be used in his profession ; also the typewriter of a stenographer, the typewriters of a newspaper reporter and the typewriters or other mechanical contrivances employed for writing in type, actually used by the owner thereof for making his living ; also one bicycle when the same is used by the owner for the purpose of carrying on his regular business, or when the same is used for the purpose of transporting the owner to and from his place of business. . . .

§ 690.5 All prosthetic and orthopedic appliances personally used by the judgment debtor. . . .

§ 690.6 Exemptions; miners' cabin, tools, equipment, draft animals, etc. . . .

§ 690.7 Two horses, two oxen or two mules, and their harness, and one cart or wagon, one dray or truck, one coupe, one hack, or carriage, for one or two horses, or vehicle for hire, by the use of which a cartman, drayman, truckman, huckster, peddler, hackman, teamster, chauffeur or other laborer habitually earns his living; and one horse with vehicle and harness or other equipments, used by a physician, surgeon, constable or minister of the gospel, in the legitimate practice of his profession or business; with food for such oxen, horses or mules for one month. . . .

§ 690.8 One fishing boat and net, not exceeding the total value of five hundred dollars, the property of any fisherman, by the lawful use of which he earns his livelihood. . . .

§ 690.19 All moneys, benefits, privileges, or immunities, accruing or in any manner growing out of any life insurance, if the annual premiums paid do not exceed five hundred dollars ($500). . . .

§ 690.20 All moneys, benefits, privileges, or immunities, accruing or in any manner growing out of any disability or health insurance, if the annual premiums do not exceed five hundred dollars. . . .

§ 690.24 One motor vehicle of a value not exceeding two hundred fifty dollars ($250). One house trailer actually occupied by debtor and his family of a value not exceeding two thousand five hundred dollars ($2,500). . . .

§690.51 All lots of land, not exceeding one-quarter of an acre in size, owned, used, or occupied by any person . . . in any graveyard, cemetery, or other place for the sole purpose of burying the dead, together with the railing or fencing enclosing the same, and all gravestones, . . . and other appropriate improvements thereon erected, are exempt from levy and forced sale by virtue of any writ, order, judgment, or decree or by any legal process whatever. . . .

Not more than one lot owned, used, or occupied . . . in any one cemetery, graveyard or other place is exempted by this section.

§690.52 All pews in churches and meeting-houses, used for religious purposes, owned and claimed by any person, or held, in accordance with the rules and regulations of such churches, are exempt from levy and sale on any writ or legal process or by operation of any law whatever. . . .

NOTE 2.

RECHT v. KELLY
82 Ill. 147, 148, 25 Am. Rpts. 301 (1876)

MR. JUSTICE SCOTT delivered the opinion of the Court:

. . . The owner may, if he chooses, sell, or otherwise dispose of any property he may have, however much his family may need it, but the law will not aid him in that regard, nor permit him to contract, in advance, his creditor may use the process of the courts to deprive his family of its benefit and use, when an exemption has been created in their favor. Laws enacted from considerations of public concern, and to subserve the general welfare, can not be abrogated by mere private agreement.

NOTE 3.

MICKENHEIM v. CATHCART
228 La. 890, 84 So. 2d 449 (1955)

HAMITER, JUSTICE.

[46 U.S.C.A. § 601 provides:]

"No wages due or accruing to any seaman or apprentice shall be subject to attachment or arrestment from any court, * * * *Provided*, That nothing contained in this * * * shall interfere with the order by any court regarding the payment by any seaman of any part of his wages for the support and maintenance of his wife and minor children."

*   *   *

In view of the purpose of exemption laws generally, and since the present one evidences a specific intent to benefit the debtor's family as well as the debtor, it would seem to follow that the objective of the statute relied on by this defendant would be defeated if his wife cannot enforce collection from his wages of the attorneys' fees and costs expended by her which were incidental to and necessary for the obtaining of an alimony judgment. As plaintiff's counsel appropriately comment:

"* * * To rule otherwise would, in effect, nullify the specific exception found in the instant statute; for the husband by forcing the wife into court each time she sought to collect alimony would cause her to incur legal expenses which would only reduce the alimony necessary for her support if the wife had to pay them out of the alimony she recovered."

NOTE 4.

BANKRUPTCY ACT—SEC. 17
Debts Not Affected by a Discharge*

a. A discharge in bankruptcy shall release a bankrupt from all of his provable debts, whether allowable in full or in part, except such as . . . (2) are liabilities for . . . alimony due or to become due, or for maintenance or support of wife or child, or for seduction of an unmarried female, or for breach of promise of marriage accompanied by seduction, or for criminal conversation. . . .

c.   Bankruptcy Exemptions: Critique and Suggestions†

State exemptions, sired by the nineteenth-century economy and later adopted by the Bankruptcy Act, have failed to grow up. The dollar has depreciated. Wealth forms and occupational patterns have changed. Economic stability at high living standards has been achieved. New attitudes toward governmental responsibility for financial disaster have developed. But state exemptions have inadequately responded to these phenomena. Nonetheless, their incorporation in bankruptcy goes virtually unchallenged. . . .

Although the exclusion of specified assets from creditors' claims may have seemed to be the only proper means of debtor rehabilitation in an era which emphasized individual incentive and responsibility, the recent development of welfare legislation suggests that the community, rather than creditors, ought to bear the burden of ameliorating the effects of bankruptcy. State welfare programs, financed from general tax receipts, would spread the costs of economic misfortune more widely, and perhaps more equitably. Extension of credit is a necessary economic function, and except insofar as they knowingly allow a borrower to overextend himself, lenders are no more responsible for the debtor's financial embarrassment than other members of the community. Moreover, trained welfare personnel could more effectively foster rehabilitation, by helping the bankrupt secure a new job or acquire new skills. Family protection would also be bolstered, since funds would be expended under staff supervision, thus not subject to the debtor's control and possible improvidence. Finally, governmental assistance would presumably be geared to need, while the exemption system permits some debtors to emerge from bankruptcy with more property than is necessary and does not provide for the

bankrupt who has no assets out of which to claim an exemption.

But presently existing welfare legislation, as classified into categorical . . . assistance, administered by the state and frequently supported by the federal government, helps only those persons who, because of status or prior contributions, qualify for payments. Typically, these programs aid the aged, the blind, the disabled, the unemployed, and the uncared-for child, and are not, as a rule, predicated on an individual showing of need. Unless the discharged bankrupt happens to fit in one of these favored groups, he will receive no benefit from such statutes. Although unemployment insurance might appear to offer sustenance to many bankrupts, recent statistics indicate that the overwhelming majority are employed wage earners at the time proceedings are initiated. Thus, the average bankrupt desiring state aid is relegated to reliance on general assistance.

Derived from the English poor laws, general assistance programs furnish temporary cash or commodity allowances to eligible persons. Although the statutory tests of eligibility vary widely, all require the recipient to demonstrate "need," and some retain the criteria of "pauperism" or "destitution." In practice, a relief applicant must have so little property that he is unable to sustain himself and his family, although the more liberal jurisdictions will give aid to those holding some cash and life insurance, or even a modest homestead. Additional limitations on general assistance as an effective mode of social welfare are the residency requirements in all but eight jurisdictions. One-year residence is most common, but some statutes demand as much as five years. Even if the applicant can surmount the residency and necessity barriers, however, he will often find that the relief allowance is inadequate to maintain a standard of living above the most meager subsistence level. Most programs are designed to enable the recipient to meet only his most immediate and basic needs, with a view toward his early removal from the relief rolls. Many state legislators and relief administrators are seemingly wedded to the puritan philosophy that public aid encourages moral weakness, and it should be denied wherever possible. In fact, some jurisdictions retain the Elizabethan requirement of a "pauper's oath," cause recipient's names to be published and disenfranchise them. . . .

* * *

While a revamping of these programs, or the introduction of new ones, could conceivably furnish a complete alternative to exemptions, such a course would place upon the government a dual burden of providing interim support and replacing

---

* 11 U.S.C. Sec. 35a.

† Comment, 68 YALE L. J. 1459, 1497-1502, 1507, 1513-14 (1959). Reprinted with permission of the publisher.

those necessaries surrendered to creditors. Household furnishings, cooking utensils and wearing apparel, for instance, would have to be restored. Substitute housing would have to be secured for those bankrupts whose homestead is surrendered. In addition, when a debtor's livelihood depends upon an automobile, tools, or farm acreage, they would have to be furnished if he is to continue his occupation. Not only would this involve large expenditures of funds and talent, but it would inevitably impose unwanted governmental controls upon many individuals who could, with the aid of exemptions, reconstruct their lives without additional assistance. In striking a balance between laissez-faire and a welfare economy, legislators have sought to relieve personal misfortune with a minimum impairment of self-reliance and initiative. The welfare alternative to exemptions would seem to undercut the philosophy implicit in most welfare legislation: help only to those who cannot help themselves.

With complete reliance on social welfare an inadequate substitute, it is clear that exemptions still have utility in a modern economy. . . .

* * *

Abolition of the exemption of specific assets is the most fundamental step in the attainment of a modern exemption system. The bankrupt should surrender all of his property to the trustee and be accorded a dollar allowance out of its value. He could realize this allowance or use it in whole or in part to "repurchase" any relinquished items he wishes to retain. With the cash, he could procure items necessary for his family's support or start a new life—perhaps by moving to another community, acquiring a skill or trade, or investing in a business venture. This course has several advantages. It treats bankrupts equally, without regard to whether their assets—either by chance or by design—meet the statutory description of exempt property. . . . Secondly, it avoids all problems of recovery of exempt assets under the avoiding sections of the Bankruptcy Act, for there would no longer be a distinction between "exempt" and "nonexempt." Thirdly, exemptions would never become anachronistic, for money, unlike animals and turnips, always measures wealth accurately. Moreover, a cash exemption can reflect alterations in the dollar's purchasing power, either by periodic amendment, or more profitably, by automatic annual changes, geared to some economic indicator such as per capita income or a retail price index. . . .

* * *

Problems of the exemption system itself aside, the Bankruptcy Act should be amended to realize more effectively the exemption goal of security

for a bankrupt's dependents. At present the discharged family is insufficiently protected: the debtor can dispose of his exempt assets irresponsibly. Under the proposed uniform cash exemption system, the typical bankrupt—neither pauper nor entrepreneur—would get unsupervised control of the funds. Although a few states have attempted to safeguard the family, the methods of control are imprecise and some of the consequences undesirable. For example, state statutes barring alienability of homesteads without the consent of both spouses only prevent the debtor from encumbering or disposing of one type of property, and in so doing serves to clog credit.

A more comprehensive approach to family protection might be based on the British example. Under the English bankruptcy act, the trustee may grant the debtor periodic allowances for family support during pendency of the proceedings, subject to review by a creditors' inspection committee. The American statute could adopt this approach by substituting the bankruptcy court for the inspection committee. The court could advise the bankrupt's dependents of the availability of periodic allowances. If special protection is needed, they could petition for guardianship, and the necessity thereof would be decided by the court. Supervisory jurisdiction following discharge might similarly be ordered, if necessitated by an irresponsible head of a household. Such a case could be referred to a local welfare agency, which would return any remaining assets to the debtor or his spouse when solvency is achieved.

* * *

NOTE

BLACK, H.

Buy Now, Pay Later*

. . . In an alarming number of instances . . . people find that no matter how hard or how long they labor they can't meet their debts. The result has been a sharp increase in family bankruptcies. During the fiscal year of 1959 nearly 89,000 families failed financially, a 300 per cent increase over the past decade and more than the total number of bankruptcies filed during the height of the Depression. These families represented 88.3 per cent of all failures filed under the United States Bankruptcy Act and that includes all business, farm and professional bankruptcies. Thousands of others avoid failure by the expeditious means of extending the number of payment periods, which only puts them deeper into debt.

* From *Buy Now, Pay Later* by Hillel Black, p.7. Copyright © 1961 By Hillel Black. By permission of William Morrow & Company, Inc.

According to the statisticians the average American family is only three months away from financial failure.

6.

IN THE ADMINISTRATION OF SOCIAL SERVICES—THE FAMILY AS AN ENCLOSURE FOR ASSISTANCE, HEALTH, AND MORALITY

a. Workman's Compensation

PITTSBURGH PIPE AND COUPLING CO.
v.
UNEMPLOYMENT COMPENSATION BOARD OF REVIEW
401 Pa. 501, 165 A. 2d 374 (1960)

OPINION BY MR. JUSTICE MUSMANNO:

From 1951 to December, 1957, Charles P. Savage was employed as a machine operator at the plant of the Pittsburgh Pipe and Coupling Company in Allison Park (near Pittsburgh). His home was in Hastings 60 miles distant from the plant. In order to avoid the burden of a 120-mile round trip between these two points every day, he stayed at the home of his sister in Gibsonia (near Allison Park), paying her $25 a week for room and board. Every weekend he returned to his wife and four children (the oldest being 10 years of age) in Hastings.

On December 19, 1957, Savage now receiving wages amounting approximately to $22 a day, the plant shut down for a two-week period and Savage was directed to return on January 6, 1958, but at laborer's wages at $2 per hour for a four-day week, activity at the plant having slackened. This reduction in pay and work-week (which was in accordance with a labor-management agreement) effected a lowering of Savage's income to about $64 a week.

On January 2, 1958, Savage notified his employer that his wife had suffered a disabling spinal injury and for that reason he was compelled to remain at home to take care of her and the children. His employer recommended that he take a three-month leave of absence. Savage refused to accept this offer and made claim for unemployment compensation. The Bureau of Employment Security found that he was entitled to unemployment compensation benefits. The company appealed to the unemployment compensation referee who reversed the board on the basis that the claimant had not terminated his employment for reasons of a necessitous and compelling nature as specified in Section 402(b) of the Pennsylvania Unemployment Compensation Law. . . .*

---

*Act of December 5, 1936, P.L. (1937) 2897, Art. IV, Sec. 402, as amended.

. . . The only question for determination by this Court is whether the facts establish that the claimant was, as a matter of law, ineligible to receive compensation benefits on the basis that he terminated his employment without cause of "a necessitous and compelling nature."

To answer this question it is necessary to pass in review, briefly, the legislative history of the Pennsylvania Unemployment Compensation Act. The first enactment of this law in 1936 was silent on the topic of necessitous abandonment of one's job. It contained no exception to the provision that: "An employee shall be ineligible for compensation for any week in which his unemployment is due to . . . (b) voluntarily leaving work . . ." . . .

In time it became apparent that this wording deprived meritorious employees from unemployment compensation where, although ostensibly voluntarily leaving employment they were in reality compelled to do so by circumstances beyond their determination. Thus, in 1942 the Legislature amended the act to read: "An employee shall be ineligible for compensation for any week . . . (b) in which his unemployment is due to voluntarily leaving work without good cause . . ." (Act of April 23, 1942, P.L. 60 § 402.)

What constituted "good cause" became a matter of judicial interpretation. In 1944, the Superior Court in the *Teicher Unemployment Compensation Case*, 154 Pa. Superior Ct. 250, held that the action of the claimant there involved, in voluntarily quitting her employment and moving to another city to live with her husband who was a member of the Armed Forces in time of war was "good cause."

In the *Sturdevant Unemployment Compensation Case*, 158 Pa. Superior Ct. 548, 557 (1946), Judge RENO, in a masterful opinion, said: "If a worker leaves his employment when he is compelled to do so by necessitous circumstances or because of legal or family obligations, his leaving is voluntary with good cause, and under the act he is entitled to benefits. The pressure of necessity, of legal duty, or family obligations, or other overpowering circumstances and his capitulation to them transform what is ostensibly voluntary unemployment into involuntary unemployment."

In the *Mooney Unemployment Compensation Case*, 162 Pa. Superior Ct. 183 (1948), the claimant, a married woman with small children, had been employed at a job which started in the evening; her shift was then eliminated and she was offered work which began at 11:30 a.m. She refused to accept the change, stating she desired to continue on the night shift or be assigned to work starting a 9 a.m., because she could not otherwise take care of her children. When the employer would not or could not offer her the hours of work she requested, she quit her employment and made claim for unemployment compensation. The Superior Court affirmed unemployment compensation because she had "good cause" for leaving her employment, pointing out: "She [the claimant] was legally obligated to care for her three small children. Family obligations cannot be considered as mere whim or fancy but, on the contrary, are real and compelling reasons. . . ."

*   *   *

In 1953 the Legislature amended the Act to exclude marital, filial and domestic circumstances as "good cause" within the meaning of the Act. . . .

Two years later, however, the Legislature reconsidered the subject and, by an amendment enacted on March 30, 1955 (P.L. 6, § 5), declared that: "An employee shall be ineligible for unemployment compensation for any week . . . (b) in which his unemployment is due to voluntarily leaving work without cause of a necessitous and compelling nature."

By this amendment the Legislature removed the specific exception it had placed in the Act of 1953 and thereby indicated its intent to adopt the judicial construction of the language of the 1942 amendment which had caused it to enact the 1953 exception. . . .

*   *   *

When an employed person becomes unemployed, he is, by that fact in itself, potentially a beneficiary of the Act. The law was passed to protect society itself as much as the individual involved because the cumulative distress of vast numbers of unemployed can wreck the stoutest and most solid economy. Thus, the Legislature in its wisdom, provided a formidable bridge over which the recently dismissed employee may pass unharmed (or as slightly harmed as possible) from one job to another.

The Act has wiped out the acute and almost unbearable hardships which heretofore accompanied unanticipated loss of employment. The employee does not need to fear now that suddenly, because he has been "laid off", the bread will be taken off his table and his wife and children will be bereft of adequate heat, light, raiment and perhaps even a roof over their heads. The Unemployment Compensation Act is proof that mankind is on the march toward an ever-increasing concern over one's fellow-man who, through no fault of his own, falls into the waters of want and privation because of economic floods which he can no more control than the rains and the snows.

*   *   *

. . . The employee in the case at bar is desirous of work, he needs it, he wants it, but he lives 60 miles away from the job and his wife is ill, and there are four children of tender age who require his attention and care. It would be difficult to conjure up a reason of a more necessitous and compelling nature to leave the job which he cannot reach and at the same time discharge the obligations which he owes to his family through law, love, and the loyalty which in America one expects of a husband and father.

*   *   *

The appellant argues . . .: "This Court has in many instances recognized the wife's moral and legal obligation to arrange her work schedule to meet her family requirements. . . . But it has never held that a husband has such a legal obligation to move to the wife's abode. Indeed, the contrary is true, that the wife's legal duty is to follow her husband's selection of residence. . . ."

But here again it must be asserted that Hastings is not the abode of Mr. Savage's wife. It is the residence and permanent domicile of the Savage family. This is not the case of an employee voluntarily and without reason choosing a new domicile too distant from his place of employment and using that distance as a reason for abandoning his job. It is to be repeated that in this case, the claimant is returning to what has always been his domicile and returning there because his wife's illness and the care of his minor children demand his presence.

NOTE

P.E.P.

Family Needs and the Social Services*

A Government handbook on the social services says of Britain's comprehensive system of social welfare that the basic idea has remained the same throughout the post-war years.

> . . . social services should not be regarded as a form of charity but rather as one of the natural benefits available to citizens of a civilized state, ranking equally with defence, justice and law and order.

> . . . every child or citizen of Britain whatever the circumstances of his birth shall be assured freedom from want and insecurity, and equal opportunities in regard to health, education and employment.[1]

---

* London: George Allen & Unwin Ltd., 1961, pp. 18-21. Reprinted with permission of the publisher.

1. COI Reference Pamphlet No. 3, *Social Services in Britain*, 1958 ed., pp. 2 and 8.

This was the view taken during the planning years when it was widely believed that the services in their reorganized form should concern themselves positively with the welfare of all sections of the population, and not simply with the needs of special groups who were in difficulties.

The separate plans were then seen as parts of a co-ordinated whole, forming "the main pillars on which our post-war social structure will rest—education, health, housing, social insurance".[2]

Statements made during the planning years illustrate the more specific aims in each of the different fields. It was the Government's intention in health

> . . . to ensure that everybody in the country—irrespective of means, age, sex, or occupation—shall have an equal opportunity to benefit from the best and most up to date medical and allied services available.[3]

Talking of old age Lord Beveridge said:

> I suggest that our aim should be that every British citizen who works while he can and contributes while he is working and earning, should be assured of an old age without want, without dependence on the young, and without the need for charity or assistance.[7]

Family allowances would be introduced for the first time since

> . . . the first principle should be that we should regard it as a primary aim of social policy to ensure every child against want, against going hungry, cold, ill-clad, and ill-housed, not because the parents are spending their money badly, but because the family income is not sufficient to provide the bare necessities of healthy life.[8]

. . . The new approach was to be universal and comprehensive. The social services were no longer to be considered primarily important to underprivileged groups in the population.

> Today we are moving towards a more equalitarian society, and the principal social services are provided and paid for by the community as a whole for the benefit of all its members.[11]

The prime function was no longer the prevention or alleviation of hardship, but the "furtherance of the well-being of the individual citizen".[12] The emphasis was upon extending the range of services and improving their quality.

During the past few years the broad aims of social policy have remained unchanged but the background of public comment has been characterised as one "compounded of uneasiness and complacency".[13] There is no longer the same degree of agreement about either the aims or the achievements of particular policies. . . . It is often couched in general terms rather than in relation to particular services, and is sometimes concerned with the possible larger effects upon the public:

> It is generally recognized that decline in initiative and repudiation of private and public responsibility are among the dangers arising from the multiplicity of statutory services.

and sometimes with the possible effects upon the services themselves:

> A further problem arising from the greatly increased scope of the social services, and associated with the assumption of statutory responsibility for them, is the danger of their mechanisation.[14]

b. Taxation

BITTKER, BORIS I.
Federal Income Estate and Gift Taxation*

* * *

Joint returns of husband and wife. The issue of geographical uniformity in federal income taxation came to a head during the Congressional hearings on the Revenue Act of 1948. Proposals for mandatory joint returns . . . found no support, but the so-called "split-income" plan (permitting a married couple to file a joint return and pay twice the tax that would be paid by a single taxpayer having one-half the combined income) gained ground rapidly. It had obvious political appeal, and the Treasury . . . implied that it would be acceptable. . . .

The statutory scheme is simplicity itself. Husband and wife may file a joint return on which they aggregate their income and deductions; this procedure is open to them even though one of them has no income or deductions. Their status is determined at the end of the taxable year; if there is a decree of divorce or of legal separation at that time, they are not to be considered as married. . . . It has been held that separation under an interlocutory decree of divorce does not bar the filing of a joint return. . . . If hus-

---

2. Willink, March 1944, *Hansard*, Vol. 398, Col. 428.
3. *A National Health Service*, Cmd. 6502, p. 47.
7. Beveridge, November 1944, *Hansard*, Vol. 404, Col. 1127.
8. *Ibid.*, Col. 1125.
11. M. Penelope Hall, *The Social Services of Modern England* (Routledge), 1952, p. 6.
12. *Ibid.*, p. 7.

13. R. H. Titmuss, "The Social Division of Welfare," Eleanor Rathbone Memorial Lecture, 1956 (Liverpool University Press), p. 4.
14. M. Penelope Hall, *op. cit.*, p. 7.
* Boston: Little, Brown & Co. 1958, pp. 282-286. Reprinted with permission of the publisher.

band or wife dies during the taxable year, a joint return may be executed by the decedent's executor or . . . by the surviving spouse. . . .

The tax on a joint return is computed by cutting the aggregate taxable income in half, computing a tax at the usual rate on one-half, and then doubling that amount. § 2(a). The result is that the tax paid by husband and wife on a joint return is twice what a single person would pay on one-half their taxable income. Liability for the tax is joint and several. § 6013(d)(3). This joint and several liability is for the tax actually due on the true aggregate taxable income, not merely for the amount of tax reported on the return itself; and it includes liability for interest on any deficiency and penalties for negligence or fraud if applicable, even if the misconduct is attributable to only one spouse.

*   *   *

Heads of households. Although the 1948 Act produced geographical uniformity by giving married couples in the common law states the opportunity to split their income, it brought to the common law states a disparity between married couples and unmarried persons with similar family responsibilities, which had formerly existed only in the community property states. In an effort to correct this disparity, Congress in 1951 enacted the head-of-household provision of § 1(b), described in the following extract from Pechman, "Individual Income Tax Provisions of the 1954 Code," 8 *Nat'l. Tax J.* 114, 126-128 (1955): *

This curious provision was enacted to mitigate the harsh treatment accorded to widows, widowers, and other single persons with family responsibilities under income splitting. The problem it was designed to alleviate may be illustrated by the following example: Assume two executives, each with a wife and two children, have identical homes. They receive the same incomes and, in general, spend their incomes in substantially the same manner. Now, suppose that the wife of one of the executives dies. In the following year, he is required to pay much higher taxes than his neighbor— even though he must incur even larger expenses to run the household than when his wife was alive—because he is automatically denied the benefits of income splitting by virtue of his status as a single person. If his income is $25,000, the tax increase (under present rates and assuming he elects the standard deduction) is $2,610, or over 43 per cent. The loss of an exemption is worth only $324 in tax at this level so that income splitting accounts for $2,286 of the tax increase. The tax penalty due

to the denial of income splitting rises to a maximum of $25,180 at the highest income levels.

*   *   *

As originally enacted, the provision set up a category of unmarried taxpayers, called "heads of households," who were permitted to compute their tax liabilities on the basis of a special rate schedule which gives them half the advantage of income splitting. A head of household was defined as a single person who "maintains as his home a household which constitutes . . . the principal place of abode" for an unmarried child or grandchild (whether or not they qualify as dependents), or any other person who is a dependent for tax purposes.

The provision was clearly defective in several respects. In the first place, it did not really solve the problem which it was designed to cure. True, the widow or widower with small children receives a portion of the benefits of income splitting, but it is only half a loaf. Second, the fact that a dependent may not be able, or willing, to live in the home of the taxpayer may increase, rather than decrease, the expenses of supporting him, yet the taxpayer is denied half the benefits of income splitting because of the "place of abode" requirement. Third, a taxpayer is entitled to the benefits of the provision even though the child or grandchild who makes him eligible for it is self-supporting. In extreme cases, the combined tax liability of the taxpayer and the child may be less than the tax of a married couple having the same total income. Fourth, and by no means least important, the provision adds several columns to the simplified tax table, thereby making it unwieldy, and confuses millions of taxpayers by confronting them with a choice between two rate schedules.

The House version of the 1954 Code made a frontal attack on all of these problems. It substituted a new category of taxpayers—heads of families—for the old heads of households. Heads of families would have been permitted to split their incomes for tax purposes, as if they were married. In this way, the complaints of the widows and widowers would have been quieted and, at the same time, the separate rate schedule would have been eliminated. In addition, the dependent giving the taxpayer head of family status would not have been required to live in his household. On the other hand, the taxpayer would have been required to support the dependent giving him head of family status, thus eliminating the bonus to those who happened to live with self-supporting children or grandchildren. Only taxpayers supporting parents, children, grandchildren, and brothers and sisters would have been eligible, presumably to limit the benefits to the most deserving cases.

The Senate Finance Committee disagreed with the House and restored the old head-of-household provision. . . .

---

* Published by the National Tax Association. Reprinted with permission.

NOTE

REILLY, T. J.

An Approach to the Simplification and Standardization of the Concepts "The Family," "Related Parties," "Control," and "Attribution of Ownership"*

The Revenue Act of 1934 was the first taxing statute to recognize "members of a family" as a definitive group for tax purposes. In that Act the concept was deemed essential in reaching two types of alleged tax-avoidance schemes: (1) claimed losses between closely-related (family) taxpayers, and (2) the use of personal holding companies. . . . In each instance the family was defined to include *brothers and sisters, whether of the whole or half blood, spouse, ancestors, and lineal descendants.*

With respect to losses between members of a family, [two Committee] Reports[9] stated, "It is believed that this provision will operate to close this loophole of tax avoidance."

* * *

. . . It was in section 212 of the Revenue Act of 1950 that Congress enacted strong legislation to overcome the growing practice of converting ordinary income into capital gain through the device of corporate liquidations, aptly described as "collapsible" corporations. Rules attributing stock ownership among members of the family were needed "in order to prevent any one shareholder's disguising his interest by the placement of the stock of the corporation among the different members of his family."

The "family" in this section . . . includes *spouses of brothers and sisters and spouses of lineal descendants,* in addition to the usual provisions of spouse, brothers and sisters, whether by the whole or half blood, ancestors, and lineal descendants

. . . In other sections of the 1954 Code and also in the Technical Amendments Act of 1958, contractions have been made in the definition of "the family," the usual contraction being the elimination of brothers and sisters, whether by the whole or half blood, as members of the family. This contraction exists in section 318 of the 1954 Code, relating to the constructive ownership of stock, section 382, relating to net operating loss carryovers, and section 1235, relating to the sale or exchange of patents. . . . In addition, in section 318 and section 382, which adopts section 318 by reference, "the family" does not include

ancestors other than a parent. In its narrowest concept (section 1551), "the family" consists solely of an individual, his spouse, and minor children.

* * *

. . . Because of the many additions and changes to the taxing statute over a long period of years, the concept of "the family" is scattered throughout the Code, but with disturbing lack of uniformity. The confusion that has resulted from this incredible diversity in the use of the concept suggests the desirability, in so far as it is practical, of a uniform definition of the term. . . .

. . . Although a uniform definition of "the family" seems both warranted and desirable, there exists the further question as to the scope of such a definition. Should the concept be a narrow one or should it be broad? Argument could be made for a narrow concept if its function were to enlarge a taxing area or to impose a further tax. However, its primary use is to the contrary, *i.e.,* to prevent tax avoidance by related persons and within existing statutes. . . .

* * *

. . . When used in this defacto sense of preventing tax-saving collaborations, the need for a uniform and broad statutory concept of "the family" rather than a narrow one becomes axiomatic. Its uniformity will tend to an equal application of the taxing statute. The narrower the definition, the more likelihood of avoidance. . . . These considerations suggest a definition that would include *brothers and sisters* and their spouses, as well as *spouse, ancestors, lineal descendants, and their spouses,* in order to prevent collaboration with its tax-saving incidents. However, "spouse" would not include one separated by an interlocutory or final decree of divorce or separate maintenance. Further, a legally adopted child would be considered as a child by blood.

In addition, "the family" should include any corporation, partnership or trust which a member of the family controls and also any trust or estate of which he is a substantial beneficiary. . . .

c. Aid to Dependent Children

PEOPLE v. SHIRLEY
55 Cal. 2d 521, 360 P. 2d 33 (1961)

GIBSON, C. J.—After a jury trial, defendant was found guilty of grand theft under an indictment charging that she unlawfully took $1,811 of funds of Tulare County between October 1, 1958, and April 30, 1959. Imposition of sentence was suspended for three years, and she was granted probation. She has appealed. . . .

---

* 15 TAX L. R. 253, 260-263 (1959-60). Used by permission of the publishers.

9. H.R. REP. No. 704 and S. REP. No. 558, 73d Cong., 2d Sess. (1934), 1939-1 CUM. BULL. (Part 2) 607.

Defendant received welfare aid for herself and minor children periodically commencing in 1948. She was informed repeatedly that it was her duty to keep the county welfare department advised of any changes in the family status or income and that anyone moving into or out of the house would affect her welfare budget. On October 21, 1958, defendant reported to a county social worker that her only income was the money she received from the welfare department, plus the occasional earnings of two of her children, and that there were no unrelated adults living with the family. She was again advised of her duty to keep the welfare department informed regarding income and household members, and she agreed to report any change in income or other financial conditions.

The social worker visited defendant at her home on April 14, 1959, and found a Mr. Shirley there, fully clothed but wearing bedroom slippers. Two days later, at the request of the welfare department, investigators from the district attorney's office called at the defendant's home about 2:30 a.m. and found Shirley in bed in her bedroom. Defendant told the investigators that Shirley had been living in her home for at least six months and that during this time he had averaged spending $20 a week for household expenses and in addition had given her $10 a week in cash. Thus his total contributions during that period were approximately $800. She said that he had also helped with payments on a refrigerator. She admitted knowing that she should report all income received by her and any changes in the number of persons in the home. On April 23, 1959, she reported to the welfare department that she had married Shirley on the previous day. The department recomputed defendant's budget for the period in question and determined that she had been overpaid $1,811.

The evidence is sufficient to support the implied findings of the jury that defendant made false representations of fact with intent to defraud and that, when she promised to report any change in her household and financial condition, she had no intention of keeping her promise. It is also clear that the welfare payments were made in reliance upon the false representations and that the county was defrauded.

The jury was instructed, pursuant to section 1508 of the Welfare and Institutions Code, that where a needy child lives with his mother and stepfather, the amount of the grant shall be computed after consideration is given to the income of the stepfather and that a stepfather is bound to support, if able to do so, his wife's children if without support from such stepfather they would be needy children eligible for aid. The jury

was also told that under regulations of the State Board of Social Welfare a stepfather living in the home is responsible for the support of the mother of a needy child unless incapacitated and unable to support, that a man living in the home assuming the role of spouse has the same responsibility as that of a stepfather for the mother and the needy children, and that the income of a stepfather or other man assuming the role of spouse that is to be used in determining his ability to contribute is his take-home pay plus his income from all other sources except his wife's earnings.

The regulations set forth in the instructions are designed to assist welfare workers in the determination of need, which is one requirement of eligibility for assistance. . . . Under both the state and federal laws a needy child is defined as a needy person under the age of 18 years who has been deprived of parental support. . . . The federal act requires the state plan to provide that the state agency, in determining need, shall take into consideration any other income and resources of a child claiming aid. . . . The administration of the public assistance programs, including aid to needy children, presents many complex problems. . . .

Under its express terms the provisions of the Welfare and Institutions Code are to be administered fairly, with due consideration not only for the needs of applicants but also for the safeguarding of public funds. . . . If children are not in need, they are obviously not eligible for assistance regardless of who is paying for their support. As we have seen, the welfare department is authorized by section 1508 of the code to consider the income of a stepfather in computing the amount of aid to be granted, and it is unlikely that the financial need of a child will vary substantially depending upon the legality of the relationship between his mother and a man living in the home and assuming the role of spouse. It is reasonable to infer that a man assuming the role of spouse will contribute to the support of the mother and her needy child and will thus reduce their need, but it would be difficult and perhaps impossible for the department to ascertain the amount of contributions in each case. A practical solution of the difficulty is offered by the regulations which authorize the department to consider the income of such a man in the same manner as it would consider that of a stepfather. A decision declaring the regulations invalid would place a premium upon an illegal relationship and operate as a deterrent to marriage of the mother and the man assuming the role of spouse. The regulations are in accord with the primary purpose of the program, which is to aid needy children, and they are valid insofar as they direct the welfare department, in determining the amount of aid to be granted, to consider the man's income without regard to the existence of a lawful marriage.

To the extent that the instructions may have indicated that a man assuming the role of spouse, although not married, had an obligation to support the mother and her children, they went beyond the issues and were erroneous. It does not appear, however, how the jurors could have been misled, since the question of such a man's liability for support had no bearing on whether defendant was guilty of theft by false pretenses, and the jurors were fully informed of the elements of that offense which they must find in order to return a verdict of guilty.

* * *

The evidence of defendant's guilt is clear and convincing, and we are satisfied that there was no miscarriage of justice. . . .

PETERS, J.—I dissent.
The conviction in this case was based, in part at least, on erroneous instructions to the jury and on inadmissible evidence. . . .

* * *

The effect of the majority opinion is to hold that the Board of Social Welfare, by a regulation adopted by it, can determine that a needy child, who is otherwise entitled to state aid, can be deprived of a certain portion of that minimum aid which the Legislature has determined to be necessary to support him . . . solely because the mother is engaged in an extramarital relationship with a man who has no legal obligation to support the child, and who may, in fact, legally refuse to do so. To uphold such a regulation is to uphold the usurpation of legislative power by an administrative board.

The majority uphold this regulation because, so it is asserted, it affords a "practical solution" to the problem of determining whether a man living with the child's mother is actually contributing support money. It is contended that "[i]t is reasonable to infer that a man assuming the role of spouse will contribute to the support of the mother and her needy child." This reasoning is obviously unsound.

* * *

It is elementary law, of course, that the Legislature may confer upon an administrative board the power to "fill up details" of a legislative policy by enacting rules and regulations, as long as the Legislature establishes an adequate standard. . . . But it is equally elementary that the administrative agency can neither vary, enlarge, or change the scope of a legislative enactment, nor may it adopt regulations which lie outside the scope of the statute. . . . Certainly, the administrative agency has no authority to remedy or supply even an involuntary omission by the Legislature. . . . It is obvious that the regulation here under consideration violates all of these fundamental rules.

* * *

The Welfare and Institutions Code is most specific in defining those instances in which a child otherwise entitled to aid may be deprived of that aid because of the acts of other persons. The child may be denied support if the custodial parent refuses to cooperate with law enforcement officers charged with enforcing the legal obligation of the absent parent (§ 1523), or refuses to accept vocational rehabilitation (§ 1523.5), or refuses to accept reasonable employment (§1523.6). These are the only situations that the Legislature determined should be sufficient to withdraw aid from a needy child.

These sections are exclusive. . . .

* * *

[T]he reason why the Legislature provided that a stepfather's income may be used in computing the amount of aid granted to the child is that section 1508 carefully makes the stepfather legally obligated to support his stepchildren up to an amount representing his wife's community property interest in his income. The support of the child, the paramount concern of the statute, is thus assured. The child is given, as a substitute for aid, the legal right to enforce his right to support from a stepfather. But a "quasi spouse" has no legal obligation to support the child, and the woman with whom he is living has no legal right to any part of his income. . . .

. . . The fundamental purpose of the ANC program is to help the innocent child who has been caught in the web created by the adults around him, not to punish the child for the misdeeds of these adults.

. . . Certainly, the state should not be required to support children who are, in fact, being supported by others. It is equally true that deliberate attempts to subvert and defraud the welfare program should be prevented. But the existence of the need for reform cannot create in the Board of Social Welfare the authority to pass regulations to correct abuses that have developed in a plan evolved by the Legislature. It is for the Legislature and not for the board to determine policy. It is for the Legislature and not the board to determine whether a needy child is to have his allotment curtailed because his mother is living with a man who assumes "the role of spouse," whether such a man shall be legally obligated to support the child, and whether the child shall receive ANC aid unless a legal stepfather relationship has been established. Such policy decisions are not to be made by an administrative board without guidance from the Legislature.

This does not mean that appellant cannot be convicted of grand theft if she misrepresented her actual income. The vice of the present case is that the jury was misdirected and improper evidence was admitted. These matters were clearly prejudicial.

I would reverse the orders appealed from.

NOTES

NOTE 1.

MAY, EDGAR
A Way Out of the Welfare Mess*

A few miles from where you live there is a part of America nobody wants. It may be a group of ramshackle farm houses or the gray, weather-worn tenements of a city street. Row on row they shelter the culls of society whose togetherness is marked by frayed collars and the musty smell of the poor.

Their subsistence is a government check and their guardian is a civil servant, who, more often than not, has too little education, too many responsibilities, and too few dollars in his own pay envelope. For a number of months I was one of these untrained dispensers of public charity in the city of Buffalo.

During this stint I helped waste some of the millions of dollars and vast quantities of human energy which go into the program called public welfare. Today my counterparts range from the smallest village to our nation's largest cities. And wherever they hold the purse strings of the slums, they are—with few exceptions—setting new spending records that are dismaying taxpayers and instilling the fear of voting-booth retaliation in politicians.

. . . My . . . metropolitan relief operation— the Erie County Welfare Department—this year will spend $34 million—more money than it

---

* *Harper's*, Oct., 1961, pp. 37-38. Reprinted with permission of the publisher.

costs to educate every child in the public schools of Buffalo.

Similar industrial centers mirror the same fiscal dilemma. . . . Yet our national effort to be our brother's keeper is as erratic as the Manhattan skyline. In Mississippi the average family receiving aid-to-dependent-children funds lives on $36.41 a month while a New York State family gets almost five times as much. In Alabama the caseworker who authorizes checks is the provider of 349 families; in New Jersey the figure is 86.

Behind these statistical disparities and monetary woes is a question asked with increasing frequency by legislative investigating committees in many states: Just what does this flood of money buy? The traditional answers always have been that it keeps families together, prevents children from starving, and blocks a wholesale increase in crime because otherwise people would have to steal to eat. But are these adequate answers when in almost every year since the war, the population of this public-dependent society has expanded through good times and bad?

"What you givin' me is okay," Mrs. A, one of my relief cases said. "But you gives the landlord most twice as much as this heap is worth and then I gives the grocer more than he should get 'cause he allows me credit when that check don't come on time. The money is here okay, but it ain't goin' to be no different next month, is it?"

. . . Secretary of Health, Education, and Welfare, Abraham A. Ribicoff, recently explained her problem this way: "I've come to feel that we have just been drifting in the field of welfare. Many welfare workers have become mere conduits between state treasuries and those they seek to help—neglecting prevention, rehabilitation, and protective services." . . .

After a week of training lectures on the job of a caseworker, my supervisor offered me the first of several helpful hints: "The main thing is to get the aid out," he said. "You can always check things later if you have suspicions." But "later"—as it turned out—I had more and more cases and there never was any time. Within two months, in fact, I was the government-assigned head-of-household for 160 families. "I'm sorry that you've got so many cases because you shouldn't really have them," my supervisor said, "but there just isn't anybody else." . . .

The effect of such case loads was written in the records. One report, for instance, showed that at least five recipients had not been visited at home by a caseworker in three years although the mailman was delivering checks every month.

For ten others the "home call" lapse was two years. Yet the rule book said they should be visited at least once every three months.

"If you see a visitor once a year, my, that's a lot," one of my clients told me after she had hesitated to open her door to me. "That's why when you first rang I didn't have any idea who you might be." Her record, which I had inherited, showed a home call eight months earlier, but the client could not remember seeing a caseworker for a year and a half. My predecessor apparently had reported a call that never was made. In all these cases the "conduits" described by Secretary Ribicoff dutifully kept on channeling dollars from the treasury to the needy. No one has starved. Few have committed crimes. But fewer still have been helped.

* * *

. . . Judges who might be lenient to a convicted welfare chiseler because he doesn't even have money to pay a fine should hand down a jail sentence if the amount stolen warrants it. When a shoplifter goes to the penitentiary and a major relief cheat is placed on probation, the public's confidence is not enhanced.

But unless the key element—help—accompanies the future flow of relief checks, the tax of being our brother's keeper may become prohibitive. Beyond this, the human price may be too high. When government charity began on a major scale, the political patron saint of social work, President Franklin D. Roosevelt, said in his 1935 message to Congress:

> "Continued dependence upon relief induces a spiritual and moral disintegration fundamentally destructive to the national fiber. To dole out relief in this way is to administer a narcotic, a subtle destroyer of the human spirit."

NOTE 2.

5A, Mississippi Supp. § 7171 (1962 Supp.)

§ 7171. Dependent children, aid to.

Assistance may be granted under this act to any dependent child who is living in a suitable family home meeting the standards of care and health fixed by the laws of this state, and the rules and regulations of the state department of public welfare. Provided, however, a home will not be considered suitable in which the parents of the children living in the home for whom they are requesting aid are living together and are not husband and wife by virtue of a statutory ceremonial marriage or by a legal common-law marriage. . . .

NOTE 3.

MISSISSIPPI DEPARTMENT OF WELFARE
Manual of Instruction—Special Factors in Aid to Dependent Children*

PURPOSE OF THE PROGRAM

The purpose of aid to dependent children is to provide financial assistance and services for children who have lost wholly or partially the support and care normally provided for them by their parents. When one parent is incapacitated or absent, the assistance payment is to help the remaining parent to maintain the home for the children by providing basic necessities. When both parents are dead or absent, the assistance payment goes to a relative within a certain degree of relationship who will share his home with the child and will give him the care and guidance he needs, but who cannot provide financially for the child without help.

* * *

BASIC ELIGIBILITY REQUIREMENTS

The Mississippi statute provides that assistance may be granted to a dependent child who:

1. Is living in a suitable family home meeting the standards of care and health fixed by the laws of this state and the rules and regulations of the State Department of Public Welfare; and
2. Is a needy child who is under the age of sixteen, or under the age of eighteen if found to be regularly attending school or disabled to attend; and
3. Has been deprived of parental support or care by reason of the death, continued absence from the home, or physical or mental incapacity of a parent; and
4. Is living in the home of relatives within a specified degree of relationship.

SUITABLE HOME PROVISIONS

The state statute . . . sets out as an eligibility requirement that a child for whom aid is requested be living in a suitable family home, and thus calls for a definition of such a home.

Much is known about the qualities and material means which families need in order to provide the best opportunities for the physical growth and the intellectual, emotional, and social development of children. Much less is known about the degree to which these qualities are needed. For example, families which lack one or more of these qualities or elements, or which are weak in some of them, still are able to help their children grow up to be well adjusted, useful, and well equipped adults.

_____

* Vol. III, Section D, revised 1 June, 1960. (pp. 4500-4515).

Although these variations exist and exact measurement is not possible, there is agreement on the essential functions of the family. These functions are recognized as being:

1. The provision of physical security and protection, and of material opportunities for living and for growth;
2. The transmission from one generation to another of the special way of life that makes up the civilization of the nation;
3. The provision of opportunities for spiritual development and for affiliation with some religious body;
4. The provision of a place where both the parents and the children have their emotional needs met;
5. The development in its members of socially desirable character traits;
6. The maintenance of order and the division of responsibilities and duties; and
7. The development of sound relationships between the members of the family and the outside community.

Thus a suitable family home can be defined in terms of these functions and can be said to exist when these functions are performed in whole or for the most part reasonably well. However, since this is still an inexact definition, it is easier to describe the conditions which will result in a decision that a home is unsuitable. Therefore the material which follows will define unsuitable conditions, will discuss principles to be kept in mind in considering such conditions, give criteria for evaluating the effect of the condition on the care of the children, and direct the staff in steps to be taken with regard to the granting or denial of aid.

The following steps are to be taken in evaluating the home for suitability or unsuitability:

1. Test the current situation in the home; that is, the present provisions for the care of the children, the way in which their physical needs are met, the present conduct of the adults in the home, what effect the conduct of the adults has on the children, and the plans of the parent or other relative for the future care and development of the children. While the social history will show the way in which the parent or other relative has provided or failed to provide a suitable environment and care for the children, it is the present plan and intentions of the parent or other relative that are to be taken into consideration.
2. Identify the strengths in the home that are meeting the needs of the children and on which the worker can build in helping the parent or other relative improve conditions.
3. Locate the problem which raises a question on the suitability of the home, getting facts on what the problem is specifically, the extent of the problem, and how long it has existed.
4. Evaluate the extent to which the factor causing unsuitability is affecting the children, the parent's ability to use help to change the situation, and what action he can take to make the correction.
5. Determine what plan, if any, the agency can make to provide care for the children if it is clear that the parent or other relative cannot or will not try to make the necessary changes.
6. In most instances the plan which is needed for the care of the children will indicate whether initial or continuing eligibility exists. The material below discusses eligibility under each heading.

* * *

Principles Involved in Helping with Change. Because of the responsibility which the county workers and county welfare board members have in making decisions on the suitability or unsuitability of homes in ADC, principles are being included for use in considering these situations. These principles set out some of the facts which are necessary for understanding the difficulties encountered by a person in making a change, and also factors involved in planning for and carrying through a change in living patterns.

1. In working with people in any capacity, one must believe in human worth, accept each person as an individual different in many ways from all other persons, and as having value. While people have many similarities, many of the same needs, and certainly many of the same problems, they cannot be classed as certain types and be expected to respond in the same way. Keeping alert to individual differences and responses will help to find clues to intentions and reasons for behavior.
2. Each person has the ability to change, but can change only as he has the opportunity to change and sees an advantage in doing so. This is seen every day in families in which the children behave almost exactly in the same way in conducting their lives as their parents have and even as their grandparents did. In working with clients, the visitor must remember to inquire into

what opportunity for change the parent or other relative has had, and whether he has seen any benefit from doing so. So in either gathering or reviewing material about a person's intent about his way of living, it is helpful to look for information on these points.

3. There is no one rule for evaluating the desire and ability of a person to change his behavior or condition, and there is no set time period at which it can be expected that people are ready to change. Each person's readiness or ability or opportunity must be discovered and the decision as to his sincerity and real intent made on this basis.

4. As people are affected adversely or favorably by those with whom they associate, one should examine carefully the kind of environment in which the person lives, and if it is undesirable, whether the person has had any chance of moving or has any definite plans for doing so if he can manage financially. Environment includes not only the location of the home itself but one's associates, as family, neighbors, and community. Environment also includes the school and the church.

5. Since changing one's habits, ideas, or physical location is hard for almost everybody, it is necessary to ask what help the person has had in making changes in his way of living and whether he can sustain a different way of conducting himself alone or with the assistance of others.

6. Changes are most easily and lastingly made when they come from a person's inner urge to live differently. However, this society is one in which the good deeds of its citizens are recognized and their bad acts punished or at least disapproved. If the only incentive for change on the part of the parent or other relative is the wish to receive assistance, it should not be disregarded, as the necessity for money to live on is sometimes as strong and impelling as a set of standards for one's self.

7. The best information about a person is obtained through forming a good relationship with him and discussing the matter in question directly with the person. In instances in which references should be used in obtaining information about a parent or family, the grocer, the landlord, and sometimes the employer are usually helpful sources of information. Both neighbors and members of the family may be prejudiced either for or against the family

and their information if secured must be carefully evaluated.

UNSUITABLE HOME CONDITIONS

Certain conditions in the home have been identified as interfering with the normal functioning of the family, and certain treatment of the child as being detrimental to his well-being. . . .

* * *

Abuse, Exploitation, or Neglect of the Child. The protection of abused, exploited, or neglected children is a legal responsibility of the agency. . . .

* * *

Should court action be necessary and the court remove the child from the home, aid cannot be granted or reinstated in the name or home of the same relative until the court has returned the child to the custody of this relative.

The following questions may be helpful in making a decision as to the effect of the parent's behavior on the care of the children:

1. Does the parent leave the children alone and uncared for, not fed, during the period of absence?

2. Does the parent engage in his misconduct in the home so that the children are subjected to the degrading influences and bad conditions resulting from the behavior?

3. Has the mother or other relative been arrested for prostitution? If not, is her activity known in the community, so that the children are also singled out by this behavior?

4. Have facts been obtained to determine that such conduct exists? That is, are reports of such behavior based on rumor, malicious gossip, or other unreliable forms of information, or have the facts been checked? Facts may be checked by discussion with the parent and observation of the home, by court records, discussion with conscientious persons concerned about the care of the children and the conditions in the home, and the like.

Inadequate Provision for Physical Needs of the Child. One of the expected functions of the family has been listed as that of provision for meeting the physical needs of the child. Although sometimes conditions in a home may on first observation appear to exist because of neglect as described above, more inquiry into the situation will reveal the problem not to be of sufficient severity to warrant calling it a protective service case. That is, the situation may arise from poor household management, ignorance, temporary illness on the part of the parent, or some less serious problem.

* * *

Inadequate Provision for Supervision of the Child. In order for the family to carry out its recognized functions, the parent must as a minimum supervise and control the children, see that they attend school regularly, and provide opportunities for spiritual development. Certainly a great need exists for all children to get as much education as possible, and spiritual growth is a need of each person. It is detrimental for the children to be left unsupervised and uncared for during the absence of the parent or other relative, and for limits not to be set for their behavior and experimentation.

* * *

Again as in inadequate provision for meeting physical needs, the decision about the inadequacy of care of the child will be based on the severity and may result in a finding of neglect in the sense of protective service as a child welfare case. For example, the parent or other relative may be feeble-minded or so ill that he is incapable of giving the child minimum care and no improvement can be expected in the situation. In that event plans would have to be made for the care of the child, whether in foster care, by removal to another relative's home, or through court action.

Aid to dependent children grants may be continued through the period of exploration of the problem and the planning with the adult responsible for the child.

Inadequate Provision for Social and Moral Standards. Listed among the recognized functions of the family are the passing on from one generation to another of the special ways of life that make up the civilization of the nation, and the development of socially desirable character traits. Parents are expected to help each child to develop moral and social standards through example, training, and education. The development of moral and ethical standards not only provides a safeguard against wrongdoing of various kinds, but determines the kind of citizens the children will become.

Failure of the parent or adult to provide even minimum opportunities for a child to develop such standards will raise the question of the suitability of the home. Flagrant and continued violation of the moral and social standards of the community usually results in emotional and sometimes actual physical damage to the child.

Involved here also is the failure of the family to develop and to assist the child to develop sound relationships between the members of the family and the outside community.

1. *Failure to provide legal marriage.* The contracting of a legal marriage is the accepted custom in this country, and failure to formalize a marriage deprives the child of certain rights and privileges as well as damages his emotional and social development. Lack of legal status deprives a child of his legal rights of the inheritance of property, and of eligibility for benefits such as veterans compensation payment and survivors insurance under the Social Security Act.

For these reasons if the mother and the father, or the mother and a father-person, are in the home with the children and have formed a continuous union without legal status, the environment cannot be considered as providing adequately for the development of social and moral standards.

When the worker finds that the parents have failed to form a legal union, or have failed to terminate a previous marriage and so cannot form a legal one, the worker will discuss with them the requirements for a statutory ceremonial marriage. . . .

A grant cannot be placed or continued in this home until the marriage is given legal status.

2. *Casual relations and birth of illegitimate child.* It is obvious that parents fall below a minimum standard for provision of moral and social training when they engage in sexual relations with other than the legal spouse, and fail even more completely when such relations are casual ones or the parent must be termed promiscuous. The birth of an illegitimate child is evidence of an illicit relationship or promiscuity.

In addition to the failure of the parent or other relative to teach moral and ethical standards, such conduct jeopardizes the health of the child by exposing him to the danger of venereal disease. Parents who are careless about their sexual relationships are many times equally careless about provision for meeting the physical and emotional needs of the child or about protecting him during their absence. Others engage in their behavior in the home where the children are.

When the worker finds on an initial application, a reapplication or a determination of continuing eligibility, that the parent or other relative is engaging in casual relations or relations with other than the legal spouse, the question of the suitability of the home must be resolved.

* * *

If the worker finds that the moral standards of the mother or other adult relative are not acceptable and she is not interested in making a change in them or in showing that she is making a change, then the application must be denied or the grant discontinued on the basis that the home is unsuitable because of inadequate provision for social and moral standards.

*   *   *

[I]n instances in which the problem is the failure of the adult relative to correct unacceptable moral and social standards, but the care of the child is adequate or in general in accordance with the care afforded children in the community, then the responsibility of the worker will be that of making other plans, if possible, for meeting the family's requirements for basic maintenance. Local resources may exist, or the worker may have to request emergency help from other agencies, organizations, civil clubs, churches, or individuals, for food for the children.
. . . These questions may be helpful in evaluating the statements of the parent or other relative that she has a bona-fide intent to make a change in the environment, or that she has already done so. All questions will not apply to all cases, but some of the questions will be pertinent to some situations and others to different ones.

1. What is the meaning of this way of living to the mother or other relative? That is, what benefits does she derive from the relationship: financial assistance, feeling of status, companionship and emotional support, physical gratification, unplanned following in the pattern set by her parents, etc.

2. Does the mother or other relative say that these benefits are important to her and she cannot see any way of relinquishing them? If so, the prognosis for change is unfavorable.

3. If the mother says that she will relinquish the relationship, how will the needs of the family be met? What plan can the worker and mother make to meet the needs not supplied even if ADC can be granted?

4. If the mother says that she has given up the relationship, how have the needs of the family for the necessities been met? If no explanation of how food has been bought, the rent paid, and fuel supplied, can be given, then apparently someone has been helping the family. The mother will be asked for a reasonable explanation of how economic needs have been met.

5. If the mother has engaged in casual relationships or formed a non-legal union after having had a legal marriage, is she

able to state the reason for this action? For example, a woman after the loss of her husband, whether by death, desertion, or divorce, may be quite lonely and form a relationship with another man without consciously deciding on this way of living, and may then be able to be helped to make another decision for herself.

6. If the pattern of having unacceptable social and moral standards is well-established, the incentive and reason for making a change must be stronger than if the conduct was of short duration. In cases of this sort, in addition to being able to present a reason for the resolution to live differently, the mother must be able to show definite plans to avoid the danger of falling into the previous way of living. For example:

a. Does the mother plan to move out of the home or neighborhood in which she has been living? If not, has she been unable to do so because of lack of money, and if she receives ADC and has help in locating another place, does she really intend to move, and if so what other place does she have in mind?

b. What constructive activities does she have in mind for herself and children? That is, work, church affiliation, improvement of the home, even returning to school if the mother is a young girl.

c. Has she informed her associates of her intentions and asked their help in making a change in her way of living? Will her parents and other relatives support her in this intention?

d. Is she concerned that her own children not follow her pattern of living, or does she show no interest in or concern about this question?

7. Is the mother sincerely interested in having help from the worker in making plans for a better life for herself and the children? Since both resolving to change and sticking to it are hard, it is obvious that the mother must have help from her family, neighbors, or the worker in her resolution unless of course she has already demonstrated her ability to stand alone.

8. If one man has been the father of more than one of the children, is there any tie between him and the mother that could be built on for a marriage? A marriage between the mother and this man might be a better way of life than the mother alone on ADC. If no such tie exists, what

assurance can the mother give that the relationship will not be resumed? In other words, where is the man, why did they stop seeing each other, and has the mother advised him of her resolve to terminate?

9. Does the mother believe that having relations with a man is necessary for her health? If so, it is not likely that she intends to discontinue such relationships. Would she be willing to discuss this matter with her doctor or a doctor and receive advice regarding it?

10. What protection does the mother have from the advances of men? That is, women who have had relations with men and who may have a real desire to discontinue may lack actual physical protection, and may need planning to provide it. This ties back to the location of the home and living arrangments discussed above.

11. If the mother feels she cannot give up her relationships but is concerned about maintenance for her children, what can she suggest about some plan? That is, can other relatives take the children in their home and care for them or receive ADC, or does the mother plan to obtain work, make an arrangement for the care of the children while she is away, and thus be independent?

Procedures in Cases Involving Birth of Illegitimate Child. Because of legal requirements in the state statute, special procedures are required in two instances: (1) reapplication made by a mother who had an illegitimate child while receiving assistance or was found illegitimately pregnant while receiving aid; and (2) cases receiving aid when the mother is found to be illegitimately pregnant or to have given birth to an illegitimate child.

* * *

On active cases when the mother is found to be illegitimately pregnant or to have given birth to an illegitimate child, the county department must take action to stop payment either temporarily or finally. The worker will advise the parent or other relative of the steps necessary to remedy the situation, but the family can receive no payment during the time that the evidence is being evaluated and the county welfare board is reaching its decision.

* * *

Effect of Conduct of Other Adults in the Home. The same question about the stability of the home will arise when an adult other than the parent or other grantee relative engages in such conduct as endangers the well-being of the children. The same principles will apply and the same plan of working with the grantee relative will be followed as when the grantee's conduct is in question.

* * *

Effect of Conduct of Child . . .

If the parent or other adult relative has plans or can enter into plans for correcting the situation and preventing its recurrence, the grant will be continued. In instances in which one of the children in the grant has had an illegitimate baby, if the best plan is for the young mother to keep the baby, the baby may be added to the grant provided the question about suitable home has been resolved.

* * *

NOTE 4.

CALHOUN, ARTHUR W.

A Social History of the American Family*

[S]laves could have no guarantee of family ties. There was no such thing as legitimacy of children. The attorney-general of Maryland declared: "A slave has never maintained an action against the violation of his bed. A slave is not admonished for incontinence, or punished for fornication or adultery—never prosecuted for bigamy . . ." Marriage was a temporary contract dissoluable at any time at the caprice of the master. Booker Washington wrote:

In the days of slavery not very much attention was given to . . . family records—that is, black family records. . . . Of my father I know even less than of my mother. I do not even know his name. I have heard reports to the effect that he was a white man who lived on one of the near-by plantations. . . . I never heard of his taking . . . interest in me or providing in any way for my rearing.

The full property right of the master involved, of course, the right to break up families and sell the members apart, and this right was frequently exercised. When Miss Martineau asked a southern lady, "Is it possible that you pair and part these people like brutes?" the lady looked surprised and asked what else could be done. When slave mothers wished to keep their children quiet they threatened them with the negro buyer. One woman had three husbands sold from her in three years by reason of the straightened circumstances of the master. . . .

* New York: Barnes & Noble, Inc. (University Paperbacks), Vol. II, 1960, pp. 251, 253-4, 256, 259. Reprinted with permission of the publisher.

Professor Andrews, sometime of the University of South Carolina, inquired of a slave-trader near Washington, "Do you often buy the wife without the husband?" "Yes, very often ; and frequently too they sell me the mother while they keep the children. I have often known them to take away the infant from its mother's breast, and keep it whilst they sold her." Farmers near Washington bred slaves like cattle for market and cared no more for mother's agony than for the lowing of a cow. A standing advertisement in Charleston papers read: "Several small boys without their mother." . . .

* * *

. . . The Synod of Kentucky (a state where slavery had a precarious hold) confessed in 1834 that

> The system produces general licentiousness among the slaves. Marriage, as a civil ordinance, they cannot enjoy. . . . Until slavery waxeth old, and tendeth to decay, there cannot be any legal recognition of the marriage rite, or the enforcement of its consequent duties. For, all the regulations on this subject would limit the master's absolute right of property in the slaves. In his disposal of them he could no longer be at liberty to consult merely his own interest. . . . Their present quasi marriages are continually . . . voided [at the master's pleasure] They are, in this way, brought to consider their matrimonial alliances as things not binding, and they act accordingly. . . .

* * *

Demand for slaves put a premium on fecundity, especially after the African trade was outlawed. . . .

NOTE 5.

FURMAN, BESS

U.S. Seeks to Bar Aid for Louisiana*

Hearings were opened . . . on whether Louisiana should be denied further Federal aid to dependent children. The Department of Health, Education and Welfare argued that funds should be cut off.

The department held that Louisiana's action in cutting 23,000 children off its rolls "required withholding further Federal grants."

* * *

Former Gov. Robert F. Kennon, counsel for Louisiana, said his state had violated no part of the Social Security Act and that the department

---

* *The New York Times,* 15 Nov. 1960 (c. 6, p. 42). © 1960 by The New York Times Company. Reprinted with permission.

therefore had no right to cut off funds. He said that until Congress amended the act to rule out "suitable home" laws, Louisiana would stand on its new law. He said it had been merely "borrowed from a neighbor state."

* * *

He insisted the law was not anti-Negro in nature, but intended only to uplift the morals of the state.

* * *

Representative Otto E. Passman, Democrat of Louisiana, a member of the House Appropriations Committee, testified that the writers of the Social Security Act had ruled out Federal interference in the conduct of state affairs. He read a lengthy statement on the mounting Federal debt to justify his state's action in reducing the relief rolls.

NOTE 6.

MAINOR v. MIDVALE CO.
192 Pa. Super. Ct. 367, 162 A. 2d 27 (1960)

OPINION BY GUNTHER, J.

Mary B. Mainor, claiming to be the common law wife and widow of William Mainor, filed a fatal claim petition on December 6, 1956 under the Occupational Disease Act as a dependent. In this petition she set forth that her marriage to William Mainor took place in 1940. Both appellants filed answers to this petition denying, in effect, that claimant was a common law wife. . . .

* * *

The basic question raised here . . . is whether there was a valid common law marriage. If there was no valid common law marriage proved, the corollary is whether the court below properly remitted the record to the board.

Upon the death of William Mainor, a claim petition was sent to claimant from Harrisburg. She sought the aid of one of the men in charge of the Philadelphia office of the Workmen's Compensation Board in filling out the petition and she gave the information which was used to file the petition. The fourth paragraph of the printed petition required information as to the marital status of the claimant and in answer to this requirement, she stated that the marriage was a common law marriage in 1940. . . .

Claimant stated that she first met William Mainor between 1940 and 1941 and that she lived with him since 1940 from which time she was known as Mrs. Mainor. She admitted that she knew that William Mainor had a legal wife living when they began living together. It was shown that William Mainor obtained a divorce from his legal wife, Blanche Square Mainor, on April 22, 1953 and that immediately after that date he returned to her, at which time the following is alleged to have taken place: "Q. Tell us, what happened after that? Where was the divorce secured? A. North Carolina. So he came home about five o'clock in the morning. Q. Was that on the 22nd or 23rd? A. That was on the 22nd; yes. Q. Yes. Then he came home—well, the same morning he got home so that had to be the 24th. A. 23rd. So he met me and said. Q. Tell us whether he had his papers. A. He had his papers. He told me I was his wife. Q. Did he give you anything at that time? A. Gave me the ring. Q. Is that the ring (indicating)? A. That's the ring. Q. That you are wearing now? 3. Yes." Over objection, she was permitted to testify further: "Q. Tell us what took place at that time? A. Well, we kissed and we didn't have time—he went to work—we both had to go to work, and he said as I told you. Q. Tell us what he said. A. He said, 'Now you are my wife,' and I said, 'You are my husband.' Q. On April 23, 1953? A. That's right."

*　*　*

It is clear from the evidence that the commencement of this so-called common law marriage was meretricious at its inception and continued that way at least until 1953. Such a relationship is presumed to be illicit unless and until clear and convincing evidence is produced to show a change of circumstances. . . .

d. Social Security

ROBLES v. FOLSOM
239 F. 2d 562 (2d Cir. 1956)
cert. den. 353 U.S. 960 (1957)

CLARK, CHIEF JUDGE (dissenting).

As Judge HAND'S opinion points out, this child from birth was accepted by the father as his own and a part of his family; and while the parents were eligible to marry, they just did not bother to do so. No bar to either inheritance or receipt of social security benefits could have arisen had father and son remained in Puerto Rico; but removal to New York now results in denying these benefits to the recognized child. This very harsh result comes, in my opinion, from forcing Anglo-Saxon moral patterns on a family having its origin in the more tolerant atmosphere of Puerto

Rico and the civil law it follows.[1] And this, in turn, comes about from an emphasis on names or labels, rather than on substance, in translating civil law concepts into New York equivalents.

Whereas New York classes all children born out of wedlock as "illegitimates," legal systems influenced by the Code Napoleon distinguish "natural children" from others—a natural child being one whose parents were not legally barred from marrying each other at the time of the child's birth or conception. By informal voluntary acts a parent can raise a natural child to the status of "recognized (or acknowledged) natural child," thus giving it rights of inheritance and certain social benefits. Or, by formal acts prescribed in the local civil code, the parent can "legitimate" the child, elevating it above recognized natural children to the level of those born in wedlock. In these civil law countries there are three categories of children—"legitimates," "acknowledged natural children," and others, i.e., bastards; and there are two different processes for changing status—"legitimation" and "acknowledgment."[3]

I cannot agree that the New York law prevents an acknowledged child from taking personal property if his father dies intestate while domiciled in New York. It is clear that the status of the child would be determined by the law of the place where he was born. . . . In that case a child born out of wedlock in Wurttemberg attempted to take real property in New York by intestacy upon the death of his father. His parents had subsequently married each other, and the law of Wurttemberg entitled him to inherit real property there. Under the then law of New York, however, subsequent marriage did not "legitimate" children born out of wedlock and they could not inherit. The Court of Appeals applied the Wurttemberg law of inheritance and found for the child.

In the most recent New York case discussed by my brethren a child born out of wedlock in Louisiana whose parents never married was considered eligible to inherit in New York. In re Slater's Estate, 195 Misc. 713, 90 N.Y.S. 2d 546. Louisiana's Civil Code derived from the Code Napoleon and had the concept of acknowledged natural child. Under the Louisiana cases, which were cited in the New York opinion, the father's informal acts of attending his daughter's christening and later referring to her as his own were sufficient to confer this status on the child, despite

---

1. "The common law of England, which is also the American common law, is more unfavorable to the illegitimate child than the civil law of Rome, on which the continental legal systems are based, mainly in two respects: It does not recognize a legal relationship even between the mother and the child and it does not allow legitimation by subsequent marriage." Freund, Illegitimacy Laws of the United States and Certain Foreign Countries 9 (1919).

3. "The relation less than legitimation, that of recognized natural child, may arise by the law of several European states, between a parent and a natural child." 2 Beale, A Treatise on the Conflict of Laws Sec. 140.2 (1935).

the literal wording of Art. 203 of the LSA-Civil Code. . . . Under other Louisiana cases, which were also cited in the New York opinion, such informal acts of the father were insufficient to "legitimate" the child and elevate it to full legal equality with children born in wedlock. . . .

These cases held that both acknowledged and legitimated children had rights of intestate succession, and the distinction between the two groups was significant only if the child's claim was contested by an heir with rights superior to an acknowledged child, but not superior to a legitimated one. The New York Surrogate in In re Slater's Estate, supra, 195 Misc. 713, 90 N.Y.S. 2d 546, properly did not distinguish between acknowledged and legitimated children, but rather classed both types together and contrasted them with children born out of wedlock and never elevated —a group which has no rights of inheritance or social position. When he spoke of acknowledged children as "legitimate" or "legitimated," he used these words in their New York, and not their Louisiana, sense.

From the cases he cited it is clear the Surrogate understood that Louisiana courts would have called the Slater child "acknowledged," and not "legitimated." All commentators who have discussed the Louisiana cases have noticed that such informal acts create the first status, rather than the second. My brethren say these cases are irrelevant, and they prefer to interpret the Surrogate's opinion in the light of four Louisiana statutes. But the cases which the Surrogate selected to support his decision seem a far better indication of his meaning than the naked text of these statutes —two of which he did not cite, and all of which are discussed in these cases.

Thus the result reached by the Surrogate appears to be good sense, as well as good law. Since civil law jurisdictions have three categories of children and New York has only two, the "acknowledged natural child" must be likened to either New York "legitimates" or New York "bastards." The chief similarity to the New York bastard, for purposes of intestate succession, is a mere semantic identity—neither is labeled "legitimate." On the other hand, the acknowledged child is one whom the father claimed as his own with knowledge that the act would confer on it rights of inheritance and greater social status.

* * *

Since, as I believe, acknowledged natural children may take by inheritance in New York, the plaintiff should prevail. The Puerto Rican Civil Code, which derives from the Louisiana and Spanish Civil Codes, has the same three categories of legitimates, recognized natural children, and

others.[9] Like the Louisiana law cited in the Slater case . . . Puerto Rican law distinguishes between natural children who have been "recognized" and those who have been "legitimated." The former have limited rights of inheritance and social status; the latter are raised to full equality with children born in wedlock.[10] It is true that the Puerto Rican procedures for raising natural children to full legitimacy are somewhat different from the procedures in Louisiana;[11] but the difference cannot distinguish the Slater case from this one, since in both cases the child was only "acknowledged" under local law, and in neither case did the parents utilize the local procedure for elevating their child to full equality with children born in wedlock.

I think we should reverse and direct judgment for the plaintiff.

NOTES

NOTE 1.

HAMMOND v. PENNSYLVANIA R. R. CO.
31 N.J. 244, 156 A. 2d 689 (1959)

WEINTRAUB, C. J.

The single question presented is whether illegitimate children are "children" within the meaning of the Federal Employers' Liability Act, 45 U. S. C. A. §51. . . .

The complaint alleged the deceased John Ham-

---

9. Sec. 442 is the same as Secs. 178-180 of the La. Civil Code of 1870, and defines legitimate and illegitimate children. Secs. 461-466 further define legitimate children and state their rights. Secs. 481-486 govern the process of "legitimation." Secs. 501-506 define natural children, prescribe the modes for recognizing them, and state the rights of recognized natural children. Secs. 507-514 govern the right of other children to support.

10. See U.S. Dept. of Labor, op. cit. supra note 6, at 2: "The law of Louisiana differs from that of other States in being based on the Napoleonic Code. Only the child of persons who might legally have married at the time of the child's conception, may be legitimated on marriage of his parents. Such children, called natural children, are the only children born out of wedlock whose interests are protected by the Louisiana law. In addition to legitimation on formal acknowledgment of paternity and marriage of the parents, such a child may be 'legitimated' for purposes of inheritance by either the natural mother or father on declaration of intentions before a notary public or two witnesses. The law of Puerto Rico is similar in origin and similarly defines a natural child."

11. In Puerto Rico at the time when the plaintiff was born, full legal equality for children born out of wedlock was possible only if the parents subsequently married. . . . In Louisiana at the time of the Slater child's birth such equality was conferred only if there were formal acts, either before a notary or in the marriage contract. . . . In both jurisdictions later legislation has made it much easier for children born out of wedlock to attain full equality. See Oppenheim, Acknowledgement and Legitimation in Louisiana—Louisiana Act 50 of 1944, 19 Tulane L. Rev. 325 (1945); Laws of Puerto Rico Ann. tit. 31, Sec. 441 (1954), passed in 1952.

mond was survived by his five children, all under the age of 21 years, who "were dependent upon the said John Hammond for support, maintenance, nurture and education, all of which have been lost by his death." The federal statute provides that an employer railroad shall be liable in damages for negligence in the case of the death of an employee "for the benefit of the surviving widow or husband and children of such employee ; and, if none * * * then the next of kin dependent upon such employee." Illegitimacy of the infants was conceded.

Defendant urges that who are "children" must be determined by state law. . . .

But plaintiffs argue that "children" may readily be identified on the basis of physical relationship. Hence, there being no need to look to state law, it is urged the word should receive an interpretation which will fully satisfy the congressional purpose to compensate the dependent for financial loss caused by a defendant's wrong. Reliance is placed upon Middleton v. Luckenbach S. S. Co., Inc., 70 F. 2d 326, 328 (2 Cir. 1934), certiorari denied 293 U. S. 577, 55 S. Ct. 89, 79 L. Ed. 674 (1934). There the action was brought under the Death on High Seas Act, 46 U. S. C. A. §761, which provides for recovery "for the exclusive benefit of the decedent's wife, husband, parent, child, or dependent relative." . . . The court held "children" to mean children in fact, whether or not legitimate under state law, a result it found consonant with the purpose of Congress to compensate for deprivation of support, saying (70 F. 2d, at page 329):

"There is no right of inheritance involved here. It is a statute that confers recovery upon dependents, not for the benefit of an estate, but for those who by our standards are legally or morally entitled to support. Humane considerations and the realization that children are such no matter what their origin alone might compel us to the construction that, under the present day conditions, our social attitude warrants a construction different from that of the early English view. The purpose and object of the statute is to continue the support of dependents after a casualty. To hold that these children or the parents do not come within the terms of the act would be to defeat the purposes of the act. The benefit conferred beyond being for such beneficiaries is for society's welfare in making provision for the support of those who might otherwise become dependent. The rule that a bastard is nullius filius applies only in cases of inheritance. Even in that situation we have made very considerable advances toward giving illegitimates the right of capacity to inherit by admitting them to possess inheritable blood. 2 Kent's Commentaries (12th Ed.) 215."

* * *

In the light of the foregoing we cannot say with confidence that "children" here was intended by Congress to refer solely to a physical relationship without regard to any impact on the local policies of the several states. For the reason about to be stated, we need not decide the question, for, if we assume a reference to state law was intended, the infants nonetheless are entitled to prevail.

* * *

NOTE 2.

Commissioners' Prefatory Note to 1950 Uniform Reciprocal Enforcement of Support Act*

* * *

Commissioners studied the subject of non-support as early as 1909 and in 1910 approved the Uniform Desertion and Non-Support Act. This act, adopted in 24 jurisdictions, made it a punishable offense for a husband to desert or willfully neglect or refuse to provide for the support and maintenance of his wife in destitute or necessitous circumstances or for a parent to fail in the same duty to his child under sixteen years of age. The defects of the 1910 act were that it sought to improve the enforcement of the duties of support through the criminal law only and it made no reference to enforcement as against husbands and fathers who fled from the state.

With the increasing mobility of the American population the problem of interstate enforcement of duties of support became acute. A deserting husband was beyond the reach of process in the state where he had abandoned his family and the family had no means to follow him. Welfare departments saddled with the burden of supporting destitute families were often prevented from enforcing the duty of support in the state where the husband could be found by decisions holding that the duty existed only as to obligees within the state.

The avenue of criminal enforcement was not more fruitful. Charges could be preferred against the fleeing husband but he had to be returned for trial to the state where the offense was committed. Extradition was both expensive and narrowly technical, and it was often impossible to prove that he had "fled from justice" for frequently he supported his family until he left the state and only left in order to get a job. Even if he were brought back and successfully prosecuted the result was disappointing. The proceedings rendered

---

* Uniform Reciprocal Enforcement of Suppport Act, 9C U.L.A. (p. 13). Printed with the express permission of the Edward Thompson Company, Brooklyn, New York.

reconciliation with the family improbable, took him away from his job in the state to which he had fled, and by branding him a convicted criminal lessened the probabilities of gainful employment in the home state.

In June 1949 the Social Security Administration announced that the total bill for aid to dependents where the father was absent and not supporting was approximately $205,000,000 a year for the nation and the states.

* * *

The 1950 act attempted to improve and extend by reciprocal legislation the enforcement of duties of support through both the criminal and the civil law. Its provisions are in addition to remedies now existing for the enforcement of duties of support within the state. Each state will enforce its own laws as before so long as the husband remains in the state, and the new act is meant to improve enforcement where the parties are in different states.

The only extension of the duties of support is the principle stated in Section 4 that the duty shall bind the obligor regardless of the presence or residence of the obligee. The purpose here is to overcome the rule in some states that the duty of support runs only in favor of obligees within the state, and to overcome the indifference of many states which would refuse or neglect to enforce support in favor of out-of-state dependents on the theory often tacitly admitted, that one state has no interest in helping another state rid itself of the burden of supporting destitute families.

The criminal provision of Section 5 purports to relieve the extradition process from the narrow requirements that the person whose surrender is demanded must have been in the demanding state at the time of the commission of the crime and must have fled from justice therefrom. These requirements have been heretofore a constant stumbling block to the successful extradition of deserting bread winners, and the act marks a distinct advance in this respect.

Section 6 provides necessary relief from extradition if the obligor complies with support orders of the state. This is designed to encourage voluntary compliance which will be much more profitable to both states than the expensive procedure of extradition.

In the provisions on civil enforcement (Part III of the Act) it is to be noted that the duties of support enforceable are those now existing in the several states (Section I). In other words the act does not attempt to dictate to the states what duties shall be enforced. This seems a wise provision, for it is little realized how different are the duties existing in our 48 states. Some enforce a duty toward illegitimate children, others do not. Forty jurisdictions require children to support their parents, the others do not. A dozen states require support between brothers and sisters, the others do not. Seventeen states require a wife to support a husband under certain circumstances, the others do not. And even in the duty of a parent to support his child the several states require this support up to different ages, varying from 14 to 21 years. This Act is therefore suitable for wide adoption for it attempts not to impose a new pattern of duties of support but to enforce this varied pattern as it now exists. Of course the destitute's family (the obligee) may exercise rights under the act. But the state or political subdivision thereof may also seek reimbursement for support already furnished to the family (Section 8). This section will allow the states to recapture a good part of the $200,000,000 a year now spent in supporting deserted families and is perhaps the most important provision of the act.

Sections 9 to 24 cover details of what is known as the two-state proceeding. In the past, the greatest difficulty in enforcing support where the parties are in different states has been the expense of travel to a distant state to litigate the rights of the destitute obligee. Under this Act this expense can be reduced to filing fees plus a few postage stamps. In a nutshell, this two-state proceeding is as follows: It opens with an action (Section 9) which normally will be commenced in the state where the family has been deserted (the initiating state). A very simplified petition is filed (Section 10). The judge looks it over to decide whether the facts show the existence of a duty of support and if they do he sends the petition and a copy of this Act to a court of the responding state to which the husband has fled or in which he has property (Section 13). That court will take the steps necessary to obtain jurisdiction of the husband or his property, will hold a hearing (Section 17) and if the court finds that a duty of support exists, it may order the defendant to furnish support (Section 20) and will transmit a copy of its order to the court in the initiating state (Section 21). To enforce compliance with its orders the court may subject the defendant to such terms and conditions as it may deem proper, may require him to furnish bond or make periodic payments or, in case of refusal, may punish him for contempt (Section 22). It has the duty to transmit to the initiating court any payments it receives and upon request to furnish a certified statement of those payments (Section 23). The initiating court must receive and disburse these payments (Section 24).

This simple two-state procedure can be carried out with a minimum of expense to the family or the state—the usual court costs and postage for the transmission of papers and money. Yet it preserves due process, for each party pleads in his own court. Provisions covering other details of procedure have been kept out of the Act so that the usual rules for obtaining jurisdiction for carrying on the procedure and for appeals may be held to govern.

The remaining sections cover minor matters. Section 25 makes husband and wife competent and, if thought advisable, compellable witnesses as to confidential communications. This is already law in many states. Section 26 (a bracketed and hence an option section) provides for the simplified rules of evidence that may already exist in certain courts of the state. A few states have courts with simplified rules of evidence and this section is included to make the act suitable for adoption in such states. Section 29 is the standard severability provision.

* * *

NOTE 3.

STATE BD. OF CHILD WELFARE v. P.G.F.
57 N.J. Super. 370, 154 A. 2d 746 (1959)

BELLFATTO, J. J. D. R. C.

The question presented is whether under R.S. 44:1-140, a person may be compelled to support the illegitimate child of his illegitimate daughter. R.S. 44:1-140, is L. 1924, c. 132, sec. 74, which is "An Act for the settlement and relief of the poor," etc. The section in question provides that:

> "The father, grandfather, mother, grandmother, children, grandchildren, and husband or wife, severally and respectively, of a poor, old, blind, lame or impotent person or other poor person or child not able to work, shall, if of such sufficient ability, at his or their charge and expense, relieve and maintain the poor person or child in such manner as the overseer of the poor shall order, or the court upon its own initiative or the information of any person, after notice to the person or persons chargeable and hearing the overseer, may so order.
> "The provisions of this section shall apply to the minor children of a mother whose husband shall fail properly to support and maintain such children when by reason thereof they are likely to become a public charge upon the municipality in which they have gained a legal settlement."

Section 1 of the act consists of a number of definitions of the words used in the act. However, the words "father, grandfather, mother, grandmother, children, grandchildren, * * * poor person or child" or any similar words used in sec. 74 as noted above have not been defined.

Unquestionably under the common law neither the "father" nor the so-called grandfather were under any obligation to support an illegitimate child, and there is no such obligation today where the common law has been expressly changed by statute. . . .

A study of the act . . . does not indicate any legislative intent to burden a so-called grandfather of an illegitimate child with the burden of supporting that child. The act does not attempt to alter the relations between a child and its ancestors. . . . The express purpose of the act is to provide welfare service for all dependent and neglected or needy children and to provide home life for them. This burden of providing welfare service for such neglected or needy children is assumed by the State itself, and quite naturally in doing this it would not have been appropriate for the State to discriminate between legitimate and illegitimate children. This is quite different, however, from concluding that the State thereby intended to impose upon a person not theretofor obligated under the common law the duty to support a child not legally his grandchild

* * *

e. Immigration

POSUSTA v. UNITED STATES
285 F. 2d 553 (2d Cir. 1961)

HAND, CIRCUIT JUDGE.

This is an appeal from an order of the District Court for the Southern District of New York denying a petition of Marie Posusta to be naturalized. The petitioner is a Czechoslovakian by birth and was admitted into the United States for permanent residence in 1952. She married Posusta in this country on January 24, 1959, and filed her petition on April 20 of that year. The question is whether she had proved that she was a person of "good moral character" from April 20, 1954 to April 20, 1959. The facts are as follows.

She had become Posusta's paramour in Czechoslovakia some time in 1936 when she was about nineteen, and she bore him one child in August, 1940, and another in January, 1947. Posusta had himself married a woman, named Krausova, on December 30, 1939, by whom he had previously had a child. It is to be assumed that the petitioner's relations with Posusta remained the same from 1937 or 1938, until he took his wife and her child with him to France in 1948. The petitioner followed them with her two children, and later took them to this country in 1952. After a visit back to France in January, 1953, she returned to the United States in July, 1954, Posusta having preceded her in May of that year. His marriage with Krausova ended in a divorce in March, 1954, so that there was not, and indeed could not have been, any adultery between them after April 20, 1954—five years before the petition was filed. On October 27, 1954, he and the petitioner took out a marriage license, and, although they did not marry until January 24, 1959, they continued their former relation with occasional interruptions.

Their explanation for the delay in marrying after Posusta had been divorced, was that he "wanted to take charge of" the education of Krausova's son which he thought he "could do better than" Krausova, and that, if he married again, "she would not give me the child at all." This child was apparently still a minor which to some extent confirms the avowed reason for their failure to marry for more than five years after they had the license. Moreover, the judge appears to have accepted this explanation of the delay. Upon this record the Naturalization Examiner recommended that the petition be granted, but the Regional Commissioner found otherwise, and Judge Levet agreed with him, and dismissed the petition on the ground that the petitioner had not proved that she was a person of "good moral character" for five years before she filed her petition.

. . . Much has been written as to the scope of that phrase, and, as was inevitable, there has been disagreement as to its meaning. However, it is settled that the test is not the personal moral principles of the individual judge or court before whom the applicant may come ; the decision is to be based upon what he or it believes to be the ethical standards current at the time. . . .

In the case at bar we think it enough that during the five years before she filed her petition the petitioner on the whole did what, as things stood, was consonant with "good moral character." We do not indeed mean that her relations with Posusta are to be condoned, or indeed that persistent incontinence may never preclude having "a good moral character" ; but during the probationary period there were greatly extenuating circumstances. So far as appears, Posusta was her only lover and she had been true to him for over twenty years. Her relations with him were not concealed ; indeed when they were both in this country they lived under the same roof. People will of course differ in their degree of condemnation of such breaches of the moral code ; we can say no more than that even a continued illicit relation is not inevitably an index of a bad "moral character." If she married Posusta, he would lose all power over his son to the son's great disadvantage. True, she would legitimatize her own children, but she could do that anyway after the boy grew up, as she did in fact. It seems

at least a reasonable solution to let things stand as they were until the boy became old enough to be independent of his mother. We do not forget that she was not obliged to continue her relations with Posusta ; but these had been in all respects connubial for many years except for the absence of a legal marriage. We cannot think that good "morals" compelled her to separate from him and leave her children fatherless in substance as they already were in law. Any decision was complicated, but situated as she was, the better course in 1954 was to accept the situation until Krausova lost her power over Krausova's son.

. . . The petitioner's conduct before the probationary period certainly showed that in her youth she disregarded the accepted rules of sexual conduct ; but by April 1954 she was over the age of 35 and it was to the last degree unlikely that after the experience she had had, she was still likely to engage in new illicit amatory adventures. "Good character" we measure by the probable responses to provocations.

The statute is not penal ; it does not mean to punish for past conduct, but to admit as citizens those who are likely to prove law-abiding and useful. . . . We hold that the petitioner was a person of as "good moral character" as is necessary in order to become a citizen.

NOTE

JOHNSON v. UNITED STATES
186 F. 2d 588 (2nd Cir. 1951)

L. HAND, CHIEF JUDGE.

. . . We must own that the statute imposes upon courts a task impossible of assured execution ; people differ as much about moral conduct as they do about beauty. There is not the slightest doubt that to many thousands of our citizens nothing will excuse any sexual irregularity, for some indeed this extends even to the subsequent marriage of an innocent divorced spouse. On the other hand there are many thousands who look with a complaisant eye upon putting an easy end to one union and taking on another. Our duty in such cases, as we understand it, is to divine what the "common conscience" prevalent at the time demands ; and it is impossible in practice to ascertain what in a given instance it does demand. We should have no warrant for assuming that it meant the judgment of some ethical élite, even if any criterion were available to select them. Nor is it possible to make use of general principles, for almost every moral situation is unique ; and no one could be sure how far the distinguishing features of each case would be morally relevant to one person and not to another. Theoretically, perhaps we might take as the test whether those who would approve the specific conduct would outnumber those who would disapprove; but it would be fantastically absurd to try to apply it. So it seems to us that we are confined to the best guess we can make of how such a poll would result.

f. Education

COCHRANE v. MESICK BD. OF EDUCATION
360 Mich. R. 390, 103 N.W. 2d 569 (1960)

KELLY, J. (*for reversal*). The attorney general intervened and appeals from a decision of the trial court holding that defendant school district did not violate the statute guaranteeing to all students an equal right to public educational facilities by excluding married high school students from participation in "co-curricular activities."

Intervenor and appellant states:

"The attorney general, in the exercise of his duty, respectfully requests the Supreme Court to provide an authoritative determination of the questions referred to, and takes the initiative in this appeal for the purpose of resolving these important public questions. * * *

"It is submitted by the attorney general that the action of the school board, in taking what it frankly admits is punitive action, designed to humiliate and ridicule the plaintiff students before their classmates so as to discourage other marriages, is violating the public policy of the State by attacking the married status of these students as 'wrongdoing', and that the rule in question is clearly void for that reason alone. The concern of the law is to protect, not to attack, the state of matrimony, and to exalt, not to undermine, the security of legal marriages. * * * They are entitled, by law and public policy, to the respect and security of community acceptance in their married status, as well as to all the benefits of equal access to all public educational facilities, including their earned status in the co-curricular activities. To deprive them of the intangible security of their pride of achievement in the 'glamor' titles and offices so important to the high school student, at a time of life when they are peculiarly sensitive to acceptance and approval by their contemporaries, is to interfere not only with their education but also with their marriages, by undermining their morale in this respect, thus condemning their marital status through the exclusionary rule. Instead of making the status of marriage itself an occasion for stripping students of achievement and rank, so as to deprive them of the admiration of fellow students, it is the duty of the school board to respect and exalt the status of matrimony. * * * If, however, the community is to take a position against high school marriages, the way to do it is through legislation, as by raising the age limit for marriage, not through school board interference with the pre-

rogatives of the legislature, the parents, and the church."

* * *

There was introduced in evidence an exhibit entitled, "Reasons for Adoption of Board Policy Concerning Married Students," containing the following:

"1. Adopted for the possible bad influence when married students are forced to be closely associated with their unmarried peers in any way other than the more formal circumstances; that is, classrooms, under the immediate supervision of a teacher.

"2. Students today are more ready to accept the actions of their peers as the thing to do. If any married students are in a position of idolization the more desirous is the group to mimic.

"3. It is felt that married students need all the extra time available to provide a proper family life and time spent in co-curricular activities is not conducive to this end.

"4. When a student enters into marriage he assumes adulthood and consequently enters into another society, removed from the less mature students and also removed from parental guidance."

Sections 355 and 356 of the school code . . . provide that all students over 5, if resident of a school district, shall have an equal right to attend school. . . .

* * *

The right to contract marriage at an age when the majority of our youth are attending high school was granted by the legislature when it provided . . . :

"Every male or female who shall have attained the full age of 18 years shall be capable by law of contracting marriage."

Extensive research has failed to disclose a decision of this, or any other supreme court, dealing with the right of a school board to deny married students an opportunity to participate in extracurricular activities. We shall comment on and quote from the only 3 known supreme court decisions dealing with the right to expel or suspend solely on the ground that the student is married (Mississippi, Kansas, and Tennessee).

In *McLeod* v. *State, ex rel. Colmer, District Attorney* (1929), 154 Miss. 468 (122 So. 737, 63 ALR 1161), an ordinance adopted by the school trustees barring married persons, otherwise eligible, from public schools, was held unreasonable and void under the statute giving the school trustees authority "to prescribe and enforce rules, not inconsistent with law or those prescribed by the State board of education, for their own government and government of schools, and * * * to suspend or dismiss pupils, when the best interest of the school makes it necessary."

The Mississippi supreme court, at pages 474, 475, said:

* * *

"The question . . . is whether or not the ordinance in question is so unreasonable and unjust as to amount to an abuse of discretion in its adoption. * * * The ordinance is based alone upon the ground that the admission of married children as pupils in the public schools of Moss Point would be detrimental to the good government and usefulness of the schools. It is argued that marriage emancipates a child from all parental control of its conduct, as well as such control by the school authorities; and that the marriage relation brings about views of life which should not be known to unmarried children; that a married child in the public schools will make known to its associates in schools such views, which will therefore be detrimental to the welfare of the school. We fail to appreciate the force of the argument. Marriage is a domestic relation highly favored by the law. When the relation is entered into with correct motives, the effect on the husband and wife is refining and elevating, rather than demoralizing. Pupils associating in school with a child occupying such a relation, it seems, would be benefited instead of harmed. And, furthermore, it is commendable in married persons of school age to desire to further pursue their education, and thereby become better fitted for the duties of life. And they are as much subject to the rules of the school as unmarried pupils, and punishable to the same extent for a breach of such rules."

In *Nutt* v. *Board of Education of the City of Goodland* (1929), 128 Kan. 507 (276 P. 1065), a writ of mandamus was granted against a board of education compelling it to admit the plaintiff's daughter to the public high school as a pupil despite a ruling of the board declining to admit her for the reason that she was married. . . .
The Kansas supreme court stated (p. 509):

. . . Other than the fact that she had a child conceived out of wedlock no sufficient reason is advanced for preventing her from attending school. Her child was born in wedlock and the fact that her husband may have abandoned her should not prevent her from gaining an education which would better fit her to meet the problems of life."

In *State, ex rel. Thompson,* v. *Marion County Board of Education* (1957), 202 Tenn. 29 (302 S.W. 2d 57), mandamus proceedings sought to compel restoration to enrollment of a high school student expelled for remainder of term during which she

married. The chancery court of Marion county denied the relief sought. The Tennessee supreme court stated:

* * *

"If the representations made to the county board of education by every high school principal in Marion county as to their respective observations and experiences on this subject is at all accurate, then married students, and by virtue of the psychological effect thereof, for a few months immediately following marriage, have a detrimental influence upon fellow students, hence, a detrimental effect upon the progress and efficiency of the school. Therefore, if these principals know whereof they speak, the attendance during such period of such married students in the schools is within the bounds of reasonable regulation by the board.

"We are accustomed to accept the testimony of experts in the various fields of human activity as to what is reasonably necessary for the welfare of the particular activity as to which this expert therein is testifying. No reason is suggested as to why this practice should not be followed when the witness is an expert in the field of operating public high schools. Certainly the principals of the high schools in question should be regarded by reason of training, experience, and observation as possessing particular knowledge as to the problem which they say is made by the marriage and uninterrupted attendance of students in their respective schools. * * *

"Boards of education, rather than courts, are charged with the important and difficult duty of operating the public schools. So, it is not a question of whether this or that individual judge or court considers a given regulation adopted by the board as expedient. The court's duty, regardless of its personal views, is to uphold the board's regulation unless it is generally viewed as being arbitrary and unreasonable. Any other policy would result in confusion detrimental to the progress and efficiency of our public school system. * * * The decree of the chancellor will be affirmed."

The students denied the right to full participation in school activities were "top-notch boys from the standpoint of their being good students in a school," and their behavior was "above reproach." They were denied educational privileges allowed to other students even though they had not "improperly conducted themselves about the school premises in any way since their marriage" or had "been guilty of any indiscreet language around the school, or in the presence of students, since their marriage."

The reasons advanced by the board, endeavoring to justify its action, are not persuasive or convincing. The board refers only to "possible bad influence" and assumes that married students enter "into another society" requiring all of their available time "to provide a proper family life and time spent in co-curricular activities is not conducive to this end."

Denying a married student the right to education, whether a partial denial such as denying the right to participate in extracurricular activities, or a complete denial such as expulsion or suspension, was not a reasonable exercise of authority by a school board or school officials.

There was no reason for denying plaintiffs the right to participate in extracurricular activities, other than the fact that they had married. The action of the school board was arbitrary and unreasonable.

The order of the lower court should be set aside. . . .

KAVANAGH, J. (*for affirmance*). . . .

What were the reasons given by the local school board in arriving at the decision to adopt such a rule? In addition to the reasons given in the formal resolution, Mrs. Sprague, president of the school board, in reply to a question as to some of the reasons the board had adopted this policy, said:

> "Well, we adopted the policy because of a possible bad influence on the unmarried students at that age when they were not in a formal classroom and in direct supervision of an instructor. Also, in these co-curricular activities they oftentimes get to a position where they are more or less of a hero and the others—particularly the younger students—might think that, or be influenced to think that, the thing to do was to get married. Also, that they themselves had entered, more or less, into responsibilities of adulthood; that they needed, maybe, extra time, whether they were a man or woman, for their responsibility as a homemaker and their scholastic work as well. Then one of the main points, I think, is that our students are minors and under their parents' guidance, and when they enter into a position of marriage they are more or less their own boss, which could cause problems. Now, it's been stated here that they are mingled with other children, which they are in this particular respect: In the classroom seniors are pretty much with seniors, juniors with juniors, and so on down, but in the band they can be any grade in high school, and on occasions even junior high, on certain projects."

Mr. Howard Weston, a member of the school board, testified as follows:

"Q. . . . What led you to consider and adopt this policy?

* * *

"A. Well, we were under the impression that when you get married you enter into another phase of life, and it was mainly we were looking

out for the protection of the other students, which number about 400. We weren't doing anything that would harm—we didn't feel that we were doing anything that would harm the basic education of the students involved.

NOTES
NOTE 1.

In re ROGERS
36 Misc. 2d 680, 234 N.Y.S. 2d 172 (1962)

LISTON F. COON, JUDGE.

The issue submitted to the Court by the parties to this proceeding is plainly this, "Do the compulsory education laws require school attendance by a female child under sixteen years of age, against her will, when that child is married and resides with and maintains a household for her husband?"

* * *

The real issue here, to this Court, goes beyond whether this child is in need of supervision or should be compelled to go to School against her will under the circumstances. There remains a very real problem as to the effect resulting from the association of a married fifteen-year-old in school with other children of the same age.

Times and the modes of people have changed since the Legislature first created compulsory education. It is doubtful that any thought was given then to the existence of a situation such as is now before the Court relative to school attendance.

The unquestioned advantages of school attendance by minors below sixteen years of age must therefore be equated against the harmful effects, if any, of forcing the association of a married fifteen-year-old female with school children of such young and impressionable ages, especially where the former is not disposed to attend school. It seems to the Court that the issue goes to the health, safety and welfare of more than just this respondent.

An analogy can be drawn to the cases which hold that children may be excluded from school unless they have first been vaccinated on the basis that the health and welfare of all the children are concerned. . . .

It seems ludicrous indeed that a school district can, on one hand, exclude pupils for not having been vaccinated against a practically non-existent disease and, on the other hand, compel a married fifteen-year-old to attend school and associate with other fifteen-year-olds. . . .

This Court feels that the purpose of the Family Court Act was not to adhere so much to legalistic theories as to balance the relative merits and demerits of domestic relationships within the framework of the facts presented in a given situation.

The Family Court Act recites that one of the purposes of the article dealing with juveniles is to provide a due process of law "for devising an appropriate order of disposition for any person adjudged a juvenile delinquent or in need of supervision." . . .

This Court interprets that statute to provide power to make an appropriate order in any case short of adjudication.

On the basis of the facts and circumstances of this case, the Court finds that respondent is not a person in need of supervision and the petition is accordingly dismissed.

NOTE 2.

STATE v. GANS
168 Ohio St. 174, 151 N.E. 2d 709 (1958)
cert. den. 359 U.S. 945 (1959)

MATTHIAS, JUDGE.

The complaints herein charge that defendants "did act in a way tending to cause the delinquency of * * * Kay Gans, age 11 * * * in that [said defendants] did consent to said child securing a marriage license and misrepresenting her age."

These complaints charge an offense under the provisions of Section 2151.41, Revised Code, which reads as follows:

> "No person shall abuse a child or aid, abet, induce, cause, encourage, or contribute to the dependency, neglect, or delinquency of a child or a ward of the juvenile court, *or act in a way tending to cause delinquency in such child.* No person shall aid, abet, induce, cause, or encourage a child or a ward of the court, committed to the custody of any person, department, public or private institution, to leave the custody of such person, department, public or private institution, without legal consent. Each day of such contribution to such dependency, neglect, or delinquency is a separate offense." (Emphasis added.)

* * *

[T]he complaints herein are based upon the *second* clause of the first sentence of Section 2151.41, referring to acts "*tending* to cause delinquency."

It is apparent that the purpose of that clause is to prevent a delinquency before it occurs rather than to await such delinquency and then punish the adult offender. The purpose of the clause is to avoid the undesirable result which might arise if an adult is permitted to pursue a course of conduct which tends to cause a child to become a delinquent. It is the old theory of preventive

medicine. A disease is much easier to prevent than to cure. . . .

* * *

Subdivision (D) of Section 2151.02, supra, provides that a delinquent child is one "*who so deports himself as to injure or endanger the morals or health of himself or others."*

Even if we were to assume for the purpose of argument that it is not probable that Kay's schooling will be frustrated by her marriage, and were to assume that she will continue to attend school, it is at once apparent that she will, by virtue of her marriage, have certain knowledge and attitudes which will be far more mature than those of her classmates and about which most of her classmates will, if at all, only have begun to think seriously. It is such knowledge and attitudes that, even in more mature years, tend to keep married groups and single groups separate.

It is unfortunate but true that, assuming that Kay *should* remain in school, the more successful her marriage would be the more it could tend to cause her to act so as to adversely affect the morals of her classmates.

NOTE 3.

FREUD, SIGMUND
Introductory Lectures on Psychoanalysis (1915)*

. . . No doubt you will feel inclined at first to deny . . . that children have anything that can be described as sexual life, . . . So allow me to begin by explaining to you the motives for your opposition, and then to present you with the sum of our observations. To suppose that children have no sexual life—sexual excitations and needs and a kind of satisfaction—but suddenly acquire it between the ages of twelve and fourteen, would (quite apart from any observations) be as improbable, and indeed senseless, biologically as to suppose that they brought no genitals with them into the world and only grew them at the time of puberty. What *does* awaken in them at this time is the reproductive function, which makes use for its purposes of physical and mental material already present. You are committing the error of confusing sexuality and reproduction and by doing so you are blocking your path to an understanding of sexuality, the perversions and the

---

* Reprinted from *The Standard Edition of the Complete Psychological Works of Sigmund Freud.* Vol. 16. London: The Hogarth Press, 1963 (pp. 311-13, 364-65). Used with permission of the publisher. Also from *A General Introduction to Psychoanalysis* by Sigmund Freud. By permission of LIVERIGHT, Publishers, N.Y. Copyright © R, 1963 by Joan Riviere.

neuroses. This error is, however, a tendentious one. Strangely enough, it has its source in the fact that you yourselves were once children and, while you were children, came under the influence of education. For society must undertake as one of its most important educative tasks to tame and restrict the sexual instinct when it breaks out as an urge to reproduction, and to subject it to an individual will which is identical with the bidding of society. It is also concerned to postpone the full development of the instinct till the child shall have reached a certain degree of intellectual maturity, for, with the complete irruption of the sexual instinct, educability is for practical purposes at an end. Otherwise, the instinct would break down every dam and wash away the laboriously erected work of civilization. Nor is the task of taming it ever an easy one ; its success is sometimes too small, sometimes too great. The motive of human society is in the last resort an economic one ; since it does not possess enough provisions to keep its members alive unless they work, it must restrict the number of its members and divert their energies from sexual activity to work. It is faced, in short, by the eternal, primaeval exigencies of life, which are with us to this day.

Experience must no doubt have taught the educators that the task of making the sexual will of the new generation tractable could only be carried out if they began to exercise their influence very early, if they did not wait for the storm of puberty but intervened already in the sexual life of children which is preparatory to it. For this reason almost all infantile sexual activities were forbidden to children and frowned upon ; an ideal was set up of making the life of children asexual, and in course of time things came to the point at which people really believed they were asexual and thereafter science pronounced this as its doctrine. To avoid contradicting their belief and their intentions, people since then overlook the sexual activities of children (no mean achievement) or are content in science to take a different view of them. Children are pure and innocent, and anyone who describes them otherwise can be charged with being an infamous blasphemer against the tender and sacred feelings of mankind.

Children are alone in not falling in with these conventions. They assert their animal rights with complete *naïveté* and give constant evidence that they have still to travel the road to purity. Strangely enough, the people who deny the existence of sexuality in children do not on that account become milder in their educational efforts but pursue the manifestations of what they deny exists with the utmost severity—describing them as 'childish naughtinesses'. It is also of the highest theoretical interest that the period of life which contradicts the prejudice of an asexual childhood most glaringly—the years of a child's life up to the age of five or six—is afterwards covered in most people by the veil of amnesia which is only completely torn away by an analytic enquiry, though it has been permeable earlier for the construction of a few dreams. . . .

* * *

[This has] a certain interest from the point of view of education, which plans the prevention of neuroses by intervening at an early stage in children's sexual development. So long as one focuses attention principally on infantile sexual experiences, one must suppose that one has done everything for the prophylaxis of nervous illnesses by taking care that the child's development is delayed and that it is spared experiences of the sort. We already know, however, that the preconditions for the causation of neuroses are complex and cannot be influenced in general if we take account of only a single factor. Strict protection of the young loses value because it is powerless against the constitutional factor. Besides, it is more difficult to carry out than educationists imagine and it brings with it two fresh dangers which must not be underestimated: the fact that it may achieve too much—that it may encourage an excess of sexual repression, with damaging results, and the fact that it may send the child out into life without any defence against the onrush of sexual demands that is to be looked for at puberty. Thus it remains extremely doubtful how far prophylaxis in childhood can be carried with advantage and whether an altered attitude to the immediate situation may not offer a better angle of approach for the prevention of neuroses.

NOTE 4.

FREUD, SIGMUND
Three Essays on the Theory of Sexuality (1905)*

. . . In so far as educators pay any attention at all to infantile sexuality, they behave exactly as though they shared our views as to the construction of the moral defensive forces at the cost of sexuality, and as though they knew that sexual activity makes a child ineducable: for they stigmatize every sexual manifestation by children as a 'vice', without being able to do much against it. . . .

---

* Reprinted in VII *The Standard Edition of the Complete Psychological Works of Sigmund Freud.* London: The Hogarth Press, 1953 (p. 179). Used with permission of the publisher and of Basic Books, Inc., New York.

NOTE 5.

FREUD, SIGMUND
Civilization and Its Discontents (1930)*

That the education of young people at the present day conceals from them the part which sexuality will play in their lives is not the only reproach which we are obliged to make against it. Its other sin is that it does not prepare them for the aggressiveness of which they are destined to become the objects. In sending the young out into life with such a false psychological orientation, education is behaving as though one were to equip people starting on a Polar expedition with summer clothing and maps of the Italian Lakes. In this it becomes evident that a certain misuse is being made of ethical demands. The strictness of those demands would not do so much harm if education were to say: 'This is how men ought to be, in order to be happy and to make others happy; but you have to reckon on their not being like that.' Instead of this the young are made to believe that everyone else fulfils those ethical demands—that it, that everyone else is virtuous. It is on this that the demand is based that the young, too, shall become virtuous.

C.
The Family as Perceived in Many Disciplines

1.

BY A PSYCHOANALYST

FREUD, SIGMUND
Civilization and Its Discontents (1930)†

*   *   *

The last, but certainly not the least important, of the characteristic features of civilization remains to be assessed; the manner in which the relationships of men to one another, their social relationships, are regulated—relationships which affect a person as a neighbour, as a source of help, as another person's sexual object, as a member of a family and of a State. Here it is especially difficult to keep clear of particular ideal demands and to see what is civilized in general. Perhaps we may begin by explaining that the element of civilization enters on the scene with the first attempt to regulate these social relationships. If the attempt were not made, the relationships would be subject to the arbitrary will of the individual: that is to say, the physically stronger man would decide them in the sense of his own interests and instinctual impulses. Nothing would be changed in this if this stronger man should in his turn meet someone even stronger than he. Human life in common is only made possible when a majority comes together which is stronger than any separate individual and which remains united against all separate individuals. The power of this community is then set up as 'right' in opposition to the power of the individual, which is condemned as 'brute force'. This replacement of the power of the individual by the power of a community constitutes the decisive step of civilization. The essence of it lies in the fact that the members of the community restrict themselves in their possibilities of satisfaction, whereas the individual knew no such restrictions. The first requisite of civilization, therefore, is that of justice—that is, the assurance that a law once made will not be broken in favour of an individual. This implies nothing as to the ethical value of such a law. The further course of cultural development seems to tend towards making the law no longer an expression of the will of a small community—a caste or a stratum of the population or a racial group—which, in its turn, behaves like a violent individual towards other, and perhaps more numerous, collections of people. The final outcome should be a rule of law to which all—except those who are not capable of entering a community—have contributed by a sacrifice of their instincts, and which leaves no one—again with the same exception—at the mercy of brute force.

The liberty of the individual is no gift of civilization. It was greatest before there was any civilization, though then, it is true, it had for the most part no value, since the individual was scarcely in a position to defend it. The development of civilization imposes restrictions on it, and justice demands that no one shall escape those restrictions. What makes itself felt in a human community as a desire for freedom may be their revolt against some existing injustice, and

* Reprinted in XXI *The Standard Edition of the Complete Psychological Works of Sigmund Freud*, London: The Hogarth Press, 1961 (p. 134 n.1). Used with permission of the Hogarth Press and W. W. Norton & Company, Inc. Copyright © 1961 by James Strachey. First American Edition 1962.

   † Reprinted in *The Standard Edition of the Complete Psychological Works*, Vol. 21, London: The Hogarth Press, 1961 (pp. 94-133). Used with permission of the Hogarth Press and W. W. Norton & Company, Inc. Copyright © 1961 by James Strachey, First American Edition 1962.

so many prove favourable to a further development of civilization ; it may remain compatible with civilization. But it may also spring from the remains of their original personality, which is still untamed by civilization and may thus become the basis in them of hostility to civilization. The urge for freedom, therefore, is directed against particular forms and demands of civilization or against civilization altogether. It does not seem as though any influence could induce a man to change his nature into a termite's. No doubt he will always defend his claim to individual liberty against the will of the group. A good part of the struggles of mankind centre round the single task of finding an expedient accommodation—one, that is, that will bring happiness—between this claim of the individual and the cultural claims of the group ; and one of the problems that touches the fate of humanity is whether such an accommodation can be reached by means of some particular form of civilization or whether this conflict is irreconcilable.

. . . This 'cultural frustration' dominates the large field of social relationships between human beings. As we already know, it is the cause of the hostility against which all civilizations have to struggle. It will also make severe demands on our scientific work, and we shall have much to explain here. It is not easy to understand how it can become possible to deprive an instinct of satisfaction. Nor is doing so without danger. If the loss is not compensated for economically, one can be certain that serious disorders will ensue.

But if we want to know what value can be attributed to our view that the development of civilization is a special process, comparable to the normal maturation of the individual, we must clearly attack another problem. We must ask ourselves to what influences the development of civilization owes its origin, how it arose, and by what its course has been determined.

The task seems an immense one, and it is natural to feel diffidence in the face of it. But here are such conjectures as I have been able to make.

After primal man had discovered that it lay in his own hands, literally, to improve his lot on earth by working, it cannot have been a matter of indifference to him whether another man worked with or against him. The other man acquired the value for him of a fellow-worker, with whom it was useful to live together. Even earlier, in his ape-like prehistory, man had adopted the habit of forming families, and the members of his family were probably his first helpers. One may suppose that the founding of families was connected with the fact that a moment came when the need for genital satisfaction no longer

made its appearance like a guest who drops in suddenly, and, after his departure, is heard of no more for a long time, but instead took up its quarters as a permanent lodger. When this happened, the male acquired a motive for keeping the female, or, speaking more generally, his sexual objects, near him ; while the female, who did not want to be separated from her helpless young, was obliged, in their interests, to remain with the stronger male. In this primitive family one essential feature of civilization is still lacking. The arbitrary will of its head, the father, was unrestricted. . . . In overpowering their father, the sons had made the discovery that a combination can be stronger than a single individual. The totemic culture is based on the restrictions which the sons had to impose on one another in order to keep this new state of affairs in being. The taboo-observances were the first 'right' or 'law'. The communal life of human beings had, therefore, a two-fold foundation: the compulsion to work, which was created by external necessity, and the power of love, which made the man unwilling to be deprived of his sexual object— the woman—and made the woman unwilling to be deprived of the part of herself which had been separated off from her—her child. . . .

[M]an's discovery that sexual (genital) love afforded him the strongest experiences of satisfaction, and in fact provided him with the prototype of all happiness, must have suggested to him that he should continue to seek the satisfaction of happiness in his life along the path of sexual relations and that he should make genital erotism the central point of his life. [I]n doing so he made himself dependent in a most dangerous way on a portion of the external world, namely, his chosen love-object, and exposed himself to extreme suffering if he should be rejected by that object or should lose it through unfaithfulness or death. For that reason the wise men of every age have warned us most emphatically against this way of life ; but in spite of this it has not lost its attraction for a great number of people.

* * *

The love which founded the family continues to operate in civilization both in its original form, in which it does not renounce direct sexual satisfaction, and in its modified form as aim-inhibited affection. In each, it continues to carry on its function of binding together considerable numbers of people, and it does so in a more intensive fashion than can be effected through the interest of work in common. The careless way in which language uses the word 'love' has its genetic justification. People give the name 'love' to the relation between a man and a woman whose genital needs have led them to found a family ; but they also give the name 'love' to the positive feelings between parents and children, and between the brothers and sisters of a family, although *we* are obliged to describe this as 'aim-inhibited love' or 'affection'. Love with an inhibited aim was in fact originally fully sensual love, and it is so still in man's unconscious. Both—fully sensual love and aim-inhibited love—extend outside the family and create new bonds with people who before were strangers. Genital love leads to the formation of new families, and aim-inhibited love to 'friendships' which become valuable from a cultural standpoint because they escape some of the limitations of genital love, as, for instance, its exclusiveness. But in the course of development the relation of love to civilization loses its unambiguity. On the one hand love comes into opposition to the interests of civilization ; on the other, civilization threatens love with substantial restrictions.

This rift between them seems unavoidable. The reason for it is not immediately recognizable. It expresses itself at first as a conflict between the family and the larger community to which the individual belongs. We have already perceived that one of the main endeavours of civilization is to bring people together into large unities. But the family will not give the individual up. The more closely the members of a family are attached to one another, the more often do they tend to cut themselves off from others, and the more difficult is it for them to enter into the wider circle of life. The mode of life in common which is phylogenetically the older, and which is the only one that exists in childhood, will not let itself be superseded by the cultural mode of life which has been acquired later. Detaching himself from his family becomes a task that faces every young person, and society often helps him in the solution of it by means of puberty and initiation rites. We get the impression that these are difficulties which are inherent in all psychical—and, indeed, at bottom, in all organic—development.

Furthermore, women soon come into opposition to civilization and display their retarding and restraining influence—those very women who, in the beginning, laid the foundations of civilization by the claims of their love. Women represent the interests of the family and of sexual life. The work of civilization has become increasingly the business of men, it confronts them with ever more difficult tasks and compels them to carry out instinctual sublimations of which women are little capable. Since a man does not have unlimited quantities of psychical energy at his disposal, he has to accomplish his tasks by making an expedient distribution of his libido. What he employs for cultural aims he to a great extent withdraws from women and sexual life. His constant association with men, and his dependence on his relations with them, even estrange him from his duties as a husband and father. Thus the woman finds herself forced into the background by the claims of civilization and she adopts a hostile attitude towards it.

The tendency on the part of civilization to restrict sexual life is no less clear than its other tendency to expand the cultural unit. Its first, totemic, phase already brings with it the prohibition against an incestuous choice of object, and this is perhaps the most drastic mutilation which man's erotic life has in all time experienced. Taboos, laws and customs impose further restrictions, which affect both men and women. Not all civilizations go equally far in this ; and the economic structure of the society also influences the amount of sexual freedom that remains. Here, as we already know, civilization is obeying the laws of economic necessity, since a large amount of the psychical energy which it uses for its own purposes has to be withdrawn from sexuality. In this respect civilization behaves towards sexuality as a people or a stratum of its population does which has subjected another one to its exploitation. Fear of revolt by the suppressed elements drives it to stricter precautionary measures. A high-water mark in such a development has been reached in our Western European civilization. A cultural community is perfectly justified, psychologically, in starting by proscribing manifestations of the sexual life of children, for there would be no prospect of curbing the sexual lusts of adults if the ground had not been prepared for it in childhood. But such a community cannot in any way be justified in going to the length of actually *disavowing* such easily demonstrable, and, indeed, striking phenomena. As regards the sexually mature individual, the choice of an object is restricted to the opposite sex, and most extra-genital satisfactions are forbidden as perversions. The requirement, demonstrated in these prohibitions, that there shall be a single kind of sexual life for everyone, disregards the dissimilarities, whether innate or acquired, in the sexual constitution of human beings ; it cuts off a fair number of them from sexual enjoyment, and so becomes the source of serious injustice. The result of such restrictive measures might be that in people who are normal—who are not prevented by their constitution—the whole of their sexual interests would flow without loss into the channels that are left open. But heterosexual genital love, which has remained exempt from outlawry, is itself restricted by further limitations, in the shape of insistence upon legitimacy and monogamy.

Present-day civilization makes it plain that it will only permit sexual relationships on the basis of a solitary, indissoluble bond between one man and one woman, and that it does not like sexuality as a source of pleasure in its own right and is only prepared to tolerate it because there is so far no substitute for it as a means of propagating the human race.

This, of course, is an extreme picture. Everybody knows that it has proved impossible to put it into execution, even for quite short periods. Only the weaklings have submitted to such an extensive encroachment upon their sexual freedom, and stronger natures have only done so subject to a compensatory condition, which will be mentioned later. Civilized society has found itself obliged to pass over in silence many transgressions which, according to its own rescripts, it ought to have punished. But we must not err on the other side and assume that, because it does not achieve all its aims, such an attitude on the part of society is entirely innocuous. The sexual life of civilized man is notwithstanding severely impaired; it sometimes gives the impression of being in process of involution as a function, just as our teeth and hair seem to be as organs. One is probably justified in assuming that its importance as a source of feelings of happiness, and therefore in the fulfilment of our aim in life, has sensibly diminished. Sometimes one seems to perceive that it is not only the pressure of civilization but something in the nature of the function itself which denies us full satisfaction and urges us along other paths. This may be wrong; it is hard to decide.

* * *

We have treated the difficulty of cultural development as a general difficulty of development by tracing it to the inertia of the libido, to its disinclination to give up an old position for a new one. We are saying much the same thing when we derive the antithesis between civilization and sexuality from the circumstance that sexual love is a relationship between two individuals in which a third can only be superfluous or disturbing, whereas civilization depends on relationships between a considerable number of individuals. When a love-relationship is at its height there is no room left for any interest in the environment; a pair of lovers are sufficient to themselves, and do not even need the child they have in common to make them happy. In no other case does Eros so clearly betray the core of his being, his purpose of making one out of more than one; but when he has achieved this in the proverbial way through the love of two human beings, he refuses to go further.

So far, we can quite well imagine a cultural community consisting of double individuals like this, who, libidinally satisfied in themselves, are connected with one another through the bonds of common work and common interests. If this were so, civilization would not have to withdraw any energy from sexuality. But this desirable state of things does not, and never did, exist. Reality shows us that civilization is not content with the ties we have so far allowed it. It aims at binding the members of the community together in a libidinal way as well and employs every means to that end. It favours every path by which strong identifications can be established between the members of the community, and it summons up aim-inhibited libido on the largest scale so as to strengthen the communal bond by relations of friendship. In order for these aims to be fulfilled, a restriction upon sexual life is unavoidable. But we are unable to understand what the necessity is which forces civilization along this path and which causes its antagonism to sexuality. There must be some disturbing factor which we have not yet discovered.

The clue may be supplied by one of the ideal demands, as we have called them, of civilized society. It runs: 'Thou shalt love thy neighbour as thyself.' It is known throughout the world and is undoubtedly older than Christianity, which puts it forward as its proudest claim. Yet it is certainly not very old; even in historical times it was still strange to mankind. Let us adopt a naive attitude towards it, as though we were hearing it for the first time; we shall be unable then to suppress a feeling of surprise and bewilderment. Why should we do it? What good will it do us? . . .

* * *

The . . . truth . . . which people are so ready to disavow, is that men are not gentle creatures who want to be loved, and who at the most can defend themselves if they are attacked; they are, on the contrary, creatures among whose instinctual endowments is to be reckoned a powerful share of aggressiveness. As a result, their neighbour is for them not only a potential helper or sexual object, but also someone who tempts them to satisfy their aggressiveness on him, to exploit his capacity for work without compensation, to use him sexually without his consent, to seize his possessions, to humiliate him, to cause him pain, to torture and to kill him. *Homo homini lupus.* Who, in the face of all his experience of life and of history, will have the courage to dispute this assertion? As a rule this cruel aggressiveness waits for some provocation or puts itself at the service of some other purpose, whose goal might also have been reached by milder measures. In circumstances that are favourable to it, when the mental counter-forces which ordinarily inhibit it are out of action, it also manifests itself spontaneously and reveals man as a savage beast to whom consideration towards his own kind is something alien. . . .

The existence of this inclination to aggression, which we can detect in ourselves and justly assume to be present in others, is the factor which disturbs our relations with our neighbour and which forces civilization into such a high expenditure [of energy]. In consequence of this primary mutual hostility of human beings, civilized society is perpetually threatened with disintegration. The interest of work in common would not hold it together; instinctual passions are stronger than reasonable interests. Civilization has to use its utmost efforts in order to set limits to man's aggressive instincts and to hold the manifestations of them in check by psychical reaction-formations. Hence, therefore, the use of methods intended to incite people into identifications and aim-inhibited relationships of love, hence the restriction upon sexual life, and hence too the ideal's commandment to love one's neighbour as oneself—a commandment which is really justified by the fact that nothing else runs so strongly counter to the original nature of man. In spite of every effort, these endeavours of civilization have not so far achieved very much. It hopes to prevent the crudest excesses of brutal violence by itself assuming the right to use violence against criminals, but the law is not able to lay hold of the more cautious and refined manifestations of human aggressiveness. The time comes when each one of us has to give up as illusions the expectations which, in his youth, he pinned upon his fellowmen, and when he may learn how much difficulty and pain has been added to his life by their ill-will. At the same time, it would be unfair to reproach civilization with trying to eliminate strife and competition from human activity. These things are undoubtedly indispensable. But opposition is not necessarily enmity; it is merely misused and made an *occasion* for enmity.

*   *   *

It is clearly not easy for men to give up the satisfaction of this inclination to aggression. They do not feel comfortable without it. The advantage which a comparatively small cultural group offers of allowing this instinct an outlet in the form of hostility against intruders is not to be despised. It is always possible to bind together a considerable number of people in love, so long as there are other people left over to receive the manifestations of their aggressiveness. . . .

If civilization imposes such great sacrifices not only on man's sexuality but on his aggressivity, we can understand better why it is hard for him to be happy in that civilization. In fact, primitive man was better off in knowing no restrictions of instinct. To counterbalance this, his prospects of enjoying this happiness for any length of time were very slender. Civilized man has exchanged a portion of his possibilities of happiness for a portion of security. . . .

*   *   *

. . . I return to my view that [aggression] constitutes the greatest impediment to civilization. . . .

*   *   *

. . . What means does civilization employ in order to inhibit the aggressiveness which opposes it, to make it harmless, to get rid of it, perhaps? [The] aggressiveness is introjected, internalized; it is, in point of fact, sent back to where it came from—that is, it is directed towards his own ego. There it is taken over by a portion of the ego, which sets itself over against the rest of the ego as super-ego, and which now, in the form of 'conscience', is ready to put into action against the ego the same harsh aggressiveness that the ego would have liked to satisfy upon other, extraneous individuals. The tension between the harsh super-ego and the ego that is subjected to it, is called by us the sense of guilt; it expresses itself as a need for punishment. Civilization, therefore, obtains mastery over the individual's dangerous desire for aggression by weakening and disarming it and by setting up an agency within him to watch over it, like a garrison in a conquered city.

*   *   *

[W]e know of two origins of the sense of guilt: one arising from fear of an authority, and the other, later on, arising from fear of the super-ego. The first insists upon a renunciation of instinctual satisfactions; the second, as well as doing this, presses for punishment, since the continuance of the forbidden wishes cannot be concealed from the super-ego. We have also learned how the severity of the super-ego—the demands of conscience—is to be understood. It is simply a continuation of the severity of the external authority, to which it has succeeded and which it has in part replaced. We now see in what relationship the renunciation of instinct stands to the sense of guilt. Originally, renunciation of instinct was the result of fear of an external authority: one renounced one's satisfactions in order not to lose its love. If one has carried out this renunciation, one is, as it were, quits with the authority and no sense of guilt should remain. But with fear of the super-ego the case is different. Here, instinctual renunciation is not enough, for the wish persists and cannot be concealed from the super-ego. Thus, in spite of the renunciation that has been made, a sense of guilt comes about. This constitutes a great economic disadvantage in the erection of a super-ego, or, as we may put it, in the formation of a conscience. Instinctual renunciation now no longer has a completely liberating effect; virtuous continence is no longer rewarded with the assurance of love. A threatened external unhappiness—loss of love and punishment on the part of the external authority—has been exchanged for a permanent internal unhappiness, for the tension of the sense of guilt.

* * *

[I]f the human sense of guilt goes back to the killing of the primal father, that was after all a case of 'remorse'.* Are we to assume that [at that time] a conscience and a sense of guilt were not, as we have presupposed, in existence before the deed? If not, where, in this case, did the remorse come from? There is no doubt that this case should explain the secret of the sense of guilt to us and put an end to our difficulties. And I believe it does. This remorse was the result of the primordial ambivalence of feeling towards the father. His sons hated him, but they loved him, too. After their hatred had been satisfied by their act of aggression, their love came to the fore in their remorse for the deed. It set up the super-ego by identification with the father; it gave that agency the father's power, as though as a punishment for the deed of aggression they had carried out against him, and it created the restrictions which were intended to prevent a repetition of the deed. And since the inclination to aggressiveness against the father was repeated in the following generations, the sense of guilt, too, persisted, and it was reinforced once more by every piece of aggressiveness that was suppressed and carried over to the super-ego. Now, I think, we can at last grasp two things perfectly clearly: the part played by love in the origin of conscience and the fatal inevitability of the sense of guilt. Whether one has killed one's father or has abstained from doing so is not really the

decisive thing. One is bound to feel guilty in either case, for the sense of guilt is an expression of the conflict due to ambivalence, of the eternal struggle between Eros and the instinct of destruction or death. This conflict is set going as soon as men are faced with the task of living together. So long as the community assumes no other form than that of the family, the conflict is bound to express itself in the Oedipus complex, to establish the conscience and to create the first sense of guilt. When an attempt is made to widen the community, the same conflict is continued in forms which are dependent on the past; and it is strengthened and results in a further intensification of the sense of guilt. Since civilization obeys an internal erotic impulsion which causes human beings to unite in a closely-knit group, it can only achieve this aim through an ever-increasing reinforcement of the sense of guilt. What began in relation to the father is completed in relation to the group. If civilization is a necessary course of development from the family to humanity as a whole, then—as a result of the inborn conflict arising from ambivalence, of the eternal struggle between the trends of love and death—there is inextricably bound up with it an increase of the sense of guilt, which will perhaps reach heights that the individual finds hard to tolerate. . . .

2.
BY A PROFESSOR OF LAW

LLEWELLYN, KARL N.

Education and the Family: Certain Unsolved Problems*

[D]espite the huge expansion of officially organized government, the family remains an organization with its internal legal, governmental, political side, in which the basic lessons are learned even when they are not consciously taught; and this holds true even though as against the outside world the individual adult is supposed to operate today largely as an individual and no longer primarily as a member of an organized, politically recognized family unit. Indeed a discrepancy here presents the unsolved problem. For if the family is the political unit or one main political unit, then rearing in the family almost of necessity produces conscious political education—consider the situation in a city ward where a numerous solid bloc of family votes is a manipulable asset. But, where the governmental scheme is viewed primarily from the standpoint of the individual,

---

* . . . When one has a sense of guilt after having committed a misdeed, and because of it, the feeling should more properly be called *remorse*. It relates only to a deed that has been done, and, of course, it presupposes that a *conscience*—the readiness to feel guilty—was already in existence before the deed took place. Remorse of this sort can, therefore, never help us to discover the origin of concience and of the sense of guilt in general. . . .

---

* From "Education and the Family" by Karl N. Llewellyn in *The Family: Its Function and Destiny*, Revised Ed., edited by Ruth Nanda Anshen (Harper & Bros., 1959), pp. 334-35.

the family's contribution to legal and political education is likely to drop out of sight.

Order backed by authority, fairness in procedure plus decency in result, reasonable compromise of conflicting interests and desires ; a hearing in a trial, a voice by petition or by vote in regard to any change ; the pledged word kept and to be kept, acquired rights respected, but each of these things limited by recognition of the meaning of materially changed circumstance, each (like the action of authority) taking account of the full range of interests within the team and of the felt needs of the whole team as such—these are the legal, governmental, and political lessons to be had from the modern family. The resulting attitudes have the same power of carry-over as has the attitude of fair play ; like fair play, too, they have the priceless value, so lacking in most of the "finer" values as we learn them, of ready carry-over into application to outsiders. But to be seen and felt as general attitudes, as general goals of all types of law and government of *any* team, up to and including a world in which team-consciousness is still to build, such attitudes and standards require that a touch of conscious instruction be added to mere experience. For mere experience is too likely to concentrate its lesson upon what the family does and should do and to limit that lesson to one in a "family life" as contrasted with great government and official law, and, above all, with politics.

The problem is unsolved, and likely to remain so into the indefinite future, because the legal and governmental aspects and implications of the family remain as yet unexplored, unseen, too obvious to stir attention. Of course, should an effort ever be made to highlight them and bring them to bear upon the problem, it would be no less obvious that like the moral values of family education they rest first on the principle of learning by doing and only second on conscious instruction. And by such a process of doing they are effectively inculcated in any crisis case. The pained outrage of tone in "Dad—don't I get a chance to say *my* say?" is fundamental education for Dad, in the meaning of the term "due process of law". The fact that a promised trip to the circus is called off because Mummy is sick is fundamental education in the meaning of contract as limited by supervening circumstance and the welfare of a whole. If the prohibition on going into the jam closet is literally adhered to though a jar of jam has been fished out with a sand shovel, there is education for the young fisherman in the fact that rules have purposes, that law is *for* something, and that what rules and law are for is an inherent part of them ; but it is education for parents, too, in the need for making

the purpose clear and the prescribed measure definite as to its purpose.

* * *

3.

BY A POLITICAL ECONOMIST

ROUSSEAU, JEAN JACQUES
The Social Contract (1762)*

I mean to inquire if, in the civil order, there can be any sure and legitimate rule of administration, men being taken as they are and laws as they might be. . . .

* * *

Man is born free ; and everywhere he is in chains. One thinks himself the master of others, and still remains a greater slave than they. How did this change come about? . . .

* * *

The most ancient of all societies, and the only one that is natural, is the family ; and even so the children remain attached to the father only so long as they need him for their preservation. As soon as this need ceases, the natural bond is dissolved. The children, released from the obedience they owed to the father, and the father, released from the care he owed his children, return equally to independence. If they remain united, they continue so no longer naturally, but voluntarily ; and the family itself is then maintained only by convention.

This common liberty results from the nature of man. His first law is to provide for his own preservation, his first cares are those which he owes to himself ; and, as soon as he reaches years of discretion, he is the sole judge of the proper means of preserving himself, and consequently becomes his own master.

The family then may be called the first model of political societies : the ruler corresponds to the father, and the people to the children ; and all, being born free and equal, alienate their liberty only for their own advantage. The whole difference is that, in the family, the love of the father for his children repays him for the care he takes of them, while, in the State, the pleasure of commanding takes the place of the love which the chief cannot have for the peoples under him.

* * *

* Reprinted in Vol. 38, Great Books. Chicago: Encyclopaedia Britannica, Inc. 1952 (pp. 387-388). Translated by G. D. H. Cole for Everyman's Library. Used with permission of E. P. Dutton and Co. and J. M. Dent and Sons Ltd.

C. THE FAMILY AS PERCEIVED IN MANY DISCIPLINES

4.

BY A PHILOSOPHER

RUSSELL, BERTRAND

Marriage and Morals (1929)*

[T]he family . . . affords the only rational basis for limitations of sexual freedom. . . . The subject we have now to consider is the degree of stability in sex relations demanded by the interests of children. That is to say, we have to consider the family as a reason for stable marriage. This question is far from simple. It is clear that the gain which a child derives from being a member of a family depends upon what the alternative is: there might be institutions for foundlings so admirable that they would be preferable to the great majority of families. We have also to consider whether any essential part in family life is played by the father, since it is only on his account that feminine virtue has been thought essential to the family. We have to examine the effect of the family upon the individual psychology of the child—a subject dealt with in a somewhat sinister spirit by Freud. We have to consider the effect of economic systems in increasing or diminishing the importance of the father. We have to ask ourselves whether we should wish to see the State taking the place of the father, or possibly even, as Plato suggested, of both father and mother. And even supposing that we decide in favour of both father and mother as affording the best environment for the child in normal cases, we still have to consider the very numerous instances in which one or other is unfit for the responsibility of parenthood, or the two are so incompatible that separation is desirable in the interests of the child.

* * *

The family is a pre-human institution, whose biological justification is that the help of the father during pregnancy and lactation tends to the survival of the young. . . . The primitive father does not know that the child has any biological connection with himself; the child is the offspring of the female whom he loves. This fact he knows, since he has seen the child born, and it is this fact that produces the instinctive tie between him and the child. At this stage he sees no biological importance in safeguarding his wife's virtue, although no doubt he will feel instinctive jealousy if her infidelity is thrust upon

his notice. At this stage, also, he has no sense of property in the child. The child is the property of his wife and his wife's brother, but his own relation with the child is merely one of affection.

With the development of intelligence, however, man is bound sooner or later to eat of the tree of the knowledge of good and evil. He becomes aware that the child springs from his seed, and he must therefore make sure of his wife's virtue. The wife and the child become his property, and at a certain level of economic development they may be very valuable property. He brings religion to bear, to cause his wife and children to have a sense of duty towards him. With children this is especially important, for although he is stronger than they are when they are young, the time will come when he will be decrepit while they will be in the vigour of manhood. At this stage, it is vitally necessary to his happiness that they should reverence him. The Commandment on this subject is deceitfully phrased. It should run: "Honour thy father and thy mother that *their* days may be long in the land." The horror of parricide which one finds in early civilization shows how great was the temptation to be overcome; for a crime which we cannot imagine ourselves committing, such as cannibalism for example, fails to inspire us with any genuine horror.

It was the economic conditions of early pastoral and agricultural communities that brought the family to its fullest fruition. Slave labour was, for most people, unavailable, and therefore the easiest way to acquire labourers was to breed them. In order to make sure that they should work for their father, it was necessary that the institution of the family should be sanctified by the whole weight of religion and morals. Gradually primogeniture extended family unity to collateral branches, and enhanced the power of the head of the family. Kingship and aristocracy depend essentially upon this order of ideas, and even divinity, since Zeus was the father of gods and men.

Up to this point, the growth of civilization had increased the strength of the family. From this point onward, however, an opposite movement has taken place, until the family in the Western world has become a mere shadow of what it was. The causes which brought about the decay of the family were partly economic and partly cultural. In its fullest development, it was never very suitable either to urban populations or to seafaring people. . . .

* * *

The decay of the family in quite recent times is undoubtedly to be attributed in the main to the industrial revolution, but it had already begun

* Reprinted from pp. 134-38, 141-47, 148-49, and 171-74 by permission of the publishers: Liveright, New York, and George Allen and Unwin, London. Copyright © R, 1957, by Bertrand Russell.

before that event, and its beginnings were inspired by individualistic theory. Young people asserted the right to marry according to their own wishes, not according to the commands of their parents. The habit of married sons living in their father's house died out. It became customary for sons to leave home to earn their living as soon as their education was ended. So long as small children could work in factories, they remained a source of livelihood to their parents until they died of overwork; but the Factory Acts put an end to this form of exploitation, in spite of the protests of those who lived on it. From being a means of livelihood, children came to be a financial burden. At this stage, contraceptives became known, and the fall in the birthrate began. There is much to be said for the view that the average man in all ages has had as many children as it paid him to have, no more and no less. At any rate this seems to be true of Australian aborigines, Lancashire cotton operatives, and British peers. . . .

The position of the family in modern times has been weakened even in its last stronghold by the action of the State. In its great days, the family consisted of an elderly patriarch, a large number of grown-up sons, their wives and their children—perhaps their children's children—all living together in one house, all co-operating as one economic unit, all combined against the outer world as strictly as the citizens of a militaristic modern nation. Nowadays the family is reduced to the father and mother and their younger children, but even young children, by the decree of the State, spend most of their time at school, and learn there what the State thinks good for them, not what their parents desire. (To this, however, religion is a partial exception.) So far from having power of life and death over his children, as the Roman father had, the . . . father is liable to be prosecuted for cruelty if he treats his child as most fathers a hundred years ago would have thought essential for a moral upbringing. The State provides medical and dental care, and feeds the child if the parents are destitute. The functions of the father are thus reduced to a minimum, since most of them have been taken over by the State. With advancing civilization, this is inevitable. In a primitive state of affairs, the father was necessary, as he is among birds and anthropoid apes, for economic reasons, and also to protect the young and their mother from violence. The latter function was long ago taken over by the State. A child whose father is dead is no more likely to be murdered than one whose father is living. The economic function of the father can be performed, in the well-to-do classes, more efficiently if he is dead than if he is living, since he can leave his money to his children,

without having to use up part of it on his own maintenance. Among those who depend upon earned money, the father is still economically useful, but so far as wage-earners are concerned this utility is being continually diminished by the humanitarian sentiment of the community, which insists that the child should receive a certain minimum of care, even if he has no father to pay for it. It is in the middle classes that the father is at present of most importance, for so long as he lives and earns a good income, he can give his children those advantages in the way of an expensive education which will enable them in their turn to preserve their social and economic status, whereas if he dies while the children are still young, there is a considerable chance that they may sink in the social scale. The precariousness of this state of affairs is, however, much diminished by the custom of life insurance, by means of which, even in the professional classes, a prudent father can do much to diminish his own utility.

In the modern world, the great majority of fathers are too hard-worked to see much of their own children. In the morning they are too busy getting off to work to have time for conversation; in the evening, when they get home, the children are (or ought to be) in bed. One hears stories of children who only know of their father as "that man who comes for the week-end". In the serious business of caring for the child, fathers can seldom participate; in fact this duty is shared between mothers and education authorities. It is true that the father often has a strong affection for his children in spite of the small amount of time that he can spend with them. On any Sunday, in any of the poorer quarters of London, large numbers of fathers may be seen with their young children, evidently rejoicing in the brief opportunity of getting to know them. But whatever may be the case from the father's point of view, from that of the child this is a play relation, without serious importance.

In the upper and professional classes, the custom is to leave children to nurses while they are young, and then send them to a boarding-school. The mother chooses the nurse, and the father chooses the school, so that they preserve intact their sense of power over their offspring, which working-class parents are not allowed to do. But so far as intimate contact is concerned, there is less, as a rule, between mother and child among the well-to-do than among wage-earners. The father has a play relation with his children in holidays, but has no more part in their real education than a working-class father. He has, of course, economic responsibility and the power of deciding where they shall be educated, but his personal contact with them is not usually of a very serious kind.

When a child reaches adolescence, there is very apt to be a conflict between parents and child, since the latter considers himself to be by now quite capable of managing his own affairs, while the former are filled with parental solicitude, which is often a disguise for love of power. Parents consider, usually, that the various moral problems which arise in adolescence are peculiarly their province. The opinions they express, however, are so dogmatic that the young seldom confide in them, and usually go their own way in secret. It cannot be said, therefore, that at this stage most parents are much use.

So far we have been considering only the weakness of the modern family. We must now consider in what respects it is still strong.

The family is important at the present day, more through the emotions with which it provides parents than for any other reason. Parental emotions in men as well as in women are perhaps more important than any others in their power of influencing action. Both men and women who have children as a rule regulate their lives largely with reference to them, and children cause perfectly ordinary men and women to act unselfishly in certain ways, of which perhaps life insurance is the most definite and measurable. The economic man of a hundred years ago was never provided in the textbooks with children, though undoubtedly he had them in the imagination of the economists, who, however, took it for granted that the general competition which they postulated did not exist between fathers and sons. Clearly, the psychology of life insurance lies wholly outside the cycle of motives dealt with in the classical political economy. Yet that political economy was not psychologically autonomous, since the desire for property is very intimately bound up with parental feelings. Rivers went so far as to suggest that all private property is derivative from family feelings. He mentions certain birds which have private property in land during the breeding season, but at no other time. I think most men can testify that they become far more acquisitive when they have children than they were before. This effect is one which is, in the popular sense, instinctive, that is to say, it is spontaneous, and springs from subconscious sources. I think that in this respect the family has been of incalculable importance to the economic development of mankind, and is still a dominating factor among those who are sufficiently prosperous to have a chance to save money.

There is apt to be on this point a curious misunderstanding between fathers and children. A man who works hard in business will tell his idle son that he has slaved all his life solely for the benefit of his children. The son, on the contrary, would much rather have a fiver and a little kindness now than a fortune when his father dies. The son notices, moreover, quite correctly, that his father goes to the City from force of habit and not the least from parental affection. The son is therefore as sure that his father is a humbug as the father is that his son is a wastrel. The son, however, is unjust. He sees his father in middle age, when all his habits are formed, and he does not realize the obscure, unconscious forces which led to the formation of those habits. The father, perhaps, may have suffered from poverty in his youth, and when his first child was born his instinct may have made him swear that no child of his should endure what he had had to suffer. Such a resolution is important and vital, and therefore need never be repeated in consciousness, since without the need of repetition it dominates conduct ever after. This is one way in which the family is still a very powerful force.

From the point of view of the young child, the important thing about parents is that from them the child gets an affection not given to anyone else except his brothers and sisters. This is partly good and partly bad. . . .

* * *

Perhaps the greatest importance of the family, in these days of contraceptives, is that it preserves the habit of having children. If a man were going to have no property in his child, and no opportunity of affectionate relations with it, he would see little point in begetting it. It would, of course, with a slight change in our economic institutions, be possible to have families consisting of mothers only, but it is not such families that I am considering at the present time, since they afford no motives for sexual virtue, and it is the family as a reason for stable marriage that concerns us in the present work. It may be—and indeed I think it far from improbable—that the father will be completely eliminated before long, except among the rich (supposing the rich to be not abolished by Socialism). In that case, women will share their children with the State, not with an individual father. They will have such number of children as they desire, and the fathers will have no responsibility. Indeed, if the mothers are at all of a promiscuous disposition, fatherhood may be impossible to determine. But if this comes about, it will make a profound change in the psychology and activities of men, far more profound, I believe, than most people would suppose. Whether the effect upon men would be good or bad, I do not venture to say. It would eliminate from their lives the only emotion equal in importance to sex love. It would make sex love itself more trivial. It would make it far more difficult to take an interest in anything after one's own death. It would make men less active and probably cause them to retire earlier from work. It would diminish their interest in history and their sense of the continuity of historical tradition. At the same time it would eliminate the most fierce and savage passion to which civilized men are liable, namely the fury which is felt in defending wives and children from attacks by coloured populations. I think it would make men less prone to war, and probably less acquisitive. To strike a balance between good and bad effects is scarcely possible, but it is evident that the effects would be profound and far-reaching. The patriarchal family, therefore, is still important, although it is doubtful how long it will remain so.

* * *

The substitution of the State for the father, so far as it has yet gone in the West, is in the main a great advance. It has immensely improved the health of the community and the general level of education. It has diminished cruelty to children, and has made impossible such sufferings as those of David Copperfield. It may be expected to continue to raise the general level of physical health and intellectual attainment, especially by preventing the worst evils resulting from the family system where it goes wrong. There are, however, very grave dangers in the substitution of the State for the family. Parents, as a rule, are fond of their children, and do not regard them merely as material for political schemes. The State cannot be expected to have this attitude. The actual individuals who come in contact with children in institutions, for example school-teachers, may, if they are not too overworked and underpaid, retain something of the personal feeling that parents have. But teachers have little power: the power belongs to administrators. The administrators never see the children whose lives they control, and being of an administrative type (since otherwise they would not have obtained the posts they occupy), they are probably peculiarly apt to regard human beings, not as ends in themselves, but as material for some kind of construction. Moreover, the administrator invariably likes uniformity. It is convenient for statistics and pigeon-holing, and if it is the "right" sort of uniformity it means the existence of a large number of human beings of the sort that he considers desirable. Children handed over to the mercy of institutions will therefore tend to be all alike, while the few who cannot conform to the recognized pattern will suffer persecution, not only

from their fellows, but from the authorities. This means that many of those who have the greatest potentialities will be harried and tortured until their spirit is broken. It means that the vast majority, who succeed in conforming, will become very sure of themselves, very prone to persecution, and very incapable of listening patiently to any new idea. Above all, so long as the world remains divided into competing militaristic States, the substitution of public bodies for parents in education means an intensification of what is called patriotism, i.e. a willingness to indulge in mutual extermination without a moment's hesitation, whenever the Governments feel so inclined. Undoubtedly patriotism, so-called, is the gravest danger to which civilization is at present exposed, and anything that increases its virulence is more to be dreaded than plague, pestilence, and famine. At present young people have a divided loyalty, on the one hand to their parents, on the other to the State. If it should happen that their sole loyalty was to the State, there is grave reason to fear that the world would become even more bloodthirsty than it is at present. I think, therefore, that so long as the problem of internationalism remains unsolved, the increasing share of the State in the education and care of children has dangers so grave as to outweigh its undoubted advantages.

[T]he substitution of the State for the father would be a gain to civilization if the State were international, but that so long as the State is national and militaristic it represents an increase of the risk to civilization from war. The family is decaying fast, and internationalism is growing slowly. The situation, therefore, is one which justifies grave apprehensions. Nevertheless, it is not hopeless, since internationalism may grow more quickly in the future than it has done in the past. Fortunately, perhaps, we cannot foretell the future, and we have therefore the right to hope, if not to expect, that it may be an improvement upon the present.

5.

BY A PSYCHOANALYST

FLUGEL, J. C.

The Psychoanalytic Study of the Family (1921)*

[T]he causes which have led to the strong attachment of the individual to the family are probably connected with certain necessary con-

* London: The Hogarth Press and The Institute of Psychoanalysis, 1950 (pp. 218-220). Reprinted with permission of the publisher and The Humanities Press, Inc.

ditions of human growth and development—the long period of helplessness and immaturity, the dependence upon others (and especially the parents) for the very necessaries of life, the need to learn from others, the need for an early arousal and outward direction of the love impulse, *etc*. The causes which underlie the tendency away from the family—such as the need of casting off the dependence on the family in order to attain a full measure of individuality, the antagonism between the family attachments and the wider social bonds, the value of sexual sublimation for the advance of culture, the possible dysgenic effects of inbreeding—these are in the main connected with less pressing and immediate conditions of existence ; conditions which are no doubt of great importance for the ultimate fate of the individual and the race, but which are not essential for the immediate preservation and growth of the individual in his early life, and which frequently involve a diminution rather than an increase in immediate benefit or pleasure ; representing, as they do, biological values of a higher and more complex order, which come into operation only when those of a more primitive kind have been attained.

If this is so, it would seem fairly clear that our practical efforts must on the whole be directed to aid the process of weaning the individual from his family attachments rather than to any attempt at preventing or destroying these attachments themselves. The tendencies that bind the individual to the family are probably too deeply rooted in Man's nature to yield to any such direct attack ; and in any case, in spite of a character in some respects archaic, it is almost certain that they still perform a necessary and beneficial part in the process of psychical development—a part for which no adequate substitute could easily be found ; so that it would be undesirable to eliminate the operation of these tendencies, even if such elimination were within the bounds of possibility. Thus it would seem that all schemes and attempts that have been made, from Plato onwards (and probably long before him), with a view to preventing the development of the feelings that centre in and are aroused through connection with the family, are doomed to failure: —practical failure, because these feelings are too strong, too intimate and essential a part of human nature to be successfully and permanently inhibited by any alteration of environment ; moral failure, because the development of certain of the most important aspects of human character are, in their origin and first appearance, bound up with these feelings and would probably fail to ripen if these feelings were abolished.

6.
BY A POLITICAL SCIENTIST

KEY, V. O.
Public Opinion and American Democracy*

The family is obviously a major agency in the formation of basic political attitude. In addition to whatever qualities he inherits, the child acquires in the family circle social outlooks of varying political content and relevance. . . .

Estimation of the relation of family experience as a child to the political opinions of the adult meets formidable research obstacles. First, available data about the early family environment of adults are limited. They also depend upon the individual's recall of his family situation, which may be colored by projection of his own attitudes back to his family. Further, there is the problem of disentangling family influences from other factors that mold political outlook. Children come under the influence of other children, of the schools, and often early in life they begin to sense the political stimuli that play upon the community generally. Ordinarily these factors may reinforce the family ; its circumstances may determine what kinds of peer influences, what types of school environment, and what sorts of media reach the child. In some instances, though, these external influences may weaken the effect of the family. As a person grows older, his early family experience becomes remote and other considerations enter into his political outlook. They may again either reinforce or weaken the political orientation a person had at, say, age eighteen. Withal, one must take with a large grain of salt correlations between present political outlooks of adults and their memories of the politics of their families. Nevertheless, the data strongly suggest that early family experiences have important consequences in adult political behavior.

Given the significance of party identification in the behavior of the American electorate, any institution that contributes to the shaping of party loyalties is an important political agency. Family evidently plays a major role in the fixing of attachments to political parties. Children acquire early in life a feeling of party identification ; they have sensitive antennae and, since they are imitative animals, soon take on the political color of their family. . . .

* * *

While the evidence about the bearing of family experience on the subsequent political activities

* New York: Knopf, 1961, pp. 293-294, 313-314. Copyright, 1961 by V. O. Key. Reprinted by permission of Alfred A. Knopf, Inc.

and outlooks of children is scant, it is consistent with the view that the family must be regarded as a conserving factor in the political system. The family is conserving in that it tends to project into the future the prevailing pattern of social and occupational status with the associated political outlooks. It is conserving in that it tends to perpetuate the prevailing system of identifications with political parties and other politically relevant groups. To a degree offspring probably also take on attitudinal orientations in the general direction of those of their parents. Yet to say that the family is a conserving influence is not to say that it is necessarily conservative in the usage of our day. A radical father may also have a radical son, but collectively families tend to project the existent national pattern of party loyalties and to a lesser extent the existent attitudinal pattern on policy into the future where it becomes subject to reinforcement or alteration by new forces.[1] Families may or may not develop in the offspring an interest in and concern about politics. Doubtless the family indoctrinates the child with a variety of social norms and values some of which in the long run have an importance for the nature of the political order.[2]

This broad interpretation of the place of the family in the political order receives recognition, if not verification, in the practices of revolutionary regimes—and reactionary regimes as well. Those orders—be they communist, fascist, Nazi, or whatnot—that seek to break with their political past establish special youth organizations to separate the young, even the very young, from family influences and to impress the new political orthodoxy upon the youth. And they may go to the contemptible extreme of converting the child into a political spy to ferret out parental deviationism.

One of the most significant political functions of the family is almost completely missed as the few cases concerned slip through the tines of the apparatus for sampling national populations—the function of producing political leaders, political activists, politicians. Evidence on the sources from which political activists come, though thin, indicates the families of politicians, of public officials,

of bureaucrats, and of officeholders contribute a disproportionate share of those who run for office and otherwise provide leadership within the community. It would be unexpected if full evidence established that this relationship did not prevail. Conspicuous political families—the Adamses, the Tafts, the Lodges, the Kennedys, the Roosevelts, the Longs, the Talmadges—come to mind, but doubtless sprinkled through the population are many families in which there runs a political activism of a less spectacular sort.

7.

BY AN ECONOMIST

KYRK, HAZEL

The Family in the American Economy*

If the family is defined as a unit of mutual responsibility based upon a recognized relationship, the family in primitive societies is the extended kinship group, and each member has a responsibility for and claims upon a larger group than is the case today. Today the family as a unit of responsibility is created by the marriage bond and by the biological linking of parent and child. Two adults assume in certain respects the same responsibilities as does the larger clan or gens under other systems. Margaret Mead argues that the family as it now stands is a weak form of organization for the purpose of child nurture and support. She points out that it can be shattered by either death or divorce, leaving the child "in an indeterminate position economically, socially and affectionally."[9] It is true that the parental responsibility remains in spite of divorce, but the power and willingness to meet it grow weak especially if a new family is established of which the children in question are not a part. She also argues:

> Were state responsibility for children substituted for the present family organization we would obtain a type of guarantee for children which the present weak bilateral family group fails to give. In the clan, or any of its modifications, a child's status and subsistence is assured as long as there are members of the clan alive. Under the state, a child would again claim a relationship to a large group of adults—a group too large to be dissipated by a single blow. . . . Our present narrow definition of adult responsibility towards children as being limited to own or legally adoptive parents has robbed the child

---

1. Alex Inkeles, on the basis of a study of Russian defectors, concludes that parents who have themselves undergone the experience of extreme social change may not, in rearing their own children, simply recapitulate their own experience but may attempt to adjust their child rearing practices "the better to prepare their children for the life" they expect "those children to lead."—"Social Change and Social Character: The Role of Parental Mediation," *Journal of Social Issues*, XI, 2 (1955), 12-23.

2. See the provocative discussion, based on prolonged interviews with 15 New Haven adults, by Robert E. Lane: "Fathers and Sons: Foundations of Political Belief," *American Sociological Review*, XXIV (1959), 502-11.

---

* Chicago: University of Chicago Press, 1953, pp. 51-56, 12-17. Reprinted with permission of the publisher.

9. "Contrasts and Comparisons from Primitive Society," *Annals of the American Academy of Political and Social Science*, CLX (March, 1932), 28.

of that security which was assured by all primitive societies not primarily organized about the marriage tie.[10]

*   *   *

Not only does the system of complete parental responsibility without claims upon others constitute a threat to the child's security if the marriage between its two adult protectors is broken, but while it endures, the adequacy of the provision for his needs is entirely a function of their ability, knowledge, foresight, and good fortune.

*   *   *

The social and economic arrangements that came to characterize the great societies of the Western world inevitably brought changes in the relation of the family to the larger economy of which it is a part. It is now a contractual and pecuniary relationship established by one or more of the family members. In their major work activities individuals are not characteristically associated with persons related to them by blood or law. Few of the goods and services they enjoy are the direct product of their own labors. The modern family is not self-sufficing, but it is supposed to be and ordinarily is largely self-supporting. The presumption is that the members do not look outside the immediate family circle for the wherewithal to purchase food, clothing, and shelter. Correspondingly, the family's responsibility tends to stop with its own members. Sharing with others is not obligatory, except as an act of generosity or charity, very different in character from the discharge of an obligation. Collective responsibility for children, the aged, the disabled, the economically unfortunate, manifests itself largely through the impersonal agency of the state.

*   *   *

What are the human needs and social values that account for the persistence and universality of the family? Is the American family system in accord or in conflict with the culture pattern in other respects? Is the dwindling in size to near the basic minimum as a group living together and as a unit of mutual responsibility to be encouraged or discouraged? Does this dwindling foreshadow its disappearance, and what would this disap-

pearance mean in terms of human personality and welfare and in terms of new social arrangements that would be necessary?

A variety of evidence could be assembled to indicate how strongly life in small family groups is entrenched in our standard of living. The assumption is that all individuals, young and old, will live in that way except for special circumstance. Attempts to make other ways of living with a lesser degree of exclusiveness possible and attractive have not been successful. Recognition of its costs, and it has its costs, does not deter us from choosing it. Even when families are forced to live at public expense, this way of living is usually allowed for ; even the so-called subsistence budget is drawn up on the basis of life in small family groups.

Is this pattern of living so widespread and persistent because of its economic values in the sense that the family members are thereby better fed, better clothed, and better housed than would otherwise be the case? . . . It is evident that production for small family units is inefficient and wasteful in many respects as compared with production differently organized. The overhead costs of housing, feeding, and otherwise providing for such small groups are relatively high, especially if at least one able-bodied person is withdrawn from the paid labor force to devote full time to the tasks involved. Only a weak case could be made for family living if it were based only on the greater abundance of material goods thereby provided.

The bases of the preference of the family as a way of living could not be adequately arrived at without intensive analysis of human needs and interests. The preference seems to represent both a desire for withdrawal from others, a desire for privacy and exclusiveness, and a desire for close association with a selected group closely bound by affectional and other ties. The place of the individual in this group and the relation of others to him are unlike those in any other. The effect upon personality development is profound. As in all forms of human association, conflicts and tensions are inevitable. In fact, in the modern family they are so great and numerous as to seem to constitute a major source of human misery. . . .

*   *   *

The institutional changes in the Western world previously reviewed are often described as a change from a regime of status to one of contract. The obligations and claims that come from contract grew and were extended to a wider and wider group. As contractual rights move with and measure freedom and opportunity, rights due to

---

10. *Ibid.*

family and civil status represent security. If the two great demands of our age are for more opportunity and more security, the great problem of our age may be described as how to limit and define the area of contractual rights and of those derived from family relationship and from citizenship. The recurrent question is: What shall the state assure to its members—to the young, to the old, to the sick, to everyone? How far can rights based on civil status be extended without the assumption of controls that decrease various forms of economic and personal freedom? The security represented by the clan or great family system carried with it a high degree of control of the individual by the group.

Another related but unresolved question is: How far should the claims and obligations of family relationship extend? What group should the family comprehend as a system of rights and duties? What does a man "owe" his parents? His brother or his brother's children? What, correspondingly, do they "owe" him? Can the standard for responsibility differ greatly from the standard as to what persons should live under the same roof? Should services given and support provided for others be entirely a matter of affection and free choice? The kinship bond still carries a sense of obligations to and of claims upon others outside the immediate family circle, the degree varying from family to family and from community to community. Should we try to stay its weakening? Or should the ethical emphasis be upon developing solicitude for all children, related or nonrelated, all aged, and all needy?

. . . As a system of rights and obligations the family represents a status system surviving and functioning in what is otherwise largely a regime of contract. A major issue of social policy is at what point and in what degree rights based on civil status shall be substituted for those once based upon family status. . . . What should be the property rights of each spouse during the marriage and when it is broken? The family system as it now stands makes for a high concentration of the burden of support of children. The social investment in human resources correspondingly is made by a limited group, and the investment itself is correspondingly limited. The family system also makes for inequality in opportunity and wealth in a society attempting to promote equality therein. The family attempts to give its children advantages; society to give all an equivalent chance to get what is desired out of life. The family attempts to accumulate an inheritance for its children, thus further reducing the chance that all will have an even start and that, later, incomes will be equal.

8.
BY ECONOMIC HISTORIANS

MARX, KARL and ENGELS, FRIEDRICH
Manifesto of the Communist Party*

* * *

The bourgeoisie has torn away from the family its sentimental veil, and has reduced the family relation to a mere money relation.

* * *

Abolition of the family! Even the most radical flare up at this infamous proposal of the Communists.

On what foundation is the present family, the bourgeois family, based? On capital, on private gain. In its completely developed form this family exists only among the bourgeoisie. But this state of things finds its complement in the practical absence of the family among the proletarians, and in public prostitution.

The bourgeois family will vanish as a matter of course when its complement vanishes, and both will vanish with the vanishing of capital.

Do you charge us with wanting to stop the exploitation of children by their parents? To this crime we plead guilty.

But, you will say, we destroy the most hallowed of relations when we replace home education by social.

And your education! Is not that also social, and determined by the social conditions under which you educate, by the intervention of society, direct or indirect, by means of schools, etc.? The Communists have not invented the intervention of society in education; they do but seek to alter the character of that intervention and to rescue education from the influence of the ruling class.

The bourgeois claptrap about the family and education, about the hallowed co-relation of parent and child, becomes all the more disgusting, the more, by the action of modern industry, all family ties among the proletarians are torn asunder and their children transformed into simple articles of commerce and instruments of labour.

But you Communists would introduce community of women, screams the whole bourgeoisie in chorus.

The bourgeois sees in his wife a mere instrument of production. He hears that the instruments of production are to be exploited in common, and, naturally, can come to no other conclusion than that the lot of being common to all will likewise fall to the women.

---

* Reprinted in Vol. 50 Great Books of the Western World. Chicago: Encyclopaedia Britannica 1952 (pp. 420, 427-28). Used with permission of the publisher.

He has not even a suspicion that the real point aimed at is to do away with the status of women as mere instruments of production.

For the rest, nothing is more ridiculous than the virtuous indignation of our bourgeois at the community of women which, they pretend, is to be openly and officially established by the Communists. The Communists have no need to introduce community of women; it has existed almost from time immemorial.

Our bourgeois, not content with having the wives and daughters of their proletarians at their disposal, not to speak of common prostitutes, take the greatest pleasure in seducing each other's wives.

Bourgeois marriage is in reality a system of wives in common and thus at the most what the Communists might possibly be reproached with is that they desire to introduce, in substitution for a hypocritically concealed, an openly legalized, community of women. For the rest, it is self-evident that the abolition of the present system of production must bring with it the abolition of the community of women springing from that system, i.e., of prostitution both public and private.

*   *   *

9.

BY A POLITICAL SCIENTIST

MOORE, BARRINGTON, JR.

Thoughts on the Future of the Family*

Among social scientists today it is almost axiomatic that the family is a universally necessary social institution and will remain such through any foreseeable future. Changes in its structure, to be sure, receive wide recognition. The major theme, however, in the appraisal American sociologists present is that the family is making up for lost economic functions by providing better emotional service. . . .

In reading these and similar statements by American sociologists about other aspects of American society, I have the uncomfortable feeling that the authors, despite all their elaborate theories and technical research devices, are doing little more than projecting certain middle-class hopes and ideals onto a refractory reality. If they just looked a little more carefully at what was going on around them, I think they might come to different conclusions. . . . While personal ob-

servations have some value, one can always argue that a single observer is biased. Here all I propose to do, therefore, is to raise certain questions about the current sociological assessment of the family on the basis of such evidence as has come my way rather casually. In addition, I should like to set this evidence in the framework of an intellectual tradition, represented, so far as the family is concerned, by Bertrand Russell's *Marriage and Morals,* that sees the family in an evolutionary perspective, and raises the possibility that it may be an obsolete institution or become one before long. I would suggest then that conditions have arisen which, in many cases, prevent the family from performing the social and psychological functions ascribed to it by modern sociologists. The same conditions may also make it possible for the advanced industrial societies of the world to do away with the family and substitute other social arrangements that impose fewer unnecessary and painful restrictions on humanity. Whether or not society actually would take advantage of such an opportunity is, of course, another question.

It may be best to begin with one observation that is not in itself conclusive but at least opens the door to considering these possibilities. In discussions of the family, one frequently encounters the argument that Soviet experience demonstrates the necessity of this institution in modern society. The Soviets, so the argument runs, were compelled to adopt the family as a device to carry part of the burden of making Soviet citizens, especially after they perceived the undesirable consequences of savage homeless children, largely the outcome of the Civil War. This explanation is probably an accurate one as far as it goes. But it needs to be filled out by at least two further considerations that greatly reduce its force as a general argument. In the first place, the Soviets, I think, adopted their conservative policy toward the family *faute de mieux.* That is to say, with their very limited resources, and with other more pressing objectives, they had no genuine alternatives. Steel mills had to be built before crèches, or at least before crèches on a large enough scale to make any real difference in regard to child care. In the meantime the services of the family, and especially of grandma (*babushka*), had to be called upon. In the second place, with the consolidation of the regime in the middle thirties, Soviet totalitarianism may have succeeded in capturing the family and subverting this institution to its own uses. At any rate the confidence and vigor with which the regime supported this institution from the early thirties onward suggests such an explanation. Thus the Soviet experience does not constitute by itself very strong evi-

* Excerpts reprinted by permission of the publishers from Barrington Moore, Jr., *Political Power and Social Theory*, 1960, pp. 160-178. Cambridge, Mass: Harvard University Press, Copyright 1958 by the President and Fellows of Harvard College.

dence in favor of the "functional necessity" of the family.

If the Soviet case does not dispose of the possibility that the family may be obsolete, we may examine other considerations with greater confidence, and begin by widening our historical perspective. By now it is a familiar observation that the stricter Puritan ethics of productive work and productive sex have accomplished their historical purposes in the more advanced sections of the Western world. These developments have rendered other earlier elements of Western culture and society, such as slavery, quite obsolete, and constitute at least prima facie evidence for a similar argument concerning the family. Let us ask them to what extent may we regard the family as a repressive survival under the conditions of an advanced technology? And to what extent does the modern family perform the function of making human beings out of babies and small children either badly or not at all?

One of the most obviously obsolete features of the family is the obligation to give affection as a duty to a particular set of persons on account of the accident of birth. This is a true relic of barbarism. It is a survival from human prehistory, when kinship was the basic form of social organization. In early times it was expedient to organize the division of labor and affection in human society through real or imagined kinship bonds. As civilization became technically more advanced, there has been less and less of a tendency to allocate both labor and affection according to slots in a kinship system, and an increasing tendency to award them on the basis of the actual qualities and capacities that the individual possesses.

Popular consciousness is at least dimly aware of the barbaric nature of the duty of family affection and the pain it produces, as shown by the familiar remark, "You can choose your friends, but you can't choose your relatives." Even if partly concealed by ethical imperatives with the weight of age-old traditions, the strain is nevertheless real and visible. Children are often a burden to their parents. One absolutely un-Bohemian couple I know agreed in the privacy of their own home that if people ever talked to each other openly about the sufferings brought on by raising a family today, the birth rate would drop to zero. It is, of course, legitimate to wonder how widespread such sentiments are. But this couple is in no sense "abnormal." Furthermore, a revealing remark like this made to a friend is worth more as evidence than reams of scientific questionnaires subjected to elaborate statistical analyses. Again, how many young couples, harassed by the problems of getting started in life, have not wished that their

parents could be quietly and cheaply taken care of in some institution for the aged? Such facts are readily accessible to anyone who listens to the conversations in his own home or among the neighbors.

The exploitation of socially sanctioned demands for gratitude, when the existing social situation no longer generates any genuine feeling of warmth, is a subtle and heavily tabooed result of this barbaric heritage. It is also one of the most painful. Perhaps no feeling is more excruciating than the feeling that we ought to love a person whom we actually detest. The Greek tragedians knew about the problem, but veiled it under religion and mythology, perhaps because the men and women of that time felt there was no escape. In the nineteenth century the theme again became a dominant one in European literature, but with the clear implication that the situation was unnecessary. Even these authors, Tolstoi, Samuel Butler, Strindberg, and Ibsen, in exposing the horrors and hypocrisies of family life, wove most of their stories around the marital relationship, where there is an element of free choice in the partner selected. Kafka's little gem, *Das Urteil,* is a significant exception. With magnificent insight into the tragedy on both sides, it treats the frustrations of a grown-up son forced to cherish a helpless but domineering father. Henry James's short story, *Europe,* is an effective treatment of the same relationship between a mother and her daughters. Despite some blind spots and limitations, the artists, it appears, have seen vital aspects of the family that have largely escaped the sociologists.

In addition to these obsolete and barbaric features one can point to certain trends in modern society that have sharply reduced rather than increased the effectiveness of the home as an agency for bringing up children. In former times the family was a visibly coherent economic unit, as well as the group that served to produce and raise legitimate children. The father had definite and visible economic tasks, before the household became separated from the place of work. When the children could see what he did, the father had a role to be copied and envied. The source and justification of his authority was clear. Internal conflicts had to be resolved. This is much less the case now.

It is reasonably plain that today's children are much less willing than those of pre-industrial society to take their parents as models for conduct. Today they take them from the mass media and from gangs. Radio and television heroes, with their copies among neighborhood gangs, now play a vital part in the socialization process. Parents have an uphill and none too successful struggle against these sources. Like adult mobs, children's groups readily adopt the sensational, the cruel, and the most easily understood for their models and standards. These influences then corrupt and lower adult standards, as parents become increasingly afraid to assert their own authority for fear of turning out "maladjusted" children.*

The mass media have largely succeeded in battering down the walls of the social cell the family once constituted in the larger structure of society. Privacy has greatly diminished. Newspapers, radios, and television have very largely destroyed the flow of private communications within the family that were once the basis of socialization. Even meals are now much less of a family affair. Small children are frequently plumped down in front of the television set with their supper on a tray before them to keep them quiet. Since the family does less as a unit, genuine emotional ties among its members do not spring up so readily. The advertising campaign for "togetherness" provides rather concrete evidence that family members would rather not be together.

The mother, at least in American society, is generally supposed to be the homemaker and the center of the family. Has she been able to take up the slack produced by the change in the father's role? Is she, perhaps, the happy person whose face smiles at us from every advertisement and whose arts justify the sociologists' case? A more accurate assessment may be that the wife suffers most in the modern middle-class family, because the demands our culture puts upon her are impossible to meet. As indicated by advertisements, fiction, and even the theories of sociologists, the wife is expected to be companion, confidante, and ever youthful mistress of her husband.

If the demands could be met, many wives might feel very happy in this fulfillment of their personality. The actual situation is very different. The father is out of the house all day and therefore can be neither overlord nor companion. With the father absent, radio and television provide the mother with a watery substitute for adult companionship. A young colleague told me recently that his wife leaves the radio on all day merely to hear the sound of a grown-up voice. The continual chatter of little children can be profoundly

irritating, even to a naturally affectionate person. The absence of servants from nearly all American middle-class households brings the wife face to face with the brutalizing features of motherhood and housework. If she had the mentality of a peasant, she might be able to cope with them more easily. Then, however, she could not fulfill the decorative functions her husband expects. As it is now, diapers, dishes, and the state of the baby's bowels absorb the day's quota of energy. There is scarcely any strength left for sharing emotions and experiences with the husband, for which there is often no opportunity until the late hours of the evening. It is hardly a wonder that the psychiatrists' anterooms are crowded, or that both husband and wife seek escapes from psychological and sexual boredom, the cabin fever of the modern family. For the wife, either a job or an affair may serve equally well as a release from domesticity.

A further sign of the modern family's inadequacy in stabilizing the human personality may be seen in the troubled times of adolescence. This stage of growing up has been interpreted as a rejection of adult standards of responsibility and work by youngsters who are about to enter adult life. It seems to me that this period is more significantly one of pseudo-rebellion, when the youngsters copy what they see to be the real values of adult life instead of the professed ones. Even in the more extreme forms of youthful rebellion, relatively rare among respectable middle-class children, such as roaring around in noisy cars to drinking and seduction parties, the adolescents are aping actual adult behavior. Adolescents then do things they know many grown-ups do when the latter think they are escaping the observant eyes of the young. A "hot-rod" is, after all, nothing but an immature Cadillac. Where the Cadillac is the symbol of success, what else could be expected? Adult standards too are made tolerable through commercialized eroticism that lures us on to greater efforts and greater consumption from every billboard and magazine cover. Thus the whole miasma of sexual and psychological boredom in the older generation, pseudo-rebellion and brutality in the younger one, is covered over by a sentimental and suggestive genre art based on commercial sentiment.

No doubt many will think that these lines paint too black a picture. . . .

To refute the appraisal offered in these pages it would be necessary to demonstrate that they misrepresent basic structural trends in the family in advanced industrial countries. The most important argument of this type that I have encountered asserts that the proportion of married people in the population has steadily risen while

---

* It is sometimes claimed that the modern family still represents a bulwark against mass and totalitarian pressures. No doubt this is true in the best cases, those few where parents are still able to combine authority and affection. These are, however, mainly a relic of Victorian times. By and large it seems more likely that the family constitutes the "transmission belt" through which totalitarian pressures toward conformity are transmitted to the parents through the influence of the children.

the proportion of single individuals has steadily dropped. Therefore, people obviously prefer family life to bachelorhood, and the gloomy picture sketched above must be nothing more than vaporings of sour-bellied intellectuals thrown on the dump-heap by the advance of American society.

* * *

The figures do show a rise in the proportion of married persons and a decline in the proportion of single ones. They also show that the proportion of married persons is overwhelmingly larger than the number of divorced ones. But the biggest change has been in the proportion of divorced people. For men it has risen ninefold since 1890 and for women more than fivefold. A bigger proportion of people are married now than in 1890, but a *much* bigger proportion have abandoned the marital state. In the long run, the latter change might turn out to be the more important one.

* * *

. . . It is perfectly possible that conditions exist, perhaps even now, that permit better institutional arrangements than most people would be willing to accept. The word better, of course, implies a definite standard of judgment. One can debate such standards endlessly, and perhaps cannot reach agreement without at some point making arbitrary assumptions. I shall not enter this debate here except to say that any social institution is a bad one that imposes more suffering on people than is necessary when they have sufficient material resources and scientific knowledge to do away with this suffering. This standard, anthropologists tell us, is that not only of Western culture, but of all culture.

What then, are the prospects for the future? We need not take a completely determinist view. Indeed, the perceptions that both plain people and opinion-makers have about the present enter in as a significant component among the forces shaping the future and thereby provide an entering wedge for rational adaptation.

Among those who accept a substantial part of the preceding image of the family as basically correct, one frequently hears the prescription that what American culture really needs is a higher evaluation of the social role of the housewife and of motherhood. The trouble with this prescription, I would suggest, is that it merely increases the element of self-deception already so prevalent in our culture. Under present conditions motherhood *is* frequently a degrading experience. There is nothing to be gained by concealing the facts in the manner of an advertising campaign designed to raise the prestige of a particular occupation. We

would not think of trying to eliminate the hazards of coal mining in this way. Why should we try to do it with motherhood? If it is true that under present circumstances the experience of motherhood narrows and cramps the personality rather than promotes the development of its capacities, some other way will have to be found if it is to be a real solution.

The trend towards a continually more efficient technology and greater specialization, which dominates the rest of our culture, may conceivably provide an answer. In regard to the division of labor it is important to recall one widely known but neglected fact. In the past, whenever human beings have acquired sufficient resources and power, as among aristocracies, they have put the burden of child-rearing on other shoulders. Twenty years ago Ralph Linton pointed out that "aristocrats the world over . . . are reluctant to take care of their own children. Anyone who has had to take care of two or three infants simultaneously will understand why. This arduous business is turned over to slaves or servants. . . ."

Since the decline of slavery, a basic trend in European society has been to transfer to machines more and more tasks formerly carried out by slaves. By and large, this change has been accompanied by the growth of large organizations to perform tasks formerly scattered among many small groups. This trend may well affect the family. Specialized human agencies, developing from such contemporary forms as the creche, play school, and boarding school, might assume a much larger share of the burden of child-rearing, a task that could in any case be greatly lightened by machinery for feeding and the removal of waste products. Can one sensibly argue that the technical ingenuity and resources required to solve this problem are greater than those necessary for nuclear warfare? Are we to regard as permanent and "natural" a civilization that develops its most advanced technology for killing people and leaves their replacement to the methods of the Stone Age?

Against this viewpoint it is usually argued that human infants require some minimum of human affection, even fondling, if they are to survive, and that therefore some form of the family is bound to remain. The premises may be correct, but the conclusion does not follow. A nurse can perform these tasks of giving affection and early socialization just as well as the parents, often better. The argument does not prove anything therefore about the inevitable necessity of the family.

At the same time this point of view does call attention to certain important problems. Industrial society is not likely to produce household nurses, or any form of "servant class" in abundance. On the other hand, as everyone knows who has been in a hospital, nurses in a bureaucratic setting have a strong tendency to treat persons under their care "by the book," without much regard for their individual tasks and requirements. This is a well-known trait of bureaucracy, which tends to treat people and situations alike in order to achieve precision and efficiency. Infants and small children on the contrary require individual attention. For some years they may need to feel that they are the center of the universe. How then can the characteristics of bureaucracy be brought in line with those of maternal affection?

Though this may be the most difficult problem facing any qualitative transformation of the family, it is not necessarily insoluble. In the first place, as Bertrand Russell points out, a good institutional environment may be better for the development of the human personality than a bad family one. In the second place, an increase in the resources allocated to a bureaucratic organization can greatly increase its flexibility and capacity to satisfy variations in individual temperament. Any first-class hotel knows how to cope with this problem. In a few of the best ones in Europe the guest can have privacy and the illusion of being the center of the universe. Finally, one might legitimately expect that the persons who are drawn to serve in any such child-rearing institutions of the future would have more than the average amount of fondness for children, as well as general human warmth and kindliness. Under proper circumstances and management such institutions could give full scope to these benevolent sentiments.

Certain other considerations suggest an alternative that has at least the merit of being much more palatable to the vast majority of people today, since it is more in line with our deep-rooted cultural traditions. These considerations are essentially two. One is the possibility of some innate biological trait roughly resembling the "maternal instinct." The other lies in technological developments that might allow for wider dissemination of machinery to lighten household tasks and to take over the more routine aspects of child rearing. The dish-washing machine, laundromat, and, as a much more extreme device, the "Skinner box" represent prototypes of this technological development that could strengthen decentralized arrangements for rearing children.

I do not know what students of human physiology now believe about the maternal instinct. Common observation is enough to show that it cannot be an instinct like sex or hunger. There are many women who never become fond of children, or who soon cease to be fond of

them. For them the institutional outlet just sketched would be the most satisfactory way of providing for their offspring. But for others, possibly the majority, the gestation period with its trials and burdens may be enough to create in the mother a desire to retain the infant under her care, after which she could become reluctant to give it up. If machinery were available to lighten child-rearing and household tasks on a far wider scale than is now the case, mothers might be able to satisfy the more positive desires of motherhood. One that seems to be quite important in the middle class is the desire to mold the child according to some ideal image, though it is now contradicted by fears of damaging the child that derive from superficial popularizations of Freud.

For the home to become again the place where human beings take the first important steps toward realizing their creative potentialities, parents would have to become willing once more to assert their authority. In turn this authority would have to acquire a rational and objective basis, freed of current attempts to revive religious taboos. Thus there would have to be a philosophical as well as a social revolution whose implications we cannot here pursue. One aspect, nevertheless, deserves to be stressed. Rational arguments can be given only to persons competent to understand them. For obvious reasons children are not able to absorb all rational arguments at once, though the present system of education undoubtedly postpones the development of this faculty where it does not destroy it altogether. Therefore parents will have to learn not to be afraid of saying to a child, "You are not old enough yet to understand why you have to do this. But you must do it anyway." The "progressive" family, where every decision turns into an incoherent and rancorous debate, actually contributes to reactionary tendencies in society by failing to equip the next generation with adequate standards of judgment.

There are, however, some grounds for doubting that this conservative solution will eventually prevail as the dominant one. The disappearance of the wider economic functions of the family would make it very difficult, and probably impossible, to restore the emotional atmosphere of a co-operative group in which the father has a respected authority. Furthermore, the bureaucratic division of labor has proved the most effective way of solving recurring and routine problems in other areas of life. Though a considerable part of the task of raising children is not routine, a very great portion is repetitive. For these reasons one may expect that semi-bureaucratic arrangements will continue to encroach on the traditional structure of the family. No doubt many individual variations, combinations, and compromises will remain for some time to come. Yet one fine day human society may realize that the part-time family, already a prominent part of our social landscape, has undergone a qualitative transformation into a system of mechanized and bureaucratized child-rearing, cleansed of the standardized overtones these words now imply. As already pointed out, an institutional environment can be warm and supporting, often warmer than a family torn by obligations its members resent.

Such a state of affairs, if it comes at all, is well over the visible horizon now. Quite possibly it may never come at all. If it does come, there is not the slightest guarantee that it will solve all personal problems and land us in a state of air-conditioned euphoria. Values that many people hold high today may go by the board, such as the affection older couples show for one another who have shared the same pains in life until they have grown but a single scar. It is also possible that a

world of reduced family burdens might be one of shallow and fleeting erotic intrigues, based really on commercial interests. Hollywood could conceivably be the ugly prototype of such a future world, especially in its earlier transitional phases. The most that might be claimed by any future apologist for such institutions, if they ever come to pass, is that they gave greater scope to the development of the creative aspects of the human personality than did the family, which had begun to damage rather than develop this personality under advancing industrialism. And the most that can be claimed for the arguments supporting this possibility is that they correspond to some important trends visible in the family itself as well as in the rest of society. Nevertheless, it would appear that the burden of proof falls on those who maintain that the family is a social institution whose fate will differ in its essentials from that which has befallen all the others.

D.

The Family of the Future—A Glimpse from Law and Science

Much in the world of science, from increasing longevity on this planet, to procedures for artificial procreation and banking of human germinal material, to programs for outer-spacial and subterranean living, are bound to have an impact on the meaning and function of family. How and to what extent these and future developments are to be met by lawmakers is something for which lawyers must plan.* The materials in this section have been selected to illustrate the complexity and potentiality of communication between law and science, as well as to identify new problems that raise fundamental questions about the relationship of the state to the family.

1.

A FRAME OF REFERENCE

LASSWELL, HAROLD D.

The Political Science of Science†

. . . Long before atomic weapons were introduced we were well aware of the importance of scientific knowledge for the technology of fight-

---

* The New York *Times*, Aug. 31, 1964, p. 27, 1: "Congress took the first significant step today toward establishing the advisory machinery for reviewing and resolving the multiplying scientific problems confronting it.

"The Library of Congress announced it was creating a Science Policy Research Division within its Legislative Reference Service to advise Congress and Congressional committees on scientific and technological developments."

† *The American Political Science Review*, Vol. 50 (1956), p. 961. Reprinted with permission of the publisher, The American Political Science Association, and the author.

ing. . . . Since technical developments were not explicitly anticipated we did not clarify in advance the main policy alternatives open to decision makers in this country or elsewhere. We did not create a literature or a body of oral analysis that seriously anticipated these issues. [W]e should have anticipated fully both the bomb and the significant problems of policy that came with it.

* * *

Plainly there were not enough political scientists [and lawyers] trained in physics, or sufficiently aware of the implication of impending scientific developments, to do much forward thinking and planning. This points to a failure of professional . . . training, and calls in question the then-prevailing conception of the political scientist's [and lawyer's] role. . . . Part of our role, as the venerable metaphor has it, is scanning the horizon of the unfolding future with a view to defining in advance the probable import of what is foreseeable for the navigators of the Ship of State. It is our responsibility to flagellate our minds toward creativity, toward bringing into the stream of emerging events conceptions of future strategy that, if adopted, will increase the probability that ideal aspirations will be more approximately realized.

*   *   *

As clarifiers of the goals and alternatives implicit in a decision process and as advisers of the participants we have an opportunity to reduce the amount of unnecessary friction by establishing a frame of reference in advance of the facts. When factual details appear they will of course exhibit some novel elements; common goals and principles will not. . . .

It is, of course, essential that in taking advantage of this opportunity we deal with the entire context of value goals and principles as they relate to potential facts. . . .

*   *   *

When we think configuratively about . . . problems raised in reference to the new resources it is clear that instead of relying on blanket principles . . . the most fruitful policy alternatives are likely to emerge when we anticipate the appearance of characteristic factual contexts, and consider how the values chiefly at stake in them can be maximized. . . .

*   *   *

One way to jar "cakes of custom" out of the mind is to draft specifications for the first Mayflower expedition to establish continuing occupation outside the earth. . . . What proportion of men, women and children of which culture or combination of earth cultures shall we select? What ideological traditions, secular and sacred? What class backgrounds (elite, mid-elite, mass)? What individual and group interests? What personality structures?

By asking questions of this kind we are in a position to assess our present stock of knowledge concerning the interdependence of institutions specialized to power, and all other institutions in the social process of any community, together with the forms of personality involved. . . .

[W]e are [not] even . . . well prepared to anticipate developments in genetics, experimental embryology and related disciplines. Taken together these fields signify that, as Julian Huxley has often put it, man is on the threshold of taking evolution into his own hands. By influencing the genes that constitute the key units in man's bio-logical inheritance we affect the entire potential of future generations.

*   *   *

It has been pointed out that perhaps the most satisfactory index of genetic damage is the sum of tangible defects existing among living individuals. We are speaking of such stigmata as "mental defects, epilepsy, congenital malformations, neuromuscular defects, hematological and endocrine defects, defects in vision or hearing, cutaneous and skeletal defects, or defects in the gastro-intestinal or genito-urinary tracts." We are informed that about 2 per cent of the live births in the United States have defects that are of "simple genetic origin and appear prior to sexual maturity." If mankind were subjected to a "double dosing" of radiation the present level of genetic defects would rise, and would eventually be doubled.

Regulatory measures are obviously needed against wars and weapon tests; and they are essential to the disposition of nuclear waste from industrial plants. (It has been remarked that a nuclear power plant is to be viewed as a large scale production of both highly poisonous gas and explosives under a single roof.)

The principal questions to which I desire to call attention . . . have already come up in controversies over artificial insemination. They have embarrassed the champions of the orthodox prescriptions that prevail in several fields (theology, ethics, jurisprudence). Shall we call a child legitimate whose biological father is not identical with the sociological father? Even with the consent of the latter? With spermatozoa from a known or unknown source? (A possible international question is whether a nation state like the United States can claim the child as a citizen if the spermatozoa employed originated with an American mail order house and was sent by air mail for use abroad.)

Poignant as these issues are in specific cases they do not confront us with the consequences for public order that are to be anticipated if the progress of biology separates insemination and child bearing from genital contact. The assumption is often made that the continuation of sexual rectitude and even civic order depends upon charging every genital contact with the blessings and perils of procreation. The impending improvement of oral contraceptives, joined with other recent advances, are factors that already suggest the wisdom of other norms and sanctions of public order.

Other developments are threatening current ratios of the influence and power of the sexes. Given the millions and millions of spermatozoa produced by one male and the technique of canning by refrigeration, any very large number of males becomes relatively redundant for purposes of procreation. Must the male rest his future upon other values such as the strictly aesthetic appeal of the male contour? Before the female of the species becomes too complacent in this context it may be worth recalling the significance of some current experiments for the removal of the primordial female function from the body and into other receptacles. (Women, too, may have to rely upon their charm, a role for which their experience has provided extensive preparation.)

Apparently we are closer than most of us like to think to the production of species that occupy an intermediate position between man and the lower animals (or even plants). It is sometimes said, even in august quarters, that "one has not yet succeeded in making a species from another species." Theodosius Dobzhansky notes, however, that "the feat of obtaining a new species was accomplished more than a quarter of a century ago." In recent decades a fair number of new species have been brought into being. It is also true that some species that exist in nature have been recreated experimentally. A garrison police regime fully cognizant of science and technology can, in all probability, eventually aspire to biologize the class and caste system by selective breeding and training. Such beings can, in effect, be sown and harvested for specialized garrison police services or for other chosen operations.

Great strides have been taken in brain design. Experimental models of robots have been built who solve problems of a rather complex order in a given environment. Some of these machines look after themselves to a degree, obtaining and using the raw materials required for energy and repairs. Already it is claimed that the function of reproducing its kind, and of interacting with others, can be in-built.

The question then rises: Given our concern for human dignity when do we wisely extend all or part of the Universal Declaration of Human Rights to these forms? When do we accept the humanoids—the species intermediate between lower species and man, and which may resemble us in physique as well as in the possession of an approximately equivalent central nervous and cortical system—as at least partial participants in the body politic? And at what point do we accept the incorporation of relatively self-perpetuating and mutually influencing "super-machines" or "ex-robots" as beings entitled to the policies expressed in the Universal Declaration?

It is obvious that we are not too well equipped by cultural tradition to cope with these problems. A trait of our civilization is the intense sentimentalization of superficial differences in the visible format of the groupings to be found even within the human species. Recall the theologians, ethicists and jurists who have devoted themselves to the elaboration of symbols to show that the while race alone is genuinely human and hence solely entitled to the dignity of freedom. Recall, too, the counter-assertions, nourished in the soil of humiliation, that have arisen among ethnic groups that seek to overcome their contempt for themselves by dragging down the pretensions of the white imperialist.

* * *

The most disturbing question, perhaps, arises when we reflect upon the possibility that super-gifted men, or even new species possessing superior talent, will emerge as a result of research and development by geneticists, embryologists or machine makers. In principle, it is not too difficult to imagine a superior form. For instance, our sensory equipment does not enable us to take note of dangerous radiation levels in the environment. We have no inborn chattering of a Geiger counter.

. . . It is plain that if we bring certain kinds of living forms into the world we may be introducing a biological elite capable of treating us in the manner in which imperial powers have so often treated the weak. A question is whether the cultivation of superior qualities ought to be limited to intellectual capability. The answer, I feel confident you will agree, is in the negative. We need to be sufficiently vigilant to prevent the turning loose on the world of a hyper-intelligent species driven by an instinctual system especially inclined toward predation. The blood-stained story of our own species is only too familiar (the stories about succulent missionaries whose bodies were more readily incorporated than their messages are not wholly without foundation). Can we improve the prospects of developing a form of intelligent life copied not after our own image, but after the image of our nobler aspirations?

It is not to be overlooked that the problem of human capability can become acute if in the years ahead we escape from our present habitat on the earth, or are visited by other forms of intelligent life. . . . It would of course be embarrassing, at least, to discover that we are the savages or that we are put together on a markedly inferior biological plan.

The fact is that many of the problems to which I have been referring will be upon us long before we can make great changes in the ideological outlook or the socio-political patterns of life in this country or elsewhere. The same point applies to ourselves in our role as individuals and as [lawyers]. . . . Considering our present predispositions how can we improve the likelihood of contributing to the decision process at every level, from the neighborhood to the world as a whole?

* * *

Our first professional contribution, it appears, is to project a comprehensive image of the future for the purpose of indicating how our overriding goal values are likely to be affected if current policies continue.

. . . Our traditions have not been life-centered, but man-centered. We possess various paranoid-like traditions of being "chosen." Clearly a difficult task of modifying these egocentric perspectives lies ahead.

* * *

2.
FOREBODINGS IN TORTS AND GENETICS

a.   ZEPEDA v. ZEPEDA
        49 Ill. App. 2d 240, 190 N.E. 2d 849 (1963)

MR. PRESIDING JUSTICE DEMPSEY DELIVERED THE OPINION OF THE COURT.

The plaintiff is the infant son of the defendant. He seeks damages from his father because he is an illegitimate child. He appeals from an order dismissing his suit and striking his complaint for its failure to state a cause of action.

. . . During the oral argument in this court Mr. Hugh M. Matchett, the plaintiff's attorney, said he thought the defendant's viewpoint should be represented. He suggested that Professor Max Rheinstein, an internationally recognized authority in family law, be asked to participate as amicus curiae. Dr. Rheinstein accepted our appointment. We are indebted to Mr. Matchett for his generous suggestion and to Dr. Rheinstein for his gracious acceptance.

The factual averments of the complaint, which were admitted by the motion to strike, are: the defendant is the plaintiff's father; the defendant induced the plaintiff's mother to have sexual relations by promising to marry her; this promise was not kept and could not be kept because, unbeknown to the mother, the defendant was already married. The complaint charges that the promise was fraudulent, that the acts of the defendant were willful and that the defendant injured the plaintiff in his person, property and reputation by causing him to be born an adulterine bastard. The plaintiff seeks damages for the deprivation of his right to be a legitimate child, to have a normal home, to have a legal father, to inherit from his father, to inherit from his paternal ancestors and for being stigmatized as a bastard.

In describing this complaint, Dr. Rheinstein stated:

> "Such a claim is novel. There is no statutory or judicial recognition of such a claim in Illinois or elsewhere in the United States. There is no adverse decision either. In fact, no such claim seems ever to have been raised in any court in Illinois, of any other Common Law jurisdiction, or any Civil Law country either."

The plaintiff . . . presents two theories of recovery, one in tort and the other in contract. . . .

The contract theory is that the plaintiff should be regarded as a third party beneficiary of the agreement made by his father and mother to marry each other. This contention, even if it were tenable, is not available to the plaintiff because his complaint sounds in tort. Therefore, the only theory of recovery to be considered on this appeal is whether the complaint states a cause of action in tort.

The first of the many interesting questions prompted by the unique averments of the complaints is this: was the act of the defendant a legal wrong, a tortious act? From the admitted facts we can draw the conclusion that the defendant's act was willful and, perhaps, criminal. It was willful in that the defendant was completely indifferent to the foreseeable consequences of his act. He pursued a course of conduct which showed a conscious disregard for the rights of others. He knew he could not marry the woman and he knew that if a child were born as a result of his act he could not legitimatize that child. The act may have been criminal in that the defendant, a married man, and the mother, an unmarried woman, were living together in the mother's apartment. If this cohabitation as husband and wife was openly done, it was a criminal offense: adultery on the part of the defendant, fornication on the part of the mother. . . . The criminal aspect of the act accentuates its gravity. It was not only a moral wrong but was, under the aggravated circumstances of this case, tortious in its nature.

. . . Our problem is whether a tort was committed upon the child. Thus, the second question to confront us is, can a tort be inflicted upon a being simultaneously with its conception?

The law of torts has been hesitant in recognizing what medical science has long known, that life begins at the moment of conception, and what theology has longer taught, that for the moment of conception every human being has the rights of a human person. . . . Although other branches of the law, such as property and inheritance, recognized the legal existence of a child from the moment of conception, in tort a child was not regarded as a being separate from its mother until it was born. In the last few years a change has taken place in the law pertaining to prenatal physical injuries. From 1884 to 1946 it was universally held that under the common law there could be no recovery for such injuries. . . . There were occasional dissenting opinions ; judges were troubled by the unfairness of holding that a child *en ventre sa mere* was a human being for inheritance and property rights and not one if it suffered tortious physical injury. It was not until 1946 that a major breakthrough was made under the common law. . . . Gradually thereafter various jurisdictions permitted actions for prenatal injuries if a child was viable at the time of injury and if it survived birth. [G]enerally the viability of the child at the time of injury became the criterion upon which recovery rested. However, the exact time when viability occurs is uncertain. No medical authority can say with accuracy just at what moment a child can live when separated from its mother. Babies have survived in incubators even further removed from the time of normal birth. The law has slowly come to realize these uncertainties and the viability test is being abandoned. Now complaints are being sustained where the pleaded facts show that the child was not, or might not have been, viable when the injury ocurred. . . .

The case at bar seems to be the natural result of the present course of the law permitting actions for physical injury ever closer to the moment of conception. In point of time it goes just a little further. The significance of this course to us is this: if recovery is to be permitted an infant injured one month after conception, why not if injured one week after, one minute after, or at the moment of conception? It is inevitable that the date will be further retrogressed. How can the law distinguish the day to day development of life? If there is human life, proved by subsequent birth, then that human life has the same rights at the time of conception as it has at any time thereafter. There cannot be absolutes in the minute to minute progress of life from sperm and ovum to cell, to embryo to foetus, to child.

But what if the wrongful conduct takes place before conception? Can the defendant be held accountable if his act was completed before the plaintiff was conceived? Yes, for it is possible to incur, as Justice Holmes phrased it in the *Dietrich* case [138 Mass. 14 (1884)], "a conditional prospective liability in tort to one not yet in being." It makes no difference how much time elapses between a wrongful act and a resulting injury if there is a causal relation between them. Let us take the hypothetical case of an infant injured after birth by a defective household device. Sup-

pose, before the child was conceived, a manufacturer negligently made a space heater and sold it to a retailer who retained it in his store. After the infant's birth his mother purchased the heater and used it in the room of her child who was burned because of its faulty preparation. Would there not be a right of action against the manufacturer despite the fact the negligence took place before the child was conceived? In the hypothetical case the child was injured after birth. Lest this fact be given undue importance, let us proceed a step further. Suppose a manufacturer prepared and sold a drug for human consumption which had not been adequately tested ; that, while it was beneficial for the purpose intended, it proved to be harmful if taken by women in the very early stage of pregnancy in that it arrested the development of infants' bodies, causing them to be born with abnormal arms or legs. Would not a child so born have a right of action in tort? In the second case the child was injured soon after conception. So let us go still further and take a third suppositive case, where the wrongful act also takes place before conception but the injury attaches at the moment of conception. Physicists and geneticists declare that thermonuclear radiation can so affect the reproductive cells of future parents that their offspring may be born with physical and mental defects. Schubert and Lapp, Radiation—What It Is And How It Affects You, p. 181 (1957) ; Crow, The Genetic Effects Of Radiation, p. 20, Bulletin Of Atomic Scientists (January 1958) ; Grobman, Our Atomic Heritage, pp. 68, 135 (1951) ; Weaver, Radiations And The Genetic Threat, p. 733, Treasury of Science (1958). If a child is born malformed or an imbecile because of the genetic effect on his father and mother of a negligently or intentionally caused atomic explosion, will he be denied recovery because he was not in being at the time of the explosion?

*   *   *

[I]t is not too important whether the plaintiff's life began during or subsequent to the act of procreation. There is no certainty as to the exact moment conception takes place. It occurs when the male semen contacts and fertilizes the female ovum and this may happen at the time of coition or within a few hours thereafter. . . . If the plaintiff was conceived before the completion of the act he became a living, human organism concurrently with the wrongful act. If his conception took place after the act, he was a potential being with essential reality at the time of the act. The seed was planted, the life process was started, life ensued and birth followed. The defendant's wrongful act simultaneously procreated the being whom it injured.

In neither event was the plaintiff a "person" as that word has been historically understood in the law of torts. We do not think this is too material for we are not concerned with some abstract ontological proposition as to the instant a human entity becomes a person. The plaintiff is a person now and he was a potential person with full capacity for independent existence at the time of the original wrong. As he developed biologically from potentiality to reality the wrong developed too. It progressed as did he, from essence to existence. When he became a person the nature of the wrong became fixed. From a moral wrong and a criminal act against the public, it became a legal wrong and a tortious act against the individual.

This brings us to the next question to be considered, the character of the plaintiff's injury. Injuries other than physical or to property are compensable in law and the plaintiff in the case at bar endeavors to come within the coverage of two of them: mental suffering and defamation. This court, in the first case in Illinois involving the right of privacy, considered the interrelationship between right of privacy and mental suffering and concluded that actions were permissible for Intentionally caused mental suffering. . . . In *Knierim v. Izzo*, 22 Ill. 2d 73, 174 N.E 2d 157 (1961), a complaint was upheld where the cause of action was based upon the mental anguish of the plaintiff occasioned by the threat of the defendant to kill her husband and the carrying out of this threat. The court held that peace of mind was an interest of sufficient importance to receive protection from the law against intentional invasion. The present complaint, however, does not charge mental distress. The nearest approach to this is the allegation that "His father has wilfully injured and wronged him . . . in stigmatizing him as an adulterine bastard." To some persons the shame of being an adulterine bastard might cause as genuine and severe emotional distress as that resulting from other serious provocation. However, in the absence of proper and adequate averments, we must hold that the complaint states no cause of action for this tort. If it did outline such an action, it would be an interesting speculation whether a charge of mental distress and emotional suffering could be made and sustained in behalf of an infant.

Likewise, the complaint does not state a cause of action for defamation. The averment that the plaintiff has been damaged in reputation is akin to this tort because defamation is the invasion of reputation and good name; but to be actionable the derogatory appellation or statement must have been communicated by the defendant to third persons, and there is no allegation of publication. Also ignored is the fact that the truth, if published

under certain conditions (with good motives and for justifiable ends), can be a complete defense to the charge. . . . The complaint, which is based on the truth, does not negative the conditions.

The plaintiff further complains of being deprived of the normal home that might have been his and of equality with the legitimate child he might have been. A legitimate child has the natural right to be wanted, loved and cared for. He also has an interest in preserving his family life and he may protect this interest against outside disturbance. . . . However, a legitimate child cannot maintain an action against his own parents for lack of affection, for failure to provide a pleasant home, for disrupting the family life or for being responsible for a divorce which has broken up the home. An illegitimate child cannot be given rights superior to those of a legitimate child, and the plaintiff has no cause of action on this account.

But it would be pure fiction to say that the plaintiff suffers no injury. The lot of a child born out of wedlock, who is not adopted or legitimatized, is a hard one. The community itself has come to understand this hardship. After centuries of stagnation, an evolution has been taking place and illegitimate children are now being treated with more consideration. The contrast between the common law and present day statutes is striking.

Under the common law an illegitimate child was called "filius nullius" son of no one, or "filius populi" son of the people. . . . His position in the community was one of ignominy and he had no rights in law. Since he was the child of no one he was without a name; his parents had no right to his custody and no subsequent act of theirs could make him legitimate, only a special act of Parliament could do so. . . . He could not compel his parents to support him, he could not inherit and he could have no heirs except his widow and the issue of his own body. . . .

In most American jurisdictions illegitimate children were also treated harshly, but in recent years a more compassionate sense of social justice has brought about the enactment of beneficent legislation which has alleviated some of the oppression long visited upon these unfortunates. The whole climate has changed nationally, with variations in degree from state to state. . . . More euphonious terms are also being used in the statutes. "Bastard" is giving way to "illegitimate child," to "a child born out of wedlock," and to "a natural child"; "Bastardy Acts" have yielded to "Family Acts" and "Paternity Acts."

This liberalization is reflected in the statutes of Illinois: an illegitimate child has the right to his father's surname; either or both of his parents may be compelled to support and educate him until he becomes 18 years of age; his parents have custodial rights; he may be legitimatized by the marriage of his parents; if a birth certificate has been issued a new one is issued in the same form as for a legitimate child and the old certificate is impounded; if he is born following an attempted marriage, where some form of a lawful marriage has been performed, he is considered legitimate; if he is born of an adulterous relation he may be legitimatized if his parents intermarry and his father acknowledges him to be his child; in order to facilitate his legitimation, the certificate of negative finding as to venereal disease in his parents, a prerequisite to marriage, is waived; he is not considered as illegitimate if, after his conception or birth, the marriage of his parents is declared void; the consent of his father is not necessary for his adoption; the word "illegitimate" and the phrase "born out of wedlock" cannot be used in his adoption petition or decree; he may inherit from his mother and his maternal ancestors; if his mother has died he may inherit from those from whom she might have inherited; his issue may take what he would have taken if he were living; not only his wife and descendants inherit from him, but his mother and her descendants can also.

The developing concern in Illinois for illegitimate children is also illustrated by the support provisions of the 1957 Paternity Act. (Ill. Rev. Stat. 1957, ch. 106-3/4.) Since 1827 putative fathers have been obliged to contribute to the support of their children, but from 1827 to 1919 the maximum obligation imposed by law was $550.00; from 1919 until 1957 the statutory maximum was $1,100.00. This single amount was "held applicable whether the mother gave birth to one child, twins, triplets or quadruplets." . . . Under the 1957 Act there is no limitation; the purpose of the Act is to see that the same care is provided for illegitimate as for legitimate children.

All these measures spring from the conscience of man disturbed by the severity of the common law and the patent injustices long suffered by innocent children, damned by the sins of their parents. By these benign statutes an illegitimate child's material inequality has been lessened, his legitimation made easier and his succession rights improved. Praiseworthy as they are, they do not, and no law can, make these children whole. Children born illegitimate have suffered an injury. If legitimation does not take place, the injury is continuous. If legitimation cannot take place, the injury is irreparable.

The injury is not as tangible as a physical defect but it is as real. This is acknowledged by the State itself. The statutory provisions that a child's illegitimacy must be suppressed, in certain public records, is an admission of the hardship that can be caused by its disclosure. How often during his life does an illegitimate try to conceal his parentage and how often does he wince in shame when it is revealed? Public opinion may bring about more laws ameliorating further his legal status, but laws cannot temper the cruelty of those who hurl the epithet "bastard" nor ease the bitterness in him who hears it, knowing it to be true. This, however, is but one phase, one manifestation of the basic injury, which is in being born and remaining an illegitimate. An illegitimate's very birth places him under a disability.

It is of this that the plaintiff complains. His adulterine birth has placed him under a permanent disability. He protests not only the act which caused him to be born but birth itself. Love of life being what it is, one may conjecture whether, if he were older, he would feel the same way. As he grows from infancy to maturity the natural instinct to preserve life may cause him to cherish his existence as much as, through his next friend, he now deplores it. Be that as it may, the quintessence of his complaint is that he was born and that he is. Herein lies the intrinsic difficulty of this case, a difficulty which gives rise to this question: are there overriding legal, social, judicial or other considerations which should preclude recognition of a cause of action?

Bearing in mind that an action for damages is implicit in any wrong that is called a tort . . . it may be inconsistent to say, as we do, that the plaintiff has been injured by a tortious act and then to question, as we do, his right to maintain an action to recover for this act. This is done deliberately, however, because on the one hand, we believe that the elements of a willful tort are presented by the allegations of the complaint and, on the other hand, we approach with restraint the creation, by judicial sanction, of the new action required by the complaint.

Recognition of the plaintiff's claim means creation of a new tort: a cause of action for wrongful life. The legal implications of such a tort are vast, the social impact could be staggering. If the new litigation were confined just to illegitimates it would be formidable. In 1960 there were 224,330 illegitimate births in the United States, 14,262 in Illinois and 10,182 in Chicago. Vital statistics of the United States 1960, Vol. 1, secs. 1, 2 (1962). Not only are there more such births year after year (in Illinois and in Chicago the number in 1960 was twice that of 1950) but the ratio between illegitimate and legitimate births is increasing. . . .

That the doors of litigation would be opened wider might make us proceed cautiously in approving a new action, but it would not deter us. The plaintiff's claim cannot be rejected because there may be others of equal merit. It is not the suits of illegitimates which give us concern, great in numbers as these may be. What does disturb us is the nature of the new action and the related suits which would be encouraged. Encouragement would extend to all others born into the world under conditions they might regard as adverse. One might seek damages for being born of a certain color, another because of race; one for being born with a hereditary disease, another for inheriting unfortunate family characteristics; one for being born into a large and destitute family, another because a parent has an unsavory reputation.

The present case could be just a forerunner of those which may confront the courts in the future. Without stimulating them, we may have suits for wrongful life just as we now have for wrongful death. Cases are appearing in the domestic relations field concerning children born as a result of artificial insemination. Walker, Legitimacy and Paternity, 14 Ark. L. Rev. 55 (1960). How long will it be before a child so produced sues in tort those responsible for its being?

Will there be public sperm banks such as the blood banks we now have? Presently, a private sperm bank is said to exist. The author of an article in the American Bar Association Journal wrote:

> ". . . to protect the issue of the astronauts from mutations resulting from ionizing radiation in space, a technique has been developed for them to deposit their sperm in a sperm bank and to preserve it indefinitely through a refrigeration process. (See New York Times, July 16, 1961, p. 57; August 29, 1961, p. 26. 'Survival'—The American Institute of Biological Sciences Bulletin, October 1961, p. 15.)" Leach, Perpetuities in the Atomic Age: The Sperm Bank and the Fertile Decedent, A.B.A.J., vol. 48, No. 10 (1962).

If there are public sperm banks in future years and if there are sperm injections like present day blood transfusions, with donors and donees unknown to each other, will there not be a basis for an action for wrongful life?

As man's knowledge increases he will wield ever greater control over the functions of nature. Where this may lead and what its consequences may be are unpredictable. As one biologist observed, "Some would-be architects of our future look toward a time when it will be possible to alter the human germ plasma by design." Carson, Silent Spring, p. 8 (1962). In the event it becomes possible to produce departures from normally-to-be-expected, inheritable qualities, would not action lie for wrongful life by a victim of inten-

tional gene mutation who was dissatisfied with the result?

We shall include another example, farfetched to be sure, but illustrative of the point being discussed. Dr. George Wells Beadle, president of the University of Chicago and an eminent biologist, is quoted as saying, "No one has yet synthesized life, but biologists say it should be possible." Manly, University of Chicago, Chicago Daily Tribune, April 28, 1961. Under the title "Modern Creation" the medical editor of the same newspaper wrote this:

> "What is the nature of life? To answer this question scientists first must create life in a test tube and research along this line is being done in many laboratories thruout the world. They are down to the basic chemical ingredients and the code could be broken at any time by the right manipulation and recombining of different molecules." Van Dellen, Modern Creation, Chicago Tribune, January 20, 1963.

If such awesome experiments are successfully pursued and their ultimate goal, the abiogenesis of human life achieved, would a being so created have a cause of action for wrongful life against those whose knowledge and skill were so employed?

If we are to have a legal action for such a radical concept as wrongful life, it should come after thorough study of the consequences. This would be so even if the new action were to be restricted to illegitimates or even adulterine illegitimates. A study, of the depth and scope warranted by the gravity of this action, can best be made by the General Assembly which, as we have seen, has been steadily whittling away at the legal handicaps shackling bastards and has given them rights almost equivalent to those born legitimate. Changing economic, social or political conditions, or scientific advancements, produce new problems which are constantly thrust upon the courts. These problems often require the remolding of the law, the extension of old remedies or the creation of new and instant remedies—but no recent development is presented by this case which demands an immediate remedy to keep abreast of progress. Although the legal questions unfolded are new, the problem is not; the social conditions producing the problem have existed since the advent of man.

We have decided to affirm the dismissal of the complaint. We do this, despite our designation of the wrong committed herein as a tort, because of our belief that lawmaking, while inherent in the judicial process, should not be indulged in where the result could be as sweeping as here. The interest of society is so involved, the action needed to redress the tort could be so far-reaching, that the policy of the State should be declared by the representatives of the people.

Affirmed.

b.   MULLER, HERMANN J.

The Guidance of Human Evolution*

Even though natural selection has been the great guiding principle that has brought us and all other higher organisms to their present estate, every responsible student of evolution knows that natural selection is too opportunistic and short-sighted to be trusted to give an advantageous long-term result for any single group of organisms. Mankind constitutes one of those relatively rare, fabulously lucky lines whose ancestors did happen to win out—else we would not be here—while the incalculably vast majority of species sooner or later vanished, without now living descendants. That is, of all the species existing at any one time, only a relatively few ever function as conveyors of germ plasm that is to continue indefinitely, but most of these few branch and rebranch to more than compensate for the far greater number that are lost. Do we have reasons for believing that our species belongs in that very limited category that is to continue into the geologically distant future?

In examining this question we may first note that man is virtually excluded from ever again splitting into diversified species on this earth, so long as his technological culture remains. For that culture has the effect of shrinking the earth and removing ever more effectively the barriers to migration and interbreeding. Moreover, besides lacking the multiple chances for success which multiple speciation confers, our single species is undergoing, genetically, something analogous to an increase in entropy within itself. For its diverse sublines—hitherto numerous, partly isolated, and to some extent subject to ultimate competition with one another—are increasingly dissipating their separate individualities by merging genetic combinations, so that ever less opportunity is afforded for the intra-species selection among many small groups that has been so potent an evolutionary force. Finally, the remaining intra-group selective processes are becoming subject to modification in their direction of operation through the influence of social processes which, left to themselves, tend to preserve and in some ways even to aid the multiplication of characteristics that are disservicable to the welfare of the

group as a whole—that is, of the species. For all these reasons it seems to follow that the one final remaining line of man will, if he retains or amplifies his technological culture, meet with biological extinction long before the earth grows too hot or too cold to support him.

The question arises here, May not this very culture that man has made effect some further alterations in the working of the principles of selection or add features to them that will, after all, permit man's indefinite survival as a civilized being? The answer seems clear. Cultural interference can bring about the survival of man and his culture only if it makes consummate use of man's most distinctive characteristic, his foresight, so as *consciously* to evade the otherwise inevitable decline.

I. *Genetic Benefits Resulting from Past Cultural Evolution*

Before discussing what such purposeful action would imply, we may first acknowledge that cultural factors, operating *without* man's realization of the evolutionary effects they would ultimately produce—that is, without long-range foresight—have in fact exerted major influences on human evolution in the past. And most, although not all, of the changes wrought thereby are of kinds that we would nowadays classify as good.

Prime examples are man's facility in using tools, thereby better manipulating the environment, and his facility in communicating, mainly through speech. Tools and speech themselves are, of course, cultural developments, improved through many generations of extragenically transmitted experience. The possession of these aids to living, even in their more primitive forms, gave increasing scope for the exercise of the faculties that produced them and thereby strengthened and sharpened the selection that elaborated further the genetic bases of these faculties. . . .

*   *   *

II. *Genetic Inadequacies of Cultural Evolution*

*   *   *

[T]he family, long before the arrival of man, must have afforded the primary unit for intergroup selection whereby the genetic basis of altruistic proclivities became developed. Then, as the groups came to include a number of families, they were still small enough and numerous enough to allow effective selection for the traits that predisposed their members for the wider cooperation and altruism here in order. Even if the individual sacrificed himself for the small group, he tended to foster the multiplication, through the others of that group, of genes like those that

* *Perspectives in Biology and Medicine*, Vol. 3 (Autumn, 1959), pp. 1-42. Copyright 1959 by The University of Chicago. Reprinted by permission of The University of Chicago Press.

had predisposed him to this behavior. With the formation of towns and large civil units in general, this kind of influence on selection tended to disappear.

It is doubtless true, that, even today, co-operation *within* the family results in some positive selection in favor of genes conducive to intra-familial aid. In the setting of large-scale communities, the operation of these same genes can to some extent be adapted through cultural practices for the purposes of mutual aid in these larger communities. The very success of such adaptation, however, spells a corresponding decline in the selection. Moreover, so far as those proclivities are concerned that would tend to broaden the basis of the co-operation, by making a man really feel toward men in general as toward his brothers, there is no longer an automatic mechanism for enhancing their genetic basis. At the same time the characteristically human tendencies to feel antagonistic toward those outside one's "circle" keep seeking an outlet and are not effectively selected against. This situation has left men very imperfectly constructed to live by the utopian precept "Love one another." Yet any other basis of behavior for a form of living that depends on our modern global technologies must result in even greater disharmonies, whereby these technologies themselves become turned against their users.

* * *

[I]t is indisputable that, as man's control over matter advances, more and more of his bodily structure and functioning can be amended and even replaced by artificial means. Thus, even as primitive man found his body hair largely dispensable and replaced it by coverings, future man will require less and less heat regulation, antibody production, natural hormone generation, digestive juice secretion, and so forth. He can use scooters for locomotion and computers for calculation. And he can finally do without himself!

Primitive man could replace his natural faculties by artifices only in certain limited aspects of his living, as in protection against weather, wild animals, and certain vicissitudes in food supply. The techniques needed for these purposes were not too burdensome, and they actually gave him much better means of meeting the given requirements than did his inherited specializations. Hence it was these biological endowments rather than his cultural devices which ultimately became too burdensome to be maintained. Certainly in the case of modern and future man this situation will apply in many more areas of living. But to acknowledge this fact is not the same as to say that there would, in general, be a net gain in

substituting for our genetic endowment everything that would now or in the future be devised to take its place. Where should we draw the line?

A given natural endowment is better lost than retained if all the following three conditions hold. First, the artificial substitute should be more effective and dependable than the natural endowment. Second, the net burden to the community involved in maintenance and operation should, for a given return, be less for the artificial substitute than for the natural endowment. Third, the maintenance of the natural endowment as a supplement to the man-made contrivance should be more trouble than it is worth before its lapse can be considered justifiable.

Today, of course, no attempt is made to assess these balances when procedures are instituted which, in helping individuals, may contribute to the relaxation of selection in given directions. It is regarded as ethical to employ every available artificial aid to enable an individual to reproduce or to enable him to live and thereby reproduce, even when his reproduction would be likely to perpetuate the genetic condition that had occasioned the given difficulty. So far as the immediately treated generation is concerned, mutual aid of this kind is unquestionably a social obligation. Its over-all cost is very small in comparison with its benefits to the community in well-being, general efficiency, harmonious interrelations, sense of security, and enjoyment of life. The real issue is not whether society should in this way help the individuals themselves to live better, as if that were where the matter stopped. It is whether the acts of society should be so ordered as actually to facilitate the perpetuation of defective genetic equipment into later generations. Should we give with one hand while taking away with the other?

* * *

III. *Results of the Continuation of Present Practices*

On the average, the counterpressure of selection, consisting in the elimination of individuals with excess detrimental genes, almost exactly equals the pressure of mutation in producing these genes. There is evidence from more than one direction that man at least one person in five, or 20 per cent, carries a detrimental gene which arose in the immediately preceding generation and that, therefore, this same proportion—one in five —is, typically, prevented by genetic defects from surviving to maturity or (if surviving) from reproducing. This equilibrium holds, only when a population is living under conditions that have long prevailed. Modern techniques are so efficacious that, used to the full, they might today (as judged by recent statistics on deaths and births) be able to save for life and for a virtually normal rate of reproduction some nine-tenths of the otherwise genetically doomed 20 per cent. Assuming this to be the case, there would in the next generation be 18 per cent who carried along those defects that would have failed to be transmitted in the primitive or equilibrium population, plus another 20 per cent (partly overlapping the 18 per cent) who had the most recently arisen defects. At this rate, if the effectiveness of the techniques did not diminish as their job grew, there would after about eight generations, or 240 years, be an accumulation of about 100 "genetic deaths" (scattered over many future generations) per 100 persons then living in addition to the regular "load of mutations" that any population would ordinarily carry. It can be estimated (on the supposition that human mutation rates are like those in mice) that this amount of increase in the load is about the same as would be brought about by an acute exposure of all the parents of one generation to 200r of gamma radiation, a situation similar to that at Hiroshima, or by a chronic, low-dose-rate exposure of each of the eight generations to 100r.

* * *

[I]t is absurd to assume that environmentalist techniques alone, dealing purely with the phenotype, can in the long run keep ahead of mutations so as indefinitely to enhance or even preserve human well-being. The assumption bears a close analogy to that made by anti-Malthusians when they suppose that means can be found of continuing to increase the earth's supply of food, goods, and living room to accommodate a population that keeps on growing at its present rate. That rate, some 1.75 per cent per year, would amount to a thousand fold increase every 400 years. The accumulation of mutations is an inordinately slower process than the expansion of population. Yet in either case the process will inevitably come to a halt too late, as a result of the misery and disorganization which it brings about, unless it is forestalled through long-range foresight that exercises a conscious control over reproduction. In the case of the population problem, that control need be exercised only over the total quantity of reproduction, whereas, to meet the mutation problem, the control must be exercised in a qualitative way—a much more difficult and still more important matter.

A favorite cliche with those who do not understand this situation is the statement that, by definition, natural selection must always be acting and must always be favoring the fitter. This statement overlooks the fact that the degree of genetically occasioned difference in reproductive rate—that is, the intensity of selection—can be far less in some situations than in others. But the major point disregarded here is that what is fitter in the immediate acts of life is not always fitter for a group or a species as a whole in the long run. In such a case the group is running a race toward debasement and sometimes toward extinction, in this respect following the great majority of species of the past. In the case of man, the trick factor in this connection is a very unusual one: culture. Although culture did serve to sharpen salutary types of human selection in the past, as we have seen, it has now reached a point at which its very efficiency, when not yet involving foresight in regard to genetics, has placed upon society the burden of supporting almost indiscriminately the ever increasing genetic failings of its members.

If in accordance with the above cliche we define fitness in the narrow (but erroneous) sense, by the criterion of leaving a larger number of immediate offspring, then, of course, later generations of man must, by definition, be increasingly fit. Yet this type of fitness is no longer the same as fitness in regard to the qualities conducive to the well-being and survival of mankind in general. In fact, it seems not unlikely that, in regard to the human faculties of the highest group importance—such as those needed for integrated understanding, foresight, scrupulousness, humility, regard for others, and self-sacrifice—cultural conditions today may be conducive to an actually lower rate of reproduction on the part of their possessors than of those with the opposite attributes. Is it not too often true that today, when birth control is available, those persons most lacking in perspective or dominated by superstitious taboos or unduly egotistical or unmindful of others' needs or shiftless or bungling in techniques are the very ones with the largest retinue of children, whether legitimate or otherwise? These considerations raise the possibility that a much faster-acting and more serious cause of genetic deterioration than the previously discussed accumulation of detrimental mutations occurring in the wake of relaxed selection is an actual reversal of selection in regard to those psychological traits that are of the highest social importance. Objective data are badly needed on this question.

* * *

Statesmen, economists, social scientists, and men of affairs are seldom interested in such remote matters. Yet, as evolutionists, we know that the greatest and most creative, as well as the most destructive, operations of the living world have been of this creeping, secular character. Unless we are willing to remain, when viewed in larger perspective, helpless creatures of circumstances, we must take these insidious operations into account, master their principles, and devise ways of dealing with them.

IV. *The Protection of Our Genetic Heritage*

The crux of the problem is the interference with salutary types of selection in man that has arisen incidentally as a by-product of the widespread and increased effectiveness of mutual aid when it utilizes the tools supplied by science. What means can be used to protect our genetic heritage from this paradoxical situation? Occasional reactionary voices are to be heard calling upon us to reduce our mutual aid in the name of "rugged individualism," "private enterprise," or the like, and others are asking for a moratorium on science and even for a return to a fancied golden age.

However, it has been exactly the combination of intelligence with cooperative behavior that has made culture possible and raised men above beasts, and these propensities brook no stopping point. The enormous advances opening to men in consequence of the further extension of science (representing intelligence) and of a worldwide social organization (representing mutual aid) so utterly overshadow, in their potential effects within the next few hundred years, the damage that may be done in that period to men's genetic constitution that none but the unbalanced would consider now giving up, for genetic reasons, the march of civilization.

* * *

The main role of science in this matter is the discovery of the situation, but it will be important to get much more information concerning its details, both qualitative and quantitative, and concerning the kinds of strategies that would be effective in meeting it. However, the choice and implementation of these strategies is largely bound up with men's attitudes in regard to mutual aid.

Although the mores of our society approve the extension of society's aid to individuals for the purpose of saving their lives and thereby enabling them to reproduce, they do not yet, reciprocally, recognize a duty on the part of individuals to exercise their reproductive functions with due regard to the benefit or injury thereby done to society. So long as illegitimacy is avoided, the individual is not considered to be under any genetic obligation but deems it his right to have as many or as few children as he personally wishes. This being the case, his choice in the matter is largely determined by irrational factors

and by shortsighted aims. Such practices worked out well enough genetically only so long as, in matters of survival, the families or the small groups were in large measure on their own.

What is most needed in this area of living is an extension of the feeling of social responsibility to the field of reproduction: an increasing recognition that the chief objective in bringing children into the world is not the glorification of the parents or ancestors by the mere act of having children but the well-being of the children themselves and, through them, of subsequent generations in general. When people come to realize that in some measure their gifts as well as their failings and difficulties—physical, intellectual, and temperamental—have genetic bases and that social approval or disapproval will be accorded them if they take these matters into account in deciding how much of a family to beget, a big step forward will have been taken in the motivation of human reproduction.

It can become an accepted and valued practice to seek advice, though not dictation, in these matters, even as it is today in matters of individual health. Although no one enjoys admitting his faults, he can learn to take pride in exercising humility and ordering the most important of his biological functions—reproduction—in such ways as to win the approbation of himself and his fellows. This is, to be sure, a higher type of mutual aid, a superior moral code, than exists at present, but it can be just around the corner for people who have been alerted from early youth to the facts of genetics and evolution and who have been imbued with a strong sense of their participation in the attainment of human well-being.

Those for whom it seems wiser, in the interests of the coming generation, not to play as active a part as they might in producing people plagued by the very shortcomings that they have seen bring trouble to themselves can still find plenty of meritorious and satisfying work to give them a sense of fulfilment. Nearly everyone is above average at something and should be given opportunity to exercise his aptitudes in ways that do him credit and aid society. He may be a skilled teacher or custodian of the the young, although, because of some unfortunate defect or combination of weaknesses, he is less suitable than the average for personal reproduction. If instructed from the beginning regarding the nature of the human effort and the interdependence of man, he can take this realization in his stride and devote himself to kinds of activity in which he can take pride.

That is not to say, of course, that there can be hard-and-fast rules and that any one or a few known genetic defects should enjoin a person from reproduction. Everyone has many minor and some more serious inherent imperfections. In conscious decisions, as in the process of primitive natural selection, it is the total balance of these that should count, and the answer need seldom be an all-or-none one.

Contrariwise, for those clearly better endowed, this kind of social motivation should lead them to place special importance on creating children, even though in such cases especially there will be much temptation to expend disproportionately much effort in other directions. It is true that economic and other aids could be of value here. However, the underlying mores will inevitably exert the most powerful influence. The main job, if the situation is to be rectified, consists in laying the foundations for these mores.

This does not mean that we can expect ever to specify just what would be the optimal number of children for any given individual to have, in view of his genetic constitution. Natural selection would never have succeeded in the past if such precision were necessary. Environmental influences always complicate, sometimes inextricably, the determination of developed traits. It is enough, from a long-range point of view, if only the trend is in a salutary direction. And that is the result that must be sought in the attempt to protect man's most invaluable possession—his own genetic material.

Two developments of our present period are powerful positive influences toward the needed change in motivation. One is the sudden realization of the damaging effects of radiation on heredity. This, by reason of having been made a political football, has done more to arouse the public and its leaders to the fact that our genetic constitution requires protection than all the propaganda that eugenists have ever put forth. Characteristically, the danger has been greatly exaggerated. . . . Nevertheless, the over-all effect of the controversy has been highly educational and has helped to make people far more genetics-conscious than they ever were before. It so happens that this same radiation problem is one of the proper faces of the ax which is here being ground. Thus it is fitting to take advantage of the receptivity created by political circumstances to awaken the public to the more general need for a reformation of attitude toward reproduction.

The other relevant development of our time is the menace of over-population. Even publicists are at last becoming alarmed at the smothering of cultural advance and the disaster to democratic institutions that it can bring about in a generation or two if unchecked. Its checking absolutely requires not only that birth-control techniques be made available but also that large masses of people execute an about-face in their attitudes toward having children. They must recognize that to have or not to have children, and how many, should be determined primarily by the interests of the children themselves—that is, of the next and subsequent generations. If this change in outlook is effected—as it must be sooner or later—it is a relatively short step to the realization that the inborn equipment of the children also counts mightily in their well-being and opportunity for happiness.

V. *The Genetic Offensive*

Thus far I have emphasized conserving the genetic goods we have. As in most defensive operations, it is a dreary, frustrating business to have to run as fast as one can merely to stay in the same place. Nature did better for us. Why can we not do better for ourselves? For both psychological and material reasons, the best defensive in this as in other matters is the offensive.

A man finds little incentive to take steps to ward off a hidden danger that is a thousand or ten thousand years away. But when there is a definite possibility of tangible improvement in the conditions of life within a period such that he or his wards can directly experience it, then a man's efforts can be enlisted far more effectively.

Why should we or anyone else who has become aware of the marvelous advances that have been made in biological evolution consider it sufficient merely to keep things as good as they are if we can do much more than that? Certainly, the majority of mankind have come, within a few generations, to set their objectives much higher in the case of cultural evolution, now that they have learned how astonishingly amenable it can be to their own contrivings. They are also making considerable progress in the genetic reshaping of organisms of service to them. It seems almost inevitable that, if civilization avoids its present opposite pitfalls of mutual extermination and over-population, men will in the not too distant future want to utilize also, for their own benefit, the vast, though more unwieldy, possibilities of their own biological advancement. But, to make this advance, false gods will have to fall along the way.

It is sometimes objected that our cultural evolution has superseded our biological evolution. Nothing in either of these processes is inherently exclusive of the other, even though, as we have seen, culture is now developing in a way that does tend to run counter to biological progress. It is also asserted that biological progress is no longer necessary, since so much more rapid, radical, and diverse improvements can be effected by cultural means—not only with physical and chemical techniques and educational and sociological methods but ultimately too, no doubt, in embryological, including neurological, ways of modifying patterns.

The vast potentialities of cultural advance (subject to the mutational limitations previously discussed) are not to be denied. On the contrary, they need to be emphasized even more. But we should not think of phenotypic and genotypic operations as rivals. They can do best when they proceed in the same direction, even as they did in the formative days of our species. It is culture that chiefly distinguishes the scientist from the witch doctor, but it is genes that distinguish man from protozoon or virus and make his mastery of culture possible. In fact, the genetic and the cultural advances cannot even be considered additive; they are related more like the factors in a product formed by multiplying one by the other. Thus a small improvement in the genes may, in effect, work out as an enormous advance when there is already a high type of culture. Conversely, when acting with a high genetic endowment, a relatively small cultural advance can attain far more significance than otherwise.

The same kind of change in attitude toward reproduction as needed to insure the preservation of our genetic heritage is also the necessary basis for its improvement. If once it is accepted that the function of reproduction is to produce children who are as happy, healthy, and capable as possible, then it will be only natural for people to wish each new generation to represent a genetic advance, if possible, over the preceding one rather than just a holding of the line. And they will become impatient at confining themselves to old-fashioned methods if more promising ones for attaining this end are available. As the individualistic outlook regarding procreation fades, more efficacious means of working toward this goal will recommend themselves. In time, children with genetic difficulties may even come to be resentful toward parents who had not used measures calculated to give them a better heritage. Influenced in advance by this anticipation and also by the desire for community approval in general, even the less idealistic of the parental generation will tend increasingly to follow the genetic practices most likely to result in highly endowed children.

But before discussing these questions of biological means, it is important to consider ends—or, rather, objectives. We may start by a brief dismissal of the contention sometimes raised that one cannot recognize merits higher than one's own, nor lift one's self by one's bootstraps. If this were true, there would be no use in self-criticism, and persons of exceptionally high ability would never be identified except by each other. However, given the thesis that men can come to realize in some measure their own limitations and can conceive of beings superior to themselves, this question must be faced: By what criteria should they decide what changes would be desirable? For without some consensus on this ultimate question of values, men's efforts in biological—and, for that matter, also in cultural—directions can only be at cross-purposes.

VI. *Values.*

* * *

Despite the carpings and quibblings of some philosophers, the most generalized rational formulation of human aims that most persons concerned with the subject can agree upon is the promotion of the greatest over-all happiness. We need not define happiness more precisely here than as the sense of fulfilment derived from the attainment, or from approaching the attainment, of whatever is deeply desired. (Any one of a number of other terms might, of course, be substituted for "happiness" here, provided that it be defined in this way.) Granted that in given cases one man's meat can be another's poison and that some find fulfilment in actually giving pain to others, most men recognize that, from a longer-range standpoint, these interpersonal disharmonies are undesirable, in that they allow less over-all happiness. In the same class would come a one-sided attachment to subsidiary aims—such as the satisfaction of pride in the building of pyramids or in the unlimited accumulation of luxuries—that reduces the capacity to contribute to the over-all welfare and thereby hinders the survival, expansion, and long-term happiness of the group.

The will to self-development—hedonism—the urge to achieve—functionalism—the ideal of service—altruism—and a spiritual attitude toward existence—consecration—all these modes of approach to living, when followed up logically, become finally resolved into the pursuit of the same objective. The reason that self-development can be included among these orientations is that man is a naturally social animal in whose individual personality a major role is played by his regard for others. The final objective, likewise, may be thought of and designated in different ways, such as human happiness, richness of life, welfare, increasing survival, or advancement, since these are all diverse aspects of one great combination that in practice remains inseparable.

* * *

This question must then be raised: What genetic and cultural backgrounds are conducive to the highest success, as judged by the ulterior criterion of their promotion of over-all happiness? First, it is evident that the distribution of relative strengths of different drives that was most appropriate to the success of people when they were divided into many small, nearly autonomous groups is far from that most suitable for men organized into a vast society engaged in scientific and technological advances, mechanized production, transportation and communication, predominantly common interests, and rational, democratically guided decisions. Surely in this society most of us could do better if, by nature as well as by training, we had less tendency to quick anger, blinding fear, strong jealousy, and self-deceiving egotism. At the same time we need a strengthening and extension of the tendencies toward kindliness, affection, and fellow feeling in general, especially toward those personally far removed from us. These impulses should become sufficiently dynamic to issue in helpful action. As regards other affective traits, there is much room for broadening and deepening our capacity to appreciate both natural and man-made constructions, to interpret with fuller empathy the expressions of others, to create ever richer combinations of our own impressions, and to communicate them to others more adequately.

Another direction in which an advance is needed is in those traits of character that lead to independence of judgment and its necessary complement, intellectual honesty. We need to strengthen the drive to see things through to as near the bottom as possible and also the drive to coordinate the elements rationally. Just as important are the will and ability to take fair criticism with good grace and, further, to search and criticize ourselves until we recognize and discard, if need be publicly, judgments based on wishful or faulty thinking or on defective data. Of course, a great deal of all this may be taught, but there seem also to be great inborn differences in the facility and degree with which such emotion-fraught mental operations are learned and in the strength of feeling behind them.

Turning now to more purely intellectual matters, it is obvious that tomorrow's world makes desirable a much greater capacity for analysis, for quantitative procedures, for integrative operations, and for imaginative creation. With more and more of the daily grind taken over by automation, the human being will be increasingly freed for higher mental jobs; yet most of our population today would be by nature ill-adapted for such activities, even if they had the desire to pursue them.

How ignoble and inadequate for its potentialities is a society in which the material operations are conducted by the utilization of the equations of Willard Gibbs, Rutherford, Einstein, and Planck, while most of the human beings who are served thereby have hardly a glimmering of what is involved—while seeking to turn these forces chiefly to such purposes as broadcasting television commercials, football games, burlesque shows, and revival meetings, or seeing Europe in a week or accurately dropping H-bombs nine thousand miles away. Missed are the opportunities for those profound stirrings which would be theirs if they could and would follow the inner workings of these forces that the combined efforts of a relatively few among them have put at their disposal. Missed also is the thrilling awareness of what vastly enlarged possibilities a more rational use of these and other powers could open up to everyone. If men are not to be mere cogs in their work and pawns in their play, they must have deeper and broader vision as well as a more virile, broadly based comradeliness. Then their machines and science can give them increasing freedom for further achievement and further savoring of the bounties of our expanding universe instead of deeper enslavement in routines.

How are men to attain the higher intelligence and enhanced fellow feeling and sensitivity that will better fit them to the modern world? Certainly there can and must be reforms in the ways and mores of society, and especially in the bringing-up and teaching of children, that will work major improvements. Some enthusiasts for biological techniques even hope that some day, by means of suitable elixirs, the growing brain may be influenced favorably during its embryonic development. But we cannot rest in the precarious hope for such a miracle. And it would be beyond reason to expect that cultural methods alone, powerful though they are, could bring to the average man that ability to understand, appreciate, and exploit the forces of nature and artifice which is today reserved for the specialist in his respective field. Yet a considerable measure of that ability, in every field at once, must become the property of the common man if he is to enter into the great cultural inheritance that will make him a really voluntary agent, led by the mind and not by the nose.

Correspondingly, a man's nature must also have at its very core a genuine warmth of feeling for his fellows if, despite the personal difficulties, compromises, and renunciations that inevitably beset everyone, he is to derive an adequate sense of fulfilment from his and their joint day-by-day efforts and achievements, and also from the larger contemplation of grand-scale human progress. This, too, is a situation which calls for not only cultural methods but also genetic ones.

That genetic methods could be effective is illustrated by the vast individual differences in native intellectual capacity, temperament, and emotional pattern that exist among human beings, even as among other higher animals. Studies of twins and people brought up in institutions and foster homes have shown clearly the high, though far from absolute, importance of their heredity in the determination of psychological as well as so-called physical traits. Undoubtedly, even seemingly minute features of the personality can be strongly influenced by the genes. More important, there are abundant instances of extremely high mental ability, of a generalized kind, reappearing conspicuously in some members of families while missing other members. Certainly, there is already genetic material on hand, recognizable through its expressions, which, if conferred on the population at large, could enable men in general to find freedom and release by engaging in great co-operative as well as individual assaults against the seeming inexorabilities of the outer world and their own stubborn natures and by giving the feelings thus engendered creative and artistic expressions.

For achieving this end, which, after all, would be only another beginning, it is imperative that men think through their values to the point at which they recognize the primary importance for themselves of these two essentials: deeper mental insight and the feelings that give them joy in common action and in individual creation that can be shared. At present they are likely to place equal or greater emphasis on nonessentials. If genetic methods are to be used, men must come to realize that at this stage of their development they still have many divisive tendencies, provincial attachments to styles, features, and peculiarities of their own particular group. They must learn that such predilections, about which they could now wrangle endlessly, must be discounted and set as much in the background of their thoughts as possible, in order that emphasis may be placed on the key faculties mentioned—which, after all, count the most for everyone. No people, no caste or class, has a monopoly on these essentials. But there is everywhere a dearth of them, in relation to present needs. Let men become more conscious of this dearth and, conversely, of the richer life that later generations may have in proportion to the degree to which that dearth is remedied. In the meantime, no one need fear that there will be a danger of men's really salutary diversities becoming wiped out. And later, in a wiser, kindlier age, men may more safely and calmly consider how this spice of life—variety—can be turned to better account.

VII. Motivations in Reproduction

It cannot be denied that the technological and social innovations of our age combined with the influence of the scientific world view, are weakening the hold of ancient taboos and superstitions, loosening the rigidities of the family system, and greatly liberalizing the attitude of large numbers of people in regard to matters of sex. Within the twentieth century, in fact, the change has been so pronounced as to justify the application of the term "sexual revolution" to this situation, even though the ostensible, officially proclaimed standards are still much the same as in Victorian times. As yet this revolution has been of a predominantly individualistic kind. It has concerned itself chiefly with making people freer of the natural reproductive consequences of sex and therefore less rigorously bound sexually, as well as less burdened with excessive childbearing and childrearing. But it has not concerned itself with the converse matter—allowing the decisions leading to parenthood to become more rational from a genetic viewpoint and to be guided in greater measure by the type of native endowment that would be valuable for the children themselves. A further break with tradition is necessary before such a viewpoint can lead to perceptible changes in this respect.

The way to such a reform in viewpoint is paved by several groups of circumstances. One of these is the sexual revolution itself. A second is the trend toward a more social outlook in general, brought about by the increasing degree of cooperation in our society consequent upon the impact of scientific and technological advances on our economic and political system. A third, more specific, influence is brought to bear as the pressure of too rapidly increasing population causes increasing numbers of people to realize that the interests of the potential children themselves must be taken into account in decisions whether to reproduce and that the implementation of these decisions requires their using artificial controls for preventing reproduction where advisable. At the same time, sterility is becoming increasingly remediable. Finally, and still more pertinent, although not yet operative, will be the realization that artificial means are already at hand, and others nearly at hand, whereby the likelihood of the child's receiving a superior genetic endowment can be greatly improved without individual sex practices being thereby interfered with. It is this fourth factor that must increasingly turn the scales.

Nevertheless, it remains true that some long-intrenched attitudes, especially the feelings of proprietary rights and prerogatives about one's own germinal material, supported by misplaced egotism, will have to yield to some extent. This feeling does not represent a natural instinct, since there are primitive tribes yet alive who do not have even the concept of biological fatherhood and others that, although having it, readily and without their parental relationships being affected thereby, adopt, confer, or exchange infants. That is, their egotism does not extend to their stirps. Actually, they are more logical in this respect than are most of the persons in more advanced societies who pride themselves on their ancestry or inborn constitution. For that is the one thing they themselves have been least—in fact, not at all—responsible for. Moreover, paradoxically, this kind of pride is today likely to be more intense in persons who are less, rather than more, fortunately endowed.

To more than balance the necessary weakening of this time-worn vanity in regard to one's stirps, other feelings will tend to develop that are of equal or greater potency. Among them will be justifiable pride in accomplishment of a far more exacting and laudable kind than that of procreation: namely, having made children of especially high endowment possible and having brought them up. Deep attachments to these children will develop, and a justified sense of identification. These new reproductive mores will come into being only very gradually. At first, only those with freer and more daring spirits will venture on these alien-seeming paths (to be indicated in the following two sections). There will be no clear break, and in the same family children of choice and children of tradition will grow up side by side in mutually helpful familial association. But "nothing succeeds like success," and the successes in these instances will often be outstanding.

VIII. *Presently Available Genetic Techniques*

*   *   *

What now are the means that would make such positive selection possible in man? The most effective method presently feasible is, of course, artificial insemination. Many thousands of people have already been begotten in the United States by this procedure—a considerable proportion of them, although not most, by sperm of donors other than the husband when the husband was sterile. Here is an excellent opportunity for the entering wedge of positive selection, since the couples concerned are nearly always, under such circumstances, open to the suggestion that they turn their exigency to their credit by having as well-endowed children as possible.

Unfortunately, most of the physicians in such cases, deterred by the fear of public and legal censure and having little appreciation of genetic matters, seem to be chiefly concerned with hiding their operations and avoiding a conspicuous result or failure that they might be blamed for, and they furtively attempt to produce a child as nearly as possible like that which might have been born if the father had been fertile. With this aim, they choose a donor resembling the husband in physique and even in religion, free from readily detectable defects, of course, and they are careful to keep the identity of this donor as secret as possible. Often a medical student or intern, if he is discreet and close at hand, serves, for a consideration, as a multiple donor, without regard for the fact that U.S. Army I.Q. tests have indicated this group to have the lowest mental ratings of all professions tested. But cases have been reported of out-of-work men, originally picked up in bars, who make an easy living by regularly selling their semen on what amounts to a mass scale. Thus opportunities for introducing a substantial genetic leaven into the population at large are flouted.

Insemination by an outside donor has now gone on for so long and become so prevalent that it is high time for it to come out into the open, even in individual instances. A judge in Chicago branded the procedure "adultery," but a number of precedents in which the children were begotten by consent of both husband and wife have been held to be legal. It is highly important for the genetic paternities of the children thus produced to be properly recorded. Not only would invaluable data be provided in human genetics and selection but, more specifically, better judgments could thereafter be made concerning the genetic potentialities of the given donors and their descendants. It should be recognized that the couple concerned in such a case, as well as the physician, have performed a service to mankind meriting not disgrace but honor. With such an outlook, even before it was generally held, both physician and couple would be armed with better incentives to take genetic considerations into account. They would be encouraged to make the best use possible of such a chance to engender the most precious thing we know of: a worthy human being.

Perhaps university teachers in scientific subjects are, through their personal experiences, better aware than any other large group of persons of the enormous differences in over-all intelligence between the average and the best endowed and of the fact that training, though essential, cannot be an adequate substitute for high native endowment. For real competence in understanding and dealing with the world as known by science, only a mind that is truly exceptional in terms of the now existing distribution will suffice. However, general intelligence is complex and multi-factorial, despite the existence of rare genes that individually have a decidedly enhancing influence on intelligence (shown by cases of long-persisting, sharply segregating effects in given pedigrees). Because of this complexity, the progeny of individuals of exceptionally high intellectual endowment tend to exhibit considerable regression and variability, even among the better-endowed segregants. This by no means signifies that selection in this area is futile—it can, in fact, have a high over-all degree of success. Rather, it underlines the importance of choosing as donors individuals of the most outstanding native mental ability—that is, those at the extreme end of the positive tail of the distribution—so far as possible, and when they do not have serious defects in other directions. Moreover, those individuals should be preferred as donors whose relatives give considerable evidence that the superior qualities are highly inheritable.

Fortunately, such a high degree of selection as here indicated is made possible by the method of artificial insemination, by reason of the large number of spermatozoa that each individual usually produces. Recently the technique of freezing spermatozoa to very low temperatures was introduced into practice, and, thanks to the accumulation of sperm thus made possible, the frequency of successful conceptions has been raised considerably above that following either natural insemination or artificial insemination of the more usual type. The deep-frozen spermatozoa can be stored virtually indefinitely without deterioration. Thus a considerable supply can in time be gathered from a chosen donor and preserved for any desired length of time. For purposes of selection, there would in such cases be enormous advantages in postponing the use of most of this supply until, say, twenty years after the donor's decease. In retrospect and after much emotionally based pressure and prejudice, both pro and con, that had arisen out of the donor's personal relationships had faded, much less biased judgments could be made concerning his actual merits as well as shortcomings. During the "probationary period," a limited but significant amount of progeny testing could be carried out to afford a sounder estimate of the donor's genetic potentialities.

Such a procedure would also have considerable psychological advantages, for it would eliminate that bane of present-day gynecologists who practice artificial insemination—the fear of intrigue arising between the donor and the woman concerned if either one learns the identity of the other. The motivation for possible jealous reactions of the husband would at the same time be greatly diminished. Moreover, both members of the couple, as well as all other persons, would be much more likely to recognize the donor's exceptional worth, a worth that would usually put him out of a class with living competitors. Finally, the chief present objections to have the identity of the donor known would be removed. Instead, all interested persons would wish to have the relationships concerned entirely above-board.

As was recently pointed out by Dr. Richard Meier, of the Mental Health Research Institute of the University of Michigan, another method of genetic upgrading is the outright adoption of children by those who otherwise cannot or do not wish to bear children or wish to have less than the average quota of their own genetic progeny. Since such practice does not involve as radical a departure from present-day customs and attitudes as does artificial insemination, it might recommend itself more readily in wide circles. This procedure presupposes, of course, that couples of high native endowment would be willing to bear more children than they could bring up and give them out for adoption. Those consenting to do this would truly be socially minded.

Perhaps in the long run, though, this method would interfere more with people's personal lives and occasion more risk of undesirable personal entanglements than the half-adoption represented by artificial insemination. Certainly the outright adoption method here suggested would not allow selection to be as rigorous, even though the eggs as well as the sperm are to some extent specially selected. Then, too, this method would lack the psychological advantage, operative in the earlier transitional period of feelings on the subject, of at least half the genetic material having been derived from those who are to bring up the child. But there is no doubt that the method would be better adapted than artificial insemination for some situations and could thus serve a useful function.

IX. Technical Advances in the Offing

We are surely just around the corner from other advances in artificial techniques concerned with production that might extend the possibilities of positive selection much further. For example, there have as yet been only a few abortive attempts to cultivate either male or female germ cells outside the body. An energetic program of research on the subject would probably be successful within a few years in enabling spermatogonia, at least, to be multiplied indefinitely in vitro and to be induced, when desired, to undergo the processes of maturation into spermatozoa. If this could be done, then spermatogonia instead of spermatozoa might be preserved in the deep-frozen state, a technique that has already proved successful with some types of somatic cells. Later, at any desired date, the spermatogonia could be multiplied and caused to mature so as to furnish an unlimited supply of mature spermatozoa from an originally small amount of material derived from any given donor. Only our present superstitious attitudes prevent such research from being actively pursued today.

As for the female germ cells, means are already known whereby the multiple release of mature eggs can readily be effected within the female with the aid of pituitary hormones. Only a little research would be required to develop methods of flushing out these eggs from the female reproductive tract, to be fertilized in vitro with chosen sperm and then implanted in selected female hosts at the appropriate stage of their reproductive cycle. This procedure is parallel to artificial insemination. It permits the multiple distribution of eggs of a highly selected female into diverse recipient females, yet allows the child to be derived, on its paternal side, from the recipient's husband.

It is not unlikely that techniques involving mature eggs could be combined with deep freezing to allow indefinitely prolonged storage. Thus similar advantages, selectional as well as psychological, might be gained for the female germ cells as are already available, even though not yet in use, for spermatozoa.

Such techniques applied to the eggs could, of course, be combined with artificial insemination by sperm of a donor other than the recipient's husband when the couple desired it. This would be another method equivalent to outright adoption. However, it would afford the opportunity for far more powerful selection than adoption of the relatively primitive sort previously discussed and would avoid the possible psychological and social difficulties that might attend such adoption.

*   *   *

When one considers how much the world owes to single individuals of the order of capability of an Einstein, Pasteur, Descartes, Leonardo, or Lincoln, it becomes evident how vastly society would be enriched if they were to be manifolded. Moreover, those who repeatedly proved their worth would surely be called upon to reappear age after age until the population in general had caught up with them. In this way, then, mankind would be able to reap the benefit of that alternation of asexual reproduction, for reliably multiplying types of tested worth, with sexual reproduction, for trying ever new combinations, that has been so advantageous in some other classes of organisms. Later generations will look with amazement at the pitifully small amount of research now being carried on to open up such possibilities, even though for years specialists have realized that they lie just around the corner.

Just as our economic and political system is inevitably, although too slowly, being modified to fit our present technological capabilities of large-scale automatic production, despite the fervor with which men try to cling to their ancient preconceptions of how business and government should operate, so too on the biological side of human affairs the time-honored notions of how reproduction should be managed will gradually give way before the technological progress that is opening and will further open up new and more promising possibilities. Practices that today are confined to couples afflicted with sterility will be increasingly taken up by people who desire to improve their reproductive lot by bestowing on themselves children with a maximal chance of being highly endowed, and thereby to make an exemplary contribution to humanity. . . .

But recently there has been a tendency in some circles to bypass the arguments for positive selection by countering that instead means will be found of making direct alterations or substitutions of a desired kind in the genetic material itself while leaving it in the main unchanged. Such proposals range from the idea of substituting individual chromosomes or parts of chromosomes, derived from selected donors, in the chromosome set of a given person's germ cell to the idea of inducing by a mutagenic agent or ultra-fine manipulative process a given chemical change in a given gene. It would be very rash to deny that some day such extraordinary feats may be possible, but they are definitely not around the corner in the sense that the developments discussed above are.

Dismissing for the moment the unparalleled advances in technique that would here be necessary, we must take into account that such procedures would also require the most minute knowledge of the role played by individual genes in the inordinately complex economy of the human organism, including its highest, most multifactorial functions, such as general intelligence. It would also be necessary to know the locations of these genes in the genetic map. And if mutations were actually to be induced or nucleotide substitutions made, we should have to know the internal constitution of these genes and the functions in them of each of their tens or hundreds of thousands of nucleotides. Though the nucleotides are of only four kinds, it is their precise arrangement in line that counts. It is not likely that all this will be worked out before men are on a much higher genetic as well as cultural level than they are today.

*   *   *

X. More Distant Prospects

Evolution in the past has been for the most part a matter of millions of years. In this larger view, what we have been discussing is but a matter of today—the step we are just about to take. So great are the present psychological impediments to this step, arising out of our traditions, that we have not had time to consider the enormous vistas beyond.

The rapid upgrading of our general intelligence must be accompanied and co-ordinated as closely as possible with a corresponding effort to infuse into the genetic basis of our moral natures the springs of stronger, more genuine fellow feeling. At the same time, especially interested groups will see to it that diverse abilities and proclivities of specific types will here and there be multiplied, both those of a more purely intellectual nature and those making possible more far-reaching and poignant appreciation of the varied kinds of experiences that life may offer. As all these genetic resources of mankind grow richer, they will increasingly be combined to give more of the population many of their benefits at once. Observation shows that these faculties are not antagonistic but rather mutually enhancing. Finally, increasing attention can be paid to what is called the physical side: bettering the genetic foundations of health, vigor, and longevity; reducing the need for sleep; bringing the induction of sedation and stimulation under better voluntary control; and increasing physical tolerances and aptitudes in general.

In many physical respects there are optimal degrees of development for given types of organisms, beyond which other functions tend to be too much interfered with. Yet these optima are seldom absolute, for there are often ways of breaking through the seeming limits by means of novel developments that open new directions for solving the old problems. These directions of inquiry are so advanced that we may leave them to the more competent minds of the future to tackle.

But at least so far as intelligence is concerned, there are no indications that we are now approaching any physiologically set limit or optimum. It is quite evident that we could benefit indefinitely by a continued increase in our mental powers: to enable us to analyze more profoundly; to recognize more readily common features when they lie deeply buried; to grasp more and more elements of a situation at once and co-ordinately; to see more steps ahead; to think more multi-dimensionally; and to imagine more creatively. Here too it is to be hoped that new breakthroughs will eventually be found; otherwise, limits will in time appear. If only we take the first, most obvious steps that we have here been considering, we will be preparing the way for making our successors capable of planning ahead much further and more soundly than we ourselves of this fumbling generation can.

It is so easy to sit smugly back in the conceit that we have now reached nearly the acme of biological evolution and that, except for eventually bestowing on everyone the genetic advantages already enjoyed by the most favored, we can hereafter confine our advances to cultural evolution, including the manipulation of things outside our own genetic constitutions. It is true that cultural evolution in this broad sense, is far more diversified, rapid, and explosive, both figuratively and literally, than biological evolution can be. There is every reason to extrapolate, along with "science-fiction" enthusiasts (despite their frequent unbalance!), that if men do not destroy each other, they will cultivate the deserts, jungles, poles, and oceans, extend their domain successively to ever more distant worlds, and perhaps even, as first suggested by Bernal, build colonies in space itself. Along with the increasing understanding and mastery over physico-chemical forces that such expansion implies, there will be corresponding advances in the biological and social realms. That is, there will be spectacular progress in means of reshaping and controlling bodily structures and functions by operations repeated in each generation anew, and also in means of interrelating people psychologically to achieve higher, more harmonious, and more constructive interactions of their feelings, thoughts, and doings. Yet all this does not mean that genetic advances beyond the stage represented by the happiest possible combinations of the best endowed of present-day humanity would be either supererogatory, unimportant, or relatively limited.

If their genetic constitution is so unimportant for beings with such advanced means of extragenic control as envisaged for our successors of, say, 500 years from now, why could they not just about as well use apes or even lowlier creatures instead of men and duly reconstruct and train them? Or, if the genetic difference between apes and men is really so important in determining their amenability to profit by culture and to contribute to it, why would not beings as far beyond present-day men, genetically, as we are beyond the apes be inordinately better suited still for exploiting the benefits of culture? The biological distance from apes to men is a relatively slight one, yet how potent! And do we hastily made-over apes really believe that, having attained this makeshift form, further steps of this kind are to be despised? Our imaginations are woefully limited if we cannot see that, genetically just as well as culturally, we have by our recent turning of an evolutionary corner set our feet on a road that stretches far out before us into the hazy distance.

Of course, the genetic changes that would be desirable for us in the future are not, in the main, developments like fur, wings, photosynthetic ability, or anything else that would be less effective or less adaptable than our own artifices. They would not be replacements for cultural devices, but the very opposite: means of better gearing together the biological and the cultural, of making still more out of our culturally enhanced propensities, and of more effectively advancing our culture. As we have seen, this evolutionary trend actually began with the advent of man, although he was unaware of it as a long-term phenomenon. But now we may carry it forward consciously and with ever longer foresight.

Although the most important genetic advances for any creature who creates a culture are obviously those that suitably extend and enhance his psychological faculties, it is a mistake to conclude that corporeal changes of diverse kinds would be of little account—such as, for example, further developments of the senses, on the one hand, or of effector organs, on the other hand. Unfortunately, spelling out radical possibilities along these lines is likely to provoke more merriment than understanding at the present stage of purblindness in this field. For evolutionary biological developments would, in general, appear utterly fantastic to a group in whom they had not yet occurred, whereas, of course, after the event they are taken for granted as being the only reasonable arrangement.[1]

It would be presumptuous to try to specify here just what form the long-range developments are likely to take and in what sequence they will occur. Intellectual and moral developments of the types mentioned as most important now will probably continue to occupy the center of the

stage for a long time to come, if not indefinitely. The faculties here concerned could probably be extended and enhanced in many ways which our present ignorance of their structure does not permit us to even guess at.

Only after we humans have advanced considerably toward the higher level to which the rough-and-ready empirical methods now available can raise us, will we be in a position to make firmer, more definite plans envisaging longer-range possibilities. Only then, when we have developed superior intelligence and greater co-operativeness, can we expect to reach a workable degree of agreement on these plans. Only then can we begin to use more exact methods and to co-ordinate them better. It is too early for blueprints.

If we are to preserve that self-determination which is an essential feature of human intelligence, success, and happiness, our individual actions in the realm of genetics must be steps based on our own personal judgments and inclinations. They should be as voluntary as our other major decisions of life. Although these decisions are all conditioned by the mores about us, these mores can be specifically shaped and channelized by our own distinctive personalities. The immediate job, then, is to make a start at getting this genetic "Operation Bootstrap" incorporated into our mores, by precept and, where feasible, by example. But we must remember that the highest values to be sought in it are, in essence, those so long proclaimed but seldom actualized: wisdom and brotherhood, that is, the pursuit of "the true and the good." When it is realized that the genetic method offers simply an additional but indispensable approach toward this ancient ideal,

1. For this reason I will give only one illustration of how a biological, genetically based series of developments could be important to a species with an already highly advanced culture. This example has to do with the means of personal communication. At present these are largely confined, in man, to gestures and to some form of speech (including its derivative, writing). Speech, marvelously effective though it has been in the long run, is pitifully slow and plodding compared with the inner flow of ideas. It has special tendencies to be misleading, and it requires forcing everything into an inappropriate one-dimensional order. Wishful thinkers, mystics, and pseudo-scientists have long dreamed of telepathy to escape from the bondage of spoken forms. However, telepathy is a species of magic for which, so far as can be seen, no biological possibility exists. It might therefore appear unlikely that any biological kind of communication better than speech could arise in evolution.

Yet such a development, involving a combination of already known biological phenomena, is in fact conceivable. Many different types of organisms have developed light-emitting tissues. In some, such as the squid, the spatial and temporal pattern of the luminescence may be very complex and subject to considerable voluntary control. In some fish the light is projected through a special lens with reflector. However, a more eyelike structure, if its retinal surface were provided with luminous cells, might serve even better. The

main development, then, would be the suitable connection of the visually imaginative portion of the brain, point by point, with the luminescent layer in such wise that the visual patterns imagined in the cerebrum become transferred into luminescent patterns that can be seen by other individuals. In effect, this would be the reverse of the transference that occurs in seeing, when the image produced by light focused on the retina is transmitted, via impulses in the fibers of the optic nerve, so as to give rise to a corresponding pattern of stimulated cells in the occipital cortex. Now the actively radiating pattern in the luminescent layer could either be projected onto a screen in a darkened inclosure outside, where it might in turn be subject to amplification or recording, or, alternatively, it could be seen directly by a close-up inspection of the transmitting "eye" by the receiving eye.

In addition to direct visual representations of things, subject to motion as in a cinema, there would doubtless be diverse symbolizations of conceptual thoughts. All in all, such communication could be raised to a level of facility, directness, speed, multidimensionality, comprehensiveness, and precision so much higher than is afforded by speech as to inaugurate far more advanced processes of communing, of learning, of thinking itself, of appreciation, and of resulting action. But for bringing these potentialities to fruition, further improvements of a neurological and psychological nature would be in order, even as was the case with speech.

then our voluntary genetic efforts, scattered and disjointed though they must now be, will tend in a common direction.

There are sure to be powerful attempts to pull in diverse directions, in genetic just as in other matters, but we need not be afraid of this. The diversities will tend to enrich the genetic background, increasing the resources available for recombination. These partial attempts can then be judged by their fruits, and these fruits, where sound, will be added to our bounty.

It seems highly unlikely that, in a world-wide society at an advanced level of culture and technology, founded on the recognition of universal brotherhood, such diversities would proceed so far and for so long as again to split humanity on this shrunken planet into semi-isolated groups and that these groups would thenceforth undergo increasing divergence from one another. It is because man is potentially master of all trades that he has succeeded. And if his culture is to continue to evolve indefinitely, he must retain this essential placticity and with it the feeling that all men are, at bottom, of his own kind.

Through billions of years of blind mutations, pressing against the shifting walls of their environment, microbes finally emerged as men. We are no longer blind ; at least, we are beginning to be conscious of what has happened and of what may happen. From now on, evolution is what we make it, provided that we choose the true and the good. Otherwise, we shall sink back into oblivion. If we hold fast to our ideal, then evolution will become, for the first time, a conscious process. Increasingly conscious, it can proceed at a pace far outdistancing that achieved by trial and error—and in ever greater assurance, animation, and enthusiasm. That will be the highest form of freedom that man, or life, can have.

NOTES

NOTE 1.

BETTELHEIM, BRUNO
The Informed Heart*

The universal success of the Diary of Anne Frank suggests how much the tendency to deny is still with us, while her story itself demonstrates how such denial can hasten our own destruction. It is an onerous task to take apart such a humane and moving story, arousing so much compassion for gentle Anne Frank. But I believe that its world-wide acclaim cannot be explained unless we recognize our wish to forget the gas chambers and

* New York: The Free Press of Glencoe, 1960, pp. 252-254. Copyright 1960 by The Free Press, a Corporation. Reprinted with permission of the publisher.

to glorify attitudes of extreme privatization, of continuing to hold on to attitudes as usual even in a holocaust. Exactly because their going on with private life as usual brought destruction did it have to be glorified ; in that way we could overlook the essential fact of how destructive it can be under extreme social circumstances.

While the Franks were making their preparations for going passively into hiding, thousands of other Jews in Holland and elsewhere in Europe were trying to escape to the free world, the better to survive or to be able to fight their executioners. Others who could not do so went underground— not simply to hide from the SS, waiting passively, without preparation for fight, for the day when they would be caught—but to fight the Germans, and with it for humanity. All the Franks wanted was to go on with life as nearly as possible in the usual fashion.

Little Anne, too, wanted only to go on with life as usual, and nobody can blame her. But hers was certainly not a necessary fate, much less a heroic one ; it was a senseless fate. The Franks could have faced the facts and survived, as did many Jews living in Holland. Anne could have had a good chance to survive, as did many Jewish children in Holland. But for that she would have had to be separated from her parents and gone to live with a Dutch family as their own child.

Everybody who recognized the obvious knew that the hardest way to go underground was to do it as a family ; that to hide as a family made detection by the SS most likely. The Franks, with their excellent connections among gentile Dutch families should have had an easy time hiding out singly, each with a different family. But instead of planning for this, the main principle of their planning was to continue as much as possible with the kind of family life they were accustomed to. Any other course would have meant not merely giving up the beloved family life, but also accepting as reality man's inhumanity to man. Most of all it would have forced them to accept that going on with life as usual was not an absolute value, but can sometimes be the most destructive of all attitudes.

* * *

. . . [I]nfantile thought processes such as wishful thinking in place of a more mature evaluation of reality, and an infantile disregard for the possibility of death . . . led many to think that they of all others would be spared and survive, and many more to simply disbelieve in the possibility of their own death. Not believing in its possibility, they did not prepare for it, including no preparation for how to defend their lives even when death became inescapable. Defending their lives before such time might have hastened their death. So up to a point, this "rolling with the punches" that the enemy dealt out was protective of life. But beyond that point it was destructive of both one's own life and that of others whose survival might be more certain too if one risked one's own life. The trouble is that the longer one "rolls" with the punches, the more likely it becomes that one will no longer have the strength to resist when death becomes imminent, particularly if this yielding to the enemy is accompanied not by an inner strengthening of the personality (which it would require) but an inner disintegration.

Those who did not deny validity to death, who neither denied nor repressed its possibility, who embraced no childish belief in their indestructibility, were those who prepared for it in time as a real possibility. . . .

NOTE 2.

DUNN, L. C., and DOBZHANSKY, THEODOSIUS
Heredity, Race, and Society*

The essence of Mendel's discovery lay in his identification of the units of heredity. . . .

. . . Mendel first recognized genes from the manner in which specific visible characters of plants, such, for example, as flower color, reappeared in their offspring. His method was so simple that it can be repeated by anyone who can observe the results of controlled matings in any kind of animal or plant. When a plant of a pure purple-flowered variety of pea is crossed with a white-flowered plant, the seeds so produced always yield only purple-flowered plants. When these purple-flowered plants are allowed to produce their progeny these are found to consist of *two* kinds of plants with respect to flower color: about $\frac{3}{4}$ of them have purple flowers, and $\frac{1}{4}$ have white flowers. When seed from these plants, the grandchildren of the original purple-flowered and white-flowered plants, was planted, it was found that although the grandchildren comprised two visibly different types, they consisted of *three* different types in respect to their ability to transmit hereditary differences in flower color. Of all of the grandchildren, $\frac{1}{4}$ were like the purple grandparents, transmitting purple to all their offspring; $\frac{1}{2}$ were like the purple parents, transmitting purple to some of their offspring, white to others, while $\frac{1}{4}$ were like the white grandparents, transmitting white only to all their offspring. Actually, in one of

Mendel's experiments the grandchildren consisted of 705 purple- to 224 white-flowered plants (about 3:1); while of 100 of these purples tested 36 had only purple offspring, 64 had both purple and white, i.e., about 1:2. Thus, the whole generation consisted of about $\frac{1}{4}$ pure purple, $\frac{1}{2}$ hybrid purple, $\frac{1}{4}$ white. Since white is not expressed in the hybrid, Mendel called it *recessive* in contrast to the *dominant* purple which is expressed in the hybrid.

* * *

The essence of the theory he proposed was that traits like flower color are transmitted by means of units in the sex cells. One of these units can be purple *or* white, *never* a mixture. From a pure purple parent only purple units are transmitted; from a white one only white units, but a *hybrid,* that is, a plant whose parents were of different colors, such as purple and white, transmits two kinds of units, purple ones and white ones in equal numbers. When these two kinds of eggs in large numbers are fertilized by the two kinds of pollen, there result combinations of purple with purple, purple with white, white with purple and white with white. The first three types develop into purple plants, the last into white plants; hence the ratio $\frac{1}{4}$ like one grandparent (pure purple), $\frac{1}{2}$ like the parents (hybrid purple), $\frac{1}{4}$ like the other grandparent (pure white).

Often the ratio of $\frac{1}{4}: \frac{1}{2}: \frac{1}{4}$, which is the fundamental one in all heredity, is directly observable. . . .

* * *

Mendel found that this theory held true for every pair of characters which he studied in the pea plants; and it has been confirmed by experiments with hundreds of other kinds of animals and plants. In all cases, it has been shown that the genes contributed to the hybrids by the parents do not mix but are segregated into the different sex cells of the hybrid, so that in the progeny of hybrids a character of the parent will reappear uncontaminated by its passage through the hybrid. This law of heredity discovered by Mendel is known as the law of segregation.

* * *

Eugenical measures may be positive and negative. Positive eugenics programs urge people who are regarded as carriers of desirable gene combinations to undertake the responsibilities of parenthood. . . .

More enthusiasm has been shown in many places for negative eugenics, which urges elimination of undesirable genes by discouraging or making it impossible for persons who show the

---

* From *Heredity, Race, and Society* by L. C. Dunn and Theodosius Dobzhansky, pp. 44-47, 85-93. Copyright 1946, 1952 by New American Library. Published by arrangement with The New American Library of World Literature, Inc., New York.

effects of such genes to have children. . . .

Many eugenists believe that putting this program into practice would improve the physical and mental qualities of mankind within a few generations, and some of the more enthusiastic ones have put forward quite extravagant claims. For example, one of the speakers at the International Congress of Eugenics held in New York in 1932 asserted that "there is no question that a sterilization law, enforced throughout the United States, would result, in less than one hundred years, in eliminating at least 90 per cent of crime, insanity, feeblemindedness, moronism, and abnormal sexuality, not to mention many other forms of defectiveness and degeneracy. Thus within a century, our asylums, prisons, and state hospitals would be largely emptied of their present victims of human woe and misery." However, let us not be carried away by big promises without a careful examination of the possibilities of their fulfillment.

The purpose of negative eugenics is to do away with hereditary diseases and other traits which are considered harmful or undesirable. There is no practical possibility of sending away the carriers of undesirable genes, since our neighbors probably would not desire to receive them either. The program of negative eugenics must, then, prevent or discourage child-bearing by the possessors of undesirable traits.

Nature itself applies the negative eugenics method to traits which are disabling or crippling. Many hereditary disabilities and diseases, which are clearly undesirable, like amaurotic idiocy in which the child loses its mind and goes blind, kill the persons who inherit them before they can have children. If a gene with such an effect is dominant, it will quickly be purged from the population, and its frequency in the population can only be maintained by new mutations of normal to abnormal genes. . . .

But not all dominant abnormalities and diseases interfere with reproduction, and it is proposed to eliminate these by sterilizing or otherwise preventing the reproduction of persons who have such genes. Where such an undesirable trait can be diagnosed before the age of reproduction, and where it is certain that it is due to a defective gene, sterilization can be a dependable method for quickly getting rid of bad dominant genes. It obviously requires the consent of the state or other authority in preventing reproduction. If for some reason we should consider ability to taste PTC as undesirable and had the power to control human mating, we could easily produce a race which could not taste PTC. Tasting ability is, as we know, dominant. Just sterilize or otherwise prevent reproduction of all tasters and the job is done. Only non-tasters can have children and all

their children will be non-tasters. The problem would seem to be solved in one generation.

In practice it is not quite so simple. Some persons with dominant hereditary afflictions may remain undetected and may thus slip through the sterilization dragnet. It has been supposed, for example, that only about 10 per cent of all the persons who inherit a dominant gene for diabetes actually develop the disease. A severe disease like Huntington's chorea (which is due to a dominant gene) often does not manifest itself until relatively late in life after the gene has already been passed on to the next generation. Nevertheless there is no doubt that prevention of reproduction on the part of possessors of bad dominant genes would quickly reduce the number of such genes.

But not all of bad heredity is due to simple dominant genes. Some hereditary abnormalities depend upon interactions between more than one gene and certain environmental conditions. Take for example "Mongoloid" idiocy. Many children with the marks of this abnormality (short stature, broad skull, stubby hands, and other external features) are born each year. There are a number of cases in which both members of a pair of identical twins are idiots, while among fraternal twins it often happens that one is affected and the other is normal, suggesting that the disease is hereditary. It also tends to occur in more than one child in a family. It is possible that more than one gene, perhaps two different genes together, determine the abnormality. But the remarkable thing is that in a family with the hereditary tendency to produce "Mongoloid" children, it is much more frequent after the mother has passed the age of 35. There is something in the older mother that brings these genes to expression. Children of younger mothers undoubtedly inherit these same genes but since they are quite normal, they would escape any law designed to prevent the reproduction of such idiots.

The prospects for getting rid of bad heredity due to recessive genes are poorer than those for controlling undesirable dominant genes.

[E]very human being must fall into one of three categories in regard to each gene. We can call these categories AA, Aa and aa. If A stands for a dominant gene producing a certain trait, it can be recognized by its effects in AA and Aa people. But if the trait is recessive, like amaurotic idiocy, for example, it can be recognized only in the aa class, while it will be hidden in the Aa class. Now it happens that children afflicted with recessive diseases and abnormalities are born mostly to parents who are only heterozygous for the defective genes, and are themselves quite normal. Thus amaurotic idiots come only from Aa parents who are quite normal. That is to say, most of the recessive genes we might want to eliminate occur in hidden form in heterozygotes, in people who do not show them at all, instead of in homozygotes who could be identified and whose reproduction might consequently be prevented.

What proportions of the recessive genes are carried in hidden form in *Aa,* and in visible form in *aa* people depends on how common or how rare a given gene is in the population. . . .

. . . [I]f a gene for a recessive disease or abnormality is rare, nearly all of the genes will be found in *Aa* people who are themselves perfectly normal, although, of course, they transmit the disease to their offspring. In England, for example, about one in every 20,000 babies is an albino. This means that in the gene pool a little more than ninety-nine per cent of the genes are *A* (the gene for normal pigmentation) and less than one per cent are *a* (the gene for albinism). In this case about one and a half per cent of people will be *Aa* (normally pigmented carriers of albinism). The carriers are, hence, about 280 times as numerous as are the albinos.

Now suppose that we are seized with a desire to have a race of people who can all taste PTC. Taste-blindness for PTC is to be regarded as a harmful trait, a defect which is to be purged from the race for good (actually, those who can taste PTC are, of course, neither superior nor inferior to those who cannot). To realize this desire we should sterilize or otherwise prevent the taste-blind people from having children. Since taste-blindness behaves in heredity as a recessive trait, all the taste-blind persons are in the *aa* category. Thus, we can stop all of the *a* genes in the *aa* people from going on to the next generation. But the gene for taste-blindness is found in *Aa* people as well, and *Aa* persons happen to be about twice as numerous as are *aa* people. Thus, even if all the taste-blind people are sterilized, the gene for taste-blindness will be perpetuated through the *Aa carriers*. Some taste-blind children will be born in the next generation.

*   *   *

One generation after the introduction of the sterilization program the frequency of the defectives is cut to less than a half. So far, so good. But . . . to depress the frequency of the defectives from 6 to 3 per cent requires two generations. To reduce it further from 3 to about 1 per cent five generations will be needed. Ten more generations of an unrelenting sterilization program would carry the defectives down to 2 per 1000 ; ten more generations to 1 per thousand ; seventy generations more to 1 per 10,000. The average length of a human generation is about 25 years. The reader can see for himself how much time is needed for the benefits of such a program to be felt.

*   *   *

Now, we have tacitly assumed that the sterilization program is absolutely thorough, so that not a single defective ever escapes sterilization. It is, of course, doubtful if any program could be so airtight in practice. But even if we were able to enforce complete compliance with a sterilization program, the dependence of the effects of genes on the environment would be another stumbling block. . . .

Assume, for example, that in a certain population 10 per cent (1000 per 10,000) of individuals have a recessive defect. If all such individuals are eliminated from parenthood, the frequency of the defect in the next generation will be reduced to 576 per 10,000. But if only half of them are eliminated, the defect will appear in 790 per 10,000 ; if only 10 per cent are sterilized the defect will be present in 961 individuals out of each 10,000.

This impotence of programs of negative eugenics to cope with rare defects is stressed for the very good reason that, strange as it may seem, genes for most hereditary defects are individually rare. This surely does not mean that there is little human wretchedness in the world, or for that matter little wretchedness due to defective heredity. But the fact is that there are so many *different* defects that relatively little can be blamed on each one taken separately. . . . For example, no fewer than 100 different hereditary eye diseases are known, so that the incidence of most of them taken separately is quite low.

Mental diseases present a human problem even more serious than blindness. Here again, a certain proportion of cases have little or nothing to do with heredity. Cases attributable to defective heredity are of many kinds which can be more or less easily distinguished by a specialist and are almost certainly due to different genes. Each gene is rare if its frequency is computed for the total population of the country. . . . This is a great difficulty which advocates of sterilization do not always take account of.

NOTE 3.

MEDAWAR, P. B.

The Future of Man*

The idea scientists now have in mind when they speak of "fitness" can be explained like this. All the people alive 100 years from now will be our descendants, but not all of us will be their ances-

---

* New York: Mentor Books, 1959, pp. 29-34. Reprinted with permission of Basic Books, Inc., publisher.

tors. In retrospect, therefore, it will be possible to give us scores or marks according to the share we took in being the ancestors of those future people; and those who took a larger share will be described as fitter than those who took a lesser share. The word "fitness," then, has come to mean *net reproductive advantage,* and students of heredity, geneticists, do not deliberately use it in any other sense. One hears bitter complaints about this newer use of "fitness," because it neglects so much of what is deeply important in human life: for example, the influence of good or evil people who happen to have no children but who are so obviously fit or unfit members of society in everything except this narrow genetic sense. But the contempt we may feel for the word must on no account be transferred to the idea that it embodies, an idea which has a central place in modern evolutionary thought.

The argument that advances in medicine and hygiene are undermining the overall fitness of mankind is based on the belief that there is a hereditary or genetic element in all human ills and disabilities, even if it amounts to no more than a predisposition. This is known to be true of some diseases and not known to be false of any, so there can be no disagreement here. In its simplest form, the argument then runs as follows: because of the discovery of insulin, antibiotics, and so on, we are preserving for life and reproduction people who even ten years ago might have died. We are therefore preserving the genetically ill-favoured, the hereditary weaklings, who can intermarry with and therefore undermine the constitution of normal people; and as a result of all this, mankind is going downhill.

If by "going downhill" is meant "declining in biological fitness," with the implication that mankind will probably die out, this argument is simply a museum of self-contradictions. It is true that we preserve for life people who even ten years ago might have died; but then we do not live ten years ago; we live today. It is also true that if some disaster were to destroy the great pharmaceutical industries to which diabetics and the victims of Addison's disease literally owe their lives, then a great many of them might die; but what could be deduced from this, except the lunatic inference that people who might conceivably die tomorrow might just as well be dead today? So let me put the argument in a form in which it might be put by a humane and intelligent person. He might say something like this:

I live in a country with a National Health Service, and the effect of this is that, in a sense, I myself suffer from diabetes and rheumatoid arthritis, and so on—from mental deficiency too. Of course my sufferings are only economic, in the sense that it is my taxes that help to pay the bill; but, as a result of them, I can afford to have only two children, though I very much wanted three. Now I am a sound and healthy person, and though I'm all for helping other less lucky people, it is clear that what you call their "biological fitness" is being bought at the expense of mine.

There are two arguments here, and they cannot be considered apart. The first is that people of a genetically sound constitution are being crowded out by the inferior. My spokesman was too humane to resent the idea that the inferior should survive and have children, but he saw some danger in the fact that the population of the future would contain fewer of his descendants because it would contain more of theirs. The second point he makes is that inborn resistance to a disease can be taken as evidence of a *general* soundness of body, of fitness in some rounded and comprehensive sense; so that even if the people he described as unlucky could all be cured of their particular disabilities, there would still be a deep-seated, though hidden, deterioration of mankind.

The arguments I have just outlined are serious and respectable, but they are not generally valid; they may sometimes represent the very opposite of the truth. Consider one of the forms of inborn resistance to a very severe form of malaria, subtertian malaria. It is now known that people can enjoy a definite inborn resistance to subtertian malaria if their red blood corpuscles contain something between 30 and 40 per cent of an unusual form of haemoglobin, haemoglobin S as opposed to haemoglobin A. One of the consequences of possessing haemoglobin S is that the red blood cells tend to collapse if deprived of oxygen; they become sickle shaped instead of remaining rounded, and people whose blood behaves in this way are said to show the "sickle cell trait." Sickle cell trait can be found in parts of Africa, in some Mediterranean countries, and in parts of India— always in places where malaria has been or still is rife. It is not a disabling condition, so its victims should not be said to "suffer" from it; and, in any event, it confers a high degree of resistance to the multiplication of the malaria organism in the blood.

This sounds like a splendid example of Nature's ingenuity in coping with a particularly murderous disease, malaria, without the help of these newfangled drugs; but until one knows the rest of the story one cannot appreciate how devilishly ingenious it is.

The formation of haemoglobin S instead of A is due to an inborn difference of a particularly uncompromising kind, in the sense that if a person is genetically qualified to produce haemoglobin S, by possessing the appropriate "gene" or genetic factor, then he surely will. People who show sickle cell trait do so because they have inherited the gene that changes haemoglobin A to S from one, and only one, of their parents. But when two such people marry and have children, one quarter of their children, on the average, will inherit that gene from both their parents; all their haemoglobin, instead of only part of it, will be of type S; and as a result of this they usually die early in life of a destructive disease of the blood known as "sickle cell anaemia." This highly successful form of inborn resistance to malaria therefore makes it certain that a number of children will die.

The situation as a whole can be set out in the form of a balance sheet or equation. In some parts of the world where malaria is rife, people with sickle cell trait are the fittest people. Alongside them are, on the one hand, normal people, whose haemoglobin is wholly of type A; and, on the other hand, the victims of sickle cell anaemia, whose haemoglobin is wholly of type S. The proportion in which these three classes occur adjusts itself automatically to a pattern in which the loss of life due to malaria and to sickle cell anaemia nicely counterbalances the gain that is due to the greater fitness of those with sickle cell trait. Nevertheless, in malarial regions, populations which possess this genetic structure are fitter than populations which do not.

Essentially the same explanation will account for the widespread occurrence in certain parts of Italy of the disease known as Cooley's anaemia and, not impossibly, for the otherwise paradoxically high incidence of a certain fatal inborn disease of the pancreas in Great Britain and elsewhere. In all such cases it may turn out that there is, or recently has been, some special advantage in having inherited from one parent, and one parent only, the genetical factor which produces such disastrous effects when it is inherited from both.

The moral of this story—though morality seems to have little to do with it—is that mankind will improve if we stamp out inborn resistance to malaria by stamping out malaria itself. Sickle cell anaemia is in fact disappearing from the Negro population of America at about the rate we should expect if malaria had ceased to be a scourge to it 200 or 300 years agso. So the only good thing about inborn resistance to malaria is —inborn resistance to malaria: it does *not* reveal any general soundness of constitution; and this is just the opposite to what my imaginary spokesman supposed. It is simply not true to say that advances in medicine and hygiene must cause a genetical deterioration of mankind. There is more to be feared from a slow decline of human intelligence, but that is a different matter: *if* it is hap-

pening, it is because the rather stupid are biologically fitter than those who are innately more intelligent, not because medicine is striving to raise the biological fitness of those who might otherwise be hopelessly unfit.

NOTE 4.

SKINNER v. OKLAHOMA
316 U.S. 535 (1941)

Mr. JUSTICE DOUGLAS delivered the opinion of the Court.

This case touches a sensitive and important area of human rights. Oklahoma deprives certain individuals of a right which is basic to the perpetuation of a race—the right to have offspring. Oklahoma has decreed the enforcement of its law against petitioner, overruling his claim that it violated the Fourteenth Amendment. . . .

The statute involved is Oklahoma's Habitual Criminal Sterilization Act. Okla. Stat. Ann. Tit. 57, §§ 171, *et seq.*; L. 1935, pp. 94 *et seq.* That Act defines an "habitual criminal" as a person who, having been convicted two or more times for crimes "amounting to felonies involving moral turpitude," either in an Oklahoma court or in a court of any other State, is thereafter convicted of such a felony in Oklahoma and is sentenced to a term of imprisonment in an Oklahoma penal institution. § 173. Machinery is provided for the institution by the Attorney General of a proceeding against such a person in the Oklahoma courts for a judgment that such person shall be rendered sexually sterile. . . .

* * *

. . . We are dealing here with legislation which involves one of the basic civil rights of man. Marriage and procreation are fundamental to the very existence and survival of the race. The power to sterilize, if exercised, may have subtle, farreaching and devastating effects. In evil or reckless hands it can cause races or types which are inimical to the dominant group to wither and disappear. There is no redemption for the individual whom the law touches. Any experiment which the State conducts is to his irreparable injury. He is forever deprived of a basic liberty. We mention these matters not to re-examine the scope of the police power of the States. We advert to them merely in emphasis of our view that strict scrutiny of the classification which a State makes in a sterilization law is essential, lest unwittingly, or otherwise, invidious discriminations are made against groups or types of individuals in violation of the constitutional guaranty of just and equal laws. . . . When the law lays an unequal hand on those who have committed intrinsically the same quality of offense and sterilizes one and not the other, it has made as invidious a discrimination as if it had selected a particular race or nationality for oppressive treatment. . . .

Mr. JUSTICE JACKSON concurring.

[T]he present plan to sterilize the individual in pursuit of a eugenic plan to eliminate from the race characteristics that are only vaguely identified and which in our present state of knowledge are uncertain as to transmissibility presents other constitutional questions of gravity. This Court has sustained such an experiment with respect to an imbecile, a person with definite and observable characteristics, where the condition had persisted through three generations and afforded grounds for the belief that it was transmissible and would continue to manifest itself in generations to come. *Buck* v. *Bell*, 274 U.S. 200.

There are limits to the extent to which a legislatively represented majority may conduct biological experiments at the expense of the dignity and personality and natural powers of a minority—even those who have been guilty of what the majority define as crimes. But this Act falls down before reaching this problem, which I mention only to avoid the implication that such a question may not exist because not discussed. On it I would also reserve judgment.

NOTE 5.

COMMITTEE OF THE AMERICAN NEUROLOGICAL ASSOCIATION
Eugenical Sterilization*

There need be no hesitation in recommending sterilization in the case of feeblemindedness, though it need not, of course, be urged in the case of those conditions which are definitely of environmental origin. Though we hesitate to stress any purely social necessity for sterilization, it is obvious that in the case of the feebleminded there may be a social as well as a biological situation of importance. Certain of the feebleminded can only, under the most favorable circumstances, care for themselves, and a family of children may prove an overwhelming burden. However, in a world whch has much low grade work to be done, there is still room for the people of low grade mentality of good character.

NOTE 6.

A.L.I. Model Penal Code § 207.11 (2) (a) and Comments†

(2) *Justifiable Abortion.* A licensed physician is justified in terminating a pregnancy if:

---

* New York: The Macmillan Co., 1936, p. 180.
† Tent. Draft No. 9, May 1959. Copyright 1959. Reprinted with permission of The American Law Institute.

(a) . . .

(2) he believes there is substantial risk that continuance of the pregnancy would gravely impair the physical or mental health of the mother or that the child would be born with grave physical or mental defect, or the pregnancy resulted from rape by force . . . or from incest . . .

COMMENTS

. . . Current American legislation does not provide for aborting probably defective offspring, except as such a result might be reached under the half-dozen statutes that prohibit "unlawful" abortion without defining what is unlawful. Despite the uncertain legal status of eugenic as distinguished from therapeutic abortion, such operations are regularly performed by responsible physicians in hospitals throughout the country. Typical cases are where the mother contracts German measles (rubella) during the first 12 weeks of pregnancy, or where the mother has deep X-ray treatment to which the fetus is exposed. In the first instance, 30% of the offspring are born with serious abnormalities; in the second, two-thirds of the offspring may be expected to have gravely defective central nervous systems.

The criminal law should speak unambiguously on the authority of the physician to act where he believes that continuance of the pregnancy entails substantial risk that the offspring will be a physical or mental casualty. The prospective birth of a seriously defective child may even constitute a threat to the mental health of the apprehensive mother, but it seems preferable to rest the matter directly on scientific prognostication of the child's state of health rather than on the more uncertain prediction of the mother's reaction.

* * *

The case of incest involves somewhat different considerations inasmuch as this offense may be committed with the consent of the female. However, in view of the fact that a large proportion of incest cases involves fathers or other older relatives imposing on adolescent girls, this "consent" hardly justifies a legal requirement that the offspring of such relationships should be born against the wishes of all concerned or that a physician be designated a felon if he operates under such circumstances. Whatever position one may take on the broader question of aborting illegitimate children generally, the case for aborting incestuous offspring is much stronger, since there is some basis for believing that close inbreeding involves some chance of producing defective offspring. Moreover, in the case of incestuous illegitimacy, there is no possibility that the offspring can be legitimated by marriage of the parents.

* * *

NOTE 7.

VIEMEISTER v. WHITE
179 N.Y. 235, 72 N.E. 97, 98-99 (1904)

VANN, J. . . .

It must be conceded that some laymen, both learned and unlearned, and some physicians of great skill and repute, do not believe that vaccination is a preventive of smallpox. The common belief, however, is that it has a decided tendency to prevent the spread of this fearful disease and to render it less dangerous to those who contract it. . . .

The fact that the belief is not universal is not controlling, for there is scarcely any belief that is accepted by every one. The possibility that the belief may be wrong, and that science may yet show it to be wrong, is not conclusive; for the Legislature has the right to pass laws which, according to the common belief of the people, are adapted to prevent the spread of contagious diseases. In a free country, where the government is by the people through their chosen representatives, practical legislation admits of no other standard of action; for what the people believe is for the common welfare must be accepted as tending to promote the common welfare, whether it does in fact or not. Any other basis would conflict with the spirit of the Constitution, and would sanction measures opposed to a republican form of government. While we do not decide and cannot decide that vaccination is a preventive of smallpox, we take judicial notice of the fact that this is the common belief of the people of the state, and with this fact as a foundation we hold that the statute in question is a health law, enacted in a reasonable and proper exercise of the police power. It operates impartially upon all children in the public schools, and is designed, not only for their protection, but for the protection of all the people of the state. . . .

NOTE 8.

LUSH, JAY L.
Animal Breeding Plans*

1. Decide what kind or type of animal and what level of production would be ideal for the breeder's own individual circumstances and local conditions.

2. Find what living animals most nearly have the genes needed to produce that ideal animal.

---

*Reprinted by permission from *Animal Breeding Plans*, Third Edition, by J. L. Lush, pp. 427-429, published by the Iowa State University Press, 1945.

a. By judging and testing each animal.

b. By paying some attention to the merit of recent ancestors and close collateral relatives.

c. By studying the progeny of each animal.

3. Obtain, as far as can be done at reasonable prices, those animals which come nearest to having the ideal genes and let each have offspring in numbers proportional to the closeness with which its heredity approaches the ideal.

* * *

The first step in any animal breeding program is to decide what is ideal. Until a breeder knows what kind of animal he wants, he is stopped in his tracks and can neither select the best nor discard the worst. Somewhat indefinite words, such as best, worst, poorer, better, more productive, meritorious, etc., have intentionally been used . . . instead of more precise words in discussing selection and kindred problems because the purpose was to discuss ways of attaining the goals the breeder wants and not to enter into the subject of what ideal for each kind of animal would be most profitable. Each breeder needs to consider his own physical and biological resources, his own markets and his own personal inclinations to decide what characteristics his ideal animals should possess. Naturally a beginning breeder would defer somewhat to the opinions of those who have had more experience under somewhat similar conditions, but his own conditions may be different from those of the men from whom he is receiving advice. It seems likely that the matter of local adaptability will receive more attention in the future than it has in the past. Probably there will always be at least enough interchange of breeding stock to keep that from being overdone. The ideal must often be a compromise between satisfying the market and satisfying one's own local conditions most completely. Conceivably the butcher's interest in high dressing percentage and high quality of meat, if carried too far, might result in animals with vital organs too small for them to be as healthy and thrifty as the farmer wishes, while the animals which would suit the farmer best because they were healthiest, most robust, largest, and quickest growing might be too big, bony, and coarse to suit the butcher. . . .

NOTE 9.

Girl Says She Had Baby for Another*

A Japanese girl was reported recently to have lent herself to a childless married couple for 1 million yen (about $3,000) and bore the husband a daughter by artificial insemination.

---

*The New York *Times*, April 30, 1964 (p. 30, col. 1); © 1964 by Reuters. Reprinted by permission.

The report was published by The Mainichi Daily News, a national English language newspaper here, which said the story was originally carried by a journal published for Japanese teenagers.

The newspaper said the girl was looking for a job to help her through college when she heard of a wealthy married couple who wanted to have a child but were unable to do so.

According to the paper, the couple sought a "beautiful, healthy intelligent woman from a good family" to bear the husband's own child. The college student fitted the description and agreed to bear the child.

"I figured that with one million yen I could easily manage at college for two years," the girl was quoted as saying. "And if this could be done without seeing the man's face or being told his name, then I thought it can be taken as a purely medical and thoroughly rational albeit [part-time job] for women."

The paper said the student signed a contract in which she promised not to demand custody of the child.

It quoted her as saying toward the end of her pregnancy: "No longer could I see the baby as wrapped in 10,000-yen notes.

"As soon as the baby was delivered, the nurses carried it away behind a screen. That was the last time I saw it. The doctor came to me with sympathetic eyes and told me the baby was a pretty girl.

"Now I feel I was robbed by the rich—robbed of my baby. I didn't loan my womb for 1 million yen to a stranger.

"I am returning to school to study hard and graduate from college," the girl was quoted as saying.

NOTE 10.

NEW YORK PUBLIC HEALTH LAW
Blood Donating (1953)

§ 3120. *Blood donating; license required; procedure*

1. No person, firm or corporation shall engage in the business of procuring persons to donate human blood for the purpose of transfusion into another human being unless a license first be obtained from the local health officer.

* * *

3. Upon receipt of an application for a license, accompanied by a fee of five dollars, the local health officer shall conduct an investigation into the character of the person, firm or corporation applying for a license and if satisfied that the interest of public health will be promoted, he shall issue a license to such person, firm or corporation to conduct such business for one year from the date of such license.

* * *

§ 3121. *Blood donating; physician's certificate required*

It shall be unlawful for any person engaged in the business of donating human blood to donate such human blood for transfusion unless the donor thereof present a certificate from a physician registered under the laws of this state showing that the said donor has complied with the requirements of the sanitary code. . . .

* * *

§ 3122. *Blood donating; violations; penalties*

Any violation of sections three thousand one hundred twenty and three thousand one hundred twenty-one, of this chapter, shall constitute a misdemeanor, punishable on conviction by a fine of not exceeding fifty dollars or by imprisonment for not exceeding six months, or both such fine and imprisonment.

NOTE 11.

ARKANSAS STATUTES
Blood Transfusions (1959)

82-1601. Blood labeled as to race.—All human blood . . . to be used in the State of Arkansas for transfusions of blood, except such units of blood which will have been transported across the State line into Arkansas, shall be labeled with the word "Caucasian," "Negroid," or "Mongoloid" or some suitable designation so as to clearly indicate the race of the donor of such blood. No human blood not labeled in accordance with the provisions of this act . . . shall be used for transfusions in the State of Arkansas. . . .

* * *

82-1603. Emergency circumstances—Exceptions from act—In the event that there are, in the opinion of the doctor, emergency circumstances existing, a transfusion may be given without regard to the provisions of this act. . . . An emergency shall be deemed to exist when in the opinion of a medical attendant . . . it is necessary that immediate action be taken. . . .

NOTE 12.

NEW YORK CITY HEALTH CODE
Artificial Human Insemination §21 (1959)

§21.01 Physician to perform artificial insemination and collect seminal fluid

No person other than a licensed physician shall perform an artificial insemination or collect, offer for sale, sell or give away human seminal fluid for the purpose of causing artificial insemination.

* * *

§21.03 Examination of donor and recipient

(a) A proposed donor of seminal fluid shall have a standard serological test for syphilis and a smear and culture for gonorrhea within one week before his seminal fluid is taken and, immediately prior to taking his seminal fluid, he shall be given a complete medical examination with particular attention to his genitalia.

(b) A proposed donor and a proposed recipient of seminal fluid shall each have a blood test to establish their respective Rh factors before artificial insemination is attempted. Such test shall be made by a laboratory operated pursuant to Article 13 and classified for hematology, including blood grouping and Rh typing. If the proposed recipient is negative for the Rh factor, only seminal fluid from a donor who is also negative for the Rh factor shall be used.

* * *

§21.05 Disqualification of donors

A person who is affected with a venereal disease, tuberculosis, brucellosis or who has any congenital disease or defect shall not be used as a donor of seminal fluid for artificial insemination.

* * *

§21.07 Records; contents and confidentiality

(a) A physician who performs an artificial insemination shall keep a record of (1) the names and addresses of the physician, donor and recipient, (2) the results of the medical examination and serological and all other tests, and (3) the date of artificial insemination.

(b) Records kept by a physician pursuant to this section shall not be subject to inspection by persons other than authorized personnel of the Department. A person who has access to these records shall not divulge any part thereof so as to disclose the identity of the persons to whom they relate.

NOTE 13.

MASSEY, ALBERT P.

A Proposed Artificial Insemination Statute*

Statement of Purpose

The express purpose of this statute is to regulate the human activity known as artificial insemination by the sperm of a third party donor (A.I.D.).

---

* 9 VILL. L. REV. 77, 90-93 (1963).

This statute is drawn to correct the problems and confusion now existing regarding the legal status of children born by the use of this method of conception, the legal status and responsibility of the donor of sperm, the marital status of the mother of such child and the legal status and responsibility of her husband, whether or not consenting thereto. This statute is drafted in view of the dangers to health that may exist if A.I.D. remains unregulated and to establish a method of conduct for those persons in any way participating in A.I.D.

Article I. Definitions

Sec. 1. The Donor: Any male, twenty-one years of age or over, being of sound mind and body may be qualified as a donor of sperm for the purposes of artificial insemination.

Sec. 2. The Husband: Under this act the husband is the lawful spouse of any woman applying for artificial insemination.

Sec. 3. The Mother: The mother is the lawful spouse of the husband defined in Section 2 and the applicant for artificial insemination.

Sec. 4 The Physician: The physician referred to in this act must be a licensed medical practitioner. A person is acting as a physician within the meaning of this act when such person is examining the parties, extracting or administering sperm for the purposes of artificial insemination.

Sec. 5. The Child: The child under this act is the offspring produced through artificial insemination.

Article II. The Donor

Sec. 1. Any male donating sperm for the purposes of artificial insemination must do so willingly, without coercion or pressure from any source and in compliance with all the sections of this Article.

Sec. 2. Any donor must file an application, as required under Article VIII of this act, containing his name, address, age, race, color and marital status.

Sec. 3. To be eligible each donor must complete a physical examination by a physician as defined under this act finding him free of syphilis and other venereal disease as well as any physical or mental defect transmittable through the reproduction process. A copy of the results of such examination shall be made, dated and signed by the examining physician and filed with the Board of Artificial Insemination as required under Article VIII of this act.

Sec. 4. Each donor must complete, sign and file a form stating that he is giving freely and of his own accord, that all sections of this article have been fully and adequately performed, that the donor has no knowledge of any physical or mental defect not discovered upon physical examination, and that the donor understands that should conception and birth take place donor, and his wife, should he have one, has no claim or relationship whatsoever to the child or its mother, now and forever. The wife as a donor shall complete a form which shall contain a statement that she is fully aware of the donation and gives her consent thereto willingly and knowingly, that she is unaware of any physical or mental defect not discovered upon physical examination which would render the donor ineligible for donation and that she and donor shall have no claim or relationship to the child and its mother, now and forever. This form must be signed by the donor, his wife, and one witness.

Sec. 5. A donor may become eligible only as provided in Article VIII, and may not donate without the proof of eligibility.

Sec. 6. Any donor not complying with all the sections of this article shall be deemed in violation of this act.

Article III. *The Husband*

Sec. 1. Before the wife of any husband within the meaning of this act can become qualified for artificial insemination said husband must submit for filing a written, dated and signed consent conforming to the provisions set forth in Section 2 of this Article and Section 1 of Article IV.

Sec. 2. The written consent of the husband must contain statements evidencing voluntary consent on his part, knowledge of the procedure involved and the method of administration, assumption of all risks regarding the health and possible infirmities of the child except as provided in Section 2 of Article VI, knowledge that any child born as a result of artificial insemination conforming with this Act shall be his legitimate child and lawful heir with all rights, privileges and duties owing thereto as are owing to any child by his natural father, and that artificial insemination under this act is not a marital offense except as provided in Article IX, and all duties owing to the mother are as if the child were the natural offspring of them both.

Article IV. *The Mother*

Sec. 1. A mother shall apply for artificial insemination by filing an application stating her name, the name of her husband, her address, age and reasons for so applying. Such application must be accompanied by the written consent of the husband as required in Article III.

Sec. 2. To be qualified the mother must submit to a physical examination by a physician as provided in this act finding her free of syphilis and other venereal disease as well as any physical or mental defect transmittable through the reproduction process. A copy of the results of such examination shall be carefully made, dated and signed by the examining physician and filed with the Board of Artificial Insemination as required under Article VIII of this act.

Sec. 3. The mother shall complete a form stating that she is submitting willingly and of her own accord, that all Sections of Article III and IV have been fully performed, that she and her husband have no knowledge of any physical or mental defects not discovered upon her examination, that she and her husband have knowledge and agree that any child produced shall be their legitimate child and lawful heir, now and forever. This form shall be signed by the mother, her husband and one witness prior to filing.

Sec. 4. From the date of filing of the statement described in Section 3 there will be a waiting period of thirty (30) days before a proof of eligibility can be issued. Such proof shall be then issued according to Article VIII.

Sec. 5. After issuance of proof as provided in Article VIII, the mother and husband together shall select the sperm to be used in the insemination.

Sec. 6. Any mother failing to meet all the provisions of this article shall be in violation of this act.

Article V. *The Physician*

Sec. 1. Any physician within the meaning of this act shall be held to the ordinary standard of care required of medical practitioners engaged in this type of activity and is not held to otherwise guarantee or warrant the quality of the sperm, success of the insemination, or health of the child.

Sec. 2. No physician is qualified to extract or administer sperm, unless a proof of eligibility can be exhibited by the relevant parties.

Sec. 3. Failure by a physician to comply with all the sections of this article and all sections of this act dealing with physical examinations shall be a violation of this act.

Article VI. *The Child*

Sec. 1. Any child born in conformity with this act shall be deemed the legitimate child of the mother and husband and the lawful heir of both.

Sec. 2. Under this act a child shall be illegitimate only when the mother violates those sections of this act pertaining to the consent of her husband and the selection of the sperm.

Article VII. *Classification of Sperm*

Sec. 1. Any institution whether publicly or privately owned or operated, housing, storing or distributing sperm for the purposes of artificial insemination shall mark each container with the name, address, age and physical characteristics of the donor including race, color and educational background.

Sec. 2. Each such institution shall guarantee and warrant that the sperm is as healthy and of as high quality as when received by it and that it has exercised the ordinary standard of care required in housing, storing, and distributing a product of this nature.

Sec. 3. No institution shall receive or distribute sperm without the exhibition of a proof of eligibility by the party donating or requesting sperm.

Sec. 4. Each institution shall keep and file complete records of all its transactions and shall surrender them only upon issuance of a court order.

Sec. 5. Failure to conform to all the sections of this article is a violation of this act.

Article VIII. *Filing and Recording*

Sec. 1. This article provides for the establishment of a Public Board of Artificial Insemination to function under the auspices of the State Bureau of Health and Welfare for the purposes of filing, recording and issuing proofs of eligibility in conformance with all the sections of this article. Such Board shall consist of a physician, a psychiatrist and a lawyer.

Sec. 2. All statements and records required to be filed as a requisite to eligibility shall be filed only by the Board and copies thereof issued only through a court order.

Sec. 3. The Board shall issue proof of eligibility only when all statements are in order and on file.

Sec. 4. Each proof of eligibility shall contain the name, address and age of the applicant and his (her) physical characteristics, including race and color, for the purpose of identification.

Sec. 5. Each proof shall be dated and shall be valid for a period of six (6) months.

Article IX. *Sanctions*

Sec. 1. Any donor violating this act through his own negligence shall be liable for all the necessary and foreseeable consequences to the mother and child resulting therefrom.

Sec. 2. Any donor knowingly violating this act except as provided in Section 3 of this article shall be liable for all consequences to the mother and child resulting therefrom, subject to $1,000 fine, up to one (1) year imprisonment or both.

Sec. 3. Any donor failing to acquire the consent of his wife as provided in Article II shall be guilty of a marital offense sufficient to constitute grounds for a civil divorce.

Sec. 4. Any mother failing to comply with the sections of this act dealing with her physical examination shall be barred from recovering from any person(s) in violation of this act except where such violation in no way contributed to the injury to her or to her child.

Sec. 5. Any mother failing to comply with the sections of this act pertaining to the consent of her husband and selection of the sperm shall render the child illegitimate and be guilty of a marital offense sufficient to constitute grounds for a civil divorce and subject her to a $1,000 fine, up to one (1) year imprisonment or both.

Sec. 6. Any husband aware of or aiding in the violation of any section of this act, except those sections pertaining to procedural requirements and the consent of the wife of the donor, shall be barred from recovering under this act and from enforcing Section 5 of this Article and shall be deemed the lawful father of the child as if no violation occurred.

Sec. 7. Any physician failing to meet the standard of care required under Section 1 of Article V shall be guilty of malpractice.

Sec. 8. Any physician extracting or administering sperm without requiring proof of eligibility or while knowing of any violation of this act shall be liable for all consequences to the mother and child resulting from such violation, subject to a $1,000 fine, up to one (1) year imprisonment or both.

Sec. 9. Any institution under Article VII violating its standard of care shall be liable for the necessary and forseeable consequences to the mother and child resulting therefrom.

Sec. 10. Any institution knowingly violating any Section of this act or knowing of any violation of this act shall be liable for all consequences to the mother and child resulting therefrom and subject to fines up to $50,000.

Sec. 11. All persons within this act shall be liable jointly and severally.

NOTE 14.

Report of the Departmental Committee on Human Artificial Insemination*

. . . It has been supposed that one of the greatest dangers of A.I.D. is that children sired by the same donor may afterwards meet and marry. It is now clear to us, however, that this danger is at present minimal. We have been informed that if 2,000 live children per year were to be born in Great Britain as a result of the successful usage of A.I.D. and if each donor were responsible for 5 children, an unwitting incestuous marriage is unlikely to occur more than once in about fifty to a hundred years. Thus even if there were a twenty-fold increase in the use of A.I.D., as compared with our estimate of its present incidence, the possibility that two children having the same father would marry would be remote, although if a much wider use were made of each donor and if practitioners drew their patients from small areas, the possibility would increase. But careful selection of donors could reduce the possibility below what might otherwise occur. It should at the same time be noted that the number of incestuous marriages occurring as a result of A.I.D. would be much smaller than that resulting from fornication and adultery.

NOTE 15.

BOHN, Z. STEPHEN
Artificial Insemination†

[W]e may consider the possible adverse psychologic effects on the resultant children. How will they feel and react on discovering the nature of their procreation? It has been said that there is a parallel between these children and those who were adopted. However, one can speculate about the probability of the former having a tendency to feel closer to the mother while developing a feeling of skepticism toward his "father". Certainly he will have some of the personality characteristics of his mother but none of his "father" and this may very well result in a rift between the two. Should the husband and wife already have difficulty in adjusting to each other such a child would more than likely "take sides" with his mother and tend to widen the breach. One also might speculate that should artificial insemination become commonplace and extend over a period of many years that this period of "mass

production" which "reminds us somehow of breeding cattle"[7] would eventually result in a confusion of identity and that there could develop a certain amount of "inbreeding" by the marriage of individuals with related blood lines.

NOTE 16.

STRNAD v. STRNAD
190 Misc. 786, 78 N.Y.S. 2d 390 (1948)
cited in *Gursky v. Gursky*
39 Misc. 2d 1083, 242 N.Y.S. 2d 406 (1963)

Action by Julie Strnad against Antoine Strnad involving, inter alia, the custody of Antoinette Strnad, the minor child of plaintiff. On motion to fix defendant's right to visit child.

GREENBERG, JUSTICE.

The court has assumed, for the purpose of this disposition in the light of the record and the concessions made by the defendant, that the plaintiff was artificially inseminated with the consent of the defendant and that the child is not of the blood of the defendant. Predicated on that assumption the court concludes as follows:

(1) The defendant is entitled to rights of visitation as heretofor allowed, namely, every Sunday between the hours of 11 a.m. and 4 p.m., and during such visitations the child will be in the custody of the maternal grandmother . . .

(2) The court holds that the child has been potentially adopted or semi-adopted by the defendant. In any event, in so far as this defendant is concerned and with particular reference to visitation, he is entitled to the same rights as those acquired by a foster parent who has formally adopted a child, if not the same rights as those to which a natural parent under the circumstances would be entitled.

(3) In the opinion of this court, assuming again that plaintiff was artificially inseminated with the consent of the defendant, this child is not an illegitimate child. Indeed, logically and realistically, the situation is no different than that pertaining in the case of a child born out of wedlock who by law is made legitimate upon the marriage of the interested parties.

(4) The court does not pass on the legal consequences in so far as property rights are concerned in a case of this character, nor does the court express an opinion on the propriety of procreation by the medium of artificial insemination. With such matters the court is not here concerned; the latter problem particularly is in the fields of sociology, morality and religion.

---

* Cmnd. 1105, London: Her Majesty's Stationery Office, 1960 (p. 112), Reprinted by permission of the Controller of Her Britannic Majesty's Stationery Office.

† 34 U. Det. L. Rev. 397, 402 (1957).

---

7. Lovset, *Artificial Insemination. The Attitude of Patients in Norway.* 2 Fertility and Sterility (1951).

NOTE 17.

NEW YORK DOMESTIC RELATIONS LAW (1957)
Adoption

Sec. 109. Definitions

When used in this article, unless the context or subject matter manifestly requires a different interpretation:

1. "Foster parent" shall mean a person adopting and "foster child" shall mean a person adopted.

* * *

Sec. 110. Who may adopt ; effect of article

An adult unmarried person or an adult husband and his adult wife together may adopt another person. An adult or minor husband and his adult or minor wife together may adopt a child of either of them born in or out of wedlock and an adult or minor husband or an adult or minor wife may adopt such a child of the other spouse. No person shall hereafter be adopted except in pursuance of this article.

Adoption is the legal proceeding whereby a person takes another person into the relation of child and thereby acquires the rights and incurs the responsibilities of parent in respect of such other person.

* * *

Sec. 112. Voluntary adoption

In voluntary adoption the following requirements shall be observed:

1. The foster parents or parent, the foster child and all persons whose consent is required . . . must appear for examination before a judge . . .

2. The foster parents or parent . . . must present to such judge or surrogate (a) a petition stating the names and place of residence of the petitioners ; whether they are of full age ; whether they are married or unmarried and, if married, whether they are living together as husband and wife ; the name, date and place of birth of the foster child as nearly as the same can be ascertained ; the religious faith of the petitioners ; the religious faith of the foster child and his parents as nearly as the same can be ascertained ; the facts, if any, which render unnecessary the consent of either or both of the parents of the foster child ; the manner in which the foster parents obtained the foster child ; the period of time during which the foster parents obtained the foster child ; the period of time during which the foster child has resided with the foster parents ; the occupation and approximate income of the petitioners and the new name, if any, by which the foster child

is to be known ; that no previous application has been made to any court or judge for the relief sought or if so made, the disposition of it and a statement as to whether the foster child had been previously adopted, all of which statements shall be taken prima facie as true ; (b) an agreement on the part of the foster parents or parent to adopt and treat the foster child as their or his or her own lawful child ; (c) the consents required by section one hundred eleven of this article.

3. Where the petition alleges that either or both of the natural parents of the child have been deprived of civil rights or have been judicially declared incompetent or have been adjudged to be habitual drunkards, proof shall be submitted that such disability exists at the time of the proposed adoption.

* * *

8. Before making an order of adoption the judge . . . shall make or cause to be made an investigation by some person or agency specifically designated by him to examine into the allegations set forth in the petition and to ascertain such other facts relating to the foster child and foster parents as will give such judge . . . adequate basis for determining the propriety of approving the adoption. . . .

* * *

Sec. 113. Adoption from authorized agencies

An authorized agency may consent to the adoption of a minor in its lawful custody. Except as hereinafter provided an adoption from an authorized agency shall be effected in the same manner as provided in relation to voluntary adoptions. . . . In making orders of adoption the judge . . . when practicable must give custody only to persons of the same religious faith as that of the foster child. . . .

NOTE 18.

BOAS, FRANZ
Anthropology and Modern Life*

The eugenist who tries to do more than to eliminate the unfit will first of all be called upon to answer the question what strains are the best to cultivate. If it is a question of breeding chickens or Indian corn, we know what we want. We desire many eggs of heavy weight, or a large yield of

* New York: W. W. Norton & Co., 1932, pp. 116-117. Reprinted with permission of the publisher. Copyright 1928 by W. W. Norton & Co., Inc. Renewed 1956 by Norman Boas. Copyright 1932 by W. W. Norton & Co., Inc. Renewed 1960 by Helene Boas Yampolsky. Copyright © 1962 by W. W. Norton & Co., Inc.

good corn. But what do we want in man? Is it physical excellence, mental ability, creative power, or artistic genius? We must select certain ideals that we want to raise. Considering then the fundamental differences in ideals of distinct types of civilization, have we a right to give to our modern ideals the stamp of finality, and suppress what does not fit into our life? There is little doubt that we, at the present time, give much less weight to beauty than to logic. Shall we then try to raise a generation of logical thinkers, suppress those whose emotional life is vigorous, and try to bring it about that reason shall reign supreme, and that human activities shall be performed with clocklike precision? The precise cultural forms that would develop cannot be foretold, because they are culturally, not biologically, determined ; but there is little doubt that within certain limits the intensity of emotional life,—regardless of its form,—and the vigor of logical thought,—regardless of its content,—could be increased or decreased by organic selection. Such a deliberate choice of qualities which would modify the character of nations implies an overestimation of the standards that we have reached, which to my mind appears intolerable. Personally the logical thinker may be most congenial to me, nevertheless I respect the sacred ideal of the dreamer who lives in a world of musical tones, and whose creative power is to me a marvel that surpasses understanding.

Without a selection of standards, eugenic practice is impossible ; but if we read the history of mankind aright, we ought to hesitate before we try to set our standards for all time to come, for they are only one phase in the development of mankind.

NOTE 19.

OSMUNDSEN, J. A.

Tribe in New Guinea is Isolated to Halt Spread of Rare Disease*

About 30,000 tribesmen in New Guinea are reported to have been sealed off from the rest of the world by the Australian territorial government to halt the spread of a deadly hereditary disease that they alone carry.

The severe action of quarantining an entire tribe resulted from recent studies of the problem, which came to medical attention only five years ago.

Announcement of the territorial administration's intentions appeared in a recent issue of *South Pacific Post,* according to a letter to the journal,

---

* The N. Y. Times (July 18, 1960), p. 45, col. 2 of late city edition. © 1960 by The New York Times Company. Reprinted by permission.

Science. The letter was written by Dr. Theodosius Dobzhansky, the Columbia University geneticist, who is visiting the University of Sydney, Australia.

The disease is known as kuru, a rapidly progressive disorder of the nervous system. Its cause—save that it is hereditary—is a medical mystery.

The victim receives no warning that he has inherited the disease until the first symptoms of paralysis appear. Then it is too late. Death usually comes within nine months. There is no known cure.

The mystery that surrounds kuru is deepened by an apparent caprice of nature that has made the disease a problem exclusive to the Fore tribe of New Guinea.

Those primitive war-like people live in huts, usually five or six in a group on the summit of a ridge. Their tribal territory consists of about 880 square miles in the rugged highlands east of Mount Michael.

The rest of the world's good fortune that kuru is so confined merely accentuates the Fore tribe's tragedy, for the disease is their leading cause of death.

Kuru kills about half the women and one-tenth of the men born to the tribe. Some die very young, and others after they have transmitted the disease factor to their children.

The disease also causes the deaths of some tribesmen who may not carry the trait. These innocents die in a murder ritual known as "tokabu," which befalls them as a result of their having been named sorcerers by close relatives of kuru victims.

The disproportionate death toll of kuru among women has left some portions of the Fore tribe with a great excess of men. In some areas there are up to two and a half times as many men as women.

Some of the Fore men have felt obliged to move to neighboring tribes or to seek work as contract laborers in other parts of New Guinea. Some of these emigrants undoubtedly carry the kuru trait, which they can transmit to populations of other districts. Consequently, the territorial administration has decided to prohibit emigration from the tribal area.

All Fore men who have moved out will be returned, Dr. Dobzhansky reported.

Just how such a deadly hereditary trait can be as persistent as the one that produces kuru is a perplexing scientific problem.

Normally, such genetically based defective traits disappear a few generations after they spring up. This disappearance can be averted only if those who carry the trait, and live long enough to have children, have some adaptive advantage over those who do not carry the trait.

"The nature of this advantage is, however, completely unknown," Dr. Dobzhansky wrote.

*   *   *

Dr. Dobzhansky remarked that the government's isolation decree was severe, but that other measures were being taken to lessen the blow to the Fore tribe.

The territorial administration plans for example, to develop the Fore area to provide enough work for its people, making emigration unnecessary.

Meanwhile, scientists are studying the disease in hopes of discovering a treatment for kuru. They also hope to develop a way of identifying carriers of the trait before they can bear children and before the now irreversible symptoms appear.

NOTE 20.

KUBIE, LAWRENCE S.
Hidden Brainpower*

The infinite creative potential of the human brain is housed in a potentially indestructible body. The animal body is the only machine which has a built-in replacement system, its own self-replenishing devices! And among all animals the human being stands alone in this respect, because of the scientific use of his creative potential may solve the problems of disease. We have learned that as long as the supply system is intact the body continuously takes itself apart and puts itself together, not merely organ by organ and tissue by tissue or cell by cell, but literally molecule by molecule. Potentially, therefore, it is constantly renewed and never ages. Consequently there is no *a priori* reason why an human being need ever die. Once we conquer the problem of arteriosclerosis (as we surely will), thus maintaining the integrity of the supply system of the body ; and once such internally generated destructive diseases as cancer are eliminated (as will surely happen) ; and once the modern control of and prophylaxis against bacterial infection are paralleled by a similar mastery of viral infection ; and once a few other problems are solved it will be hard to conceive how anybody who does not have the accident habit can cease to live. Some day men and women will—except for murders, suicides, and accidents —stop dying.

Hold your breath for a moment and ask what this is going to mean. Think of space, and air, and fuel, and food and water, and housing, and trans-

portation. Think of the search for new worlds begun in desperate earnest. Think of family organization. Who is going to license young folk to exercise the precious right to procreate? What will happen to industry and employment, an enormous population, automation, and endless leisure? What of the idle undertakers? What is going to happen to the Hereafter, when no one graduates into it through death? And what of the clergy who guard its emptying portal?

I could pursue my fantasy in many directions, for I do not doubt that we will reach this point if we do not first destroy our world. Indeed, we would be well advised to start now to use that enormous brain power to which I have alluded to do a little planning in advance, planning for the day when Man conquers Death. For when that day comes, or even during these immediate years of rapidly lengthening life-span, it is vital that life itself should become more meaningful. Otherwise the mere prolongation of life will mean that the Ultimate Enemy will be Murder and Suicide out of the Desperation of Longevity. Would it not be wise to give some thought to this now, and not to wait for the redemption of life in some increasingly remote and always hypothetical Hereafter?

NOTE 21.

ARISTOTLE
Politics* (333 B.C.)

§15. The question arises whether children should always be reared or may sometimes be exposed to die. There should certainly be a law to prevent the rearing of deformed children. On the other hand, there should also be a law, in all states where the system of social habits is opposed to unrestricted increase, to prevent the exposure of children to death *merely* in order to keep the population down. The proper thing to do is to limit the size of each family, and if children are then conceived in excess of the limit so fixed, to have miscarriage induced before sense and life have begun in the embryo. (Whether it is right or wrong to induce a miscarriage will thus depend on whether sense and life are still to come, or have already begun.)

NOTE 22.

United Nations Convention on Genocide†

The Contracting Parties,

Having considered the declaration made by the General Assembly of the United Nations in its

---

* *The Saturday Review*, Oct. 13, 1956, p. 26. Reprinted with permission of the publisher and the author.

* Reprinted from *Politics* by Aristotle (Barker translation), p. 327, by permission of the Clarendon Press, Oxford.

† *Journal of the General Assembly*, No. A/PV 178, at 2-3 (Dec. 9, 1948).

resolution 96 (1) dated 11 December 1946 that genocide is a crime under international law, contrary to the spirit and aims of the United Nations and condemned by the civilized world;

Recognizing that at all periods of history genocide has inflicted great losses on humanity; and

Being convinced that, in order to liberate mankind from such an odious scourge, international co-operation is required:

Hereby agree as hereinafter provided.

Article I

The Contracting Parties confirm that genocide, whether committed in time of peace or in time of war, is a crime under international law which they undertake to prevent and to punish.

Article II

In the present Convention, genocide means any of the following acts committed with intent to destroy, in whole or in part, a national, ethnic, racial or religious group as such:

(a) Killing members of the group;

(b) Causing serious bodily or mental harm to members of the group;

(c) Deliberately inflicting on the group conditions of life calculated to bring about its physical destruction in whole or in part;

(d) Imposing measures intended to prevent births within the group;

(e) Forcibly transferring children of the group to another group.

Article III

The following acts shall be punishable:

(a) Genocide;

(b) Conspiracy to commit genocide;

(c) Direct and public incitement to commit genocide;

(d) Attempt to commit genocide;

(e) Complicity in genocide.

Article IV

Persons committing genocide or any of the other acts enumerated in Article III shall be punished, whether they are constitutionally responsible rulers, public officials or private individuals.

Article V

The Contracting Parties undertake to enact, in accordance with their respective Constitutions, the necessary legislation to give effect to the provisions of the present Convention and, in particular, to provide effective penalties for persons guilty of genocide or any of the other acts enumerated in Article III.

NOTE 22

JENNINGS, H.S.

The Biological Basis of Human Nature*

[B]ad living conditions often produce the same kinds of results that bad genes do. . . . So long as living conditions are bad, we do not know what ills are due to poor genes. We must therefore correct the bad living conditions, not only for their directly beneficial effect, but also for the sake of eugenics. When this is done, it will be possible to discover what defects are primarily the result of defective genes, and then to plan measures for getting rid of these genes: measures for stopping the propagation of their carriers. That is, as a preliminary to the effective work of eugenics other reforms must be carried through. Measures of public health must be carried out, overwork and bad conditions of living done away with, faults of diet, both quantitative and qualitative, corrected; economic ills conquered, grinding poverty abolished. When these things are done, when the human plant is given conditions under which it can unfold its capabilities without stunting, poisoning and mutilation by the environment, then it will be possible to discover what ills are due primarily to defective genes, and to plan such measures as are possible for their eradication. Acting on such precise knowledge, far more rapid and effective results may be hoped for than from the present blind action in merely encouraging the propagation of certain classes, discouraging that of others.

3.

FATHER WILLS SELECTIVE BREEDING

a. The Will of Wilson Cox Brady (1954)†

I hereby establish the Brady Eugenics Trust, a non-profit welfare and educational organization.
. . .

The purposes of the Brady Eugenics Trust shall be

a) To promote genetic betterment in general.

b) To further the improvement of the human race by improved breeding and to encourage the practical application of the science of eugenics— a science which finds expression in the areas of physical, intellectual, motivational inheritance and in the field of social behavior.

c) To demote eugenic interest from the altruis-

---

* New York: W. W. Norton & Co., 1930, pp. 250-251. Reprinted with permission of W. W. Norton & Co., Inc. and Faber and Faber Ltd. Copyright 1930 by W. W. Norton & Co., Inc. Copyright renewed © 1958 by Burridge Jennings.

† The family name has been fictionalized. Printed with permission.

tic level of racial betterment to the more intimate and understandable level of betterment of one's own family and of his own children.

d) To perpetuate itself. . . .

e) To handle and safeguard its securities and to take all lawful steps in the pursuit of its purposes.

In carrying out these purposes the trustees are to exercise all the privileges open to them under the laws of the State of California, or other State if so incorporated, as to the publication and dissimulation of knowledge, as to employing doctors, psychologists, geneticists, lawyers, etc., as to control over the properties of the trust, as to receiving legacies from sundry sources for the promotion of the purposes of the trust, and as to any other matters permissible to a charitable and educational non-profit organization.

Pari passu with the establishment of the Brady Eugenics Trust I establish the Brady Specific Eugenics Trust. . . . The purposes of this specific trust are

f) to promote the eugenic marriage of my sons Rulon Wilson and Victor Wilson through counseling, marriage and birth awards as herein described.

g) To promote the eugenic marriage of others, as designated by the Board of Trustees, provided the necessary funds for awards become available.

h) To promote, as the trustees may see fit, any unfinished or unpublished studies of mine, as selected by Faith Winston with the counsel of Edward Jensen. Some of these have professional importance and financial promise, such as the Brady Activity Preference Test, the Brady Universal Grading Scheme, the Brady proposed Reasoning versus Information, Skills and Factual Knowledge scoring for the Stanford Achievement Test, Brady statistical and measurement tests, texts, tables, etc. Earnings from any of these shall accrue to the capital funds of the Brady Specific Eugenics Trust.

. . .

*   *   *

j) To dissolve itself after the mentioned purposes have been met and in any case not later than 21 years after the decease of Rulon Wilson and/or Victor Wilson, and at this time it is to assign its assets to the charitable, educational and non-profit Brady Eugenics Trust. . . .

Being well aware of the retarding influence of rigid stipulations as to future functioning I make such only with reference to the Brady Specific Eugenics Trust. The trustees are directed, upon the recommendation of its Technical Committee, to offer two sorts of awards,—a marriage award to a son of mine and his wife, if they meet certain conditions herein laid down, and a birth award

to this same couple when a child is born. The magnitude of these awards depends upon a quantity E (eugenic fitness) as determined by the Technical Committee, hereinafter defined, of the Board of Trustees. To be eligible for the marriage award son and bride must make available, *prior to marriage*, information called for by the Technical Committee so that it can determine prior to marriage an E score for the couple. As the purpose of the trust it to induce young people to concern themselves with eugenic fitness prior to marriage the couple become totally ineligible for a marriage award (but not necessarily as to a later birth award) if the information needed by the Technical Committee is not available to it prior to marriage. It is the duty of the Chairman of the Board of Trustees to inform Rulon Wilson and Victor Wilson (and perhaps others) not less frequently than once a year of the provisions of this trust.

*   *   *

. . . It is the duty of the Technical Committee to determine an eugenics fitness score for each couple in question. This score, E, is given by

$$E = (P_f + I_f + C_f + P_m + I_m + C_m)$$
(biological and social compatibility index)

in which the subscript f stands for the prospective father, m for the prospective mother, P for physical fitness, I for intellectual fitness, and C for the character fitness.

The Technical Committee shall prescribe a questionnaire and examination, with the assistance (paid as may be appropriate) of medical and genetic experts (e.g. Dr. Kenneth Sloan, Univ. of Cal., as pertaining to the rhesus factor, parental conjunction in illness predispositions, etc.) which boy and girl shall take and from which the Technical Committee shall determine a P score for each party, the units of which shall have the following meaning (assuming a normal distribution):

—100 = 1 standard deviation below the American white population average

0 = average

100 = 1 standard deviation above the average etc.

It shall similarly prescribe an examination to yield an I score.

—100 = 1 standard deviation below the population average

0 = average

100 = 1 standard deviation above the average etc.

It shall similarly prescribe an examination to yield a C score.

−100=1 standard deviation below the population average

0=average

100=1 standard deviation above the average etc.

It shall determine a boy-girl compatibility index, based upon the joint medical records of boy and girl and upon joint appraisal of achievement, interest and activity patterns. As a preliminary estimate it is assumed that this index will usually fall within the limits 2/3 and 3/2. I profess to the Technical Committee that my basis for this estimate is inadequate and I hope the Technical Committee will at a later date be able to determine whether this compatibility factor should be large or small and whether it should be a multiplicative factor, an additive factor, or some combination of the two. After such determination the formula giving E should be revised.

Having followed the medical and school histories of my boys, as well as their social behavior, I offer to the Technical Committee my estimates of their P, I and C scores.

For Rulon Wilson

P=100

I = 90 This may be an underestimate due to Rulon's indifference as to his scholastic record.

C= 90 This may be an underestimate, Rulon can, when the spirit moves him, show excellent cooperativeness, responsibility, and even generosity.

For Victor Wilson

P= 80

I = 60 This is probably an underestimate with reference to mechanical and manipulative abilities and an overestimate with reference to scholastic abilities.

C=140 Characteristically Victor shows excellent cooperativeness and generosity and at times sense of responsibility.

The P, I and C scores, as estimated, are to assist the Technical Committee, but not to replace its own endeavors to get such scores.

The capital funds of the Brady Specific Eugenics Trust should increase pari passu with inflation, so the awards as stipulated at this date should be modified in accordance with the fluctuations of the Bureau of Labor Consumers' Price Index, which is now about 115 on the base 100 for the 1947-49 average.

The marriage award in dollars=4 E and is a joint award to husband and wife.

The birth award, at the time of the birth of a child=6 E and it also is a joint award. The collection of data in order to determine an E score for a birth award calls for the cooperation of husband and wife with the Technical Committee at some reasonable time as stipulated by the committee.

I hereby earmark $1000 of the capital funds of the Brady Specific Eugenics Trust for awarding to one or more child and spouse of Martin Michael, under conditions for promoting eugenics which Martin Michael may stipulate. If this $1000 is not so expended within ten years it is to revert to the capital funds of the Trust.

I similarly earmark $1000 for Faith Winston similarly to hold directive right to. If not expended within ten years it is to revert to the capital funds of the Trust.

* * *

With due regard to administrative funds available this privilege to use the testing techniques of the Trust may be extended to others as the Board of Trustees may designate. The funds available for testing do, of course, depend upon the earnings of the invested funds and upon the fees which the Board establishes for its members, its officers, and its test administrators. Presumably the greatest expense will attach to obtaining the C scores (perhaps via interviews and questionnaires to associates of the couple in question) and the compatibility measures. In this matter I have confidence in the ingenuity of the Technical Committee.

I favor a certain publicity in channels interested in eugenics of the intent and general terms of the two trusts herein established. . . .

Nov. 15, 1954.

I, Wilson Cox Brady, . . . declare this to be my last will, revoking all former wills. . . .

b.   UNITED STATES NATIONAL BANK

v.

SNODGRASS

202 Ore. 530, 275 P. 2d 860 (1954)

WARNER, JUSTICE.

The United States National Bank of Portland (Oregon) in its capacity as trustee under the last will and testament of C. A. Rinehart, deceased, brings this suit against Merle Rinehart Snodgrass, the decedent's married daughter and sole heir, and 17 other defendants who are relatives and contingent beneficiaries of C. A. Rinehart. Plaintiff prays for a declaratory judgment establishing the validity and correct interpretation of the trusts set up by the testament and the rights, if any, of the defendants as beneficiaries thereunder.

On May 31, 1929, at a time when his daughter Merle was about 10 years old, Mr. Rinehart executed the instrument now before us for construction. Paragraph 7 of his will provides:

"I give and bequeath to the United States National Bank of Portland (Oregon), but in trust nevertheless, the sum of Fifteen Thousand ($15,000.00) Dollars, or one-half (½) of residue if sum is more than Thirty-Thousand ($30,000.00) Dollars, to pay to my daughter Merle from the net income derived therefrom the sum of Fifty ($50.00) Dollars each month beginning with the date of my death and until she attains the age of eighteen years, excluding, however, any period prior to the date of my death; Seventy-Five ($75.00) Dollars each month to her from the time of attaining the age of eighteen years and until she attains the age of twenty-five years; the whole of such net income to her from age twenty-five years and until she attains the age of thirty-two years. When my said daughter shall have attained the age of thirty-two years and upon my death, that is to say, when these two events occur, my trustee is authorized and directed to transfer . . . to my said daughter Merle the whole of the trust fund of Fifteen Thousand ($15,000.00) Dollars, or the one-half (½) of the entire estate if sum is more than Thirty Thousand ($30,000.00)) Dollars, provided she shall have proved conclusively to my trustee and to its entire satisfaction that she has not embraced, nor become a member of, the Catholic faith nor ever married to a man of such faith. In the event my daughter . . . becomes ineligible to receive the trust fund then I direct the principal of such trust fund to be divided as follows: . . . To my Mother Louise Rinehart, and my Sisters, Cordelia, Minnie and Mildred, and their children, and the children of my deceased brother Howard Rinehart, and my sister-in-law Bertie Rinehart. . . .

The testator died in January 1932. It was stipulated that his daughter Merle became 32 years old on May 18, 1951; that sometime in 1944 she married a man who was a member of the Catholic faith; and that at the time she knew of the provisions of the foregoing paragraph 7 of her father's will.

The lower court concluded that the conditions of the bequest . . . declaring a forfeiture of her rights in the corpus of the trust if she married a Catholic before her 32nd birthday, were valid. . . .

The appellant asserts that . . . such a provision violates public policy.

Mrs. Snodgrass did not join the Catholic church and therefore the clause restraining membership in that faith is not before us. Her loss, if any, accrues by reason of the restriction on her marriage to a Catholic within the time limitation. . . .

*　*　*

Litigation springing from religious differences, tincturing, as here, every part and parcel of this appeal, tenders to any court problems of an extremely delicate nature. This very delicacy, together with the novelty of the legal questions in this jurisdiction, warrants pausing before proceeding further and reorienting our thinking in terms of the real legal problem which we must resolve. As a first step we rid ourselves of some erroneous definitions and the smug acceptance of conclusions arising from the too-frequent and inept employment of such terms as "religious freedom", "religious intolerance" and "religious bigotry". We also disassociate ourselves from the erstwhile disposition of many persons to treat any opposition to a religious faith as a prima facie manifestation of religious bigotry, requiring legal condemnation.

The testamentary pattern of Mr. Rinehart may offend the sense of fair play of some in what appears as an ungracious and determined effort to bend the will of another of an acceptance of the testator's concept of the superiority of his own viewpoint.

In terms of common parlance, "bigotry" and its concomitant "intolerance" are ordinarily odious and socially distasteful. They usually connote some intrusion upon or a variance with our traditional thoughts on religious liberty and religious tolerance; but we find nothing in the law declaring religious bigotry or intolerance to be mala in se. It is not until actions motivated by the intolerant extremes of bigotry contravene the positive law or invade the boundaries of established public policy that the law is quickened to repress such illegal excesses and in proper cases levy toll upon the offenders as reparation to those who have been damaged thereby. It is the quality of the act or expression of the bigot—not one's bigotry—which determines the necessity, if any, for legal interposition.

*　*　*

While one may personally and loudly condemn a species of "intolerance" as socially outrageous, a court on the other hand must guard against being judicially intolerant of such an "intolerance", unless the court can say the act of intolerance is in a form not sanctioned by the law. We are mindful that there are many places where a bigot may safely express himself and manifest his intolerance of the viewpoint of others without fear of legal restraint or punishment. With certain limitations, one of those areas with a wide latitude of sufferance is found in the construction of the pattern of one's last will and testament. It is a field wherein neither this court nor any other court will question the correctness of a testator's religious views or prejudices. . . .

*　*　*

The right to espouse any religious faith or any political cause short of one dedicated to the overthrow of the government by force carries with it the cognate right to engage as its champion in the proselytization of followers or converts to the favored cause or faith. To that end its disciples are free to emphasize and teach what is believed by them to be its superior and self-evident truths and to point out and warn others against what its votaries deem to be the inferior, fallacious or dangerous philosophical content of opposing faiths or doctrines. No matter how specious, how intolerant, how narrow and no matter how prejudiced or how dogmatic the arguments of the devotees of one belief may appear to others of different persuasion, the right of either to so express himself is so emphatically a part and parcel of our public policy that it will be defended and protected by the courts of the land to the uttermost, unless it is found that the fanatical and unrestrained enthusiasm of its followers results in acts offensive to the positive law.

* * *

We therefore have no intention or disposition to disturb the provisions of Mr. Rinehart's will unless it can be demonstrated that they do violence to some legal rule or precept. Two general and cardinal propositions give direction and limitation to our consideration. One is the traditionally great freedom that the law confers on the individual with respect to the disposition of his property, both before and after death. The other is that greater freedom, the freedom of opinion and right to expression in political and religious matters, together with the incidental and corollary right to implement the attainment of the ultimate and favored objectives of the religious teaching and social or political philosophy to which an individual subscribes. We do not intend to imply hereby that the right to devise or bequeath property is in any way dependent upon or related to the constitutional guarantees of freedom of speech.

We will first give attention to appellant's claim that the provision for Mrs. Snodgrass is at odds with the public policy of both the state and national governments. We preface this phase of our inquiry with the following statement from 57 Am. Jur. 1017, Wills, § 1503, approving it and adopting it as a guide in the evaluation of the respective contentions of the parties to this appeal:

> "The right of a testator to attach to a gift in his will any lawful terms he sees fit, no matter how whimsical or capricious, is widely, if not universally, recognized. Conditions which are regarded as contrary to law or public policy, which are impossible of performance, or which are too vague and uncertain in their phraseology to disclose the actual intention of the testator, will not, however, be enforced, although it is established that in considering any testamentary condition the court must indulge a presumption in favor of its validity. When questions arise as to conditions or provisions being void as being against the public good or against public policy, great caution is necessary in considering them; at different times very different views have been entertained as to what is injurious to the public."

[T]here is nothing in our organic or statutory law or in prior decisions of this court which would strike down or limit a testamentary expression in the form that Mr. Rinehart elected to use in providing for his daughter.

* * *

As early as 1853 our legislature conferred upon every person of qualified age and sound mind the right to devise and bequeath all his estate, real and personal, saving such as is specially reserved by law to the decedent's spouse. . . . This generous latitude in testamentary disposition conferred by statute is emphasized and expanded in the often-repeated statement of Mr. Justice Wolverton in Holman's Will, 1902, 42 Or. 345, 356, 70 P. 908, 913:

> "The right of one's absolute domination over his property is sacred and inviolable, so that he may do what he will with his own, if it is not to the injury of another. He may bestow it whithersoever he will and upon whomsoever he pleases, and this without regard to natural or legitimate claims upon his bounty; * * * And this court has held, in effect, that while it seems harsh and cruel that a parent should disinherit one of his children and devise his property to others, or cut them all off and devise it to strangers, from some unworthy motive, *yet so long as that motive, whether from pride or aversion or spite or prejudice, is not resolvable into mental perversion, no court can interfere,* * * * " (Italics our.)

* * *

To sustain the contention that the contested provision of the will is against the public policy of the United States, appellant depends upon the First and Fourteenth Amendments to the United States Constitution; 42 U.S.C.A. §§ 1981-1983, relating to civil rights . . . and Shelley v. Kraemer, 334 U.S. 1. . . .

The First Amendment prohibits Congress from making any law respecting the establishment of a religion. . . . That amendment is a limitation upon the power of Congress. It has no effect upon the transactions of individual citizens and has been so interpreted. . . . Neither does the

Fourteenth Amendment relate to individual conduct. The strictures there found circumscribe state action in the particulars mentioned and in no way bear on a transaction of the character now before us. . . .

Shelley v. Kraemer, supra, is authority only for the proposition that the enforcement by state courts of a covenant in a deed restricting the use and occupancy of real property to persons of the Caucasian race falls within the purview of the Fourteenth Amendment as a violation of the equal protection clause, but, said the court, "That Amendment [Fourteenth] erects no shield against merely private conduct, however discriminatory or wrongful." 334 U.S. 1, . . .

We turn to an examination of the controverted provision and note that the condition is not one of complete restraint, in which character it might well be abhorrent to the law. It is merely partial and temporary and, . . . is not in terrorem. Mr. Rinehart's daughter is not thereby restrained from ever marrying a Catholic. This inhibition as a condition to taking under the will at the age of 32 lasts only 11 years, that is, from the legal marriageable age without parental consent (in this state, 21 years). After the age of 32 she is free to marry a Catholic or become a Catholic if she so pleases and have her estate, too. Moreover, the condition imposed does not restrict the beneficiary from enjoying marital status either before or after attaining the age of 32. Here, unfortunately, appellant would eat her cake and have it, too.

* * *

The phrase "in terrorem" is not new to the law of wills, although infrequently applied. It has been defined as "In terror, or warning ; by way of threat. The term is applied to gifts or legacies given on conditions subsequent, because it is said that the possibility of losing the gift tends to inspire fear or dread." 42 C.J.S. p. 491. It is a rule designed to test the validity of gifts with certain conditions subsequent.

Generally, conditions in restraint of marriage are said to be in terrorem and therefore invalid when the subject of the gift is personal property and *there is no gift over* ; but such a condition is not void as being in terrorem when there is a gift over. It is the absence of a gift over which supplies the quality of a coercive threat necessary to bring the condition under the in terrorem rule. . . .

Because of its irrational quality and its indefensible character as a "convenient phrase * * * to stand in place of a reason", we cannot recognize it as having any proper place in our jurisprudence and therefore decline to apply it as a

medium for testing the validity of the . . . will.

* * *

The appellant here is in a rather anomalous position when she attempts to invoke the rule of "terror", for her very act in marrying a Catholic before becoming 32 attests its innocuous effect as an inspiration to fear so far as the full exercise of her own judgment was concerned.

* * *

NOTE

LEACH, W. BARTON

Perpetuities in the Atomic Age: The Sperm Bank and the Fertile Decedent*

. . . Any first-year law student would consider it elementary that a bequest "to such of my grandchildren as shall reach the age of 21" is valid. The lives in being are the testator's children, as we school teachers have been telling our trusting pupils, and the grandchildren must reach 21 within 21 years after these lives plus one or more periods of gestation. But this is no longer true. Either the testator or his sons can have children years after their respective deaths. The explanation is this: . . . a technique has been developed for them to deposit their sperm in a sperm bank and to preserve it indefinitely through a refrigeration process. . . . Muller . . . states that experiments with mice have shown that a somewhat similar technique can be effective with females ; but, if I correctly understand how this works with the female, there is no perpetuities problem.[3]

My daughter, who is the mother of two fine prehumous[4] boys asks: "But suppose an astronaut is killed in orbital flight, why should his widow *want* to have a child after his death?" I have had to tell her that her question is immaterial, since it is the *possibility* that counts. Still this did not satisfy her, so I proceeded: "Consider the bride of some future astronaut. He is a junior officer, and prudently he and his bride feel that they should not have children until he gets a few promotions so that he can finance their future education. He makes his deposit in the sperm bank. Then he is incinerated in orbital flight. She is devastated. Devoted to him as she is, she wants a child by him. Further, Professor Muller explains to her that she has a genetic responsibility to continue the bloodline of this remarkable man. She does."

---

* 48 *A.B.A.J.* pp. 942-944 (Oct. 1962).

3. This situation has been designated, by one of my young lady students, as the child *en ventre sa frigidaire* . . .

4. This is a word which I now introduce into the legal vocabulary, believing as I do that the language of the law should keep abreast of scientific progress.

One easy escape from facing the tough legal issue would be to declare the resulting child illegitimate. But would you, sitting on any bench you care to name, put this stigma on the child thus conceived, deprive him of a share in his grandfather's estate, and bring down social obloquy on the courageous widow? Since the sperm bank program is government-sponsored, would you not be swayed by this[?] . . . If you still would rule for illegitimacy, can you be sure that the appropriate legislature, with all deliberate speed, will not take appropriate action to reverse your heartless historicity? Also, since the sperm bank is available not only to astronauts but to others who might be subjected to fallout in the event of nuclear war or even nuclear tests, wouldn't it be natural to have a clause in any will (analogous to the standard "Reno Clause" which protects technical illegitimates where there has been out-of-state divorce) causing sperm-bank children to be included in such class designations as "children" or "issue"?

* * *

Permit me to offer a draft opinion for any court before which the sperm bank issue arises. "We hold that a posthumously conceived sperm bank child of the donor's widow is the legitimate child of her and her late husband, at least if she has not remarried at the time of conception. We also hold that the duration of a male 'life in being' under the Rule against Perpetuities should be defined as the period of his reproductive capacity, including any post-mortem period during which his sperm remains fertile. In the *Duke of Norfolk's Case,* 3 Ch. Cas. 1 (1682), which is the fountain-head of the Rule against Perpetuities, Lord Nottingham was faced with the question where he would draw the line, where he would stop if he validated the gift in that case. He answered, 'I will tell you where I will stop: I will stop wherever any visible inconvenience doth appear.' We consider this a sage observation establishing a sound test. It is true that, through the centuries, the Rule has become crystallized into what the great John Chipman Gray described as 'a well-established, simple and clear rule' which he then expressed in thirty-two words requiring 833 pages of explanation. But neither this nor any other rule is so rigid in its application that judges who made the rules cannot adapt them to medical and scientific change. The period of the Rule has become greatly extended since Nottingham's day by the lengthening of the life expectancy of a person of any age ; thus the advances in medical science have already affected the practical impact of the Rule, and this will continue. Yet no one

has found a 'visible inconvenience' in this development, or suggested that the period of the Rule should be reduced to half a life or a third of a life or a period of years measured by life expectancies of the seventeenth century. We also find no 'visible inconvenience' in extension of reproductive capacity (which is what counts) by a refrigeration process, and we doubt that the extension will be any greater than the future increase in life expectancies which can be anticipated. Use of the sperm bank will probably be limited to relatively young men who, apart from the risks of the nuclear age, would normally far outlive the fertility of the deposited sperm. We therefore rule that gifts are as valid as if the sperm bank had never been thought of."

. . . One thing that can be done is to procure the enactment of legislation similar to that which now exists in Vermont, Kentucky, Washington, and perhaps Idaho, substantially as follows:

> Any interest in real or personal property which would violate the rule against perpetuities shall be reformed, within the limits of that rule, to approximate most closely the intention of the creator of the interest. In determining whether an interest would violate said rule and in reforming an interest the period of perpetuities shall be measured by actual rather than possible events, provided that the measuring lives must have a causal relationship to the vesting or failure of the interest.

The second thing that can be done is to protect wills and trusts by a clause appropriate to cure any perpetuities violation, either in the basic instrument or in a later instrument exercising powers of appointment. To this end Dean James K. Logan and I have proposed a Standard Perpetuities Saving Clause in 74 *Harv. L. Rev.* 1141 (1961) and are informed that it is being widely used in several states.

But, by whatever means, the result must be accomplished. Let it not be recorded in history that the American Institute of Biological Sciences has defeated the American Bar Association—and by our own rules!

4.
A FUTURE FROM THE PAST

PLATO
The Republic V (365 B.C.)*

[H]ow can marriages be made most beneficial? —that is a question which I put to you, because I see in your house dogs for hunting, and of the

---

* Reprinted in: Great Books of the Western World, Chicago: Encyclopaedia Britannica, Inc. 1952 (pp. 361-366). Used with permission of the Clarendon Press, Oxford.

nobler sort of birds not a few. Now, I beseech you, do tell me, have you ever attended to their pairing and breeding?

In what particulars?

Why, in the first place, although they are all of a good sort, are not some better than others?

True.

And do you breed from them all indifferently, or do you take care to breed from the best only?

From the best.

And do you take the oldest or the youngest, or only those of ripe age?

I choose only those of ripe age.

And if care was not taken in the breeding, your dogs and birds would greatly deteriorate?

Certainly.

And the same of horses and animals in general?

Undoubtedly.

Good heavens! my dear friend, I said, what consumate skill will our rulers need if the same principle holds of the human species!

Certainly, the same principle holds; but why does this involve any particular skill?

Because, I said, our rulers will often have to practise upon the body corporate with medicines. Now you know that when patients do not require medicines, but have only to be put under a regimen, the inferior sort of practitioner is deemed to be good enough; but when medicine has to be given, then the doctor should be more of a man.

That is quite true, he said; but to what are you alluding?

I mean, I replied, that our rulers will find a considerable dose of falsehood and deceit necessary for the good of their subjects: we were saying that the use of all these things regarded as medicines might be of advantage.

And we were very right.

And this lawful use of them seems likely to he often needed in the regulations of marriages and births.

How so?

Why, I said, the principle has been already laid down that the best of either sex should be united with the best as often, and the inferior with the inferior, as seldom as possible; and that they should rear the offspring of the one sort of union, but not of the other, if the flock is to be maintained in first-rate condition. Now these goings on must be a secret which the rulers only know, or there will be a further danger of our herd, as the guardians may be termed, breaking out into rebellion.

Very true.

Had we not better appoint certain festivals at which we will bring together the brides and bridegrooms, and sacrifices will be offered and suitable hymeneal songs composed by our poets; the number of weddings is a matter which must be left to the discretion of the rulers, whose aim will be to preserve the average of population? There are many other things which they will have to consider, such as the effects of wars and diseases and any similar agencies, in order as far as this is possible to prevent the State from becoming either too large or too small.

Certainly, he replied.

We shall have to invent some ingenious kind of lots which the less worthy may draw on each occasion of our bringing them together, and then they will accuse their own ill-luck and not the rulers.

To be sure, he said.

And I think that our braver and better youth, besides their other honours and rewards, might have greater facilities of intercourse with women given them; their bravery will be a reason, and such fathers ought to have as many sons as possible.

True.

And the proper officers, whether male or female or both, for offices are to be held by women as well as by men——

Yes——

The proper officers will take the offspring of the good parents to the pen or fold, and there they will deposit them with certain nurses who dwell in a separate quarter; but the offspring of the inferior, or of the better when they chance to be deformed, will be put away in some mysterious, unknown place, as they should be.

Yes, he said, that must be done if the breed of the guardians is to be kept pure.

They will provide for their nurture, and will bring the mothers to the fold when they are full of milk, taking the greatest possible care that no mother recognises her own child; and other wet-nurses may be engaged if more are required. Care will also be taken that the process of suckling shall not be protracted too long; and the mothers will have no getting up at night or other trouble, but will hand over all this sort of thing to the nurses and attendants.

You suppose the wives of our guardians to have a fine easy time of it when they are having children.

Why, said I, and so they ought. Let us, however, proceed with our scheme. . . .

* * *

[H]ow will they know who are fathers and daughters, and so on?

They will never know. The way will be this:— dating from the day of the hymeneal, the bridegroom who was then married will call all the male children who are born in the seventh and ten month afterwards his sons, and the female children his daughters, and they will call him father, and he will call their children his grandchildren, and they will call the elder generation grandfathers and grandmothers. All who were begotten at the time when their fathers and mothers came together will be called their brothers and sisters, and these, as I was saying, will be forbidden to intermarry. This, however, is not to be understood as an absolute prohibition of the marriage of brothers and sisters; if the lot favours them, and they receive the sanction of the Pythian oracle, the law will allow them.

Quite right, he replied.

Such is the scheme, Glaucon, according to which the guardians of our State are to have their wives and families in common. . . .

*　　*　　*

But would any of your guardians think or speak of any other guardian as a stranger?

Certainly he would not; for every one whom they meet will be regarded by them either as a brother or sister, or father or mother, or son or daughter, or as the child of parent of those who are thus connected with him.

Capital, I said; but let me ask you once more: Shall they be a family in name only; or shall they in all their actions be true to the name? For example, in the use of the word "father," would the care of a father be implied and the filial reverence and duty and obedience to him which the law commands; and is the violator of these duties to be regarded as an impious and unrighteous person who is not likely to receive much good either at the hands of God or of man? Are these to be or not to be the strains which the children will hear repeated in their ears by all the citizens about those who are intimated to them to be their parents and the rest of their kinsfolk?

These, he said, and none other; for what can be more ridiculous than for them to utter the names of family ties with the lips only and not to act in the spirit of them?

*　　*　　*

And this agrees with the other principle which we were affirming—that the guardians were not to have houses or lands or any other property; their pay was to be their food, which they were to receive from the other citizens, and they were to have no private expenses; for we intended them to preserve their true character of guardians.

Right, he replied.

Both the community of property and the community of families, as I am saying, tend to make them more truly guardians; they will not tear the city in pieces by differing about "mine" and "not mine"; each man dragging any acquisition which he has made into a separate house of his own, where he has a separate wife and children and private pleasures and pains; but all will be affected as far as may be by the same pleasures and pains because they are all of one opinion about what is near and dear to them, and therefore they all tend toward a common end.

Certainly, he replied.

And as they have nothing but their persons which they can call their own, suits and complaints will have no existence among them; they will be delivered from all those quarrels of which money or children or relations are the occasion.

Of course they will.

Neither will trials for assault or insult ever be likely to occur among them. For that equals should defend themselves against equals we shall maintain to be honourable and right; we shall make the protection of the person a matter of necessity.

That is good, he said.

Yes; and there is a further good in the law; viz., that if a man has a quarrel with another he will satisfy his resentment then and there, and not proceed to more dangerous lengths.

Certainly.

To the elder shall be assigned the duty of ruling and chastising the younger.

Clearly.

Nor can there be a doubt that the younger will not strike or do any other violence to an elder, unless the magistrates command him; nor will he slight him in any way. For there are two guardians, shame and fear, mighty to prevent him: shame, which makes men refrain from laying hands on those who are to them in the relation of parents; fear, that the injured one will be succoured by the others who are his brothers, sons, fathers.

That is true, he replied.

Then in every way the laws will help the citizens to keep the peace with one another?

Yes, there will be no want of peace.

And as the guardians will never quarrel among themselves there will be no danger of the rest of the city being divided either against them or against one another.

None whatever.

I hardly like even to mention the little meannesses of which they will be rid, for they are beneath notice: such, for example, as the flattery of the rich by the poor, and all the pains and pangs which men experience in bringing up a family, and in finding money to buy necessaries for their household, borrowing and then repudiating, getting how they can, and giving the money into the hands of women and slaves to keep—the many evils of so many kinds which people suffer in this way are mean enough and obvious enough, and not worth speaking of.

Yes, he said, a man has no need of eyes in order to perceive that.

And from all these evils they will be delivered, and their life will be blessed as the life of Olympic victors and yet more blessed.

*   *   *

You agree then, I said, that men and women are to have a common way of life such as we have described—common education, common children ; and they are to watch over the citizens in common whether abiding in the city or going out to war ; they are to keep watch together, and to hunt together like dogs ; and always and in all things, as far as they are able, women are to share with the men? And in so doing they will do what is best, and will not violate, but preserve the natural relation of the sexes.

I agree with you, he replied.

The enquiry, I said, has yet to be made, whether such a community will be found possible—as among other animals, so also among men—and if possible, in what way possible?

NOTES

NOTE 1.

MULLER, HERMANN J.

Relations between Cultural and Biological Evolution*

No one knows better than the geneticist how uncertain the knowledge of any given individual's genetic constitution is, at best ; how much the effects of environment are interwoven with heredity in molding any individual, and how much randomness enters into the determination of what genes any new individual shall have. And no one knows better than the social scientist how vicious and self-defeating would be any attempt at dictation in matters of reproduction. What counts in evolution, however, is not the individual case but the general trend, for overall selection in a given direction eventually works. And consciously directed selection works much faster than does the unconscious kind.

The important thing then is the kind of trend. Here the madness of the racists has taught the world by terrible object lessons the dangers of

---

* Statement made in discussion "Social and Cultural Evolution," Panel V, Nov. 28, 1959, Univ. of Chicago, Darwin Centennial Celebration, pp. 2-3 (mimeo). Copyright 1959 by the University of Chicago. Reprinted with permission of The University of Chicago Press, publishers.

egotism, ethnocentrism and particularism in general. One of the main antidotes to this is a better, more vivid teaching of evolution, with its emphasis on the fundamental unity of man and the overriding importance of the species as a whole, and with its underscoring of the paramount values that men the world over have already come to cherish: especially genuine warmth of fellow feeling and a cooperative disposition, depth and breadth of intellectual capacity, moral courage and integrity, appreciation of nature and art, and aptness of expression and communication. It is the exercise of these faculties that has brought man to his present estate but most people, if they are honest, will grant that these qualities have never been in oversupply, and that, as our culture advances ever further, we can make increasingly good use of a higher quality of them. At the same time the furtherance of specialized abilities, developed in response to particular predilections, as for music, will also help to enrich the whole.

Unless men sink into the hands of mad or ignorant dictators there is, I think, no danger that in the overall run they will fail to recognize their fundamental values. After all, the same problem arises, of what shall we aim for, whenever we educate our children. And just as most of us are getting to recognize these same aims in education so we will naturally do so in genetics. Nor is there a danger that we can have too much of these faculties.

NOTE 2.

MEYER v. NEBRASKA
262 U.S. 390 (1923)

MR. JUSTICE MCREYNOLDS delivered the opinion of the Court.

Plaintiff in error was tried and convicted in the District Court for Hamilton County, Nebraska, under an information which charged that on May 25, 1920, while an instructor in Zion Parochial School, he unlawfully taught the subject of reading in the German language to Raymond Parpart, a child of ten years, who had not attained and successfully passed the eighth grade. The information is based upon "An act relating to the teaching of foreign languages in the State of Nebraska,"
. . .

"Sec. 2. Languages, other than the English language, may be taught as languages only after a pupil shall have attained and successfully passed the eighth grade. . . .

*   *   *

The problem for our determination is whether the statute as construed and applied unreasonably infringes the liberty guaranteed to the plaintiff in error by the Fourteenth Amendment. "No State shall . . . deprive any person of life, liberty, or property, without due process of law."

While this Court has not attempted to define with exactness the liberty thus guaranteed, the term has received much consideration and some of the included things have been definitely stated. Without doubt, it denotes not merely freedom from bodily restraint but also the right of the individual to contract, to engage in any of the common occupations of life, to acquire useful knowledge, to marry, establish a home and bring up children, to worship God according to the dictates of his own conscience, and generally to enjoy those privileges long recognized at common law as essential to the orderly pursuit of happiness by free men. . . . The established doctrine is that this liberty may not be interfered with, under the guise of protecting the public interest, by legislative action which is arbitrary or without reasonable relation to some purpose within the competency of the State to effect. Determination by the legislature of what constitutes proper exercise of police power is not final or conclusive but is subject to supervision by the courts. . . .

*   *   *

[T]he legislature has attempted materially to interfere with the calling of modern language teachers, with the opportunities of pupils to acquire knowledge, and with the power of parents to control the education of their own.

It is said the purpose of the legislation was to promote civic development by inhibiting training and education of the immature in foreign tongues and ideals before they could learn English and acquire American ideals. . . .

That the State may do much, go very far, indeed, in order to improve the quality of its citizens, physically, mentally and morally, is clear; but the individual has certain fundamental rights which must be respected. The protection of the Constitution extends to all, to those who speak other languages as well as to those born with English on the tongue. Perhaps it would be highly advantageous if all had ready understanding of our ordinary speech, but this cannot be coerced by methods which conflict with the Constitution—a desirable end cannot be promoted by prohibited means.

For the welfare of his Ideal Commonwealth, Plato suggested a law which should provide: "That the wives of our guardians are to be common, and their children are to be common, and no parent is to know his own child, nor any child his parent. . . . The proper officers will take the offspring of the good parents to the pen or fold, and there they will deposit them with certain nurses who dwell in a separate quarter; but the offspring of the inferior, or of the better when they chance to be deformed, will be put away in some mysterious, unknown place, as they should be." In order to submerge the individual and develop ideal citizens, Sparta assembled the males at seven into barracks and intrusted their subsequent education and training to official guardians. Although such measures have been deliberately approved by men of great genius, their ideas touching the relation between individual and State were wholly different from those upon which our institutions rest; and it hardly will be affirmed that any legislature could impose such restrictions upon the people of a State without doing violence to both letter and spirit of the Constitution.

The desire of the legislature to foster a homogeneous people with American ideals prepared readily to understand current discussions of civic matters is easy to appreciate. Unfortunate experiences during the late war and aversion toward every characteristic of truculent adversaries were certainly enough to quicken the aspiration. But the means adopted, we think, exceed the limitations upon the power of the State and conflict with rights assured to plaintiff in error. The interference is plain enough and no adequate reason therefor in time of peace and domestic tranquility has been shown.

*   *   *

PART SIX

THE FAMILY LAW PROCESS— THE FUNCTION OF THE STATE IN ESTABLISHING, ADMINISTERING, AND REORGANIZING THE FAMILY AND ADMINISTERING THE REORGANIZED FAMILY

Since their divorce the Lessers have been courting each other. We have selected for study only a few of the many documents in their post-divorce legal file. In addition to the hearings and decisions reproduced here, this file is filled with diaries, motion papers, and correspondence with their attorneys, judges, children, inlaws, doctors, and school teachers.

In returning to the Lesser case and in bringing this Chapter to a close, we ask—with the aid of hindsight and a code of another culture—What, if anything, should have been done differently by the state in the pre- and post-divorce proceedings, and why? These questions should be considered in the light of Herbert Gold's observations: "For the pulse of marriage is not broken by divorce's hemp. With children we cannot even conceive of breaking it—that eternal physical presence of the new and unending family we have created, children having children having children, long after we have died. Our being in them is never dead. ('When, now you tell me, when are you coming to live at home again, Daddy?' 'Never. But I'll come to see you every day, unless, unless—' 'Will I have to get a new daddy?' 'I'm your daddy and you're my daughter, and we won't change that.') The state of being father and child, having children, having a parent, never changes, although the manner of that being is hurtfully altered.

"Even without children, we have become ourselves only together and in our marriage and we go toward what we are becoming only together and in our divorce. Divorce is not a dissolving fluid, although it may be a corroding acid. It is like marriage but extremer: it is to marriage as an explosion is to rust. Under certain circumstances an oily cloth may smolder and decay under slow oxidation; in a tight closet it bursts into fiery life. But all that is metaphor: marriage and divorce are kind in that we have formed ourselves together within them."*

A.

The Lesser Families Revisited—Separate but Entangled—
Resolving Disputes about the Agreement.

i.

"HUSBAND" INVOKES CONTEMPT PROCEEDING TO PUNISH "WIFE" FOR VIOLATION OF VISITATION RIGHTS

a. Letter from Sadie Lesser (Ressler)

December 23, 1961

Hon. Henry Epstein
Justice of the Supreme Court of the State of New York

Dear Judge Epstein:

There is presently a proceeding pending before you wherein the defendant (my former husband) claims I violated the Judgment of this Court, dated January 30, 1960, in that I obstructed and interfered with the religious education and training of the infant, Larry; failed to afford the defendant visiting rights, and interfered with the dental treatment of the infant, Larry

Defendant has asked for an Order of this Court punishing me for Contempt.

As I cannot afford legal counsel, and as the defendant refused to pay counsel fees for me, I appeared in this matter personally.

In reply to defendant's affidavit, sworn to October 5, 1961, I state that any and all statements made by the defendant to the effect that our marital difficulties were as a result of my change of religion are absolutely false. If the Court will look at the complaint in this action and the find-

ings and decision of Justice Saul Streit, it will be seen that the defendant's cruel and inhuman treatment of me, bestial attacks upon my body, antedated my change of religion.

As a result of the cruel and inhuman treatment and abandonment of me by the defendant, I was awarded a Decree of Separation and custody of Larry. I promised Justice Streit that I would at all times permit Larry to have whatever medical treatment the defendant requested for him and I have always lived up to that promise.

At no time has the defendant obeyed the judgment and Orders of this Court. He consistently retains the child beyond the visiting time permitted by the Judgment and as amended by the agreement of January 23, 1960. He does not return the child to me at sundown on Sundays, as in said agreement provided, in Par. Fourth (B) (3). He has not permitted Larry to attend the Hebrew School serving the Community in which the child resides, as per the agreement (2) of the same paragraph in the contract. He does not provide transportation to and from the religious school as also set forth in the contract, in the same paragraph (2). He does not confer with me on matters pertaining to the children's welfare, as provided in the contract subdivision (E). He does not permit me to visit Benjamin, as set forth in the contract, subdivision (A). He does not permit me to talk on the telephone to Larry at any of the times that the child is with the defendant, but on the contrary, he and members of his household hang the telephone up on me.

He has constantly threatened me that he would break me both financially and otherwise.

From November 3rd to November 13, 1957, he flouted the Order of this Court by wilfully, delib-

* Gold, H., *The Age of Happy Problems*. Copyright © 1952, 1962 by Herbert Gold. Reprinted with permission of the publishers, The Dial Press, Inc., and Laurence Pollinger Ltd.

erately and unlawfully retaining the infant Larry from my custody. Mr. Justice Streit on a Motion brought by me found the defendant guilty of Contempt of Court.

With constant litigation facing me, I finally gave in and on January 23, 1960, signed the amended contract believing it would appease the defendant and end all litigation by my permitting him to send Larry to Hebrew School, notwithstanding the fact that the child was opposed to it and further that legally I could have brought the child up in my adopted faith, while in my custody.

There were occasions when I kept the child home from Hebrew School on account of his illness on that day. At another time, the child had to go to the dentist due to a mishap with his teeth brace. In one of his absences, he was with his father, and it was beyond my control. I myself have frequently driven the child to the Hebrew School in inclement weather to avoid his having to wait on the street for a bus, which is the only transportation provided for by the defendant.

Likewise, I have taken the child to the dentist, notwithstanding the fact that it was the defendant's obligation to arrange for that. Only once did I refuse to have Larry keep an appointment with the dentist, which was due to the fact that the defendant had unlawfully retained Larry from my home beyond the lawful time in which he should have been visiting with the father (defendant), and further because the defendant had unlawfully deducted some money from the amount allowed to me by the Court for Larry's support.

At the end of the summer vacation, 1961, the Defendant, in violation of Paragraph "Fourth" (B) Subdivision (7) of the contract of January 23, 1960, retained the child for four days overtime, and during this time it was one of the days when the child should have gone to Hebrew School, but the defendant failed to send him. During a six weeks' period in the summer of 1961, the child was with the defendant, and at no time during that period did he inform me where the child was, he having taken him away to the country, notwithstanding the fact that Mr. Justice Klein of this Court instructed the defendant to permit me to talk to the child on the telephone every day.

On October 2nd and 3rd, 1961, I retained Larry to get a return of at least two of the days out of the four overtime days when Larry was withheld by Mr. Lesser, and because of those two days, the defendant now claims in his moving papers that I have failed to afford him visiting rights.

On December 3rd, 1961, the defendant again took the law into his own hands and retained Larry deliberately and unlawfully from my custody until December 15. I served him with Motion papers to punish him for Contempt of Court. The Motion came on to be heard before Justice Louis Capozolli. Mr. Herbert Spencer Leman, who had represented me at the time of the making of the agreement of January 23, 1960, again represented me in this procedure. Mr. Leman told me that the Court would no doubt award me a Counsel fee in this proceeding.

At the request of defendant's attorney, Joseph Tiefenbrun, the Motion was adjourned to December 15th. On December 14th the defendant promised to return the child to me, but failed to do so. On the night of the 14th, Mr. Tiefenbrun telephoned to Mr. Leman and informed him that the defendant had dismissed him as his lawyer. On the morning of the 15th, I attended Court with Mr. Leman. Neither the defendant nor his attorney appeared, but the defendant telephoned to the Court and stated he was snow-bound in Westchester. This was false, because Mr. Leman and I both live in Westchester and had appeared in this Court in this Contempt proceeding, both on the 13th and 15th, and besides, the defendant had been at his place of business in New York City the entire day of the 14th and even late in the evening.

Mr. Leman pointed this out to Justice Capozolli, who thereupon directed his Clerk to telephone to the defendant and inform him that unless he appeared in Court on the 16th with the child, Larry, an Order would be issued for his arrest. This directive of the Judge was effective in that on the night of the 15th, the defendant returned the child to me, after withholding him for 13 days. At the time defendant surrendered the child, he came into my home, extended a hand of congeniality to both me and my present husband, Mr. Ressler, and stated that he had had enough quarreling, desired to stop all litigation and enmity and just wanted both parents, himself and myself, to carry out the terms of the agreement for the peace of the child. I told him that that was what I always wanted and worked toward.

We both agreed that each of us would permit the other to talk to Larry on the telephone, at least three times a week, whenever he was at home with me or visiting at the home of the defendant. I also agreed, as I always had done, to live up to the letter of the agreement with respect to the Hebrew School education and dental appointments, provided the defendant carried out the terms of the agreement on his part. In fact, on Saturday, December 17th, I took Larry to the doctor for his weekly injection for asthma.

The defendant agreed to pay my attorney Mr. Leman $150.00 for this Contempt proceeding against defendant.

I asked the defendant to withdraw the present Contempt proceedings pending before your Honor, in view of his statement that he was sick of litigation, but he refused to so do.

In view of the foregoing. I believe the Motion made by the defendant and now pending before your Honor should be terminated. If the defendant does not agree, then I respectfully ask your Honor to have a hearing in this matter on or about April 5th, 1962, postponing the proceedings until I can have Mr. Leman attend with me. Mr. Leman is presently out of New York and will not return until April. I feel that no harm can come from any delay, as both the defendant and I have come to an understanding with respect to the agreement, if adhered to.

I have sent a copy of this letter to the defendant's attorney, Joseph Tiefenbrun.

Respectfully yours,

Sadie Lesser Ressler

b. Letter from Joseph Tiefenbrun, Attorney for Perry Lesser

January 11, 1962

Dear Judge Epstein:

I am the attorney for Perry Lesser, the moving party in a motion to punish for contempt which is now pending before you since October 25, 1961. I have just returned from Europe yesterday and on my return found a copy of an eight page letter, addressed to you dated December 23, 1961, purportedly written by the respondent.

When this motion came on it was adjourned two or three times at the request of the respondent because she did not have an attorney and apparently has not retained one to this date in this proceeding. On the final adjourned date you directed that the matter be sent to the Family Counselling Unit for a report in connection with the welfare and condition of eleven year old Larry, the son of the parties. I assume that on the filing of the report there will be a hearing following which a determination will be made.

In her letter of December 23, 1961, Mrs. Ressler has requested that there be a hearing but has asked that it be deferred to April 5, 1962. Neither my client nor I can agree to this in view of the nature of the motion and the fact that it is of the

utmost importance that the boy be made secure and the conflict and uncertainties be removed. Therefore, we most strenuously oppose any such long adjournment.

The crux of the motion to punish for contempt is the failure on the part of the respondent, who has converted from Orthodox Judaism to Christian Science, to send the boy to his Father's home for the Jewish Holy Days, to permit him to attend Hebrew School and to permit him to follow an orderly sequence of medical and dental treatments, all in violation of the agreement between the parties and the decree.

The boy is not doing well in his school work and is kept in a constant state of turmoil by respondent's actions in changing her mind about the things he may or may not do, when he may attend Hebrew School or services, whether he will go to his father's home, whether he will be permitted to attend a boy scout's meeting and other similar matters.

A decision in this matter should be made as soon as practicable.

I will make no attempt to reply to the various allegations in the letter of respondent which the Court will note is not sworn to as in the affidavit of the moving party, except to state on behalf of my client that it is not truthful. All of these matters can be disposed of at the time of the hearing.

I respectfully request that the application for the long adjournment be denied and the Court set the matter down for hearing at its earliest convenience following the receipt of the report of the Family Counselling Unit.

Respectfully yours,

Joseph Tiefenbrun

CC: Sadie Ressler

c. Trial Court Decides—February 9, 1962

EPSTEIN, J.

This bitter family dispute has been within the study of the Family Counselling Unit since 1956 when ordered by the Appellate Division. Both parents are remarried yet their bitterness knows no surcease and the victim from both sides is Larry, their son, aged 11 years. Respondent father is an Orthodox Jew who seeks to impose his wishes on the young boy. The mother, petitioner, is a Christian Scientist. Young Larry has been compelled by the prior rulings of this Court and the commands of the parents to attend day school, religious school and Sunday School. The result of this strain upon him and the effect of the parental battles over him have been his failing in practically all subjects in day school, poor grades in religious school and a bitter resentment against respondent, his father.

The court has before it a full and comprehensive study of all factors involved by the Family Counselling Unit, with supporting data from schools, etc. The only possible decision here is that which will restore some mental ease to this unfortunate lad. He hates his father. This can be eased by removing the cause of that hatred. The mother now recognizes that some changes are needed. Attendance in the Boy Scouts movement has been helpful. The choice of a school for Larry must be left to his mother, petitioner, in whose custody he is placed and confirmed. Since Larry dislikes attending Orthodox Jewish religious school, and prefers the choice of his mother—he should be allowed that freedom of choice. Once a month Larry may be with his father from Friday evening 7 P.M. to Sunday evening 6 P.M. During the summer Larry shall be allowed to attend a boys' camp where he can develop independence, the cost of such camp to be borne by respondent father. This child must not be victimized by the hatred of the father and mother to each other. The father is well able to bear the expense of the schooling, camp and maintenance of Larry. Nor shall this support be lessened by reason of the bitterness engendered by thoughtless and estranged parents. Submit order embodying the foregoing provisions. This decision and the papers are ordered sealed. Copies of this opinion are to be available for the parties on application to the Clerk of Part XII.

d. Appellate Court Reverses and Orders a Rehearing—July 7, 1962

BREITEL, J. P.: Orders, entered on March 24, 1962, and May 25, 1962 reversed, on the law, and in the exercise of discretion, and a hearing directed on the issues involved (see People ex rel. Kaufman, 9 App. Div. 2d 375). The record indicates that both parties have upon occasion violated the terms of the agreement. The joy of battling seems to have taken precedence over what should have been of primary concern to these parents, that is, the welfare of the infant. Upon a motion by defendant-appellant, brought on by an order to show cause, to punish plaintiff-respondent for contempt, the court, in denying the motion and without a hearing, modified the custody provisions and also restricted and later suspended certain rights of visitation by the father as provided for in the agreement. While it may be that some changes are desirable and should be made, it is our view that such drastic action should not be taken by judicial fiat, but only after a full and comprehensive hearing is accorded the parties.

2.

FATHER INVOKES HABEAS CORPUS PROCEEDINGS TO RELEASE CHILD FROM MOTHER

a. Application for Writ

September 6, 1962

In the Matter of the Application
of
Perry Lesser, for Writ of Habeas Corpus
to Determine the Custody of Larry Lesser
a Child, Now Held by Sadie Lesser (Ressler).
Defendant

TO THE SUPREME COURT OF THE STATE OF NEW YORK:

The petition of Perry Lesser respectfully shows this to the Court:

1. The reason for this petition is that the respondent has failed and refused to permit your petitioner any visitation rights and your petitioner has not seen his son since April 1962. During that time numerous efforts have been made to see him, all unsuccessful. Respondent has secured an unlisted telephone number, has prevented any conversation between your petitioner and Larry, refused to divulge the name of the summer camp to which she had sent the infant until approximately the last ten days of the summer and has otherwise in every way obstructed and prevented your petitioner from having any contact with his son.

2. That your petitioner verily believes that the health and welfare of his child is being endangered. Respondent has adopted the religion of Christian Science and has failed and refused to send the infant for medical, orthodontic or other treatment. Your petitioner has no knowledge of the health of his son and has been unable to secure any.

WHEREFORE, your petitioner prays for a Writ of Habeas Corpus, directed to the respondent, Sadie Ressler, commanding her to produce the said child, Larry, before this Court, and for such other relief as may be just and proper.

b. Subpoena

September 6, 1962

SUPREME COURT OF THE STATE OF NEW YORK

In the Matter of the Application
of
Perry Lesser, for Writ of Habeas Corpus

THE PEOPLE OF THE STATE OF NEW YORK TO: Sadie (Lesser) Ressler

WE COMMAND you that you have the body of Larry Lesser, by you imprisoned and detained, as it is said, together with the time and cause of said detention and imprisonment, by whatsoever name he shall be called or charged, before a Special Term, Part I of the Supreme Court, to be held at the County Courthouse, on the 14th day of September, 1962 at ten o'clock in the forenoon of that day, to do and receive what shall then and there be considered concerning him, and have you then and there this Writ.

WITNESS Hon. George Tilzer, one of the Justices of this Court this 6th day of September, 1962

c. Trial Court Decides—September 11, 1962

MCCULLOUGH, J.

After consultation held in Chambers, at which the boy was produced, the Writ is disposed of as follows:

The father of the boy is to have custody of the son, Larry, from 7.30 P.M. September 10, 1962 until 8:00 P.M. September 12, 1962. The remaining matters at issue are respectfully referred to Mr. Justice Aurelio for his determination at a hearing scheduled to be held before him in the City of New York on September 14, 1962.

3.

REHEARING THE CONTEMPT— INFORMING THE JUDGE FOR DECISION

NEW YORK SUPREME COURT
September 14, October 10 & 16, 1962

Before: Hon. Thomas A. Aurelio, Justice

THE COURT. Do you wish to put on the record the motion you want to make?

MR. ERDHEIM. Nothing is stipulated. There is the order of the Appellate Division. He is moving to vacate an order made by Judge Epstein on May 26, 1961. The order of the Appellate Division of July 6, 1961 specifically said that the orders appealed from are reversed on the law and a hearing is directed on the issues involved, and nothing else. That becomes academic. I do not want to stipulate.

MR. TIEFENBRUN. We now have a situation where there is outstanding at this moment an order of June 9, 1962, punishing the defendant for contempt. It is this order that I seek to have vacated. If counsel will stipulate——

MR. ERDHEIM. I won't stipulate.

MR. TIEFENBRUN.——that this order is academic

and of no affect——

MR. ERDHEIM. That is ridiculous. The Appellate Division said that Judge Epstein should not have summarily granted the plaintiff's application and should have ordered a hearing. That is what the Appellate Division did in this order.

THE COURT. What do you suggest?

MR. ERDHEIM. I suggest this, Judge, since this is Judge Epstein's order, since he is familiar with it, and since the Appellate Division directed a hearing, I submit, your Honor, after you read the papers, without wasting a lot of your Honor's valuable time, that you refer it to Judge Epstein. He is familiar with this matter, he had it all the way down the line, and the Appellate Division ordered a hearing.

THE COURT. I cannot send it to Judge Epstein because he is not here now. This is before me and I do not think I have the right to send it to him.

I will say that this motion is withdrawn, it is academic. What is next?

MR. TIEFENBRUN. The other motion is a motion for leave for the father of this 12-year-old boy to have him for a minimum period of six weeks. A year ago I made a motion to punish Mrs. Ressler for contempt for the failure to deliver the boy on Yom Kippur, for failure to have orthodontia treatment and various other things. This was the motion that Judge Epstein summarily disposed of without any hearing and without any testimony, without any argument, just disposed of.

We took an appeal and it was reversed, and the Appellate Division ordered a hearing.

Before we get to that, however, an application was made before Judge Epstein for an adjournment so that we could get the boy examined psychiatrically and medically because she has consistently refused to permit the father to see the child. The father had not seen the child since March—in spite of these provisions I have told you about—since March or April of this year.

We were here last week and I was arguing against an adjournment on this particular thing and your Honor directed if she did not turn the boy over he was not required to pay the $50 a week. That did not get the boy. I had to—after having a lot of gentle and polite conversation with Mr. Erdheim—get a writ of habeas corpus returnable in Westchester on the Friday preceding. This woman has apparently left her second husband.

MR. ERDHEIM. Wait a minute. I submit the statement by counsel just made to the Court not only is unwarranted but untrue and has no part in this proceeding. I tell it to you now.

MR. TIEFENBRUN. I am glad of that. That was said on that night.

THE COURT. Pardon me for a moment, sir. I want to see where I stand on this. If there is to be a hearing on this matter why don't we proceed with the hearing. When we come to arguing these things as to what happened or did not happen, that can all be developed at the hearing.

MR. TIEFENBRUN. There is something before the hearing. We want the boy for a period of time to live with his father so we can arrange for psychiatric examinations and medical examinations. There has been a report of the Family Counselling Unit.

THE COURT. I will tell you quickly what came to my mind. I will determine that upon the hearing as to whether the child requires, or whether there is any need for those things. There may be no need for it. If there is need for it I will adjourn the matter for further hearing pending the psychiatric investigation.

a. Perry Lesser—Defendant

[i]
Direct Examination

BY MR. TIEFENBRUN

Q. On January 30, 1959, did you enter into an agreement with Mrs. Ressler—an agreement of separation dealing with the custody of Larry, among other things? A. Yes.

MR. TIEFENBRUN. I offer the agreement in evidence.

MR. ERDHEIM. I object to that. At a later date very shortly I am going to vitiate this agreement and the order which approved this agreement. This agreement was for the purpose of Section 51 of the Domestic Relations Law. This was an agreement in contemplation of a divorce, and a divorce did take place a couple of days later. When Judge Gold signed an order approving this agreement he did not know that this was an agreement in contemplation of a divorce. I submit that it was this type of agreement that caused the enactment of that section in the Domestic Relations Law. I submit that it is wholly improper.

THE COURT. You may argue that question later on, but I will receive it. The agreement is contained in the record on appeal to the Appellate Division on this matter. As I understand it, your client claims that Mrs. Ressler, the plaintiff here, the former wife, violated some provision of this agreement.

MR. TIEFENBRUN. That is correct.

THE COURT. Ask him in what respect that agreement was violated.

Q. In what respects has Mrs. Ressler violated the terms of this agreement? A. Mrs. Ressler violated the agreement in many respects. I will mention them as I go along.

THE COURT. Go ahead.

A. In reference to the observation of the Jewish Holy Days.

Q. Did the agreement provide that you were to have Larry on all the religious holidays required for observance by the Orthodox faith? A. Yes.

Q. Were there any times when Mrs. Ressler failed, or refused, to send Larry over for any of these Holy Days? A. Yes.

Q. Will you tell us what occasions were involved? A. As I recollect in the moving papers there were a number of occasions. One was the High Holy Days.

MR. ERDHEIM. May we have the date for the record?

THE COURT. Give us the date. A. June of 1960 was the Feast of Weeks.

MR. ERDHEIM. I object to that. It is not set forth in the papers.

MR. TIEFENBRUN. May I say this, if your Honor please, the crux of this situation is not just one violation but repeated and repeated violations.

THE COURT. You have enough here. If you establish what you have in here you don't have to fight about the other little details.

MR. TIEFENBRUN. The other little details show a distinct course of conduct.

THE COURT. Don't be difficult. You have enough here without inviting trouble. Do it my way.

Q. On Yom Kippur . .

THE COURT. You say the Day of Atonement, start off with that.

Q. On the Day of Atonement, 1960, did Mrs. Ressler send Larry over to your home?

A. No, she did not.

Q. Will you tell us the circumstances surrounding that Holy Day with respect to Larry? A. As on most Holy Days I never know whether Larry is coming to my house.

MR. ERDHEIM. I object to that.

THE COURT. Sustained. When the child did not come over did you call her up or speak to her about it?

THE WITNESS. I tried to get in touch with Mrs. Ressler. I don't remember if it was this occasion or fourteen others.

MR. ERDHEIM. I move to strike that out.

THE COURT. Please tell us about this and make it simple. If you establish this you have established your case. Do not talk about other things because you are only inviting trouble.

THE WITNESS. I sent her a telegram and it read as follows, "Will pick up Larry tomorrow after school about 4:00 P.M. for Jewish Holy Days, Yom Kippur."

THE COURT. Did you get any response to the telegram?

THE WITNESS. No. When I came to pick him up there was nobody home, no lights. I tried to get him on the telephone, but could not,

(Recess)

THE COURT. I want to call your attention to one thing, that there is an order of the Court which compels you to turn over the child to the father regardless of what the boy thinks until the issue is tried. If the Judge decides otherwise then it is all right. We have cases where a child does not want to go with the mother or the father. After we hear the case we make a decision compelling him to go where he should go. What I am trying to impress on you and the little boy is that until the order is changed, it is binding. If you were found guilty of contempt of Court I could impose a jail sentence. I am not using that as a threat, but the power of the Court is to impose a fine or anything like that. Once an order is made it should be respected until it is changed. It is up to the lawyers to change the order, if it can be changed. I do not know if it can or cannot be changed. Until it is changed it should be complied with.

MR. ERDHEIM. I have explained to Mrs. Ressler that there was an agreement made by her, and there was an order of the Court, and we hope in this hearing to change that. That is why I told Judge McCullough last week that I would recommend . . .

THE COURT. I want to call another thing to your attention. I think we are barking up the wrong tree. I think you do not understand what is before me. I am going to proceed in accordance with the direction of the Appellate Division to find out if this lady violated this order.

MR. ERDHEIM. Nothing else.

THE COURT. The matter of change of custody is not before me.

MR. TIEFENBRUN. Except for this . . .

THE COURT. You can tell me except, but I have studied it and I haven't the power. I am not making haphazard decisions, and you don't want to go up to the Appellate Division and come down here again.

MR. TIEFENBRUN. I want to resolve this once and for all.

THE COURT. I do not disagree with you, but that is not before me. I cannot be trying this man for murder or for speeding. I am only trying whether or not this lady violated the agreement.

MR. TIEFENBRUN. I think your Honor has the right to . . .

THE COURT. I will put on the record that I will not hear anything involving the change of custody but only the matter of whether or not she violated the order by not producing the child at the required times; that is all I will do. That is all there is to it.

MR. TIEFENBRUN. All I want to add is this, Judge Epstein in the order that was reversed went far beyond this and, therefore, actually was reversed, sustaining your position. However, in the course of that the situation changed so radically as a result of his order during the period of time that it does call for a review.

THE COURT. I want to make it clear again, I will only hear the issue of whether or not she failed to let the father see the boy at the time specified in the order to show cause.

MR. TIEFENBRUN. My feeling, however, is that as long as we are all before the Court that we might have an opportunity to resolve the whole question, and it would be proper for you to . . .

THE COURT. No, I won't do it. I only want to hear that one issue. The most I can do when I get through with this matter is to say that I find she violated the order. I can say ten days, or thirty days, a fine of $250, or something like that, or suspend sentence, or tell her not to do it again, or something of that sort.

MR. TIEFENBRUN. It is for this reason that I say to you—and perhaps, apparently, the Appellate Division has indicated it when they say that maybe some changes should be made, but only after a full hearing. I say to you that because—we would have to be in court every other day with a motion to punish for contempt.

THE COURT. If she is violating this order, and I give her a stiff sentence, she will obey it. That is all I can do about it. Then if she persists in doing that why don't you move then to take the custody away from her entirely? Why don't you do that now?

MR. TIEFENBRUN. We will have to.

THE COURT. You are a lawyer but I don't think you fully appreciate what you are up against. The only thing I can say is, "Guilty of contempt, thirty days or $250 fine," that is about all. Every time she does it we can impose these sentences. If she does it again bring a motion to take the child away from her entirely, understand?

MR. TIEFENBRUN. Yes. I can't talk now in view of the infant being here.

THE COURT. Don't try to sell me a bill of goods to hear something that is not before me.

MR. TIEFENBRUN. Will your Honor give me five minutes without Larry's presence?

THE COURT. All right.

(Larry Lesser, the infant, retired from the room.)

MR. TIEFENBRUN. After all, Mr. Lesser's interest is in the boy. We have this kind of a problem— and I must give you a little of this if you will give me three or four minutes. One of the principal issues in the case, of course, has been the issue of religion.

THE COURT. That is not before me.

MR. TIEFENBRUN. But this is what has been leading up to all of this, because with the failure to send the boy to Hebrew School, and failure to send him for the Holy Days, failure to get orthodontia, the kid has blotches on his legs and she won't send him to a doctor. I mention all of these things to you, and I tell you that time and again this order was violated. We have been in court three times in eighteen months. I cannot force this . . .

THE COURT. You can force it by getting out a writ of habeas corpus or by making a motion to take him away from her. I would not hesitate to take the child away from her if she is doing things that are detrimental to him. Do you see why an order should not be made for punishing her for contempt of court?

MR. TIEFENBRUN. We are here now to . . .

THE COURT. You are not. This is all that is before me, only this one issue.

MR. TIEFENBRUN. Will your Honor direct that she turn the boy over for this week-end, with the order in front of you?

THE COURT. I have suggested it.

MRS. RESSLER. I haven't any ill feeling toward my former husband. This has nothing to do with him at all. I am concerned only for the boy.

THE COURT. I have suggested to this lady that it is her duty to comply with every lawful order of this court and that her failure, notwithstanding my calling it to her attention, should be considered by the Judge who hears the motion for taking the custody of the child away from her entirely and reversing the custody.

MR. TIEFENBRUN. Do I understand that Mrs. Ressler is refusing to send the boy?

MR. ERDHEIM. She hasn't refused anything.

MR. TIEFENBRUN. Let's find out.

THE COURT. Will you let him go for the week-end?

MRS. RESSLER. The Holy Day is for one day.

THE COURT. Does the agreement so provide?

MRS. RESSLER. I may be wrong on that.

THE COURT. I want you to do what the agreement says.

MR. ERDHEIM. Judge, she will obey the agreement to the letter of the law.

MR. TIEFENBRUN. Page 56, sub-paragraph 3 says, "The father shall have the right to have Larry with him at his home every third week-end."

THE COURT. Suppose we start to consider this the third week-end. He hasn't had him for a long time.

MRS. RESSLER. He had him last week-end.

MR. TIEFENBRUN. Judge McCullough ordered it on the basis of the order.

THE COURT. Those others he is entitled to separately in addition.

MR. ERDHEIM. Mrs. Ressler, I recommend, so that we don't take up the Court's time—I know you have the boy's welfare at heart, and I think Judge Aurelio is going to give you all the time you need in this case. I recommend—and I know you will not like what I say, but you will follow the letter of the law and I recommend that you let your former husband have the child over the week-end.

THE COURT. And every third week-end until this is changed.

MR. ERDHEIM. Then there can be no question as to your conduct and whether you are violating the agreement. I would say that he return the child on Sunday night.

THE COURT. If he violates it then she has a right to refuse him. He has to comply, too.

MR. ERDHEIM. We understand that the child will be returned Sunday night.

MR. TIEFENBRUN. Yes, Friday night to Sunday night.

MR. ERDHEIM. Then to be returned on Tuesday evening and also on Sunday evening, is that correct?

MR. TIEFENBRUN. Yes. Is that all right, Mrs. Ressler?

MR. ERDHEIM. She said yes.

THE COURT. Is it all right?

MRS. RESSLER. I will answer Judge Aurelio. Yes, sir, I will be obedient to the law.

THE COURT. Here is another suggestion I want to make to both sides—and I am thinking out loud now—let's assume that you do prove a case she violated the order, let's say I or some other Judge says she is guilty, then the Judge does what? As I said before, he might fine her, or send her to jail, or suspend sentence, or something like that.

MR. TIEFENBRUN. The Judge can do more than that, too.

THE COURT. What?

MR. TIEFENBRUN. The Judge can say that under these circumstances he can review the entire situation.

MR. ERDHEIM. No, he can't, you have to follow the judiciary law.

MR. TIEFENBRUN. I know I am right.

THE COURT. I disagree with you. I think perhaps the better course would be to try this full issue in this fashion: you, for instance, could bring on a proceeding to take custody away from the mother because of a flagrant violation of the agreement. Under the law the agreement will be disregarded if the welfare of the child is concerned. He, on the other side—see what I mean—could then counterclaim we will say, or cross-move, on that same proceeding, to set aside this agreement which he claims was improvidently made, both with respect to terms——

MR. ERDHEIM. It violates the Domestic Relations Law.

THE COURT. ——both with respect to terms of visitation and also with respect to terms.

MR. ERDHEIM. It is against public policy.

THE COURT. Then you would have the two issues tried at once and you would resolve it once and for all.

MR. TIEFENBRUN. Just last Friday I brought on a writ. Judge McCullough gave it to the father for two days and referred the rest to you. If you don't want it then I will go back to Judge McCullough.

THE COURT. I only have an order to show cause to try here. What do you want me to do with the present motion?

MR. TIEFENBRUN. We would like a decision on it.

THE COURT. Then you will have to have a trial.

MR. TIEFENBRUN. Yes.

THE COURT. In order to make it easier for yourselves then each of you will know where you stand, if you will move to take this child away from her because of flagrant violations, he will cross-move to have the agreement changed and we will know where you stand.

MR. TIEFENBRUN. In view of the Appellate Division opinion we have to have a decision on this.

THE COURT. We will adjourn this without date.

Appearances   October 10, 1962
David T. Goldstick, Attorney for the plaintiff,
Same appearance for the defendant as previously.

THE COURT. Let the record show that the plaintiff, Mrs. Ressler, is in the courtroom. What is your motion?

MR. TIEFENBRUN. I have two motions. One is the hearing in the Appellate Division on a motion to punish for contempt. The second one is to have the boy for six weeks, because of the fact that she failed to deliver him or have anything to do with him during the summer.

MR. GOLDSTICK. On the second motion, with regard to the six weeks, it was my understanding, first, that this hearing was only to be addressed solely to the question of contempt. As to the second motion, the six weeks, I respectfully ask that again there is no prejudice at all to the defendant here with regard to whether or not the boy will go to him for the six weeks. I should be allowed a proper amount of time to prepare myself on this motion. He is going to have his contempt hearing today. Give me the opportunity to represent this woman adequately for the other motion.

THE COURT. The trouble is that this lady—I received a letter from her lawyer two weeks ago.

MR. GOLDSTICK. On the twenty-fifth she discharged him.

THE COURT. Twenty-fifth of September?

MR. GOLDSTICK. That is right.

THE COURT. Now here it is two weeks later. She still isn't ready to proceed. You see, after all, she has rights, but the husband has rights also, and her rights are not superior to her husband's rights.

MR. GOLDSTICK. I am not in any way trying to abrogate the rights of the husband. She retained me on Saturday.

THE COURT. She was careless in not doing it sooner. Your claim is what now? What is the contempt that you want to punish her for now?

MR. TIEFENBRUN. This is the original contempt that was before the Appellate Division. It involves the failure on her part last year, in 1961, the end of 1961, to deliver the boy for Jewish holidays. It involves a failure, a deliberate attempt on her part to cancel all orthodontia treatments because she is a Christian Scientist.

THE COURT. You, of course, deny that is the idea?

MR. GOLDSTICK. Your Honor, I deny it completely. On the second motion, that is what I ask not be heard today.

THE COURT. I will come to that later on. Let's go on with this.

Direct Examination (cont'd)

Q. Mr. Lesser, I direct your attention to last year, the latter part of September and October of 1961, on that day I believe that the Jewish day of atonement, Yom Kippur, was on October 1, 1961 ; is that correct?   A. Yes.

Q. Did you see Larry on October 1, 1961?   A. No, I did not.

Q. Will you tell us what efforts you made to get Larry at that time?

MR. GOLDSTICK. Objection.

THE COURT. Objection to what?

MR. GOLDSTICK. The form of the question.

THE COURT. What is wrong with it, for my information? I like to learn something.

MR. GOLDSTICK. I am sorry, your Honor, efforts. I object to the form of the question. The word "efforts", it is implying that he had difficulty. He can tell us what it was, and not use the word.

THE COURT. You are afraid I am going to be influenced by the use of a big word, instead of saying, "What did you do?" Go ahead. Objection overruled.

A. On September 29, 1961 I sent Mrs. Ressler a telegram, and this it what was in it: "Will pick up Larry tomorrow after school four p.m. for Jewish holidays, Yom Kippur." I did this because I always had trouble.

MR. GOLDSTICK. Objection.

THE COURT. Overruled. Go ahead.

A. I have always had trouble with Mrs. Ressler in reference to getting Larry, whether it was a holiday or a dentist appointment. So I sent this telegram to her recognizing this fact.

Q. Has she previously made claims that she didn't know the existence of certain Jewish holidays? A. Yes, sir.

THE COURT. What happened after that?

THE WITNESS. On the day that I was supposed to pick up Larry I came to the house, range the bell—

Q. This is Mrs. Ressler's house? A. Yes, Mrs. Ressler's house. I came to the house, rang the bell, stayed outside, tried to call up, tried to get somebody on the telephone. No answer, and nobody was available. So I went directly to my house.

Q. Did you see Larry after that? A. No. In fact, the next day after the holiday my son had come home from college, the oldest son, Benjamin. I had him call up Mrs. Ressler to find out why Larry wasn't over to the house and why he wasn't coming over to the house Sunday. Mrs. Ressler spoke to my son, and told him——

MR. GOLDSTICK. Objection as to any conversation.

THE COURT. Objection sustained.

Q. Did you get an explanation as to why he wasn't with you on the Jewish holiday and the Sunday? Did Mrs. Ressler ever tell you anything about that? A. When I asked her I never got any direct answer.

THE COURT. Let's do this systematically. You did not get the child on that holiday?

THE WITNESS. No.

THE COURT. Did you have occasion to talk to Mrs. Ressler at any time after that on that subject?

THE WITNESS. Yes.

THE COURT. If so, when?

THE WITNESS. I don't have the time I spoke to her.

THE COURT. How long, after a few days?

THE WITNESS. A few days after that.

THE COURT. Where did you speak to her?

THE WITNESS. On the telephone.

THE COURT. Now you may tell us what you said to her and what she said to you.

THE WITNESS. I spoke to Mrs. Ressler, and asked why Larry wasn't available on the particular high holy day and wasn't available for me on the Sunday. I got no answer or no intelligent answer.

THE COURT. What did she say?

THE WITNESS. She said it was none of my business or that it was up to her to do what she felt like.

Q. Did you discuss with her what she said to your son, Benjamin, on that day? A. Yes, I asked her why she didn't allow Benjamin to see Larry and why she insulted him over the telephone. She said that also was none of my business, and that she could do as she felt as far as Larry was concerned and as far as Benjamin was concerned. Nobody was going to tell her what to do.

Q. Have you had any difficulty in speaking with your son, Larry, on the telephone at Mrs. Glasser's house at that time? A. At that time and for many, many weeks after I tried to get Larry on the phone, but he was forbidden to speak to me, and also forbidden to call me.

THE COURT. Let me ask you. On these occasions, I take it, you telephoned?

THE WITNESS. Yes.

THE COURT. Let's do this so we get an understandable situation.

THE WITNESS. I would telephone the house.

THE COURT. Who would answer the phone?

THE WITNESS. I would telephone, and Mrs. Ressler would answer the phone, and I would say, "Can I speak to Larry?" She would say, "You can't. What do you want to tell him? I'll tell him what you want to tell him," or she would say, "You can't speak to him," and hang up. That was the general run of the treatment. He wasn't allowed to call me up.

Q. The agreement and order also provided that you are to have charge of the medical and dental regimen of Larry. In the fall of 1961 was Larry receiving any dental treatment? A. He was receiving dental treatment until September 27th.

Q. What type of dental treatment? A. Orthodontia treatment.

Q. What happened on or about September 27, 1961? A. I made an appointment for him on September 27th at the orthodontist, Dr. Fingeroth. He was to be there at 4:45.

Q. Did you notify Mrs. Ressler of this fact? A. Yes, she was notified, both through me and through the orthodontist, who sent out postcard memos, notices. At 6:15 he did not arrive. Dr. Fingeroth's assistant called up. She spoke to Mrs. Ressler directly. Mrs. Ressler told her that there was to be no more appointments, no more treatments, and this nurse or assistant asked her what was the reason for this. She said she had no reason and didn't have to give any. Then the girl said would she kindly talk to Dr. Fingeroth, because she knew that Larry was in the middle of the orthodontia work. He had one year of it, and it was silly not to finish it. It was paid for. She spoke to Mrs. Ressler, and Mrs. Ressler said she wasn't interested, she wouldn't speak to Dr. Fingeroth, she would have nothing to do, and she hung up.

Q. Has there been—had Larry been receiving any medical treatment at that time? A. Yes.

Q. What type of medical treatment was it? A. Larry has had treatment for allergies. He is supposed to get his shots every week or every other week or every ten days. But the same problem arose with Mrs. Ressler and the doctor. When he is supposed to be there I couldn't get him. When he supposed to be taken there he would be taken elsewhere. On these particular days there was a question of was he going to be there, and if he wasn't the doctor would get in touch with me and I would try to get in touch with Mrs. Ressler, but to no avail.

Q. Under the terms of the order and decree, Larry is supposed to attend Hebrew school, is he not? A. Yes.

Q. Was he registered in Hebrew school? A. Yes.

Q. Do you have any knowledge of how often Larry was present or absent from the beginning of the Hebrew school semester in September of 1961? A. Larry was absent in the Hebrew school four times in the month.

[ii]
Cross Examination

BY MR. GOLDSTICK

Q. Mr. Lesser, in the month of September, 1961, would you please tell this Court the days of the month that Larry was at your home, or in your custody?

THE COURT. Pardon me, sir? (The question was read by the stenographer.) A. I can't . . .

MR. TIEFENBRUN. Excuse me. Actually, if your Honor pleases, I don't think that is material at all.

MR. GOLDSTICK. I will refresh his recollection.

Q. Would it refresh your recollection, Mr. Lesser, if I were to tell you that on September seventh, eighth, ninth and tenth, which is a Wednesday, Thursday, Friday and Saturday, the boy was with you? Would that refresh your recollection? A. That is the time we were supposed to have half and half on the holiday. It may be so.

Q. Would it refresh your recollection if I were to tell you that at the end of August, 1961, to the eleventh day of September, 1961, the boy was with you, the first eleven days in the month of September? A. No . . . I can't recall that.

Q. Do you remember in one of these conversations in September when you spoke to her, and she spoke to you, did she say to you these words, in effect: "Larry ran in the bathroom, he is afraid to speak to you." Do you remember her ever saying that to you? A. No. It is a figment of her imagination.

MR. GOLDSTICK. I move to strike out.

THE COURT. Motion granted.

MR. GOLDSTICK. I move for a dismissal for failure to prove a prima facie case with regard to contempt in the month of September. As to the Hebrew School, there is nothing in the record whatsoever, and as to the mother's failure to allow the boy to see Benjamin, there is nothing. The boy is twenty years old and has a car. There is no testimony at all with regard to Benjamin not being able to visit the boy at home. There is no testimony on those two grounds at all. I am sorry, your Honor, I am unfamiliar with this but I am trying to acquaint myself with it, and have been trying in the last few minutes. On this refusal to speak to the boy on the telephone, your Honor, no dates were mentioned. "I had conversations—the whole allegation is for—it is only a month. They drew up an affidavit last year, no notes. I asked him to give us a date, no dates, nothing. In the first place, it makes it almost impossible to cross examine. There are no material facts here with regard to the serious charge of contempt.

THE COURT. I will reserve decision.

b. Sadie Ressler—Plaintiff

[i]
Direct Examination

BY MR. GOLDSTICK

Q. I am going to refer you to the month of September, 1961, and only that month, going into the first five days in October of 1961. First, let me ask you, Mrs. Ressler, for the first eleven days in September, 1961, where was your son Larry, to the best of your knowledge? A. At his father's house.

Q. During those eleven days did you at any time see the boy? A. Yes, sir, I saw him at the school which is behind my home.

Q. What day was this? A. I think on the 9th, sir, I am not sure, 9th or 10th.

Q. What did you say to the boy, and what did the boy say to you? A. I asked him to come home because he should have been home on the 6th, as I arranged with the father. He said he was afraid to.

Q. Afraid to come home? A. Yes, sir.

MR. TIEFENBRUN: If your Honor please, I think I must object to what the boy said to her.

THE COURT. Overruled.

Q. Mrs. Ressler, you just mentioned that you had arranged with the father that the boy was to be home the sixth. Would you explain that to the Court? What do you mean by "arranged with the father?" A. According to the agreement, we were to divide the time up before the summer vacation and after and figure out the number of days, and he was to have him half the time and I was to have him half the time.

Q. Did you discuss this with Mr. Lesser? A. Yes, sir, on the telephone.

Q. What day was the boy to be returned, under this agreement, to your home? A. On the 6th of September, the day before school opened.

Q. What day did he return to your house? A. The following Sunday night, September 11th.

Q. In other words, the boy stayed with the father four more days than he was allotted to under the agreement? A. Yes, sir.

Q. Were you to receive weekly allowance payments from your former husband for the support of the boy? A. Yes, sir.

Q. How much were those payments to be? A. $50 a week.

Q. The first week in September, how much did you receive? A. I received $25.

Q. Let me ask you as to the Jewish Holy Days of Rosh Hashana and Yom Kippur. Rosh Hashana is for one day—rather two days and Yom Kippur is for one day. Did you have any discussions with your former husband with regard to giving him the child for those three Jewish Holy Days? A. I have the very words here. Shall I read it? I wrote here, "I called Larry's daddy to find out why he took $5 off Larry's money."

Q. This is another $5? A. Yes. "He said because I had kept him out of Hebrew School one day two weeks previously, and I answered there was a very bad hurricane, I had not kept him out but the weather was so bad he could not go. I said 'You are not obeying the contract. The Judge has ordered, if you won't obey the contract I shall not take him to the orthodontist,' and he hung up on me."

Q. Mrs. Ressler, do you remember in that conversation whether there was any discussion between you and your husband with regard to he having kept the boy for four days? A. Yes, sir.

Q. In the first week of September, and that is the reason you were not allowing the boy to go for the Jewish Holy Days? A. Yes, sir.

Q. Would you tell the Court what you said to him and what he said to you? A. Yes, sir. I had asked him to take care of his moral obligations and not to withhold the boy.

Q. Not to continue to withhold the boy from you? A. Yes.

Q. When he was to return him? A. Yes, sir.

Q. You mentioned an orthodontist. Let me ask you to refresh your recollection by looking in your diary, and I refer you to the date of September 20th, September 27th, and October 3rd. Did the boy go to the orthodontist on those days? A. Yes, sir, he did.

Q. He went to the orthodontist for treatment? A. Yes, sir.

Q. Were there any other days during that period that he was supposed to go to the orthodontist? A. No, sir.

Q. Were there other appointments made with the orthodontist, or that the orthodontist asked to be made during that time? A. To the best of my recollection there weren't any other appointments that were not kept.

[ii]
Cross Examination

BY MR. TIEFENBRUN

Q. Mrs. Ressler, you did not send the boy over to his father on October 1st, Yom Kippur, is that correct? A. That is correct.

Q. On the following day, that was a Sunday, October 2nd, did the boy see his father on October 2nd? A. No, sir.

Q. And that was a Sunday when he was supposed to have been with him according to the terms of the agreement, is that correct? A. He withheld him four days.

Q. Please answer my question. That is a Sunday when he was supposed to have been with him, is that correct? A. Yes, sir.

Q. It is your claim that he withheld him for four days longer than he should have, is that correct? A. Yes, sir.

Q. Will you tell us why you picked these two particular days, Yom Kippur, to withhold him, to try to get even? A. That was the next visitation time as far as I recall it.

Q. But you told him he had been with him September 11th, up to September 11th.

MR. GOLDSTICK. She testified from September 1st to September 11th inclusive.

Q. That included the extra four days, did it not?

THE COURT: In other words, you wanted to get even on September 18th or the 25th.

MR. GOLDSTICK. Because she wanted to see the boy. It was every third week, your Honor.

Q. You are not Jewish now, are you, Mrs. Ressler?

MR. GOLDSTICK. Objection. Your Honor, this counsel, as I have read the record, has attempted to make, in every hearing and proceeding, the one basis for any application, no matter how he turns it around, that she is Christian Scientist and he is Jewish. It is stipulated in the record, so let it lie. This is enough of that.

MR. TIEFENBRUN. Let her answer the question, please.

THE COURT. You say it is admitted?

MR. GOLDSTICK. Let's let it lie.

THE COURT. Go ahead. If it has a bearing on the case I will consider it, if not, I will disregard it.

Q. You are not now Jewish, are you? A. No,

sir.

Q. You are a Christian Scientist, is that correct? A. Yes, sir.

Q. Are you desirous of having Larry brought up a Christian Scientist? A. I am desirous of having Larry have whatever is best for himself.

Q. Please answer my question. You can answer that Yes or No.

MR. GOLDSTICK. Objection to the question, as to relevance.

THE COURT. This may have a bearing on the question of whether or not she did send him to Jewish school.

MR. GOLDSTICK. Your Honor, my point is on relevance as to whether or not she wants the boy to be Christian Science or not is immaterial. The question is whether or not she sent him to the orthodontist. If she didn't, she didn't.

THE COURT. And whether or not she did not turn him over to the father on the Jewish Holy Days, Yom Kippur, and whether it is because she is opposed to his celebrating those days, or whether it is for some other reason. It may have a bearing.

MR. GOLDSTICK. I will withdraw my objection. I am more than happy to have that in the record.

Q. Will you answer that question, Mrs. Ressler? A. I don't think anyone's religion can be imposed on them. I don't proselyte whatever the boy wants.

THE COURT. What are you doing about it, one way or the other?

THE WITNESS. Absolutely nothing.

Q. My question is, what is your desire? A. My desire?

Q. With respect to Larry. A. I love my religion.

Q. Are you desirous of having Larry brought up as a Christian Scientist? A. Not any more than his father is to have him brought up as a Jew.

Q. Madam, I think now you can answer it Yes or No. Do you wish him to be a Christian Scientist when he grows up?

THE COURT. Would you prefer?

THE WITNESS. I would prefer.

Q. Would you be opposed to his being confirmed as a Jew? A. If he wanted it I would not oppose him.

THE COURT. You still haven't answered the question of why you did not let your husband have the child on Yom Kippur, which was October 1, 1960.

MR. GOLDSTICK. Excuse me, your Honor, she did answer the question. Her answer was that the father kept the boy for four extra days in September and these were the first full days that she was able to withhold the boy from the father.

THE COURT. That is the excuse. I haven't read the agreement. I understand he was entitled to visitation rights, how often?

MR. TIEFENBRUN. Every Sunday and every third weekend and every Jewish Holy Day. May I go a step further?

THE COURT. Go ahead.

Q. Madam, Rosh Hashana, as your counsel pointed out, is another High Jewish Holy Day, the New Year. A. Yes.

Q. You did send the boy over for those two days, did you not? A. Yes.

Q. You didn't attempt to take back the two days at that time, did you? A. I don't know.

Q. Your excuse is that you wanted to get back the two days therefore you took Yom Kippur, the Day of Atonement? A. I wanted to get back the four days, sir, not two.

Q. May I see the diary to which you refer? (Witness hands over her book.) A. Yes.

Q. You told us about this conversation of September 27th and I think you read from this diary that you said if you—meaning Mr. Lesser, "won't obey the contract I shall not take him to the orthodontist," is that correct? A. Yes, sir. I had warned him many times that he was breaking the contract.

Q. And you felt that this was in the best interests of Larry with respect to the care of his teeth? A. Yes, sir, I took him . . .

MR. GOLDSTICK. Objection.

Q. To discontinue the orthodontia treatment because you claimed his father took off $5 from your money. A. They were not discontinued, they were continued four days later.

Q. But you did threaten to discontinue? A. I did but I didn't do so.

Q. This diary—do you keep this regularly, Mrs. Ressler? I am referring to the diary you handed me. A. I, truthfully, haven't kept it up too well lately. It is fairly close.

Q. How long have you been keeping such diaries? A. I guess you will find the first date there.

Q. Generally how long do you keep such diaries?

THE COURT. This is for one year?

THE WITNESS. Yes, sir.

Q. At whose instructions have you been keeping this diary? A. My former attorney.

Q. I call your attention now to the entry in the diary dated September 18th, which reads as follows "if he had returned Larry September 6th as contract states, his third week-end would be the 25th, but he kept him on the 10th and 11th inclusive, so his week-end would be October 1st, but because he kept him on the 24th and 25th I did not give him to Perry on the first, and besides he owed me four days and I only took one day. Tricky!" Why was this entry put in twice?

THE COURT. What did you say there?

MR. TIEFENBRUN. It says "Tricky!" All the rest

is in hand writing, but the "Tricky!" is printed.

Q. Why were there two entries made four days apart dealing with exactly the same thing? A. I probably wanted to establish the dates in my mind, the proper dates that he was to have him, so as not to breach the contract.

Q. I call your attention to the diary entry for September 20th that has in printing "Orthodontist. L's wife came to pick up Larry for orthodontist. I sent her home. I am capable of taking him and willing to follow contract." Is that the entry? A. Yes.

Q. Does that refresh your recollection? A. Yes, sir.

Q. She did come and you sent her home? A. Yes, I took the boy myself.

Q. Your know that the agreement provides that Mr. Lesser is to be responsible for his medical and dental regimen. A. But that is not Mrs. Lesser.

Q. And he is responsible for transportation in such event. A. Yes.

Q. If he wants to send him a certain way in order to make sure he gets there, he has that right under the agreement; do you agree with that? A. I thought the agreement was between Mr. Lesser and myself, Mr. Tiefenbrun.

Q. Was that true, Mrs. Ressler, that on September 27th you notified the dentist's secretary that you were discountinuing the orthodontia treatment? A. I informed the secretary only once, and I don't know if that was the 20th or 27th. If this is the second time then it is not so. I informed her one time that until Mr. Lesser took care of his obligations Larry was not coming there until I can take him. I took him four days later.

Q. Did Benjamin ask to see Larry? A. Yes.

Q. Did you refuse? A. I never refused Benjamin visitation.

Q. What did you tell Benjamin at that time? A. At that time, I don't know, but I always invite him to my home.

THE COURT. He is your son, is he not?

THE WITNESS. Yes, sir, I always welcome him.

Q. When is the last time he visited you at your home?

MR. GOLDSTICK. Objection. I again ask counsel to limit himself to the time in question.

MR. TIEFENBRUN. I think this is a fair question.

THE COURT. I will let her answer. Go ahead A. Sometime during the summer.

THE COURT. Of what year?

THE WITNESS. 1962.

Q. When would you say was the time before that? A. I would guess a few months before, but I am just guessing. He rarely comes.

Q. I call your attention to an item in this diary under date of October 1st, "At 9:00 P.M. Benjamin called and asked to talk to Larry." I will skip toward the bottom of the page, and he did speak to him, according to this, "He asked me whether he would see Larry the next day. I said, 'That needs to be straightened out between your father and myself. Your dad has a few moral obligations to work out with me, days, money, etc., and until he works them out you cannot see Larry.' He said, 'Hold the wire.' I hung up. He called back and chastised me for hanging up. I said, 'I am busy and have nothing further to say to you.'" Is that a substantially accurate transcript of your conversation with your son, Benjamin? A. Yes, sir.

THE COURT. What is the other motion before me now?

MR. TIEFENBRUN. The agreement provides that the boy is to go to camp for the summer, provided both parties agree. Both parties did not agree. Mrs. Ressler sent him off to camp all by her little old self. Mr. Lesser at that time had not seen the boy since April. She kept him away since April. So, there was May, June, July, and August. We tried to get the name of the camp. I wrote a letter to her, I called, and so on. On July 27th I wrote a letter to her then attorney saying I had not received the camp name. He replied, "I am informed that Larry is in camp and is very happy. I have counselled Mrs. Ressler to inform Mr. Lesser of the address."

We did not get the address until the last week of August just before the boy was coming home from camp. The summer session is approximately twelve weeks. If the boy does not go to camp the parties are entitled to divide it equally. We want that six weeks for this man to re-establish some contact with his son and the boy to re-establish contact with the father. They live in the same general area and he will send him to school and do everything necessary, as he has done.

MR. GOLDSTICK. What counsel has forgotten to tell you is that Judge Epstein had a hearing in the spring of this year and he took the boy away from the father for ninety days and took visitation away for ninety days and gave the boy to the mother for religious training, completely abrogating that part of the agreement, coming to a conclusion, after a social worker had done an investigation and the Judge heard testimony from the boy, that it was for the best interest of the child that the mother have complete supervision. This was reversed in August by the Appellate Division.

MR. TIEFENBRUN. It was reversed the first week in July.

MR. GOLDSTICK. Your Honor, again for two minutes. I have had to talk to my client with regard to this motion. There was this decision by Judge Epstein giving the control of the religious upbringing to the mother. She sent him away to camp after asking Judge Epstein whether or not she could send him, and the Judge said the father would have to pay for the camp. She sent him away to camp.

MR. TIEFENBRUN. This is all news to me.

MR. GOLDSTICK. I do not know what the situation is, I have not had a chance to prepare affidavits. I have not had a chance to have reply affidavits and that is why I ask that on this motion we have an adjournment. If he is to get his six weeks, if he is entitled to them, we wouldn't want him to take it while the boy is going to school.

THE COURT. Is there any harm in letting him have him for six weeks so as to bring peace and harmony and make it easier for everybody concerned?

MR. GOLDSTICK. Before your Honor does anything so drastic as to give this boy to his father for . . .

THE COURT. I am not saying I am going to do it, what I say is why can't you agree on it.

MR. GOLDSTICK. The harm is to the boy. I have a letter in my briefcase from the boy, he wanted to hand it up to the Court today, begging this Court not to make him go to his father.

THE COURT. The boy said so?

MR. GOLDSTICK. The boy is in mortal fear of his father. I plead with this Court, before you decide anything like to speak to the child. He is almost thirteen and is certainly able to express himself to the Court.

MR. TIEFENBRUN. We just went through this in Westchester before Judge McCullough.

MR. GOLDSTICK. She wasn't represented.

MR. TIEFENBRUN. She was represented by Mr. Erdheim. The issue was the religious Holy Day of Rosh Hashana of this year. The Judge had a long interview with the boy and directed her then and there, forthwith, to turn him over. The Judge, after the long interview with the boy, directed Mrs. Ressler, then and there, to turn him over to his father for those Holy Days. What kind of mortal fear is this?

THE COURT. The boy indicated that he did not care to go with the father?

MR. TIEFENBRUN. The boy did not, and the Judge was satisfied.

THE COURT. What do you want me to do?

MR. GOLDSTICK. I want you to speak to the boy. I want you to adjourn this motion.

THE COURT. When can the boy be here?

MR. TIEFENBRUN. I want to point out that you must remember that the father has seen this boy for three days in the last six months; that is all he has seen him. The boy has been under the influence of Mrs. Ressler during this entire time.

THE COURT. What day do you wish to adjourn this to?

MR. GOLDSTICK. May we bring the boy in?

THE COURT. Yes.

MR. GOLDSTICK. I can bring the boy in tomorrow, but as to the motion, I cannot be ready.

THE COURT. We will adjourn until tomorrow at two o'clock. Bring the boy in.

c. Larry Lesser in Judge's Robing Room

BY THE COURT

Q. Your name is. . . .   A. Larry Lesser.

Q. How old are you?   A. Twelve.

Q. You go to school?   A. Yes.

Q. What class are you in?   A. Seventh grade.

THE COURT. I think the boy has reached an age —he is over twelve—where he is capable of understanding the oath. I am going to ask you to please stand up. I want you to swear that you will tell us the truth and nothing but the truth so help you God. You will do that, won't you?

THE WITNESS. Yes.

THE COURT. I want you to make yourself comfortable. I want you to know who I am. I am a Judge of the Supreme Court of the State of New York and I am trying to settle a little dispute that exists here. These things happen. It happens in the best of families in the world. After awhile these things blow over and the sun shines again. I need your assistance to help me to decide what is before me. Do you understand, Larry?

THE WITNESS. Yes.

Q. What school do you go to?   A. Westmont Junior High.

Q. Do you want to answer some questions that the two lawyers will ask you?   A. Yes.

Q. It will help everybody; do you understand? A. Yes.

Q. Speak out freely, openly and without fear of any kind. This gentleman here (indicating Mr. Goldstick), you know him, don't you?   A. Yes.

Q. He is your mother's lawyer, right?   A. Yes.

Q. He may want to ask you some questions, which I will permit him to do now.

BY MR. GOLDSTICK

Q. Larry, over the past year with your mother, have you ever discussed about going to Hebrew School?   A. Yes.

Q. Did you talk with your mother about it; what would you tell your mother, how you felt? A. I told her I thought that Hebrew School was a waste of time because I didn't like it, and it took up time after school in which I used to play with my friends, and I had homework to do, and I felt that after I came from school that I didn't want to spend two hours in a hot Hebrew School. I didn't like it.

Q. Were you getting other religious education?

A. No, I wasn't.

Q. You were getting no other religous education. A. No.

Q. Did you ever speak to your father about Hebrew School? A. I would have told him I didn't like it, but I don't think it made any impression.

Q. What did he say to you? A. He didn't answer me.

Q. Did he ever yell at you? A. Not about that, he wouldn't answer me, he told me I had to go.

Q. He yelled at you about other things? Would your dad scream at you? A. Yes, he would yell.

Q. About what? A. Certain times when I didn't come over, why I missed getting my shots, if I missed an orthodontist appointment, or if I had a cough why I didn't take medicine, and things like that.

Q. When was the last time you were at your daddy's house? A. I saw him last weekend.

Q. What did you do then? A. Let's see, Saturday . . .

Q. Let me ask you this, before you would go to your daddy's house would you talk about it with your mother at all, about whether you wanted to go or didn't want to go, or anything like that? A. She knows I didn't want to go.

Q. How does she know that? A. I told her.

Q. Why don't you like to? What happens, does anything happen while you are there? A. I don't get along with anybody; I don't know, I just don't get along.

Q. Could you give us an example? A. I don't get along with May, Ronny, and Gail.

Q. Who are they? A. They are his . . .

MR. TIEFENBRUN. May I help him? Ronny, May, and Gail are the children of the present Mrs. Lesser. Gail is a girl away at college. May is about twelve years old, or so.

THE WITNESS. Thirteen.

MR. TIEFENBRUN. And Ronny is about nine.

THE COURT. Are they older or younger?

MR. TIEFENBRUN. The two children are younger, and one is at college.

THE COURT. They are from her first husband, is that it?

MR. TIEFENBRUN. Yes.

THE COURT. Two are with the present husband?

MR. GOLDSTICK. That is right; he remarried.

MR. TIEFENBRUN. They are staying there.

BY MR. GOLDSTICK

Q. When you were visiting your daddy's house would he ever talk about your mother? A. Yes.

Q. What would he say? A. He would call her names and say she didn't know what she was doing.

Q. How did that make you feel? A. It didn't make me feel very good. I don't like to have people calling my mother names.

Q. What is this incident about sweet potatoes that you wrote to your attorney about? A. I don't like sweet potatoes, they don't stay down, they come up.

Q. Why do you say that? A. I don't know.

Q. What happened? A. My dad said I had to eat them, and I did, but they came up and so I had to leave the table.

THE COURT. Was this at your father's home?

THE WITNESS. Yes.

Q. Larry, if you had a choice to make as to how you would like to live out these next few years with your parents, what you would like your future to be—what would that be?

MR. TIEFENBRUN. I must object to that at this stage of the game.

THE COURT. Overruled. Go ahead.

A. I want to live with my mother, that is just it, I just want to live with my mother.

Q. Larry, does your mother, when it comes time to go to Hebrew School—did your mother physically prevent you from going to the School? A. She wouldn't physically stop me from going. Most of the time she would take me over there by car, that is the only way I could get there.

Q. She would take you? A. She would take me to the Hebrew School and take me back. Sometimes she wouldn't be able to take me so I would take the bus. But sometimes I just didn't want to go so it was really me who didn't want to go, it had nothing to do with my mother, I just didn't want to go and she didn't make me go.

Q. Who would take you to the orthodontist? A. I do go there.

MR. GOLDSTICK. That is all.

BY MR. TIEFENBRUN

Q. Larry, I think you remember me. A. Yes, I do.

Q. I am your father's lawyer. I would like to ask you a couple of questions. When you are over at your father's house, what kind of things do you do with your father and the other kids for fun? A. Well, we go horseback riding, we play baseball, and we go to the movies, or we take walks.

Q. Do you go bowling? A. Yes.

Q. Do you enjoy going bowling with your father? A. Yes.

Q. And do you enjoy horseback riding? A. Yes.

Q. And do you enjoy going to the movies? A. Yes.

Q. And the other things that you do? A. Yes.

Q. Do you enjoy having dinner with this

whole group of people when you all sit down at the table? A. A dinner is a dinner.

Q. During dinner do you laugh and joke? A. Yes, I guess we do, everybody does it.

Q. Do you have any trouble sleeping at your father's house? A. I sleep the same way at everybody's house, I go to bed and I sleep.

Q. Occasionally at table did your father scold you for bad manners? A. He tells me what to do and what not to do, yes.

Q. Does he scold you for using—I withdraw that. If you ever use bad language does he ever scold you for that? A. He tells me not to use bad language I suppose.

Q. These are some of the times when he yells at you. A. Yes.

Q. Does he scold you for other things? A. Yes.

Q. What kind of other things does he scold you for? A. I just told you before.

Q. Are there other things more than you have told us that he would scold you about? A. I couldn't. . . .

Q. Did he scold you for getting bad marks in school? A. No, he just said I have to do better.

Q. Did he get you a tutor when you weren't doing so well in school? A. A tutor?

Q. Did he get somebody to help you study, to give you special help? A. No.

Q. He insisted that you do better in your school work? A. It was my brother who had a tutor.

Q. I knew somebody had one. A. Yes.

Q. At home do you have any fights with Mrs. Lesser—Ida? A. Once in a while, yes. For instance, I would ask her—daddy told her to tell me I wasn't allowed to play with one of my friends and I think I should have a reason why I can't play with someone.

Q. Did she ever scold you for bad language and bad manners? A. Yes.

Q. Does she scold you if you are absent from school? A. No.

Q. She doesn't get into that? A. No, she doesn't.

Q. Does she take you out shopping with the other kids when she goes out with them? A. She doesn't take me shopping.

Q. Wherever the other kids go, you go along. A. If I want to, yes.

Q. If you don't want to you don't go? A. I stay in.

Q. Does your mother ever scold you? A. Yes, she tells me the right things to do and the wrong things.

Q. Does she yell at you? A. Once in a while, you know, it hardly ever happens.

Q. Does your mother ever reprimand you?

A. No.

Q. Does your mother scold you if you don't get good marks at school? A. No, she doesn't.

Q. Does your mother scold you if you have bad manners at table? A. No, she just tells me what to do.

Q. But she never scolds you or insists that you do what you are supposed to do. A. No.

Q. Did your mother ever punish you in any way other than by scolding? A. Yes, the way most mothers would do, they would take away certain privileges.

Q. Did she ever forbid you to go out of the house? A. If I was sick, yes.

Q. But as a punishment for something or other that you did. A. No.

Q. Did she ever lock you in a room and insist that you stay there? A. No.

Q. Did she ever take away your allowance? A. No.

Q. Has your mother taken you to church with her? A. Yes, she has.

Q. How often in the past year or so? A. For the past year or so I was going to Hebrew School. After I stopped Hebrew School in April I went fairly often with her.

Q. Would you say a couple of times a week? A. No, it is only one time a week.

Q. While you were going to Hebrew School, when you were actually in Hebrew School, did you enjoy being there when you were in the class itself? A. No.

Q. You resented the fact that it cut into your playtime? A. Yes.

Q. Are you afraid of your father? A. Yes.

Q. Afraid of him in what way? A. I don't think I could give you that.

Q. Let's try it this way, you don't like it when he scolds you, do you? A. No.

Q. Does he hit you? A. Yes.

Q. Has he hit you hard? A. He has.

Q. Has he really beaten you up? A. Yes.

Q. Have you ever had black and blue marks as a result of it. A. I never looked to see.

Q. Have you ever had a doctor called as a result of it? A. No.

Q. Have you ever had any broken bones as a result of it? A. No.

Q. By and large, when you go to your father's house and you play with the kids, and go bowling, and go horseback riding, would you say you have some fun? A. Yes.

Q. And you would like to have this fun? A. I have it at home, too.

Q. Do you do horseback riding at home? A. Yes.

Q. Do you go bowling at home? A. Once in a while.

Q. So, there is very little difference between the two, except that in one place they make you go to Hebrew School and such. A. And they have children and we don't.

Q. That is really the major difference? A. Yes.

MR. TIEFENBRUN. That is all.

BY MR. GOLDSTICK

Q. Larry, coming to this major difference between your mother's house and your father's house, do I understand that the major difference is simply that in one place you go to Hebrew School and in the other you don't, or are there other differences? A. There are other things.

Q. Where do you enjoy yourself, where do you feel that you want to stay and why? We are interested in knowing why. It is very important. If you can, could you express to us at least why you have these feelings? A. Well, I prefer staying with my mother because I feel freer, I can play with my friends, I don't have to worry about the next day I am going to be in Hebrew School, or that the next day I have to go to my father's. When I am in one place I have to think of what I will have when I am going to the next place. When I am at my mother's I worry about what is going to happen when I go to my father's house.

Q. Why do you worry? A. It is not good, this switching back and forth is not much fun.

Q. Other than what you are going to do, take your two parents, do you find any difference with the parent at one house or the other, do they both give you equal love and attention? A. I guess so; they are both my parents.

Q. When you do these things on the week-end over at your father's house, is your father with you most of the time? A. Most of the time.

Q. When you were having difficulty in school what did your mother do? A. She took me out of school and took me to a private school.

Q. Were you still staying home at night at your mother's house? A. Yes.

Q. How did your grades go when you went to private school? A. They improved.

MR. GOLDSTICK. That is all.

BY THE COURT

Q. How does your father hit you? A. With his hand.

Q. What part of your body? A. I guess in the back, over the seat.

Q. Do you know what Bar Mitzvah is? A. Yes.

Q. Are you going to be Bar Mitzvahed? A. No.

Q. Why not? A. He wants me to but I haven't gone to Hebrew School, and you have

to do something extra to be Bar Mitzvahed and I haven't done it. For every part of the year there is a certain thing you have to read to be Bar Mitzvah. You are supposed to go to Hebrew School a little earlier, you have a special class. Before you go to the School you go to the Rabbi and he teaches you the paragraph so you learn it and at the Bar Mitzvah you have to repeat it.

Q. Doesn't your mother force or urge you to go to Hebrew School so that you could prepare yourself to be Bar Mitzvah? A. She knows I don't want to be Bar Mitzvah.

Q. She doesn't compel you to go? A. No.

BY MR. TIEFENBRUN

Q. Larry, if you were to get private tutoring perhaps instead of going to Hebrew School for a little time specially so you could learn what was necessary for your Bar Mitzvah, would that change your mind? A. No, I don't want it period.

Q. I mean, you have indicated that the reason you didn't was because you didn't know enough and might be embarrassed. A. No.

MR. TIEFENBRUN. That is all.

BY THE COURT

Q. I want to ask you another thing. You go to church where your mother does, right? A. Yes.

Q. What is the name of it? A. First Church of Christ Scientist.

Q. How long are you there on these occasions? The service is how long? A. About an hour, they take an hour.

Q. What instructions do you get there? A. It is a Sunday School. We have five or six boys and girls in the class and we have a teacher.

Q. Teaching you what? A. Teaches things from the Bible and from this book that we have.

Q. You mean about the Christian Science religion, is that it? A. Yes.

Q. Do you like that religion? A. Yes.

Q. Do you like that better than the Hebrew? A. Yes.

Q. How often do you have to go there? A. Once a week.

Q. What day of the week do you go there? A. Sunday.

Q. With whom do you go? A. With my mother.

Q. Your mother takes you there every Sunday? A. She hasn't taken me recently because she hasn't gone. We were told we were not supposed to go.

Q. How do you go there? A. By car.

Q. Who takes you there? A. My mother.

Q. Your mother takes you there and leaves you

there? A. No, she goes upstairs.

Q. That is what I mean, you go with your mother every Sunday. A. Yes.

Q. What time do you have to be there? A. Eleven o'clock.

Q. You have been going there since April or May, which is it? A. April.

Q. And you like to go there? A. Yes.

BY MR. TIEFENBRUN

Q. Why haven't you gone there in the last few weeks? A. Sunday School?

Q. Yes. A. We were told I was not supposed to go to the Sunday School.

Q. Who told you that? A. Somebody told my mother.

MR. GOLDSTICK. Your Honor, if I may say, the judgment was reversed by the Appellate Division. Judge Epstein gave the mother the right to give him whatever religious education she wanted. I take it that she was advised by her attorney that the old agreement was reinstated so that he could not go to the Christian Science School.

MR. TIEFENBRUN

Q. Since you stopped going to Sunday School have you gone to Hebrew School at all? A. No.

Q. Who lives in your house? A. My mother and her husband and me.

Q. Are you all three living together now? A. Yes.

Q. Is Mr. Ressler there now, too? A. Yes.

Q. Had he been away for a while? A. Yes.

Q. How long had he been away, if you remember? A. Two or three weeks.

Q. When did he return? A. About a week ago.

THE COURT. Your stepfather, does he go to church also?

THE WITNESS. Yes.

THE COURT. So that the three of you go every Sunday, is that it?

THE WITNESS. Yes.

THE COURT. And he is a Christian Scientist, is that right?

THE WITNESS. Yes.

(Witness excused)

(At this point the hearing was continued in the courtroom)

THE COURT. Proceed, gentlemen. We are now proceeding, let us say, with another phase of the case, another application connected with the matter.

MR. GOLDSTICK. The testimony given by the boy and the purpose for adducing that testimony inside was to determine whether or not the mother was consciously and purposely in con-

tempt. That was the sole purpose of that testimony and that is why it is being considered.

THE COURT. One thing at a time, sir. He is urging upon me now to conduct a hearing on his application for the father to get custody of the boy for six weeks, which he claims he was unlawfully deprived of. Are you ready to proceed on that?

MR. GOLDSTICK. No, I am not.

THE COURT. When will you be ready?

MR. GOLDSTICK. I will have my affidavits ready next week.

THE COURT. You are going to serve your affidavits by Tuesday, I think you said?

MR. GOLDSTICK. That's right, your Honor.

THE COURT. And you can have a day or so.

MR. TIEFENBRUN. I will have mine in by Thursday, the 19th.

THE COURT. Decision reserved.

d. The Trial Court Decides

[i]
Judgment—October 26, 1962

MR. JUSTICE AURELIO: By its order dated July 6, 1962, the Appellate Division has directed that a hearing be had on the order to show cause dated October 5, 1961, why plaintiff wife should not be punished as and for a contempt of this court for her alleged violations of the provisions relating to the custody and religious training of an infant contained in a decree of this court entered on the 30th day of January, 1960.

It appears from the hearing held before me that plaintiff and defendant married in 1935 and lived together as Orthodox Jews; that they had three children; that Larry, the infant here involved, the youngest is twelve years of age; that the parties separated and a judgment of separation was entered herein on December 15, 1956, giving plaintiff wife the custody of the infant with certain rights of visitation to defendant husband; that, thereafter, on January 23, 1960, the parties entered into an agreement in writing which, pursuant to its terms, was incorporated in the decree divorcing the parties; that on June 30, 1960, the judgment of separation dated December 15, 1956, was amended and modified to include all of the terms and provisions of the agreement by stipulation of the parties. Among other things, the agreement provided (par. fourth); "(1) The Father shall have full charge of the religious education of Larry and may bring him up in the Orthodox Jewish faith, notwithstanding any different religion which the Mother may have. The Mother agrees that she will not obstruct any such religious education and will not teach the child, directly or indirectly, any other religion. (2) The Father will, at his own cost and expense, provide the religious education, including school and transportation to and from any school for religious training. The religious training shall be such as is provided by an Orthodox Hebrew School serving the community in which Larry resides. (6) The Father shall have the right to have Larry on all religious Holy Days required for observance by the Orthodox Jewish faith. For these Holy Days, the Father shall have the right to have Larry visit at the Father's home and stay over for any nights that may be involved. The Holy Days include New Years (two days), Day of Atonement (one day), Feast of Tabernacles (first two days and seventh and eighth days), Passover (first two days and seventh and eighth days) and the Feast of Weeks (two days)."

Thus, it clearly appears the parties have solemnly agreed that the infant shall be reared as an Orthodox Jew. Each of the parties has remarried, and plaintiff wife has become converted to Christian Science, the religion of her present husband. No doubt the infant is being reared in a home not of his religious faith. Both plaintiff wife and the infant testified that she takes him to a Christian Scientist church every Sunday to attend the services. The infant himself testified that he does not care to be instructed in the Jewish faith and prefers to be a Christian Scientist, his mother's adopted religion.

I am of the opinion that this infant should not be permitted to abandon so easily the faith he was born in. He has not reached the age of discernment and understanding to fully appreciate the significance of this momentous decision. I am firmly of the opinion that his father should be permitted to try to rear his boy as an Orthodox Jew in accordance with the provisions of the agreement as above set forth. I am convinced that plaintiff has greatly influenced this infant's thinking and present desire to become a Christian Scientist and that she has wilfully and deliberately violated the terms of the agreement relating to the infant's religious training and bringing up.

Defendant claims that plaintiff wife has not cooperated in carrying out the true purpose and intent of the agreement adduced before me. Suffice it to say that her attitude throughout has been to thwart the agreement she made and that she wants to do as she pleases in disregard of defendant's rights. It is apparent that if she intended to carry out the agreement there were ways and means of doing so. In sum, I conclude she has contemptuously violated the agreement and the decree of this court. Accordingly, she is adjudged in contempt of court and is fined the sum of $250.

Whether or not there should be a change of custody in order to give effect to the agreement of the parties to rear the infant as an Orthodox Jew is not before the court. If defendant father is so advised, such an application should be made in a separate proceeding.

Settle order.

Lesser (Ressler) v. Lesser—Motion for counsel fee to defend an appeal taken by defendant husband is granted. The record discloses that this application was timely made before the appeal was heard in the Appellate Division. Counsel fee is allowed in the sum of $300. Settle order.

[ii]
Order—November 10, 1962

MR. JUSTICE AURELIO: Upon the record and testimony before me it appears to my satisfaction that it is for the best interests of the infant that a temporary change of custody be ordered, the motion is granted and custody of this infant is awarded to defendant father for the temporary period of six weeks as prayed for in his affidavit, the order to be effective upon personal service made upon the plaintiff and custody to begin at such time. It is further directed that the plaintiff is to deliver Larry Lesser to the defendant upon the service of the order to be made herein. Upon expiration of the six-week period from the time defendant gets custody of Larry pursuant to this decision defendant is directed to restore custody to the plaintiff in accordance with decree of this court which incorporates the agreement the parties have made.

[iii]
Order—November 14, 1962

MR. JUSTICE AURELIO: On motion of Joseph Tiefenbrun, Esq., attorney for defendant, it is

ORDERED, ADJUDGED AND DECREED, that the plaintiff, Sadie Ressler, has committed the offenses charged and is guilty of a contempt of court in that she has obstructed and interfered with the religious education and training of the infant Larry, and in that she has failed to afford the defendant the visitation rights provided for in the order dated January 30, 1959, as amended, and has interfered with the dental treatment of the infant Larry, and it is further appearing that her misconduct was calculated to and did actually defeat, impair, impede and prejudice the rights and remedies of the defendant herein, and it is further

ORDERED, ADJUDGED AND DECREED, that the plaintiff Sadie Ressler, be and she hereby is fined the sum of $250.00 for such contemptuous misconduct, and it is further

ORDERED, that the plaintiff herein may purge herself of the aforesaid contempt by paying the fine within five (5) days following the service of a copy of this order with notice of entry thereof, and it is further

ORDERED, ADJUDGED AND DECREED, that in the event of a default by the plaintiff in making any payments of the fine at the time and in the manner herein ordered, the defendant Perry Lesser, shall be entitled without any further notice, upon application to this Court, and upon proof of the due and timely service of a copy of this order with notice of entry, on the plaintiff or her attorney, either personally or by mail, and proof by affidavit of the defendant or his attorney of the failure of the plaintiff to comply with the terms and provisions hereof, to an order of Commitment directed to the Sheriff of the County of New York or the Sheriff of any County in the County of New York or the State of New York wherein the said plaintiff may be found, directing the said Sheriff to take the plaintiff, Sadie Ressler, into custody and commit her to the Civil Jail of said County and there detain her in close custody until she shall have paid the sums of arrears to be paid by her as aforesaid, or any unpaid balance thereof, together with the Sheriff's fees and charges, or until otherwise discharged according to law.

4.

FATHER SEEKS CUSTODY—INFORMING THE JUDGE FOR DECISION

New York Supreme Court

Before: Hon. Henry Clay Greenberg, Justice

November 21, 1962

THE COURT: Let the record indicate that this motion appeared on the calendar of November 9, 1962; that Mrs. Ressler appeared without an attorney on that date, and the Court informed her that in view of the seriousness of the issue involved that she ought to obtain an attorney. She stated she did not have any funds, all her money was exhausted, and she would like to present a statement of her own. I advised her to attempt to get an attorney, nevertheless, and to that end, adjourned the motion until the 17th of November for hearing.

On the 17th she appeared again without an attorney, and I advised her again of the seriousness of the issue involved, and the motion was adjourned for hearing until the 20th of November at 2 P.M. At that time her name was called, she did not appear.

The Court thereupon instructed counsel for the defendant to send a registered letter to Sadie Ressler, informing her that the matter would proceed this morning, November 21st, at 11:30 A.M.

Counsel, under oath, has stated to the Court that he not only sent a registered letter, a receipt for which has been marked in evidence, but also a telegram informing Mrs. Ressler that she should appear in Court in connection with the hearing.

It is now twenty minutes of twelve on the 21st, and she has not appeared.

Call your first witness.

a. Perry Lesser—Defendant

Direct Examination

BY MR. TIEFENBRUN

Q. Mr. Lesser, you are the father of Larry, the infant involved in this proceeding? A. Yes, sir.

Q. Did you have Larry on September 30, the Day of Atonement? A. Yes, I did.

Q. How did that come about? A. That was at the direction of Judge Aurelio. We were in Court a week before, and we had told the Judge our problems, and he had turned around and directed Mrs. Ressler to make sure that she was going to bring the boy or I could pick him up for the Day of Atonement.

Q. In the meantime there were intervening Sundays on which you were entitled to have Larry with you, under the terms of the agreement, is that correct? A. Yes.

Q. Did you see him on any of those Sundays. A. After the Day of Atonement the Judge did not direct Mrs. Ressler, and we didn't have a writ out for her, so on the 24th of September I didn't see him, I didn't see him on the 25th, and I didn't see him on the 26th.

Q. September 25th and September 26th were also High Holy Days, were they not? A. That is right.

Q. You did not see him at all on those days? A. No, I did not.

Q. October second and third were the last of the High Holy Days, did Larry come over to your house then? A. No.

Q. So that from the end of camp, which was August twenty-fifth, through October fifteenth, I think you said October eighth and October fifteenth were the only days that you were able to see Larry without the intervention of a Court. A. That is right.

Q. October twenty-second, 1962, was a Sunday. What happened then? A. I did not see Larry on the 22nd, in fact, I have a memorandum here that I went to call for him on the 22nd, and I was there at 9:30 A.M. I rang the bell, stayed around for about ten minutes, and then left.

Q. In the meantime, while this was going on, there was a motion pending before Judge Aurelio to punish the plaintiff for contempt for similar events which had occurred in 1961, is that correct? A. Yes.

Q. According to the records, Judge Aurelio's decision came down October 24, 1962. October 27th was the week-end immediately following this decision, in which Judge Aurelio punished the plaintiff for contempt, and found her guilty of contempt. What happened on that week-end with respect to your seeing Larry? A. That week-end I called up my attorney, and he told me to pick Larry up at six o'clock Friday, the 27th.

Q. Did you go over to pick him up or did Mrs. Lesser, your present wife? A. Mrs. Lesser went there to pick him up.

Q. Was Larry brought to your house? A. No.

Q. Do you know what school Larry is now attending? A. Yes, Westmont Junior High School.

Q. Do you know whether Larry has been absent from school this semester? A. He has been absent a great deal. Since the beginning of the term, September sixth, he has been absent eighteen days.

Q. Of these eighteen days I believe he was with you on Yom Kippur one day, is that correct? That explains one absence? A. That is right. All the others are unexplained.

Q. How did you feel about these absences? A. I had been talking to Larry and I asked him how he got along in school, and he told me he had a little problem in one or two of his subjects. So I took him to school last week, saw his adviser and spoke to her.

Q. Is he now doing better at school? A. He is improving. For one thing, his adviser told me that the reason he wasn't doing too well was because of his absence. She said he was absent practically a whole month in the beginning of the term.

Q. Has Larry discussed with you his conduct when he was at your house? I mean by that did Mrs. Ressler ever tell Larry about how he was to behave when he was at your house? A. Yes, that was quite a problem, because Mrs. Ressler —in fact, not only did she tell him, but she also told the maid and she also told Mrs. Lesser that Larry didn't have to obey anybody except Mrs. Ressler.

Q. Did Larry ever say to you that he was told he didn't have to obey anybody except Mrs. Ressler? A. Yes.

Q. During the time in the last year that Larry has been with Mrs. Ressler has he attended Hebrew School with any degree of regularity prior to the summer? A. Prior to the summer, I think Larry attended school about fifty per cent of the time, Hebrew School, that is.

Q. Is Larry now attending Hebrew School? A. He now attends Hebrew School regularly.

Q. Have you had any conversations with Larry concerning his confirmation or Bar Mitzvah? A. Yes. I told him he would have to buckle down and to attend all the classes and learn everything so that when his Bar Mitzvah comes he would know what he has to do and be able to do it well.

Q. Has Larry said to you that he wants to be Bar Mitzvah? A. He definitely has.

Q. Larry is with you now, isn't he? A. That is right.

THE COURT. Where does he attend school? A. In Westmont. That is about a mile and a quarter from us, right close to us. The same junior high school he was going to before.

THE COURT. In my examination of the record, counsel, I see that a full hearing was held before Judge Aurelio with respect to an application made to punish Mrs. Ressler because she didn't comply with the decree which incorporated the agreement with respect to raising Larry in the Jewish religion.

MR. TIEFENBRUN. That is right.

THE COURT. And after the hearing he found her guilty of flagrant contempt of Court, and fined her the sum of $250?

MR. TIEFENBRUN. Correct.

THE COURT. Thereafter I understand there was another hearing before Judge Aurelio in which testimony was taken in regard to the fact that the father had been deprived of certain visitation rights, and following that hearing the father was given temporary custody of the boy, Larry, for a period of six weeks. The boy is at the present time with the father?

MR. TIEFENBRUN. That is correct. I may add that in the first hearing before Judge Aurelio, on the motion to punish for contempt, Mrs. Ressler was represented by counsel. Everybody was present, and there was a full-dress hearing on it.

THE COURT. What about the second?

MR. TIEFENBRUN. She defaulted about the six weeks, with the same situation prevailing here, where it had been adjourned for the purpose of getting counsel, an exact duplication of what happened here.

THE COURT. The first hearing was a full and complete hearing before Judge Aurelio?

MR. TIEFENBRUN. That is right.

THE COURT. Have you talked with the boy

frequently since—how long has he been with you? A. Approximately two weeks.

THE COURT. Is he happy? A. He is very happy.

THE COURT. Has he discussed any of his problems with you? A. The only problems he has discussed were boy problems, or some coat he needed or a pair of sneakers.

THE COURT. Has any question arisen about Christian Science? A. No, none whatsoever.

THE COURT. Not even mentioned? A. No.

THE COURT. Does his mother call him? A. Not that I know of. But I do know that his mother was to see him at school during lunch, he told me that, during the lunch period, and that she did call him during a study period. I don't know how many times.

THE COURT. How does he feel toward you now? A. I think he feels the way a son should feel toward a father.

THE COURT. I know Judge Epstein stated in his opinion, which was reversed because of the lack of hearing, that the boy hates his father. You say that situation no longer exists? A. I think it never existed, your Honor. He is very happy in the house.

THE COURT. What does your household consist of now? A. Right now my wife, myself, my daughter, May, fourteen.

THE COURT. She is fourteen? A. Fourteen years old; a son, Ronny, who is ten; Larry, who is twelve.

THE COURT. These are not your children, are they? A. Two of them are not.

THE COURT. First, who of your flesh and blood are with you at the apartment? A. My big older son, in college, comes home.

THE COURT. Has your oldest son seen Larry since he has been with you since the third of November? A. No, he has been away. He is coming home tomorrow.

THE COURT. What about your married daughter? A. She comes around about once a week. She has been there last week and the week before.

THE COURT. What is the relationship? A. Very nice. She is here in Court.

THE COURT. In addition to your own family you have the family of your present wife, is that it? A. That is right.

THE COURT. Consisting of what? A. A youngster of ten, a boy, Ronny.

THE COURT. And your son is age what? A. Twelve. So they get along very well together. A girl of fourteen, and another girl who is at college now, she is over eighteen.

THE COURT. Is there any feeling, so far as your son is concerned, with these other children that you have been able to observe in two weeks' time? A. Feeling of what?

THE COURT. Resentment. A. No, your Honor, in fact, the other day, if I may say so, my young son, who has a little Mazusa around his neck—he broke it, this is Ronny. He wears a Mazusa on a chain, and he broke it. He said to me, "Dad, I want to have another Mazusa and a new chain, I am getting bigger, I don't want a baby chain, I want a heavy chain." I turned around, and Larry said, "Can I have one?" I said, "Do you want a chain and a Mazusa?" He said, "Yes." I bought two heavy chains, and they both wear them.

THE COURT. They are all living in the house? A. Yes.

THE COURT. How large is the house? A. I don't know, fourteen or fifteen rooms and about five baths.

THE COURT. You are not cramped. A. No, your Honor. If I may say so, we have two extra bedrooms. When he came there I said, "Do you want to sleep in one of the bedrooms all by yourself, or do you want to sleep in the big room with Ronny?" He said, no, he didn't want to sleep in a room by himself. We had a double bed in there, and we got an extra dresser, and he has his own desk and dresser and his own bed.

THE COURT. One day before the hearing is over I would like to have a talk with him. How does the boy get along with the present Mrs. Lesser? A. Very nicely. They go bowling together and horseback riding together, your Honor.

Q. Have you taken Larry bowling? A. Yes, I have.

Q. Have you taken his friends bowling with him? A. Yes, I have. We do everything so that we can participate with not only him, but everybody.

Q. In your family do you all have dinner at the same time, as a rule? A. Most of the time.

MR. TIEFENBRUN. I think that is about all from Mr. Lesser.

THE COURT. Are your earnings adequate to take care of this household? A. Yes, sir.

THE COURT. Do I understand that this is an application to change custody?

MR. TIEFENBRUN. Yes, and to punish Mrs. Ressler for contempt.

THE COURT. Never mind about the latter; the other is more important. Regarding the application for change of custody, is that on two grounds, one because of her violation and refusal to comply with the agreement, and the decree of the Court, and also because you feel it is in the interest of the boy's welfare?

MR. TIEFENBRUN. That is correct. Let me explain a few things.

Q. Have you had occasion to call for the boy at different times, Mr. Lesser? A. Yes, I have.

Q. When you drive up what is the condition of Mrs. Ressler's house, for example, is the doorbell answered? A. No, not only is the doorbell not answered, there is no way for me to contact them whatsover. I don't have the phone number, and many times, I can say safely, 50 per cent of the time when I come up there the most I can do is toot the horn and toot it again and stay around, after two or three or four minutes, go out and ring the bell in order to get Larry to come.

THE COURT. Do you know if Mr. Ressler has any children? A. No, he doesn't.

Q. Do you know Mr. Ressler's religion? A. Yes, Christian Science.

Q. Do you know whether Mr. Ressler has been ill? A. I know that Mr. Ressler has been ill.

THE COURT. How do you know that? A. His brother called me up about . . .

MR. TIEFENBRUN. No, that is enough.

THE COURT. I happen to know the tenets of Christian Science, so you don't have to bring out any testimony in that connection. What does Mr. Ressler do? A. He hasn't worked for six months.

THE COURT. Who supports the household? A. I don't know.

THE COURT. By the way, were you paying anything for the support of Larry while he was with his mother? A. Yes.

THE COURT. How much were you paying? A. Fifty dollars a week.

b. Ida Lesser—For the Defense

Direct Examination

BY MR. TIEFENBRUN

Q. Mrs. Lesser, you are married to Perry Lesser, is that correct? A. Yes.

THE COURT. When?

Q. When were you married? A. March, 1960.

THE COURT. What is your relationship with Larry, how does he feel toward you and you toward him? A. I think it is a very warm relationship. He feels very comfortable with me.

THE COURT. Do you think he would say that if I asked him? A. I think he would.

Q. When Larry came over on the night of November third, what happened with respect to his going to sleep, for example? Did you put him to bed; did you see that he went to bed? A. Yes.

Q. Where did he sleep? A. In the same room with Ronny.

Q. How did he come to select that room, or how was he put in that room? A. He selected

that room a long time ago, when he first started coming over, he wanted to be with Ronny, and not by himself.

THE COURT. On his own, without any suggestion from you or Mr. Lesser? A. No, there were rooms available, but that is what he chose.

Q. He has always slept with Ronny, is that right? A. Yes.

Q. Hebrew School, does he go to Hebrew School with Ronny? A. On Sunday. During the week he has separate days.

Q. How did that Sunday business come about that they are in the same class? A. Ronny went in the morning from nine to eleven, and Larry went from eleven to one, and he asked me if I could change it so they could both go together.

Q. Larry asked? A. Yes.

Q. How long ago was that? A. A few weeks ago.

THE COURT. You mean even before he came to live with you? A. He has wanted this, but I never have been able to manage it before. This time the arrangements were made.

THE COURT. Since the third of November? A. Yes, I spoke to the principal in the Hebrew School.

THE COURT. Is this a Hebrew School or Sunday School? A. This is a Hebrew School.

Q. When the boy is gone to sleep at night do you go into their room? A. I go in to see that they are in bed.

Q. Will you tell us about Larry, his eating habits when he came here since the third of November, and what has happened since? A. His appetite has picked up, I can say that much. He just enjoys his eating.

Q. Has there been any change in his appearance? A. I should say so.

Q. In what manner? A. He told me that he lost six pounds, and I think he must have gained it back in one week. He just looks generally much better.

THE COURT. Does he have any allergies? A. Yes, he has.

THE COURT. Are they being taken care of by a doctor? A. When he was with us he went for his shots.

THE COURT. I am an expert on allergies. I have a grandson who used to have about twenty, but they are cut down to two now.

Q. When Larry came over on November third was there anything wrong with his legs? A. He had sores on them.

Q. What kind of sores? A. I can't answer what kind. They have practically healed up, but underneath the skin there are lumps, they were open sores, which we treated.

Q. Previously? A. Yes.

Q. Mr. Lesser has mentioned about your going bowling with Larry, for example. Will you tell us what happens then, is that more than one occasion? A. This has been going on since I first met Larry, about four years ago, when I made a trip here.

Q. And recently have you been going bowling with him? A. We have made a deal where we go once a week, according to his wishes. I must say he is very good.

Q. I believe there was some incident about if he made a certain score he would get a prize, or you would give him a bag, or something. Tell the Court about that.

THE COURT. We don't need that.

MR. TIEFENBRUN. It is just that the funniest part is that he wanted a bag like Mrs. Lesser's and no other kind.

THE COURT. For the bowling ball?

MR. TIEFENBRUN. That is the significant point, he wanted sneakers, shoes just like hers, not any other kind.

THE COURT. I don't think you need go into that. Are you pleased to have the boy with you at your home? A. I love having him. I think he is a fine boy, and I hope he can stay with us.

THE COURT. How do you account for the fact that a few weeks ago—little more than a few weeks ago—he told Judge Aurelio, according to Judge Aurelio's opinion, that he wanted to be a Christian Scientist? Are you familiar with that? A. I don't think he wants to be a Christian Scientist, he wouldn't complain of stomachaches and want bandages and medicines if he were thinking about Christian Science. He is just not part of it at all.

THE COURT. Whatever the situation may have been in the past, you say he is happy at the present time about going to Hebrew School? A. He talks to me about the Bar Mitzvah and which one should we invite and how we will do everything. He is a Jewish boy, and that is it.

THE COURT. Anything else, counsel?

MR. TIEFENBRUN. I think that is all.

THE COURT. You may step down.

(Witness excused)

MR. TIEFENBRUN. If I may, I would like to put Dee on, to testify to her relations with him.

THE COURT. Does she live in the same house?

MR. TIEFENBRUN. No.

THE COURT. We don't need that.

MR. TIEFENBRUN. The husband and she are here, they just want to corroborate.

THE COURT. We will adjourn this until Tuesday, November 28th at 4 o'clock, at which time I should like to have the boy in Court. In the meantime, I am going to ask a friend of mine, to appoint him as a Guardian, to see the boy, talk with him, and to protect his interests in this proceeding.

c. Sadie Ressler, Plaintiff

November 29, 1962
2:00 P.M.

[i]
Direct Examination

THE COURT. Let the record show that this is a continued hearing of Ressler vs. Lesser, which was commenced last week, in the absence of the plaintiff, Mrs. Ressler, who defaulted.

THE COURT. Mrs. Ressler, I understand you are not represented by counsel today.

MRS. RESSLER. No. I am sure you are aware of the circumstances. I have no longer any funds with which to fight, and I would like to represent myself as the mother of this child, and to prove why I should continue custody of him.

THE COURT. You have a perfect right to do that under our law, but there are certain dangers inherent in it, which I am sure you appreciate. The Court will try, as best it can, to protect you in every way possible.

MRS. RESSLER. Thank you.

THE COURT. The hearing that we had consisted primarily of the testimony of the father in connection with the making of the agreement, which provided that the boy should be raised in the Jewish faith, and your signing the agreement and your being represented by an attorney at that time; and the testimony further covered the field where you had violated the order of the Court from time to time to produce the boy and to deliver him for visitation rights with the father.

Your former husband testified also, as I recall it, that the main difficulty arose because of the fact that although you were Jewish you had adopted, as you, of course, had a right as an adult to do, the faith of the Christian Science Church, and that contrary to the agreement and the order of the Court, you were raising the boy as a Christian Scientist, rather than in the Jewish faith. We are at that point.

Are there any questions you wish to ask of the father or anyone at this time? Any statement you would care to make?

MRS. RESSLER. Yes.

THE COURT. All right. Do you want to take the witness stand? In view of the fact that the plaintiff is appearing without counsel, although afforded the opportunity on several occasions by the Court to obtain counsel, the Court will accept her testimony in narrative form. You may go ahead.

THE WITNESS. I would like to state to this

Court that I have never broken the agreement regarding the father's rights of visitation, or any other of his rights. The only time that the agreement seemed to be broken was when the child was ill, or when he was away at camp, at which time I did not have him myself, and at the time when the child was so afraid of the father when he saw him strike me that he was afraid to go out to him or open the door to go out to the car. I couldn't force him to do so.

MR. TIEFENBRUN. Excuse me, I don't like to interrupt, but if the Court will ask Mrs. Ressler about the periods of time that are involved here it might be helpful.

THE COURT. All right. Approximate times when these things you say took place. A. The time when the father struck me?

THE COURT. Yes. A. I think the date was September third.

THE COURT. What year? A. 1962, in my home.

THE COURT. Go ahead.

MRS. RESSLER. I believe the Court has stated that the child was—besides the visitation rights you said I broke the agreement in some other manner. May I ask about that?

THE COURT. Not raising the child according to the agreement, in the Jewish faith.

MRS. RESSLER. I can answer that. Judge Streit, at the time of the separation in 1956, had stated that the child could have the religion of his mother, and that was the time he went to the Sunday School.

This year, in March, Judge Epstein had agreed that the child could go to the Sunday School. Those were the only two times that he went, with the permission of the Court, proving that I have never broken the agreement. At all other times I have kept to it, he has gone to the Hebrew School.

THE COURT. Do you want to ask any questions, Mr. Tiefenbrun?

MR. TIEFENBRUN. Yes, several.

[ii]
Cross Examination

BY MR. TIEFENBRUN

Q. As a result of Judge McCullough's order, Larry was sent over to Mr. Lesser for the first of the High Holy Days of this year, is that correct? A. Yes.

Q. Then another application was made before Judge Aurelio on September 14, 1962, in order to have him for the next High Holy Day, is that correct? A. I don't know what the application was for, but you may be right.

Q. September 24th and September 25th were High Holy Days, Mrs. Ressler. Did Larry go over to his father on that occasion? A. Your

Honor, may I get my notes?

THE COURT. Yes, will you let her have her notes?

THE WITNESS. I think I have a copy of the dates. (Some papers were handed to the witness.) A. Was that September 24th?

Q. Yes, September 24th and 25th. A. Will you please state that again?

Q. Was Larry with his father on those days? A. No, sir, he was ill. I have an affidavit to prove it.

Q. October second and third were, again, Jewish High Holy Days, was he with his father on those days? A. No, sir, he was in bed.

Q. Was he with Mr. Lesser during any of those intervening Sundays between the end of camp and October third? A. Except for the time that Judge Aurelio ordered him to be, no, sir.

Q. And you did not send him over on any of those Sundays in that interim period? A. No, sir.

Q. Larry was with his father then October 8, 1962, and October 15, 1962, is that correct? A. You mean the week-end of October sixth, do you not?

Q. Was he there for the week-end or was he there just for the day? A. He was there for the week-end. I drove him there myself. No one came for him.

Q. The next Sunday, October 22, 1962, was Larry there? A. No, sir, he was ill again.

Q. October 24, 1962 is the day that Judge Aurelio's decision came down punishing you for contempt. Were you advised of that decision by your lawyer? A. On October what?

Q. October 24th it came down. Were you advised of that decision by your lawyer? A. No, sir, my attorney had left the case, I believe, in the middle of the case, and I had no one to advise me.

Q. I am talking now of the day that Judge Aurelio's decision came down. Did your lawyer at that time call you and tell you that there had been a decision on the motion to punish you for contempt? A. I couldn't honestly answer that. I don't know.

Q. How did you learn that there had been a decision? A. When the father came that evening and took the child, with three detectives.

Q. I am talking about earlier. I am talking of October 24th, which is almost a month ago— Mr. Goldstick did not withdraw from the case until October 30th—does that help you? A. Yes, sir, I have that here, but I am not 100 percent sure that he called to advise me. He may have.

Q. He may have? A. Yes.

Q. Do you recall a conversation that you had with Mr. Goldstick on the telephone concerning the weekend of October 27th? Would you look at your notes or whatever information you have? A. Yes, sir. What is it you want to know?

Q. In the course of that conversation did Mr. Goldstick ask you whether there would be any problem with sending Larry over to his father that very weekend, October 27th? A. Yes, he did.

Q. What did you say? A. I can't recall the exact answer, but I believe it was something to the effect that I would try to see to it that the child was there.

Q. Did Larry get to his father's house that week-end? A. No, sir.

Q. This is the week-end immediately following Judge Aurelio's decision? A. The child was afraid to go. He said his father would kill him for not going to Hebrew School the previous Tuesday, when no one came for him.

Q. Did you say no one came for him? A. No one transported him. We stayed home until four o'clock, and no one came for him.

Q. And then you left? A. Then we left.

Q. Mr. Goldstick told you that someone would be there at four o'clock? A. That we must be home until four o'clock, which we were.

Q. You are sure that is what Mr. Goldstick said? A. I am positive about it.

Q. If you want to correct your answer on that, please do so now. A. No, sir.

Q. Then Mr. Goldstick left the case October 30th, is that right? A. Yes.

Q. Prior to that time you had been represented by Mr. Erdheim, prior to Mr. Goldstick? A. Yes.

Q. And he left the case during the hearings before Judge Aurelio? A. Yes, sir.

Q. And shortly prior to the time Mr. Erdheim represented you you had been represented by Mr. Herbert Spencer Lehman? A. Yes, sir. Mr. Lehman is a dear friend, and helps me out whenever I ask him to.

Q. Has he helped you in connection with this application? A. This particular one?

Q. Have you discussed this matter with him? A. No, sir.

THE COURT. Madam, while the boy was with you did you take him to a Christian Science Church every Sunday to attend the services? A. At what particular time do you mean, your Honor?

THE COURT. Up to the time you delivered the boy to the father, pursuant to the direction of Judge Aurelio, the end of October. A. No, sir. I only took him when Judge Epstein had given me permission.

THE COURT. There was a full hearing before Judge Aurelio, wasn't there, a lot of testimony taken? You testified; Mr. Lesser testified. A. Well, there was a little bit of testimony taken,

yes, sir.

THE COURT. You say a little testimony. This record is 136 pages. And after that testimony was taken Judge Aurelio said, "Both plaintiff wife and the infant testified that she takes him to a Christian Scientist Church every Sunday to attend the services. The infant, himself, testified that he does not care to be instructed in the Jewish faith, and prefers to be a Christian Scientist, his mother's adopted religion." Did you testify before Judge Aurelio that you take the boy to Christian Science Church every Sunday? A. Only since Judge Epstein . . .

THE COURT. Don't tell me about Judge Epstein, his order was reversed. A. Then I stopped.

THE COURT. Listen to what Judge Aurelio said: "I am convinced that plaintiff has greatly influenced this infant's thinking and present desire to become a Christian Scientist, and that she has wilfully and deliberately violated the terms of the agreement relating to the infant's religious training and bringing up." A. It is my conviction that the Court was prejudiced. All I want is justice, your Honor, and the agreement enforced. The father has not been obeying the ruling of the Court. It now stands that the father is to see the child every Sunday and every third week-end, but he deliberately disobeyed the order.

THE COURT. According to the agreement that you signed at the time you were represented by counsel, and which agreement was incorporated in the decree, it said: "The father shall have full charge of the religious education of Larry Lesser, and may bring him up in the Orthodox Jewish Faith, notwithstanding any different religion which the mother may have." A. He has done so.

THE COURT. You have done so? A. He has done so.

THE COURT. What about you? A. I have never stood in the way, your Honor, never.

THE COURT. Do you realize you are under oath, Mrs. Ressler? A. Yes, sir.

THE COURT. "The mother agrees she will not obstruct any such religious education and will not teach the child, directly or indirectly, any other religion." A. The only time I did was when Judge Epstein changed the order, and said the child could have his own freedom of religion.

THE COURT. Your boy testified that you take him to a Christian Science Church. Was he telling the truth? A. At the time, yes, sir, from March until the time the order was rescinded.

THE COURT. Do you have any further questions?

Q. Mrs. Ressler, on this weekend of October 27th, where you said that Mr. Goldstick had told you that you were to wait until four o'clock that

Friday afternoon . . . A. I don't recall the time.

Q. Were you at home at six o'clock on that day? A. I don't have it down here, but I am sure I was.

Q. Did you see the present Mrs. Lesser come up to your house, drive up to your house? A. I don't know who was in the car, but I was protecting my boy. He was frightened and intimidated.

Q. Did you see a car drive up? A. Yes, sir.

Q. Did you answer the doorbell? A. No, sir.

Q. Did you make any reaction from the house, in reply to the honking of the horn? A. No, sir.

Q. Nobody came out? A. No, sir.

Q. Although you were in the house? A. Yes, sir.

Q. And the boy was in the house? A. Yes, sir.

Q. And Mr. Lesser did not see the boy that week-end, is that right? A. No, sir.

Q. Do you know how many days Larry was absent from school this present semester? A. No.

Q. If I told you he had been absent eighteen days beginning with September sixth would that surprise you? A. No, Larry has been ill quite a bit.

Q. How many doctors have called for him? A. Two.

Q. Who are they? A. Dr. Corsada and Lupatkin.

Q. How many times did they see him, each? A. Dr. Corsada was there once, and Dr. Lupatkin was there.

Q. But Larry was absent eighteen days from school. A. I am taking your word for it.

Q. And two doctors came once each during that entire period, is that right? A. Yes, sir.

Q. And the absences were, in the main, due to illness, right? A. They were due to illness.

THE COURT. Mrs. Ressler, could you remember one occasion when you were here with your husband, standing at the bench, and I asked you why you didn't obey the orders of the Court, why you didn't comply with the agreement which was incorporated in the decree of the Court? Why you didn't deliver the boy to the father, as required by the orders of the Court? Remember at that time your husband and you said you were obeying a higher law? A. Yes, sir.

THE COURT. Is that the principle on which you are acting at this time? In other words, is it your concept that you don't have to obey the orders of the Court? A. No, sir, we are very law-abiding people, and we have fixed principles, too, which would keep us from being disobedient.

THE COURT. It so happens, doesn't it, that on two occasions you were found guilty of ruthless contempt of Court because of your failure to comply with the agreement to raise the boy in the Jewish faith, and your further failure to give visitation rights to your former husband? A. I never never failed to agree that the child could be brought up in the Jewish faith, and he has been, your Honor, at any time that the agreement was in effect.

THE COURT. You are a practicing Christian Scientist, aren't you? A. Yes.

THE COURT. And you say in spite of that the boy has been raised while in your custody in the Jewish faith? A. Yes, sir.

THE COURT. Your boy didn't so testify when he appeared before Judge Aurelio. A. How could he not have been? We live our own religion, but we don't press it on the boy.

THE COURT. Did you ever take him to Hebrew School while he was with you? A. Most of the time, because there have been no arrangements for his transportation; when no one came for him I took him myself.

THE COURT. Mrs. Ressler, the truth of the matter is—I want you to be honest with the Court—that you did want to raise this boy in the Christian Science faith? A. I want what the boy wants. It has nothing to do with my desire. The boys wants to be raised as such.

THE COURT. And you had no influence on him at all? A. Only an influence for good.

THE COURT. That is not answering my question. Did you say anything to him or influence him in any way in his wanting, impressing upon him that it would be desirable to follow the Christian Science faith? A. Never.

THE COURT. He just did that on his own? A. Yes, sir.

THE COURT. And you are saying that under oath? A. Under oath.

THE COURT. Go ahead, counsel.

MR. TIEFENBRUN. That is all.

[iii]
Redirect Examination

THE COURT. Do you have anything else to say? A. I would like to say, your Honor, that I would like perpetual custody of my child. I am not a bad mother. I am not an adulteress: I don't drink and I don't smoke, and I don't see why I should be deprived of my child. I have not seen him for over three weeks. I am not allowed to talk to him on the telephone; the phone is hung up. I think that something should be done about it. The father has already taken two of my children, and now he wants the third.

THE COURT. You say the father took two of them. Wasn't it their choice to go with the father? A. The Judge had awarded the older girl to me, but she decided to go with the father because I did not have as much to offer her as the father had.

THE COURT. What about the son, the older boy? A. The older boy chose to be with his father at the time.

THE COURT. Apparently these two children wanted to go with the father, he couldn't have been too bad could he? A. Well, I just want the father to obey the ruling, your Honor.

THE COURT. You are only concerned about the father obeying the ruling. What about imposing that same obligation on yourself? A. I have been obedient. The boy is afraid of the father, your Honor, and he doesn't want to be with him. If I am to be condemned for protecting my child that isn't fair.

THE COURT. It isn't a question of protecting the child, obviously, but the father wants to protect his child, too. A. But the boy is afraid of the father.

THE COURT. Let's find out about that. You step down for a few minutes, and ask the boy to come in, please.

(The Court conferred with the infant in Chambers.)

THE COURT. I have had a brief talk with the boy, and he said he is comparatively happy. He says he has been well since he has been with his father, and he plays. He has been fed well, clothed. He said his father has been kind and considerate to him. He didn't say anything against his mother, you needn't worry about that.

He made a point, which I can understand, that he was confused by the existing situation. I think a more mature mind would be confused also. It is unfortunate when marriages flounder that the children become the unfortunate victims of the misdeeds of either parent or both of the parents. It is equally unfortunate there isn't some way that parents should be made to pay for the situation which results in inflicting such harm and frustrations on innocent victims.

As Larry indicates in this case, and as I found to be the fact in a number of other matters over the years I have been in the Court, and particularly since I have been on the bench, I don't think we have any Solomons around. I don't believe sociology has developed to a point where we can control these things so far as youngsters are concerned, and there are enough problems involved in the ordinary routine of family life to cause frustrations when to those are added a divided family.

If parents would only realize how utterly important it is to submerge their own feelings and likes and dislikes and emotions and interests for the welfare of the children, and cooperate, in spite of their feelings one toward the other, to the end of making life more bearable for youngsters.

Here is a boy, who is a nice-looking lad, bright and alert, healthy looking, and who wants to be happy, yearning for happiness, for love and affection, and yet he finds himself in a position where he is confused. As he put it, he doesn't know what to do. I can well understand his feelings and the distortions that are in his mind.

I asked him how he happened to go to the Christian Science Church, and he said, well, he was in the home, his mother and father practiced it, and he just sort of drifted into it, which of course, is understandable. It is like you walk along the street sometimes and you see a three-year-old child speaking Spanish, you look at him in wonder. When you remember the Spanish are of Spanish extraction you understand, and it is not such a wonder.

This case has given me considerable pause, and it isn't [sic] a difficult one to decide. I will give it some thought. I know it is not easy to deprive a mother of the custody of a child, especially one of immature years, as Larry is. At the same time, we always try to teach youngsters to obey the law and to live up to concepts of honesty and decency, and yet when a boy finds himself in the atmosphere of a home where the parents pay so little attention to the orders of the Court, it would be small wonder if the boy grew up in such an atmosphere, without the proper concepts of dignity, decency, law and order, develop a high order of integrity. I said that to Mr. & Mrs. Ressler when they were here last week, that children learn by precept, by concept, by environment. If they do become, as I am sure that they do, aware of the fact that the parent has been found guilty of contempt of Court—and it is in no way measured by the $250 fine which Judge Aurelio imposed in this case—how can you expect the child to have any respect for law and order? The child will soon, all things being equal, develop a code of his own, which might well be the code of the jungle.

He thinks, my parents don't pay any attention to the order of the Court, why should I pay attention to a policeman or to other laws which have been established.

I have much respect for any religious faith or any concept a person has. The fact nevertheless remains that the highest law of the State is as it is administered by the Courts, and no person has a right to say that he or she is abiding by a higher law, which while perfectly laudable, perhaps, in a sociological or moral or religious world, is something which cannot be tolerated as our society is constituted today.

You have to bear those things in mind, Mrs. Ressler. Unless you want to forfeit the right of custody, that there are more important things, particularly in so far as your boy is concerned, than satisfying your own feelings or in wreaking revenge or displaying an animosity towards grievances, true or untrue, that you may have against your husband.

The paramount consideration on the part of the Court is the welfare of the child. Adults have lived their life, have, to use an old expression, made their beds, and may lie in them or otherwise, but a parent has no right to mold a child in any way that is calculated to lead him or her in a path that can only bring hazard and unhappiness and confusion, dismay and mental disturbance. That is what is happening now.

First, because of the separation, then the divorce, and later, because of his being taken from one religious household and suddenly thrown into another religious orbit. An older mind couldn't withstand that traumatic psychological assault which this boy has been subjected to, and he ought not to be.

In so far as this Court can protect him against both parties wherein each may be guilty of infractions of accepted norms, this Court expects to do so.

I am going to read the record of the testimony of both hearings before Judge Aurelio, and I shall read the testimony taken here, as well as the testimony of Mrs. Ressler and the other testimony and statements submitted by her, together with—I think there have been reports from the Family Counseling Unit—and after such consideration, render a decision to the best of my ability.

This matter is now closed.

Decision reserved.

MRS. RESSLER. May I see the boy?

THE COURT. Sure. Do you want to talk to him?

MRS. RESSLER. May I have some visitation rights with the boy?

THE COURT. Counsel, step up a minute.

(At Bar discussion.)

(Hearing adjourned.)

May 2, 1963.

MR. SEAVER. Your Honor will recall that hearings were conducted in this matter before you, and that at a certain point in the hearing you determined that the plaintiff who had not appeared by counsel should be represented by counsel, and that at the Court's suggestion that I take an assignment on her behalf. I accepted such an assignment and served a notice of appearance, which I now desire to file.

I have given my client certain advice in connection with the conduct of these proceedings, all with a view, if your Honor please, to bring this strife—more than just legal controversy—to an end.

d. Doris Penman—For the Defense

[i]
Direct Examination

BY MR. TIEFENBRUN

Q. What is your occupation, Miss Penman?
A. I am a Dean at the Westmont Junior High School.

Q. Is that the school that Larry Lesser attends?
A. Yes, sir.

Q. After Larry was entered in your school did you have any contact with him? A. Yes, sir, I did.

Q. Approximately how often between September and November? A. About four times.

Q. Is that an abnormal amount for you to have contact with a child?

MR. SEAVER. The question is objected to.

Q. In your capacity.

MR. SEAVER. The question is objected as to form.

THE COURT. I will allow it.

MR. SEAVER. The question is objected to as to form.

THE COURT. Let's say unusual, if not abnormal.

Q. Is that an unusual amount of visits for you to have with a child? A. It's very little more than usual. Depending on the situation.

Q. Since November, how often have you had occasion to see Larry? A. Once.

Q. Have you noticed or are you aware of any differences in Larry's general conduct and demeanor over the period of time that you have seen him? A. He was a very concerned boy when I first saw him. Now, the fact that I haven't seen him recently might indicate that he is not quite as concerned as he was at that time. I sent for him first for an initial interview which I do routinely, and then when I recognized that he was quite concerned about his new school and his situation, and a little wondering at that time which school he would finally go to. He wasn't sure whether he would stay in our school or go to some other school. I sent for him a few more times so that he could talk it out and feel a little bit better about his position in our school. It's a kind of first-aid treatment.

THE COURT. By the way, how has he been doing in school? A. There has been an improvement on the English, a few points dropped off on Citizenship Education, a dropoff, if you compare the first and the third quarters in Science, a two point increase in Math, one point increase in

Industrial Arts, and an improvement in effort in Physical Education.

[ii]
Cross Examination

BY MR. SEAVER

Q. Are there many other boys in the school whose records are not dissimilar to this, showing, for example, the equivalent rating of progress in one subject such as English, and an equivalent rate of falling down as in citizenship and in science? Are there other boys in school—— A. There are other boys.

Q. ——who fall in the same pattern? Would you say that this happens to boys who come to school without problems of concern as well as with boys who have things to be concerned about, on the basis of your experience? A. Usually, with a youngster who is as bright as this child we have a better performance unless there is something that the child is concerned about. Now, this is a pattern and not——I cannot break this out specifically.

Q. Based on your experience, would you say that the presence of a pupil in court or in any other areas of dispute between parents would create a matter of concern for the boy in relation to his school work? A. Yes, sir, it usually has an effect.

THE COURT. Will you please tell us what the achievement tests were in the various areas and what they indicated on the basis of your experience? A. Yes. (Reading): Seventh grade, fifth month ; word meaning, seventh grade, seven months, and I would like to mention that this is a Stanford Achievement Test. Average reading sixth grade, seven months ; spelling, seventh grade, five months ; language, seventh grade, four months ; arithmetic reasoning, seventh grade, two months ; arithmetic comprehension, sixth grade, four months ; average arithmetic, sixth grade, eight months ; social studies, seventh grade, nine months ; science, seventh grade, eight months ; study skills, sixth grade, five months, and the medium for the whole battery is seventh grade, four months.

MR. SEAVER. What grade had he completed at the Westmont School when he left? A. That would have been sixth grade, sir.

Q. And the achievement test indicated that his achievements were equivalent to an average to a boy in the seventh grade, four month period ; is that correct? A. Based on national norms, yes.

Q. Seven years and four months, and he had completed the sixth grade, is that correct? A. Yes, sir. He hadn't—he had not quite completed the sixth grade at that time.

[iii]
Redirect Examination

BY MR. TIEFENBRUN

Q. Miss Penman, in connection with mathematics, was there any improvement so far as your records go in effort or attitude towards it? A. We have a record here for the second quarter that says, "U," and "U" in mathematics, which means poor effort and poor production, poor performance in relation to his ability to perform. In the third quarter we have "Fair," so there has been an improvement over the second quarter.

Q. In his effort and attitude towards his work in this field? A. Yes, sir.

Q. With respect to the achievement test that Mr. Seaver referred to and the records that you received from the Westmont School, you told us that this indicated that he was in the seventh year four-month rating of achievement, and that is measured by the national norm? A. Yes.

Q. In your opinion, from your experience, considering this boy's intelligence, and considering this boy, this boy's potential of achievement, was that normal for him? A. No, sir. Normal for him would be in our school situation, in our cultural background, in our community, we would anticipate that he would run more to two years ahead.

e. Ida Lesser—For the Defense

[i]
Cross Examination

BY MR. SEAVER

Q. Larry has been with you constantly since November 1962 ; is that correct? A. Yes.

Q. And he has been with you on prior occasions? A. Yes, he has.

Q. During the time that he has been with you have you found him to be a gentlemanly young man? A. On occasions.

Q. Do you mean by that that he is unruly on most occasions? A. It depends on the situation. I'd say he is an average boy.

Q. Average enough for him to be in the company of your own son of ten years of age? A. I would say so.

Q. You never hesitated at any time to have your boy in his company? A. No, I wouldn't.

MR. TIEFENBRUN. You better raise your voice.

Q. Now, in the month of February of this year while Larry was residing in your home, was Mr. Lesser away? A. Yes, he was.

Q. As a matter of fact, you were away with him ; isn't that right, Mrs. Lesser? A. Yes ; that is right.

Q. Where were you? A. In Miami.

MR. TIEFENBRUN. If your Honor please, I object to this. I don't know what this is going into.

MR. SEAVER. The charge has been made here that there ought to be a change of custody because the mother is a violator of the agreement. I want to point out through the testimony of this witness that the father himself was a violator.

MR. TIEFENBRUN. May I just correct something? The charge is made here and the request is made for a change of custody, not because the mother is a violator of the agreement, but because of the fact that the boy is going to be far better off under the care of his father, and that the violation of the agreement evidences this fact.

May I just continue this, your Honor? If the purpose of this testimony is to try to prove that because the father has custody of a boy, that the father may not go away from the house or leave or anything like that, then I think we ought to change the whole order so that the boy has custody of the father.

MR. SEAVER. Let's see in whose care the boy was left. This is important.

THE COURT. Let's go ahead.

EXAMINATION BY MR. SEAVER (cont'd.)

Q. Mrs. Lesser, in whose care was Larry left during this period when you were in Miami Beach, Florida? A. With the maid.

Q. Who in your household prepares breakfast? A. Who? The maid does.

Q. Do you prepare breakfast? A. On occasion.

Q. You make it when the boy does not have to leave early; is that correct? A. That's right. She is up earlier and she makes the breakfast for all of them.

Q. Who prepares the boy's lunch? A. Either the boys do or the maid does.

THE COURT. Mr. Seaver, I have got a grandson. Why don't you ask me who prepares his breakfast, and if you do I will tell you he does himself. A. They would rather do it themselves.

MR. SEAVER. There are various views on that.

Q. Now, do you know that Larry is going to be confirmed on Saturday? A. He is going to be Bar Mitzvahed Saturday.

Q. And invitations have been issued to the ceremony? A. Yes, they have.

Q. Who prepared those invitations?

MR. TIEFENBRUN. If your Honor please, I don't see how it is material.

MR. SEAVER. It is very material.

THE COURT. Was the first Mrs. Lesser invited? That is what he is getting at.

MR. SEAVER. I'm sure she is not.

THE WITNESS. No, she wasn't, according to my list.

MR. SEAVER. I want to point out—the point is very plain—that this defendant would prefer to let the world know that the former Mrs. Lesser is not the mother of these children, and I think this indicates it.

[ii]
Redirect Examination

BY MR. TIEFENBRUN

Q. When you and Mrs. Lesser left on this vacation to Florida, you left the other children at home too? A. Yes, certainly.

BY THE COURT

Q. How does Larry get along with your children? A. They get along very nicely.

Q. Does Larry appear to you to be happy where he is now? A. I would say very much so.

f. Dee Shiff—For the Defense

[i]
Direct Examination

BY MR. TIEFENBRUN

Q. Mrs. Shiff, you are the daughter of Mr. Lesser and Mrs. Ressler; is that correct? A. Right.

Q. Larry is your brother? A. Yes.

Q. Are you married? A. Yes.

Q. Do you have any children of your own? A. Yes. Three.

Q. Have you visited at your father's home over the years since you have been married? A. Yes, I have.

Q. Have you been in contact with Larry over this period of time? A. Yes.

Q. Have you visited at your father's home in the last six months that Larry has been living with your father? A. Yes, up until the last three months I saw him about every week or certainly once every two weeks.

Q. About three months ago I think that you gave birth; is that right? A. Right.

Q. And since that time you have seen him how often? A. I have seen him at my house about once a week or two times every three weeks.

Q. Have you seen any change in Larry? A. Yes, I have.

MR. SEAVER. That is objected to, if your Honor please.

THE COURT. I will allow that.

Q. What nature of change have you seen in the last six months or so? A. I would say in the last six months he has come out of a shell, and he used to be very quiet, and I think he acted old for his age. He was quiet and seemed a little nervous, you know, rather than easy-going.

Q. Do you feel that he is more stable at this

point? A. I think he acts more like other children his age should.

Q. Do you think he is happier than he was? A. I think so.

THE COURT. How old are your children? A. Two years and three months. I have twins three months old, and a girl three.

Q. Have you noticed any physical change in Larry in the past six months? A. He has gotten bigger and seems to have gained a little weight.

Q. What is the relationship between Larry and your father? How does that seem to you? A. It seems very normal.

Q. And the relationship between Larry and the rest of the children in the household? A. Excellent.

Q. Have you had any conversation with your mother recently concerning this case, the issue that is before this Court? A. Yes.

Q. Would you tell us when that took place and what was said? A. It took place about a week ago. I had told her that I was going to appear in court again if it was needed, if I was needed, and that the only reason I was going is because I thought Larry would be happier living with my father, and she had asked me how, what makes me feel this way, and if I was really interested in Larry why I don't ask Larry how he really feels, and I said the only reason I didn't ask Larry is because I think he has been questioned enough by people.

MR. TIEFENBRUN. That is all.

[ii]
Cross Examination

BY MR. SEAVER

Q. Mrs. Shiff, so that I may understand your testimony correctly, is your view of Larry's attitude in regard to the questions whether he would be better off wtih his mother or father based on your feelings and not on anything that Larry had said to you; is that correct? A. Right.

Q. Now, do you recall some years ago when the separation trial occurred in this case? A. Yes.

Q. When the question of custody first came up? A. Yes.

Q. And Judge Streit at that time interviewed you with regard to your desires? A. Yes.

Q. And at that time you made the choice, did you not, to remain with the father? A. Yes.

Q. You thought that that would be better for you? A. Yes.

Q. And you feel that it would be better for Larry too; is that right? A. Yes.

Q. Would I not be correct in inferring that your thoughts as to what might be better for Larry really rests on the fact that you made a choice for yourself? A. In other words, because I

choose the way I felt.

Q. Because you found it was better for you, that that is really the reason it would be better for Larry? A. No.

Q. You are sure of that? A. Yes, because at the time I made the decision my father wasn't even married. It was an entirely different situation.

THE COURT. How old were you at that time? A. Seventeen, eighteen.

MR. SEAVER. So that you were satisfied to remain with your father even though he had no other wife; is that right? A. Yes.

Q. And you think that it would be better for Larry or that your feeling with regard to what is better for Larry is aided by the fact that your father is now married? A. I think it would help him, yes.

Q. In other words, you would prefer to have your brother live with a lady who is not his mother in preference to residing with his mother; is that your view? A. Well, yes, I suppose so.

THE COURT. Mrs. Shiff, would it embarrass you—you don't have to answer this question—if I asked you why at this separation trial you made your decision to go with your father instead of your mother? If you don't want to answer that question, I will forget about it. A. It is a long involved——

THE COURT. All right.

g. Perry Lesser—Defendant

Cross Examination (continued)

BY MR. SEAVER

Q. Have you taken Larry to a psychiatrist? A. No.

Q. Or to a psychologist in the time he has been with you, since November of 1962? A. No.

Q. May I take it that you haven't taken him there because in your judgment you didn't believe it was necessary to do so? A. Yes.

Q. Is that correct? A. Yes, sir.

Q. Now, would you say that Larry has gone to a physician since he has been with you at least a half dozen times? A. Approximately.

Q. Did you report to his mother any occasion on which you took him to a physician? A. No.

Q. Did it occur to you that the mother should be entitled to know this? Just did it occur to you? A. No, it didn't.

Q. In February when you went away to Miami, did it occur to you to inform the Court or Mrs. Ressler's attorney that you were going to go away and find out whether it was all right to leave the boy with the maid? A. No.

Q. It did not occur to you? A. No.

Q. Did you believe that you were the sole judge

of what was best for the boy? A. It didn't enter my mind to question or ask about leaving the boy because I left the rest of my family within the same confines and the house and everybody else.

Q. But, of course, with regard to the other children in the house this was agreeable to Mrs. Lesser, who was the mother of the other children; is that right? A. Naturally.

Q. May I assume that you discussed with Mrs. Lesser whether it would be all right to leave her children behind with the maid while you and Mrs. Lesser went to Florida? A. No, we didn't. We assumed that this entire unit is a family, and that Larry and that Ronny and May is no different and it is treated as such.

Q. You mean you felt you had a right to disregard at that time, and just follow me carefully now, that Larry had his own mother? A. It is not a question of whether he had his own mother or not. It was a question of that our house is capable of taking care of whoever is in it.

Q. You knew, did you not, that custody of the boy had not been transferred to you and that the boy was left in your care pending the hearing of this proceeding? A. Yes.

Q. Did you know that Mrs. Ressler, his mother, has been taking him from public school to the Hebrew school during the time he has been living with you? A. Not all the time.

Q. Did you know that she does it on occasions? A. Yes, on occasions, he has told me this.

Q. He has been truthful with you then? A. He always has.

Q. Have you found him to be truthful? A. Well, he is like a little boy, if he feels like he doesn't——

Q. Can't you tell me whether or not in your opinion your own son has been truthful since he has been living with you? A. Yes, he has, and I am trying to state the reasons why he isn't sometimes.

Q. Do you give his mother any credit for having instilled the ideals of truth in him as a result of all the years that he has lived with her? A. I don't give the mother the credit.

Q. Has the boy been obedient to you during the time he has lived with you? A. When he first got there he had a little time to adjust, because Mrs. Ressler——

Q. Don't give me the because.

MR. TIEFENBRUN. Please.

THE WITNESS. I want to state the reason.

THE COURT. Wait a minute. Let the lawyer bring it up.

MR. SEAVER. I move to strike out anything after the word "because."

THE COURT. Strike it out.

BY MR. SEAVER

Q. He hasn't balked about going to Hebrew School since he has been with you, has he? A. No, sir.

Q. You are pleased to note that, were you not? A. Yes, sir.

Q. He went bowling with you, can he bowl? A. In fact, he bowls about 130. In fact, I gave him a pair of shoes, because I said when he bowls a hundred he will get a pair of shoes, when he bowls 125 he will get a bag, and in fact, I think four weeks ago he bowled 150 or something.

Q. Was he that good when he came to live with you? A. No, he wasn't able to bowl 80.

Q. In November he couldn't bowl 80? A. He couldn't even bowl 80.

Q. Could he bowl? A. I wouldn't say he could bowl. If he couldn't bowl 80, that is pretty low.

Q. Was he able to ride a horse when he came to you? A. Yes, he was able to.

Q. As a matter of fact, he has been riding a horse for several years before? A. I don't know, but he was riding.

THE COURT. Let's don't spend any more time on that.

MR. SEAVER. Judge, I want to show that this boy has been well raised while he has been with his mother. He learned all the skills a boy normally learns.

THE COURT. I don't have any impression the boy has been abused. I don't think you need go into that.

MR. SEAVER. I'm not talking about abuse on his part. I am trying to point out the boy has been well raised. This has to do with the question of the transfer of custody.

May 3, 1963

h. Sadie Ressler—Plaintiff

[i]
Direct Examination

BY MR. SEAVER

Q. Larry is your natural child; is he not? A. Yes, he is.

Q. He lived continuously with you for how long? A. Up until November 3, 1962.

Q. During those years did you nurse him when he was ill? A. Yes, I did.

Q. And you fed him? A. Yes.

Q. And he lived in your home, whatever it was? A. Yes.

Q. And was he during that period of time under the care of any other person, any person other than yourself? A. No.

Q. During the month of April, did Mr. Lesser communicate with you by telephone? A. No.

Q. There came a time, did there not, when you terminated your telephone number? A. Yes.

Q. Did anything happen as between you and Mr. Lesser before you terminated your telephone number? A. Yes. I was constantly threatened.

Q. How? A. Cursed, insulted.

Q. When? A. I was told I was crazy.

Q. Let's pause for a moment. You say you were told. By whom were you told? A. By Mr. Lesser.

Q. Did he tell you this face-to-face? A. On the telephone.

Q. On the telephone to your home? A. Yes.

Q. And these were on the occasions of telephone calls made by you or by him? A. Either way.

Q. What was the tone of his voice during the course of these telephone conversations? A. Usually it was quite violent, and nasty insulting.

MR. TIEFENBRUN. I think we ought to have these whole conversations.

MR. SEAVER. You want them?

Q. Counsel has asked, and I am perfectly agreeable, Mrs. Ressler, that you inform the Court of the statements that you made. A. You are putting me on the spot here. That I was crazy; I don't know—I don't ever know what I am talking about, and general insults that a person doesn't usually recall.

Q. What other phrase? A. "Drop dead."

Q. During the month of April did Larry go to Mr. Lesser's—— A. I would think so.

Q. Is there anything here that you can refresh your recollection from as to the precise times? A. The black book.

Q. You say a black book. Is this a diary which you kept during the year? A. Yes.

Q. Did you keep it on the advice of anyone? A. Yes, sir, a former attorney.

Q. Do you recall the testimony that Mr. Lesser gave about a visit to your home for the purpose of picking up the boy? A. Fairly well.

Q. Can you tell the Court what happened on that occasion? A. Mr. Lesser rang the bell. My husband let him in.

Q. Did you have a conversation with Mr. Lesser? A. Yes.

Q. Who was present at that conversation? A. At the beginning my husband was, but then he went to the telephone.

Q. What was said between you and your husband? Tell us everything. A. I told him that Larry would not object to seeing him if he could come to him on his own time, on his own terms, but he wanted to come. And he said he wanted the boy. He called the boy down. He was upstairs, had locked himself in the bathroom.

Q. Who was upstairs? A. Larry had locked himself in the bathroom. He had refused to come out when he knew that his father's car was outside.

Q. Now, did Mr. Lesser call for the boy in any manner? A. Yes, he screamed for him.

Q. How did he do it? Just what did he say, if you remember? A. He said, "Come down here."

Q. Was that in the normal voice as you are uttering it or was it a shouting voice? A. He was shouting. He screamed up the stairs and the child came down in his robe.

Q. What happened when the boy was downstairs? A. He sat right close to me on the sofa, Larry sat down close to me on the sofa, and the father asked him if he didn't want to go with him, and the boy didn't answer, in my recollection.

And I said that he should not intimidate the child; "The child is afraid of you and would not—doesn't want to go with you."

And the father pushed me in the chest and—or struck me.

Q. What else did the father do besides push you? A. He said he was going to call the police and wanted to use our phone. And Mr. Ressler said if he didn't leave he would have to put him out, and then he tried to put him out, and he eventually did leave.

THE COURT. Mrs. Ressler, do you recall during November or December, at one of your many appearances in court up at the bench here with your husband, Mr. Ressler, I asked you why you didn't obey the order of the Court, and you said to me in essence you did but that you responded to a higher law than the law of the State of New York? A. That was Mr. Ressler who said that.

THE COURT. Do you remember his also saying that every time the boy was supposed to go to the father that you opened the Bible and went to the bathroom or some room and read it, and then concluded that you ought not to comply with the order? A. He did say something like that, yes. I believe that is the reason he is in a mental institution at the moment.

BY MR. SEAVER

Q. Do you believe in compliance with the law of the State of New York and the law of the country? A. I do. I have said that before under oath, and I certainly mean to keep my word, and have always kept my word since I am a Christian Scientist.

Q. Do you believe in compliance with contracts that you enter into? A. I certainly do, sir.

Q. In this case, in this case——

MR. SEAVER. And may I digress for a moment, as long as your Honor brought it out.

Q. In any instance, was any of your actions

with regard to Larry or this contract with which we are here concerned motivated by an intent on your part to violate the terms of that agreement?

MR. TIEFENBRUN. I object to that. A. No.

THE COURT. Yes.

MR. SEAVER. We are speaking on a matter of intent, if your Honor please.

THE COURT. No. I have to determine that from the facts, counselor.

MR. SEAVER. Judge, we are in a court of equity. We deal with the question of wilful behavior.

THE COURT. I know, but even in a court of equity there is a limit to the elasticity of the chancellor.

MR. SEAVER. I recognize that. Your Honor does not have to believe the word of any witness, but I believe it is perfectly proper for a witness to express what her intent was.

THE COURT. The best evidence of that fact is what you did and not what your intentions may have been.

BY MR. SEAVER

Q. Now, what happened in your relations with Mr. Lesser after September 3rd? Were you served with a writ of habeas corpus to produce the boy before a Justice in Westchester County? A. That's correct.

Q. When you got that writ of habeas corpus did you go up to Mr. Erdheim's office? A. Yes.

Q. Did you act on some advice which he gave you at the time? A. Yes. He said go into the court and ask for an adjournment.

Q. Did he tell you why you should ask for an adjournment?

MR. TIEFENBRUN. I will object to that at this point. I think we ought to bring Mr. Erdheim in if you want to.

THE COURT. What is the point?

MR. SEAVER. They made a big to do in the papers about the fact that she didn't produce the boy before a Justice of the Supreme Court.

THE COURT. All right. You don't need to go into that. Those things don't influence me.

Mr. Erdheim, I regret to say, has made a practice of advising clients in other matters, which I thought was clearly in violation of ethics and propriety of conduct the lawyer should employ in a case. Of course, he could well have been engaged at that time. He is busy. I know that to be a fact.

MR. SEAVER. Of course, I am concerned with the client's behavior.

THE COURT. I am only concerned about two or three things in this proceeding, Mr. Seaver. One is whether or not this lady complied with the agreement, which agreement by the way was made a part of the Mexican decree which she herself obtained; and two, whether she intends to comply with it; and three, how would the best interests of the boy be served. That is all. That is elementary Mr. Watson.

THE COURT. Did I understand you to say before that your husband was in a mental institution at the present time? A. Yes, sir.

THE COURT. How long has he been there? A. Since November.

THE COURT. What is the nature of this mental illness, do you know? A. I don't. They haven't told me.

THE COURT.. Do you know how long he will be confined there? A. No, sir.

BY MR. SEAVER

Q. Did you have anything to do with his commitment? A. No, sir, I did not. He committed himself.

Q. Did you know when you married him that he had any difficulty from an emotional point of view? A. No, I found out after we were married that he had in 1947 had the same problem and had been away.

THE COURT. Let me ask you this: Suppose he comes out of the mental institution. Do you expect him to come home to you? A. If it will mean that I cannot have my son back I definitely will not take him back. It has to do with his— even if he is healed, which he is not at the moment.

THE COURT. Do you know it would be a rather unwholesome thing for the boy to be in that atmosphere even if he is discharged? Frequently such cases have a recurrence of the illnesses. That is why I asked you the type, because I would be able to determine what the chances are of his complete recovery.

But you said he had been confined on some other occasion? A. Yes, in 1947. I found this out afterward. He had defrauded me in that respect. And if it means that—his being at home would deprive me of my child, I will not take him back because my son comes first.

THE COURT. All right.

BY MR. SEAVER

Q. Is your own health good? A. Perfect.

Q. Have you certain skills by which you could procure employment if need be? A. Yes. I can't model at the moment, but I can——

Q. When you say you can't model at the moment, you mean you once worked at modeling? A. I once worked at modeling, but I can do speed-writing, typing, and I can sell.

Q. Do you believe, on the basis of the income you received from your house and compensation that you would be expected to receive for the support of Larry if he were with you from the father who is responsible for it, that you would have sufficient to maintain yourself and Larry in respectable circumstances? A. Very nicely.

Q. At least so long as he is attending grade school without the expense say of a private school? A. Yes, sir. I would do anything to keep my child.

Q. Would you also go to work part-time if that is necessary? A. Yes, sir, I certainly would.

Q. Mrs. Ressler, during the time of the operation of Judge Epstein's order, you did take Larry to Christian Science services of some kind? A. Yes, sir.

Q. Over how long a period of time? A. Until the order was rescinded.

Q. Are you familiar with what he was taught there? A. Yes.

Q. What was he taught? A. He was taught——

MR. TIEFENBRUN. I object.

THE COURT. Where is that?

MR. SEAVER. In the Christian Science school. I want to show there has been no genuine interference.

THE COURT. There is no need to go into that.

BY MR. SEAVER

Q. Let me put it this way: Do you know whether or not there was anything in the teaching which he obtained in the Sunday School which was critical of his Hebrew faith?

MR. TIEFENBRUN. I object.

THE COURT. I'm not sure. I know something about the Christian Science.

MR. SEAVER. No further questions.

THE COURT. I have some friends of mine who are the most wonderful people in the world who are Christian Scientists. It isn't a question of whether Christian Science is good or bad.

In the first place, I express no opinion on it. In the second place, the principal issue here is whether or not there were violations of some orders or agreements.

BY MR. SEAVER (cont'd.)

Q. Regardless of your own personal predilections, Mrs. Ressler, do you intend to abide by your agreement so long as that agreement is in force and effect? A. Yes, sir.

THE COURT. All right.

[ii]
Cross Examination

BY MR. TIEFENBRUN

Q. Where is Mr. Ressler now? You told us in a mental institution.

MR. SEAVER. That has been testified to and I object to the pursuit of the question.

Q. Creedmore? A. Yes.

Q. Do you consider that he is ill?

MR. SEAVER. I object to that. The question is bad as to form.

MR. TIEFENBRUN. This is very important.

THE COURT. She already testified that if the mental health of the husband interferes with her procuring the custody of the child, she will give up her husband.

MR. TIEFENBRUN. There is another reason for this, because under her Christian Science belief she will not consider that he is ill.

MR. SEAVER. Then I certainly object.

MR. TIEFENBRUN. This has a bearing on the fitness of the mother.

THE COURT. We've got enough troubles in this case without getting into Christian Science.

BY MR. TIEFENBRUN

Q. In the last six months, Mrs. Ressler, you have seen Larry quite often, haven't you? A. No.

THE COURT. Let's say since last November, when the boy went to live with his father, you have seen him quite frequently, haven't you, during school periods? A. No, sir, just lunch time, 15 minutes.

THE COURT. Almost every day while he was in school? A. Almost, yes, but he just had barely time to eat and runs back.

THE COURT. I didn't say how long it is. Don't be grudging in your testimony. You see him, don't you? A. Yes.

BY MR. TIEFENBRUN

Q. And you see him in the afternoons after school a number of times a week, don't you? A. I guess you could say yes to that.

Q. You take him to Hebrew School, you told us? A. I guess you could say yes to that.

Q. Have you ever discussed with Larry the terms of the agreement between yourself and Mr. Lesser? A. Only when they weren't adhered to.

Q. Don't you feel that when Mr. Lesser doesn't pay you money during the current period, that is a violation of the agreement? A. Yes, I do.

Q. Have you discussed that with Larry? A. I can't recall.

Q. You mean you don't recall at all whether you discussed this recent six-month period and the failure to pay money with Larry? A. I may have said I found it hard to make ends meet, but I can't recall what else I might have said.

Q. Did you tell him that it would be easier if he were living with you? A. No. I told him that it was difficult to make ends meet regardless, because the father had generally not adhered to the agreement.

Q. You told him that you would dearly love to have him with you? A. Perhaps once.

Q. Did you tell him that you relied upon him in any way? A. Well, I told him that I felt that I would need him when I would get older.

Q. When did you tell him that? A. Not too long ago. Maybe about a month.

Q. Will you tell us what the conversation was? A. I could not recall.

Q. Give it to us to the best of your recollection. A. Well, it may have gone something like this: that Mr. Lesser had four or five or six children there, and I would like to feel that I have him to rely upon when I get older.

Q. What did he say? A. Nothing. To my recollection.

Q. I want to clarify one more thing, Mrs. Ressler, about when Mr. Ressler comes out of the hospital. If he comes out of the hospital without regard to the result of this inquiry, do you intend to live with him or not? A. Everything hinges upon the result of this inquiry, Mr. Tiefenbrun.

Q. Suppose he went out today, what would you do? A. If he were healed well, and did not—and could make my home happy, and I could be permitted to have my child, with Mr. Ressler, I would think about it.

Q. If he were healed then you would—is it fair to say if he were discharged as healed, that you would probably want to live with Mr. Ressler with your son? A. Only if Judge Greenberg agreed that it was all right to have him there.

Q. Assuming that he is discharged. I am not interested in what Judge Greenberg thinks at this moment. I am interested in what you think and your feelings. Assume that he were discharged as healed. You would then like to live with him and with your son; is that right? A. I really cannot say, Mr. Tiefenbrun. My mind is not made up. Because it all hinges upon the outcome of this case.

Q. He is your husband; isn't he?

MR. SEAVER. If your Honor please, I object to the pursuit of this argumentative fact.

THE COURT. I have got the picture. You don't need to pursue that any further.

[ii]
Recross Examination

BY MR. TIEFENBRUN

MR. TIEFENBRUN. We rest except for Benjamin and Larry to come in late Monday afternoon.

THE COURT. I don't know that I want Benjamin. What do you want him for?

MR. TIEFENBRUN. I think that he should— he is anxious to tell the Court what he knows about the way his brother has grown and the

way his brother feels, and he is 21 now. He is almost 21 years old now.

THE COURT. If you want to bring him in, I'll talk to him.

MR. SEAVER. Judge, there is one concession, to the effect that the husband of the young lady, Mrs. Shiff, who testified yesterday, the daughter of the parties, her husband, that girl's husband, is employed by Mr. Lesser.

May 7, 1963

THE COURT. Then both sides rest?

MR. TIEFENBRUN. Yes.

THE COURT. Decision reserved.

MR. TIEFENBRUN. Is it conceded that both sides consent that the Court may interview Larry without either one of us being present?

MR. SEAVER. Oh, yes.

THE COURT. Which the Court has already done. The Court also spoke to the older boy.

i. The Trial Judge Decides—May 18, 1963

GREENBERG, J.

An unhappy picture of human relations has been presented by this custody proceeding, which has plagued the Courts for the past six or seven years. The instant application, one of a long series of contests between the father and mother of a thirteen year old child, seeks to modify an order of this court, dated January 30, 1960, by changing custody from the mother to the father with rights of visitation to the former.

Immediately prior to the institution of this proceeding, the mother had been held in contempt of court because of her failure to comply with its order relating to visitation rights for the father. In addition, the question of the religion of the child was tendered, the father claiming that, under a written agreement which was incorporated in a divorce decree, the wife was required to rear the child in the Jewish faith, when, as a matter of fact, she raised the child in the faith of Christian Science, the mother claiming that although she was a Christian Scientist as well as her present husband, she did not violate the order of the court. On this issue another justice ruled against her.

For several months now, the father, pursuant to the order of the court, has had temporary custody of the boy with adequate rights of visitation to the mother. The boy received instructions in the Jewish faith and just recently had his Bar Mitzvah (confirmation). He seems quite reasonably happy in his present surroundings. He attends school regularly, has many friends, is healthy, sees his mother frequently and has completely adjusted in the new household, his father having remarried.

The court interviewed the boy, as well as his older brother, who is a student in college, and also heard the testimony of his sister, the eldest child, who herself is now a mother.

Weighing all of the testimony and factors in the case and considering primarily the welfare of the child, the court must conclude that over-all custody be awarded to the father and the mother be allowed to see the boy from time to time as indicated hereinafter.

Paramount is the welfare of the child; his physical, moral and mental condition must be appraised in order to determine what the future course should be. Both mother and father are genuinely devoted to this boy and he shares his love equally between them. When the court saw the boy six months ago, he was confused and unhappy, having been confronted with the strife between his parents and not knowing whether he preferred to be with one or the other.

The mother, as pointed out previously, has re-married and at the present time her husband, unfortunately, is confined to a mental institution. She occupies a small apartment which is temporary in character and her economic condition is deplorable. Even her state of mind is unsettled. In spite of her devotion to her child, to place him in such a position and condition would be harmful and prejudicial to his best interest. She clearly is not in a position to raise the boy under existing circumstances.

The Court is determining the issue of custody solely on the basis of the welfare of the boy—completely aside from the order of contempt which was entered against the mother and com-pletely removed from the issue raised that she violated the order of the court in not rearing the boy in the Jewish Faith.

Accordingly, custody is awarded to the father, with the right of the mother to visit with the child two alternate weekends a month, from Friday at 6:00 P.M. until Sunday at 4:00 P.M. The mother will be permitted to telephone the boy once a day if she is so advised. In addition, she may have the boy with her one week before the commencement of the new school term. If the boy should go to camp, then the mother may visit with him under the rules of the camp. If the boy does not go to camp, the weekend visits, as herein-before provided, shall prevail.

The father is directed to continue to pay the mother $25.00 a week for the support of the boy and to pay all sums due to date.

MEMORANDUM ONLY

ADDENDUM:

The court expresses its grateful appreciation to Irving Seaver, Esq., for accepting the assignment to represent the mother without compensation and for performing a job of exceptional quality.

5.
DECISIONS OF THE LESSERS—"UNTIL DEATH DO US PART"

a. Sadie Ressler Files Appeal

SUPREME COURT: NEW YORK COUNTY

SADIE RESSLER
　　　　　　　　　Plaintiff

　　against　　　　　　　*Notice of Appeal*

PERRY LESSER,
　　　　　　　　　Defendant

SIRS:

PLEASE TAKE NOTICE that the plaintiff above-named hereby appeals to the Appellate Division of the Supreme Court, First Judicial Department, from so much of the order made herein on June 13, 1963 and entered in the office of the Clerk of New York County on June 14, 1963, as (a) grants the motion of the defendant above-named to modify the order of this Court dated January 30, 1960, so as to give custody to said defendant of the infant, LARRY, (b) amends and modifies said order dated January 30, 1960, by awarding custody of said infant to said defendant, and (c) reduces the amount payable to said plain-tiff by said defendant for the support of said infant under said order dated January 30, 1960.

Dated: New York, July 12, 1963.

　　　YOURS, &c.,

　　　　　IRVING J. SEAVER
　　　　　Attorney for Plaintiff

To:

　　JOSEPH TIEFENBRUN, Esq.
　　Attorney for Defendant

　　CLERK OF THE SUPREME COURT,
　　NEW YORK COUNTY

b. Perry Lesser Cross Appeals

SUPREME COURT: NEW YORK COUNTY

SADIE RESSLER
　　　　　　　　　Plaintiff

　　against

PERRY LESSER
　　　　　　　　　Defendant

SIRS:

PLEASE TAKE NOTICE that the defendant above-named hereby cross-appeals to the Appellate Division of the Supreme Court, First Judicial Department, from so much of the order made herein on June 13, 1963 and entered in the office of the Clerk of New York County of June 14, 1963, as directs the said defendant Perry Lesser to continue to pay to plaintiff Sadie Ressler the sum of $25 a week for the support of the infant Larry.

Dated: New York, July 17, 1963.

YOURS, etc.

JOSEPH TIEFENBRUN
Attorney for Defendant

TO:
IRVING J. SEAVER, Esq.
Attorney for Plaintiff

CLERK OF THE SUPREME COURT,
NEW YORK COUNTY

B.

China's Family Code—A Model for State Intervention?

In presenting this code out of its societal context, we are aware of Margaret Mead's significant *caveat:* "[The] uninformed use of cultural material is often mistakenly called cultural relativity, but that is exactly what it is not, for cultural relativity demands that every item of cultural behavior be seen as relative to the culture of which it is a part. . . . The science of culture can insist . . . that when we consider contrasting types of behavior we shall attend always to the complete system, and that random, indiscriminate citations of cultural contrasts in detail be strictly recognized for what they are . . ."* *Therefore, we ignore the cultural origins of this document and consider it only in terms of our own culture and as a source of ideas for legislative decisions.*

THE MARRIAGE LAW OF THE PEOPLE'S REPUBLIC OF CHINA—MAY 1, 1950†

Chapter One: GENERAL PRINCIPLES

ARTICLE 1.

The arbitrary and compulsory feudal marriage system, which is based on the superiority of man over woman and which ignores the children's interests, is abolished.

The New Democratic marriage system, which is based on free choice of partners, on monogamy, on equal rights for both sexes, and on protection of the lawful interests of women and children, shall be put into effect.

ARTICLE 2.

Polygamy, concubinage, child betrothal, interference with the remarriage of widows and the exaction of money or gifts in connection with marriage shall be prohibited.

---

* Mead, Margaret, "The Comparative Study of Culture and the Purposive Cultivation of Democratic Ideals," *Second Symposium Conference on Science, Philosophy and Religion*, New York: Harper & Bros. 1942 (p. 56).

† Reprinted from Yang, C. K.: *The Chinese Family in the Communist Revolution*, Cambridge, Mass.: The Technology Press, 1959 (pp. 221-226). Reprinted with permission of the publisher.

Chapter Two: CONTRACTING OF MARRIAGE

ARTICLE 3.

Marriage shall be based upon the complete willingness of the two parties. Neither party shall use compulsion and no third party shall be allowed to interfere.

ARTICLE 4.

A marriage can be contracted only after the man has reached twenty years of age and the woman has reached eighteen years of age.

ARTICLE 5.

No man or woman in any of the following instances shall be allowed to marry:

(a) Where the man and woman are lineal relatives by blood or where the man and woman are brother and sister born of the same parents or where the man and woman are half-brother and half-sister. The question of prohibiting marriage between collateral relatives by blood within the fifth degree of relationship is to be determined by custom.

(b) When one party, because of certain physical defects, is sexually impotent.

(c) Where one party is suffering from venereal disease, mental disorder, leprosy, or any other disease which is regarded by medical science as rendering the person unfit for marriage.

ARTICLE 6.

In order to contract a marriage, both the man and the woman shall register in person with the people's government of the subdistrict or village in which they reside. If the marriage is found to be in conformity with the provisions of this law, the local people's government shall, without delay, issue a marriage certificate.

If the marriage is found to be incompatible with the provisions of this law, no registration shall be granted.

Chapter Three: RIGHTS AND DUTIES OF HUSBAND AND WIFE

ARTICLE 7.

Husband and wife are companions living together and shall enjoy equal status in the home.

ARTICLE 8.

Husband and wife are in duty bound to love, respect, assist, and look after each other, to live in harmony, to engage in production, to care for the children, and to strive jointly for the welfare of the family and for the building up of a new society.

ARTICLE 9.

Both husband and wife shall have the right to free choice of occupations and free participation in work or in social activities.

ARTICLE 10.

Both husband and wife shall have equal rights in the possession and management of family property.

ARTICLE 11.

Both husband and wife shall have the right to use his or her own family name.

ARTICLE 12.

Both husband and wife shall have the right to inherit each other's property.

Chapter Four: RELATIONS BETWEEN PARENTS AND CHILDREN

ARTICLE 13.

Parents have the duty to rear and to educate their children; the children have the duty to look after and to assist their parents. Neither the parents nor the children shall maltreat or desert one another.

The foregoing provision also applies to stepparents and stepchildren. Infanticide by drowning and similar criminal acts are strictly prohibited.

ARTICLE 14.

Parents and children shall have the right to inherit one another's property.

ARTICLE 15.

Children born out of wedlock shall enjoy the same rights as children born in lawful wedlock. No person shall be allowed to harm or to discriminate against children born out of wedlock.

Where the paternity of a child born out of wedlock is legally established by the mother of the child, by other witnesses, or by other material evidence, the identified father must bear the whole or part of the cost of maintenance and education of the child until it has attained the age of eighteen.

With the consent of the natural mother, the natural father may have custody of the child.

With regard to the maintenance of a child whose natural mother marries, the provisions of Article 22 shall apply.

ARTICLE 16.

A husband or wife shall not maltreat or discriminate against a child born of a previous marriage.

Chapter Five: DIVORCE

ARTICLE 17.

Divorce shall be granted when husband and wife both desire it. In the event of either the husband or the wife insisting upon divorce, it may be granted only when mediation by the subdistrict people's government and the subdistrict judicial organ has failed to bring about a reconciliation.

In the case where divorce is desired by both the husband and wife, both parties shall register with the subdistrict people's government in order to obtain a certificate of divorce. The subdistrict government, after establishing that divorce is desired by both parties and that appropriate measures have been taken for the care of children and property, shall issue the certificate of divorce without delay.

When only one party insists on divorce, the subdistrict people's government may try to effect a reconciliation. If such mediation fails, it should, without delay, refer the case to the district or city people's court for decision. The subdistrict people's government shall not attempt to prevent or to obstruct either party from appealing to the district or city people's court. In dealing with a divorce case, the district or city people's court must, in the first instance, try to bring about a reconciliation between the parties. In case such mediation fails, the court shall render a verdict without delay.

In the case where, after divorce, both husband and wife desire the resumption of matrimonial relations, they should apply to the subdistrict people's government for a registration of re-marriage. The subdistrict people's government should accept such a registration and issue a certificate of remarriage.

ARTICLE 18.

The husband shall not apply for a divorce when his wife is with child. He may apply for divorce only one year after the birth of the child. In the case of a woman applying for divorce, this restriction does not apply.

ARTICLE 19.

The spouse of a member of the revolutionary army on active service who maintains correspondence with his (or her) family must first obtain his (or her) consent before he (or she) can ask for a divorce.

As from the date of the promulgation of this law, divorce may be granted to the spouse of a member of the revolutionary army who does not correspond with his (or her) family for a subsequent period of two years. Divorce may also be granted to the spouse of a member of the revolutionary army who has not maintained correspondence with his (or her) family for over two years prior to the promulgation of this law and who fails to correspond with his (or her) family for a further period of one year subsequent to the promulgation of the present law.

Chapter Six: SUPPORT AND EDUCATION OF CHILDREN AFTER DIVORCE

ARTICLE 20.

The blood ties between parents and children do not end with the divorce of the parents. No matter whether the father or the mother acts as guardian of the child or children, they still remain the children of both parties.

After divorce, both parents still have the duty to support and educate their children.

After divorce, the guiding principle is to allow the mother to have custody of a baby still being breast-fed. After the weaning of the child, if a dispute arises between the two parties over the guardianship and an agreement cannot be reached, the people's court shall render a decision in accordance with the best interests of the child.

ARTICLE 21.

After divorce, if the mother is given custody of a child, the father shall be responsible for the whole or part of the necessary cost of the maintenance and education of the child. Both parties shall reach an agreement regarding the amount of the cost and the duration of such maintenance and education. In the case where the two parties fail to reach an agreement, the people's court shall render a decision.

Payment must be made in cash, in kind, or by tilling the land allocated to the child.

Such an agreement reached between the parents or decision rendered by the people's court in connection with the maintenance and educational expenses for a child shall not prevent the child from requesting either parent to increase the amount above that fixed by agreement or by judicial decision.

ARTICLE 22.

In the case where a divorced woman remarries and her husband is willing to pay the whole or part of the cost of maintenance and education for the child or children by her former husband, the father of the child or children is entitled to have such cost of maintenance and education reduced or is entitled to be exempt from bearing such cost in accordance with the circumstances.

Chapter Seven: PROPERTY AND MAINTENANCE AFTER DIVORCE

ARTICLE 23.

In case of divorce, the wife shall retain such property as belonged to her prior to her marriage. The disposal of other household properties shall be subject to agreement between the two parties. In the case where an agreement cannot be reached, the people's court shall render a decision after taking into consideration the actual state of the family property, the interests of the wife and the child or children, and the principle of benefiting the development of production.

In the case where the property allocated to the wife and her child or children is sufficient for the maintenance and education of the child or children, the husband may be exempt from bearing further maintenance and education costs.

ARTICLE 24.

After divorce, debts incurred during the period of marriage shall be paid out of the property acquired by husband and wife during this period. In the case where no such property has been acquired or in the case where such property is insufficient to pay off such debts, the husband shall be held responsible for paying these debts. Debts incurred separately by the husband or wife shall be paid off by the party responsible.

ARTICLE 25.

After divorce, if one party has not remarried and has difficulties in maintenance, the other party should render assistance. Both parties shall work out an agreement with regard to the method and duration of such assistance; in case an agreement cannot be reached, the people's court shall render a decision.

Chapter Eight: BYLAWS

ARTICLE 26.

Persons violating this law shall be punished in accordance with law. In the case where interference with the freedom of marriage has caused death or injury, the person guilty of such interference shall bear criminal responsibility before the law.

ARTICLE 27.

This law shall come into force from the date of its promulgation. In regions inhabited by national minorities . . . the provincial people's government may enact certain modifications of supplementary articles in conformity with the actual conditions prevailing among national minorities in regard to marriage. . . .

C.

Epilogue

A conservative estimate of the money expended for administering and reorganizing the relationships of the Lesser families was between $10,000 and $15,000, measured in judges and court personnel. To obtain this state service, the Lessers spent approximately $45,000 in counsel fees.

CHAPTER II

Problems for Decision in Establishing, Administering, and Reorganizing Wife-Husband Relationships

This Chapter is a search for guides to decision concerning what ought to be the extent and nature of state intervention in establishing, administering, and reorganizing wife-husband relationships. It is designed to evaluate what the law should and can contribute to the creation, nourishment, and redefinition of the rights and duties attributed to these "family" relationships.

At each point in the family law process (from the promulgation of legislation through its invocation, application, and appraisal), a series of problems which seldom achieve meaningful definition confront decisionmakers who answer without consciously posing the question: What ought to be the functions and consequences of procedures for granting or denying authorization to marry, to annul, to separate, and to divorce? In an effort to force these problems into focus we ask in each of the four parts of this Chapter: For whom, to what extent and why are economic gratification (Part One), sexual gratification (Part Two), health, happiness, and respect (Part Three), and procreative opportunity (Part Four) relevant to decisions concerning the establishment, administration, and reorganization of wife-husband relationships as well as the administration of reorganized relationships? In responding to these questions it is hoped that definition can be given to establishment, administration, and reorganization as functions of the state in the family law process.

To the extent possible, materials have been selected which are free of the complications that may arise when children are part of the family. But children, the subject of Chapter III, are almost always implicitly, if not explicitly a consideration. The questions set forth in the Introduction should be reread.

PART ONE

FOR WHOM, TO WHAT EXTENT, AND WHY IS PROVIDING OR OBTAINING ECONOMIC GRATIFICATION RELEVANT:

A.

To Decisions Concerning the Establishment of Wife-Husband Relationships?—Gifts and Promises With Love

1.

AVNET v. AVNET
204 Misc. 760, 124 N.Y.S. 2d 517 (Mun. Ct. of N.Y.C. 1953)

CHIMERA, JUSTICE

Plaintiff-wife institutes this suit in conversion, against defendant-husband, to recover the value of furniture, household furnishings and personal effects, claimed by the former to be her exclusive property. The basis of her contention rests upon her story that she alone purchased the items in question from her own personal funds (with the exception of some $200 worth of linens admittedly brought into the household by the husband); that all wedding gifts were in cash and delivered to her personally almost entirely by friends and relatives on the bride's "side"; that they amounted to $1,000 approximately; that a goodly portion of this amount was spent on the honeymoon and the balance was absorbed by the husband in

the purchase of personal items of clothing and other expenses.

All of plaintiff's important assertions are sharply contested by the defendant, particularly the amount of cash gifts and the source from which the money came. Defendant-husband claims that the total amount was closer to $2,400 and that most of it was given by friends and relatives on the groom's "side". Neither denies that the wife had the ultimate control of the funds or such of them as were left over after the honeymoon, and both agree that a substantial portion of the cash was deposited in the wife's personal bank account and commingled with her own monies. No statement is made by either party that any of the donors attached any conditions or requests to their gifts.

This is the pathetic and often repeated story of the bride who could not tear herself away from her parental domicile and of the groom who did little if anything to make her assume her proper place and responsibility in the new home. Their marriage has degenerated into a game of "who shall torture whom" . . . The game was started in some other tribunal and this Court is only a stopping place on their weird journey.

Both counsel move for a directed verdict at the end of the case, the plaintiff contending as a matter of law that the chattels are the property of the wife because they were purchased with her own funds, or, in any event, if purchased by gift monies, the gifts were the property of the bride and therefore the purchases were hers. The defendant on the other hand contends that the purchases were made from gift monies as a matter of law belonging to both parties and that, in any event, the complaint must fall because plaintiff has failed to establish the value of the chattels at the time of the alleged conversion. On these motions the jury was discharged and decision was reserved by the Court.

Ever since man came to abandon the nomadic life, settled in communities and divided the land so that each had his own property, he began to select his women and from that day to this marriage in some form or other has become an honored institution bringing with it myriad questions, moral and legal.

One would think that, after so many centuries of marital experience, all of the rights of the parties to a marriage will have been determined by some judicial tribunal and that at least the question who is entitled to possession of the household furniture and effects will have been settled by now, so clearly that many of the popular misconceptions of the day will have been avoided.

Prior to the enactment of Chapter 200, Laws of 1848, Chapter 140, Laws of 1860 and Chapter 172, Laws of 1862—("Enabling Acts")—the issue would have been simple of solution. Then a femme couvert was little more than a chattel herself (juridically speaking) and everything she owned became the property of the privileged male, her spouse. Advancing civilization brought with it some refinements however, for even then the Courts came gradually to the view that she should be allowed exclusive possession of the things peculiarly adaptable to her own use—such things as her wearing apparel and other items of female adornment. Valuable jewelry however, even though given to her as a gift by the husband, continued to be his property and subject to distraint by his creditors. . . .

With the advent of the "Enabling Acts" woman become free to own her own property and from that day to this the popular misconceptions above-referred to have come into being. Lawyers and laymen alike have been heard to say at one time or another that household furniture and effects are presumed to be the property of the husband, the property of the wife, and then again the property of both jointly, this without regard to who purchased it or who brought it into the marital domicile.

One things is clear and that is that no presumption in law exists as to the ownership of such items used in common by husband and wife where they were purchased with the funds of the husband or the wife or with the funds of both of them. In each case title depends on the facts.

* * *

In re Springarn's Estate, 111 N.Y.S. 2d 172, 173, . . . clearly indicates that there is no presumption of ownership of household furniture in the wife and if a gift is claimed, title must rest upon clear proof of delivery and acceptance. The case concerned household furniture in an apartment and in a farmhouse part of which was the husband's before the wife came into the picture. Sufficient proof of gift of the apartment furniture within the meaning of the law was predicated upon the following facts: 1. Declaration by the husband. 2. Exercise of control and dominion by the wife. 3. Active participation by the husband in a sale by the wife, and 4. Transfer by the husband of the fire policies on the furniture from his name to that of his wife. The rule was against the wife in connection with the farm furnishings, evidence of acts of dominion and of delivery not having been proven to the satisfaction of the Surrogate.

* * *

All of the foregoing is true in spite of the tendency of the legislature in recent years to reserve to the surviving spouse an inalienable quantum of household effects, Surrogate's Court Act, § 200, and rightly so, for the rules that apply to the disposition of decedent's estates are grounded on considerations other than the facts of title or gift to be gleaned from the conduct and acts of the living.

But what of household goods and furniture purchased with money wedding gifts or which came as gifts in kind? Does it make a difference whether the money or the object itself was delivered into the hands of the bride or of the groom—whether it came from the bride's "side" or from the groom's "side". This is the most intriguing question which this Court is called upon to answer.

The authorities . . . are few and elusive to put it mildly. Indeed I find that only Emily Post pre-

whosoever's wedding gifts?

sumes to speak with confidence in this regard. *Etiquette,* Emily Post, New and Enlarged Edition, Funk and Wagnalls Company, page 322.

> "Wedding presents are all sent to the bride, and are, *according to law, her personal property."* (Italics ours.)

It may be that in "polite" society all wedding presents are sent to the bride and as Miss Post goes on to say:

> "The bridegroom seldom receives presents. Even those who care about him in particular and have never met his bride, send their presents to her, unless they send two presents, one in courtesy to her and one in affection to him. * * *"

The fact is however that not all wedding guests have been trained in the niceties of "polite" society and unfortunately many of them have never read Miss Post's book.

More than that —there is a tendency to give money instead of things these days and in the average wedding, it is not unusual for each "side" to deliver the money gifts into the hands of its own.

While no one will challenge Miss Post's eminence as an arbiter of good taste, I doubt that her pronouncement on the law in this regard may be accorded the dignity of stare decisis. It would have been nice had she cited a competent judicial decision of such sweeping magnitude. Had she done so there would be no need for this opinion.

* * *

I cannot and do not agree however with the . . . opinion to the effect that "if a gift be made to a bride-to-be, or to a married woman, from whomever or from whencever it may come, it is hers absolutely, without any valid claim thereto by any other person whatsoever."

Donors send wedding gifts to the bride for one of three reasons: (1) Because they wish the gift to be the exclusive property of the bride in which case the character of the gift may be a clue to the intention, or the intention must be otherwise unequivocally expressed ; (2) because as Miss Post says, supra, etiquette dictates that "wedding presents are all sent to the bride" ; and finally (3), because by indicating the bride-to-be's residence on the invitation notices, the donor is politely told where to send the gift.

Whom to give the gift is dictated by custom and usage but title to the thing itself must rest on the intention of the donor and sometimes on the receivers themselves.

* * *

Shulman v. Shulman . . . N.Y. Law Journal Dec. 31, 1951, p. 1634, col. 1. This was an action by a husband for conversion by the wife of funds on deposit in a joint savings account, with a counterclaim by the wife for the value of a half interest in an automobile purchased with monies from the account in question. Here the Court dismissed both the complaint and counterclaim, saying: "* * * This account was created with funds supplied by the plaintiff and the defendant and from *wedding gifts.* * * *It is impossible to determine how much each put into this bank account.* * * *" (Italics ours.) Certainly, if nothing else, the amount of the cash wedding gifts could have been determined. Implicit in this determination no presumption of single ownership in either party was indulged in by the Court as regarded the wedding gift feature of the case.

Falk v. Falk . . . N.Y. Law Journal, March 15, 1947, page 1036, col. 1. Here too the ownership of household furniture was in issue. The Court found as facts that a wedding gift of $10,000 given by the bride's parents was given to both ; that the funds of both went into the purchase of the real estate and the furniture, and that the parties intended that the property and furniture be jointly owned. This ruling was made in spite of the fact that the husband was a young doctor and the Court was "* * * not unmindful of the practice among Jewish people (the litigants are Jews) for the bride's parents to bestow a dowry upon the groom. * * *" This is but another example of the application of the rule that no presumption as to ownership may be indulged in the case of wedding gifts and that not only the expressed intention of the giver must be taken into consideration but the intention of the wedded couple as well.

[C]ounsel for the parties has offered this Court citations . . . [which] have a value in this opinion, if only to place in true perspective certain other popular misconceptions affecting joint and trust bank accounts, and title to the contents of safe deposit boxes held in the joint names of husband and wife.

No clearer statement could have been made on the law as it affects joint bank accounts than that appearing in Marrow v. Moskowitz, 255 N.Y. 219, 174 N.E. 460, Cardozo, J.:

> "When a bank account is opened in the form prescribed by statute (Banking Law, § 249, subd. 3.), a presumption at once arises that the interest of the depositors is that of joint tenants. Upon the death of one of the depositors, this presumption becomes conclusive in favor of the survivor in respect to any monies *then* left in the account. *It continues to be a mere presumption in respect of any monies previously withdrawn."* (Italics ours).

So that it would seem that even a joint account is not conclusive on the question of ownership during the life of the depositors named.

With regard to ownership of the contents of a safety deposit box held in the joint name of husband and wife, it was held in Matter of Squibb's Estate, 95 Misc. 475, 160 N.Y.S. 826, that the commingling of securities originally separately owned, raises no presumption of gift or ownership in the survivor. They hold as tenants in common and not as joint tenants. If gift is claimed it must be proven by delivery and acceptance . . .

* * *

Coming back to the facts and issues at bar—these are my findings:

I am convinced that neither side told the full truth; that everything, except the personal effects of the wife and some $200 worth of linens was purchased with the wedding gift monies which were sufficient to cover the entire cost even after the honeymoon expenditures; that plaintiff has failed in her burden of proof to satisfy me by a fair preponderance of the credible evidence that the money wedding gifts amounted to as little as she claims or that they came entirely from the bride's "side". Moreover I find no specific proof that any such gifts came "earmarked" to be the exclusive property of the bride. Finally, there is no evidence of value as to the plaintiff's personal effects and indeed no clue to what they consisted of. Consequently, I am in no position to fasten a figure on any judgment which she may have been entitled to recover in that connection.

Accordingly, the complaint must be dismissed on the merits as to every item except the personal effects of the plaintiff, and dismissed as to those without prejudice to a new suit upon proper proof of value. Plaintiff's remedy is elsewhere but certainly not on the theory of conversion, except in the case of her personal effects.

In passing I might say that more so than in any other period in the long history of mankind, this is the age of "50-50" marriages. The time has come to say clearly that all wedding gifts whether from the bride's "side" or from the groom's, excepting such items which are peculiarly adaptable to the personal use of either spouse, and those gifts which are specifically and unequivocally "earmarked" as intended exclusively for the one or the other of the spouses, commonly intended for general use in the household, are the joint property of both parties to the marriage. This reasoning should apply as well to the things of like use purchased with cash wedding gifts not otherwise "earmarked".

NOTES

NOTE 1.

SAMSON v. SAMSON
[1960] 1 All E.R. 653, 656

. . . Where there is evidence of intention on the part of the donor it may well be that wedding presents may be found to have been given either to one spouse or to the other, or to both; but where no intention is clear the court is fully entitled to draw the inference . . . that money and gifts in kind originating from one side of the family were intended for the husband and those from the other side, from friends of that party, were intended for the wife.

NOTE 2.

GIKAS v. NICHOLIS
96 N.H. 177, 71 A. 2d 785 (1950)

KENISON, JUSTICE.

The main issue in this appeal is whether the donor of an engagement ring may recover it from the donee who terminates the engagement. By the great weight of authority recovery is allowed . . . The basis for recovery is quasi contractual, as it is considered that it is unjust for a donee to retain the fruit of a broken promise. . . .

It is not necessary and in the natural course of events it would be unusual for the donor to give the engagement ring upon the expressed condition that marriage was to ensue. Such a condition may be implied in fact or imposed by law in order to prevent unjust enrichment. . . . In this case the defendant did not testify but there is evidence from the plaintiff's testimony from which it can be found that the engagement ring was a token of the expected marriage and was given only as such.

R.L. c. 385, § 11 reads as follows: "Breach of contract to marry shall not constitute an injury or wrong recognized by law, and no action, suit, or proceeding shall be maintained therefor." . . . It is the theory . . . that the so-called heart-balm statutes not only bar breach of marriage contracts but any other proceeding which directly or indirectly arises out of the breach. Under that view gifts in contemplation of marriage may not be recovered even though unjust enrichment may result to the donee. The results of these cases have been almost uniformly criticized as being unnecessary and undesirable. . . .

It was not the intention of the New Hampshire Legislature in outlawing breach of promise suits to permit the unjust enrichment of persons to whom property had been transferred while the parties enjoyed a confidential relationship. To so construe the statute would be to permit the unjust enrichment which the statute is designed to prevent. . . .

The miscellaneous gifts of personal property other than the engagement ring stand on a different footing. While the plaintiff seeks their return neither his testimony nor the evidence takes them out of the category of absolute gifts. They were personal gratuities upon which the law imposes no condition of return and are more nearly akin to a Christmas present. . . . Such personal gratuities are considered incidental to the marital quest and recovery is not usually expected and if requested is denied. . . . The plaintiff is entitled to maintain his action for the return of the engagement ring or its value but not for return of the other personal property.

* * *

NOTE 3.

BROWN, NORMAN O.
Life Against Death*

The archaic institution of the gift is the clue to the psychology of the whole sector of the sacred-superfluous. In the archaic economy gift and countergift organize the division of labor; prestige and power are conferred by ability to give; gifts are sacred and the gods exist to receive gifts (*do* ut *des*). Hence the principle of nonenjoyment, the compulsion to work and to produce an economic surplus, is contained in the need to give. An economic surplus is created in order to have something to give; archaic man does not enjoy because he needs to give.

. . . According to Mauss, the fundamental problem is to determine what obligates the recipient of a gift to make a return gift. He assumes that the original giver needs such an assurance before he will give, an assurance that he will not lose in the transaction; here we see the assumption of a psychology of egoism. But the psychology of egoism is incapable of explaining the institution of gift exchange. For gift exchange in the archaic economy is broadly governed by the principle of reciprocity, so that although the giver may not lose, he does not gain. The psychology of egoism cannot explain activities resulting in no gain, merely no loss. The question is not what obligates the recipient of a gift to return a gift, but why give in the first place? In the end Mauss has to take the same position on the gift as Durkheim took on the division of labor: gift exchange is a primal act of social solidarity.

* Reprinted from *Life Against Death*, pp. 264-265. Copyright © 1959 by Wesleyan University. Reprinted by permission of Wesleyan University Press and Routledge & Kegan Paul Ltd.

It is a great step forward to indicate that the concrete institution of the gift creates social solidarity, and therefore that the basic psychology of human social organization may be contained in the psychology of giving. But we are not going to understand either the gift or social organization if we simply derive the gift from a not-further-analyzable principle of social solidarity.

What then is the psychology of the need to give? We have . . . postulated a connection between the need to give and the principle of nonenjoyment: that is to say, the psychology of giving takes us beyond egoism, beyond the desire for individual happiness—in Freud's phrase, beyond the pleasure-principle. Archaic gift-giving (the famous potlatch is only an extreme example) is one vast refutation of the notion that the psychological motive of economic life is utilitarian egoism. Archaic man gives because he wants to lose; the psychology is not egoist but self-sacrificial. Hence the intrinsic connection with the sacred. The gods exist to receive gifts, that is to say sacrifices; the gods exist in order to structure the human need for self-sacrifice.

NOTE 4.

KUGLING v. WILLIAMSON
231 Minn. 135, 42 N.W. 2d 534 (1950)

MATSON, JUSTICE.

In an action for damages for breach of promise to marry, wherein the jury gave plaintiff a verdict for $5,000, defendant made a motion for judgment *non obstante* or a new trial, which was granted *unless* plaintiff filed a written remittitur consenting to a reduction of $1,000 in the amount of the verdict. Plaintiff consented to the remittitur, and in consequence thereof defendant's motion for a new trial stood denied, and from this order of denial defendant appeals.

Plaintiff, of the age of 47 years, immigrated to this country from Germany in 1924 with her husband and one child . . . Her husband procured an absolute divorce from her on June 17, 1946. In the latter part of the same month, upon defendant's request, she moved to his farm, where she cooked, kept house, and assisted with the chores, garden, and field work. Defendant was then a widower with minor children. Apparently, on various occasions defendant expressed a desire to marry plaintiff. According to plaintiff defendant made a definite promise of marriage on December 15, 1946, which was two days short of the expiration of the six-month period following her divorce. That a mutual promise of marriage then existed between the parties is admitted. On December 19, 1946, the parties obtained a marriage license. Marriage, however, did not then take place, but the parties continued to live and work together on the farm as before. Plaintiff failed to get along with defendant's children, and in the latter part of December 1947 she struck one of them in defendant's presence. As a result of the altercation which followed, plaintiff left the farm on January 5, 1948. Defendant gave her a check amounting to $3,300 at that time. She spent two weeks in the hospital and then, at defendant's behest, returned to the farm, where she stayed until May 1948 when she and defendant separated for good. Clearly, the evidence will sustain a finding that plaintiff had loaned defendant a sum of money varying from $3,300 to $3,500, and that the $3,300 payment which she received from defendant was in payment of this loan. It is defendant's contention, however, that when he gave her the check for $3,300 plaintiff accepted the sum in complete settlement, pursuant to a mutual agreement whereby the parties released each other from the contract of marriage.

* * *

Defendant assigns as error the trial court's refusal to admit in evidence a marriage license issued to plaintiff and Jacob Klooz about 11 months after defendant's breach of promise. Although the general rule seems to be that plaintiff's declarations and acts, *occurring after the marriage contract was broken,* are inadmissible in mitigation of damages, whether it be by way of showing plaintiff's lack of affection for defendant at the time of their engagement or to show that she has subsequently made satisfactory marital arrangements with another . . . it is unnecessary here to determine whether such rule ought to be adopted. In the instant case, even if we were to hold such evidence admissible, there would, nevertheless, be no prejudicial error, in that the marriage license was issued about 11 months after defendant's breach and, as such, constituted evidence of so remote a character as to have little if any weight. No hard and fast rule can be laid down to fix the limitation of reasonable time as to remoteness. Whether evidence should be excluded for remoteness rests largely in the discretion of the trial court. . . . It also goes without saying that a woman may recover substantial damages for breach of promise of marriage notwithstanding her subsequent marriage to another. . . .

Is the verdict excessive as the result of passion and prejudice? . . .

An action for breach of promise is in form on contract ; but in respect of damages it is in general governed by the law applicable to tort actions . . . The amount awarded cannot be measured by any fixed standard, but in general is such sum as will compensate plaintiff for the benefits, losses, or detriments suffered as a result of the broken promise to marry. There was no error in instructing the jury that in assessing plaintiff's damages it could take into consideration defendant's financial worth, his social position, the pecuniary and social advantages plaintiff would have enjoyed had he performed his contract, as well as the mental pain and anguish she suffered as a result of the breach. . . . In view of the fact that the evidence sustains a finding that defendant owned 320 acres of farm land, of the reasonable value of $75 per acre, plus a full line of farm machinery, which was subject to an encumbrance of only $3,500, damages in the sum of $4,000 do not appear unreasonable.

* * *

NOTE 5.

FEARON v. TREANOR
272 N.Y. 268, 5 N.E. 2d 815 (1936)
cert. den. 301 U.S. 667 (1937)

HUBBS, JUDGE.

By Chapter 263 of the Laws of 1935 a new article (2-A) was added to the Civil Practice Act (section 61-a et seq.), by which civil actions to recover damages for alienation of affections, criminal conversation, seduction, and breach of promise to marry are declared to be against public policy and are abolished, . . .

* * *

The Legislature, acting within its authority, has determined as a matter of public policy that marriages should not be entered into because of the threat or danger of an action to recover money damages and the embarrassment and humiliation growing out of such an action.

We are convinced that the Legislature, in passing the statute, acted within its constitutional power to regulate the marriage relation for the public welfare. . . .

2.

SHONFELD v. SHONFELD
260 N.Y. 477, 184 N.E. 60 (1933)

CROUCH, J.

The action is to annul a marriage for fraud. . . .

Any fraud is adequate which is "material, to that degree that, had it not been practiced, the party deceived would not have consented to the marriage" and is "of such a nature as to deceive an ordinarily prudent person." (Di Lorenzo v. Di Lorenzo 67 N.E. 63, 64-65).

With so much premised, we turn to a consideration of the case at hand. The action was undefended. Plaintiff testified that for some years prior to the marriage he had been keeping company with the defendant. On several occasions when the question of marriage was brought up by the defendant, the plaintiff had stated plainly that he was in no position to marry because he was not able to make a living; that he was working on and off with his father without a regular salary and just managed to keep himself going. In May, 1930, the subject was again broached by the defendant, who suggested that if it was merely a matter of sufficient money to establish him in a business of his own, she had enough, if such an opportunity presented itself. A month later there came such an opportunity. An acquaintance, aware that the plaintiff desired to go into business, suggested a partnership in a jewelry store to be leased in the Hotel McAlpin, in the city of New York. Seven thousand dollars was required. The acquaintance was able to contribute only $1,500 or $2,000. The defendant was made acquainted with this and she told the plaintiff that she had $8,000 which would be available. From that point on she took part in the discussions with respect to the proposed business and approved the partnership arrangements and the plans of the store. A lease of the store was to be closed on July 21. Before the execution and delivery of the lease, a deposit by way of security was required. The defendant refused to furnish any money before marriage. There was a civil marriage on July 15. It was not consummated. Each party returned to the parent's home where each lived. On July 19 the plaintiff went to defendant's home to secure the amount of the required deposit on the lease. He then discovered that the defendant did not have and never had had any such money or the means of getting it. The trial court found as facts that the representations thus made were false, were believed and relied upon, did induce the plaintiff's consent to the marriage, and that if they had not been made he would not have consented. A decree was refused upon the ground that the representations did not go "to the essence of the marriage contract."

For reasons stated above, the ground of the decision is untenable. If the proof shows that the representations were of a nature to deceive an ordinarily prudent man who, but for the representations, would not have consented to the marriage, there is an adequate basis for a decree. The primary consideration in every case is the materiality of the representation viewed in the light of all circumstances by the mind, not of the individual plaintiff but of an ordinarily prudent man. To be material, the representation "must not only have induced the action taken, it must have been adequate to induce it by offering a motive suffi-

cient to influence the conduct of a man of average intelligence and prudence." 1 Bigelow on Fraud, 497. Present in every case as a circumstance which such a mind would necessarily consider is the important and irrevocable nature of the contract of marriage, affected, as it is, with a public interest and with resultant rights and duties unalterably fixed by law. The trier of fact in testing materiality by this objective standard on such a background is no doubt justified in rejecting, as immaterial, representations which in the case of other types of contract might lead to a different conclusion. Generalizations other than these may not be made. The boundaries of materiality must be pricked out by individual decisions. The question here is whether it can be said as matter of law that the representations made by defendant were not material. The Appellate Division by a divided court has in effect so said. We reach the opposite conclusion. The obligation of a husband to support a wife is no less lightly to be entered into than the other obligations of the marital relation. The ability to support is correspondingly important. While plaintiff's attitude may have been something less than heroic, realization of the responsibilities of marriage need not be condemned as sordidly mercenary. The business which defendant's mythical money was to establish was plaintiff's only prospect of supporting her. The misrepresentation was not a mere exaggeration or misstatement of her means or prospects, which might or might not be an incentive to marriage. It was a definite statement of an existing fact without which, as defendant clearly understood, no marriage was presently practicable. It cannot be said as matter of law that either reliance or materiality hang upon an unreasonable or whimsical attitude on plaintiff's part. No public policy outlaws a marriage settlement agreement . . . , and no public policy demands that prudent consideration of ability to fulfill the duty of support shall not have a legitimate place in the determination by a party of whether or not to marry.

The judgment of the Appellate Division and that of the Special Term should be reversed, and an interlocutory judgment of annulment directed in favour of plaintiff.

CRANE, J. (dissenting).

The marriage in this case was a mere matter of bargain and sale. The woman bought the man for $6,000, and because she failed to have the money the man seeks to have the marriage annulled The question really is whether the marriage ceremony in this state is of any binding force or whether it is an empty ceremony. . . .

* * *

. . . Even in annulment actions one is not to be relieved by the courts if he is so stupid and foolish as to believe statements which his own eyes or ears could have discovered to be false in the exercise of a little care. Neither are the judges and the courts to be fooled in an undefended annulment action by the whimper of a party that he was deceived, when he has no one to blame but himself. The law makes no adjustments of those marital difficulties brought about by a person's own indifference to, and disregard of, his own welfare. Care and caution are required and have been emphasized in all the cases dealing with this subject of annulment for fraud.

* * *

For failure to exercise the ordinary caution of a reasonably prudent and careful man dealing in financial matters this plaintiff can obtain no relief in equity, . . .

* * *

We must recognize that the marriage contract can never be on a par with other civil contracts because of its very nature. Other contracts deal with money values or property interests ; not so, the marriage contract. Money damages can be ascertained, at least by approximation, for the breach of a civil contract, and even for the breaking of a promise to marry, but no such element finds place in the contract of marriage itself. The utmost the law can do is to dissolve the status for fraud or for disability. Every jurisdiction recognizes that marriage procured by false and fraudulent representations may be annulled in equity. What are the false and fraudulent representations which the courts will consider material? The difference in opinion, as found in the decisions, is over this question of materiality. Surely every representation leading up to marriage cannot be material—the fact that a brunette turned to a blond over night or that the beautiful teeth were discovered to be false, or the ruddy pink complexion gave way suddenly to pallor, or that a woman misstated her age or was not in perfect health, would lead no court to annul the marriage for fraud. . . .

Fraud assumes many different forms and it has always been impossible to predict just how it will appear. No definite rule can be stated for matrimonial actions any easier than it can be stated for any other class of fraud actions. We may say, however, that because of the importance of the marriage contract and the status established thereby the courts will not treat the matter lightly and will only deal with those representations which are serious, grave, and important ; the representations must be proved by clear and convincing evidence to have been a vital and dominant element in entering into the contract. What induces a man to marry a woman? Who can tell? Are the judges wiser than other men? This is a matter which better not be inquired into too inquisitively, as it has baffled the philosophers of all ages. Law moves not upon supposition or guess, but upon evidence. The false representations inducing a marriage must be so weighty and material that the courts can say that they would have influenced the consent of a man of average intelligence and prudence. . . .

* * *

Most of the annulment cases upon the ground of fraud are defaults. The parties seek by this easy means to obtain a decree dissolving the bonds of matrimony. In a divorce case based upon adultery the innocent party is prohibited from testifying. Whatever he or she knows about the guilt of the other cannot be told. Not so in annulment cases. The plaintiff becomes a ready witness and glibly recites his or her story in the absence and default of the other party. This has led the courts to say that the proofs should be strong and convincing in these annulment cases, and that the false representations must go to a vital part of the marriage contract. It should clearly appear not only that the representations were made but the facts stated were of such weight and seriousness as to induce reasonable persons similarly situated to rely and act upon them.

* * *

NOTES

NOTE 1.

MONTAGU, M.F.A.

Marriage—A Cultural Perspective*

Perhaps one of the most striking characteristics of marriage in our culture is the fact that it is based upon the concept of romantic love. This concept of love, developed in the twelfth and thirteenth centuries among the nobility of France, was characterized by a complete abdication of all selfish motives, complete fealty and a complete idealization of the beloved. Love was held to be a matter of free exchange, and that which was freely given was conceived to be vastly superior to the dutiful relationship supposed to exist be-

* Reprinted in Eisenstein, V.W.: *Neurotic Interaction in Marriage*. New York: Basic Books, Inc., 1956, pp. 4-5. Reprinted with permission of the publisher.

tween husband and wife in marriages that were arranged by parents or overlords.

The concept of romantic love, appealing as it did to women, has been handed down through the centuries and is now held by most women in our own culture—but not by most men. Romantic love does, of course, govern the male's courtship behavior. During this period he behaves much like the adoring lover described by the twelfth-century troubadours. But after marriage, the male—because he has never been culturally conditioned to it—cannot maintain the role of romantic lover, and the wife's disillusionment at the change in him is one of the causes of marital dissatisfaction. Such disillusionment does not occur, of course, in other cultures, in which romantic love plays no part.

Closely related to the romantic ideal is the notion that a principal function of marriage is to increase one's personal happiness. . . . Since happiness is not likely to be achieved by purposeful pursuit, this hedonistic view leads almost inevitably to some degree of disappointment and disillusionment in marriage. . . .

NOTE 2.

TUCHSHER v. TUCHSHER
16 Misc. 2d 1, 184 N.Y.S. 2d 131 (1959)

BENJAMIN BRENNER, JUSTICE

Action to annul a marriage for fraud.

Plaintiff wife was fifty-six years of age when she married her husband and lived with him for about two months when she discovered that he did not earn $200 weekly, as represented, and that he did not possess a paid-up insurance policy for $16,000, relative to which he had promised to name her beneficiary. These representations, she insists, were the all important conditions of the marriage. Plaintiff readily testified that hers was no love match but that she could get used to the defendant in time. Apparently even this minimal requirement for marital happiness was unattainable because the $100 weekly house and table money was not forthcoming and the $16,000 paid-up policy turned out to be a cancelled $1,500 policy.

* * *

Plaintiff undoubtedly expected her second matrimonial venture to be her last. Factors taken into account by younger or more romantic women, such as affection and compatibility, could but take second place in her thoughts, and while I suspect that there were some aspects of bargain and sale here, plaintiff's prime consideration was that of security in a not too distant old age. To this plaintiff, representations of good earnings and ownership of a substantial paid-up policy were most important. Certainly their falsity constituted no mere disappointment in the material wealth of the spouse. Average prudence and intelligence vary with each classification of persons and often the age, sex, physical and financial condition of the party determine the weight and impact of the misrepresentation claimed as grounds for the sought after dissolution. Thus, if average prudence and intelligence be the test of the materiality of promises made to induce a marriage, this plaintiff has met that test.

I find on the evidence that the plaintiff is entitled to a judgment dissolving the marriage. This opinion shall constitute the findings of fact and conclusions of law.

NOTE 3.

Delaware Code, Tit. 13, § 101(c) (1953)

A marriage between paupers is prohibited, and is void from the time its nullity is declared by a court of competent jurisdiction at the instance of the innocent party.

NOTE 4.

KERSHNER v. KERSHNER
244 App. Div. 34, 278 N.Y.S. 501 (1935)
aff'd. 269 N.Y. 655, 200 N.E. 43 (1936)

MARTIN, PRESIDING JUSTICE.

The plaintiff seeks to annul a marriage contracted between the parties more than ten years prior to the commencement of this action. The alleged basis for said annulment is that the marriage was induced by false and fraudulent representations on the part of the defendant.

It is alleged that prior to the marriage the plaintiff was engaged in the study of medicine with the intention of preparing himself to follow the profession of surgeon, involving a number of years training and study after being licensed to practice as a physician, and that the defendant had full knowledge of that intention and knew that during such period of preparation the plaintiff would have no income or earnings. To induce the plaintiff to consent to the marriage, defendant represented that she was a person of independent means and able to support herself, and that, if plaintiff married her, she would not demand of plaintiff any support or maintenance for a number of years following the marriage, and would not require the plaintiff to engage in any income-producing employment until after plaintiff qualified as a skilled and fully competent surgeon, and would not demand of plaintiff that he establish a home, but would continue to reside with her parents; further promising that in the interim she would cohabit with the plaintiff and perform her marital duties in the same manner as if he had established a home and provided for her support and maintenance. Shortly after the performance of the marriage defendant demanded that plaintiff abandon his plans to qualify as a surgeon, and demanded that he practice as a physician in order to earn an income to establish a home; defendant in the meantime refusing to consummate the marriage by sexual cohabitation with the plaintiff. It is further alleged that defendant took available steps to, and did, compel the plaintiff to abandon certain courses of training. It is asserted that the defendant had no intention at any time of fulfilling her aforesaid promises, but, on the contrary, intended at all times to endeavor to compel the plaintiff to give up his surgical training and to devote his efforts to providing a home for the defendant. The complaint finally alleges that the falsity of the aforesaid representations was but recently discovered and could not have been discovered sooner, due to the defendant's concealment of her state of mind.

* * *

The order was properly granted, since the promise upon which the plaintiff relies is invalid because contrary to public policy and one which will not receive the sanction of the courts. Conditional marriages are not tolerated in this state. This action is only another instance of the extent to which these annulment actions have gone.

The contract of marriage is not alone a personal contract between the parties. It creates a status which is a matter of public interest and incidental to which arise certain quasi public duties and obligations which may not be altered or abrogated by any agreement of the parties. Among these is the obligation of the husband to maintain and support his wife. Not only is it against the settled public policy of the state to permit such obligation to be abrogated or suspended by agreement of the parties, but it is expressly prohibited by the Domestic Relations Law, § 51, which provides in part as follows: "But a husband and wife can not contract to alter or dissolve the marriage or to relieve the husband from his liability to support his wife."

* * *

In the case at bar, an adequate excuse for defendant's refusal to cohabit is presented by the failure of the plaintiff to perform his marital obligations of providing a home and maintenance for the defendant, and such failure and refusal on his part . . . is a bar to the maintenance by him of this action.

* * *

NOTE 5.

HENLEY v. FOSTER
220 Ala. 420, 125 So. 662 (1930)

BOULDIN, J. . . . .

Annulment proceedings differ materially from those for divorce. Divorce with us is statutory. Annulment rests upon general equity powers. Divorce fixes the future marital status; annulment, that of the past and present. Still, they are kindred proceedings. Both relate to the marriage status; both concern the social order.

3.

TROHA v. SNELLER
169 Ohio St. 397, 159 N.E. 2d 899 (1959)

ZIMMERMAN, JUDGE.

A decision in this case turns on an interpretation of the prenuptial agreement between Pauline Troha and the decedent and on the surrounding facts existing before and after its execution and following the death of Philip.

[I]n 1946 Philip Troha and Paulina or Pauline Yerkic, being adult persons and each having a substantial amount of property and each having four grown children by prior marriages, decided to enter the bonds of matrimony. On July 29, 1946, Philip Troha, as party of the first part, and Paulina Yerkic, as party of the second part, executed a prenuptial agreement, witnessed and notarized, the material parts of which read as follows:

"Whereas, each is seized of property real and personal, said parties have agreed and do hereby agree as to their property as follows:

"Now, therefore, in consideration of said marriage and of the covenants of the said first party and second party hereinafter contained, the said first party hereby covenants and agrees to relinquish all right, title, interest, or claims of dower, in and to the real property of said second party now owned or hereafter acquired, and in lieu of any and all rights or claims to a distributive share of said second party now owned or hereafter acquired and in lieu of any and all rights or claims in or to the estate of the said second party which may arise by virtue of said marriage.

"And the said second party, in consideration of said marriage and of the convenants of said first party hereinafter contained, covenants and agrees to relinquish all rights or claims of dower in and to the real property of said first party now owned or hereafter acquired, and in lieu of any and all right, title, interest, or claims to a distributive share of first party's personal property now owned or hereafter acquired, and in lieu of any and all rights or claims in or to the estate of the said first party which may arise or accrue by virtue of said marriage, and both parties mutually agree that at no time will they claim any right, title or interest in the real or personal property now owned by them previous to their marriage, and in the event either party to this agreement should sell any of their real property and acquire other real property, each party to this agreement waives all their right, title and interest in and to the same, and that at the death of either party to this agreement said real property shall go to the children of the respective parties to this agreement.

"It is further agreed that each party to this agreement shall pay their own taxes, insurance and upkeep of their own premises.

* * *

"It is further agreed by and between the parties to this agreement that in the event there should be a dissolution of this marriage, either by law or by death, that then the respective parties to this agreement agree to give instruments of conveyance releasing any and all of their right, title and interest in each other's property.

* * *

Philip and Pauline decided on a trip to Europe in the summer of 1957. In late June, he withdrew $2,058.78 from a joint and survivorship bank account, carried in the names of himself and his son, to pay expenses connected with the trip. Philip and Pauline embarked for Paris on July 1, by airplane, and he died during the flight. On July 2, his children were advised of his death by cablegram from Paris. Although it is not wholly clear, the conclusion seems warranted that through a Cleveland undertaker the Troha children made arrangements for the return home of their father's body for burial, and that the total funeral expenses amounted to $2,169.98.

Pauline continued on the European trip, apparently exhibiting little interest concerning her husband's remains or his funeral. If she disclosed her whereabouts, such fact does not appear from the evidence. At any rate, she did not return to America until about the middle of October 1957, and she was not a witness in the Probate Court hearing.

. . . It was the view of the Court of Appeals that, by her conduct and protracted absence, the widow forfeited any right she may have had to administer her deceased husband's estate, and, furthermore, that under the terms of the prenuptial agreement she possessed no interest in the estate which entitled her to administer it.

The Court of Appeals also held that by the clear and unambiguous language of the prenuptial agreement each of the parties thereto surrendered and relinquished all possible rights in the property of the other . . .

* * *

Although strong and unmistakable language in a prenuptial agreement is necessary to deprive a surviving spouse, and particularly a widow, of the special benefits conferred by statute, we think that the agreement herein was designed and intended to do just that, and that it was the plain intention of the parties to accomplish that object.

We know of no public policy in Ohio and no statutory enactments or court decisions which prevent the parties to a prenuptial agreement, situated as were Philip and Pauline, from cutting one another off entirely from any participation in the estate of the other upon the death of either.

* * *

Judgment affirmed.

B.

To Decisions Concerning the Administration of Wife-Husband Relationships?—From Love to Support

1.

BLACK, HILLEL

Buy Now, Pay Later*

As Ralph Homer placed his wallet on the night table, he reflected on the good life. He was blessed with a lovely wife and two fine children. A rising young executive employed by a growing

* New York: William Morrow and Co., 1961, pp. 3-8, Copyright 1961 by Hillel Black. By permission of William Morrow and Co.

company, he had just moved his family into a new Cape Cod House. Though the future was understandably vague, Ralph Homer was secure in his belief that nothing but the best would happen. It seemed that he had every reason to be a man contented. Take today as an example. It had been, as he had remarked to his wife Alice, one of those complete, well spent days. Indeed it had.

The day began when Ralph drove downtown to work. He had stopped at a service station to buy gasoline. Ralph discovered his wallet was empty, but paid the $3.40 with his petroleum credit card.

At noon Ralph met Alice in the office lobby. Their first stop was an elegant restaurant. Lunch including drinks and tip cost $15.80. Ralph paid the bill with his all-purpose credit card.

Ever since they had moved to the suburbs Alice had been complaining that they needed a second car. So after lunch the Homers dropped in on an auto dealer. They had seen an ad in the Sunday paper offering one of those new "compacts" for no money down and thirty-six months to pay. The salesman told Ralph the car would cost him only $63.50 a month. Ralph decided he could manage the payments and signed the sales contract with no more than a glance before returning to work.

Alice planned to spend the remainder of the afternoon shopping. She carried no cash. Instead, her handbag contained a half-dozen bank charge-it cards and charga-plates. She also had four pocketbook-size directories which listed all the stores she could shop at without cash.

At a little after five Alice met Ralph at the garage near the office. She wore the smile of a triumphant woman. She had just bought a $90 dress for $59.95, a pair of $42 blue suede shoes for $29.50 and a $39 smoking jacket (for Ralph's birthday) for $28. The way Alice figured it, her bargain hunting had saved the Homer household $53.55. In reality, she had just added $177.45 to the Homer debt. But neither Ralph nor Alice would be aware of it immediately. Various revolving credit plans through which Alice made her purchases meant that the Homers would be paying only $9.78 a month for the next year. Of course, they would also be paying 18 per cent true annual interest on the declining balance. But Alice and Ralph never calculated finance charges, service charges or interest.

When Ralph started the car, he noticed a slip of paper on the windshield. It was a reminder that the garage bill was overdue. Although neither Ralph nor Alice had any money with them, Ralph decided to pay the bill—it came to $30—with an *Instant Money* check. The Homers did not possess any of the usual checking accounts since they no longer could afford to maintain even a minimal balance. But they did have an *Instant Money* check book with which they could write almost as many checks as they wanted and then pay back the amounts of the checks in monthly installments. It was the same as borrowing money without going to the bank. Ralph made out an *Instant Money* check for $50, which not only paid the garage bill but gave him $20 in cash.

As the Homers returned in their still-to-be-paid-for car to their mortgaged home with its still-to-be-paid-for washer, dryer and living room furniture, they might have considered the fact, that already weighed down with debts, they had increased their obligations by $2472.65. They had not only managed seven transactions without exchanging a penny of cash but had ended the day with twenty dollars "more" than they had started with. If you had asked them about the state of their finances, they would have told you that theirs is an expertly managed, intelligently budgeted family. All of which was true the day the Homers married. But it wasn't long before they began building their nest on credit. And as their hopes and needs expanded, so did their debts. Today, the Homers' future is pinned to the salary Ralph has yet to make. As a homeowner and man who has so far paid his bills, he has no trouble obtaining more debt. Now, six years after Ralph and Alice's marriage, the Homers not only have no liquid assets but have mortgaged their future for years to come. In effect, they are practicing a sort of family financial brinkmanship. Perhaps what is most disturbing is that they do not even know it.

* * *

Currently about one hundred million Americans are participating in the buy-now, pay-later binge. Furthermore, they can, if they wish, do anything and everything on credit. Babies are being born on the installment plan, children go through college on time, even funerals are being paid for on what the English quaintly call "the never never." Through debt people are buying hairpins, toothpaste, mink coats, girdles, tickets to baseball games, religious medallions, hi-fi equipment, safaris in Africa. Most of these items were sold for the first time on *time* only during the last decade. For example, half of all the furniture, TV sets, washing machines and outboard motorboats are bought on *time,* in addition to two-thirds of all new cars. The result has been a consumer credit explosion that makes the population explosion seem small by comparison.

The enormous force of this explosion can be measured by these figures. All consumer debt, that is debt owned by individuals as distinguished from business or the government, totals a staggering $195 billion, nearly a 200 per cent increase over the past ten years. In the same period consumer's disposable income increased only 60 per cent. A breakdown shows that Americans currently owe $139 billion in home mortgages and $56 billion in intermediate and short term debt, or what the Federal Government calls "consumer credit." This $56 billion debt includes money owed on cars, appliances, home repairs, small loans, charge accounts, revolving credit and credit cards. Consumer credit—the key to the rise in private debt—has increased over 550 per cent since 1940. In the last ten years it has more than doubled. By 1970 experts predict consumer credit will reach $107 billion, or nearly double again.

And how is all this credit being paid for? The money comes not only out of people's current but also future earnings. As we enter the nineteen sixties the American people must work over two months out of twelve to reimburse their creditors . . .

* * *

Companion with the consumer credit explosion has been the emergence of a new type of entrepreneur, the debt merchant. Although people throughout the ages have made profit through the sale of debt, this is the first time that debt merchandising has been conducted on such a gigantic scale. Today, every auto dealer, commercial bank, department store, small loan operator, sales finance company, as well as nearly every Main Street retailer is in the business of selling debt.

NOTES

NOTE 1.

SPELLMAN v. SPELLMAN
[1961] 2 All E.R. 498

DANCKWERTS, L.J., . . . : This is a case which has raised some interesting points and may perhaps be said to illustrate the complexities caused by modern life and the practice of obtaining property on hire-purchase [credit]. [T]he subject-matter of the controversy concerns a certain motor car, an Austin Healey Sprite. The complications are very considerable. It is a dispute between husband and wife and the proceedings before us are a summons taken out under the provisions of the Married Women's Property Act, 1882, s. 17. The parties were married on Mar. 24, 1957, and there is a child of the marriage. Their relations became less happy than it was hoped they would be, and matters were in rather a serious state in the early part of 1960. There was some idea—I do not want to put it any higher than that—that the purchase of another motor car might bring the parties together perhaps in the same manner as it is often suggested that the birth of a child may effect a similar result. The idea does not appear to have been successful. The purchase of a motor car was discussed, and the evidence seems to establish that it was agreed between the husband and wife, by which phrase I do not mean to describe any legal condition, but the colour was chosen and the car was acquired. It was delivered to the home of the parties by the agent or car dealer; the wife saw it through the window and asked whether that was the car which the husband had bought for her and he said that it was. The registration book or log book, as it is sometimes called, was put in the name of the wife and this was done by the husband for reasons which were not entirely clear, but which may possibly have had something to do with the question of insurance. The parties again fell out and the husband left his wife, taking the car with him. The wife in fact had never driven the car because apparently it had a kind of gear change with a gear lever to which she was not accustomed. She was in fact driving at the time a Ford Zephyr motor car with the operation of which she was acquainted and which for the time being suited her purpose, but the intention undoubtedly was that the wife should be taught to drive the Austin Healey in course of time. It was only a matter of some three weeks before the break up occurred and the husband went off taking the car with him.

* * *

. . . The wife . . . claimed that the motor car was a gift from her husband to her and she denied that there was any understanding at any time that she held the motor car in trust for him. It is probable that the parties originally had no conception of the position of the motor car except that of an ordinary gift of a motor car, a chattel, from the husband to the wife. But it turned out, . . . that it was the subject of a hire-purchase agreement . . . and that was really a fatal obstacle to the delivery of the motor car as a gift in the ordinary way. The hire-purchase agreement was in the usual form in which such things are drawn up, and the property in the motor car was in the hire-purchase company and not in the husband at all. Consequently it was impossible for him to make a delivery of what he did not own. . . . There were provisions that the car should be kept in repair, that the hirer should pay the rent in respect of the premises where the car was kept, there was a provision against assignment of the hire-purchase agreement or the benefit thereof, and there was a prohibition against the hirer parting with possession. . . . [N]o gift could be made until the husband had acquired the car by the final payment. On that view of the matter it is impossible to sustain the claim of the wife based on the theory of a gift of the car. . . .

NOTE 2.

CALIFORNIA CIVIL CODE
Husband and Wife (1957)

§155. *Mutual Obligations of Husband and Wife.* Husband and wife contract towards each other obligations of mutual respect, fidelity, and support.

§156. *Rights of Husband, as Head of Family.* The husband is the head of the family. He may choose any reasonable place or mode of living, and the wife must conform thereto.

§157. *Separate property; dwelling.* Neither husband nor wife has any interest in the property of the other; but neither can be excluded from the other's dwelling.

§158. *Husband and Wife May Make Contracts.* Either husband or wife may enter into any engagement or transaction with the other, or with any other person, respecting property, which either might if unmarried. . . .

§159. *Contracts; property; separation.* A husband and wife cannot, by any contract with each other, alter their legal relations, except as to property, and except that they may agree, in writing, to an immediate separation, and may make provision for the support of either of them and of their children during such separation.

§160. *Consideration for Agreement of Separation.* The mutual consent of the parties is a sufficient consideration for such an agreement as is mentioned in the last section.

§161. *May be Joint Tenants, etc.* A husband and wife may hold property as joint tenants, tenants in common, or as community property.

§161a. *Community property*; interests of parties *defined.* The respective interests of the husband and wife in community property during continuance of the marriage relation are present, existing and equal interests under the management and control of the husband . . .

§162. *Separate Property of the Wife.* All property of the wife, owned by her before marriage, and that acquired afterwards by gift, bequest, devise, or descent, with the rents, issues, and profits thereof, is her separate property. The wife may, without the consent of her husband, convey her separate property.

§163. *Separate Property of the Husband.* All property owned by the husband before marriage, and that acquired afterwards by gift, bequest, devise, or descent, with the rents, issues, and profits thereof, is his separate property.

§166. *Separate personal property; effect of recording inventory.* The filing of the inventory in the recorder's office is notice and prima facie evidence of the title of the party filing such inventory.

§168. *Wife's earnings; husband's debts; necessities.* The earnings of the wife are not liable for the debts of the husband; but, except as otherwise provided by law, such earnings shall be liable for the payment of debts, heretofore or hereafter contracted by the husband or wife for the necessities of life furnished to them or either of them while they are living together.

§169.1 *Separate property; earnings and accumulations after separate maintenance judgment.* After the rendition of a judgment or decree for separate maintenance the earnings or accumulations of each party are the separate property of the party acquiring such earnings or accumulations.

§170. *Wife's premarital debts; non-liability of husband's earnings and separate property.* Neither the separate property of the husband nor his earnings after marriage is liable for the debts of the wife contracted before the marriage.

§172. *Community personal property; management and control; restrictions on disposition.* The husband has the management and control of the community personal property, with like absolute power of disposition, other than testamentary, as he has of his separate estate; *provided, however,* that he can not make a gift of such community personal property, or dispose of the same without a valuable consideration, or sell, convey, or encumber the furniture, furnishings or fittings of the home, or the clothing or wearing apparel of the wife or minor children that is community, without the written consent of the wife.

* * *

§174. *Support of Wife; necessaries.* If the husband neglect to make adequate provision for the support of his wife, . . . any other person may, in good faith, supply her with articles necessary for her support, and recover the reasonable value thereof from the husband.

§175. *Support of wife on abandonment or separation.* A husband abandoned by his wife is not liable for her support until she offers to return, unless she was justified by his misconduct, in abandoning him, and the earnings of the husband during the period of unjustified abandonment, prior to such offer, are his separate property; nor is a husband liable for his wife's support when she is living separate from him, by agreement, unless such support is stipulated in the agreement.

|§176. *Support of husband.* The wife must support the husband, when he has not deserted her, out of her separate property, when he has no separate property, and there is no community property, and he is unable, from infirmity, to support himself.

§177. *Rights of Husband Governed by What.* The property rights of husband and wife are governed by this Chapter, unless there is a marriage settlement containing stipulations contrary thereto.

2.

LESTER v. LESTER
195 Misc. 1034, 87 N.Y.S. 2d 517 (Dom. Rel. Ct. 1949)

PANKEN, JUSTICE.

* * *

A marriage procured in consequence of coercion or fraud will be regarded ab initio as if the marriage had not been entered into at all. Marriages procured by coercion or in consequence of fraud may in a court having jurisdiction be annulled. An annulment of a marriage is a determination that the conventional relationship of man and wife had not been established despite and in face of a marriage ceremony.

Marriage presumably is a relationship into which individuals enter upon freely and voluntarily. Environmental influences, and that means education, conventions at a given time and in a given place, and economic status of the parties sometimes control the character of the freedom and the voluntary attitudes of the parties entering into the marriage relationship. To that extent the freedom exercised in a marriage contract is limited.

Under our form of government the right of the individual is supreme. He may not be coerced to do that which the law does not permit or which society does not sanction. Rights are limited to the extent that their exercise impinges upon the rights of others. Individual liberty and desires are limited when in their exercise they trespass upon the rights of others, the community of individuals; freedom of the individual is circumscribed to avoid and prevent hurt to those amongst whom and with whom one lives. That defines public policy.

The welfare of most is the purpose of all democratic government. In authoritarian regimes or in absolute governments the welfare of the governing group is made by them supreme and so the welfare of the many is disregarded; the many do not participate in establishing governmental

policies and the dictates of government. Public policy reflects the need of the many, nevertheless, protecting the few. It is the expression of the need and the will of the majority and the conservation of the rights of the minority. That is public policy as conceived in and as part of democracy.

The state and the community are interested in and concerned with the institution which marriage creates. Man enters a marital relationship to perpetuate the species. The family is the result of marital relationship. It is the institution which determines in a large measure the environmental influences, cultural backgrounds, and even economic status of its members. It is the foundation upon which society rests and is the basis for the family and all of its benefits.

The character of the culture and civilization, the morals, conventions, law and relationship in the life of a community are what man develops. The community, man, has a vital interest in the marriage institution, for the present generation is father to the succeeding one, and that generation will be the determinant as to the advance of civilization, morals, law and relationships of the future. The character of the succeeding generation is influenced by the permanence and decency of the family institution. Public policy enlists and commands the need of regulation of marriage, and the course that the family institution is to pursue. Though marriage is a free institution to be entered into freely and voluntarily because of the community's interest in that institution, the state has a right to regulate and insist upon decency and morals in its maintenance.

Agreements entered into ante-nuptially between parties which do violence to the accepted conventions and laws of the state and the community are unenforceable as a matter of public policy.

The petitioner and the respondent were married according to law. The respondent claims that no valid marriage was entered into; that it was never intended to be a real marriage. He introduced in evidence two documents bearing upon his claim. One exhibited in part reads, "Know all men by these presents that whereas C.L. can no longer bear to continue her relationship with N.C.L. in the same way as in the past, but at the same time is not willing to give him up; and whereas she is desirous of reestablishing herself in the good graces of her relatives and friends; and whereas considering all things, this cannot be done unless said relatives and friends are given the impression that N.C.L. has married her; and whereas, for personal reasons, she can no longer continue staying with her sister, B.C., but must seek a place of her own; for these and other reasons important only to herself, * * * " and then the document proceeds to set forth that that was the reason and purpose for the marriage between the parties. Another portion of the same document reads, "N.C.L. hereby states, and C.L. hereby admits, that the pretended and spurious marriage contract and ceremonies, and simulated marriage relationship, is taking place against N.C.L.'s wishes, and only because of serious and dire threats of all types made against him and against herself by C.L. ; and because of the understanding that the relationship being thus established is only for the benefit of C.L., and hence is not to be interpreted under any conditions as an actual marriage; and that the said relationship involves no obligations of any kind whatsoever, now or at any time in the future, on the part of N.C.L. * * *." Upon those grounds the respondent bases his claim that the marriage is not valid and the obligations which naturally flow from a marriage relationship in favor of the petitioner do not exist. He accepted the benefits of that relationship. He cannot blow hot and cold.

The other exhibit in part reads that both the petitioner and the respondent "do hereby declare that the marriage ceremony we went through at Elkton, Maryland, is in pursuance of our agreement and contract of August 27, 1938," (the date of the other exhibit) "and we therefore consider the marriage ceremony and contract performed between us at Elkton, Maryland, null and void in all its parts and implications whatsover, ab initio."

Contracts resulting from force or fear, or procured by coercion are unenforceable. Contracts to be valid must be entered upon voluntarily, freely.

This court partakes of the nature of a civil tribunal. In Kane v. Necci, 269 N.Y. 13, 198 N.E. 613, the Court of Appeals of our State has definitely construed the Act creating the Domestic Relations Court of the City of New York to be a court partaking of the nature of a civil forum. Under civil law contracts procured by force or fear or coercion may be set aside by courts of equity. However, it must be clear that the contract was entered into in consequence of oppression, coercion, fright or fear. An assertion that a contract was procured because of coercion is not sufficient to set aside the contract by a court of equity nor can this court disregard it. Particularly is that true in the case where the contract contemplates a marriage.

Has the marriage contract entered into between the parties before me been the result of coercion, threat, force, fraud or other taint? That question must be determined from the evidence in the case and the surrounding circumstances attending the relationship between the parties.

It has been held by our courts that a formal marriage ceremony of itself does not constitute a binding marriage if it is shown that the marriage ceremony was the result of coercion, force, fraud or some other taint.

* * *

The testimony as well as the documentary evidence submitted herein negatives the assertion that this marriage was entered upon as the result of threat or coercion.

Private individuals may not by agreement set aside the law of the land. They may not declare that which is valid in law null and void. Law is and should be the expressed will of the majority. It is binding upon those who agree as well as upon those who disagree with the effects, force and purposes of the law. Persons may not enter upon a marital relationship in conformity with the law and then dissolve that marriage in violation of law. As a matter of public policy the regulation of divorce is as important as is that of marriage. The parties hereto did sign a paper which is in evidence that they both declared their marriage to be "null and void" in all its parts and implications whatsover "ab initio." What they have signed and sealed after they have entered into a marriage relationship is not enforceable as a matter of law when the purport of that agreement runs counter to the established law and to the morals and mores and conventions of the society in which they live.

The respondent's claim of coercion or threat seems to be unfounded in the light of his relationship for about ten years with the petitioner subsequent to the agreements upon which he rests his claim to invalidity of the marital relationship.

* * *

In the course of the hearing before me it was testified by the respondent repeatedly that he had been under duress during the entire period of their marital relationship. He testified, for instance, that he had had intimate relations with her, sexually, under duress. In other words he was coerced by her to have sexual relations with her. His explanation when asked what the duress was which she exercised, was "The constant fear of committing suicide and leaving me, blackening my name at the College and blackening my name so that I would lose my employment." The respondent before me is a teacher in some college and oddly he teaches the law of family relations. Evidently he thought himself familiar with the law when he caused the petitioner to sign the two documents above referred to. It is quite odd. He prepared the documents in anticipation of a claim by him that the marriage was entered into by him because of coercion and threat.

I find as a matter of fact and as a matter of law for all purposes that the petitioner has established by fair preponderance the allegations in her petition. She is the wife of the respondent and continues to be such until the marriage is annulled by a court of competent jurisdiction, if at all. In this case the respondent claims that there has been no marriage and the only method in which he might be relieved of his obligation as the petitioner's husband is by an annulment of the marriage. It is very questionable indeed whether he could possibly prevail. Indeed, I think he could not.

The petitioner testified that she is unable to work because of illness. The testimony of her spouse supports her statement that she is too ill to work. He testified of her extreme nervousness.

The respondent who is represented by able counsel argues that the petitioner herein is entitled to support on the basis of her likelihood to become a public charge; that she is not entitled to support according to the means of which the respondent is possessed or is able to gather.

It is incredible that a man who teaches in a college and who lectures and counsels on family relations would continue to live and have relations with a woman for a period of ten years under duress. It is inconceivable that a man may by duress be compelled to have intimate relations. It is peculiar counsel which he gave himself. The petitioner is undoubtedly a very nervous person and so is the respondent. They probably should not have entered upon any marital relationship at all, but they did, and when the respondent entered upon that relationship he assumed certain obligations, duties and responsibilities. He obligated himself to provide for his wife according to her needs or his means. The testimony does not permit a finding that her conduct was such as would justify the respondent's leaving her. His testimony is that he left her and that he had on quite a number of occasions indicated his desire to leave; there was an abandonment by the respondent of the petitioner. The law is that one must not live with his wife or she with her husband if conditions were made unbearable by the acts of one or the other parties to the relationship. I find in this case that there was an abandonment by the respondent of the petitioner, and so direct that the respondent contribute to her support according to his means. See order filed.

NOTES

NOTE 1.

COMMONWEALTH v. LAZAROU
180 Pa. Super. 342, 119 A. 2d 605 (1956)

ROSS, JUDGE.

This is an appeal by Louis Lazarou from a support order entered in favor of his wife under the provisions of section 733 of the Act of June 24, 1939, P.L. 872, 18 P.S. § 4733.

The parties were married in September 1952 while Louis was in medical school and his wife, Rita, was but one month short of graduating from college. After her graduation, the wife obtained employment as a teacher in the Philadelphia school system and is earning about $2,800 a year gross salary. From that time until the separation, she supported herself and her husband while he continued his schooling. Louis earned nothing while going to school and contributed nothing toward the maintenance expenses. The parties separated in February 1955 and have since lived apart. At the hearing held on June 8, 1955, it developed that Louis was graduating in four days and that he was then leaving to serve his internship at a California hospital where he would earn $75 a month plus room and board. After the hearing, the lower court entered an order of $100 a month and this appeal followed.

Appellant contends that (1) under the circumstances there has been no failure or neglect to support appellee, therefore, *no* order should have been entered, and (2) if there is basis in fact and law for *some* order, the present one is excessive. Initial proceedings for the support of a wife are essentially two-fold in nature: to establish in the first instance the obligation to provide support, and in the second instance, the amount which is reasonable and proper for her comfortable support and maintenance. Subsequent proceedings are generally only concerned with changes in the amount by reason of changed circumstances. . . .

The obligation of appellant has more than adequately been settled here. The Act provides: "If any husband * * * being within the limits of this Commonwealth separates himself from his wife * * * without reasonable cause, or neglects to maintain his wife * * *" the court may order him, "* * * being of sufficient ability, to pay such sum as said court shall think reasonable and proper * * *." Appellant never contributed to the support of his wife; he separated himself from her within the limits of Pennsylvania; he attempted at the hearing but failed to show that he left with reasonable cause. Nothing was produced indicating any conduct on the part of his wife which would entitle him to a divorce and consequently relieve him of the duty to support. . . . Whether the separation was consensual or not is immaterial. . . . The record amply supports the lower court's finding that appellant left without reasonable cause. Appellant also contends that his limited income and that his wife's earnings are a complete bar to his obligation to support. There is no duty upon a married woman to reduce the liability of her husband for support by obtaining employment, . . . nor does the fact that she has some earnings deprive her of her right to support from her husband. . . . Where she is employed and has a separate income, then of course her earnings should be considered in fixing the amount which is reasonable to maintain her. . . . But it does not follow as appellant contends that her separate earnings will completely relieve him of that which is his primary duty. Under the circumstances here presented there was no error in finding that the appellant has a legal obligation to support his wife. However, we believe that the order must be modified.

The lower court quite agrees that the order is excessive if based upon appellant's earnings as an intern, but concluded that he had a far greater earning capacity than that of an intern, stating that "a graduate of a medical school has ample opportunity to earn more than seventy-five ($75.) per month. Among such opportunities are pharmaceutical manufacturing companies which to our own knowledge are happy to pay non-graduates of a medical school well over One Hundred Dollars ($100.) per week." Appellee cites in support of this reasoning Commonwealth ex rel. Wieczorkowski v. Wieczorkowski, 155 Pa. Super. 517, 38 A. 2d 347. There the husband was a pharmacist who was working in his mother's small drug store. His defense to the support action by his wife was that he earned nothing more than his room and board. This Court affirmed an order based upon his present earning *capacity* because: "* * * qualified as he is as a registered pharmacist, he could find employment elsewhere sufficiently remunerative to support himself and to comply with the moderate order from which he has appealed. In determining what a husband reasonably should pay for the support of his wife the court may consider the earning power of the husband and is not restricted to his actual earnings. * * *" 155 Pa. Super. at pages 518, 519, 38 A. 2d. at page 347. The distinction is obvious. In the present case the husband is a medical student who is in the process of obtaining his education. Rita married him while still in medical school, knowing his ambition and in fact consenting to it to the point of actually obtaining employment herself to run the household during the lean years. The appellant has no choice, if he is to become a doctor, than to serve an internship. He is only continuing in the process of gaining an education in the profession to which his wife consented when she married him. He certainly is not like the husband in the Wieczorkowski case. He is not a *qualified* physician who is working at a particular job which purportedly pays him meager wages while other jobs are in existence *in his* qualified field. Nor are there present the highly suspicious

circumstances pointing to a deliberate design to minimize the obligation to support his wife which are usually present in those cases where the court is moved to consider earning capacity rather than actual earnings. . . . The bona fides of appellant's ambition to become a doctor is unquestioned.

Under the circumstances then, there would seem to be no justification for requiring appellant to give up his medical training just short of completion merely because of marital difficulties. Appellant's reasons for leaving his wife do not justify a prohibitive order. The support laws were meant to provide reasonable support for a wife, not to penalize an erring husband. . . .

Even though the appellant is going to California, the court below will retain jurisdiction, and it is well established that support orders may be increased where the financial conditions of the parties change. . . . When appellant has completed his training and becomes a qualified physician his financial situation of course will be greatly improved and this will enure to the benefit of his wife. Until that time, however, he has only limited resources and his wife must bear this hardship which she would have borne had they not separated. The fact of their parting cannot have the effect of accelerating his station in life and corresponding income from that of a medical student to that of a practicing physician. Under all the attendant circumstances here, we believe that the order should be reduced to the nominal amount of $15 a month, and the order of the court below is so modified.

NOTE 2.

ROBINSON v. ROBINSON
186 Misc. 974, 61 N.Y.S. 2d 859 (1945)
rev'd. 271 App. Div. 98, 62 N.Y.S. 2d 785 (1946)
aff'd. 296 N.Y. 778, 71 N.E. 2d 214 (1947)

WALTER, JUSTICE.

May 26, 1938, a husband and wife entered into an agreement which, after reciting the fact of their separation . . . provides that the husband . . . shall pay to the wife a stated sum weekly for one year, and at the expiration of said one year if the parties cannot agree on the amount to be paid, the amount shall be fixed by arbitration under Article 84 of the Civil Practice Act of the State of New York.

By subsequent agreements the weekly payments were fixed at stated sums to and including December 31, 1944. Differences then arose as to what the weekly amount should be after that date. The wife demanded arbitration, but the husband refused, and he now opposes this motion by the wife to compel arbitration, not upon the ground that he did not agree to arbitrate or that differences have not arisen, but upon the ground that the controversy is not arbitrable in character. His argument is that no controversy is arbitrable unless it is one which may be made the subject of an action, and that our courts cannot entertain an action simply for the fixation of the amount a husband shall pay for the support of his wife and children.

To my mind the contention so advanced is startling in the extreme. Fixing the amount which a husband shall pay for the support of his wife and children is something which our courts are doing practically every day, and the discouragement of litigation over that subject is so plainly in the public interest that I would have supposed that no question could be raised as to the right of the parties to agree upon another tribunal to do the same thing.

*   *   *

. . . The husband's obligation of support arises from the marital and parental status, and all that is here sought is that that existing obligation be measured and defined in terms of a stated number of dollars according to the situation of the parties ; and the judicial nature of such measurement and definition is not lessened by the accident that in the courts of this state such measurement and definition are made only in connection with an application for a divorce or separation.

*   *   *

NOTE 3.

TROSSMAN v. TROSSMAN
24 Ill. App. 2d 521, 165 N.E. 2d 368 (1960)

McCORMICK, JUSTICE.

The questions presented to this court by this appeal are whether an action for a declaratory judgment will lie during the lifetime of the parties to declare valid an antenuptial agreement and whether the complaint presents an actual and justiciable controversy.

. . . By the terms of the carefully drawn antenuptial agreement it was agreed that the property rights of the parties to the contract should be and remain absolutely and forever separate and distinct as though marriage had not taken place, and that the contract should remain in full force and effect whether the marriage was terminated either by death or divorce. . . . The complaint . . . avers that a case of actual controversy now exists between the parties, the defendant asserting that the agreement is invalid and of no force and effect and that she will, notwithstanding it, in the event of plaintiff's prior death, seek dower and an

intestate share in the plaintiff's estate ; that plaintiff's position is that the said antenuptial agreemen is valid and binding upon both and that it must be observed in their lifetime and in the event of the death of either ; and that it is necessary that the court render a declaratory judgment declaring the rights and other legal relations of the parties with respect to the said antenuptial agreement and the positions of the respective parties thereto with respect to the same. . . .

*   *   *

The purpose of the Declaratory Judgment Act is well expressed in the Notes by Messrs. Jenner and Tone to section 57.1 of the Civil Practice Act found in the Annotated Statutes (Smith-Hurd Ill. Anno. Stat. ch. 110, § 57.1):

"The remedy is not designed to supplant existing remedies, nor afford a new choice of tribunals. It supplies a new form of relief where needed. It is designed to afford security and relief against uncertainty with a view to avoiding litigation, rather than in aid of it, and to settle and fix rights before there has been an irrevocable change of position of the parties in disregard of their respective claims of right, and thus promote peace, quiet and justice, with the end always constantly in view that one of the chief purposes is to declare rights rather than to execute them. . . .

*   *   *

In the case before us there was an actual controversy, definite and concrete. The parties had adverse legal interests. In actions for declaratory judgments, "just as in equitable actions to quiet title or *quia timet,* no wrong need be proved but merely the existence of a claim or record which disturbs the title, peace, or freedom of the plaintiff, so any claims, assertions, challenges, records, or adverse interests, which, by casting doubt, insecurity, and uncertainty upon the plaintiff's rights or status, damage his pecuniary or material interests, establish a condition of justiciability. * * * While actions for declaratory judgments may be brought either after wrong done or threatened, or prior thereto, the fact that the court must be convinced that its judgment will settle the controversy and quiet the disputed or endangered rights is an assurance against abuse of a remedy which has simplified the administration of justice and admirably served a considerable part of the civilized world." Borchard, Declaratory Judgments, 2nd Ed., pp. 39, 40. Here the controversy was neither moot nor based on a hypothetical state of facts. The contention of the defendant that the antenuptial contract was invalid would prevent a comprehensive plan being made on the part of the plaintiff to dispose of his estate either by will or otherwise. Here are present the ripening seeds of litigation. Such a dispute under the declaratory judgment statute "may be tried at its inception before it has accumulated the asperity, distemper, animosity, passion, and violence of the full-blown battle which looms ahead. It describes a state of facts indicating 'imminent' and 'inevitable' litigation, provided the issue is not settled and stabilized by a tranquilizing declaration. The dispute may be determined before the *status quo* has been altered or disturbed by physical acts of either party." Borchard, Declaratory Judgments, 2nd Ed., p. 57.

The judgment of the Circuit Court of Cook County is reversed and the cause remanded for further proceedings. . . .

3.

Ex Parte THREET
160 Tex. 482, 333 S.W. 2d 361 (1960)

GREENHILL, JUSTICE.

This is a habeas corpus case filed in this Court by Bobby Gene Threet. He has been held in contempt by a district court for refusing to make support payments pending a divorce action. He denied that he had been married, and here contends that the district court was without power to require such payments because there was no evidence introduced at the hearing that there had ever been any marriage.

The alleged wife contended that there had been, in effect, a secret common law marriage. Since the question of marriage had been put in issue, and since the person seeking support had failed to introduce proof tentatively establishing such a common law marriage (i.e., proof that the couple lived and held themselves out publicly as husband and wife), we here hold that the trial court was without power to require the making of support payments. Threet will therefore be discharged.

We shall refer to the alleged wife as the plaintiff. Threet will be called the defendant.

It is conceded that there had been no ceremonial marriage. The plaintiff at the time of the alleged common law marriage was 15 years old, a student in junior high school. She began dating the defendant, then 20 years of age, around December of 1958. She testified that on February 14, 1959, she and the defendant entered into an agreement to become husband and wife. The agreement was followed by sexual intercourse at her mother's house. She and the defendant, she testified, continued to engage in acts of intercourse

from February 14 until the middle of April, 1959, which was the last time she "dated" him.

All of the acts of intercourse, she said, occurred at her parents' house or at the home of defendant's parents. After such meetings, the one away from home would "go home." The couple was together mainly after school while the parents were working. They never spent an entire night together. When her parents were away for a weekend, the defendant stayed at her house until dawn.

The plaintiff candidly admitted that she and the defendant never established a home together. She never moved in with defendant at his house, nor he into hers. She continued to give her parent's residence as her residence. Neither moved any of his or her clothes or personal effects into any common room or apartment.

* * *

A valid marriage is a prerequisite to a support order in an action for divorce. The existence of the marriage must be admitted or shown before such a decree or order properly can be made. Where the marriage is denied, as it was here, the marriage must be at least tentatively established. Stated differently, when the marriage is put in issue, the burden is upon the party seeking support to establish at least a prima facie case of marriage. . . .

What elements, then, need be shown to make a prima facie or tentative showing of a common law marriage?

In Texas, three elements must exist: (1) an agreement to be husband and wife; (2) living together as husband and wife; and (3) a holding out to the public that the couple are husband and wife. . . .

In the Grigsby case [153 S.W. 1124] this Court announced that the marriage was more than a contract; it is a status. The living together *as man and wife* and the public and open holding out that the two are man and wife are as essential to a valid common law marriage as the agreement itself. Without these elements, there is no common law marriage.

It is our opinion that the facts above set out do not constitute evidence that the couple lived together *as man and wife* or that they held out to the public that they were man and wife. As a matter of fact, the plaintiff apparently wanted to keep the alleged marriage a secret except from four or five of her closest friends. They never moved into or occupied, publicly, a common residence or room. She continued using her own name and publicly represented to those at her school and at her place of work that she was a single person. . . . [T]he introduction of defendant as her husband to two close friends, and telling two or three others that she was married to defendant, constituted no evidence that plaintiff and Threet were living together as husband and wife and holding themselves out to the public as man and wife. Under the Texas decisions, there can be no secret common law marriage as such. The secrecy is inconsistent and irreconcilable with the requirement of a public holding out that the couple are living together as husband and wife.

This opinion is, of course, not determinative of whether there was or was not a common law marriage. That question will be determined when the action is tried on its merits. This opinion does hold that on the preliminary hearing for support, where the question of marriage was put in issue, there was no evidence of two vital elements of a common law marriage. Under those circumstances, the trial court was without power to require Threet to make support payments pending the trial of the divorce action.

* * *

SMITH, JUSTICE (dissenting).

. . . There is no evidence that the unborn child mentioned in the record is not the natural result of the prima facie common law marriage.

This habeas corpus proceeding is a collateral attack on the judgment, declaring that a common law marriage existed. This court has no jurisdiction to weigh the evidence to determine whether it preponderates against the judgment. . . .

The court states that its opinion is not determinative of whether there was or was not a common law marriage. It is difficult for me to conceive of a more effective manner that the court could adopt to effectually preclude a finding in favor of the respondent on the question of common law marriage. It is for the legislature and not this court to decide whether or not common law marriages will continue to have legal sanction in Texas.

* * *

NOTES

NOTE 1.

Ex Parte THREET
One Year Later

(a) After the Supreme Court tore us up with its opinion, I felt that I could not establish a common law marriage. So the case never went to trial on its merits. My client was left with her child without support. Fortunately a very fine young man met her and they married and I presume the new husband will adopt the child. This was a very upsetting case to handle, since I proceeded in the preliminary hearing on the

proposition that it was necessary to prove only a prima facie case of marriage. If the case had been later tried on its merits, I could not show any open and notorious living together; at least not any stronger than on the preliminary hearing. I always will feel that a common law marriage was proved. [Letter dated May 8, 1961 from Everett B. Lord, attorney for the plaintiff.]

(b) I represented the defendant, Bobby Threet. . . . When Threet was served in said action, I filed a sworn answer in his behalf denying under oath that there had ever been any type of marriage contract between the parties.

Texas, being a community property state, does not have any alimony after a final decree, but a woman in necessitous circumstances is entitled to ask for alimony, pendente lite. The pleadings filed by me challenged the jurisdiction of the court, but the court in effect found that there was a common law marriage and ordered my client to pay the sum of $25.00 per week. Inasmuch as there is no appeal from an interlocutory order, my only remedy was to allow my client to disobey the order and be held in contempt of court, so that I might test the validity of the marriage, which was jurisdictional, by means of habeas corpus. . . . [Letter dated May 9, 1961 from Joe B. Goodwin, attorney for the defendant.]

NOTE 2.

HOUG v. HOUG
159 Misc. 894, 289 N.Y.S. 27 (1936)

PANKEN, JUSTICE

. . . Public policy would be shocked beyond mention if in an instance such as is before me an order should be made to require the respondent to contribute to the support of the dependent spouse. . . . The uncontradicted testimony in this case discloses a situation which shakes faith in human beings. Petitioner was convicted of prostitution and served a term of 100 days for having committed the act of prostitution. After she was discharged from the workhouse she contracted a bigamous marriage; and I might say, brazenly and unconcernedly admits it. The report submitted to me by the clinical department of the Court indicates the dread disease of syphilis in the petitioner and which finding is supported by a blood test made under the Wasserman System by the board of health in the city of New York. I cannot bring myself to sign an order requiring the respondent here to support the petitioner, even if the petitioner will continue to be a public charge. It is much better that the community should continue to provide for her than to do violence to decent instincts, conscience, and justice which an order upon the respondent would be tantamount to. Accordingly, petition is dismissed, and corporation counsel is given exception to the dismissal.

NOTE 3.

KUSEL v. KUSEL
147 Cal. 57, 81 P. 295 (1905)

SHAW, J.

The plaintiff is the wife of the defendant, and the action is brought to obtain a decree to compel the defendant to maintain her while living separate and apart from him. . . .

We think the court erred in awarding plaintiff the sum of $10,000 for her support and maintenance, instead of a periodical allowance. The action is maintained under the provision of section 137 of the Civil Code, which is as follows: "When the husband wilfully deserts the wife, she may, without applying for a divorce, maintain in the superior court an action against him for permanent support and maintenance of herself or of herself and children. * * * The final judgment in such action may be enforced by the court by such order or orders as in its discretion it may from time to time deem necessary, and such order or orders may be varied, altered or revoked at the discretion of the court." Section 140 provides: "The court may require the husband to give reasonable security for providing maintenance or making any payments required under the provisions of this chapter, and may enforce the same by the appointment of a receiver, or by any other remedy applicable to the case." It will be observed that there is nothing in the statutory provisions above quoted expressly authorizing the court in suits for maintenance to divide the property of the husband, or to give to the wife, in lieu of periodical payments for her support, a gross sum out of the husband's estate. Originally "alimony," in its technical significance, meant an allowance of money payable in periodical installments, not in gross. "Alimony is not a sum of money nor a specific proportion of the husband's estate given absolutely to the wife, but it is a continuous allotment of sums, payable at regular intervals, for her support from year to year." 1 Bouvier's Dict. (Law Ed.) 131; . . . The same rule applies in actions for maintenance, or in the similar action for a judicial separation without an absolute divorce. . . .

. . . The action does not contemplate a divorce, but, on the contrary, that the parties shall continue to remain as they were before—husband and wife. The rights of the wife in the remaining property of the husband are not destroyed or affected in the least by the decree or judgment. The necessity for the separate maintenance may terminate at any time by reconciliation of the parties, or by the death of one of them. The law favors the reconciliation of the parties, and it should not be construed so as to afford a temptation for the wife to press an action for maintenance, rather than to seek restoration to her marital rights. There is nothing in the statute which requires us to depart from the prevailing rule that the right to alimony or maintenance, where the marriage is not dissolved, contemplates periodical payments during such time as the necessity for the maintenance continued, and not an absolute allowance out of the estate.

* * *

4.

MATTER OF CYBULSKI
8 Misc. 2d 119, 163 N.Y.S. 2d 495
(Surr. Ct., Nassau Cty. 1957)

JOHN D. BENNETT, S. The executrix has petitioned for the judicial settlement of her account.

The Department of Public Welfare has presented a claim against the estate for assistance rendered to the decedent's husband between the period of April 1, 1953 and December 12, 1955, the date of death of the decedent. The executrix rejected the claim "because she doubts the justice and validity of same".

The testimony at the hearing showed that the decedent and her husband were married in 1940; that they lived together for short periods for about a total of seven or eight months during the first few years of the marriage, and that he then disappeared for about 10 years, after which the family was informed that he had been picked up for vagrancy; that he never contributed to the support of the family; that he "never held a job or anything", and that during the few months that he did live with the decedent, "whatever she had he would take from the house".

On these facts the executrix rejected the claim and now urges that the decedent's estate is not liable to the Department of Public Welfare for the assistance given the husband. On the other hand, the claimant contends that the statutory obligation of a wife to support her husband as contained in sections 101 and 104 of the Social Welfare Law is absolute, and that there is no exemption from its application because of the misconduct of the spouse.

Section 101 (subd. 1) of the Social Welfare Law provides that a "wife * * * of a recipient of public assistance or care * * * shall, if of sufficient ability, be responsible for the support of such person". Section 104 of the Social Welfare Law provides that "A public welfare official may bring action against * * * the estate * * * of a person who dies leaving real or personal property, if such person, or any one for whose support he is or was liable, received assistance and care during the preceding ten years". This section was amended to provide that no claim of a public welfare official against the estate or the executors of the estate "shall be barred or defeated, in whole or in part, by any lack of sufficiency of ability on the part of such person during the period assistance and care were received." . . .

The ability of the decedent to support her husband is not in issue, as the claim of the Department of Public Welfare against the estate may not be barred or defeated because of any lack of sufficiency of ability. . . . The Social Welfare Law, however, is silent as to the obligation of the wife or of her estate where the husband abandoned her or was guilty of some other moral delinquency.

* * *

The court in *"Mendelsohn"* v. *"Mendelsohn"* (192 Misc. 1014) ruled . . . "Unlike some other States, in New York there is no statutory provision which relieves otherwise legally liable relatives from the duty of indemnifying the public against the burden of maintaining a poor relative whose conduct has forfeited all moral claims against them. . . ."

For the court to allow the claim here makes this a "hard case" and a disturbing one. The reluctance to arrive at such a result, however, must yield before the direction implicit in the language of the Court of Appeals in *People* v. *Schenkel* (258 N.Y. 224, 227-228): "In this State the penal statute leaves no discretion to the Courts. A person is 'disorderly' who leaves wife or children in danger of becoming a burden upon the public or who neglects to provide for them according to his means. Duty of provision is absolute and regardless of the wife's fault. The public interest, in the opinion of the Legislature, requires that the husband, not the taxpayer, shall bear the burden of her support as long as the relationship of husband and wife is not altered or dissolved by decree of the court. * * * Whether the obligation of maintenance continues after the wife has been guilty of adultery is not now before us. . . . Perhaps even there the ancient rule has been changed, and only dissolution of the marriage relation can destroy its incidents. . . .

The language of the Court of Appeals is equally applicable where the duty of maintenance is imposed upon the wife. In *Hodson* v. *Stapleton* (248 App. Div. 524, 525) the court said: "Of course, it has always been the husband's duty to support his wife, even in the absence of statute.

. . . But at common law there was no corresponding duty on the part of the wife. . . . However, it cannot be denied that there exists a moral obligation on the wife, if she has the means, to support her husband when he is in need. It is that obligation which the statute (§§ 125, 128), in the public interest, has transformed into law. As between the wife and the State, the support of the husband is primarily the responsibility of the wife. If the State discharges her obligation, it is not unreasonable that the State should be reimbursed by her for the expenditure. Nor is it true that the statute is retroactive even though applicable to marriages contracted previously, for it does not create any liability for relief received before the enactment of the law. It merely attaches a new incident to the marriage relationship."

Considerable significance should be attached to the fact that when subdivision 1 of section 101 of the Domestic Relations Court Act was amended (L. 1950, ch. 786, §3) no exculpatory matter was inserted or condition attached to the duty of a wife to maintain her husband because of a breach of his marital duties. The sentence added read: "A wife is hereby declared to be chargeable with the support of her husband who is or is likely to become a public charge, and, if possessed of sufficient means, may be required to pay such sum, or any part thereof, as may be necessary to prevent his being or becoming a public charge." . . . Had it been the Legislature's intention to excuse a wife (or her estate) from supporting her husband because of his immoral or unconscionable actions, the Legislature could have added this to the conditions found in the amendment. Its failure to do so in this court's opinion should be called to its attention so that "hard cases" such as this need not continue to occur.

It is with considerable reluctance that the court holds that the claim of the Department of Public Welfare must be allowed.

NOTE

Comment by the Deputy County Attorney

In the subject case, the claim of the Nassau County Department of Public Welfare was filed against the estate of the wife, Veronica Cybulski, in the amount of $2,995.00. However, when the said claim was upheld by the Surrogate's Court of Nassau County the assets in the estate were only sufficient to partially satisfy the claim and my office collected the amount of $583.33, which closed this matter as far as the estate was concerned. [Letter dated May 22, 1961 from Aaron D. Samuels, deputy county attorney, Nassau County, N.Y.]

C.

To Decisions Concerning the Reorganization of Wife-Husband Relationships?

1.

ECONOMIC CONDUCT AS A CAUSE OF ACTION

GOLLINS v. GOLLINS
[1962] 3 All E.R. 897

WILLMER, L. J.: . . .The nature of the wife's case was that throughout the marriage the husband had run up debts and had persistently failed to maintain her and the two children of the marriage. As a result of this she had, she said, since 1957 been compelled to earn her own living by running the matrimonial home as a guest-house for elderly people, and this enabled her to provide financial support not only for herself and the children but also for the husband. In September, 1960, she wrote him a letter informing him that she could not stand the strain of his debts any longer, and warning him that if he did not get work and clear himself of debt she would have to take proceedings. As this letter produced no effect, she issued a summons before the justices asking for a maintenance order on the ground of the wilful neglect of the husband to provide reasonable maintenance for herself and her children; and on Jan. 5, 1961, the justices made an order in her favour at the rate of £3 per week for herself and £1 per week for each of the two children. The husband never paid more than a trivial fraction of the amount of maintenance so ordered. In April, 1961, the wife consulted her doctor, who found that she was suffering from a moderately severe anxiety state, which he attributed to her financial and marital difficulties. Armed with this, the wife issued a summons for variation of the previous order by the insertion of a non-cohabitation clause on the ground of persistent cruelty on the part of the husband. . . .

* * *

The argument on behalf of the husband which prevailed before the Divisional Court . . . may be briefly summarised as follows. The justices, it is said . . . never really looked at the case as a whole, and never stood back, as it were, at the end of the case in order to consider whether in the circumstances the husband's conduct could fairly be described as amounting to cruelty in the ordinary sense of that word. It was submitted that the husband's conduct amounted to no more

than a manifestation of his own not very attractive character and temperament, and was in no sense directed at the wife; that the wife, thanks to her own efforts, was never really in need; and that the facts disclosed no more than what was described as a "marginal" failure on the part of the husband to provide maintenance. It was not denied that in some circumstances a failure to provide maintenance might amount to cruelty. Such a case, however, it was said, would be exceptional and the present was certainly not such an exceptional case.

* * *

. . . The gravity of the husband's behavior is not, in my judgment, to be measured in pounds, shillings and pence. It is perfectly true that the wife was not actually in need; but this was entirely due to her own efforts, and does not reflect any merit on the part of the husband. The gravamen of the wife's charge is that the husband had been neglecting to maintain her or the children throughout the whole of the marriage. Thanks to the husband's behavior, she had had to endure unnecessary financial anxieties for years. It was the husband's conduct which ultimately drove the wife to run a business for herself in an effort to make her own living, and to endure the financial anxieties inseparable therefrom, to the ultimate detriment of her health. It is not, I think, to be put against her that it took fifteen years to wear her down and bring about injury to her health.

In these circumstances, it appears to me that there was abundant material to justify the finding of cruelty at which the justices arrived. . . .

HARMAN, L. J.: I have felt constrained to reach a different conclusion from that just expressed. . . .

* * *

How do the facts stand with relation to that state of the law? Shortly put, this man is bone idle. He may be described in a modern slang phrase as a lay-about. He married a competent active woman and has made no effort ever since. He was in debt when he married, though he did not tell his wife so. He sold his farm to pacify his creditors. With what was left out of the wreck a new house was bought, which he either caused or allowed to be put in his wife's name, she being thus saddled with the mortgage, and all that he has done is to hang up his hat in the hall. He started by keeping some poultry, but these seem to have been sold off and the proceeds have gone into or through his pocket. He does a little gardening and suggests that that is quite enough. The wife has gone on from year to year shouldering the burdens of the establishment, carrying on a business at the house, by which she has succeeded in keeping down the mortgage, educating her daughters and maintaining the family. She has also from time to time staved off his creditors. Her complaint is not that she cannot carry on the business, nor that she is in want of money, but that the continual irritation of his debts, though she is not responsible for them, and the exasperation she feels at his continued refusal to help her and her sense of injustice that she should do all the work and he none, have driven her to revolt and have produced what her doctor calls a "moderate anxiety state". As to the business, she says "I shall have to give it up as I am getting so impatient". She also says: "I don't claim that I am short of money. I have to work to raise money to pay for the mortgage and keep myself. One expects the husband to pay."

There was no direct evidence at all that the husband sought to injure his wife, nor even that he knew that his conduct might be injurious to her health. . . .

Counsel for the wife has argued that the true inquiry is: (a) was there injury to health? and (b) can the blame for it be attributed to the other spouse? If so, he says, that is cruelty. I cannot accept this. The cause of the spouse's ill-health may be entirely trivial, but to be cruelty the conduct must be something serious which can be properly so described. In this case there is an absence of conduct directed at the wife, and that is why the Divisional Court describes it as "negative". I am not enamoured of this word, nor indeed of other descriptive phrases. I think the court or the jury must be asked: "Was this man cruel to his wife?" I think the answer is "No". As a husband, he was everything he should not be. Above all, he exasperated his wife, who feels a husband ought to bear his share of the burden. Many husbands have felt the same about their wives, but that has never been counted cruelty, unless it results in damage to the home or the family. These conditions do not exist here. Whatever opprobrious names one may give to this husband, I do not think that "cruel" is one of them. . . .

DAVIES, L. J.

. . . The first comment which I would respectfully make on that passage is that for myself I do not find the contrast between "positive" conduct and "negative" conduct either readily comprehensible or helpful, although these expressions are undoubtedly to be found in the decided cases. Almost any sort of conduct can at one and the same time be described both as positive and as negative. An omission in most cases is at the same time a commission. But much more important is the fact that the Divisional Court appear to have attached great weight to the absence of any wish or desire to injure the wife. The presence of such a wish or desire is no doubt of cardinal importance in such cases and may well be decisive. . . .

* * *

. . . There was evidence in the present case, and the magistrates found, that the husband had been told and knew that his conduct was injuring his wife's health and that nevertheless he persisted in it. The absence of any wish or desire on his part to injure her was, therefore, irrelevant.

Another of the reasons which influenced the decision of the Divisional Court was the fact that the husband's conduct could not be called "cruelty", in the ordinary sense of the word:

> ". . . they [i.e., the magistrates] did not ask themselves whether the conduct amounted to cruelty in the ordinary sense of that term . . . we do not consider that the husband's conduct, however reprehensible, can properly be stigmatised by the word 'cruelty' in its ordinary acceptation."

This seems, with all respect, to be a dangerous test. . . . Any conduct—intentional in the sense which I have described—by one spouse towards the other, provided that it can properly be described as ill-treatment and provided that it is sufficiently grave and weighty and not merely trivial, can amount to cruelty if such conduct causes injury or reasonable apprehension of injury to life, limb, or health, bodily or mental. Whether it does so amount is a question of fact in each case.

* * *

2.

ECONOMIC STATUS AS AN AGGRAVATING OR MITIGATING FACTOR

HOPES v. HOPES
[1949] P. 227, 235

DENNING, L. J.: Since the housing shortage, the innocent party in a matrimonial dispute is often forced to remain in the same house as the guilty party, because he or she has nowhere else to go or has not the means to go elsewhere. This has given rise to a number of cases where the innocent party has claimed maintenance or a divorce whilst they are both living under the same roof. The matrimonial offences of cruelty and adultery can, of course, be committed by the guilty party (and be not condoned by the innocent party) whilst they are living under the same roof ; but, can the matrimonial offence of desertion be committed? One of the essential elements of desertion is the fact of separation. Can that exist whilst the parties are living under the same roof? My answer is: "Yes". The husband who shuts himself up in one or two rooms of his house, and ceases to have anything to do with his wife, is living separately and apart from her as effectively as if they were separated by the outer door of a flat. They may meet on the stairs or in the passageway, but so they might if they each had separate flats in one building. If that separation is brought about by his fault, why is that not desertion? He has forsaken and abandoned his wife as effectively as if he had gone into lodgings. The converse is equally true. If the wife ceases to have anything to do with, or for, the husband and he is left to look after himself in his own rooms, why is not that desertion? She has forsaken and abandoned him as effectively as if she had gone to live with her relatives. . . .

3.

PROVIDING FUTURE ECONOMIC GRATIFICATION AND DIVIDING THE SPOILS—WITHOUT LOVE

a.   PHILLIPS v. PHILLIPS
1 App. Div. 2d 393, 150 N.Y.S. 2d 646 (1956)
aff'd. 2 N.Y. 2d 742, 138 N.E. 2d 738 (1956)

BOTEIN, JUSTICE

An otherwise routine application for examination during trial poses a question that has not yet been presented foursquare to any appellate court in this state.

Plaintiff wife, having been granted an interlocutory judgment of divorce against defendant husband, moved during trial to examine the husband concerning his income and assets. Thereupon the husband moved to examine the wife as to their standards of living during the marriage, her contributions thereto, and *her* property, assets and current income. Special Term granted the motion of each party for examination of the other. The wife appeals, insisting that her present assets and current income are, as a matter of law, wholly

irrelevant to any determination of the amount of alimony to be fixed in the final decree.

It is true that during marriage a husband is obliged to support his family in accordance with his financial ability, and a wife is not legally obligated to use her independent assets to maintain her husband and children. . . . She may choose, however, to contribute towards raising their joint standard of living. "If, with the aid of her funds, they have been living beyond what he alone could afford, then, in event of a separation, he should not be required to support her on that basis wholly out of his own income or property." Van Voorhis, J., in Judd v. Judd, 1 Misc. 2d 965, 59 N.Y.S. 2d 680, 681. There can be no question as to the propriety of an inquiry into the contributions the wife has made towards the standard of living of the parties during their marriage. Query, and more troublesome: In determining the amount of permanent alimony to be paid by a husband, should the court also consider the current income and assets of the wife who obtained the divorce?

At common law it was held that "the very being or legal existence of the woman is suspended during the marriage" (1 Blackstone, Commentaries on the Laws of England 442 [1758]), and that the husband, as the one in control of his wife's property and income, was obligated for her debts and her support. The convention that a divorced husband is responsible for the full and unrelieved support of his wife had its origin back in the days when courts in England could grant no absolute divorce—only a limited divorce, or what we recognize as separation. Since the marriage survived the limited divorce, the husband at fault still retained control of his wife's property ; and any support provisions for the wife would be borne out of their joint assets and income. Therefore, there was no practical reason for separately taking cognizance of the wife's property in fixing allowances for support as an incident to a limited divorce.

This view undoubtedly carried over after the legislature made statutory provision for the absolute divorce which had not been obtainable at common law. Absolute divorce released the parties from the mutual obligations imposed by marriage, but society demanded that even a divorced wife should be appropriately maintained by her ex-husband so that she would not become a charge on the community. Hence, alimony was created as a statutory substitute for the marital right of support. . . .

The position of the wife has changed, however. Her role as a frail, sheltered, ineffectual person—if ever authentic—is as much a thing of the past as her crinoline and whalebone. By statute she has been given exclusive right to hold her own property, § 50, Domestic Relations Law, and her coequal status with her husband has been recognized in law as well as in fact.

"From her old position as an identity merged in him and not separable from him, she has advanced to a position of independence in most respects fully equal with his. Whereas in the period when the law of alimony was largely shaped and fixed she had no property apart from her husband and had no means of securing help if she left him or called him to a legal accounting of his husbandry, today she has her separate property, and ways and opportunities at least as many, if not more, of earning a livelihood outside the home and independently of her spouse." (The Changing Social Setting of Alimony Law, 6 Law and Contemporary Problems, 186, 192-193.)

The number of married women who work in gainful occupations has increased twenty-eight-fold, from 515,260 in 1890 to 14,305,000 in 1954, so that despite continued family responsibilities, almost one third of all married women are now in the labor force (Historical Statistics of the U.S. 1789-1945, p. 63 ; 1955 Statistical Abstract of the United States, p. 195). Millions of women own their own property. With the advance in the legal and social status of the married woman have come concomitant responsibilities.

> "* * * until recent years, a divorced wife had little prospect of being able to work and earn a livelihood, and it was essential to a well-ordered society that she be appropriately maintained by her estranged husband so that she would not become a charge on the community. Times have now changed. The broad, practically unlimited opportunities for women in the business world of today are a matter of common knowledge. Thus, in an era where the opportunities for self-support by the wife are so abundant, the fact that the marriage has been brought to an end because of the fault of the husband does not necessarily entitle the wife to be forever supported by a former husband who has little, if any, more economic advantages than she has." Kahn v. Kahn, Fla. 1955, 78 So. 2d 367, 368.

* * *

The courts of almost every American jurisdiction are in accord in taking the assets of the wife into consideration in fixing the amount of alimony. . . . In some of the states, statutes require expressly that the court consider a wife's separate estate in awarding alimony. Others operate under statutes that provide for the fixation of alimony as justice requires or after taking into consideration the circumstances of the parties.

The rule generally applied in other states is that a husband who has been divorced as a result

of his wrongdong should not be relieved of his marital obligation to support his wife, despite her proven ability to provide for herself. However, the courts usually take the realistic view that the amount of such support should be fixed with an eye to the ex-wife's resources or abilities for self-support.

The abiding interest of the state is in the preservation of the family, and in maintaining it as a self-sufficient, independent unit. Even when the familial entity has been destroyed, however, the state has a continuing interest in allocating the economic burdens fairly, so that members of the former family group, including the husband, are not individually destroyed by crushing economic and psychological pressures. Alimony must therefore be measured largely by the need for support rather than the desire for vengeance, although in weighing the various factors many states avowedly use the fault element as a counterpoise.

Therefore, the financial circumstances of the wife, while not controlling, are relevant as one of the factors that must guide the court's discretion in determining the amount of maintenance which justice requires. The ultimate determination in each case must depend upon a balancing of several factors—the financial status of the respective parties, their age, health, necessities and obligations, their station in life, the duration and nature of the marriage, and the conduct of the parties. . . .

Special Term therefore properly permitted the examination of the plaintiff as to her property, income, and assets and correctly refused to limit the examination of the plaintiff to the time when the parties lived together, since one of the criteria is the wife's continuing need for support, and her resources as of the present time are clearly relevant thereto. The order appealed from should be affirmed.

* * *

NOTES

NOTE 1.

BARNETT v. BARNETT
158 Okla. 270, 13 P. 2d 104 (1932)

CULLISON, J.

* * *

The record discloses that the defendant and his wife had lived together as husband and wife for over fifteen years. Each had allotments when they were married. Later, oil was discovered on the allotment of the plaintiff, and from her vast income she bought more land and the defendant looked after it and helped work and care for the property of the plaintiff faithfully for many years.

The record discloses that he was a model husband. At the time the petition was filed there were two children, aged seven and nine. The trial court found, in substance, that George Barnett had given fifteen years of his best life in making and keeping a Christian home together for himself and family, until broken up by the adulterous acts of the wife, and that he now found himself destitute and dependent upon the judgment of the courts for existence by reason thereof, and that he should be granted alimony. . . .

Under the laws announced, in cases growing out of the same facts, the court will look at the question: "What is the nature and extent of the pecuniary change operated by the wife's criminality?" If the union has been abandoned by the criminality of the wife without the fault of the husband, it seems just that the innocent husband should not, in addition to the grievous wrong done by the breach of the marriage vow, be wholly deprived of means to support himself and children; nor, viewing the matter from another standpoint, does it seem either just or equitable that funds which were intended at the time of the marriage for the use of both should be borne off by the guilty wife and perhaps transferred to the hands of the adulterer as the dowry of a second marriage. The interests of society point in the same direction.

After a careful study of the record and the law applicable to the facts involved, we are of the opinion, and hold, that the trial court did not err in granting the husband a reasonable amount of the wife's separate property, for the support of the husband and minor children.

NOTE 2.

FAUSONE v. FAUSONE
75 Nev. 222, 338 P. 2d 68 (1959)

BADT, JUSTICE.

This is the wife's appeal from a judgment awarding the husband a divorce and refusing to award any alimony to her.

*   *   *

In denying alimony the court said: "There is no reason in the world why a man should support a woman, unless she has something obligating her such as with the care and support of children, why he should have to support her any more than I should support him because he needs it. If he has imposed obligations on her as a result of her marriage, she has suffered an illness, or become disabled during her life with him, then she is entitled to alimony. I can see no other reason. A woman is not entitled to alimony just because she has been his wife."

Appellant assigns error in two respects: first, that the evidence clearly shows that she was entitled to a divorce on the ground of her husband's extreme cruelty to her, and that in any event she was the least at fault, and, secondly, that the court abused its discretion in refusing to grant the wife any alimony.

*   *   *

The theory of "comparative rectitude" was adopted in 1931 (and amended in 1957, by adding the condition expressed in the last clause) in the following words now appearing as NRS 125.120, "In any action for divorce when it shall appear to the court that both husband and wife have been guilty of a wrong or wrongs which may constitute grounds for a divorce, the court shall not for this reason deny a divorce, but in its discretion may grant a divorce to the party least in fault, if both parties seek a divorce, otherwise to the party seeking the divorce."

Appellant contends that it was error for the court to fail to apply the doctrine of comparative rectitude. . . .

*   *   *

We feel that the court was in error in its refusal to award alimony to appellant. The parties were married in Michigan in 1939 and continued to reside there. In 1953 and 1954 marital difficulties arose. While these apparently grew out of the husband's attention to another woman, the trial court was of the opinion that this situation was in turn caused by the wife's attitude toward the husband. The parties separated in January of 1954 and for a period of approximately a year the husband voluntarily sent the wife sums for her support of $50 to $75 every two weeks. In January 1955 the husband sued for divorce in Michigan and the Michigan court awarded temporary alimony to the wife in the sum of $135 a month. This amount the husband paid for about two years. . . . At the time of trial the wife was 56 years of age, the husband 48 years. The wife is in general poor health and suffers from severe degenerative arthritis of the left ankle and arthritis of the left wrist. She has no provision or prospects for employment and has only an eighth grade education. She had not worked during marriage, is presently in debt, and has no sources of income other than charity of friends and relatives. She owns a 1955 Chevrolet car subject to monthly payments of $42.40, which a niece had been paying for her. The husband had been employed in Michigan as a radio sports announcer and advertising salesman in which he earned some $4,500 a year or more. At the trial it developed that he expected to return to similar work, although he was then earning $8 a day as a handy man or kitchen employee. Under such a situation the necessities of the wife for her support and the ability of the husband to contribute a reasonable sum definitely appear. While we agree with the court's conclusion that "a woman is not entitled to alimony just because she has been his wife," we cannot agree with the court's other conclusion that she is not entitled to support "unless she has something obligating her such as with the care and support of children" or "obligations imposed on her as a result of her marriage" such as "illness or becoming disabled during her life with him." At the time of the separation the parties had been married some fifteen years, at the time of the trial some nineteen years.

The community home . . . is situated in the country seven miles from the nearest shopping center, with no transportation available other than by private car. Under these circumstances we cannot say that the ownership of a three year old Chevrolet for the transportation of a woman of the age of 56 years suffering from severe degenerative arthritis of the left ankle must be characterized as an extravagance, as stated by the trial court.

* * *

The judgment of divorce in favor of respondent is affirmed . . . and the case is hereby remanded to the district court wtih instructions to amend the judgment by providing a reasonable amount for the wife's support. Appellant will recover her costs in this court.

NOTE 3.

FAUSONE v. FAUSONE
Three Years Later

After winning the appeal as to the alimony, I felt that it would be dangerous to the interest of my client to leave the amount of the award up to the District Judge. We therefore stipulated with the husband to pay $100 per month for a period of 24 months.

The decision of the lower court did reflect a policy of the District Judge to only award alimony in cases where there were minor children. However, in this case, I felt that the decision was so unjust, since the wife was incapacitated from arthritis and was nearing 60 years of age, I carried the matter to the Supreme Court without any fee except what was awarded by the Supreme Court against the husband. The District Judge rendering the decision had not been reversed before, to my knowledge, mainly for the reason that in such cases, as was the case here, the wife

did not have sufficient finances to carry the matter to the Supreme Court on an appeal. [Letter from Mr. Joseph O. McDaniel, attorney for the wife, dated May 16, 1961.]

b. The Boschettos

[i]
Establishing the Relationship—1947

Saints Cyril and Methodius' Bulletin
June 29, 1947

BANNS of the forthcoming marriage: BEN BOSCHETTO, Sr. son of late John Boschetto and Mabel Bazanella, of this parish

and

Frieda Kob, daughter of Charles Kob and Rose Montel of the parish in Salorno, Bolzano, Tyrol. First time.

If anyone knows of an impediment, let that be made known.

[ii]
Reorganizing the Relationship—1959

BOSCHETTO v. BOSCHETTO
80 Wyo. 374, 343 P. 2d 503 (1959)

MR. CHIEF JUSTICE BLUME delivered the opinion of the court.

This action, which is one for divorce, was instituted by Ben Boschetto, appellee herein, on March 30, 1956, asserting that Margaret Boschetto, his wife and appellant herein, had offered such indignities to the appellee as to render his condition as husband of defendant intolerable. Margaret Boschetto answered, generally denying the allegations of the petition, and filed a cross-petition alleging that the plaintiff had been guilty of extreme cruelty to the defendant and that the plaintiff had offered such indignities to defendant as to render her life with plaintiff intolerable and further alleging that plaintiff and defendant had, by their joint efforts and as joint adventurers and partners, acquired property in excess of $200,000 in value. She asked that she be divorced from the plaintiff. The case was tried to the court without a jury and at the close of the trial the court rendered judgment granting a divorce to the plaintiff, Ben Boschetto, and dividing the property of the parties as hereinafter mentioned. From that judgment Margaret Boschetto has appealed. She will be referred to hereafter as the appellant and Ben Boschetto will be referred to as the appellee.

[F]rom 1941 to August, 1947, the parties herein lived together as husband and wife and held themselves out as such but were not in fact married. They were married, however, in August,

1947, and lived together as husband and wife except as hereinafter indicated until February, 1956, when the appellee left the appellant, and the parties have not lived together since that time. The appellee had been married previously and by that marriage had three children, namely, a son named Ben, born in 1927, Alfred, a son born in 1930, and one daughter named Verlee born in 1932. The appellant also had been previously married and had one daughter who died in 1949.

* * *

Division of the property. Section 3-5916, W.C.S. 1945, provides as follows:

> "In granting a divorce, the court shall also make such disposition of the property of the parties, as shall appear just and equitable, having regard to the respective merits of the parties and to the condition in which they will be left by such divorce, and to the party through whom the property was acquired, and to the burdens imposed upon it, for the benefit of the wife and children, and the court may also decree to the wife reasonable alimony out of the estate of the husband having regard for his ability, and to effectuate the purposes aforesaid, may order so much of his real estate or the rents and profits thereof, as is necessary to be assigned and set out to the wife for life, or may decree a specific sum to be paid by him to her, and use all necessary legal and equitable processes to carry its decrees into effect."

In Lovejoy v. Lovejoy, 36 Wyo. 379, 256 P. 76, 79, Id., 38 Wyo. 358, 267 P. 91, this court stated:

> "It is conceded that in making a division of property under the statute the trial court exercises a discretion. There are no hard and fast rules to control its action. The statute does not require an equal division. A just and equitable division is as likely as not to be unequal. The decision of the trial court should not be disturbed, except on clear grounds, as that court is usually in a better position than the appellate court to judge of the respective merits and needs of the parties. * * *"

Inasmuch as a trial court's judgment cannot be disturbed except on clear grounds, we have seldom interfered with the action of the trial courts and whenever we have done so we have interfered only to a very limited extent. It is readily seen that unless we adhere to that course we should be apt to have before this court a plethora of appeals in divorce cases involving a division of property and asking us to virtually constitute ourselves as a court of the first instance to divide the property. We do not think that this is the function of this court.

The court awarded to the appellant Lots 5 and 6, Block 10, in the Clark Addition to Rock Springs, Sweetwater County, Wyoming, valued at $23,000. This property was the home of the parties and contained in addition a number of apartments which were rented out to other parties. The court further awarded to the appellant the sum of $10,000 in cash, a 1955 Oldsmobile sedan and attorneys' fees of $2,500. It awarded all other property to the appellee. The net worth of appellee, according to the stipulation of the parties, was approximately $199,000, so that after deducting what was awarded to the appellant and considering the attorneys' fees, the property left to the appellee would be approximately in the sum of $160,000 as against about $37,000 awarded to the appellant. Counsel for the appellant claim that their client should have half of the appellee's property.

Appellant and appellee, as heretofore indicated, started living together in a meretricious relationship in July, 1941, holding themselves out, however, as husband and wife. This relationship continued until they were married on August 22, 1947. The evidence fairly discloses, we think, that appellant was aware that the relationship was meretricious. She was 25 years of age in 1941, had been married before, and had a child by that marriage. . . . We do not think that on account of public policy we are justified in overruling Willis v. Willis, 48 Wyo. 403, 49 P. 2d 670, 681, Id., 49 Wyo. 296, 54 P. 2d 814, where we stated:

> " 'A wife is not entitled to compensation for services rendered her husband. And where a woman lives with a man as his mistress or concubine, she cannot recover for such services as are incidental to the relation in which they live, unless a contract for payment is shown.' " 40 Wyc. 2823.

In Annotation, 31 A.L.R. 1255, 1259, it is said:

> "Where a woman cohabits with a man and has actual knowledge of the unlawful nature of the relationship, she does not by such cohabitation alone acquire any rights in the accumulations of the man during such relationship * * *. She may, however, acquire certain rights where it is established that there was an agreement to pool earnings or an agreement of partnership or joint adventure, or where there are circumstances adequate to establish a constructive trust. * * *"

Counsel for appellant claim that there was an agreement to pool earnings as partners or joint adventurers and that there were circumstances adequate to establish a constructive trust.

It appears herein that the appellant had $500 which she gave to the appellee about 1942 and which was used to pay unpaid bills. The court appears to have regarded that as a loan and we cannot say that we disagree. The court took this loan into consideration in making its award of property. Appellant also did the housework for the parties and rented the apartments connected with their home, occasionally cleaning an apartment if it became vacant, and doing occasional painting in that connection whenever it was necessary. But the main stress of counsel for appellant is laid on the fact that she signed notes with appellee aggregating some $75,000 during the period here in question. Counsel for appellee dispute this and say that many of the various notes were signed in order to pay off other and previous notes. We need not, we think, go into the matter. Counsel for appellant say and stress the fact that she was just as much responsible for the payment of these notes as appellee. Theoretically that is true. Practically speaking, it is not. She had no visible property of any kind. She was earning no money. She had no financial standing whatever. Hence, she cannot be said to have helped the appellee financially by signing notes with him. The addition of her name to the notes was substantially merely a formality. We find no sufficient evidence in the record to justify us in holding that there was any agreement or pooling of property as partners or joint adventurers or that there is any basis for a constructive trust.

However, the appellant stands in this case before the court not as a courtesan but as the lawful wife of the appellee so that Willis v. Willis, supra, has only a limited bearing in this case, and we must determine whether or not this court can be justified in modifying the awards made by the trial court in view of the fact that the appellant was the wife of appellee for a period of nine years before the commencement of this action. The home and the apartment awarded to appellant had been acquired by the appellee long before 1941. The appellee started his grocery business in 1931, to which a locker business was added in 1948 and 1949. Appellee worked hard, as is admitted by the appellant herein, often working late at night and on Sundays. He built up his business until now it is a substantial, well-paying one. Our statute provides that in dividing property in the case of divorce the derivation of the property is an item to be considered. Hence, what his children helped him to acquire is relevant herein. The testimony shows that his boys commenced to work for him in the store at hours when not in school from the time when they were about eight years of age, that they worked hard and got only their spending money. The daughter too, who was 15 years of age in 1947, helped in the store and helped the appellant in taking care of the housekeeping and the washing necessary for the store. The appellant during the marriage continued to take care of the renting of these

apartments and matters incidental thereto as she did before the marriage. In addition she worked about two weeks in the store in 1948, possibly a little more, and ran a trailer and hamburger and popcorn stand in conjunction with her husband for about two months in 1949 during the evenings. She kept house during this time but the oldest boy, Ben, went into military service in 1945 to 1946 and was married in 1949. The second boy, Alfred, went to military service in 1951 and was married during that time. The girl, Verlee, was married in 1953. None of the children lived with the appellant after being married and Verlee helped considerably in the housework before 1953. So the burden of housekeeping from and after 1951 could not have been very great. In 1951 the appellee and his two boys formed a partnership, the boys each receiving a 20 percent interest in the store and locker business and the appellee retaining a 60 percent interest therein. The property which he has left is, in the main, this 60 percent interest.

The apartments awarded to appellant herein would bring an income as far as we can judge, taking into consideration necessary repairs from time to time, of approximately $2,000 per annum. If she invests the $10,000 awarded her by the court at 4 percent, that would bring in an additional income of $400 per annum. The care of the renting of the apartments should not take much of appellant's time. She is now 43 years of age, still a comparatively young woman. She should not expect to be able to spend her life in idleness. If she quits her excessive drinking of intoxicants, as she should, she should be able for many years to increase the above income by a considerable amount so as to enable her to live in comparative comfort. She has neither chick nor child dependent upon her. Appellee has three children. We do not think that we should be justified in depriving the latter of their expectancy to inherit from their father the property to the acquisition of which they devoted much of their time.

The majority of the court is in doubt as to the wisdom of modifying the award herein. They do not believe that a clear case has been presented to justify this court to do that. They believe that the trial court had a better opportunity to judge as to how the property of the parties should be divided and that its judgment in that connection should stand. The whole of the judgment of the trial court, accordingly, is affirmed.

[iii]
Maintaining a Reorganized Relationship—1961

Mrs. Boschetto is, and has been, managing the apartments since the disposition of the divorce case. She occasionally drinks to excess, but not as often as she did prior to the divorce. To my knowledge she has not been engaged in any gainful employment since the divorce case, but is satisfied to live off the rentals.

The husband and sons continue to operate the grocery business. This business has grown considerably and now does over a million dollars a year gross business. The percentages of the sons as partners has been increased. Also Mr. Boschetto's daughter now has an interest in the partnership. [Letter dated May 15, 1961 from Albert E. Nelson, attorney for Mr. Boschetto.]

c. RICHARDS v. RICHARDS
44 Haw. 491, 355 P. 2d 188 (1960)

MARUMOTO, JUSTICE

* * *

Upon the granting of libellant's motion, libellee announced that he would not offer any evidence in support of his cross-libel. The judge thereupon heard so much of libellant's testimony as he deemed sufficient to establish the ground for divorce, and rendered an oral decision dismissing libellee's cross-libel, granting absolute divorce to libellant on the ground [of grievous mental suffering] alleged in the libel, and reserving the questions of temporary and permanent alimony, expenses of the proceeding, and division of property, for decision at a later date. . . .

The judge took voluminous evidence bearing on the questions of alimony, expenses of the proceeding, and division of property at extensive hearings held over a period of seven months. Upon consideration of such evidence, he filed a decision in which he made an award of permanent alimony of $600 per month, commencing as of February 1, 1956; an allowance of $3,036.99 for expenses; and a division of household furniture, silver, works of art, and other paraphernalia, whereby the bulk of such property went to libellant. He denied temporary alimony for the period between June 30, 1955, and February 1, 1956, and division of property other than household paraphernalia. The allowance of $3,036.99 for expenses was in addition to the sum previously advanced for the taking of depositions, but did not include attorneys' fees and fee and expenses of expert witness. A supplemental decree of divorce in accordance with such decision was entered on September 27, 1957.

The case is before this court on appeals by libellant and libellee from the supplemental decree of divorce. On these appeals, the propriety of the granting of the divorce is not in question. Nor is there any question regarding the division of household paraphernalia.

On her appeal, libellant charges that the judge erred in entering the decree of divorce before deciding the remaining issues of the case; in denying temporary alimony, temporary and final attorneys' fees, and fee and expense of expert witness; in failing to award adequate permanent alimony; and in failing to make a division of property other than household paraphernalia.

Libellee, on his appeal, specifies but one error, namely, that the judge erred in ordering him to pay libellant's expenses other than atttorneys' fees and fee and expenses of expert witness.

* * *

Libellant's charge of error regarding the denial of temporary alimony is well taken. . . .

[E]ntirely apart from the stipulation of the parties, the application of pertinent statutory provision to the facts of this case leads to the same conclusion. This point may be considered in connection with libellant's charge that the judge erred in denying her request for attorneys' fees and fee and expenses of expert witness, and libellee's charge that the judge erred in ordering him to pay libellant's expenses other than attorneys' fees and fee and expenses of expert witness. These charges involve the application of R.L.H. 1955, § 324-34, which reads as follows:

> "After the filing of a libel for divorce or separation the judge may make such orders relative to the personal liberty and support of the wife pending the libel as he may deem fair and reasonable and may enforce such orders by summary process. The judge may also compel the husband to advance reasonable amounts for the compensation of witnesses and other expenses of the trial, including attorney's fees, to be incurred by the wife and may from time to time amend and revise such orders."

* * *

[A] showing of wife's destitute circumstances is not a prerequisite to an award of temporary alimony or allowance of expenses of trial. The [statute] leaves the judge with discretion to make an award of temporary alimony limited only by the standard that it be fair and reasonable. The same is true with respect to expenses of trial.

Under R.L.H. 1955, § 324-34, we think that a wife who has sufficient means to live in her accustomed manner, and to prosecute her libel for divorce, without impairing the capital of her separate estate, is not entitled to temporary alimony or expenses of trial. . . . But, in our opinion, the statute does not require a wife to impair her capital, and if her income is insufficient for the maintenance of her accustomed standard of living and for the efficient prosecution of her libel, she may be awarded temporary alimony to supplement her income and may be allowed reasonable expenses of trial. Of course, due consideration must be given to the financial resources of the husband. . . .

In Harding v. Harding [144 Ill. 589, 32 N.E. 208] . . . the supreme court made the following statement, with which we are in accord:

> "It would seem equitable and just that the wife, who is prosecuting her suit in good faith, should be placed upon an equality with the husband; and if her income be insufficient to maintain her, and to carry on the litigation, his income should be required to contribute, before she should be required to exhaust her estate. . . ."

* * *

[H]ere, despite libellant's cash position, the judge ordered libellee to pay libellant's expenses other than attorneys' fees and fee and expenses of expert witness. The judge gave two reasons for such action, first, that such expenses were expenses reasonably incurred by libellant as a direct and proximate result of the divorce proceedings which stemmed from libellee's misconduct, and, second, that libellant's income was insufficient to enable her to meet her costs of living during the pendency of the proceeding and still pay such expenses without impairing her capital.

We think that the reasons given for the allowance of libellant's expenses other than attorneys' fees and fee and expenses of expert witness are sound and valid. But these reasons are equally applicable to attorney's fees and require that such fees be allowed. Libellant needed the services of her attorneys in order to assert her rights in the divorce proceeding. The uncontroverted evidence is that the proceeding arose out of libellee's misconduct. Libellant had no means of paying her attorneys except by dipping into her capital.

* * *

Libellant's contention with respect to periodic alimony is that, under R.L.H. 1955, § 324-37, she is entitled to periodic alimony which, added to her income, will enable her to maintain the standard of living to which she was accustomed during her marriage to libellee, and that the monthly sum of $600 which was ordered to be paid as alimony is so inadequate that the judge abused his discretion in failing to order the payment of a larger monthly sum.

At the hearings, libellant claimed that the sum required for the maintenance of her accustomed standard of living was $1,813 per month, or $21,756 per year, net after Federal and Terri-

torial income taxes; that she had only $2,400 of "pure income" per year of her own which might be applied to her living expenses, consisting of $600 in bank interest, $200 in dividends, and $1,600 from annuity; that she received $7,875 annually from an annuity provided by her mother but only $1,600 of such annual sum was pure income and the balance was return of wasting asset.

With respect to division of property, libellant contends that she is entitled to a reasonable share of libellee's property, which she claims to be one-third, and that the judge abused his discretion in failing to award such share or, in the alternative, to make an equivalent cash award as property settlement or as alimony in gross. The basis of her claim to such share is that she considers it to be in the nature of a substitute for dower. She argues that her marriage to libellee would not have been dissolved except for libellee's misconduct, that if the marriage had continued she would have been entitled to dower upon libellee's death, and that she is entitled to "receive at least financially that which would have been hers but for the Husband's cruel and inhuman treatment."

Libellant also urges upon us that R.L.H. 1955, § 324-37, makes the personal conduct of a husband toward his wife a material consideration in the determination of the extent of relief thereunder in view of the requirement that the judge have "regard to the respective merits of the parties" in granting the relief, and, consequently, the undisputed facts regarding the grievous mental suffering inflicted upon her by libellee furnished compelling reasons for the exercise in full measure of the equitable powers under the statute.

We shall begin our consideration of libellant's foregoing contentions with an examination of the relief available under R.L.H. 1955, § 324-37. For an understanding of the nature and scope of such relief, a study of prior statutes and decisions of this court on the subject will be of assistance.

The original statute on the subject was C.C. 1859, § 1328, which provided that upon the granting of a divorce "the court may make such further decree or order against the defendant, compelling him * * * to provide such suitable allowance for the wife, for her support, as the court shall deem just and reasonable, having regard to the ability of the husband, the character and situation of the parties, and all other circumstances of the case." Under it, the amount of alimony was determined by the circuit court, the determination of the court was reviewed on exceptions, and upon such review the determination had the effect of a jury verdict. . . .

* * *

The original statute was construed as being sufficient to authorize an award of alimony in gross, as well as in periodical payments, but not broad enough to sanction an award of specific property in a divorce proceeding. . . .

The amount of periodic alimony was subject to modification for change of circumstance of either party, both by statute and under the decisions of this court. R.L.H. 1955, § 324-37, par. 2. . . .

On the other hand, alimony in gross was not subject to modification because its award constituted a final settlement of the financial affairs of the parties. . . .

In Farm v. Cornn, 31 Haw. 574, 585, a case in which the principal issue was whether periodic alimony was subject to reduction although no power to do so was reserved in the decree, this court made the following statement in answer to the wife's contention that alimony was in lieu of dower and that therefore it became, upon its award, a property right which could not be subsequently disturbed: "In our opinion alimony is not granted in lieu of dower. The latter is a provision made by the law for the support of a wife after the death of the husband. The former is a provision which courts are authorized to make for the support of the wife during the life of the husband. The fact or the quantity of the dower is never affected by the fact whether the wife has or has not had alimony. The fact or the amount of the alimony is never affected by the fact of whether the husband owns or is likely to own at the time of his death property which is subject to dower."

With regard to the considerations to be taken into account in determining whether periodic alimony or alimony in gross should be awarded, this court stated in Nobrega v. Nobrega, 14 Haw. 152, 155: "As a rule the alimony should be payable periodically. The court can then control its amount more effectually and change it from time to time according as the means and needs of the parties change. An award in gross may be made appropriately when the husband is likely to vexatiously delay or withhold payments, and of course, there are other circumstances to be considered." It also stated in Santos v. Santos, supra, 40 Haw. at page 647: "An award of alimony in gross accomplishes a more equitable result than periodic alimony in circumstances where a wife has contributed real or personal property owned by her at the time of marriage, or where property has been accumulated after marriage by the joint efforts of husband and wife. In such cases, it is generally held that a wife's contribution should be restored out of the estate of the husband so acquired." However, in the latter case it recog-

nized that there was no criterion which embraced all of the possible circumstances in which an award in gross was proper and that such award "should properly be confined to those cases wherein the presence of special circumstances might require it or render it advisable."

* * *

Some of the considerations involved in determining the amount of alimony in gross were set forth in Nobrega v. Nobrega, 14 Haw. 152, 158, where it was stated: "A further contention is that there was not sufficient evidence to support a decree for alimony, in that it was not shown how much was necessary for the wife's 'support' per month or year, &c., or what her expectation of life was. In the nature of things it could not, nor does the statute require it to be shown exactly how much she would need, nor in awarding an allowance in gross was it necessary to estimate the amount of tables of annuities and mortality. The statute provides as to the amount, that it shall be such 'as the court shall deem just and reasonable, having regard to the ability of the husband, the character and situation of the parties, and all other circumstances of the case.' * * * Courts elsewhere do not seem as a rule to make use of such tables or to require exact proof of the wife's needs in estimating alimony in gross," and that "As a rule allowances in gross are less than one-third of the estate, and in estimating the amount the property that the wife already has is taken into account and especially that part of it which came from her husband, and, on the other hand, any contributions she may have made."

In Santos v. Santos, supra, 40 Haw. at page 652, this court stated that the last statement in Nobrega v. Nobrega did not "mandate an inflexible apportionment, but the ratio of the amount of the award to the husband's estate may be considered as one of the primary factors in determining the amount of the award in gross."

Such was the state of the law when S.L.H. 1955, c. 77, was enacted to amend the original statute.

A feature of the original statute, of significance in connection with libellant's contentions regarding permanent alimony and division of property, was that it empowered the judge to order a husband to provide "suitable allowance for the wife, for her support" but did not give him the authority to effect a property settlement, as such, in a divorce proceeding. This did not mean that a wife who had a meritorious claim to a share of the property held by her husband, by reason of her contribution to its acquisition or otherwise, was wholly without relief. On the ground that the quoted phrase was broader in meaning than the term "alimony," as known at common law, this court construed the statute as authorizing an award of alimony in gross. Nobrega v. Nobrega, 13 Haw. 654, 658. Such judicial construction of the statute enabled the judge to give some measure of recognition to the claim of the wife by making an award of alimony in gross based on "the amount, character and reasonable value of the property owned by the husband." Chong v. Chong, 35 Haw. 385, 395.

However, this court at no time deviated from its position in Nobrega v. Nobrega, 14 Haw. 152, 156, that alimony, whether periodical or in gross, is not considered a part of the husband's estate and that the "Power to award alimony in gross does not, any more than power to award it as an annuity, permit a division of even personal estate *in specie*."

S.L.H. 1955, c. 77, was enacted for the sole purpose of enabling the judge to effect a property settlement in a divorce proceeding, thus saving the parties the bother of resorting to a separate civil action to obtain such settlement. It did not change the pre-existing law regarding alimony. The Judiciary Committee of the House of Representatives and the Judiciary Committee of the Senate. Twenty-eighth Legislature of the Territory of Hawaii, stated:

> "1. The purpose of this bill is to confer upon the Judge who grants a final decree of divorce the power to make property settlements between the parties of all property, real, personal, or mixed, whether held as community, joint or separate property.
>
> * * *
>
> "3. At present, because of the lack of power by the judge to order property settlements, two or three trials may be necessary before the interests of the parties to a divorce are finally settled. In addition to the trial for divorce, a trial to partition the real estate and a trial to divide his personal property may be necessary. Court costs and attorney's fees may mount and much time may be wasted. The provisions of this bill are intended to solve these problems and correct injustices which arise under the present law.
>
> * * *
>
> "5. This bill will not in any way affect the awarding of alimony. It is the intent of this bill that, depending on all the circumstances, in addition to a property settlement, the aggrieved party may be entitled to alimony." Standing Committee Report No. 356, House Journal 1955, p. 697; Standing Committee Report No. 595, Senate Journal 1955, p. 632.

This statute was inartistically drawn. After empowering the judge to grant two types of relief, namely, an order compelling a husband to provide suitable allowance for his wife's support and an order for a just and equitable division of property, it set forth the considerations to be taken into account in determining the extent of the relief which the judge may grant in the following words: "having regard to the respective merits of the parties, to the ability of the husband, to the condition in which they will be left by such divorce, to the burdens imposed upon it for the benefit of the children of such marriage, and all other circumstances of the case." From the position in which those words are placed, it is not clear whether all of the considerations are applicable to both types of relief, or whether some are applicable only to one type of relief and some to the other.

Here, our concern is with the phrase "the respective merits of the parties." Libellant's position is that the phrase applies to both types of relief and that it has reference to personal conduct of the spouses toward each other. We think otherwise. We think that in the context in which the phrase is used, it means the merits of the respective claims of the spouses to the property sought to be divided and is pertinent only in connection with division of property. We do not think that it has any reference to personal conduct of the spouses. The phrase is used in statutes of Vermont, Washington, and Wyoming. . . . In none of these States has it been interpreted to mean personal conduct of the spouses toward each other.

Personal conduct of the spouses toward each other is material to the establishment of a ground for divorce. But it has no bearing on the question as to which spouse has a better claim to the property sought to be divided in a divorce proceeding.

Likewise, personal conduct of a husband toward his wife should have no bearing on the determination of the amount of alimony. Alimony is not awarded as reward for virtue and punishment for wrongdoing. Under the statute, it is a "reasonable allowance for the wife, for her support." The reasonable need of a wife for her future support does not depend on whether her husband was kind or inconsiderate to her in the past. . . .

The foregoing discussion disposes of libellant's contention that personal conduct of a husband toward his wife is a material consideration in the determination of the extent of the relief that may be granted . . . and we see no need for reviewing the evidence regarding the grievous mental suffering inflicted upon libellant by libellee.

Coming now to libellant's contentions regarding permanent alimony and division of property, we shall first consider the contention with respect to division of property before we take up the contention about alimony. We do so because, as we construe R.L.H. 1955, § 324-37, it empowers the judge to order a division of property independently and without regard to his action on alimony, but, in determining the amount of alimony, it requires the judge to take into account the resources of the wife, including the property apportioned to her in the divorce proceeding.

At the time of the divorce, libellee had under his control, at his residence and in storage at a commercial warehouse, a considerable amount of household furniture, silver, works of art, and other paraphernalia, which libellant though† was worth about $50,000. We shall hereafter refer to all of such property as household paraphernalia.

* * *

We think that R.L.H. 1955, § 324-37, empowers the judge to make a cash award in lieu of division of property in kind where a spouse establishes a meritorious claim but specific division is either impracticable or does not bring about a fair and equitable result.

Here, the record does not show that libellant established a meritorious claim to division of property other than household paraphernalia. Except as to household paraphernalia, it cannot be said from the evidence adduced at the hearings that libellant contributed any property of her own to the building up of libellee's estate or that she lent any effort to the accumulation of any portion of such estate.

Libellant owned considerably more property at the time of the divorce than at the time of the marriage. At the time of the marriage, her property consisted of $25,205.89 in bank deposits; a claim of $12,436.77 against her former husband for insurance adjustments; household paraphernalia which she valued at $25,587.04; and personal jewelry and effects of unspecified value. During the marriage, she acquired additional jewelry and household paraphernalia. At the time of the divorce, she had bank deposits, traveler's checks, United States Treasury bonds, and current credits which totaled $42,045.04; securities of the approximate value of $4,827; and personal jewelry of a market value of $52,925 and a replacement value of $83,140. The judge apportioned to her in the divorce proceeding household paraphernalia of the approximate value of $35,000.

Libellant argues that, although she might not have contributed directly to the acquisition or accumulation of libellee's estate, other than household paraphernalia, she is entitled to a substantial cash award as a property settlement because she assisted in the conservation of such estate to the extent that she used her funds to pay the living expenses which libellee was bound to provide.

We see at least two difficulties in libellant's argument. First, it assumes that libellee was legally obligated to provide the entire sum which the parties expended for their living during the marriage. During the period of the marriage, libellant had cash receipts of $225,264.81 from sources not attributable to libellee, as follows: $138,490.05 from annuity; $82,004.42 as salaries, bonuses, and perquisities from Reader's Digest; and $4,770.34 from dividends and stock sales. Libellant used the receipts to pay part of her living expenses and to purchase furniture. Also, during the same period, about $400,000 of libellee's funds was used to defray the living expenses of the parties. Such evidence merely indicates that the parties lived expensively. It is no proof that libellee had the legal obligation to pay all the expenses of such living. Second, there is no proof that libellee's estate was conserved by the manner in which libellant used her receipts. If the living expenses of the parties during the period of the marriage exceeded their joint income, which remained after the payment of Federal and Territorial income taxes, libellee's estate would not have been preserved. The record is devoid of evidence showing the amount of the aggregate net income of the parties during the marriage. There is evidence that at least since 1948, the living expenses of the parties exceeded their joint net income and that libellee expressed his concern about the situation to libellant.

We shall now turn to libellant's contention regarding the periodic alimony awarded by the judge. Here, the question is whether the monthly sum of $600 which was ordered to be paid as periodic alimony was so inadequate that we can say that the judge abused his discretion in failing to order the payment of a larger monthly sum.

As we noted previously, libellant claimed at the hearings that she needed $1,813 per month, or $21,756 per year net after Federal and Territorial income taxes, to live in the manner to which she was accustomed during the marriage. She conceded that $2,400 of her income was applicable to her living expenses. Even with such concession, an alimony of at least $50,000 per year, or more than $4,000 per month, would have been required to provide libellant with a net sum of $21,756 after the payment of Federal and Territorial income taxes under the existing rates. But libellee's income was considerably less than such required amount. Libellant figured libellee's total annual income at the time of the divorce to be $29,855.55. Libellee figured it to be $28,737.49. In either case, the figure is close enough to $30,000, and so we shall assume that libellee's total annual income was $30,000 for the purpose of further discussion.

From [his] total annual income of $30,000, libellee was required to pay alimony of $300 per month, or $3,600 per year, to his first wife. Under the supplemental decree entered in the instant case, he was required to pay alimony of $600 per month, or $7,200 per year, to libellant. These payments would have left $19,200 before Federal and Territorial income taxes. The net balance left to libellee after the payment of such taxes would have been approximately $13,000.

At the time of the divorce, libellant had a total annual income of $15,875, including the alimony awarded in this divorce proceeding. Such income consisted of the following items: annuity, $7,875; interest, $600; dividends, $200; and alimony, $7,200. With respect to the annuity of $7,875, we reject as being without merit libellant's argument that only $1,600 was pure income and the balance was return of wasting asset. If Federal and Territorial income taxes were deducted from such total annual income of $15,875, libellant would have had approximately $11,500 left for her living expenses.

In other words, the alimony of $600 per month, or $7,200 per year, added to her other income, provided libellant with a net sum of approximately $11,500 per year available for her living expenses as compared with a net sum of approximately $13,000 per year available to libellee. The amount of alimony which was awarded to libellant was not a liberal allowance. We think it was on the low side. But, our function here is limited to a review for abuse, and considering all the circumstances as they appear in the record, we cannot say that the judge abused his discretion in not awarding a larger alimony.

Libellant based the amount of periodic alimony she claims on the scale of living of the parties during their marriage. The parties were married in 1938. At that time, libellee was president of Hawaiian Pineapple Company, Limited, and had an annual income of more than $125,000, of which approximately $70,000 was from salary and bonus and the balance was from dividends. His net worth was $941,000. The parties lived on a scale commensurate with libellee's income. Three years later, libellee was let out as president of the company, and his income was drastically reduced. Thereafter, he suffered business losses in excess of $640,000. Nevertheless, the parties continued to live expensively to the time of the divorce. In the last years of the marriage, the expenditures for such living which were paid out of libellee's funds exceeded his income.

It is frequently stated as a general proposition that a wife, who is divorced by reason of her husband's misconduct, is entitled to live in the manner to which she was accustomed during the marriage and that the divorced husband is obligated to provide the funds required for such living. The statement is too broad to be true in all cases. The amount of alimony is to be determined upon a realistic appraisal of the situation of the parties at the time of the divorce. Such appraisal involves a consideration of the respective resources and revenues of the parties, their accustomed manner of living, and the manner of living which is appropriate on the basis of such resources and revenues. We think that normally the principal consideration in determining the amount of periodic alimony should be the respective income of the parties. There may be situations which require consideration of factors other than income in arriving at a just result, such as where a substantial portion of the capital of either party is kept in non-productive form, or where either party, though in good health, malingers or otherwise fails to use his or her talent in income-producing endeavors. Also, ill health of either party may require extraordinary medical expenses which justify an invasion of capital.

Here we cannot say that libellee's capital was not properly employed in income-producing enterprises and investments, nor can we say that libellee avoided the use of his personal talent to advantage in earning income. There is evidence that libellant was in poor health and was hospitalized immediately before the divorce, but the evidence was insufficient to establish libellant's continuing future need for hospitalization and other medical expenses.

Libellant argues that the judge should have made a larger award because, in addition to his actual income, libellee enjoyed "the possibility of prospective income of a very substantial nature." She also argues that a larger award should have been made because of her precarious health which required frequent and lengthy hospitalization in the past. In answer to such argument, it suffices to say that they are based on conjecture. If the possibility of libellee's prospective income or the concern about libellant's need for future medical expenses materializes, it will be time enough for the judge to order appropriate relief upon such change of circumstance.

Libellant urged in her brief that the evidence in this case justified an award of a liberal alimony in gross as an alternative to periodic alimony and division of property. A short answer to such proposition is that the record does not show that it was presented to the circuit judge. Libellant specifically prayed for "a reasonable sum of money each month as permanent alimony" in her libel. Even if the proposition were presented to the judge, its rejection would not have constituted reversible error. Periodic alimony is generally preferred over alimony in gross because it allows the judge to "control its amount more effectually and change it from time to time according as the means and needs of the parties change." Nobrega v. Nobrega, 14 Haw. 152, 155.

The supplemental decree of divorce appealed from is affirmed, except insofar as it denies temporary alimony, attorneys' fee and fee and expenses of expert witness. . . .

NOTES

NOTE   1.

RICHARDS v. RICHARDS
One Year Later

Please be advised as follows:

1. Following the entry of the decision in the Supreme Court of the State of Hawaii in *Richards* v. *Richards,* we negotiated a compromise settlement which was reduced to writing in the form of a Property Settlement Agreement. . . . You will note that [the] significant compromise provisions provided for the continuation of alimony even after the death of the husband, in the event that the wife should survive the husband. In addition, the $600.00 per month alimony became a fixed obligation without any power of modification. In agreeing to this, we were aware of the fact that we were giving up the likelihood of an increase in periodic alimony based upon continuing expenses attributable to Mrs. Richards' health and further based upon the increased income of Mr. Richards.

The Supreme Court, of course, had intentionally commented on these two factors and in effect, had mandated the lower court to increase the alimony if the existence of these factors was proven, especially since it in effect said that the original award was niggardly.

We believed the compromise to be advantageous to Mrs. Richards since (a) she would not have to return from New York City, where she is now living, and go through continuing agony of additional court hearings, (b) Mr. Richards could not later seek to modify or eliminate the alimony based on any reduction in his income, (c) Mrs. Richards can now live serenely knowing that the earlier death of Mr. Richards will not impair her income, and (d) she was the owner of two policies of life insurance on the life of Mr. Richards, which policies had an aggregate cash value in

excess of $31,000.00, and in view of the alimony becoming a charge upon his estate, she will now be free to cash the policies and enjoy the use of those funds.

Our thinking, of course, was tempered by her poor health, and by the fact that she was also receiving her annuity of $656.25 per month and other modest income, the aggregate of which, together with the alimony, would be ample to support her, even in poor health, during her remaining years.

2. With respect to attorney's fees, we had charged our client in the trial court $13,500.00, a sum which we believe to be very much on the low side, since we had 52 separate court hearings, (most of them half days or less, however) together with a tremendous amount of outside preparation and numerous consultations with the client in order to provide her peace of mind throughout the dismal days of trial. In setting the fee, we had left the door open to charging an additional amount as a part of our Appellate fee in the event that we received substantial concessions in the Supreme Court. We had also set a minimum fee of $3,000.00 for handling the appeal. In the interest of settling the matter, however, we adhered to our minimum fees, both in the lower court and on appeal. Both of these fees were paid by the husband as a part of the compromise property settlement, and thus Mrs. Richards was reimbursed the $13,500.00 that she had paid us. We did not feel that our efforts had been sufficiently rewarding to Mrs. Richards to charge her any additional fees over and above what the husband was required to pay.

I might add that, although I thereafter concluded successfully several "carriage trade" divorces on the basis where an adequate fee could be obtained, I am no longer handling domestic relations matters of any type. Most of the cases we have handled, including the Richards case, were taken reluctantly in order to do a special favor at the request of an attorney (in this case, an attorney in New York) or for a special client. I have come to the firm conviction that the typical divorce case results in the following circumstances:

1. Both parties tend to blame and usually blame the other spouse's attorney for the acts and attitudes of the opposite party, and consequently are bitter toward the other attorney for the rest of their lives.

2. Both parties tend to blame their own attorneys for the predicament they are now in financially and the wife can't understand why the attorney is able to produce such a small slice of

the pie for her comfort, whereas, the husband blames his attorney for recommending that he give such a large slice of the pie to his wife. The parties together have usually been exhausting their incomes in maintaining their joint household, and it pinches dreadfully to have to support two households from the same income. The attorneys therefore become the scapegoats.

3. Because the parties are so emotionally involved, they usually and frequently call their attorneys at all hours of the day and night and put everything on a high priority basis. As a consequence, one's peace of mind and business practice suffer.

4. When the shouting is all over, the parties are both so hard up financially that it is difficult to charge and collect an adequate fee.

Consequently, you will probably not be seeing the name of this firm in future domestic relations cases. [Letter dated May 12, 1961, from William W. Saunders, attorney for Mrs. Richards.]

NOTE 2.

GORDON, RICHARD E. ; GORDON, KATHERINE K. ; *and* GUNTHER, MAX

The Split-Level Trap*

Diane Weber would have been better able to assert herself with Link if, during their marriage, she had made herself indispensable to him, if she had seen to it that the house and bank account were in her name as well as his, and had in other ways created for herself a position of power. But like many mobile wives she had failed to do this. Her only hold on him was that of a romantic "being in love," which, as it sometimes will, dried up and disappeared.

When Link came to her a year later and asked that the separation be transmuted to divorce, however, the tables were turned. Link needed his freedom in order to marry his wealthy divorcee friend, who had indicated to him that their relationship could not continue otherwise. Diane was now in a position of greater power, and she had learned how to use it well. She carefully controlled her vindictive feelings toward Link ; she saw no point in arguing about guilt or blame or sin, or in making Link repent. Those are not forward-looking concepts. They are related to the past. Diane saw that if she acted vengefully toward Link, he would answer with anger of his own ; and the result might be a long, bitter battle

* Reprinted with permission of Bernard Geis Associates from *The Split Level Trap* by Dr. Richard E. Gordon, Katherine K. Gordon and Max Gunther, pp. 780–81. © 1960, 1961 by Dr. Richard E. Gordon, Katherine K. Gordon, and Max Gunther.

in the courts, expensive to both sides in money and emotional wear. Instead of dwelling on the past, Diane moved forward from it. She used past unhappiness as a lesson for the present. She asserted herself with Link, firmly and fairly. Their lawyers quickly arranged a cash and alimony settlement that protected her financially and provided for the children until they had finished college. The agreement seemed reasonable to both sides.

Diane demonstrated that self-assertiveness doesn't have to be unpleasant. When it is unpleasant, it begets anger. Anger is contagious, and when anger is boiling up on all sides it is hard to think clearly or work out mutually useful solutions.

NOTE 3.

California Civil Code § 146 (1954)

Community property and homestead ; disposition on divorce or separate maintenance

Order. In case of the dissolution of the marriage by decree of a court of competent jurisdiction or in the case of judgment or decree for separate maintenance of the husband or the wife without dissolution of the marriage, the court shall make an order for disposition of the community property and for the assignment of the homestead as follows:

One. Community property, cases of adultery, cruelty, or insanity. If the decree is rendered on the ground of adultery, incurable insanity or extreme cruelty, the community property shall be assigned to the respective parties in such proportions as the court, from all the facts of the case, and the condition of the parties may deem just.

Two. Community property, other cases. If the decree be rendered on any other ground than that of adultery, incurable insanity or extreme cruelty the community property shall be equally divided between the parties.

Three. Homestead from community property. If a homestead has been selected from the community property, it may be assigned to the party to whom the divorce or decree of separate maintenance is granted, or, in cases where a divorce or decree of separate maintenance is granted upon the ground of incurable insanity, to the party against whom the divorce or decree of separate maintenance is granted. The assignment may be either absolutely or for a limited period, subject, in the latter case, to the future disposition of the court, or it may, in the discretion of the court, be divided, or be sold and the proceeds divided.

Four. Homestead from separate property. If a homestead has been selected from the separate property of either, in cases in which the decree is rendered upon any ground other than incurable insanity, it shall be assigned to the former owner of such property, subject to the power of the court to assign it for a limited period to the party to whom the divorce or decree of separate maintenance is granted, and in cases where the decree is rendered upon the ground of incurable insanity, it shall be assigned to the former owner of such property, subject to the power of the court to assign it to the party against whom the divorce or decree of separate maintenance is granted for a term of years not to exceed the life of such party.

Homestead, temporary assignment. This section shall not limit the power of the court to make temporary assignment of the homestead at any stage of the proceedings.

Partition or sale. Whenever necessary to carry out the purpose of this section, the court may order a partition or sale of the property and a division or other disposition of the proceeds. . . .

NOTE 4.

THOMASSET v. THOMASSET
122 Cal. App. 2d 116, 264 P. 2d 626 (1954)

VALLEE, JUSTICE.

Property acquired during marriage and taken in the name of the husband is presumed to be community property. . . . The presumption is rebuttable. . . . The burden rests on the party asserting that property acquired after marriage is separate to establish that fact. . . . There are expressions in the decisions to the effect that the separate character of property acquired after marriage is to be established by "clear and convincing evidence," "clear and decisive proof," "clear and satisfactory proof". . . .

Moneys earned by defendant prior to, but collected after, marriage were not community funds. . . . Whether property acquired by a man during marriage is separate is determined by the time of its acquisition. If it was separate then, it remains so with the exception of such increase thereof as may have been due to the contribution of the community by virtue of capital or industry, unless by agreement of the spouses it is transmuted into community property. . . . Separate property does not lose its character as such by reason of a change in form or identity. . . . Property that is purchased with separate funds ordinarily continues to be separate property. . . .

It appears to be plaintiff's contention that if a dollar which is separate property is deposited in a bank account in which there is a dollar which is community property, the dollar which was separate property becomes community property; and if a dollar which is community property is deposited in a bank account in which there is a dollar which is separate property, the latter dollar becomes community property; and that, in either case, all property purchased with the deposited funds is community property. That is not the law. Where separate and community funds are so commingled that it is *impossible* to trace the source of the funds, the whole will be treated as community property. . . . The presumption that property acquired during marriage is community is controlling only when it is impossible to trace the source of the specific property. . . .

* * *

It is presumed that expenses of the family came from community earnings. . . . Where the husband, charged with the support of a ·family, has income derived from his separate property and income from his earnings which are community property, there is no presumption that he has supported the family out of the separate property and preserved intact the community funds. He is at perfect liberty to devote all that is necessary of the community earnings to the family support and to preserve his separate property intact. . . .

If a husband pays community indebtedness out of his separate funds at a time when the community funds are exhausted, he is entitled to reimbursement when the community account is replenished. . . .

. . . There was evidence that the money defendant had on hand at the date of marriage, plus fees received after marriage for services performed before marriage, plus his pension, were sufficient to enable him to purchase the property which the court found to be his separate property. The source of every dollar deposited in the bank accounts was shown. Defendant's separate funds were traced into the items of property decreed to be his separate property. There was evidence that . . . defendant expended all of the income which originated after marriage from his practice in the expenses of his practice and the living expenses of the parties. There was evidence that from the date of marriage to the end of 1951 the community income was $50,807.57 and that the community expense, not including office expense, was $59,160.46, an excess of expenses over income of $8,352.89. An accountant testified that at the time the various items adjudged to be defendant's separate property were purchased, there were no community funds available. Evidence that there was no excess of community income over community expenses is as effective to prove that all assets in the name of the defendant are separate property as a specific showing from which separate source each asset flowed. . . . On this evidence the court was warranted in concluding that the items of personal property in question are the separate property of defendant. . . .

NOTE 5.

BENOM v. BENOM
173 Cal. App. 2d 286, 343 P. 2d 632 (1959)

HERNDON, JUSTICE.

* * *

As stated in Socol v. King, 36 Cal. 2d 342, 345, 346, 233 P. 2d 627, 629: "* * * it is well settled in this state that the form of the instrument under which a husband and wife hold title is not conclusive as to the status of the property and that property acquired under a joint tenancy deed may be shown to be actually community property or the separate property of one spouse according to the intention, understanding or agreement of the parties. [Citations.] * * * When there is an oral or written agreement as to the ownership of the property [citations], or where such an understanding may be inferred from the conduct and declarations of the spouses [citations], it is true that the terms of the deed are not controlling. But where such circumstances do not exist, a true joint tenancy is created by a conveyance to husband and wife in that form, although the property is purchased with community funds [citations] or with the separate funds of the husband [citations]. When property is purchased with community funds and title is taken in joint tenancy at the request of the wife, the secret intention of the wife that the property shall remain a part of the community is not effective. 'She cannot defeat her act by testimony of a hidden intention not disclosed to the other party at the time of the execution of the document.' [Citation.] The same rule should be applied where joint funds are used to buy the property."

Civil Code, section 164 provides that: "* * * when any * * * property is acquired by husband and wife by an instrument in which they are described as husband and wife, unless a different intention is expressed in the instrument, the presumption is that such property is the *community property* of said husband and wife." (Emphasis added.) This provision of Civil Code, section 164 would clearly be applicable to the three parcels of property which the parties in 1953 conveyed to themselves as husband and wife, and in the absence of evidence to the contrary the statutory presumption would apply to require a finding that these parcels were community property. . . . But that presumption is of course rebuttable. . . .

NOTE 6.

TAYLOR v. TAYLOR
331 S.W. 2d 895 (Ky. 1960)

PALMORE, JUDGE.

This is an appeal by the wife from a judgment granting to the husband an absolute divorce, custody of the children, all of the furniture owned by the parties, and a residence bought by them in the wife's name, and denying relief of any sort to the wife.

* * *

The parties were married in 1940 and have a son and daughter whose approximate ages at this time are 19 and 16, respectively. The husband earns $70 per week at a laundry. The wife earns $40 per week as a saleslady in a department store. They have a home purchased in 1953 for $9,500 with a down payment of $1,000, which included $975 saved by the wife out of her own earnings. The wife being, according to the husband's testimony, "a lot younger than me" (12 years) and therefore expected to live longer, the title was taken in her name only. The home is furnished with 5 rooms of furniture accumulated by their joint efforts. Apparently there is a balance of some $6,000 owing on the house mortgage and $600 against the furniture.

Conceiving the wife's fault to be the sole cause for the divorce, the trial court awarded everything to the husband. This was error, for under any circumstances the wife was entitled to restitution in the amount of her contribution to the purchase of the home. Under the statutes providing for restoration KRS 403.060(2) and KRS 403.065, the matter of fault is of no consequence. . . . Therefore, the home cannot be restored to the husband without provision for restitution of the $975 contributed by the wife to the down payment, together with such additional sums as she may have paid on the principal of the mortgage debt. Upon the same principle we think she is entitled to a fair division of the furniture, since some of her earnings went into it.

It is argued further on this appeal that under the facts of the case the judgment should have been in favor of the wife, thereby entitling her to alimony, and that . . . she would be entitled to alimony even if it be conceded that she was primarily responsible for the breach. The rule . . . is that when the wife has not been guilty of moral delinquency and the husband has not been entirely free of fault the wife *may* be entitled to alimony even though the divorce is rightly granted to the husband. But such entitlement is not mandatory. It is a matter within the discretion of the chancellor, the exercise of which would not be disturbed on appeal unless the results were clearly unconscionable.

In this case the evidence indicated that the wife had been going with another man for some 5 years, during the course of which, among other things, she had received from him a slobbering love letter which fell into the husband's hands. Although she and the other man denied any knowledge of or connection with this literary effort, the other man's wife, who subsequently divorced him, testified that it was in his hand-writing. On one occasion the other man's wife and her brother visited the appellant in an effort to persuade her to give up this association, but appellant merely denied its existence. This and other evidence certainly created an issue sufficient to support the trial court's factual conclusion to the effect that the wife and the other man had been keeping "steady company" and its legal conclusion to the effect that this conduct constituted cruel and inhuman treatment. . . .

The trial court's direct finding against the wife on the issue of her association with the other man necessarily stigmatizes her testimony. The fact that she denied the relationship is strong evidence that it was an improper one, and if it was improper it would be sufficient basis for denial of alimony, particularly when coupled with the giving of false testimony.

Affirmed except as to the restoration of property, . . .

NOTE 7.

DE BURGH v. DE BURGH
39 Cal. 2d 858, 250 P. 2d 598 (1952)

TRAYNOR, JUSTICE.

. . . When a divorce is granted to both, alimony may be awarded to either, for the basis of liability for alimony is the granting of a divorce against the person required to pay it. See Civil Code, §139. Section 146 of the Civil Code provides that if the divorce is granted for extreme cruelty, the court may apportion community property as it deems just, but that statute has been interpreted to permit an award of more than half of the community property only to an innocent spouse. Eslinger v. Eslinger, 47 Cal. 62, 64. When a divorce is granted to both parties, neither is innocent within the meaning of this rule, and the community property must be equally divided.

NOTE 8.

GARVER v. GARVER
184 Kan. 145, 334 P. 2d 408 (1959)

WERTZ, JUSTICE.

* * *

We are of the opinion that alimony and property division are completely separate and that a wife who prevails in a divorce action is entitled to both alimony and division of property. The right to alimony is separate and distinct from the right to division of the property jointly acquired by the parties during the marriage. The doctrine of alimony is based upon the common law obligation of the husband to support his wife, which obligation is not removed by her obtaining a divorce for his misconduct. Division of property, on the other hand, has for its basis the wife's right to a just and equitable share of that property which has been accumulated by the parties as a result of their joint efforts during the years of the marriage to serve their mutual needs. In this sense, the marital relationship is somewhat analogous to a partnership, and when the relationship is dissolved the jointly acquired property must be divided, regardless of which party has been at fault. . . .

d.   BEDINGER v. GRAYBILL'S EXECUTOR AND TRUSTEE
302 S.W. 2d 594, 596-600 (Ky. 1957)

STANLEY, COMMISSIONER.

The case presents what may be said to be, as a popular expression of today, "A $64,000 question." Is it lawful for a man to adopt his wife as his child and heir at law? The amount involved is approximately $64,000.

By her will, executed in August, 1914, Mrs. Luella Graybill set up a trust for her son, Robert E. Graybill, for his life. The trustee was authorized to pay him one half the corpus. The third paragraph of the will reads:

> "After the death of my said son, I direct that the trust estate in the hands of the Trustee be paid over and distributed by the Trustee to the heirs at law of my said son, Robert E. Graybill, according to the Law of Descent and Distribution in force in Kentucky at the time of his death."

A holographic codicil dated December 12, 1922 provided. "If my son, Robert, dies without heirs, the estate is to be divided between Foreign Missions and Ky. Mountain School."

The son and the appellee, Louise W. Graybill, were married on December 25, 1922. He was then 39 and she was 26 years old. The testatrix died on April 9, 1923. On March 18, 1941, when he was 58 and she was 45 years old, by a proceeding in the Fayette County Court, Robert E. Graybill adopted his wife. The judgment recited she was adopted "as his legal heir at law and child and after this date she shall be deemed to all legal intents and purposes the legal heir at law of said Robert E. Graybill."

Robert E. Graybill died October 28, 1955, without a child having been born to him. This suit is to have the court declare whether Mrs. Graybill, as his adopted heir, or his cousins, as his natural heirs, or "Foreign Missions & Ky. Mountain School" are entitled to the remaining corpus of the trust. The court, in a learned opinion, concluded that the adoption of the wife was lawful and adjudged her entitled to the trust estate. The appeal by the decedent's cousins challenges the judgment. . . . There is no contrary intention apparent in Mrs. Luella Graybill's will. . . .

* * *

. . . Adoption, in the sense of voluntarily taking a child of other parents as one's own child, is of ancient origin. The history and development of adoption reflect its use as the means of establishing not only the social relationship of parent and child but as well its use for the exclusive purpose of making the adoptee eligible to inherit property the same as one born to a party in lawful wedlock. . . .

* * *

The appellants would bring the present case within that rule of interpretation. They submit that the state's interest in and control of its social institutions deny the right of this adoption since it vitiates the common law unity of husband and wife, and that as a man cannot marry his adopted child, the reverse must be the same, that a man cannot adopt as a child a woman whom he has married.

A husband and wife are indeed united in wedlock, yet they remain two distinct personalities. Adoption for the purpose of inheritance of an estate does not change them or unite them by nature. Public policy might be invoked in case of a marriage between the parties after adoption, but we are concerned here not with policy as it pertains to marriage after the status has been created, but, as stated, concerned only with the clear, unqualified statutory authorization of adoption. . . .

The suggestion or implication that public policy is offended by interpreting the statute so that it sanctions such an adoption rests on the idea that it results in an incestuous relation. This point disappears when it is noted that the statute declares to be incestuous only marriages between persons who are of "kin to each other by consanguinity" in specified degrees. [T]his has been construed as embracing only one of blood relationship, so that the crime is not committed by sexual relations between a stepfather and stepdaughter. It has been held in Mississippi that an adopted child is not a "daughter" within an incest statute and that the court by way of construction could not ingraft such a meaning or application into the statute.

Neither the cleverness of the scheme of Graybill to establish his wife as the ultimate beneficiary of the trust estate, nor the incongruity of the legal status of parent and child, can lead the court away from the fact that the adoption was within the authorization of the statute. It follows, therefore, that Mrs. Graybill became and was the sole heir of the life beneficiary of the trust— not by flesh and blood, but an heir by operation of the law.

The judgment is affirmed.

D.

To Decisions Concerning the Administration of Reorganized Wife-Husband Relationships?

1.

MODIFICATION

a.   WALTERS v. WALTERS
341 Ill. App. 561, 94 N.E. 2d 726 (1950)

TUOHY, JUSTICE.

Plaintiff, divorced wife of defendant, appeals from an order of the Superior Court of Cook County terminating installment payments of money, payable under a divorce decree, after and because of the divorced wife's remarriage, and from an order dissolving a rule on defendant to show cause why he should not be held in contempt for failure to make certain installment payments. The matter comes here on the pleadings.

. . . The property settlement agreement of the parties, made part of the decree, in material portions is as follows:

"1. As a lump sum property settlement and alimony in gross, in full of her right, title and interest of every kind, nature, character and description whatsoever, in and to the property, income or estate which the Husband now owns or may hereafter acquire.

"(a) The Husband shall pay to the Wife the sum of Thirty-four Thousand Five Hundred Forty Dollars ($34,540.00), payable in periodic payments during a period ending more than ten years, as follows:

"Twenty-five Hundred Dollars ($2500.00) in cash on the date of the entry of the contemplated decree for divorce hereinafter mentioned; and

"Two Hundred Sixty-seven Dollars ($267.00) per month for a period of one hundred twenty (120) months, first payment to be made on August 1, 1946.

"(b) In the event of the death of the Husband prior to the completion of the payments set forth in sub-paragraph (a) above, any unpaid balance thereof, shall be a charge against his estate.

"(c) The Husband shall by his Will provide as follows: To bequeath to the Wife the sum of Ten Thousand Dollars ($10,000.00) to be paid to her upon his death in the event she survives him and has not remarried; in the event the Wife has predeceased him or has remarried, such sum shall be paid to the son of the parties, Carl Clark Walters; and in the event the Wife has remarried and their said son has predeceased the Husband, such legacy shall be cancelled.

*   *   *

On October 27, 1947, plaintiff filed a petition charging the defendant with being in arrears under the terms of the decree in the sum of $801, being payments due on August 1st, September 1st and October 1st, 1947, in the amount of $267 each. Petitioner asked for attorney's fees for services in connection with preparing and prosecuting the petition. Defendant answered, setting out that on July 2, 1947, plaintiff married one John T. Wheeler, by reason of which fact her right to periodic payments of alimony ceased. . . .

. . . On December 6, 1948, the court entered the order appealed from, finding in part material here that the payments provided for in the decree were "periodic alimony" to which plaintiff ceased to be entitled after and by virtue of her remarriage. . . .

The primary question raised by this appeal is whether the amount required to be paid "as a lump sum property settlement and alimony in gross" became a vested property right of plaintiff upon the entry of the decree. Whether or not it did so become necessitates an examination into the provisions of the decree to determine whether the provision was in fact a lump sum property settlement payable partially in installments or whether it was merely a provision for the pay-

ment of periodic alimony. If it was a lump sum settlement, then it is not modifiable; but if it was periodic alimony, then it is modifiable, and under section 18 of the Divorce Act plaintiff's right to payment of the installments accruing after remarriage is extinguished.

Section 18, paragraph 19, chapter 40, Illinois Revised Statutes, in force at the time this decree was entered, provided as follows:

"When a divorce shall be decreed, the court may make such order touching the alimony and maintenance of the wife or husband, the care, custody and support of the children, or any of them as, from the circumstances of the parties and the nature of the case, shall be fit, reasonable and just; * * * and provided further that a party shall not be entitled to alimony and maintenance after remarriage. * * *"

*   *   *

"Alimony" has been defined as an allowance in a decree of divorce carved out of the estate of the husband for the support of the wife. . . . Many . . . Illinois cases . . . indicate that the term "alimony" bears certain distinguishing characteristics. It is for an indefinite period of time and usually for an indefinite total sum. It is based upon the husband's income and the needs of the wife determined from the standpoint of the manner in which they have been accustomed to live. It is modifiable after decree when the wife's needs increase or decrease, or when the husband's ability to pay increases or decreases. This is so because it takes the form of periodic allowances which do not vest until they become due. It usually terminates upon the death of the husband, although by agreement payments may be made a charge upon the husband's estate after they become due. They are never a charge on a husband's estate in advance of the due date because they are not, prior to that time, vested. Payments of alimony from husband to wife are not based upon any consideration moving from wife to husband, but are based upon the common law duty of the husband to support his wife. "Alimony" in this sense of the word, is modifiable.

On the other hand, the phrase "alimony in gross" or "gross alimony" is always for a definite amount of money; the payment is always for a definite length of time; it is always a charge upon the husband's estate and has uniformly been held by our courts to be not modifiable.

*   *   *

That the award may be payable in installments is not determinative of the question as to whether it is gross alimony or periodic alimony. Gross alimony may be payable in installments—whether all cash or all or partly on credit does not affect the essential nature of the transaction. *The principle involved is that gross alimony becomes a vested right from the date of the rendition of the judgment, and the manner of its payment in no wise affects its nature or effect.* It would be a harsh rule that would deprive parties of the right to make final property settlements merely because the one furnishing the money was unable to meet the entire obligation in one payment. It would favor the affluent over the one less fortuitously circumstanced. . . .

* * *

The parties here described the purpose that they had in mind, in the preamble to their agreement, wherein it was recited:

> "Whereas, the parties hereto consider it to their best interests to settle between themselves now and forever the respective rights of property, dower rights, homestead rights, and any and all other rights of property and otherwise growing out of the marriage relationship existing between them, and which either of them now has or may hereafter claim to have against the other, in and to any property of every kind, nature or description, real, personal or mixed, now owned or which may hereafter be acquired by either of them; and
> "Whereas, a full and complete disclosure has been made by each of the parties hereto to the other of all property, real, personal and mixed, owned by either of them, and each of the parties has had the benefit of his and her respective counsel" etc.

This statement of purpose indicates that the parties were entering into an agreement having to do, not with an arrangement for the support of the wife which would take the form of monthly payments, but with rights which each had or might have in the property of each other, and were attempting to work out an arrangement whereunder neither would have any further claim to the property of the other. . . .

* * *

It thus appears that the parties entered into a property settlement for a definite amount of money for a definite length of time, which was to be a charge on the husband's estate, payable partly in installments. The language used in the agreement and decree supports the construction that the wife was to receive $34,540 as a lump sum property settlement which was not subject to future modification upon remarriage or for any other cause.

* * *

Reversed and remanded with directions.

NOTES

NOTE 1.

WALTERS v. WALTERS
Eleven Years Later

. . . Subsequent to her divorce from Mr. Walters she married a man of considerable means. She insisted on receiving the balance of payments allegedly due her because she thought she was entitled to them as unpaid installments on a property settlement agreement. . . . [Letter from Mr. Addis E. Hull III—attorney for defendant, dated May 19, 1961.]

NOTE 2.

JAMES v. JAMES
14 Ill. 2d 295, 152 N.E. 2d 582 (1958)

DAILY, JUSTICE.

* * *

The law is well settled that parties to an action for divorce may adjust between themselves the amount required for the future support of a wife by a husband, and that they may, if such a course is desired, voluntarily effect a settlement of their property interests. . . . When such agreements are made a part of the divorce decree, they become merged in such decree and are regarded as contracts between the parties which, if fairly made and in good faith, will be accepted and enforced by the courts. . . . They will, however, be set aside and vacated for fraud or coercion practiced by either party, or if contrary to any rule of law, public policy or morals. . . .

NOTE 3.

HULL v. SUPERIOR COURT OF LOS ANGELES COUNTY
54 Cal. 2d 139, 352 P. 2d 161 (1960)

PETERS, JUSTICE.

Geraline Hull secured an interlocutory decree of divorce from her husband, Thomas E. Hull. About eleven months later Geraline moved the trial court to bar the entry of the final decree if her husband should seek to have such a decree entered. Shortly thereafter, and after the required one-year period had elapsed, Thomas moved for entry of the final decree. The trial court granted Geraline's motion. Thomas petitions for a writ of mandate to compel the entry of the final decree, contending that he is entitled to such entry as a matter of right. With this contention we agree.

The facts are as follows: On September 3, 1958, after an uncontested hearing, Geraline secured an interlocutory decree of divorce. The decree incorporated an integrated property settlement agreement previously negotiated by the parties. This agreement provided, among other things, for the conveyance of property then in escrow (subject to an exchange agreement by virtue of which Thomas was to convey certain property owned by him and receive the particular property specified in the settlement) to Geraline, alimony, child support, vacation payments for the children, and execution by Thomas of an irrevocable will creating trust funds for Geraline and the children.

On February 13, 1959, Geraline initiated a contempt proceeding against Thomas, alleging that he had failed to convey the property to her, had failed to execute his will as agreed, and had remarried in Mexico in February and was transferring valuable property to his new "wife." Geraline did not appear at the hearing and no evidence was introduced. The contempt proceeding was dismissed.

* * *

Thomas, by counter-affidavit, admitted noncompliance with the contract, but alleged . . . that the escrow had not been completed because the other parties to it had disapproved of the covenants attached to his property, and not through any wilful action on his part. He moved for entry of the final decree.

After several hearings, the trial court granted Geraline's motion to bar entry of the final decree of divorce. It is this order which gives rise to the present petition for a writ of mandate to compel the court to enter the final decree.

[1] If Thomas is entitled to entry of the final decree as a matter of right then mandate is the proper remedy. . . .

. . . The refusal to enter the final decree forces the continuation of a marriage which is no longer a going unit, and has not been such for a period of more than one year. There are no allegations of reconciliation or cohabitation. There has been neither mistake nor fraud. The parties are simply involved in a property dispute arising from a contract which they freely executed, each being represented by counsel, in an attempt to settle all property obligations resulting from their marriage. The marital relationship is severable from the property rights which it creates, and final settlement of the relationship should not be dependent upon final settlement of corollary property interests.

The concept of divisible divorce has become established in our law. Beginning with Estin v. Estin, 334 U.S. 541, 68 S.Ct. 1213, 92 L.Ed. 1561, many cases have held that a divorce action which severs the personal relationship of the parties does not necessarily determine their property rights. . . . It is true that these cases were concerned with the question of jurisdiction, but they recognize the basic proposition that severance of the personal relationship is divisible from a determination of property and support rights.

The divisible divorce is more than a jurisdictional concept. Severance of a personal relationship which the law has found to be unworkable and, as a result, injurious to the public welfare is not dependent upon final settlement of property disputes. Society will be little concerned if the parties engage in property litigation of however long duration ; it will be much concerned if two people are forced to remain legally bound to one another when this status can do nothing but engender additional bitterness and unhappiness. If the parties choose to enter into a property agreement, termination of their personal status should not be conditioned upon compliance with this agreement. If they enter into an integrated property settlement which provides for support payments as well as property allocation the entire agreement is considered a property agreement . . . and should be divisible *in toto* from the final dissolution of their personal status. Otherwise property disputes, real and specious, could continue for years, effectively preventing the legal establishment of any other relationship by either party. . . .

Geraline also contends that the court should deny Thomas a final judgment of divorce because he has flouted the authority of the court by "remarrying" in Mexico during the interlocutory year and is now living in "sin" in a bigamous relationship within the state. There is no merit to this contention. Entry of the final decree is not a reward for good behavior nor is the refusal to grant it a punishment. Its purpose is to finally dissolve a relationship which has been severed in fact. It would serve no legitimate purpose to compel Thomas to continue to live in a state of bigamy as punishment for already having done so. . . .

NOTE 4.

SLEICHER v. SLEICHER
251 N.Y. 366, 167 N.E. 501 (1929)

CARDOZO, C. J. Plaintiff and defendant were married in 1908. By a separation agreement made in 1923, the defendant, the husband, promised to pay to his wife, the plaintiff, for her support and maintenance $400 monthly from April, 1923, to June, 1924, and $350 monthly thereafter. In case of divorce, he consented that allowance for alimony at the same rate be incorporated in the decree, "to continue so long as she remains unmarried." A court of competent jurisdiction in Nevada gave judgment for divorce in October of the same year. By the judgment, "all demands for alimony, maintenance and support" were declared to be "fixed and prescribed" by the separation agreement, which was made part of the decree as if incorporated therein.

Plaintiff contracted a second marriage with one Hannum on August 16, 1924, and thereafter brought suit in this state to annul it on the ground of fraud. Judgment of annulment was granted on August 17, 1927; the basis of the decree being the fraud of the husband "in fraudulently concealing from the plaintiff that fact that prior to, up to and including the time of said marriage, he was insane." Alimony payments ceased upon the second marriage, and have never been resumed. This action, begun in February, 1928, is brought to recover the unpaid installments. The plaintiff claims that the right to alimony revived when the second marriage was annulled for fraud avoiding it from the beginning, and that the effect of the revivor was not merely to charge the defendant with a prospective liability for installments falling due from the time of the annulment, but to charge him retrospectively with installments lawfully withheld while the second marriage was in force. We think the liability should be adjudged as to the future, but denied as to the past.

A marriage procured by fraud is voidable, not void. Even so, annulment when decreed, puts an end to it from the beginning. . . . It is not dissolved as upon divorce. It is effaced as if it had never been. . . .

The retroactive effect of rescission from the beginning is not, however, without limits, prescribed by policy and justice. These limits are not unknown even in controversies between parties or privies to the rescinded act . . . but they have their typical application to the rights and duties of a stranger. For the stranger, rescission from the beginning is a watchword to be heeded when an act to be thereafter done with reference to one or other of the parties may be governed or affected by the time or quality of the severance. It does not express a rule that reaches back into the past and lays upon innocence the opprobrium of guilt. The defendant, the first husband, must now comply with the mandate of the judgment of divorce and provide for his former wife as for one who has not remarried. This does not mean, as we view it, that he must provide for her during the years when the voidable marriage was in force and unavoided.

. . . The defendant was not at fault when he failed to make his monthly payments of alimony from August 16, 1924, the date of the second marriage, to August 17, 1927, the date of the annulment. If the plaintiff had been unwilling to take advantage of the fraud, the second marriage might have continued while the parties to it were alive. The defendant could not know that it would ever be annulled, still less the time or cause. During all the years that it continued, or

at least till action was begun, the second husband was chargeable with a duty of suitable support. There is a presumption, if nothing more, that the duty was fulfilled. . . .

. . . The purpose of an award of alimony is support for a divorced wife not otherwise supported. This purpose is perverted by imputing a dual obligation. In the case at hand, the wife might have waited to annul the marriage to her second husband till the first was in his grave. If that had been her choice, we cannot bring ourselves to believe that she could have recovered from his estate the installments accruing during life on the theory that . . . he had been in default from the beginning. The test must be the same, however, whether the suit for installments overdue is brought during life or postponed till after death. . . .

NOTE 5.

MARK v. MARK
248 Minn. 446, 80 N.W. 2d 621 (1957)

MATSON, JUDGE.

[I]t is not to be overlooked that the subsequent remarriage of a divorced husband, as his own voluntary act, is not *of itself* a circumstance which justifies a revision of alimony. Despite many sweeping statements to the contrary, a trial court obviously does not, and cannot, wholly ignore the needs of innocent children who are born of a divorced husband's remarriage. Their needs, especially where the children of the prior marriage have become self-sustaining and the divorced wife is capable of pursuing gainful employment, is a circumstance which may indirectly bear upon the propriety of a revision in alimony despite the fact that the father himself, by his voluntary act in begetting another family is usually entitled to little judicial consideration when he seeks relief from the burdens of his former marriage. A trial court's sound discretion in solving marital problems should not be shackled by rigid rules which prevent a recognition of the needs of innocent children whether they be born of a first or of a second marriage. Children born of the second marriage, like the children of the first, are not responsible for their existence and are equally dependent upon their father for support. . . . Consideration of the needs of such children does not mean that the necessities or wants of the first wife will be unreasonably curtailed or ignored. Several other courts have been realistic enough likewise to recognize the rights of second-marriage children, as innocent third parties, as a circumstance to be considered in passing upon an application for the revision of alimony.

* * *

NOTE 6.

New York Domestic Relations Law
§ 248 (1963 Supp.)

Where . . . a final judgment of divorce has been rendered in favor of the wife, or a final judgment annulling the marriage or declaring its nullity has been rendered, the court . . . upon the application of the husband . . . on proof of the marriage of the wife after such final judgment, must modify such final judgment . . . by annulling the provisions . . . directing payments of money for the support of the wife. The court in its discretion upon application of the husband on notice, upon proof that the wife is habitually living with another man and holding herself out as his wife, although not married to such man, may modify such final judgment . . . by annulling the provisions . . . directing payment of money for the support of such wife.

b.   NORTON v. COFFIELD
                      357 P. 2d 434 (Okla. 1960)

BERRY, JUSTICE.

A. W. Coffield, who at one time was also known as Abe Walker, hereafter referred to as "testator", died testate in Creek County, Oklahoma on October 5, 1954. In his will testator bequeathed a life estate in all of his properties to his wife, Eunice, whom he had married in 1921. The remainder was bequeathed to his six living children . . . Eunice elected to take under the will which was admitted to probate in November, 1954. On January 30, 1956, Rose Walker Norton, hereafter referred to as "Rose", filed a petition in the probate proceedings in which she alleged that she and testator were married in 1893 in Cherokee County, Georgia ; that one child, Dollie, was born of this marriage ; that Dollie died in 1936 ; that she (Rose) was the lawful wife of testator at the time of his death and, as testator's wife, elected to take her statutory interest in testator's estate.

A hearing was had on Rose's petition in . . . which her asserted claim of share in testator's estate was denied. . . .

Testator first married a woman in Texas in the 1890's whose given name was Mary. . . . As a result of personal involvement in Texas . . . testator hurriedly left Texas and went to Georgia where he matriculated in a college under the name of "Abe Walker." While a student in Georgia he became acquainted with Rose. In 1893 he and Rose were married. [T]estator became involved with a young woman and hurriedly left Georgia. He subsequently completed his medical education and apparently practiced medicine in a number of states and in a great many localities from the late 1890's to date of his death.

After leaving Georgia, testator used his true name. In 1905 testator married a woman whose name was Emma. . . . In 1921 this marriage was terminated by a divorce. In 1921 testator married Eunice. Testator and Eunice lived as husband and wife from date of their marriage to date of testator's death. . . . The sole grounds upon which the validity of testator's marriages to Emma and Eunice is questioned are that as of dates of said marriages testator and Rose were husband and wife.

In 1907 Rose married Andrew Norton in Georgia. Thereafter Norton and Rose lived together as husband and wife in the community in which Rose was born and in which testator and Rose had lived together as husband and wife. Norton, Rose and their families and friends at all times treated this marriage as a valid marriage.

Rose learned that testator was alive and that he was married to Emma as early as 1917. She also learned of his divorce from Emma and his subsequent marriage to Eunice. Following her marriage to Norton, Rose at no time prior to filing her petition herein claimed to be testator's wife. The claim that she here asserts was therefore only asserted 61 years after testator deserted her, 51 years after testator's marriage to Emma, 49 years after her marriage to Norton, 35 years after testator's marriage to Eunice and 2 years after testator's lips were sealed by death. . . .

*   *   *

That her interest has always been solely commerical is evidenced by the fact that upon learning in 1917 or before that testator was alive, she made no effort to obtain a divorce from him and thus, in keeping with her present position, validate her marriage to Norton. Rose's attorneys, of course, predicate Rose's asserted rights to share in testator's estate upon the proposition that she was in fact his lawful wife at the time of testator's death. Rose's testimony shows that to her way of thinking her marriage to Norton was a valid marriage.

*   *   *

One of the issues presented by this appeal is whether the evidence overcomes the strong presumption that three ceremonial marriages of long standing are valid . . . We refer to (1) Rose's marriage to Norton in 1895 ; (2) Emma's marriage to testator in 1905 . . . (3) Eunice's marriage to testator in 1921. . . .

It is settled law that where a marriage has been consummated in accordance with the form of the law, the law indulges a strong presumption in favor of its validity ; that one who asserts the invalidity of such marriage because one of the parties thereto has been formally married and the spouse of such marriage is still living, has upon him the burden of proving that the first marriage has not been dissolved by divorce or by lawful separation. . . .

* * *

The validity of Rose's marriage in Georgia to Norton is here involved and we, therefore, think it appropriate to refer to the law as promulgated by the Supreme Court of Georgia. In Azar v. Thomas, 206 Ga. 588, 57 S.E. 2d 821, 822, the statement is made that the "presumption of the dissolution of the previous marriage grows stronger with the passage of time where the second marriage is not questioned or attacked. . . ."

When it is remembered that Rose's marriage to Norton was consummated some 49 years prior to her attack on testator's marriage to Eunice, the presumption in Georgia of validity of said marriage is surely so strong that proof showing the invalidity thereof must be "so clear, strong and unequivocal as to produce a moral conviction" that said marriage is invalid.

The evidence supporting Rose's contention that she at no time obtained a divorce from testator, is her testimony to said effect. Prior to 1956 the courthouse in each of the counties in Georgia where Rose would be expected to obtain a divorce from testator burned destroying all court records. While this is a coincidence, this fact tends to show the wisdom of the rule to the effect that the presumption under consideration should strengthen with the passage of time. . . .

* * *

We are of the opinion that the trial court's basic finding that the evidence did not overcome the strong presumption of the validity of testator's and Eunice's marriage is clearly sustained by the evidence.

Affirmed.

WELCH, JUSTICE (dissenting).

The reason for dissenting is that, as I view it, we have several times heretofore held to the contrary as a matter of law, and those former decisions have not been overruled, and, though not followed, are not overruled here ; so that until this decision, I thought we had come to the view and legal philosophy in this state, and so announced in our decisions, that when a ceremonial marriage had been fully consummated between two wholly competent parties, that the marital relationship would exist and continue on and on, until dissolved by death of one of the parties, or until dissolved by judicial decree of annulment or divorcement, and that such marital relationship could not be canceled out merely by the voluntary acts of the parties, whether those acts were by agreement, or whether they were wrongful acts, and that neither party to such matrimonial relationship could interrupt the continued existence of the same merely by some voluntary act of such party, even though such voluntary act was a wrongful act, or even if it was the act of purporting by ceremony to marry some other person followed by their living together as though legally married.

* * *

I would direct special attention to the late case of United States v. McCarty, 10 Cir., 144 F. 2d 341, where the holding of the court is set forth in . . . the syllabus:

"Under Oklahoma law the statutory law of succession or descent is not controlled by equitable considerations, and a surviving spouse is not estopped from inheriting from deceased spouse because surviving spouse abandoned deceased spouse long before and entered into a pretended marriage relationship with another. 84 O.S. 1941, § 213."

* * *

This court persistently held before the new statute in 1915 that a man could not be prevented from inheriting from his wife though he murdered her. . . .

All these holdings are founded on the legal philosophy that inheritance is based on the expressed provisions of statutes, and upon nothing else, and those statutory rules cannot be changed upon any equitable consideration or any equitable principle.

In this case Rose the woman claimant is entitled to inherit from this man by our former decisions, and by statute, if she was legally his wife when he died (though, in the opinion of some, not then his wife equitably or in good conscience), since this is purely a matter of statutory law.

I really do think that this rule and the rule of the above cited Oklahoma cases should be followed and applied in this case, in the interest of administering even justice to all alike, since those cases have not heretofore been overruled and are not overruled in this case.

So the question is was Rose legally the wife of decedent at time of his death?

They were certainly legally married in 1893. That was the evidence. The trial court so found and the majority opinion does not question that finding.

How long then did that legal marriage exist? When did it terminate? Did that legal marriage cease to exist on the happening of any one or all of the things emphasized in the majority opinion, that is:

> One—When the decedent remarried in the year 1905?
>
> Two—When Rose remarried in the year 1907?
>
> Three—When decedent married again in 1921?
>
> Four—When future children were born to decedent or to Rose?
>
> Five—When Rose and decedent each discovered that the other was living with a subsequent spouse?
>
> Six—When she failed to *claim* that she was his wife for a period of years before he died?

*   *   *

None of these things or items above listed are sufficient to terminate this legal marriage under our former decisions and by statute. The only way a legal marriage may terminate before death is by judicial annulment or divorcement.

NOTES

NOTE 1.

ERNST, MORRIS L.

Foreword To "The Last Caprice*"

In a lawyer's office, Will Time is an occasion for unmasking and for all kinds of spiritual undressing. As each client concedes his mortality and faces up to the problems of disposition, the lawyer's desk becomes the psychologist's couch. Face to face, many of the wealthy who have hated the government give instructions which make bequests to the state and Federal treasuries—in the form of inheritance taxes—rather than leave the money to a pet charity or cause. Then there is the dominant male, often a delightful and casual philanderer, who expresses a desire to have his dead hand control the love life of his surviving wife. She is to receive substantial income until the day of her remarriage. Thus does the testator induce his widow to live in so-called "sin" with a lush income from the estate rather than get married to an impecunious male and have her income cut off.

However, in our society wives may not be totally disowned; even husbands often may not be

*Reprinted from Menchin, Robert S., *The Last Caprice*, New York: Simon & Schuster, 1963, pps. 12-13. Copyright © 1963 by Robert S. Menchin. Reprinted with permission of the publisher.

cut off without a sou. This so-called "dower" is the sovereign state's answer to the testator, preventing the too great expression of hate that would leave the surviving spouse without that guessed-at compromise between duty and affection —often, one-third of the will-maker's estate.

NOTE 2.

DAVIS v. DAVIS
167 Wisc. 360, 167 N.W. 819 (1918)

VINJE, J. . . .

. . . Under our statutes a single act of adultery on her part is cause for divorce from the bonds of matrimony, and such a decree bars her dower. That a husband for religious or other reasons may not desire to avail himself of the remedy given him by law and divorce his wife is no reason why the rights and obligations flowing from a continuance of the marital relation should be abrogated and ancient remedies substituted therefor. The law gives him a remedy. It is optional with him to use it or not. . . .

*   *   *

[T]he only inference we can draw from his conduct is that he did not wish to sever the relation of husband and wife. At any rate he did not sever such relation. Not having done so, she remained his wife during his lifetime, and became his widow upon his death, with all the legal rights attaching to such relation.

*   *   *

ESCHWEILER, J. (dissenting). I think the claimant should be held to be barred of her dower by the rule of the common law, and also as having been waived by her own deliberate act, and the judgment be affirmed.

*   *   *

In this case her right was based solely upon the marriage relationship. That it was a known right is quite apparent from the filing of her claim in the month of July following his death. Knowingly she voluntarily abandoned all the relative duties and obligations on her part, and lived away from her husband from 1871 until his death in September, 1914. During these 43 years that she "lived her own life," as the saying is, she bore ten children, begotten by others than the deceased. Such an accumulation of cumulative repudiations of the marital obligations ought to require a judicial declaration that her repudiation thereof was entire and absolute. The faithless ought not now to be rewarded as though faithful.

NOTE 3.

DARTER v. MAGNUSSEN
172 Cal. App. 2d 714, 342 P. 2d 528, 531-32 (1959)

BRAY, PRESIDING JUSTICE.

* * *

The death of one of the parties to a suit for divorce abates the action and terminates the jurisdiction of the court to proceed with the action or to make any *further* determination of property rights, alimony, costs or attorney's fees. . . . However, the death of a party does not affect the court's power to take such action as may still have to be taken to enforce the property rights adjudicated by the interlocutory decree.

. . . In Gould v. Superior Court, 1920, 47 Cal. App. 197, 191 P. 56, the court in denying a petition for rehearing, . . . stated: "It was held that, although the court may have lost jurisdiction to make a final decree, after the death of the husband, dissolving the marriage status, the property rights fixed by the agreement and confirmed by the interlocutory decree still remained in existence, and that as to them the court retained jurisdiction to enter the final decree in the manner specified in the interlocutory decree." 47 Cal. App. at page 204, 191 P. at page 59. The rationale of the decision was the contract basis of the interlocutory decree in respect to the division of the property. And contract rights may endure beyond death. . . .

NOTE 4.

KNIGHT v. MAHONEY
152 Mass. 523, 25 N.E. 971 (1890)

FIELD, C. J. . . . The first clause of the will of Wheaton T. Knight is as follows: "I give and bequeath to my beloved wife, Sabra A. Knight, all my real estate and personal property of every kind and description, after paying all my debts and legal charges, and paying out to my children the allowances hereinafter made, so long as she remains my widow." . . . The principal question of law is whether, under the will, Mrs. Knight took an estate in fee or for her life, or during her widowhood. . . . The weight of authority is in favor of treating as valid limitations or conditions which are annexed to devises and bequests to the wife of the testator, although they tend to restrain her from marrying again, and although the will does not dispose of the property by a gift over to other persons in the event of her marrying again. . . . [T]he right of a widow to receive certain portions of the estate of her deceased husband is secured by statutes, if she chooses to avail herself of them. If a widow prefers to take under the will of her husband, and he has chosen by his will to give her the use of property during her widowhood only, intending that if she marry again she should rely thereafter for her support upon her future husband, we think that his intention ought not to be defeated on any ground of public policy, and the decisions on this question do not proceed upon any distinction between a limitation of the duration of the estate given to the widow and a condition subsequent whereby the estate given is divested on her remarriage. . . .

NOTE 5.

MILBOURN v. MILBOURN
384 P. 2d 476 (Id. 1963)

McQUADE, JUSTICE.

The opinion of this court filed herein July 5, 1963, is withdrawn and this opinion is substituted therefor.

This appeal is taken from a decree of divorce.

The parties hereto were married in June, 1933, in the State of Iowa; no children were born of the marriage. The respondent, husband, brought this action against the appellant, wife, for a decree of divorce and division of property.

* * *

The trial judge entered judgment that the bonds of matrimony between the parties be severed; that the respondent have the farm machinery and his personal effects; that the appellant be awarded the household furniture and furnishings in her possession; that the appellant have a judgment against the respondent in the sum of $4,000, payable $100 per month; and that the appellant shall have additional attorney fees in the sum of $150.

Appellant has taken her appeal from this judgment. Subsequent to entry of judgment by the trial court the respondent died from injuries suffered in an automobile accident. Death of respondent presents the question as to whether or not the action was abated thereby. This question was fully presented to the court by briefs and oral argument. Our statute pertaining to abatement of actions is I.C. § 5-319.

> "An action or proceeding does not abate by the death or any disability of a party, or by the transfer of any interest therein, if the cause of action or proceeding survive or continue. In case of the death or any disability of a party, the court, on motion, may allow the action or proceeding to be continued by or against his representative or successor in interest. * * *"

This question of abatement was disposed of in Weisgerber v. Prescher, 37 Idaho 653, 217 P. 615.

> "A simple action for divorce is extinguished by the death of one of the parties. [citing authorities] On the other hand, if the issues in the action expressly involve property rights, the action is

not extinguished by death so far as that issue is concerned, but survives." [citing authorities]

The action between respondent and appellant concerned property rights. Division was made by the trial court of the property and this appeal was taken from the judgment. Therefore, because this action involves property rights it is not abated by death of the respondent.

* * *

c.   COMMONWEALTH v. CASE
200 Pa. Super 200, 189 A. 2d 756 (1963)

PER CURIAM.

The order of the court below is affirmed on the opinion of Judge Monroe of the Court of Quarter Sessions of Bucks County.

WOODSIDE, JUDGE (concurring in part and dissenting in part).

I concur with this court's conclusion that an order for the support of the defendant's wife was properly made for the reasons set forth in Judge Monroe's scholarly opinion, but I think under the circumstances the amount of the order was exorbitant.

Orders for the support of a wife are limited to one-third of the husband's income or earning power. This is the maximum allowed to the most worthy wife—one who has spent her life sacrificing to help an ungrateful husband accumulate his capital, develop his earning capacity and rear his children only to be cast aside when she has become needy, ill and old.

In the case before us, the relatrix owned and operated a dress shop for 12 years, going out of business *after* she left the defendant. At the hearing a few months later, she first denied, and then reluctantly admitted, that she had leased a storeroom to go back into the business. She lived with the defendant—in luxury—for less than a year. In order to marry him, she left and divorced her former husband after many years of married life, cooperated with the defendant in his leaving and divorcing his wife after many years of married life, and committed a fraud upon the courts of Alabama to get her divorce. Certainly, this relatrix is not entitled to the most liberal order possible. Nevertheless, her desertion and fraud proved to be a good investment for her. The defendant is ordered to pay $120 a week, plus taxes and mortgage installments, making a total of $8280 a year.

The defendant's income tax return shows gross income of $25,983 in the last reported year. He pays his first wife $7200 a year under an agreement entered into with the relatrix's knowledge, and undoubtedly with her consent and for a purpose which she then thought was for her benefit. (The defendant paid both his wife and the relatrix's husband, who thereupon entered no objections to the fraudulently obtained divorce.) The trial judge concluded that the defendant had income in excess of the amount he returned for income tax purposes, and set his gross income at $34,823 and his net income, after taxes and the payments to his first wife, at $19,123.

A sound argument might be made that the order exceeds one-third of the defendant's earning capacity, but whether or not it does, I think it is excessive. I would reduce the weekly order to $75, which, added to the mortgage and real estate tax payments, would constitute an order of $5940 a year.

The opinion of Judge Monroe follows:

The defendant, Russell J. Case, is being charged with violation of Section 733 of the Penal Code of the Commonwealth of Pennsylvania in that he has failed to support his wife, Hellene R. Case. The defendant was formerly married to Elma Case; on the third day of February 1961, he secured a "Final Decree of Divorce" from her in Geneva County, Alabama. The prosecutrix was formerly married to Robert Lanning Kulp; on the fourth day of February, 1961, she secured a "Divorce Decree" from him in Covington County, Alabama. A general appearance for both spouses is noted in the decrees which are incorporated in the record. On February 17, 1961, Russell J. Case and the prosecutrix were married in Morrisville, Bucks County, Pennsylvania.

The defendant denies that the divorce decrees obtained by the parties in Alabama were valid because of the fraud committed on the Courts in Alabama and hence contends that he is not now legally married to the prosecutrix. Both the divorce decrees contained a provision prohibiting each party thereto from remarrying except to each other for a period of sixty days.

* * *

In the instant case, Mr. Case admits that it was his idea that he and Mrs. Kulp should go to Alabama to obtain their divorces. And on the strength of those divorces, he married her. Since Mr. Case would be estopped in Alabama from attacking the validity of the Kulp's divorce, he is estopped in Pennsylvania from collaterally attacking it.

Mr. Case and Mrs. Kulp were married in Pennsylvania within the sixty day prohibited period specified by their decrees. Pennsylvania follows the general rule that the validity of a marriage is determined by the law of the place where it was contracted. . . . It is abundantly clear that Pennsylvania is the domicile of the parties, the marriage occurred in Pennsylvania and there is nothing in the laws of Pennsylvania which requires, as a matter of public policy or otherwise, a waiting period after a divorce decree.

The New York courts have had occasion to explore the meaning of the prohibition. Marzano v. Marzano, Sup., 154 N.Y.S. 2d 507 (1956), in the absence of proof of Virginia law, dealt with the validity of a Virginia marriage contracted in violation of Alabama's sixty day proscription as though the problem was governed by New York law. "Marzano held that in New York the determining factor was whether the foreign decree was interlocutory or final, and after carefully analyzing the Alabama cases, concluded that the Alabama decree was final, and the Virginia marriage valid notwithstanding the prohibition." Olsen v. Olsen, 27 Misc.2d 555, 209 N.Y.S. 2d 503, p. 505 (1960). . . .

* * *

While we do not condone the action of Mr. Case and Mrs. Kulp in working a fraud on the Alabama courts, we will leave them in the position in which they put themselves.

Having determined the liability of the defendant to support his wife, we turn to the function of this court to fix an amount which is reasonable and proper for her comfortable support and maintenance, not exceeding one-third of the defendant's income, and taking also into consideration the nature and extent of his property and other financial resources. . . .

* * * .

According to our calculations . . . defendant's gross income approximates $34,823.13. His Federal and New Jersey tax liability approximates $8500 per year, his annual liability to his former wife $7200, netting to him approximately $19,123.

The order for the support of the wife may not exceed one-third of the husband's total income. . . .

[W]e are not persuaded that the relatrix requires one-third of either the gross or net income of the defendant in order to live as she comfortably did the few months she and her husband resided together. . . .

The relatrix lists expenses of $894.03 per month or $208.60 per week as reasonably necessary for her comfortable support and maintenance. Included therein are monthly payments of $133.03 and $37 for mortgage liquidation and taxes on the entireties home, both of which obligations are being paid by the defendant. Eliminating extended discussion, the bona fides of her expenditures for car rental, clothing and accessories, food, cleaning and laundry, beauty parlor, and miscellaneous items, was considerably shaken by her cross-examination and later testimony. For example,

her testimony discloses (P. 30) that during the eight blissful marital months during which she resided with defendant and he with her, the defendant paid her $125 per week from which she paid all of the expenses which she has listed in this case, including the mortgage installments and part of the taxes, but excepting the gardener's pay, the doctor's bills, donation and car rental.

2.

ENFORCEABILITY

VANDERBILT v. VANDERBILT
354 U.S. 416 (1957)

MR. JUSTICE BLACK delivered the opinion of the Court.

Cornelius Vanderbilt, Jr., petitioner, and Patricia Vanderbilt, respondent, were married in 1948. They separated in 1952 while living in California. The wife moved to New York where she has resided since February 1953. In March of that year the husband filed suit for divorce in Nevada. This proceeding culminated, in June 1953, with a decree of final divorce which provided that both husband and wife were "freed and released from the bonds of matrimony and all the duties and obligations thereof. . . ."[1] The wife was not served with process in Nevada and did not appear before the divorce court.

In April 1954, Mrs. Vanderbilt instituted an action in a New York court praying for separation from petitioner and for alimony. The New York court did not have personal jurisdiction over him, but in order to satisfy his obligations, if any, to Mrs. Vanderbilt, it sequestered his property within the State. He appeared specially and, among other defenses to the action, contended that the Full Faith and Credit Clause of the United States Constitution compelled the New York court to treat the Nevada divorce as having ended the marriage and as having destroyed any duty of support which he owed the respondent. While the New York court found the Nevada decree valid and held that it had effectively dissolved the marriage, it nevertheless entered an order, under § 1170-b of the New York Civil Practice Act,[4] dir-

1. It seems clear that in Nevada the effect of this decree was to put an end to the husband's duty to support the wife—provided, of course, that the Nevada courts had power to do this. . . .

4. "In an action for divorce, separation or annulment, . . . where the court refuses to grant such relief by reason of a finding by the court that a divorce . . . declaring the marriage a nullity had previously been granted to the husband in an action in which jurisdiction over the person of the wife was not obtained, the court may, nevertheless, render in the same action such judgment as justice may require for the maintenance of the wife." Gilbert-Bliss: N.Y. Civ. Prac., Vol. 6A, 1956 Cum. Supp., Sec. 1170-b.

ecting petitioner to make designated support payments to respondent. . . . The New York Court of Appeals upheld the support order. . . . Petitioner then applied to this Court for certiorari contending that § 1170-b, as applied, is unconstitutional because it contravenes the Full Faith and Credit Clause. . . .

In *Estin* v. *Estin,* 334 U.S. 541, this Court decided that a Nevada divorce court, which had no personal jurisdiction over the wife, had no power to terminate a husband's obligation to provide her support as required in a pre-existing New York separation decree. The factor which distinguishes the present case from *Estin* is that here the wife's right to support had not been reduced to judgment prior to the husband's *ex parte* divorce. In our opinion this difference is not material on the question before us. Since the wife was not subject to its jurisdiction, the Nevada divorce court had no power to extinguish any right which she had under the law of New York to financial support from her husband. It has long been the constitutional rule that a court cannot adjudicate a personal claim or obligation unless it has jurisdiction over the person of the defendant.[6] Here, the Nevada divorce court was as powerless to cut off the wife's support right as it would have been to order the husband to pay alimony if the wife had brought the divorce action and he had not been subject to the divorce court's jurisdiction. Therefore, the Nevada decree, to the extent it purported to affect the wife's right to support, was void and the Full Faith and Credit Clause did not obligate New York to give it recognition.

MR. JUSTICE FRANKFURTER, dissenting.

The question in this case is whether Nevada, which was empowered to grant petitioner a divorce without personal jurisdiction over respondent that must be respected, by command of the Constitution, by every other State, *Williams* v. *North Carolina,* 317 U.S. 287, was at the same time empowered by virtue of its domiciliary connection with petitioner to make, incidental to its dissolution of the marriage, an adjudication denying alimony to which sister States must also give full faith and credit. Whatever the answer to the question may be, *Estin* v. *Estin,* 334 U.S. 541, does not supply it. What the Court now states to be "not material" was crucial to the decision in that case, namely, the prior New York support order, which the Court held Nevada was required to respect by virtue of the Full Faith and Credit Clause, Art. IV, § 1, of the Constitution. That this fact was crucial to the Court's decision in that case is made

clear by the Court's reference to the prior New York judgment in its two statements of the question presented and more than a half dozen times throughout the course of its opinion. The Court rightly regarded the fact as crucial because of the requirement of Art. IV, § 1, that Nevada give full faith and credit to the prior New York "Judicial Proceedings."

The Court now chooses to regard the existence of a prior New York support order as "not material," holding for the first time that "the Nevada divorce court had no power to extinguish any right which [respondent] had under the law of New York to financial support from her husband. It has long been the constitutional rule that a court cannot adjudicate a personal claim or obligation unless it has jurisdiction over the person of the defendant [citing for this proposition, *Pennoyer* v. *Neff,* 95 U.S. 714, 726-727]." We have thus reached another stage—one cannot say it is the last—in the Court's tortuous course of constitutional adjudication relating to dissolution of the marriage status. Whereas previously only the State of "matrimonial domicile" could grant an *ex parte* divorce and alimony, now any domiciliary State can grant an *ex parte* divorce, but no State, even if domiciliary, can grant alimony *ex parte* when it grants a divorce *ex parte.*

*   *   *

. . . The Court . . . solves all with the statement, "It has long been the constitutional rule that a court cannot adjudicate a personal claim or obligation unless it has jurisdiction over the person of the defendant." This is an artful disguise for labeling the action with the question-begging phrase, "in personam." A dogmatic, unanalyzed disregard of the difficulties of a problem does not make the problem disappear. Strictly speaking, all rights eventually are "personal." For example, a successful suit in admiralty against a ship results of course not in loss to the ship but to its owner. The crucial question is: what is the fair way to proceed against these interests? May a State deal with the dissolution of a marriage comprehensively, or must it chop up the normal incidents of the cause of action for divorce?

No explanation is vouchsafed why the dissolution of the marital relation is not so "personal" as to require personal jurisdiction over an absent spouse, while the denial of alimony incident thereto is. Calling alimony a "personal claim or obligation" solves nothing. I note this concern for "property rights," but I fail to see why the marital relation would not be worthy of equal protection, also as a "personal claim or obligation." It may not be translatable into dollars and cents, but

---

6. *Pennoyer* v. *Neff,* 95 U.S. 714, 726-727. If a defendant has property in a State it can adjudicate his obligations, but only to the extent of his interest in that property. . . .

that does not make it less valuable to the parties. It cannot be assumed, by judicial notice as it were, that absent spouses value their alimony rights more highly than their marital rights. Factually, therefore, both situations involve the adjudication of valuable rights of an absent spouse, and I see no reason to split the cause of action and hold that a domiciliary State can *ex parte* terminate the marital relation, but cannot *ex parte* deny alimony. "Divisible divorce" is just name-calling. I would therefore hold that Nevada had jurisdiction to make the determination it made with respect to alimony and that New York must give full faith and credit to the whole Nevada judgment, not just to part of it.

It should also be noted that the Court's decision, besides turning the constitutional law of marital relations topsy-turvy, has created numerous problems whose solution is far from obvious. The absent spouse need no longer appear in the divorcing State in order to be present when an adjudication is made. She (or he) may sue wherever she can serve the other spouse or attach his property. What will happen in States that grant alimony only as incident to a divorce? Most States do not have statutes like the New York statute involved in the present case. Would this Court require any State in which one spouse catches another to entertain a cause of action for alimony? . . . Also, it is not even settled what the relation of a State to an ex-wife and an ex-husband must be for the State, as a matter of due process, to be able to grant support on the basis that the parties were once man and wife.

* * *

For me, the rigorous commands of the Full Faith and Credit Clause are determinative. I cannot say that the Nevada judgment denying alimony is more "obnoxious" to New York policy (as expressed in § 1170-b of its Civil Practice Act) than its judgment of divorce. Since New York is required to give full faith and credit to the one, it is to the other.

MR. JUSTICE HARLAN, dissenting.

The Court holds today, . . . that Nevada, lacking personal jurisdiction over Mrs. Vanderbilt, had no power to adjudicate the question of support, and that any divorce decree purporting so to do is to that extent wholly void—presumably in Nevada as well as in New York—under the Due Process Clause of the Fourteenth Amendment. . . .

I cannot agree with such a holding. . . .

* * *

. . . I see no reason why we should extend that, for me, already somewhat unpalatable mediation

to the limits of its logic in order to hold that Nevada's views as to support as well as divorce must be forced onto other States, and that Nevada can not only compel wives domiciled elsewhere to become single against their will, but to be pauperized against their will as well. Of course, the reason for the distinction is not that the wife's right to support is "worth" more than her interest in remaining a wife. But the interest of the wife in not becoming single *and* penniless is greater than her interest in not becoming single. In other words, merely because it is held that the wife must be deprived of one benefit *ex parte,* in the interest of national uniformity, does not *compel* us to hold that the other benefit must vanish with it, where the interest in national uniformity is not as compelling.[2]

In deciding this case we must always remember that the *reason* why the Nevada *ex parte* divorce has the effect of a judgment in New York even on the question of status is because this Court found, in measuring the competing interests, that uniformity should prevail. It will not do, therefore, to say that once that is done the Court is foreclosed from weighing competing interests in determining the effect of the Nevada adjudication as to questions other than status. One cannot rest on the inexorability that the Nevada decree is a "judgment" and eliminate the fact that it was held to be a judgment outside Nevada as to status for reasons which do not necessarily apply to the question of support, any more than one can solve the problem by labeling support as a "property" right.

Quite a different case is presented, it seems to me, where a wife becomes a domiciliary of New York after the *ex parte* divorce and is then granted support. In such a case New York could not pretend to be assuring the wife the mere survival of a pre-existing right, because the wife could have had no pre-divorce rights in New York at all. New York would merely be *granting* the wife a marital right in the teeth of a valid Nevada adjudication that there is no marriage. And, of course, at the time of the divorce New York would have had no interest in the situation of any kind. In such a case, therefore, it seems to me that the Full Faith and Credit Clause would require New York to respect the Nevada judg-

---

2. "It is easier to have a flat rule than to make distinctions based on judgment. Yet, from the standpoint of partitioning power among the several states, there may well be wisdom in having a gap between what due process will not forbid and what full faith and credit will not require. Certainly in suits over property and money there may be grounds that are thought good enough to justify a state in exerting its power so far as it relies wholly on its own strength and yet not so good that other states should be bound to lend a hand." Powell, *supra,* at 936; . . .

ment as to support rights. Furthermore, even aside from the judgment, as a matter of choice of law I should think New York would be forced to look to the law of a State which had a substantial contact with these parties at the time of the divorce in determining the effect to be given to the divorce decree. It seems to me unfortunate that this Court should permit spouses divorced by valid decrees to comb the country, after the divorce, in search of any State where the divorcing spouse has property and which has favorable support laws, in order there to obtain alimony. I would therefore by no means hold the Nevada adjudication "void" and therefore of no effect in any State.

Thus decision here, as I see it, turns on the domicile of Mrs. Vanderbilt at the time of the divorce. On this question I am left in some doubt. Section 1165-a of the New York Civil Practice Act makes one year's residence necessary to suits for support. This is amenable to the interpretation that New York would not recognize Mrs. Vanderbilt as domiciled in that State until the lapse of a year, that is, after the decree of divorce here involved. . . . On the other hand, the opinion below intimates that the one-year residency can be regarded as merely a procedural prerequisite to filing suit under § 1170-b, and does not affect Mrs. Vanderbilt's status as a domicilary of New York *ab initio*. In view of this uncertainty in the state law, I would remand to the state court for reconsideration in light of the above-stated principles.

NOTES

NOTE 1.

HUDSON v. HUDSON
344 P. 2d 295 (Cal. 1959)

TRAYNOR, JUSTICE.

* * *

The crucial question in this case . . . is whether the law of California permits plaintiff to obtain support following the entry of an ex parte divorce. . . .

* * *

In Dimon v. Dimon, 40 Cal. 2nd 516, 254 P. 2nd 528 [1953] . . . a majority of this court held that a wife's right to recover alimony or support for herself is limited to the period when the parties are husband and wife. . . .

The broad proposition of the Dimon case that alimony cannot be granted if the marriage has been dissolved cannot be denied, if the marriage was dissolved in this state and the court had jurisdiction over both spouses. . . . But the Dimon

case extended this proposition to cover a case where the marriage had been dissolved by an ex parte Connecticut decree procured by the wife. The wife's right to support from her husband had not been adjudicated prior to the divorce decree as in the Estin case. After Estin, but before Vanderbilt, the argument could have been made that by terminating the marriage the ex parte divorce automatically terminated all rights, including the non-adjudicated right to support that grew out of that marriage. But after the Vanderbilt case, such a proposition cannot be maintained, for it is now clear that the ex parte proceeding does not affect the wife's support rights. By treating the Connecticut decree as terminating any possibility that the plaintiff in Dimon could secure a support award in this state, we gave that decree more weight in this state than it is now constitutionally entitled to receive. To follow Dimon after Vanderbilt in a case involving a foreign ex parte divorce is to permit the court of another state to preclude the courts of this state from deciding a question of California law that the foreign court had no jurisdiction to determine. Under Vanderbilt the conclusion is inescapable that the issue of alimony, which could not be decided by the divorce court, remains open for determination in a proper forum. The Dimon case is therefore overruled.

The doctrine of divisible divorce set forth in Estin and Vanderbilt provides a sensible solution to the problems engendered by ex parte divorces. Its repudiation in this case would compel collateral attacks upon such divorces to protect rights to support, with resulting confusion as to marital status, property rights, rights of innocent third persons who may have relied upon the decree, and the legitimacy of children. See Powell, And Repent At Leisure, 58 Harv. L. Rev. 930. California has a dominant interest in the well-being of her domiciliaries, and the courts of this state are open to adjudicate their support rights following an ex parte divorce.

Since plaintiff may maintain her action for permanent alimony without attacking defendant's Idaho decree, it follows that she may receive temporary alimony, costs, and fees to enable her to continue the suit when she has shown that she needs such relief and that defendant has the ability to provide such assistance. . . .

NOTE 2.

LIGHT v. LIGHT
12 Ill. 2d 502, 147 N.E. 2d 34 (1958)

SCHAEFER, JUSTICE.

This is an appeal from a decree of the circuit court of McLean County, entered in a proceeding brought to register in that court, under the Uniform Enforcement of Foreign Judgments Act, a divorce decree of the circuit court of the city of St. Louis, Missouri. The case is properly here because the appeal, and particularly the cross appeal, call for a construction of the full-faith-and-credit clause of the Federal constitution.

The Missouri decree was entered May 1, 1944. It granted a divorce to the plaintiff . . . ordered the defendant to pay gross alimony of $3,600, and thereafter to pay . . . alimony of $50 a month. On September 28, 1953, the plaintiff filed her petition to register the Missouri decree under the Uniform Act. (Ill. Rev. Stat. 1957, chap. 77, pars. 88-105.) The defendant was personally served with summons. After evidence was heard before a master in chancery, the court entered a decree which directed that the Missouri decree be registered in the circuit court of McLean County "as to past due installments as of September 28, 1953, of alimony. . . ." The decree also awarded interest on the amount found due, allowed the plaintiff $1000 for attorney's fees and taxed the costs of the proceeding against the defendant.

The Uniform Act, which was adopted in Illinois in 1951, is intended to make it easier to enforce judgments across State lines. To that end it establishes a procedure for registering the foreign judgment in an appropriate court in this State (sec. 2), and authorizes the levy of execution at once upon a judgment so registered. (Sec. 6.) Sale under the levy is postponed, however, until the judgment debtor has an opportunity, after service of process, to assert whatever defenses he may have to the enforcement of the judgment. (Secs. 4, 5, 8, 13.) Upon default, or if the asserted defenses are not sustained, the registered judgment becomes a final judgment of the court in which it is registered. The judgment so rendered is binding either personally or *quasi in rem,* depending on the kind of service had upon the defendant. (Secs. 7, 12.) The act applies to "any judgment, decree or order of a court of the United States or of any State or Territory which is entitled to full faith and credit in this state." (Sec. 1.) . . .

The first contention that the defendant makes in this court is that registration of the judgment is barred by the Illinois five-year period of limitations for actions on foreign judgments. (Ill. Rev. Stat. 1957, chap. 83, par. 16.) That limitation period is incorporated in section 2 of the Uniform Act. We have long since held, however, that in the case of a judgment for the payment of money in periodic installments a right of action accrues on each installment as it becomes due, and that the period of limitations runs on each installment only from the time it becomes due. . . .

The main thrust of defendant's effort to reverse the decree centers upon the Missouri statute which enacts a conclusive presumption of payment after ten years from the entry of a judgment, in the absence of its revival upon personal service, and in the absence of payments "duly entered upon the record thereof." (Mo. Rev. Stat. sec. 516.350, V.A.M.S.) This action was commenced well within the ten-year period, but it was not concluded until after that period had elapsed. . . .

* * *

. . . The act . . . contemplates that the vitality of the foreign judgment is to be determined as of the date that it is registered. And in this case the judgment was registered under the statute several months before the ten-year period expired.

Since we conclude that the Missouri decree is not barred from registration by the statutes of this State or of Missouri, we are brought to the questions raised concerning the extent to which its various aspects are entitled to full faith and credit. The defendant concedes, as indeed he must, that the decree is entitled to full faith and credit insofar as it awarded plaintiff a divorce and to the extent that it awarded alimony in gross. But to the extent that it awarded . . . and ordered monthly payments by way of . . . alimony, he argues that it is subject to modification in Missouri and therefore is not entitled to full faith and credit. . . .

The provisions of the decree that ordered the defendant to make periodic payments for . . . alimony are entitled to full faith and credit as to amounts already accrued unless they are subject to retrospective modification in Missouri. . . .

The plaintiff contends, upon her cross appeal, that the decree is entitled to full faith and credit as to future installments of alimony . . . and that the trial court erred in failing to register the decree as an Illinois judgment insofar as it concerned future payments. There are indications in the leading cases on the subject . . . that a decree for alimony which is subject to modification in the future by the court in which it was rendered is not entitled to full faith and credit. There are also intimations to the contrary in those cases and particularly in the concurring opinion of Mr. Justice Jackson in Barber v. Barber, 323 U.S. 77, 65 S.Ct. 137. . . .

Policy considerations argue strongly that such decrees are entitled to full faith and credit. Unless they receive interstate recognition, the insulated judicial systems of the several States may become sanctuaries within which obligations that have been fully and fairly adjudicated in another jurisdiction may be escaped. These policy considerations have found expression in the decisions of many State courts which, on the grounds of comity, have given full effect, including equitable enforcement, to foreign decrees awarding alimony in the future. . . .

* * *

The practical problems that might arise in the enforcement of a decree subject to modification by the courts of more than one forum are no more difficult under the full-faith-and-credit clause than they are when foreign judgments are given full effect as a matter of comity. If anything, they are less complicated . . . We hold . . . that the decree is entitled to full faith and credit as to future payments.

* * *

Because the statute is new, we think that it is appropriate to say a word as to the kind of judgment or decree that it contemplates. What is registered is the foreign judgment or decree, to the extent that no defense to it exists. If there is a defense that bars its enforcement completely, the final judgment must be for the defendant. Where a partial defense exists, as by partial satisfaction or limitations, that defense must be recognized in the final judgment. This can conveniently be done by first setting out the foreign judgment or decree in full in the final order entered in the Illinois court, and then indicating clearly the portions of it that are entered as a judgment of the Illinois court.

The decree of the circuit court of McLean County is reversed, and the cause is remanded to that court, without costs in this court to either party, with directions to enter a decree in accordance with this opinion.

* * *

3.
ENFORCEMENT

BRADLEY v. SUPERIOR COURT
48 Cal. 2d 509, 310 P. 2d 634 (1957)

SCHAUER, JUSTICE.

A writ of certiorari was issued for the purpose of reviewing an order of the superior court adjudging petitioner to be in contempt for refusing to make certain payments to his former wife in accordance with the provisions of their property settlement agreement and decree of divorce, and directing that petitioner be imprisoned if he fails to comply with the court's order of payment. We have concluded that although upon the record before us certain of petitioner's contentions concerning interpretation of the provisions of the property settlement agreement cannot be upheld, the order directing his imprisonment for contempt upon his continued failure to make payment should nevertheless be annulled as in violation

of the constitutional prohibition against imprisonment for debt. (Cal. Const., art. 1, § 15.)

* * *

Although, "As in the case of all constitutional provisions designed to safeguard the liberties of the persons, every doubt should be resolved in favor of the liberty of the citizen in the enforcement of the constitutional provision that no person shall be imprisoned for debt" (11 Am. Jur. 1128, § 327 . . .) a court may nevertheless punish by imprisonment as a contempt the willful act of a spouse (or former spouse) who, having the ability and opportunity to comply, deliberately refuses to obey a valid order to pay alimony or an allowance for the support of the other spouse (or former other spouse). It is held that the obligation to make such payments is not a "debt" within the meaning of the constitutional guaranty against imprisonment for debt. . . .

Where, however, the payments provided in a property settlement agreement constitute an adjustment of property interests, rather than alimony, support, or maintenance, the more generally prevailing rule is stated to be that decrees based thereon are not enforceable by contempt proceedings. (154 A.L.R. 466, 468-469.) . . . In Maryland it has been held that only modifiable alimony payments may be enforced by contempt, and that both child support and unmodifiable payments based on the parties' written agreement (even though such payments might be characterized as "alimony" in the court's order in the divorce proceedings) fall within the constitutional provision prohibiting imprisonment for debt. . . . Further, it appears that in Michigan "The fact that the court's award, made pursuant to or in accordance with the parties' agreement, includes both alimony and a property settlement (or a settlement in lieu of dower, or other obligation not enforceable by contempt proceedings) commingled in such a way that it does not appear, from the provisions of the decree, what amount of the award is alimony and what amount property settlement (or other obligation), has been deemed to preclude the enforcement of such award by contempt proceedings." (154 A.L.R. 475.)

No California case has been cited or discovered in which the point has been squarely presented. . . .

* * *

We are satisfied that the better view is that payments provided in a property settlement agreement which are found to constitute an adjustment of property interests, rather than a severable provision for alimony, should be held to fall within the constitutional proscription against imprisonment for debt. That is, if the obligation sought to be enforced is contractual and negotiated, as distinguished from marital and imposed by law, even though the contract relates to marriage obligations, the remedy must be appropriate to the right asserted. Payments which fall into the category of law-imposed alimony or separate maintenance are based upon the statutory obligation of marital support, may be modified by the court upon a proper showing, ordinarily terminate with the death of either party, and may properly be held not to constitute a "debt" within the meaning of the constitutional provision. No such case for special exemption from the constitutional proscription can be made where the payments represent the result of a bargain negotiated by the parties in adjustment of their respective interests. . . .

TRAYNOR, JUSTICE.

I dissent.

The majority opinion concedes that an alimony award based on the agreement of the parties is enforceable by contempt, . . . since it is sufficiently related to the statutory duty of support incident to the marriage relationship as to be outside the constitutional prohibition of imprisonment for debt. Cal. Const. art. 1, § 15. Rights and duties with respect to property growing out of the marriage relationship and crystallized in a court order are likewise outside the scope of that provision. Such an order has not less a special character because it is based on an agreement of the parties than an alimony award based on such an agreement. Indeed, in some states the very theory underlying use of contempt to enforce awards of alimony is that alimony is itself an adjustment of property rights. . . .

* * *

Even if the statutory duty of support were the sole justification for enforcing such court orders by contempt, the majority opinion would still be in error in stating that an order to make payments pursuant to an integrated bargain cannot be so enforced, when the wife has not remarried. In Dexter v. Dexter, 42 Cal. 2d 36, 41-42, 265 P. 2d 873, 876, we stated: "When, as in this case * * *, the parties have made the provision for support and maintenance an integral part of their property settlement agreement, the monthly payments will ordinarily have a dual character. To the extent that they are designed to discharge the obligations of support and maintenance they will ordinarily reflect the characteristics of that obligation and thus have the indicia of alimony. [Citations.] On the other hand, to the extent that they represent a division of the community property itself, or

constitute an inseparable part of the consideration for the property settlement, they are not alimony, and accordingly cannot be modified without changing the terms of the property settlement agreement of the parties." So long as the wife has not remarried, the characteristics of the support and maintenance obligation remain and alone justify enforcement by contempt. . . .

* * *

. . . There may be practical considerations for an order that community property, such as a going business, remain intact and that the wife receive her share in periodic payments. Whether such payments are also intended to discharge a duty of support, they may actually be the wife's only means of support. As in the case of wages, the payments may be difficult to collect by repeated executions. The enforcement of the obligation by contempt is no more tantamount to imprisonment for debt than criminal punishment for the wilful refusal to pay wages.

I would adhere to the settled law of this state and affirm the order holding petitioner in contempt.

* * *

NOTES

NOTE 1.

POLITANO v. POLITANO
262 N.Y.S. 802 (Sup. Ct. 1933)

BONYNGE, JUSTICE.

The defendant, an ignorant and penniless Italian, has been continuously imprisoned for two years and seven months for nonpayment of alimony to a young and childless wife, capable of and actually earning her own living. He enjoys the unique, if unhappy, distinction of being the senior inmate of the sheriff's alimony colony.

The parties hereto were married in October, 1927. As their union was blessed with no children, the plaintiff atoned for this by installing her mother and sister as permanent members of the household. The defendant expended his cash savings of $3,000 in fitting up and supporting the home. At the end of eleven months the money was gone and the parties separated. The plaintiff sued for separation and was awarded temporary alimony of $10 a week, which was regularly paid. In September, 1929, a decree was rendered in plaintiff's favor fixing the permanent alimony of $12 a week. The defendant is a bricklayer by trade, and, in common with most of the artisans in the building industry, has suffered severely as a result of the economic depression. His payments fell in arrears commencing in the fall of 1929, with a consequent adjudication of contempt and warrant of commitment. Successive adjudications of like kind followed, including an order requiring defendant to file a bond of $1,000 to secure payments to the plaintiff. There is nothing in the record to show that the defendant has fraudulently concealed or divested himself of property or has ever been able to comply with the court's orders. In his plea for release the defendant says: "I am very proud to state that I am an American citizen, and I have also fought for democracy in the front trenches of the World's Great War, and in which war I have not endured the misery, heartache, nervousness and worry as I am during this dreadful incarceration. Your Honor can realize what a Godsend it would mean, were you to give me my freedom and liberty."

This case presents the bold question of whether, and under what circumstances, life or even moderately prolonged imprisonment is permissible for the nonpayment of alimony, where the default is not due to sheer willfulness or obstinacy. The denials by other justices of previous applications for discharge by this defendant, as well as the present recommendation of the learned official referee, suggest the necessity for careful consideration of the matter.

*   *   *

Granting that even a lowly alimony prisoner has constitutional rights, it still remains to be determined whether such rights of this defendant have been violated, bearing in mind that he is a victim of misfortune and not of obduracy. In Weems v. United States, [217 U.S. 349], the court, in considering whether a sentence of fifteen years at "painful labor" and other penalties of infringement of a statute of the Philippine Islands, was violative of the constitutional inhibition against "cruel and unusual punishment," viewed the sentence in the light of comparable statutes of the United States and thus reached the conclusion that the constitutional rights of the prisoner had been invaded. It will be instructive to apply a similar test to the plight of this defendant. Sections 750 and 751 of the Judiciary Law deal with criminal contempts, which exceed in gravity the civil contempt of which the defendant stands adjudged guilty. Under these sections if an intruder disturbs the serenity of a courtroom by disorderly or insolent behavior, or interrupts the proceedings of the court or willfully resists its lawful mandate, the limits of judicial displeasure are circumscribed by statute to a jail sentence of thirty days and a fine of $250. However, let a waspish woman pluck the sleeve of the judicial gown, or nudge the elbow concealed therein and this temperate restraint is immediately cast aside, and the delinquent spouse

faces the possibility of unending imprisonment through successive adjudications of contempt (Civil Practice Act § 1172). This carries the supposed rights of women to absurd, not to say unconstitutional, lengths. Through the ages man has yielded authority in the home to the opposite sex and accepted the consequences with humility. With a blend of humor, resignation, and affection the relationship has come to be known as petticoat government. While the institution has functioned reasonably well, there are those who doubt the expediency of its extension into a form of petticoat justice.

The correct disposition of this case requires only a candid answer to a single question. Punishment for contempt is a deserved and salutary rebuke to one who has affronted the dignity of a court. If an evildoer invades my courtroom and reviles me or my ancestors or my country with indecent or blasphemous utterances, a penalty of thirty days is the straight-jacket of my righteous wrath. Can I truthfully say that this defendant who shouldered arms when the need was great, and now, through poverty or misfortune, omits to pay alimony to a vindictive and relentless wife, has offered my court an affront more than thirty fold greater? The answer being obvious, the report of the learned official referee is set aside and the defendant ordered discharged from imprisonment forthwith.

NOTE 2.

Ex Parte TODD
119 Cal. 57, 50 P. 1071 (1897)

PER CURIAM   Petitioner's wife obtained a decree of divorce, including an order for the payment of permanent alimony, in weekly installments. After paying $280 the petitioner ceased making further payments, and, at the instance of the plaintiff in the divorce suit, was cited by the superior court to show cause why he should not be punished for contempt of the order of the court in failing to pay the sum of $200 in arrears, and also to show cause why he should not pay to plaintiff said sum of $200. Petitioner appeared in response to the citation, and, after hearing testimony pro and con, the court found, among other facts, that he had no money or other means of payment, and that he had made no disposition of any property in fraud of his creditors. The court found, in other words, that it was not in the power of the petitioner to pay the money, or any part of it; but, at the same time, the court found that petitioner, having been allowed a month or thereabouts to seek employment by which he might have earned money to make the weekly payments of alimony as prescribed in the order, had wholly failed and neglected to make any effort to obtain employment, and therefore ordered him to be imprisoned in the county jail until he paid the $200 due. This order was clearly in excess of the power of the court, which cannot compel a man to seek employment in order to earn money to pay alimony, and punish him for his failure so to do. Prisoner discharged.

* * *

NOTE 3.

Rhode Island Public Laws
Ch. 3721 (1956)

Sec. 38. Every person who shall have been imprisoned in [the] adult correctional institutions for a period exceeding 6 months, by virtue of an execution issued in any civil suit, may, at his request, during the remaining time of his detention therein, be kept at labor, as prisoners are under section 37 of this chapter, for the benefit of his creditor or creditors by virtue of whose execution he is imprisoned.

Sec. 39. Such execution-debtor shall be allowed by the state for every day's actual labor by him done the sum of 35 cents, if the state shall receive or be benefited to that amount by his labor, if not, the amount which the state shall receive therefor or be benefited thereby.

Sec. 40. The warden shall keep against every such execution-debtor an account, in the name of the state, in which he shall charge him with the cost of board, if any, provided for him by the state, and any other necessaries furnished to such debtor by the state, and shall credit him with the price of the value of his labor as aforesaid, and the balance, if any, shall, as often as once a month, be paid over by said warden to the creditor detaining such debtor, or if there be more than one creditor so detaining him, be divided amongst such detaining creditors, in equal proportion to the amount of their debts, in liquidation of the same.

NOTE 4.

Minnesota Session Laws, Ch. 715 (1957)

AN ACT relating to offenders sentenced for one year or less, authorizing their employment at their customary work, and defining the powers and duties of sheriffs in relation thereto.

* * *

(631.425) Employment of offenders at their customary work.

* * *

(Subd. 2.) *Discretion of court.* Any convicted prisoner sentenced to jail may in the discretion of the sentencing court be committed under this act. If so committed, the sentence shall so provide.

(Subd. 3.) *Continuation of employment.* If the person so committed has been regularly employed, the sheriff shall arrange for a continuation of the employment insofar as possible without interruption. If the person is not employed on any job, the sheriff or any suitable person or agency designated by the court shall make every effort to secure some suitable employment for him. Any prisoner so employed shall be paid a fair and reasonable wage for such work and shall work at fair and reasonable hours per day and per week.

(Subd. 4.) *Confinement when not employed.* Unless the court otherwise directs, each prisoner shall be confined in jail during such time as he is not employed, or, if employed, between the times of employment.

Subd. 5.) *Earnings.* The earnings of the prisoner shall be collected by the sheriff, probation department, welfare board or suitable person or agency designated by the court. From such earnings the person or agency designated to collect them shall pay the cost of the prisoner's maintenance, both inside and outside the jail, but the charge for maintenance inside the jail shall not exceed the legal daily allowance for board allowed the sheriff for ordinary prisoners, and, to the extent directed by the court, pay the support of his dependents, if any, and court costs and fines, if any. Any balance shall be retained until his discharge when it shall be paid to him.

NOTE 5.

BLUMENTHAL v. COMMISSIONER OF INTERNAL REVENUE
183 F. 2d 15, n. 3 (3rd Cir. 1950)

KALODNER, CIRCUIT JUDGE.

[The divorce decree] provided, *inter alia,* that Sara was entitled for her support and maintenance to receive from the taxpayer $100 per week until her death or lawful remarriage, and as security for the payments the taxpayer was required to assign his salary, dividends and bonuses. And,

"Ordered, Adjudged and Decreed, that plaintiff is entitled to have delivered . . . for the purpose of securing and protecting the plaintiff in the payments to be made for her sole support . . . in the event of the death of defendant . . . policies of life insurance aggregating Sixty-five thousand (65,000) Dollars in face amount . . . and plaintiff is entitled to be named in said life insurance policies as irrevocable beneficiary for her life or until her death or lawful remarriage, . . . plaintiff is entitled to have the defendant maintain the premiums on said policies of insurance. . . .

NOTE 6.

BLANC v. BLANC
21 Misc. 268, 47 N.Y.S. 694 (1897)

RUSSELL, J. The substantial thing in controversy is the use of a name by the former wife, now divorced on account of her adultery. In the first case the motion is to punish for contempt, for her continued use of the name "Baroness Blanc," in defiance of the judgment of divorce providing:

"... that the defendant be prohibited from using the name of 'Blanc,' or 'Frederic N. Blanc,' as her name, or any portion of her name."

*   *   *

It is strenuously urged by the defendant's counsel that the judgment of divorce exceeded the jurisdiction of the court, in prohibiting the use of the name of her former husband, and therefore, while using her real name, "Elizabeth L. Waters," in private life, she has, under the advice of counsel, used the name of "Baroness Blanc" for theatrical purposes, in her vocation of an actress, presumably believing that thereby more prominence would be given to her in that vocation. . . .

Is the question of name borne by the wife one of those matters which come from the inception of the marriage relation, and which ought to terminate when she has, by misconduct, lost her right to its use? . . .

. . . How can she further claim the right to identify herself with her former husband, when all relations between them are so broken? Courts have a right to regard her use of the name as of serious consequence to the innocent husband. There are higher rights flowing out of the marriage than the pecuniary part, as affecting either of the persons concerned. The unoffending party ought certainly to have the privilege of preventing the claim directly made, or so urged upon the public as to deceive it, that the other is still the lawful spouse, and still has the right to bear the name of that spouse. Such a husband may be affected in a pecuniary way. Out of the marital obligation comes the duty to provide the necessaries for the wife; and while, after a decree of divorce, he may not be legally liable to persons from whom she purchases on his credit, yet others may be deceived, and they may be the losers, and he be subjected to annoying and vexatious litigations. And, if such unoffending party desires to remarry, the use by the former wife of his name might be a serious impediment in gaining the consent of some worthy woman, who might not want to be one of two women bearing the name of the husband. I think the court did not transgress its power when it held that the use of the name was a subject fairly within its consideration . . . The motion therefore is granted to punish the defendant for contempt. . . .

E.

Reservations and Proposals

1.

DOYLE v. DOYLE
5 Misc. 2d 4, 158 N.Y.S. 2d 909 (1957)

HOFSTADTER, JUSTICE.

Motion to resettle order of December 4, 1956, is granted to the extent of making the increase of the weekly alimony effective from and as of July 1, 1956. . . .

. . . This action is a classic example of the type of matrimonial litigation that has given rise in recent years to so much concern on the part of judges, lawyers, social agencies and the community at large. The suit, commenced 13 years ago and now reopened on a question of modification of an alimony award, was an apparently simple one confined to the trial court level. It involved no complicated questions of either fact or law requiring the attention of an appellate tribunal. Despite this, however, the matter has occupied the time and efforts of some half-

dozen lawyers and at least twelve judicial officers of our court.

In addition, this case had a prior history of marital maladjustment back almost a quarter of a century, and of hearing and rehearing in the Domestic Relations Court—one of the busiest and most useful of our city—where both judicial intervention and social aid were employed in an attempt to solve the legal and underlying marital problems.

This is, in short, a typical case where the parties have "shopped" from court to court seeking help. For matrimonial litigation clings to its victims with all the tenacity of the Old Man of the Sea. Even when the substantive matter of the action is terminated—by dissolution or otherwise—the question of support persists, often throughout the lifetime of the parties, and is a continuous source of vexation and legal controversy. In the interest of the litigants and of the efficient administration of justice, there must be a renovation in the procedures for handling family matters in the court and, more particularly, in the principles relating to alimony and support.

From the point of view of procedure, it is manifest that there is a dire need of an integrated court, properly staffed and equipped with social aids, to handle all family matters . . . so that a court dealing with the family will be able to prescribe comprehensive and final relief rather than piecemeal and temporary palliatives. . . .

Further, in an effort to reduce the numerous applications for rehearings and modifications of support allowances, consideration must be given to the use of more efficient methods employed in other jurisdictions to determine the financial capacity of the husband and the need of the wife. Standardized budgets for various income groups, court auditing offices equipped with accountants and investigators, sworn financial statements, etc. should be instituted.

However, changes in procedure alone are not sufficient; a shift in the basis of awards is requisite. The perverse system which now obtains for the fixing of alimony and support is unjust in concept and faulty in application. It is unfair to men and to women. Honest and deserving women get too little—their children likewise—and others far too much for their own good and that of society.

In evolving a modern system for fixing alimony and support the elements of (1) fault, (2) financial capacity and (3) need must be reappraised.

Alimony should not be a reward for virtue nor a punishment for guilt. The element of fault should be de-emphasized. Fault should not be a bar to alimony except in cases of gross culpability, such as infidelity or abandonment. In most cases neither party is at fault or both are in some degree. Generally, family break-ups are not due to specific acts of either spouse, legal fictions notwithstanding. They result rather from general malaise to which both have contributed. Fault usually comes after malaise has set in; it is the symptom not the cause of domestic discord.

The factor of need, too, must be adjusted to women's new position in our society. The married woman has come a long way since the days of Blackstone when she had no legal identity apart from her husband's; she is no longer the Victorian creature, "something better than her husband's dog, a little dearer than his horse." She is now the equal of man, socially, politically and economically. It is time that consonant with this new approach to woman's status we develop a modern basis for fixing alimony and support which will have its roots in reality.

A practical approach in awarding alimony would be to proceed on the basis of what we may term "net need," the wife's actual financial requisite less her current assets and earning potential in relation to her husband's capacity to pay. If a woman proves need she should have support —but when she can, she should also be required to mitigate her husband's burden either by her own financial means or earning potential or both. The want alimony seeks to solve is economic—for alimony is basically the statutory substitute for the marital obligation of a husband to support his wife.

Each case must be treated as its particular circumstances indicate for there are many variables that should be taken into account in the determination of alimony. If a woman has contributed however indirectly to her husband's career and helped to increase his substance she may rightfully be regarded as entitled to a share of his gain. A woman who has devoted the greater part of her time to caring for a home and children has had little opportunity to learn the skills necessary to earn a living in our competitive society. The court should and will take cognizance of her plight.

But the same considerations do not operate in the case of a young woman who in all but form has remained alien to her husband's interest. Why should ex-wives and separated women seek a preferred status in which they shall toil not, neither shall they spin? Alimony was originally devised by society to protect those without power of ownership or earning resources. It was never intended to assure a perpetual state of secured indolence. It should not be suffered to convert a host of physically and mentally competent women into an army of alimony drones.

Ironically, inflated alimony awards are frequently not only financially disastrous to the man but psychologically deleterious to the woman. She remains hopelessly entangled in the web of the past, never establishing a new and independent life but "wandering between two worlds, one already dead and the other powerless to be born."

In the field of matrimonial litigation and alimony awards the husband and wife are not the sole parties. Society itself has locus standi for it is deeply affected in vital aspects. For the benefit of all concerned, we must proceed in a climate of sanity that will reflect modern reality and in a spirit of sympathetic understanding that will achieve justice and equity.

Settle re-settled order accordingly.

NOTES

NOTE 1.

New Hampshire Revised Statutes 458:19 (1955)

Alimony. Upon a decree of nullity or divorce, the court may restore to the wife all or any part of her estate, and may assign to her such part of the estate of her husband, or order him to pay such sum of money, as may be deemed just, provided that in cases in which no children are involved, or in which the children have reached the age of majority, said order shall be effective for not more than three years from the date thereof, but such order may be renewed, modified or extended if justice requires for periods of not more than three years at a time; and may compel the husband to disclose, under oath, the situation of his property; and before or after the decree, may make such orders and use such process as may be necessary.

NOTE 2.

California Civil Code § 139 (1954)

Except as otherwise agreed by the parties in writing, the obligation of any party in any decree, judgment or order for the support and maintenance of the other party shall terminate upon the death of the obligor or upon the remarriage of the other party. . . .

2.

PEELE, CATHERINE GROVES

Social and Psychological Effects of the Availability and the Granting of Alimony on the Spouses*

It is not surprising that generally there is much emotion associated with the giving or receiving of alimony. Alimony perpetuates, in most instances, a relationship passionately undesired and in a way that continues and even increases former antagonisms. Although we can safely assume that the average individual will react emotionally to an alimony decree, it is difficult to know in advance what slant this will take, so many elements are involved. It easily becomes a sort of legal poultice that draws to a head the underlying domestic poison that the divorce is expected to drain away.

Naturally, of first importance in determining the reaction spouses will have to the matter of alimony is their existing attitude toward each other. Other things that have to be taken into account are: the individual's viewpoint on alimony in general, his attitude toward legal proceedings of any kind, and his feeling in regard to money. These various factors can not be isolated. One often reinforces another. Thus, a man who harbors a great deal of resentment towards his wife for her part

* Reprinted from a symposium, *Alimony*, in 6 *Law and Contemporary Problems* 283 (1939). Copyright © by Duke University Press. Reprinted by permission of Duke University School of Law, Durham, North Carolina, publisher.

in bringing about their separation, will become convinced that it is most unjust to expect a man to continue to support an able-bodied woman after he has separated from her, and will in the end become antagonistic toward the court which forces him so to do. Such a man may put up a tremendous fight to keep from paying alimony in spite of the fact that his friends try to get him to see that he is losing more in prestige by his contest than he can ever gain if he wins.

Alimony is a concrete thing around which all the feelings concerning the divorce or separation are likely to gather. To the man who has always told his cronies how extravagant his wife is, the amount of alimony she demands is proof that he is right. To the woman who keeps her bridge club up-to-date on instances of her husband's inconsiderate behavior, his attitude toward giving her alimony is the most flagrant example of all. Also, alimony goes on after the divorce suit has been settled. Animosities that might otherwise have burnt out with the passing of time may be rekindled each time a check is mailed. The memory of other wrongs may fade, but the husband may find the paying of the alimony a constant source of annoyance, while the wife may be irritated each time the check arrives because it is no larger.

Another thing that has to be considered is that the payment of alimony is not a thoroughly accepted thing throughout our society, appearing mainly in cases of divorce or separation among those in the higher economic groups, seldom in those among the lower. Therefore, although alimony may be taken for granted in certain circles, it can not be said to be so regarded among the public as a whole. In general, alimony in cases of separation or divorce seems to be the accepted thing among those whose economic status is such that the wife usually has some property of her own at the time of marriage. It is not as accepted in those groups where the wife seldom adds more to the economic aspect of the marriage partnership than her own wage-earning ability.

Thus a man who would expect legal means to be taken to force him to pay off his creditors, to give his employees their wages, and to support the wife with whom he lived, may take a very different attitude toward the payment of alimony, and he may be backed up in his resistance by the opinion of his friends.

* * *

[A] woman may think of alimony as meaning power, not her former husband's power over her, but her power over him. She may cherish this power merely for its nuisance value, hoping that having to pay it constitutes a constant source of annoyance to him. Or she may know that as long as he has to pay alimony he can not afford to marry again, or to live in accordance with the style in which he would like to live. Her desire to punish him may be a much more important factor in her insistence on receiving alimony than is her need for financial support.

> A woman came to a Legal Aid Society demanding that her divorced husband be forced to pay her alimony. Investigation revealed that the man was quite ill, had not worked in some time, and was being supported by his second wife. This made no difference to the woman, who did not question these facts but who insisted that he be taken into court anyway, and she became very angry with the agency when this was not done.

It would appear from the public's generally skeptical attitude toward women who seek alimony that this punishing drive is considered to be the almost universal motive for a woman's desire to get support from a former husband. It is not uncommon to find that men who have been generally condemned in the eyes of their community for their treatment of their wives become suddenly the object of pity as soon as the wife gets a divorce and is awarded alimony. Legislators, too, seem to have assumed that women have more desire to punish than to get support, for what other basis could there be for laws which enable a woman to jail her husband or former husband for non-payment of alimony when we have long ago outgrown the idea that creditors should be allowed to imprison debtors?

Perhaps the wives who are out for vengeance make themselves the most conspicuous, but as a matter of fact a woman may be humiliated by the knowledge that she is receiving support only because of a legal decree as frequently as the man may balk at the threat of compulsion contained in the decree. Anybody who comes into contact with cases of separation and divorce knows that there are many more women who do without what they need rather than take legal means to force their former husbands to support them, than there are women who use the courts to harass their ex-spouses.

Then again it may be not a desire for vengeance that makes a woman resort to the courts more than perhaps is necessary, but a new-born sense of power. A woman who has always felt completely helpless as far as her husband is concerned may get her first taste of being able to hold her own against him when she uses the court to force him to pay alimony. Then, glorying in this newly gained sense of authority, she may continually threaten her former husband with this power of the court until he rises in open rebellion.

Nor does the woman always wait until a divorce is granted before using alimony as a threat, and there is no telling in how many domestic spats women tauntingly remind their husbands of the obligation to support them even though they should separate, which in the majority of instances of course they do not do. A few men, the type who grow up with the notion that the female represents a lower type of the human species than does the male, may treat their wives as more on a par with themselves on being thus threatened, for to such men women gain in prestige in so far as they have legal rights that they are not afraid to enforce. Also, some men, who value highly the things that money can buy, may put up with a great deal of domestic wrangling rather than to try to support two households. However, in very few instances would the reluctance to pay alimony be a deciding factor in keeping a man from seeking a divorce or separation.

When one considers the woman's side of the question, however, alimony may be of prime importance. The effect of alimony is to give the non-income-producing spouse (who of course is generally the woman) a chance to decide on a divorce or separation without thereby having to relinquish all the economic rights that she would have as a wife.

If there were no alimony laws many spouses would reach a voluntary agreement as to division of property if they both desired the separation, but the existence of such laws gives the woman who desires a marital break more nearly the same ability to achieve it in spite of her husband's opposition as a man has to get a divorce even though his wife may not want one. The mere right to sue for divorce would mean nothing to some women if they would have no way of procuring support, for economic reality may make it very difficult for a woman, if untrained and middle aged or older, to support herself in anything like the style to which she is accustomed. Having no provision for enforcing payment of alimony would be in some cases the same thing as allowing the man alone to decide whether there should be a divorce or not.

Thus, on the whole, alimony operates to place the woman on a more equal footing with her husband when a decision must be made as to the point at which they shall cease to try to live together as man and wife. There is no way of knowing how many of the women now receiving support from a former mate would have made another attempt to get along with their husbands if there had been no such thing as alimony, but probably the main effect of alimony on the divorce rate arises from the fact that it puts a premium on legal separations as against informal ones. Couples no longer wishing to live together, but with no desire to remarry, who might otherwise merely live apart without making public avowal of the fact, may take steps to make the separation a legal one in order to get the court's backing for the property settlement. In so far as this factor operates to increase the number of divorces, however, it does so without actually increasing the number of broken homes.

This is not to say that the allure of alimony never leads a woman to the divorce court; it may even have led her to the altar in the first place. Nevertheless, the number of women who marry very rich men, live with them a short period of time and then demand huge sums as alimony is certainly much smaller than their ability to make newspaper headlines would lead one to suppose. Their importance is mainly the influence that a few such instances can have on public opinion.

Indeed, so widespread is the idea that alimony is just another racket that it is not uncommon to hear people say that it should be done away with entirely. This, however, is an unsound conclusion. If alimony laws work a hardship in certain cases, it would seem that it should be possible to amend them so that the abuse could be done away with, rather than to let the defects blind us to the essential justice of the principle involved, that of making a fair division of the economic assets that a married couple have built up over a period of years. The only asset may be the husband's earning power, and whether or not the wife has directly or indirectly helped to increase this over a period of time, if she has spent the best years of her life at the job of being a wife she may have thereby reduced her own potential earning power considerably. If it were not for the fact that anything connected with the breaking up of a marriage arouses emotional reactions in most of us, we should probably look upon alimony in the same light as we do the procedure of dividing property among the former partners of a concern that is going out of business.

* * *

NOTES

NOTE 1.

WEBBER v. WEBBER
33 Cal. 2d 153, 199 P. 2d 934 (1948)

SPENCE, JUSTICE.

. . . Here plaintiff, a woman fifty-three years of age, the mother of eight children, having been occupied solely with her household duties during some thirty-six years of married life with defendant, and without training or experience in the industrial or business world to fit her for earning her own livelihood, was allowed no provision for support because the trial judge thought "they [plaintiff and defendant] can both get a job" and so declared his intent not to make an alimony award before plaintiff presented her evidence of need therefor. It is true that defendant, a man sixty-one years of age, was dependent on his daily labor as a means of support, but it has been said: "A man past middle age can usually rehabilitate himself in life in case of a break in the marriage relations. A woman of that age seldom can; and the courts may very properly safeguard her financial future where, by the fault of her husband, the marriage is dissolved." Farrar v. Farrar, 41 Cal. App. 452, 457, 182 P. 989, 991.

Although after the trial judge's untimely comment on the alimony issue plaintiff was allowed to present evidence thereon, the record shows that he considered it "time wasted," and that his predetermined state of mind continued to exist. Thus, at the end of the trial, he stubbornly declared to plaintiff's counsel: "I have told you that I am not going to award any support. I have told you that several times." Accordingly the finding was made that "defendant has no ability to earn more than sufficient for his own support and maintenance * * * and has no ability to pay further for the support and maintenance of plaintiff or for her attorney's fees or Court costs herein." Such finding appears to be inconsistent with defendant's own testimony as to what he had actually been doing in the way of support for himself and family in previous years by virtue of his wages from daily labor—"$40 to $47 a week * * * take-home pay." It is true that at the time of trial defendant was not employed, but he had been "laid off" only "a short time" and he had purposely refrained from taking "a new job" because of the imminence of the trial. Defendant freely admitted that work was available, that he "could have gone to work at $140 a month, but [he] knew that this was coming up," and he was "not afraid" that he could not "get a job again." Not only the "husband's [actual] earnings" but "his ability to earn money" by the use of reasonable effort will affect the propriety of an alimony award. . . .

. . . Here it plainly appears that there was no exercise of discretion in resolving the conflicting inferences . . . but rather an arbitrary determination of the opposing considerations in line with the biased and prejudiced attitude of the trial judge as reflected in his announced prejudgment of the issue. . . .

NOTE 2.

ROYAL COMMISSION ON MARRIAGE AND DIVORCE
Report, 129-138 (1956) (Cmd. 9678)*

486. Some witnesses considered a complete change of principle to be necessary—each spouse should primarily be liable to support himself or herself. It was contemplated, however, that the wife should still be able to apply for maintenance from her husband (or former husband) but the burden would be upon her to satisfy the court that she could not support herself, for instance because age or ill-health prevented her from working, or because she had young children to look after; it might also be reasonable to allow her maintenance while she was training to take up work.

3.

BRADWAY, J. S.

Why Pay Alimony?†

It is comparatively simple to find fault with nearly any rule of law. One who attempts to formulate a remedy offers himself to make a Roman holiday. The value of the proposal need not be judged by its ultimate acceptance as the ideal solution. . . .

* * *

[W]e come to the present proposal which involves the following steps:

A. Marriage has several aspects—spiritual, physical, economic. The economic aspect has received modern legislative and judicial attention with respect to married women's property rights, but not enough with respect to support and alimony. This phase of it should be segregated and studied in isolation.

B. Marriage as a sacrament or a status was not bewildering to a medieval ecclesiastical jurist. The legal concept fitted into a social and economic scheme in which the mutual obligations for the spouses were both clear and, in general, enforceable. But the mutual obligations of modern spouses are not so clear or enforceable. Common law administrative machinery is more effective in enforcing a contract with business sanctions behind it than a status in which spiritual values are inextricably involved. If the obligation of a husband to support his wife can be isolated from the rest of the status and a business sanction substituted the result may be a material gain for the spouses with little or no disturbance of the spiritual relationship.

C. A third difficulty to be removed is the antagonism engendered by the litigation process. Some other device should be found which will enable the spouses to adjust their differences.

Let us first consider the substitution of a new set of concepts. The marital relation has been likened to a partnership. It approximates more closely a corporation because most marriages must have the approval of the state before they are valid and a divorce may be obtained only by permission of the state. If the legal concepts in the economic aspect of family life were expressed in terms now applied to a corporation the subject would be clearer and ready for critical study and improvement.

A corporation deals with three groups of persons—creditors, stockholders and employees. To the first it pays its debts under well recognized legal rules. To the second go dividends in orderly fashion. To the third are awarded wages for services rendered. The economic relations of the wife to the husband can be expressed in terms of debts, dividends and wages without doing violence to her legal rights or his. If she brings to the marriage money or property amassed elsewhere, her rights in it may be defined as those of a creditor. If she contributes to the social or economic improvement of the family by extraordinary services or skills a dividend could reward her insofar as such imponderables may be translated into material values. But for her ordinary services wages would seem a businesslike return.

The use of the wages concept has been urged by many feminists, but apparently not as a part of the analogy between the family and the corporation. The market value of wages is determinable. As long as the family remains a going concern the wife's wages ordinarily would be a matter of domestic adjustment. But when the family disintegrates, the wife's rights might be protected by something like unemployment insurance.

2. *Modifications in Administrative Machinery.* There is nothing unusual in utilizing the insurance device to solve social problems. A long list of precedents show that it is practicable and that it has an inherent flexibility which should make possible an adaptation to a somewhat novel situation. The question is whether it can be adapted to the domestic relations field. An illustration will suggest some of the administrative problems and bring up tentative proposals for their solution.

Let us assume that an insurance fund has been established with all the necessary administrative

---

* Reprinted with permission of the Controller of Her Britannic Majesty's Stationery Office.

† Reprinted by special permission of the *Illinois Law Review* (Northwestern University School of Law), Vol. 32, No. 3, pp. 301–306, Copyright © 1937, by the Illinois Law Publishing Corporation.

details; that it offers a policy or variety of policies of insurance to husbands and wives promising to pay the wife a certain sum or sums upon the event of the dissolution of the family; that it will function when the wife, unable to live adequately upon the normal returns for her services in the home, is faced with an appeal to the charity of friends or the public authorities administering the poor laws; that the wife must elect either the present system, or the insurance plan, but not both.

M and W, planning to marry, or already married, and being convinced that the possibility of domestic dissolution with the consequent unemployment of the wife for an uncertain period is a contingency as worth guarding against as the illness or death of the breadwinner, the burning of the residence or the theft of the family possessions, come to the office of an insurance company and make application. They have decided that it is more businesslike to accept the insurance protection than to rely upon the older methods.

They desire to know, first of all, the nature of the fund out of which the insurance will be paid. Public and private insurance funds, sustained by premiums, by taxation and otherwise, have engaged the attention of experts in the field for a sufficiently long time so that several working models are available, any one of which geared to the local conditions of a particular jurisdiction, should offer adequate service.

The second question will relate to the cost of the protection. After a reasonable period of experimentation it is possible for any insurance company to arrive at an actuarial figure for premiums, on certain classes of risks. While it is usual for the insured to pay the premiums, it is not unknown for the beneficiary to undertake the burden. In cases where the individual does not have sufficient funds to meet the payments, group insurance, paid by the employer, or a group of individuals on a cooperative basis or even by the state is not unknown.

The nature of the policy next engages attention. This would be in the form of a promise by the insurance agency, public or private, to pay certain monies in a certain manner upon the happenings of the contingency. The amount of the policy may be a matter for individual agreement. There is much to be said, however, for the arrangement, now in effect in workmen's compensation policies, which provides for a return to the beneficiary or his family at a schedule based upon the wages earned, and the nature of the disability, whether temporary or total. The manner of distribution of the money upon the happening of the contingency, whether in a lump sum or installments, may also be the subject of individual

preference. It is likely, however, that the state may desire some voice in the matter since the purpose of the plan is to protect the public from the need to pay for the wife's support. The duration of the liability of the fund, whether for a term or an endowment basis or otherwise, may be adjusted to fit the particular family.

The next step is to make the application. From a business standpoint this is important because it presents the facts which enable the insurance fund to determine whether or not the applicant is an insurable risk. It is the practice of insurance companies not to accept the application at its face value, but to make a thorough investigation of the applicant to prevent fraud, and for other reasons. Hence one finds physicians on the staffs of insurance companies. Other business organizations also probe into the financial ability of a prospective customer, his credit rating and other personal matters. Some of the small loan companies of the country employ a social worker to aid in obtaining the social background of the prospective borrower and to investigate any difficulties which occur during the continuance of the loan.

In the light of these established practices there is little novelty in the proposal that part of the application procedure for unemployment insurance for the wife should be an investigation by a trained social worker as to the social stability of the family. There seems no better way to determine whether it is an insurable risk. The technique of such an investigation is well known to trained social workers, and they are able to secure a maximum of information with a minimum of annoyance to those being investigated. Experience should permit the erection and maintenance of reasonable standards here as in other business relations. It is possible that during an experimental period the executives of the insurance fund will require periodic renewals of the application on which occasions the fund may relieve itself from liability in the event of fraud or a threatened domestic instability. During the continuance of the policy there may be occasional social investigations and perhaps we may hear the slogan, "See your social worker twice a year," just as we now find life and health insurance companies advising their clients to have periodic conferences with physicians and dentists. When group insurance in this field has become well established there may be organized supervision which will tend, by preventive means, to keep families from disintegration. The analogy is to preventive work in the medical field.

The insured will look forward to certain contingencies: the ending of the term when the contract will cease and determine; the death of the husband when the policy may provide a payment to the wife as in ordinary endowment life insurance; the death of the wife, when the policy may provide an endowment return to the husband; the continuance of the marriage for a certain number of years, when an endowment may be payable to both parties. Such matters may render the plan more attractive to individual families.

What will happen when the family breaks down? A break down may mean a domestic quarrel, a desertion, or a divorce. Through its periodic social investigations the insurance fund should have advance notice, and it is assumed that all sorts of preventive efforts will have been made. When the contingency, in spite of everything, does occur, the following steps are in order:

1. A filing of a claim by the wife.
2. A social investigation of the claim by the insurance fund.
3. The approval or rejection of the claim.

If the claim is approved, payments will be made at once. If it is rejected, the wife may sue the insurance company presenting such facts as she may have to support the contention that the contingency has occurred and that it is bona fide. . . . This, roughly, is the plan both as to theory and practice. Attention should now be given to some obvious criticisms.

* * *

The first possible snag is the problem of regimentation. Will people voluntarily submit their personal affairs to investigation by social workers and others, no matter how tactful and able? There are several reasons why they may. The applicant may come to believe that the business advantages of the plan outweigh considerations of privacy. Since, in an earlier day, individuals submitted to supervision by families and church officials, the proposal is not novel, rather it is a return to fundamentals. If standards of living were more clearly defined and the causes of breakdown statistically presented, individuals might be aroused to a sense of pride in keeping the rate of marriage dissolutions in their home community at a lower rate than in the neighboring city.

A second snag is the possibility that frauds may be perpetrated upon the fund so extensive and ingenious as to discourage its operation. It is difficult to see how such frauds would be greater than those now attempted in other forms of insurance. Since they are being met and insurance companies still show a profit, it is likely that ingenuity, backed by an enlightened self interest, will find a solution. The social work investigation should reduce the possibility of fraud to a minimum and the offenders could be prosecuted criminally with more effect than a wife can bring to bear upon her husband.

A third snag is the possibility that romantically inclined persons will resent what may appear to them a commercialization of the marriage relation. If this were the only occasion dragging the domestic intimacies before the light of publicity, the argument would be stronger. Domestic matters are spread abroad in the columns of every newspaper and many magazines. Court proceedings receive wide attention. A generation which has learned to discuss sex without distress of mind or spirit, and to seek aid from advice-to-the-lovelorn columnists is not likely to be frightened by the instant proposal. When an engagement is announced insurance agents flock to the prospective bridegroom and discuss with him such dismal subjects as death, illness, accidents. Since young love can see a business value in protecting the family from such spectres, it would seem that there is nothing scandalously shocking in the suggestion that protection should be afforded the wife, if a family dissolution should occur.

The fourth snag is the possibility that the proposed device will free the husband from a sense of obligation to his family, and that a general exodus will ensue. There seems to be no real reason to fear such a catastrophe. While the present proposal is not intended to solve the whole problem of family disintegration, it is not so revolutionary as to upset established habits. The proposal is voluntary, not compulsory. If the husband and wife do not elect it, there are still the existing rules and machinery. If they take the insurance it does not necessarily mean that they abandon all marital ties. No doubt some men will seek their freedom who today are restrained by a fear of the consequences. Yet one cannot call this an unmitigated evil. A family held together only by fear is not a healthy social organism such as the state desires. How can it perform adequately the tasks which the state requires of it, such as the rearing of children?

* * *

4.

TOMPKINS, ROGER

Report of the Subcommittee on the Family Law Process—Marriage Insurance*

Society has become uncomfortably aware of the contradictory purposes of the law in relation to the family. The legislature, desiring to focus on

---

* Excerpts from a paper submitted by Roger Tompkins, following a hearing in a class on The Family and the Law, during his third term as a student at the Yale Law School (1962). Printed with permission of the author.

given areas in order to achieve a coherent synthesis and, to receive suggestions for the implementation of these goals in practice, has appointed this committee "to consider the problems raised, for nearly one million citizens annually, by alimony decrees and more specifically to advise the legislature concerning the establishment of state or private alimony insurance."

The Committee was guided in its deliberations by acknowledging that the functions, or purposes of awarding periodic payments by one party to another subsequent to divorce include: (1) Punishment of the party "at fault," that is, the party held responsible at law "for causing" the divorce or breakup; (2) Maintaining continued contact between the parties so that they might be induced to reconcile and to remarry; (3) Supporting either party with or without fault, and any children of the marriage.

The stimulating and rewarding task of ordering and summarizing the ideas rising from this committee's discussion fell to me, as secretary.

*   *   *

The Committee proposed that each couple—subsequent to the marriage ceremony—should apply for a marriage insurance policy for a certain minimum coverage. Premium payments should be determined by actuarial standards taking into account: age, homogeneity of religious and cultural background, prior status, and any other factors statistically related to the divorce rates. In the event of divorce, insurance payments should be paid to either or both parties or to any party awarded alimony, thereby relieving the party obligated to provide alimony of such payments to the extent of coverage.

The Committee found no serious legal barriers to the insurance plan; our legal system has long upheld insurance as a manifestation of the freedom to contract.

(1) Some members, while accepting wholeheartedly the principles underlying freedom of contract, pointed out that since no one can have a business or property interest in divorce, alimony insurance cannot be "an insurable interest" and must, therefore constitute a wager. They reminded the committee that wagering contracts in the form of insurance have been banned in England since the early seventeenth century and that the American courts early adopted this proscription. In striking down a marine "insurance" contract in which the policy holder was held to have no insurable interest, the court in *Amory v. Gilman*, 2 Mass. 1 (1806), quoted Sergeant Marshall (1 Marsh 95), saying that

"The practice of gaming, by nourishing a constant hope of gain, excites the mind in interest which engrosses the attention, and withdraws the exertions of men from useful pursuits. By pointing out a speedy, though hazardous, mode of accumulating wealth, it produces a contempt for the moderate, but certain profits of sober industry. It perverts the activity of the mind, taints the heart, and depraves the affections. By frequent and great reverses of fortune, it becomes not only the source of great private misery, but suggests constant temptations to fraud, and to the perpetration of atrocious crimes."

The minority further argued that the dangers are even greater in the case of life insurance. They quoted the Supreme Court in *Warnock v. Davis*, 104 U.S. 755 (10), which struck down an agreement giving nine tenths of the policy's proceeds to a trust association because the association had no insurable interest.

It is not easy to define with precision what will in all cases constitute an insurable interest . . . [but must be such] as will justify a reasonable expectation of advantage or benefit from the continuance of [the insured's] life [: for example] either pecuniary or of blood or affinity. [O]therwise the contract is a mere wager, by which the party taking the policy is directly interested in the early death of the assured. Such policies have a tendency to create a desire for the event. They are, therefore, independently of any statute on the subject, condemned, as being against public policy. [*Id.* at 779].

It is preposterous some members argued, to think that divorce or alimony constitute an insurable interest.

But the majority of the Committee replied that not alimony or divorce, but rather marriage was the interest to be insured. Such insurance contains certain elements of investment, as well as indemnity insurance. As Professor Vance, discussing life insurance, noted: "[W]hen made in good faith, for the purpose of accumulating a fund for the support after the death of the insured, of those dependent upon him, the contract is one that encourages industry and thrift, and tends to relieve society of the burden of caring for its helpless members." [*The Law of Life Insurance* 8-27 (2d ex. 1930)] When a couple insures their marriage they invest against the contingency of its dissolution at the same time they protect the property interest of continued support in case of dissolution. By gearing premiums and payments to earning power, and by setting a maximum, as well as minimum schedule of payments, it is possible to make the continuation of marriage more lucrative than its dissolution. Moreover, the affection and security which many held to be the essence of marriage, will no doubt be an incentive to continuation of the marriage. And it may be possible to induce such continuation further by allowing the policy to be converted into a retirement or life insurance scheme at a set date. All of these interests not only constitute property and more, which one may wish to insure or invest, but also serve to offset any inducement to dissolve the marriage. Thus the Committee concluded that any such plan should be called MARRIAGE not alimony, insurance.

(2) Nevertheless, even if one has an insurable interest in post-divorce support, it was objected that such a scheme might be an incentive to divorce by inducing marriage solely for the purpose of financial gain. Arguing by analogy to support this causal effect, a dissenting member quoted opponents of the social security acts, stating that,

> the instinct of self preservation and the desire to save will be destroyed if men can waste . . . their earnings and then call upon the central government for help. [Workers will] sit idly by . . . even though there is no hope that their former jobs will ever be revived. [Strawn and Calderini, *The Social Security Act* (Chicago, 1936) at 10, 26.]

To avoid inducing such fraud the Committee recommended a clause allowing a two year period from its operative date during which the insurer could establish a reasonable presumption of fraud. The insurer shall have the burden of pleading and proving the charge, unless the accused party alone shall have access to necessary evidence or unless the court shall call forth the accused on a doctrine of *res ipsa loquitur*. After the two year period, however, there shall be an irrebuttable presumption of non-fraud.

(3) Another member switched the argument to a less obvious danger. He reasoned that if the scheme does not induce fraud, it will certainly remove an effective deterrent to divorce. The couple's financial problems cared for, they will surely not think twice about divorce. They will make no effort to stay together, to make the marriage work. The overriding interest insured would be in divorce in order to collect, and not in the continuation of the marriage. Furthermore, since there is no deterrent to divorce in the form of authorized sanction, as the crime of arson in fire insurance or murder in life insurance, the proposed policy would surely induce, or fail doubly to deter, contemplated divorce.

He further reminded the committee of the words of Henry Ford who, believing that unemployment insurance would only serve to stimulate the evil it insured, commented:

> To regard the present conditions as permanent and then to legislate as if they were, is a serious

mistake. It is the surest way to keep these wrong things with us. I would not insure unemployment; to me that looks like the surest way of establishing unemployment as a permanent evil. What we should do is to abolish it. And that can be done. . . . In every case where it exists, unemployment insurance is simply taken out of industry's pay envelope in advance. The men can do that for themselves if they want to, as well as any government can do it. . . . Somebody has to earn everything that is paid. No amount of juggling can change that fact. There is no exempt class. Establish unemployment insurance and you simply remove the pressure toward abolishing unemployment. The people then accept unemployment as a not too serious fact. But it is useless to discuss that, because if you insure unemployment it is only a matter of time before the insurance collapses under the load of unemployment it creates. [From an article in *The New York Times*, Nov. 8, 1931.]

The Committee acknowledged that financial considerations as a deterrent to divorce might be weakened in some cases. But in others the financial security offered by the policy might enable the parties to make an unclouded decision concerning their capacity to live together in a meaningful relation. Insofar as people have control over whether they can continue living together, by minimizing the risk of financial pressure, the scheme allows the parties to view their position with somewhat less anxiety than is already imposed upon them. The increased burden of insecure financial future might actually cause persons to leap into divorce—without considering whether their relationship is or could become meaningful—simply in order to reduce anxiety or to secure punishment to satisfy severe guilt feelings. Moreover, because of affection and stability that constitute a meaningful relation, it was felt that the parties would always struggle to attain that relationship even though they could receive certain minimal payments upon dissolution of the marriage. And, furthermore, failing the establishment of such a relationship parties should not be deterred from or handicapped in establishing another marriage.*

---

* The Committee notes with approval the views of John Locke.

[There] are ties upon mankind which make the conjugal bonds more firm and lasting in man than the other species of animals, yet it would give one reason to inquire why this compact, where procreation and education are secured and inheritance taken care for, may not be made determinable, either by consent, or at a certain time, or upon certain conditions, as well as any other voluntary compacts, there being no necessity, in the nature of the thing, nor to the ends of it, that it should always be for life—I mean, to such as are under no restraint of any positive law which ordains all such contracts to be perpetual. [Locke, *Second Essay Concerning Civil Government*, ch. vii at 43 (1690).]

(4) Even if the inducement and non-deterrent arguments are not true, some argued, is it not possible that by admitting the possibility of divorce through providing for it, the state is tacitly sanctioning the moral evil of a family dissolution? And in doing so, is not the state cutting against its primary interest of keeping the parties together in their marital relation? The law has always been averse to interfering with the marital relation, either to promote or obstruct it. In *White v. Equitable Nuptial Benefit Union*, 76 Ala. 251 (1884), the court refused to allow any contracts inducing or deterring marriage and in speaking of a marriage-broker contract for the purpose of procuring a marriage partner declared:

> Although they may not be a fraud on either party, such contracts are held to be void, and a public mischief, forasmuch as they are calculated to bring to pass mistaken and unhappy marriages, to countervail parental influence in the training and education of children, and to tempt the exercise of an undue and pernicious influence, for selfish gain, in respect to the most sacred of human relations. (*Id.* at 258.)

In that case the court struck down an insurance policy—providing that after three months, the insured, upon marrying, would receive monthly benefits—as an inducement to postpone marriage indefinitely, declaring that,

> all conditions in deeds or wills and all contracts, executory or executed, that create a general prohibition of marriage, are contrary to public policy and to "the common weal and good order of society." The rule rests upon the proposition, that the institution of marriage is the fundamental support of national and social life, and the promoter of individual and public morality and virtue; and that to secure well-assorted marriages, there must exist the utmost freedom of choice. Neither is it necessary there shall be positive prohibiting. If the condition is of such nature and rigidity in its requirements as to operate as a probable prohibition, it is void.

Moreover, the law absolutely refuses to sanction any agreement tending to disrupt the harmony of a marriage. In *Metropolitan Life Ins. Co. v. Smith*, 22 Ky. Law Rep. 868, 59 S.W. 24 (1900) the wife obtained a life insurance policy on her husband without his consent and paid the premiums out of her housekeeping money which he had given her. The court declared that,

> it was against public policy for . . . the wife [to] obtain insurance upon her husband's life without his knowledge and consent. . . . [I]f such practice was indulged in, it might be a fruitful source of crime. . . . It seems to us that it is not only illegal and against public policy for any insurance company to engage in such insurances as unquestionably existed in this case, but it is also to

be condemned for the further reason that the tendency is to induce the wife to use money for insurance purposes that ought to be applied to the purchase of food and raiment for the family. It is also likely to produce discord in the family. [59 S.W. at 25.]

The majority of the Committee however argued that marriage insurance comports with the overall objective of minimal state intervention in the family—whether to encourage or discourage marriage or its dissolution. By insuring minimal alimony payments the insurance plan will reduce state intrusion by eliminating substantive enquiry into the fault of either party The Committee observed that the lack of funds arising either because a party cannot pay alimony or because he must pay alimony, may well be the very sort of detriment to *re*-marriage which the dissenting member abhors.

(5) Finally it was argued that since the law forbids insurance covering loss caused by the wilful destruction of the property insured, benefits to any person found at fault in a divorce action should be forbidden because the insurance would be for "wilfully destructive" conduct.

In *Burt v. Union Central Life Ins. Co.*, 187 U.S. 362, a case concerning a life insurance contract, the court declared:

> It cannot be that one of the risks covered by a contract of insurance is the crime of the insured. There is an implied obligation on his part to do nothing to wrongfully accelerate the maturity of the policy. Public policy forbids the insertion in a contract of a condition which would tend to induce crime, and as it forbids the introduction of such stipulation, it also forbids the enforcement of a contract under circumstances which cannot be lawfully stipulated for. [*Id.* at 574.]

The majority of the Committee replied that it was erroneous to equate the concept of "fault" in crime and tort with the concept in divorce. Whatever a finding of fault in divorce may mean, it cannot be relied on as a finding of *the cause* of the breakdown of so highly a complex interrelationship as marriage. Except in rare instances, placing the burden of wilful marital destruction exclusively on one party, oversimplifies the nature of the relationship and is clearly unrelated to defrauding the insurer, which is already met by the two-year provision of the plan.

The Committee recognized the apparently unromantic aspects of the marriage insurance plan, but nevertheless believed that it is responsive to a reality which must not be denied. Furthermore it provides a partial solution to the unanticipated and crippling financial risks accompanying marriage. Many problems remain. Nothing in this plan resolves the difficulties of distributing family assets at the time of divorce. Moreover, we have not considered whether payments should cease for the beneficiaries who remarry; how long payments should continue; whether marriage insurance should be extended to provide for the care and education of children, or for optional medical expenses or for its conversion to a retirement or a life insurance plan.

Whether the policy—whatever its coverage—should be compulsory or voluntary; whether it should be administered by the state—in a deductible payment scheme similar to social security—or operated solely by private companies are important decisions requiring further study.

Of course, we have assumed that alimony is desirable; we have only argued about its form. If the goal of welfare legislation is to secure minimum financial standards for each individual, we might ask why alimony payments, in any form, should be allowed to raise divorced persons above that minimum. Should alimony therefore be abolished, or does something in the nature of the marital relationship compel us to retain it?

NOTES

NOTE 1.

MONAHAN, THOMAS P.

When Married Couples Part: Statistical Trends and Relationships in Divorce*

Duration of marriage to *separation* varies from area to area, from time to time, and from one

------

* *American Sociological Review*, Vol. 27 (1962), pp. 625, 633. Reprinted with permission of the American Sociological Association.

population class to another. It has been found that couples have longer durations of marriage to separation when they are in their first marriage, have children, are in higher socio-economic occupational groups, generally, and live in less metropolitan but middle-sized population areas. [I]t is likely that race, educational achievement, premarital pregnancy, and other elements also bear a relationship to this measure of marriage duration. . . .

NOTE 2.

Cairo Seeks Pensions for Divorced Women*

The Ministry of Social Affairs submitted a bill to the National Assembly today for the granting of life pensions to divorced wives.

Social Affairs Minister Hussein el Shafei said that under the measure, all working men, married or single, would be required to pay 1 per cent of their salaries into a fund handled by a "divorce insurance bank," which would be set up soon.

He said the bill was designed to protect the women and children of men who have discarded wives as easily as old garments.

The controversial measure would provide fixed monthly payments of from $11 to $33 to divorced wives, the amount to be determined by the number of their children. The children's fathers will still be required to pay for the upkeep of each child.

------

* *The New York Times*, Feb. 5, 1961, p. 4. © 1961 by The New York Times Company. Reprinted by permission.

PART TWO

FOR WHOM, TO WHAT EXTENT, AND WHY IS SEXUAL GRATIFICATION RELEVANT:

A.
To Decisions Concerning the Establishment of Wife-Husband Relationships?

1.

ANONYMOUS v. ANONYMOUS
49 N.Y.S. 2d 314 (Sup. Ct. 1944)

SHIENTAG, JUSTICE.

This is an action brought by the husband to annul a marriage on the ground that when a civil ceremony was entered into on August 10, 1940, both parties, who were then twenty-four years old, agreed that the ceremony was not to be considered valid and binding and the marriage was not to be consummated until a religious ceremony was performed.

After the civil ceremony husband and wife lived separately; they returned to the homes of their respective parents; the wife continued to work and to use her maiden name and the marriage was disclosed only to some members of the immediate families and to a few close friends.

Thereafter and before a date was set for the performance of the religious rites, the wife, on October 12, 1940, met with an accident resulting in serious injury to the spinal cord. In consequence of the injury sustained, which caused

paralysis, the wife has been and still is confined to a hospital. The accident occurred in a synagogue which the wife visited for the purpose of making arrangements for the religious ceremony. Both parties are of the Orthodox Jewish faith.

The basis of the husband's complaint is that the parties agreed that the civil ceremony was not to be considered valid unless and until a religious ceremony was performed; that the marriage was, in fact, never consummated; that as a result of the injuries she sustained in the accident, the wife became physically incapable of consummating the marriage, of performing the marital act; and for the plaintiff, under the circumstances, to go through a religious ceremony would be the performance of a futile act and the ceremony itself would be an idle one. "The defendant", he urges, "cannot be a wife to the plaintiff in every sense of the word nor can she fulfill the obligations of a true marriage."

Thus we are confronted with one of life's tragedies where two young people about to start on their journey together are plunged in an instant into the depths of misery and despair. The case on its facts may be a novel one but the principles of law involved have been firmly established.

We start with the proposition that there was no fraud or misrepresentation practiced in the inception of the marriage. Undoubedly both parties intended that a religious ceremony was to be performed before they would live together publicly or hold themselves out as man and wife. It is doubtful, however, whether they or either of them believed that the civil marriage was not valid or binding until the religious ceremony would be performed. This civil ceremony was more than an empty gesture. They wanted a valid and binding marriage; otherwise they could well have waited until the husband was in a position to assume the financial obligations of marriage and have it solemnized in accordance with the rites of their religious faith.

The defendant herself says that at the suggestion of the bridegroom's mother, they both promised her that the marriage would not be physically consummated until the religious ceremony. The wife says that promise was not kept; the husband says that it was, and that there never has been a consummation of the marriage. I accept the wife's testimony on that point. But, whichever version is adopted, the legal consequences remain unchanged.

The civil ceremony was legal and binding under the laws of this State. There being no fraud in the inception of the marriage, the law recognizes no privately imposed conditions that would alter the marital status. That status is too much a matter of public concern to allow the parties to tinker with it according to their own notions of what is expedient or proper. . . .

The husband himself, by numerous acts, acknowledged the validity and the binding effect of the civil ceremony and of the marital status established thereby. In his dealings with the hospitals in which his wife was cared for, in his income tax returns, his registration for selective service, in communications had at his instance with his draft board, in his suit for the injury sustained by his wife in which he asserted his claim as the husband for loss of consortium, in his application to the Navy, in which he now serves, for an allotment to his wife—in all these and in other ways he avowed the marriage to be valid and subsistent.

By his tender devotion for almost three years to his stricken wife, his invariably regular and frequent visits to her in the hospital, his endearing letters of love and encouragement and faith in their ultimate happiness, he recognized that they were, in fact as in law, truly wedded husband and wife.

In the summer of 1943 he met another woman, fell in love with her, told this to his wife and asked to be released from his marriage. She refused, at least until the war was over. The wife was in a sad plight. Her father and mother had passed away. She had no one on whom to lean for strength and guidance, other than her husband to whom, in the full vigor of young womanhood she had plighted her troth.

It is not intended to convey the impression that there was anything vicious about this young man; quite the contrary. For several years he displayed a devotion which left nothing to be desired. Then the weakness of human nature asserted itself. His nobler feelings succumbed to the craving of youth for the joy of life, for what he believed to be his right to happiness. After the long interval of time, he says, he had despaired of his wife's recovery.

The law inexorably sets its face against granting him the relief he now seeks. The right to annulment in this State is derived from statutory enactment and its scope is limited thereby. . . . From an early date it has been held that for what takes place after a valid marriage, there is no right to an annulment unless subsequent events reflect the situation existing at the time the marriage was entered into. The only exception to this was created by law in 1928 by an amendment to the Domestic Relations Law permitting an annulment under certain conditions where either of the parties to a marriage "has been incurably insane for a period of five years or more." Domestic Relations Law, § 7, subd. 5.

*   *   *

The law does not recognize conditions subsequent or even conditions precedent in marriage. The parties are either married or not. There is no intermediate condition known to the law. Marriage, to be sure, is a contract, but it is something more than an ordinary contract. It is a contract resulting in a status to which certain unalterable rights and obligations are attached which cannot be changed by the parties themselves. . . . Conditions arising altogether after the performance of a valid civil ceremony of marriage, even if they result in destroying the physical capacity to perform the marital act, are misfortunes which the parties have to bear.

Judge Crane, speaking for a unanimous court, expressed this thought in language which I cannot hope to rival:

"The man and woman who marry take each other for better or worse, richer or poorer, to cherish in sickness or in health. If this be old fashioned according to some moderns, it is still the hope and joy of pledged loyalty. The law of this state affords no relief to subsequent disappointment. Sickness and misfortune are common to mankind, and must be borne with courage and resignation." Lapides v. Lapides, 254 N.Y. 73, 80, 171 N.E. 911, 913.

The wife in this case has borne her sickness and misfortune with courage and resignation. She says she has faith in her gradual improvement, and faith has wrought great miracles.

* * *

In the exercise of discretion the court ordered . . . an examination and appointed for that purpose a neurologist of high standing in his profession. . . . His testimony on the stand was a model of thoroughness, completeness and scientific accuracy. He testified that, notwithstanding the condition of paralysis and its consequences which he described in detail, the wife, from a medical standpoint, was capable of performing the marital act. The psychological aspects, in such a situation, he held must vary with the individuals concerned.

I accept these conclusions but even if they had been the other way, my decision would have been the same.

* * *

2.

DONATI v. CHURCH
13 N.J. Super. 454, 80 A. 2d 633 (1951)

BIGELOW, J.A.D.

The appellant husband instituted the action to annul his marriage with respondent on the ground of her impotence. The advisory master to whom the case was referred in the Chancery Division, after hearing the proof, dismissed the complaint.

Our statute, R.S. 2:5C1(c), N.J.S.A., authorizes a decree of annulment where "The parties, or either of them, were at the time of marriage physically and incurably impotent, provided the party making the application shall have been ignorant of such impotency or incapability at the time of the marriage, or has not subsequently ratified the marriage".

Impotence is not sterility or inability to beget or bear a child. It is inability to have sexual intercourse. . . . We are satisfied that respondent is and was at the time of the marriage, incurably impotent. The introitus or opening of the vagina is infantile in type and too small to allow of copulation, although her husband was able to, and did frequently, insert the tip of his penis. This imperfect intercourse is not enough to rebut a finding of the defendant's impotence. . . .

. . . What will bar relief in a case of this sort was suggested by the Lord Chancellor in G. v. M., 10 App. Cas. 171, at 186 (H. of L. 1885): "Conduct on the part of the person seeking this remedy which ought to estop that person from having it; as, for instance, any act from which the inference ought to be drawn that during the antecedent time the party has, with a knowledge of the facts and of the law, approbated the marriage which he or she afterwards seeks to get rid of, or has taken advantages and derived benefits from the matrimonial relation which it would be unfair and inequitable to permit him or her, after having received them, to treat as if no such relation had ever existed." And he gave as illustrations, "taking pecuniary benefits for example, living for a long time together in the same house or family with the status and character of husband and wife, after knowledge of everything which it is material to know." In the same case (p. 197), Lord Watson expressed the rule in these terms, "that in a suit for nullity of marriage there may be facts and circumstances proved that so plainly imply, on the part of the complaining spouse, a recognition of the existence and validity of the marriage, as to render it most inequitable and contrary to public policy that he or she should be permitted to go on to challenge it with effect."

The parties now before us were married in July 1947. Plaintiff instituted his suit May 31, 1949, while he was still living with his wife, and he continued to live in the same small apartment with her until August or September. He testified, and his wife denied, that right after instituting the action, he ceased occupying the same bed with her, and instead slept on a couch. The last day of the year 1949, plaintiff returned to his wife's apartment and continued to live there one week, according to his own testimony, or until February 6, 1950, according to his wife. He returned to her because he thought they could "make a go of it," although "I knew I would never get the thing I wanted." But after a few days or weeks, he consulted his lawyer, who told him, "You're making a big mistake." So he left his wife for the second time, but still continued to visit her occasionally. While living with defendant in the early days of 1950 and whenever he called on her later, they had sexual intercourse of the kind and to the extent that her condition permitted. The advisory master who heard the case, found that this occurred as late as two weeks before the final hearing.

The conduct of the plaintiff toward the defendant can be defended only by reason of the marriage relation between them, and clearly constituted a ratification of the marriage. The judgment dismissing the petition must therefore be affirmed.

NOTES

NOTE 1.

DONATI v. CHURCH
Nine Years Later

a. The effect of the decision was to condemn a vigorous young man to a life of sexual frustration through no fault of his own; but rather the congenital fault of his wife, of which he was not aware before he married her.

The irony in the case is that the very virtues of the man, in trying every conceivable medical remedy, and in trying to be charitable to the wife when she begged for friendship, should be construed by the court as "condonation".

The husband went to another jurisdiction, obtained a divorce, returned to New Jersey, remarried, had a child, and was indicted for bigamy at the instigation of his first wife (Church).

Mr. Irving Youngelson, a lawyer in Dover, represented Mr. Donati after the appeal was lost. [Letter dated Dec. 12, 1960 from Paul Colvin, attorney for Mr. Donati.]

b. Following the entry of the judgment by the Superior Court of New Jersey in the above citation, Alvino Donati married another woman in the very same Church where he had married his first wife. When this news reached the first wife, she caused a complaint for bigamy to be made against her husband. It was then that Mr. Donati retained me to represent him.

Mr. Donati was a very peculiar individual. He had served in World War II in the U.S. Navy and two ships on which he saw service were sunk and he was rescued from the Pacific waters. On one of these occasions he was rescued after being in the icy waters for over one entire day.

Mr. Donati had a Catholic religious background and when I questioned him as to why he had committed bigamy, his answer was, "God intended that I should be married to a normal woman, with whom I could have sex relations and have children, but my first wife did not fulfill these provisions and I could not consider that I was properly married in the eyes of God. That is why I married my second wife".

Following the finding of the Grand Jury of an indictment for bigamy, I thereupon took Mr. Donati to the office of the County Prosecutor. I felt that it was necessary for the State to know the true facts involved in this matter. There was no question that the act of bigamy had been committed. Mr. Donati, however, felt that the court had made an improper decision and that he was technically not bound by it, because he felt that he was not actually married to his first wife, because she was unable to consummate sexual relations.

After a discussion of the merits of this matter, it was decided that if the second wife would secure an annulment of the marriage, the charge of bigamy would thereby be abated.

Consequently, the second wife did file her suit for an annulment of the marriage under the Statutes of New Jersey granting relief in cases involving a previous marriage still in force and effect, and as a result, the annulment of the second marriage was then granted to the second wife.

Therefore, by virtue of an annulment being entered, the status of the matter was that the second marriage actually did not take place, since the annulment made the second marriage void from its inception. Therefore, upon my motion in the Criminal Court that the charge of bigamy be dismissed by reason of the fact that the second marriage had been annulled, my motion was granted and Mr. Donati was thereupon completely exonerated of the charge of bigamy.

As a result of this technical maneuver, Mr. Donati was still legally married to his first wife. It was his desire to still marry his second wife, as and when he was legally able to do so. He therefore left the jurisdiction of the State of New Jersey and went to Nevada where he secured his divorce from his first wife. Thereafter, he obtained employment in the State of California, and sent for his second wife and they were subsequently married in California, and as far as I know, they are still residing there.

From my knowledge of this matter gained from a complete history and investigation of the family of Mr. Donati, I had ascertained that prior to his first marriage, he had never actually been in the company of any girl or woman prior to his enlistment in the Navy. He had told me that during his service in the Navy, his comrades would kid him about his refusal to go out with a girl and enjoy some sex life during their leave periods. It seemed that his parents had been very strict with him during his youth and never permitted him to associate with any female. After he returned from his service in the Navy and had been discharged, he went into a tavern and there met his first wife. She played up to him and he bought her a couple of drinks and he told me that when he found out that she was single, his desire to have sexual relationship was so great that he then and there proposed to her and she immediately accepted his proposal of marriage. Subsequent events proved that this girl (first wife) knew of her physical defect and inability to have sexual relations. As a matter of fact, her mother was constantly trying to unburden her daughter upon some man in the hope that her daughter would get married and perhaps effect a cure of her physical defect. That is why the first wife tried to hold on to her marriage as long as she was legally able to do so. [Letter dated Dec. 22, 1960 from Irving Youngelson, attorney for Mr. Donati.]

NOTE 2.

RICKARDS v. RICKARDS
53 Del. 134, 166 A. 2d 425 (1960)

WOLCOTT, JUSTICE.

This is an appeal by the husband from a judgment of the Superior Court of New Castle County granting an annulment of marriage at the suit of the wife. . . .

The action was based upon 13 Del. C. § 1551, which provides as one ground for annulment of marriages:

> "Incurable physical impotency, or incapacity for copulation, at the suit of either party; if the party making the application was ignorant of such impotency or incapacity at the time of the marriage."

*   *   *

[T]he wife had sustained the burden of proving that the husband was sexually impotent, at least as to her, was probably incurable as a "pure form" sexual deviate, and by reason thereof had an incapacity for copulation with the wife.

We think it also established beyond doubt that the husband's incapacity was entirely due to psychic causes. The evidence is clear that he suffered from no physical defect of a sexually incapacitating nature. We think it apparent that psychogenic causes had made the husband physically unable to copulate, at least with the woman he had married.

The question before us, therefore, is whether 13 Del. C. § 1551 permits the annulment of a marriage when the cause of impotency is psychic rather than physical in origin.

The wife argues that the statute, being in the alternative, permits proof of either "incurable physical impotency" or "incapacity for copulation" for any recognized medical reason. . . .

We think this statutory ground for annulment of marriage is an incurable physical inability on the part of one spouse to copulate with the other. This being so, it follows that whether the inability stems from physical or mental defects, provided in either case that the resulting condition is incurable, the requirement of the statute is met.

*   *   *

[W]e affirm that portion of the judgment appealed from granting an annulment, and the resumption by the wife of her name prior to the marriage.

NOTE 3.

MORE, SIR THOMAS
Utopia (1517)*

. . . In choosing mates [The Utopians] favour seriously and strictly a custom which seemed to us very foolish, and extremely ridiculous. For the woman, whether maiden or widow, is shown naked to the suitor by a worthy and respectable matron, and similarly the suitor is presented naked before the maiden by a discreet man. We laughed at this custom and condemned it as foolish; but they on the other hand marvelled at the notable folly of other nations, who in buying a pony, where it is only a question of a little money, are so cautious that though it is almost bare they will not buy until they have taken off the saddle and removed all the harness, for fear some sore may be concealed under these coverings, and yet in choosing a wife, when pleasure or disgust will follow them all their lives in consequence, they are so careless, that while all the rest of her body is covered with clothes, they estimate the value of the whole woman from a single handsbreadth of her, the face only being visible, and take her to themselves not without great danger of their agreeing ill together, if something afterwards gives offence to them. For all men are not so wise as to regard the character of the woman only, and even in the marriages of wise men bodily attractions are no small enhancement to the virtues of the mind. Certainly such foul deformity may be hidden beneath these coverings, that it may quite alienate a man's mind from his wife, when bodily separation is no longer lawful. If such a deformity arise by chance after the marriage has been contracted, each must bear his own fate; but beforehand the law ought to protect him from being entrapped by guile. This provision was the more necessary, because the Utopians are the only people in that part of the world who are satisfied with one wife, and matrimony is seldom broken except by death, unless it be for adultery or intolerable offensiveness of disposition.

NOTE 4.

MOORE, K. L., and EDWARDS, C. H. C.
Medico-Legal Aspects of Intersexuality: Criteria of Sex†

Relatively recent developments concerning the criteria of sex have raised questions that have medico-legal implications. Society and the law

---

* Translated by G. C. Richards, Oxford, Clarendon Press, 1923, (86-87). Reprinted by permission of the publisher.
† *Can. Med. Assoc. J.*, Vol. 83 (1960), pp. 709-711. Reprinted by permission of the publisher.

recognizes only two sexes. Usually the differences are obvious, partly because cosmetic and garment manufacturers make it easy for females to accentuate or falsify their characteristics.

At birth the physician assigns sex from the appearance of the external genitalia. If these organs are equivocal, other criteria must be used. In the past a final decision was usually not made until the type of gonads had been determined. Often this was not done until contradictory sex characteristics appeared at puberty; frequently in such cases sex was changed, resulting many times in unhappy confused patients.

During the past decade much has been learned about the diagnosis and management of intersex. New laboratory procedures have made it relatively easy to make a credible diagnosis without exploratory surgery. Sex may now be assigned with confidence fairly soon after birth; corrective surgery and hormone therapy may be carried out later. As a result, intersexes may lead fairly normal lives. Many can be made marriageable; some will be fertile.

*   *   *

[T]he criteria of sex that should be used in forming a correct judgment . . . (1) chromosomal sex, (2) gonadal sex, (3) hormone pattern, (4) internal sex organs, (5) external genitalia, (6) habitus, (7) sex of rearing, and (8) gender role and orientation. In the newborn, the first five criteria are used.

NOTE 5.

S. v. S. (otherwise W.) (No. 2).
[1962] 3 All E.R. 55, 62

WILLMER, L. J.: I shall for convenience refer to the parties as the husband and the wife. It is not to be thought that in taking this course I am begging the question that has to be decided. By his petition, dated May 6, 1959, the husband prayed for a decree of nullity, alleging that his marriage had never been consummated and that the wife was incapable of consummating it. . . . The judge found himself unable to say that the wife, if given medical treatment, was incapable of consummating the marriage, and on that ground dismissed the petition. . . .

*   *   *

. . . It is admitted . . . that inability to conceive a child is no ground for saying that the marriage cannot be consummated. It is also admitted that the degree of sexual satisfaction that may be obtained by either or both of the parties makes no difference. As to this point, however, it seemed to me that some inconsistency was to be detected in the argument for the husband. For

we were pressed to consider certain physiological differences between the natural and the artificial vagina; for instance, the absence in the latter of the natural membrane, of the normal secretions and of the special sensory quality of the former. It may be that the absence of these would affect the degree of sexual satisfaction that could be obtained by a wife with an artificial vagina. But, once it is admitted that sexual satisfaction is not a determining factor, it appears to me that these distinctions are largely irrelevant. In any case much the same could be said of a natural vagina artificially enlarged by a surgical operation of the same type. Moreover, it is to be remembered that in the present case it is not the wife, but the husband, who is the complaining party, and according to the evidence of Miss Bottomley the degree of sexual satisfaction to be obtained by the husband would not be very materially affected.

If neither the ability to conceive nor the degree of sexual satisfaction to be obtained is a determining factor, what else, it may be asked, remains to differentiate between intercourse by means of an artificial vagina and intercourse by means of a natural vagina artificially enlarged? In either case full penetration can be achieved, and there is thus complete union between the two bodies. Counsel for the wife conceded (no doubt rightly) that an artificial cavity created in some other part of the wife's body, into which the husband's organ could be inserted, would not be appropriate. But there is no question of that in relation to the operation suggested by Miss Bottomley. What would be created would be a vagina, albeit an artificial one, and it would be located precisely in the position where a natural vagina would be. In such circumstances I do not see why intercourse by means of such a vagina should not be regarded as amounting to "vera copula", so as to satisfy the test laid down by Dr. Lushington.

In reaching this view I have derived some assistance from the decision of the House of Lords in *Baxter v. Baxter*. In that case on every occasion when intercourse was attempted between the parties the wife insisted on the husband wearing a contraceptive sheath. Yet the House of Lords decided that such intercourse was sufficient to consummate the marriage. That was a case, if ever there was one, where the natural act of sexual intercourse was artificially interfered with; for the effect of the persistent use of such a contraceptive was that the husband's organ was permanently prevented from ever coming into contact with the wife at all. In the case of intercourse by means of an artificial vagina, on the other hand, the husband's organ would at least be united, in physical union, with the appropriate part of the wife's body.

I would only add one further observation on this part of the case. If it is to be held that a wife with an artificial vagina is incapable in all circumstances of consummating her marriage, it can only be on the basis that such a woman is incapable of taking part in true sexual intercourse. If that were right, the strangest results would follow. It would involve, for instance, that such a woman might be to a considerable extent beyond the protection of the criminal law, for it would seem to follow that she would be incapable in law of being the victim of a rape. What is perhaps even more startling would be that a woman with an artificial vagina would be incapable in law of committing adultery. Consequently, the wife of a man engaging in intercourse with such a woman would be left wholly without remedy. I should regard such a result as bordering on the fantastic; yet it is accepted as being the logical conclusion of the argument presented on behalf of the husband.

* * *

NOTE 6.

LAIDLAW, ROBERT W.

The Psychiatrist as Marriage Counselor*

[A] girl of 21 . . . presented herself to the counselor in a marked state of tearful agitation. She felt that she must break her engagement. She loved her fiance deeply, but she felt that she would wrong him by marrying him. There was something in her past life which she had been trying to shut out of her mind, but now, as marriage approached, this "thing" was haunting her more and more and branding her as "unfit" for marriage. This "thing" proved to be the usual sort of history of masturbation in a girl brought up in a hidebound environment where all sex was anathema. Two hours of counseling melted away this patient's guilt and provided her with a correct concept of the normality of such a history of masturbation. Other guilt feelings in regard to minor physical intimacies with boys were also ventilated. The patient was found to be completely ignorant in regard to sexual anatomy and physiology, and, through the excellent drawings in Dickinson's "Human Sex Anatomy" and by his three-dimensional models of the pelvis, she was given a working orientation in this field. She was referred to a gynecological colleague for pelvic examination (which was normal) and for instruction in self-dilatation of the hymen (which allowed her to be fitted contraceptively before marriage). The fiance was also interviewed. The patient's difficulties were interpreted to him and his cooperative understanding was secured. In the

* *American Journal of Psychiatry*, Vol. 106 (1950), p. 732, 734. Reprinted by permission of the publisher.

final interview both were seen together and an easy, candid discussion of the psychosexual aspects of marriage took place. The total time of counseling was 4 hours. Two months later they were married and the marriage has proved to be a successful one.

3.

MORGAN v. MORGAN
[1959] 1 All E.R. 539

MR. COMMISSIONER LATEY, Q.C., read the following judgment: This is an undefended petition for nullity of marriage brought by the husband on the ground of his own impotence at the time of the ceremony of marriage. When the marriage took place on Jan. 25, 1958, at Ramsgate Register Office, the husband was a bachelor seventy-two years of age, and the wife was a spinster fifty-nine years of age. They had first met in 1953, at Richmond. He was on holiday there and he saw her every evening until he returned to his abode at Margate. When he left she kissed him goodbye at the station. She often visited him at Margate. On these occasions he booked a room for her at a hotel, spent the days with her, and saw her to her hotel, where she spent the night, he returning home. Apart from greeting and goodbye kisses, there was no manifestation of affection between them. The husband gave me to understand that this form of friendship continued for several years. He said that he loved her to some extent, and that they liked each other's company. On various occasions she suggested that they should buy an annuity and that they should live more or less together, from the point of view of company, as she put it. She intended to go to Australia after they married, and she told him to find a flat where they could live on her return. They were to marry on the basis of companionship. Toward the end of 1957 they agreed to marry and that he should buy an annuity in her name, and that she was to continue at her work. He had a small income from an annuity and the old age pension.

His evidence went on as follows:

"Q.—You have made the remark that she wanted a companionship marriage with you. At that stage when you were discussing this matter and indeed right up to the date of this ceremony, were you agreeing to that situation or not? A.—Yes. Q.—Yes. I want you to listen very carefully to my next question and consider your answer carefully. Tell my Lord this: did you ever hope that any change might take place in that situation as far as the relationship between you was concerned? A.—Well, naturally as time goes on and we live together, I might possibly have thought possibly connexion might be had, but otherwise—— Q.—You had that in mind? A.—I had that in mind, certainly, like any man would do. Q.—You had it in mind like any man would, after you had lived with her for some time. A.—Lived with her for some time. Q.—As husband and wife? A.—Quite."

The husband, who had never had sexual intercourse with any woman, said that, at the time of the marriage in January, 1958, he did not know that he was incapable of sexual intercourse. After the ceremony they went to the wife's hotel, where she had a room for two nights. He took his meals at his own address and then went to see her at the hotel, and he saw her off to London on the day after the ceremony. On the night after the ceremony she had slept at the hotel, and he at his home. After the ceremony he gave her a cheque for £2,000 for the annuity. Soon after, she said: "I am worried. If I leave you, you shall have your money back". He tried to calm her down, but wanted the marriage to go on as arranged. His evidence continued as follows:

"Q.—You told us that she wanted a marriage on what you called 'companionship terms'—something like that? A.—Yes, exactly. Q.—What did you understand her to mean by that? A.—Well, to put it bluntly to you she made it quite obvious to me—I said to her 'Can I take you a cup of tea up in the morning?' She said, 'No, I will lock the door first'. That was obviously the attitude she was in. Q.—Let us do it completely. Did you understand or not that she did not want to have sexual relations when you were married? A.—Exactly, yes."

*   *   *

[I]n the ordinary case . . . the husband would be entitled to a declaration of nullity of marriage on the ground of his own impotence. There were, however, extraordinary circumstances in connection with this contract of marriage raising difficulties affecting the public interest which caused me to seek the assistance of the Queen's Proctor. The question which arose was whether the husband was debarred from the relief which he claimed by reason of his having entered into this marriage on the basis of mere companionship and without any intention of marital intercourse, and whether this court, which must always treat nullity cases as of national importance irrespective of the wishes of the parties, can accept the husband's mental reservations as to the bare possibility of marital intercourse in the future. On the facts as to the pre-marital arrangement and what followed, I accept the husband as a truthful witness. I also assume that he was not aware of the law as to nullity of marriage until at any rate some months after the marriage. But for his assertion of his own impotence, and possibly the companionship understanding, it is clear that he

might have obtained a decree of nullity on the ground of the wife's wilful refusal to consummate the marriage. That remedy was barred, however, the moment his legal advisers became aware of his assertion of impotence.

[U]nder the pre-Reformation canon law an impotent spouse could plead his or her impotence, provided that (a) he did not know of such impotence when the ceremony took place and had not deceived the other spouse, and (b) the other spouse did not know at that time of such impotence ; and that neither the statute law nor common law had interfered in this respect with the pre-Reformation canon law, which, . . . is still operative. In *Harthan v. Harthan* the husband petitioner, who was granted a declaration of nullity, had made futile attempts at intercourse within the first five years of his marriage. In arguendo in that case, counsel incidentally drew attention to a phrase which has been employed from time to time in nullity cases, namely, of a man marrying a woman "tam quam sororem"—as if a sister. Counsel for the Queen's Proctor has illustrated its use in various cases: for example, . . . *Brown v. Brown* (1828), 1 Hag. Ecc. 523, in which SIR JOHN NICHOLL said in the Court of Arches (ibid., at p. 524):

". . . a man of sixty who marries a woman of fifty-two should be contented to take her 'tanquam soror'."

. . . In my view, this phrase became a convenient verbal vehicle in the context of some cases of nullity in the ecclesiastical courts, but does not embody any legal principle.

. . . Counsel submitted that, on the facts as we know them, the husband ought to have been very doubtful of his sexual capacity and of the likelihood of having marital intercourse, and, as a reasonable man, should have been put on inquiry as to his own condition. He pointed out that, if the marriage were valid, it was a clear case of desertion by the wife immediately after the ceremony, for which desertion the husband could obtain a divorce after the expiry of the three years laid down by statute.

Counsel maintained that the husband must show that the non-consummation was due to his own misfortune, but his incapacity was purely incidental to the married status. Suppose that a man married a woman knowing that she was incurably stricken with poliomyelitis or was so crippled that sexual intercourse was impossible: he could not claim nullity on the ground of his own impotence. Having regard to the circumstances in which this marriage was contracted, the husband could not make a grievance now of what did not appear to him a grievance then. . . . LORD MERRI-

MAN, P., said ([1948] 2 All E. R. at p. 651):

"... the reaction of the respondent to the situation created by the impotence of the petitioner should be taken into account in considering whether the circumstances of the case as a whole, including the respondent's attitude, are such as to debar the impotent spouse from suing."

Pausing at this stage of the argument put forward on behalf of the Queen's Proctor, I should be disposed to regard this statement of principle as irrelevant in the circumstances of this case, insomuch as the wife never put the husband's potency to the test and has abstained from any defence, so that I must assume that her reaction to the petition was favourable.

Counsel for the Queen's Proctor urged that the petition failed for lack of sincerity and bona fides, and that it would be inequitable and contrary to public policy to grant the husband the relief which he sought. He pointed out that, when the cohabitatio triennalis of olden days—the period during which spouses in a certain type of case were expected to try and try again—was discarded by our courts long ago, there was left a discretion in the court to decide whether it was just or right to annul a marriage, and that that discretion still survives.... Counsel submitted that from the standpoint of public interest it was a vitally important case. Having entered into the marriage on the basis of companionship, the husband should not in equity or justice be allowed to claim relief from the marriage on the ground of his own impotence.

* * *

The whole pith of the present case is the premarital companionship agreement. In the ordinary case of a younger couple, the agreement itself would be void as against public policy.... Many elderly and aged people intermarry on the basis, implied or agreed on, that they come together merely for companionship and without any thought of sexual relations. In some such cases, owing to advanced age or physical infirmity one or other of the spouses might be able to prove after the marriage his or her impotence, without having had any thought of it when the marriage was arranged or solemnized, and without putting it to the test afterwards. Supposing one of these elderly or aged spouses in that condition found that he or she was not happy in the union, would it be just or right to allow him or her to plead impotence for the purpose of getting rid of the marriage? Having regard to their agreement, I should say that that was an act, though premarital, which would bar the remedy.

* * *

... I cannot accept the husband's somewhat vague mention of his mental reservation as to perhaps having sexual intercourse in the future as reliable. It was the only point in his evidence which I felt was unreliable.

On this point I adopt the words used in the REPORT OF THE ARCHBISHOPS' COMMISSION ON THE LAW OF NULLITY OF MARRIAGE (1955) at p. 27:

"In English ecclesiastical law no agreement or private determination is allowed to nullify a marriage, even though it involves the frustration of one of the principal ends of matrimony. English law looks to the consent as expressed, and will not allow the parties privately to derogate from their public professions."

In other words, mental reservations cannot in English law invalidate a marriage duly celebrated.

* * *

NOTES

NOTE 1.

NEWMAN, G., and NICHOLS, C. R.

Sexual Activities and Attitudes in Older Persons*

... Little has been reported concerning the sexual activity and attitudes of older people. There have been many misconceptions, certainly, about the role of sex in the lives of older people in our society. One commonly recognized belief among younger people in our society is that older persons, especially grandparents, have no sexual feelings. As we now recognize, the feelings and attitudes of people are directly related to the expectations of the society in which they live. Thus, it is common for the physician to see in his daily practice older persons who feel guilty about having sexual feelings; often these feelings are not acceptable to the older person, to the physician, or to other people in the environment in which the older person is living. Guilt or anxiety over sexual feelings may interfere with the adjustment of the older person and with his interpersonal relations, among which is the doctor-patient relationship. Guilt or anxiety on the part of the patient may thwart the therapeutic efforts of the physician.

* * *

In the comprehensive, interdisciplinary study of geriatric subjects living in the Durham, N.C., community, data have been gathered and assessed regarding the sexual activity and attitudes of older people. Subjects averaged 70 years of age and ranged from 60 to 93 years. The study included both caucasoid and negroid men and women. Analysis of these data shows little correlation of

* J.A.M.A., Vol. 173 (1960), pp. 33-35.

sexual activity with age, but in this study, negroid subjects were more active than caucasoid and men more active than women. The subjects also rated themselves on the relative strength of their sexual urge in youth and old age, and a comparison of the two ratings shows a remarkable constancy of the experiencing of the sexual drive within individual persons throughout life. Although older people experienced a decline in sexual activity and strength of sexual drive, these data show that, given the conditions of reasonably good health and partners who are also physically healthy, elderly persons continue to be sexually active into their seventh, eighth, and ninth decades.

NOTE 2.

PETTIT v. PETTIT
[1962] 3 All E.R. 37, 41-43

DAVIES, L.J. . . .

[T]he present case is in my opinion entirely different and to be distinguished from all . . . petitions by a potent petitioner on the grounds of the respondent's incapacity. Here it is the petitioner who is incapable. Counsel for the husband submits that this makes no difference and that the principles on which the court should act in granting or refusing a decree are the same in both cases. He relies in support of this contention on the words of LORD NORMAND (Lord President) in the Inner House of the Court of Session in F. v. F. The judge said this:

> . . . it can hardly be questioned that the impotent spouse has an equal interest with the potent spouse in a question which vitally affects his or her status. The bond of a marriage which cannot be consummated, it may be added, can be as irksome and humiliating to the impotent as to the other spouse. If, therefore, the impotent spouse is to be denied the remedy, it is necessary to inquire what is the supposed ground for this denial. LORD FRASER speaks of the potent spouse as the party aggrieved. But, with respect, both alike are aggrieved; and to treat the potent spouse as alone aggrieved is to imply that the impotent spouse is in some sense a defaulter, as though he or she had failed to implement a contract and was debarred from founding on his or her default. The condition of impotency which is a ground of nullity is not voluntary; and the voluntary refusal to have intercourse, though it may be dealt with as desertion, is not a ground for an action of nullity. Where the incapacity results from a physical or temperamental condition, for which the sufferer is not responsible, he cannot be debarred from the remedy on the ground that he has defaulted in his obligations. There may, of course, be circumstances which will bar the potent spouse. If, for example, he or she entered into marriage knowing the defect, the other spouse would indeed

be entitled to complain, and to plead the suppressio veri in bar of the action. . . .

It is no doubt true that both parties have an equal interest in putting an end to a marriage which has not been consummated. But I cannot accept that the spouse whose defect or misfortune is the cause of the non-consummation is entitled as of right in all circumstances to insist on a decree, regardless of the wishes, rights and interests of the spouse against whom no defect can be alleged. I use the words defect or misfortune advisedly. In the older cases the impotent spouse is not infrequently described as a wrongdoer ; . . . If, however, one looks on impotence as a defect or misfortune rather than as a fault, the fact still remains that the potent spouse is not in any way responsible for the non-consummation, and is therefore on any fair view entitled to be heard as to the justice and equity of granting a decree to an impotent spouse.

*   *   *

If the husband were to obtain a decree, she is apprehensive about her position in regard to a widow's pension. She takes the view that a decree would have a very bad effect on her daughter, as one can well understand. She is a Roman Catholic, and, if the court were to pronounce a decree, she would have to put the whole matter before the authorities of her church. These are some of the factors which have to be borne in mind. On the whole of the case I have come to the conclusion without any doubt whatsoever that it would be unfair, inequitable and unjust to grant this husband a decree against the wishes of the wife. I would accordingly dismiss the appeal.

4.

LEVY v. LEVY
309 Mass. 230, 34 N.E. 2d 650 (1941)

DOLAN, JUSTICE.

This is a libel for nullity of marriage. G. L. (Ter. Ed.) c. 207, § 14. The case was referred to an auditor. . . . [It] was heard upon the auditor's report, and certain affidavits and counter affidavits. . . . After hearing, the judge . . . ordered that the libel for nullity be allowed. . . .

Material facts found by the auditor may be summarized as follows: The parties first met in August, 1937, when the libelee, while standing on Harvard Street, Brookline, waiting for a street car, motioned to the libelant, who was seated in an automobile which was "stopped in traffic," and requested him to drive her to Commonwealth Avenue. He acquiesced. From that time on during that year they associated together on frequent occasions. On December 23, 1937, the libelant told the libelee that he was going to New York on vacation. She suggested that she go with him. He consented and she "arranged for the transportation, which consisted of tickets for the boat to New York." On December 24, 1937, they travelled together on the boat to New York, and during the voyage had sexual relations. At that time the libelee employed a certain artifice, which need not be here described, to convince the libelant that, as she had previously represented to him, she was a "virgin." At some prior time she had told a third person that she intended to marry the libellant by "hook or crook," and to make him believe that she was a virgin, and to that end to employ the artifice in question. Arriving in New York City they registered as man and wife at a hotel in which they occupied a room. The libelee informed the libelant that she was pregnant as a result of their relations, and said that she could not go back to Boston unless he married her. For two or three days she appeared to be hysterical and "threatened to jump out of the window unless the * * * [libelant] married her." On December 31, 1937, the parties filed an application for a marriage license with the "New York State Department of Health," in which the libelee, who was thirty-seven years of age represented her age to be twenty-nine years. The libelant was then thirty-eight years of age, was president of an electric service corporation, and had accumulated over $5,000 in cash. The libelant did not know that the libelee was thirty-seven years of age. The parties were married in the city of New York on January 3, 1938, and returned to Boston on that day. On March 15, 1938, they went to live together in an apartment in Brookline. In the interim they had gone to New Hampshire for a week's vacation, during which time they occupied the same room. They lived together in Brookline until late in May. Prior to the separation the libelant had given the libelee $421 to pay for a "so-called engagement ring," and had turned over to her "by way of orders on banks" $4,550.42, a substantial part of which she used to purchase "furniture and other things connected with the housekeeping." She had promised the libelant that she would "return to him on demand such money as was left after using it for said purpose."

When the libelee represented to the libelant that she was a "virgin" she had pending in the Superior Court four actions, in each of which allegations were made by her that one of the defendants had had intercourse with her with resulting pregnancy, and against other defendants that they had performed an abortion upon her at the persuasion of the first defendant without her knowledge or consent. These actions were settled in September 1938, after the libelant and libelee had separated, by the payment to her of $3,000. She signed releases "in the name of Helen Bornstein" running to all the defendants. She was not pregnant when she so represented to the libelant nor at any time thereafter to the conclusion of the hearings before the auditor in the summer of the year 1939. Her statement to the libelant in December, 1937, that she was a "virgin" was "knowingly and falsely" made. Although she intended to procure his "monies and properties" by means of the marriage, she intended to live with him as his wife, and subsequent to the marriage so lived with him and had intercourse with him. The finding of the auditor as to the reason why the libellant consented to marry the libelee is that "he feared that because of the pregnancy, she would commit suicide if he did not marry her." The parties at all times "had their place of domicile in Massachusetts." The auditor found and ruled that "Insofar as it * * * [was] within * * * [his] province * * * the law of Massachusetts is applicable to the facts * * * found" by him, and found for the libelee.

. . . It is settled that, if the laws of this Commonwealth govern the determination of the case, the libelant cannot prevail since he had criminal intercourse with the libelee before his marriage to her. . . . It is also settled that, with certain exceptions based on public policy which do not affect the present case, the law governing nullity of marriage is that of the place where the marriage contract was entered into. . . .

Section 1139 of the Civil Practice Act of the State of New York, so far as here material, provides as follows: "An action to annul a marriage on the ground that the consent of one of the parties thereto was obtained by force, duress or fraud may be maintained at any time by the party whose consent was so obtained. * * * But a marriage shall not be annulled on the ground of force or duress if it appears that, at any time before the commencement of the action, the parties thereto voluntarily cohabited as husband and wife, with a full knowledge of the facts constituting the fraud."

. . . In the Shonfeld case, 260 N.Y. at page 481, 184 N.E. at page 61, the court said: "If the proof shows that the representations were of a nature to deceive an ordinarily prudent man who, but for the representations, would not have consented to the marriage, there is an adequate basis for a decree. The primary consideration in every case is the materiality of the representation viewed in the light of all circumstances by the mind, not of the individual plaintiff but of an ordinarily prudent man."

Applying these principles to the present case we are of opinion that, on the facts, it would not be found properly that the representations and artifice employed by the libelee were such as to deceive an ordinarily prudent person, and hence not such as he would have a right to rely upon. The auditor has not found that the libelant married the libelee in reliance upon her representations that she was chaste and, in our opinion, the facts found would not warrant an inference by the judge that as an ordinarily prudent man the libelant would be warranted in so doing. In view of the manner of the meeting of the parties, the arrangement by the libelee with the consent of the libelant for the passage on the boat by which they traveled together to New York, and in the progress of which they had intercourse without, so far as appears, any intention to talk of marriage, we think that it could not be found properly that the libelant as an ordinarily prudent man would be deceived by and have a right to rely on these representations and the artifice employed as an inducement to marriage.

*   *   *

It follows that the order of the judge that the libel for annulment be allowed was erroneous.

NOTES

NOTE 1.

FREUD, SIGMUND

The Taboo of Virginity (1917)*

. . . The demand that a girl shall not bring to her marriage with a particular man any memory of sexual relations with another is, indeed, nothing other than a logical continuation of the right to exclusive possession of a woman, which forms the essence of monogamy, the extension of this monopoly to cover the past.

. . . Whoever is the first to satisfy a virgin's desire for love, long and laboriously held in check, and who in doing so overcomes the resistances which have been built up in her through the influences of her milieu and education, that is the man she will take into a lasting relationship, the possibility of which will never again be open to any other man. This experience creates a state of bondage in the woman which guarantees that possession of her shall continue undisturbed and makes her able to resist new impressions and enticements from outside.

The expression 'sexual bondage' was chosen by von Krafft-Ebing (1892) to describe the phenomenon of a person's acquiring an unusually high degree of dependence and lack of self-reliance in relation to another person with whom he has sexual relationship. This bondage can on occasion extend very far, as far as the loss of all independent will and as far as causing a person to suffer the greatest sacrifices of his own interests; the author, however, does not fail to remark that a certain measure of such dependence 'is absolutely necessary, if the tie is to last for any length of time'. Some such measure of sexual bondage is, indeed, indispensable to the maintenance of civilized marriage and to holding at bay the polygamous tendencies which threaten it, and in our social communities this factor is regularly reckoned upon.

*   *   *

[D]efloration has not only the one, civilized consequence of binding the woman lastingly to the man ; it also unleashes an archaic reaction of hostility towards him, which can assume pathological forms that are frequently enough expressed in the appearance of inhibitions in the erotic side of married life, and to which we may ascribe the fact that second marriages so often turn out better than first. The taboo of virginity, which seems so strange to us, the horror with which, among primitive peoples, the husband avoids the act of defloration, are fully justified by this hostile reaction.

NOTE 2.

BLANDING, SARAH G.

The Day I Spoke off the Cuff to the Girls of Vassar*

. . . In April, at a college assembly, I spoke of the standards of behavior expected of Vassar students. I laid it on the line that the college does not condone and will not tolerate the excessive use of alcohol, premarital sexual indulgence, or offensive, vulgar conduct on the part of students, at Vassar or away from the campus. . . .

*   *   *

Our culture is built around the monogamous family unit, sanctified by Hebraic-Christian tradition. I believe that it is the responsibilty of parents and educators to prepare young people to live within this cultural framework, not as something that is repressive and imprisoning, but as a background for creative development and responsible freedom. The Kinsey report to the contrary, I believe that pre-marital sexual relationships, espec-

* Reprinted from: *The Standard Edition of the Complete Psychological Works of Sigmund Freud.* London: The Hogarth Press, 1957 (pp. 193-194, 208). Reprinted with permission of the publisher and of Basic Books, Inc., New York.

* *McCall's,* Nov., 1962, pp. 91, 162. Reprinted with permission of the publisher.

ially if casual or promiscuous, set the stage for later extra-marital relationships, which weaken or destroy family life. I believe, further, that premarital chastity on the part of young women is conducive to the stability of marriage.

Conscience and moral attitudes are individual matters. Conduct and behavior—except for someone alone on an island—are not. A college has the responsibility and the right to lay down ground rules for the behavior of the young people who are voluntarily enrolled.

It is easy to forget that late teenagers know considerably less than they think they do. The perspective of youth is necessarily limited, and prestige, popularity, romance, sex, passion, and love are easily and frequently confused.

* * *

But the highest standards of behavior referred to in the handbooks and matriculation pledges of most colleges and universities are not subject to the same subtle, individual interpretation as one's personal code of moral values. They are a reflection of the best of our cultural traditions, modified gradually and thoughtfully in terms of changing social needs and conditions. . . .

NOTE 3.

TRAVIS v. TRAVIS
183 Pa. Super. 273, 130 A. 2d 724 (1957)

HIRT, J.

* * *

In a marriage contract there is no implied warranty by either party of premarital chastity. A man may make a woman's previous continence a condition of his promise to marry her; but if her virginity is a controlling consideration as to him it is incumbent on him to make due inquiry in an effort to ascertain the fact and not ask the law, later, to relieve him from his marriage contract because of his wife's premarital lapse from virtue. Accordingly the general rule is that failure to divulge an antenuptial incontinence by a woman does not in itself constitute fraud, upon which an annulment of the marriage by judicial decree can be predicated. . . . In *Allen's Appeal*, 99 Pa. 196, Chief Justice Sharswood in referring to the principle (which however was not the controlling issue in that case), said: "in this country—certainly in this state—adultery is a ground for divorce a vinculo matrimonii; so that if there should be a relapse after marriage, the marriage can be annulled"; and further, after referring to the rule that prior unchastity supplies no ground for avoiding the contract, " . . . if ante-nuptial incontinence be a sufficient ground of nullity as against the woman, it is not easy to see why it

should not be so likewise against the man, and the consequences of such a doctrine it is not difficult to predict."

* * *

NOTE 4.

Code of Virginia—1950

§20-91. *Grounds for divorce from bond of matrimony.* A divorce from the bond of matrimony may be decreed:

(8) Where prior to the marriage the wife had been, without the knowledge of the husband, a prostitute, such divorce may be decreed to the husband. . . .

NOTE 5.

CLARKE v. CLARKE
159 N.Y.S. 2d 263 (Sup. Ct. 1957)

GOLD, J.

[The] defense alleges that the plaintiff, at the time of her marriage to defendant, represented that she had been married only three times, whereas, the fact is that she had had four prior marriages. There is no allegation as to whether or not the parties continued to cohabit after defendant's discovery of the true facts. In any event, the court holds as a matter of law that the alleged misrepresentation was immaterial and furnishes insufficient basis for defeating this action. A false representation that plaintiff had never been married would be material. It may be that a representation that plaintiff had been married only once would be material if she had been, in fact, married three or four times or more. But the difference between three and four prior marriages is so insignificant that it must be held to be unsubstantial to permit defendant to escape his marital obligations to plaintiff. It is difficult to believe that defendant, who was willing to marry a thrice-married woman, would have balked at one who had been married four times. The defense is insufficient.

NOTE 6.

CLARKE v. CLARKE
Four Years Later

While an appeal was pending from the decision the omniscient Providence interfered, and the fourth husband of the plaintiff died. The plaintiff then figured that if she accepted the decision she saved the costs of appeal and further costs in getting rid legally of apparently unsavory fifth husband. Leaving the decision, whether legally right or wrong, stand left her legally unfettered matrimonially, and free to hunt for a sixth candidate for wedded bliss. [Letter dated Jan. 14, 1961 from Borris M. Komar, attorney for plaintiff.]

NOTE 7.

GAMBACORTA v. GAMBACORTA
136 N.Y.S. 2d 258 (Sup. Ct. 1954)

AURELIO, JUSTICE.

*   *   *

I am satisfied that plaintiff would not have married defendant had he known she was divorced by her prior husband for adultery. Plaintiff is hence entitled to a decree of annulment in his favor. . . .

NOTE 8.

RICHARDSON v. RICHARDSON
200 Misc. 778, 103 N.Y.S. 2d 219 (1951)

LAPHAM, OFFICIAL REFEREE.

. . . Annulment appeals to the popular mind more strongly than absolute divorce in that it does not bear the stigma of the ugly charge of adultery (the sole ground in our State), and the foreign decree is both inconvenient and burdensome, not to say ineffective and futile in many instances. Then, too, the requirements for procuring an annulment have been more easily met than in the case of divorce, since an action to annul does not seal the lips of the complaining spouse as to the heart of the issue. The fruits of annulment are not only present freedom, but release ab initio, and life begins anew with the granting of such a decree. An analysis of the unending procession of annulment actions on the calendars of our Courts, gives rise to the conviction that many persons who would not stoop to frame a false charge of adultery, fall prey to the temptation of magnifying pre-marital assurances and post-marital words and acts to satisfy the technical requirements of the law, thus shielding themselves from the necessity of disclosing the real cause of the rift—causes which all too often are but minor discords that would not serve as a key to open the legal door to freedom.

*   *   *

NOTE 9.

WORDEN v. WORDEN
231 Ark. 858, 333 S.W. 2d 494 (1960)

MCFADDIN, JUSTICE.

*   *   *

This is a suit to annul a marriage because of alleged fraudulent representations. The Chancellor denied the prayed relief. . . .

. . . Harry was in the military service, and returned to Jonesboro for a 15-day leave about the first of November, 1958. He had a date with Genevive, and coition occurred . . . on several occasions. . . . In December 1958 Genevive wrote Harry that she was pregnant and that he was the father of the expected child. Harry came home at the end of his military service . . . and on March 1, 1959 he and Genevive were married and lived together until the birth of the baby on May 16, 1959. Then Harry's mother concluded that it was a full 9-months baby and that Harry could not have been the father of the baby. Thereupon, Harry filed the present suit for annulment, alleging that he had married Genevive because she had represented to him that he was the father of her unborn child, and that such representation was known by her to be false. In her answer to the complaint, Genevive insisted that Harry was the father of the child ; and also that he had entered into the marriage of his own free will and accord.

*   *   *

. . . Harry did not sufficiently establish that he married Genevive *in reliance on her representation to him that he was the father of the expected child,* even if it be conceded that the representation was false. In a suit to set aside an ordinary business contract on account of false representations, the person who seeks to set aside the contract has the burden of establishing: (a) that the representation was false ; (b) that the person making the representation knew it was false ; (c) that it was made for the purpose of inducing the contract ; (d) that the person to whom the representation was made relied on the false representation ; and also (e) *that he would not have entered into the contract except for the false representation.* . . .

[We have] held that the burden was on the party seeking the annulment to establish the alleged fraud by clear and convincing evidence:

> ". . . Indeed, since marriage is a solemn contract, entered into by license from the State, it is clear that the same *quantum* of evidence is required to set aside a marriage contract for fraud as is required to set aside any other written contract. . . ."

*   *   *

NOTE 10.

MORRIS v. MORRIS
13 A. 2d 603 (Super. Ct., Del. 1940)

RODNEY, JUDGE, delivering the opinion of the court :

*   *   *

The ground for the present annulment suit is that the defendant, at the time of the marriage to the plaintiff, was with child by another. As said by Morse, J., in Sissung v. Sissung, 65 Mich. 168, 31 N.W. 770, 773,

> "The essence of the marriage contract is wanting when the woman, at the time of its consummation, is bearing in her womb, knowingly, the

fruit of her illicit intercourse with a stranger; and the result is the same whether the husband is ignorant of her pregnancy, and believes her chaste, or is cognizant of her condition, but has been led to believe that the child is his."

* * *

NOTE 11.

Israeli Draft Family Code § 41 (1956)*

Second Marriage of a Woman

No marriage shall be celebrated of a woman whose former marriage was dissolved within the preceding six months, unless she has given birth during that period or presents a physician's certificate that she is not pregnant.

Comments

* * *

We propose a waiting period of six months. We do not believe (as did those who established the said rule in Jewish law) that after three months the question "as to whether or not she is pregnant" can already be answered by external symptoms. On the other hand, we do not accept the Roman and modern view that the waiting period must be the same as the longest period of pregnancy. We consider a period of six months as adequate. Since a waiting period is required "to distinguish between the issue of the first husband and that of the second" and only for that purpose, there is no need to wait further where the woman has given birth after the dissolution of the former marriage or where it has otherwise been established that she is not pregnant. This fact can nowadays be proved by medical examination with absolute certainty, or, in any event, with a degree of certainty sufficient for the purpose of the present provision.

* * *

The non-compliance with the waiting period constitutes a violation of criminal law on the part of the individual who solemnizes the second marriage, and only on his part. The validity of the marriage is not affected. . . .

5.

WHITE v. WHITE
[1948] 2 All E.R. 151

WILLMER, J.: This case started with a petition by the wife for the decree of nullity on the ground

* Cambridge: Harvard Law School–Brandeis University Cooperative Research for Israel's Legal Development. Copyright 1956 by the President and Fellows of Harvard College. Reprinted with permission.

of the alleged wilful refusal of the husband to consummate the marriage. The petition . . . was amended by adding an alternative plea, namely, that, assuming the marriage to be a valid marriage, the husband was guilty of cruelty so as to justify the court in pronouncing a decree of dissolution. The ground on which both the prayer for nullity and the alternative prayer for dissolution are based is an allegation that from beginning to end the husband practised what is known as *coitus interruptus*. It is said, in the first place, that in those circumstances the marriage has never been consummated and that the non-consummation was due to wilful refusal on the part of the husband, and, in the alternative, assuming the marriage to have been consummated, that the conduct of the husband in relation to his sexual behavior has amounted to cruelty so as to warrant a decree of dissolution. The husband, by his answer, merely denies each and every allegation. . . . There is no cross prayer for relief on his part. I have had the benefit of hearing the evidence of both the parties. I have also heard some valuable medical evidence called on behalf of the wife, and I have had the additional advantage of hearing evidence from the wife's sister, with whom the parties resided for a considerable period of the married history. I would like to say at once—because this conclusion influences all the other conclusions at which I have arrived—that, having heard the evidence of the parties, I was left in no doubt that the husband was a witness on whose statements I could place no reliance. : . . I approach this case on the basis that the wife's account of what happened is substantially to be believed, and the husband's account, where it differs from the wife's, is not to be believed.

That being so, I can state the salient facts quite briefly. The parties were married, or went through a ceremony of marriage, in September, 1937. It is common ground that no intercourse at all took place for six months and that about six months after the marriage what is called *coitus interruptus* took place. The wife's case is that thereafter, throughout the married life, intercourse was rarely resorted to—only about once in every three or four months or so—and that whenever it was resorted to it always took the form of *coitus interruptus*. She says—and I believe her—that she showed her husband quite plainly that she did not approve of it and made it clear to him that she wanted children, but that she received an answer from him either that he did not want to risk children because he could not afford them or that he was too tired. . . .

The wife was a woman of somewhat nervous disposition. She had, before marriage, had a nervous breakdown, and I think that there is no doubt, in view of the medical evidence which I have received, that the practice of *coitus interruptus* (which also deprived her, if not of the possibility, at least of the likelihood, of having children, and, therefore, led to a certain amount of friction between the parties) had its effect on her health, and in the later years of the marriage she was repeatedly having to go into hospital suffering from nervous complaints. I need not go into detail about these visits to hospital. [T]he wife was sent to visit Dr. Strauss, a specialist in nervous diseases, who has given evidence before me. . . . The significance of his report is that the wife's own medical adviser summoned the husband to see him and read to him extracts from the report so that the husband could be left in no doubt of the view which had been taken, namely, that it was his conduct to a large extent which had brought about the bad state of health of the wife. I have no doubt that the husband fully understood exactly what the specialist had to say.

*   *   *

. . . The interview resulted in nothing. The husband was un-cooperative and continued as he had previously conducted himself. In May, 1946, the wife again had to go to hospital. She was advised then not to go back to her husband, but she did so and remained with him until she once more had to go into hospital in November, 1946. During the period between May and November there was no intercourse whatsoever. When she was in hospital in November, 1946, the wife made up her mind that she could not go back to the husband again, and there has been no co-habitation since that date.

I should state that in this case there is evidence from Dr. McLean that, when *coitus interruptus* is practised, the possibility of conception none the less remains. . . . That may or may not be of some materiality. It seems to me a significant piece of evidence, because, if I came to the conclusion that in such circumstances a decree of nullity could be pronounced on the ground of non-consummation, one might get a very curious result. The marriage would be annulled on the supposed ground of non-consummation, notwithstanding the fact that the wife might have borne, not one child, but many children. It seems a curious position that that which might very well produce a child or children should at the same time be a reason for obtaining a decree of nullity on the ground of non-consummation.

In those circumstances, the points which I have to determine are (i) whether the wife is entitled to a decree of nullity on the ground of wilful refusal of the husband to consummate the mar-

riage, such non-consummation consisting of the practice which he followed of having only *coitus interruptus* and never complete intercourse. If I decide that in the affirmative, the other question does not arise. If, on the other hand, I decide that there is no ground for a decree of nullity, then I must go on to consider (ii) whether the husband's practice of *coitus interruptus* and his persistence in that practice, which he knew his wife resented and was undermining her health, is sufficient to constitute cruelty so as to entitle the wife to a decree of dissolution.

Let me deal with the question of nullity first. . . .

*   *   *

[I]t is not the consent to marry; as it relateth to the procreation of children, that is requisite; for it may consist, though the woman be far beyond that date; but it is the consent whereby ariseth that conjugal society, which may have the conjunction of bodies as well as of minds; as the general end of the constitution of marriage is the solace and satisfaction of man.

. . . The question, therefore, is what is meant by this "conjunction of bodies" or, to use the Latin phrase, *vera copula*. There is no question in this case, but that full entry and penetration has been achieved. It is submitted on behalf of the wife that there is no *vera copula* unless there is not only full entry and penetration, but also completion of the act within the body of the woman, whether with or without the use of mechanical contraceptives. On the other hand, it is contended that there is a complete conjunction of bodies, a *vera copula*—which means literally "true conjunction"—as soon as full entry and penetration has been achieved. What follows goes merely to the likelihood or otherwise of conception.

In my judgment, the latter contention must be correct. . . . I find it impossible, having heard this matter fully argued, to say that this marriage has not been consummated. . . . I feel bound to say that I cannot pronounce a decree of nullity in this case.

That makes it necessary for me to consider whether a case of cruelty has been made out. I introduce the discussion on that by . . . referring to *Baxter v. Baxter*. In the concluding passage of his speech the Lord Chancellor says this ([1947] 2 All E.R. 886, 892):

I take the view that in this legislation Parliament used the word "consummate" as that word is understood in common parlance and in the light of social conditions known to exist, and that the proper occasion for considering the subjects raised by this appeal is when the sexual life of the spouses, and the responsibility of either or both for a childless home, form the background to some other claim for relief.

It seems to me that the House of Lords was there saying that questions arising out of imperfect intercourse of one sort or another may very well arise in connection with allegations of cruelty. Similarly, they may arise in desertion cases where matters of that sort are put forward by the opposite party as constituting reasonable cause, and that, in the view of the House of Lords, is the proper place to consider sexual irregularities of the sort contemplated. What the House of Lords was saying in relation to intercourse with the use of contraceptives seems to me to apply equally to the case of *coitus interruptus*—a proper place to consider the effect of that is in relation to claims that may be made for dissolution on the ground of cruelty or desertion.

My attention was drawn to the case of *Rice v. Raynold-Spring-Rice* [(1948) 1 All E.R. 188] in which the Divisional Court came to the conclusion, in agreement with the view of the justices, that *coitus interruptus,* practised by one party against the will of the other, was a good ground for the other spouse separating from the offending party, that is to say, was such as to constitute a good defence to a claim based on desertion. In argument I asked counsel for the husband whether, on the basis of the facts as I have now found them, the wife would have a good defence if sued by the husband for desertion, and, as I understood him, he was not prepared to contend that she would not. That, of course, is not sufficient by itself to make out a case of cruelty, although it goes some way along the road. Here, however, I have, as it seems to me, all the necessary facts which would entitle me to pronounce a decree on the ground of cruelty. I have a course of conduct persisted in by the husband, notwithstanding the objection and repeated complaints of the wife. I have a course of conduct which, according to the medical evidence, is calculated to impair the health of a woman of nervous disposition such as the wife in the present case. I have a course of conduct which did, in fact, according to the medical evidence, result in serious injury to the health of the wife. There may well have been other causes contributing to the wife's breakdown in health. Her health did, undoubtedly, break down, but I am left in no doubt, having heard the wife's evidence and the medical evidence, that, at any rate, one of the potent factors contributing to the breakdown in health was the persistent refusal of the husband to have full intercourse in the normal way. I am not saying by any means that the practice of *coitus interruptus* is a ground in every case for pronouncing a decree on the ground of cruelty. The evidence of the doctor which I have heard is that there are many cases, where the parties are a normal man and a normal woman, in which it does no harm to either of them, but where one gets a woman of a nervous disposition like this the practice, as I understand it, may be most damaging to health. A husband must take his wife as he finds her, and, if she is a woman of a type who needs the full and natural completion of the act, to persist in withholding it from her, in the face of her repeated complaints and objections, is in itself an act of cold, calculated cruelty . . . I, therefore . . . pronounce a decree *nisi* of dissolution. . . .

NOTES

NOTE 1.

C. v. C.*

. . . The husband alleged that that child was the result of marital intercourse early in 1954. The wife's case was that the child was conceived by *fecundatio ab extra*.

The parties met in 1948, when the husband was 29 and the wife 21. . . . At the time of the engagement, the husband told the wife that he could give her only a funny sort of love, but that he would do his best. . . . For about 18 months [after the marriage] on some half-dozen occasions, the husband attempted consummation, but each attempt failed because of *ejaculatio praecox*.

. . . In January, 1954, there was an occasion when, according to the wife, the husband returned from a party rather "merry", and attempted intercourse. Although the attempt followed the same pattern as on previous occasions, some three months later the wife discovered she was pregnant. . . .

. . . Her version . . . was strongly supported by the evidence of her family doctor, who found that, even after conception, gynaecological exploration of the wife was unusually difficult.

* * *

It has been established that the marriage had never been consummated owing to the husband's incapacity—not a general impotence, but incapacity *quoad hoc*. There would therefore be a decree *nisi* of nullity. . . .

---

* London: *The Times*, July 12, 1960, p. 3, col. g. Reprinted with permission of the publisher.

NOTE 2.

MACLEOD, DOUGLAS, and READ, CHARLES
Gynaecology*

Coitus Interruptus ... There is little doubt, ... that many couples practise this successfully, and it would appear that provided there is no pre-cipitancy on the part of the husband it may be an effective and harmless method of birth control. Many failures, however, are recorded. The Roman Catholic Church does not countenance *coitus interruptus,* but allows "carezza," which implies penetration of the male organ without intent to ejaculate. Should ejaculation, however, occur after withdrawal, provided there was no previous intent to ejaculate, this is condoned.

---

* London: Churchill & Co., 5th ed., 1955, pp. 172-173. Reprinted with permission of the publisher.

B.

To Decisions Concerning the Administration of Wife-Husband Relationships?

MIRIZIO v. MIRIZIO
242 N.Y. 74, 150 N.E. 605 (1926)

HISCOCK, CH. J. This action is brought under the provisions of section 1162 of the Civil Practice Act, alleging that the defendant as plaintiff's husband has abandoned and refused to support her and demanding judgment of separation with provision for support. The defense which thus far has been sustained is that the plaintiff has refused to live with the defendant and discharge her marital obligations and that, therefore, he has been relieved from any duty of support. There is little dispute of fact. Plaintiff and defendant were united in marriage by a civil ceremony but they were observers of the Catholic religion and, therefore, entered into an agreement that they would not live together or consummate the marriage until performance of a religious ceremony. The plaintiff has been willing and ready to have this ceremony performed and then consummate the marriage but defendant has refused to do this and, under these circumstances, the former has never lived with her husband.

*   *   *

. . . Our State as a matter of long-continued policy, by many statutes and innumerable decisions has fixed the status of the marriage contract as a civil contract which when once executed becomes binding and carries with it certain rights, duties and obligations and the real question presented to us in this case is whether the parties to such a contract lawfully and completely entered into may modify its effect, postpone its consummation and lessen its undoubted and fundamental obligations by private agreements between themselves. In this particular case the private agreement embodies religious observances and from that standpoint is of high order. In the next case the agreement may be based on less meritorious and more selfish considerations and it requires no fertile vision to see where we may be led if the views now being urged shall prevail, that the parties by private agreement may permanently annul or indefinitely postpone the obligations which they assume when they enter into the marriage contract and defeat the policy of the State and the views which have so long and definitely prevailed in a right-minded society. In my opinion such a course as it is now suggested we ought to set out upon of recognizing modifications of the marriage contract by private agreement would lead to disruption of that contract and disaster in the attempt to enforce it. The danger always is that a court may be led by what seem in some particular case to be equitable considerations into adopting some principle which when carried to subsequent and logical application to other facts leads to results which are unfortunate and unjust.

This plaintiff with her religious scruples concerning the consummation of a marriage contract had the situation in her own control. She was not obliged to submit to a civil marriage and then rely upon her husband to carry out a religious ceremony which would satisfy her scruples. I find no evidence that he unduly persuaded or misled her into this course. She could have had a religious ceremony first and thus avoided either discomfort to herself or impairment of her marriage contract. And while she has been drawn into an unfortunate situation by what seems to be the failure of her husband to keep his promise, her agreement in my opinion furnishes no just reason for allowing her in violation of all contractual considerations to compel enforcement of a contract which she, for inadequate legal reasons, refuses to observe. Public policy in such a vital matter as the marriage contract should not be made to yield to subversive private agreements and personal considerations. . . .

For these reasons I think the judgment should be affirmed. . . .

CRANE, J. (dissenting). . . .

. . . She swears that she is willing to live with the defendant if he provides her a home, and that he has never given her any support or offered to provide her with a place to live. As I read this record, the defendant will not do this unless the plaintiff consents to cohabit with him. His duty is to provide a home in the first instance, and take his wife into it. After that, matters may adjust themselves. A little tact and kindness upon the part of the defendant would probably remove the necessity for appearances in court. The position of the defendant is in my judgment unreasonable and unjustifiable. That he is the plaintiff's husband he does not deny. That he is bound to support her and provide her with a home the law makes emphatic. The defendant has failed and refused to provide this home. He tries to excuse his failure upon the ground that his wife *says* and *declares* that she will not cohabit with him. This is not a case where the man and wife are living together, and the wife so refuses after solicitation. The defendant has first failed in his duty as a husband. He justifies his failure and breakdown of all matrimonial obligations because of what his wife *threatens* to do. A little knowledge of womankind would be more helpful to defendant than a lawsuit. It is the proverbial privilege of women to change their minds. A little forbearance, gentleness and consideration for the feelings of others will accomplish what force will fail to do.

* * *

LEHMAN, J. (dissenting). . . .

An agreement not to consummate the marriage might well be considered as an agreement to "alter" the marriage forbidden both by our public policy and by the spirit if not the letter of section 51 of the Domestic Relations Law, but no agreement that the marriage shall not be consummated has been asserted here ; no obligation to consummate the marriage is wholly repudiated or denied by the plaintiff. She recognized that obligation but asserts a right to postpone until such time as the defendant will comply with his promise to perform these preliminary rites which will change sexual intercourse from an act which according to her view is morally illicit, to one which is sanctioned by the guardians of her conscience. Even in those jurisdictions where refusal of marital intercourse is regarded ordinarily as equivalent to desertion, the courts are impelled at times to consider whether reasonable, moral or psychological factors have determined such refusal. . . . Marriage should constitute a bond, but rigid rules of law which decree that religious, moral and other psychological factors which determine human conduct must be disregarded in the measurement of the performance of marital obligation will tend to make the marriage contract not a bond but a chain.

NOTES

NOTE 1.

HIS HOLINESS POPE PIUS XII
Moral Questions Affecting Married Life*

The Creator Who in His goodness and wisdom has willed to conserve and propagate the human race through the instrumentality of man and woman by uniting them in marriage has ordained also that in performing this function, husband and wife should experience pleasure and happiness both in body and soul. In seeking and enjoying this pleasure, therefore, couples do nothing wrong. They accept that which the Creator has given them.

Nevertheless, even here couples must know how to restrict themselves within the limits of moderation. As in eating and drinking, so in the sexual act, they must not abandon themselves without restraint to the impulse of the senses. The right norm therefore is this:—The use of the natural inclination to generate is lawful only in matrimony, in the service of and according to the order of the ends of marriage. From this it follows that only in marriage, and by observing this rule, the desire for and the fruit of this pleasure and satisfaction are lawful. Hence, enjoyment is subordinated to the law of action from which it derives and not the other way about, the action to the law of enjoyment. And this law, so reasonable, concerns not only the substance but also the circumstances of the act, with the result that although the substance of the act be unimpaired, one may sin in the manner of performing it.

Transgression of this rule is as old as original sin. But in our times there is the risk of losing sight of the basic principle. At present it is the custom to maintain in word and writing (and some Catholics do it too) the necessary autonomy, the proper end, and the proper value of sexuality and its performance independently of the object

---

* Address given October 29, 1951 to the Italian Catholic Union of Midwives. Washington: National Catholic Welfare Conference (undated), pp. 21-22. Reprinted with permission of the publisher.

of procreation. People want to reexamine and find a new rule for the order established by God. They do not want to admit any other check on the manner of satisfying instinct than observing the essence of the instinctive act. Thus, for the moral obligation to dominate the passions there is substituted license to follow blindly and without restraint the caprices and impulses of nature, a line of conduct which sooner or later can but lead to the damage of man's morals, conscience, and dignity.

If nature had aimed exclusively or even primarily at a mutual gift and mutual possession of couples for pleasure, if it had ordained that act solely to make their personal experience happy in the highest degree and not to stimulate them in the service of life, then the Creator would have adopted another plan in the formation and constitution of the natural act. But this act is completely subordinated to and ordered in accordance with the sole great law of *"generatio et educatio prolis,"* the fulfilling of the primary end of matrimony as the origin and source of life.

Unfortunately, never-ending waves of hedonism sweep over the world and threaten to drown all married life in the rising flood of thoughts, desires, and acts, not without grave dangers and serious damage to the primary duty of man and wife.

NOTE 2.

GUYON, RENÉ

Sex Life and Sex Ethics*

Criticism of Sexual Conventions.— If we submit sexual morality to a critical examination . . . we find that it is based:

(a) On false associations of ideas; for to attribute *moral* value to *physiological* organs is a false association. It is equally false to attribute purity or impurity to the exercise of a sense or a function, even though it be sexual. Such things as the testicles, the neck of the womb, or the act of coitus can be neither good nor bad; valuations of this kind rest entirely on convention, and in no wise on reason and necessity.

(b) On false reasonings, derived from false associations which have become converted into postulates. Thus it is false reasoning to condemn people who freely exercise their sexual sense as morally inferior, even when this exercise involves no violence or deceit, and is carried out with the full consent of their partners: for

* London: The Bodley Head, 1939, pp. 129-132. Reprinted with permission of the publisher. Reprinted with permission of Alfred A. Knopf, Inc., from *Ethics of Sexual Acts* by René Guyon, translated by J. C. & Ingeborg Flugel, copyright 1934, 1948 by Alfred A. Knopf, Inc.

such exercise is only in accordance with the demands of physiology and hygiene; nor is abstinence in any way a sign of superior morality. To place "the honour" of a woman in her sexual organs is . . . a childish conception originated by our primitive ancestors, who possessed a lively gift for metaphysics, but who were very ignorant of biology, of evolution, and of the true nature of living beings.

*   *   *

(d) In the last resort, on a complete confusion between physiology, which is one thing, and morality, which is another. It is strange indeed that morality should have been able to take possession of certain physiological manifestations and erect them into a criterion of good behaviour. The sexual act is in reality as a-moral as are eating, breathing, or sleeping; and it is self-sufficient. There can therefore be neither honor nor dishonor when two beings agree to give each other sexual pleasure: There is merely the deliberate exercise of a perfectly admissible physiological need.

Positive Rules.— If, now, we try to extract certain positive teachings from this critical examination, we may summarize such teachings in the following rules:

(i) *The convention which regards the sexual organs as shameful is without any foundation in reason, logic or physiology; it would be just as possible and just as foolish to regard the nose, the tongue, or the act of swallowing, as shameful.*

(ii) *The acts accompanying sexual pleasure find their only and sufficient justification in the pleasure that they bring; sexual pleasure is therefore just as admissible as any other natural satisfaction, and its exercise, in whatsoever form may be preferred, has nothing to do with the morality, the virtue or the dignity of either sex.*

(iii) *There should therefore be no disgrace, either for the man or for the woman, in procuring or giving sexual pleasure; it is the lawful and natural exercise of a physiological act.*

(iv) *Sexual pleasure is always lawful, whether it is obtained with a view to reproduction or as an end in itself, i.e. for the mere purpose of obtaining a specific satisfaction.*

(v) *Everybody has the right to exercise quite freely his own preferences in matters of sex, so long as he is guilty of no violence or deceit to others; the right to sexual satisfaction is just as inalienable as the right to eat.*

(vi) *The hygiene of the sexual sense and sexual organs is a matter of science and of personal responsibility, just as is the hygiene of the nutritive function.*

Thus we are led to realize what inestimable advantages would be gained by a substitution of the term *"neural pleasure"* for that of *"sexual pleasure."* Not only should we, in so doing, re-establish a physiological truth, but with one stroke we should abolish all those conventional and ethical prejudices which so distort the observations of psycho-analysts and independent moralists within this field. So-called sexual morality would retire in favor of the natural laws of biology, physiology and hygiene; and the confusion between neural pleasure and the function of reproduction would automatically cease.

* * *

A critical examination of the facts, therefore, fails utterly to give any support to the theory (itself based on a faulty physiology) which maintains that men and women who abjure sex enjoy more dignified lives than those who freely lend themselves to sexual pleasure. Dignity is no more concerned here than it would be in the question as to whether we should travel by foot or in a car. This imaginary *dignity* is only the counterpart of the imaginary *defilement*: the latter was a punishment, the former a reward; the aim of both being to ensure the triumph of false conceptions. It is just as ridiculous for a person to consider himself worthy or respectable because he abstains from neural pleasure as it would be to consider himself morally superior for going without one of his daily meals. These supposed moral values are, every one of them, distorted: they only exist as so many arbitrary and artificial categories for those who are incapable of understanding physiological truth.

NOTE 3.

REIK, THEODOR
Of Love and Lust*

. . . We want to discriminate between sex and love as the chemist would isolate the sodium element from chloride in the combination, salt. To make the difference clear and clean-cut it is the best to contrast love and sex in their extreme manifestations, where they do not yet appear fused.

Sex is an instinct, a biological need, originating in the organism, bound to the body. It is one of the great drives, like hunger and thirst, conditioned by chemical changes within the organism. The time is not far distant when we shall think of libido in chemical terms, and in chemical terms only. The sex urge is dependent

---

* Reprinted from *Of Love and Lust* by Theodor Reik, by permission of Farrar, Straus & Company, Inc. Copyright © 1941, 1957 by Theodor Reik.

on inner secretions. It can be localized in the genitals and in other erogenic zones. Its aim is the disappearance of a physical tension. It is originally objectless. Later on the sexual object is simply the means by which the tension is eased.

None of these characteristics can be found in love. If we do not accept the opinion of the ordinary man and woman that love lives in the heart we are unable to place it. It certainly is not a biological need, because there are millions of people who do not feel it and many centuries and cultural patterns in which it is unknown. We cannot name any inner secretions or specific glands which are responsible for it. Sex is originally objectless. Love certainly is not. It is a very definite, emotional relationship between a Me and a You.

What is the aim of sex? the disappearance of a *physical* tension, a discharge and a *release*. What is the aim of the desire we call love? Disappearance of a *psychical* tension, *relief*. In this contrast between release and relief lies one of the most decisive differences. Sex wants satisfaction; love wants happiness.

Sex appears as a phenomenon of nature, common to men and beasts. Love is the result of a cultural development and is not even found among all men. We know that the sex urge is subject to periodic fluctuations of increase and decrease. This is of course quite obvious among the beasts, but survivals of its original nature are easily recognized in men. Nothing of this kind is known about love. Sex can be casual about its object. Love cannot. Love is always a personal relationship. This is not necessarily so with sex.

NOTE 4.

BRODIE v. BRODIE
[1917] P. 271

HORRIDGE, J.

[P]etitioner . . . sought a decree for restitution of conjugal rights, to which the respondent has put in a plea that he relies upon a written agreement drawn up and signed by both parties before marriage and signed by them after marriage whereby it was agreed that he and the petitioner should live apart. . . .

[B]efore the marriage the petitioner was expecting to be delivered of a child by the respondent and pressed him to marry her, and he agreed to marry her if, and only if, she would sign an agreement to separate after marriage, and on the day before the marriage was celebrated an agreement in writing, dated December 19, 1913, was signed whereby it was agreed that after the solemnization of the marriage it should be lawful for the respondent at all times to live separate and apart from the petitioner as if he were un-married, and the petitioner should not require or compel, or endeavour to compel, the respondent to cohabit or dwell with her by any legal proceed-ings for desertion or for restitution of conjugal rights or otherwise howsoever, and she would not take any proceedings against the respondent to obtain judicial separation.

The parties were married on December 29, 1913, and on the same date at the registry office, a further agreement dated December 20, 1913, endorsed upon the previous agreement, was entered into whereby it was mutually agreed between the parties that each of them thereby confirmed the terms of the within written inden-ture and agreed to perform and observe the covenants and conditions thereof so far as they were to be observed and performed by them respectively.

*   *   *

. . . Such an agreement is void and against public policy. . . .

*   *   *

For these reasons there must be a decree in this case for restitution.

NOTE 5.

COMMONWEALTH OF AUSTRALIA
Matrimonial Causes Act No. 104 of 1959
Division 4.—Restitution of Conjugal Rights.

60. A petition under this Act by a party to a marriage for a decree of restitution of conjugal rights may be based on the ground that the parties to the marriage, whether or not they have at any time cohabited, are not cohabiting and

that, without just cause or excuse, the party against whom the decree is sought refuses to cohabit with, and render conjugal rights to, the petitioner.

61. An agreement for separation, whether entered into before or after the commencement of this Act, does not constitute a defence to proceedings under this Act for a decree of restitution of conjugal rights.

62. The court shall not make a decree of restitution of conjugal rights unless it is satisfied—

(*a*) that the petitioner sincerely desires con-jugal rights to be rendered by the respondent and is willing to render conjugal rights to the respondent; and

(*b*) that a written request for cohabitation, expressed in conciliatory language, was made to the respondent before the institution of the proceedings, or that there are special circum-stances which justify the making of the decree notwithstanding that such a request was not made.

63. Where the court makes a decree of restitu-tion of conjugal rights on the petition of a hus-band, the petitioner shall, as soon as practicable after the making of the decree, and at such other times as the rules so require, give to the respondent notice, in accordance with the rules, of the provision made by the petitioner, or which the petitioner is willing to make, with respect to a home for the purpose of enabling the respon-dent to comply with the decree.

64. A decree of restitution of conjugal rights is not enforceable by attachment.

C.

To Decisions Concerning the Reorganization of Wife-Husband Relationships?

1.

SEXUAL CONDUCT AS A CAUSE OF ACTION

a. Adultery

MACLENNAN v. MACLENNAN
[1958] Scots Law Times 12

LORD WHEATLEY.—The pursuer seeks decree of divorce from the defender on the ground of her adultery, and *prima facie* his case is essentially

simple. The parties were married on 25th August 1952 and it is a matter of agreement that they have not lived together or had marital relations since 31st May 1954. On 10th July 1955 the defender admittedly gave birth to a female child in Brooklyn, New York, and on that his-torical narrative of events the pursuer asks the Court to find proven facts, circumstances and qualifications from which an inference of the defender's adultery can be drawn. In the un-complicated days before science began to innovate on the natural process of procreation, the lapse of time between the last act of marital intercourse and the birth of the child would have led to the inevitable inference that the defender had been guilty of an adulterous act with another man by means of the normal and natural physiological mechanism as a result of which the child was conceived. The defender, however, has tendered an explanation by way of defence, which is unique in the annals of our law, and which seeks to establish that she conceived the child not as a result of sexual intercourse with another man, as that phrase is commonly understood, but as a result of artificial insemination from a donor. She does not aver, however, that the pursuer was a consenting party to such an artificial process of conception, and the pursuer maintains that he never agreed to the defender adopting it, if in fact it ever took place. The defender submits that artificial insemination by a donor even without the consent of the husband is not adultery as the law understands and has interpreted that term, and that proof of conception by such means would rebut the inference which would otherwise be raised from the 14 months' period of non-access followed by the birth of a child. . . . [T]he term "artificial insemination by a donor" is glibly used without any explanation of the process in the pleadings, it being apparently assumed that such unusual practices and interference with the natural processes of procreation fall within that omniscience on all worldly matters which is described, sometimes euphemistically and sometimes with a complimentary but quite unjustified faith, as "judicial knowledge". My own particular knowledge of this subject is culled from the articles thereon in some of the journals to which I was referred in the course of the debate. . . .

Artificial insemination is the process whereby the seed of the male is extracted from the male body, enclosed in a receptacle, and subsequently inserted into the female sexual organ, presumably by means of a syringe, thereby reproducing in the end the same result as follows from the natural and unrestricted act of full sexual intercourse. This scientific innovation on the natural processes substitutes a syringe containing male seed for the male sexual and reproductive organs, and the act of conception, if the seed eventually fertilizes, is achieved without the presence of the male body. Technically, although I have no particular knowledge of this, I presume that the woman could acquire the seed and operate the syringe herself, thereby excluding the presence of any other person during the actual insertion. There are apparently three recognized systems of artificial insemination. The first is A.I.H.

which is insemination in the manner indicated by seed extracted from the husband. The second is A.I.D. which is effected by the introduction into the female organ of seed extracted from a male known as the "donor", and who in practice seems to be a man unknown to the recipient, although there would appear to be no reason why the donor should not be known to or indeed selected by the recipient, if the latter preferred it that way and the donor was agreeable. This method may be employed either with or without the consent of the husband. If such a practice constitutes adultery on the part of the wife, the fact that the husband has consented would not prevent the act from being adultery, but it would not be adultery on which the husband could found since he had connived at it. The third method is somewhat cynically known as C.A.I. or confused artificial insemination, wherein there is used for the impregnation of the woman a mixture of the seed of the husband and the seed of a donor.

There are manifestly grave moral, ethical, social and personal considerations involved in the practice of artificial insemination in its various forms which will no doubt be fully deployed elsewhere. It is almost trite to say that a married woman who, without the consent of her husband, has the seed of a male donor injected into her person by mechanical means in order to procreate a child who would not be a child of the marriage has committed a grave and heinous breach of the contract of marriage. The question for my determination, however, is not the moral culpability of such an act but is whether such an act constitutes adultery in its legal meaning. A wife or a husband could commit an act of gross indecency with a member of the opposite sex which would be a complete violation of the marital relationship, but which could not be classified as adultery. It would indeed be easy, according to one's personal viewpoint, to allow oneself to be influenced by the moral, ethical, social and personal considerations to which I have referred and to reach a conclusion based on these considerations, but this problem which I am called upon to solve must be decided by the objective standard of legal principles as these have been developed and must be confined to the narrow issue of whether this form of insemination constitutes adultery in the eyes of the law. If it is not adultery, although a grave breach of the marriage contract, that is a matter for the legislature if it be thought that a separate legal remedy should be provided.

In determining whether the marital offence (which I opine it to be whatever view one takes of its nature) of being impregnated by the seed of another man without the husband's consent constitutes adultery in its legal sense, one naturally seeks a solution from the definitions of "adultery" in the works of our leading legal writers or in reported decisions. Some of our great legal writers however do not even seek to define it, while others, in referring to it, use terms which are more descriptive than definitive. This may be due to the fact that in earlier days when life was regulated by the natural rather than the scientific order of things, people knew what was meant by adultery and what its concomitants were. Where, however, attempts were made to describe adultery if not to provide an exhaustive definition of it, the idea of *conjunctio corporum* seems to be an inherent concomitant— a conception of the process which incidentally can likewise be found in the book of Deuteronomy, the writings of St. Paul and the works of the Canonists. The idea that adultery might be committed by a woman alone in the privacy of her bedroom aided and abetted only by a syringe containing semen was one with which the earlier jurists had no occasion to wrestle. Certainly this form of perpetuation of the species does not conform to the common conception of adultery. Nonetheless the argument advanced in support of the contention that it does constitute adultery was powerfully advanced. I accordingly turn to consider the views of the earlier jurists on the meaning of the term "adultery".

The Scots Act of 1563, cap. 10, which was passed shortly after the Reformation and introduced divorce into the law of Scotland for the first time, prefaces the enactment of divorce for adultery with a condemnation of the practice in denunciatory terms, and castigates those who have been guilty of the offence as people who had no regard to the commandments of God but only to their sensualities, filthy lusts and pleasure.

Neither Stair nor Erskine defines adultery but Sir George Mackenzie in his treatise on *Criminal Law* at page 86, describes it as the violation of another's bed, and is committed by a married person lying with one who is unmarried or an unmarried person lying with one who is married.

*   *   *

Baron Hume in his *Lectures* (vol. I Stair Society Publications at page 83) states that: "the second obligation of the married pair is that of fidelity to the marriage bed" and continues "This, though certainly true of both parties, is more especially so on the part of the female, whose infidelity may . . . impose a spurious offspring on the husband. . . ." . . .

*   *   *

Taking a line through these various definitions or descriptions of what constitutes adultery there runs the basic conception that adultery involves sexual intercourse or carnal connection. While Bankton refers to deeds inconsistent with the nature of matrimony, which is a much wider phrase than adultery, this phrase must be read in its context, and when so read it obviously refers to adultery when related to divorce. When Baron Hume in his *Lectures* refers to the possibility of infidelity to the marriage bed by a wife resulting in the imposition of a spurious offspring on the husband he is not in my view thereby laying down that the result of the infidelity is the test of adultery, but is merely pointing out the possible aggravation which might ensue from the primary act of unfaithfulness. If, then, as I deem it to be, sexual intercourse or carnal connection between a consenting spouse and a member of the opposite sex who is not the other spouse is the basic criterion of adultery, the question arises—what is sexual intercourse or carnal connection, and in particular can artificial insemination fall within such a definition? Certainly no assistance can be obtained directly on the latter point from the earlier jurists whose minds were uncomplicated by the type of scientific expedient with which we are dealing here and whose conception and understanding of such terms as sexual intercourse and carnal knowledge were based on the normal and natural methods of sexual relationship. It is not surprising, therefore, that one finds in their writings none of the physiological and biological considerations and none of the metaphysical distinctions which studded the arguments presented to me. Nonetheless I am satisfied that the solution to the present problem can be found in the basic principles which these earlier writers have enunciated.

In the normal and natural method of performing an act of sexual intercourse there is a mutual surrender both of the sexual and reproductive organs. While the primary purpose of sexual intercourse is procreation, in the eyes of the law surrender of the reproductive organs is not necessary to consummate the act of intercourse. Expedients may be used by the parties to secure birth prevention or the woman may have previously undergone an operation by which her reproductive organs were removed, or they may have ceased to function from natural causes and yet the conjunction of the sexual organs involving at least some degree of penetration would constitute intercourse and, in the circumstances under consideration, adultery. Thus impregnation *per se* cannot be a test of adultery, since in the eyes of the law the act of intercourse can be consummated without impregnation either as a result of natural causes or by the parties resorting to artificial expedients. ... It would seem, therefore that in determining such questions as consummation of marriage or adultery, the law looks at the act and not the result. It is perhaps interesting to note ... a passage from Stair's *Institutions,* 1681 ed., book 1, title IV, paragraph 6, where Lord Stair said: "So then, it is not the consent of the marriage as it relateth to the procreation of children that is requisite; for it may consist though the woman be far beyond that date; but it is the consent, whereby ariseth that conjugal society, which may have the conjunction of bodies as well as of minds, as the general end of the institution of marriage, is the solace and satisfaction of man."

... Although not presented in syllogistic form the pursuer's argument seemed to be that in the given circumstances while undoubtedly all cases of penetration of the female organ by the male organ were adultery even if impregnation did not take place, so too all cases of impregnation were adultery even if there was no such penetration. This to my mind is a legal *non sequitur.* The argument seems to me to confuse the method with the result. Impregnation may be the result of sexual intercourse, but is not necessarily an essential part of it, and if it is achieved by other means which do not involve the physical presence of the male and his sexual organ, it is difficult to see how such other means can be classified as sexual intercourse or to use the more significant phrase "carnal connection". The sheet anchor of the pursuer's argument was an *obiter dictum* of Lord Dunedin in *Russell* v. *Russell,* [1924] A.C. 687 at page 721, where his Lordship said, after dealing with the question of the wife having been fecundated *ab extra* "and fecundation *ab extra* is, I doubt not, adultery." There is no doubt that this dictum was *obiter,* but any dictum by Lord Dunedin is always worthy of the closest consideration and greatest respect. The argument which prayed it in aid, however, seemed to divorce it from its context. Briefly that argument stated that if fecundation *ab extra* in the given circumstances in adultery, it matters not whether the fecundation was at short or long range, and artificial insemination was merely a case of long range fecundation. That facile argument, however, seems to me to ignore the circumstances in regard to which Lord Dunedin opined his view. In the circumstances which he was contemplating there was a close conjunction of the bodies even although there was no penetration of any sort of the female organ by the male organ, but the close juxtaposition of the respective organs enabled an ejaculation of semen from the male organ

to enter into the female organ and fertilize. I am satisfied that what his Lordship meant was that where there was a mutual surrender of the bodies to an illicit passion and there was sufficient proximity of the respective organs to enable seeds to pass from one to another, it did not preclude the act from being an adulterous one merely because there had been no penetration. There would be present in such circumstances not only the two bodies, but physical intimacy and sexual stimulation, which resulted in the transfer of seed, and from which the fact of adultery could be inferred. As there can be penetration without emission (which would be adultery) and emission following penetration without fertilization (which would likewise be adultery) it seems to me that these factors are merely incidentals or accidentals of the adulterous act, which consists of the mutual surrender of the bodies and is evidenced by the degree of familiarity thereby occasioned, which is a complete transgression and violation of the contract of marriage. Whether such a degree of familiarity would require to be established by evidence of some degree of penetration, as recent English decisions seem to suggest, or whether it could be established by evidence of something less as Lord Dunedin contemplated, does not seem to me to be of vital importance in the present issue, since whatever view is taken there is involved in both cases the mutual surrender of the bodies to each other for the purposes of carnal gratification in breach of marital obligations. If the view be taken, as I think it must, that gross indecency short of sexual intercourse is not adultery, however reprehensible it may be, then there must be some defining line between the two, and it is for that reason that the Courts in England seem to have insisted that some degree of penetration must have occurred before sexual intercourse can be said to have taken place. The point does not seem to have arisen for consideration in Scotland but that may be due to the traditional formula whereby all that the Court has to find are facts, circumstances and qualifications relevant to infer adultery, a course which normally absolves the Court from entering into the distasteful minutiae of evidence of the adulterous act. The genesis of the suggestion that something less than penetration—or at least full penetration—might suffice to constitute adultery is to be found in a dictum of Viscount Birkenhead in *Rutherford* v. *Richardson* [1923] A.C. 1 at page 11, where the then Lord Chancellor said: "Some suggestion was made in argument in this House that the condition (of the woman's private parts) even though inconsistent with penetration, was not inconsistent with some lesser act of sexual gratification. If there was evidence of such an act, it cannot be doubted that, whatever view may have been taken in the past ages by the Ecclesiastical Courts, a decree based upon adultery might issue. But it is not open now to the petitioner to rely on some lesser sexual act."

* * *

. . . I . . . derive . . . the following propositions, according at least to the law of England.

1. For adultery to be committed there must be the two parties physically present and engaging in the sexual act at the same time.

2. To constitute the sexual act there must be an act of union involving some degree of penetration of the female organ by the male organ.

3. It is not a necessary concomitant of adultery that male seed should be deposited in the female's ovum.

4. The placing of the male seed in the female ovum need not necessarily result from the sexual act, and if it does not, but is placed there by some other means, there is no sexual intercourse.

* * *

. . . Just as artificial insemination extracts procreation entirely from the nexus of human relationships in or outside of marriage, so does the extraction of the nexus of human relationship from the act of procreation remove artificial insemination from the classification of sexual intercourse. If my views be correct, then it follows logically that artificial insemination by a donor without the consent of the husband is not adultery as the law interprets that term. The only case cited to me wherein a contrary view was reached was the unreported American case of *Doornbos* v. *Doornbos,* which was a declaratory form of action unknown to our procedure. Not having had the benefit of the judgment on which the decision was based, I cannot comment on it, but for the reasons which I have given I must express the view that the decision is one which cannot be followed or supported in our law. It is perhaps not inappropriate however to consider the implications of the contrary view. If artificial insemination by a donor without the husband's consent is to be deemed adultery, the first question which seems to call for a decision is whether the donor whose seed has been used has himself been guilty of adultery. If the answer is in the affirmative, the further question arises, at what point of time has he done so? If it be at the point when the seed is extracted from his body, certain interesting considerations would arise. I gather that seed so obtained can be retained for a considerable time

before being used, and in some cases it may not be used at all. If the donor's seed is taken merely to lie *in retentis,* it surely cannot be adultery if that seed is never used. Thus, if his adultery is to be deemed to take place at the time of the parting with the seed, it can only be an adultery subject to defeasance in the event of the seed not being used. Such a statement need only be stated for its absurdity to be manifested. If, on the other hand, his adultery is deemed to take place when the seed is injected into the woman's ovum, this latter act may take place after his death, and in that case the woman's conduct would constitute not only adultery but necrophilism. Such a proposition seems to me to be equally absurd. The third alternative is that the whole process should be regarded as an act of adultery, but as this might in certain cases result in the act covering a period of say two years, and be committed partly during the lifetime and partly after the death of the donor, I cannot distinguish between the absurdity of such a proposition and the absurdity of the other alternatives. Senior counsel for the pursuer appreciated the illogicality and absurdity of these consequences of the proposition that the donor had committed adultery and accepted that he had not. This then forced him to argue that the wife could commit adultery by herself. One need not consider the interesting point whether the administrator could be said to commit adultery, because the administrator might be a woman or the seed might be self injected by the wife herself operating the syringe. The idea that a woman is committing adultery when alone in the privacy of her bedroom she injects into her ovum by means of a syringe the seed of a man whom she does not know and has never seen is one which I am afraid I cannot accept. Unilateral adultery is possible, as in the case of a married man who ravishes a woman not his wife, but self-adultery is a conception as yet unknown to the law. The argument of pursuer's counsel was that adultery meant the introduction of a foreign element into the marital relationship. That, however, seems to me to beg the question, because what has still to be determined is what is the foreign element? For the reasons which I have already explained, that foreign element is the physical contact with an alien and unlawful sexual organ, and without that element there cannot be what the law regards as adultery. The introduction of a spurious element into the family, with all its consequences, may be the result of such conduct, but is not a necessary result, and it is by the means and not by the result that this issue is to be judged. If artificial insemination by a donor were to be regarded as adultery, then I opine the view that it would be adultery whether the seed germinated or not, and yet in the latter case there would be no resultant adulteration of the strain. At the root of the argument for the pursuer was the proposition that impregnation is at the basis of adultery, and it was argued that the view of the English judges that there must be penetration indicated that there must be the possibility of insemination. Whatever the moral and ethical aspects of that argument may be, the Courts have now accepted that adultery can take place when the possibility of insemination has been excluded either by natural causes or artificial expedients, and so that argument must fail.

NOTES

NOTE 1.

BLAKE, NELSON M.
The Road to Reno*

[E]asy divorce has roots in the remote past. Athenian husbands might put away their wives at will; Athenian wives could shed their husbands with only moderately greater difficulty. In the early Roman Republic several different types of marriage evolved. In most of these the husband enjoyed a right to divorce his wife at will as part of his general patriarchal authority. Under the strictest patrician form of marriage (conferreatio), divorce was very difficult, even for the husband. But long before the birth of Christ a less stringent form of marriage had become almost universal. This was based upon the principle of free contract, from which either party might obtain release without court proceedings by a simple declaration before witnesses.

* * *

Jewish custom strongly resembled that of early Rome in recognizing the full authority of the husband and allowing him to divorce his wife at will. As codified in Deuteronomy, the traditional Mosaic law provided that if a wife found no favor in her husband's eyes because of something unseemly in her, he was to give her a bill of divorce and send her out of the house, after which she might marry another man. The prevailing school of broad construction held that this power of the husband was unlimited: he could divorce his wife for any reason at all; a strict constructionist minority argued that the husband could do so only on the grounds of the wife's adultery.

* New York: The Macmillan Co., 1962, pp. 9-11, 22-24, 32-33, 36-37. Reprinted with permission of the publisher. © Nelson M. Blake 1962.

It was against this background of Jewish controversy that a Pharisee, according to Matthew's Gospel, challenged Jesus by asking: "Is it lawful to divorce one's wife for any cause?" The reported reply has been of momentous consequence in the history of divorce:

He answered, "Have you not read that he who made them from the beginning made them male and female, and said, 'For this reason a man shall leave his father and mother and be joined to his wife, and the two shall become one'? So they are no longer two but one. What therefore God has joined together, let not man put asunder." They said to him, "Why then did Moses command one to give a certificate of divorce, and to put her away?" He said to them, "For your hardness of heart Moses allowed you to divorce your wives, but from the beginning it was not so. And I say to you: whoever divorces his wife, except for unchastity, and marries another, commits adultery."

Unfortunately for Christians trying to follow the letter of their Lord's teachings, the exact meaning of these words has been vigorously disputed by theologians and commentators, beginning with the earliest Church Fathers and continuing to the present. The passage from Matthew just quoted contains ambiguities, and these points become still more doubtful when Matthew's account is compared with those of Mark and Luke. For each of the following statements some reputable ancient or modern authority could be cited:

1. Christ taught the indissolubility of marriage and forbade all divorce.
2. He allowed divorce, but only to the husband, and only for one cause, adultery.
3. He allowed divorce for adultery to both husband and wife.
4. Neither party to a divorce may marry again while his former mate is still alive. To do so is adultery.
5. The innocent party may remarry, but not the guilty.
6. Both parties may remarry, after sincere repentance.
7. Adultery means only one thing, the sexual intercourse of a married person with someone other than the husband or wife.
8. Adultery is a symbolic word, standing for any sin that violates the marriage contract.

* * *

Both conservatives and radicals drew comfort from the writings of Martin Luther. The great German explicitly denied that marriage was a sacrament. Asking the question, "What is the proper procedure for us nowadays in matters of marriage and divorce?" he answered that "this should be left to the lawyers and made subject to the secular government." . . .

In commenting on Jesus' teachings on divorce, Luther explains: "Christ is not functioning here as a lawyer or a governor, to set down or prescribe any regulations for outward conduct; but He is functioning as a preacher, to instruct consciences about using the divorce law properly, rather than wickedly and capriciously, contrary to God's commandment."

Luther accordingly distinguishes sharply between what the law may permit and what the Christian ought to do. The law may sensibly permit rather liberal divorce, since it is better to allow "wicked and unmanageable people" to be divorced than to let them do worse by "vexing or murdering each other or by living together in incessant hate, discord, and hostility." But he goes on to admonish: "Those who want to be Christians should not be divorced, but every man should keep his own spouse, sustaining and bearing good and ill with her, even though she may have her oddities, peculiarities, and faults." This is not an absolute principle; Luther interprets the Scriptures to sanction the Christian's right to seek absolute divorce in cases of adultery or desertion, and limited divorce without the privilege of remarrying for other causes. According to Luther, the Christian ought to practice forgiveness and reconciliation whenever possible, but if the guilty party persists in his bad conduct, it is he who has dissolved the marriage and the innocent party should be completely free.

In a characteristically blunt passage, Luther extends desertion to cover the case of the husband or wife who unreasonably refuses to meet his partner's sexual needs:

> One spouse may rob and withdraw himself or herself from the other and refuse to grant the conjugal due or to associate with the other. One may find a woman so stubborn and thickheaded that it means nothing to her though her husband fall into unchasteness ten times. Then it is time for the man to say: If you are not willing, another woman is; if the wife is not willing, bring on the maid. But this is only after the husband has told his wife once or twice, warned her, and let it be known to other people that her stubborn refusal may be publicly known and rebuked before the congregation. If she still does not want to comply, then dismiss her. . . .

* * *

. . . The eighteenth century point of view is amply illustrated by the famous Dr. Samuel Johnson's remarks upon the subject of adultery:

. . . Confusion of progeny constitutes the essence of the crime: and therefore a woman who breaks her marriage vows is much more criminal than a man who does it. A man, to be sure, is criminal in the sight of God: but he does not do his wife a very material injury, if he does not insult her; of, for instance, from mere wantonness of appetite, he steals privily to her chambermaid. Sir, a wife ought not greatly to resent this. I would not receive home a daughter who had run away from her husband on that account. A wife should study to reclaim her husband by more attention to please him. Sir, a man will not, once in a hundred instances, leave his wife and go to a harlot, if his wife has not been negligent of pleasing.

* * *

. . . The act of 1692 for "the Orderly Consummating of Marriages," allowed ministers as well as justices of the peace to perform the ceremony, laid down strict requirements for registering all marriages with the civil authorities, and specified that "all controversies concerning Marriage and Divorce shall be Heard and Determined by the Governeur and Council."

Two or three years later the Cambridge Association, composed of the most influential clergymen in the colony, took up the question: "In what cases is a divorce of the Married justly to be pursued and obtained?" The divines agreed that "to judge, determine and accomplish a divorce . . . the civil magistrate is to be addressed or concerned." They then specified seven grounds upon which a marriage might be dissolved: impotence, bigamy, adultery, incest, fornication before marriage with a relative of the present husband or wife, malicious desertion, and long absence with the presumption of death. On two questions controversial among Christian theologians, the Massachusetts group took forthright positions. On one of these, they declared:

> In the case of a *malicious desertion* by a married person, who is obliged and invited to return, a divorce may be granted by lawful authority unto the forsaken. For the word of God is plain, "that a man is not bound in such cases" by the marriage unto one which has thus willfully violated the covenant; and tho' our Saviour forbids "a man's putting away his wife, except it be for fornication," yet he forbids not rulers to rescue an innocent person from the enthralling disadvantages of another that shall sinfully go away.

And on another oft-disputed point, they said:

> A divorce being legally pursued and obtained, the innocent person that is released may proceed unto a "second marriage in the Lord;" otherwise the state of believers under the New Testament would in some of these cases be worse than what

the God of heaven directed for his people under the Old.

NOTE 2.

THOMPSON v. THOMPSON
[1938] P. 162

LANGTON, J. This has proved a difficult, anxious and most distasteful inquiry. Evidence was given at the hearing by two domestic servants, working in a house at Peppard, near Henley-on-Thames, proving that Major Thompson and Miss Causton had stayed together at this house and together occupied the same bedroom. This evidence was supplemented by evidence from two hall-porters from Cumberland Mansions proving further association between Major Thompson and Miss Causton at the latter's London address. . . .

[[T]he solicitor acting for Miss Causton had sent to the petitioner's solicitors copies of two certificates which purported to have been obtained from two eminent gynaecologists, . . . to the effect that they had separately and on different days examined Miss Margaret Causton and found that her hymen was intact.] . . .

Accordingly, at the same time that I granted Lady Hulton her decree, I directed that the papers should be sent to the King's Proctor to enable him to inquire into the case, with the special object of discovering what were the true facts. . . .

On March 4 last the Solictor-General and Mr. Barnard, appearing on behalf of the King's Proctor, presented a plea alleging: (1) that the decree nisi which I had granted had been obtained contrary to the justice of the case; (2) that the respondent had not committed adultery with the intervener; and (3) that the intervener was at all material times a virgin. . . .

* * *

In the present case I have had useful evidence from Dr. Beckett Overy, a well-known gynaecologist, upon the general question of the various forms of sexual gratification which might be obtained without rupturing the hymen. . . .

* * *

. . . I have deliberated long and carefully upon this subject, and in spite of the strong presumption in her favour, I cannot escape the inference which arises from the fact that Major Thompson and Miss Causton, who are admittedly on terms of deep affection, have certainly slept together in the same room at Peppard, and almost certainly slept together in the same bed in London and have been at great pains to deceive both the world and this Court in the matter of their behaviour. I am regretfully forced to the con-

clusion that the respondent and the intervener in this case have had mutual intercourse amounting to adultery in law.

NOTE 3.

COHEN v. COHEN
200 Misc. 19, 103 N.Y.S. 2d 426 (1951)

PECORA, OFFICIAL REFEREE.

Presented, in this action by a wife for absolute divorce, is the question whether an act of sodomy alleged to have been committed by defendant constitutes an act of adultery. Plaintiff has proven that she married defendant in 1930. . . . The complaint alleges: "That on or about the 20th day of March, 1946, the defendant herein committed adultery with a person unknown to plaintiff in the Township of Mahwah, County of Bergen, State of New Jersey." In support of that allegation, plaintiff offered in evidence the record of defendant's conviction, upon his plea of guilty, of the crime of sodomy [upon a male person]. . . . Defendant was sentenced to a term of imprisonment of not less than seven nor more than ten years in the New Jersey State Prison. . . .

* * *

The statutes of this state assign only one ground for divorce, i.e., adultery. . . . Whether the commission of an act of sodomy may constitute adultery is a question which does not seem to have been decided by the courts of this or any other state. See 1 Bishop—Marriage, Divorce and Separation, § 1832, p. 756. Adultery is defined in the Penal Law as "sexual intercourse of two persons, either of whom is married to a third person". In Section 690 of the Penal Law, defining sodomy, "carnal knowledge" is used in one portion of the statute, while the words "sexual intercourse" are given their usual meaning when reference is made to a dead body. I am of the opinion that the words "sexual intercourse" do not include the acts of carnal knowledge coming within the scope of the definition of sodomy. I am fortified in this conclusion by the fact that in England and in two sister states, sodomy and crimes against nature are specifically made distinct grounds for divorce, in addition to adultery. . . .

While sympathetic with plaintiff's plight in the instant case, the court is powerless to alleviate it in the present action. The complaint should, therefore, be dismissed.

NOTE 4.

Code of Alabama Title 34, § 20 (5) (1959)

. . . The circuit court in equity has power to divorce persons from the bonds of matrimony, upon bill filed by the aggrieved party, for the causes following: . . . 5. The commission of the crime against nature, whether with mankind or beast, either before or after marriage. . . .

NOTE 5.

RUSSELL, BERTRAND
Marriage and Morals*

Adultery in itself should not, to my mind, be a ground of divorce. Unless people are restrained by inhibitions or strong moral scruples, it is very unlikely that they will go through life without occasionally having strong impulses to adultery. But such impulses do not by any means necessarily imply that the marriage no longer serves its purpose. There may still be ardent affection between husband and wife, and every desire that the marriage should continue. Suppose, for example, that a man has to be away from home on business for a number of months on end. If he is physically vigorous, he will find it difficult to remain continent throughout this time, however fond he may be of his wife. The same will apply to his wife, if she is not entirely convinced of the correctness of conventional morality. Infidelity in such circumstances ought to form no barrier whatever to subsequent happiness, and in fact it does not, where the husband and wife do not consider it necessary to indulge in melodramatic orgies of jealousy. We may go farther, and say that each party should be able to put up with such temporary fancies as are always liable to occur, provided the underlying affection remains intact. The psychology of adultery has been falsified by conventional morals, which assume, in monogamous countries, that attraction to one person cannot co-exist with a serious affection for another. Everybody knows that this is untrue, yet everybody is liable, under the influence of jealousy, to fall back upon this untrue theory, and make mountains out of molehills. Adultery, therefore, is no good ground for divorce, except when it involves a deliberate preference for another person, on the whole, to the husband or the wife, as the case may be.

In saying this I am, of course, assuming that the adulterous intercourse will not be such as to lead to children. Where illegitimate children come in, the issue is much more complicated. This is especially the case if the children are those of the wife, for in that case, if the marriage persists, the husband is faced with the necessity of having

another man's child brought up with his own, and (if scandal is to be avoided) even as his own. This goes against the biological basis of marriage, and will also involve an almost intolerable instinctive strain. On this ground, in the days before contraceptives, adultery perhaps deserved the importance which was attached to it, but contraceptives have made it far more possible than it formerly was to distinguish sexual intercourse as such from marriage as a procreative partnership. On this ground it is now possible to attach much less importance to adultery than is attached to it in the conventional code.

*   *   *

. . . The good life cannot be lived without self-control, but it is better to control a restrictive and hostile emotion such as jealousy, rather than a generous and expansive emotion such as love. Conventional morality has erred, not in demanding self-control, but in demanding it in the wrong place.

*   *   *

. . . The substitution of a new moral code for the old one can never be completely satisfactory, unless the new one is accepted with the whole personality, not only with that top layer which constitutes our conscious thought. To most people this is very difficult if throughout their early years they have been exposed to the old morality. It is therefore impossible to judge a new morality fairly until it has been applied in early education.

*   *   *

The doctrine that I wish to preach is not one of licence; it involves nearly as much self-control as is involved in the conventional doctrine. But self-control will be applied more to abstaining from interference with the freedom of others than to restraining one's own freedom. It may, I think, be hoped that with the right education from the start this respect for the personality and freedom of others may become comparatively easy; but for those of us who have been brought up to believe that we have a right to place a veto upon the actions of others in the name of virtue, it is undoubtedly difficult to forego the exercise of this agreeable form of persecution. It may even be impossible. But it is not to be inferred that it would be impossible to those who had been taught from the first a less restrictive morality. The essence of a good marriage is respect for each other's personality combined with that deep intimacy, physical, mental, and spiritual, which makes a serious love between man and

---

* Reprinted from pp. 182-83, 188, 245-46, and 249-50, by permission of the publishers: Liveright, New York, and George Allen & Unwin, London. Copyright © R, 1957, by Bertrand Russell.

woman the most ̄fructifying of all human experiences. Such love, like everything that is great and precious, demands its own morality, and frequently entails a sacrifice of the less to the greater; but such sacrifice must be voluntary, for, where it is not, it will destroy the very basis of the love for the sake of which it is made.

NOTE 6.

ROYAL COMMISSION ON MARRIAGE AND DIVORCE
Report 1951-1955*

Our terms of reference do not embrace a consideration of the moral and social implications of artificial insemination, but we have felt it right to consider in what, if any, circumstances artificial insemination by a donor should constitute grounds for divorce. In our view, if a wife accepts artificial insemination by a donor without the consent of her husband she is doing him a grave injury, an injury which, in its possible consequences, is as serious as that of adultery. The intention is, and the result may be, to father a child on the husband without his knowledge. It was in fact suggested to us that this conduct should be deemed to be adultery for the purpose of the divorce law, whether or not it can accurately be described as adultery. We think that this would not be desirable. Instead, we recommend that acceptance by a wife of artificial insemination by a donor without the consent of her husband should be made a new and separate ground of divorce.

b. Cruelty

[i]

H. v. H.
59 N.J. Super. 227, 157 A. 2d 721 (1959)

CONFORD, J. A. D.

This is an action for divorce by the plaintiff-husband for extreme cruelty of the defendant-wife consisting of her maintenance of an active homosexual relationship with another woman, one E. F. Another count in the complaint charging the same acts to constitute adultery was withdrawn at the trial. The case was uncontested.

* * *

At the conclusion of plaintiff's case, no opposition proofs being tendered, the court . . . concluded that: "Nothing has been shown to indicate any lewd, lascivious or indecent act engaged in by either defendant or E. F. * * *"; that plaintiff's testimony of alleged acts of cruelty

* Cmd. 9678. London: Her Majesty's Stationery Office, 1956, pp. 31-32. Reprinted by permission of the publisher.

"is unsupported and is not corroborated"; and that the proofs failed to establish that defendant's conduct "had a deleterious effect" upon plaintiff's health or safety or that "his life or health would be endangered if he continued the marital relationship." The case was regarded as "factual," turning "solely on the question of credibility of the plaintiff, his witnesses and exhibits."

* * *

In June 1956 plaintiff came home one evening unexpectedly early to find the apartment dark. When he turned the lights on he found the defendant in bed with a young woman by the name of E. F. Asked on direct examination as to his reaction to this occurrence, he testified: "Well, I just don't like the word 'queers.' I just don't like Lesbians of any form. * * * When I seen that they were together I knew right away who she was and it just bothered me very much. I got mad, sick and nervous and everything all at once. * * * Well, right then and there I knew I just couldn't live with her any more. * * * After her being like that for so long, just changed my opinion of her as a woman." He moved out of the apartment at once and never lived with defendant since.

* * *

. . . Plaintiff's position is that homosexual activity is extreme cruelty *per se,* requiring no specific proof of adverse affect upon the injured spouse. . . . [W]e entertain no doubt as to the fact of such practices by this defendant and the sufficiency of the proof and corroboration thereof. Nor need we determine whether they constitute extreme cruelty *per se,* as in the case of adultery in the marital home. . . .

It is difficult to conceive of a more grievous indignity to which a person of normal psychological and sexual constitution could be exposed than the entry by his spouse upon an active and continuous course of homosexual love with another. Added to the insult of sexual disloyalty *per se* (which is present in ordinary adultery) is the natural revulsion arising from knowledge of the fact that the spouse's betrayal takes the form of a perversion. . . .

. . . Few behavioral deviations are more offensive to American *mores* than is homosexuality.[1] Common sense and modern psychiatric knowledge concur as to the incompatibility of homo-

1. Kinsey, Pomeroy and Martin, *Sexual Behavior of the Human Female* (1953), Ch. II, p. 476; George W. Henry (Associate Professor of Clinical Psychiatry, Cornell Medical School), *All the Sexes*, pp. 583-586; Ploscowe, *Sex and the Law* (1951), p. 213; Kirkpatrick, *The Family* (1955), p. 43.

sexuality and the subsistence of marrage between one so afflicted and a normal person.[2]

In the case before us we need not indulge presumptions as to the inward turmoil produced in plaintiff by his discovery of his wife's perversion. Within his limited powers of articulation, he forcefully expressed . . . his disgust at what he had learned about defendant and his resulting instinctive antipathy toward any further matrimonial relationships with her. This was a credible and reasonably expectable reaction of a normal husband and father. It required no further probative embellishment. In order to dispel any question about this related to plaintiff's subsequent visits to defendant's apartment, we took the testimony of the plaintiff at the oral argument, in exercise of our original fact-finding jurisdiction, and he emphatically stated he had had no sexual relations with the defendant since he left her in 1956. We so find.

* * *

Although no point was made of the circumstance in the opinion of the trial court, it will be noted that most of the acts of cruelty charged took place after the parties separated. . . . However, the general rule is that the fact that the parties happen to be living in a state of separation at the time the acts occur does not operate as a bar to their being assigned as a basis for a charge of extreme cruelty. . . . This principle is sound and we accept it. The state of separation may, in the particular circumstances presented, affect the capacity of the acts to injure the plaintiff, but this is a matter to be decided in each case on its own facts. . . .

The judgment is reversed and the cause remanded with directions for the entry of a judgment *nisi* in favor of the plaintiff.

NOTE

CORY, D. W.

The Homosexual in America*

At the age of twenty-five, after determining that I was capable of consummating a marriage, I was wedded to a girl whom I had known from childhood, a lovely and outgoing person, who brought deep understanding to our union and who shared many interests with me. I resolved that marriage would be the end of my sins, that I would sever my ties with the homosexual circles and with my dear friends therein, and build what appeared to be the only life that might be fruitful for me.

I was not long in learning that marriage did not reduce the urge for gratification with men and that I could not have the energy and peace of mind to continue a fecund career while I was in constant struggle with something that was living within me. I needed my former companionships, but I would not allow myself to admit, even in the silence of the thought process, that I wanted them.

Compelled to solve the problem and convinced that the only way to solve it was to rid myself of the homosexual urge, I visited a well-known psychoanalyst, who assured me that I could be helped.

Gradually, as the long analysis proceeded, it became apparent to me that he was going to help me overcome my feelings of shame, guilt, remorse, rather than overcome the impulses which brought forward these feelings. I fought bitterly against this plan. I wanted my shame and was proud of it. In fact, I needed it. But my battle only served to prove to myself, with the doctor's aid, that shame and guilt were props that I had been using to make possible a continuation of the homosexual life I claimed to be in revolt against. By feeling guilty and remorseful, I exonerated myself of all responsibility, proving to my own self that homosexuality was a compulsion carried out against my will; and this exoneration made it possible to continue the very same homosexual life. But the price I was paying was severe.

Today, after many years of a successful marriage, with a happy home and with children, and with a firm bond of friendship that has developed with a man who has been an inspiring person in my life, I sit down to relate what it means to be a homosexual. This is not the thinking of a bitter and unhappy person. It is the accumulated experience and outlook of one who has been through the struggle with himself and with society.

[*ii*]

BAMPTON v. BAMPTON
[1959] 2 All E.R. 766

HODSON, L. J. This is an appeal from a judgment of BARNARD, J., sitting at Winchester on Nov. 27, 1958, when he dismissed a petition for divorce presented by Mrs. Doris Eileen Bampton against her husband founded on sodomy and cruelty. The learned judge found that the cruelty

---

2. "If a person has developed a well-established homosexual pattern, the probabilities are that he will not have a genuine desire for marriage. It is doubtful that the interests of the individuals concerned, or of society are well served by contracting marriage with a homosexual." Henry, *op. cit.*, supra, at p. 347.

* Reprinted with permission from *The Homosexual in America* by Donald Webster Cory, pp. xv-xvi. Copyright 1951, Chilton Company, Philadelphia & New York.

was not proved, partly because he did not find that the wife's health had been injured, or that she was in reasonable apprehension of injury to health, but he also held in respect of the serious allegation of cruelty as opposed to sodomy, that the wife was a consenting party to some disgusting sexual perversions which had taken place between them, the husband using the wife's mouth. The sodomy charge was dismissed on the ground that the wife had consented to sodomy, and therefore was not entitled to relief. The husband by his pleading had denied the charges of sodomy and the charges of cruelty, and in the alternative had pleaded that his wife had condoned both by living with him until Sept. 10, 1957, when he left this country for Jamaica in the course of his service as a steward on board a merchant ship. . . .

The question which falls for decision (and it is the main ground of appeal) is whether the consent of the wife to the act of sodomy, as opposed to the cruelty, was a bar to her obtaining relief ; and, if such consent is a bar, whether it is right to say that there was here a real consent. In considering the second question, the relationship of husband and wife lies in the background. It should be recognized that the relationship of husband and wife being what it is, and the obligations of one to the other being what they are, it is not readily to be taken against a wife in a situation such as exists in this case, especially a young wife, that there has been a real consent. If the same acts were under consideration between two persons, not being husband and wife, where this relationship did not exist, the presence or absence of consent would have to be considered in a different way.

First as to the facts. Was there a real consent? The learned judge held that, as to the act of sodomy, there was. The parties were married in the year 1953 when the wife was only nineteen years of age, and the husband twenty-five ; and the acts of sodomy which were proved took place from 1955 onwards, beginning with an attempt made in April, 1955, before the birth of the younger child on June 6, 1955. That attempt was rejected and was successfully opposed by the wife ; but, as the judge found, subsequently, during the next two years of the married life, there were attempts which were successful. In this connection I should say that the wife was a witness who was obviously a straightforward witness, frank and simple in character, and moreover intelligent, able to appreciate the questions which were put to her, and fully alive to her obligations to her husband which she had taken on herself on marriage. She was by no means anxious to bring this marriage to an end ; she was very much in love with her husband,

and was anxious to keep it in being not only for her own sake, but for that of the children. . . . The husband's evidence, in so far as it was in conflict with that of the wife, was rejected by the learned judge ; but in finding the sodomy proved, he was supported in his finding by an admission which the husband himself made that he may have penetrated the back passage of the wife on one occasion. Another witness, a friend of the parties, gave evidence that the husband made an admission to him which supported the wife's case. . . .

As to consent, I think that it is necessary to read what the wife said in her evidence about this. First, as to the attempt. She was asked to say when her husband first made the desire to enter her rectum apparent, and she answered:

"In 1955. . . . We were lying in bed, and I had my back to him, and he started messing around with himself on my buttocks, and he said he had always fancied some of that. . . . I said, 'Well, you are not going to get it from me'. . . . He then said something to the effect, 'Let me have a little try'. . . . He continued to mess around with me. He was trying to insert his penis into my rectum."

"Q.—Did you object to that, or consent to it, or what? A.—I told him it was very painful, and that I wouldn't consent to it, but he was always so affectionate to me at those times. That was the only thing I enjoyed. He was always very affectionate with it and before and during the time he was working up to it. Q.—It may be said that you should have fought him off, or something of that kind. I think you agree you didn't fight him off? A.—I didn't fight, no. Q.—Tell my Lord why. A.—Well, because for one thing I was glad of the affection he was showing me, and he always bragged what other women did. I was worried if I might lose him if I didn't let him try."

She was then asked her age, and she said twenty-four, so that in 1955 she was just twenty-one, the husband being six years older. She was asked why she had not complained, and her answer was:

"Because I thought that was something I could handle myself . . . I thought that once I was sterilized, my husband would stop those things."

She had had a very difficult confinement on the birth of each of her children, and the danger of her having any further children was so great that it was thought right, with the consent of both the husband and the wife, that she should be sterilized, and that had been done in 1957. The last occasion when sodomy was committed, she said, was in August, 1957, which was the year that she left. She had sexual intercourse with her husband after the last occasion. It was on Sept. 10 that he actually went to sea, and she would not have anything more to do with him.

With regard to the question of consent, so far as ordinary sexual intercourse was concerned, it is clear that the wife was able, when she wished, to refuse the husband sexual intercourse because she said that sometimes, when he required sexual relations, she did refuse it. In another part of her evidence, in cross-examination—the cross-examination was not directed, of course, to the question of consent because the husband's case was that the sodomy had not been committed—she was asked to remember the particular occasion when she complained that he was hurting her, and she . . . said:

"There was a time when he started in my rectum and I asked him to carry on in a normal fashion, which he did, and there was a time,"

and then she refers to another occasion. That answer indicates that he did not continue in the act of sodomy, or attempt to commit the act of sodomy, when she asked him to do otherwise. In that state of the evidence, bearing in mind not only the relationship between husband and wife which I have mentioned, but also the fact that there was still other disgusting activities which took place between these two people which the wife, whether she disliked them or not, assented to over a period of time, I feel it impossible to find myself in disagreement with the learned judge in holding that there was consent—and when I say consent, I mean a real consent. There was no question of consent being compelled by fraud or duress; there was no threat, nothing of that kind. There is nothing in the case, having regard particularly to the number of occasions when this act was successfully achieved, which enables me to form an opinion different from that which the learned judge, in my view, rightly formed, namely, that there was here the element of consent which would bar the wife's claim to relief.

So far as the law about consent is concerned, the submission made was (i) that consent in itself is no bar . . . it was pointed out that in the statute (and, indeed, in all the statutes relating to this offence) there is no reference to consent. . . . [I]n the ecclesiastical courts divorce a mensa et thoro could be granted on the ground of adultery, cruelty or unnatural offences, and sodomy would be an unnatural offence. When the matter came to be regulated by statute in 1857, divorce a vinculo matrimonii was for the first time made available, and the grounds which were open to a wife were these, that the husband had been guilty of adultery coupled with such aggravated enormity as incest, bigamy, rape, sodomy, bestiality, cruelty or desertion without reasonable excuse for two years or upwards. The

word "sodomy" appears there between the words "rape" and "bestiality", which would not involve the relationship of husband and wife; and it may be that the legislature had in mind sodomy committed by the husband with a third party. But there were cases brought by wives on the ground of sodomy with themselves, as appears from a decision of BARGRAVE DEANE, J., in C. v. C. . . . ((1905), 22 T.L.R. 26), where the point was taken on behalf of the husband that sodomy with a wife was not a matrimonial offence under s. 27 of the Act of 1857, which included an offence with a third person; and the learned judge said that within his own knowledge "many decrees have been pronounced in similar cases".

GREER, L. J., said [in *Statham* v. *Statham* [1928] All E.R. Rep. 219, 224]:

"It seems to me impossible to say that where two people commit sodomy together, either of them is entitled to ask the court for a decree based on an act to which he or she was a party, and if the facts appear in the evidence, the judge . . . cannot shut his eyes to them."

The learned lord justice deals with the question of condonation and consent to some extent together, although no doubt he recognized that the question of consent would arise before or contemporaneously with the act charged, and condonation would arise subsequently. RUSSELL, L. J., in his judgment analyzed the wife's evidence, which . . . ([1929] P. at. p. 156), made it quite clear:

"(1) that her husband explained to her quite plainly the exact physical act which he wished to do upon her; (2) that she assented and placed her body at his disposal for the purpose of that act being committed; (3) that no compulsion of any kind was brought to bear upon her; and (4) that the only reason given by her for refusing subsequent invitations to a similar act was fear of pain. It thus appears that the wife was a consenting party to the only act upon which a decree for divorce could be founded. It is immaterial whether or not she knew that the act to which she consented was called sodomy or that it was a crime. The act was accurately explained to her beforehand, she must have known that it was against nature, yet she consented of her free will to its commission. In these circumstances it is impossible for her to obtain a decree for divorce based solely upon an act of the husband to which she was a consenting party. The husband is entitled, in my opinion, to have the petition for divorce dismissed."

* * *

. . . I think that this petition was rightly dismissed, and I would dismiss the appeal.

NOTES

NOTE 1.

FREUD, SIGMUND
Three Essays on Sexuality (1905)*

The normal sexual aim is regarded as being the union of the genitals in the act known as copulation, which leads to a release of the sexual tension and a temporary extinction of the sexual instinct—a satisfaction analogous to the sating of hunger. But even in the most normal sexual process we may detect rudiments which, if they had developed, would have led to the deviations described as "perversions". For there are certain intermediate relations to the sexual object, such as touching and looking at it, which lie on the road towards copulation and are recognized as being preliminary sexual aims. On the one hand these activities are themselves accompanied by pleasure, and on the other hand they intensify the excitation, which should persist until the final sexual aim is attained. Moreover, the kiss, one particular contact of this kind, between the mucous membrane of the lips of the two people concerned, is held in high sexual esteem among many nations (including the most highly civilized ones), in spite of the fact that the parts of the body involved do not form part of the sexual apparatus but constitute the entrance to the digestive tract. Here, then, are factors which provide a point of contact between the perversions and normal sexual life and which can also serve as a basis for their classification. Perversions are sexual activities which either (a) extend, in an anatomical sense, beyond the regions of the body that are designed for sexual union, or (b) linger over the intermediate relations to the sexual object which should normally be traversed rapidly on the path towards the final sexual aim.

* * *

The use of the mouth as a sexual organ is regarded as a perversion if the lips (or tongue) of one person are brought into contact with the genitals of another, but not if the mucous membranes of the lips of both of them come together. This exception is the point of contact with what is normal. Those who condemn the other practices (which have no doubt been common among mankind from primaeval times) as being perversions, are giving way to an unmistakable feeling of *disgust*, which protects them from accepting sexual aims of the kind. The limits of such dis-

---

* Reprinted from: *The Standard Edition of the Complete Psychological Works of Sigmund Freud*, London: The Hogarth Press, 1953 (pp. 149-52, 160-61). Reprinted with permission of the publisher and of Basic Books, Inc., New York.

gust are, however, often purely conventional: a man who will kiss a pretty girl's lips passionately, may perhaps be disgusted at the idea of using her tooth-brush, though there are no grounds for supposing that his own oral cavity, for which he feels no disgust, is any cleaner than the girl's. Here, then, our attention is drawn to the factor of disgust, which interferes with the libidinal overvaluation of the sexual object but can in turn be overridden by libido. Disgust seems to be one of the forces which have led to a restriction of the sexual aim. These forces do not as a rule extend to the genitals themselves. But there is no doubt that the genitals of the opposite sex can in themselves be an object of disgust and that such an attitude is one of the characteristics of all hysterics, and especially of hysterical women. The sexual instinct in its strength enjoys overriding this disgust. . . .

Where the anus is concerned it becomes still clearer that it is disgust which stamps that sexual aim as a perversion. I hope, however, I shall not be accused of partisanship when I assert that people who try to account for this disgust by saying that the organ in question serves the function of excretion and comes in contact with excrement—a thing which is disgusting in itself—are not much more to the point than hysterical girls who account for their disgust at the male genital by saying that it serves to void urine.

* * *

It is natural that medical men, who first studied perversions in outstanding examples and under special conditions, should have been inclined to regard them, like inversion, as indications of degeneracy or disease. Nevertheless, it is even easier to dispose of that view in this case than in that of inversion. Everyday experience has shown that most of these extensions, or at any rate the less severe of them, are constituents which are rarely absent from the sexual life of healthy people, and are judged by them no differently from other intimate events. If circumstances favour such an occurrence, normal people too can substitute a perversion of this kind for the normal sexual aim for quite a time, or can find place for the one alongside the other. No healthy person, it appears, can fail to make some addition that might be called perverse to the normal sexual aim; and the universality of this finding is in itself enough to show how inappropriate it is to use the word perversion as a term of reproach. In the sphere of sexual life we are brought up against peculiar and, indeed, insoluble difficulties as soon as we try to draw a sharp line to distinguish mere variations within the range of what is physiological from pathological symptoms.

Nevertheless, in some of these perversions the quality of the new sexual aim is of a kind to demand special examination. Certain of them are so far removed from the normal in their content that we cannot avoid pronouncing them "pathological". This is especially so where (as, for instance, in cases of licking excrement or of intercourse with dead bodies) the sexual instinct goes to astonishing lengths in successfully overriding the resistances of shame, disgust, horror or pain. But even in such cases we should not be too ready to assume that people who act in this way will necessarily turn out to be insane or subject to grave abnormalities of other kinds. Here again we cannot escape from the fact that people whose behaviour is in other respects normal can, under the domination of the most unruly of all the instincts, put themselves in the category of sick persons in the single sphere of sexual life. On the other hand, manifest abnormality in the other relations of life can invariably be shown to have a background of abnormal sexual conduct.

In the majority of instances the pathological character in a perversion is found to lie not in the *content* of the new sexual aim but in its relation to the normal. If a perversion, instead of appearing merely *alongside* the normal sexual aim and object, and only when circumstances are unfavourable to *them* and favourable to *it*—if, instead of this, it ousts them completely and takes their place in *all* circumstances—if, in short, a perversion has the characteristics of exclusiveness and fixation—then we shall usually be justified in regarding it as a pathological symptom.

NOTE 2.

GUYON, RENÉ
Sex Life and Sex Ethics*

There are no sexual aberrations, there are only differences of procedure, cunningly combined according to individual variations of taste, together with preferences for particular persons or classes of person; and that is all. These considerations allow us to draw up the following principles:

(i) It is wrong to suppose that ordinary coitus is the only normal mode of sexual satisfaction:

---

* London: The Bodley Head 1933, pp. 338-339. Reprinted with permission of the publisher. Reprinted by permission of Alfred A. Knopf, Inc., from *Ethics of Sexual Acts* by René Guyon, translated by J. C. & Ingeborg Flugel, copyright 1934, 1948 by Alfred A. Knopf, Inc.

it is the only normal mode of reproduction, but that is quite a different thing.

(ii) Every mechanical means of producing sexual pleasure is normal and legitimate; there is no room for moral distinctions between the various available methods; all are equally justifiable and equally suited to their particular ends.

(iii) The personal characteristics of the sexual partner have nothing to do with the physiological manifestations of sexual pleasure itself; the importance attributed to these characteristics is a matter of convention, and varies from age to age; indeed, even though the personality of the partner were totally unknown, this would make no difference to the sexual act, the specific pleasure of which would remain completely unaffected.

NOTE 3.

ELLIS, ALBERT
Marriage Counseling with Couples Indicating Sexual Incompatibility*

Mrs. Carre's chief complaint in her marriage was not that her husband wanted sex relations too often, but that he desired certain types of relations, including oral and anal participation, which she considered "unnatural." Said, eventually, the counselor: "Actually, Mrs. Carre, *you*, and not your husband, are the unnatural partner or, to use a misleading but widely employed term, a 'sexual pervert.' For sexual perversion consists, from a scientific standpoint, of anyone's being able to derive satisfaction from only *one* specialized mode of sex activity, and from no other method. It is true that homosexuals, masochists, exhibitionists, and other deviants are perverted when they *exclusively* or *mainly* derive sex enjoyment from their one particular mode of sex conduct. But it is just as true that any man or woman who can *only* enjoy face-to-face intercourse, particularly in the one position with the man surmounting the woman, is as much a pervert as the homosexual or sadist. Since you tell me that you can enjoy only so-called 'normal' intercourse, while your husband desires several so-called 'abnormal' variations, the truth of the matter is that you, apparently, are 'perverted' while he is perfectly 'normal.' Not until you get rid of this silly fetich about 'normal' coitus will you actually become 'normal' and 'non-perverted.' "

Mrs. Carre, as the counselor had intended her to be, was quite shocked. But, with a few more sessions of reorientation about "normality" and "abnormality" in sex relations, and with some sexual experimentation with her husband, she

---

* 15 *Marriage and Family Living* 53 (1953).

got entirely over her "normal intercourse" fetich, and she and Mr. Carre no longer are sexually incompatible.

[iii]
RECORD v. RECORD
244 Iowa 743, 57 N.W. 2d 911 (1953)

* * *

LARSON, JUSTICE

Plaintiff alleges as ground for divorce that "the defendant * * * has been guilty of such cruel and inhuman treatment as to impair her health and endanger her life."

Plaintiff, age 50, and defendant a year older, were married June 5, 1950 and lived together until March, 1952, when plaintiff filed her petition for divorce. Both had been previously married and plaintiff . . . was employed at Wilson & Co. as a jowl press operator, earning $1.35 per hour. She continued to work after marriage. Defendant was employed by the Chicago, Northwestern Railroad Company as a yard clerk and last year earned $3626 which was used for household and living expenses. . . .

Apparently there was no serious trouble between the couple until nearly a year after the marriage. On this occasion, while plaintiff was at home on a four month sick leave in the summer of 1951, the defendant became over amorous in midday and in the scuffle that followed, plaintiff complained that she suffered a twisted neck, and some two inch scratches on her legs. Defendant desisted on plaintiff's stern warning.

Plaintiff had suffered from nervousness and severe headaches for some years. During the past year she claims her condition became worse due to the actions of the defendant. Plaintiff further complained that defendant was unclean, but admitted that he never had struck her or threatened her; never drank, gambled, or stayed out nights; never called her names or shouted or swore at her; and did not embarrass her in the eyes of the neighbors. He did get meals, do washings and bring home the groceries; worked in the yard and attended her when she was ill in bed. Plaintiff maintained her normal weight of 128 pounds, but stated she had been under the care of an osteopath and a medical doctor for some time.

The defendant relies solely, as basis for reversal, on the allegation that plaintiff failed to prove that defendant had been guilty of cruel and inhuman treatment such as to endanger the life of plaintiff. [T]wo questions are thus involved: 1. The treatment complained of by plaintiff, and 2. the effect thereof on plaintiff, To determine whether or not plaintiff brings

herself under the statutory requirements we shall apply them here, for the rights to divorce is not a natural one but is purely statutory. . . .

Code Section 598.8 Code 1950, I.C.A., provides: "Divorces * * * may be decreed against the husband for the following causes * * * 5. When he is guilty of such inhuman treatment as to endanger the life of his wife."

. . . The only such acts complained of by plaintiff of this nature related to a scuffling or wrestling when defendant sought relations with his wife. No blows were ever struck. . . . There were no other assaults of any nature, unless the complaint by plaintiff that defendant had "B.O." is so held. We think that complaint trivial, indeed.

It is difficult to provide corroborative testimony regarding the reasonableness or unreasonableness of defendant's demands for physical relations. In marriage there are certain marital obligations and duties. The contemplated love and affection of the parties presume reasonable relations of that nature. Having each been married before it must have been contemplated. The burden rests, as always, with the complainant. . . . Medical testimony would aid us if the results injured plaintiff's health, but no such evidence was offered. As to the number of defendant's requests, there was some dispute. Plaintiff said, "Well, once a week or so, maybe." Defendant said "once a month." Plaintiff claimed the requests were at unreasonable hours in the night when she was tired and exhausted from a hard day's work. To the question, why she refused, she answered: "Well, I was sick, working long hours, I was tired, exhausted, I would have to get to bed early and he would wake me up in the middle of the night * * *."

We note that on these occasions defendant did not persist, but believed himself abused, sulked and became silent, sometimes for days, and on one occasion "two or three weeks." This is not a case of sexual abuse. The facts here related to defendant's request, plaintiff's refusal and defendant's pouting. The effect, if any, was mental. We do not believe such actions by defendant amount to cruelty or inhuman treatment.

* * *

[I]n this case there is an apparent loss of mutual love and affection. It is not so apparent as to the cause. Was it disappointment by the plaintiff because defendant did not insist that she quit her job at the packing plant? Was it disappointment by the defendant because plaintiff was unresponsive to his desire for physical relations? Did defendant thereby sulk in silence and neglect his appearance? Do all of these actions add up to more than incompatibility? We think not. Incompatibility is not a ground for divorce in this state. . . .

We are aware that plaintiff claims mental distress because of these acts of defendant and claims she suffered serious headaches and nervousness, stating: "I just can't take it, I am so nervous and irritable." Many instances that are conclusions rather than facts appear in plaintiff's testimony, as well as those who furnish corroboration for her.

When it appears that the inhuman treatment complained about refers to mental torment, two factors become important. 1. The nature of the acts complained of and 2, the sensitiveness or mental and physical makeup of the complaining spouse. . . .

In Thompson v. Thompson, 186 Iowa 1066, 173 N.W. 55, 5 A.L.R. 710, we said: "Life may be endangered by treatment, though it involves no physical violence. * * * The mind can grasp the possibility of inhuman treatment that does not endanger life. Whether it does or not, depends, not only upon the physical, but upon the moral, mental, or spiritual quality of the one made subject to the treatment."

In the case before us the plaintiff contends that the treatment she received so worried her as to endanger her life.

The record is lacking in evidence to prove that plaintiff is a frail, sensitive person. Her work for years at the packing plant at "hard fast work" where odors are known not to be sweet, and the prior ailment and nervousness do not bespeak of frailty. Employment from 7 A.M. until 6 or 7 P.M. could exhaust, tire and fray the nerves of strong persons. We conclude that she has not shown herself in the delicate class . . . entitling her to special consideration in cases of this kind.

*   *   *

. . . In Olson v. Olson, . . . [130 Iowa 353, 106 N.W. 759], we said: "A little patience, a spirit of forgiveness, and a measure of toleration for the frailties of human nature will do more for these parties than a decree of divorce. * * * while we may not compel husband and wife to live together, we can at least make it so difficult to obtain a divorce as to encourage another effort at observance of the matrimonial vows." We think the same is applicable here, and urge upon the parties to make another effort to understand and sympathize with each other's problems.

*   *   *

The claimed aggravation of her nervousness and headaches we feel falls short of endangering

her life, so as to justify the court's action in dissolving this marriage to society's detriment.

. . . We are satisfied that the case should be and it is reversed. . . .

NOTES

NOTE 1.

RECORD v. RECORD
Eight Years Later

Following the reversal by the Supreme Court of Iowa there was no reconciliation and two years later Mr. Record secured a divorce from Mrs. Record on the charge of desertion.

Mrs. Record has been in good health since the divorce and is still working daily at a local meat packing company.

An interesting sidelight on the case was that Mr. Record became engaged to marry another woman prior to the time that the Supreme Court of Iowa reversed the lower Court and of course, after the reversal of the lower Court he found that he was still married and had to break the engagement. [Letter dated Jan. 19, 1961 from Richard F. Nazette, attorney for the wife.]

NOTE 2.

KINSEY, ALFRED C.; POMEROY, WARDELL B.; and MARTIN, CLYDE E.

Sexual Behavior in the Human Male*

In the population as a whole . . . the highest frequencies of marital intercourse occur in the youngest age groups. Males who are married between 16 and 20 start with frequencies which average 3.9 for the population as a whole . . . and many individuals at that age have intercourse on an average of 5, 7, 10 or more times per week. There is considerable individual variation, and the 15 per cent of the group who are capable of multiple orgasm . . . may regularly secure 14, 21, or more climaxes per week from intercourse with their wives. Frequencies drop steadily from the teens to about 2.9 at age 30, to 1.8 at age 50, and to 0.9 at age 60. . . .

NOTE 3.

EISENSTEIN, V. W.

Neurotic Interaction in Marriage†

CLINICAL EXPERIENCE indicates that a good sex life does not assure a happy marriage, nor do sexual difficulties necessarily cause marital breakdowns. Sexual symptoms occur in the context

---

* Philadelphia: W. B. Saunders Co., 1948, p. 569. Reprinted with permission of the Institute for Sex Research, Inc.
† New York: Basic Books, Inc., 1956, pp. 101-102. Reprinted with permission of the publisher.

of either manifestly harmonious or frankly discordant relationships. There is no question, however, that happy marriages, by and large, are marked by a greater degree of sexual satisfaction, while unhappy marriages have a much higher incidence of sexual conflicts.

The sexual symptom is only one of many indicators of individual emotional problems which find numerous avenues of expression in a marriage. Disturbances in the sex life are related to the individual neurosis, to the neurotic choice of a mate, and to the resultant type of neurotic interaction between partners.

* * *

Since the marital union is a dynamic rather than a static relationship, circumstances are bound to arise through which unconscious infantile conflicts may be revived and find expression in sexual disorders. Premature ejaculation or impotence in the male, for instance, may appear after the wife has given birth, or has undergone surgery. Or it may occur following a death in the family, or after an injury to self-esteem in a business or professional matter. What is popularly known as sexual incompatibility may arise when the partner acquires a new meaning in the unconscious life of the affected individual, thus reactivating deepseated conflicts centered around a parent or sibling in early childhood.

NOTE 4.

DEUTSCH, HELENE
The Psychology of Women*

Woman's frequent fear of coitus originates in the fact that it implies an injury to her physical integrity; it can be compared to man's fear of castration. Under special circumstances, the pain and masochistic character of the experience also mobilize destructive tendencies that lend this fear the character of the fear of death. In this connection, the following observation of an obsessive neurotic proved enlightening. This young woman constantly tormented herself with feelings of guilt; she accused herself of having caused the deaths of various relatives by acts of negligence. After she married and overcame the first difficulties of coitus, she achieved full orgastic gratification. But after achieving the orgastic eclipse of consciousness, she was seized by the fear of never being able to awaken from this state. During each following coitus she convulsively watched herself in order "not to go too far," and as a result became frigid. The destructive elements intensified

her masochistic readiness and transformed her pleasure into fear of death. Usually such a fear of death is mobilized only during childbirth or during the expectation of childbirth. However, there are many women who cannot experience and enjoy the sexual act without conscious or unconscious ideas about childbirth, and in such cases the associative connection between the two acts has a disturbing effect.

Naturally, the justified fear of undesired pregnancy must not be termed pathologic, but it can produce the effect of a direct inhibition, particularly if it is obsessively exaggerated, as is often the case. The other form of the conscious association with the reproductive function, the wish for a child, particularly if its fulfillment is beset with difficulties, can also exert an inhibiting effect on the orgasm and perhaps even make conception difficult.

NOTE 5.

WOODWARD, L. E.
Discussion Following Murdock's "A Comparative Anthropological Approach"*

[W]ith regard to sexual behavior, two men may each have five orgasms a week. One may do so to boost his insecure ego and convince himself that he is a regular man, prostituting his partner completely while he affords himself this psychological tonic. The orgasm of another may be achieved as the expression of a deep and abiding affection and as a part of a mutually enriching experience which gives him and his partner both a profound sense of belongingness and of shared purpose. If orgasms are the only measure, or if conformance to the heterosexual pattern is the only norm, the two men would appear alike. Yet their experiences are fundamentally different and have very differing kinds of value just as the sun and a tallow candle are very different and have widely different value though the light from each vibrates at the same rate.

NOTE 6.

KRAMPE v. KRAMPE
339 S.W. 2d 447 (Ky. 1960)

BIRD, CHIEF JUSTICE.

Beatrice Krampe sued for divorce on the ground that her husband, Edward Krampe, had habitually behaved toward her "in such a cruel and inhuman manner as to indicate a settled aversion to her and to destroy permanently her peace and happiness."

---

* New York: Grune & Stratton, 1945, Vol. II, pp. 92-93. Reprinted with permission of the publisher.

---

* *Journal of Social Hygiene*, Vol. 36 (1950), p. 156. Reprinted with permission of the American Social Health Association.

The husband, without seeking affirmative relief, denied the allegations of the complaint.

The trial court refused to grant the divorce and dismissed the complaint. The wife appeals.

Under the authority of Coleman v. Coleman, Ky., 269 S.W.2d 730, Mrs. Krampe must have proven at least one of two things to entitle her to a divorce upon the grounds alleged. She must have shown either that the acts of her husband indicated a settled aversion to his part or that his acts were such as would destroy her peace and happiness during the marriage.

All of Mrs. Krampe's complaints against her husband originate in his insistence on sexual intercourse. There is nothing in the record to indicate that his desires were abnormal or that his demands, under normal circumstances, were unreasonable. His conduct not only refutes the idea of aversion but rather shows a keen desire for his wife's attention. Mrs. Krampe has failed to show an aversion. Therefore, if she is entitled to the relief sought upon the grounds alleged she must not only show that his acts constituted cruelty under the circumstances but that her peace and happiness have been destroyed by these acts.

The Court is reluctant to go into the unpleasant and embarrassing details of the evidence and we shall therefore state conclusions only.

It is apparent from the whole record that Mrs. Krampe is so allergic to sexual intercourse that she becomes both mentally and physically disturbed by the thought of sexual intercourse with her husband. We have concluded that, if her peace and happiness have been destroyed, it has resulted from her state of mind. We are unable to say from the record that the husband's conduct contributed to that state of mind. There is convincing evidence in the record that this state of mind existed before the marriage. The trial court could, from the evidence, have concluded that her peace and happiness were destroyed because of her state of mind, a condition for which her husband was not responsible. She would not be entitled to relief upon the ground asserted unless her husband was responsible for the loss of peace and happiness.

* * *

The judgment is affirmed.

c. Desertion

WILLIAMS v. WILLIAMS
121 Mo. App. 349, 99 S.W. 42 (1906)

BLAND, P. J.   The action is for divorce. . . . It is alleged that from the date of the marriage until the date of separation, about 11 years, plaintiff treated defendant with kindness and affection, but that defendant without any just cause has persis-

tently refused to permit plaintiff to have any sexual intercourse with her whatever. . . . After hearing the evidence the circuit court found against plaintiff and dismissed his bill. Plaintiff's evidence is that at no time during the marriage would the defendant consent or submit to sexual intercourse with him, though often at proper times and places importuned by him to do so, and that he never did have sexual intercourse with her; that he was gentle and kind with her when he importuned her to concede to him his matrimonial rights, as well as at all other times; that the only excuse defendant ever made for not doing so was that "she could not." There is no direct evidence that defendant was incapable of having sexual intercourse on account of any physical deformity or want of proper development. But there is evidence tending to show that she was suffering from organic disease of the heart, was nervous, feeble, and subject to fainting spells. Plaintiff testified that he understood before he married defendant that she had some sort of heart trouble; that he saw her faint one time, but did not know that the faint was caused from heart trouble or weakness. His evidence tended to show that after the marriage the defendant had fainting spells on an average of one in every three to four months; that she recovered from the effects of these spells in from one to two days, and would be able to go about her ordinary duties; that she attended dances and danced, played on drums and triangles in an amateur orchestral company, and attended the World's Fair frequently in July and August; that aside from her refusal to have sexual intercourse with him she was a kind, attentive, and affectionate wife.

. . . Dr. Pittman, defendant's family physician, testified that she was suffering from organic disease of the heart, from which there was very little, if any, hope of recovery, and gave it as his opinion, from his knowledge of her condition and knowledge of her heart trouble, that any excitement would produce a disturbance to the general nervous system, and that the act of sexual intercourse would certainly be a disturbance of the action of the heart and to her general condition, and that she was not in a condition to have sexual intercourse; that she was a small delicate woman, weighing not over 110 pounds, and requires constant rest. Other expert evidence on the part of the defendant tended to corroborate that of Dr. Pittman. On behalf of the plaintiff the expert evidence tended to show that the exercise of sexual intercourse by her before or after recovery from one of the fainting spells would not be injurious to her health, but that, if she had intercourse, the hazard of conception would be present, and conception would be injurious to one in her physical condition. The defendant did not testify.

Impotency at the time of marriage continuing thereafter is a statutory ground for divorce, but the refusal of either to have sexual intercourse with the other is not made a specific cause for divorce. Section 2921, Rev. St. Mo. 1899. So, also, if one of the parties absent him or herself without reasonable cause for the space of one year, the other party is, under the statute, entitled to divorce. Plaintiff contends that under the evidence he is entitled to a divorce on the ground of impotency, or of desertion, or on both grounds.

* * *

. . . Nelson says: "Where there is no peculiar form of statute indicating a contrary definition or term desertion is believed to be that the statutory term desertion, as applied to husband and wife, means a cessation of the marital relation, and * * * it means the ceasing to live together as husband and wife. Marriage is the union of opposite sexes, and sexual intercourse is the distinguishing feature of the union." Paragraph B. vol. 14, p. 612, Enc. Law & Procedure, it is said: "In some states a persistent and continued refusal of marital intercourse by one of the spouses without cause or justification, constitutes desertion, although the parties still live beneath the same roof . . . By the weight of authority, however, the mere withdrawal from the marital bed is not sufficient to constitute the offense. There must be a substantial abandonment of other marital duties also"— . . .

. . . In Davis v. Davis, 60 Mo. App. 545, and State v. Weber, 48 Mo. App. 500, it was held, to establish desertion, three things must occur— "cessation from cohabitation continuing over a year, intention in the mind of the deserter not to resume cohabitation, and absence without the consent of the other party." Hence to establish desertion under our statute (section 2921, supra) there must not only be a cessation of copula, but the husband and wife must not live together under the same roof. . . .

The evidence is that the husband abided with his wife under the same roof, and there is none to show they did not sleep in the same room to within a few days before the petition was filed. Hence plaintiff is not entitled to a divorce on the ground of abandonment or desertion. It is neither directly or indirectly charged in the petition that the defendant at the time the contract of marriage was entered into was impotent and has continued so. Hence this ground for divorce is not before us for consideration, though there is some evidence in the record tending to prove it. The petition charges, in substance, that defendant's conduct in refusing to have sexual intercourse

with him injured his health. Cruel and barbarous treatment is a ground for divorce. This is not charged in the petition, nor is there any evidence tending to show that the plaintiff's health was injured by the refusal of the defendant to have sexual intercourse with him. The evidence is not clear or convincing in respect to the condition of the defendant's health at the date of the marriage, or for several years thereafter. In justification of her conduct for the last three or four years it is proper to state that the evidence tends to show the exercise of sexual intercourse would injure her health, and that the condition of pregnancy would be hazardous to her life.

It seems to us that, viewed from any standpoint, the evidence is insufficient to warrant a divorce on any ground stated in the petition, or intended to be stated in it. But we do not wish to be understood as holding that plaintiff is barred by the judgment in this action from prosecuting another action against his wife for divorce on grounds other than those alleged in his petition in this case, and the judgment of the circuit court is modified to read: Plaintiff's bill is dismissed without prejudice to resume on grounds not alleged in the bill.

NOTES

NOTE 1.

BUXTON v. ULLMAN
147 Conn. 48, 156 A. 2d 508 (1959)
(dismissed 367 U.S. 497 (1961). See Ch. I, p. 377)

BALDWIN, C. J.:

* * *

The complaints in these four actions seek declaratory judgment as to the constitutionality of § 53-32 of the General Statutes, prohibiting the use of any drug, medicinal article or instrument for the purpose of preventing conception, and § 54-196, prohibiting the counseling or abetting of such use. The plaintiff C. Lee Buxton is a licensed physician. The plaintiff Jane Doe is a married woman living with her husband. The plaintiffs Paul and Pauline Poe, as well as the plaintiffs Harold and Hanna Hoe, are husband and wife. . . . They are patients of Dr. Buxton. . . .

* * *

. . . In Buxton v. Ullman, the complaint alleges, in substance, and the demurrer admits, that the plaintiff, a licensed physician, has a patient, Jane Doe, a married woman twenty-five years of age, living with her husband. She had been admitted to the obstetrical service of the hospital where the plaintiff, an eminently qualified obstetrician and gynecologist, was in charge. She was three and one-half months pregnant and developed a condition which brought her to the very brink of death. Her physical condition is now such that conception and another pregnancy would be exceedingly dangerous to her life. She needs and requires advice as to what preventive measures can be taken to avert a recurrence of the experience she suffered. She claims a right to live a normal married life with her husband. She has asked the plaintiff for medical advice, and he has knowledge of drugs, medicinal articles and instruments which could be used by her to prevent conception and avoid the serious consequences of another pregnancy. . . .

* * *

. . . It may well be that the use of contraceptives is indicated as the best and safest preventive measure which medical science can offer these plaintiffs. That fact does not make it absolutely necessary for the legislature to accept such a solution in all cases, where there is . . . another alternative, abstinence from sexual intercourse. We cannot say that the legislature, in weighing the considerations for and against an exception legalizing contraceptive measures in cases such as the ones before us, could not reasonably conclude that, despite the occasional hardship which might result, the greater good would be served by leaving the statutes as they are.

* * *

NOTE 2.

MENNINGER, KARL

Psychiatric Aspects of Contraception*

Clinical experience brings us as psychiatrists to the very definite conclusion that while in the lower animals sexual pleasure is primarily a means to an end, in human beings it is not only a means to an end but also a very important end in itself. With a much more elaborate central nervous system and a far more complicated social environment, the human being no longer reacts as animals do in a simple reflex way to the sensory indications of a reproductive opportunity. The impulse for sexual union travels a long, complicated path and becomes entwined, as Havelock Ellis says, with all the highest and subtlest human emotions and activities, with the refinements of social intercourse in every sphere, with art, with religion, with all the facets of that which we call love between human beings. The thwarting of this means the interference with productivity and creativeness in all spheres and the interference with the harmony of human affection which law,

_____

* Reprinted with permission from the _Bulletin of the Menninger Clinic_, Vol. 7, pp. 36-40. Copyright 1943 by The Menninger Foundation.

religion and social custom are at such pains to nurture.

2.

SEXUAL CONDUCT AS AN AGGRAVATING OR MITIGATING FACTOR

a. In Adultery

[i]

HENDERSON v. HENDERSON
[1944] 1 All E.R. 44

VISCOUNT, SIMON, L.C.: . . .

The testimony as to condonation was contained in the appellant's own evidence in chief. He stated that, after his wife had admitted to him her adultery, he told her that she must entirely break off all acquaintance with the co-respondent if he (the husband) were to remain with her, and that she promised to do so. Thereupon the husband and wife went to bed together; he forgave his wife and had sexual intercourse with her that night at her suggestion. Early the next morning her attitude changed and she said she did not see why she should stop seeing the co-respondent, and that, if she denied the adultery, the co-respondent ought to do so too. Upon this, the appellant left the house and never lived with her again.

It was argued that there was no condonation, since the appellant's forgiveness of his wife was conditional on her promise to have no more to do with the co-respondent and this promise was withdrawn after he had had intercourse with her.

* * *

. . . The essence of the matter is (taking the case where it is the wife who has been guilty of the matrimonial offence) that the husband with knowledge of the wife's offence should forgive her and should confirm his forgiveness by reinstating her as his wife. Whether this further reinstatement goes to the length of connubial intercourse depends on circumstances, for there may be cases where it is enough to say that the wife has been received back into the position of wife in the home, though further intercourse has not taken place. But where it has taken place, this will, subject to one exception, amount to clear proof that the husband has carried his forgiveness into effect. The exception is that, if the intercourse was induced by a fraudulent misstatement of fact by the wife, that circumstance will prevent the husband's actions from having the effect of condonation; . . . where the husband petitioned for a dissolution of his marriage on the ground of the wife's adultery and it appeared that she had confessed the adultery but had denied, in answer to his question, that she was pregnant in consequence of it, where upon the husband forgave her and had marital relations with her. It was held . . . that, since the wife knew she was pregnant and had induced the acts of her husband by false and fraudulent statements, he had not condoned her adultery and was entitled to his decree. . . .

* * *

Counsel for the appellant in his ingenious argument advanced the proposition that condonation by the husband is not established by the resumption of intercourse, if that intercourse was obtained by a promise given by the wife to the husband as to her future conduct which is not genuine or sincere at the time when it was given. To that contention there are two answers. In the first place, the facts in the present case and the findings of the trial judge do not involve the view that the wife was not genuine and sincere at the time when she made the promise to her husband that she would keep away from the co-respondent's company. HODSON, J., negatives the view that the respondent when she made the promise was making a fraudulent misstatement as to her future intentions. On the contrary, he finds that in the morning, after the promise had been given and intercourse had taken place, the respondent changed her mind.

But further, the proposition is itself unsound in law. There cannot be such a thing as contingent condonation by a husband of his wife's adultery—certainly not when the condonation includes the irrevocable act of sexual connexion. It is, of course, quite true that condonation is subject to one implied condition, but that is the condition that, if the spouse who has been forgiven past matrimonial offences is proved to commit a further matrimonial offence in the future, then the past offences are revived and become available as further ground for a divorce. But condonation cannot be treated as cancelled because an erring wife who makes promises as to her future conduct withdraws the promise later on. Condonation is not a contract in which one party may claim to be discharged by the other's repudiation.

Condonation is not a contract at all; it is the overlooking of past wrongs accompanied by action on the part of the aggrieved spouse which shows that they are really forgiven, and the circumstance that the guilty party, before or at the time of condonation, makes promises as to future conduct cannot lead to the consequence that previous offences are no longer condoned, if and when the promises are afterwards repudiated. The result might be different if it could be shown that the husband's forgiveness and taking back of his wife was procured by the wife deliberately misrepresenting her true state of mind, for, . . . the state of a person's mind, when it can be definitely ascertained, may be as much a fact as the state of his digestion . . . But that is not the same thing as saying that the husband is not to be treated as condoning if he believed in the wife's promise to behave as she should in the future. [B]elief is not the test. It is fraudulent misstatement of fact, not assurances as to future conduct, which may remove the disabling consequences of condonation.

I move that this appeal be dismissed.

NOTE

W. v. W.
[1961] 2 All E.R. 626, 633-34

BAKER, J.: . . .

The husband was convicted at the Monmouth Assizes at Newport on his own confession of the crime of incest, committed on a child of the marriage, Freda, between Mar. 30 and Apr. 6, 1959. He asked for an offence to be taken in consideration and the evidence shows that that offence was of incest with the daughter Kathleen. Freda was fourteen and Kathleen was in her early twenties. In his evidence before the magistrates the husband admitted both these offences. It has to be remembered that incest is a vile form of adultery.

* * *

There remains the short question whether the sexual intercourse which admittedly took place between these parties on two occasions, and which the magistrates found, as I read their reasons, probably took place on more occasions but in the open air, constitutes either condonation, or a resumption of the life together which brings desertion to an end. I do not propose to discuss the question of which one ought to consider and I shall use "condonation" to cover both because it seems to me, putting the matter shortly, that unless driven by authority to hold that the sexual intercourse amounts to the "something" which . . . must follow an antecedent oral forgiveness, the sexual intercourse in the present case can have no effect. . . . I have heard and I know of no authority which drives me to the conclusion that this intercourse amounts to condonation. If the wife had been asked at the time: "Do you consider that you are forgiving what he has done and reinstating him?", there having been no completed agreement to forgive, although there had been negotiation, her answer would have been "That thought has never entered my mind. I have never gone beyond the stage of considering forgiveness". To my mind it would be wrong to attribute to her any intention to condone. . . .

* * *

[I]t would be absurd to hold that the wife by this intercourse was condoning what the husband had done. I agree that this appeal should be dismissed.

* * *

[ii]

The Trial of Nims v. Nims *

NEW YORK SUPREME COURT,

Kings County.

Special Term—Part 5.

Before: GOLDEN, J.

Brooklyn, February 1, 1947
11:20 o'clock

[ii-a]

Dr. Saul Nims—Plaintiff

DIRECT EXAMINATION BY MR. STRYKER

Q. Are you the plaintiff in this action?   A. Yes.

Q. When were you married to the defendant Louise Nims?   A. December, 1932.

Q. Are there any children of the marriage?   A. Two daughters, one thirteen and one eleven.

Q. Were the acts of adultery alleged in the complaint committed with your consent, connivance, privity or procurement?   A. Yes.

Q. You didn't understand me. Were the acts of adultery charged here committed with your consent?   A. No.

Q. Or your connivance or procurement?   A. No.

Q. Have five years elapsed since you discovered the commission of the alleged adultery? (Pause.) Five years have not passed since then, have they?   A. No.

Q. Have you forgiven or condoned the offense alleged in the complaint?   A. No.

Q. Have you cohabited with the defendant since you discovered the alleged adultery?   A. No.

Q. You are asking for the custody of your two children, are you not?   A. Yes.

[ii-b]

Dr. Paul Rebar—For Plaintiff

DIRECT EXAMINATION BY MR. STRYKER

Q. Are you a nephew of the plaintiff Dr. Nims   A. Yes.

Q. Do you remember October 12, 1946?   A. Yes, I do.

Q. At about 5:50 P.M. did you go to the St.

---

* This is an excerpt from an actual record. Dates, the names of the parties and their residence have been changed. Without indicating deletions we have edited the record primarily to focus on the issue of divorce. Additional excerpts concerning the disposition of the Nims' children are reproduced at 928 in Chapter III.

Moritz Hotel at 50 Central Park South, City of New York?   A. Yes.

Q. Did you on that occasion, in company with others, enter Room 1922 of the hotel at somewhere after 5:40 P.M. on that day, together with the plaintiff Dr. Nims?   A. Yes.

Q. Will you describe to his Honor, please, what you saw in the room when you entered the room?   A. I was the fourth individual to enter this room. Three men preceded me, one of whom was my uncle Dr. Nims. As I entered the room, I saw two individuals lying in a bed, a female—one was a male and one was a female. The female individual I recognized immediately as being my aunt Mrs. Louise Nims.

Q. The male was not the plaintiff in this action?   A. No.

THE COURT. Your aunt is the defendant in this case?

THE WITNESS. Yes. As soon as we walked in, a flash bulb went off, indicating that a picture had been taken. The sheets or the sheet was ripped off the bed and a man nude jumped out of the bed and proceeded to dress himself. My aunt covered her face with her hands. Pictures were taken. Questions were asked of me as to the identity of both individuals. I looked about the room, saw the condition of the room and then, in company with the other men, left.

Q. Did you hear the defendant speak on that occasion?   A. Yes.

Q. What did she say?   A. She was asked several questions, one of which was whether this man who was found with her in this room was her lover. She answered that he was not; that he was her intended husband. She insisted that we all leave and that she would confess to everything.

Q. Did you see her apparel on a chair by the bed?   A. I did.

Q. I show you this group of pictures (indicating) and ask you whether they properly depict what you observed there in that room on that occasion—eight pictures.   A. Yes, they do.

[ii-c]

Laura Raines—For Plaintiff

DIRECT EXAMINATION BY MR. STRYKER

Q. Are you a niece of the plaintiff in this case?   A. Yes.

Q. How old are you?   A. Twenty-three.

Q. Are you engaged in the teaching profession?   A. Yes, Psychology.

Q. Do you know the defendant in this case?   A. Yes.

Q. How long have you known her?   A. Approximately fourteen-and-a-half-years.

Q. Were you present at the wedding when she was married to the plaintiff? A. Yes, I was.

Q. Were you present at the Hotel St. Moritz on the afternoon of October 12, 1946 ; that is, last October? A. Yes, I was.

Q. Did you enter the room together with the previous witness? A. Yes.

Q. As a matter of fact, he is related to you, isn't he? A. Yes, he is my cousin.

Q. Perhaps it will shorten this if you turn to his Honor and tell in the briefest way just what you saw and heard. A. I saw my aunt in bed with a man whom I couldn't identify but whom she identified as her intended husband, when questioned. When we entered the room, a series of flash bulbs went off. I assume pictures had been taken. And the gentleman whom we couldn't identify but who was in bed with my aunt, both of whom were undressed completely, got out of bed and began to clothe himself ; that is, he put on a pair of trousers. My aunt however remained in bed and was asked several questions. She identified herself and said that she would confess everything if we would please leave her alone.

[ii-d]
Louise Nims—Defendant

DIRECT EXAMINATION BY MR. MURRAY

Q. You are the defendant in this action, Mrs. Nims, are you not? A. Yes, I am.

MR. MURRAY. I might say to your Honor that your Honor recalls that we withdrew the answer that denied the adultery, and the issue now before your Honor is one of consent on the part of the plaintiff.

THE COURT. Was it consent and condonation, or just consent?

MR. MURRAY. Consent, your Honor.

Q. Where were you educated? A. Part of the time in New York, and part of the time in the State of Ohio.

Q. Have you got any college degrees? A. Yes.

Q. From where? A. Toledo University.

Q. And what degree have you? A. Bachelor of Science.

Q. Did you ever follow any vocation after you left college? A. For one semester, I taught at Waite High School.

Q. Now, Mrs. Nims, I am going to ask you some questions as a basis for our contention here that there was consent in the issue of adultery. How did you and your husband get along the first years of your marriage? A. We had a great deal of difficulty from the very beginning of our marriage, Mr. Murray.

Q. Would you be more specific and tell His Honor in what respect? A. Yes. From the very beginning of our marriage, even before our marriage, we started to look for an apartment—my husband and I decided on a five-room apartment —and he asked me to go with his sister, to look for apartments. We did. After going around, the wind-up was that we got a four-room apartment. Then the problem of furnishing a home arose and my husband told me that his sister was going to go shopping with me for furniture, so we went together and her taste and my taste were worlds apart.

MR. STRYKER: I don't want to interrupt a natural sequence of events, but it does seem to me that this hasn't very much to do with the issue.

MR. MURRAY: Would your Honor permit me to suggest, as I said before, we are not trying a separation action, but the attitude of the husband of indifference, lack of love, and a course of conduct which would be consistent with the subsequent consent in this case. That is the only purpose for which I offer it. I know it is a long way back, your Honor, and I will just skim over that briefly and then come down to the issues, if your Honor will permit.

THE COURT: I will take it.

A. And so we went shopping for furniture and one night I came home and I told my husband that I saw something that I liked very much and that I would like to have. It was a bedroom suite, and he said to me, "Yes, I heard all about it, and you are not going to get it", and I asked him why. He said, "Because my sister Gertie said it is not worth the money and I will not let you buy anything that isn't a good value." The first time this happened, I accepted it. Then——

Q. Now, Mrs. Nims, I know how difficult it is for you, but if you will try to curtail in as brief a space as possible the attitude of your husband so far as his family were concerned, without going into great detail, you see we will save a lot of time. Would you try to do that? A. I will try, Mr. Murray, I will try to take just a few minutes on this. This customary pattern prevailed many times until one time—one evening when I came home and told him I like something, and again he offered the same answer, "that my sister Gertie says it is not worth the money." I understood what was happening, that everything she didn't like she said wasn't worth the money, and I told him that I didn't feel that it was fair that her tastes should be imposed upon me ; after all it was our house and we should choose the things that we would like, and he told me, "Look Louise, you will have to abide by what she says because she knows best, you are only a child, you don't know what is good, and you don't know what is bad, and you will have to do what she says—she knows best."

Q. Did you say anything to him then about the intervention of his family? A. Yes, I did. I told him that I didn't think that his family had a right to impose their ideas upon our way of living.

Q. And what was his reply? A. His answer was, "You will have to listen to what they say, they know more than you know about everything, you can't know, you are a young girl and I will not let you make the decisions, you will have to take what they say." The family intervention continued for five years at a very, very extreme pitch, they meddled in everything, they told him how much money to give me to live on.

Q. Now we will leave that subject and go to something else. You were how old when you were married? A. I was twenty-three—a little under twenty-four.

Q. I take it that sexually you are a normal woman, are you? A. I believe I am, Mr. Murray.

Q. Was there any difference or disagreement or talk between you and your husband about any sexual inadequacy on the part of anybody? A. Yes, throughout our married life, Mr. Murray. In the beginning of our marriage, we had intercourse and he was very quick in the act—I don't even know what you call it, I would complain very bitterly, because I was left suspended in air and I was very, very irritable and very nervous and very upset, and I would plead with him that I felt that he should give a little more attention to trying to give me time, to arouse me, in trying to prepare me, and he told me that I am frigid, he said that all men are this way, and in the first few years of my married life I thought perhaps he was right, and while I was very bitter about it, I accepted it, but as years went on and I did speak with certain of my friends,—my women friends,—I heard different stories and I heard that not all men are quick and that it doesn't have to take one or two minutes and that there is happy sexual relationship, and so later on, after a few years of my marriage, when the same conversation always took place, because every time the intercourse took place the same question arose, then I approached him and I said that "I had heard it is not true, Saul, it is not true that all men are quick and are fast and there is such a thing as a happy relationship and I think you ought to learn something, you ought to read and you ought to inquire and find out what is to be done, because I cannot go on this way. You tell me I am nervous and I am irritable. Yes, I am, but I am beginning to understand why."

Then he said to me, "Look, Louise, this is the way I am, and this is the way most men are. You are the frigid one and I don't give a damn if you feel that you are not satisfied and that I am not keeping you happy," he said, "You just go to somebody else."

CROSS EXAMINATION BY MR. STRYKER

Q. What was the date of this talk? A. These conversations began around 1940, about that time.

He said—I told him, rather, that "I can understand why women go to other men, if this is the way their husbands treat them, I can understand it, and one of these days, Saul, I am going to go to somebody else, too," and he said, "Go ahead, go ahead," and I said, "Yes, you say go ahead, but if I do it you would hold it against me."

He said, "No, I will not hold it against you, if you are unhappy with me and if I am not satisfying you and you think somebody will, you go ahead."

Well, I didn't go ahead, and later on, when the conversations continued and I told him that—this conversation of "Go ahead" was repeated countless times. He finally said, "'Now, look here, you are getting on my nerves, I cannot stand this from you, you are driving me crazy, I don't give a good God damn what you do, you can do whatever you wish. If you want to go, go ahead.

All I want from you is, don't bother me, I don't want—just leave me alone. If I am not taking care of you, you go to somebody else, and I don't give a damn what you do."

REDIRECT EXAMINATION BY MR. MURRAY

Q. From 1940 and up to the period of the commencement of this action for a divorce against you, what was the attitude of your husband toward you so far as showing you any love or affection or interest? A. My husband—the way I interpreted it, my husband did not love me, because he worked twenty-one hours out of every twenty-four hours of the day.

Q. Did you complain about that? A. I complained bitterly about that.

Q. What did you say? A. I told him that I didn't think it was fair, that I was a young woman, and that I didn't get married to be alone all the time, that he was never home, and when he came home for a few minutes for meals, he was so tired, he fell asleep right after he ate, if he lasted in the house until he finished the meal, and that, what was he offering me, he was never home, and when he came home, the few minutes he was asleep, and I said that after all, I was a young person, there was something more to life than just practice of medicine, and that not only haven't I got a husband, but I have two children who never saw their father, they didn't even know what their father was, and when he comes in the only thing they know of him is that he was irritable and nasty, that he yelled at them, he can't stand the least of talk and noise, and that is all they know of their father is the irritableness.

I said I thought that this is not any kind of marriage at all and if he had intended to live that kind of life, he never should have gotten married and then not only didn't he ever take me out, but in the first ten years of our marriage, aside from our delayed honeymoon, which took place about two years after our marriage—we had a week's honeymoon two years after the marriage——

Q. When you got married, you had a honeymoon, didn't you? A. No, I did not, Mr. Murray.

Q. Didn't you go some place? A. Yes, we went to the Waldorf Hotel, we came about three o'clock in the morning, and eight o'clock in the morning my husband left, and he left to go to work, and his sister called for me later in the morning to take me shopping to buy pots and pans, but that vacation, that honeymoon, we had two years after, about two years after our marriage, and after that, the man didn't have one day's vacation in ten years—not one day in ten years.

Q. Could that have been because his medical practice was such that he couldn't spare the time? A. Well, Mr. Murray, I don't think so, because if he were in a field of medicine where you have to deal with emergencies, I might be able to understand it, but this is obstetrics and obstetrical cases, you take these—you register these cases seven or nine months before the baby is born.

Q. Didn't you talk to him about his duties to you as a husband? A. Yes, I did. Mr. Murray, there is one thing that I told him a thousand times. At this time when he—the later years when this started in, he was earning about seventy-five or a hundred thousand dollars a year, and I told him, "Saul, for God's sake, I beg you, we are married, I think we should have some kind of life together, you never take me out, and if you take me out twice a year to a show, you have some temper tantrums, you eat me up alive, before we even go there, there is such a scene, and I cry so much, I don't even want to go, and when we go and there are friends there, you don't hesitate with your temper tantrums on the street because you resent so much that you had to take me out this once or twice, that you carry on so badly on the street, I am even ashamed to be with you. Why must you do this? Give up your work, I don't need a hundred thousand dollars a year, I will live on a fraction of what you make, I want a husband—I want a husband and my children want a father, and I want to live together. I got married for companionship and what are you giving me? You are giving me lonesomeness. I am always alone, I am neglected, I always go alone, what

did I have to get married for in the first place?"

I said, "We don't use all this money, so you will save less, and if we have to live on less, I will be content to live on less, I want a husband," but it was to no avail, he always said next year, next year, and next year, and it never came.

Q. Mrs. Nims, you claim that that is a resume of your relations through the years, and now let us get to 1944. In 1944, were you interested in any particular work? A. Yes. I did two pieces of work that were very close to my heart. During this terrible Hitler period, when they were killing all these millions of Jews, because I was so alone, because my husband left me so much alone, I got myself interested in some charitable work, in some humanitarian work. I felt that as long as I had some time, I couldn't sit while people were being destroyed and not help them.

Q. What was that venture, in a word? A. To try to rescue as many of the Jewish children of Europe as I could and to rehabilitate them.

Q. And did you meet someone, a man who is named the corespondent in the adultery charge? A. Yes, I did.

Q. What was his name? A. His name was Mr. Claude Blum.

Q. Was he a citizen of the United States? A. No, of Algeria.

Q. What was the man's background? A. This man had come to this country also interested in helping the political status and the rescue and rehabilitation work of the Jewish people.

Q. Did you know anything about the man's education, his culture, his financial standing, or anything else? A. I learned that he was a man in very good financial circumstances—very comfortable. He was a graduate attorney from one of the universities in Paris, he came from one of the best families of Algeria, he was a man who was so—who was a man of very wide cultural background, he was very well informed in many aspects of cultural interests.

Q. And eventually, did you invite him to your home? A. Yes, I did. He came to my home in the first week of December, 1944.

Q. He met your husband? A. That's right.

Q. On any other occasion, did he meet your husband? A. Yes.

Q. Where? A. We went out together twice and then I made another party in my home for him, and some of the other delegates to this Congress.

Q. Did you have any talk with your husband about this man, Claude Blum? A. Yes.

Q. When was it you had the talk with him? A. It was after the second party that I gave in my home.

Q. You see, Mrs. Nims, no one knows when the second party was. It may have been A.D. or B.C.

A. I believe it was Christmas Eve, about that time, in 1944.

Q. 1944? A. Yes.

Q. Did you have any talk with your husband about this man? A. Yes, I did.

Q. When, what year? A. It was that same night of the party. My husband said to me, "I don't see what you see in this man, what are you so excited about?" I told him that I thought he was a very fine man and a very nice man and perhaps if he were able to speak to him at greater length, he, too, would understand what I saw in him, and he said, "Well, what is he, he seems like nothing at all?"

I said, "Well, you can't very well say that. He is a man who has been a leader of the entire Jewish community of his country for many years; he is a man who is an official of the Chamber of Commerce in his country; he is a man who, when the Jewish rights were taken away, when they were disenfranchised in Algeria under the Vichy regime, he was the one who was chosen by the country to negotiate with the minister of the interior and it was through his efforts primarily and his negotiations that Jewish rights were restored to the French citizens; that when there was a meat famine in the country during the North African campaign and people were starving because of the black market, the Government chose him to go in and try to control it and he put meat back through his efforts—the people got meat back on their tables. This is a view of the accomplished things." When I finished telling him some of these things, he said, "My, it sounds like you are in love with this man", and I said, "Perhaps I am", and then after that—or I should say that prior to that time, when he refused to go out with us, some of the times pleading that he was busy, he told me to go out with him and to say that he was stuck in the hospital.

Then he said, "Now, look, Louise, if that is the way you feel about that man, you go out with him, you can do anything. If you are in love with him, go ahead, I give you the freedom to do whatever you wish. All I want from you is that you leave me alone, just don't bother me, don't insist that I come along on your parties, and as far as you are concerned, you can do whatever you wish—just leave me out of it."

Q. I assume the friendship and relationship between you and Claude Blum grew and grew, did it? A. Yes, that's right.

Q. Was there any talk after this incident with your husband concerning a divorce? A. That was in May 1945, and before I left, I had spoken with the head of my children's school about my contemplated divorce, and I was concerned about the welfare of the children, whether or not they would be better off to remain on in school during this divorce discussion, or whether we should have them home, and while I was in San Francisco, my husband went up to the school and this head of the school, thinking that I had already discussed it with him, gave him the answer. I had not yet told him my plan, but my sister phoned me and told me that he had learned about my plan to divorce, and I had better come home, and so I came home a week before I had expected.

That night, on June 8, 1945, when I came home, we spoke of divorce. He asked me whether it was true, and I said yes, it was true, and he asked me why I wanted the divorce and I told him that I no longer loved him and I didn't think he loved me. He said, "Well, I will not consider any divorce." He said, "You know divorce is against my principles, and I will not give you any divorce."

I said, "But, Saul, I don't know why. In all these years, the way you acted toward me, first with your family and then all our quarrels about money, that you made a beggar out of me, I never had the freedom, you such a rich man, and I never had the freedom to buy a penny's worth of something without coming to you for everything I had to buy, I had to ask your consent and your permission, and if I didn't get your permission, you screamed at me and you made me return it, or there was a terrible fight—you made a beggar out of me, you left me alone, did you ever take me out, and those times when you took me out, you know what went on, you never showed any interest in me, you never cared when I had friends in my house, you insulted me, you called me names, you even said in front of my friends many a time, 'You stink'."

I said, "What kind of talk is that from a husband to a wife? How can you say such things? You don't even have any respect for yourself, certainly you have no respect for me and for my children, and all the quarrels before the children and every minute you came in the house, when you came into the house, you never came in quietly, it was always yelling and always slamming things, you broke things and you slammed things, and everything that you did in all these twelve and a half years led me to believe that you didn't love me—as a matter of fact, I thought you hated me—and I don't see, if that is how you felt in all these years, why you should refuse to give me the divorce if you don't love me, and if you don't love me, why do you insist?"

So he turned around and then he asked me, "Are you in love with somebody else?" and I said, "Yes."

He said, "With whom, that Blum, by any chance?"

I said, "Yes."

He said, "Well, I still won't give you the divorce, I don't give a damn. I cannot afford any divorce. I cannot afford the scandal, I have been working all these years toward life at a certain position and you are not going to destroy it for me. If you want to carry on an affair with this man, you go ahead. If you want to stay with him, you want to live with him"—by "live", he didn't mean that I should leave my home—"you want to stay with him, go ahead, as long as you keep up the face of this marriage, you are free to do whatever you wish, but I will not give you a divorce."

Q. Did you have a subsequent conversation with your husband about a divorce? A. That next day, we resumed the conversation and he told me that he had been thinking about everything that I had said, and that he knew that he had not behaved properly, he knew that he was wrong, and his excuse was that he didn't know that I was so sensitive and that it meant so much to me, his behavior toward me, but that if I would try to keep this marriage together, he would change.

When he spoke that way to me, I told him, "Look, Saul, I am not anxious to destroy this marriage, I understand, I appreciate what this is going to mean with our children, and if there is any chance of holding this marriage together, I want that chance", and we agreed that we would have a three months' period, trial period, during which time he would try to make amends and I would try to forget Claude, but I told him that if I knew myself at all, that once my love for somebody was destroyed, that there wasn't much chance or much hope for re-establishing it, but that I would try, but that he would have to make me a promise that at the end of that time, if I still felt the way I did, he would give me the divorce, and he promised me that he would, and he told me at that time—we discussed the conditions.

He said that he would give me the children. And in order for me, since all my life I was unhappy that I never could do anything on my own, that I never had the feeling of independence, that I had to go to beg, here when my husband had a half a million dollars that he saved, I didn't have one penny, but I had to beg for everything, he said, "All right, I'll see to it that you can have your own income." That apartment house on Elmwood Avenue, in which he had a $65,000 investment, he would give it to me so that I would never have to be dependent upon anybody, and that was the conclusion of the divorce discussion.

Q. This was what month and what year? A. This was the next day, June 9, 1945.

Q. Was there any understanding reached between the two of you at that time? A. Yes, that I would wait the three months, and that at the end of that time, if I still felt the same way, that he would give me the divorce and would give me those two things—the custody and this apartment house.

Q. That was June, 1945? A. That's right.

Q. After that, how did you get along together? A. Well, he had made an effort to stop his ugliness toward me, but I was very unhappy and the truth is that I was struggling terribly between my love for this Mr. Blum and the fact that I felt that I should try to hold my marriage together and try to keep it, and I was torn between the two and I didn't say anything at the end of the three months.

He spoke with my sister and he asked her if he should speak to me and she said, "Saul, do you want the divorce?" He said, "No." So she said, "Then if she is not bothering you, why should you talk to her?" And the truth was that I couldn't decide, I was not ready with my decision, but one day in April of 1946—It was on a Saturday afternoon my husband phoned me from the hospital and said he wants to talk with me, would I stay home, and I said yes.

When he came home he said, "Now, look here, I see that something is troubling you and that you are not very happy. I want to know what it is. Is it anything new?"

I said, "No, it is nothing new, it is the same thing."

He said, "Well, before this you told me all the transgressions that I committed against you and I felt you were right and so I tried to change. What is your complaint now?"

I said, "It is true that you have changed in a good measure in certain outward aspects, but on the question of sex, Saul, with all the talk that you told me, I am still very unhappy, you haven't changed at all, you are still the same"—there are certain expressions which I don't want to use here, but I said, "It still takes you a minute or two and you have been telling me again that I am so nervous and so irritable. Yes, I am, I am a human being and if I weren't sleeping in the same bed with you and I didn't have any desires—I have the desire, I want to be loved and you either don't want me, weeks go by that you don't even try to touch me," I said, "you know that there were times even when I came home from certain of my trips that I went on a mission and when I came back you didn't even try to approach me for almost three weeks after I came home."

I said, "Either you don't have any interest in me and when you do, it doesn't seem to me that you are interested in me, you are just interested in your own physical relief and you don't give a damn about me. Well, this can't go on. I am going—I can't take it," and I said, "You haven't changed that way and I am still unhappy."

I told him at that time that the way I felt, I thought that the best thing for me to do would be to go away, that I was very unhappy, and I couldn't see clearly ahead of me and if he pressed me now on whether I still wanted the divorce, my answer would be yes, but if he wanted to wait a little while longer, that I would go away and try to think things out clearly, and I said I thought if I went away for about six or eight weeks, perhaps I would see and understand more what I wanted out of life.

He said to me, "if you want to go away for six months, it doesn't even—you can go away for six months. I will tell you what I will do: I will foot all the bills, you can go anywhere you want, I won't even ask you where you will go, if you want to go, stay in America, if you want to go to Mexico, if you want to go to Europe, if you want to go to North Africa, you can go anywhere you want, you don't even have to write me a postcard, and you will go and you can go wherever you want and go with whomever you want and do whatever you want, and then you will see that it is not my fault, that you are the frigid one, that you are frigid," and he told me at that time that if I wanted to go with Claude, go ahead with Claude; if I wanted to go with somebody else, go with somebody else, "but you will see that you are the frigid one."

Q. Where was Claude during those discussions with your husband? A. Claude was in North Africa, in Algeria.

Q. Now, let me ask you something, Mrs. Nims, or rather a delicate question: In all your life had you ever had sexual intercourse with anyone besides your husband and Claude? A. Never.

Q. Now, did a time come when Claude returned to the United States? A. Yes, that was July, 1946.

Q. Do you know whether or not your husband was apprised of the fact that he was returning to the United States? A. Yes. A cable was phoned in by Western Union and my husband received that call.

Q. And did he give it to you? A. He left it on his night table for me.

Q. Whose name was signed to the cable? A. Claude's.

Q. Did you have any discussion then or the next day about Claude and the cable? A. Yes.

Q. What was it? A. That night when I got into bed he asked me what did Claude have to say. I said, "Claude cabled that he was coming on Friday," and that was all that took place that night. He had been half asleep and I didn't want

to discuss it.

Q. I just asked you what was said. A. The next day when I saw my husband I told him that—we resumed the conversation and he asked me what Claude—what my plans were and I told him that Claude was coming on Friday and that I was going to go away for the week-end, and he said, "All right," and that was the end of that conversation.

Q. And you did go away for the week-end? A. Yes, I went away for the week-end.

Q. And then did you leave again? A. Not at once, but I had a conversation with my husband and I told my husband that I was still in love with Claude and he told me—and at that time I told him that I couldn't see any other way except —of holding my marriage together unless I would try to live with Claude. I told him that if it were true what the world says, that the only way to know a man is to live with him, then I felt that the only possibility of perhaps holding our marriage together was to go away with Claude and if I would go away with him and live with him twenty-four hours out of the day, perhaps I would get so sick and tired of him, perhaps I would get so fed up, perhaps he wouldn't be the wonderful person that I think he is, and that I would find out differently and if I get tired out and fed up with him and I could get him out of my mind, I felt I could come back, and now that my husband was showing me his attempt to be nicer to me than he was in those twelve and one-half years before, I felt certain that we could make a go of our marriage.

He told me that I could go, that if I thought that would be the way to come to a solution that he wanted to hold the marriage together, and if I felt that that would be the way, that I could go ahead, and so I planned to go but my father became very ill, as my husband knows—he was operated on and he had several attacks and I couldn't go at the time—and the summer was going away—I had wanted to go when my children were in camp and the time was drawing close. We decided that since I couldn't go away for any length of time, we would go away for over the Labor Day holiday.

Q. What did your husband say? A. He said that if I felt that that would help me, getting me to know him any better, or if that would make me happier, go ahead. When I came back from this vacation with Claude, I spoke with my husband and I told him that I had made up my mind definitely that I was going through with the divorce. He tried to convince me to the contrary and I said no, and that night he agreed to the divorce, he said he would keep his promise, he agreed to give it to me. He left the house after our discussion and went to his sister's and brother-in-law's home and he came back about an hour and a half later and said that he was not going to leave me in the house, he was not going to give me the money and he was not going to give me the children, he reneged on every promise that he had made on our divorce discussions.

These conversations continued back and forth several days—one day it was yes, one day it was no, and he kept stalling me to keep me from going on. The Jewish holidays were coming and I thought I would respect the family, because they were a religious family, and I felt I wouldn't create disgrace to the whole family, and I said I would wait until after the Jewish holiday, and then after the Jewish holiday I spoke with him again, I said, "Now, Saul, you have to make up your mind." We spoke in terms of a Reno divorce and he said, "Well, this would be a terrible birthday present to give your daughter. Why don't you wait until after the 18th of October?", which was my daughter's birthday. He said, "You wait until then."

I said, "All right, Saul, I will wait, but I'm telling you now that next day you will have to make up your mind—either this will be a Reno divorce, according to the terms that we have agreed, or I will sue for separation. I will wait no longer," and he said, "All right."

Q. Your position is that your husband told you to go with Claude. A. That's right.

Q. And then he headed a raid on the room in which you were with Claude? A. That's right. On the 12th of October.

Q. Eventually were you able to get in a position where you had a conversation with him about the raid and the subsequent conversations that you had about going with this man Claude? A. Yes, on December 22. When I came into the room, he fell on my neck and he kissed me——

Q. You see, Mrs. Nims, we are just asking for conversations and you burden the record by going into all the details, to no end. A. O.K.

Q. Did you tax him with having let you go with this man and then pulling a raid on you? A. I asked him how he could have done such a cruel and such a wicked thing to me when he knew all the time that I was in love with Claude and he knew that I was going with Claude and he told me to go ahead and he even told me not only to sleep with him, but he told me to go ahead and go on a vacation with him, and that after giving me his consent and after telling me that I could, why did he resort to such a nasty trick; that if he really wanted to divorce me and give me the divorce, why that way, and he answered me that that is the way it had to be because I wanted

the children and I wanted too much and he wasn't going to give it to me, and he did that so that he could get what he wanted; in other words, to turn me out without anything, and that that was his object.

I said, "But how could you do such a thing to me? Here in these last few months when you knew you didn't love me, you protested that you did. If you had any love for me or for your children, how could you do this to them, even if you didn't think of me, and was this necessary, such an uncivilized way? After all, I told you that if you would not agree to my terms, I would sue for separation, which would have meant it would be your terms. Now, as long as I was ready to go without money, why did you have to do this to me?"

And he said that a Reno divorce is not a secure divorce, "You could come back and later ask for money from me, you could say that it was not legally gotten and you could come back, you would still be my wife," and then at another conversation—well, as far as the money and that, we had other conversations which I will explain what he said to me further about why he wanted this type of raid and why he did this thing to me instead of going through with a decent and clean divorce that wouldn't bring any scandal to him and to me and to the children, above all, and that night we spoke and he told me that he still doesn't want the divorce and that he was going to Florida.

I asked him with whom he was going to Florida. He said with his brother-in-law but that he doesn't want to go with him, he doesn't want to go himself.

I said, "That sounds like an invitation, Saul," and then he said—oh, frankly, he started to cry— he said, "I don't want a divorce. If you want to come with me, we will drop them behind and we will go away together," and I told him that I wasn't quite ready, for everything that he had done to me, and I couldn't see it that way, and why doesn't—and then he started to speak Reno divorce to me and he told me, "All right, my family wants this divorce, they want this so badly, they want to break us up. Perhaps if we go through with a Reno divorce"—he said, "Why don't you take this divorce and then afterwards we will get together again, we will be reconciled and we will remarry?"

I said, "Saul, you can't expect me to have you take me through and drag me through a dirty divorce and then expect me to come back with you. If you really want to hold this marriage together, and there must be a divorce, then let us have a clean divorce, a Reno divorce, and at least you will leave an open door, you will leave some kind of cleanliness between us and not bitterness between us, and then if you want to call on me and take me out again, perhaps we will start all over again", and he was thrilled with the idea and he said, "Yes, that is the way it will be".

He went to Florida and when he left that night, he said, "You know, my brother Irving is the only one in the family who wants a Reno divorce—the rest of them want a New York divorce".

He said, "I understand you spoke to a Rabbi and that the Rabbi was against the New York divorce."

He said, "You get the Rabbi together with my brother Irving and let them work on the women in my family so that you can get this thing and when I come back, and when I have worked on the family, I will say yes, I want a Reno divorce", and then he said, "And then we will start all over again, I will start taking you out, I will court you and maybe we will start a new life, we will have profited by our very bad experience", and he went to Florida and the next thing I heard from him—two days later was my birthday——

Q. After his return from Florida, did you have any more talks with him, or didn't you? A. Yes, I did. When he came back from Florida, I think it was the day after he came back from Florida, another meeting was arranged and it was in somebody's house that we met, and he referred to certain things he had sent me, and he told me that he was very happy that he had seen me.

BY THE COURT

Q. You say he referred to certain things he sent you. What do you mean by that? A. He sent me flowers on my birthday and he was very happy that he had seen me before he left because then he was able to enjoy his vacation more.

Q. When was your birthday? A. December 24.

Q. And he sent you these flowers? A. That's right.

Q. That was December 24 following the raid? A. Yes, this was two days after our first conversation after the raid.

CROSS EXAMINATION BY MR. STRYKER

Q. Will you tell us again exactly what your husband said to you when this matter of having sexual intercourse with men was first discussed with you in 1940? Q. My husband said—I told my husband that I can see why women go to other men and I was so unhappy and that I was so upset and that if I didn't sleep with him in the same bed, it wouldn't matter, but I was human and I felt he wasn't doing the right thing and that one of these days, I might go to another man or I would go to another man and he shouldn't be surprised. It was something to that effect. These were constant conversations and the words may have varied but the thought was the same, and he told

me to go ahead, that if I thought I would be happy that way and if I would be happier that way and if he didn't satisfy me, I could go ahead, and when I told him that "Yes, you say go ahead and then if I did, you would hold it against me", he said, "No, I will not hold it against you."

Q. Did you find in 1946 that the power of attorney that you have told us about that was given to you in 1940 had been revoked and therefore needed renewal? A. No.

Q. You understood that that general open power for you to go out and sleep with any man you wanted was still in existence and effect? A. Yes.

Q. Then what was the occasion of discussing it again in April, 1946? A. Oh, a very great occasion—a question of divorce.

Q. You had had intercourse with the correspondent before the time when you last had intercourse with the doctor, your husband; is that right? A. Yes.

Q. Now, did you tell your husband on that occasion that you had already had intercourse with this man, the correspondent; yes or no; just yes or no, please. A. No.

Q. Didn't you feel any sense of shame? A. No.

Q. No shame? A. My husband had told me that I could, and it was with his consent, and I felt that I was absolutely within my rights.

Q. You felt no shame as a woman, the mother of daughters?

Q. Some time in July, you spent several days with this Frenchman at the Warwick Hotel, didn't you? A. That's right.

Q. Before you went, did you not tell your husband where you were going? A. I said I was going to visit with some friends.

Q. Did he not ask you where you were going to visit and who the friends were? A. No.

Q. And you didn't tell him? A. No.

Q. As a matter of fact, you weren't going to visit with some friends, were you? A. As a matter of fact, I told him on Thursday, the 25th, that Mr. Blum was coming and I was going away with him for the week-end.

Q. I thought you told me a minute ago that you told your husband you were going to visit some friends. A. That's right, and I did visit some friends, too.

Q. You mean at the Warwick, you visited some friends? A. We had some friends come to the Warwick, and we also went to visit some friends.

Q. Did you tell him that you were going into the Hotel Warwick to sleep with this man? A. No, I did not.

Q. In other words, you, a married woman, supported by your husband, and with growing daughters, thought that you would see how you liked living with this Frenchman who himself had a wife in France and children? A. Well, that is one way of putting it.

Q. Did you have talks with your husband about wanting a substantial cash settlement from him? A. I said that I felt that since he had acquired— saved a half a million dollars during the course of our marriage, there were four of us in the family, I thought that I was entitled to my share. However, I would settle for much less, all that I wanted was that the same feeling, the suffering that I went through those twelve and a half years where I had to come to him for every penny, I wanted to have independence, so I wouldn't have to go to any man for everything.

REDIRECT EXAMINATION BY MR. MURRAY

Q. There has been an imputation here, Mrs. Nims, that you spent your money to entertain Blum. Will you tell his Honor what Blum spent while he was entertaining you? A. He spent many thousands of dollars while he was here in the four months, and not one penny of my money went for that—not one penny—and I could give a complete report of where my money went, if that would be necessary, and that can be checked.

MR. MURRAY: If your Honor please, I would like to see this letter, Plaintiff's Exhibit 10 for Identification, and show it to the defendant so that she may read it in its entirety.

MR. STRYKER: Certainly.

Jan. 23, 1947

My dear Fakir,

Always seeking an excuse to bluff your way out of a tough spot! But you know the old adage "You can fool some of the people some of the time, etc. etc."

I straightened Y out on this latest lie. And let me straighten you out, so that if you have an iota of a conscience (which I completely doubt) you won't try to "pass off" on others the story you gave to Y. for not giving me any money. The truth is that you never intended to give me any money. That Monday morning conversation (Jan. 13th) was only a "fake". Was it part of the game to feel me out? It was just the final act to the whole month of treachery you played with me. It is my conviction that you played that month-old game with me because not only didn't you want me, but you wanted no one else to have me. You hoped to break us up.

If there was one speck of truth in all your talk—the fact that you now offer me a low-down and dirty New York divorce is no justification for denying me what you offered me with a clean Reno divorce. Which fact, all adds up to the cheap liar you are.

So you think there won't be any trial on Monday? Well, my dear I hate to disappoint you, for there will be one and when it is over, it will be just as your family predicted. I'll hate your guts (as I already do) and you'll hate mine. Shall I be foolish enough to tell you that you are going to encounter a few delightful surprises?

Before I give you the accounting of my financial affairs (which by the way should now reverse your reason for not providing for me. Now you can argue—she still has $7500—She doesn't need my money. Let her use that!)

Let me tell you what I think of you in just a few words——

I think you are the "lowest life" that ever lived. You have no brains, no heart, no guts, no soul, no conscience and no respect for anyone and no human decency. Your god is the Almighty Dollar. Which all makes you no more than an amoeba. My only great regrets are that I ever knew you, that I ever wasted my life with you, that I ever wasted a tear on you and above all, that you are the father of my children.

Now for the accounting, you gave me

	$15,000 bonds (I have ½ left)
I had	5,500 plus cash
	$20,500 Total assets
	13,000
I spent	7,500 bond—balance
	5,000 lawyers—because you wanted N.Y. divorce
	1,100 rent—because you threw me out
	400 children—because you didn't provide
	1,000 payment your debts
	5,500 jewels—purchased while your wife
	$13,000

I had a few hundred dollars which I spent on myself since Dec. 1st—Actually I spent $500 on myself in all this time. What excuse will you give now?

Goodbye, my love—forever

Louise.

Q. Mrs. Nims, you wrote the letter to your husband, didn't you? A. Yes, I did.

Q. Now, was there any conversation between

you and your husband that inspired you to write this letter, Defendant's Exhibit A, to him? A. Yes.

Q. Would you tell his Honor what it was? A. Yes. The night before my husband went to Florida—

Q. Now that doesn't mean anything. What date? A. December 22.

Q. Without going into the utmost detail, did you break off any arrangements with Blum concerning marriage? A. Yes, Mr. Murray. That night, on December 27, I told him to stop all action, that I was going to consider a reconciliation with my husband, or even if it was a Reno divorce, he shouldn't because I might go back with my husband and I didn't want to break his marriage.

RECROSS EXAMINATION BY MR. STRYKER

Q. You had been advised, had you not, Mrs. Nims, that if you succeeded in getting the doctor to come back with you, that he would condone, thereby condone the adultery and put an end to his own case? You knew that, didn't you? A. I had been advised that?

Q. You knew that, didn't you? You didn't understand me? A. That what?

Q. Had you not been told that if the doctor went back to you and lived with you, that that act would end his divorce case, because it would be deemed by the law to have condoned your adultery? Didn't you know that? A. No, I wasn't advised to that effect.

Q. You weren't told that? A. No, I wasn't advised. I understood later.

Q. But you knew that was so? A. From later subsequent conversations, I understood there was a possibility.

Q. In other words, you understood it would be ruinous to his case against you if you succeeded in getting him to come back to you; you knew that? A. And yet when he offered reconciliation, I didn't accept it.

Q. Did you know that? Answer that question. A. I knew that it would be condonation, yes.

Q. One other question: Didn't you, knowing that, suggest a reconciliation to your husband? A. No, I did not.

[ii-e]
Dr. Saul Nims—Plaintiff

DIRECT EXAMINATION BY MR. STRYKER

Q. At the very outset, Doctor, I want to ask you this question: Did you at any time or place in any way say or suggest to your wife that as far as you were concerned, she was at liberty to live with any other man, either this man Blum, or any other man? A. No, sir.

Q. Did you ever tell her that she was at liberty to have sexual intercourse with any other man in the world? A. Definitely not.

Q. Did you say to her at or about that time, "My, it sounds like you are in love with this man," and did she say, "Perhaps I am," and did you tell her to go out with Blum because you were stuck in the hospital so much? Did you say anything like that? A. That was never brought up.

Q. And did you say, "Now, look Louise, if that is the way you feel about that man, you go out with him, you can do anything. If you are in love with him, go ahead, I give you the freedom to do whatever you wish. All I want from you is that you leave me alone, just don't bother me, don't insist that I come along on your parties, and as far as you are concerned you can do whatever you wish—just leave me out of it." A. That is absolutely not true.

Q. Did she ever complain to you in regard to the manner in which you performed the sex act? A. On two occasions.

Q. Did you on any such occasion say to her, "Look, Louise, this is the way I am, and this is the way most men are. You are the frigid one and I don't give a damn if you feel you are not satisfied and that I am not keeping you happy, you just go to somebody else."

Q. Did you say that or anything like that; yes or no? A. Never.

Q. Did there come a time, Doctor, when your wife went to San Francisco in May, 1945, to attend the U.N. Conference? A. Yes, sir.

Q. When she returned home did you then relate to her what Mr. Kaye, the head of this girl's camp, had said to you; did you tell your wife that? A. Yes, sir. I told her that Mr. Kaye told me something very shocking, "Your wife is breaking up your home." I was shocked and I stopped at that, and I wasn't able to stay there much longer except spend the day by myself. I asked her why she had to tell it to him first instead of talking to me directly. She told me that it was her mistake and "it is too bad that he told you," that she was going to tell me herself at a later date. Then we discussed the statement and she said "It is very true, I am going to break away from you, I don't like you any longer, I can't love you as a husband, I admire you as a character," and we had quite a discussion which lasted three or four hours, trying to convince her that it is foolish to do it at this stage of the game, after being married fourteen years and having two children.

Q. Take your time, Doctor, it is all right. A. She said it wouldn't do any good, she must go through with it. Well, we cried, both of us, and she finally decided to continue with the discussion next morning, and the next day, we decided to compromise, that we will try to make this thing——

Q. Make the marriage a success? A. Work properly and make it a success and give it another chance for a year. I promised her that I will try to give her more time and take her out more frequently, to make her happier, if that is the thing that makes her unhappy, and she agreed to wait another year.

Q. Your wife testified that you turned to her and asked her, "Are you in love with somebody else?" and that she said "Yes". Did that happen? A. No, sir.

Q. Your wife has testified, Doctor: "Q. Did a cable come from Claude?" She said "Yes," and she was asked, "How was it delivered?" and she said it was phoned in by Western Union. Then she was asked, "To whom?" and she said, "My husband received that call."

Then she was asked, "Did he write it as it was phoned," and she said, "Yes, he wrote it out."

"Q. And did he give it to you? A. He left it on on his night table for me.

"Q. Whose name was signed to the cable? A. Claude's."

Is that true? A. No, sir.

Q. When she returned from this August trip, did she tell you that she had been away with Blum and had been having sexual intercourse with him? A. No, Sir.

Q. Do you remember the conversation of September 11, 1946, the conversation you had with your wife then? A. That was two days after she had returned from her vacation in Massachussetts, and I approached the subject again. I asked her how she feels about our married life. She told me at that time that she definitely decided to break it up, that she cannot any longer stay with me, that she is not in love and that she is unhappy.

I asked her what she expects to do. She said she expects to go away, if possible, to get an apartment for herself, she wants to have the kids, and by herself, with nobody else.

I said, "What kind of a life is that?"

She said, "That is the kind of a life I need, I want to forget everybody, I just want to be by myself with the children, relax, concentrate, and take it easy."

I said to her, "That, to me, sounds like a psychopathic individual, you want to be by yourself, it is not normal. I would suggest that you see a psychiatrist, perhaps he can straighten you out."

She then told me that she is quite sane, she does not need any psychiatric help, and that she wants to go through with it in the worst way.

I said, "Suppose I don't cooperate with you?"

She said, "If you don't cooperate with me, I will have papers for separation served on you, but I will give you a week or two time to decide. I don't want to drag you into court, I want to make it as quiet as possible, but if you force me to, I will have the papers served."

Q. Did she on that occasion say anything to you relative to men, that if she got a divorce, as to whether she wanted to or not to have anything to do with men for a long time? Was anything said like that? A. It didn't sound right to me from the way she spoke, that she wants to be by herself and she wants to be divorced. I said, "If you want to be by yourself, take two months' vacation, and you will be by yourself. Why do you have to be divorced? Why go through that ceremony, because I hate that word 'divorce.'"

She said, "Well, if you are divorced, you are free."

I said, "Free to do what?"

She said, "Just free."

I said, "To me, it sounds like the only way that is looking like would be to have relations with other men."

Q. What did she say to that? A. She said, "Well, I don't mean that, but I don't see anything wrong in it."

I said, "How can you have relationship with other men if you are not going to be married?"

She said, "Well, the next time I get a man, I am going to try out and see if I really like him before I marry him. If he satisfies me, I will marry him."

I said, "Suppose that man is married?"

She said, "That wouldn't make any difference."

Q. Did you, directly or indirectly, by words, expression or anything else, say or indicate to her that this thought of hers of having sex relations with another man was in any way acceptable to you? A. For a moment, I was shocked, and then I reprimanded her, I said, "How can you say such a thing?"

Q. You reprimanded her? A. Yes, sir. "How can you say such a thing, that you would like to try out with a man that you are not married to?"

She said, "Well, it's nothing serious."

Q. Did you tell her, "Go ahead and do that," or anything like that? A. No, sir.

Q. Now, in the course of that conversation— if I am right, that is the conversation—did she discuss how much money she wanted out of you? A. She was talking terms.

Q. Were you in the room when this raid was made and your wife was found? A. Yes, sir.

THE COURT. The testimony would be inadmissible so far as the adultery is concerned, but if it has any bearing on the question of consent, it would be received for that purpose.

Q. Your wife testified, in effect—I can't put my finger right on it—that you were bludgeoned into going to this place. Is that true? A. No, sir.

Q. Without saying a word about what you saw —we have had the photographs here and the testimony—I ask you this, Dr. Nims: Did you tell your wife at any time before this occurrence when she was found under the circumstances that are in evidence, did you tell her that it was all right with you for her to go and sleep with Blum and have sexual intercourse with him ; yes or no? A. No.

Q. Now, Doctor, following the occurrence of October 12, you went to Florida, did you not? A. Yes, sir.

Q. Before you went to Florida, did your wife, unannounced call on you at your office? Did she call on you? A. She called on me, but she told me that she was coming to see me that night. She met me at the office, and the purpose of this meeting was because I was going away, and I was afraid, due to the fact that the children were going to be away from school, that there will be some sort of friction between the governess, and the children and my wife. Before I left, we met and we decided that she is going to have more freedom of visitation, that she will not interfere with the governess, that she will not try to get home and that everything will be quiet in a most respectable manner.

I also called her attention to the fact that it is unfortunate that I have to go to Florida with my brother-in-law instead of with her, because she had created a situation of this type, and then she approached the subject of reconciliation, a Reno divorce, and all other matters, but I was not able to answer her anything.

Q. You did send her flowers from Florida? A. I did not.

Q. Did you send her a telegram, your wife, on her birthday? A. Yes, sir.

Q. Did the telegram read, "Happy Birthday and Happier Birthdays to come. I hope you liked the weeds." A. Yes, sir.

Q. Referring to the flowers, I suppose? A. Yes, sir.

Q. Did you know that the children would probably learn of the flowers, and the telegram, and were you anxious to make them happy? A. Yes, sir, for that purpose they were sent.

Q. Did you also write to your wife from Havana, in which you said, "The President and I wish you a happy New Year"? A. I am not sure. I think I did.

Q. Do you remember when you returned from the south, your wife calling upon you at your office? A. Yes, sir.

Q. Did she say something to you about the divorce case and a jury trial? A. Yes, sir. She tried to impress upon me the disgrace of having gone through with this trial, and she was pleading for reconciliation. I told her that the question of reconciliation is out, that she will have to go through this trial, that if she wants to make it in private chambers, I thought it could be arranged. She said no, she will not go through any trial in private chambers, if I want to force this nasty divorce on her, it will have to go through before a jury.

Q. Anything about photographers being there? Did she say anything about that? A. She said, "As soon as that is announced, I will be photographed," and "It will be in all the papers, all smeared up."

I told her that it is up to her to do it in a nicer way without any public spectacle.

Q. Did she say anything further in that talk about the kids would be there crying, or something like that? A. Well, she said I will have to point out to her that she is the guilty woman in front of the children and in front of the jury, and I said that I can't help it, it is up to her to make it as easy as possible.

Q. Did she say anything about having to fight you or about having to lie, or anything of that kind? Did she say anything about that? A. Yes, sir.

Q. What did she say about that? A. She said, "I may have to tell something that is not true, but that will be in defense of my case."

CROSS EXAMINATION BY MR. MURRAY

Q. You bear in mind, don't you, that you told us that when you met Mrs. Nims in your office before your trip to Florida, that you had made up your mind you were done with her forever? A. Yes, sir.

MR. MURRAY: I offer this, if your Honor please.
MR. STRYKER: I have no objection.

Miami 12/26/46

Dear Louise,

I wonder if you were surprised to get both items on your birthday. However something within me prompted me to do so and I was happy to take the advantage of the occasion.

Things are rather dull for a Captain whose ship is in storm, but I am trying to make the best of the situation and hoping for clearer weather some day.

It is the rest that I went down here for, and not for sports. Rest I get sufficiently and believe it will do me some good.

I wrote a letter to Y.S. and I assume you read it. I hinted to the meeting of "The Revival of the Misfitted."

I was unable to get into any better hotel so I parked here as a last resort, I guess it will do for what I need.

I read your letter several times and found it very interesting. You thought that certain phrases would anger me but nothing really caused me any discomfort.

Be well and take it easy! God above us will guide his children and steer them straight.

Louis.

P.S. Please do not answer this communication because I have a co-pilot here.

L.A.B.

Q. Did you tell Mrs. Nims that you dreamt about your father while you were in Florida? And that your father came to you and told you not to listen to the family? A. Yes, sir, that's right.

Q. And that you should go back to Louise? A. No, sir.

Q. But you did tell her that you dreamed of your father, is that right? A. That's right.

Q. And that he told you not to listen to the family? A. That's right.

Q. Would you explain to us what you remember of this dream where your father had told you not to listen to the family?

MR. STRYKER: Are you asking what the conversation was, Mr. Murray?

MR. MURRAY: With his father, yes.

MR. STRYKER: Just a minute. I don't care—not being a Mr. Freud or anyone else, I don't care to explore this gentleman's dreams. I suppose whatever he may have, or whatever it is claimed he may have said to his wife, it is proper to interrogate about. If Mr. Murray will make it clear that he is not asking about the dream except as related to the wife, I won't object.

MR. MURRAY: Well, your Honor, I submit I first have to find out what his dead father said to him in this dream before I can interrogate him as to what he said to his wife about it.

THE COURT: I think it is the other way around. I think you must first find whether or not he told Mrs. Nims about this dream.

MR. STRYKER: I think the conversation with the father would be hearsay.

MR. MURRAY: I know, but that is for the protection of Mrs. Nims, and not your client, the hearsay rule.

Q. You did? What did you tell Mrs. Nims about your mental reaction to what your father told you in the dream about not listening to the family? A. That if it is only possible, I shall try and give her a Reno divorce.

Q. That is what you told her? A. That's right.

Q. Isn't it a fact Doctor, that you were sensitive and remorseful because you yourself had brought about by your conduct toward Mrs. Nims and your talk to her about going with other men the situation that resulted in the raid in the St. Moritz Hotel? A. I was not remorseful.

Q. It didn't bother you at all? A. No, sir.

Q. And that had no part in your reasons for discussing the Reno divorce? A. No part.

Q. Or the dream of your dead father that you related to Mrs. Nims about a Reno divorce? A. That's right.

Q. Did you tell Mrs. Sharp to convey to Mrs. Nims this: that your mother would die if there was a Reno divorce and that your mother went to your father's grave to ask your father's intervention in keeping you from arranging a Reno divorce?" A. No, sir.

Q. On the first talk of divorce between you and your wife, didn't she beg you to cut down on your practice so that you might act as a husband to her? A. Yes, sir.

Q. Didn't she ask you to take 200 cases a year instead of 700 a year? A. That's right.

Q. Didn't she say that you were getting a minimum of $200 a case and there would be plenty to live on and there was no use of piling up money? A. That was not discussed. Money was never discussed in this situation.

Q. Well, will you tell us what led up to her request to you that you cut down on the number of cases, which I understand was fixed at 700 a year? What led up to that? A. She said that I can do less work and give her more time.

Q. What did you say? A. I told her that the responsibility is too great in time of war to give up the obstetrical practice, that I will do that in a year or two, perhaps, after the war.

Q. She was begging you to take her out, wasn't she? A. Yes, sir.

Q. To take her to a theatre once in a while? A. That's right.

Q. To take her visiting friends, isn't that right? A. Yes, sir.

Q. To spend some time with her? A. Yes, sir.

Q. To go to a restaurant with her? A. Yes, sir.

Q. But you were too busy to do it, weren't you? A. No, sir, I did go.

Q. How frequently did you go, Doctor, say, in the year 1944? A. About twice a week.

Q. And yet at the same time, is it true that she was begging you to cut down the amount of your practice so that you could act as a husband to her? A. Yes, sir.

Q. And yet you say you went out with her twice a week? A. That is right.

Q. Didn't you tell her, in effect, that you were wedded to your profession and that that came first? A. I told her the responsibility is much greater than some of the time that I can give her at home.

Q. And she kept on importuning you, didn't she, to have your company and society, isn't that right? A. That's right.

Q. Was sexual inadequacy discussed between the two of you? A. Just casually.

Q. Just casually? A. That's right.

Q. Did she leave you to believe that that wasn't of much moment to her in motivating her in seeking a divorce? A. Yes, sir.

Q. Before that, had she mentioned to you her painful situation on account of the sexual inadequacy on your part? A. No, sir.

Q. Never? A. Occasionally, but not as an important issue.

Q. Did you have a talk with Mrs. Nims after your return from Florida in which you said to her that you wanted no divorce and you wanted to arrange a Reno divorce, to go along with the wishes of your family, and, in substance, that afterwards, when they were satisfied, you would woo her again and that you wanted to marry her? A. No, sir.

Q. Did you say anything at all, in substance or words along those lines, to Mrs. Nims? A. Yes, sir.

Q. When? A. In January, and on a few more occasions, but after the raid, she was trying to convince me that a Reno divorce is the most logical thing in the interests of the children, to spare the children's reputation. I, for one, thought that she was correct, and I was willing to go with her on this issue until I consulted the lawyers, and they convinced me that I will not be divorced if I do get a Reno divorce.

[ii-f]

Louise Nims—Defendant

REDIRECT EXAMINATION BY MR. STRYKER

Q. Will you tell us as briefly as you can whether you wish to modify your presentation? A. What I said is the true story, and everything else that was said here to contradict that is absolutely untrue, and it is unfortunate that the person who could testify to all this is in a position where, because of bread and butter, they cannot come to testify to the truthfulness of every word that I am saying, and that is all I have to say.

[ii-g]

Colloquy

MR. STRYKER: Well, step down. I don't want to ask any questions.

MR. MURRAY: That is the defense, if your Honor please.

MR. STRYKER: You rest?

MR. MURRAY: Yes.

THE COURT: Both sides rest?

MR. STRYKER: Yes, your Honor.

THE COURT: Are there any suggestions which counsel may wish to make to the Court?

MR. MURRAY: Well, if your Honor will give me time, I would like to submit a brief.

MR. STRYKER: My suggestion would be that there is no question of law that I think would intrigue the Court or counsel. The facts are quite plain. Your Honor has had very adequate opportunity to do the one thing that, as I see it, is involved in this case—to weigh the credibility of the witness with respect to the issue that is before you, and I would really feel, your Honor, that it was supererogation on my part, although I would be glad to do it, if you would care to have me, to marshal and arrange, not alone dilate upon the testimony concerning this woman.

You have seen her, you have heard what she did, you have heard her say that when she came back to her little children, after her escapades and her intercourse with this married man, that she had no sense of shame or degradation. That, coupled with the undisputed facts, would to me, at least, and I would imagine surely, the more so, to your Honor, give you all the index I would need to weigh the testimony of a brazen adulteress with no shame.

On the other side, you have the testimony of an unimpeached doctor, whom you have seen, and you have, as I may say, the preposterousness of the contention, of the palpable falsity of this acknowledged adulteress, that this husband, a man of decent standing in this community, doing a useful service for humanity here in Brooklyn, would say to his wife, "Go out and sleep with any man you want to, I don't care, I don't even care if you bring disease back into the home of these daughters, I don't care if you come back and bring the bastard into the home, it is all right, go anywhere you want.

If I filed fifty briefs, I don't think I would want to say more than that.

MR. MURRAY: Now, your Honor, I could call names too. I could call a woman names, too, but I won't. Perhaps I could say something, too, that would make the folds of the American flag flutter, but I won't do that either, because I know I am talking to a Judge who is not impressed by that character.

You see, there is more in this case, your Honor, than my learned opponent sees. He may be in the position of the farmer who had no hay for his cow and put green glasses on his eyes and gave it sawdust and the cow was deceived, but I, your Honor, without being dramatic without any perorations here, I would like to submit a question to any reasonable person in the world, and it is this: If this high-minded Dr. Nims, this man who has rendered a great service to humanity, and probably at a minimum of $200 a case, if this man, without any fault on his part, did not bring about a situation where this woman was found in the arms of another man for many many reasons that appear in this record, I would like to have some reasonable person explain to me the letter that he sent to her from Florida. Your Honor, that is more expressive and eloquent than anything that anyone can say.

[ii-h]
Opinion of Trial Court

(*New York Law Journal*)

Nims v. Nims—This is an action for an absolute divorce. The issue of adultery was not contested and the proof offered by the plaintiff established the commission of the adultery by a preponderance of the credible evidence. The defendant raised the issue that the plaintiff consented to the adultery. The defendant has failed to establish such defense. There must be a judgment in favor of the plaintiff on the merits.

NOTES

NOTE 1.

PIKE v. PIKE
100 N.J. Eq. 486, 136 A. 421 (1927)

BENTLEY, VICE CHANCELLOR. On petition for divorce, filed by the wife, on the ground of desertion, and a counterclaim charging adultery.

* * *

The parties were married in December, 1922, when the defendant was 26, and the petitioner 20. He appears to be a man of education and refinement. Unlike the usual marriages, these parties never took up their residence together, and neither one of them was held out to society as the other's spouse. He continued to reside at the home of his parents in this state, while his wife took up her abode with her mother as a single woman. While living in this state of physical separation, she was discovered by her husband in a room, at night, with a man named Mandell, under circumstances that were ample to convince anybody that she had been guilty of adultery with him. That act was condoned, and her husband afterwards supported her by payments of a weekly stipend until the 2nd day of October, 1925, when she unquestionably again committed adultery with a man named Proctor, in her bedroom in a New York hotel, where she was living, to the knowledge of her husband, as an unmarried woman.

This man is not entitled to any relief at the hands of this court, because of his own conduct. It will have been observed that, although he had gone through the marriage ceremony with this woman, he never discharged any of his obligations incident to his status as her husband, except the mere, material, financial means of animal sustenance. Added to that is the further fact that he knew, when he married his wife, that she was a weak vessel and required unusual protection. At the close of his cross-examination, he was engaged in the following conversation:

"Q. Was she [at the time of marriage] engaged in theatrical work? A. She had been on the stage before, and when she wasn't on the stage she was a model.

"Q. Did you know, before your marriage, of any sexual intercourse she had ever had, either with you or any one else? A. Yes.

"Q. If you knew of her weakness, why didn't you do something to protect her from the likelihood of her committing adultery? A. Well, it was rather difficult to do that without living with her, you see.

"Q. Were you willing to risk the destruction of the soul of the woman you married, rather than to face some other consequence? A. (The witness does not answer.)"

The explanation given, either by the defendant or his counsel, to explain the former's failure to make a home for his wife was that he had recently entered upon the export business at the time of his marriage and was still dependent upon his father for his support and perhaps the capital that was required in his vocation. His marriage had been a secret one, and he was apprehensive that, if the fact became known to his parents, he would be cast adrift to fend for himself. A sorrier excuse could hardly be given.

Under the circumstances of this case, a husband is under a peculiar duty to protect his wife against her own weakness. The defendant knew at the time of his marriage that his wife had been unable to resist temptation and had been the victim of seduction. Not only did he fail to give her a home, but he never even gave her his name. He never threw around her the protection that every husband is supposed to give his wife, however moral she may be. He did not give her the comfort of his society, as a man is supposed to do. She was left, under all these circumstances, with abundant opportunity to seek the solace of the companionship of others, and the inevitable came to pass. . . .

* * *

. . . His neglect of his wife renders her misconduct no less reprehensible, morally or criminally, but when he complains of his private injury, produced in large part by his failure to perform his duties to her, his complaint falls on deaf ears so far as this court is concerned.

Of course, it is not to be deduced from anything said herein that in ordinary marriages an innocent party is under any duty to interfere with an act of adultery by his or her spouse after suspicion is aroused in the former's breast, but where the opportunity and desire are entirely the creation of the latter and the paramour, and the former had no reason to suspect the chastity of the latter at the time of the marriage. The former may spy and watch the movements and the actions of the other without an effort to frustrate the guilty desire . . . But when a husband is put upon his guard, the peculiar duty mentioned above devolves upon him, and he cannot be recreant to it and then expect the assistance of this court.

* * *

It was urged upon the argument that this man's position is an impossible one. That may be so, unless he shows himself to be the man he did when he forgave her first adultery, recognizing his own shortcomings, and makes an earnest effort to carry out the solemn vow he expressed at the time the petitioner became his wife. He was not an ignorant boy at the time of his marriage. He was a fully matured man of 26, sound of body and mind, who should have experienced no fears of his ability to earn a livelihood for her and himself. There would be few marriages if every young man should postpone his wedding until he had amassed a fortune or established a successful business. But whether his lot be a hard one or not, the policy of our law forbids this court to give him any relief, and, if such is to be had, it must be secured from that branch of the government to whom is committed the authority to declare the policy of the state. Whether relief should be given in a case like this is, at least, problematical, in view of the lightness with which this solemn ceremony is so frequently entered.

The petition should be dismissed for lack of any evidence, and the prayer of the counterclaim denied.

NOTE 2.

BROWN v. BROWN
[1956] P. 438, 452-455

LORD MERRIMAN, P.

[D]esertion in the nature of things almost invariably involves total deprivation of sexual intercourse, in addition to comprising the wider intention permanently to disrupt the marriage, although it is well settled that the refusal of sexual intercourse does not by itself constitute desertion. . . . Thus, desertion is clearly a graver matrimonial offence than refusal of sexual intercourse; and if the greater includes the less, it is not altogether clear, on principle, how it is that refusal of sexual intercourse can, but desertion cannot, amount to conduct conducing.

It was suggested in argument that there is a distinction between desertion and the deprivation of sexual intercourse while the parties are living together, inasmuch as the natural instincts of the deprived spouse are more habitually invoked by the presence of the other. While this may be true in certain cases, it is difficult to distinguish between the deprivation caused by the resolute withdrawal for years to a separate room, and that caused by desertion.

* * *

NOTE 3.

LLOYD v. LLOYD AND LEGGERI
[1938] P. 174, 183-196

LANGSTON, J.

* * *

It is impossible to argue that there was nothing which the petitioner could have done [about his wife's adultery], and, indeed, one is driven here to contemplate the question whether a man can ever be entitled to say, as the petitioner appears to have said to himself: "The mere matter of adultery does not seem to me to be of crucial importance. Of course, I greatly dislike my wife committing adultery, and wish she would not do it, but I am not going to part company with her, or seek the assistance of the Divorce Court on that ground. I will wait and see whether I can get her back, whether my circumstances will not improve." Can he, to put it in another way, make his own law in the matter, and say: "The test with me is whether her affection has changed, not whether she commits adultery, and I will ask the Court to give me a decree on the ground of adultery when I find that what I really care about has taken place, namely that her affection has now been taken from me?" That is not, as I understand it, the law. . . . A man comes here for the remedy of a wrong. The wrong is adultery, and it would be going further, as I see it, than I have ever yet seen any other judge go, to say that a man may take the law into his own hands in this matter and make his own selection of what he thinks to be the real grievance that enables him to come here.

* * *

. . . The petitioner appears to have taken the view that if he could get his wife back in the end, it was worth while—not shutting his eyes to it, that would be putting it too high—but tolerating his wife's infidelity for the time being. . . . Is it fair to say that the petitioner was guilty of lethargy? It certainly is a toleration of a very lengthy and a very complete kind.

It is not in dispute that the parties continued their marital relations when they met. There is something to be said for a man who is endeavouring to win his wife back. The petitioner's attitude was "well, if we continue relations when we meet there is some chance that she will return." Against that it is quite obvious that toleration becomes contentment. In such a case it can hardly be said that the husband was really strongly disapproving if he was for all this time prepared to share his wife with another man.

* * *

[T]he matter stands in this way: Is this toleration for nine months on the part of the petitioner fatal to his case? As I understand the law of connivance it is fatal to his case. The respondent comes before the Court with no merits at all. . . . A man may not stand by and tolerate his wife's adultery, meeting her, conversing with her, having intercourse with her, as this man did, and then thereafter, because of some private view of his own as to what a woman owes to her husband, complain of her violation of that private view and come here to seek a remedy at the hands of this Court.

b. In Cruelty

WILLAN v. WILLAN
[1960] 2 All E.R. 463

WILLMER, L. J. . . . . This is an appeal by a husband against a decision of Mr. Commissioner GALLOP of Oct. 13, 1959, whereby, on a petition for dissolution of his marriage . . . on the ground that the cruelty had been condoned. The husband appeals to this court, inviting us to find that in the circumstances there was no condonation and that the husband is entitled to the relief claimed . . . there is now no dispute as to the fact of the wife having been cruel to the husband.

The relevant facts lie within a comparatively small compass. The parties were married on June 2, 1925, and there are two children of the marriage, one born shortly after the marriage and the other born soon after the war in 1946. The husband was away on military service during the war, but cohabitation was resumed on his demobilization, and he continued to live with his wife until the morning of Sept. 29, 1958.

The husband's case against the wife is that throughout the marriage, and more particularly in the latter part of it, she frequently and persistently assaulted him and showed violence to him and that she was immensely jealous of his relations with other women ; and it was also said that she habitually used offensive and obscene language, calling him by horrible names and so forth. It is also alleged—and this is the real gravamen of the charge—that she frequently demanded sexual intercourse with him at times when he did not wish to have it, obliging him to conform to her wishes by indulging in various types of violence in order to bend his will to hers. In particular, it was said that she would pull his hair, catch hold of him by the ears, and shake his head violently to and fro ; and, at any rate on one occasion, it was said that she kicked him on his injured leg, causing him great pain. She would also pester him far into the night to have sexual intercourse, so that eventually he was compelled to comply as the only means of getting his rest. That is the nature of the husband's case of cruelty which, as I have said, was found in his favour. I have referred to the details of it only because the alleged act of condonation is very largely bound up with the kind of conduct which is complained of by the husband as cruelty on the part of his wife.

It appears that for some time before the final separation the parties were on bad terms, although sexual intercourse was continuing in the circumstances which I have described. The husband at least was for some time in the hands of solicitors, and we know that on or about Aug. 13, 1958, the solicitors wrote on his behalf to his wife, complaining of her cruel conduct and informing her that the husband would be obliged to leave her. Even after that, however, life went on very much as before, the husband continuing to reside in the matrimonial home with his wife, and continuing to share the same bed with her. He said in the course of his evidence that two or three weeks before the final separation he voluntarily and willingly had intercourse with his wife. A distinction is drawn in the evidence between that occasion and certain others when he had intercourse with his wife, not because he wanted to, but for the sake of peace, in the circumstances to which I have alluded. It is not without significance, I think, that even after the solicitors' letter was written the husband is still found to be willingly and voluntarily having intercourse with his wife.

It is said (and this much is common ground between the parties) that, on the night of Sept. 28/29, i.e., the night before the husband left for the last time, an act of sexual intercourse took place between the parties. The husband says that that act, like many other acts previously, was induced by the wife pestering him far into the night, showing some degree of violence to him, pulling his hair and so forth and, finally, as I understand it, rolling on top of him, so that eventually, towards the small hours of the morning, and for the sake of peace, he did have intercourse with her. Thereafter, the parties appear to have gone straight to sleep, and the next thing that happened was the alarm clock going off at a quarter to six in the morning. The husband promply got up, dressed and left the house at six o'clock in order to go to work. He kissed his wife and said goodbye, all in accordance with his usual procedure, the wife saying good-bye to him. I mention those facts as to what took place after the last act of intercourse because it was at one time suggested that, if that act of intercourse did amount to condonation, conduct subsequent thereto on the part of the wife was sufficient to bring about a revival. Clearly, however, on the evidence there never could have been any merit in that suggestion. The only question is whether or not the husband, by having intercourse with his wife in the circumstances which I have described on the night of Sept. 28/29, must be held to have condoned the prior cruelty found against the wife.

When the case came on ultimately in this court . . . the first ground . . . was in the following terms:

> "That the learned commissioner misdirected himself in law in that the last act of intercourse which occurred between the parties on the night of Sept. 28, 1958, could not have constituted condonation by reason of the fact that it constituted an important element of the cruelty complained of, and/or by reason of the fact that it took place when the petitioner was under duress and/or was not a free agent."

So stated, that ground of appeal runs two or three arguments together, and I will do my best to keep them separate. In the first place, it is said that this act of intercourse on the part of the husband could not be held to amount to condonation, because it was one and the same with an act which was of itself relied on as part of the cruelty alleged. . . . Certainly there is no finding by the learned commissioner that the last act of intercourse relied on as condonation was one with the cruelty alleged by the husband against the wife. Furthermore, as it seems to me, and as I indicated during the argument, the contention is really the result of muddled thinking, because it confuses the actual act of sexual intercourse, which constitutes the evidence of condonation, with the prior conduct complained of on the part of the wife, whereby she induced the act of intercourse. I can well understand that pestering in such circumstances on the part of the wife, in such a way as to deny the husband sleep, more particularly if accompanied by the pulling of his hair, might very well be capable of amounting to cruelty. But, whether that be so or not, I find it impossible to say that the subsequent action of the wife in submitting herself to an act of sexual intercourse could in any circumstances amount to an act of cruelty against the husband . . . .

Then it was said that this act of intercourse was induced by duress on the part of the wife, and that the husband was not to be regarded as a free agent. It is well established that, whatever may be the position of a wife, in the case of a husband the fact of having intercourse with the wife, with full knowledge of the matrimonial offence of which complaint is made, is conclusive evidence of condonation by the husband of the wife. It is conclusive evidence because it is the best possible way of showing that the wife has been reinstated as a wife. Only one exception to that rule was accepted by the House of Lords . . . and that is the case where the act of intercourse is induced by fraud on the part of the wife. Subject to that . . . intercourse by a husband with his wife after knowledge of the matters complained of is conclusive evidence of condonation.

*   *   *

[T]he learned commissioner expressed this view:

> "Leaving aside questions of hysteria or hypnotism, or other such matters, if a man, through whatever blandishment or irritation, decides to have sexual intercourse, that must be a voluntary act, and I must hold that the act of intercourse in this case was a voluntary act."

I agree with the learned commissioner, and I doubt whether the matter can be better stated than in the commissioner's own words.

All that has been proved in this case is that the wife used means, to which exception may well be taken, for the purpose of persuading her husband to have intercourse with her. He was free to submit or to resist. He was free, I suppose, to have run away, but in the end he decided that the best course to take was to submit to her wishes. I dare say he did show unwillingness, but to say that he showed unwillingness is not to say that he acted involuntarily. It might be otherwise in the case of a wife; but in the case of a husband who has sexual intercourse it can only be said of him that what he does he does on purpose, and that sexual intercourse with his wife must be a voluntary act on his part.

*   *   *

c. In Desertion

[i]

SMITH v. SMITH
198 Md. 630, 84 A. 2d 890 (1951)

MARKELL, JUDGE.

This is an appeal from a decree granting the wife a divorce *a mensa*.

The parties were married in 1924, when they were both under twenty. They have two sons, both adults and married. Since 1940 they have frequently quarreled. One or more previous bills for divorce were filed. They both live in the same house, not now as husband and wife. When they had an "argument", she would strike him and he would strike her, apparently without lasting harm to either. His net earnings have ranged from zero to five hundred dollars or a thousand dollars a year. They both were practically supported by his mother, whose second husband's death in 1950 has reduced her income. For some years the mother had employed the husband at twenty dollars a week at a tavern which she sold about 1945. The mother owns, but does not collect, a ground rent on the house owned by husband and wife as tenant by the entireties. The mother gave the wife forty dollars a week, allowed the husband to collect a rent of two hundred and fifty dollars a month from a property of the mother's, and frequently paid bills for him and made him other gifts. The husband suffers from deafness and, he says, from heart trouble and stomach ulcers. The wife is skeptical about his ill health, but the trial judge did not definitely discredit it. He owns a boat on which he takes out fishing parties, for hire, in Florida in winter and from Annapolis in summer. For some years he has gone to Florida (without his wife) in winter, for his health or for fishing or for both, and has frequently gone fishing in the boat in summer, staying days at a time. In these respects his conduct in 1950, apart from statements ascribed to him by the wife, was not appreciably different from their manner of living in former years.

Neither husband nor wife drew a prize in their matrimonial lottery. For industry and either zeal or capacity to support his wife his pecuniary value is low. In his testimony he was disposed to rhapsodize about their happy home and family— if the wife would refrain from excessive drink— but there seems to be little in him to hold a wife's affection. She admits she drinks beer, but denies that she becomes intoxicated. If, as she says, she could drink eight bottles, at a protracted sitting, without becoming intoxicated, it may be that, as the husband says, their bedroom smelled like a brewery and she was not a pleasant companion. However, neither non-support nor drunkenness is a ground for divorce.

In the bill of complaint, filed October 2, 1950, the wife alleged that on June 23, 1950 the husband deserted her without just cause or reason, declaring his intention to live with her no longer, that this abandonment and desertion has continued uninterruptedly until the present time, is deliberate and final and the separation is beyond any reasonable hope or expectation of a reconciliation. . . .

One night the last week of August she came home about two or three o'clock, had no key and had to climb through the back window. Her husband came in. "He gave me the devil. We had come in and we were both feeling good"; she had been drinking. Having testified that the desertion on June 22, 1950 had "continued uninterruptedly until the present time" and on cross-examination, that on the August night "nothing [else] that I can recall" happened, she was asked, "You say you don't recall anything else that happened?" She answered, "* * * Yes, there was something else that happened. We had intercourse, and, he told me at the time, he says, 'I am still leaving'." He says she was the aggressor, but both were willing. In response to leading questions by her own counsel (not her counsel in this court) she testified: "Q. You say this act of intercourse took place between you and your husband in August, 1950. I think you said you tried to make up to him? A. Yes. [She had not in fact said so.] Q. Is that the reason you performed the act of intercourse with him? A. Yes."

[T]he marital relations in August not only (a) amounted in law to a termination of any existing desertion and a condonation of any previous marital offenses of either against the other, but (b) show that in fact neither party considered that there had been any desertion. If he had deliberately and finally deserted her, there was neither excuse nor occasion for him to "give her the devil" for coming home late drunk. To constitute condonation, other conduct may require evidence of intent, but we think the sound view is that the law itself ascribes to marital relations the conclusive effect of condonation and specifically of terminating desertion. . . . Such relations are legally compatible only with marriage, not with separation. The concept of "constructive desertion", when the deserter and the deserted continue to live under the same roof, cannot make out of marriage a hybrid status of separation with occasional concubinage. . . .

. . . We think the trial judge was in error in granting a divorce *a mensa*, without adequate ground for divorce, because he thought such a disposition of the case would be beneficial to the parties. In his opinion the judge said, "* * * You are not dealing here with a young married couple with children who are infants, and I realize, of course, that the State is interested in keeping the marriage a going concern, so to speak. . . . Intercourse can be conditional, of course—conditional on a reconciliation. She said that is why it took place. She was hoping it would effect a reconciliation, and when the intercourse was over, he said it was over, and left. He said she got up out of bed and went into the other room. Be that as it may, I think that the practical and proper solution is as I have said, a divorce *a mensa* for Mrs. Smith."

For the reasons stated, we think this view is not in accord with the law.

NOTES

NOTE 1.

SMITH v SMITH
Ten Years Later

This is to advise you that these parties went back to live together and as far as I know are living happily. [Letter dated Jan. 17, 1961, from Meyer Reamer, attorney for the husband.]

NOTE 2.

BAGULEY v. BAGULEY
[1961] 2 All E.R. 635

HODSON,, L. J.

. . . The authorities, as I understand them, have consistently proceeded on the basis that the law of condonation is the same for the wife as for the husband in that sense—namely, that, if she has reinstated him by submitting voluntarily to his embraces without any extraneous circumstance weighing against the inference to be drawn from that submission, she must be held to have condoned the offence.

There has been, no doubt, some talk about the desirability of the law of condonation being altered, in the sense that it might be thought to be desirable that some interval should elapse—some probationary period might be allowed to supervene—before it could be said that the party could not rely on complaints previous to that condonation. That talk has not resulted in legislation. And the law, as I understand it, is as I have stated it—that once the reinstatement has taken place it cannot be said: "Oh, well, it was only a short reinstatement: in this case it was only one act of intercourse: it did not even take place in the matrimonial home, it took place in a living room in somebody else's house: therefore it can be treated as of no consequence." This was not a submission to the embraces of someone of the opposite sex who had no ties with her. It was a submission of a woman to her husband; and . . . it is repugnant to regard that act of submission as if it were some sort of casual commerce between two persons of opposite sexes, when in fact one knows that it is an act of intercourse of a wife with her husband—indeed, following conversations at which they had agreed to reconciliation.

*   *   *

NOTE 3.

RASGAITIS v. RASGAITIS
347 Ill. App. 477, 107 N.E. 2d 273 (1952)

SCHWARTZ, JUSTICE.

. . . Cohabitation means the living together as husband and wife, People v. Burke, 400 Ill. 240, 79 N.E. 2d 488, but does not necessarily imply sexual intercourse.

Condonation is a question of intent and not a defense that can be reduced to any exact formulae. It is defined as a full and free "forgiveness of an offense upon condition that it will not be repeated * * *." Abbott v. Abbott, supra, 192 Ill. at page 441, 61 N.E. at page 351. Cohabitation is evidence of condonation, but it is not conclusive evidence thereof. . . . The Illinois Supreme Court has held that even an act of intercourse does not necessarily constitute condonation when it is not accompanied by an intent to resume the marital relation in full. . . . [T]he court held that condonation would not be found as a matter of law, even though the parties continued to live together right up to the filing of the bill; that cohabitation, the living together as husband and wife, although evidence of condonation, is not conclusive evidence thereof. Condonation, said the court, "depends upon the intention of the injured person to forgive the offender, to overlook the wrong and to continue or renew the conjugal relation."

[*ii*]

PERRY v. PERRY
[1952] P. 203

Appeal from Judge Emlyn Jones sitting as a commissioner in divorce.

The husband and wife were married on July 2, 1939. On July 6, 1944, the wife left her husband and went to live with her mother. From July to October, 1944, the husband paid weekly visits to the wife in an endeavour to persuade her to return to him. He did not see his wife again until December, 1949, when he received a letter from her asking for money. As a result of that letter he went to see her and visited her at fortnightly intervals from December, 1949, to March, 1950; on each occasion he pressed her to return but she always refused. On two or three of those fortnightly visits he had sexual intercourse with her and as a result a child was born on December 6, 1950. The husband did not visit the wife again after March, 1950. On November 8, 1950, she wrote to him as follows: "Bob, it isn't any use asking me to live with you again because I have fully made up my mind I never will. It is nearly six years since you and I parted and I have never felt at any time as if I wanted to return to you. You know we never get on well together. The love was all on your side. I made a big mistake when I married you. I am sorry, but never ask me again. Goodbye."

On May 15, 1951, the husband presented this petition for divorce alleging that the wife had . . . deserted him without cause for a period of "at least three years" . . . [i]mmediately preceding the presentation of the "petition". The wife did not defend the petition. Of the husband's evidence the commissioner said: "The husband impressed me, and I place this on record, as a truthful and completely honest man, and he told me that even now he was anxious to effect a reconciliation with his wife. It is clear to me that he loved her and still does." The commissioner then proceeded: Upon these facts I am satisfied and so hold that the wife was guilty of desertion on or about July 6, 1944. I am also satisfied that the state of desertion, thus commenced, continued up to the presentation of the petition in the ordinary sense of the word 'desertion.' That is to say, both the fact of separation and the necessary animus on the wife's part so continued. By 'separation' I mean here only that there was no full resumption of cohabitation in a matrimonial home. Of the wife's animus I need only say that I find that at no time since July, 1944, has she formed any intention to resume married life."

* * *

EVERSHED, M. R.

[D]esertion as a ground for divorce differs from the statutory grounds of adultery and cruelty in one important respect. The offence founding the cause of action is not complete, is (as it were) inchoate, until the action is constituted. If one spouse has committed adultery or has treated the other with cruelty, the latter has an accrued right to petition for divorce. He or she may at once repudiate the marriage and is no longer bound to affirm it and reinstate the offending spouse. The deserted spouse has no such right, no such election. If the deserting spouse genuinely desires to return, his or her partner cannot refuse reinstatement. It is, moreover . . . , contrary to public policy that the deserted spouse, desiring a resumption of cohabitation and bound to affirm the marriage, should be embarrassed in efforts for reconciliation.

It is because of these essential characteristics that, according to Mr. Bingham, [for the husband] what is known as "condonation" cannot be properly applicable to the offence of desertion prior to presentation of the petition. And Mr. Duncan [Queen's Proctor] has not indeed con-

tended to the contrary. The burden of his argument is not that an act (or, as in this case, two or three acts) of sexual intercourse should be taken to amount to "condonation" by a husband of a deserting wife (involving directly or by analogy the conditions and consequences attaching to "condonation" as applied to adultery or cruelty) but rather that such an act or acts must involve necessarily such a resumption of cohabitation, or the marital relationship, that the preceding desertion is altogether ended and its consequences wiped away.

. . . [I]t is convenient, first, to observe that it is clear—and also agreed between Mr. Bingham and Mr. Duncan—that "desertion" postulates both (i) the factum of separation and (ii) a continuing animus deserendi on the part of the deserting spouse. . . .

The conception of condonation as understood in England is older than that of divorce according to statute, to which it is now related. Historically it could not have been applied to continuing desertion as a ground for divorce; but that is no necessary reason why it should not applied now. . . . It involves, . . . forgiveness confirmed or made effective by reinstatement. But by the law of England it is no less clearly established that the so-called "forgiveness" is conditional, conditional upon the "condoned" spouse thereafter fulfilling in all respects the obligations of marriage, so that if any matrimonial offence is afterwards committed by him or her—whether or not the same as that "condoned," and whether or not in itself giving ground for divorce—the "condonation" ceases to have effect; the offence "condoned" and all its consequences are for all purposes "revived." . . . So in the present case Mr. Duncan was content to submit that by "condonation" was implied a "conditional sacrifice of an accrued right."

At any rate the notion of "forgiveness made effective by reinstatement" implies, in my judgment, a right of election on the part of the injured spouse and does not fit the case of a deserted spouse who must always (until presentation of the petition at least) affirm the marriage and be ready to take back the deserting spouse. It is, moreover, naturally applicable to an act committed or to a course of conduct rather than to a state of mind (which is the second characteristic of desertion). Finally, the conditional quality of "condonation" and the liability of the condoned offence to be "revived" by subsequent misconduct cannot be made to fit with continuing but (as regards remedy) incomplete desertion; for it seems to be established that a period of desertion once terminated cannot afterwards be relied upon, when added to a later period of desertion or otherwise, to satisfy the requirements of . . . the Act of 1950. In this connexion it is to be noted that under the Act of 1857, where a husband had committed adultery and had also committed the offence of desertion without reasonable cause for two years, but the wife had condoned the adultery, subsequent matrimonial misconduct by the husband was held to revive not only the adultery but the desertion. . . .

Whatever, therefore, may be the situation where acts which in the case, for example, of adultery would have constituted condonation had taken place after presentation of a petition for divorce on the ground of desertion . . . , the conception of condonation has, in my judgment, no application, either in strictness or by analogy (save perhaps indirectly to the extent later mentioned in regard to resumed cohabitation), to a current period of desertion. I do not forget that desertion, though of a character not sufficient to give grounds for divorce, is nevertheless a matrimonial offence. But even if such an offence could be said to be "condoned" by some act or conduct not involving a resumption of the marital relationship, such a condonation should be in principle "conditional" so that the offence would be for all purposes revived by subsequent misconduct. . . .

* * *

[S]exual intercourse is conclusive proof of condonation of adultery by a husband who has knowledge of the adultery and, in the absence of fraud by the wife, whatever may have been in fact the intention of either spouse. That it may not be so in the case of an injured wife depends on the proposition that the situations of a husband and wife are not entirely the same. Historically they plainly were not; and modern legislation may be said not effectively to have been capable of eliminating all biological differences. Still, the difference in situation is not obvious in a case where the wife has voluntarily left her husband and has for years been living entirely separate from, and independent of, him.

* * *

There remains, however, the question . . . whether an act of sexual intercourse, or at least two or three acts such as were proved in the present case, should not be treated (against a husband petitioner) as constituting such a resumption of the marital relationship as puts a stop, for good and all, to the precedent period of desertion by the wife.

There is no doubt (as I have earlier stated) that resumption of marital relationship or resumption of cohabitation (for this purpose I treat the two formulae as synonymous) puts an end to desertion. . . . Approaching the matter as res integra and without regard to authority, I should have thought that the question whether cohabitation or marital relationship has or has not been resumed is a question of fact and degree to be determined according to common-sense principles. Sexual intercourse is beyond doubt a most important incident in the relationship, though its significance will obviously vary, for example, according to the age of the spouses. Still, I should not have thought (again treating the matter without reference to authority) that an act or two or three acts of intercourse without more could sensibly be regarded as necessarily determining the question; and I should also have thought that mutual (or "bilateral") intention was in this matter essential. Without attempting a definition, the implication of desertion is a rejection of all the obligations of marriage. It has been held by the House of Lords . . . that absolute refusal of sexual relations by one spouse, who in other respects fulfils the duties of marriage, could not amount to desertion; and, if this is so, it does not seem to me shocking or unreasonable that participation in one or two acts of intercourse by a husband or wife, who in all other respects repudiated the marital relationship, should not be regarded as necessarily constituting a resumption of that relationship. If this view be right, then on the facts found in the present case I should conclude that there had been no such resumption.

[M]utual intention is of the essence of the matter. . . . [I]n Bartram v. Bartram[57] . . . Bucknill L. J. said: "But, in the present case, the husband has established actual desertion by the wife for many months. That being so, it seems to me that the husband is entitled to say that the desertion, once established, continues until it is proved that it has been brought to an end. The wife did not suggest at any time that she had brought it to an end. The question is, do the facts proved establish that it was brought to an end? In my view, it can only be brought to an end if the facts show an intention on the part of the wife to set up a matrimonial home with the husband. . . . If the facts do not establish any intention on the part of the wife to set up a matrimonial home, the mere fact that, as a lodger, she came to live under the same roof as her husband, because she had nowhere else to go, does not remove the desertion

---

57. [1950] P. 1, 5, 6.

which she had already started and which continued to run."

* * *

There remains Mr. Duncan's point that—particularly having regard to the birth of the child in December, 1950—it is contrary to common sense to suppose that at the time of the proved acts of intercourse and of the conception of the child its parents were separated in fact and truth. I am unable to agree. If the right view is that there must be some reality of resumed cohabitation to stop the running of desertion, common sense is by no means offended by my conclusion. The question is of the inference to be drawn from acts of intercourse: to that question the birth of the child appears to me to be an irrelevant misfortune. The quality of the acts of intercourse cannot be affected by the accident of their result. Nor can I think it would as a matter of public policy be desirable that matters of this kind should involve possible questions of dispute about the use of contraceptives.

* * *

. . . I think that the appeal should be allowed and that the petitioner is entitled to his decree.

d. In the Distribution of Property

KEENE v. KEENE
57 Cal. 2d 657, 371 P. 2d 329 (1962)

PETERS, J.—I dissent:

The majority opinion adopts a double standard that is neither moral nor legal. It tells us that a woman who has "sinned," by knowingly entering into a meretricious relationship, is not to be permitted to share in property that she helped to accumulate, and that all such property is to go to the man involved, even though he has also "sinned," at least in equal degree. In other words, the majority opinon says that even though the property before the court may have been acquired, in part, as a result of the nonmarital and valuable services of the plaintiff, as a matter of law, she has no legal or equitable right in that property because she knowingly entered into a meretricious relationship. That is not and should not be the law.

The facts, generally, are correctly set forth in the majority opinion, although the key facts are there under-emphasized. These parties lived together as husband and wife for nearly the entire period from 1938 to 1956. Undoubtedly, the relationship was meretricious, and the finding that both parties knew that it was is supported by the evidence. During this period the plaintiff managed the household and performed all the customary duties of a housewife. But the court found, and the finding is supported, that she did much more. It found that from 1938 to 1946 "plaintiff did perform work and labor for the mutual benefit of defendant and plaintiff on a certain ranch situate in Butte County, California, standing of record in the name of and owned by defendant, said services consisting of helping in the performance of farm labor, including the raising of turkeys, chickens, sheep, cattle, the clearing of land, the sowing, raising and harvesting of grain crops and the growing and harvesting of nut crops. The court further finds that on a few occasions during the years 1947 through 1956, the plaintiff assisted defendant in connection with the operation of his real estate brokerage business, furniture business and the buying and selling of real estate, timber and timber lands."

This finding is amply supported by the record. Even the defendant testified that some such services were rendered.

There is substantial evidence that during the period the parties resided on defendant's ranch—1938 to 1946—a large commercial turkey flock was purchased and maintained by them, and that this flock was entirely cared for by the plaintiff. . . . There is substantial evidence that she helped to clear certain areas of the ranch by working with the men to clear off rocks, and thus made these areas available for cultivation. There is also substantial evidence that she not only grew and maintained a large vegetable garden, but that she helped sow and harvest the commercial crops, including not only grain but nut crops as well. These are not the customary duties of a housewife.

In 1946 defendant sold the ranch, which he had owned prior to the inception of his relationship with plaintiff, and from then until 1956, engaged in the real estate and furniture businesses, or spent his time traveling about the country for pleasure with plaintiff. There is evidence that during this period the plaintiff assisted defendant to some extent in those businesses.

* * *

The trial court found and concluded that, as a matter of law, plaintiff was entitled to no portion of this jointly earned fund. The majority opinion affirms this result. It reasons that, in the absence of an agreement of joint venture or partnership, the plaintiff is without remedy because she knowingly entered into the meretricious relationship. In reaching this result the majority opinion purports to follow the rule of *Vallera* v. *Vallera*, 21 Cal.2d 681 [134 P.2d 761]. That case announced no such rule, but, in fact, announced a rule quite to the contrary.

* * *

In *Vallera,* after holding that a woman who lives with a man in the good faith belief that a valid marriage exists may share in the property acquired by them during the existence of the relationship, the court posed the specific problem involved as follows: "The controversy is thus reduced to the question whether a woman living with a man as his wife but with no genuine belief that she is legally married to him acquires by cohabitation alone the rights of a co-tenant in his earnings and accumulations during the period of their relationship. It has already been answered in the negative. [Citation.)]" (21 Cal. 2d at p. 684.)

This is the rule that the majority believes is controlling in the present case. But note that the quoted rule merely holds that the plaintiff is not entitled to share in their accumulations by reason of "cohabitation alone." [W]here, in addition to "cohabitation alone" the woman contributes to the joint acquisition her own funds or property, she is entitled to share in the property in the proportion that her funds or property contributed towards its acquisition. . . . The exact words used by the court were these (p. 685):

"Plaintiff's lack of good faith in alleging the belief that she had entered into a valid marriage would not, however, preclude her from recovering property to which she would otherwise be entitled. If a man and woman live together as husband and wife under an agreement to pool their earnings and share equally in their joint accumulations, equity will protect the interests of each in such property. [Citations.] Even in the absence of an express agreement to that effect, the woman would be entitled to share in the property jointly accumulated, in the proportion that her funds contributed toward its acquisition. . . ."

The key word in that quotation, so far as the instant problem is concerned is "funds." By the use of that term did the majority in *Vallera* intend to include extramarital services as well as money and perhaps negotiable paper? The word "funds" could, of course, mean only money, and perhaps negotiable paper. The majority, in the instant case, so interpret the term by referring at some length to its dictionary definitions, and by disregarding the holdings of the . . . cases. . . .

The theory of these cases is sound and is based on sound public policy. Obviously, if the two were not illegally living together, the woman could recover. In that event it would be a plain business relationship and a contract would be implied. Illicit cohabitation does not invalidate an otherwise valid relationship. The man is not entitled to benefit from such nonwifely services simply because the two have illegally cohabited.

The majority opinion, with some apparent reluctance, concedes that where the sinful plaintiff contributes money or property towards the joint acquisition she may proportionately recover in spite of the meretricious relationship. It reaches this conclusion not only by adopting a very limited definition of the term "funds" as used in *Vallera,* but also purports to reach the same result by an interesting but inapplicable discussion of the law of trusts. The majority would permit a recovery, apparently on the theory of resulting trust, when the plaintiff contributes money or tangible property towards acquisitions taken in the name of defendant. In other words, if the woman contributes cash or tangible property worth $1,000 towards the creation of a fund of $2,000, she could, upon termination of the relationship, recover one half of the property. But if she renders nonmarital services worth $1,000 and the man contributes $1,000 in property towards the fund, she can recover nothing. In such event, the majority would say that she has furnished no "consideration" towards the acquisition of the property that is before the court. Services, of course, as well as money or property, can constitute "consideration."

* * *

D.

To Decisions Concerning the Administration of Reorganized Wife-Husband Relationships?

1.

PEARCE v. PEARCE
37 Wash. 2d 918, 226 P. 2d 895 (1951)

HAMEY, JUSTICE.

The propriety of a commitment for contempt . . . [is] questioned on this appeal.

We are here concerned with the aftermath of a divorce action in which the trial court found that the plaintiff wife, Veva Marie Pearce, had no grounds for divorce, but awarded a divorce to the defendant husband, Leo E. Pearce, on his cross-complaint.

* * *

As a part of the interlocutory decree, the trial court restrained the wife "from in any way associating or communicating with Art Kringel and from seeking employment * * * or being employed where he is employed." Mr. Kringel, although not a party to the action, was likewise restrained "from in any way associating or communicating with" Mrs. Pearce, and "from seeking employment or being employed where she may be employed."

Mrs. Pearce and Kringel did thereafter associate and communicate with each other. As a result, Mr. Pearce, on May 9, 1949, and prior to the entry of a final decree, instituted this proceeding requiring Mrs. Pearce and Kringel to show cause why they should not be punished for contempt. A show cause order was duly entered, and a hearing was set for May 24, 1949.

* * *

The hearing was held before the same judge who had heard the original divorce proceedings and had entered the interlocutory decree and restraining order. Numerous witnesses testified, including Mrs. Pearce and Kringel. The evidence was in conflict as to the extent of the association and communication which had been carried on between Mrs. Pearce and Kringel since entry of the interlocutory decree. The trial court's finding on this, as recited in the order of commitment, was as follows:

> "That said Veva Marie Pearce and Art Kringel on May 1, 1949, were sitting together in the Blue Bell Tavern, in Spokane and were drinking, smoking and conversing with each other; that they were in the Pleasure Inn, in Spokane, at the same time on the 30th day of April; that they were in a drugstore at Napa and Mission in Spokane, on the 26th day of December, 1948 * * *."

Whether that association and communication was casual and unpremeditated, or was planned and willful, was disputed at the hearing and is hotly and extensively debated in the briefs. The trial court, in its oral opinion, expressed the view that these meetings were not mere accidents, and a finding to this effect is to be implied from the recitals of the order of commitment.

Following the hearing, and on May 31, 1949, two orders were entered. In one order the trial court found Mrs. Pearce and Kringel guilty of contempt, by reason of a violation of the restraining order, and committed them each to the county jail for ten days. . . .

It is our view that the trial court had no authority to enter the restraining order, the violation of which was the basis for the contempt proceeding.

We recognize and approve the modern tendency to protect personal rights by injunctive relief where there is no adequate remedy at law. We have found cases where husbands have enjoined third parties from associating with their wives; . . . where wives have enjoined third parties from associating with their husbands; . . . and where fathers have enjoined third parties from associating with their daughters; . . . but we have found nothing comparable to the present situation.

The husband here was not asking for the protection of the society and affection of his wife against interference by Mr. Kringel; he apparently did not want the one and had acquiesced in the loss of the other. He asked for a divorce and was awarded an interlocutory decree.

* * *

We are of the view that the restraining order was an attempted extension of the equity power beyond any proper limits, and that it amounted to an unwarranted and unjustified interference with the personal rights of Mrs. Pearce. (Kringel has not appealed.) As was said in Snedaker v. King, supra: "The decree in this case is an extreme instance of government by injunction. It attempts to govern, control, and direct personal relations and domestic affairs." 111 Ohio St. at page 228, 145 N.E., at page 16.

While we hold that the trial court exceeded its authority in entering the restraining order on which the contempt order is predicated, we cannot but feel that it was intended for the wife's protection, and that she would have been much better off had she obeyed it. However, courts cannot stand in *loco parentis* to adults like Mrs. Pearce, and, under the pains and penalties of contempt, restrain them from doing those things which they ought not to do, except as those things come within the orbit of matters which affect the welfare of the child or children concerned. . . .

* * *

NOTES

NOTE 1.

BRANCH v. BRANCH
188 Pa. Super. 587, 149 A. 2d 573 (1959)

WOODSIDE, JUDGE.

* * *

The question is whether a person named correspondent in a divorce action can appeal from a decree granting the plaintiff a divorce on the ground of adultery.

* * *

The reputation of one named as a corespondent in a divorce action suffers thereby, and the social consequences may be serious.[1] But the effect of the decree upon the appellant is an argument that must be directed to the legislature.

Although the decree may have serious social and personal consequences, it should be noted that it is not an adjudication *against* the corespondent, and has no legal effects upon him, except the indirect one that the defendant cannot marry him as long as the plaintiff lives.

Of course, if the defendant committed adultery with the corespondent, it follows that the corespondent must have had sexual intercourse with the defendant. But this is not a legal conclusion. Judicial fact finders, having no absolute wisdom to know the truth, must make their determination solely from the evidence bearing upon the issue before them. They may rely upon *only* such evidence as is properly admitted. The evidence admissible against the defendant to determine her wrongdoing, would not always be admissible against the corespondent if the issue were his wrongdoing. As the corespondent is not a party and the issue upon which evidence is admitted is not *his* guilt, a divorce decree is not an adjudication against the corespondent.

NOTE 2.

BRANCH v. BRANCH
Two Years Later

It is my impression that the corespondent appealed because he was a school teacher . . . and feared that his acquiescence might be held against him. . . . [Letter dated April 7, 1961 from Matthew W. Bullock, Jr., attorney for appellee.]

NOTE 3.

14 McKinney's Consolidated Laws of New York Art. 2, § 8 (1959 Supp.)

Marriage after Divorce for Adultery

Whenever a marriage has been or shall be dissolved, the complainant may marry again during the lifetime of the defendant. But a defendant for whose adultery the judgment of divorce has been granted in this state may not marry again during the lifetime of the complainant, unless the court in which the judgment

---

1. "Who steals my purse steals trash, 'tis something, nothing;
   'Twas mine, 'tis his, and has been slave to thousands;
   But he that filches from me my good name
   Robs me of that which not enriches him,
   And makes me poor indeed."
   Othello, Act III, Scene 3.

of divorce was rendered shall in that respect modify such judgment, which modification shall be made only upon satisfactory proof that three years have elapsed since the decree of divorce was rendered, and that the conduct of the defendant since the dissolution of said marriage has been uniformly good; and a defendant for whose adultery the judgment of divorce has been rendered in another state or country may not marry again in this state during the lifetime of the complainant unless three years have elapsed since the rendition of such judgment and there is no legal impediment, by reason of such judgment, to such marriage in the state or country where the judgment was rendered. But this section shall not prevent the remarriage of the parties to an action for divorce. As amended L. 1915, c. 266; L. 1919, c. 265, eff. May 3, 1919.

NOTE 4.

FISHER v. FISHER
250 N.Y. 313, 165 N.E. 460 (1929)

KELLOGG, J. In this action for a separation the complaint alleges "that the parties hereto were duly married on the 24th day of October, 1925." The answer denies the allegation. Concededly, on the day named the parties to the action were on board the steamship *Leviathan,* then on the high seas, bound from the port of New York to Southampton, England. When the ship was forty miles out from the port of New York, its captain performed a marriage ceremony, wherein these parties were the principals. In the course of the ceremony the captain asked the plaintiff if she took the defendant for her husband; asked the defendant if he took the plaintiff for his wife; received an affirmative answer from each; and thereupon pronounced them man and wife. Cohabitation of the principals followed the ceremony. The ultimate question for decision here is this: Were the parties upon the occasion in question lawfully united in marriage?

* * *

The defendant, prior to the performance of the marriage ceremony in question, was already a married man. His former wife had procured, in this jurisdiction, a decree of divorce against him, dissolving the marriage on the ground of adultery. According to the terms of the decree, and the laws of this State, the defendant was forbidden to remarry during the life of his then wife. The wife, who procured the decree, is still living. It is well settled that the provisions of our statute forbidding the remarriage of a party who has been divorced for adultery have no extraterritorial effect; that a subsequent marriage of the guilty party, during the life of the innocent party, in a sister State, if valid in that State, will be recognized here as a lawful marriage. . . . The question then arises, did the laws of the State of New York follow the steamship *Leviathan* in its journey upon the high seas?

* * *

NOTE 5.

GOLD, HERBERT
Divorce as a Moral Act*

It is said that the widow who was truly devoted to her husband is the one who has faith in marriage, believes in love, marries again. The unhappily married, unfulfilled man or woman, having his problem fantastically solved by a death he only dreamed of, must mourn forever— guiltily, regretfully, guiltily. He must even invent a justificatory bliss in the past. Gray-faced, always in mourning, his life is over.

No! cries the grief-stricken true lover when the time of sharpest bite is finished. This *no* is a *yes* to life. No, no, love is too important to pass out of my life by this accident. My dead lover tells me this: he wants me to have the best part of his legacy, and this is the power to give and take love. This widow or widower inspires love, deep and sensual love, at any age ; and gives and takes it. A new sharing occurs on earth— the best gift which earth offers everyone in the democracy of blood.

May it not be, in the same way, that only the divorced couple who sometimes were truly happy and loving have the chance to find love again? The good divorce is that between two who have once loved each other. Justly they may pity the bad divorce—that of beings who have merely made mistakes, merely rectified mistakes, merely repeated old errors bred in the family. The bad divorce is the one of diminished decision: submission to a painful pattern, a deathly cure by living through the sins of the fathers. The good divorcee dares to love again—as only the widow who was happy can dare to give up her fabricated memories.

2.

WELLS v. WELLS
79 N.Y. Super. 388, 191 A. 2d 763 (1963)

CONFORD, S. J. A. D. This is an uncontested action for divorce on the ground of the defendant's

---

* *The Atlantic Monthly*, Nov., 1957, p. 118. Reprinted in *The Age of Happy Problems* by Herbert Gold. Copyright © 1957, 1962 by Herbert Gold. Reprinted with the permission of the publishers, The Dial Press, Inc.

desertion of the plaintiff. Judge Hand, sitting in the Chancery Division, denied relief on the ground of plaintiff's adultery, he having married another woman after his wife left him and cohabited with her continuously up to and at the time of the trial. (For aught we know that cohabitation continues to this day.)

* * *

Although the trial court did not rest its decision on the cohabitation of plaintiff and Ruby during the years before he learned that Mattie was still alive, but only on the subsequent relations between them, plaintiff is at pains on this appeal to develop the point that the earlier period of cohabitation was not adulterous because of the entry of plaintiff and Ruby into the ceremonial marriage relationship in good faith and armed with an asserted statutory presumption that Mattie was dead. For purposes of this appeal it will not be necessary to determine whether, under the facts presented, the relationship with Ruby was adulterous prior to the coming to light of Mattie's continued existence. A persuasive argument can be made that it was not if one assumes that which here is attended by considerable doubt—that plaintiff made such reasonably thorough inquiries concerning the whereabouts of his wife as justified him in a *bona fide* belief that she was actually dead when he remarried. . . .

Obviously, any arguable presumption . . . as to Mattie's death prior to the marriage to Ruby was dissipated upon the establishment . . . of Mattie's survival in 1961. . . .

* * *

We find Judge Hand's determination . . . to have been a conscientious and correct discharge of his responsibility notwithstanding his sympathies admittedly lay with the plaintiff. The State is a third party in every divorce case, interested in the maintenance of the marriage relationship, and it is the duty of the trial judge, even in an uncontested case, to see to it that a divorce is not granted except where warranted on the statute and the proofs. . . .

Although generally the defense of recrimination must be pleaded to be availed of by a defendant, a recognized exception is that "the relief prayed for by the petitioner will not be granted, notwithstanding that recrimination is not set up as a defense, if he in putting in his case shows his own guilt." *Young v. Young,* 94 N. J. Eq. 155, 157, (E. & A. 1922). . . .

* * *

. . . Here plaintiff's unclean hands are aggravated by his continued cohabitation with Ruby, not merely after learning that she was certainly not his wife, but even after filing an action for divorce acknowledging that fact and while awaiting favorable action from the court on his complaint. The court is practically treated as a ministerial agency expected to rubber-stamp approval of a *fait accompli,* as it were, and this on no stronger ground than that plaintiff did not know any better.

We cannot accede to plaintiff's cynical argument that this decision will merely encourage perjurious denial of cohabitation by plaintiffs in similar future cases. It is not unreasonable to expect a plaintiff in such a situation to cease cohabitation with the other woman temporarily when he learns the facts and while awaiting the court's decision on his prayer to be freed from the ties of his lawful existing marriage. . . .

*   *   *

GAULKIN, J. A. D. (dissenting). Judge Hand said "[a]s a practical matter, it does seem that plaintiff might well deserve favorable, equitable consideration after some 18 years of a compatible matrimonial relationship with Ruby and that this relationship might well be invested with legality, rather than being consigned to the status of an illegal relationship." (73 N. J. Super., at p. 549) Let us look at the facts which led him to express such sympathy and regret.

Plaintiff is a working man with a third grade education. He married Mattie Belle Robinson (hereafter Mattie) in Vero Beach, Florida in 1929. She bore him a son, but she nevertheless deserted him in 1933, leaving the child with him. He continued to reside in Vero Beach until his marriage with the second Mrs. Wells (Ruby) in 1944. It is not disputed that plaintiff married Ruby in good faith believing Mattie dead.

Plaintiff and Ruby established a good home, made friends and a place in the community as husband and wife, worked hard, saved, and in 1957 bought a home. During his handling of the purchase, Mr. Brach, plaintiff's attorney, learned of Mr. Wells' previous marriage. Mr. Brach advised plaintiff, as he says in his brief, to commence this action "in order to permanently and finally determine his status, remove questions as to title and property, permit in the future determination as to social security rights and other rights between himself and Ruby Wells and finally to provide Ruby Wells as well as himself with the basis of knowing that their marriage was valid and subsisting." Mr. Brach made inquiry in accordance with the rules of court and was unable to locate the defendant, but, while the divorce action was pending, Mattie's whereabouts was discovered when she made a condolence call upon a relative of Mr. Wells. Thereupon Mr. Brach had her served personally with a copy of the summons and complaint in Detroit, but she entered no appearance.

As behooves an ethical lawyer, Mr. Brach told Judge Hand the foregoing facts. For this, Judge Hand properly commended Mr. Brach "for his forthrightness and diligence" and refused his client the divorce.

No one told this simple unlettered plaintiff to leave Ruby and their home when he learned that Mattie was still alive. As might be expected, it never occurred to him that the law required him to do so after having lived with Ruby for 18 years.

Mr. Wells has been denied the divorce, not because he lived with Ruby for 18 years, but because he continued to live with her for the few months after he knew that Mattie was still alive. The effect of this is that plaintiff remains married to Mattie, who does not want him, did not appear to contest the divorce, and showed no interest in the proceedings. For all that appears, she may have obtained a divorce from plaintiff and/or she herself may have again married.

A plaintiff's condoned adultery is not a defense. Since Mattie kept sufficiently close watch over the Wells family to know of the death of one of them, it is reasonable to assume she knew of plaintiff's remarriage and cared nothing about it. Certainly she did not expect him to be celibate since 1933, and she no more expected him to leave Ruby when he learned of her existence than she expected to change her own way of life because she was sued for divorce. Mattie, in turn, is (at least so far as New Jersey is concerned) indissolubly wedded to plaintiff. The innocent Ruby, who has been a faithful wife for 18 years, must either separate herself from Mr. Wells or live with him in sin, and, of course, the same is true of Mr. Wells.

Now let us see whether we are really compelled to do this "injustice according to law." Our precedents have committed us to the acceptance of the defense of recrimination, but only when it is pleaded and proved by the defendant or appears affirmatively in the plaintiff's case. . . .

*   *   *

The history of the law teaches us that mechanical rules spawn arbitrary exceptions, to avoid the harshness which arises out of their universality. . . .

It does not seem to me that what the denial of the divorce does to plaintiff and his wife of 18 years advances our public policy. On the contrary it seems to me opposed to the public policy declared when parallel situations are presented in other courts. For example, had Mr. Wells been killed in the course of his employment, we would hold that there was the strongest possible presumption that the marriage to Ruby was valid, and we would draw all possible inferences to rebut any attack on the validity of that marriage, even after Mattie's reappearance.

In short, I would reverse and order the entry of judgment of divorce in favor of plaintiff.

PART THREE

FOR WHOM, TO WHAT EXTENT, AND WHY IS BEING HEALTHY, HAPPY, AND RESPECTED RELEVANT:

A.

To Decisions Concerning the Establishment of Wife-Husband Relationships?

1.

LICENSING THE MARRIAGE—ON STATES OF MIND, BLOOD, AND PIGMENTATION

a.   F. A. MARRIAGE LICENSE
            4 Pa. D. & C. 2d 1 (Pa. 1955)

KLEIN, P. J. and LEFEVER, J., May 19, 1955.—
Application for a marriage license was filed by
the applicants on April 30, 1955. It appears from
the statements made by the female applicant
(herein referred to as F. A.), that she was a mental
patient in St. Mary's Hospital, Philadelphia, for
a period of two months in 1951.

Mr. MacDonell, assistant orphans' court clerk,
pursuant to the provisions of section 9[1] of the

Marriage Law of August 22, 1953, P. L. 1344,
48 PS § 1, et seq., refused to issue the license
and certified the matter to this court for hearing.

This is the first time that this court has been
asked to construe the provisions of the new
marriage law, pertaining to the issuance of a
marriage license to a person who has been
afflicted with mental illness within a period of
five years prior to the date of application for the
license.

For years the marriage statutes of this Commonwealth had lacked clarity and had been out
of adjustment with advances in medical science
and our changing approaches to social problems.

---

1. "Section 9: Orphans' Court to Pass Upon Refusal of
Clerk to Issue License.—

"In those cases where the right to a license is not made to
appear, the clerk of the orphans' court shall refuse to issue
the same. Upon request of the applicants, the clerk of the
orphans' court, immediately after such refusal, shall certify
the proceedings to the orphans' court of the county without
formality or expense to the applicants.

"Such application for a license to marry shall thereupon,

at the earliest possible time, be heard by a judge of said
court, without a jury, in court or in chambers, during the
term or in vacation, as the case may be. The finding of the
court that a license ought to issue or ought not to issue
shall be final, and the clerk of the orphans' court shall act
in accordance therewith.

"The true intent of this section is to secure for applicants
an immediate hearing before the orphans' court without
delay or expense on the part of the applicants."

The old statutes were defective in three principal respects.

1. The legislature had failed to designate with particularity the persons who were authorized to perform marriages. . . .

2. Refugees who had fled from totalitarian terrorism, whose spouses had died in concentration camps, labor camps, gas chambers or otherwise, under circumstances which made efforts to obtain death certificates or other positive proof of death almost hopeless, found it virtually impossible to remarry and reestablish themselves in normal family relationships. There was no provision in the law for issuance of licenses in such cases.

3. Section 15 of the Act of July 24, 1913, P. L. 1013, provided that:

> ". . . no license to marry shall be issued where either of the contracting parties is an imbecile, epileptic, of unsound mind, or under guardianship as a person of unsound mind."

The statute did not define the prohibited sicknesses nor give the court any discretion as to the manner in which the statute was to be administered.

The discovery of new drugs has dramatically reduced the ill effects of epilepsy. Enlightened medical opinion now regards the absolute bar to marriage of epileptics as harsh, unjust, and unnecessary. Tremendous strides have also been made in the care of the mentally ill, resulting in cures in many cases and substantial improvements in others. It is now possible for some of these people to marry without serious risk to themselves, their spouses, their offspring, or the community generally.

The Marriage Law of 1953 recognized these advances in medicine, and in a large measure, corrected these long existing, entrenched deficiencies in our marriage laws.

The uncertainty with respect to officials who are permitted to solemnize marriages has been removed. Section 13 of the act designates with particularity the persons in whom such authority is now vested.[4]

---

4. "Section 13: Persons Qualified to Solemnize Marriages. The chief justice and each justice of the Supreme Court, the president judge and each judge of the Superior Court, the president judge and each judge of the court of common pleas, the president judge and each judge of the orphans' court, the president judge and each judge of the Allegheny County and the Philadelphia Municipal Court, each magistrate, alderman, justice of the peace, mayor of any city, and burgess of any borough of this Commonwealth, and each minister, priest or rabbi of any regularly established church or congregation, is hereby authorized to solemnize marriages between such persons as produce a marriage license issued by the clerk of the orphans' court. . . ."

The judges of the orphans' courts now have jurisdiction, under certain designated circumstances, to decide that the spouse of an applicant is a presumed decedent. . . .

. . . Under the 1953 statute a marriage license may be issued to a person who is suffering from epilepsy or who has been, within five years preceding the time of the application, an inmate of an institution for epileptics, but only if authorized by a judge of the orphans' court. Likewise, if the applicant has been an inmate of an institution "for weakminded, insane, or persons of unsound mind" within five years preceding the time of the application, the license may be issued only if authorized by a judge of the orphans' court.

The legislature has thus placed a great social responsibility on the orphans' court. It is our duty to determine whether "it is for the best interest of such applicant and the general public to issue the license." Yet, the statute contains no criteria, standards or rules for determining this fact; and no definition of crucial terms used in the statute. This is perhaps necessary, for the broad discretion vested in the courts, will enable them, in true common-law tradition, to progress with the advances of science in this difficult and inexact field of law and medicine and decide each case on its own facts.

A vast, hazy shadowland exists between mental health and mental illness. The gradations of abnormalities are as varied and diffused as the merging colors of the rainbow. The most illustrious and respected psychiatrists often disagree radically in their opinions with respect to the sanity of an individual.

The following extract from the Encyclopaedia Britannica, vol. 12, p. 383 (14th ed.) points up the difficulty very sharply:

> "INSANITY. This term ordinarily connotes more or less severe unsoundness of mind. Though its loose usage is almost synonymous with mental disease, scientifically the term should only be applied to the mental condition of an individual who, through socially inefficient conduct, has to be placed under supervision and control. The mind is the mechanism by means of which we adapt adequately to our environment and when, through its derangement, conduct is exhibited which the community looks upon as evidence of disease and as implying irresponsibility, the individual concerned is said to be insane and the law steps in to certify him as such. Strictly speaking, then, insanity is really a social and legal term and not medical. Mental illness is a broad concept which may include very efficient members of society. No satisfactory definition can therefore be arrived at, since it would be necessary to define what we mean by sanity, which would involve us in equal difficulties."

The phrase "an inmate of an institution for weakminded, insane, or persons of unsound mind" is, likewise, subject to interpretation. Institutions for the insane are no longer regarded merely as places in which persons of unsound mind are confined as custodial cases to rid the general public of their troublesome presence. Today, great progress is being made toward curing the mentally sick and the establishments in which they are housed are usually called "hospitals". In fact, many general hospitals have departments set aside for the care of the mentally sick. Furthermore, in present day usage the word "inmate" has been generally replaced by the more charitable word "patient". The language of the statute is general, but we believe that the legislature intended to include all cases in which the applicant has been hospitalized for treatment of some form of mental illness or deficiency in any mental institution, including a general hospital which conducts a department for the care of the mentally sick.

Basically, the problem which confronts us is one for the medical profession. A diagnosis by judicial decree should not be made except with the advice, and upon the recommendation of, trained psychiatrists.

The statute does not in so many words state that an applicant who has been in a mental institution must be cured permanently at the time the application is made. However, because the issuance of a license to a person who is weakminded, insane or of unsound mind is absolutely prohibited by the statute, the legislature must have intended that a license is to be issued only to a person who has been completely cured of his mental illness or whose condition has so improved that he can be expected to lead a normal life and to take his place in society without serious risk to himself or to the community generally.

Leading members of the medical profession freely admit that the science of caring for the mentally ill is in its infancy. Much research and investigation has been undertaken recently which has resulted in tremendously enhancing the chances of curing or, at least, improving the condition of persons suffering from mental sickness.

It seems clear that under no circumstances should a marriage license be issued to persons having a mental deficiency of severe degree, e.g., an idiot or imbecile. It is also apparent that persons suffering irremedial brain injury, or deteriorating organic brain syndromes which are of progressive or irreversible nature, e.g., senile dementia, should not be permitted to marry.

On the other hand, many persons who are unable to cope with the intense pressures of the modern age, suffer what is commonly designated as "mental breakdowns" and are institutionalized.

Most of these people respond favorably to therapy ; many are completely cured. These obviously are the persons whom the legislature intended to benefit primarily and furnish no serious problem when they apply for marriage licenses.

The real difficulties arise with respect to persons who suffer moderate mental deficiency or who have been hospitalized because of the more serious mental illnesses, such as manic-depressive psychosis, schizophrenia (dementia praecox), post-partum psychosis, and involutional melancholia. Although many of these cases are completely hopeless, a great number show marked improvement under modern therapy, such as shock treatment, psychotherapy, and the use of newly discovered drugs. Some of these persons are able to leave the mental hospitals and, at least temporarily, take their places in society as useful citizens. Some apparently have complete remission from their malady. Whether they have recovered sufficiently to assume the responsibilities of marriage presents an extremely delicate question.

No general rule can be handed down. Each case is sui generis and must be decided upon its own facts. The discretion vested in the orphans' court must be carefully exercised in order to protect not only the applicants and their issue, but the general public as well.

Three preliminary requirements seem to be indicated in every case before a license should issue : (1) Full disclosure must be made to both applicants of all of the details of the case history of the applicant who has been mentally afflicted ; (2) the court must be satisfied that such applicant has recovered sufficiently to adjust normally to the problems of everyday living, particularly those arising from the marriage relationship, and (3) the court must be reasonably assured that if children are born of the marriage, such children will be normal, healthy children, free from the taint of mental illness or deficiency.

With these principles in mind, let us examine the factual situation existing in the present case.

No question is raised concerning the sanity of the male applicant. He was present at the hearing, fully cognizant of the history of F. A.'s mental sickness, and is, nevertheless, not only willing, but eager, to marry her.

F. A. is 30 years of age. She was graduated from a Catholic parochial grade school and attended Little Flower High School for two years. She left school when she was about 17 years old and took a job in a hosiery mill, "sewing on piece-work". She continued in the hosiery industry until, apparently, the pressure of "piece-work" caused her to have a mental breakdown. She was hospitalized at St. Mary's Hospital in Philadelphia for a period of eight weeks with a diagnosis of dementia praecox. While in the hospital she received a full course of electric shock treatments, following which she received treatments as an outpatient until December 1953, when she was pronounced well. It appears, further, from the testimony that since her discharge from the hospital she has managed the household of her invalid sister satisfactorily and efficiently and has given no evidence of any recurrence of her malady.

Dr. William L. Long, the physician who treated F. A., was the principal witness in her behalf. Dr. Long has specialized in neuropsychiatry since 1928 and is well and favorably known to the court. He is chief neuropsychiatrist at St. Mary's Hospital, and is on the psychiatric staff at Nazareth Hospital, Doctor's Hospital, and the Philadelphia General Hospital. Dr. Long examined F. A. shortly before the date of the hearing. He testified:

> "I am satisfied that she is fully recovered from her illness and I think she now has a well-adjusted emotional life."

He testified further that, in his opinion, if she had children they would be normal. He recommended that the marriage license be issued.

* * *

After a careful study of the record in this case we make the following findings of fact:

* * *

4. That F. A. is not at this time weak-minded, insane, or a person of unsound mind;

5. That the male applicant is fully aware of the entire history of F. A.'s mental illness, and

6. That there is no compelling evidence that children, if any, born of this marriage will be mentally deficient or predisposed to mental illness.

This is a borderline case and we confess that we are beset with doubts. However, life at its very best is uncertain. Probably in a strictly disciplined society persons of defective mentality would be deprived of the blessing of matrimony. This, however, is an imperfect world. It is difficult to foretell the unhappy consequences which might result from our refusing to issue a marriage license in this case in view of the fact that the marriage banns have been posted, and all of the arrangements for the marriage have been made. The applicants are obviously in love with each other. If they cannot be married in this State, they may be tempted to live together without the benefit of marriage, or to seek a marriage license in another State where the re-

strictions are less stringent. Under all of the existing circumstances, we are of the opinion that it is for the best interest of the applicants and the general public to issue the marriage license.

* * *

NOTES

NOTE 1.

STAR, SHIRLEY A.

The Public's Ideas about Mental Illness*

. . . By the way of background, let me say that this research is a pioneering attempt by the National Opinion Research Center, University of Chicago, to subject to thorough analysis the nature of popular thinking about mental illness. The study is based on thirty-five hundred intensive interviews—interviews of about an hour and a half's duration—with a representative cross-section of the American public and is, so far as we know, the only such study attempted on a national scale. The goals of the research are, first, to describe in some detail the characteristic ideas about mental illness current in our society and, second, to explain—so far as we can—the reasons why popular conceptions of mental illness assume the form they do.

* * *

In practice, people make it clear that they do not generally regard behavior as proof of mental illness, unless three interrelated conditions obtain. First of all, they look for a breakdown of intellect, an almost complete loss of cognitive functioning or, in short, a loss of reason. And so, in explaining why a particular example is not mentally ill, they frequently say things like, "A lot of people who are nervous, their minds are as good as they ever was" or "She knows what she is doing, so her *mind* can't be affected." Second, people expect, almost as a necessary consequence of this loss of rationality, that the behavior called mental illness must represent a serious loss of self-control, usually to the point of dangerous violence against others and certainly to the point of not being responsible for one's acts. Here people say an example is mentally ill because "He isn't in control of himself" or because "He's getting dangerous for the people who live with him," or someone else is not mentally ill because "He isn't doing things he shouldn't be doing" or because "He isn't

_____

* Paper presented to the Annual Meeting of the National Association for Mental Health, Sheraton-Lincoln Hotel, Indianapolis, Indiana, 1955. Reprinted by permission of the author and the National Opinion Research Center.

really out of control—he could stop acting that way if he wanted to."

* * *

Now, all of this, I am sure, has a most familiar sound to all of you. . . . It is, of course, about the same set of moral norms and premises about man and his nature that underlies all of our legal codes, governing who shall be held responsible and punished for his acts and who shall be exempt from punishment by reason of insanity. Or, in other words, it is an expression of an internally-consistent, rather well-organized, morally-grounded view of human nature and of human conduct that is deeply engrained in Western civilization.

According to this view of man, rationality and the ability to exercise self-control are the central, basically human qualities. From this, it follows that the normal person *is* rational, he *is* able to control himself and *is* responsible for his acts, and his acts are reasonable—appropriate to the circumstances in which he finds himself and intelligible to others in the light of those circumstances. Given this view of normalcy, it follows quite consistently that if mental illness represents the loss of normalcy or its opposite, it must necessarily turn out to be a rather extreme form of psychosis.

* * *

[T]he typical psychotic patient is viewed as dangerous by more than two-thirds of the American public and, more for this reason than for considerations of treatment, about the same proportion feel that *all* psychotics should be institutionalized. The interesting thing is that when people make clear what it is they mean when they say psychotics are dangerous, it turns out that they are not primarily or exclusively thinking in terms of physical violence. Running through what people say, there are, more frequently, expressions of the kind of anxiety generated in people when they are forced to deal with persons who have lost their crucially human qualities, persons whose behavior can neither be understood or controlled by the means which are applied in every-day interpersonal relationships. Over and over again, the element of "danger" is described in terms of the psychotic person's being unpredictable, irrational, and not responsible for his acts. He is dangerous, not so much because of his overt acts, but because— to quote some typical responses—"You never know what they are going to do" or "They *might* do anything," and this very uncertainty constitutes the real threat.

In a very real sense, too, people view a psychotic illness as irremediable, despite the fact that . . . most people say psychotics get better again. But, when we look at it more closely, the most frequent position is that, though they can get better again, they can never again be the same. In fact, only a third of the American people believe that psychotics can generally recover again to a point where they will show no signs of their former illness, whereas 37 per cent believe that most will always show signs of the illness. . . . We failed to ask exactly what these stigmata were that the recovered patient would always bear, but if I had to venture a guess or an interpretation, I would say that the very presence of a former patient reminds people of the existence of a threat they would rather forget, and the resulting disquietude is attributed to something about the ex-patient. And, again in a very real sense, given people's premises, there *is* something different about the patient. He is a kind of skeleton at the feast who has, in having become ill at all, exposed a potentiality, which he, at least, can never thereafter deny and his presence makes everyone too acutely conscious of it.

It certainly seems to be something along these lines that accounts for the fact that 60 per cent of the American people indicate that they would not feel or act normally toward an ex-patient, even if they did not learn this fact about him until after they had known him for a while without noticing anything wrong with him. This group indicates that they would be afraid and would feel a kind of unease and uncertainty in dealing with him quite akin to their feelings about the dangerousness of psychotics. Knowledge of the fact of his former illness introduces, for the majority of the public, a precariousness into the relationship: people feel, as they put it, "a dread that they might go off again" or "unsafe, not knowing when it's going to happen again" and, as a result, prefer to avoid contact or, if in it, would act awkwardly and unnaturally in their efforts to avoid what they fear. Again, in people's own words, "The very thought of their having been insane would always be with me, I'd always be thinking about it and feel I had to be cautious in anything I might say or do." Or, "I'd be careful not to say anything that might disturb or irritate her." And, although some 38 per cent of the public deny that they personally would respond like this, only 15 per cent believe that freedom from such reactions would be typical of the general public.

This complex of attitudes toward psychosis is, I suppose, the sort of thing people have in mind when they talk about a kind of atavistic fear.

Certainly, the attitudes go beyond any set of rational considerations we can uncover. Take, for instance, people who said that most psychotics can recover completely with no signs of their former illness and that most psychotics aren't dangerous in any sense, even when ill. Then why should it be that two-fifths of this group still feel the same hesitancy, fear and discomfort at the idea of associating with an ex-patient that I have just described? It is true that this figure is a good deal lower than that for the other extreme of the population—people who believe recovery is generally impossible and that psychotics are usually dangerous—where the distrust of the ex-patient might be viewed as a reasonable outcome of beliefs that he is not really or wholly cured and is dangerous when ill. But there still remains the question of what bothers the people who say nothing about psychosis that might explain their fears of the ex-patient. It is just the evidence of such paradoxes as these which lead us to feel that the totality of the many different kinds of data we have all points to a very basic and widespread fear, however buried it may be—a fear in each individual that he too may be overwhelmed by irrationality—and a consequent withdrawal from and avoidance of anything that activates that fear.

*   *   *

Where this leaves us today is something like this: on the one hand, there is an old, socially-sanctioned, well-established set of views which supports the identification of mental illness only with violent, extreme psychosis and, within this context of ideas, mental illness emerges more or less as the ultimate catastrophe that can befall a human being. This is the orientation people are using when they deal with or think about other individuals or human behavior generally and when they respond emotionally to the term mental illness. On the other hand, ours is a literate, educated population, and they have encountered in the various channels of information a rather different point of view. According to this doctrine, and it is usually presented as a fact rather than as a point of view, all manner of emotional disturbances belong within the general category of mental illness. So, when we ask people to consider abstractedly and intellectually, the question of just what mental illness is supposed to cover, it is this modern definition that they give us. We are, in other words, in a period of transition in which the modern definition of mental illness has been rather widely disseminated without anything like an equal ac-

ceptance of the point of view about the nature of mental illness and about the roots of human personality and behavior which lies back of this usage of the term. It is a definition which people simply cannot work with in practice within the context of their fundamental beliefs about human behavior. Most people simply don't try to; once having stated the definitions in answer to our questioning, they thereafter revert to their own more familiar way of thinking. . . .

NOTE 2.

JACKSON, DON D.

A Critique of the Literature on the Genetics of Schizophrenia*

. . . Although it seems likely that hereditary factors do play a part in at least some of the schizophrenias, it remains to be established in what forms, how vital is a hereditary "vulnerability," and what the phenotypical expression is of the genotypical defect. It seems to me that with the exception of the painstaking population studies carried out in the Scandinavian countries and some of the Swiss work genetic studies in mental illness have not been of the caliber of such investigations in certain other areas of medicine. . . .

Statistical studies can impress the unwary with their "scientific," "impartial" look, but it must never be forgotten that however one juggles the figures with dazzling mathematical techniques, they can never be any more accurate than the original observations upon which they are based. And impressive-looking statistics have a way of haunting investigators for years; J. de Sauvage Nolting collected extremely impressive figures to show that the majority of schizophrenics were conceived in March. Although no other investigator has confirmed these figures independently, many have tried to explain them on one basis or another.

For example, it is statistically curious that the most genetically loaded families produce the majority of patients with "atypical" or "schizophreniform" psychoses with relatively good prognoses. Genetically, this finding is contrary to that for other medical disorders. But from a psychological viewpoint, it is easy to conceive of openly disturbed families allowing the individual to become more floridly psychotic. . . .

Although the statistics that have been gathered in twin studies are impressive, there are . . . reasons to suppose that they have been inade-

* Reprinted from Jackson, D. D., ed.: *The Etiology of Schizophrenia.* New York: Basic Books, Inc., 1960, pp. 80-81. Reprinted with permission of the publisher.

quately controlled for nongenetic factors. Possible environmental causes and particularly psychic identification have been ignored in favor of possible genetic causes.

But, however much the geneticists may ignore the cultural, they have been able by their figures to convince many people to such an extent that they have led to unwarranted confident genetic counseling and in some cases to sterilization laws. . . .

NOTE 3.

HIGGINS, JOHN W.

Schizophrenia as a Consideration in Annulment of Marriage*

In connection with this whole question of prognosis, a judge may ask "is it true: once a schizophrenic, always a schizophrenic?" We would have to say that "it depends—". . . . [V]arious levels of improvement are possible. A severely and chronically ill person may lose his bizarre behavior, hallucinations and delusions but remain grossly impaired in his ability to relate to others and to think in any organized fashion, or he may improve to the level of "good hospital adjustment"; a markedly disturbed person with a short history of illness and a reasonably sound past history may to all intents and purposes recover, or retain pathology discernible only by the most acute observer; or a person with only subtle signs to begin with may remain unchanged, getting neither better nor worse, or he may go very far in either direction. A person like the last, incidentally may in the proper circumstances lead an active life, including scientific and artistic creativity, and with varying degrees of personal satisfaction to himself and to others.

The variety in levels of improvement is pertinent also to an evaluation of medical reports of "improved" or "recovered" or "unchanged" as applied to particular cases. "Recovered" in one institution may refer to a level of improvement which in another place may be rated as "slightly improved." . . .

NOTE 4.

North Dakota Revised Code § 14-0307 (1960)

Marriage by a woman under the age of forty-five years or by a man of any age, unless he marries a woman over the age of forty-five years, is prohibited if such man or woman is a chronic alcoholic, an habitual criminal, an imbecile, a feebleminded person, an idiot, an insane person,

* Bulletin of the Guild of Catholic Psychiatrists, Vol. 7 (1960), p. 87, 92-93. Reprinted with permission of the publisher.

a person who has been afflicted with hereditary insanity, or with any contagious, venereal disease.

NOTE 5.

SCHAEFFER v. SCHAEFFER
20 Misc. 2d 662, 192 N.Y.S. 2d 275 (1959)

NICHOLAS M. PETTE, JUSTICE.

This is an action by plaintiff for a judgment annulling his marriage to the defendant upon the ground of fraud.

* * *

The crux of the plaintiff's complaint is:

"That at and before the marriage of the parties hereto, the Defendant fraudulently concealed from the Plaintiff that she had been an inmate of the Islip Mental Hospital, Islip, Long Island, New York", and

"That Plaintiff married the Defendant believing her to be a woman without taint, mental disability and that she was on the date thereof and at the time prior thereto mentally normal", and

that plaintiff would not have married defendant had he known that she had prior to the marriage been confined in a mental institution. . . .

* * *

[T]he Court finds that the parties hereto were married on October 13, 1951, . . . that there are three children the issue of said marriage, . . . all three being presently in the custody of the plaintiff; that there has been no judgment of divorce, separation or annulment granted between the parties hereto. . . .

* * *

Dr. Jeptha R. Macfarlane, a physician at Creedmore State Hospital testified that defendant was oriented and presently lucid, and that she would understand and appreciate the importance of an oath. When asked by the Court in his opinion whether it would be proper for defendant to testify under oath, he answered: "Well, I feel that it is proper that she can testify, but her testimony must be evaluated in the light of the fact that she is a patient". He also testified: "The one big problem we have had with her is responsibility. She will have periods of alternating with very bizarre behavior; and she will go through periods in which she withdraws from reality completely, and the effect, the emotional tone in which she faces things is usually inappropriate". He further testified that the diagnosis was Schizophrenia, Catatonic type, and stated "This Catatonic type is an impulsive type. She will suddenly have outbursts and over activity, and then they will withdraw right in a shell. She does this many times, she has admitted." He also testified that defendant was presently on medication, "which does modify to a certain extent her behavior at this time".

* * *

. . . The Court finds that plaintiff first discovered that defendant has been confined to Central Islip State Hospital on October 11, 1956 at the Aftercare Clinic on Schermerhorn Street, Brooklyn, when she told him that she had been confined to the Central Islip State Hospital prior to their marriage, and that from the time of such discovery he has never lived with the defendant as husband and wife. The Court is of the opinion that the requirements of Section 1143 of the Civil Practice Act as to the proof necessary for granting a judgment annulling a marriage have been sufficiently met by the plaintiff.

* * *

Permanent custody of the infant children is awarded to plaintiff.

NOTE 6.

Israeli Draft Family Code §39 (1956)*
Medical Examination

No marriage shall be celebrated unless each of the parties has been medically examined within two months before the marriage and a physician has explained to the parties in the presence of both so much of the result of the examinations as is likely to affect their marital life or their issue.

Comments

* * *

We should not be content with declarations by the parties that each knows the other's state of health; the law must assure that this knowledge does in fact exist. Nor should we be satisfied with the knowledge as such, but should require knowledge coupled with an understanding of the medical and eugenic significance of the findings. Only a medical examination, followed by medical explanation, is likely to bring home to the couple the real state of affairs knowledge of which is imperative; ignorance of which may prove

dangerous thereby preventing illusions on the one hand and unjustified fears on the other hand.

After the parties have been examined and have received the explanation they are entitled —and are bound—to decide themselves whether or not to contract marriage. The responsibility for their own fate and for that of their issue is theirs. Although we do not purport to approach this problem from a medical point of view, medical progress on the one hand (treatment of venereal diseases, of mental disturbances, etc.) and the theory of heredity on the other, do not justify in our opinion intervention of the law by way of prohibitions of marriage in cases of certain diseases.

NOTE 7.

ERICKSON, MILTON S.

A Clinical Note on Indirect Hypnotic Therapy*

A young couple in their early twenties, much in love and married for a year and close friends of several of the writer's medical students at that time, sought psychiatric help.

Their problem was one in common—life-long enuresis. During their fifteen-month courtship, neither had the courage to tell the other about the habitual enuresis.

Their wedding night had been marked, after consummation of the marriage, by a feeling of horrible dread and then resigned desperation, followed by sleep.

The next morning each was silently and profoundly grateful to the other for the unbelievable forbearance shown in making no comment about the wet bed.

This same silent ignoring of the wet bed continued to be manifested each morning for over nine months. The effect was an ever-increasing feeling of love and regard for each other because of the sympathetic silence shown.

Then one morning, neither could remember which made the remark, the comment was made that they really ought to have a baby to sleep with them so that it could be blamed for the wet bed. This led at once to the astonishing discovery for each that the other was enuretic and that each had felt solely responsible. While they were greatly relieved by this discovery, the enuresis persisted.

After a few months more . . . they sought an appointment, [and] earnestly asked if they could be given help.

---

* Cambridge: Harvard Law School-Brandeis University Cooperative Research for Israel's Legal Development. Copyright 1956 by the President and Fellows of Harvard College.

---

* *Journal of Clinical and Experimental Hypnosis* (1954). Reprinted with permission of the publisher.

NOTE 8.

REIDER, NORMAN
Problems in the Prediction of Marital Adjustment*

. . . If we keep in mind the degree of subjectivity in the designation of a good marriage and what constitutes a good marriage, we can see the uselessness of trying to establish any criteria by the study of diagnostic categories. Two schizophrenics who marry may get along miserably. Others marry and often get along quite well. Reviewing both my clinical experience and my observations among people of my acquaintance, I have to conclude that I've seen "mixed marriages" between one diagnostic category and another both succeed and fail. Nor am I impressed with the possible predictive value in such diagnoses, with the one possible exception that I have known few marriages between male paranoid characters and female hysterical characters to succeed, by almost any criterion of success. The nature of the sado-masochistic struggle in these settings is of an unbearable quality. From a purely nosological attitude, therefore, one may as well attempt to find correlations of the success in marriage between the color of men's eyes with the color of women's hair.

Nor does the typology arising from consideration of character structure provide data more amenable to our investigation. . . . I know of no studies from the point of view of whether the partners got along better if they were both oral characters, or got along poorly if one was an oral character and the other an anal character. What might at first appearance seem to be more valuable, descriptions of character types such as "passive-dependent" or "aggressive," also fail, on closer examination, to provide any worthwhile working hypothesis. Clearly the phenomenon to be studied is too complicated for any base provided by diagnostic classifications. Other considerations, therefore, must be looked into.

* * *

One conclusion, at the present state of our research, would be to the effect that many a marriage could be saved if one or the other or both partners went into psychiatric treatment, and such a conclusion would be warranted on the basis of experience. It implies that treatment would be the primary way of meeting the problem. Obviously, this is not always feasible. Therefore, it is justifiable to anticipate some sort of

prophylactic devices for meeting problems before they arise, and this thought is back of all kinds of planning toward making marriages more effective. Suggestions and advice range from trial marriages to giving courses in domestic science, and encouraging children to "play house." The theory back of this is clear. By way of anticipation, there may be some working through a situation and thus an actual preparation for mastery of a future area of difficulty. This leads to a consideration of the whole area of education, which ranges from courses in family life in high schools and colleges to premarital counseling, and the efficacy of the use of marriage manuals.

[M]any individuals use the material in the marriage manuals as measuring rods and construct artificial levels of aspirations to which they feel they have to conform, especially in regard to sexual activity and behavior. Yet despite the artificialities that may result from certain types of conformities in sexual behavior, we frequently overlook a positive gain that may come from the so-called educative devices. We are usually so accustomed ourselves to the use of conceptual approaches to the problem on a highly sophisticated level that we lose sight of the fact that many people do have a great deal of curiosity and quest for definite types of information. We overlook the fact that many people can use simple knowledge about anatomy and physiology as an aid to master, in some belated sort of way, troublesome problems. To be sure it is no accident that courses and books in marital relations often provoke anxiety instead of allaying it; but again, whether they produce adverse effects is frequently influenced by an already existing tendency in the individual toward anxiety. It is these failures in the popularization of knowledge that we come across as clinicians; and because the beneficial effects of popular education rarely come to our attention, we tend to forget them.

* * *

And so if one wants to talk about the general problem and ways of educating and of preparing people for marriage, one must also consider the multiple motives of authors and teachers which are reflected in their educative policies, often unconsciously. Some of these educative trends are clearly moralistic, others express pressure toward conformity, still others have a pragmatic trend that seems to promise a person that the more information he has the happier he will be. It thus seems fair to say that such educational methods have a value insofar as they give information. What they might do to help a person overcome neurotic trends, and thereby equip him better for marriage would be largely accidental and indirect.

* Reprinted from Eisenstein, V. W., ed. *Neurotic Interaction in Marriage.* New York: Basic Books, 1956, pp. 311-325. Reprinted with permission of the publisher.

b. *Sharp*

PEREZ v. LIPPOLD
32 Cal. 2d 711, 198 P. 2d 17 (1948)

TRAYNOR, J.

In this proceeding in mandamus, petitioners seek to compel the county clerk of Los Angeles County to issue them a certificate of registry (Civ. Code, sec. 69a) and a license to marry (Civ. Code, sec. 69). In the application for a license, petitioner Andrea Perez states that she is a white person and petitioner Sylvester Davis that he is a Negro. Respondent refuses to issue the certificate and license, invoking Civil Code section 69, which provides: "* * * no licence may be issued authorizing the marriage of a white person with a Negro, mulatto, Mongolian or member of the Malay race."

Civil Code section 69 implements Civil Code section 60, which provides: "All marriages of white persons with Negroes, Mongolians, members of the Malay race, or mulattoes are illegal and void." . . .

Petitioners contend that the statutes in question are unconstitutional on the grounds that they prohibit the free exercise of their religion and deny to them the right to participate fully in the sacraments of that religion. They are members of the Roman Catholic Church. They maintain that since the church has no rule forbidding marriages between Negroes and Caucasians, they are entitled to receive the sacrament of matrimony.

The provision of the First Amendment to the Constitution of the United States that Congress shall make no law "respecting an establishment of religion, or prohibiting the free exercise thereof" is encompassed in the concept of liberty in the Fourteenth Amendment. State legislatures are therefore no more competent than Congress to enact such a law. . . . Although freedom of conscience and the freedom to believe are absolute, the freedom to act is not. Cantwell v. Connecticut, supra, 310 U.S. at pages 303, 304, 60 S. Ct. at page 903.

The regulation of marriage is considered a proper function of the State. It is well settled that a legislature may declare monogamy to be the "law of social life under its dominion," even though such a law might inhibit the free exercise of certain religious practices. . . . If the miscegenation law under attack in the present proceeding is directed at a social evil and employs a reasonable means to prevent that evil, it is valid regardless of its incidental effect upon the conduct of particular religious groups. If, on the other hand, the law is discriminatory and irrational, it unconstitutionally restricts not only religious liberty but the liberty to marry as well.

The due process clause of the Fourteenth Amendment protects an area of personal liberty not yet wholly delimited. "While this court has not attempted to define with exactness the liberty thus guaranteed, the term has received much consideration and some of the included things have been definitely stated. Without doubt, it denotes not merely freedom from bodily restraint but also the right of the individual to contract, to engage in any of the common occupations of life, to acquire useful knowledge, to *marry,* establish a home and bring up children, to worship God according to the dictates of his own conscience, and, generally, to enjoy those privileges long recognized at common law as essential to the orderly pursuit of happiness by free men." Italics added. Meyer v. Nebraska, 262 U.S. 390, 399, 43 S.Ct. 625, 626, 67 L. Ed. 1042, 29 A.L.R. 1446. Marriage is thus something more than a civil contract subject to regulation by the state; it is a fundamental right of free men. There can be no prohibition of marriage except for an important social objective and by reasonable means.

* * *

The right to marry is as fundamental as the right to send one's child to a particular school or the right to have offspring. Indeed, "We are dealing here with legislation which involves one of the basic civil rights of man. Marriage and procreation are fundamental to the very existence and survival of the race." Skinner v. Oklahoma, supra. 316 U.S. at page 541, 62 S. Ct. at page 1113. Legislation infringing such rights must be based upon more than prejudice and must be free from oppressive discrimination to comply with the constitutional requirements of due process and equal protection of the laws.

Since the right to marry is the right to join in marriage with the person of one's choice, a statute that prohibits an individual from marrying a member of a race other than his own restricts the scope of his choice and thereby restricts his right to marry. It must therefore be determined whether the state can restrict that right on the basis of race alone without violating the equal protection of the laws clause of the United States Constitution.

Distinctions between citizens solely because of their ancestry are by their very nature odious to a free people whose institutions are founded upon the doctrine of equality. For that reason, legislative classification or discrimination based on race alone has often been held to be a denial of equal protection. . . .

* * *

A state law prohibiting members of one race from marrying members of another race is not designed to meet a clear and present peril arising out of an emergency. In the absence of an emergency the state clearly cannot base a law impairing fundamental rights of individuals on general assumptions as to traits of racial groups. It has been said that a statute such as section 60 does not discriminate against any racial group, since it applies alike to all persons whether Caucasian, Negro, or members of any other race. . . . The decisive question, however, is not whether different races, each considered as a group, are equally treated. The right to marry is the right of individuals, not of racial groups. The equal protection clause of the United States Constitution does not refer to rights of the Negro race, the Caucasian race, or any other race, but to the rights of individuals. . . .

In determining whether the public interest requires the prohibition of a marriage between two persons, the state may take into consideration matters of legitimate concern to the state. Thus, disease that might become a peril to the prospective spouse or to the offspring of the marriage could be made a disqualification for marriage. . . . Such legislation, however, must be based on tests of the individual, not on arbitrary classifications of groups or races, and must be administered without discrimination on the grounds of race. . . . It has been suggested that certain races are more prone than the Caucasian to diseases such as tuberculosis. If the state determines that certain diseases would endanger a marital partner or offspring, it may prohibit persons so diseased from marrying, but the statute must apply to all persons regardless of race. Sections 60 and 69 are not motivated by a concern to diminish the transmission of disease by marriage, for they make race and not disease the disqualification. Thus, a tubercular Negro or a tubercular Caucasian may marry subject to the race limitation, but a Negro and a Caucasian who are free from disease may not marry each other. If the purpose of these sections were to prevent marriages by persons who do not have the qualifications for marriage that the state may properly prescribe, they would make the possession of such qualifications the test for members of all races alike. By restricting the individual's right to marry on the basis of race alone, they violate the equal protection of the laws clause of the United States Constitution.

* * *

. . . Many courts in this country have assumed that human beings can be judged by race and that other races are inferior to the Caucasian, Respondent's position is based upon those premises. He justifies the prohibition of miscegenation on grounds similar to those set forth in the frequently cited case of Scott v. State, 1869, 39

Ga. 321, 324: "The amalgamation of the races is not only unnatural, but is always productive of deplorable results. Our daily observation shows us, that the offspring of these unnatural connections are generally sickly and effeminate, and that they are inferior in physical development and strength, to the full blood of either race."[2] Modern experts are agreed that the progeny of marriages between persons of different races are not inferior to both parents.[3] Nevertheless, even if we were to assume that interracial marriage results in inferior progeny, we are unable to find any clear policy in the statute against marriages on that ground.

* * *

The Legislature . . . permits the mixing of all races with the single exception that white persons may not marry Negroes, Mongolians, Mulattoes, or Malays. It might be concluded therefrom that section 60 is based upon the theory that the progeny of a white person and a Mongolian or Negro or Malay are inferior or undesirable, while the progeny of members of other different races are not. Nevertheless, the section does not prevent the mixing of "white" and "colored" blood. It permits marriages not only between Caucasians and others of darker pigmentation, such as Indians, Hindus, and Mexicans, but between persons of mixed ancestry including white. If a person of partly Caucasian ancestry is yet classified as a Mongolian under section 60 because his ancestry is predominantly Mongolian, a considerable mixture of Caucasian and Mongolian blood is permissible. A person having five-eighths Mongolian blood and three-eights white blood could properly marry another person of preponderantly Mongolian blood. Similarly, a Mulatto can marry a Negro. Under the theory of In re Estate of Stark, supra, that a Mulatto is a person having one-eighth or more of Negro ancestry, a person having seven-eighths white ancestry could marry a Negro. In fact two Mulattoes, each of four-eighths white and four-eighths Negro blood, could marry under section 60, and their progeny, like them, would belong as much to one race as to the other. In effect, therefore, section 60 permits

2. Respondent refers to the following language in State v. Jackson, 80 Mo. 175, 179, 50 Am. Rep. 499, although stating that "we have not found any other statement to bear out the biological claims" therein: "It is stated as a well authenticated fact that if the issue of a black man and a white woman, and a white man and a black woman intermarry, they cannot possibly have any progeny, and such a fact sufficiently justifies those laws which forbid the intermarriage of blacks and whites, laying out of view other sufficient grounds for such enactments."

3. See, Castle, "Biological and Sociological Consequences of Race Crossing," 9 Am. J. Physical Anthropology, pp. 145, 152-153.

a substantial amount of intermarriage between persons of some Caucasian ancestry and members of other races. Furthermore, there is no ban on illicit sexual relations between Caucasians and members of the proscribed races. Indeed, it is covertly encouraged by the race restrictions on marriage.

Nevertheless, respondent has sought to justify the statute by contending that the prohibition of intermarriage between Caucasians and members of the specified races prevents the Caucasian race from being contaminated by races whose members are by nature physically and mentally inferior to Caucasians.

Respondent submits statistics relating to the physical inferiority of certain races. Most, if not all, of the ailments to which he refers are attributable largely to environmental factors. Moreover, one must take note of the statistics showing that there is a higher percentage of certain diseases among Caucasians than among non-Caucasians. The categorical statement that non-Caucasians are inherently physically inferior is without scientific proof. In recent years scientists have attached great weight to the fact that their segregation in a generally inferior environment greatly increases their liability to physical ailments. In any event, generalizations based on race are untrustworthy in view of the great variations among members of the same race. The rationalization, therefore, that marriage between Caucasians and non-Caucasians is socially undesirable because of the physical disabilities of the latter, fails to take account of the physical disabilities of Caucasians and fails also to take account of variations among non-Caucasians. The Legislature is free to prohibit marriages that are socially dangerous because of the physical disabilities of the parties concerned. (See, Civ. Code §§ 79.01, 79.06.) The miscegention statute, however, condemns certain races as unfit to marry with Caucasians on the premise of a hypothetical racial disability, regardless of the physical qualifications of the individuals concerned. If this premise were carried to its logical conclusion, non-Caucasians who are now precluded from marrying Caucasians on physical grounds would also be precluded from marrying among themselves on the same grounds. The concern to prevent marriages in the first category. and the indifference about marriages in the second reveal the spuriousness of the contention that intermarriage between Caucasians and non-Caucasians is socially dangerous on physical grounds.

Respondent also contends that Negroes, and impliedly the other races specified in section 60, are inferior mentally to Caucasians. It is true that, in the United States, catalogues of distinguished people list more Caucasians than members of other races. It cannot be disregarded, however, that Caucasians are in the great majority and have generally had a more advantageous environment, and that the capacity of the members of any race to contribute to a nation's culture depends in large measure on how freely they may participate in that culture. There is no scientific proof that one race is superior to another in native ability. The data on which Caucasian superiority is based have undergone considerable re-evaluation by social and physical scientists in the past two decades. Although scientists do not discount the influences of heredity on the ability to score highly on mental tests, there is no certain correlation between race and intelligence. There have been outstanding individuals in all races, and there has also been wide variation in the individuals of all races. In any event the Legislature has not made an intelligence test a prerequisite to marriage. If respondent's blanket condemnation of the mental ability of the proscribed races were accepted, there would be no limit to discrimination based upon the purported inferiority of certain races. It would then be logical to forbid Negroes to marry Negroes, or Mongolians to marry Mongolians, on the ground of mental inferiority, or by sterilization to decrease their numbers.

Respondent contends, however, that persons wishing to marry in contravention of race barriers come from the "dregs of society" and that their progeny will therefore be a burden on the community. There is no law forbidding marriage among the "dregs of society," assuming that this expression is capable of definition. If there were such a law, it could not be applied without a proper determination of the persons that fall within that category, a determination that could hardly be made on the basis of race alone.

Respondent contends that even if the races specified in the statute are not by nature inferior to the Caucasian race, the statute can be justified as a means of diminishing race tension and preventing the birth of children who might become social problems.

It is true that in some communities the marriage of persons of different races may result in tension. Similarly, race tension may result from the enforcement of the constitutional requirement that persons must not be excluded from juries solely on the ground of color, or segregated by law to certain districts within a city. . . .

The effect of race prejudice upon any community is unquestionably detrimental both to the minority that is singled out for discrimination and to the dominant group that would perpetuate the prejudice. It is no answer to say that race tension can be eradicated through the perpetuation by law of the prejudices that give rise to the tension. . . . In the present case, however, there is no redress for the serious restriction of the right of Negroes, Mulattoes, Mongolians, and Malays to marry; certainly there is none in the corresponding restriction of the right of Caucasians to marry. A member of any of these races may find himself barred by law from marrying the person of his choice and that person to him may be irreplaceable. Human beings are bereft of worth and dignity by a doctrine that would make them as interchangeable as trains.

* * *

In summary, we hold that sections 60 and 69 are not only too vague and uncertain to be enforceable regulations of a fundamental right, but that they violate the equal protection of the laws clause of the United States Constitution by impairing the right of individuals to marry on the basis of race alone and by arbitrarily and unreasonably discriminating against certain racial groups.

Let the peremptory writ issue as prayed.

NOTES

NOTE 1.

NAIM v. NAIM
197 Va. 80; 87 S.E. 2d 749 (1955)

BUCHANAN, J.

Virginia statutes regarding the intermarriage of white and colored persons in effect at the date of the marriage, and now in effect, provide that all marriages between a white person and a colored person shall be absolutely void (§ 20-57); that if a white person and a colored person go out of the State for the purpose of being married and with the intention of returning, and after being married return and reside here, and cohabit as man and wife, they shall be punished as provided in § 20-59, and the marriage shall be governed by the same law as if it had been solemnized in this State. Section 20-59 provides that they shall be guilty of a felony and confined in the penitentiary for not less than one nor more than five years.

As stated in appellant's brief, the only question at issue is whether the marriage of the appellant and appellee could be annulled on the ground of their racial ineligibility to marry one another.

* * *

In State v. Gibson, 36 Ind. 389, 10 Am. Rep. 42, a statute prohibiting the intermarriage of Negroes and white persons was held not to violate any provision of the Fourteenth Amendment or the Civil Rights laws. In the course of a well-

reasoned and well-supported discussion of the powers retained by and inherent in the States under the Constitution, the court said:

> "* * * In this State marriage is treated as a civil contract, but it is more than a mere civil contract. It is a public institution established by God himself, is recognized in all Christian and civilized nations, and is essential to the peace, happiness, and well-being of society. * * * The right, in the states, to regulate and control, to guard, protect, and preserve this God-given, civilizing, and Christianizing institution is of inestimable importance, and cannot be surrendered, nor can the states suffer or permit any interference therewith. If the federal government can determine who may marry in a state, there is no limit to its power. * * *" 36 Ind. at pages 402-403.

It was said in that case that the question was one of difference between the races, not of superiority or inferiority, and that the natural law which forbids their intermarriage and the social amalgamation which leads to a corruption of races is as clearly divine as that which imparted to them different natures.

* * *

More than half of the States of the Union have miscegenation statutes. With only one exception they have been upheld in an unbroken line of decisions in every State in which it has been charged that they violate the Fourteenth Amendment: . . .

The exception is California, where a divided court held to the contrary with three of the seven judges dissenting, in Perez v. Sharp, 32 Cal. 2d 711, 198 P. 2d 17 (sub nom. Perez v. Lippold). In one of the two concurring opinions it was pointed out that since California recognized a marriage performed in another State between persons of the white and colored races, such marriage could not be considered vitally detrimental to public health and morals, and that the California statutes forbidding miscegenetic marriages were distinguished from such statutes in other States in that they were entirely declaratory, while all the others carried with them punishments for violations, indicating an attitude of comparative indifference on the part of the California legislature and the absence of any clearly expressed sentiment or policy. However that may be, the holding is contrary to the otherwise uninterrupted course of judicial decision, both State and Federal. . . .

* * *

Brown v. Board of Education, supra [347 U.S. 483, 74 S.Ct. 691], reached its conclusion that segregation in the public schools was contrary to the Equal Protection clause on the basis that education is perhaps the most important function of State and local governments, "the very foundation of good citizenship", and that the opportunity to acquire it, "where the state has undertaken to provide it, is a right which must be made available to all on equal terms."

No such claim for the intermarriage of the races could be supported ; by no sort of valid reasoning could it be found to be a foundation of good citizenship or a right which must be made available to all on equal terms. In the opinion of the legislatures of more than half the States it is harmful to good citizenship.

* * *

We are unable to read in the Fourteenth Amendment to the Constitution, or in any other provision of that great document, any words or any intendment which prohibit the State from enacting legislation to preserve the racial integrity of its citizens, or which denies the power of the State to regulate the marriage relation so that it shall not have a mongrel breed of citizens. We find there no requirement that the State shall not legislate to prevent the obliteration of racial pride, but must permit the corruption of blood even though it weaken or destroy the quality of its citizenship. Both sacred and secular history teach that nations and races have better advanced in human progress when they cultivated their own distinctive characteristics and culture and developed their own peculiar genius.

Regulation of the marriage relation is, we think, distinctly one of the rights guaranteed to the States and safeguarded by that bastion of States' rights, somewhat battered perhaps but still a sturdy fortress in our fundamental law, the tenth section of the Bill of Rights, which declares: "The powers not delegated to the United States by the Constitution, nor prohibited by it to the states, are reserved to the states respectively, or to the people."

The decree appealed from is affirmed.

NOTE 2.

MEDAGLIA v. GILL
Circuit Court for Baltimore County
Feb. 13, 1964 (unpublished)

W. A. MENCHINE, JUDGE.

ELIZABETH MEDAGLIA has filed a Petition for a Writ of Mandamus to compel the Clerk of this Court to issue a marriage license to permit her to marry one DR. BENJAMIN A. deGUZMAN. The Clerk of Court, acting under Article 62, §12 of the Annotated Code of Maryland, refused to issue the license upon the ground that Article 27, §398 prohibited their marital union.

The Petition recites that the refusal of the Clerk of Court was illegal, arbitrary and unreasonable and contends also that Article 27, §398 is unconstitutional and void.

Article 27, §398 reads in pertinent part as follows:

"All marriages between a white person and a member of the Malay race * * * shall be void."

The phrase "member of the Malay race" is not defined in the Statute.

Webster's New International Dictionary (1958) defines "Malayan Race" as follows:

"One of the five varieties of mankind discriminated by Blumenbach in 1775, and comprising the non-negritic inhabitants of the Malay Peninsula and Oceania.
The five varieties of mankind delineated by Blumenbach are:

1. Caucasian
2. Mongolian
3. Ethiopian
4. American
5. Malay."

The evidence established the following facts:

1. The Petitioner was of the white race.
2. The other party to the proposed marriage was a Filipino, was born in Manila, P.I., one grandmother of whom was of the white race.

Assuming, without deciding, that *in general* a Filipino is a member of the Malay Race, it is very clear that *in particular,* this Filipino is not. The evidence shows that he is a person of mixed races —white and Malay—and the marriage of such a person to a member of the white race is not proscribed by §398.

The Court will, on presentation, issue the Writ of Mandamus requiring the Clerk to issue the marriage license in accordance with law.

The suggested Constitutional question is not reached under the facts of this case.

NOTE 3.

VAN HOUTEN v. MORSE
162 Mass. 414, 38 N.E. 705 (1894)

MORTON, J.   The defense principally relied on in this case is that the promise which the jury have found was made was induced by fraudulent conduct and representations and concealments on the part of the plaintiff with reference to various matters relating to her past life, to her parentage and family, and to her position and circumstances. The defendant contends that the instructions of the court as to what constituted fraudulent concealment were not sufficient, and that certain requests which he made should have been given.

The jury were correctly instructed that it was not the duty of a party, before making or accepting an offer of marriage, to communicate all the previous circumstances of his or her life ; and that the parties would be bound, if they became engaged without making any investigation, and without receiving any assurances or representations which led to the engagement, even though matters were discovered subsequently which, if known at the time, would have prevented the engagement, unless they were such as gave a right to the other party to terminate the contract upon their discovery. Whether the only matters which would give the defendant such a right were those relating to the chastity of the plaintiff, we have no need now to consider. No question was made by him as to the plaintiff's chastity ; and the fact, if it was a fact, that the plaintiff had some negro blood in her veins, or that her motives were mercenary, or that there was a want of affection on her part, or that there was an incompatibility resulting from disparity of age, difference in character and disposition, and other causes, which, apart from fraud, were the things relied on by the defendant, would not justify him as a matter of law in breaking the contract. . . .

* * *

. . . with regard to her parentage and family. She was under no obligation to tell the defendant about them in the absence of inquiry by him. But, if she voluntarily undertook to make any statements concerning them, she was bound not only to state truly what she told, but also not to suppress or conceal facts which would materially qualify those which she stated. If, for instance, as the evidence tended to show, she told the defendant that her father and mother were both of the best white families in Charleston, South Carolina ; that her father was a distinguished lawyer ; that her mother was equally high bred ; and that after his death her mother married a man by the name of Smith, with which marriage her mother's folks were dissatisfied, and that on that account the family moved to California ;—but if she suppressed the facts that Smith was a colored barber and an octoroon and her reputed father, and that her mother had negro blood in her veins, and was about one-eighth negro, the impression as to the standing of herself and family, and the credibility of her statement respecting her parentage, would or might be quite different from that which would be likely to be the case if she had told the whole truth. These facts, if they were facts, were necessary to a correct understanding of the real state of the circumstances of her family and of her previous history, and were or might be found to be material ; and a willful suppression of them

on her part, in view of what there was evidence that she told, would constitute, or might be found to constitute, a fraud upon the defendant. . . .

NOTE 4.

ANONYMOUS
Will You Marry Me?*

Dear Charles,

It is with the greatest concern that I await an answer from you on November first, and lest you make, from insufficient knowledge, an irretrievable decision that will leave me long regretful, let me present what persuasion I can word in my own behalf.

Of all my best traits—tolerance, humor, adaptability—perhaps the most valuable in a chosen companion would be that of a strong zest for living, a desire to fill life with intensity, color and variety. I fear for many months after I met you this characteristic of mine was thoroughly but temporarily subordinated by unexplainable circumstances ; but I have recovered it as the polarstar of my existence ; and hope to live again with imagination, to design living with a view to orderly and graceful backgrounds of white fireplaces and silver-edged mirrors ; socially with teas by candlelight, culturally with recordings of *Jewels of the Madonna* and translations of Villon, practically with good waffles, and emotionally with a warm understanding of the needs of companionship.

My inheritance is an unbrokenly American one since 1723. I will fall heir to the ancestral house (nothing to brag about) and to the . . . stock (not a bad legacy). I have sufficient income for my needs, aside from food and shelter. I have no interfering or dependent relatives, have contracted no debts and have a genius for living well without money. My education includes one college, two universities and a business school ; a little French, much music and no art ; much Latin and no Greek. I have travelled up and down the Atlantic coast (U.S.) and thus enjoyed the broadening influence of varied contacts, and appeased youth's craving for single-handed adventure. Though well and kindly guarded I have thus made valuable acquaintances from my father's law-associates in New York through Charleston's renegade socialites to Florida's politicians.

I love children and dogs and have been instructed by my friends in the proper training of both. I have good health and no objections to perpetuating the species. I wish to make C. my

* Reprinted from: Scheu-Riesz, H., ed. *Will you Marry Me*? New York: Island Workshop Press, Co-op. Inc., 1940, pp. 94-96.

home, so have interested myself in many of its activities, joined its Country Club ; been careful, though therefore slow, to choose friends, I swim excellently, ride horseback well, dance nicely, play bridge indifferently and read aloud abominably. I no longer desire to become the despair of the Saints Above and I can follow the Episcopal service without a prayer book.

Most notably, I am reasonable, keep my word and arrive at conclusions without the necessity of argument. On the basis of affection, admiration and common interests I should find marrying you a delightful pact for mutual benefit. Should it, as a contract, prove otherwise, I assure you I would be entirely tractable and undemanding ; if a mistake emotionally speaking, I assure you—"that I can go like snow and leave no trace behind."

ALICE

NOTE 5.

MONTAGU, ASHLEY

Man's Most Dangerous Myth*

The phenomenon of increased vigor following upon hybridization has been long recognized by biologists and is known as *heterosis,* or hybrid vigor. By "hybrid vigor" is mean the phenomenon frequently observed as a result of the crossing of the members of two distinct inbred lines derived from different species, varieties, or groups, in which the hybrid, that is, the offspring resulting from the union of a sperm and an egg which differ in one or more genes, exceeds both parents in size, fecundity, resistance, or other adaptive qualties.

From this definition it will be perceived that all possible matings between human beings must result in hybrids, since all potential human matings, whether they occur in the same or in different ethnic groups, are necessarily between individuals who differ from one another in many more than one gene. In practice, however, the term "hybrid" is used to refer to the offspring of two individuals who differ from each other in their genetic constitution for one or more distinctive characters or qualities. The essential difference between these two conceptions of a hybrid is an important one ; we shall return to it upon a later page. In what follows we shall abide by the latter conception of a hybrid because it is the sense in which the term is most commonly used.

Evidence of hybrid vigor in man is difficult to obtain because the gene differences between human ethnic groups for the majority of traits are not sufficiently marked. For the same reason we would not expect, and do not find, any degeneration, disharmonies, or infertilities in so-called "race crosses." Inbred plants and animals, on the other hand, constitute highly homozygous strains, often characterized by different chromosome numbers and other genetic differences, which frequently produce genetic disharmonies in the offspring. But this is not the case in man, for the varieties of man are characterized by a high degree of heterozygosity. Heterozygotes are characterized, on the whole, by greater stores of both genotypic and phenotypic plasticity and variability. It has been suggested that hybrid vigor, in the form of benefits which accrue to the offspring and eventually to the group as a result of crossing, occurs because each parent supplies dominant genes for which the other parent may be recessive. . . .

The new types which emerge in this way generally exhibit something more than merely the blended sum of the properties of the parental types. That is, they show some characters and qualities which are in their way somewhat novel, characters not originally possessed by, although potentially present in, the groups from which the parents have been derived. We have here the emergence of novelty, the emergents of hybrid syntheses.

* * *

It is, indeed, a sad commentary upon the present condition of Western man that when it is a matter of supporting his prejudices he will distort the facts concerning hybridization so that laws are caused to be instituted making it an offense against the state. But when it comes to making a financial profit out of the scientifically established facts he will employ geneticists to discover the best means of producing hybrid vigor in order to increase the yield of some commercially exploitable plant or animal product. Should, however, such a geneticist translate his scientific knowledge to the increase of his own happiness and the well-being of his future offspring, by marrying a woman of another color or ethnic group, the probability is that he will be promptly discharged by his employer.

NOTE 6.

ANDERSON, R. C.

The Influence of Heredity on Family Health*

If there is anyone who closes his eyes to heredity, it is probably the courting individual. He or she sees phenotypically rather than genotypically. In other words, he selects a partner on the basis of individual appearance, not on

---

* New York: World Publishing Company, 1964, pp. 188-192. Reprinted with permission of the publisher.

* *Marriage and Family Living,* Vol. 19 (1957), pp. 138-139.

family performance. It is somewhat akin to crop or animal judging, as constrasted with the more scientific method of pedigree studies and performance tests. Unconsciously, however, consideration is given in selection to such genetically influenced factors as height, musical aptitudes, intelligence, complexion, emotional makeup, eye color, nose shape, physique, hair color, and many less specific features. . . .

The law imposes certain restrictions on marriage, some of which are of genetic importance. The marriage of close blood relatives is forbidden. In the majority of states, the marriage of first cousins is forbidden, while the others permit first cousins to marry, but not closer relatives. This restriction against the marriage of blood relatives is observed in all societies, either by edict or taboo. There is, of course, biological justification for such restriction because blood relatives tend to share more genes in common. Therefore, since all people probably possess one or more hidden deleterious recessive genes, the marriage of blood relatives would increase the chances of a child being born with a double dose of one of these harmful genes, and he would exhibit the undesirable trait.

* * *

Just as the marriage of blood relatives is inadvisable, so too are the marriages of individuals whose families are harboring the same recessive hereditary disease. Thus, diabetics or members of families where there is diabetes are usually advised to marry into families where diabetes is unknown, in order to lessen the chances of having diabetic children. Diabetes is perhaps the most common of the major hereditary diseases of man, and about one person in every sixty-five is either a diabetic or will become one at some time during his life. It is now thought that diabetes may represent several distinct diseases, rather than a single disease. The diabetic gene or genes are very common in the population and the diabetic person may marry a "carrier" of the predisposing gene, even if he marries into a family in which none of its members have the disease. The second most common of the major diseases which is generally considered to be caused by recessive genes is schizophrenia and perhaps one person in one hundred is predisposed to this disease. And the same recommendation regarding marriage applies as in the case of diabetics.

* * *

Where hereditary disease has already manifested itself in the marriage partners or their families, it is possible to make predictions as to the likelihood of its appearance in the next generation. If the mother's father had hemophilia, then the chances of her sons having the disease would be fifty-fifty; of her daughters, zero. If one parent has syndactyly (webbing of the digits), or polydactyly (extra digits), future children may have a fifty-fifty chance of also having it because these often behave as dominant hereditary traits. Some of the genetic traits or diseases are relatively unimportant, such as syndactyly or polydactyly. Others are literally devastating. For example, retinoblastoma (a type of eye cancer due to a dominant gene) generally allows only two alternatives: death in early childhood or blindness which results from surgical removal of the eyeball or from radiation treatment. . . .

If one were to review critically all families for genetic "taints," there would be relatively few that would escape criticism. There would be few ideal marriage candidates. The exposure of taints and the exaggeration of risks would undoubtedly do more harm in precipitating anxieties than good in the eugenic sense. . . .

NOTE 7.

FRASER, F. C.
Heredity Counseling*

. . . A 23-year-old albino French-Canadian man was referred by the Institute for the Blind because he was considering marriage and wanted to know the risk of his children being albino. Two of this nine siblings were also albinos. It was explained to him that the statistical risk for his children was low, but that the crucial point was whether or not the prospective wife was a carrier, the risk being 50 per cent if she was, but 0 per cent if she was not. In view of Waardenburg's claim that albino "carriers" may often be identified by trans-illumination of the iris (cited by Falls, 1953) we suggested that the fiancee should come in for examination. The patient reacted so strongly against this that further delving into his feelings about the fiancee was undertaken, and it was found that she was eight years older than he, that she, not he, had done the proposing, and that, in short, he was not at all keen on getting married and was hoping to use the poor outlook (as he thought) for the children as a reason for not going into the marriage.

. . . Mr. Dixon consulted me because his son, Alan, was intent on marrying Mr. Dixon's sister's daughter. He did not seem opposed to this, but wanted to know if there was anything to the idea that first cousins shouldn't marry. The

---

* Eugenics Quarterly, Vol. 3, (1956), pp. 48-50.

genetic disadvantage of consanguineous matings was explained, and it was pointed out to him that although marrying a first cousin certainly increases one's chance of having defective children, we really do not know what the actual risk is—if we had to guess it we might say about a 10 per cent risk for each child of developing a recessively inherited disease. This risk constitutes an argument against the marriage which would have to be balanced against the arguments for the prospective marriage, and the decision taken accordingly. Shortly afterwards Mrs. Andrews, Mr. Dixon's sister, consulted me, not knowing of Mr Dixon's visit, because her daughter was thinking of marrying Alan Dixon. Exactly the same advice was given to her.

The result was that Mr. Dixon went away saying "The geneticist says the risk is low, and there is no objection to the marriage," while Mrs. Andrews went away saying " The geneticist says the risk is high, and the marriage would be ill-advised." Both interpreted the information to suit their own ends.

NOTE 8.

GROUP FOR THE ADVANCEMENT OF PSYCHIATRY
Emotional Aspects of School Desegregation*

. . . According to the distortions of myths the Negro male has great sexual prowess, the Negro female is invariably responsive. This concept of the aggressive, primitive, potent Negro represents all that is bad and forbidden, all that the white adult, when reared to conform to middle-class social mores, has been denied. Because these adults fear to allow themselves to play the leading roles in fantasies of violent primitive sexual behavior, they more readily assign such roles to the Negro.

Unacknowledged white male jealousy of the Negro male's fantasied advantage as a sexual rival for the white female is an emotional source of power behind the extreme taboo, maintained by the white-supremacy code, ostensibly to protect white womanhood. This code sanctions the most savage reprisals for Negro male violation, or even the most realistically flimsy suspicion of it, as in the Emmett Till "wolf whistle" case. The irrational emotionality of a lynch mob reveals the terrible antisocial power of racial myth. The white-supremacy code also provides immunity to the white male from Negro resistance or retaliation for the white's sexual freedom with Negro females. And so, fear and

* New York: Group for the Advancement of Psychiatry, Report No. 37-A, 1960, pp. 10-18. Reprinted with permission of the publisher.

hate, founded and maintained by racial sex mythology, breeds ever more fear and hate within members of both races.

The stereotype of the sexual Negro has entered deeply into the emotions of many white people. To such people this image is very real, although objectively it is groundless. . . .

c. Should the State Sponsor Counseling for Marriage?

[i]
Wisconsin Family Code Ch. 245 (1963)

245.05 Marriage license . . .

MARITAL INFORMATION

Your marriage license will be issued to you under the provisions of chapter 245 of the Wisconsin statutes, which is part of "The Family Code." For your information and advice, section 245.001 of that chapter includes the following provision:

Intent. It is the intent of chapters 245 to 248 to promote the stability and best interest of marriage and the family. Marriage is the institution that is the foundation of the family and of society. Its stability is basic to morality and civilization, and of vital interest to society and the state. The consequences of the marriage contract are more significant to society than those of other contracts, and the public interest must be taken into account always. The seriousness of marriage makes adequate premarital counseling and education for family living highly desirable, and courses thereon are urged upon all persons contemplating marriage. The impairment or dissolution of the marriage relation generally results in injury to the public wholly apart from the effect upon the parties immediately concerned.

* * *

[ii]
KARPF, M. J.
Marriage Counseling and Psychotherapy*

At various times and in different connections, this writer has advanced the view that marriage counseling is considerably different from psychiatry and psychoanalysis and even from psychology. The point was made that unlike practitioners in other fields, the marriage counselor deals mostly with normal people who, on the whole, manage their affairs quite adequately but occasionally find themselves confronted by a set of circumstances or a constellation of prob-

* *Marriage and Family Living*, Vol. 13 (1951), pp. 169-178.

lems which are too much for them, either because of their own emotional involvement or because they do not possess the necessary information to handle the situation, or both.

This view of marriage counseling problems leads to several rather important conclusions: First, that the marriage counselor, while holding himself alert to evidence of abnormalities and to hidden motivations, need not necessarily probe too deeply and need not indulge in extended analyses or attempt fundamental personality changes. In many, if not most, situations requiring his professional services, he can safely deal with the problems as they present themselves on a surface or conscious level after making certain that he is not dealing with a displacement, i.e., that the client is not withholding the real problem from him by substituting a different problem, perhaps one of lesser significance and importance.

Second, the marriage counselor must make certain, so far as possible, that he is not dealing with deep-seated psychotic or neurotic situations which are beyond his ability to cope with. This implies that the marriage counselor should be sufficiently well trained to recognize a neurosis or psychosis when he is confronted with it. This is admittedly not always easy or certain for there are situations which will puzzle or escape even the better trained psychiatrist who is not especially well trained or experienced in differential diagnosis. But it means also that the marriage counselor need not be prepared to handle deep seated neuroses or psychoses.

The wise counselor will, of course, call a competent psychiatrist into consultation whenever he is uncertain about the nature of the problem he is dealing with.

Similarly, the conscientious counselor will take proper precaution that he does not overlook or ignore somatic factors and will utilize the skills of the medical profession whenever the situation seems to require it.

Incidentally, practiced on this level, marriage counseling becomes a professional service within the financial means of many who could not possibly afford it if longer and more involved analysis and therapy were resorted to. In this way, many marriages that would end in divorce might be saved. It also means that the already heavily burdened professions of psychiatry and social work would be free to concentrate on the many serious and frequently more involved problems coming to their attention, for which, as it is, the needed time and personnel are not available for adequate service.

This writer holds that the marriage counselor can best make his important contribution by equipping himself to function not as a pseudo psychiatrist or analyst but as one who has made a special study of the problems and inter-relationships of family life ; the bonds, loyalties and conflicts ; the loves, rivalries and hostilities ; the need for identification and the conflicting desire for independence ; the wish for security and the urge for adventure ; in brief, the stresses and strains involved in membership in a family and the psycho-social factors and influences of such membership on the personality.

* * *

CASE 1. PREMARITAL COUNSELING—INTERRACIAL PROBLEM

This case first came to the counselor's attention through the girl's father, Mr. X, a lawyer of broad, liberal views on social and economic questions, interested in good race relations and active in several organizations promoting them. He was a member of the N.A.A.C.P., the Urban League and other organizations promoting civic unity. His daughter, a senior in a local university, shared his views, mingled freely with white and coloured classmates of both sexes, and brought them home with the encouragement of her father until she announced that she was in love with a colored boy, a first year graduate student in chemistry, and intended to marry him.

The father stated that Z is an only child, had a fairly happy childhood, was a rather good student in elementary and secondary schools as well as in college where she is majoring in literature with special interest in drama, has a fine social conscience and has always been interested in the underdog. She has shown considerable interest in minority groups and responded to agitation on the campuses of the Junior College and University, opposing discrimination. She resigned from a sorority because of her opposition to discrimination.

He reported that she was not active in church groups and had no special interest in church activity or attendance. The family as a whole is not religiously inclined although the mother would prefer a greater degree of religious identification. The family life was tranquil and happy until this problem arose. While it has not reached the conflict stage it has caused tension which may result in strife.

The father said he had no objection to racial intermarriage on principle ; that he would not oppose the marriage of his daughter to a Negro except that he does not believe that she will be happy, as society is not so constituted at the present as to make it possible for such a couple to be happy. He is deeply hurt by his daughter's accusations that he was insincere in his activities in favor of racial understanding and good will and by her saying that, like all good conservatives, he draws the line at intermarriage. She has even charged that he would draw the line at having Negro neighbors.

Mrs. X upbraids her husband with the charge that he is responsible for their difficulties, that she foresaw trouble when their daughter associated with colored boys and girls and wanted to put a stop to it, or at least discourage it, but could not stand up against the two of them. She insists that if this marriage goes through she will not be able to face her friends and relatives. Mr. X fears that if this marriage takes place they will have to leave the city, if, indeed, it does not cause his wife's nervous collapse or a rupture in their own marriage.

He was inclined to doubt the depth of his daughter's love for the boy. It seemed to him that at first the relationship was something of an adventure with her and that later it became a "cause." He requested advice as to what to do and how to handle the problem. When it was suggested to him that no advice could be given without discussing the matter with his daughter and perhaps also with his wife, Mr. X doubted whether his daughter would agree to come to see the counselor but thought she might do so because she knows of his interest in interracial problems. He promised to try to get her to come.

First Interview: Z, an attractive, high spirited, intelligent and somewhat impulsive girl, stated that she knew that her father had been to see the counselor and had no doubt prejudiced him against the marriage, that the only reason she agreed to come was her regard for the high reputation of the counselor on account of his attitude or face relations but if he had any intention of persuading her against the marriage, he might as well save himself the time and energy. It was apparent that she was aggressively hostile, and that in her present mood little insight could be obtained into her real feelings and motivations. It seemed necessary, therefore, to divert her attention to a different problem, to gain her confidence on a different level, and in a different area.

She was assured that nothing was further from the counselor's mind than to persuade her to give up her plan to marry the boy she loves, that I was concerned with a different problem she was facing, perhaps not known to her, on which I might need her help; that it was up to her whether she should discuss the forthcoming marriage with me; that I had no desire to force her confidence and that, in fact, I did not share her father's fears and particularly her

mother's conviction, that she would wreck her life with this marriage, as I have known several intermarriages which turned out quite happy; that it all depended on the personalities involved and the circumstances. The important thing at the moment was quite a different problem— one which, unless wisely handled, might not only hurt a number of people whom she loved, but might even become a serious obstacle to her own marital happiness.

By this time the girl was considerably calmer, was more at ease and interested in the problem on which I wanted her help. Despite her request that I tell her what the problem was, I told her that I was not yet ready to confide in her, that I would like to know a little more about her, her interests, the kind of books she reads, her outlook on life, the courses she took, and her reactions to them, the insights she has acquired into human behavior, etc.

We then discussed her courses at the University, especially those in psychology and sociology, her teachers whom we knew in common, books she has read, and so on, so that by the time the first interview was drawing to a close we had established a very good rapport. She then asked what problem I wanted to discuss with her and how she could help me.

I told her that it was too late to go into that but I could tell her that the problem concerned her family, that I was especially concerned about her mother and that I would greatly appreciate it if she would observe her mother most carefully during the next few days and give me the results of her observations and her opinion as to whether there was a problem there, what it is due to and what can be done about it.

She wanted to stay on and discuss it at once but it was explained to her that this was both undesirable and impossible. It would be better if she had an opportunity to observe the situation and make up her mind after this special observation. An appointment was made for a week hence.

The Second Interview with Z consisted mainly of a discussion of the problem presented by the mother, about which the girl became greatly concerned. She recognized that her mother was facing a nervous breakdown, ascribed it to her own involvement with the colored boy, was still defiant and insisted that she would go through with the marriage but was hesitant and deeply concerned about its effect on her mother. She saw no solution because the only thing that would set her mother up, she thought, would be to give up her plans of marriage, which she was unwilling to do.

Several times during this interview she asked whether she was not right in her attitude and whether she did not have a right to her own happiness and whether it was right for her parents to interfere. These questions were studiously avoided by me until she challenged me for an answer.

The reply was that she really did not want an answer to these questions because she knew the answers herself and in fact would most likely not accept anyone else's view on the matter, if it differed from hers. I offered to change places with her and have her answer these questions for me. But since the period was almost up we might leave this subject for our next discussion if she wished to come again. This she was eager to do and another appointment was made a week hence.

The Third Interview began with a discussion of the parents' attitude but quickly turned to the questions left unanswered at the last session, i.e., whether she did not have a right to her own happiness and whether her parents had a right to deny it to her by interfering with her intended marriage.

Again it was suggested that she answer the questions. At first she was very resistive, but when it became clear that I would not answer them until, at least, she had attempted to do so she finally yielded.

The first question she answered in the affirmative, i.e., that she had every right to her own happiness. Without challenging that right in any way, she was led to reexamine that right when it involved the unhappiness of others. This led to a discussion of her relation to her parents, theirs to her, the interrelation of their happiness as individuals and as a family group and whether she or they had a right to purchase their own happiness at the cost of the unhappiness of the others.

At the end of the hour she was by no means certain that she would or could be happy if she knew that she would thereby cause extreme unhappiness to her mother or father or both.

Again she was asked whether she wanted to continue to discuss the second question and when she declared her eagerness to continue, another appointment was made for her.

The Fourth Interview began by a review and some further discussion of her right to happiness without regard to its cost to her parents. She said that she had thought about it all week and was very much disturbed by the question and the trend of her own thinking. At several points she started to discuss it with her father and boy friend but could not get herself to do so for fear of being misunderstood or being influenced by either or both. She had as yet reached no conclusion and thought that a discussion of the second question might throw some light on the first.

Again she sought my answer and again I refused to give it. She finally saw that she might be better off if she thought the question through as she had the first.

It was not long before she recognized and freely admitted that never before had her parents interfered with anything she desired or wanted to do when she was able to convince them that she really wanted it; that whenever they resisted her it was because they feared that it was not to her best interests. An examination of a number of incidents made it clear that they were usually right and that where they yielded to her insistence she was usually proved wrong. There was never any "I told you so" and each situation was dealt with on its own merits regardless of how wrong she may have been in the previous one. This naturally made her question whether it was interference on their part or a desire to save her from making a serious mistake. Their greater and more persistent opposition she recognized as due to the seriousness of the step contemplated. This led to the question whether she or they are right and how this question might be answered.

At first she was quite certain that she knew her mind and was sure about her feelings. Her parents, she was convinced, had never been willing to be objective about the matter and always looked upon the dark side of the situation. They saw no possibility for a successful marriage in this for her and only saw the difficulties for her and the heartbreak for themselves. This made it impossible for her to give their objections the weight she otherwise would have attached to them.

Her mother was especially difficult about it. She would burst into tears the moment the situation was mentioned or when she thought about it by herself. She insisted that she would not survive the marriage, that she could not face her friends and that she did not want to be grandmother to colored children. She had forbidden her home to the young man, which only made matters worse because the daughter was forced to meet him outside the home and developed a strong sense of guilt about it.

While her father was somewhat more objective about the matter and did not throw the "temper tantrums" that her mother did, he too, was deeply involved and, she felt, took refuge behind the plea that she spare her mother. In fact this was the first calm and more or less objective discussion she has ever had about her problem and she was very grateful for the opportunity. She only wished that she could get some advice instead of doing all the talking.

When doubt was expressed as to whether she wanted advice or confirmation of her own attitude and intentions, she admitted somewhat shamefacedly that she guessed she had not been "too objective" herself and had perhaps "acted like a spoiled brat when crossed." But the problem still remained, what should she do? Was she right or wrong? How could she find out?

This led to a consideration of the problems and issues involved in intermarriage in general and this type of intermarriage in particular. Since the hour was almost up it was suggested that if she wanted to pursue the matter further she might read up on the subject before the next session and see whether her reading would throw some light on how she might proceed to find out. She asked for some references as to what to read, but it was suggested that she get a list of readings from her sociology professor or the librarian.

Although Z was a little rebellious at the delay she admitted that this was a good idea and promised to work on this lead. She skipped the next week, after calling up, on the ground that she would like to do more reading before discussing her next steps, and made an appointment for the following week.

The Fifth Interview opened with Z's statement that although she had not yet resolved her problem she was much clearer about it than she had ever been, and knew now that she must consider it not only from her own point of view and emotional involvement but from the standpoint of the others involved. She now realized that this type of intermarriage is much more serious in its implications and consequences, whether it proves a success or failure, than other marriages or intermarriages. She had not realized before that she would be practically limited to living in a colored area, that she would virtually have to give up her white friends and associates, or would have to be prepared to face a life in which she would always imagine herself being pitied or considered peculiar. She seemed particularly concerned about the effect of the marriage upon her boy friend and the color of the children born in this marriage. She was no less resentful of society for imposing restrictions and handicaps upon people simply because of the color of their skin, but she wondered whether the best way of fighting this discrimination was by flying in the face of society or whether she could accomplish more

by fighting discrimination without being charged with having an axe to grind.

These and other thoughts, she said, made her feel that she had gained more objectivity. She was particularly pleased with two aspects of her new attitude: First, she could discuss the matter with her parents, and especially her mother, without either of them 'flying off the handle,' so that she was able to reassure her mother that she would not act precipitously, as a result of which her mother has become a different person and something of their former relationship has been reestablished; Second, she has come to look upon her boy friend in a somewhat different light. Whereas formerly she saw him as the embodiment or personification of his unfairly persecuted race she now looks upon him as a person in his own right, and as her future husband, the man with whom she will spend the rest of her life.

But despite her new attitude she still did not know what to do, or rather, she corrected herself, what would be the wisest and best thing to do, everything and everybody considered. She expressed the wish that it were possible for her to look into the future and see what it holds in store for her.

When it was suggested to her that this might be possible, at least to a limited extent, she was startled and eagerly asked how this might be accomplished. She was reminded that her new attitude which has given her so much satisfaction is not due to anything that anybody had told her but rather the result of her own thinking. She readily saw that this, too, is something she might think through for herself and that whatever conclusions she arrived at would be more acceptable to her. She agreed to think about it and asked for another appointment.

The Sixth Interview was devoted to a consideration of a plan she had worked out which would enable her to see what life in a Negro environment, if she had to live in one, would be like. Briefly the plan called for her to go to New York, obtain quarters in Harlem and live there as she might have to live there, or in some other city under similar conditions, after marriage. After further discussion it was agreed that upon graduation, which was only a few weeks off, she would go to New York City, enter Columbia University for graduate study, secure living quarters in Harlem, preferably with a colored family, and endeavor to live as normal a life as the circumstances would permit. She had acquainted her friend with her plan without revealing her purpose in full. He tried to dissuade her but although she assured him that she would think the matter over, she admitted that she had the feeling that he was afraid that "she couldn't take it" and that this might be the end of their friendship. Hence he tried to keep her from going. His fears only served to strengthen her resolve to do this unless "our discussion should produce a better method of looking into the future."

I promised to facilitate her contacts with colored people in New York through several friends who were highly placed in the Negro community there. In addition her boy friend has some relatives there to whom he promised to write although he seemed rather reluctant to do so on the ground that they might misunderstand and think she was out slumming. I told her that I would write my friends frankly the nature of her interests and something of her background. At first she refused to give me permission to reveal her motive but gradually realized that I could not do otherwise if I were not to violate their friendship and confidence and that in the long run it would also be the best thing for her because she and they could act more naturally than would be possible otherwise.

I saw her only once more before she left. She seemed much better poised and much more certain of herself. She had handled the matter of getting her parents' consent in excellent fashion and had also obtained the active co-operation of her friend.

She wrote me several letters from New York. The first few were mainly descriptions of what she did, the people she saw, their mode of life, accounts of the cordiality with which my friends had received and treated her, her utilization of every opportunity to meet and get to know as many colored folks, on as intimate as possible a social level, as came within her orbit, and how much she was learning from these contacts. In every letter she expressed appreciation of what our sessions did for her.

Then came a letter in which she announced that she had practically made up her mind that the venture was too much for her and that she did not possess the pioneering spirit which such a marriage required. She said that she did not want to hide behind pious declarations that it was because she felt that she could do more to right the wrongs our society inflicted upon the colored people, as she probably would have done some months ago. She preferred to face the situation frankly and honestly by admitting that she just did not have the courage to go through with it. She asked whether she should write her friend of her decision or wait until she came back. She added that she did not intend to finish the year in Columbia but would finish the semester.

My reply neither approved nor disapproved her decision. My only query was whether she was certain of herself and what she wanted to do. It also suggested that the manner in which she should acquaint her friend with her decision must be her choice based on her own sense of right and wrong, her knowledge of the young man's character and personality, which we had not discussed very much, and what is best in this situation.

It only remains to be added that she decided to wait until she returned home and told her friend in person. He made it rather easy for her by saying that he expected this outcome, once she told him that she wanted to go to New York.

She has completed her graduate work here and maintains contacts with both white and colored folks, and sees her former boy friend occasionally. Her mother, too, has regained her emotional balance and has less violent objections to colored people visiting her home, although she is still not happy about it. The girl will soon complete her work for the doctorate and feels that she is much richer for the experience.

* * *

As already suggested in the introduction, some readers may feel that the foregoing presentation leaves a number of questions unanswered. What about the boy? Why was he not seen? Was the counselor prejudiced against the marriage *ab initio*? Else, why did he not try to see the mother or win her over to the marriage? In agreeing to the plan proposed by the girl, did the counselor throw the weight of his authority in the direction of a separation because it was fairly certain that the girl would most likely "not be able to take it"?

The psychoanalytically inclined will question whether the neurotic element in the girl's make-up, which prompted her to seek an alliance with a Negro and which was neither probed nor treated, will not break forth in some other form of neurotic or deviant behavior. Similar questions may be asked about the boy, etc.

Space does not permit an adequate discussion of these and other questions which might be raised. In the absence of a more detailed discussion it can only be stated that the counselor had and has no prejudice against interracial marriages; that his only requirement is that the social and psychological factors be such as to make possible a happy and successful marriage—a condition required in all premarital counseling. Had he been satisfied that "the girl could take it," something which seemed in doubt because of her tendency to dramatize herself and her situations, he would have seen the mother and the young man. As it was, the time had not come for it. Moreover, it did not seem that the young man was very deeply involved emotionally, but that he was more or less swept off his feet by the girl and the prospect of marrying a white girl of good family with all its implications. Needless to add, this was never mentioned to the girl in order not to prejudice her against the young man.

As for the neurotic trend in the girl which remained unexplored and untreated, this, of course, goes to the heart of the matter. To be sure, it is possible that such a trait exists in the girl. It is possible, also, that had it been inquired into, it would have been uncovered and would have required extensive analysis and therapy. However, a number of years have elapsed since her last visit and since this case was first reported. The girl has secured her doctorate, is teaching in a junior college, is married, and has combined a fairly successful teaching career and motherhood without any neurotic trait having manifested itself thus far. May it not be assumed, therefore, that it is not impossible that she may live to a ripe old age without any neurotic trait presenting itself? And may we not say also that in this case, at least, treating the situation on a conscious level was justified and was a service to the client?

NOTES

NOTE 1.

HILTNER, SEWARD
Discussion*

In his own discussion of this case, Dr. Karpf has anticipated most of the questions which can be raised; and we can surely not blame him for this evidence of elementary self-protection. . . .

Nevertheless, there seem to me to be three types of issues raised by his account: the nature of the difference between depth and therapy and marriage counseling, the place of "direction" in counseling, and the specific handling of this case. As to the first, Dr. Karpf seems to see the difference in two ways: on the one hand, the depth therapist deals with people who do not, on the whole, manage their affairs adequately; on the other hand, he deals at a deep or, presumably, "unconscious" level. But this represents a confusion which clouds the very issue. The fact is that any of us deals with the people who come to us because of what *they* think we repre-

---

* Reprinted from: Vincent, C. E.: *Readings in Marriage Counseling.* New York: Thomas Y. Crowell Co., 1957, pp. 246-247. Reprinted with permission of the publisher.

sent. Referral is as important as Dr. Karpf says; but if on the criterion of whether they can "handle their affairs quite adequately," . . . . And on the question of unconscious material, the question in any counseling is not whether we deal with it (we always do), but whether it will be forced, encouraged, permitted to emerge, or pushed back.

This leads to the second issue, the place of "direction." Directiveness is involved if dissociated material is forced, encouraged, or pushed back, i.e., something other than the person, within his frame of reference, is deciding what is discussible, i.e., what is permitted. This means that the question of direction, as found in Dr. Karpf's discussion, is finally a moral one. He is concerned lest the girl make a decision which will be, for practical purposes, irreversible; he wants her to maintain freedom until it is clear that that decision can be freely made and the consequences accepted. That is, he wants the moral growth in her necessary to accept the consequences of her decision. I do too, i.e., I favor this as the moral objective. But how can we promote the most basic kind of freedom, moral freedom, unless it is arrived at by the person on his own initiative although, to be sure, with our help?

These issues become clear in the case itself. It is not so much a question whether the girl is neurotic or not. But the counselor was not square with her. He asked her "opinion" when this was not really what he wanted at all. "She finally yielded" and answered his questions. He "diverted her attention." If he had told her in so many words at the beginning that he doubted her understanding of the consequences was therefore in this sense prejudiced, but he'd found a lot of people knew more about their own insides than was apparent, and therefore he wanted to help her if he could even though he was making his own position clear—he might very well have been expressing a confidence in her which would be the dynamic agent of therapy. I suspect that, beneath Dr. Karpf's description, he probably did communicate something of this kind. But in that case, the direction had nothing to do with the result, and the therapy was better than the description of its dynamics.

I would hope, in a case of this kind, to be more "eductive" than Dr. Karpf precisely because I would not want to have deep material emerge which I was unprepared to handle, and because I would want any dealings I have with a person to strengthen his moral automomy. There may indeed be life situations in which intervention is needed, although I doubt whether they should fall under the heading of either psychotherapy or marriage counseling. But as many have pointed out, what good does it do to solve an immediate problem if the moral and psychic autonomy of the person is weakened by the process through which the solution occurs?

NOTE 2.

LONDON, PERRY

The Morals of Psychotherapy*

It is obvious that, in most therapeutic situations, there are choice points at which the therapist must manifest some very real concern with the life the patient leads outside the therapy situation proper, and that some of that concern will be directed towards how the patient ought or ought not to act.

Considering the foregoing as a purely technical problem forces the theoretical and basic issue into bold relief: What does the therapist wish to accomplish? What are the goals of his therapy? What does he wish to see happen to this person? In what way does he, as therapist, want his ministrations to alter the clients' life?

Ultimately, I believe, this is a moral question which, posed to the therapist, is always answered by him in practice, and in terms of some superordinate, if unvoiced, moral code of his own. Sometimes the nature of the answer is masked in the impersonal scientistic language of mental health—but it is not hard to see, in the minister who counsels against premarital intercourse because of its "unfortunate psychological consequences"; in the Catholic caseworker who opposes his client's divorce because of its "mentally disrupting effect"; in the libertarian who helps his clients accept the "psychological legitimacy" of extra-marital affairs. These therapeutic goals represent personal morals rather than scientifically validated conclusions.

Perhaps the most general, and accurate, answer that sensitive and self-conscious therapists might offer to the question of their goals could be put so: "I want to help reshape this person's existence so that he will emulate values which I cherish for myself, aspire to what I wish humanity to be, fulfill my need for the best of all possible worlds and human conditions."

It is a truism that the therapist is himself a human being, that he does, in fact, live in society, and that wisely or unknowingly, responsibly or casually, he has made moral commitments to himself and that society. But the pre-

sent argument carries this platitude to its own logical conclusion—that the very nature of his interaction with the people he serves makes some kind of moral confrontation, or at least communication of his own moral commitments, an inescapable part of his therapeutic work.

* * *

. . . To any given incident revealed by his client, the psychotherapist must make some kind of response. He may carefully avoid making a very emphatic positive or negative response—he may manifest a studiedly neutral attitude, and he may sincerely and devoutly feel neither censure nor approval of the situation at hand. But to regard this neutrality as an amoral position, to salve his own democratic, egalitarian, or relativistic conscience, to convince himself that he "is not imposing his own value system upon his client"—by the simple fact that he does not want to impose it—is ultimately to deceive both the client and himself. For this belief implicitly denies the essence of the psychotherapeutic relationship, i.e. that its most critical points are those involving the *interactions* between participants, not the private experiences of either of them. In other words, psychotherapy is a social, interpersonal action, characterized by an *exchange* of individual, personal ideas and feelings. The verbal content of the exchange differs with the respective roles of client and therapist, but the relationship is, in its most vital respects, a reciprocal one.

The very fact of the exchange relationship dictates, I believe, the inevitability of the therapist's functioning practically as a moral agent for three reasons:

1) He influences the moral decisions of the client because the client necessarily *interprets* the therapist's response to his moral concerns. If the therapist approves his behavior, he may reinforce it. If the therapist disapproves, he may change it. If the therapist appears neutral, he may interpret this as either tacit approval or disapproval—and in many instances, it may be either one, complicated by the therapist's fears of upsetting the client or his reluctance to "dictate" ground rules of propriety. In any case, the very fact that the therapist permits any discussion of these issues largely legitimizes the attempt on the client's part to interpret the therapist's reaction to his remarks.

* * *

3) Therapists have personal value systems, and it is difficult to see how they could possibly form relationships with clients even for the sole pur-

---

* *Columbia University Forum*, Vol. 4, No. 38 (1961), pp. 41-43. Reprinted with the permission of the author. For a further development see *The Modes and Morals of Psychotherapy* by Perry London. New York: Holt, Rinehart & Winston, Inc., 1964.

pose of understanding them, never mind helping them, without being cognizant of their own values and making implicit comparisons between themselves and their values and those of their clients. The failure to respond in any way to those comparisons, by some process of suspension of his own beliefs, may eventually commit the therapist to suspending his very interaction—for it is hard to see how he can respond to his patient without cognizance of himself, and once cognizant of his own values, how he can completely withold communicating them and still continue to interact.

*   *   *

It becomes apparent, for one thing, that not all of the matters dealt with in therapy are mental health matters, even within the broadest meaning of that term. Some of these matters refer to religion, politics, and social and economic behavior of the broadest importance both to individuals and society. Psychotherapists cannot claim special knowledge or competence in the discussion of such issues, but neither are they apparently free on that basis to disengage themselves from their patients' concerns.

I do not believe that this is an entirely soluble dilemma, but certainly a first step towards its solution would require that the therapists become vividly aware of what their personal commitments are. . . .

NOTE 3.

MERTON, ROBERT K.
Intermarriage and the Social Structure: Fact and Theory*

Speaking literally, all marriage is intermarriage in the sense that the contractants derive from different social groups of one sort or another. This follows immediately from the universal incest taboo which forbids marriage at least between members of the same elementary family unit and derivatively restricts marriage to members of different family groups. Marriage contractants invariably come from different elementary family groups; often from different locality, occupational, political, nationality groups; and at times from different religious and linguistic groups, races and castes. Thus, if the term intermarriage is used to denote all marriage between persons of *any* different groups whatsoever, without any further specification of the groups involved, it becomes virtually synonymous with the term marriage and may well be eliminated. In other words, differences in group-affiliation of the con-

tractants may occur, but if these affiliations—for example, political, neighborhood, social clubs—are not defined as relevant to the selection of a spouse, then the case is one of marriage, not intermarriage. The fact is, however, that certain types of marriage are sufficiently distinctive with respect to the group-affiliations of the contractants as to mark them off as a special category. Intermarriage, then, will be defined as *marriage of persons deriving from those different in-groups and out-groups other than the family which are culturally conceived as relevant to the choice of a spouse*. Thus, a given marriage may be, within one frame of reference—for example, the caste—in-marriage, and within another frame of reference—for example, social class—intermarriage. The distinction is analytical.

*   *   *

In the case of intercaste mesalliances, . . . the problem is not solved by . . . makeshift "escapes" to another community, for here the problem of establishing new social relationships is encountered. This problem becomes almost insuperable in cases of racial-caste intermarriage where ineffaceable physical badges of affiliation with different castes bar the way to a reintegration of the conjugal pair with new social groups. Similarly, when status differences are correlated with marked cultural differences leading to high visibility of another kind, flight from the native community fails to solve the problem. Under these conditions, new relationships can no more satisfactorily be established than the old relationships could be maintained. In cases of intermarriage where both physical and cultural visibility are absent, the temporarily atomized pair may gear into a satisfactory set of new social relationships as a conventional family group. But all such adjustments by the deviant pair which, in the optimum case, may attain some measure of personal success are still at the expense of the social relationships which have been sloughed off by ostracism and mobility. Successful evasions indicate loopholes in the structure of community control, not modifications of the marriage structure. Hence, although a segmented, mobile society may reduce the animus directed toward certain types of cacogamy, it is functionally necessary to maintain such effective antagonism if the going arrangement of social relationships is not to be endangered.* Metaphorically, intercaste marriage

---

* *Psychiatry*, Vol. 4 (1941), pp. 361-370.

---

* This functional statement does *not* imply a value-judgment favoring or rejecting the current social arrangements. Only a perversion of functional analysis systematically results in rationalizations of the *status quo* in various areas of social life.

may be viewed as a catalyst which activates and intensifies group consciousness. It symbolizes the repudiation of standardized cultural values which have been defined as sacrosanct and inviolable. A cultural axiom is being challenged. Cultural orientations are, by virtue of this challenge, presumably no longer secure. The response is immediate and familiar. The violation is intensely condemned; the nonconformists are stigmatized; the cultural norms are reaffirmed. All this has little of design, of the predetermined plan. It resembles rather the automatic, the prompt trigger-like response ensured by socialization and rooted in sentiment. The pattern is an integrated arrangement of action, sentiment and reaction serving to order social relationships. It may suggest a premeditated structure but it is more nearly reminiscent of the ordered integration of reflexive behavior. The crisis arouses self-consciousness; in this instance, consciousness of self as a member of the in-group.

NOTE 4.

JOHNSON, NORA

A Marriage on the Rocks*

Instead of expending all this missionary zeal in saving marriages, we might do better to make it harder to get married in the first place. Most people get married in a state of emotional blindness. Thereafter the family concept is torn between glorification and degradation, and both parties to it suffer from the discrepancy between expectation and reality. We are so deluded by the mass communications glorifying love and marriage and parenthood that we believe solutions to our problems will be found in the institutions rather than in ourselves. It is a fearful age; we fear ourselves as much as anything else, and trying to build love on fear never works.

2.

REVOKING THE LICENSE—ON THE MEANING OF CONSENT

a. PHIPPS v. PHIPPS
216 S.C. 248, 57 S.E. 2d 417 (1950)

TAYLOR, JUSTICE.

Appellant in this action sought to have annulled and declared void, on the ground of duress, a marriage entered into with the respondent, Ethel Louise Phipps, on September 9, 1947.

The matter was referred to Honorable J. K. Dorman, Master for Horry County, for the pur-

_____
* The Atlantic Monthly, Vol. 210 (July, 1962), p. 49. Reprinted with permission of the author.

pose of having him take the testimony and report the same, together with his findings, both of law and fact. After taking the testimony, the Master made his Report, dated December 17, 1948, in which he recommended that the Complaint be dismissed.

* * *

Appellant and respondent first met each other in September, 1946. From that time they saw each other regularly about three times a week up until March or April when the visits were reduced to approximately once every two weeks. In November, 1946, they became engaged and planned to be married the first of the year.

In January of 1947, appellant induced the respondent to have improper relations with him, which resulted in her becoming pregnant and giving birth to a child on October 15, 1947.

When the respondent realized her condition, she informed the appellant, who stated that he would marry her and continued to promise that he would up until August 22nd, when he informed her that he was not going to do so.

The respondent's parents learned of her condition on September 7, 1947. That night the respondent and her parents rode into Conway and tried to find the appellant, but were unable to do so. The following morning, the respondent's father, Mr. George Spivey, and two of her brothers went to the home of the appellant's sister with whom he lived. Upon being informed of the situation, appellant attempted to run, but was restrained by Mr. Spivey, who held him by the belt. Upon being questioned about a prior statement to respondent that he had procured a marriage license, he denied having done so and it was then that appellant, according to his testimony, was placed in Mr. Spivey's car and they proceeded to the Courthouse, whereupon Mr. George Spivey went into the Courthouse and returned shortly, when the following transpired, according to appellant's testimony:

"Q. Goes in where? A. In the courthouse. He comes back out and he said: 'You are a little bit smarter than I thought you were.' He was speaking to me. Preston said: 'You know what we should do with him?' I said: 'What, shoot me?' He said: 'That's exactly right.' Mr. George said: 'This is too good for him. We should take him to the river and tie a rock around his neck and toss him in.' "

It certainly doesn't sound reasonable that appellant was actually in fear of being injured or he would never have suggested that he be shot. Further, the father of respondent, after returning to the car from the Probate Judge's office told appellant that he was correct in stating that he had not procured a marriage license and that he was going to have him arrested and went back into the courthouse. Appellant with respondent and three of her brothers were in the car and it was at this time that Mr. Preston Spivey, one of the brothers, proposed that the appellant and respondent get married, and he would pay the cost of a divorce if appellant stayed with respondent until the child was born.

As to this, appellant testified as follows:

> "Q. How did you finally agree to go to the Probate Court and get a license?   A. We agreed that if he would put it in writing, that if I would marry her, I wouldn't have to live with her and that as soon as the child was born, he would pay for the divorce, all doctor bills and hospital bills and support her. . . ."

Appellant and respondent then proceeded to the Probate Judge's office alone and applied for a marriage license. The testimony further shows that while they were parked at the courthouse all of the occupants left the car except appellant and respondent and that appellant then went to the drug store and procured soft drinks for himself and respondent and were sitting in the car. When the others returned, they then proceeded to appellant's home where he went into the house alone and got his clothes. There was a telephone there but he made no attempt to call for help but rejoined the party in the car and accompanied them to the respondent's home. Being questioned as to his intent at this time, appellant said:

> "Q. Isn't it a fact, that having made this agreement, you intended to stick up to it like a gentleman?   A. If they had done like they said they would do.
> "Q. You are willing to go ahead and carry out your part of the agreement if they had done what they said they would do?   A. That's right.
> "Q. That is, put it in writing?   A. That's right. . . ."

It appears from the testimony that when they all went back to the home of Mr. George Spivey, several of the men, if not all of them, left the house, and the plaintiff remained at the house and slept in a room by himself that night, with the windows open.

. . . These facts are cited for the purpose of showing that if the plaintiff had wished to run away, he had ample opportunity for doing so. . . .

It is therefore seen that appellant was willing to comply with the agreement provided that it be reduced to writing before the marriage. This is strong evidence that he was exercising his own will and not being coerced.

The next morning appellant accompanied respondent's father to the office of a Mr. Cartrette where the agreement was to be reduced to writing. Not finding Mr. Cartrette in, Mr. Spivey left the appellant there alone. Returning some time later and finding that Mr. Cartrette had not yet arrived at his office, they proceeded to the courthouse, Mr. George Spivey going in while appellant remained outside with others. Shortly thereafter, Mr. Spivey came out, accompanied by Mr. Lonnie D. Causey, a reputable member of the Conway Bar. Mr. Causey suggested that the thing for appellant to do would be to go ahead and get married and then in ten or twelve days come in and get "divorce papers." The original agreement was that the appellant, after the marriage, would return to the Spivey home and remain until the child was born, but, at the suggestion of Mr. Causey, the agreement was not put in writing as he informed them that such a contract would not be binding. Appellant and respondent then decided to have the marriage ceremony performed and each to go separate ways, whereupon they proceeded to the office of the Probate Court alone where the marriage ceremony was performed by the Probate Judge. Appellant then escorted the respondent back to the car and returned to his home, while she returned to the home of her father.

If duress, as is contemplated by the law, was at any time during the negotiations exercised by respondent or her family, it must clearly have dominated throughout the transaction to such an extent that appellant could not and did not act as a free agent. The violence or threats must have been of such a nature as to inspire a great fear of bodily harm. There is ample evidence to the contrary in the case at bar. . . .

The Master in his Report to the Circuit Court recommended that the complaint be dismissed. . . .

*   *   *

Judgment affirmed.

NOTES

NOTE 1.

PHIPPS v. PHIPPS
Eleven Years Later

I went over to Conway, and talked to the lady who was Mrs. Phipps, and learned the following from her and from others: The Phipps procured the divorce, and Mrs. Phipps married a [man] who was killed in an automobile accident. She, thereafter, married. . . . The little girl lives with her mother and step-father and she is doing nicely in the Conway graded school.

Mrs. [Phipps] has a new baby girl by her last husband, and she tells me that she, her husband and daughters are all well and happy.

I do not know what happened to Mr. Phipps. The father of Mrs. [Phipps] who induced the original marriage, so that the little child, to be, "could have a name," is still living out in the country, and with another of his married children. [Letter dated January 21, 1961 from R. D. Epps, counsel for Mrs. Phipps.]

NOTE 2.

MOSS v. MOSS
[1897] L.R.P.D. 263

SIR F. H. JENNE, PRESIDENT. . . .

. . . Ayliffe in his Parergon, p. 361, says: "Matrimony ought to be contracted with the utmost freedom and liberty of consent imaginable, without fear of any person whatsoever; for matrimony contracted through any menace or impression of fear is null and void ipso jure; . . . for marriages contracted against the will of either of the parties are usually attended with very bad and dismal consequences. . . . I have just now observ'd that the principal thing required to a legal marriage is the consent of the parties contracting, which is sufficient alone to establish such a marriage. And tho' there is nothing more contrary to consent than error, yet every error does not exclude consent. Wherefore I shall here consider what kind of error it is, according to the canon law, that hinders or impeaches a matrimonial consent and renders it null and void ab initio. Now there are four species of error, which are hereunto referr'd. The first is stiled error personae, as when I have thoughts of marrying Ursula; yet by my mistake of the person I have marry'd Isabella. For an error of this kind is not only an impediment to a marriage contract, but it even dissolves the contract itself, through a defect of consent in the person contracting. For deceit is oftentimes wont to intervene in this case; which ought not to be of any advantage to the person deceiving another. A second species is stiled an error of condition; as when I think to marry a free woman, and through a mistake I have contracted wedlock with a bondwoman and so vice versa; for by the canon law such an error is an impediment to a matrimonial contract. But as there is now no such thing among Christians as persons that are truly bondmen or bondwomen (this kind of bondage or servitude being now abolish'd among us by the advantage of the Christian religion) I shall not long insist on this head. But if a freed man marry'd a bondwoman, knowing her to be such, the Church did not dissolve such a marriage. And thus we read that the marriage

between Abraham and Agar the handmaid was a true and valid marriage. The third species is what we call error fortunate; and is when I think to marry a rich wife and in truth have contracted matrimony with a poor one. But this error does not, even by the canon law, dissolve a marriage contract made simply and without any condition subsisting. But 'tis otherwise by that law if I have contracted with a person to marry her upon condition that she is worth so many thousands pounds, and the condition is not made good. The last species is stiled an error of quality—viz., when a person is mistaken in respect of the other's quality, with whom he or she contracts. As when a man marries Berta, believing her to be a chaste virgin, or of a noble family and the like, and afterwards finds her to be a person deflower'd or of a mean parentage. But according to the common opinion of the doctors this does not render the marriage invalid; because matrimony celebrated under such kind of error, in point of consent, is deem'd to be simply voluntary as to the nature and substance of it, though in respect of the accidents 'tis not voluntary'. "

NOTE 3.

STONE v. STONE
159 Fla. 624, 32 So. 2d 278 (1947)

BUFORD, JUSTICE.

In a suit to annul a marriage it was alleged in effect that appellant's younger brother had an affair with appellee which resulted in appellee becoming pregnant with child. Both parties were of tender years, the girl being only fourteen and the boy about seventeen years of age. The families were friendly with each other and were of equally good standing. The alleged father of the unborn child had become involved in other trouble and was not available to take on the responsibility of marriage.

To prevent the child from being born out of wedlock, it was agreed between appellant and appellee, and the respective families, that the appellant and appellee would go through a civil marriage ceremony for that and no other purpose and that appellant and appellee would not consummate the marriage by cohabitation. This agreement was kept and performed. There was no cohabitation between the parties. There was no consummation of a legal marriage. . . .

* * *

In Anders v. Anders, 225 Mass. 438, 113 N.E. 203, L.R.A. 1916E 1273, the Court said:

"In the case at bar the libellee went through the marriage ceremony with an intention never to perform any one of the duties of a wife. She went through the ceremony solely to secure a right to bear the name of a married woman and in that way to hide the shame of having had an illegitimate child, intending to leave her husband at the church door and not see him again. That plan she carried into effect. It is settled that a contract for the sale of goods is induced by fraud and for that reason voidable where the purchaser had an intention when the contract was made not to perform his promise to pay for them. If any intention not to perform his promise renders a contract for purchase of property voidable, a fortiori the same result must follow in case of a contract to enter into 'the holy estate of matrimony.' "

Such pretended marriages as these, while they may be laudible when viewed from the standpoint of the participants, thinking of the interest of the innocent unborn child, are contrary to public policy and are without the sacred elements on which the estate of matrimony is founded. The courts should not hesitate to annul such marriages at the behest of either party on clear and unequivocal proof that the purported marriage was so entered into and that the marriage status was never consummated by any cohabitation. This rule would not apply in cases where the reputed father of the child marries the mother without any fraud or deceit being practiced on him.

For the reasons stated, the decree is reversed with direction that same be vacated and a decree of the annulment of the marriage be entered.

NOTE 4.

VERNON, DAVID H.

Annulment of Marriage: A Proposed Model Act*

Section 8. *Jest or Dare.*

A. A marriage is annullable in an action brought by either party if both parties entered the marriage as a jest or on a dare, or if one party entered the marriage as a jest or a dare and this fact was known, or should have been known, to the other party, provided the parties do not thereafter live together as husband and wife.

B. A marriage is annullable in an action brought by the party who entered the marriage with a serious contractual purpose if the other party entered the marriage as a jest or on a dare and this fact was not known, nor should it have been known, to the other party, provided the parties do not after the marriage live together as husband and wife.

C. An action to annul a marriage on the ground that it was entered into as a jest or on a

---

* 12 J. Pub. Law 143, 179-180 (1963).

dare must be brought within one year of the marriage.

Section 12. *Marriages of Minors to Which Parental Consent May Be Given.*

A. A marriage is annullable if, at the time of the marriage, the male party is eighteen, nineteen or twenty years old or the female party is sixteen or seventeen years old, unless consent to the marriage is given by a parent, guardian or person in charge of the underage party.

B. The consent contemplated by subsection A of this section shall be deemed given if the parent, guardian or person in charge of the underage party

(1) is present at the marriage and does not protest ; or
(2) signs a written consent to the marriage which is authenticated before a competent authority. Such written consent may be given either before or after the marriage.

NOTE 5.

Israeli Draft Family Code § 43 (1956)*

Consent of the Parties

No marriage shall be celebrated unless both parties have expressed their consent in person before the person solemnizing the marriage.

Comments

This provision seeks to ensure that the parties agree in person and of their free will to get married to each other. No marriage shall be solemnized without the consent of the parties nor by proxy. On the other hand, the Bill does not require the personal presence of both parties ; where the personal law of the parties permits consent in writing, the proposed Law does not derogate from such a rule. The consent of the parties is required as a formal condition only. . . .

NOTE 6.

UNITED NATIONS

Universal Declaration of Human Rights†

Article 16

2. Marriage shall be entered into only with the free and full consent of the intending spouses.

---

* Cambridge: Harvard Law School—Brandeis University Cooperative Research for Israel's Legal Development. Copyright 1956 by the President and Fellows of Harvard College.

† Adopted by the General Assembly, Dec. 10, 1948.

b.
MAHAN v. MAHAN
88 So. 2d 545 (Fla. 1956)

THORNAL, JUSTICE.

Appellant Mary Agnes Mahan, who was plaintiff below, seeks reversal of a decree of the Chancellor denying the annulment of her marriage to appellee James J. Mahan, who was defendant below.

The sole question before us is whether the evidence was sufficient to sustain the allegations of the complaint.

The complaint sought annulment of the marriage on the ground that at the time of the alleged ceremony the appellant was so intoxicated by the use of "alcoholic stimulants" that she was not in possession of her mental faculties and was incapable of forming conscious consent to the alleged marriage. The defendant answered that he could neither admit nor deny the allegations of the complaint because at the time of the alleged marriage, he was so intoxicated that he could not even state whether he was ever married to the plaintiff. The parties stipulated for the appointment of a Special Master to hear the testimony and report his findings.

There was no conflict in the testimony and if it is to be believed, it would appear that the allegations of the complaint were proved.

The record shows that on July 2, 1955, after an afternoon and evening devoted to drinking a combination of such stimulants as beer, whiskey and gin at an establishment bearing the foreboding name of "The Caribbean," the parties, accompanied by another man, in some fashion wound up in Folkston, Georgia, late in the evening. At this point they were united in wedlock by an Ordinary of the State of Georgia. Folkston, Georgia, incidentally, appears to be the "Gretna Green" of Florida couples who are either not inclined to comply with the requirements of our laws stipulating various conditions precedent to matrimony, or for other reasons find themselves incapable of completing the marriage contract in our state. Experience has suggested that, although there are of course fortunate and happy exceptions, many of these "Folkston-Green" marriages terminate as did this one. Be this as it may, the record shows that the plaintiff was not conscious of the fact that she was married until she came to her senses at the home of her mother the afternoon of July 3, 1955.

. . . Her knowledge of her marriage was conveyed to her by her mother who received the information from the attending witness. There is testimony also that the marriage did not culminate in cohabitation of the parties and that they had never lived together as husband and wife.

[T]he Master found that the allegations of the complaint had been sustained by the evidence and recommended annulment. At final hearing, the Chancellor declined to approve the recommendations of the Master and dismissed the complaint with prejudice to the plaintiff, who now seeks reversal of that decree.

* * *

One condition precedent to a valid and binding marriage contract is that the parties be mentally competent to enter into the contractual engagement. A party lacking the essential requirement of mental capacity may in a proper case obtain the annulment of the contract absent ratification or confirmation during a lucid interval, or upon regaining mental competency. . . .

* * *

This court approved this general rule in the early case of Prine v. Prine . . . 18 So. 781, 785. . . . Although in the Prine case it was held that cohabitation subsequent to the recovery of reason precluded annulment, nonetheless, the rule as to the effect of intoxication on the validity of the marriage contract was stated as follows:

> "* * * As to the law applicable to the facts, it cannot be doubted that if the party, at the time of entering into the contract, is so much intoxicated as to be non compos mentis, and does not know what he is doing, *and is for the time deprived of reason,* the marriage is invalid; but it is not invalid if the intoxication is of a less degree than that stated." (Emphasis added.)

* * *

. . . However, reluctant as we always are to disturb the conclusions of a Chancellor on the sufficiency of the evidence, we cannot in this case escape a decision that the uncontradicted evidence established the allegations to the effect that at the time this marriage was performed the appellant and, for that matter apparently, the appellee were so thoroughly and completely dethroned of their mental faculties by the use of alcohol that they were not conscious of what they were doing and that they were mentally incapable of forming the intent to enter into the contract which was essential to its validity.

The marriage contract is one of the most sacred of compacts. It should not be set aside or dissolved in the absence of clear and substantial proof that annulment or dissolution is justified under the law.

* * *

Finding as we do, and finding further that there is no evidence of ratification or confirmation of the marriage, it is our view that the prayer of the complaint for annulment should have been granted. . . .

NOTES

NOTE 1.

FREUD, SIGMUND
Group Psychology and the Analysis of the Ego (1921)*

In connection with this question of being in love we have always been struck by the phenomenon of sexual overvaluation—the fact that the loved object enjoys a certain amount of freedom from criticism, and that all its characteristics are valued more highly than those of people who are not loved. . . . If the sensual impulses are more or less effectively repressed or set aside, the illusion is produced that the object has come to be sensually loved on account of its spiritual merits, whereas on the contrary these merits may really only have been lent to it by its sensual charm.

The tendency which falsifies judgment in this respect is that of *idealization*. But now it is easier for us to find our bearings. We see that the object is being treated in the same way as our own ego, so that when we are in love a considerable amount of narcissistic libido overflows on to the object. It is even obvious, in many forms of love-choice, that the object serves as a substitute for some unattained ego ideal of our own. We love it on account of the perfections which we have striven to reach for our own ego, and which we should now like to procure in this roundabout way as a means of satisfying our narcissism.

If the sexual overvaluation and the being in love increase even further, then the interpretation of the picture becomes still more unmistakable. The impulses whose trend is towards directly sexual satisfaction may now be pushed into the background entirely, as regularly happens, for instance, with a young man's sentimental passion ; the ego becomes more and more unassuming and modest, and the object more and more sublime and precious, until at last it gcts possession of the entire self-love of the ego, whose self-sacrifice thus follows as a natural consequence. The object has, so to speak, consumed the ego. Traits of humility, of the limitation of narcissism, and of self-injury occur in every case of being in love ; in the extreme case they are merely intensified, and as a result of the withdrawal of the sensual claims they remain in solitary supremacy.

---

* Reprinted from: 18 *The Standard Edition of the Complete Psychological Works of Sigmund Freud.* London: The Hogarth Press 1955, pp. 112-113). Reprinted with permission of The Hogarth Press and Liveright, Publishers, New York.

NOTE 2.

FREUD, SIGMUND
Civilization and its Discontents (1930)*

. . . Normally, there is nothing of which we are more certain than the feeling of our self, of our own ego. This ego appears to us as something autonomous and unitary, marked off distinctly from everything else. That such an appearance is deceptive, and that on the contrary the ego is continued inwards, without any sharp delimitation, into an unconscious mental entity which we designate as the id and for which it serves as a kind of façade—this was a discovery first made by psycho-analytic research, which should still have much more to tell us about the relation of the ego to the id. But towards the outside, at any rate, the ego seems to maintain clear and sharp lines of demarcation. There is only one state— —admittedly an unusual state, but not one that can be stigmatized as pathological—in which it does not do this. At the height of being in love the boundary between ego and object threatens to melt away. Against all the evidences of his senses, a man who is in love declares that 'I' and 'you' are one, and is prepared to behave as if it were a fact. What can be temporarily done away with by a physiological [i.e. normal] function must also, of course, be liable to be disturbed by pathological processes. Pathology has made us acquainted with a great number of states in which the boundary lines between the ego and the external world become uncertain or in which they are actually drawn incorrectly. There are cases in which parts of a person's own body, even portions of his own mental life—his perceptions, thoughts and feeling—, appear alien to him and as not belonging to his ego ; there are other cases in which he ascribes to the external world things that clearly originate in his own ego and that ought to be acknowledged by it. [For example, in psychosis]. . . .

NOTE 3.

KUBIE, LAWRENCE S.
Psychoanalysis and Marriage†

. . . It will be my basic thesis that a major source of unhappiness between husband and

---

* Reprinted from: 21 *The Standard Edition of the Complete Psychological Works of Sigmund Freud.* London: The Hogarth Press, 1961 (pp. 65-66). Reprinted with permission of The Hogarth Press and W. W. Norton & Company, Inc. Copyright © 1961 by James Strachey. First American Edition 1962.

† Reprinted from Eisenstein, V. W., ed.: *Neurotic Interaction in Marriage.* New York: Basic Books Inc., 1956, pp. 10-43. Reprinted with permission of the publisher.

wife is to be found in the discrepancies between their conscious and unconscious demands on each other and on the marriage, as these are expressed first in the choosing of a mate and then in the subsequent evolution of their relationship.

The only way to clarify this thesis is through example. Men and women are infinitely ingenious in their ability to find new ways of being unhappy together; so that even with unlimited space it would be impossible to illustrate every variety of marital misery. Therefore, I will restrict myself almost entirely to one aspect of the problem: namely, the unconscious forces that make it difficult for people to know what they are seeking in marriage, and how this confusion influences both the initial choice of a mate and the fate of the marriage.

A young woman had been left fatherless at an early age. Over a number of years it was evident to all of her friends, but not to herself, that she was driven by an obvious need to find in marriage a substitute father and an ally against her mother. She ran through a series of engagements with older men, and finally married one who was within a year or so of her father's age only to discover that a substitute is never more than a substitute, and that in spite of the age discrepancy he wanted to be mothered as much as she wanted fathering. Since each felt cheated, they ended in a snarl of bitter recriminations.

* * *

Two youngsters had grown up insecure and lonely, seclusive and bookish in their tastes, in various ways apart from the general run of adolescents. They drew together through mutual sympathy and the compatibility of their intellectual and artistic interests, through their understanding of each other's needs and problems, and in some measure just because misery loves company. During their courtship the sense of loneliness was gone. Each had an ally. Almost for the first time each had some place to go, and someone with whom to share life. Each was literally all the world to the other.

Unfortunately, when they married they discovered that when they faced the world together something quite unexpected happened. They could no longer be the whole world to each other. Instead, they had to reach out to the world to bring it into their joined lives. Yet each was still frightened of this outside world. In a sense each pushed the other, saying "You go first." But neither could. So they became angry at each other. The separate and private misery that each had brought into the marriage and that originally had drawn them together was now compounded in a marriage that had been contracted in an unrealistic expectation that it would lessen that misery. Instead, in marriage the unresolved neurosis of one was added to the neurosis of the other. That social shyness which had united them became something hampering, which one resented in the other, and which ultimately drove them apart.

They were learning bitterly and painfully a lesson that humanity as a whole has never learned —that no one has ever married himself out of a neurosis. Instead, when two young people are drawn into marriage by the lure of the other's illness, one will add the weight of his own neurotic infirmity to that of the other, with growing pain and resentment.

* * *

Many marriages illustrate the fatal discrepancy between conscious, attainable needs and unconscious, unattainable goals as a major source of marital discord. A widely prevalent example of this is seen among the many men and women who marry with the major unconscious purpose of finding a parent. This may take varied forms. Unconsciously, the woman may be marrying not her fiance but his father or mother; the man may be marrying his fiancee's mother or older sister or aunt, or, for that matter, her father.

During the courtship, while the marriage is still in the offing any vague feelings of discontent or incompleteness will be balanced by the reassuring hope that fulfillment merely waits on the next step—the marriage itself, or a new home, or the advent of a child or of ten children, or more money, and so on. After marriage, however, the time comes when all such milestones will have been reached without dispelling the feelings of emptiness and unfulfillment. If we keep in mind the unconscious and unattainable goal of the marriage, then this discontent is almost mathematically predictable. It has nothing to do with the potential compatibility of the couple's interests and standards.

* * *

Thus the difficulties of maintaining a happy relationship may start the moment the period of courtship is over—indeed, the moment uncertain pursuit has turned into victory. Two people who have been completely happy during a thoughtful and serious courtship can become equally unhappy once this relationship is established in marriage.

I hope I have made it clear that the choosing of a mate is one of the most confused steps a human being takes in life, and this not primarily because he chooses a mate whose interests and habits are incompatible with his own, but because each of the pair is ignorant of the unconscious purposes that determine their respective choices. This is why hasty and impulsive unions may stand up as well as those which have been made with the greatest possible conscious foresight. Both miscarry whenever unconscious goals exercise a preponderant influence which has been left out of account and which is at variance with conscious and perconscious goals.

NOTE 4.

TAUBER, EDWARD S., and GREEN, MAURICE R.

Prelogical Experience*

Psychically, man is constantly registering a huge manifold of percepts which never enter awareness as conscious knowledge, as demonstrated by recent investigations into the perceptual activity of the mind at sub-threshold levels of awareness. The results of these investigations also strongly suggest that below the levels of awareness, the prelogical processes go on night and day. The prelogical processes build out of the innumerable subthreshold percepts the foundations of one's everyday thinking, relating man to the world about him in many subtle and elusive ways that are not given concious, logical formulation.

It is also a peculiarly human phenomenon that a person presents much more information about himself than he is capable of recognizing. At any moment in time each of us reveals to the outside world a huge manifold of cues out of which only a small number are experienced within awareness. Man realizes very little of what is taking place within him. He senses unformed feelings, gropings for words, efforts to put things into rational forms. But he is largely unmindful of the preliminary nonrational states ushering in his later ordered mentation.

* * *

In everyday life the prelogical processes are operative in all inter-personal relationships and form the vast backdrop to every variety of human enterprise and contact. In effect, the most important thing that goes on within man and between man and man is involved with these covert referential processes. A great deal of what we do among one another consists in apprehending nonpropositional emotional responses and reacting to them. Most interpersonal interaction, in fact, goes on in the prelogical mode. We are constantly negating prelogical processes and converting them unwittingly into logical syntactical

---

* New York: Basic Books, Inc., 1959, pp. 1-4. Reprinted with permission of the publisher.

propositions, with a consequent falsification of security and communication.

One must infer that nonverbal subthreshold "arrangement" is frequently the determining factor in highly significant decisions such as marriage, friendships, and sexual collaboration where unusual or sophisticated nuances are called for. In the negative sense, aversions to collaborations with others achieve their destination in like fashion.

. . . In marriage we see, at least in those married people who visit the psychiatrist, the type of mating which exquisitely defines the neurotic needs of the partners. This capacity to pick out the partner is rooted in subthreshold perception and has little to do with the official explanation of the choice made. . . .

c.   GOLDMAN v. GOLDMAN
169 Cal. App. 2d 103, 336 P. 2d 952 (1959)

FRED B. WOOD, JUSTICE.

Defendant appeals from a judgment annulling the marriage of the parties upon the ground that defendant was of unsound mind at the time of the marriage.

(1) *Was the finding insufficient because it declared that defendant "was of unsound mind" at the time of the marriage and "incapable of legally consenting to" the marriage? No.*

Defendant claims this finding was insufficient because it failed to specify the particular type of unsound mind here required, the lack of sufficient mental capacity to understand the nature of the marriage contract and its duties and responsibilities.

It is not necessary to specify with such particularity either in a pleading or in a finding on this issue. The statute is not that specific. It uses merely the words "that either party was of unsound mind." Civil Code, § 8. . . .

(2) *Does the evidence support the finding of unsoundness of mind and lack of capacity to consent to the marriage? No.*

The marriage was solemnized on the 18th of June, 1943. Defendant was committed to Agnew State Hospital in March of 1950 and has remained there ever since except for a period of two months when she was paroled to one of her sisters. Plaintiff filed this action on July 16, 1956.

Three witnesses gave evidence tending to support the questioned finding. A summary of their testimony follows.

Plaintiff testified that about four months before the marriage he had discussions with defendant about the purchase of a home. He asked her aid in making a selection but her attitude was one of great indifference. She gave him no suggestions as to what she wanted. She had no ideas for him to carry out. When looking at possible homes she did not indicate what she liked or did not like. The same occurred in selecting furniture and furnishings for the home. She would just shrug her shoulders and say, "well I don't care." She exhibited an attitude of total indifference. Upon their wedding day they agreed to meet at a bus station at a certain hour and take the bus to the place where the marriage was to be solemnized. She did not show up until about an hour after the time appointed. She gave no explanation why she was late.

At first they occupied the same bed. After three or four months she would prevent his sleeping by vibrating the bed, jumping up and down on it while he was trying to sleep. He would remonstrate and get no response. After a while it got so bad he had to use another bed. She suggested that he take the bed in their spare room, which he did.

For a period of about six months after the marriage he and she went shopping together on a Saturday and she prepared the meals. At the end of this period she refused to go shopping and to do any more cooking, and he had to do the shopping and prepare her meals as well as his own. The only reason or explanation she gave for not shopping or cooking was the remark "Why should I?" About four to six to eight months after the marriage she remarked that she was very unhappy in the home and wanted to move. Asked why, she said "I consider this place a prison ; I feel like I am confined. I cannot stand it."

On several occasions she would take a paper of matches, light them and throw them on the rug and say to him she was going to burn the house down. He would then go over and step on them and she would go to her room and lock the door. She would lock herself in quite frequently.

Plaintiff's official duties required him to work until a late hour upon occasion. Upon several such occasions in 1943 when he arrived at home the doors were locked. Though he had a key he was unable to get in because the inside latch was turned. He would ring the bell and knock on the door, and nothing would happen. The latch on one of the doors was a chain latch which he found he could open by cutting the chain with a hacksaw. On at least two occasions defendant was awake and, when asked what the problem was, laughed and said nothing. Not long after the marriage defendant falsely accused plaintiff of infidelity, of double-crossing her in everything she did and claimed that on the nights he was out at work he was not at work at all and probably was either in some political

deal of some kind or out with somebody he should not be with. About two years after their marriage she denied he was married to her.

* * *

It was about one and a half or two years after the marriage when he began to suspect that defendant was mentally ill. Earlier than that he realized that there was something wrong but could not diagnose it himself. He had not had any experience with persons who were mentally ill, nor any opportunity to observe mental illness.

Defendant finally consulted a psychiatrist and was given shock treatments toward the end of 1949. After a period at a private institution she was committed to Agnew State Hospital in March of 1950.

The psychiatrist who examined defendant in the fall of 1949 and prescribed electric shock treatments testified that his initial diagnosis was a depression. After the shock treatments his diagnosis was schizo-affective psychosis, which he described as "a combination of dementia praecox and a psychosis combination," adding that to the layman it signifies insanity. It is not a disease of sudden onset, "the very meaning of the term 'schizo' means gradual onset." He further testified that on the basis of information given him by the plaintiff in 1949 and information some one gave to a physician at the hospital when she was admitted for shock treatments, she was showing inappropriate and withdrawn disinterested behavior developing over a period of many years. Upon the basis of this and other information thus furnished, the witness said it would be consistent to say that the ailment "started back some several or many years before I saw her in 1949." This was a long standing condition at the time he saw her. Asked if in his opinion the defendant was of unsound mind on June 18, 1943, the witness said it was his opinion that "she was not mentally healthy at that time, that this ailment for which I treated her had started at the time of or at the terminaion of her first marriage, which I presume would go back before 1940 * * * ." From information made available to the witness, he expressed the opinion that defendant was already becoming somewhat withdrawn and disinterested in her surroundings at the time of the marriage, i.e., at that time her present illness had already begun. She was beginning to be disinterested in her surroundings, withdrawn, less active, "and that isn't a healthy state of mind." The witness did not know whether this unhealthy mental condition had at that time developed to such a degree as to render her incapable of understanding what she was doing.

As late as 1949 when he saw her she was not totally out of contact with things. She still had a certain amount of understanding. She knew the day. She recognized the witness when he saw her at the hospital. She knew she was in the hospital. She wanted to go home. She was oriented as to time and place.

Defendant's daughter, who was born in 1929, testified that she shared a room with her mother prior to the latter's marriage to plaintiff. Beginning in about 1935 or 1936 her mother would laugh and mumble to herself in the dark and would have sudden alterations in mood. The witness could remember being awakened at night and her mother would be laughing and kind of mumbling, talking to herself. Her mother seemed rather withdrawn a lot of the time and then would suddenly become very cheerful and make some very cheerful remarks. By "withdrawn" the witness meant "sort of day-dreaming and far away."

* * *

From this evidence the trial court concluded that at the time of the marriage defendant lacked mental capacity to understand the nature of the marriage contract, its duties and responsibilities. The question before us is whether or not this was enough evidence, substantial evidence, to justify that conclusion. Any of it that may be subject to differing inferences must be read in the light most favorable to the plaintiff, the prevailing party below. In such an inquiry we are not to consider evidence unfavorable to the trial court's finding. Such evidence merely created a conflict which the trier of the facts resolved in favor of the plaintiff.

In ascertaining whether or not the favorable evidence furnished substantial support for the finding of incapacity, we must bear in mind that the day of the marriage is the critical date for determination of lack of capacity. It may, of course, be determined from proof of the party's condition before and after that date. . . .

We must also bear in mind that the "presumption is always that a person is sane * * * Insanity exists as a matter of law only from the time it is shown to exist and proof of subsequent insanity will not create nor carry a presumption of its past existence * * * " In re Estate of Perkins, 195 Cal. 699, 703, 235 P. 45, 46.

The psychiatrist's diagnosis in late 1949, the determination made at the time of defendant's commitment to the state hospital in March, 1950, and her continuation at the hospital constitute substantial evidence in support of an inference that the defendant lacked the requisite mental capacity as early as the latter part of 1949. But

that does not take us back to the date of the marriage, June 18, 1943.

NOTES
NOTE 1.

GOLDMAN v. GOLDMAN
Two Years Later

The plaintiff had a new trial and an annulment was denied on all grounds set forth in the opinion of the Appellate Court and also on the ground of laches in commencing the action 13 years after the marriage.

After the annulment was denied on the retrial, an action was commenced for a divorce under the provisions of section 92, subd. 7, of the California Civil Code. While such action was pending Mrs. Goldman died of a heart attack, which was some time in December of this year just past.

* * *

Of course in each trial of the case on annulment a guardian ad litem was appointed to handle the defense for Mrs. Goldman, and also a guardian ad litem was appointed in the divorce case, and under California law the husband, Mr. Goldman, would be entitled to a divorce, subject to the obligation to continue to support Mrs. Goldman so long as she lived, which obligation ceased on her decease. [Letter dated Jan. 21, 1961 from Marvin C. Hix, attorney for Mr. Goldman.]

NOTE 2.

HIGGINS, JOHN W.

Schizophrenia as a Consideration in Annulment of Marriage*

In general preface, the existence should be recognized of many unsettled issues about Schizophrenia. . . . For example, there are some who say that the etiology of Schizophrenia is understandable on experiential, developmental, psychological grounds, and those who say that it is an illness which springs essentially from some kind of physiochemical imbalance. . . .

* * *

[T]here is disagreement about the validity of the clinical concept since there are some who say that "Schizophrenia" as a clinical entity does not exist, on the grounds that included under this rubric is too much that is changing and indefinite. . . . However proper the contention against the clinical concept may turn out to be, there is actually a working consensus that the term "schizophrenic reactions" . . . is a clinically useful and reasonably reliable concept.

* *Bulletin of the Guild of Catholic Psychiatrists*, Vol. 7 (1960), pp. 87-95. Reprinted with permission of the publisher.

From the clinical viewpoint, the schizophrenia reactions are psychoses "characterized by fundamental disturbances in reality relationships and concept formations, with affective, behavioral, and intellectual disturbances in varying degrees with mixtures"— and "marked by a strong tendency to retreat from reality, by emotional disharmony, unpredictable disturbances in stream of thought, regressive behavior, and in some, by a tendency to 'deterioration'. . . ." [If] we take a sample group of patients from various parts of a mental hospital, from the psychiatric wards of a general hospital, and from psychiatrists' offices, all of which patients have been properly diagnosed as "schizophrenic" we will have a most heterogeneous seeming group. At one extreme, there will be individuals showing dramatically bizarre behavior in action and dress and—if they are verbally communicative at all—speaking either completely incoherently, or voicing strange delusions and hallucinatory experiences; at the other extreme may be found individuals who to the ordinary observer seem no different in any respect from any other human being, and who indeed may for the most part be active, contributing members of society. Between the two extremes, and depending on the size of our sample, will be all sorts of gradations of severity and variety of symptoms. We still lack a wholly satisfactory description of the pathognomonic phenomenon common to these widespread manifestations. In the opinion of most, the disturbances in the organization of thought, and the ability to relate to others tend toward the nuclear. With the stipulation that this by no means covers the matter, the thought disorder can be considered as one in which the usual fairly orderly distinctions between present experience and past experience, the real and the fantasied, and between inner perception and outer perception begin to break down. The reaction to this disintegration will be reflected in the type and severity of the more outward manifestations. Of considerable importance to us is the question of the implication of this kind of disorder for a free, human act, or for the ability to "consent". In some states of severe affliction, as far as we can tell, the individual seems wholly incapable of *any* human act. In decreasingly severe states, some actions according to deliberation of will seem probable. But *always* there will be some actions wholly open to serious contamination by the pathological thought processes. At a given time, this may or may not specifically affect, for example, the consent to the marital vow. The disturbance in the ability to relate to others connotes roughly a deficiency in the ability to invest real and meaningful interest in

another as a separate person. An explication of this would involve considerations of the theories of "self" and of "identity". For our purposes, we should mainly be aware that the intimacy of the married state and perhaps especially the intimacy of the sexual act can be critically threatening to a schizophrenic, although by no means is this universally true.

I will evade any discussion of whether or not it is appropriate to include all the motley manifestations under one heading: the fact we have to face is that current systems and methods of diagnosis provide us with this scope and I believe it has implications for us. . . . [T]wenty-five to 40 years ago, our task would in some ways be simpler. In such circumstances, it is highly likely that the only "schizophrenia" we would be talking about would be a more or less stereotyped complex of hallucinations, delusions, and "deterioration" of thinking and behavior. But in the intervening years, clinical experience, refinements of theory, and especially the rapid growth of interest in active treatment of all sorts has fostered a sharpening of diagnostic acumen so that as therapists we no longer await the appearance of a gross picture to make our diagnosis. I do not mean for a moment to lose sight of the picture of a full-blown and chronic schizophrenia. We should keep this clearly in mind for two reasons: One is that visualizing it helps to convey the severity of the illness in its worse form. Few experiences are more disheartening and even shocking than the sight of an inaccessible, regressed, almost inhuman hebephrenic schizophrenic barely existing in what is often euphemistically called the "continued treatment service" of a mental hospital. The second reason for keeping this picture in mind is to be aware of the contrast with someone at the other end of the scale. Here may be a patient to whom has been applied the diagnosis only after a considerable number of interviews, and furthermore where the diagnostic balance may have been tipped only because of subtle findings in a battery of psychological tests. Toward this end, will be the patients called "ambulatory" or "latent" or "borderline" schizophrenics. Two points are worth emphasizing about this group. The first point is that despite the difficulty some observers may have in uncovering the diagnostic criteria, the diagnosis can be quite valid. The second point is, in effect, a corollary of the first: because the criteria in question will often be subtle, we must recognize that diagnostic error is possible to a degree it is not with more blatant cases; the error can be either in the direction of missing the diagnosis or making it incorrectly. Certainly the scope of possible clinical pictures and the difficulties in the diagnosis of "mild" or "early" cases should be kept in mind when a marital partner is dubbed "schizophrenic" and annulment proposed.

Since the problem in question is illness, some kind of consideration has to be given to the outlook with and without treatment. First, it is to be granted that prognosis in any behavioral disorder in the present state of our knowledge is exceedingly difficult since the course is open to influence by various factors, including, but not restricted to therapeutic intervention. In regard to any given individual case, projecting a "natural course" of the illness is hazardous. However, this can be done if it is remembered that the projection is hypothetical; at least one has the right to think of early (mild, unformed), middle, and late stages. Also there may be cycles of remission and exacerbation.

Evaluation of the stage is an exercise in professional judgment, but it seems relevant to specify the set of factors whose interaction influences the prediction of outcome. These may be conceived of in various ways, but they will include: the status of the illness, the total personality of the individual, the environment whence he comes and in which he must live, and the availability of treatment. Of these let me mention first "the environment" because in some ways it is superordinate to the others, or at least impinges on them. It has been commonplace to recognize that the individuals surrounding a patient, with their demands, standards, and ability to provide satisfactions are important. But the parameter of the patient's social status has until recently not received explicit attention. In order to discuss this, I draw upon the work of Hollingshead and Redlich in New Haven. Recall that the schizophrenic reactions may include disorders of varying degree; also, it should be noted that the making of the diagnosis already represents medical intervention. Actually the making of the psychiatric diagnosis is the last of nearly the last of four steps in the path to the psychiatrist, which are: the occurrence of behavior judged to be "abnormal" by the society members immediately around the patient; the judgment of the "abnormality" as "mental illness"; the decision to seek psychiatric treatment; and, only last, the carrying out of the decision. Hollingshead and Redlich demonstrated that as one descends the social scale this path significantly lengthens. This means that those in the lower social echelons will usually be "sicker" by the time they reach a medical treatment facility. Likely related to this, but a highly probable thesis which stands by itself, is that there is a higher absolute incidence of severe mental disorder (including schizophrenia) toward the lower end of the social scale. . . .

Once psychiatric treatment becomes a possibility, the response of interest in the psychiatrist will be affected, even unwittingly, by other subsidiary factors within the patient; e.g. his personal attractiveness, wit, charm, intelligence, level of accomplishment, and so on. Incidentally, these, too, although by no means completely reliant on social status are not unconnected with it.

The last of the specific factors influencing prognosis will be the availability of treatment and the nature of it. In medicine, we often like to think of treatment as being based on etiologic grounds, after the model of the treatment of infectious diseases. Many would hold that this model is rarely if ever appropriate, on realistic or humanistic grounds, to *any* significant illness, much less mental illness. It seems likely that the full treatment of a schizophrenic patient will always be a complex matter, even if ultimately some pathophysiological phenomenon is incriminated. . . .[I]t would be terribly erroneous to foster any illusion that there is *a* "treatment" applicable in *all* instances, to *all* patients, and by *all* physicians. As I have indicated, the treatment plan must be derived from apprising at least the four factors I have listed. The one I am addressing here is the availability of treatment and its quality. In regard to the former, we must acknowledge that for geographic and personal financial reasons, good in-patient and out-patient treatment are simply not available to many. In the absence of treatment facilities even a "mild" or "early" case may have a dim future. When we attempt to grapple with the question of the quality of treatment, we encounter a still more elusive issue. Even if we sidestep therapeutic allegiances and think of only vigorous, imaginative, emphatic treatment as "good quality" treatment, this can be scarce, indeed. To recast a previous point the more severe a case, the less available will be "quality" treatment. Depending on the severity and the environment, hospitalization may or may not be necessary.

In regard to outlook and treatability, I must particularly single out the group of patients who are regarded as in need of chronic hospitalization. How to define "chronic" may be a question we would like to try to settle in further discussions. It may be two years, or it may be five, but in most institutions, some kind of time span of hospitalization will be in the minds of the staff, which if exceeded, denotes a darker, if not virtually hopeless, outlook. Partly this is a reflection of the severity of the problem, partly it is an indication of the lack of response to whatever treatment is realistically available, and partly it is a recognition of the adverse influence of the hospital experience itself. Although we are in the midst of a wave of interest in the last factor (e.g. the "open door" policies, the more flexible administrative planning, etc.) we still must accept the fact that the likelihood of ultimate remission or recovery is seriously diminished as the time passes beyond a certain critical date.

In connection with this whole question of prognosis, a judge may ask "is it true: once a schizophrenic, always a schizophrenic?" We would have to say that "it depends—". In the first place, predictions of improvement have to be made on the grounds already mentioned. Second, we must clarify that various levels of improvement are possible. A severely and chronically ill person may lose his bizarre behavior, hallucinations and delusions but remain grossly impaired in his ability to relate to others and to think in any organized fashion, or he may improve to the level of "good hospital adjustment"; a markedly disturbed person with a short history of illness and a reasonably sound past history may to all intents and purposes recover, or retain pathology discernible only by the most acute observer; or a person with only subtle signs to begin with may remain unchanged, getting neither better nor worse, or he may go very far in either direction. A person like the last, incidentally may in the proper circumstances lead an active life, including scientific and artistic creativity, and with varying degrees of personal satisfaction to himself and to others.

The variety in levels of improvement is pertinent also to an evaluation of medical reports of "improved" or "recovered" or "unchanged" as applied to particular cases. "Recovered" in one institution may refer to a level of improvement which in another place may be rated as "slightly improved." . . .

* * *

[A] word about genetics, which includes items pertaining to the history of the illness and especially of the individual. Practically any psychological study of the schizophrenic will contain emphasis on untoward experiences in early infancy and early childhood. If there is any validity in this emphasis (which I believe there is) it should be of concern to us here, not because of the litigant but because of the children who may be born. I do not necessarily suggest that a schizophrenic patient begets schizophrenic children, but the increasingly rich studies of the families of schizophrenics leave no doubt that the influence of a disturbed parent can be pervasively pathological indeed. Conservatively, the evidence supports a conclusion that the future well-being of children will not be served by their being raised in the household of a schizophrenic parent.

Before proceeding further, it may be well to allow that not all such marriages are ill-fated. Certainly, from the viewpoint of the patient, some aspects of being married can be conducive to health. Our group in New Haven has recently conducted a follow-up study of discharged patients; the data are not yet completely analyzed, but one of the early findings is that good post-hospital adjustment is more a function of living with one's marital partner than it is of diagnosis or nature of in-hospital treatment for example. The fact is that our information is sparse in connection with a good part of this whole problem. However, at the very least, we must remain skeptical about the welfare of the children of such unions.

I should like to raise the possibility of a revision in the rules of evidence. There seems to be current precedence that "when insanity is proved for the time before and after marriage, it is presumed to exist also during the interval", even when the interval is years long. In the case cited, the "proof" accepted was the medical diagnosis together with hospitalization. There seems to be less certainty about the admissibility of evidence other than of medical experts even when "strange conduct" attributed to "unusual traits of character" was seen by peers. I would hold that weight should be given to adequate description by non-professional persons of disturbed behavior especially for the period before marriage. Furthermore, I would hold that *bona fide* illness may be present *even if not recognized at all* by the surrounding community. . . . In this connection, the rules of evidence ought to allow for a proper time interval *before* the outbreak of recognized symptoms during which illness can be presumed to be present.

Another problem well worth considering is that of the "chronic schizophrenic." Specifically, I mean an individual for whom there is no satisfactory evidence of the presence of schizophrenia before marriage who, perhaps several years after marriage, becomes psychotic and whose subsequent course (severity, poor response to treatment, etc.) is reliably predictable as carrying a bad, even hopeless, prognosis. Although such cases may be uncommon, they are known to most psychiatrists. The plight of the spouse (who may be still quite young) and of the children can be most pitiable. I am not prepared to suggest what code of canon law or its interpretation is apposite, but a definition of our position seems clearly part of our concern.

NOTE 3.

JOHNSON v. JOHNSON
104 N.W. 2d 8 (N.D. 1960)

DOUGLAS, B. HEEN, DISTRICT JUDGE.

[T]he critical inquiry is whether Bennie O. Johnson, at the very date of such marriage, was of unsound mind thereby lacking sufficient mental capacity to contract a valid marriage; whether he as alleged in the complaint, was feeble-minded, was a common drunkard and afflicted with a contagious disease.

*   *   *

While there has been a hesitancy on the part of the courts to judicially define the phrase "unsound mind," it is established that such term has reference to the mental capacity of the parties at the very moment of inception of the marriage contract. Ordinarily, lack of mental capacity, which renders a party incapable of entering into a valid marriage contract, must be such that it deprives him of the ability to understand the objects of marriage, its ensuing duties and undertakings, its responsibilities and relationship. There is a general agreement of the authorities that the terms "unsound mind" and "lack of mental capacity" carry greater import than eccentricity or mere weakness of mind or dullness of intellect. . . .

*   *   *

[A]n expert testified in effect that plaintiff was not capable of entering into a marriage contract, and by letter stated,

> "In thinking this case over, I believe I may have misunderstood the question of marriage. I should like to revise that statement of mine to indicate that I believe that Mr. Johnson could marry and he may well be a happier person being married. However, this, in my opinion, does not alter the

other answer, namely that he cannot be considered competent to handle his financial affairs and that he needs a guardian."

Yet another medical witness testified that plaintiff was not competent to contract marriage as he was not employable and further basing his opinion somewhat on the conclusion that plaintiff could not be competent because of his entry into a private mental hospital.

NOTE 4.

JOHNSON v. JOHNSON
One Year Later

1) The parties did not eventually receive a divorce or annulment.
2) The guardian wished an annulment of the marriage as he was of the definite opinion that this was a marriage arranged by Mrs. Johnson for the purpose of financial security and in the belief that if the marriage continued, she would spend all of his money and property and then, unless he died, abandon him.
3) Mr. Johnson is not hospitalized at the present time although he is being taken care of by members of his family. Mrs. Johnson has never attempted to resume living with Mr. Johnson since the Supreme Court reversed the decision.

One additional factor might be interesting and that is that an action was brought by Mrs. Johnson, which is still pending, for support in which the question is involved as to whether she can legally bring such action where she is a resident and citizen of Winnipeg, Canada, and not a resident of Traill County, the county of the residence of Mr. Johnson. [Letter dated Jan. 30, 1961 from A. W. Stokes, counsel for Mr. Johnson.]

B.

To Decisions Concerning the Administration of Wife-Husband Relationships?

1.

APPLICATION OF THE PRESIDENT AND DIRECTORS OF GEORGETOWN COLLEGE, INC.,
(Misc. 2189, D.C. Cir. 1963)*

a. Memorandum

At 4:00 P.M. on September 17, 1963, Messrs. Edward Bennett Williams and Colman Stein, at-

---

* Dated Sept. 19, 1963. Reprinted as Exhibit B in Petition of Jessie E. Jones, Respondent, for Rehearing *En Banc*.

torneys representing the Georgetown Hospital, called at my chambers with an application for an order to permit the Hospital to administer blood to an emergency patient who the doctors at the Hospital represented would die without it. It appeared that the patient, age 25, mother of a seven-month-old child, and her husband were both Jehovah's Witnesses, the teachings of which sect, according to their interpretation, prohibited the injection of blood into the body.

Unsuccessful application for the order had first been made to Judge Tamm of the District Court immediately prior to counsel's appearance before me.

I called the Hospital by telephone and spoke with Dr. Westura, Chief Resident Physician, who confirmed the representations made by counsel. I thereupon proceeded with counsel to the Hospital, where I spoke to Mr. Jones, the husband of the patient. He advised me, that, on religious grounds, he would not approve a blood transfusion for his wife. He said, however, that if the court ordered the transfusion, the responsibility was not his. I advised Mr. Jones to obtain counsel immediately. He thereupon went to the telephone and returned in 10 or 15 minutes to advise that he had taken the matter up with his church and that he had decided that he did not want counsel.

I asked permission of Mr. Jones to see his wife. This he readily granted. Prior to going in to the patient's room, I again conferred with Dr. Westura and several other doctors assigned to the case. All confirmed that the patient would die without blood and that there was a better than 50 per cent chance of saving her life with it. Unanimously they strongly recommended it. I then proceeded inside the patient's room. Her appearance confirmed the urgency which had been represented to me. I tried to communicate with her, advising her again as to what the doctors had said. The only audible reply I could hear was "Against my will." It was obvious that the woman was not in a mental condition to make a decision. I was reluctant to press her because of the seriousness of her condition and because I felt that to suggest repeatedly the imminence of death without blood might place a strain on her religious convictions. I asked her whether she would oppose the blood transfusion if the court allowed it. She indicated, as best I could make out, that it would not then be her responsibility.

I returned to the doctors' room where some 10 to 12 doctors were congregated, along with counsel for the Hospital and the husband. The President of Georgetown University, Father Bunn, appeared and pleaded with Mr. Jones to authorize the hospital to save his wife's life with a blood transfusion. Mr. Jones replied that the Scriptures say that we should not drink blood, and consequently his religion prohibited transfusions. Father Bunn explained the meaning of the Scriptural passage, to which Mr. Jones referred, to no avail. The doctors explained to Mr. Jones that a blood transfusion is totally different from drinking blood in that the blood physically goes into a different part and through a different process in the body. Mr. Jones was unmoved. I thereupon signed the order allowing the Hospital to transfuse the patient.

Mrs. Jones had been brought to the Hospital for emergency care, having lost two thirds of her body's blood supply from a ruptured ulcer. She had no personal physician. She relied solely on the Hospital staff. She was a total Hospital responsibility. When death without blood became imminent, the Hospital was faced with the choice of turning the patient out of the Hospital for failure to accept medical treatment, which of course was impossible because of her condition, letting her die in bed, with whatever responsibility that would entail, or administering the blood. In their dilemma the Hospital authorities sought the advice of their counsel, who applied to the court in the name of the Hospital for permission to administer the blood. This court at the time of the application was unaware of any precise legal precedent for its action.[1] It was advised of similar cases respecting children. But here the patient was a 25-year-old adult. Because of the demonstrated imminence of death from loss of blood, this court decided to sign the order to save the patient's life, in the event that subsequent research supported its authority so to do. The court was also comforted by the apparent assurance from the patient herself as well as from her husband that if the court undertook the responsibility for authorizing the transfusion, they themselves would not be in violation of their religious beliefs.

/s/ J. Skelly Wright
UNITED STATES CIRCUIT JUDGE

September 19, 1963

b. An Appellate Judge Appraises His Role and Function in an Emergency

331 F. 2d 1000 (D.C. Cir. 1964)
(*Cert. den.* 377 U.S. 978 (1964))

WRIGHT, CIRCUIT JUDGE:

Initially, it may be well to put this matter into fuller legal context, including "the nature of the controversy, the relation and interests of the parties, and the relief sought in the instant case." The application was in the nature of a petition in equity to the United States District Court for the District of Columbia, a court of general jurisdiction. Though not fully articulated therein, the application sought a decree in the

---

1. There are, however, persuasive analogies. The Supreme Court has said that if a wife religiously believed it was her duty to burn herself upon the funeral pile of her husband, it would not be beyond the power of the civil government to prevent her carrying her belief into practice. *Reynolds* v. *United States*, 98 U.S. (8 Otto) 145, 166 (1878). . . .

nature of an injunction and declaratory judgment to determine the legal rights and liabilities between the hospital and its agents on the one hand, and Mrs. Jones and her husband on the other. Mrs. Jones subsequently appeared in the cause, in this court, as respondent to the application. The treatment proposed by the hospital in its application was not a single transfusion, but a series of transfusions. The hospital doctors sought a court determination before undertaking either this course of action or some alternative. The temporary order issued was more limited than the order proposed in the original application, in that the phrase "to save her life" was added, thus limiting the transfusions in both time and number. Such a temporary order to preserve the life of the patient was necessary if the cause were not to be mooted by the death of the patient.

At any time during the series of transfusions which followed, the cause could have been brought on for hearing by motion before the motions division of this court, and the order either vacated, continued, or superseded by an order of a more permanent nature, such as an interlocutory injunction. Neither the patient, her husband, nor the hospital, however, undertook further proceedings in this court or in the District Court during the succeeding days while blood was being administered to the patient.[8]

*   *   *

Clearly the "case of controversy" raised here is "justiciable," that is, of the type that courts may be called upon to decide. . . . Were a patient in a hospital, unable to leave, to protest its planned treatment, for the most fundamental reasons, it could hardly be questioned that the judiciary would have jurisdiction to rule upon the issue of the patient's, and the hospital's, rights and duties. In this area, failure of the courts to declare the law would not place the responsibility for decision in the executive or legislative branches of government. Judicial abdication would create a legal vacuum to be filled only by the notions, and remedies, of the private parties themselves. And if the courts are to act in this area, damage suits *post facto* are a poor

8. After the writ had become *functus officio* by its own terms, the life of the patient no longer being in danger, and more than ten days after its issuance, *cf.* Rule 65(b), F.R. Civ. P., the patient on October 14 filed a petition in this court, as respondent to the application, seeking to have the order issuing the writ reheard *en banc.* Substantive constitutional arguments as to freedom of religion, and the right of liberty, were advanced, and the question of mootness was dealt with. Georgetown Hospital filed a reply brief. After consideration, this court *en banc* denied the petition for rehearing *en banc.*

substitute for timely declaratory or injunctive relief. Thus if Mrs. Jones had brought an action to restrain the hospital from administering the transfusions, a justiciable controversy would certainly have been presented. The fact that it was the hospital which sought judicial declaration of its rights does not make the controversy less justiciable. Moreover, while the question presented is of utmost importance to those concerned, it is of such infrequent occurrence as to be unlikely to attract the attention of the legislature. Courts sit to decide such questions.

*   *   *

Reference to the Court of Appeals, immediately after the denial of the application by the District Court, was proper under the power of federal courts to issue "all writs necessary or appropriate in aid of their respective jurisdictions." 28 U.S.C. § 1651. Such "authority is not confined to the issuance of writs in aid of a jurisdiction already acquired by appeal but extends to those cases which are within its appellate jurisdiction although no appeal has been perfected." *Roche v. Evaporated Milk Assn.,* 319 U.S. 21, 25 (1943). These "common law writs, like equitable remedies, may be granted or withheld in the sound discretion of the court." *Ibid.* . . . The Federal Rules of Civil Procedure, Rule 62(g), recognize the "power of an appellate court *or of a judge or justice thereof to* *** grant an injunction during the pendency of an appeal or to make any order appropriate to preserve the status quo or the effectiveness of the judgment subsequently to be entered." (Emphasis added.) . . .

The power of a single judge to issue such emergency temporary writs cannot be disputed. 28 U.S.C. § 1651; Rules 6 and 11, General Rules, D. C. Cir.; Rule 62(g), F.R. Civ. P.; Rules 50 and 51.1, Sup. Ct. Rules. . . .

The power recognized by Rule 62(g) and the All Writs Statute, 28 U.S.C. § 1651, inheres in the Single Supreme Court Justice and the single circuit court judge equally, each exercising the same power within the "respective jurisdictions" of his court. 28 U.S.C. § 1651; 6 MOORE, FEDERAL PRACTICE ¶54.10[2] at 61, text at 6.1. . . . And Professor Moore has said: "By virtue of this provision [§1651(b)] an individual Justice of the Supreme Court can give interim relief pending action by the full Court, as by granting or staying an injunction." MOORE, JUDICIAL CODE COMMENTARY ¶0.03(53) at 603 (1949). . . .

Additionally, "if this broadly phrased subsection [(b) of § 1651] is not construed to grant this power [to issue injunctions] to individual

Justices, then the power may be found in 28 U.S.C. § 1651(a) which, although it merely confers upon 'courts' the power to 'issue all writs necessary or appropriate in aid of their respective jurisdiction and agreeable to the usages and principles of law', may nevertheless be construed as also conferring upon individual Justices *or judges* the power to issue such writs where such issuance is customary. . . .

* * *

This opinion is being written solely in connection with the emergency order authorizing the blood transfusions "to save her life." It should be made clear that no attempt is being made here to determine the merits of the underlying controversy. Actually, the issue on the merits is *res nova.* Because of the demonstrated imminence of death from loss of blood, signing the order was necessary to maintain the *status quo* and prevent the issue respecting the rights of the parties in the premises from becoming moot before full consideration was possible. But maintaining the *status quo* is not the only consideration in determining whether an emergency writ should issue. The likelihood of eventual success on appeal is of primary importance, and thus must be here considered.

Before proceeding with this inquiry, it may be useful to state what this case does not involve. This case does not involve a person who, for religious or other reasons, has refused to seek medical attention. It does not involve a disputed medical judgment or a dangerous or crippling operation. Nor does it involve the delicate question of saving the newborn in preference to the mother. Mrs. Jones sought medical attention and placed on the hospital the legal responsibility for her proper care. In its dilemma, not of its own making, the hospital sought judicial direction.

It has been firmly established that the courts can order compulsory medical treatment of children for any serious illness or injury, . . . and that adults, sick or well, can be required to submit to compulsory treatment or prophylaxis, at least, for contagious diseases. . . .

Of course, there is here no sick child or contagious disease. However, the sick child cases may provide peruasive analogies because Mrs. Jones was *in extremis* and hardly *compos mentis* at the time in question; she was as little able competently to decide for herself as any child would be. Under the circumstances, it may well be the duty of a court of general jurisdiction, such as the United States District Court for the District of Columbia, to assume the responsibility

of guardianship[16] for her, as for a child, at least to the extent of authorizing treatment to save her life. And if . . . a parent has no power to forbid the saving of his child's life, *a fortiori* the husband of the patient here had no right to order the doctors to treat his wife in a way so that she would die.

The child cases point up another consideration. The patient, 25 years old, was the mother of a seven-month-old child. The state, as *parens patriae,* will not allow a parent to abandon a child, and so it should not allow this most ultimate of voluntary abandonments. The patient had a responsibility to the community to care for her infant. Thus the people had an interest in preserving the life of this mother.

Apart from the child cases, a second range of factors may be considered. It is suggested that an individual's liberty to control himself and his life extends even to the liberty to end his life. Thus, "in those states were attempted suicide has been made lawful by statute (or the lack of one), the refusal of necessary medical aid [to one's self], whether equal to or less than attempted suicide, must be conceded to be lawful." Cawley, *Criminal Liability in Faith Healing,* 39 MINN. L. REV. 48, 68 (1954). And, conversely, it would follow that where attempted suicide is illegal by the common law or by statute, a person may not be allowed to refuse necessary medical assistance when death is likely to ensue without it. Only quibbles about the distinction between misfeasance and nonfeasance, or the specific intent necessary to be guilty of attempted suicide, could be raised against this latter conclusion.

. . . But whether attempted suicide is a crime is in doubt in some jurisdictions, including the District of Columbia.[17]

The Gordian knot of this suicide question may be cut by the simple fact that Mrs. Jones did not want to die. Her voluntary presence in the hospital as a patient seeking medical help testified to this. Death, to Mrs. Jones, was not a religiously-commanded goal, but an unwanted side effect of a religious scruple. There is no question here of interfering with one whose religious convictions counsel his death, like the Buddhist monks who set themselves afire. Nor are we faced with the question of whether the state should

16. See 21 D.C. Code Sec. 301: "The equity court shall have full power and authority to superintend and direct the affairs of persons non compos mentis ,* * * and to make such orders and decrees for the care of their persons * * * as to the court may seem proper. * * *"

17. *Compare* 22 D.C. Code Sec. 2401 (1961) ("Whoever* * * kills *another* [etc.] is guilty of murder * * *") *with* 18 U.S.C. Sec. 1111(a) (1948) ("Murder is the unlawful killing of *a human being* [etc.]") (emphasis added).

intervene to reweigh the relative values of life and death, after the individual has weighed them for himself and found life wanting. Mrs. Jones wanted to live.

A third set of considerations involved the position of the doctors and the hospital. Mrs. Jones was their responsibility to treat. The hospital doctors had the choice of administering the proper treatment or letting Mrs. Jones die in the hospital bed, thus exposing themselves and the hospital, to the risk of civil and criminal liability in either case.[18] It is not certain that Mrs. Jones had any authority to put the hospital and its doctors to this impossible choice. The normal principle that an adult patient directs her doctors is based on notions of commerical contract which may have less relevance to life-or-death emergencies. It is not clear just where a patient would derive her authority to command her doctor to treat her under limitations which would produce death. The patient's counsel suggests that this authority is part of constitutionally protected liberty. But neither the principle that life and liberty are inalienable rights, nor the principle of liberty of religion, provides an easy answer to the question whether the state can prevent martyrdom. Moreover, Mrs. Jones had no wish to be a martyr. And her religion merely prevented her consent to a transfusion. If the law undertook the responsibility of authorizing the transfusion without her consent, no problem would be raised with respect to her religious practice. Thus, the effect of the order was to preserve for Mrs. Jones the life she wanted without sacrifice of her religious beliefs.

The final, and compelling, reason for granting the emergency writ was that a life hung in the balance. There was no time for research and reflection. Death could have mooted the cause in a matter of minutes, if action were not taken to preserve the *status quo*. To refuse to act, only to find later that the law required action, was a risk I was unwilling to accept. I determined to act on the side of life.

c. On Petition for Rehearing en Banc

331 F. 2d 1010 (D.C. Cir. 1964)

Before: BAZELON, CHIEF JUDGE, and WILBUR K. MILLER, FAHY, WASHINGTON, DANAHER, BASTIAN, BURGER, WRIGHT and MCGOWAN, CIRCUIT JUDGES, *en banc,* in Chambers.

---

18. Whether or not a waiver signed by a patient *in extremis* would protect the hospital from civil liability, it could not be relied on to prevent criminal prosecution. Death resulting from failure to extend proper medical care, where there is a duty of care, is manslaughter in the District of Columbia. *Jones* v. *United States,* 113 U.S.App. D.C. 352, 355, 308 F. 2d 307, 310 (1962).

ORDER

Upon consideration of a pleading styled "Petition for Rehearing En Banc" in the above-entitled matter and an opposition thereto, it is

ORDERED by the court *en banc* that said petition is denied.

Per Curiam.

WILBUR K. MILLER, CIRCUIT JUDGE, dissenting:
. . .

Although the proposed order was styled "Application of The President and Directors of Georgetown College, Inc., a Body Corporate," there was no such proceeding pending in the District Court; there had been no complaint, petition or formal written application filed. The only "application" was the oral request of the attorneys that the tendered order be signed and entered. To this day, there is nothing on file in the District Court Clerk's office with reference to this "application." Judge Tamm endorsed on the paper the word "Denied," which of course meant that he was denying the oral application for the order. It is plain, I think, that at the very least Judge Tamm's denial was based on the fact that there was nothing before him upon which he could act, that the jurisdiction of the District Court had not been properly involved, and that there was no pending case or controversy.

About 4:00 p.m. on September 17 the same attorneys appeared, unannounced, at the chambers of a judge of this court and requested an immediate review of Judge Tamm's action denying the application for authority to administer a transfusion to a patient at the hospital, said to be in imminent danger of death from loss of blood. They did not file a written petition for review of Judge Tamm's refusal to sign the order but merely orally requested a single judge to take the action which Judge Tamm had just refused to take. The appellate judge spoke by telephone with the hospital's chief resident physician who confirmed the representations made by counsel and thereupon the judge proceeded to the hospital. There he spoke to the husband of the patient who advised that, on religious grounds, he would not approve a blood transfusion for his wife. The judge advised the husband to obtain counsel immediately but, after brief consideration, the husband declined to do so. The judge then called at the patient's room and repeated to her what the doctors had said. Her only reply audible to him was, "Against my will."

* * *

On October 14, 1963, Jessie E. Jones, the patient, filed a petition for a rehearing *en banc* and for an order vacating and quashing the order of September 17 which authorized the transfusion. The petition states the question presented as follows:

"The question is whether a free adult citizen of the United States can be forced against her will to accept medical treatment to which she objects on both religious and medical grounds.

"This case is of vital importance and rehearing should be granted due to the broad implications of the question presented. The right of free exercise of religion and the right of a free citizen to have his body inviolate are all a part of the rights guaranteed by the Constitution. The problem raised here additionally affects all doctor-patient-hospital relationships throughout the entire country. Thus, while the fact issue may be unusual, the principle is broad and vital and these important qualities make this a case which peculiarly calls for reconsideration by the full court *en banc* and the right of a rehearing."

* * *

I object to the order which merely denies the petition for rehearing, without more, because it leaves in effect the two orders of September 17, as orders of this court which may be cited hereafter as precedents, not only for the summary administration of blood transfusions against the will of the patient, but also for the proposition that one judge of this court, without summoning two of his colleagues to act with him and without any record before him, may take the drastic and unprecedented action which was taken in this matter.

Under Article III, Section 2, of the Constitution of the United States, the judicial power extends only to cases and controversies. Although the Section defines and limits judicial power, it does not prescribe the particular method by which that power may be invoked. The method of invoking it is provided by Rule 3 of the Federal Rules of Civil Procedure, which reads: "A civil action is commenced by filing a complaint with the court." As has been shown, there was no complaint filed here, so a civil action was not commenced and the power of the District Court was not properly invoked. I do not understand that one may institute a civil action merely by entering the chambers of a district judge and asking him to sign a proffered order; nor that an appeal from his refusal may be taken by orally requesting a single circuit judge to review it.

Even when a case or controversy is properly presented to a Court of Appeals, one judge thereof is not empowered to take the decisive action which was taken here. The determination of such matters is committed to a division of three judges, of which two constitute a quor-

um, or to the court *en banc*. This is provided by subsections 46(b), 46(c) and 46(d) of Title 28, U.S. Code:

"(b) In each circuit the court may authorize the hearing and determination of cases and controversies by separate divisions, each consisting of three judges. Such divisions shall sit at the times and places and hear the cases and controversies assigned as the court directs.

"(c) Cases and controversies shall be heard and determined by a court or division of not more than three judges, unless a hearing or rehearing before the court in banc is ordered by a majority of the circuit judges of the circuit who are in active service. A court in banc shall consist of all active circuit judges of the circuit.

"(d) A majority of the number of judges authorized to constitute a court or division thereof, as provided in paragraph (c), shall constitute a quorum. (June 25, 1948, ch. 646, 62 Stat. 871.)"

These sections, it seems to me, do not provide for or permit action by a single appellate judge such as that which was taken here. It has been suggested, however, that the Code provision which authorizes one appellate judge to enter an order to preserve the *status quo* pending appeal justifies the procedure employed here. The suggestion is, I think, without foundation. Even if an appeal had properly been in this court from Judge Tamm's refusal to enter the proffered order, the orders entered on September 17 by one judge of this court did not preserve the *status quo*; to the contrary, the orders completely changed the *status quo ante* by granting fully and finally all of the relief sought, thus disposing of the matter on its merits. This fact is confirmed, perhaps unwittingly, by the majority's order denying the petition for rehearing *en banc,* which implicitly relies on mootness.

I think that, instead of merely denying the petition for rehearing, we should dismiss it on the ground that there was no case or controversy presented or determined and that consequently there is nothing to rehear. But, whether the petition for rehearing be denied or dismissed, the purported orders of September 17 should be expunged so there would be nothing in our records which could be cited as a precedent for future similar action by a single appellate judge. We have inherent power to take that action *sua sponte*.

I do not mean to impugn the motives of our colleague who signed these orders. He was impelled, I am sure, by humanitarian impulses and doubtless was himself under considerable strain because of the critical situation in which he had become involved. In the interval of about an hour and twenty minutes between the appearance of the attorneys at his chambers and the signing of the order at the hospital, the judge had no opportunity for research as to the substantive legal problems and procedural questions involved. He should not have been asked to act in these circumstances.

I suggest it is not correct to suppose that, where there is a serious emergency in life, a judge of a district or a circuit court may act to meet it, regardless of whether he is empowered by law to do so. This situation shows the truth of the adage that the hard cases make bad law.

BURGER, CIRCUIT JUDGE: I believe we should dismiss the petition for rehearing en banc for want of a justiciable controversy, . . . rather than merely deny it.

* * *

The judicial power is narrow and limited is a concept deeply embedded in our System. Thus the need for external restraints on the powers of Federal Judges was plainly an important corollary to their constitutionally secured tenure. It was quite as clear in the 1780's as it is today that men are not notorious for exercising self-restraint when they possess both permanent tenure *and* plenary power. Under our System no single Branch of Government has both, and no single Branch of Government could safely be entrusted with both.

Confronted by a unique episode such as this, it seems to me we must inquire where an assumption of jurisdiction over such matters could lead us.[5] Physicians, surgeons and hospitals—and others as well—are often confronted with seemingly irreconcilable demands and conflicting pressures. Philosophers and theologians have pondered these problems and different religious groups have evolved different solutions; the solutions and doctrines of one group are sometimes not acceptable to other groups or sects. Various examples readily come to mind: a crisis in childbirth may require someone to decide whether the life of the mother or the child shall be sacrificed; absent a timely and decisive choice both may die. May the physician or hospital require the courts to decide? A patient may be in a critical condition requiring, in the minds of

experts, a certain medical or surgical procedure. If the patient has objections to that treatment based on religious conviction, or if he rejects the medical opinion, are the courts empowered to decide for him?

Some of our greatest jurists have emphasized the need for judicial awareness of the limits on judicial power which is simply an acknowledgement of human fallibility.

Cardozo, in *The Nature of the Judicial Process,* said:

> The judge, even when he is free, is still not wholly free. He is not to innovate at pleasure. He is not a knight-errant, roaming at will in pursuit of his own ideal of beauty or of goodness. He is to draw his inspiration from consecrated principles. He is not to yield to spasmodic sentiment, to vague and unregulated benevolence. He is to exercise a discretion informed by tradition, methodized by analogy, disciplined by system, and subordinated to "the primordial necessity of order in the social life." Wide enough in all conscience is the field of discretion that remains.

It is at the periphery of the boundaries of power where the guidelines are less clear that an appealing claim presents difficult choices, but this is precisely the area in which restraint is called for in light of the absolute nature of our powers and the finality which often, as here, attends our acts. . . . Some matters of essentially private concern and others of enormous public concern, are beyond the reach of judges. . . .

---

5. There is another interesting facet which needs only to be mentioned briefly: the emergent nature of the factual situation confronting the hospital demonstrates that what on its face was "interlocutory relief" was really the ultimate relief. Once granted, no more remained for any court to consider. Were we to view the claims now as moot, we would have to acknowledge their mootness as soon as the challenged order was acted upon. This was in effect not only a form of instant relief but perhaps also instant mootness. This does not appear to be a situation of preserving a status quo in order to preserve jurisdiction but rather one where the interim relief was the total relief.

2.

LILLEY v. LILLEY
[1958] 3 All E.R. 528

LORD MERRIMAN, P., read the following judgment: . . .

. . . The parties were married on Oct. 2, 1948. It is evident from one of the magistrate's findings that the marriage went reasonably smoothly until the birth of the child on Mar. 13, 1952. It appears, however, that the husband was always more interested in the sexual side of life than the wife was. The wife's confinement was very difficult. The magistrate found that thereafter the wife suffered from some mental or nervous disorder which was either caused or gravely aggravated by the birth of the child. She suffered from periods of acute depression which got progressively worse, and she developed an invincible repugnance to sexual intercourse which . . . the magistrate described as being

> "as real and as overwhelming as a physical disability which made sexual intercourse impossible"

and said that this state of things was in no way attributable to wilfulness on her part. . . .

Dr. Hendy said amongst other things that the neurosis produced an acute revulsion to sex relations, over which he believed her to have no control; that if she were to return to live with her husband he feared that the result would be disastrous. Asked by the magistrate to say exactly what he meant, he said she might go over the border into insanity, or over the border into physical disability. The effects would be comparable in any case: that there would be a serious breakdown in her health so as to make her incapable of living a normal life. The doctor did not think that living with her husband on condition that there was no sexual intercourse was a reasonable condition for either of them. He thought that the fact that the wife could not bear to be near to her husband was largely due to the sex phobia, a manifestation of the neurosis, but that it extended to proximity to men generally, and added that the very fact that a man was near her would set her in a state of anxiety. . . . He made it clear that this was apart from actual sexual acts, and that he was speaking of the mere fact of having to return and live under a communal roof; repeating that he feared that it would be disastrous to her mental health to return to her husband at all. He said that there was nothing wilful about this state of things at all; that it was an illness.

Cross-examined, he said that he accepted that the wife was rational and in normal mental health "except so far as it related to her husband"—and to other men. It seems to me that the exception goes to the root of the matter, and I will return to this later. The doctor did not think that there was any great difference in her condition as between Aug. 8, 1957, and the day on which he was then giving evidence. He also said in cross-examination that it was his firm belief that it was not possible for her to join her husband in his house on any terms whatever. Finally in answer to the stipendiary magistrate, he made it quite clear that he was satisfied that the wife could not be said to be "playing-up," and that he thought that he would have spotted the symptoms if she had been doing so; that she was probably all right living a quiet life apart from her husband, but was "just managing on very thin ice," and that the possibility of a relapse could not be ruled out.

*   *   *

[T]he wife's case is that she had been and still is prevented by the state of neurosis from which she suffers in relation to life with her husband, and that this is a grave and weighty reason justifying her in not resuming cohabitation, even though it does not emanate from any misconduct

on the part of the husband; that if she is not a deserter (there being no question of adultery) the husband is liable to maintain her by the common law of England, and therefore, his deliberate refusal to do so amounts to wilful neglect.

*   *   *

The stipendiary magistrate stated that he assumes, on the part of the wife, a physical capacity to resume cohabitation and a mental capacity to make a rational decision and to form an intention to desert. Having regard, however, to the medical evidence already mentioned, the antithesis between physical and mental capacity seems to me to be of doubtful validity. The wife's assumed capacity to make a rational decision is based on Dr. Hendy's answer to the question already quoted, which itself contains the words "except so far as it relates to her husband," in assenting to which Dr. Hendy said "and to other men." In the course of the argument we intimated that we were not convinced that a woman suffering from an illness causing the reaction to the mere presence of her husband, or anyone of the male sex, as described by Dr. Hendy, without any question of wilfulness about it, could properly be assumed to be capable of making a rational decision to return to cohabitation or to desert. I am still of that opinion. . . . [T]he undisputed medical evidence establishes that, although no longer in hospital, she was just as incapable of resuming cohabitation, whether one describes the incapacity as physical or mental. . . . For these reasons I do not agree with the stipendiary magistrate that all the elements necessary to constitute desertion were present.

*   *   *

. . . In a very forcible argument [counsel for the wife] he submitted that the wife not being in desertion, though living apart, and there being no question of adultery, the husband is liable to maintain her at common law, and that he has not done so since he deliberately stopped what was described as the voluntary allowance of 30s.; and therefore he is guilty of wilful neglect to provide reasonable maintenance within s. 4 of the Summary Jurisdiction (Married Women) Act, 1895.

In this case there was plainly no agreement, either that the wife should live apart or that she should be maintained as a separated wife. The husband is admitted not to be in desertion, and I am assuming that the wife also is not so. The wife only attempts to justify her refusal to cohabit on a ground which involves "no matter of complaint against her husband" (see 12 Halsbury's Laws (3rd Edn.) 482, para. 1077). In my opinion we should not be justified in abandoning the principles laid down . . . by the majority of the Court of Appeal in *Price v. Price,* in which case Hodson, L.J., said ([1951] P. at p. 421):

> "The question of [the wife's] right to mainten-ance may depend on whether she is a deserter or whether she is deserted or whether there is a con-tract between them. I do not think that the law recognises a sort of undefined condition where parties are living apart in conditions which may be described as of drift, or in some not very clearly defined condition in so far as rights to mainten-ance are concerned."

Nor do I think that we ought to ignore the line of decisions in this court that wilful neglect to provide reasonable maintenance involve an element of misconduct—and to do both on the strength of a dictum* that the wife is entitled to maintenance because she is a wife. . . .

National Assistance Board v. Wilkinson ([1952] 2 All E.R. 255), and *National Assistance Board v. Parkes* ([1955] 3 All E.R. 1) decided that if the wife is a deserter the huband cannot be made to contribute to any public assistance given to the wife, but that if she is not in deser-tion, and there is no question of adultery, the National Assistance Board has an independent right against the husband under s. 42 and s. 43 of the National Assistance Act, 1948. It is true that under s. 43 (5) (b) the National Assistance Board can obtain an order to pay the money to the wife but this, I emphasise, is an order made by virtue of the express liability of the hus-band to maintain his wife under s. 42 and does not necessarily impute a finding of wilful neglect. In my opinion that is the true solution of this difficult case. But I do not think that in the circumstances the husband can be found guilty of wilful neglect to provide reasonable mainten-ance. I therefore agree with the learned stipen-diary magistrate's conclusion, although I differ from some of his reasons. Accordingly the ap-peal will be dismissed.

NOTES

NOTE 1.

LILLEY v. LILLEY
[1959] 3 All E.R. 283

HODSON, L. J.

There is in this case no agreement to live apart, but there is a de facto separation which is explained by the wife's state of neurosis, be-cause of which, as the learned stipendiary found, the wife would be risking grave consequences to her mental health if she returned to her husband

at the present time. She maintains that in the circumstances if he does not maintain her apart from him he is guilty of wilful neglect to main-tain just as much as if she were separated from him by necessity. Examples of separation by necessity come readily to mind where the occupa-tion of the husband makes it necessary for him to spend long periods apart from his wife by reason of his absence at sea or otherwise away from his home. The changes and chances of life may often, where there is a separation of neces-sity, put on the husband the obligation to sup-port his wife when she is separated from him, and if he does not do so he will be guilty of the offence with which he is charged. This duty must surely subsist if separation is forced on the parties by illness which compels residence in hospital, and this would be the same whatever the nature of the illness, even if it be mental disorder, provided always that the intention of the absent spouse to return to the other contin-ues. . . . We see no reason why the obligation to maintain which exists when the husband and wife are living together should be affected by an enforced separation. If the husband does not maintain his wife while in the home he is clearly in default under the statutes, and an en-forced separation of itself can make no differ-ence. We would, therefore, with all respect to the opinion expressed by the Divisional Court and by the learned stipendiary magistrate, have been of opinion that if the wife was not in desertion the husband must, in the circumstances of this case, have committed the offence with which he is charged, subject to consideration of the rela-tive means of the parties.

The remaining question is, therefore, whether the wife is in desertion since she failed to re-spond to the husband's request to return con-tained in his letter of Apr. 17, 1957. . . . The following questions and answers are taken from the transcript of her evidence:

> "Q.—At any rate, you are determined that you cannot live with him at the present time? A.—Yes. Q.—And never can? A.—Definitely not. Q.—Do you accept that he wants to live with you? A.— Yes. Q.—That he has a home for you to go into? A.—Yes. Q.—That he has kept the home in the hope that you will go back to him? A.—I have repeatedly told him I can't go back. Surely, he should have accepted that by now. Q.—And whatever promises he made to you with regard to how he would treat you if you came back to him, you still would not have him back? A.—No. Q.—Do you think, under those circumstances, it is fair to ask him to maintain you? A.—Yes."

She then gave reasons in support of her con-tention that it was fair to ask for maintenance.

---

* Per Denning, L.J., [1955] 3 All E.R. at p. 4.

As to the wife's capacity to make a rational decision, the stipendiary said:

> "It is clear from the evidence and indeed in no way in dispute that the wife is capable of making a rational decision and of forming an intention to desert."

The learned President did not, however, consider that this finding was justified by the evidence. He based his decision on an answer given to the court in cross-examination by Dr. Hendy. The question was in this form:

> "As I understand it, you say that this lady is rational and in normal mental health except so far as it relates to her husband? A.—Yes, and as I said just now, to other men."

This question was phrased in an unfortunate form, for it contains two questions. The answer "Yes," if taken to apply to both parts of the question, no doubt qualifies in an important respect the doctor's evidence that the wife was rational, but having regard to the rest of his evidence and for the express finding of the learned stipendiary already read that the rationality of the wife was not in dispute, we cannot regard this answer as sufficient to destroy the effect of Dr. Hendy's evidence in this essential matter, consistent as it is with the view which the magistrate must have formed of the effect of the evidence of the wife herself, and of her letters and her demeanour in court. . . . In the present case we are of opinion that the conclusion of fact reached by the stipendiary on this issue was amply justified by the evidence before him. The attitude of the wife went far beyond saying "I cannot return to you at present." She added in effect "and I never will." This expression of her fixed intention appears both from the letters and her statements in court. . . . She has made a deliberate choice for all time, and she cannot properly complain of the natural consequences of her act.

This is no doubt a strong case, for the neurosis of the wife is severe and may be incurable. It may appear hard, therefore, that she should be guilty of desertion if she expresses herself as unwilling ever to return to her husband, but we think that the conclusion that she is in desertion is inevitable on the evidence as it stands at present. . . .

NOTE 2.

OPPENHEIMER v. OPPENHEIMER
20 Misc. 2d 248, 192 N.Y.S. 2d 714 (1959)

CHARLES A. LORETO, JUSTICE.

Plaintiff has brought this suit to set aside the separation agreement, to declare the divorce decree null and void and for a decree of separation with an allowance of alimony and counsel fee.

Upon the trial, it was proved that while plaintiff was a patient of the New York Psychiatric Institute, the defendant, her husband, secured her signature to a separation agreement and to a power of attorney for an uncontested divorce. With the latter he obtained a Mexican decree of divorce, incorporating the terms of the separation agreement, which provides for the payment to her of the sum of $500 in two equal installments and the further sum of $150 per month for the period of three years.

* * *

The court is satisfied from the record that shortly after their marriage the defendant became acutely aware of plaintiff's emotional instability. Later acquiring knowledge of the insanity of her mother and brother, he had doubts as to her mental competency and became determined to terminate the marriage. He often brought the subject up to her. She dreaded and feared the severance of the marital bonds. By reason of his persistence she believed that there was no alternative but to yield and in February 1956 she prepared and signed an agreement consenting to a divorce, the defendant agreeing to pay her a lump sum of $1,000 and $100 monthly for one year. Immediately after its execution the parties resumed cohabitation and that agreement was thereby terminated.

* * *

At the trial plaintiff testified that the defendant gave her papers to look at while riding in the automobile, but that she could not read as she was crying and hysterical and that she does not know what took place at the apartment of the attorney's secretary. The court finds that the plaintiff was in such a disturbed emotional and mental condition that she did not consciously give her free and willing consent to those instruments.

The court is satisfied that the defendant, realizing the plaintiff's emotional and mental condition, wanted to be free of her and to secure such freedom with the most limited financial contribution possible. The plaintiff was painfully aware of his attitude toward her, and feeling forsaken was overcome with overpowering despair, reaching the point where she was ready to surrender life itself. There is no doubt that at times her conduct was irrational. It would indeed be uncharitable to deem her culpable for such conduct. She needed psychiatric care and treatment and above all the true and abiding devotion and loyalty of her husband. There is no doubt too that living with the plaintiff was very difficult if not impossible and that it would take a person of exceptional physical and moral fiber to do so. However difficult it was for the defendant to continue to live with her, the time and circumstances under which he secured her signature to the documents is shocking and must be denounced. The plaintiff was then suffering from acute hysteria, a psychoneurosis. When the defendant planned to secure and in fact obtained plaintiff's signature to such important documents shortly after the dreadful episode of April 21, 1957 and while she was still a patient in a psychiatric hospital, was a time when she especially needed someone to protect her rights. She had no one. . . . Can it be held that her letter dated May 22, 1957 (Ex. Ll) wherein she wrote "I have full confidence in you * * * I don't know how you are going to handle this—but you have had practice * * * " is confirmation that she knew what had been done? Or that her confidence in him in that connection was well reposed?

The several letters written by her soon thereafter indicate how depressed she was and how her mind was completely filled with the fear and dread of divorce and abandonment and how she still was fighting the thought of divorce.

Contrary to statute and the public policy of this state written in the statute (Domestic Relations Law, § 51), defendant took unconscionable advantage of his wife in securing her signature to these instruments which were designed to permit the dissolution of their marriage and to relieve him of his obligation to support her. At that time she was at his mercy. In a letter dated May 31, 1957 she wrote "It is all too miserable for me to accept—but I have no choice". The court holds that the defendant is chargeable with having exercised a species of duress over his wife in connection with the execution of the documents. As both were signed at the same time and in the same circumstances, forming one transaction, they are both subject to the same infirmities.

The fact that the plaintiff was never adjudicated incompetent and that no committee of her person and property was ever appointed, is of no consequence in this case. It is sufficient to declare the instruments executed by her voidable as the court finds that the plaintiff was not rational. . . .

*   *   *

With respect to the plaintiff's action for separation, the court finds there is sufficient support therefor in the evidence of cruelty on the part of the defendant toward the plaintiff in his conduct in persistently beseeching her to give him a divorce and in seeking to be relieved of his obligation to support her except for limited small payments. This conduct on his part subjected her to great distress and mental anguish, which was aggravated when he refused to permit her to live in the same apartment on the occasions when she was discharged from the Psychiatric Institute in both 1956 and 1957. It is unnecessary to consider other evidence offered in support of this cause, as the court finds that this conduct on the part of the defendant is sufficient to warrant the granting of a decree of separation in her favor.

NOTE 3.

RIGGINS v. RIGGINS
294 P. 2d 751 (Calif. 1956)

PER CURIAM.

. . . In section 108 of the Civil Code, also enacted in 1941, it was provided that a divorce on the ground of incurable insanity might be granted "only upon proof" that the defendant had been incurably insane for a certain time and had been confined in a certain place "under the provisions" of certain sections of the Welfare and Institutions Code. The confinement referred to in those sections is confinement under order of court. It thus appears that the Legislature excluded voluntary confinement or admission in its determination as to the proof that should be required. . . .

3.

WATSON, ANDREW S.

The Conjoint Psychotherapy of Marriage Partners*

. . . I will endeavor to explain and conceptualize my recent treatment efforts with family and marriage problems.

Several specific premises regarding the nature of marital unions will be utilized but not explicitly substantiated here. They are:

1. That marriage partners choose each other for highly specific, conscious and unconscious reasons. This selection represents the summation and gratification of normal and appropriate

* American Journal of Orthopsychiatry, Vol. 33 (1963), pp. 913-921. Copyright, The American Orthopsychiatric Association, Inc. Reproduced by permission.

goals, as well as various neurotic and symbolic needs that must be met either intrapsychically or socially. . . .

2. Both partners enter into a mutually "satisfying" interlocking homeostatic balance. . . . Despite external appearances to the contrary, they reach a state of psychological equilibrium that "gratifies" both mature and neurotic needs for both partners. One of the treatment objectives in this kind of therapy will be to elucidate the details of this interlocking system, in order to open up the possibility for a different and more appropriate adjustment between them.

3. This homeostatic relationship may also be viewed as a mutually shared communication system involving many verbal as well as non-verbal communication devices. Therefore much characterological interchange will take place, and this will lead inevitably to the necessity for emphasizing the interpretation of character manifestations in this form of treatment.

4. Any therapeutic disruption in the psychological homeostasis of one partner in the marriage will inevitably force upon all other members in the family an alteration in their psychological adjustments. For this reason, it appears that often the most efficient way to impinge upon the interlocking adjustment of the partners is to have both participate in the insight-producing process. This would simultaneously tend to bring about revised homeostatic techniques for each. The family anxiety level may be kept closer to optimal limits than often occurs when individuals are treated separately and only one member has opportunity for, and access to, insight-producing experience. . . .

* * *

In conjoint psychotherapy, both marriage partners are seen together and the strategic goal of the interpretive process is to work through the central neurotic distortions of their interlocking adaptive and communication systems. This involves interpretation of the multiple transferences, utilizing all the traditional psychoanalytic concepts of personality dynamics. Because of the more complex transaction in these sessions, several specific procedures are followed.

It will be clear to all sophisticated in the theory of psychotherapy that there is an extremely complex interlocking system of transference—countertransference operations present in a therapeutic setting where three individuals participate. Because of this fact, it is essential at the very beginning of treatment to understand thoroughly the characteristics and etiology of each partner's psychological participation.

When the decision has been made to treat a couple conjointly, both parties will be interviewed separately for two or three sessions in order to obtain a thorough anamnesis and diagnostic formulation. [A]n effort is made to isolate and formulate the core psychodynamic forces operating in each spouse and relate them to precise etiological data. Early memories are obtained; family backgrounds are explored with emphasis on recollections and thoughts about significant family members; dreams and other specific historical details needed to develop the diagnostic formulation are collected. By the time these interviews are concluded, the therapist should be able to make at least a well-educated guess about the meaning of the various communications that will be present during the course of treatment. Just as the significance of communications becomes more clear as individual psychotherapy progresses, so they will become more meaningful in the course of conjoint treatment.

Some may leap to the assumption that patients in this kind of treatment setting will not talk freely about the details of their fantasy life, but this has not proved true. It is my impression that freedom to communicate in such treatment is more often than not a function of the therapist's comfort and countertransference than it is of the patient's inhibition. As Ackerman has stated (p. ix), "These so-called secrets turn out not to be real secrets at all. Far more often they are common family knowledge surrounded by a tacit conspiracy of silence." I share this view, and, when the basis for the conspiracy is worked through, the participants have no further need to avoid free discussion, or free association.

As the exploratory sessions with each partner are drawing to a close, it is usually in order to make some general statement to each about specific adaptive techniques that appear to create their difficulty. Then, when both are brought back into the conjoint setting, they will have some anticipation about their own contribution to the marriage problems.

As in all psychotherapy, conjoint treatment starts where the patients want it to start. They may or may not talk about themselves, their children or a multitude of other problems. Material is not judged "good" or "bad" but as communication relating to the significant problems or resistances. Associations are interpreted in the same way as they are in any other form of psychotherapy. However, one factor controls the interpretive choice made at any given time: *All interpretations will focus on those aspects of the material and dynamics that relate to the process of communication between the spouses.* In other words, in selecting which of several alternative interpretations to make, the therapist will choose the one that is related dynamically to the cause of the communication distortion in the marriage. Material mainly relevant to only one partner will not be interpreted.

As material is brought up by one or the other partner and its meaning is interpreted in the presence of both, it helps the listening or observing spouse to impersonalize communications and progressively see them as a function of his partner's psychic problem. This distance-producing measure facilitates improvements in the ego's perceptive capacity, progressively decreases the narcissistic identifications between the partners, and thereby improves their capacity to communicate rationally and resolve mutual problems more objectively. For example, if psychological closeness is ego-threatening to a husband, any demonstration of closeness and intimacy by his wife will cause him to withdraw and she will usually interpret this as personal rejection. When this maneuver manifests itself and is interpreted in treatment, the husband can learn to understand why he "needs" to withdraw. At the same time, the wife is learning why she views such reactions as personal and, progressively, how to objectify the meaning of the withdrawal.

Another important aspect of this technique is that the therapist must observe strict strategic neutrality. He will interpret objectively whatever he sees in the behavior of both spouses, and from time to time will focus his attention on one more than the other. Over the course of treatment, however, he will not ally with one party more than with the other. This is especially important in the beginning phases of treatment, and it is essential to establish this fact clearly to both participants. For the first several hours, this necessitates shifting interpretive focus back and forth between the partners, so that hours end with each receiving approximately equal attention from the therapist. Interpretation should also balance in terms of their positive and negative implications to the partners.

After setting forth to both partners the psychological premises stated above, the therapist then encourages the unfolding of the marital problems. Usually this happens quickly and in very vivid form. As in all transference-oriented treatment, it is possible to see at first hand the nature of the psychological participation of both partners. The therapist need not speculate about what has happened at home, since he may directly observe the interaction between them, as well as their individual transferences to him. Es-

pecially in the early phases of treatment, this is excellent material to focus upon, since it gives patients insight into the goals of treatment, provides them with sufficient gratification to offset some of the anxiety this technique produces, and thereby creates "hope" that the treatment will be worthwhile. Such an attitude is a crucial element for effective therapy. . . .

One of the principal tactical advantages of this kind of treatment lies in the fact that it is possible to make an interpretation to one spouse, though its main impact is directed toward the other one. If there is strong resistance or ego vulnerability in one, a correlated interpretation can be made to the other spouse, thus turning the interlocking nature of the marital neurosis to therapeutic advantage. For example, if there is a provocative masochistic tendency in one, coupled with sadistic-criticalness in the other, either side of this emotional axis may be interpreted. Both hear the interpretation and perceive it in terms of their own dynamics. If they have a psychological need to do so, they may, temporarily at least, be permitted to view this as "the other person's problem." Such displacement-potential is useful for regulating the timing of interpretations, while permitting the therapist to deal with current pertinent material. This considerably increases therapeutic flexibility.

This approach stirs up active psychological participation in the couple, with mounting anxiety usually related closely to the emotional stalemate that brought them to therapy. It is important to give reassurance during the early stages, while they are in the process of discovering their own powers to sustain such discomfort. The therapist, during his early experience with this form of treatment, will likewise reverberate to the patient's anxiety, until he too finds that it is possible to carry out and control such therapy. Ultimately his calmness and comfort in participating in this process, more than anything else, provides patients with the will to explore and accept what had been frightening in the past and had always caused avoidance and reinforced repression. . . .

Another characteristic of this technique is the degree of participation in the process by the therapist. In most one-to-one psychotherapy, the therapist can remain essentially passive, only occasionally making interpretive or confronting remarks. In conjoint treatment, where interpretation often centers upon some character manifestation, the "action" is fast-moving and the therapist will by necessity bring himself more into view. . . . Also, as interpretations are made, he may "lend" his identity by way of references to personal experiences that serve to underscore

his awareness of the problems as well as his belief that they may be resolved. This can be
analogized to the ego support rendered by parents to their children as they encourage the an-
nexational identifications that press them forward
in their exploration and mastery of reality.
Though this kind of support is more specific
and tangible in conjoint treatment, it is certainly
present at least by implication in the most classical psychoanalytic process. In fact, one might
say that one of the criteria for psychoanalysis
is the capacity on the part of the patient to
perceive this fact. If patients cannot, some alternative approach must be taken.

*   *   *

Once this treatment technique has been elected,
it should be the dominant therapeutic mode, at
least until the interlocking psychological problems of the couple have been resolved. However, on occasion one spouse may try to use the
therapeutic situation to act out neurotically, in
a way that would create individual problems and
disrupt the timing of the therapeutic process.
Such maneuvers should be blocked promptly by
the therapist through interpretation. If such acting out cannot be checked within the conjoint
sessions, there is reason to see that spouse
individually sufficiently often (usually one to
three sessions) to clarify and obviate the motives
for such masochistic moves. Any reactions stirred up in the partner *not* seen alone must be
dealt with actively, and occasionally he, or she,
too must be seen alone in order to retain
balance.

After the conjoint sessions have been reinsti-
tuted, the material that came out in the individual meetings can usually be worked slowly into
the discussions. Sometimes these separate sessions
turn out to have been flanking moves to avoid a
conjoint issue. In such a case it must be so interpreted to the partners, and the therapist should
view the separation as a tactical miscalculation.
At other times enormously valuable material
emerges which, when dealt with conjointly, moves
therapy forward precipitously because of the therapist's deepened understanding and the patients'
added insight.

The main problems arising in conjoint treatment
are the product of the more complex transference-
countertransference reactions. Clearly, conjoint
therapy should not be undertaken unless the therapist can comprehend quickly what is going on in the
sessions and can think freely about the material
in precise psychodynamic terms. So much occurs
during the conjoint sessions that the therapist has
no time to pause and reflect at length before

dealing with the material. Neither can he sit by
and wait for multiple confirmations of the psychodynamic theme before he decides to make an
interpretation. To do so puts him far behind the
effectively significant events, and he may never
come abreast of the significant transactions. While
there will be much reiteration of material, the
same timing problem will always exist.

Obviously there are two sets of transferences,
as well as two sets of countertransferences. . . .
Because of the presence of both marital partners and the more realistic presentation of problems, there is an increased risk of the therapist's unconsciously identifying with one or the
other spouse. However, by being aware of this
hazard and through more active involvement in
the therapeutic process, there is greater opportunity for empathic identification and a quicker
grasp of the problems unfolding before and with
him. Under these circumstances it is neither possible nor effective to have long periods of silence
nor to avoid finding answers to specific reality
problems. This does not mean that the goal is
simply to gratify. Rather, the exploration for
answers is carried on in a way that impinges
dynamically on the neurotic process of the
couple. The *act* of mutual exploration is contrived to clarify the defensive maneuvers of each
spouse in such a way as to increase insight and
maturation even as a problem is being solved.
. . .

Another common countertransference anxiety
in conjoint treatment arises when the partners
begin to make threatening remarks about getting
a divorce, or some other offer to act out. Because
both partners are present to witness the intense
affect unleashed, and because it may readily be
interpreted as more than mere transference, the
therapist is likely to wonder if he may not have
a tiger by the tail. These occasions may
be turned to good therapeutic advantage, but
only if the therapist is comfortable in taking
them up and working them through. He may very
easily assume that he has been the cause of such
an upset. While this is obviously not true, the
physical presence of both partners with their
emotional reactions to the therapeutic situation
makes this distortion easy to believe.

The therapist is also likely to react with deep
concern to other kinds of highly charged material
as it emerges and creates the specter of serious
trouble between the partners. As noted above,
such material is not truly secret, and its revelation presents an opportunity to clarify issues that
have too long been hidden just deeply enough
to prevent resolution and yet cause marriage
difficulties. To date, there have been no instances
in which truly damaging material has arisen.

Rather, it has been confirmed that the information was "known" by both parties beforehand.

Though it is often stated that the psychotherapist presents no value judgments to his patients, I do not accept this view. For example, whenever it is decided that there has been a neurotic distortion such as projection, a value judgment about reality has been made and, along with it, an estimate of the degree of distortion. All this is inferred from what the patient has said, which places a large analytical task upon the the therapist. Though he does have access to transference reactions with which to check out impressions of extra-therapy behavior, there is always the possibility of error due to observational bias, as well as the likelihood that some reactions to the therapist will be different in kind from those to other persons in the environment. In conjoint therapy there is the immediate advantage of direct observation of the participants in the family problem. This facilitates more objective evaluation of the partners' behavior and limits the need to judge distortion from more indirect data. This frees the therapist's energy to deal with the complexity of the process, and well offsets the disadvantages arising from the increased distortion potential caused by the complicated interaction.

Another marked advantage of this technique results from the pressure it places on the couple to re-examine their reality testing. When an interpretation is made to one spouse, the other has the opportunity to hear it, remember it, and re-introduce it, during the interim between therapeutic sessions. This provides the therapist with a working assistant for each of the partners, who will constantly reinforce the interpretation he makes during therapy sessions. While there is a possibility and even a probability that interpretations will be used for nontherapeutic purposes, the general summation effect is reinforcement of, and mounting pressure toward, increased reality testing by both spouses. In most individual psychotherapy there is a strong tendency for the patient to leave the hour and fall back into archaic patterns of the problems solving and old ego defenses. Ever so slowly the therapist breaks into the automaticity of the defense system, to bring about broadening of the reality testing and subsequent improvement in the patient's capacity to synthesize and manipulate current experience. The speed with which conjoint therapy improves reality testing is a distinct advantage. There is, in addition, the marked ego satisfaction that comes from the fact that both spouses are participating jointly in the solution of common problems. Here there is no untreated spouse to build up fantasies of being conspired against by the therapist. . . . Instead, there is the clear opportunity to work with the partner and share in the resolution of difficulties. Thus one of the principal problems in treating a married person may be avoided.

Another advantage in conjoint treatment is that insights are gained in the very context from which problems arise. This removes much of the need to translate from transference back to reality since reality and transference are close together in time and content and therefore more accessible to perception and learning. Such contextual analysis appears to enhance markedly the speed of such learning, even while maintaining the advantages of individual treatment to ferret out and clarify neurotic distortions. This avoids vicarious guilt in one partner for gaining something the other is not getting, and facilitates the forging of a new ego ideal that can be held jointly by both. . . .

The final advantage I would like to comment on is economic. There is ample evidence that the decision of *who* gets psychotherapy depends to a large extent on ecomomic status. . . . Obviously, if the multiple parties to a marriage problem may be successfully and simultaneously treated, the saving of professional time will have at least two immediate and practical reverberations for this group of patients:

1. Therapy will become at least twice as available, which is important in the face of an absolute shortage of treatment personnel.
2. The cost of treatment to such a couple may be halved, which can extend the availability of treatment to many who cannot now afford it.

There are other economic effects in conjoint treatment. Several writers have commented on the speed with which this process works, and I concur fully with such observations. . . . Psychodynamic elements that ordinarily take months to raise to awareness sufficient for their being re-examined and reality tested emerge and are effectively altered in a matter of four or five sessions. While these new insights are not fully integrated in such a short time, the improved adaptation that re-evaluation of attitudes and feelings carries with it begins and gains momentum. Patients can then return to their own reality testing and experience gathering with a likelihood for continued maturation. . . .

To discuss indications for conjoint therapy at length would be premature. However, there are several specific situations in which they seem clear-cut:

1. In those family relationships where the commonly held distortions are so gross and so reality-disruptive that speed in checking family

disintegration is a critical factor, conjoint treatment seems to offer an ideal way in which to slow down the destructive neurotic process and provide a chance to resolve at least the surface problems before they destroy the marriage, and often the children.

2. This technique is especially well suited to cases in which the problems are largely of an acting-out, characterological nature. It helps greatly in "trapping" these maneuvers where they can be seen, interpreted and attached to some of the underlying neurotic dynamisms and effects. This makes it very useful in just that type of case in which the parties are "poorly motivated" and "not ready" for treatment. Once they are seen in this therapeutic setting, they may very quickly be led to "discover" reason and feelings to justify continuing.

* * *

The question arises as to how far conjoint treatment can be carried. The answer to this is not yet clear, since various cases have proceeded (and are proceeding) to the handling of all levels of psychopathology from superficial to deep. It does appear, however, that when the focus of psychological emphasis shifts away from elements of mutual emotional cathexis to the partners, if further therapy is needed it should move to individual sessions. There is reason to believe that one should not leap too quickly to this alternative, since it is clear that even dreams and fantasies among marriage partners have a high degree of mutuality. These facts seem to indicate that there will be far-reaching therapeutic potential for conjoint psychotherapy.

. . . The question of contraindication [must] remain open until further experience has been accumulated.

NOTE

VINCENT, CLARK E.

Readings in Marriage Counseling*

In 1816 a Zurich experiment for curing marital incompatibility involved locking the erring couple in a single jail cell for two weeks on the assumption that they would emerge at the end of that time completely dependent on one another and thus cured of incompatibility. This experiment was based on the belief that only sin, evil, or downright stubborness prevented a happy marriage. . . .

* New York: Thomas Y. Crowell Co., 1957, p. 19. Reprinted with permission of the publisher.

4.

REIDER, NORMAN

Problems in the Prediction of Marital Adjustment*

THE VERY FACT that in the history of the human race the importance of the family as a primary social unit has almost never been questioned seemingly commits us to make every possible effort to maintain the family and remove marital discord. Yet these efforts, however worthy their purpose and aim, have not escaped all prejudicial factors; their underlying premises require careful examination.

By prejudicial I mean those irrational elements, highly emotionally tinged, that make us automatically consider possible divorce or separation with a certain amount of discomfort and anxiety. Sometimes this attitude reflects the patient's feelings; sometimes it represents conflicts which are stirred up in ourselves, over and above a rational consideration of the possible damage to result from the disruption of a marriage.

True, damage may result from one or the other or both partners, or for the children; yet it has been my observation that even though sound clinical judgment indicates that a couple will both be better off if they are divorced or separated and that even the children may be better off, elements of the irrational unconscious, or fear of what relatives, friends, neighbors and society in general may think, help to obscure the reasonable approaches. Of course, such matters as shame and embarrassment, whether justified or not, must not be ignored. They must be dealt with as any other data, realistic or neurotic—by investigation, evaluation and good clinical judgment.

Frequently, the very orientation of a study of marital problems has, whether we like it or not, a certain prejudicial character in that the therapist or counselor is committed not to investigating the individual and his whole situation, but to preserving the institution of marriage. Consider how much more catholic and comprehensive its approach if the thesis also included studies on what the definite indications for the disruption of a marriage are. To continue some marriages, given certain insoluble conditions, may be a disservice to both the marital partners and to the children as well. All too often the disruption of a marriage comes as a final admission of failure and as a last resort, rather than as the result of scientific efforts at study

* Reprinted from: Eisenstein, V. W., ed. *Neurotic Interaction in Marriage*, New York: Basic Books, Inc., 1956, pp. 311-325. Reprinted with permission of the publisher.

of the total situation. Perhaps such a traditional attitude is the proper one, however, since a calm, scientific approach to marital problems with an equal readiness for divorce as well as for correction is most difficult, and the method would lend itself to all sorts of abuse in the hands of those who capitalize on the misfortunes of unhappily married persons. The method would also require a considerable amount of courage in this age of anxiety wherein the quest for security becomes more and more ominously palpable. We live in an era wherein tightening and fortifying of bonds and ties is the order of the day rather than any lessening of them. Nevertheless, studies of human relationships should be used to benefit people and not institutions.

*   *   *

The premise that we are somehow or other, and for good reasons, largely committed to the preservation of marriage and to making it a happier institution includes other kinds of prejudices, some apparent and others implied. Although clearly, the character of marriage has no homogeneity, the trend to treat it as an entity persists ; a good marriage is considered a rather uniform phenomenon, composed of similar ingredients in each instance. But this is not true. However many social data are gathered, however many diagnostic typologies are classified, the phenomenon known as marriage in our society has no homogeneity. Instances of marriages arranged and settled by the parents of the couple still exist. Multiple and complex motivations, conscious and unconscious, exist in every marriage—the quest for security, for a repetition of a previous home life, for convenience, for changes in social status, for sexual activity in a socially approved setting, for children, for proofs of maternity or paternity, for satisfaction and needs of various kinds, including those of punishment.

Even such complex, diverse motivations in marriage would still make for a relatively simple situation if they always remained the same, but the problem is further complicated by the fact that people change and their needs change with them as they grow older. The marriage that is sound or seemingly so at its beginning because the partners have certain needs in common, may become difficult as changes occur. These changes come about not only because of disappointments or the lessening of early passion. The vicissitudes of the libidinal and interactional changes that occur in marriage introduce another kind of complexity. Many a person matures in the course of marriage and if his partner meets these qualities of maturation,

things are likely to go well, though not necessarily, because the process of maturation in one person may then uncover needs which differ greatly from those of his partner. . . .

Considered, then, from such points of view, any set of rules or injunctions seems unlikely to serve as a worthwhile guide to successful marriage. And yet a considerable body of empirical experience qualifies this statement. From time immemorial, whenever there has been any semblance or illusion of freedom in choice of a marriage partner, people have used rules, signs and tokens of one sort or another that have worked. Being in love, coming from a certain social group, bearing some particular physical characteristics, having a similar or different temperament, or being given magical signs by a fortune-teller—all have been so used. Many a marriage has withstood the pragmatic test, so that people believe the omen to be of value.

In our scientific efforts we tend to lose sight of the considerable amount of magic, let alone wishful thinking, that goes into preparations for marriage. The mores and ceremonials of courtship and betrothal, the looking for signs of auspicious days, the vows and rituals, the many and varied incantations for best wishes and good fortune, the hopes, the prayers, the gaiety and tears that attend a marriage are mainly devices attempting to insure happiness in marriage.

Of course, there is more than all this in whether a marriage succeeds or fails, and whether the magical rites work well or not. Perhaps the old rites play less of a role in our present day and age than acceptance of traditional ceremonies. But the ceremony still symbolizes the entering of a pact or contract that is to be taken seriously ; and indeed the ceremony itself and all the atmosphere of seriousness, fortified at times by legal and religious restrictions, help to insure, for most people, a certain degree of stability and permanence.

Our primary concern, though, extends further than permanence. We seek to know whether actual contentment and satisfactions exist in a more mature sense. . . .

*   *   *

Let us examine next the possible value of what is ordinarily called "marriage counseling." The field is primarily the domain of ministers, family physicians, lawyers and others not directly concerned with psychiatry. For one thing, a goodly number of people prefer to go to marriage counselors rather than to psychiatrists, and thus avoid the implication of neurosis or need for treatment. It is also easier for a person to identify himself with a group of people who have "marital difficulties" rather than an emotional illness or disturbance. Secondly, the marriage counselor is by his function more prepared to give advice and suggestions of an immediate and practical nature, and so to offer a kind of help that is often met with a comparable state of readiness in the client to accept it. In some instances that I have had the good fortune to study, an unexpected factor played a role in this state of readiness on the client's part and his submissiveness and trust in turning over the major responsibility to the counselor. The client then unconsciously acted out, according to the counselor's suggestions for improvement of the marital situation, utilizing the advice not so much as a rational plan but as a need to make what the counselor said come true.

In general, what has been said about courses and special books on marital relations may be said of counselors. People in trouble have a certain readiness to follow advice, and especially when this advice consists of information and results in increases in practical knowledge, marital situations have improved. At other times one observes that what happens as a result of advice and counseling is an increase in one neurotic partner's adaption to the other, along with an authorized diminution of the level of aspiration. Indeed this may well be what happens in many instances of marital adjustment that evolve from counseling, psychiatric treatment or the ageing process.

The matter of treatment as an aid toward improved marital relations remains to be considered. At the present time this seems to offer the best hope for the future, particularly with our increased psychiatric facilities and increasing skills of therapists in clinics and social work agencies. Nevertheless, even the excellent papers that have been written on psychiatric and psychoanalytic studies of marital difficulties provide little of any definite nature that can be used as a predictive tool. For one thing, the patient who quite willingly and readily goes into a treatment situation with the avowed intent of preserving or improving a marriage has of necessity to take some risk that the treatment might have the opposite result. Even when marital partners go into treatment with the deep conviction that they love each other and want to preserve their marriage, one or the other may come to a different conclusion; although it must be admitted on a clinical basis that in these instances the marital partners have a better chance of staying together.

As clinicians we are undoubtedly impressed with the successes we have had in helping people with their neurotic problems and thus, in turn, helping them with their marital situation. The sequence in the last statement is carefully chosen as the proper one, because logically we look at marital problems as being most likely a part of the process of neurotic interaction, so that a treatment approach should be directed toward helping a person solve his neurosis rather than his marital situation as such. And here the psychoanalytic approach offers most, while at the same time it has the disadvantage of being the most inaccessible of treatments. Hence, we must rely upon psychoanalytically oriented psychotherapy of one sort or another as the medium of choice. Yet, in any treatment, I have been impressed by the unanalyzed factors that continue to play a role even after many neurotic elements have apparently been more or less successfully treated. One of the best examples of this is the person who overcomes neurotic trends sufficiently to obtain a divorce and remarries in an undercurrent attitude of having to prove that the first marriage was a mistake and with the quiet but grim determination to make the second marriage succeed. And it frequently does.

As a final consideration I should like to comment on those accidental social influences that touch upon the psychic structure of individuals and probably have an important influence on marital relations. A realistic attitude is not necessarily a pessimistic one. External influences and realistic life situations do influence certain people in their marital lives. Good fortune and misfortune have both been accidental occurrences that have helped people mature and appreciate each other.

The question may very well be raised, in regard to the last statement, as to whether such episodes as the birth of children, success in work, prestige achieved one way or another, a misfortune which has a binding effect upon a married couple, are elements that make for real maturation, or whether these are simply the results of shifts in symptoms. The question is a valid one only for purposes of investigation and research. The fact is incontrovertible that such external forces have made sufficient changes in the internal economy so as to provide flexibility for adaptation of one neurotic partner to another.

In a similar vein one may remark that improved marriage and divorce laws and other social reforms may increase the possibilities for more felicitous marital relationships. At one extreme, as numerous examples show, the more restrictive and binding the marriage laws, the more will stringent divorce laws reflect an authoritative attitude that makes people bind themselves together in a family unit by command rather than by desire. The aggression that is manifested in divorce would not necessarily be successfully suppressed or diverted into more healthful channels, however. At the other extreme, it is true that experiences with more permissive marriage and divorce laws do show that in themselves they contribute to marital happiness by giving people a greater mobility and control over their own destinies. Such a trend is consistent with a proper setting for the functioning of mature attitudes. Yet the question can arise as to what limits have to be set even for so-called mature individuals. Obviously if social changes are to be affected that would make for a better atmosphere for marital felicity, they will have to be profound measures that take due cognizance of the complexity of interpersonal relationships.

C.

To Decisions Concerning the Reorganization of Wife-Husband Relationships—Grounds, Aggravations, or Mitigations?

1.

IN "INSANITY"

STATE v. BROWN
213 Ind. 118, 11 N.E. 2d 679 (1937)

TREANOR, C. J.—This is an appeal from a judgment . . . granting a divorce to plaintiff, Ruben C. Brown. The complaint of Ruben C. Brown . . . was for absolute divorce on the ground of incurable insanity, predicated upon Clause 8 of Chapter 87 of the Acts of 1935 which declares incurable insanity to be a cause for divorce.

The prosecuting attorney of Marion County by his deputy appeared and resisted the action pursuant to Section 3-1212 Burns Indiana Statutes 1933, section 916 Baldwin's 1934, which provides that "Whenever a petition for divorce remains undefended, it shall be the duty of the prosecuting attorney to appear and resist such petition."

The prosecuting attorney filed a demurrer to the complaint which was overruled. After the overruling of the demurrer a Guardian Ad Litem was appointed and upon the issues joined by the general denial filed by the Guardian Ad Litem and finding and judgment of the court were for the plaintiff "that he is entitled to a decree of divorce from said defendant on the grounds and cause of incurable insanity as alleged in plaintiff's complaint. . . . "

The prosecuting attorney filed a motion for a new trial. . . .

*   *   *

The complaint alleged and the evidence shows that Cora M. Brown was suffering from the disease of incurable insanity, and that she was admitted to the Central State Hospital for the Insane on the 17th day of November, 1926, and has been confined there as a patient for more than five years.

The pertinent provision of the statute regulating the granting of divorce is as follows:

"Divorces may be decreed upon the application of the injured party for the following causes, and no other:

*   *   *

"Eighth. Incurable insanity. No divorce shall be granted because of incurable insanity unless such insane person shall have been duly and regularly committed to and confined in a hospital or asylum for the insane, either in this state or in some other state or territory, for a period of at least five years next preceding the commencement of the action for divorce, nor unless it shall be made to appear to the court that such insanity is incurable. No action shall be maintained on the grounds of insanity unless the person applying for the divorce shall have been a resident of this state for a period of at least five years prior to the commencement of the action, nor shall a decree granted on the grounds of insanity relieve the successful party from contributing to the support and maintenance of the defendant."

The complaint alleges, in the very words of the statute, the facts which the statute purports to make a legal cause for divorce. Consequently if the General Assembly has the constitutional power to make incurable insanity a cause of divorce, the complaint states a cause of action, unless the attempted expression of this power is rendered ineffectual by defects in the manner and form of its expression. And appellant relies upon the latter since he makes no contention that the General Assembly does not have the power to make insanity a ground for divorce, but merely contends that the pertinent clause of the statute is "unconstitutional and void as it now stands."

Appellant urges that Clause 8 is invalid for the reason that it is "vague and indefinite"; and insists that the words "incurable insanity" have no definite and established meaning in law, and points out that there is no definition of the words in clause 8. It is true that there is no rule of law which purports to define "incurable insanity." The law, however, does recognize the reality of insanity as a mental state or condition, the existence of which is capable of being established by evidence, and attaches many legal consequences to the existence of this mental state. The existence of incurable insanity is a fact to be proved by whatever evidence the law recognizes as competent. It is essentially a matter of expert opinion, and since even expert opinion is not infallible, it may often turn out that the lawful trier of facts has erroneously determined the existence of incurable insanity. But a trier of facts might erroneously determine the existence of permanent disability or any other fact. The law accepts as realities those physical and mental conditions which authoritative medical science has determined to exist. When those who were conceded to know most about the subject believed that witchcraft was a reality, the law accepted witchcraft as a fact. Since medical science recognizes the existence of the mental condition of incurable insanity, and purports to determine its existence in particular cases, the law assumes that it is possible to establish the existence of "incurable insanity" as a fact. Consequently the words "incurable insanity" have a factual meaning which is definite and tangible enough for legislative or judicial cognizance. The law dreams of the absolute but must be content with the approximate and relative.

Appellant urges that one's becoming insane after marriage is not an injury to the other party to the marriage, but that at most results only in injury to the marital relation. And assuming the foregoing to be true, appellant contends that no one is entitled under the Act to assert the cause of action for divorce on the ground of insanity the other party since by the terms of the Act the right of action is given to an "injured party." It is true that as respects the other causes for divorce "the injured party" is presumed to suffer actual injury by the conduct which constitutes the cause for divorce. But the term "injured party" must be construed in such a way as to give effect to the obvious intent of the Act as a whole. Assuming that "incurable insanity" can be made a cause of divorce by legislative action, it follows that "injured party" must be construed to include a husband or wife who, by the plain terms of the act, is intended to have a right of action for divorce on the ground of incurable insanity.

We see no lack of definiteness in the phrase "duly and regularly committed to and confined in a hospital or asylum for the insane." "Duly and regularly committed" reasonably can mean only that the afflicted spouse must have been *committed* under legally recognized procedure; and we assume that the "hospital or asylum" must be an institution which under the law is authorized to accept insane persons for care and treatment.

Clause 8 contains the provision that a decree of divorce granted on the ground of insanity shall not "relieve the successful party from contributing to the support and maintenance of the defendant." And appellant contends that the foregoing is incomplete and unenforceable since there is no method provided to carry into effect the provision for support and maintenance. But there is no apparent need for an enforcing provision. The effect of the "support and maintenance" provision is to leave unimpaired the legal duty of the one securing a divorce under Clause 8 to support and maintain the divorced spouse; and such duty can be enforced on behalf of the insane person by whatever procedure would be available prior to the granting of the divorce.

We find no valid objection to Clause 8 on the ground of unreasonable and arbitrary classification. The basic fact of distinction is incurable insanity; and the requirements of committal to and confinement in a hospital or asylum for five years, as well as the five years' residence requirement of the plaintiff are merely restrictions on the right of the plaintiff

Prior to the adoption of our present Constitution the General Assembly possessed and exercised the power to grant divorces by special legislative enactments. The present Constitution forbids the General Assembly's granting a divorce by a special law, but places no specific limitation upon its power to declare the legal causes for divorce; and whatever limitation exists must be found in the general limitations on the power of the General Assembly. Since the General Assembly has specifically enumerated the legal causes for divorce, the courts are bound by such legislative expression and cannot increase or diminish the causes.

Prior to the General Assembly's inclusion of "incurable insanity" among the causes for divorce this court held that insanity was not a legal ground for divorce. The following is from the opinion in *Baker v. Baker*[1]:

"Insanity is no reason for dissolving the marriage. The statute does not make it one of the grounds for divorce, and surely no principle of justice or morality will justify the severance of the marital ties for any such cause. The judgment

---

1. (1882), 82 Ind. 146.

and conscience revolt at the thought that such a terrible affliction should be deemed cause for separating the wife from the husband. Divorces are granted not because of misfortune, but because of fault. It would be a barbarous code that would allow the wife to put aside the husband because stricken by such an awful calamity as the loss of reason."

We heartily concur with the sentiment of the foregoing and have no doubt that the law was correctly announced, since at that time there was no legislative sanction of insanity as a ground of divorce. But since the statute now expressly declares that incurable insanity is a cause for divorce, the holding and reasoning of the foregoing decision is no longer controlling. Courts are bound to declare the law to be that which the General Assembly, acting within its constitutional power, enacts, be it wise or foolish as measured by our personal views, and even though it shocks our sense of justice and fairness.

We conclude that the trial court did not err in overruling the demurrer to the plaintiff's complaint, and in overruling the motion for a new trial.

The judgment . . . is affirmed.

NOTES

NOTE 1.

BLEULER, EUGEN

Dementia Praecox or the Group of Schizophrenias*

Since schizophrenia may become stationary at any stage, continue to progress or develop acute symptoms, it is impossible to establish any definite, systematic outline of prognosis. Improvements even in chronic states are always theoretically possible. They can be expected inasmuch as even chronic excited states abate with time, but these abatements are usually accompanied by increased deterioration. Otherwise essential improvements of chronic states are rare and cannot be counted on. . . .

* * *

We certainly can exclude the possibility of improvement if a deteriorated patient's condition remains completely uniform and unaltered for some years, exhibiting no acute symptoms and not reacting to changes of treatment and/or environment. As long as the condition changes, extensive improvement cannot be excluded. . . .

* * *

---

* New York: International Universities Press, 1950, pp. 328-333. Reprinted with permission of the publisher.

Many writers have felt the need to be able to estimate the interval of time which must elapse beyond which improvement could no longer be expected. This problem pertains to legal matters, for instance questions of divorce. Various codes of law designate three years as the period of time beyond which a poorly developing case can be considered as practically incurable. However, improvements which may be considered as cures cannot be excluded from the realm of the possible even after several decades, even though it is quite rare. In Switzerland, where divorce for mental disease is rather frequent, I have acted as an expert witness in such matters. I have never had any unfortunate experience in using this time limit of three years. But I must admit that I have always had a very uncomfortable feeling with each case I declared to be incurable.

NOTE 2.

KATZ v. KATZ
191 Kan. 500, 382 P. 2d 331 (1963)

JACKSON, JUSTICE.

The majority of the court is of the opinion that the statute . . . means that the insane spouse must have been insane for a period of five years but that it is not necessary to show that the insane spouse has been a patient in any mental hospital or institution continuously for the five years. The statute would rather put the test upon the three physicians who must agree that the spouse is incurably insane.

We know that the Topeka State Hospital has not been filled to capacity for some time since many of its patients are allowed to live outside as "out patients." Under modern methods of treatment of mental illness, it would be a most severe case where the patient was confined during all of the first five years.

NOTE 3.

HAMAKER v. HAMAKER
18 Ill. 137 (1856)

SCATES, C. J. . . .

Now, insanity is not among the causes known to the common law, nor is it found among the new causes created and defined by our statute. . . . The pitiable misfortune of the defendant, who, for want of reason to guide her, appeared in the court below, and here, by a conservator, of the court's appointment, would hardly call upon us to make a precedent for casting her off from her only domestic stay and support. . . .

So far from presenting features appealing to our feelings of sympathy or sense of justice, for this kind of relief, it rather wears the aspect of brutal insensibility, to cast off the poor, unfortunate wife and unoffending mother. If there be a period during the marital relation, when, more than at any other, the tenderest care, support and watchfulness of an affectionate husband is demanded, it is while the wife is helpless from sickness or insanity. To make this misfortune, the greatest that can befall us, the ground of the next greatest wrong and injustice, would be truly adding insult and injury to providential misfortune. But where to put the unfeeling husband who would thrust his wife away, because she had become totally incapable of self-care, must be left to the dictates of Christian humanity.

The procreation and nurture of children being one of the objects of marriage, the law has provided that corporeal infirmity, or impotency, before marriage, shall be cause to dissolve it. This provision is made for a sound body, but none for the mind. If there be here incongruity, inconsistency, irrationality, we can only say, we do not make, but interpret and apply the rule.

NOTE 4.

MAYNARD v. HILL
125 U.S. 190, 203-206, 209-210 (1887)

MR. JUSTICE FIELD: . . . [W]as the act of the Legislative Assembly of the Territory of Oregon of the 22nd of December, 1852, declaring the bonds of matrimony between David S. Maynard and his wife dissolved, valid and effectual to divorce the parties. . . .

* * *

What were "rightful subjects of legislation" when these acts organizing the Territories were passed, is not to be settled by reference to the distinctions usually made between legislative acts and such as are judicial or administrative in their character, but by an examination of the subjects upon which legislatures had been in the practice of acting with the consent and approval of the people they represented. A long acquiescence in repeated acts of legislation on particular matters, is evidence that those matters have been generally considered by the people as properly within legislative control. Such acts are not to be set aside or treated as invalid, because upon a careful consideration of their character doubts may arise as to the competency of the legislature to pass them. Rights acquired, or obligations incurred under such legislation, are not to be impaired because of subsequent differences of opinion as to the department of government to which the acts are properly assignable. With special force does this observation apply, when the validity of acts dissolving the bonds of matrimony is assailed, the legiti-

macy of many children, the peace of many families, and the settlement of many estates depending upon its being sustained. It will be found from the history of legislation that, whilst a general separation has been observed between the different departments, so that no clear encroachment by one upon the province of the other has been sustained, the legislative department, when not restrained by constitutional provisions and a regard for certain fundamental rights of the citizen which are recognized in this country as the basis of all government, has acted upon everything within the range of civil government. . . . Every subject of interest to the community has come under its direction. It has not merely prescribed rules for future conduct, but has legalized past acts, corrected defects in proceedings, and determined the status, conditions, and relations of parties in the future.

Marriage, as creating the most important relation in life, as having more to do with the morals and civilization of a people than any other institution, has always been subject to the control of the legislature. That body prescribes the age at which parties may contract to marry, the procedure or form essential to constitute marriage, the duties and obligations it creates, its effects upon the property rights of both, present and prospective, and the acts which may constitute grounds for its dissolution.

It is conceded that to determine the propriety of dissolving the marriage relation may involve investigations of a judicial nature which can properly be conducted by the judicial tribunals. Yet such investigations are no more than those usually made when a change of the law is designed. They do not render the enactment, which follows the information obtained, void as a judicial act because it may recite the cause of its passage. Many causes may arise, physical, moral, and intellectual—such as the contracting by one of the parties of an incurable disease like leprosy, or confirmed insanity or hopeless idiocy, or a conviction of a felony—which would render the continuance of the marriage relation intolerable to the other party and productive of no possible benefit to society. When the object of the relation has been thus defeated, and no jurisdiction is vested in the judicial tribunals to grant a divorce, it is not perceived that any principle should prevent the legislature itself from interfering and putting an end to the relation in the interest of the parties as well as of society. If the act declaring the divorce should attempt to interfere with rights of property vested in either party, a different question would be presented.

* * *

. . . If the Assembly possessed the power to grant a divorce in any case, its jurisdiction to legislate upon his status, he being a resident of the Territory, is undoubted, unless the marriage was a contract within the prohibition of the federal Constitution against its impairment by legislation. . . .

The facts alleged in the bill of complaint, that no cause existed for the divorce, and that it was obtained without the knowledge of the wife, cannot affect the validity of the act. Knowledge or ignorance of parties of intended legislation does not affect its validity, if within the competency of the legislature. . . .

The organic act extends the legislative power of the Territory to all righful subjects of legislation "not inconsistent with the Constitution and laws of the United States." The only inconsistency suggested is, that it impairs the obligation of the contract of marriage. Assuming that the prohibition of the federal Constitution against the impairment of contracts by state legislation applies equally, as would seem to be the opinion of the Supreme Court of the Territory, to legislation by territorial legislatures, we are clear that marriage is not a contract within the meaning of the prohibition. . . .

NOTE 5.

SCOTT v. SCOTT
17 Ind. R. 309 (1861)

HANNA, J. . . .

We come to the question . . . [w]hether under the law declaring marriage a civil contract, 1 R.S. 1852, § 1, p. 361, a suit to annul such contract, or to dissolve the obligations thereby entered into, is now a mere action between the parties to such contract, the man and the woman, and governed by the usual and ordinary rules of procedure in civil suits.

We are not at liberty to consider the statute "declaratory of the law regulating marriages," . . . alone, but must also, in connection therewith, examine that "regulating the granting of divorces," 2 R.S. 233; the last section of which, p. 238, is, that "whenever a petition for divorce remains undefended, it shall be the duty of the prosecuting attorney to appear and resist such petition."

If the theory that the government has some interest in, and something to do with, the status of the citizen, does not prevail, we are not informed of the necessity of this latter statute. Where such a suit remains undefended, a government officer, one who stands as the representative of the government in bringing offenders against the criminal laws to justice, is thus commanded to resist such petition. Why is this? Is it not because persons not before the Court will be affected by its action in the premises? Is it not because public policy requires that government shall exercise some control in reference to this relation in life? If government can not, or should not, exercise this control, why pass laws at all to regulate marriage and divorce? Why not leave the husband, as of old, to write his wife a bill of divorcement and give it to her in her hand, and send her out of his house. Deut. XXIV, 1-4.

The marriage relation is more sacred; the obligations imposed thereby, it appears to us, somewhat different from those resting upon parties in a mere contract for the purchase of a mule or hog.

2.
IN DESERTION AND VOLUNTARY SEPARATION

a.
LANG v. LANG
[1955] A.C. 402

The parties were married in South Australia on November 8, 1924. On October 29, 1951, the wife presented a petition to the Supreme Court of Victoria praying for a divorce on the ground that her husband had without just cause or excuse wilfully deserted her and had continued in desertion for three years and upwards.

The appellant denied that he had been guilty of constructive desertion.

LORD PORTER, J.

The following are the provisions of the Marriage Act, 1928 (No. 3726) of the State of Victoria which govern the relevant transactions: "(75) Any married person who at the time of the institution of the suit has been domiciled in Victoria for two years and upwards, may present a petition to the court praying on one or more of the grounds in this section mentioned that his or her marriage with the respondent may be dissolved—(a) on the ground that the respondent has without just cause or excuse wilfully deserted the petitioner and without any such cause or excuse left him or her continuously so deserted during three years and upwards . . . If in the opinion of the court the petitioner's own habits or conduct induced or contributed to the wrong complained of . . . such petition may be dismissed."

* * *

If cruelty had been a sufficient ground for divorce in the State of Victoria, then assuming, as seems to their Lordships very probable, that the wife's health suffered from the treatment she received, the case would have presented no complications. As it is, the wife, who had been brutally ill-used and insulted over a long period, since she was the first to leave the matrimonial home, had to found her petition on desertion; and in order to succeed had to establish what is described as "constructive desertion."

. . . Both in England and in Australia, to establish desertion two things must be proved: first, certain outward and visible conduct—the "factum" of desertion; secondly, the "animus deserendi"—the intention underlying this conduct to bring the matrimonial union to an end.

In ordinary desertion the factum is simple: it is the act of the absconding party in leaving the matrimonial home. The contest in such a case will be almost entirely as to the "animus." Was the intention of the party leaving the home to break it up for good, or something short of, or different from that?

Since 1860 in England, and for a long time in Australia, it has been recognized that the party truly guilty of disrupting the home is not necessarily or in all cases the party who first leaves it. The party who stays behind (their Lordships will assume this to be the husband) may be by reason of conduct on his part making it unbearable for a wife with reasonable self-respect, or powers of endurance, to stay with him, so that he is the party really responsible for the breakdown of the marriage. He has deserted her by expelling her: by driving her out. In such a case the factum is the course of conduct pursued by the husband—something which may be far more complicated than the mere act of leaving the matrimonial home. It is not every course of conduct by the husband causing the wife to leave which is a sufficient factum. A husband's irritating habits may so get on the wife's nerves that she leaves as a direct consequence of them, but she would not be justified in doing so. Such irritating idiosyncrasies are part of the lottery in which every spouse engages on marrying, and taking the partner of the marriage "for better, for worse." The course of conduct—the "factum" —must be grave and convincing.

In the present case there is not the slightest question that the "factum" is sufficient. . . .

The whole and sole question is whether the wife has proved the necessary animus or intent on the part of the husband. How should that animus be ascertained? In particular, (1) is it enough for her to show a course of conduct on the part of the husband which in the eyes of a reasonable man would, by making her life insufferable, be calculated to drive the wife out, the husband's actual intention being immaterial on the footing that every man is presumed to intend

the natural and probable consequences of his acts? Or (2) should the objective criterion of the reasonable man's reactions be rejected on the footing that the real question is, did this particular husband (who may not have been reasonable) know that his conduct, if persisted in, would in all human probability result in the wife's departure—it being remembered that it is possible (human nature being what it is) for such knowledge on the husband's part to co-exist with a desire that she should stay, since people often desire a thing but deliberately act in a way which makes that desire unrealizable. Or again (3), should inferences which would naturally be drawn be wholly disregarded and an intention which would naturally be drawn from the husband's conduct negatived provided there is proved to exist, de facto, on his part a genuine desire (however illogical or impossible it may be to square such a desire with his conduct) that the matrimonial union should continue? On this view the husband's desire to maintain the home is conclusive whatever his conduct. All three of these views have found expression in the decided cases.

*   *   *

. . . "Caveman stuff" is not an unfair description for the treatment he had been applying to his wife for years past and which had twice caused her to leave him. However, on August 13, he planned and carried out what he referred to as the "rape of Lucrece"; in the words of the trial judge's finding he "forced sexual intercourse" on her in circumstances of "calculated and revolting indignity": and told her that he was going to "use her for the same purpose whenever he wanted to and as often as he wanted to." These last words are important. She then finally left and filed her petition, ignoring a number of letters which he wrote begging her to return but not expressing any intention to treat her differently if she did. Her patience was not unnaturally exhausted, and even if he had expressed penitential sentiments it would not have been unreasonable for the wife to doubt their sincerity.

*   *   *

In the present case the existence of conduct by the husband being of sufficient gravity to constitute the necessary factum, the question is what he intended, or must be taken to have intended, while so conducting himself. Did he intend to bring the matrimonial relations to an end? Let it be supposed that a husband intentionally persists in conduct which the hypothetical reasonable man would think calculated to cause the wife to leave him; is he necessarily guilty of constructive desertion, notwithstanding that he genuinely desires the marriage to survive? If so, evidence of his consistently expressed desire that the wife should stay with him is irrelevant and inadmissible. The formula, if satisfied, creates an irrebuttable presumption.

* * *

The other view is that no matter how reprehensible has been the husband's behaviour, if there is positive and credible evidence negativing any actual intention on his part to end the marriage, the law wll not impute such an intention to him.

The difference between the two views is . . . what meaning is to be attached to the word "intention" and what evidence is sufficient to rebut a prima facie case.

Prima facie, a man who treats his wife with gross brutality may be presumed to intend the consequence of his acts. Such an inference may indeed be rebutted, but if the only evidence is of continuous cruelty and no rebutting evidence is given, the natural and almost inevitable inference is that the husband intended to drive out the wife. The court is at least entitled and, indeed, driven to such an inference unless convincing evidence to the contrary is adduced. In their Lordships' opinion this is the proper approach to the problem, and it must therefore be determined whether the natural inference has been rebutted in the present case.

* * *

The fact that the question at issue involves a consideration of the effect of the actions of one person upon another adds to the complexities of the case. But, apart from this, the distinction between intention and desire has to be borne in mind. A man may wish one thing and intend another—"Video meliora proboque, Deteriora sequor"—and, indeed, as the High Court have pointed out, a man's intention does not necessarily always remain constant but fluctuates from time to time. Nevertheless, some general principle must be sought and adopted.

But before the question of the rebutting evidence is reached it has first to be determined what is the exact connotation of the word "intention" . . . .

* * *

Their Lordships . . . question whether as a matter of strict terminology a man can be said to entertain conflicting "intentions." A man may well have incompatible desires. He may have an intention which conflicts with a desire: i.e., he may will one thing, and wish another, as when he renounces some cherished article of diet in the interest of health. But "intention" necessarily connotes an element of volition: desire does not. Desires and wishes can exist without any element contributed by the will. What, then, is the legal result where an intention to bring about a particular result (be it proved directly or by inference from conduct) co-exists with a desire that the result should not ensure? That is the substantial point raised by this appeal. The issue may be put more concretely. What legal inference is to be drawn where the whole of a husband's conduct is such that a reasonable man would know—that the particular husband must know—that in all human probability it will result in the departure of the wife from the matrimonial home? Apart from rebutting evidence this, in their Lordships' opinion, is sufficient proof of an intention to disrupt the home: but suppose, further, a husband's hope is that in some way his actions will not produce these natural consequences, that the wife will stay and that the home will not be disrupted. Where a man's own actions are concerned and not their effect on another, the answer is easy. If he desires to resist temptation but yields to it his intention is evidenced by his acts. His better self is, it may be, overborne, yet in the end his intention is to yield. Where, however, the effect of his actions upon other people is concerned and there is no certainty but only a high degree of probability as to what the result will be, is a court to say that if he did entertain an unjustified hope that his wife would stay, the intention normally to be inferred from his acts is rebutted, and is the correct conclusion that he did not intend to drive her out? In their Lordships' opinion no such conclusion is justified. If the husband knows the probable result of his acts and persists in them, in spite of warning that the wife will be compelled to leave the home, and indeed, as in the present case, has expressed an intention of continuing his conduct and never indicated any intention of amendment, that is enough however passionately he may desire or request that she should remain. His intention is to act as he did, whatever the consequences, though he may hope and desire that they will not produce their probable effect.

To say that it is not enough unless he knows that separation must inevitably result from his actions is to ask too much. Men's actions and judgments are not founded upon certainty—in most cases certainty is unascertainable—but on probabilities. No doubt a high degree of probability is required, but no more.

With these considerations in mind, can it be said that the appellant has rebutted the natural inference, which would be drawn from his acts if no countervailing testimony was given? In their Lordships' opinion no sufficient ground has been given for rejecting the finding of the High Court.

It is true that Lowe J. founded his judgment upon the wording . . . in which one of the tests is expressed to be an intention to persist in a course of conduct which any reasonable person would regard as calculated to bring the matrimonial relationship to an end, and in their Lordships' view this is too objective a requirement. But the High Court took a more subjective standard after examining the evidence as a whole. They found, and, as their Lordships think, were entitled to find, that the appellant must have known that what he was doing would necessitate her withdrawal if she acted as any reasonable creature would. Such a finding, if warranted, is in their Lordships' opinion decisive of the case, and in spite of Lowe J.'s reliance upon what may be regarded as a purely objective test there is in their view ample ground for coming to the conclusion that the appellant must have recognized the gravity of the effect of his behaviour though he hoped and desired that it might not have its natural result.

*   *   *

[F]or the reasons they have indicated their Lordships will humbly advise Her Majesty to dismiss the appeal. . . .

b.   LLOYD v. LLOYD
            204 Md. 352, 104 A. 2d 595 (1954)

BRUNE, CHIEF JUDGE.

In this case, a husband brought suit for an absolute divorce on the ground of voluntary separation; his wife admitted the separation but denied that it was voluntary. From the dismissal of his bill of complaint, the husband appeals. The pertinent statutory provision is Code 1951, Article 16 §33, which authorizes an equity court to grant a divorce *a vinculo matrimonii* "when the husband and wife shall have voluntarily lived separate and apart, without any cohabitation, for three consecutive years prior to the filing of the bill of complaint, and such separation is beyond any reasonable expectation of reconciliation".

Appellant married appellee on July 5, 1944, at Hanover, Pennsylvania, and they spent a brief honeymoon at Starner's Dam in Carroll County, Maryland. After appellant returned to his duties in the wartime service of his country, appellee resided at her parents' home in Hanover, where appellant visited her whenever he had a leave. However, she and the appellant were able to live together for a few months first in Philadelphia, then in New London, Connecticut, and later in California. A son was born July 21, 1946. Shortly after appellant's discharge from the armed forces in November, 1947, they purchased a house . . . at Littlestown, Pennsylvania.

The wife's health, good until pregnancy, had become impaired after the birth of the child. Her condition was diagnosed, early in 1948, as multiple sclerosis. This progressive disease so handicapped her in the performance of her normal household duties that by the fall of 1949 the husband, who was attending Gettysburg College in the morning and working at the Cambridge Rubber Company at night, had to perform an increasing number of household duties. Appellee's mother came, one day a week, from Hanover to do the cleaning.

Appellee then suggested that they sell the Littlestown house and move to Hanover. This the husband declined to do. On October 21, 1949, the wife and child were taken, at her request, by her parents to their home in Hanover, where they have remained ever since.

The Chancellor has ably summarized the conflicting versions of the events leading up to the separation. First, we quote below from his summary of the husband's version: "After living there for several months, the wife became dissatisfied and wanted to sell the property and buy one in Hanover. Properties were scarce and prices were high, and he did nothing. They stayed at the Littlestown home against her wishes. He claimed that his mother-in-law interfered in every possible way because she resented him very much; that she would upset his wife and then he and his wife would have 'verbal battles.' He then testified that in October, 1949, his wife felt they 'couldn't get along' and that she would take the child and go to her parents' home. He refused to take her, and one day when he came from College he found she had gone with the baby. He learned that his father-in-law, accompanied by William Bair, had removed some furniture, including the furniture from the child's room, and all of their clothing. He objected to taking his wife to visit her mother because of the mother's interference and because she was instilling in her daughter belief in voodoo or witchcraft."

"[The husband's mother] testified she visited her son's home and that she could plainly see that her visits were displeasing to the defendant, that the wife was very much dissatisfied and wanted to go to her mother. While her son treated his wife very nice, she would nag him and she heard her curse him on several occasions."

Of the other side of the case, the Chancellor said (in part): "Mrs. Mary Berwager, the mother of the defendant [appellee] testified that her daughter * * * has multiple sclerosis and was unable to do her work and look after the child. * * * On October 21, 1949, the defendant said to her father, 'Dad, can Jim [the child] and I come home.' The father answered affirmatively and her daughter and grandson came to her home. At that time her daughter could not walk alone and could not feed herself. She is now bedfast and has been so for three years. * * * The defendant could not appear in Court, and by agreement of counsel her testimony was taken at Hanover, Pennsylvania. The reporter stated, 'It was necessary to use an interpreter (Mrs. Mary Berwager), because of the inability of the witness (the defendant) to enunciate properly.' She said she left her home in October, 1949, when she could no longer do her work. When asked if she wanted to leave her husband she said 'no' and her reply was 'no' to the question 'Did you want him to leave you?'"

* * *

No "reconciliation" (if such a term is appropriate on the facts of such a case as this) has ever been sought by either of the parties ; there has been no cohabitation for over three years, and, as the Chancellor found, "from the physical condition of the wife, it is apparent they will not live together again."

There is no question as to the existence or seriousness of the affliction from which the wife was suffering. Undoubtedly, some of the irritations and friction testified to in the case were attributable to the nature and effects of multiple sclerosis, as it is described in Alpers, Clinical Neurology (2nd Ed.) 673, 674, 687. This neurological disease, the cause of which is unknown, appears most frequently in individuals between the ages of nineteen and thirty, and is sometimes precipitated by pregnancy and childbirth. The author states that: "Emotional disturbances of some sort are usually present. Liability of emotional responses, with inability or decreased ability to inhibit emotional reactions, is probably the most common manifestation. These affective disorders are part and parcel of the disease, are very frequent, and in a fair number of instances they precede the neurological signs."

The quoted language may, in some measure, explain testimony of appellant's mother that appellee was "very nervous" since marriage, on occasions lost her temper, and argued with, "cursed," and "said nasty things" to appellant. Some light may also be shed upon the "crying spells" to which appellant testified.

It seems clear, on the other hand, that during the parties' residence at Littlestown the husband was doing all that could reasonably have been asked of him in caring for his wife and child and in helping to keep the household going. This he did in spite of the fact that outside of his college hours he was employed on an eight-hour night shift—from 11:30 p.m. to 7:30 a.m. daily.

The evidence, we think, supports the Chancellor's finding that the separation of the parties was not, at the outset, voluntary within the meaning of our divorce statute.

Although the testimony was somewhat conflicting as to the extent of the wife's disability in October, 1949, immediately prior to the separation, it is clear that it was serious and that she was unable to care adequately for herself and the child.

All of these facts faced the Chancellor in determining whether there was a voluntary separation. "The word 'voluntary' signifies willingness. When used in reference to an act of an individual, it means that he acted of his own free will ; when used in reference to a common act of two or more persons affecting their common relationship, it means that they acted in willing concert in the doing of the act." Kline v. Kline . . . 16 A. 2d 924, 926. . . .

This Court has declared, "Unless the parties agree to live apart the separation cannot be voluntary. It would hardly be contended that if one spouse is confined in a hospital as a helpless invalid that the separation is voluntary." France v. Safe Deposit & Trust Co., supra . . . 4 A. 2d at page 726. This principle would seem to govern the case at bar. The evidence, we think, was ample to support the Chancellor's finding that the wife "left home because she was physically unable to do her work and she needed help." His further conclusion that "It was not unreasonable that she would go to her mother" seems obviously sound—particularly in view of the husband's reported refusal, on the ground of expense, to hire a woman to do the cooking and cleaning.

It may also be noted that the husband had declined shortly before the separation to take the wife to her parents' home, and her actual departure was without his knowledge or consent at the time when she left Littlestown.

This Court has, however, repeatedly indicated that a separation which was involuntary when it first occurred, may later become voluntary. * * * It therefore is necessary to consider whether the separation did become voluntary at some time after its inception.

To support his contention that it did, the appellant relies on three things: (1) the fact that the wife took some household furnishings and appliances to her parents' home, agreed to the sale of others and of the home and accepted part of the proceeds of sale thereof ; (2) that her attorney at Hanover indicated that she was perfectly agreed to a divorce if the appellant would give her $4,000 in cash ; and (3) that on January 19, 1950, the appellee said to the appellant, "So far as I am concerned, we are through."

All of these matters were, of course, before the Chancellor, as were the wife's statements denying that she wished the separation, which were transcribed by the court reporter as "translated" by her mother. The appellant himself testified before the Court below.

As to the first, the physical condition of the wife would seem to have left her no such choice as to constitute an election ; and as to the second, the statement attributed to the wife's Hanover counsel would show a willingness to consent to a divorce upon a condition which was not met, not an existing mutual agreement to live separate and apart. . . .

The third point—the wife's statement testified to by the husband that so far as she was concerned "we are through"—was, of course, before the Chancellor, and this testimony was set forth in his opinion. Weighing this testimony, and any inferences to be drawn from it, and the plaintiff's other testimony against the wife's denial of the voluntary nature of the separation and the testimony relating to the illness which caused her to seek help at the home of her parents and which since then has grown progressively worse, the Chancellor held that a voluntary separation—that is, a separation based upon a mutual agreement—had not been shown. Even the realization by both husband and wife that their separation is final—and the wife's statement in this case may have meant no more than such a realization on her part—does not of itself establish an agreement that they shall live apart. . . . We do not think that the evidence is such as to warrant us in overturning the finding that "there was no voluntary separation entered into in October, 1949, or at any time thereafter."

It is strenuously urged on behalf of the appellant that no possible harm could come to anyone from the granting of a decree in this case—that the denial of a divorce would be of little value to the wife and would leave the husband under a restriction which serves no useful purpose. It is perfectly apparent from the record that the case is a pitiful one viewed from the point of view of either spouse. However, these considerations do not enlarge the causes for which the Legislature has authorized the courts to grant divorces. It was held in Smith v. Smith, 198 Md. 630, 84 A. 2d 890, that a divorce could not be granted simply because it would be beneficial to the parties. If benefit to the parties is not sufficient to support the granting of a divorce, certainly the absence of harm is not.

For the reasons above stated, the decree must be affirmed.

NOTES

NOTE 1.

LLOYD v. LLOYD
Seven Years Later

(a) The parties to this action have never been divorced, at least so far as Mrs. Lloyd has been able to determine. She has never been served with divorce papers or notices of any kind from any jurisdiction after the above action was dismissed, and so their present status would be that of husband and wife. Mrs. Lloyd has had, and still has, custody of their child, James.

Mrs. Lloyd is still bedridden with multiple sclerosis and in very poor condition. [Letter dated March 11, 1961 from Robert B. Frey, counsel for Mrs. Lloyd.]

(b) The situation still remains precisely the same as it was when the above case was decided in 1954. Mr. Lloyd advises me as follows : "We have not seen or contacted each other in any way. I can see no chance that we will, and I knew that 10 years ago. The law apparently doesn't always contribute to the well-being and happiness of people." He is of course still contributing toward the support of the child.

I maintain that the wife's acquiescence in the situation constituted at least a tacit agreement on her part to live separate and apart, and should have entitled the plaintiff in this case to a divorce on the ground of voluntary separation. [Letter dated March 21, 1961 from John Wood, counsel for Mr. Lloyd.]

NOTE 2.

MATYSEK v. MATYSEK
212 Md. 44, 128 A. 2d 627 (1957)

BRUNE, CHIEF JUDGE.

This is a divorce case in which the wife (appellee) was granted an absolute divorce on the ground that the parties had voluntarily lived separate and apart, without cohabitation, for a period of more than three years prior to the filing of the bill and that the separation was beyond any reasonable expectation of reconciliation. Code 1951, Article 16, Sec. 33, clause fifth. The husband admitted the fact and duration of the separation and the absence of cohabitation ; but resisted the suit on three grounds : (1) he denied that the separation was voluntary, asserting that it was not by mutual agreement ; . . . The Chancellor found against him on the facts. . . .

On the question of voluntary separation, the evidence, . . . was to this effect : that the husband drank quite frequently ; that he had humiliated his wife on a number of occasions; that he had repeatedly told her that she was "no good" and to "get out"; that following an argument he again made such statements to the wife at her mother's house on the night of July 25, 1952; that in response to his demand then made that she "get out,", she said "All right"; and that early on the next morning she did get out and went to her mother's home. . . .

The cases in this Court are uniform in holding that a voluntary separation as a ground for divorce under our statute imports a mutual agreement to live separate and apart. * * *

None of the . . . cases . . . holds that a voluntary agreement to live separate and apart must be arrived at either with calmness and courtesy or without anger. Courtesy certainly, and calmness probably, were lacking in the instant case, and in all likelihood anger was present. We think that a mutual agreement may be reached under such circumstances. The case which most nearly approaches the present case in the general tone of language used seems to be Miller v. Miller [11 A. 2d 630]. There the husband had threatened to leave the wife (for a reason which this Court found to be insufficient), and then replied "Well if you want to go, go on and go, but you are going to have to take care of these children." The husband claimed that this amounted to a voluntary agreement to separate. His contention was rejected because the wife's statement amounted merely to acquiescence in what she could not prevent. That was not the situation in the present case. The husband demanded that the wife leave. She could have refused. Instead, she agreed and she did leave.

We think that the language and conduct of the parties on the night of July 25th and the early morning of July 26th were sufficient to support the Chancellor's explicit finding that the separation was voluntary. At the conclusion of the testimony he said: "I think these people separated voluntarily. They were glad to get away from each other." . . .

NOTE 3.

MATYSEK v. MATYSEK
Four Years Later

I am informed that the wife did remarry. To the best of my knowledge, the husband did not.

I do not know whether or not you gleaned from the case that the wife, immediately after the separation from the husband, began living with and continued to live with another man by whom she had two children. This is the man whom she married after the divorce. [Letter dated Feb. 17, 1961 from Morton H. Perry, attorney for Mrs. Matysek.]

NOTE 4

WALKER v. WALKER
140 Miss. 340, 105 So. 753 (1925)

McGOWEN, J., delivered the opinion of the court:

C. C. Walker filed his bill for divorce against his wife, Mrs. Wincie Ann Walker, alleged as grounds for divorce that the defendant deserted her home on the 2nd day of June, 1921, and that the desertion constituted willful, continued, and obstinate desertion, for the space of and term of more than two years' time immediately before the filing of the bill.

* * *

Mrs. Walker . . . charged complainant with being to blame, with having driven her from home; and she filed a cross-bill with her answer, charging the defendant with habitually cruel and inhuman treatment, specifying in many particulars. She further charged that, actuated by his desire to rid himself of her, he (the cross-defendant) had instituted insanity proceedings, hired skilled physicians and alienists, and sought to have her committed to an insane asylum, but that upon the first hearing she was adjudged sane; that in the early part of 1921 she became a victim of influenza, and that her husband, complainant, did not summon a physician. She stated, further, that in April she had received $1,250, and charged that her husband attempted to acquire this money from her, and that he instituted a second insanity proceeding against her; that instead, as claimed in the bill of cross-complainant, of willfully and obstinately absenting herself from him, she was in truth and in fact by order of the chancery court decreed to be insane and placed under the custody of her brother, John Stringfellow, as a result of her husband's wicked design to get rid of her and squander her estate. . . .

* * *

. . . The records as to the insanity proceedings offered in evidence disclosed that a decree confirming the chancery clerk's judgment upon verdict of a jury that Mrs. Walker was insane but not dangerous and should not be confined in an asylum, and that she was committed to the care of her brother, John Stringfellow, was entered on June 21, 1922. . . .

On August 11, 1923, the same chancellor entered an order declaring Mrs. Walker had been restored to reason and discharged from the custody of her brother, John Stringfellow. On August 18, 1923, the complainant, the husband, filed the bill in this case.

* * *

It is assigned as error that defendant could not be held responsible for her conduct during the period in which she was declared and adjudicated to be insane.

Divorce is not a matter of right but is a matter of grace from the state and in this case it clearly appears that Mrs. Walker was adjudicated insane, and that this adjudication was procured by her husband, who had alienists, Dr. Buchanan, Dr. Gilbert, and others, to make examination preliminary to the trial of the insanity proceedings, and that within one week after the court entered a decree adjudicating that she was restored to reason he filed his bill for divorce.

If the defendant is to be charged with responsibility for remaining away from her husband's bed and board from the time she was committed by the decree to the care of her brother, John Stringfellow, to wit, from the date of the decree of the clerk, later confirmed by the chancellor on June 21, 1922, until August 11, 1923, then the bill in this case is sustained, and the decree granted by the chancellor dissolving the bonds of matrimony is proper.

* * *

After a careful study of this record, we have reached the conclusion that the decree of divorce in this case should not be permitted to stand against the defendant, for the reason that, as to the desertion, the major portion of the time the defendant was, by decree of the chancery court, insane; therefore not capable during that period of willfully and obstinately doing an act. . . .

Section 170, 19 C. J. p. 76, reads as follows: "The insanity of a spouse, if it existed at the time of the commission of a matrimonial offense, is a defense to an action for divorce, whether the offense is cruelty, abandonment, or desertion, non-support, or by the weight of authority, adultery, although there is some authority for the doctrine that the adultery of a wife is not excused by insanity. But a divorce may be obtained for acts happening prior to insanity, notwithstanding the subsequent insanity. Where, as in some states, voluntary separation for a specified period is a ground for divorce, the insanity of one of the spouses during the period of separation will preclude the granting of a divorce."

* * *

In the case at bar, the husband seeking the divorce from his wife fixes the time within the period within which the offending wife was decreed to be insane, or so immediately before as to make it reasonably certain that the act was the result of insanity, and not an habitually cruel and inhuman act of a sane person, and likewise that it was not the willful and obstinate act of a sane person.

Conceding then that the facts set out constitute habitually cruel and inhuman treatment in view of the statements above, we must say that the court below erred in awarding a divorce in this cause.

NOTE 5.

STEPHENSON v. STEPHENSON
191 A. 2d 248 (D.C. Ct. App. 1963)

MYERS, ASSOCIATE JUDGE: . . .

The admissions of both counsel at the end of the trial that neither party objected to the other's obtaining a divorce on the ground of desertion did not lend strength to the proof of either side. It was apparently of little importance to the parties which one prevailed, but willingness of the parties to have the bonds of matrimony severed is not a substitute for the evidentiary showing required to establish the statutory grounds upon which a judgment must rest. Though neither the husband nor the wife had any desire to further live together in a marital relationship, dissolution of their marriage must be accomplished upon proper statutory grounds. The much-quoted phrase that the 1935 amendments to the Code were designed to permit "termination in law of certain marriages which have ceased to exist in fact" was not intended to enunciate a lessened standard of proof required to sustain a divorce on one of the statutory grounds.

We cannot say that the trial judge was manifestly wrong in ruling that neither party had proved that the other was the deserting spouse or that he was required to reach a decision favoring one side or the other.

NOTE 6.

FOSTER, HENRY H., JR.
Common Law Divorce*

[A] most interesting and extreme example of extra-legal divorce is the practice which has been observed in some counties of Georgia. When Negro couples obtain a marriage license, the application is filed in a "shoehole" or box. If they have a falling out, one or both appear before the clerk and the old application is refiled in another "shoehole" or box, and thereafter a new marriage license may be issued to one or both. In addition, there have been instances where clerks or persons at the courthouse tear up the old marriage application and tell disgruntled and naive spouses that such constitutes a divorce and that they are free to remarry.

* 46 MINN. L. REV. 1961 (pp. 43, 60-61).

Another curious custom which is said to have existed at one time among American Negroes is that of "jumping over a broom." The initial "jumping" signified a marriage of the couple, and if they later decided to call it quits, each jumped backwards over the broom. This reversal of ceremony is interesting because it is analogous to the Roman *diffarreatio* which was the reverse ceremony for *confarreatio* or the religious ceremony of marriage.

NOTE 7.

BARWICK, SIR GARFIELD
Parramatta—Attorney-General

Matrimonial Causes Bill 1959—Second Reading*

There remains for mention a ground upon which there may centre a good deal of attention and discussion. It is ground (m) of clause 27, with which must be read clause 33. I shall read the principal parts of these clauses—

> (m) that, since the marriage, the parties to the marriage have been separated (whether by agreement, decree or otherwise) for a continuous period of not less than five years immediately preceding the date of the petition and there is no reasonable likelihood of cohabitation being resumed.

*   *   *

Mr. Speaker, I mentioned, in opening, that the Government has utilized the concept that there is a public interest in allowing dissolution where the parties, perhaps without matrimonial offence on the part of either, were, and have for years been, separated with no prospect of any reconciliation. This ground (m) is the result of that course ; not requiring a matrimonial offence to have been committed, nor regarding the commission of such an offence as necessarily preventing relief to the wrong-doing party. . . .

Here, the public interest in family life comes down on the side of allowing each of these separated parties to regularize their relationships or to assume regular relationships in the future. On this view, no sense is seen, in the public interest, in denying the possibility of family life to each when all is irretrievably lost between them. No sense is seen in possibly condemning either or both of them to irregular relationships which, in honour, cannot result in families. Nor is the existing capacity of an innocent party to withhold dissolution indefinitely seen as necessarily just or conformable to the public interest.

---

* Australia Parl. Deb. (Hansard) Vol. H. of R. 23 (New Series), 1959 (p. 2231).

3.

IN ADULTERY, INDIGNITY, AND INCOMPATIBILITY

a.   ANONYMOUS v. ANONYMOUS
         37 Misc. 2d 773, 236 N.Y.S. 2d 288 (1962)

BERNARD S. MEYER, JUSTICE. Involved in this divorce action is the question under what circumstances does the mental condition of an erring spouse constitute a defense. Though New York defines by statute the standard governing responsibility for criminal conduct (Penal Law, § 1120) and establishes a wholly different measure for determining when a mentally ill person may be hospitalized (Mental Hygiene Law, § 2[8]), it has enacted no statute fixing criteria for responsibility for conduct in violation of marital obligations. New York case law has recognized that an insane wife is incapable of abandoning her husband . . . and refused a divorce to a husband whose wife committed adultery while suffering from dementia praecox. . . . Some of those cases emphasize the marital obligation to provide support, including medical assistance, to an afflicted spouse ; in none was it necessary to consider the degree of affliction that would excuse infidelity.

Should the standard be that advanced in M'Naghten's Case, 10 Cl. & F. 200, and now embodied in Penal Law, § 1120: ability to distinguish right from wrong or to understand the nature and quality of the act? . . . Or should the criteria of responsibility be that suggested as a revision of the criminal rule in Durham v. United States, 94 U.S.App.D.C. 228, 214 F. 2d 862, . . . under which the defense is established by showing (a) a mental disease or defect, and (b) that the act in question was the product or result of the disease or defect ; that is—that the defendant would not have committed the act if he had not been diseased as he was. . . . New Jersey's test of ability to exercise a rational judgment at the time the adultery was committed . . . appears to fit in the latter category, and the statement in the Laudo case . . . that penalty should not be imposed "upon one who is a victim of conditions beyond her control, and not a *willing, rational actor*" (188 App. Div. p. 704, 177 N.Y.S. p. 399, emphasis supplied) suggests the Durham-Carter rule. While at first blush the conclusion of the American Bar Foundation's study of "The Mentally Disabled and the Law" appears contrary to use of Durham-Carter standards in matrimonial cases, its suggestion (at p. 203) that "serious thought should be given to the use [in divorce cases] of standards defining civil hospitalization" of necessity refers only to the presence of a mental disease or defect and is not understood as excluding causal relationship in matrimonial cases, although causal connection has no bearing on civil hospitalization.

* * *

The burden of proving mental condition relieving defendant of responsibility is on defendant. . . . Her sanity is presumed and the presumption must be overcome by a contrary showing. . . . To overcome the presumption defendant offered the testimony of her psychiatrist and the record of her hospitalization at Meadowbrook a few days after the incident which is the basis of this action. The psychiatrist testified that defendant had been under his care since September 1960; that she was even now highly unstable; that he had first diagnosed her as a character disorder, but later concluded that she was schizophrenic, affective type; that when hospitalized at Meadowbrook she was quite irrational and talking of destroying herself, but that he felt that committing her to Pilgrim State would destroy her ability for re-integration and, therefore, took her back as a private case; that in his opinion it was best for her to be working and that she, therefore, has been attending speedwriting classes since shortly after she left Meadowbrook Hospital; that after the incident he had asked her indirectly if she had committed adultery since and she had evaded the question; that prior to the incident she was aware that she was being followed since plaintiff had told her in the presence of the psychiatrist that as a result of prior infidelities he intended to have her followed; that defendant had discussed the rendezvous with the witness three days before it occurred and told him that she had sought to dissuade her paramour from going through with it and had told the paramour that he might be involved in a lawsuit; that defendant nonetheless felt compelled to go ahead with the meeting; that she was motivated by emotionality rather than rational thinking and felt justified in what she was going to do; that she was unable to determine that it was a wrong act; that it was for her primarily a means of getting even with her father, and to a lesser degree with plaintiff, both of whom considered her a "bad" person; that in his opinion she was unable to control her actions and in poor contact with reality at the time of the incident, and was then unable to distinguish the true nature of the act she was committing or to differentiate right from wrong; that although she knew vaguely that what she was doing was contrary to law and social conventions, she was not aware of the legal or social consequences; that when she had sufficient health, she would not engage in extra-marital relations and because she got as far into the act as plaintiff's proof of the incident

showed, he concluded that she was no longer capable of making a decision concerning it. The hospital record shows an initial impression of schizophrenic reaction, affective type, chronic, severe, but this was changed a few days later to character disorder. There is a notation that "she is quite aggressive sexually" and the nurse's notes of January 28, 1962 detail incidents in the ward which, apparently, form the basis for that conclusion, including overtures of a homosexual nature.

On the other side of the scale is the testimony of plaintiff's psychiatrist that in his opinion while defendant has had psychiatric difficulty and was emotionally unstable and in need of treatment, she was sufficiently intact to be able to use the ordinary standards of right and wrong; that she behaved in a manner which indicated that she was aware of those factors; that she knew at the time of the incident that she was committing adultery and that it was wrong; that she is not schizophrenic and that her stating to him that she had no recollection of the incident but being able quickly and accurately to supply data unrelated to the incident indicated to him that she was lying in an attempt to evade discussion of the incident with him. Also to be weighed are (1) the testimony of two investigators, members of the raiding party, that when they broke into the hotel room defendant jumped up from bed, cried out "Oh no" repeatedly and ran toward the bathroom, (2) the photograph of defendant standing completely nude near the bathroom door, her face covered by a towel, (3) defendant's affidavit of February 26, 1962, which recounts in detail and with coherence her problems with her parents and with plaintiff and plaintiff's finances, and among other things states that as a result of an hysterectomy "I felt the need for proving myself as a woman. I had to be assured that I was still wanted as a woman," (4) defendant's failure, though present in the courthouse, to testify or even to enter the courtroom where the trial was being held.

The court concludes that defendant has not sustained the burden of proof. Had she testified the impressions gained by the court during her testimony would have supported the opinion of one or the other of the psychiatrists. At the base of the differing opinions of the experts is their differing views of her credibility. Her credibility is also the central issue in this case. Deprived of the opportunity of forming first hand impressions concerning defendant's credibility, the court can choose between the experts' view only on the basis of the consistency of those views with the evidence as a whole. The inconsistency between the conclusion that defendant was driven into acts of adultery by an irrational necessity to get even with her father and with plaintiff and, on the one hand, the homosexual overtures at the hospital, and, on the other, the implication in defendant's affidavit that the acts of adultery resulted from the necessity of proving herself a woman, suggests to the court that the hospital overtures and the affidavit's contention are afterthoughts contrived by defendant to escape the consequences of her act. That defendant went ahead with her tryst notwithstanding she had been warned she was being followed can be interpreted as irrational but might also indicate either disbelief that plaintiff would take action or a rational conclusion on her part that her relationship with plaintiff had so far deteriorated that she didn't care whether the marriage continued or not. While her statement to her psychiatrist that she tried to talk the paramour out of going ahead with their plans is consistent with irrationality, her actions when caught and thereafter, as demonstrated by word and deed, suggest a realization of the nature of her conduct and a desire to avoid its consequences. On all of the evidence the court concludes that defendant has not demonstrated by a preponderance of the credible evidence that she was, as pleaded in her separate defense, "suffering from mental and emotional disorders so as to make her incompetent and irresponsible for the acts charged against her in the complaint."

Plaintiff is, therefore, awarded judgment of divorce. . . .

b. BOBST v. BOBST
160 Pa. Super. 340, 51 A. 2d 414 (1947)

RENO, JUDGE.

The court below approved the report of the master, and decreed a divorce upon the husband's charge of indignities.

Although duly notified, the respondent did not appear, nor was she represented, at the master's original hearing. After she received notice of the master's report recommending the decree and the final rule, she petitioned the court to reopen the case and permit her to enter a defense. Several causes, illness, imprudent advice, and her own conviction that her husband's case was without merit and would not support a divorce—the last was doubtless the moving reason—were responsible for her omission to appear earlier. The case was reopened, and when her side of the case was heard, the master and the learned judge who entered the final decree sat together.

Our conclusion based upon our independent and protracted study of the voluminous typewritten record is that the decree must be reversed. . . .

*   *   *

The parties were married in 1927. He was then 26 years old, a graduate of a noted college and divinity school, and a clergyman with a charge in Philadelphia. She was 25 years old, a graduate of a teacher's college, a teacher in public and Sunday schools in Northampton County. They were members of the same denomination, and met at a church conference in her home town of Bangor. During her married life she sang in the choir and taught in her husband's Sunday School. If a common faith, similar cultural backgrounds, equal social standards, and mutual interest in a common cause can produce marital happiness, their future was bright with promise. They lived together until 1944 ; yet if libellant's unchivalrous exposure of the whispered intimacies of the connubial chamber were authentic, the marriage was wrecked in its first six months. This he called "the seat" of the trouble between them. It has never dawned upon him that at that very moment she was bearing within her the evidence which, fructifying by the birth of a daughter six months later, irrefragably refuted his apocryphal revelation. His disclosure is spurious, and even were it true, sexual mismating is not an indignity nor a ground for divorce. . . . Nor has the law "set up standards for dissolving those [marriages] which are mistakes," as the master erroneously assumed. The divorce courts cannot rectify misalliances ; they dissolve only those marriages which have produced results which the legislature has recognized as grounds for a divorce. . . .

We shall not attempt to mention, much less discuss, all the incidents related in this bulky record. Some are trivial in themselves, and when added together amount only to the friction engendered by and almost inseparable from the married state. . . . They have been satisfactorily explained, or denied. Others bear upon their face the badge of inherent improbability. Our review will be limited to an examination of several episodes to which the master and the court attached unusual significance.

According to libellant's testimony, "the basic, underlying difficulty" was that "she thought that I was more friendly with folk of the opposite sex than I should be." To the master's question: "Are you of a jealous nature?" She answered frankly: "To the extent of keeping my husband and keeping his reputation as a good minister." The record amply justifies her answer. Time and again she admonished him concerning his close association with women of the congregation which, whether innocent or not, were clearly above and beyond the line of his professional duty. The record is replete with incidents, none denied by libellant, which would naturally arouse the suspicions of any just woman, and move a good woman to guard her husband against their consequences. The purpose of this opinion is to decide the case without injuring libellant in his profession, and no good end would be accomplished by detailing the conduct which establishes firm basis for his wife's solicitous regard for his reputation. This court has long held that where reasonable grounds for suspicion exist, admonitions and even charges of undue intimacy made in good faith, are not indignities. . . .

Possibly the most important episode is libellant's charge that at supper, in the presence of his children, respondent served him with stewed rhubarb containing ground glass. Every one knows that sugar in stewed rhubarb tends to crystallize, and resembles a glassy substance. Even libellant testified that at first he thought he had bit a lump of sugar, and only his wife's confession, still in the presence of the children, convinced him that the substance was glass. Of course she completely denies the occurrence, and even without the denial, the story will not bear rational analysis. To suppose that a woman of intelligence, to say nothing of a woman of good character, would in the presence of her children, then old enough to be witnesses against her, administer a hidden lethal substance to her husband is to war upon logic and human experience. Triers of fact are not required to accept as judges what they would reject as men, and we cannot accept this utterly fantastic tale.

Starting five years after the marriage, libellant began collating notes of his wife's derelictions against the contingency of a divorce. He exhibited them to the master at the hearing and from them he purported to refresh his recollection. Something can be said about a man who spends 10 years of his life compiling an index of his grievances, but the potent point is: How did it happen that a man who was diligently collecting evidence against his wife, did not preserve the ground glass and the rhubarb as autoptic testimony of her criminal assault upon him?

The court found, notwithstanding her vigorous denials, "that the respondent made it a practice to talk all through the church services; that she laughed loud enough for people around her to hear her laughter; that she would blow her nose vigorously and regularly while her husband was preaching and when he was leading in prayers; that she stuck her fingers up at her nose at him as he walked out of the church at the conclusion of the services". There was testimony supporting that finding; one of libellant's extravagantly enthusiastic witnesses testified that respondent thumbed her nose at libellant at most every Wednesday night prayer meeting for *five or six years*! The preponderance of the evidence coming from her witnesses who were also present at the services and saw respondent is that the odious conduct never occurred. Congregational chit-chat concentrated for centuries upon the preacher's wife, her dress, her manners, her housekeeping, and her congregational activities, has slight, if any, probative value. How significant it is, is illustrated by this record. According to one of *libellant's* witnesses, when the final rupture came "there was a distinct division between the members of the church", some for and some against the pastor, and he was not reappointed for the following year. But the complete answer is that there is not a particle of evidence that these actions had ever been reported to libellant, and consequently even if the evidence were true, they lack the prime requisite of indignities, for they could not have made his life burdensome or his condition intolerable. . . .

This is a melancholy case and its most poignant feature is reached in the testimony of respondent and her witnesses. One searches in vain in the libellant's testimony for an instance where he spoke to his wife about their difficulties, made one kindly and conciliatory advance, and sought earnestly an understanding and adjustment of their differences by which forgetfulness and complete unity would supplant the threatened estrangement. Instead of seeking peace, he was brooding upon and taking notes of his imaginary grievances. On the contrary, respondent's testimony breathes constantly her unfaltering love for him, and her repeated passionate pleas for restoration of happiness. To all this he turned a deaf ear; "something snapped in my head", he said; and the claims of his children, his position in the church, the ardent appeal of his father-in-law availed nothing. But more devastating is the testimony of the vice-president of his church. He testified that when a committee of the board of trustees interviewed him, libellant "refused to have anything to do with the woman, he is through." The committee also conferred with her, and the vice-president testified: "When we spoke to her, she was willing to do anything for a reconciliation, for the benefit of the church and her children."

Before the law all men are equal, and all men are judged by the same law. There is not one law for ministers and another for laymen. Yet in the divorce courts we deal with personalities, and their reaction with others. A charge of indignities requires an examination of behavior, and in determining what constitutes indignities courts keep in view the parties' moral perceptions, their ethical professions, their characters, their backgrounds, their social status, and even their station in life. . . . Not so long ago Judge, afterwards Mr. Justice, Parker, speaking for this court, in the case of a businessman said, "if he had displayed the same industry and tact in his home life that he did in his business, the result would have been different": Kerr v. Kerr, 115 Pa. Super. 18, 22, 174 A. 820, 821. It is our duty to decide cases, not to advise litigants, but this testimony convinces us that had libellant employed the means at his command as a minister he could have saved his marriage and his happiness. If his wife was guilty of actions which called for forgiveness, and we find no evidence of any major offense, he was vicar of a Master who commanded forgiveness, and he would not. All of us have carefully studied the testimony, and we are all of opinion that libellant failed to prove a satisfactory case.

Decree reversed and libel dismissed.

NOTE

OHLIGSCHLAGER v. OHLIGSCHLÄGER
125 Cal. App. 2d 45, 270 P. 2d 577 (1954)

SHINN, PRESIDING JUSTICE.

[W]e summarize the evidence relative to the unhappy conditions under which these young people lived, which, as the court found were such "That the marriage relationship has so far deteriorated that the parties hereto cannot even live together as friends—that their relationship to each other is that of strangers."

From time to time defendant was transferred to different [Army Air Force] fields. Plaintiff accompanied him and encountered many difficulties in finding suitable abodes. During this time it was plaintiff's desire not to have children. She believed it would be unwise, not only because of the travelling made necessary by the transfers of defendant, but also because the marriage was an unhappy one. Upon the subject of having children there was sharp disagreement. Defendant had not only desires but strong scruples on the subject, of religious origin and belief, which were in conflict with plaintiff's desire to use measures which would prevent conception. Plaintiff, against her better judgment, gave in; although not planned, a child was born while the parties were living in Tacoma, in August 1948. For the greater part of their married life the couple have never been happy together, and plaintiff believed it would be wrong to bring any more children into the family. All sexual relations were terminated in September 1949. In July 1950 plaintiff returned to her former home in Ventura, leaving defendant in Tacoma. She returned to Tacoma and again went to Ventura. In July 1951 defendant spent three weeks in Ventura, living under the same roof with plaintiff. He was sent to Labrador and returned in August 1952. Soon after, plaintiff instituted this action. There was evidence that defendant was habitually taciturn, uncommunicative, unwilling to discuss family affairs and problems, secretive with respect to his finances, reluctant to give plaintiff money which she needed, indifferent toward the forthcoming birth of the child, unsociable toward guests and unwilling to make an effort to make the marriage a successful one. All this was testified to by plaintiff and her mother. The latter visited the couple in Tacoma for six weeks and testified that they treated each other as strangers. After plaintiff had spent two months in Ventura, following the birth of the baby, she returned to Tacoma in order to make another effort to save the marriage. Fearing that she might be the one at fault she consulted a psychiatrist, seeking an answer to her problem. She urged defendant to do the same, but upon the advice of his chaplain he declined to do so. Shortly before the trial he consulted with someone in the American Institute of Family Relations. Whatever advice the parties received failed to help the situation.

The law provides a method of escape from marital relationships that have become intolerable to one or both of the parties. This was such a marriage. There were mutual desires to solve the marital problems and avoid a divorce, but the sincere efforts of plaintiff had failed and it appeared clearly from the evidence that further efforts would have been futile. It is not the policy of the law that a man and his wife should be required to live together, or be held in a marital relationship, when they have come to regard each other as mere strangers, even though one of them objects to its termination. And when it appears that honest and repeated efforts have been made by the complaining party to overcome the causes of the failure of the marriage, and that they cannot be overcome, it would be an act of injustice to withhold the relief which the law provides. Defendant had his day in court before an understanding and patient judge, and he has been found at fault. In his testimony he stoutly defended his own conduct and placed the blame for failure of the marriage upon his wife. The finding of cruelty, wrongfully inflicted, means only that it was within defendant's power to change his ways, which were the principal cause of dissention, and that his failure to do so was wrongful. . . .

. . . The court has found that continuation of the marriage would cause a serious hazard to the health of plaintiff. This finding has support in the evidence. The court denied defendant's motion for a new trial, upon which motion defendant no doubt advanced all the arguments that are made on the appeal. We are satisfied that the court reached an eminently wise and just decision and that the appeal is without merit.

The judgment is affirmed.

c.
MOORE v. MOORE
337 S.W. 2d 781 (Mo. 1960)

RUARK, JUDGE.

On the evening of November 18, 1958, what had apparently been a successful marriage exploded in the presence of neighbor friends when the husband, having discovered that his wife had failed to make a telephone call which he had requested her to make, announced that "I just want my soul back. I want my freedom." His explanation to an attempted peacemaker neighbor who was present at the time was that he wanted to be his own boss.

Later he sought this recovery of soul and freedom by filing a petition for divorce based on "general indignities." To his petition defendant filed answer and cross bill. During trial of the case, however, the defendant announced and testified that she did not want a divorce and that she believed a reconciliation could be effected, and in the argument in this court she renounced any desire for judgment on the cross bill. The judgment of the court granted a divorce on plaintiff's petition, and from that judgment the defendant has appealed.

Plaintiff rests his claim of indignities largely on two things, (a) that his wife was domineering and interfered with his personal and business affairs, and (b) that she indicated a dislike for his relatives and friends and made them feel unwelcome.

Plaintiff and defendant are middle-aged. Both have been married previously. Both have grown children by their former marriages, none by this marriage. They were married on September 16, 1952, and separated on November 18, 1958. Plaintiff husband was (since 1946) and still is a rural mail carrier. Defendant had been an "Avon" saleslady and after the marriage continued to work at such employment on a part-time basis. Financially the union was moderately successful. Shortly before the marriage plaintiff had bought, on credit, a farm located near Galena either on or near James River. He said that at the time of marriage he had no money, and he appears to have had little else, except the farm he owed for. Defendant had, at the time of the marriage, a Chevrolet automobile and some money (the amount is in dispute) which went into the furnishing and improvement of the home. During the six years of marriage the parties paid about $3,000 in reduction of the mortgage and purchased an-

other forty acres to add to it (cost $1,800). They remodeled and added to the home; added to the furnishings; redrilled the well and brought water into the house; rebuilt or repaired the barn; rebuilt the fencing; and in general made an attractive place known as "Sky Farm," complete with equipment and machinery, some cattle, riding horses, and, essential to the way of life of people living along James River, a boat and motor.

It is not disputed that defendant's efforts contributed to the prosperity of the parties and that she was a good housekeeper and a hard worker. In addition to her household duties and part-time work as Avon saleslady she sometimes did a man's work with the farm tractor and in taking care of the stock. Plaintiff conceded that she was "a good cook," "a pretty good lover and pretty good wife," "at times, when she wanted to be."

But respondent in his brief, in all sincerity, asserts that among the Four Freedoms recognized in Stone County (sometimes referred to as "The Kingdom of the James" because of the James River) are the right of a man to be master in his own house, the right of a man to fish and hunt with his friends at reasonable times without interference from the wife, and the right to deal and trade in livestock without the wife's intervention. The respondent contended, that the defendant was domineering and bossy in interferring with these rights. Running through the whole of plaintiff's testimony and the testimony of a number of his friends is the firm idea that, since the marriage, the plaintiff's old hunting, fishing, swapping (and, shall we say occasionally imbibing) cronies have gradually come to feel that they are *persona non grata* at Sky Farm. In the words of one of them, the reception they got at the Moore house "sometimes * * * was kinda cool," and of another one, "a little on the cool side, like I wasn't more or less wanted to visit with Lowell." And the occasions of plaintiff's joinder and participation in their ventures have probably become fewer as time has passed. Plaintiff and some of his witnesses testify to the effect that defendant was domineering toward the plaintiff. A number of defendant's witnesses, on the other hand, are equally firm in the belief that plaintiff *couldn't* be dominated. The sum total of their beliefs concerning him in this respect could be summed up in a good James River word by the expression "bull-headed." Such general characterizations, however, unless accompanied by specific incidents or occurrences, have very little probative value. . . . So we will attempt to take the evidence of the claimed indignities item by item. For the sake of clarity we will refer to the parties by their first names, as did most of the witnesses.

Item—The colt incident: D. I. Guilliams (or Williams), a farmer, stockman, and motel operator, who testified that prior to Lowell's marriage "we bought cattle, hogs, fished, and hunted together," and who characterized his freeborn independence by stating that "I drink when I like," said that he had been drinking on occasions when he visited the Moore farm but that he was never drunk or "out of the way" on those occasions, and virtuously affirmed that since the marriage neither he nor Lowell had *been drunk when out together*. He went to the Moore home one afternoon to see about a colt which he was buying or trading for from Lowell. Evidently Lowell was gone, but Minnie was there. Guilliams says he was "not drunk but drinking" on that occasion. (Minnie says he was drunk.) She told him she wasn't going to let the colt go, or words to that effect. The witness said, "I would have traded. I wasn't supposed to be trading with Mrs. Moore."

Item—The turkey shoot: In the fall of 1954 Guilliams and Lowell were going to a turkey shoot at Crane (on Flat Creek). "Lowell and I stopped at Jake Watts' store down here, and his wife drove up, and was opposed to him going to this turkey shoot, and said, 'I married you to be with me, and I intend for you to stay with me.' And she told him that he wasn't going to the turkey shoot, and she made a few slaps at him, and embarrassed him very much; me, also——" The witness said, however, that Lowell went on to the turkey shoot. He doesn't think he had been drinking on that occasion but he didn't remember.

We find nothing in Lowell's testimony concerning the turkey shoot. Minnie's version is that it didn't happen. She says that what happened was that, after she and Lowell had been married about three weeks, Guilliams came over to the place with a fifth of whisky and the two of them (Lowell and Guilliams) sat out in the yard and drank awhile and then left; that she was a stranger and scared, and when Lowell failed to return by 9:00 she went hunting for him. She found the two "at this end of the bridge—sitting there drinking." She says she urged Lowell to come home, and that Mr. Guilliams observed, "You know, that is funny about you women. My wife just left here. She has been hunting me too." Lowell came home "when he got ready," but afterwards apologized.

Item—Insistence on putting farm in defendant's name: Lowell said that Minnie was in-

sistent on his putting the title to Sky Farm in both their names because she was afraid "my kids would throw her off, if anything happened to me, and she would be set out in the cold," and finally, in 1953, he acceded to her demands because he "had rather do it than listen to it." After that she "started being more domineering."

Item—Refusal to sell or mortgage the home: Lowell was offered the chance to go into a Table Rock lake shore property development. Minnie refused to join in mortgaging the home in order to raise the necessary $10,000. Admittedly this was a speculative proposition, and it is doubtful that Lowell himself would have gone through with it. In a letter written to his stepdaughter he said the offer "might be a fleece job" and expressed some doubt concerning the proposition. In another letter he said he was "bowing out" because his proposed partner had promised a real estate dealer ten per cent instead of five per cent for sale of lots.

On what may or may not have been another occasion Lowell said that he wanted to sell Sky Farm and move to town, and according to Lowell they had an interested prospective buyer, but Minnie, without his knowledge, removed the property from the real estate listing.

Item—Criticism of trades: Lowell said that his wife refused to sign notes "on some of my stupid trades." He said that she criticized most of his cattle trades, and when he would buy a cow on his mail route he usually "got the devil about it" when he got home. But he bought the cows anyway. One of his witnesses (Gladys Hicks) said Minnie told her Lowell was always making stupid trades. Lowell's stepmother testified Minnie said he "wasn't any business man," that he was a good worker, but "didn't know how to handle his money, or do business, and if it hadn't been for her they wouldn't have had anything." Minnie denies she made any of these statements.

Item—Lowell says that Minnie made it disagreeable for his children to visit and at one time threatened (to him) not to cook for them any more. . . .

Item—The quail hunting incident: This is the incident which probably triggered the blowup. The parties had an old Chevrolet and a comparatively new Plymouth. On Sunday before the separation Lowell left at 4:30 in the morning to go quail hunting. He asked for the keys to the Plymouth. Minnie refused because "you are not hauling that bird dog in the Plymouth" and because she had Avon products in that car.

Lowell said he would unload it. Minnie said she would do it herself "when I get ready." With that, plaintiff "told her what to do with the car" and went in the old one.

Item—The telephone incident: Minnie's daughter and son-in-law were both employed in Detroit. The evidence, including Lowell's testimony, shows that he was fond of them and had written several letters concerning business opportunities in the Galena neighborhood, including boat dock, tourist court, and television business. Finally they decided to move to Galena and go into the television business. The correspondence indicates that Lowell, if not actually urging the move, was favorably disposed toward it, whereas Minnie says she was not so favorable because she felt her daughter and son-in-law were used to making more money than was possible in Galena. They quit their jobs and loaded their equipment in trucks. Lowell had written that he would come to Detroit and drive one of the trucks to Galena. The daughter had sent plant tickets and a neighbor had arranged to drive Lowell and Minnie to the airport at Springfield. On Monday after the quail hunting incident above mentioned, Lowell told Minnie to call the children and tell them that he and Minnie were not coming. She did not make the call because, so she says, the next morning he told her *not* to call. This precipitated the declaration of Lowell concerning his freedom. He said her failure to make the call indicated that he couldn't place dependence in what she said.

Item—Finally, the witness Gladys Hicks testified that on one occasion Minnie referred to Lowell's folks as "hillbillies."

There are still a number of other incidents which we cannot relate because of the length of this opinion. They are more trivial than those we have heretofore described, but in general they are along the same line. In concluding our statement of the evidence we should say that neither of the parties impugned the morals of the other and both proved to have excellent reputations among their neighbors.

. . . The question here is, do the acts and transactions which we have described amount to a course of conduct such as to render plaintiff's condition intolerable (Section 452.010 RSMo 1949, V.A.M.S.)? Each case of this kind must necessarily be judged on its own facts. No "indignities" case is exact precedent for another, and no hard, fast rule can be followed, because the sensitivities of people differ. . . . "It has long been established as the law that where the action is based on indignities,

such indignities, in the statutory sense, must amount to a species of mental or physical cruelty, or of injury accompanied with insult or hatred, and they must be such as cannot be relieved by any exertions of the injured party. Indignities such as to warrant the granting of a divorce, ordinarily must amount to a continuous course of conduct. A single act or word, or occasional acts or words, will not suffice. *The course of conduct must be such as to connote settled hate and a plain manifestation of alienation and estrangement.* Indignities are such acts as consist of unmerited contemptuous conduct, or words and acts of one spouse toward the other which manifests contempt, or contumely, incivility or injury accompanied with insult and amounting to a species of cruelty to the mind." (Our emphasis.) Hoffman v. Hoffman, Mo. App., 224 S.W. 2d 554, 561. . . . And the indignities sufficient to sustain a decree of divorce are wrongful acts over a course of time which are of sufficient gravity or magnitude to make plaintiff's life as defendant's spouse intolerable. . . .

Applying the general rule to the present case, we find no settled or continuous course of conduct which indicates hatred, contempt or estrangement, and we find no great injury to have been suffered by the plaintiff. The incidents which he produced are scattered out over more than six years of married life. Some of the instances of insistence upon going fishing with him occurred shortly after the marriage, and we believe that it is not unusual for a bride of short duration to insist upon her husband's presence and company at that time. Plaintiff himself said Minnie was a "pretty good lover." One instance in wihch she made an unladylike objection to his going fishing with his friends is not dated, except that it was "a good long time ago." We will agree with respondent in his definition of Stone County freedoms that a husband has a *right* to go fishing. And we will go further and say that this *right* extends to fishing without the constant and ever-present impediment of female presence and participation, if such be against the will of the husband. It is a wise wife who accords her husband that freedom—in moderation—and a foolish wife who interferes. The studied, constant, and repeated interference with that *right* over a long period of time could be, under certain conditions, an indignity, but two or three or four isolated instances of insistence upon going along, or insistence upon his not going (either fishing or turkey shooting), over a period of six years do not, in and of themselves, constitute a constant and studied course of conduct amounting to indignities which render life intolerable. Further, the record convinces us that the plaintiff did, with and without his wife's consent or presence, indulge in a fair amount of fishing, hunting and swapping.

As to plaintiff's charge of domination in financial affairs: We think it was not unusual or unseemly that defendant was insistent upon conveyance of the (then mortgaged) farm into joint title. She was putting her work and money into the venture, and we see no reason why she should not have insisted upon the record title evidencing her interest, especially in view of the plaintiff's trading proclivities. Plaintiff himself agrees that they were partners in the operation of the farm business. Neither can we say that defendant was unjustified in being unwilling to sell or mortgage the farm home to finance his proposed essay into a speculative venture.

Concerning the accusation and criticism in respect to "stupid trades": As to whether Lowell's trades were stupid we cannot say, but the evidence is, by his own statement, that he was not affluent before the marriage, and further, by his admission, he and Minnie were joint owners and "partners over there and in business together. What I owed she owed, didn't she?" Being an equal partner, she was entitled to exercise some rights of a partner in respect to partnership property. It is probable that repeated and constant harping and criticism of every act and endeavor in respect to trading could become extremely wearisome and distasteful and ultimately one form of "indignities." We are inclined to believe that Minnie did, from time to time, assume a critical, or at least an impolitic, attitude in respect to Lowell's trading and swapping activities, but we are likewise inclined to believe that some of her criticism was justified and that Lowell exaggerates when he would have it appear that it was constant. There is an old saying that criticism hurts the most when it is true. And we note he *did* continue to trade.

The accusation that Minnie made it disagreeable for Lowell's children to visit is not borne out by the evidence. The children *did* frequently visit and vacation at Sky Farm, and the evidence indicates that they *did* enjoy themselves and she *did* cook for them, along with her other chores and duties. We can find no place where she communicated any expression of ill will to plaintiff's children, and we note that neither of his children testified against her.

As to the incident concerning her having made his daughter, Sharon, cry because she forbade Sharon to go out in her negligee, we can only say that even in the pleasant and relaxed atmosphere of our clean, forthright Ozarks it is not customary for grown women (Sharon was twenty) to run around outdoors, in the daytime, in their nightgowns. We do not find that the restriction on the daughter was unreasonable.

We are satisfied that the defendant did, with only the best of intentions, attempt to channel her husband's activities into courses which she thought were best for the marriage and best for him, but that in so doing she adopted a course of conduct and attitude which occasionally tended to have a "smothering" effect on plaintiff. It is a close question and one subject to human frailties of judgment as to whether this smothering reached the degree which amounts to the "indignities" as defined by the case law heretofore stated. The defendant probably, but understandably, preferred that the plaintiff spend his time with her, or in useful or profitable occupation, rather than with his fishing-hunting-swapping-horseriding companions, and we deduce that she probably was afraid of his trades. No doubt she desired to direct him toward (what she considered to be) "a better life," and she no doubt found it difficult to compromise her sense of what was best with any great understanding or comprehension of what her husband's views, habits, and masculine desires might demand. To use a Southern Missouri expression, she wanted to tie the stake rope a little too short. But all this was without conscious desire to dominate or oppress and was with the love which promotes the complete desire to do that which was best for her husband. The trouble arose because she perhaps failed to take into account that her husband had, and was entitled to have, ideas of his own on these subjects. We are convinced that he manfully and patiently (or so he thought) submerged his somewhat unconscious desire to pull up the stake until finally the pressure proved overpowering and he "blew up" It was not wholly the fault of either one and neither of them was entirely innocent.

In respect to plaintiff's evidence that Minnie once referred to relatives of the plaintiff as hillbillies: We suggest that to refer to a person as a "hillbilly," or any other name, for that matter, might or might not be an insult, depending upon the meaning intended to be conveyed, the manner of utterance, and the place where the words are spoken. Webster's New International Dictionary says that a hillbilly is "a backwoodsman or mountaineer of the southern United States;— often used contemptuously." But without the added implication or inflection which indicates an intention to belittle, we would say that, here in Southern Missouri, the term is often given and accepted as a complimentary expression. An Ozark hillbilly is an individual who has learned the real luxury of doing without the entangling complications of *things* which the dependent and over-pressured city dweller is required to consider as necessities. The hillbilly foregoes the hard grandeur of high buildings and canyon streets in exchange for wooded hills and verdant valleys. In place of creeping traffic he accepts the rippling flow of the wandering stream. He does not hear the snarl of exhaust, the raucous braying of horns, and the sharp, strident babble of many tense voices. For him instead is the measured beat of the katydid, the loansome, far-off complaining of the whippoorwill, perhaps even the sound of a falling acorn in the infinite peace of the quiet woods. The hillbilly is often not familiar with new models, soirees, and office politics. But he does have the time and surroundings conducive to sober reflection and honest thought, the opportunity to get closer to his God. No, in Southern Missouri the appellation "hillbilly" is not generally an insult or an indignity; it is an expression of envy.

We are of the opinion that the indignities complained of were too scattered and remote, and, in general, too inconsequential, to be termed a continuous or studied course of conduct amounting to a species of cruelty, injury, insult, contempt, settled hatred or estrangement. Practically all marriages have their moments of discord. Few run their course without some occasional "indignity" offered and suffered. Most marriage ceremonies take that into account when the parties promise to take each other for better or worse. Occasional exhibition of traits which offend the other is a part of the "worse," but it is not the intolerable indignities contemplated by the statute.

Appellant's second contention is that, because of certain acts and conduct on the part of the plaintiff, he was not the innocent and injured party and was therefore not entitled to a decree Since we have held the plaintiff did not prove sufficient indignities to entitle him to a divorce, and since the cross bill has been abandoned, we see no reason to consider such alleged acts and it would be of no service to the parties to this already crippled marriage to spread them upon the published record. It is our judgment that the divorce should be denied and the whole cause dismissed. It is so ordered.

MCDOWELL, J., not sitting [fishing?].

NOTES
NOTE 1.

MOORE v. MOORE
One Year Later

. . . The parties are not living together and have never lived together since the first separation. [Letter from J. Hal Moore, attorney for plaintiff, dated December 12, 1960.]

NOTE 2.

CHAPPELL v. CHAPPELL
298 P. 2d 768, 771 (Okla. 1956)

PER CURIAM.

When incompatibility is the grounds for a divorce we think . . . that the judgment of the trial court should be based on reasoning to the effect that conflicts in personalities and disposition are so deep as to be irreconcilable and render it impossible for the parties to continue a normal marital relationship with each other. This disharmony of the marriage relationships in their common every day life must be so deep and intense as to be irremediable. It must be such a relationship that would make the conditions very unhappy on the part of both spouses should the marriage be required to continue.

It should not be grounds for divorce where only one of the parties to a marriage is incompatible. Incompatibility is a two way proposition and should not be applicable where the party seeking the divorce is the only one who is incompatible. Our statute did not intend to mean that any one could obtain a divorce on this ground merely because a divorce was desired. In all such cases there must be some conduct creating incompatibility on the part of the defendant.

NOTE 3.

MEAD, MARGARET
Male and Female*

[T]o-day with the growing recognition that divorce may come to any marriage, no matter how devoted, how conscientious, how much in love each spouse originally was, marriage is something that has to be worked at each day. As the husband has to face the possibility of losing his job, so also the wife has to face the possibility of losing hers, of finding herself companionless, out of the job she chose, often with small children to care for alone. Both husband and wife face the need to re-choose each other, to reassert and re-establish the never permanent claim of one upon the other's choice. The wife in curl-papers is replaced by a wife who puts on lipstick before she wakes her husband, and the husband with a wandering eye finds that his eye wanders less happily because at any moment it may light on some one whom he will choose instead of his wife. As it is her obligation to make herself continuingly desirable, so it is his obligation not to put himself in positions where other women may become desirable to him. . . .

. . . Quarrelling, sulking, neglectfulness, stubbornness, could be indulged very differently within a frame that could not be broken. But now over every quarrel hang the questions: "Do you want a divorce? Do I want a divorce? Does she want a divorce? Will that be the end of this? Is that where we are going?"

NOTE 4.

The Regulations and Proclamations of Travancore*

§4. A marriage may be dissolved only in one of the following ways, that is to say,—

Dissolution of marriage.

> (i) by the death of either party; or
> (ii) by mutual consent evidenced by a registered instrument; or
> (iii) by a formal order of dissolution as hereinafter provided.

§5. A husband or wife may, notwithstanding anything contained in the Civil Courts Regulation, present a petition for dissolution of the marriage, under Section 4, Clause (iii), . . . on any of the following grounds, namely, insanity, incurable disease, impotency, incompatibility of temperament, habitual cruelty, adultery or change of religion:

Provided that the wife shall herself be competent to apply for divorce if she has completed sixteen years of age.

4.

IN CRUELTY

a.   LISSACK v. LISSACK
                     [1951] P. 1

The wife petitioner married her husband, the respondent, in 1941, and there was one child of the marriage, a daughter, born in 1942. On October 25, 1948, the wife went out for the evening, leaving the child in her husband's charge. On her return she found the kitchen barricaded, and when she got in she found that the child had been strangled and that her husband had made an attempt to commit suicide by putting his head in the gas oven. In a subsequent signed statement to the police, which began: "I want to tell you how I came to do this terrible thing", the husband admitted that he had made up his mind some weeks before October 28 to kill the child, and stated that he had creeping paralysis, brought about by his habits, that the disease was hereditary, and that he had passed it on to his daughter. He said that he had decided not to

---

* Reg. 11 of 100 Secs. 4 & 5 (1924).

leave her with such a complaint, and had made up his mind to kill her and himself. His statement described in detail how he had killed the child, and referred to a note which he had written in anticipation. In that note he stated: "The reason for this terrible thing is all through my wickedness. If Barbara [the child] had lived she would have been blind and paralytic inherited through me. What kind of life would that have been for her and Rosie and everybody else concerned with our darling. A fine son I've turned out to be, and what a terrible thing to do to a wonderful girl like Rosie. Please God let my darling wife find happiness again". In a letter written from prison on November 5, 1948, to his wife's brother he said: "After what I have done to Rosie I can hardly face her. . . . I know what torment, misery and agony she is going through for she is constantly in my thoughts . . . " . He referred to the suffering of his parents, and concluded: "There doesn't seem much more I can say except that I've messed up a lot of decent people's lives".

On November 17, 1948, he was tried for murder at the Central Criminal Court and found guilty but insane and so not to be responsible according to law for his actions at the time. It was ordered that he be kept in custody as a criminal lunatic, and he was in Broadmoor when the petition for divorce was heard. From Broadmoor he wrote in December, 1948, two letters to his wife regretting the pain which he had caused her and the "terrible things" which he had done.

The husband was not incurably insane; his condition had improved, and it was possible that he might in the future be released.

*   *   *

PEARCE, J. stated the facts and continued: The medical evidence shows clearly that, as one would suppose, the shock has had a very serious effect on the wife's health and nerves, that some part of the damage will be permanent, and that some mental relief would be afforded to her by a release from her marriage tie to the husband. Apart from the question of insanity the wife has a clear right to the relief which she claims. There can be no greater cruelty to a woman than the killing of her child. Does this insanity prevent her obtaining relief?

Mr. Tyndale, for the wife, argued that insanity of the husband is no defence to a wife's petition based on cruelty. He relied on the following cases, and on the fact that such a defence had in no reported case been successful. . . .

In *Hanbury v. Hanbury* ([1892] p. 222, 224), Butt P. said in charging the jury: "I am not entirely satisfied that a mere plea of insanity is a sufficient answer to a suit. It may be that a person is so insane as to necessitate his or her confinement in an asylum or some other place of permanent detention, and the disease may be such that there is no hope of recovery or amelioration such as will allow of his or her discharge. When a disease of that sort seizes upon a person, and he or she has to be incarcerated or permanently to be placed in confinement, I should hesitate to say that in regard to an act committed in such a state of insanity a plea of insanity might not be an answer. But I think it is very different with regard to intermittent and recurrent insanity. If a man is afflicted with madness or insanity of such a nature as to necessitate keeping him in duress for the rest of his life, there is no danger of violence to his wife. I conceive that the object of the Divorce Act is not so much, or nearly so much, the punishment or retribution for a marital offence as the protection of the party who is in peril. I believe that protection, and not punishment or retribution, is the main object; and if it can be shown that the insanity is of such a nature that it will produce violence on the part of the husband, and endanger the safety of the wife, though it need not entail the permanent incarceration of the man, but only his restraint from time to time—if the mania is recurrent and comes on suddenly from time to time she may be placed in great jeopardy. In such a case I can well conceive that, although in some instances insanity may be one of those misfortunes which must be taken by a wife with her husband for better or for worse, and though it may assume the form of a disease, yet if it is such as to imperil the wife's safety she is entitled to the protection of this court. Assuming for a moment that these attacks were not brought on the respondent by his own self-indulgence, assuming that they were the result of hereditary disease, I should still be disposed to hold that acts of cruelty committed in one of these fits of mania would entitle the wife to the remedy which she asks—separation from her husband. If the mania is intermittent and recurrent, the husband is entitled to go home when he recovers from time to time—the wife cannot refuse him admission to the conjugal home; and if the mania is likely to recur accompanied with violence which would place the wife in peril, the ordinary protection which she is supposed to obtain by proceedings in lunacy is a delusion, because it does not protect her against the return home of her husband, who is liable at any moment to become a lunatic".

* * *

. . . It is for the husband to establish that a legal defence of insanity does exist in matrimonial cases. . . . In criminal matters, where the object is punishment, such a defence is obviously necessary in a just society. So, too, in a more limited form, at common law and in chancery. But I do not think it a safe analogy to assume that justice therefore requires it in matrimonial matters.

Since in petitions based on cruelty the court's duty to interfere is intended not to punish the husband for the past, but to protect the wife for the future, the question for the court is whether the wife can with safety to life and health live with the husband now. To withdraw from the ambit of legal cruelty conduct that is intolerable, but is due to insanity, is to make the court powerless to help in cases where help may be most needed. It is said that the other course may also cause hardship. Theoretically it might: if a husband is cruel to his wife owing to insanity and then recovers, it is hard for him that he should be divorced by her; but since, ex hypothesi, her affection and fortitude were not great enough to enable her in the circumstances to tolerate a continuance of married life and she wishes for divorce, it is unlikely that he would have secured happiness by maintaining the marriage tie. Moreover, since such a defence has in no reported instance ever been made out on the facts, its existence would seem to give little practical benefit to respondents.

. . . For that reason, and because in my view such a defence is not in accord with the true view of the law relating to cruelty, I hold that the defence of insanity is not open to the husband and that the wife is entitled to a decree.

In case I am held to be wrong in this view, it is desirable that I should express my opinion whether the necessary degree of insanity has been proved in this case. If insanity can be a defence, the onus of proving it must be on the respondent. The test suggested is that laid down in *M'Naghten's* case as the proper test in criminal cases, namely, "to establish a defence on the ground of insanity, it must be clearly proved that, at the time of the committing of the act, the party accused was labouring under such a defect of reason, from disease of the mind, as not to know the nature and quality of the act he was doing; or, if he did know it, that he did not know he was doing what was wrong".

The test whether he knew that he was doing wrong is a very unsatisfactory one in measuring misdeeds so dependent on the circumstances and personalities of the parties as acts of cruelty. Acts may be cruel in particular circumstances and between particular persons that are not at the time of their commission known to be wrong. To alter the test by substituting for the word "wrong" the word "cruel" would not be possible. . . . This in itself shows how unsatisfactory is such a test. To limit the test so that it accords with that applied in common law and chancery courts would make it more practical. Halsbury's Laws of England (2nd ed.), vol. 21, p. 293, §504, quoted by Bucknill L.J., in *White v. White* ([1950] p. 39, 48), reads as follows: "In an action at common law or in chancery, where the responsibility of a person alleged to be of unsound mind is in question, the issue generally directed is, 'was the person alleged to be of unsound mind at the date in question capable of understanding the nature of the act he was performing?' " Such a limitation of the test would be reasonable, since the test of the knowledge of wrong, though suitable to criminal matters where the primary object is punishment, is not suitable in matrimonial matters. . . . In this case it is agreed that the husband knew the nature and quality of his acts. If, therefore, that limited test were applied in this case, the wife would succeed.

Even if the test in *M'Naghten's* case were the true one, the husband can only defeat the wife's prayer if he did not know his acts to be wrong. On this issue there is a divergence of medical opinion. I have to decide it on the evidence before me. The opinion formed by a jury—who, incidentally, did not have before them all the evidence that I have had—does not compel me to the same conclusion. The doctor who saw the husband thirty-six hours after the crime, and thereafter from time to time for some three weeks, says that, though he cannot speak with certainty, there is a high degree of probability that, owing to schizophrenia, the husband had no knowledge that his acts were legally or morally wrong. He suggested also that the disease might have created an irresistable impulse to the deed. But in view of the man's own statement this seems most unlikely. This doctor relies on the complete flatness and absence of emotion displayed by the husband when he examined him, a condition typical of schizophrenia. But it must be remembered that the husband had been through a horrible ordeal, to which, if his statement is to be believed, he had difficulty in screwing up his courage, an ordeal which must have taken heavy toll of his nervous resources. The doctor at Broadmoor said that the husband was certifiable when he entered that institution. The opinion of the doctor called by the wife is that the husband knew that what he was doing was contrary to law and was wrong. That opinion is derived from the man's signed statement and the other documents on which this

doctor relies as showing knowledge of wrong and which at all events, as the other doctor admits, give some indication of that knowledge. All the documents show the husband's appreciation of the pain which his acts would inflict, or had inflicted, on the wife. The references in the original note to "this terrible thing" and "what a terrible thing to do to a wonderful girl like Rosie" are more consistent with an appreciation of wrong than with a failure to appreciate it. There is here no glorification of his act, no indifference to its consequences so, too, with the signed statement made the day after the occurrence, where he explains how he "came to do this terrible thing". So, too, with his difficulty in getting up his courage to do it and in his waiting to do it till his wife went out. So, too, with the contrition expressed in the letters after the event. I am asked to believe that there was an interval between these documents, namely, at the moment of the killing, when the knowledge of wrong passed from his mind. But if, as I believe, when he first planned the deed and wrote the note, he knew that it was wrong, yet determined to do it if he could muster the courage, and if, as I believe, when he made his signed statement shortly after the event (and later when he wrote the letters) he knew it to be wrong, I find it impossible to assume an intervening interval when he did not know it to be wrong. The evidence of the doctor called by the wife seems to me the more likely to be correct; but, at the highest, the matter is one of opinion and probability.

I have to consider whether the husband has proved clearly that he did not know that it was wrong. I am satisfied that on the evidence he has not proved that clearly, or at all. This case seems to me very similar to that considered in the fourth question in *M'Naghten's* case (10 Cl. & Fin. 24); and, since the husband's conduct, even if the delusions had been true, would have been unlawful, he cannot escape liability for that conduct. There will be a decree nisi in favour of the wife.

NOTES

NOTE 1.

WILLIAMS v. WILLIAMS
[1963] 2 All E.R. 994, 1002-1004

LORD REID: . . .

I have come to be clearly of opinion that it would be wrong to take McNaghten rules as a test. Not only have these rules been subject to persistent and powerful criticism for nearly a hundred years but their strict application would lead to capricious results. It appears to be the general opinion of medical men, who at least have a better understanding of insanity than lawyers, that there are types of insanity not within the rules which deprive the insane man of choice or responsibility just as much as those types which are covered by the rules. So if guilt, culpability, or blameworthiness in some degree is to be held a necessary element in cruelty, I can see no rational basis for holding that if two persons are in fact equally irresponsible one is to be divorced because his type of insanity does not come within the rules, but the other is to have a defence because his case is covered by the rules.

The second possibility is that insanity should be a defence if it is so bad that the insane person does not know what he is doing, but not otherwise. This test seems straightforward whereas the test that a man knows that his acts are wrong may seem simple, but in fact is not: it is a test which experts seem to have great difficulty in applying. Moreover I think that many people would say that if a man does not know what he is doing his acts are not really his acts at all, but they have at least a lingering suspicion that when a man does know what he is doing he cannot be wholly blameless, whatever the experts may say. I think that this is a possible half-way house, but I would not much favour it myself. It is still subject to the objection that it discriminates between people who on evidence are proved to be equally irresponsible by reason of disease of the mind. But I must recognise that, if we are thinking of protection, a man who does not know what he is doing will, except in cases of epilepsy or temporary lapses into insanity, generally be detained, whereas a man certifiable for less serious types of insanity may be released at least for a time.

So it remains for me to choose between the two clear-cut alternatives—either insanity is a defence or it is not. I think that ultimately the answer must depend on the meaning one gives to the word "cruel", and on this there are obviously two opinions, even among judges. Some think that there cannot be cruelty without some kind of mens rea and some think that there can. To my mind "cruelty" is a word that can take its meaning from its context: often it connotes blameworthiness, but quite often it does not. Let me give one or two examples. Even in comparatively recent times practically everyone, including men of the highest integrity and intelligence who were quite as civilised as any of us, firmly believed that persecution in one form or another was not only excusable, but was a moral duty. Few would deny that their acts were cruel, but I do not see how we can reasonably blame them for not having anticipated modern ideas. And is it

a misuse of language to call a cat cruel? Again, when we speak of the cruel sea, no doubt we personify the sea, but do we blame it? So the law cannot just take cruelty in its ordinary or popular meaning because that is too vague: we must decide what, if any, mental state is a necessary ingredient. . . .

If some mental or subjective element is necessary, the first possibility is that there must have been malignity or an intention to hurt. But that has long been abandoned. Such an intention may be an aggravation, and may justify holding that acts are cruel where, without that intention, they would not be sufficiently grave and weighty to amount to cruelty: but it is not essential. The next possibility is that there must be some degree of mens rea, that at least the respondent must be blameworthy for what he did—and that requires careful consideration. But opinions have been expressed that it is enough if his acts were intentional, if he knew what he was doing, although he could not be held blameworthy. That would be a basis for holding that insanity is a defence if the insane person did not know what he was doing, but not otherwise. . . .

. . . Then we come to the really difficult cases if blameworthiness is to be a test. There are many cases of husbands and wives not insane but either sick in mind or body or so stupid, selfish or spoilt that they plainly do not appreciate or foresee the harm which they are doing to the other spouse, and perhaps they are now so self-centred that nothing would ever get the truth into their heads. Certainly allowances have to be made, particularly when their condition is due to misfortune. But I suppose that no one would now maintain that cruelty cannot be proved against such a person, if his acts are sufficiently grave and really imperil the other spouse.

It is often untrue that such a man is able to exert his reason so as to control his acts in the normal way or even that he is capable of forming a rational decision about them. Yet these are often the cases where the other spouse is most in need of protection. It is difficult in some of these cases to attribute more than a speck of scintilla of blame to the respondent in the sense that he, not the reasonable man, ought to have realised the consequences of what he was doing and could have done otherwise if he had tried. If we are to make culpability an essential element in cruelty, we can really only bring in these people by deeming them to have qualities and abilities which the evidence shows that they do not possess. Surely it is much more satisfactory to accept the fact that the test of culpability has broken down, and not to treat entirely differently two people one of whom is just short of and the other just over the invisible line which separates abnormality from insanity.

In my judgment decree should be pronounced against such an abnormal person not because his conduct was aimed at his wife, nor because a reasonable man would have realised the position, nor because he must be deemed to have foreseen or intended the harm he did, but simply because the facts are such that, after making all allowances for his disabilities and for the temperaments of both parties, it must be held that the character and gravity of his acts was such as to amount to cruelty. And, if that is right for an abnormal person, I see no good reason why the same should not apply to an insane person.

* * *

NOTE 2.

KASLEFSKY v. KASLEFSKY
[1951] P. 38, 47

DENNING, L. J.

. . . This wife grossly neglected her husband and child, but her conduct was not aimed at him, nor had she any desire to injure him or inflict misery on him; she was simply lazy. It was all very wrong of her, but it was not cruelty. It was a defect of character and temperament which he, having married her, must put up with. It led, no doubt, to discord between them, but gross neglect or chronic discord is not yet a ground for divorce. Even if the wife had herself been cruel to the child, that would not by itself be cruelty to the husband unless there were in some part an intention on her side to inflict misery on him. The converse case of cruelty by a husband to the children has, like habitual drunkenness, been specially made, by statute, a ground on which a wife can obtain an order against him in the magistrates' court: but it has not yet, by itself been made a ground for divorce. In many cases, however, it will be so likely to cause distress to the wife that the husband may be presumed to have intended in some part to inflict misery on her. . . .

NOTE 3.

STEVENSON v. STEVENSON
13 Utah 2d 153, 369 P. 2d 923 (1962)

CALLISTER, JUSTICE.

* * *

An additional factor of importance is whether the granting of the divorce would conflict with the public interest our divorce statutes were designed to protect. The public has an interest in the preservation of marriages in which the parties have mutual love and respect, and where the circumstances promote the happiness, welfare, health and morality of the parties and of their children. However, there is no public interest in the preservation of a marriage where one of the parties can no longer endure the relationship without impairing his or her health; or where the conduct of one party has deteriorated the relationship to the extent that the parties will no longer continue cohabitation, and the marriage exists only in name but not in fact.

* * *

b.   DeBURGH v. DeBURGH
39 Cal. 2d 858, 250 P. 2d 598 (1952)

TRAYNOR, JUSTICE.

Plaintiff Daisy M. DeBurgh and defendant Albert Raymond DeBurgh were married in California in October, 1946. They separated in February, 1949, and in the same year plaintiff brought this action for divorce on the ground of extreme cruelty. Defendant filed a cross-complaint for divorce, also on the ground of extreme cruelty. The allegations of cruelty were denied in the answers filed by each party. The trial court found "that each of the parties to this action has been guilty of acts of cruelty towards the other, and that such acts of cruelty by each were provoked by the acts of the other." The court decided that "each party had been guilty of recrimination and neither is entitled to a divorce from the other." The court entered judgment that plaintiff take nothing by her complaint and that defendant take nothing by his cross-complaint. Plaintiff appeals. . . .

The evidence regarding cruelty is in conflict; it supports the finding that each party has been cruel to the other. Plaintiff's evidence tended to show that defendant was frequently intoxicated to excess, that he inflicted physical injury upon plaintiff on several occasions, that he boasted of his relations with other women, that he unreasonably criticized plaintiffs daughter, that he unjustly berated plaintiff concerning a former suitor, and that, although he was a lavish spender in other ways he was penurious with plaintiff. Defendant's evidence indicated that plaintiff had unjustly accused him of dishonesty and homosexuality and had communicated to his business associate similar false and malicious statements.

Since the trial court found that defendant was guilty of acts of cruelty towards plaintiff, it is clear that the judgment denying plaintiff a divorce is not on the ground that plaintiff failed to prove the allegations of cruelty in her complaint. The judgment thus must be based either on the finding that defendant's cruelty was provoked by plaintiff or on the ground that defendant established the defense of recrimination.

The finding that the cruelty of each party was provoked by the other party is inconsistent with the conclusion that recrimination was established. Cruelty that is provoked does not give rise to a cause of action. . . . To establish recrimination, however, a cause of divorce must be shown. Civil Code, § 122. . . . Provocation and recrimination, therefore, are not complementary, but mutually exclusive, defenses. To justify extreme cruelty by one spouse under the doctrine of provocation, the misconduct of the other spouse must itself be a serious violation of marital obligations. . . . The record in the present case fails to disclose any such violation on plaintiff's part that would justify the physical brutality and other misconduct of defendant. Defendant's act of cruelty, as set forth in plaintiff's evidence, took place from the date of marriage until the separation of the parties, whereas defendant freely conceded at the trial that his allegations of plaintiff's cruelty were based solely upon plaintiff's accusations that he was dishonest and a homosexual, charges that were made no earlier than two or three days before the separation. Thus, although the evidence would support the finding that defendant's cruelty provoked the false accusations made by plaintiff, there is no evidence of any earlier misconduct by plaintiff that would justify defendant's cruelty. Under these circumstances, the decision of the trial court cannot be supported upon the theory of provocation rather than recrimination.

The determinative question on this appeal, therefore, is whether the findings and conclusions in this case warrant application of the doctrine of recrimination. It is apparent from the remarks of the trial judge at the close of the trial that he believed that the transgressions of each party necessarily precluded the granting of a divorce to either. On the other hand, the language of section 122 of the Civil Code indicates that the trial court may have abused its discretion in disregarding the requirement therein that the cause of divorce of which one party is found guilty must be "in bar" of that party's ground of divorce against the other party. To resolve this conflict, we have studied the history of the doctrine of recrimination, its objectives, and the wording and legislative background of the applicable statutes.

It has sometimes been assumed that any cause of divorce constitutes a recriminatory defense. The legislative language, however, is ill-adapted to such a broad purpose. Read together, Sections 111 and 122 of the Civil Code provide: "Divorces must be denied upon * * * a showing by the defendant of any cause of divorce against the plaintiff, in bar of the plaintiff's cause of divorce."

Had the Legislature meant to make every cause of divorce an absolute defense, it could easily have provided that: "Divorces must be denied upon * * * a showing by the defendant of any cause of divorce against the plaintiff." We are bound to consider the additional requirement that such a cause of divorce must be "in bar" of the plaintiff's cause of divorce.

Much of the confusion concerning recrimination in California has proceeded from the erroneous discussion of the subject in Conant v. Conant, 10 Cal. 249, which was decided before recrimination became a part of the statutory law. It was stated in that case that this defense is based on the doctrine that one who violates a contract containing mutual and dependent covenants cannot complain of its breach by the other party. Logically, such a theory would permit the party against whom the first marital offense was committed to ignore thereafter the duties imposed by the marriage "contract" for in contract law a material breach excuses further performance by the innocent party. . . . In fact, however, the defense may be asserted without regard to whether the plaintiff or the defendant was the first at fault. . . .

The deceptive analogy to contract law ignores the basic fact that marriage is a great deal more than a contract. It can be terminated only with the consent of the state. In a divorce proceeding the court must consider not merely the rights and wrongs of the parties as in contract litigation, but the public interest in the institution of marriage. The family is the basic unit of our society, the center of the personal affections that ennoble and enrich human life. It channels biological drives that might otherwise become socially destructive; it ensures the care and education of children in a stable environment; it establishes continuity from one generation to another; it nurtures and develops the individual initiative that distinguishes a free people. Since the family is the core of our society, the law seeks to foster and preserve marriage. But when a marriage has failed and the family has ceased to be a unit, the purposes of family life are no longer served and divorce will be permitted. "[P]ublic policy does not discourage divorce where the relations between husband and wife are such that the legitimate objects of matrimony have been utterly destroyed." Hill v. Hill, 23 Cal. 2d 82, 93, 142 P. 2d 417, 422; . . .

The chief vice of the rule enunciated in the Conant case is its failure to recognize that the considerations of policy that prompt the state to consent to a divorce when one spouse has been guilty of misconduct are often doubly present when both spouses have been guilty. The disruption of family relationships, the clandestine associations with third parties, and the oppressive effect upon children and the community are intensified. It is a degradation of marriage and a frustration of its purpose when the courts use it as a device for punishment.

Moreover, the historical discussion of the doctrine of recrimination in the Conant case is inaccurate. . . .

* * *

The California Legislature, in enacting the Civil Code in 1872, did not follow the principles of the Conant case. The Code provisions on recriminations made two important departures from the existing law.

First, the Code requires that the defendant prove a cause of divorce against the plaintiff to establish this defence. The requirement of the Conant case that plaintiff be "without reproach" no longer prevails. . . .

Second, as shown by the notes of the Commissioners who drafted the Code, the Legislature rejected the strict rule of recrimination of the ecclesiastical courts. Significantly, neither the Conant case nor any other divorce cases appear among the precedents listed by the Commissioners as the basis of the statute. It is apparent from the decisions that were listed that the Legislature intended that divorce cases involving recrimination be governed by the same principles that apply generally throughout our jurisprudence. Although the plaintiff's fault has always been regarded as an important element in the decision of any case, our courts have traditionally refused to exalt that element above the public interest. . . . This respect for the public interest has formed the basis of a recognized exception to the equitable doctrine of unclean hands,[*] with which the defense of recrimination has become increasingly identified since the enactment of the Code. It is clear that the Legislature, in relying upon judicial principles of general application, intended that in divorce litigation the fault of the plaintiff should have no more significance than elsewhere in the law. Apparently with this purpose in mind it worded the statute to require

that a cause of divorce shown by defendant must be "in bar" of the plaintiff's cause of divorce. It would have defeated its own purpose had it closed the avenues to divorce when the legitimate objects of matrimony have been destroyed. The perpetuation of an unwholesome relationship would be a mockery of marriage.

The California cases decided since the enactment of the Civil Code contain little analysis or discussion of the principles governing the defense of recrimination. In Brenot v. Brenot, 102 Cal. 294, 296, 36 P. 672, this court correctly stated the rule to be that "a court of equity is *authorized* to enter a judgment dismissing an action of divorce, where both parties are seeking a decree, and the evidence discloses them to be equally guilty of the misconduct alleged." (Italics added.) Again, in Glass v. Glass, 4 Cal. App. 604, 607, 88 P. 734, the appellate court, in affirming the judgment with regard to property issues, observed without objection that the trial court had found both parties guilty of extreme cruelty but nevertheless had granted the plaintiff a divorce. In some cases, however, it has been assumed, apparently with the acquiescence of the parties themselves, that the mere showing of a cause of divorce against the plaintiff is sufficient. . . . This failure to exercise the discretion authorized by the statute has enabled the thinking engendered by the Conant case to survive by default. Important developments of the past several decades have made it increasingly clear that the courts can no longer decline to exercise the discretion inherent in the clean hands doctrine.

The rising divorce rate in the United States has compelled a growing recognition of marriage failure as a social problem and correspondingly less preoccupation with technical marital fault. This trend is strikingly exemplified by the recent amendment of Section 92 of the Civil Code designating incurable insanity as a ground for divorce. Formerly, no matter how vicious the conduct of an insane spouse, he could not be divorced, for the law refused to find in him the guilt essential to a marital offense. . . . The Legislature has come to realize, however, that when a union is dominated by insanity, fulfilment of the normal purposes of marriage is hopeless. What was once a bar to divorce is now recognized as a justification for divorce. Still more striking in recognition of this trend has been the enactment of legislation in many states authorizing divorce when the spouses have lived apart for a required number of years. Marriage failure, rather than the fault of the parties, is the basis upon which such divorces are granted. . . .

---

[*] In DeBurgh v. DeBurgh, 240 P. 2d 625 (1952): It is not unusual that both spouses in divorce proceedings make claims of cruelty or other inequitable conduct. In such event, if both succeed, relief is denied both because they have come to court with unclean hands. Divorce is a remedy for the innocent against the guilty, whereas if both parties are equally at fault, a divorce will not be granted. To serve as ground for divorce, cruelty must be unmerited and unprovoked. . . . A court of equity does not allow itself to become the handmaid of iniquity. Intervention is justified not for the sake of either party who might be thereby benefited but in order to uphold the integrity of the law.

It would be forward indeed for the court, when it is called upon to evaluate an alleged recriminatory defense, to ignore the growing awareness that a marriage in name only is not a marriage in any real sense. In other fields, equity does not deny relief on the ground of plaintiff's unclean hands when to do so would be harmful to the public interest. . . . Such a rule is even more appropriate in marital litigation, where the social consequences of the court's decree are of the utmost importance. . . .

It bears noting how frequently divorces are uncontested. In many cases neither spouse is "innocent," and yet by agreement, one of them defaults to ensure a divorce. Thus a strict recrimination rule fails in its purpose of denying relief to the guilty. Moreover, it exerts a corrupting influence on the negotiations that precede the entry of such a default. The spouse who more desperately seeks an end to a hopeless union is penalized by the ability of the other spouse to prevent a divorce through the assertion of a recriminatory defense, and the more unscrupulous partner may obtain substantial financial concessions as the price of remaining silent. Were the clean hands doctrine properly applied, it would encourage estranged couples to bring their differences before the chancellor, where the interests of society as a whole can be given proper recognition and where settlement negotiations can be supervised and unfair advantage prevented.

A mechanical application of the doctrine of recrimination is by no means universal. In some states, the defense has been limited by requiring that the plaintiff's offense be of the same type as the defendant's or that it involve equal guilt. . . . Such limitations are not entirely satisfactory, however; even when misconduct is identical the court should be permitted to exercise a sound discretion in the public interest. Several states expressly recognize judicial discretion concerning recrimination. . . .

In view of the reliance of the Conant case of what was thought to be the English rule, perhaps the most illuminating of the modern cases on the subject is Blunt v. Blunt, [1943] A.C. 517. . . . [In that case at 525] Lord Chancellor Simon reviews the factors that should govern the decision in a given case. Among these are the prospect of reconciliation and the interests of the children of the marriage. In keeping with the traditional view of the law toward both marriage and divorce, the Lord Chancellor states that the consideration of "primary importance" is the interest of the community at large. This interest is "to be judged by maintaining a true balance between respect for the binding sanctity of marriage and the social considerations which make

it contrary to public policy to insist on the maintenance of a union which has utterly broken down." . . .

In examining the doctrine of recrimination, we have given the most serious consideration not only to judicial precedent but also to the work of leading scholars and practitioners. Few rules of law have been more widely condemned by the legal profession. In 1948, a committee of experts of the American Bar Association joined with the representatives of other interested groups in the work of the National Conference on Family Life. The Bar Association's representatives, acting as the legal section of the conference, strongly recommended the elimination of the defense of recrimination, Report of Legal Section of National Conference on Family Life [1948], pp. 1, 3, 7. See also Chafee, Some Problems of Equity [1950], pp. 73 et seq. In view of the statutory provisions on the subject, we are not free to go so far. Morever, we do not believe that the comparative guilt of the parties will be without significance in every case. We do believe, however, that some of the evils pointed out by the Bar Association Committee can be avoided within the framework of the existing statute if it is kept in mind that the doctrine of recrimination, like the doctrine of unclean hands of which it is a part, is neither puristic nor mechanical, but an equitable principle to be applied according to the circumstances of each case and with a proper respect for the paramount interests of the community at large.

*   *   *

We have concluded that section 122 of the Civil Code imposes upon the trial judge the duty to determine whether or not the fault of the plaintiff in a divorce action is to be regarded as "in bar" of the plaintiff's cause of divorce based upon the fault of the defendant. Tested by the considerations discussed above, the evidence in the present case would have been ample to support a finding that the parties' misconduct should not bar a divorce. Reconciliation appears impossible. The trial judge himself observed that "the marriage here was a failure from the start" and that "there is nothing really to keep them together." There was evidence that defendant more than once inflicted bodily injury upon plaintiff; that after one severe beating plaintiff attempted to commit suicide by an overdose of sleeping pills; that defendant often boasted in the presence of plaintiff and guests of intimate relations with other women and discussed their physical attributes in detail; that defendant was often intoxicated; that defendant frequently told plaintiff that her daughter by a previous marriage had loose morals; that defendant was insanely jealous of a former suitor of plaintiff and on one occasion seized an alarm clock given plaintiff by the suitor and threw it into the toilet; and that defendant lavishly tipped waiters and spent his money freely in public, but in private life refused to give plaintiff sufficient funds to purchase clothes suitable for her station in life. On the other hand, defendant's evidence was to the effect that plaintiff had invented false accusations against him; that plaintiff had deliberately attempted to ruin his business life by writing a letter to his partner falsely accusing defendant of dishonesty and homosexuality; and that plaintiff had announced her intention of writing similar letters to other business associates of defendant. If the foregoing facts are true, it is apparent that there has been a total and irremedial breakdown of the marriage. Technical marital fault can play but little part in the fact of the unhappy spectacle indicated by this evidence, with its inevitable effect upon the family, friends, neighbors, and business interests of the parties.

Moreover, it is significant that the application of a strict rule of recrimination in the present action does not operate with equal justice. As the spouse entrusted by law with the management and control of the community property, see Civ. Code §§ 161a, 172, 172a, defendant is in a position to use that property for his personal benefit. Although he has an obligation to support plaintiff, a large discretion is customarily vested in the husband concerning the manner of performing that obligation; in the present case, disagreement and repeated legal actions to obtain support money are almost certain to ensue.

There can be no precise formula for determining when a cause of divorce shown against a plaintiff is to be considered a bar to his suit for divorce, for the divorce court, as a court of equity, . . . is clothed with a broad discretion to advance the requirements of justice in each particular case. In general, however, certain major considerations will govern the court's decision:

1. The prospect of reconciliation. The court should determine whether the legitimate objects of matrimony have been destroyed or whether there is a reasonable likelihood that the marriage can be saved. It should consider the ages and temperaments of the parties, the length of their marriage, the seriousness and frequency of their marital misconduct proved at the trial and the likelihood of its recurrence, the duration and apparent finality of the separation, and the sincerity of their efforts to overcome differences and live together harmoniously.

2. The effect of the marital conflict upon the parties. If a continuation of the marriage would constitute a serious hazard to the health of either party, as in the case of physical brutality, the court should be reluctant to deny divorce. Although financial considerations can play only a minor role in determining the propriety of divorce, even these may not be entirely ignored if the evidence indicates that marital conflicts are destroying the livelihood of the parties.

3. The effect of the marital conflict upon third parties. In every divorce case in which children are involved, their interests are of the utmost concern to the court. The disruptive effect of divorce upon children is to be deplored, but in a given case it may be preferable to violence, hatred, or immorality when these are present in the home. The community as a whole also has an interest. Adultery, desertion, or cruelty, for example, can only discredit marriage; their perpetuation is not lightly to be decreed.

4. Comparative guilt. In many ways the guilt of the parties may be unequal—in the gravity of the misconduct involved, in the frequency of its occurrence, or in its effect upon children and others. Moreover, one spouse may demonstrate substantially greater repentence and reform. Marital offenders, therefore, are not necessarily in pari delicto before the chancellor. Their comparative guilt may have an important bearing upon whether or not either one or both should be granted relief.

We have concluded that in light of the foregoing discussion the findings and conclusions in the present case are not sufficient to support the determination that recrimination was established. It is essential that findings be made on every material issue raised by the pleadings. . . . As we have seen, whether or not the cause of action proved against each spouse is to be regarded as in bar of the cause of action proved against the other spouse is a material issue and must be expressly decided by the trial court before it may be said that recrimination has been decided. To decide the issue raised by a plea of recrimination, the court must consider the prospects of reconciliation, the comparative fault of the plaintiff and the defendant, and the effect of the marital strife upon the parties, their children, and the community.

Upon remand of the case for application of the clean hands doctrine as herein indicated, the trial court may decide that one of the parties should be granted a divorce. In that event, alimony and more than half of the community property may be awarded to the prevailing spouse as in any other case. It is also possible, however, that a divorce will be granted to both parties, . . . and it seems advisable to indicate here the rules that should govern the granting of alimony and the apportionment of community property under such circumstances. When a divorce is granted to both, alimony may be awarded to either, for the basis of liability for alimony is the granting of a divorce against the person required to pay it. See Civil Code, § 139. Section 146 of the Civil Code provides that if the divorce is granted for extreme cruelty, the court may apportion community property as it deems just, but that statute has been interpreted to permit an award of more than half of the community property only to an innocent spouse. Eslinger v. Eslinger, 47 Cal. 62, 64. When a divorce is granted to both parties, neither is innocent within the meaning of this rule, and the community property must be equally divided.

The judgment is reversed. The appeal from the order denying the motion for a new trial is dismissed. Defendant is to bear the costs of this appeal.

EDMONDS, JUSTICE (concurring).

Solely upon the ground that there are contradictory, irreconcilable findings about matters material to a proper disposition of the case, I concur in the reversal of the judgment. . . . In view of the conflicting evidence, it would be inappropriate for this court to determine which finding is supported by the greater weight of the evidence and to order judgment accordingly. . . .

In my opinion, these conclusions are determinative of the appeal. If, upon retrial the evidence should disclose that each party has a cause of divorce against the other, as I read the Civil Code, the trial court will have no alternative but to deny each of them a divorce. Civ. Code § 111(4). Likewise, if it should be proved that the conduct of each was provoked by the other, a divorce must be denied either party because neither one will have shown a cause of divorce. Cruelty which is provoked by the party seeking a divorce is not actionable. . . . However, it may be that, although the evidence disclose cruelty on the part of each party, provocation for the acts of one upon the part of the other may be proved. In that event, the trial court properly might award a divorce to the party whose actions were provoked by the other.

This court cannot anticipate what the evidence upon another trial may disclose, nor can it predict what findings and conclusions the court will draw therefrom. The conclusion that the findings are in irreconcilable conflict disposes of the issue before us and the lengthy discourse upon

the doctrine of recrimination is unnecessary and unwarranted dictum. However, because of my disagreement with the interpretation placed upon the statutory law of this state, I am compelled to state my views upon that question.

"The legislature has seen fit to make the doctrine [of recrimination] an integral part of the law of this state. It is not for the courts to determine the rightness or wrongness of the doctrine so declared. That is a legislative and not a judicial function." Comfort v. Comfort, 17 Cal. 2d 736, 752, 112 P. 2d 259, 268.

In effect, the court now repeals sections 111(4) and 122 of the Civil Code. Section 111 provides: "Divorces *must* be denied upon showing: * * * 4. Recrimination; * * *." Emphasis added. Section 122 defines recrimination as "a showing by the defendant of any cause of divorce against the plaintiff, in bar of the plaintiff's cause of divorce."

Ignoring the mandatory "must" of section 111, the majority hold that the trial court may exercise its "discretion" in determining whether to grant a divorce where each party has shown a cause of divorce against the other. . . .

* * *

In the present opinion "recrimination" is not defined. However, the inevitable implication of the analysis of the problem is that there is no such thing. It is acknowledged that a cause of divorce must be proved before the doctrine of recrimination may be applied. The conclusion is then reached that, after the defendant's cause is established, the trial court must determine whether it is "in bar" of the relief sought by the plaintiff.

The fallacy of such circuitous reasoning lies in the misinterpretation of the plain language of the statute. It is assumed that the phrase "in bar of the plaintiff's cause of divorce" refers back to the words "any cause of divorce". However, the structure of the sentence precludes any such interpretation. The phrase beginning with "in bar" is a modifying one deliberately separated from the preceding modifying language by a comma. As diagramed in Klemmer v. Klemmer [42 Cal. App. 618, 187 P. 86], the sentence reads: "Recrimination is a *showing* by the defendant of any cause of divorce against the plaintiff, *in bar of the plaintiff's cause of divorce*." . . . The word "showing" is modified by two separate, and equal, phrases. The first, "by the defendant of any cause of divorce against the plaintiff", explains the kind of "showing," which must be made. Such showing, if made, is "in bar of the plaintiff's cause of divorce."

The majority say 250 P. 2d 600: "Had the Legislature meant to make every cause of divorce an absolute defense, it could easily have provided that: 'Divorces must be denied upon * * * a showing by the defendant of any cause of divorce against the plaintiff.'" They ignore the fact that section 122 is a definition of "recrimination" as used in section 111. In defining "recrimination" as a showing "in bar of the plaintiff's cause of divorce", the code commissioners simply adopted the accepted judicial definition of that term as stated in Conant v. Conant, 10 Cal. 249, 256, and the English cases there cited.

*   *   *

. . . By the decision the court did not establish a doctrine that the plaintiff be "without reproach" to secure a divorce. It held that "where the matter pleaded is such as would entitle the defendant to a decree, had it been presented in a bill brought by himself, the relief should be denied." 10 Cal. at page 256. In using the words "without reproach", it specifically limited them to "similar guilt, or an offence to which the law attaches similar consequences". 10 Cal. at page 258. Because the now abandoned doctrine of two types of divorce then existed, the court did provide a lesser guilt would bar a divorce a vinculo matrimonii. However, it is important to note that a divorce would be granted a mensa et thoro where the guilt of the plaintiff was not sufficient to have established a cause of divorce in the defendant.

In the Conant case the court also rejected the strict rule of the ecclesiastical courts. They had allowed only adultery as a bar to a suit for divorce. . . .

*   *   *

None of the decisions cited by the commissioners considered the public policy argument now presented. The full quotation from Freeman v. Sedwick [6 Gill, Md. 29, 39-40], the only one of those cases here relied upon, is as follows: "After a careful examination of the authorities, we are brought to the conclusion that Courts of equity have held, and uniformly decided, that it was both the wisdom and policy of the law to withhold all aid or relief from parties in controversies between themselves, who stood strictly in pari delicto, which might or could tend to the consummation of agreements entered into in fraud of the law, or the rights of any person. Mr. Justice Story, in his Commentary in Equity Jurisprudence, vol. 1, p. 317, sec. 298, says: 'The suppression of illegal contracts is far more likely, in general, to be accomplished by leaving the parties without remedy against each other, and by thus introducing a preventive check, naturally connected with a want of confidence, and a sole reliance upon personal honor. And so, accordingly, the modern doctrine is established. Relief is not granted, where both parties are truly in pari delicto, unless in cases where public policy would thereby be promoted.'"

*   *   *

By now saying that "the considerations of policy that prompt the state to consent to a divorce when one spouse has been guilty of misconduct are often doubly present when both spouses have been guilty", in effect, this court repeals the statutory rule of recrimination. Thus, in any case where, by the terms of the statute, recrimination is a bar, it should not be applied because of public policy. Only the embalmed corpse of the doctrine is preserved, impotent in the shroud of standards established "for determining when a cause of divorce shown against a plaintiff is to be considered a bar to his suit for divorce".

*   *   *

Whether a cause of divorce is established is simply a matter of proof. If the evidence is sufficient to sustain a decree upon any one of the statutory grounds, a cause of divorce is shown and cumulative evidence does not give it greater sanctity. Either a cause of divorce is established or it is not. Once established, it is neither more nor less effective than any other cause as the basis for a divorce or a bar to the other spouse's cause of divorce. And yet, it is now held, these causes, equal under the law, must in some metaphysical fashion be measured or weighed by the trial judge. By comparing the equal, inequality may be discovered. Beyond the superlative of "extreme" or "utmost" cruelty the court may find an indescribable infinity which is more than utmost, an unimaginable degree of cruelty which is greater than the greatest.

That the doctrine of recrimination has been repealed is made crystal clear by the suggestion "that a divorce will be granted to both parties". The code makes no provision for such a decree and the result is contrary to the requirement that a divorce "must be denied" when recrimination is proved. "Certain consequences are attached to the decree, independent of the dissolution of the marriage contract, and they are generally more favorable to the party obtaining the relief than to the contestant; but a decree can not be granted in favor of one, and afterwards in favor of the other, as the first would dissolve the marriage, and then no marriage would subsist, upon which the second decree could act; and a decree granting a divorce in favor of each, would be an anomalous proceeding." Conant v. Conant, supra.

The Civil Code contemplates that a divorce can be awarded to only one party. Section 131 provides in part: "If it determines that the divorce ought to be granted, an interlocutory judgment must be entered, declaring that *the party* in whose favor the court decides is entitled to a divorce; * * *" (Emphasis added.)

* * *

The anomaly of awarding a divorce to both parties is further stressed by the discussion of alimony and property rights. . . . No provision is made for the situation where a decree is granted against both parties. That such an eventuality was not anticipated by the Legislature is obvious from section 142, which provides: "When the *prevailing party* in the action has either a separate estate, or is earning his or her own livelihood, * * * the court in its discretion, may withhold any allowance to *the prevailing party* out of the separate property of *the other party*." (Emphasis added.) Clearly, the Legislature did not foresee a prevailing party against whom the decree might be granted.

By statute, 32 American jurisdictions allow the defense of recrimination. In only three of these may the court, in its discretion, grant a divorce after proof of recrimination. Except for these three, recrimination is, by statute, an absolute defense in the majority of states. 2 Vernier, American Family Laws, p. 87. The decisions from other states and England, here cited as recognizing judicial discretion, all rely upon different statutes or declare judicial policy in the absence of statute. The policy which underlies these exceptions to the general rule may be commendable. But this court should not usurp the legislative prerogative by the device of interpreting a statute which needs no interpretation, and which has been accepted without question for eighty years. If public policy no longer condones the doctrine of recrimination, then it is for the Legislature, and not for the court, to repeal the statute.

SHENK, JUSTICE (concurring and dissenting).

I concur in the judgment of reversal on the ground that the findings are contradictory and irreconcilable. I disagree with the meaning given to the phrase "in bar of the plaintiff's cause of divorce". . . .

Section 111 of the Civil Code reads: "Divorces must be denied upon showing * * * 4. Recrimination". The limitation of that defense in an action for divorce is continued in section 122. That section defines "Recrimination" as " a show-

ing by the defendant of any cause of divorce against the plaintiff, in bar of the plaintiff's cause of divorce." Separate maintenance is an available remedy where a cause of divorce exists, section 137, Civ. Code, but because of a showing of recrimination a divorce may not be granted. Section 111.

There is thus no warrant for disapproving or overruling prior cases. . . .

NOTES

NOTE 1.

EVANS v. EVANS
176 Ore. 403, 157 P. 2d 495 (1945)

BRAND, JUSTICE (dissenting).

* * *

Turning to considerations of public policy. I question the wisdom of applying the normally wholesome maxim of clean hands as if it were a rule of property law. Divorce is not a lawsuit between two parties. It involves the wrongs of plaintiff and defendant, but it affects the rights of innocent children and the vital interests of society. In these matters, I think the courts are still controlled by mores, now discarded, of generations long since dead. We need an injection of realism into the law of domestic relations. When husband and wife come to the parting of the ways, they are no longer bound together by a strong, if not puritanical, public condemnation of divorce. They part. Then some court, by a procedure which is often little more than a formality, confers its blessing upon the new freedom by granting a divorce. The court and the community appear to agree that the public welfare is served by freeing from the bonds of matrimony one who has been subjected to cruel and inhuman treatment. But if each spouse has subjected the other to such treatment and if the facts are made to appear, the court dooms both to the unhappy bonds and burdens of such a life—married in law, divorced in fact.

It is at this point that I think considerations of public policy are of more importance than legal rules of thumb. It is a truism to say that the sanctity of the home is the basis of Christian civilization, but I can not see why the law should be so concerned to maintain the marriage status, and theoretically the home, when both spouses are at fault, while granting wholesale dissolution of marriages when but one is at fault. The misconduct of both parties is often the result of an unfortunate incompatibility. In such a case, the legal recognition of a factual separation may restore both parties to useful and wholesome living.

Any judge who has had wide experience on the trial bench will concede that in divorce cases, theory and practice are as widely separated as the poles. I suppose that ninety-nine percent of divorces are granted on a routine ex parte hearing after the defendant has failed to appear, or has entered a general appearance and refused to plead further. In legal theory, the proceeding is an adversary action, but in a large proportion of cases, both parties are content that the divorce be granted. Frequently acquiescence reaches the verge of collusion. It has been my observation that when a divorce is contested it is seldom because the defendant hopes, or expects, that the home can be kept intact if the decree is denied. The bitter contests almost invariably involve the adjustment of property rights or the custody of children.

If, in the multitude of default divorce cases, the courts were to insist upon a bilateral disclosure of the real controversy and of mutual fault and then were sternly to apply the doctrine of pari delicto in those cases, as it does in the few instances of contest, the entire divorce system, as it now exists in fact, would become unrecognizable.

In cases of mutual fault, I think the court should be guided by two paramount considerations in determining whether to invoke the rule of pari delicto. It should consider, first, the welfare of the children, if any, and, second, what will be the probable effect on the parties and on society in general, if the divorce be denied. If, at the time of the trial, a separation has, in fact, taken place and there is no reasonable probability of a reconciliation, then we may be fairly sure that denying the divorce will not result in the re-establishment of the home. Again, if a definite separation has occurred and thereafter charges and countercharges are hurled at both litigants in the course of a contested divorce suit, so much bitterness is likely to be engendered that the possibility of re-establishing even the forms of normal domestic life in the same household will be utterly destroyed.

There may be instances in which persons with an enlightened sense of parental duty will re-establish a home if divorce be denied them in a contested suit and will carry on for the benefit of their children. If that result should appear to be within the realm of probability and the parties appear to be about equally at fault, perhaps a court would be justified in denying a divorce in the hope that the home already broken might be mended, but I have never heard of such a case. If, in the case of mutual fault, the court finds that denial of the divorce will not result in the reestablishment of the home for the benefit of the

children, then a serious problem of public policy arises. Assuming that father and mother will continue to live apart, is it for the good of society that the court should adjudge that they must forever remain married in law, when they are irrevocably unmarried in fact?

The fact that one or both parties to a marriage may have given the other one ground for divorce does not necessarily prove the offender to be of either a vicious or criminal disposition. If it did, the solution would be more simple. The causes of marital unhappiness and misconduct are often subtle and deep-seated and are better known to the social worker or to the psychiatrist than to the judge. I am convinced that in many, though of course not in all, instances the interests of the children, of society at large, and of the parties themselves would be better served if the courts were to exercise more cautious circumspection in denying relief to a seriously wronged spouse on the ground of pari delicto.

By granting a divorce in such a case, the court would be recognizing the existence of facts over the continuation of which the law has no effective control, and it could then exercise to the fullest an informed discretion as to the custody of the children, awarding them to the parent most likely to serve them well, since it can not award them to both.

*   *   *

NOTE 2.

ZAVIN v. ZAVIN
229 Ore. 289, 366 P. 2d 733 (1961)

GOODWIN, JUSTICE.

*   *   *

After four days in court, the experienced trial judge concluded that neither party had carried the burden of proof. His carefully reasoned memorandum opinion weighs and sifts the evidence and finds it substantially lacking in probative force. He summarized his conclusions by observing that at least one of the parties was lying, but he could not tell which one it was. If he had stopped there, the cause would have been dismissed. But, being of the opinion that the marriage was a failure, the judge then reexamined the pleadings. He found that the husband had charged the wife with infidelity but had produced no evidence thereof. This unproven allegation of misconduct apparently tipped the balance in favor of the wife who had made equally grave and equally unproven charges, but not quite so many of them. The court having concluded as a matter of fact that the marriage was an empty legal status without hope of rehabilitation, then granted the wife a divorce and a considerable amount of property.

The plaintiff on this appeal seeks to have the decree reversed so that he may be awarded the divorce as the prevailing party. [T]he plaintiff would then have both his property and his freedom.

The case is controlled, however, by . . . our former decisions . . . where we denied either party a divorce when the record revealed that the fault of one substantially equalled the fault of the other. . . .

Under ORS 107.030, which lists the grounds for divorce, we are not at liberty to follow the lead of those courts which have recognized marriage failure as a social problem justifying divorce without any particular consideration of grounds. . . .

* * *

NOTE 3.

BURBURY, SIR STANLEY

Some Extra-Judicial Reflections Upon Two Years' Judicial Experience of the Commonwealth Matrimonial Causes Act 1959*

Our modern divorce law is a product of our modern society ; it has in no sense caused more broken marriages, it is symptomatic of a changed outlook in society upon the institution of marriage—a society in which many no longer subscribe to the Christian concept of marriage and in which there are many who maintain that the law should readily provide for dissolution of a marriage which has in fact broken down. Modern divorce legislation must be taken to be a democratic expression of the will of the majority of the community. To abolish divorce or make it less easy would not be to repair broken marriages. In fact I believe that our modern divorce legislation has proved a considerable social benefit in regularizing many

---

* 36 AUSTRALIAN L. J. 283, 284, 286 (1963).

unions which but for it would have remained permanently illicit and in removing the stigma of illegitimacy from the offspring of such unions. The modern divorce laws give legal recognition to factual breakdown of marriages and proceed to impose safeguards as conditions precedent to that legal recognition.

We may regret the decline in spiritual, moral, and social values which has occasioned the modern legislation. But legislators must legislate in the existing social context and the law must be adjusted to social conditions as they exist ; and not even judges in their ivory towers can pretend that in their task of interpreting and applying divorce legislation they are unaffected by the prevailing social climate.

* * *

The introduction of separation as a ground has I believe removed a strong incentive to perjury and in many cases has avoided the unreality under the label of desertion (actual or constructive) of attributing the breakdown of the marriage to the fault of one party.

In my limited experience of this ground I have found that in the overwhelming majority of cases in which it has been invoked it is quite plain that the marriage has utterly broken down and divorce or no divorce there is not the slightest possibility the parties will ever live together again. In other words, divorce or no divorce the family unit has irretrievably disintegrated. I have also found that in a very large number of these cases one or both of the separated spouses has entered into a permanent illicit relationship and children have been born of the illicit union. These are cases where for one reason or another none of the traditional grounds for divorce was available. It has appeared in many cases of this kind that the result of a decree would be to regularize one and often two illicit unions and remove the stigma of illegitimacy from a number of children.

* * *

D.

To Decisions Concerning the Administration of Reorganized Wife-Husband Relationships?

ARONSTEIN v. ARONSTEIN
170 Cal. App. 2d 494, 339 P. 2d 191 (1959)

TOBRINER, JUSTICE.

This case presents the narrow issue whether the record supports an order that respondent

pay $50 per month for support of appellant from whom respondent was divorced upon the ground of incurable insanity.

The relevant facts disclose an unfortunate series of events. Married on April 14, 1949, appellant within six months became ill with tuberculosis which caused her confinement at the Belmont Sanitarium. Upon her release from the sanitarium in June, 1950, appellant again resumed living with her husband, only to suffer a miscarriage in November, 1950. In turn, this difficulty reactivated appellant's tubercular condition, and she was sent to the National Jewish Hospital at Denver, Colorado. While there, appellant became mentally ill; she was then transferred to Kaiser Hospital in Vallejo, California. On February 13, 1952, the Superior Court for the County of Solano committed appellant to the State Hospital for the Insane at Napa, California.

Respondent obtained an interlocutory decree of divorce from appellant on the ground of incurable insanity on September 26, 1955. The final decree, entered October 8, 1956, provided that respondent pay $30 per month to the Department of Mental Hygiene for her support and $5 per month to the Social Service Department at the Napa State Hospital for her personal use. The decree also required respondent to designate appellant as the irrevocable beneficiary of a $5,000 life insurance policy on his life which he was to maintain during her lifetime.

After more than five years of confinement, appellant obtained leave from the hospital in March, 1957, and went to live with her parents. Dr. Kurt S. Brock, as appellant's physician, filed an affidavit stating that during the period of her release appellant required administration of a drug under the supervision of a physician; that her tubercular condition was "arrested"; that she was not "physically or mentally capable of accepting employment."

The 67 year old father of appellant, appointed her guardian ad litem, has moved for an increase in the support provision of the final decree, stating that appellant's minimum needs call for $125 per month, of which amount $25 is required for medical expenses alone. Respondent, an unmarried man of 42 years of age, employed by the Fairmont Hotel as a headwaiter or captain at the Venetian Room, does not challenge the claimed need for support but contends that he is unable to make such payments.

Upon hearing . . . the trial court did, pursuant to respondent's offer . . . increase the payments from the original $35 to $50 per month. The order of modification provides, likewise, that if appellant is again hospitalized respondent shall, in lieu of the $50 per month, pay $30 per month to the Department of Mental Hygiene and $5 per month for appellant's personal use to the Social Service Department of the hospital in which she is confined.

Appellant appeals from the modification order insofar as it fails to provide for more than $50 per month during such periods as she is not hospitalized. Accordingly, we must first define the nature of the obligation owed by a spouse who obtains a divorce upon the ground of incurable insanity; thereafter we must determine whether the trial court applied the proper test for fulfilling that obligation, and finally examine the the record to see if it supports the court's order.

Society has been slow to recognize the propriety of a divorce granted on the ground of a spouse's incurable insanity. This reluctance probably stemmed from the concept that a divorce could rest only on "the deliberate misconduct of the defendant" and not on the "impossibility of a functioning marriage." 1 Armstrong California Family Law (1953) 177. In Great Britain only in 1937 did the Matrimonial Causes Act of that year provide for divorce upon the ground of "unsoundness of mind," regarded after five years of duration as incurable. . . . It was in the comparatively recent year of 1941 . . . that the Legislature of this state denominated insanity as a ground for divorce (Civ. Code § 108) and even then posited it upon the condition that the party seeking the divorce allege in the complaint and prove at the trial that there was "reasonable ability to support the insane spouse for the remainder of the life expectancy or that such insane spouse has property sufficient to provide support for the remainder of the life expectancy * * *." When this condition was declared unconstitutional because it created an arbitrary and unreasonable class discrimination between those of different financial resources . . . the Legislature removed it in 1951. . . . The process of relieving the innocent husband or wife from a marriage that no longer existed as a human relationship and which served only as a formality to frustrate the normal life of the sane party was halting and tortuous.

The archaic discrepancy between the divorce granted for alleged fault of the party and that based upon incurable insanity remains in the differing requirements for support of the divorced spouse. While under Civil Code, section 139, the court is empowered to "compel the party against whom the decree or judgment is granted to make such suitable allowances for support and maintenance of the other party * * * as the court may deem just, having regard for the circumstances of the respective parties * * *," section 108 by contrast contains this caveat: "No decree granted on this ground shall relieve the spouse granted the divorce of any obligation imposed by law as a result of the marriage for the support of the spouse against whom the divorce is granted, and the court may make such order for support, or require a bond therefor, as the circumstances require."

The wide latitude of discretion of section 139, permitting the consideration of such factors as the length of the marriage, the respective age of the parties, the degree of fault as to events leading up to the divorce, the separate estate of the ex-spouse seeking support, the need of the former spouse compared to the ability of the other . . . finds no counterpart in section 108. Instead, that section imposes upon the spouse who obtains a divorce upon the grounds of insanity a primary and irrenounceable duty of support.

* * *

Yet there are limits to the obligation of support in section 108. The term "obligation" is inchoate; the court must give it content. Obviously it is not absolute; the spouse cannot be saddled with an obligation which is beyond his economic capacity. The section itself states that the divorce granted on the ground of insanity shall not "relieve the spouse granted the divorce of any obligation imposed by law as a result of the marriage * * *." The obligation, then, must relate back to that of the married spouse. This obligation obviously cannot reach beyond the extent of the spouse's ability to meet or pay for the support of the partner. . . .

* * *

[T]he court expressed some concern as to the disparity of the rules of the sections, the court expressly related its findings to the respondent's ability to pay, saying: "I would be less than honest as far as the record is concerned if I didn't say I was influenced by the argument Mr. Eisler has just made, that if she had been divorced under any other circumstances she would long since now have been cut off from support as far as my philosophy of it is concerned. On the other hand, the statutory admonition is there, * * *. I just don't see the money here, counsel, to support her from this man, to support her the way she should be supported."

* * *

In the instant case, appellant contends that respondent's gross monthly wage was $360 per month; that he admitted his tips amounted to a figure of $2,100 in the year of 1956; that his Federal Income Tax Return shows an investment in vending machines of $8,792.18; that in addition he purchased an automobile for $2,450. She contends that since respondent shows expenses of only $350 per month he could well afford to meet appellant's claim for support of $125 per month.

In substance, the contrary contention of respondent is that his net earnings amount to less than $400 per month; that his expenses reach at least $350 per month; that the investment in vending machines was obtained by a loan; that the car is required for servicing and maintaining the vending machines.

. . . The court's apparent conclusion that respondent's income was in the neighborhood of $400 per month would . . . find substantiation in the evidence.

Likewise, the court's finding that respondent's expenses approximated $350 per month finds support in the record. . . . The record, then, substantiates the court's ruling that defendant's limit of ability to pay for appellant's support was no more than $50 per month.

While there was some testimony of respondent that he expected his vending machine business to do better in the future and while it is possible that respondent may increase his earnings in wages and tips to an extent which might increase his ability to pay for the support of appellant, these possibilities cannot sustain a ruling of this court that the trial court's finding is unsupported. In any event appellant may make such future application to the trial court regarding respondent's ability to pay as may be justified by change of circumstance.

We therefore affirm the order of the trial court.

NOTES

NOTE 1.

ARONSTEIN v. ARONSTEIN
Two Years Later

The husband has continued to pay the $50.00 a month ordered up to the beginning of this year. He is in default with his payments since February 1, 1961. Recently, he has filed a motion that he be allowed to borrow an amount of $1,000.00 on the life insurance policy which, under the divorce decree, he has to keep alive, so that there be some funds for the wife, should he die within 20 years from the decree. That life insurance policy was community property, and is for the amount of $5,000.00. The motion was denied. There has been no motion of the wife to increase the monthly amount of $50.00. The wife is still living with her family, and has not been recommitted. In fact, most of the support for the wife has been paid and is paid by her father. What will happen when the father dies, is a question which I cannot answer. The husband had left California for a while. Then he came back and, together with a partner, now runs a restaurant in San Francisco which is owned by a two-man corporation. The income tax return of Mr.

Aronstein for 1960 shows income in the amount of $750.00. The income tax return of the corporation is unknown to me, but it will show no profit, or a very small profit, since the initial expenses of opening the business were undoubtedly high and the border line between depreciable expenses and current expenses is rather thin in the case of such small corporations. Mr. Aronstein has remarried. I shall probably have to proceed against him for contempt of court, if payment of the arrears should not be made now. [Letter dated May 16, 1961 from Richard O. Graw, attorney for appellant.]

NOTE 2.

JASS v. JASS
255 Minn. 183, 96 N.W. 2d 30 (1959)

THOMAS GALLAGHER, JUSTICE.

Appeal from an order denying defendant's motion to have plaintiff adjudged in contempt of a decree of divorce for his failure to pay certain medical expenses incurred by defendant and for an order determining the amount due defendant therefore and directing judgment against plaintiff for such amount. The divorce decree dated March 6, 1950, included the following provision:

"* * * plaintiff shall pay to the defendant any reasonable extraordinary medical expenses which may be necessarily incurred by her."

On June 16, 1954, this was modified by the court by a provision that:

"* * * defendant, before she incur any future extraordinary medical or hospital expenses in her behalf, notify the Probation Officer of Ramsey County and obtain his approval for such expenditures."

. . . Subsequently, on two occasions she incurred additional medical expenses without first obtaining the consent of the probation officer of Ramsey County, which expenses were paid for by plaintiff.

* * *

Plaintiff refused to pay for such expenses, and . . . submitted an affidavit that . . . in his opinion the expenses now sought to be recovered were unnecessary and incurred by defendant for purposes of revenge.

Defendant denied this and submitted affidavits of her physicians to the effect that the medical expenses described were necessary. . . .

* * *

[W]e cannot conclude that the court intended that plaintiff was under no obligation to pay defendant's reasonable, necessary medical ex-

penses unless she first obtain the consent of the probation officer of Ramsey County. Obviously, the objective of the court was to prevent the incurrence of unreasonable or unnecessary medical expenditures. The final decision as to whether such services were reasonable and necessary would scarcely be left to the decision of the probation officer who was not a licensed physician or surgeon. While the court required that he be notified of intended surgery, it would still seem illogical to hold that, in the absence of his consent, defendant might not under any circumstances still establish that surgery was needed and of vital importance. This she might do by presenting evidence to such effect under the original decree. . . .

This opportunity was denied her in the present proceeding. It is our opinion that the court should have proceeded to a hearing. . . .

NOTE 3.

JASS v. JASS
Two Years Later

(a) After the Supreme Court decision the parties stipulated that an order be entered by the trial court requiring the husband to pay the medical but not the dental bills. So far he has not paid very much. The wife has had further medical expenses and has made further application to the Court. [Letter dated May 1961 from T. F. Quinn, attorney for the wife.]

(b) We represented the husband. After the Supreme Court reversed the trial court a new hearing was scheduled, but just a few hours before the hearing the other attorney and I agreed upon a reduced figure and that amount was paid.

The wife has needed additional medical treatment since the case was tried and has been averaging about $1,000 per year in medical treatment since the divorce was granted. At the time the divorce was granted it was anticipated that this woman would have some need for surgery and medical attention because of a bladder disorder. She was very bitter about the divorce and her bitterness has increased as the years go by. We feel that she is now running up medical bills solely for revenge, but of course such a contention is almost impossible to prove. [Letter dated June 1, 1961 from Thomas J. Burke, attorney for the husband.]

NOTE 4.

LAMBORN v. LAMBORN
251 P. 943 (D. Ct. of App., Cal. 1926)

PLUMMER, J. This is an appeal by the plaintiff from an order of the superior court of the county of Alameda, made and entered on the

6th day of June, 1921, reducing the amount of alimony from $45 to $30 per month. . . .

. . . The transcript shows that the respondent herein was then of the age of 33 years, was an employee of the Atchison, Topeka & Santa Fe Railway, earning a sum slightly less than $160 per month ; that the respondent desired to marry again, that the plaintiff in said action was able to earn money for her own support ; that the decree was oppressive and deprived the petitioner herein of money for his own needs ; and that the health of the plaintiff, the appellant in this proceeding, and her professional training enabled her to earn money for her own support.

* * *

[The] record indicate[s], at least, a lack of any real disposition on the part of the appellant to earn any part of her own living.

[O]ne of the physicians . . . testified that he had treated the appellant for a number of months. This, however, does not require the conclusion that the plaintiff was wholly incapacitated for work. We think it is common knowledge that many people, suffering from some ailment for which they are receiving treatment, continue their usual employment for considerable periods at a time, nor is an ailment which incapacitates a person for a particular line of work a sufficient reason why a trial court should come to the conclusion that such person is not able to earn money in other fields of labor. To determine this question the trial court must necessarily have some knowledge of the intellectual capacity of the persons in question, their intelligence, their power of adaptability. . . .

We agree with the substance of appellant's argument that trial courts should be niggardly in the matter of awarding alimony, and we also coincide with the effect of respondent's insistence that where the ex-husband is earning wages by daily labor, a trial court, in awarding alimony, should not do so in a sum inducing idleness on the part of the ex-wife. Where there are no children involved and the parties are both young in years, we think the trial court may take into consideration, in awarding alimony, the possibility, probability, and the desirability of allowing the respective parties to establish another and, perhaps, more congenial home. The prevalence of divorces may well call for judicial support of the institution of marriage, and we cannot say it is an abuse of discretion for a trial court to admit testimony and consider proof relative to future marriage. While the mere desire of a party to remarry may not, in and of itself, be a sufficient ground for reducing the award of alimony, it is

a matter to be taken into consideration, when determining whether the other party has or has not evinced a willingness to earn something toward her own support. In other words, we think the trial court was justified in considering the laudable wish of the respondent to remarry, and that he should not be so crippled in his finances that another home may not be established, unless it appeared to the trial court that the necessities of the former wife compelled such a course. The change in the industrial world which has taken place in the last few years presents to the trial court many matters for consideration and calls for the exercise of its discretion in awarding alimony. Thousands of women and girls are now employed, where formerly men and boys were once found. The employment of women in all lines of work is now so general that it may almost be said to be a mark of distinction for a woman to be self-supporting. Whether the plaintiff is sufficiently able to enter this class and become independent, or at least, to make a reasonable effort to attain that end, and so relieve the opposite party from the monthly draft upon his wages, were all equitable matters for the trial court to weigh and consider, and, unless there appears a manifest abuse of discretion, this court has no authority to interfere.

* * *

The order appealed from is affirmed.

NOTE 5.

DAKIN v. DAKIN
62 Wash. 687, 384 P. 2d 639 (1963)

HUNTER, JUDGE.

The record shows that the plaintiff has no children to support or care for ; that she was 53 years of age at the commencement of this action ; that she was extremely nervous and upset at the time of the trial ; but, otherwise, she is an able-bodied woman ; that, because of her past condition, she has been unable to maintain steady employment ; that she attended teacher's college for two years and taught school for four years thereafter ; and that she has had considerable experience as a social worker, although no formal training.

It is the policy of this state to place a duty upon the wife to gain employment, if possible. In Morgan v. Morgan, supra, we said:

"Alimony is not a matter of right. When the wife has the ability to earn a living, it is not the policy of the law of this state to give her a perpetual lien on her divorced husband's future income. Warning v. Warning, 40 Wash. 2d 903, 247 P. 2d 249 (1952); Lockhart v. Lockhart, 145 Wash. 210, 259 P. 385 (1927)."

We are of the opinion that the plaintiff in the instant case should not receive alimony until her remarriage or until her death. We think that she should be encouraged to rehabilitate herself and that, within a reasonable period, she may become self-supporting. Although she may have been nervous and upset prior to her decree of divorce, there is no evidence which indicates this condition is of a permanent nature. Except for this condition, she appears to be an able-bodied woman capable of future employment. We conclude that alimony should be awarded which is adequate for the purpose of providing for her during her transitional period. We cannot say, under the state of this record, what this period should be. Therefore, the trial court should be in a position to modify or terminate the alimony upon competent proof of changed conditions, if any, that may be established at future modification hearings. The divorce decree is therefore modified by awarding the plaintiff alimony in the amount of $300 per month until further order of the court.

NOTE 6.

ENGLISH, O. SPURGEON, and FINCH, STUART M.

Introduction to Psychiatry*

Another factor which always must be borne in mind is the degree of . . . gain which has subsequently become attached to the illness. If the patient, by virtue of his difficulty, now receives a great deal more attention, love, and support than he had previously, it may greatly diminish his desire to return to a more mature and normal way of life. Perhaps the most obvious examples of heightened . . . gain are seen in compensation cases, where as long as the individual retains his incapacitating symptoms he receives a monetary reward which he will lose the moment he returns to a more normal life. In many instances prior to any efficient therapy, it is necessary to deal with the . . . gain factor.

NOTE 7.

BLAUFARB v. BLAUFARB
9 App. Div. 86, 191 N.Y.S. 2d 785 (1959)

BENJAMIN J. RABIN, JUSTICE.

In this proceeding the plaintiff moves to amend the final decree of divorce rendered in her favor so as to provide for her support. Subsequent to the entry of that decree, which provided no alimony for her, the wife entered into an agreement waiving all claims for alimony, past,

---

* Reprinted from *Introduction to Psychiatry* by O. Spurgeon English, M.D., and Stuart M. Finch, M.D., p. 536, by permission of W. W. Norton & Company, Inc. Copyright © 1954, 1957, 1964 by W. W. Norton & Company, Inc.

present or future and at the same time executed a release in favor of her husband.

* * *

The parties were married on July 11, 1934. . . . While the wife, a school teacher, worked steadily, the husband appeared unable to earn a livelihood and was, to a large degree, supported by his wife.

The marital relationship slowly degenerated and in 1939 the parties separated. Thereafter, in 1941, the wife obtained a decree of divorce. That decree . . . made no provision for the support . . . of the wife . . . since there was no application made for such provision. The wife apparently failed to do so because of her husband's hopeless financial condition at the time. . . .

Several years after the divorce the husband remarried. His financial position took a turn for the better. For the past several years he has enjoyed and still enjoys an extraordinarily large income. In fact it was conceded upon argument that should this Court decide that the decree be modified to provide for the support of the wife, the husband is in a position to pay any sum that the Court may decide to be reasonably proper.

In 1955 the wife suffered an injury which disabled her and subsequently prevented her from teaching. As a result, she was retired on a disability pension which reduced her income to $289 per month.

During that year she commenced an action against her husband, seeking to recover the sum of $30,000 to reimburse her for moneys she claims to have expended for necessaries on behalf of the daughter. A settlement of that action was reached in December, 1955, pursuant to which she received $6,500 and she in turn executed a general release of all her claims for alimony, past, present and future. She was then represented by counsel and Special Term found that such agreement was not induced by either fraud or coercion.

* * *

What then are the standards by which we determine what is just in this case? Ordinarily we would be very reluctant to grant relief where, as here, the wife with proper representation knowingly accepted a sum in settlement of all her future claims for support—particularly after so many years had elapsed since the parties have lived together. She then expressed her readiness to look after herself and indicated by her agreement her ability to do so. However, Section 1170 envisions a change of circumstances—it looks to the future for the protection of an innocent wife whose circumstances have so changed as to put her in need. In this case the wife, a school teacher, lived on a school teacher's salary. She lived in a manner commensurate with her status. Due to the accident which made necessary her disability retirement, her income has been reduced to the sum of $289 per month. Such sum is insufficient to enable her to maintain that status particularly when we consider the reduced purchasing power of the dollar. The wife does not ask that a sufficient allowance be granted to her to enable her to live on the standard of a wife of one who enjoys the present income of the defendant. But, on the other hand, we believe that, in the circumstances of this case, she is entitled to have sufficient means to enable her to live in a manner comparable to the one prevailing at the time the parties lived together, at the time the divorce decree was entered, and at the time the agreement by which she waived further support was made. We consider the sum of $289 per month insufficient for that purpose.

* * *

BREITEL, JUSTICE PRESIDING (concurring).

* * *

While it is true that Section 1170 of the Civil Practice Act confers power on the Court to modify a final judgment, one would have thought that the parties by contract, fair and fairly arrived at, could waive their rights under the statute, except perhaps when there is danger of one of them becoming a public charge, or when one of them has become a public charge.

But the real rub is that the effect of holdings such as that here make perilous, if not nugatory, and therefore discourage, lump-sum settlements between divorced persons. I am not sure that this was ever the legislative purpose or that it is good policy. Such lump-sum settlements may frequently be of very great value to the former wife.

* * *

FOR WHOM, TO WHAT EXTENT, AND WHY IS PROVIDING OR OBTAINING PROCREATIVE GRATIFICATION RELEVANT:

In closing this Chapter's search for guides to decision in establishing, administering, and reorganizing wife-husband relationships we ask you to consider, from the vantage point of a legislator, the following comment and proposal:

There are no meaningful substantive standards, beyond the wish of either spouse to be divorced, for determining when the state should grant or deny a divorce. Existing grounds for divorce frequently stimulate state and private invasions of privacy and promote conduct offensive to the dignity of the individual participants at all points of decision in the family law process. Furthermore, grounds for divorce, coupled with the concept of fault, are irrelevant to the consequences of divorce—i.e., to decisions concerning marriageability, finances, and children. In fact, denial of divorce means for each spouse only denial of the freedom to remarry,* for issues of custody and financial status remain subject to judicial decision. Moreover, the state does not have the capacity to force individuals into meaningful interpersonal relationships. What then must be determinative in granting a divorce is only whether one spouse, after an opportunity to consider the consequences, wishes to be divorced. By thus perceiving marriage as a status of mutual respect, the state will honor rather than degrade marriage.

In the light of these comments and of the material in this Part as well as earlier Parts of this Chapter and Chapter One, determine whether and why a statute incorporating the following should or should not be enacted:

---

* This rests on the assumption that the state has adopted a policy prohibiting polygamous and bigamous relationships—a policy which the state may decide to reexamine.

Model [?] Divorce Statute

1. Any married couple or person wishing a divorce shall *request* the issuance of an *application* for divorce.

2. If one spouse does not join in the initial *request* he or she shall be given notice of the *request*.

3. A state counsellor shall receive notice of the filing of such a *request*. He shall then offer to arrange a meeting between both spouses to explore the advantages and disadvantages of the proposed course of action.

4. Three [or "?"] months from the date of notice there shall be issued to both spouses an *application* for a divorce decree, unless the initial *request* for application has been withdrawn.

5. The *application* for a divorce decree will require the following information: Date of marriage, the name of both spouses, the name and date of birth of each of their children, and whether special proceedings are needed to resolve any disputes about custody or finances. Such proceedings may also be requested by counsel for the children.*

6. Failing a private settlement about custody between the spouses and counsel for the children and, prior to the issuance of a decree, the court shall conduct a hearing designed to determine an appropriate disposition. Similarly, failing a private settlement of economic obligations, a hearing shall be held to dispose of that issue. Decisions about children and finances, whether negotiated or judicially determined, shall be part of the divorce *decree*.

7. Six [or "?"] months following the issuance of the *application* the court shall enter a *decree* of divorce in favor of both spouses despite the opposition of one spouse† unless prior to that time both spouses have advised the court that they do not wish a divorce. [Alternatively, the burden could be on either applicant to petition the court at the end of such a period to issue a *decree*.]

8. The *decree* shall restore to each of the parties eligibility for marriage.

In evaluating this proposal and its implications, official requisites for establishing a marital relationship should be re-examined in order to determine what criteria ought to be formulated for issuing licenses to marry and to have a marriage annulled. Finally, the adequacy of existing procedures and guides for state intervention in the administration of on-going and reorganized family relationships must be scrutinized.

To the extent these proposals are unacceptable and grounds for divorce and annulment continue to constitute guides for decision, the question remains: Should the family law process empower the executive or legislative branches to issue decrees or enact bills of divorcement or annulment where judicial denial constitutes a "grave injustice?"‡

In studying these proposals and before examining the materials in this Part consider the following statements.

ALEXANDER, PAUL W., JUDGE

The Follies of Divorce: A Therapeutic Approach to the Problem**

The **law** doesn't really divorce husbands and wives. It seems to think it does, but in fact

---

* See Chapter I, pp. 281 *et seq. supra*

† Assuming a goal of minimum state intervention (coercion), granting, not denying, divorce over the objection of one spouse serves this goal: divorce leaves both parties free to marry or not to marry; denial of divorce leaves the parties free not to marry and denies them the freedom to marry.

Whether antenuptial agreements setting forth different procedures or conditions for obtaining a divorce would be upheld raises many questions for judicial or legislative determination.

‡ In considering this question it may be useful to compare the place and function of the pardoning power in the criminal process.

** 36 A. B. A. J. 1950 (pp. 106-107).

they "divorce" themselves. The term is derived from **divortere** meaning "to turn apart, turn away from each other. Come to the parting of the way, separate." The law does not separate the spouses; they separate themselves—thereby bestowing upon themselves a **de facto** divorce.

All there is left for the law to do in granting a **de jure** divorce is to recognize the existence of a **fait accompli**, a fact accomplished by the spouses themselves; to undo what it has done, dissolve the status it has created, sever the bond with which it has united the parties. . . .

*   *   *

We intimated the law regards itself as divorcing spouses, thus destroying marriages and breaking homes. Consequently it looks with extreme disfavor upon divorce. It abhors divorce in general. On the other hand, almost from the beginning of recorded history the law has sanctioned some form of divorce. To meet the ever growing popular demand for divorce within the past century or so, it has sanctioned divorce as we know it in every state. But it has done so grudgingly.

The law has permitted itself to be maneuvered into an almost untenable position of striking ambivalence. . . .

*   *   *

And so it appears that the law by making guilt the index of marriage failure and by placing so much emphasis upon the grounds or forms of guilt has contributed to its own failure in its avowed purpose to preserve marriage and the family. It is not preventive; it is punitive. It does not conserve; it disserves.

TEMPLE, R. J. A., Q.C.

Discussion*

. . . I disagree that the modern divorce law has in no sense caused broken marriages. I seem to remember a phrase from Macbeth—"The means to do ill deeds makes ill deeds done", and I would prefer to say that although it may not have caused broken marriages as the immediate and proximate cause it is accurate to say it causes marriages to be broken. . . . I think that modern divorce law, and particularly our present system, leads if I may say so, to the possibility of a divorce-minded generation—people who get married with the idea that if it does not work out they can have a divorce; young persons who come together with the observation: "Well of course I know you love me, darling, and will always give me my freedom". There is a further, and to my mind, serious challenge, and that is this—it removes the pressure (such as it is) upon spouses to give and take. I am not saying anything here about sectarian matters, but it is perfectly plain that, marriage being the sum total of a most complicated human relationship, it is necessary to give and take, and to my mind, if it is felt, that a divorce is inevitable and must necessarily be granted, then the likelihood of reconciliation and the capacity to give and take and to see the other spouse's point of view is completely obliterated. I do not understand how to reconcile this particular philosophical approach to the problem with the provision for reconciliation. I should have thought that easier divorce was the nullification of reconciliation, and that it was not any good saying, "Let us have an elaborate

---

* 36 AUSTRALIAN L. J. 303-304 (1963).

machinery for reconciliation" if at the time the system itself is designed to allow a marriage to be dissolved on grounds which incidentally do not in respect of one particular section include a matrimonial offence. It would lead, to my mind, to complete circuity of action that I should have thought one would have avoided. I should have thought myself that modern society was the product of its environment. If you have a system of easier divorce, society takes its tempo and its obligations from what it finds to be politic. . . .

A.
To Decisions Concerning the Establishment of Wife-Husband Relationships?

VAN NIEKERK v. VAN NIEKERK
[1959 (4)] S.A. 658

WESSELS, J.:

Applicant . . . applies on notice of motion for certain amendments to the summons and declaration so as to enable him to claim an order declaring the marriage between the parties to be null and void on account of respondent's pre-marital sterility. . . .

* * *

[T]he purposes or *causae finales* of marriage have throughout remained substantially the same. In the course of argument counsel referred us to numerous definitions of marriage. In some of these definitions the authors make no specific reference to the procreation of children as an end of marriage while others again specifically mention the procreation and rearing of children as an end, if not the end, of the marriage union. . . .

In my opinion there can be no doubt but that the procreation and rearing of children is an end of marriage. It is not only an end of marriage but also one of the main purposes of life itself. The urge towards self preservation and reproducing the species is of vital and fundamental importance. While it is true that children may be procreated where there is no marriage, social conditions require that they should only be procreated where a man and a woman are joined in marriage.

The procreation of children is obviously not the only purpose of marriage. In this regard I respectfully adopt the following statement of the late van den Heever, J. A., in his monograph on *Breach of Promise and Seduction in South African Law* (p. 20):

"Adopting the principles of the Canon law Roman Dutch law regarded the teleological causes or *causae finales* of marriage to be: . . . (1) sexual intercourse, (2) the procreation of children, (3) mutual aid and assistance, (4) cohabitation and the enjoyment of each other's society for life and (5) the avoidance of illicit intercourse."

If there is a failure of any one or more of these causes *stante matrimonio* owing to the unlawful conduct of one of the spouses the innocent spouse may at common law obtain either a divorce or a separation *a mensa et thoro*. . . . Unless, therefore, the failure flows from unlawful conduct on the part of one of the spouses even a total failure has no effect on the continued existence of the marriage.

In this case we are, of course, not concerned (at this stage of the enquiry at any rate) with a failure of a final cause owing to the misconduct *stante matrimonio* of one of the spouses, but with a failure flowing from an incurable defect in the physical make-up of one of the spouses existing at the time of the marriage.

I consider it necessary to make certain observations in regard to the so-called teleological causes of marriage referred to above. Firstly. I doubt whether the learned author (VAN DEN HEEVER, J. A.) purported to list them in order of importance, or that any system of ranking could be based on generally accepted principles of law. In the case of a post-nuptial failure of one or more of the causes attributable to unlawful conduct on the part of one of the spouses the law apparently draws no distinction between the several causes of marriage in granting relief to the innocent spouse. In so far as the common law is concerned a post-nuptial wrongful failure of any one cause entitles the innocent spouse to relief notwithstanding the fact that other causes remain to support the marriage. I have already referred to the fact that, except where statutory relief is available, even a total post-nuptial failure of the causes of marriage cannot affect the existence of the union unless it flows from unlawful conduct on the part of one of the spouses. It seems to me that in law the marriage contract is to be regarded as a transaction between a man and a woman necessarily involving the various purposes or ends referred to, except where the parties agree to avoid one or more of them or where there is a failure of any one or more causes in circumstances where neither spouse acted unlawfully.

The emphasis to be placed on any one or any combination of final causes would, so it seems, vary not only from marriage to marriage but also from time to time during the existence of any marriage. Parties might agree to avoid all the ends of marriage and yet enter into a valid marriage which will endure until dissolved upon lawful cause. A man and a woman who indulged in pre-marital intercourse might marry in order to legitimise the child to be born while agreeing to go their separate ways after the ceremony. Although the agreement has no effect in law, its existence resulting in a total failure of the causes of marriage does not invalidate the union. A young and as yet impecunious couple might agree to avoid the procreation of children until they can afford to raise a family. In such a case the immediate emphasis is placed on the other final causes. For various reasons couples may agree to avoid the procreation of children altogether. The elderly couple may marry in the knowledge that their sexual incapacity must necessarily result in the failure of those final causes in which sexual capacity is a pre-requisite. In such a case the emphasis is placed on the remaining causes in order to support the marriage. Yet again parties may by reason of their religious beliefs agree not to have intercourse except for the purpose of procreating children. In such a case the importance of the act of intercourse is related to its result, i.e., the procreation of children.

The second observation I wish to make is that it would appear that ordinarily the only final causes which can fail on account of pre-marital circumstances are sexual intercourse and the procreation of children. (In this connection I am disregarding pre-marital agreement or unilateral intention as circumstances resulting in the failure of any one or more of the final causes of marriage, inasmuch as the failure is of no legal significance while the agreement is operative and ordinary principles relating to the dissolution of the marriage become applicable where the failure is not to be related to agreement between the parties but to unlawful conduct on the part of one of the spouses.)

The only pre-marital circumstances which can result in a failure of the two causes referred to above would seem to be defects in the physical (or psychological) make-up of one or both of the spouses. In the case of impotence (*impotentia coeundi*) there would (save possibly in very exceptional circumstances) necessarily also be a failure of the cause relating to the procreation of children. Sterility (*impotentia procreandi*) is, on the other hand, not necessarily related to impotence.

* * *

Although there is some reference in the older authorities to deceitful conduct on the part of the impotent person who contracts a marriage, it seems that in modern law a party seeking relief on the ground of impotence need not allege or prove fraud: it is sufficient to prove that the defendant was permanently and incurably impotent at the time of the marriage and that the plaintiff contracted the marriage in ignorance of this fact.

The logical justification for the existence of this ground for setting aside a marriage would seem to be the fact that sexual intercourse is so essential an element of marriage that where it cannot come about there is no marriage, i.e., the remaining purposes or causes are in contemplation of law insufficient to support the marriage unless the parties themselves are content to regard them as sufficient.

At this stage I should like to refer to another common law ground for setting aside a marriage on account of a circumstance existing at the time of the marriage, i.e., the pregnancy of the wife at the time of the marriage as a result of pre-marital intercourse with a man other than her husband. In this case, too, the true basis for relief does not appear to be the immoral pre-marital conduct of the wife or her deception in concealing her pregnancy (circumstances might conceivably arise when she honestly believes that the illicit intercourse did not result in pregnancy).

The true basis on which relief is granted on the two grounds referred to above (i.e. impotence and pre-marital pregnancy) would thus seem to be the one spouse's error as to certain qualities of the other spouse. The mistake is regarded as fundamental because the qualities to which it relates in turn relate to the essential (and not incidental) ends of marriage. Impotence must necessarily result in the failure of sexual intercourse and the procreation of children as ends of marriage and would probably give rise to illicit sexual intercourse on the part of the potent spouse. Pregnancy on the part of the wife results in at least a temporary failure of procreation of children as an end of marriage and might furthermore, throughout the marriage, seriously jeopardise the chances of harmonious cohabitation and the enjoyment of each other's society.

*   *   *

A mistake as to other qualities (e.g. age, race, nationality, religion, social standing, financial circumstances, pre-marital chastity, etc.) does not provide a basis for relief, not even where fraud is an element. . . . These mistakes are not regarded as fundamental, notwithstanding the fact that in individual cases a mistake e.g. as to religion or pre-marital chastity, may seriously affect the marriage. It cannot, however, be said that a failure of one or more of the causes of marriage must inevitably flow from such a mistake. It follows from what I have said that a mistake as to *potentia procreandi* seems to be the one exception to the rule that a mistake as to a quality which must inevitably result in a failure of at least one of the causes of the marriage (i.e. one of a fundamental nature) entitles the aggrieved party to relief.

*   *   *

It follows then that at the time the rule relating to impotence was introduced the distinction between *impotentia coeundi* and *impotentia procreandi* and their relationship with the final causes of marriage was given effect to, the first-mentioned incapacity alone being regarded as of such fundamental importance as to entitle an aggrieved party to relief. This presupposes that the various recognised final causes of marriage can be listed in order of essentiality. One can only conclude that sexual intercourse tops the list and that the remaining causes are all to be bracketed together as "not so essential" or else to be placed in some as yet undetermined order of essentiality. . . .

*   *   *

In considering procreation as an end of marriage I think one should not over-emphasise the momentary miracle of fertilisation. Seen in its proper perspective procreation relates not only to the begetting of children, but also to their maintenance and education within the family circle. In this sense, I think, procreation is not only a most important end of marriage, but also the most important single factor contributing to "the solace and satisfaction of man".

For the reasons set out above I conclude that the begetting and rearing of children is a final cause of marriage which, if it is not to be regarded as the principle end of the institution of marriage, at the time of the marriage ranks on a basis of parity with the other ends thereof. During the subsistence of the marriage the emphasis may shift from one cause to another at the instance of the parties, but in contemplation of law they remain of equal importance. . . .

*   *   *

In the result I am of the opinion that the application for the amendment of plaintiff's summons and declaration should be granted.

*   *   *

NOTES

NOTE 1.

VILETA v. VILETA
53 Cal. App. 2d 794, 128 P. 2d 376 (1942)

GOULD, JUSTICE PRO TEM.

[P]laintiff sought to have his marriage with defendant annulled upon the ground of fraud, in that, as alleged in said amended complaint, defendant prior to said marriage represented that she was normal physically and capable of bearing children, whereas, it is alleged, defendant at the time of making said representations knew they were false and untrue; that in truth and in fact defendant was then incapable of bearing children and by reason of her physical condition will suffer permanently from such disability. It was alleged that plaintiff believed defendant's representations as to her normal physical condition; that he relied upon them and would not have entered into the marriage if he had known the true facts; that he did not discover the truth until March 17, 1942, when defendant was examined by a physician, and that he has not lived with defendant since such discovery.

*   *   *

. . . A woman who accepts the hand of her suitor thereby impliedly assures him of her ability, so far as lies within her knowledge, to bear children. Her concealment of her sterility is a fraud that vitiates the marriage contract . . . and justifies annulment, when the man acts promptly upon his discovery of the fraud. . . . There is neither rule of law, principle of equity nor reason arising from public policy which requires the continuance of a marriage resulting from such a fraud as that of which defendant was guilty.

*   *   *

NOTE 2.

J. v. J.
[1947] 2 All E. R. 43

SOMERVELL, L. J., read this judgment of the case. In this case the judge dismissed a wife's petition for nullity of marriage. The case was undefended. . . .

The parties were married on June 16, 1934. Just before the marriage the husband had an operation which, while leaving him able to achieve penetration and emission, made it impossible for sexual intercourse to result in the conception of a child. He told the doctor who performed the operation that he was getting married and that there was insanity in his future wife's family. It seems that this was untrue. [A] marriage is not consummated if a husband, by his own act, prevents "intercourse" from having its natural consequence in "the passage of the male seed into the body of the woman." . . .The husband in the present case effected by the operation the same result which could have been effected by the use of a contraceptive on each successive occasion. There is no question of natural sterility. [H]e rendered himself incapable of effecting consummation by reason of a structural defect which he had himself brought about in his organs of generation.

This, however, does not dispose of the case. The doctor who performed the operation required a statement to be signed by the wife as well as by the husband setting out their understanding of the effect of the operation. This form was presented by the husband to the wife on Apr. 30, 1934. They had at this date been engaged to be married for some months. She refused to sign it, as she wanted to have children. There was an argument. Finally, she said she would sign it if he promised he would wait and not have the operation until after the marriage. She hoped she would be able to persuade him to take a different view after the marriage. He so promised, but, in fact, had the operation and this came to her knowledge on May 6, 1934, some six weeks before the marriage. The question is whether this knowledge of hers is in law an absolute bar to her petition. . . . [T]he petitioner's knowledge of impotence before marriage is not an absolute bar in law.

* * *

The next question is whether the petition should be dismissed in all the circumstances, including the wife's knowledge, for lack of what is called "sincerity." It is necessary to state further facts. Intercourse took place regularly for the first two or three years of the marriage, thereafter rarely. The marriage became increasingly unhappy. Before the marriage when the fact of the operation became known to the wife, the husband had said she could adopt children. When she suggested this later he would have nothing to do with it. She did not know that she had or might have grounds for nullity until late in 1945. She then left the husband and started these proceedings. She said she had had no material or other benefits from the marriage. Counsel submitted, first, that mere lapse of time is not by itself a bar, though of course a material circumstance in considering "sincerity." . . . Secondly, he submitted that the material date is when the petitioner, not only knows the facts, but is also aware of his or her legal rights. . . .

The judge, in dismissing the petition, did so by reason of the wife's knowledge before marriage. [W]e have come to a different conclusion. It is important to note that this is not a case where the knowledge existed at the time of the engagement. The parties had been engaged for some time. It was sprung on the wife a few weeks before the date for the marriage. She had protested against the idea. The husband had previously made her swear to say nothing about this operation to anyone. In any case it would not have been an easy reason for her to give for breaking off her engagement. The natural inference from her evidence we think is that she felt it was too late to draw back. . . .

NOTE 3.

HAFNER v. HAFNER
66 N.Y.S. 2d 442, 445 (Sup. Ct. 1946)

WALSH, JUSTICE.

* * *

The stereotyped pattern of evidence now offered in these cases, practically all undefended, and the ease with which judgments are obtained, might indicate that the State is not fulfilling its duty to protect the marriage bond. The present popular procedure is as follows: The plaintiff testifies that the defendant promised to have children, a promise which is implied in a marriage contract unless mutually excluded by the parties. Then the plaintiff testifies that the defendant insisted on using contraceptives, to which plaintiff objected or submitted to for days, weeks, months or years, after which the defendant said he or she never intended to have normal intercourse and he or she never wanted children. Corroboration is usually offered by a parent, brother, sister or other relative to prove the original promise was made, and that the defendant subsequently stated he or she never intended to keep the promise, which is simply a declaration or confession by one spouse. Usually, the testimony for the most part, consists of leading questions. The attorney testifies while the plaintiff says "yes" or "no".

In this case the parties were married in 1936 and parted in 1942 after a quarrel, allegedly over the fraud. The evidence follows the usual pattern. The Court holds that the plaintiff has not proved her cause of action. Motion for judgment of annulment denied.

NOTE 4.

BOHOK v. BOHOK
186 Misc. 991, 63 N.Y.S. 2d 560 (1946)

BERGAN, JUSTICE.

*   *   *

I know of no case in New York where an annulment has been granted because of misrepresentation of the number of children to be born. Here plaintiff contends that defendant agreed to have five children but would have only one. The defendant has been sworn and concedes this. I hold that this kind of representation based on the quantum of children to be born is not a good ground for annulment.

Assuming that the discussion was had about the number of children, I do not regard it as having been fraudulently made by defendant, although he now says it was. I think the true fact is that defendant changed his mind about the number of children after the parties were married, as the plaintiff's own testimony in several places clearly indicates. Whatever else this is, it is not fraud.

To avoid the absurdity implicit in an action to annul a marriage for a fraudulent refusal to have children where there are children, the court must carefully scrutinize any such claim.

Application for judgment denied.

NOTE 5.

LEO ABSE (PONTYPOOL)

Matrimonial Causes and Reconciliation Bill*

. . . Last year's Ministry of Health Report indicated that about a third of the illegitimate children born in this country annually—about 37,000—are born to cohabiting parents who are apparently living in permanent union but are unmarried. It is therefore reasonable to assume that a large proportion of cohabiting parents would get married if they were not under the disability of being refused a divorce from a previous partner.

From an examination of the statistics it appears likely that there are between 100,000 and 200,000 illegitimate children of such unions. These children are being brought up in an atmosphere of deceit, insecurity and guilt which, to a greater or lesser degree, is bound to pervade the household. It is wrong that the sins of the parents should be visited upon the children. It is wrong that the stigma of illegitimacy should be attached to such children and, even worse, that they should be brought up in an atmosphere which may prevent their having the confidence to which they are entitled. Just as I am concerned mainly for the children in connection with the reconciliation

---

* 671 H.C. Deb. (5th ser.) 818 (1963).

procedure, so, equally, in respect of this issue, I feel passionately that we have no right, under the guise of any rules or laws of morality, to abandon hundreds and thousands of children.

NOTE 6.

R. E. L. (Otherwise R.) v. E. L.
[1949] P. 211

Wife's defended petition for nullity of marriage on the ground of her husband's incapacity to consummate the marriage and in the alternative of his wilful refusal so to do. . . .

The following facts are taken from the judgment.

The parties were married in 1942 and at the hearing the wife was thirty-one and the husband thirty-seven. The medical examination showed that the petitioner had no impediment and that the husband was apparently capable of consummating the marriage. The trouble was psychological and for the first three years the husband made no attempt at intercourse, and evaded the matter when it was broached by the wife until in June, 1945 she made him face the question. An attempt was then made at the wife's insistence, but he was unable to have intercourse either on that or on subsequent occasions, and he did not contend otherwise at the hearing.

In the autumn of 1945 the petitioner, whose health had been affected, consulted a doctor. The doctor found no impediment, but he dilated her to make matters still easier for the husband. He impressed the seriousness of the position upon him, and tried to persuade him to have treatment.

By the end of 1945 the wife knew from the doctor that she had grounds for a decree of nullity. In 1946 another doctor took over the husband from the first doctor, but no doctor effected any improvement in him. The wife was anxious to have a child and discussed artificial insemination with her husband. At the end of 1946 she tried, under the guidance of an expert in such matters, to inseminate herself artificially with the husband's seed, but she did not become pregnant. . . . She was urging her husband to have psychological treatment, and in December, 1947, he at last agreed to pay a visit, arranged by her, to a psychologist. The psychologist advised a course of treatment but it would be long, and, in the husband's view, almost impossible for him. As an attempted short cut, the psychologist put forward suggestive treatment by Dr. L., and this treatment the husband was prepared to have. On December 1, 1947, the wife had artificial insemination by an expert from the husband's seed. On December 31, 1947, she had another such insemination. Between those two dates the husband had started a course of treatment from Dr. L., and had paid him nine or ten visits up to January 27, 1948, when the parties ceased to live together. Dr. L.'s treatment was intended to eradicate from the husband the sense of failure caused by his repeated failures to consummate, but it did not make the efforts to consummate any more effective than they had been in the past. But the treatment had an unfortunate result. It consisted largely in instilling confidence in the husband by giving him a card on which was written the information that, after reading the card, his arm would become rigid and thereafter he would feel desire. Twice he tried to consummate the marriage with that help. They were in bed, he read the card, his arm became rigid and he felt desire. Unfortunately the desire was not sufficiently strong or longlived to achieve its purpose. . . .

On January 27, 1948, the petitioner left the respondent and never returned to him. Unknown to her at that time, she was then pregnant, by artificial insemination, of a child who was born in September, 1948, and who was alive when the case was heard. . . .

PEARCE J. In most nullity cases there comes a moment when the most forbearing wife becomes sickened by the role, so unnatural to a sensitive woman, of trying to stimulate an impotent spouse sufficiently to enable him to achieve penetration. I have no doubt that that moment came when the husband added to his impotence the artificiality and crudity induced by Dr. L.'s treatment. Those experiences, on top of a difficult and trying five years, made the wife decide to leave. At the end of January, 1948, she left, determined to end the marriage, and since then they have lived apart and no persuasion has been able to get the wife to go back to him.

* * *

. . . I find it a difficult case to decide, and there is little guidance to be had from authority. The husband has not chosen to give evidence, but . . . says that the birth of the child should make me refuse a decree; that because there was a voluntary act by the wife that led to this conception, the court should consider the marriage as approbated, not only in the interest of the parties, but also of the public, and he calls public policy in aid. . . .

[T]he birth of the child is a . . . serious matter. It is important to see how this came about. The wife admitted two motives in conceiving the child: a woman's desire for motherhood and the hope that a child would help her and her husband to have proper intercourse, because she thought that it might relieve the tension caused, possibly, by her over-urgency, and so help the husband to overcome his trouble. . . .

* * *

So far as approbation of the marriage is concerned, it must be a question of degree, what acts done, with what intention, constitute approbation. Her letters and her evidence show that she never intended to approbate an abnormal marriage. Until the end she made it clear that she desired and intended to have a normal marriage. I do not regard the conception of the child, serious as it is, when done with the expressed dominant intention of producing normality in their sex relations, to be approbation of an abnormal marriage. I see no authority for saying that public policy makes it my duty to hold that she is estopped or has approbated towards the world at large. . . .

If I am right, the question of discretion does not arise, and it is irrelevant to weigh the public and private advantages of granting or refusing a decree. If I am wrong, I should, in the exercise of my discretion, grant a decree for these reasons. I see no hope of happiness by keeping these two people married. I am told by his counsel that the husband might divorce the wife for desertion when the time arrives, but there is no certainty of this. If I grant a decree it seems quite possible that the wife who seems affectionate and likely to be a good wife, may marry again, and even the husband might marry again and conquer his inhibitions and enjoy normal married happiness. The future holds better augury for the child, I think, if I grant the decree than if he is brought up by an embittered mother who may be tied for life to a marriage that has never been a real marriage, and which, only through the unnatural aid of science, has produced the fruit of a real marriage.

If the child should be made illegitimate it is most regrettable, but the stigmas of birth are of less effect than they were, and sons are not now judged by the errors of their parents. The few who know of the illegitimacy will probably also know the facts, and in them there is nothing that reflects any dishonour on either parent or on the child.

For those reasons I order a decree nisi on the ground of incapacity, with costs.

Decree nisi of nullity.

NOTE 7.

MASTERS v. MASTERS
13 Wisc. 2d 332, 108 N.W. 2d 674 (1961)

Action for annulment of marriage instituted by the plaintiff Edward Masters against the defendant Ramona Masters.

The complaint alleged that the plaintiff had been induced to marry the defendant on November 28, 1959, by reason of false and fraudulent representations that "she was pregnant with child by the plaintiff." The defendant demurred to the complaint on the ground that it failed to state facts sufficient to constitute a cause of action. . . .

The material facts brought out in the testimony are set forth in the following findings of fact of the trial court:

"During November 1959 and prior to the 28th day thereof and to induce the plaintiff to marry her, said defendant represented to the plaintiff that she was pregnant with child by him, displaying to him a certificate (of her pregnancy of several months standing) by a local well-known doctor. . . . Such representations were made to the plaintiff by the defendant deliberately and intentionally to induce him to marry her. The plaintiff believed said representations to be true and was induced thereby to marry the defendant in reliance thereon. Had such representations not been made to him he would not have married the defendant. The representations of her pregnancy by the plaintiff or anybody else were false and not true.

"On Tuesday, January 26, 1960, the plaintiff discovered that the defendant's representations of her pregnancy aforesaid were false and untrue and fraudulent and thereafter and upon such discovery he had no marital relation with the defendant, renounced her as his wife, and left their said residence. Since such discovery the plaintiff did nothing to confirm said marriage."

[T]he trial court entered the following conclusion of law:

"The defendant's representations of her pregnancy with child by the plaintiff although intentional and false and fraudulent and the sole means of procuring the marriage of the parties hereto is not sufficiently material under the applicable statutes to constitute cause for annulment of said marriage even though the plaintiff sues as the innocent and injured party who has done no act to confirm such marriage after his discovery of the character of such representations."

* * *

CURRIE, JUSTICE.

* * *

We have carefully reviewed the cases from other jurisdictions, which have denied annulment to husbands victimized by the same type of fraud as was perpetrated upon the instant plaintiff by the defendant, to ascertain the reasons advanced in support of such a determination. There appear to be two such reasons. One is that, because the parties indulged in illicit intercourse before marriage, the parties stand in *pari delicto* so that the defendant comes into court with "unclean hands." The second is that the false representation was not material, which is the view adopted by the trial court in the case at bar.

The argument that the parties stand in *pari delicto* was advanced by the defendant wife in Winner v. Winner, supra, and was rejected by this court. With respect to such contention the opinion pointed out that such intercourse constituted a mere misdemeanor. We are of the opinion that the punishment inflicted by denying an annulment in cases of this kind is out of all proportion to the offense committed. In so holding, we do not condone in the least the plaintiff's infraction of the moral code. Furthermore, by refusing an annulment the plaintiff would not be punished for the illicit intercourse, but rather for his laudable conduct in seeking to rectify a wrong he believed would result unless he did marry the defendant. There may be aggravated situations in which the doctrine of in *pari delicto* ought to be applied, such as was present in Gonduin v. Gonduin, 1910, 14 Cal.App. 285, 111 P. 756, in which the man induced the woman to submit to intercourse by his promise to marry her. This is not such a case.

Whether to apply the doctrine of in *pari delicto* poses a question of public policy. The lone justification which we can perceive for here invoking such doctrine is that it might act as a future deterrent to unmarried persons engaging in illicit intercourse. If the thought of the unpleasant consequences, which are likely to befall the male participant should pregnancy result, or the fear of a criminal prosecution for fornication, are insufficient to deter him, we doubt very much that the example which would be afforded by denying an annulment in the instant fact situation would be any more effective. On the other hand, to deny an annulment would reward the defendant for a palpable fraud and punish the plaintiff for being victimized thereby in an effort on his part to right a wrong, which he was induced by the fraud to think would result if he did not marry the defendant. When the competing policy factors are so weighed, the scales of justice tip in but one direction. Therefore, we refuse here to apply the principle of *pari delicto*.

* * *

NOTE 8.

ARISTOTLE
Politics*

§ 1. If we assume that the legislator ought, for a start, to see to the provision of a stock of the healthiest possible bodies in the nurseries of our

* Translated by Ernest Barker. Oxford: The Clarendon Press, 1946, pp. 324-325. Reprinted with permission of the publisher.

state, it follows that his first attention must be devoted to marriage; and here he will have to consider what the ages of the partners should be, and what qualities they ought to possess. § 2. The first thing to be taken into account, in legislating about matrimony, is the length of time that husband and wife are likely to live together. The right thing is that they should arrive simultaneously at the same epoch of sexual life. There should be no divergence of physical power, with the husband still able to beget but the wife unable to conceive, or the wife still able to conceive and the husband unable to beget. Such a position is apt to cause discord and difference between married persons. The second thing to be taken into account is the difference of age between children and their parents. § 3. On the one hand, there should not be too much of a gap (elderly fathers cannot give their children the benefit of parental guidance, or receive from them in return the benefit of filial piety); and yet, on the other hand, there should not be too little of a gap. § 4. That, too, leads to considerable diffi-

culties: it makes children treat parents with less respect, feeling that they are almost contemporaries, and it readily leads to quarrels about the management of the household. The third thing the legislator has to take into account—and here we return to the point from which we have just digressed—is the provision of a stock of healthy children answerable to his purposes.

Now all these objects may be secured at once by a single policy. § 5. The period of procreation finally ends, as a rule, at the age of 70 for men, and the age of 50 for women; and the beginning of marital intercourse should therefore be fixed for both parties with a corresponding interval. [The husband will thus be 20 years older than his wife at the time of marriage.] § 6. The union of young parents is bad for the procreation of issue. In the whole of the animal world the descendants of young parents have imperfections. They tend to be of the female sex, and they are diminutive in figure. We are bound to expect the same sort of result among human beings. There is evidence to warrant that expectation. . . .

B.

To Decisions Concerning the Administration of Wife-Husband Relationships?

1.

BARRETTA v. BARRETTA
182 Misc. 852, 46 N.Y.S. 2d 261 (1944)

COLDEN, JUSTICE.

Action by wife for a separation. The parties were married September 4, 1938. They have a daughter born July 23, 1940. Since the birth of their child, plaintiff has refused any sexual relations with her husband unless he would use a contraceptive. She so testified, on cross-examination, and stated that as a result of these difficulties over marital relations, they separated, she and their child going to live with her parents, she taking the furniture and household belongings, and he living with his sister.

A wife who demands benefits under the marriage contract must prove that she is willing to discharge her obligations under it. The refusal of a wife without adequate excuse to have ordinary marriage relations with her husband strikes at the basic obligations of the marriage contract. Here she seeks the benefits of that contract while violating one of the funda-

mental obligations of it. Our law does not permit her to recover. . . .

Notwithstanding widely divergent religious, sociological, economic, psychological and physiological viewpoints as to the use of contraceptives, the statutes and court decisions of the State of New York clearly indicate disapproval. Section 1142 of our Penal Law makes it a crime to sell, lend or give away, or to offer to sell, lend or give away, or to possess with intent to sell, lend or give away, or to advertise or offer to sell, lend or give away, any contraceptives. It is a crime also to give any information orally or by printing or writing as to when, where, how, of whom, or by what means a contraceptive may be obtained. A violation of this section of the Penal Law involves moral turpitude. . . . The section is constitutional. . . . A license to exhibit a motion picture illustrating a contraceptive method was held properly refused. . . . The legislature has declared that the spread of information on this subject and the sale of articles designed to accomplish its objects are acts detrimental to public morals and welfare. . . . And the detriment to public morals and welfare is not only in the acquiring of the knowledge of the means, nor in the acquisition of the material of which the means consists, but also in the use of the knowledge and the means. The insistence of a wife that her husband use such knowledge and means is contrary to the principles and policy enunciated by the statutes and decisions of the State of New York, and for a court to permit plaintiff wife to recover under the circumstances and facts in this case would be contrary to our law as it now stands.

The refusal of the plaintiff to permit her husband marital relations unless he use a contraceptive is such a violation of her obligations under the marriage contract as to preclude her from the judgment which she seeks for a separation and support. Her complaint must be dismissed. Under defendant's dèmand for other and further relief, provision may be made for custody of the child for the present with the plaintiff provided that the defendant is to have the fullest right of visitation at all reasonable hours without interference or molestation by anyone, and also to take the child with him if he wishes on holidays, on Saturdays or Sundays, and during his annual vacation, the defendant to pay the plaintiff the sum of $7 per week for the support and maintenance of the child provided that the provisions for visitation and occasional custody are strictly observed by plaintiff and those with whom she and the child may from time to time reside.

2.

ALEXANDER, FRANZ, and FRENCH, THOMAS M.

Psychoanalytic Therapy*

The patient was a beautiful young Negro woman, nineteen years of age. She was married and the mother of a four-months-old infant. She came for treatment with the complaint that since the birth of her baby she had lost all sexual feeling for her husband, although she was still in love with him. Three psychotherapeutic interviews led to a complete sexual readjustment.

In the first interview, the patient complained a great deal about the housework and frankly admitted to the (male) therapist that she would prefer to work as a salesgirl if she did not have to take care of her child. She had been married for more than a year and had become pregnant almost immediately because she and her husband wanted to have a family. Sexual relations had

been completely satisfactory until the baby was born. Since the sexual disturbance of the patient did not seem to be deeply rooted, a brief psychotherapy seemed promising.

The patient had been born in Chicago but her parents were West Indian Negroes who consider themselves an aristocracy among Negroes in general. Her mother, over thirty when she married, had been unhappy in her marriage and had obtained a divorce when the patient was two years old. From that time on, the mother took complete care of the girl. The father never assumed any responsibility nor did he show any interest in his child. The mother earned her living by working as a maid, usually keeping her daughter with her. The patient described her mother as a strict, demanding woman who had reared her daughter according to the West Indian moral tradition and seldom had time for any pleasure with her. The patient had not been allowed to mix with other children, nor, until she was sixteen, had she been permitted to go out with boys. As a young girl she had found her chief pleasure in reading; later she became very industrious, however, and when she was sixteen started to work, clerking at a soda fountain.

At this time the patient began going around with a young man two years her senior, whom she had first met in high school. He was considerate and kind and made a small income working for his father as a carpenter's helper. Her mother was not satisfied with this choice, however, because she considered him inferior to her daughter. Although she had often expressed the feeling that her daughter should marry early and avoid her own mistake of a late marriage, she had also repeatedly warned her daughter against men, teaching her to be suspicious of them all. In spite of these warnings, the patient grew very fond of the young man and, after a courtship of two years, they were married.

From the beginning, the young couple made a good sexual adjustment and planned to have a child as soon as possible. However, during the latter part of her pregnancy the patient began to show an increasing irritability toward her husband, and after the birth of the child she found, to her surprise, that she was unable to derive the former satisfaction from their sexual relations. This was the situation when the patient first saw the psychiatrist.

The patient was well poised and seemed quite aware of her stunning appearance; she evidently knew how to dress in an attractive manner with the simplest means. This secondary narcissism had apparently acted as a barrier against deeper damage which might easily have resulted from the many frustrations of her earlier life. The signifi-

* New York: The Ronald Press Co., 1946, pp. 158-161. Copyright 1946 by The Ronald Press Co. Reprinted with permission of the publisher.

cance of this pride in her beauty was revealed when the patient was undergoing a routine examination. She had been examined previously by a gynecologist, but no unusual findings were reported. To the psychologically experienced therapist, however, it was immediately apparent that the patient was extremely self-conscious and disturbed over the deformity of her abdomen caused by childbirth. She had an umbilical hernia and the abdominal walls were collapsed. The patient had never mentioned this condition to anyone and had made no attempt to get treatment for it.

To the therapist it was obvious that there was a connection between her pregnancy, the resulting deformity, and her frigidity. It seemed apparent that unconsciously she blamed her husband for this condition and that her frigidity was an expression of hostility against him. To the patient the pregnancy, and even more the unfortunate aftermath, represented a narcissistic injury for which she held her husband responsible. It was a confirmation of her early teaching that nothing good was to be expected from a man. The patient had repressed her hostility against her husband and so was not aware of this connection.

The motivation of this repression was not altogether clear. The patient had transferred to her husband a great deal of her former dependence on her mother. In spite of this, however, she had maintained some superiority to him, according to the West Indian tradition of her parents. She said that she sometimes teased him for his shyness, especially in respect to exposing his body. She would jokingly ask him if he was afraid she would take his genitals from him. This was evidently a repression of the patient's anxiety lest she be damaged by him, an attitude which reflected her own hostility against him, a result, in part, of the mother's feeling about men. It is obvious that the patient's tendency to project onto her husband the role of the aggressor diminished as she became aware of her own aggression toward him.

The treatment consisted mainly in an attempt by the therapist to verbalize for the patient this resentment against her husband. It was explained to her in simple terms that she was really blaming her husband for the deformity of her body. Simultaneously, the therapist offered her practical help; he sent her to a gynecologist for proper treatment. It should be mentioned also that the patient had been encouraged to obtain contraceptives since she was conscious that her frigidity was due in part to her fear of having another child immediately.

It is significant, however, that the patient's emotional condition did not change with the use of contraceptives. It improved only after she had gained some insight into her hostility from the three interviews with the therapist. The therapist's attitude relieved her anxiety about men, whom unconsciously she regarded as aggressors. . . .

NOTE

BRAVERY v. BRAVERY
[1954] 3 All E. R. 59

* * *

DENNING, L. J.: The parties married on Oct. 25, 1934, when the husband was twenty-five and the wife twenty-one years of age. They lived happily together for two years until a son was born to them on Dec. 19, 1936. About eighteen months later, in 1938, a shocking thing took place. The husband underwent an operation to have himself sterilised. He was the porter at a London hospital. One of the surgeons operated on him, and he was attended by the sister and staff nurse.

The operation provokes several questions. The first is: Why did the husband have this done? Let me give his answer in his own words. Counsel asked him:

> "What was the immediate cause of the operation? A.—It was because of my wife's attitude towards the boy. He was not a baby to be caressed and loved. He was a show-piece . . . Q.—Why did you agree to have an operation for sterilisation? A.—Because my wife was so installed. She was so installed with the home, and with this baby she had. Q.—You said the baby was a show-piece? A.—Yes. Q.—In what way? A.—She wanted to have him perfectly dressed, and when he was tiny, if there was the least thing missing, she would be absolutely beside herself."

Those answers throw a flood of light on the husband's mentality. Why did he object to the wife treating the baby as a show-piece? Although he did not realise it, he must in some strange way have been jealous of the place which the child had in the wife's affections, and his jealousy found expression in a determination not to give her any more children, seeing that was the way she treated this baby. But it may well be asked why go to the length of sterilisation? Why not use contraceptives? Both agreed that ever since the birth of the child they had been having intercourse using contraceptives. He was the one who used them, not she. And yet he went and had himself sterilised. It is, as the commissioner said, "an amazing story", and it was done simply because he was jealous of the baby. He did it so as to "pay her out" for making so much of it. That seems to me to be cruelty in itself.

* * *

C.

To Decisions Concerning the Reorganization of Wife-Husband Relationships?

KREYLING v. KREYLING
20 N.J. Misc. 52, 23 A. 2d 800 (1942)

MATTHEWS, ADVISORY MASTER.

* * *

The question to be decided in this case is, as far as I have been able to determine, one of novel impression in our State, namely, is the unjustified refusal by the defendant of natural sexual intercourse, persisted in willfully, obstinately and continually for a period of two years, for the purpose of preventing the petitioner from giving birth to a child, a ground for divorce for the cause of desertion, both parties being physically capable of having natural uncontracepted intercourse.

Our Court of Errors and Appeals has held in the case of Rains v. Rains, 127 N.J. Eq. 328, 12 A. 2d 857, 859: "It is well established in this state that unjustified refusal of sexual intercourse persisted in willfully, obstinately and continually for a period of two years is a ground for divorce for the cause of desertion, . . ."

* * *

In Raymond v. Raymond, N.J. Ch., 79 A. 430, at page 431 the Court said: "The controlling purpose of marriage is to enable the sexes to gratify lawfully the natural desire for procreation which has been implanted in them, that the race may be preserved upon the earth."

* * *

Now in the case of Rains v. Rains, supra, the defendant refused to have any sexual intercourse with the petitioner because he said he had a "germ" and didn't want her to become a mother. In the case sub judice the defendant did not want the petitioner to become a mother because he preferred what he called "the luxuries of life" to children, and he accomplished his purpose of not wanting the petitioner to become a mother not by refusing his wife any sexual intercourse, but by using a contraceptive device. Certainly the result of the defendant's conduct in the instant case was the same as the result of the defendant's refusal to have any intercourse in the Rains case. The defendant in the case sub judice apparently regarded the married state as mere licensed concubinage and not a relation "the controlling purpose" of which is "to enable the sexes to gratify lawfully the natural desire for procreation which has been implanted in them that the race may be preserved upon the earth."

Moreover, I think it may be said that in all of the cases in our State which lay down and follow the rule that unjustified refusal of sexual intercourse for the statutory period is a ground for divorce for the cause of desertion, the decisions rest on the principle that refusal of sexual intercourse prevents the procreation of children and thereby deprives marriage of . . . "most important object". As . . . petitioner in the instant case, said in his brief filed before trial: "It has never been held nor has it ever been suggested that either party may enter into a contract of marriage merely to legalize the performance of an act which without the marital status would be illegal. Such a construction would be tantamount to the establishment of legalized fornication."

Married persons in normal health are, by the contract and "controlling purpose" of marriage, entitled to "gratify lawfully the natural desire for procreation which has been implanted in the sexes that the race may be preserved upon the earth." In the ecclesiastical terminology of the law in olden days, marital sexual intercourse was called the "debitum", the debt owed by husband and wife, each to the other.

Prescinding, however, from all except bare legal considerations, we must recognize the modern fact that contraception to prevent or to space the birth of children for alleged therapeutic, economic, and what are modernly called "social" reasons and conveniences, is a widely accepted practice today. Erstwhile statutory prohibitions of the sale and use of contraceptive devices, medical or otherwise, for birth prevention and birth control have been more or less removed in many jurisdictions. In jurisdictions where there are statutory prohibitions against the dissemination of such information and the purveying of contraceptive devices, such prohibitions are often more obeyed in their breach than in their observance.

Where both husband and wife willingly indulge in birth prevention no legal problem arises, the matter being solely one for the individual consciences of the parties, honestly formed according to their religious and moral beliefs. Where, however, as the evidence in the instant case shows, one of the parties, the defendant, solely for his own personal selfish convenience, or, as he puts it, so that he may enjoy the luxuries of life, insists upon contraception to prevent his wife from becoming a mother, he being the active agent in the use of the contraceptive device over her continued protests and against her will, it must be said that such conduct persisted in willfully, obstinately and continually for two years is cause for divorce on the ground of desertion.

It is unthinkable that a wife, as in this case, in full health, her maternal instinct clamoring, as the evidence shows, for the realization of her desire to become a mother, may, because of the selfishness of her husband, be condemned during her marriage to him to a life of frustration of that maternal instinct and desire, with all of the deleterious physical, emotional and mental effects that follow such frustration. Such conduct by a husband is a violation of both human and Divine law.

Nor does the fact that the petitioner did not, after she left the defendant's bed in August, 1939, seek further to request or persuade him to have natural sexual intercourse with her, indicate a failure of proof of defendant's obstinacy. All of the evidence, including the statements by the defendant that he and his wife would never have a child, as well as his continued refusals to have natural intercourse with the petitioner from the very beginning of their married life, refusals culminating in his statement to the petitioner in August, 1939, that he would never indulge in natural uncontracepted intercourse with her, warranted the petitioner's statement that she finally realized, at the end of August, the absolute futility of any further requests. Moreover, I think it may be said that there are reasonable limits beyond which a wife or a husband need not go, in self-respect, in seeking such intimate relations. Under all of the evidence, I consider that the petitioner fulfilled her legal duty in this respect.

I will advise a decree of divorce for the petitioner on the ground that under the evidence the unjustified, willful, obstinate, continual refusal of the defendant over a period of two years to have natural uncontracepted intercourse with the petitioner in order to prevent her from having a child constitutes a desertion of the petitioner by the defendant.

NOTES

NOTE 1.

DEUTSCH, HELENE
Psychology of Women*

The distinction between the sexual instinct and the reproductive instinct, as well as that between

* Vol. II. New York: Grune & Stratton, 1951, pp. 22-24. Reprinted with permission of the publisher.

the instinct of self-preservation and the instinct to preserve the species, regarded as the basis of the human personality, is part of a conception that is still very debatable.

The satisfaction of sexual desire and the release of its tension are the direct goal of the sexual urge. Only gradually was impregnation recognized as a more or less regular result of the sexual act. This result of the sexual urge in the service of the preservation of the species can be deliberately wished for; more than that, the desire for sexual satisfaction can even be diverted from its true goal and be rationalized by its service to the end of reproduction. . . .

* * *

The human desire for offspring has gone through several cultural adaptations. In religious commandments to multiply, it is closely connected with the belief in immortality. These commandments derive from purely psychic sources, from primitive ideas of man and nature, life and death. In them the reproductive instinct is reflected in a spiritualized form and is connected with the deep longing to negate death and preserve life. . . .

Social and economic motives have always played an important part in reproduction and have influenced it in different ways in different civilizations. Under certain social conditions, it is useful economically to have many children. Here the motive for reproduction becomes purely practical. Sometimes social and economic reasons act inversely and restrict the will to reproduction: poverty, shortage of housing, etc., have an inhibiting effect on fertility.

It is difficult to judge to what extent woman's will to motherhood, her desire for a child, is influenced by external circumstances, to what extent it has passively and plastically adjusted to the wishes and ideas of men during various periods of civilization, and to what extent it corresponds to a primary tendency composed of motives both conscious and unconscious.

The relations between sexuality and motherliness are of a complicated psychologic nature, and this complexity seems to point to a determination beyond the purely hormonal. Sexuality and motherliness are sometimes in close harmony, yet at other times they appear completely separate. . . . In many cases the presence of one permits us to infer the presence of the other, and variations in one produce variations in the other. There are women who are both unerotic and unmotherly, and others who combine extraordinary erotic intensity with the warmest motherliness. The split between sexuality and motherliness can assume innumerable forms. For instance, each of these components can relate to different love objects. A given woman sexually desires one man or has the exciting wish to be desired sexually by him, but chooses another man as the father of her children and tenderly and faithfully loves him in this capacity. A psychically integrated woman can gratify both sexuality and motherhood through the mediation of one man.

NOTE 2.

FORBES v. FORBES
[1955] 1 W.L.R. 531

MR. COMMISSIONER LATEY, Q.C.

The main ground of the husband's case is that his wife consistently refused, with the object of avoiding conception, to allow free intercourse, and insisted on precautions which were obnoxious to him, with the result that that course of conduct on her part undermined his health.

This court always has to see that cruelty, as alleged, comes within the well-established definition—that is to say, conduct by the accused spouse of such a character as to have caused damage to life, limb or health, bodily or mental, or as to give rise to a reasonable apprehension of such danger, and the court has to be careful to watch that the range of grounds of divorce is not extended to cover mere incompatibility and such falling away from the ordinary mutual relations of husband and wife as do not come within that definition. . . .

*   *   *

. . . The husband told me that he had got into a very bad state of health, but that the tension under which he had been living gradually diminished after the final parting with his wife in the autumn of 1953. I have corroboration of this from his sister and his landlord, who described the husband's tense and emotional state when he first went to Atworth. Mr. Arnold Crowther, the husband's solicitor, described the husband's distraught condition during the proceedings before the justices and how he broke down and wept twice, and even then was still suffering from a tremendous strain.

Apparently the husband did not go to a doctor because, when on two occasions his wife suggested that he should see a psychologist owing to his restless condition, he retorted that it was no use as the cause of his condition was manifest to her, as it was to himself.

I am satisfied that the injury to his mental health was caused in the main by his wife's persistent refusal to be a wife to him in the full sense, (a) by her insistence on contraceptives, and (b) by refusing him the chance of a child.

Quite apart from the exhortation in the solemnization of matrimony that, firstly, Christian marriage was ordained for the procreation of children, I cannot ignore the fact that it is a natural instinct in most married men to propagate the species and to bear the responsibilities, and enjoy the comforts, of their own children. If a wife deliberately and consistently refuses to satisfy this natural and legitimate craving, and the deprivation reduces the husband to despair, and affects his mental health, I entertain no doubt that she is guilty of cruelty within the definition on which this court always acts.

*   *   *

Knowing her husband's feelings, knowing that the practice she insisted upon was repulsive to him, and that his desire for fatherhood had become an obsession, a legitimate obsession, an ever-growing load on his mind, taunting him as she did, she cannot in my view be acquitted of the intention to pursue her policy of obstention, whatever the result to him. Moreover . . . she definitely stated on oath before the Bath justices that she had no fear of childbirth.

In those circumstances, I find that the wife has been guilty of cruelty to the husband, and in the exercise of my discretion I pronounce a decree nisi in his favour.

NOTE 3.

FREUD, SIGMUND
On Narcissism: An Introduction (1914)*

The primary narcissism of children which we have assumed and which forms one of the postulates of our theories of the libido, is less easy to grasp by direct observation than to confirm by inference from elsewhere. If we look at the attitude of affectionate parents towards their children, we have to recognize that it is a revival and reproduction of their own narcissism, which they have long since abandoned. The trustworthy pointer constituted by overvaluation, which we have already recognized as a narcissistic stigma in the case of object-choice, dominates, as we all know, their emotional attitude. Thus they are under a compulsion to ascribe every perfection to the child—which sober observation would find no occasion to do—and to conceal and forget all his shortcomings. (Incidentally, the denial of sexuality in children is connected with this.) Moreover, they are inclined to suspend in the child's favour the operation of all the cultural acquisitions which their own narcissim has been

* Reprinted from: 14 *The Standard Edition of the Complete Psychological Works of Sigmund Freud.* London: The Hogarth Press, 1957 pp. 90-91. Reprinted with permission of the publisher and Basic Books, Inc., New York.

forced to respect, and to renew on his behalf the claims to privileges which were long ago given up by themselves. The child shall have a better time than his parents; he shall not be subject to the necessities which they have recognized as paramount in life. Illness, death, renunciation of enjoyment, restrictions on his own will, shall not touch him; the laws of nature and of society shall be abrogated in his favour; he shall once more really be the centre and core of creation—'His Majesty the Baby', as we once fancied ourselves. The child shall fulfil those wishful dreams of the parents which they never carried out—the boy shall become a great man and a hero in his father's place, and the girl shall marry a prince as a tardy compensation for her mother. At the most touchy point in the narcissistic system, the immortality of the ego, which is so hard pressed by reality, security is achieved by taking refuge in the child. Parental love, which is so moving and at bottom so childish, is nothing but the parents' narcissism born again, which, transformed into object-love, unmistakably reveals its former nature.

Table of Cases

Table of Authors

Table of Books, Articles, and Other Sources

Subject Index

ABANDONMENT
- Abiding under same roof as not constituting, 679
- As constituting more than technical separation, 75
- California law, 844
- Infant freed from parental custody and control, 1038–9
- Justification submitted, 32
- Punishment for failure to provide, California Law, 846
- Relinquishment of control over child, California law, 839
- Support, duty of husband, 581
- Surrender of child to adoption agency as, 1115ff

ABORTION
- Eugenical, 495
- Future population explosion, 504
- Incestuous offspring, 495–6
- Justifiable, 495–6

ADOLESCENCE
- Problems of home and discipline, 912–22
- Psychoanalytical study, 900ff, 907–9

ADOLESCENT COURTS
See also Juvenile Courts
- Commitment practices, 971
- Female adolescents, 970
- Girls Term, 970
- Wayward minors, 970

ADOLESCENT OFFENDERS, *see* Youthful Offenders

ADOPTION
- Agencies, California law, 841–2
- Annulment, legislative provisions for, 1127–8
- As method for improving future generations, 485
- As solution for illegitimate child, 1148–9
- Black market, 241, 1134–7
  - congressional hearing, 1137–43
  - federal legislation, 1137
  - New York Grand Jury investigation, 1143–6
  - preventive measure, 1153
- By father, of illegitimate child, 1133–4
- By step-father, with change of name, 1068–70
- By step-parent, California law, 843
- California law on, 841–3
- Case study of Cindy Brown Sims, 1034–51
  - analysis and criticism, 1051–3
  - response to analysis and criticism, 1053–4
- Child of insane parent, 1002
- Confidential report by guardian ad litem, 279
- Consent
  - California laws on, 841–2
  - mother's refusal, 278–9
  - of child, 261, 279
  - of natural parents, Israeli law, 1131
  - of natural parents, legislation, 1128
  - of natural parents, New Jersey law, 1150
  - withdrawal, 842
- Considerations, 233
- Continuation of foster care not related to, 1022–34
- County Court Practice, 278–9
- Court report, 1050–1
- Court's jurisdiction to order eligibility for, without parental consent, 1128–30
- Hearings, records, etc., New Jersey law, 1150–52
- Illegal, right of natural mother to regain custody, 1132–3
- Independent adoptions, California state bar recommendations, 1146–8
- Interracial, 1072–4
- Interracial placement program, 241
- Interstate compact on the placement of children, 1152–3
- Irrevocable nature of parents' decision to give up child, 1115ff
- Israel family code, 261
- Male adoption of female child, law on, 1105
- Mutual consent of adoptive parents, 841
- Natural parents' right to regain custody, 1115ff
  - effect on adoption procedure, 1134–6
- New Jersey law, 1149
- New York domestic relations law, 502
- New Zealand law, 1130
- Next friend, duties of, New Jersey law, 1150
- Non-adoptable children, 996
- Of wife, as child, for inheritance, 606–7
- Placement policies, New Jersey law, 1150
- Premature decision by parent subject to reconsideration, 1115–26, 1131–3
- Procedures and forms, 1040–2
- Public policy in the matter of, 1149
- Religious considerations
  - beliefs as bar to adoption, 241
  - Catholic viewpoint, 232, 242
  - Christian Science faith as bar, 253
  - Jewish viewpoint, 242
  - New York law on religion, 239–40
  - non-belief as bar, 241
  - problems, 232–3, 238–45, 253
  - Protestant viewpoint, 242
- Relinquishment by natural parent as requirement, 1038–9
- Rights of inheritance, New Jersey law, 1151
- Severance of natural ties as concomitant, 1072–3
- Suitability of adoptive environment, 1034–7
- Transfer period from foster home to adoption, 1039
- Vacating, California law, 843
- Very young infants, desirability, 1060–1
- When to inform adopted child, 1070–2

ADULTERY
- Artificial insemination as, 661–5
- As grounds for action for separation in New York, 16
- As grounds for divorce, 660ff, 667, 682ff

CHILDREN (*Cont'd.*)
Crimes against, 386–7
Criminal law for acts relating to, 846–7
Custody, *see* Custody
Difficulty in articulating problems, 261
Earliest expression of society, 833–6
Education
  California laws on, 849–56
Effect of family discord on, 919ff, 928ff
Effect of marital discord on, 800
Effect of parent's illness on, 960
Effects of preferential treatment on, 833
Father's role in development, 1100–2
Femininity, 896–7
Freed from brutal parent, 1095–6
Freed from parental control, California law, 844–5
Legislation to insure rights of children of divorce, 294–5
Maintenance, court's duty to direct in N.Y. law, 17–18
Masculinity, 896–7
Neglected, *see* Neglected children
Neuroses, prediction problems, 953–62
Offspring of polygamous marriage, 1107–9
Party status, for, 281ff
Pattern established for adult world, 833–6
Physically handicapped, 855. *See also* Deformity
Plan for provision of care of children of divorce, 297
Prior rights of children of divorce, 294–5
Psychiatric approach to, 267–8
Pupils in California schools, regulations, 852–3
Rights, physical, financial, emotional, 389–92
Schizophrenia in, 884–6
Standing to sue in tort action for damages resulting from family disruption, 388–91
CHILDREN'S COURT, *see* Juvenile Courts
CHRISTIAN CATHOLIC CHURCH OF CHICAGO
Attitude toward medicine, 248
CHRISTIAN SCIENCE FAITH
affecting custody award, 213
Anti-Semitism alleged, 43, 48
As a constant subject of home conversation, 181
As an accepted religion 250–251
As bar to adoption, 253
Attitude toward medical care, 22, 26–30, 38, 46, 54–5
Conversion to as cause of counter-complaint, 21, 26ff
Effect on child's medical care, 214ff
Faith-healing as cause for marriage break-up, 60–63
Grant of charters to, 250
Healing, 193
Healing means accepted under Pennsylvania law, 250–252
Proselytizing efforts as source of conflict in home, 30–38, 48–49, 53
Views on medicine, 190–193
CHRISTIANITY
See also Religion
Relationship to family, 218
CIVIL RIGHTS
Constitutionality of statute barring teaching of foreign languages, 514–15

Right of parents to refuse to send children to inferior, segregated schools, 1077–81
Right to be registered with correct color, 1074–7
CIVILIZATION
See also Evolution; Genetics; Happiness
And instinctual aggression, 450–2
Characteristics, 448ff
Individual sense of guilt as provided by, 452–3
Mutual aid, 477–8
Taboos, 449, 450
COMITY
Recognition of foreign divorces under, 314ff
COMMON LAW MARRIAGE
Elements, 584
Property rights of parties, 593–4
Recognition of, for purposes of death benefits, 436–7
Secrecy as bar to validity, 585
Validity, 584–5
COMMUNISM
In the nursery, 833–6
COMMUNIST PARTY
Membership in as not constituting cause for divorce per se, 66–67
COMMUNITY
Government differentiated, 348
COMMUNITY PROPERTY
California laws on, 577–9
Division, in divorce and separation, 603ff
Division, where divorce awarded to both parties, 801, 803
Elements, 604
Jointly earned, 787
CONCILIATION COURT, CALIFORNIA
Cases, examples, 143–4
Counseling, analysis of phases in 145–6
Counselors, qualifications and activities, 143ff
Procedure, 141–3
CONCILIATION COURT, NEW JERSEY
Supreme Court's Committee on Reconciliation, 151–153, 155–159, 161–162
CONDONATION, 702ff
See also Adultery; Cruelty; Desertion
CONFIDENTIAL COMMUNICATIONS
Engaged couples, 357–8
Husband-wife, 356–7
CONFIDENTIALITY
As applied to family relationships, 363–5
Children as participants, 272–4, 357
Counselor's report on psychiatric and other family conditions, 268–269
Husband-wife attempts at reconciliation, 127–8
Husband-wife communication in privacy inadmissible as testimony in divorce action, 109–10
Parent has no unqualified right to see report on basis of judge's award, 274–7
Probation reports, 274
Report by guardian ad litem in adoption proceeding, 279–80
Reports used to take child from parent, 281
CONFLICT OF INTEREST
Between parents and child, 291–3
CONFLICT OF LAWS, *see* Comity, Custody, Divorce, Full Faith and Credit, Recognition, Support

split religion as a psychological problem, 328–9
State intervention, 928–53
Supervision by court after award, proposal, 289
Teen-age potential offender, 912–25
Temporary, to effect necessary medical care, 246–7
Use of confidential psychological reports not stipulated by parties, 269–272
Visitation rights, *see* Visitation rights
Wardship cases, 274–8
Welfare of child, *see* Best interest of child, *above*
What makes a mother incompetent? 212, 928–53, 960, 998–1006, 1102–4
Where mental illness in one spouse, 720

DEATH
Abatement of actions by death, 615–16
Anguish caused by mix-up of deceased relatives as cause for action, 1188–9
Conquest of, results, 504
Denial of, 489–90
license to marry, 713ff
Presumption of
remarriage, validity, 709–11
Realization of, by child, 1014
Who has prior rights to remains of deceased? 1186–8

DEBTORS AND CREDITORS
Bankruptcy, discharge no bar to alimony or support debts, 419
Exemption laws in favor of family, 416–21
Family status in relation to, 416ff

DECEDENT ESTATE LAW
See also Succession and descent; Wills
Claim of social welfare office to, 586–7
Effect of abandonment on distributive share rights, 16
Effect of divorce on distributive share rights, 16

DECLARATORY DECREE
Court order for surgery required, 1097

DECLARATORY JUDGMENTS
On validity of ante-nuptial agreements, 582–4

DEFENSES
Defense of sister, 371
Insanity as defense to cruelty and murder, 792ff
Provocation, 797
Recrimination, 796–800
Mental incapacity, 782–4
Justification, 16
Self-defense, 369–70

DEFORMITY
Facial, 994
Parents' attitudes toward, 984–94
Psychoanalytical study of effects, 984–90, 994
State intervention to correct against parental wishes, 990–4

DELINQUENT CHILD, *see* Juvenile offenders
DELINQUENCY
See also Juvenile offenders; Youthful offenders
Determination of, in proper court procedure, 965
Prediction, 961–2

DEMENTIA PRAECOX, *see* Schizophrenia
DEMOCRACY
Public policy in, 579

DEPENDENT CHILDREN, *see* Neglected children; Social Welfare
DESCENT AND DISTRIBUTION, *see* Succession and descent
DESERTION
See also Abandonment
Act of sexual intercourse held as ending desertion, 700–2
As grounds for divorce, 697–705
As grounds for divorce, period requirement, 780–1
Australia law of, 774
Brutality as "intention" to desert, 774–7
Condonation, 703–5
Constructive desertion, 774–7
Cruel behavior as, 774–7
Insanity as bar to capacity to desert, 780–1
Intention as element, 774–7
National Assistance Act, 760
No excuse for adultery, 697–8
Poor-man's divorce, 163
Presumed death and remarriage, 709–11
Rational decision to desert as possible in mentally ill spouse, 758–61
Reconciliation unsuccessful in cases of, 156–7, 163
Refusal to cohabit as, 678–9
Refusal to cohabit under mental illness as bar to, 758–61
Separation for childrens' health as not constituting, 1007–8
Unjustified refusal to cohabit as, 826–7
While under same roof, 589–90

DETECTIVES, PRIVATE
Fees, by whom paid, 362
DISCIPLINE
See also Cruelty; Punishment
Punishment distinguished, 977–80
DISCRIMINATION, *see* Education
DIVORCE
A mensa, 700–702
Adultery requirements in New York, staged proceeding, 91–93
Agreements in contemplation of, 553
Ambivalent position of current laws, 815
Annulment contrived in New York, 92
As a happy act, 709
As nullifying reconciliation, 815
As separate from property actions, 609–10
Attorney's expenses in divorce cases, 602–3
Attorneys fees, considerations on who is to pay, and how much, 596ff
Canon law, 15
Change of name (of woman) following, 305, 306
Children, how to protect, 1107
Children's education as entering into divorce, 235
Children's rights following, 294–5
China's law on, 559–61
Christianity, early views, 665
Collusion or fraud, effect on legitimacy of child, 291
Collusive agreement, New York law, 313
Common law divorce, 781–2
Community property, division of, 603ff
Comparative guilt as consideration, 800

INHERITANCE, *see* Succession and descent
INITIATIVE
    Development of, 895–8
INJUNCTION, *see* Peace warrants
    Of third party, 132
INSANITY
    As social and legal, not medical, 714
    Bar to marriage, *see* Mental illness
    Capacity to desert as barred by, 780–1
    Defense to cruelty and murder, 792ff
    Grounds for divorce, *see* Divorce, Grounds
    Guardian for adult insane, 1002–3
    "Incurable" insanity, period requirements for determination, 770–3
    Indiana laws on divorce grounds, 770–2
    Recurrent, as a danger to spouse, divorce as a remedy, 792ff
INSTALLMENT SALES, *see* Credit buying
INSURANCE
    Divorce insurance bank, 637
    Irrevocable beneficiary policy in divorce agreement, 625
    Proposals for marriage dissolution insurance, 631ff
    Tort actions covered by auto insurance between parents and children, 399–402
INTENT
    Intention as element in desertion, 774–7
INTERMARRIAGE
    See also Miscegenation
    Biblical injunction, 63
    Problems, 738–9
INTERSEXUALITY, 643–4
INTERSTATE COMPACT ON THE PLACEMENT
    OF CHILDREN, 1152–3
INTERVIEWS
    Of adults, 78–96
    Of children, 176–8, 196–212, 261–8, 943–6
INTOLERANCE
    No bar to legality of religious provisions of testator's will, 507–10
INTOXICATION
    Bar to marriage, 719
    Grounds for divorce, 106–7
    North Dakota laws on, 719

JEHOVAH'S WITNESSES
    Attitude toward blood transfusions, 752–3
    Attitude toward flag, 237–238
    Attitude toward medicine, 245–246
    Civil disobedience upheld, 237–8
    Conversion to, as cause for family break-up, 65–66
    Refusal to accept medical emergency care for child, 291–2
JEWISH LAW
    Obligations of parents according to, 44–45
    Obligations of wife according to, 45
JEWS
    Jewishness, problems of, 116–117
JOINDER OF PARTIES
    Necessary and indispensable parties to an action 289–291
JOINT MARITAL PROPERTY
    Bank accounts, 567

    Jointly earned, 787
    Safe deposit vaults, 568
    Suits in conversion, 565–8
    Tenancy in common, joint tenancy compared, 567–8
    Wedding gifts, property rights, 565–8
JOINT VENTURES
    Distribution of property of, 705–6
JUDGES
    Arriving at a decision in matrimonial actions, 97–100
    Bias, *see* Personal prejudices, *below*
    Disqualification for personal prejudice, 113–116
    Duty in domestic relations action, 100
    Limits of judicial power, in medical cases, 757–8
    Need for more training in psychology, 1032
    Personal animosity toward attorney, example, 119–20
    Personal prejudices, 113–116, 118–21
    Reconciliation attempt by, during trial, 139
    Relevance of background, etc., to determination of qualification in matrimonial action, 113–116, 118–121
    Self-disqualification in matrimonial actions, 113–4, 118–9
JURISDICTION, *see* Custody; Divorce; Medical care
JUSTICE
    In the nursery, 833, 836
JUVENILE COURTS
    In parens patriae, concept, 966
    Parents' right to notice and hearing, 964
    Proceeding in the best interest of the child, 963ff
    Recommendations for improving justice, 972–3
    Socializing justice, problems of, 972–3
JUVENILE COURTS, CALIFORNIA, 856ff
    Jurisdiction, 858–60
    Probation officers' role, 858–61
    Records, 862
        destruction, 863
        inspection, 863
JUVENILE COURTS, NEW YORK, 967–70
JUVENILE OFFENDERS
    See also Youthful offenders
    Arrest, problems of, 971, 974
    As wards of court, fallacies, 965
    California laws on
        commitment, 850
        commitment of minors prohibited, 857
        dependent children, 861
        detention, 856–9, 863
        education, 849ff
        homes, camps, etc., 863
        neglected children, 858, 861
        separate treatment, 847, 857
        truancy, 849
        vocational training, 850
        wards of court, 861, 863–4
    Constitutional rights, 963ff, 968–9
    Court records,
        expunging, recommendation, 971
    Definition, New York, 968
    Empathic communication, 265–6
    Individualized justice, concept, 967, 970
    Institutions, California, 864

MEDICINE (PRACTICE OF) (*Cont'd.*)
  "Medical attendance" discussed, 248
  Psychological effect on patient, 255
MEGIDDO
  Belief as affecting child's personality, 216
  History of belief, 216
MEMORY
  Legal testimony and, 108ff
  Psychological factors involved in, 108ff
MENTAL ANGUISH
  Pecuniary value in the courts, 389–91, 1188–9
MENTAL HEALTH
  See also Mental Illness
  Development of personality in children, 887–904
  Prevention of neuroses, 887
MENTAL ILLNESS
  See also Insanity
  As a defense in matrimonial causes, 782ff
  Bar to marriage, 713ff, 719–20
  Determination of, for marriage license, 715–716
  Diagnosis, problems of, 714–15
  Family care provisions, 1180
  Lack of capacity to consent to marriage, 746–52
  M'Naghten rule, applicability in matrimonial
    causes, 70–74, 792–4
  Parent, possible effect on child, 998–1006
  Popular notions regarding, 716–18
  Refusal to cohabit under conditions of, not deser-
    tion, 758–61
  Related to consent in marriage, 746–51, 759–62
  Senility differentiated, 1177–9
  Sex phobia as, 758–61
  Treatment, 715
  What makes a mother incompetent?, 998–1006
MENTAL RETARDATION
  Blood test in early infancy to determine, 996
  Family problems created by, 995–6
MEXICAN DIVORCE, 305ff
MINORS
    See also Infants; Children
  Court-ordered operations upon, 293
  Crimes committed by, *see* Juvenile offenders;
      Youthful offenders
  Parents' consent to marriage, 742
  Wages, control over, 839
  Work permits, California law, 853–4
  Working for parents, California law, 854
MISCEGENATION, 722–725. *See also* Intermarriage
  California laws, 722–5
  Constitutionality of laws against, 385
  State laws, 725–6
MIXED MARRIAGES, *see* Intermarriage; Misce-
    genation
MODEL DIVORCE STATUTE, 814
MONOGAMY, 650–1
MORALS
  Development of sense of, 1112
  "Good moral character" for purposes of naturaliza-
    tion, 441–443
  Sex and, 658
MORTUARY LAWS, 1172
  Proper identification and handling of deceased,
    1188–9

MOTHER-CHILD RELATIONSHIP
  Deficient mothering as influence on neurotic de-
    velopment, 997–8
  Discontent in small child, 1055
  Effect of over-ambitious mother on child's re-
    sponses, 1086
  Gratification as prime need of very young child,
    1054–5
  Infancy, 871–5
    maternal care, importance of, 877–9
  Mixed-up infants, 1063–4
  Rejection and unwillingness by mother, 1133
MOTHER-DAUGHTER RELATIONSHIP
  Teen-age problems, 912ff
MOTHERHOOD
  Sex and, 827–8
MURDER
  See also Crimes; Homicide
  Provocation as a defense, 369

NAME
  Change of, 1068–70
    following divorce, 305–6
  Right to use of, 626
NARCISSISM, 824–5, 828
NATIONALISM
  In the nursery, 835–6
NATURALIZATION
  "Good moral character" as a problem for decision,
    441–443
NECESSITIES OF LIFE
  Definition, bestowing exemption from attachment
    of earnings, 417
NEEDY CHILDREN, *See* Neglected children; Public
    welfare
NEEDY PERSONS, *see* Aged and aging; Neglected
    children; Old age assistance
NEGLECTED CHILDREN
  See also Juvenile offenders
  California law, 844, 861
  Continued in custody of mother, 1008
  Court as *parens patriae*, 246, 253
  Court's duty to order summary provision of emer-
    gency medical care, 291–2
  Juvenile court jurisdiction, California, 858
  Mississippi plan for determination of, 432–5
  Neglect resulting in death as homicide, 371–2
  Neglect to provide medical care as crime, 247–250
  New York law, 968
  Parents' refusal to allow transfusion, 246
  Parents' refusal to correct deformity, 990–3
  Parents' refusal to send child to segregated school,
    1077–81
  Punishment of defaulting parent, California law,
    846
  Relation to juvenile delinquency, 962ff
  Religion as problem in placement, 243
  What constitutes neglect?, 870
NEGLIGENCE
  Parental neglect to control tortious acts of minor
    children, 398–9
NEIGHBORHOODS
  As focus of family, 414–415